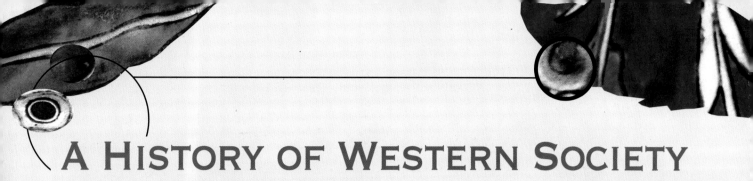

A HISTORY OF WESTERN SOCIETY

Ninth Edition

A HISTORY OF WESTERN SOCIETY

John P. McKay
University of Illinois at Urbana-Champaign

Bennett D. Hill
Late of Georgetown University

John Buckler
University of Illinois at Urbana-Champaign

Clare Haru Crowston
University of Illinois at Urbana-Champaign

Merry E. Wiesner-Hanks
University of Wisconsin–Milwaukee

HOUGHTON MIFFLIN COMPANY
Boston   New York

Publisher: Suzanne Jeans
Senior Sponsoring Editor: Nancy Blaine
Senior Marketing Manager: Katherine Bates
Development Editor: Melissa Mashburn
Senior Project Editor: Christina Horn
Art and Design Manager: Jill Haber
Cover Design Director: Tony Saizon
Senior Photo Editor: Jennifer Meyer Dare
Composition Buyer: Chuck Dutton
Editorial Associate: Adrienne Zicht
Marketing Assistant: Lauren Bussard
Editorial Assistant: Carrie Parker

Cover image: *Portrait of Christiane Kobke* by Constantin Kobke (1804–1880). Oil on canvas. © Christie's Images Ltd. All rights reserved.

Printed in the U.S.A.

Library of Congress Control Number: 2007927730

Instructor's Exam Copy:
ISBN-13: 978-0-547-05243-4
ISBN-10: 0-547-05243-X

For orders, use Student Text ISBNs:
ISBN-13: 978-0-618-94603-7
ISBN-10: 0-618-94603-9

123456789-VH-11 10 09 08 07

In Memoriam

Bennett David Hill
1934 – 2005

Bennett Hill, who authored many of the chapters in earlier editions of this book, was born in Baltimore, Maryland, the son of African American Catholics. When Bennett was ten, the family moved north to Philadelphia, where his father worked for the U.S. Postal Service and his mother for the Veterans Administration. Bennett attended public schools, and his intellectual prowess was soon evident. He won a scholarship to Princeton University, where he received an excellent education that he always treasured. Majoring in history and graduating cum laude, Bennett was a trailblazer— one of the first African Americans to receive an undergraduate degree from Princeton. He subsequently earned a doctorate in European history at Princeton, joined the history department of the University of Illinois at Urbana-Champaign, and later served as department chair. Bennett was a popular but demanding teacher with a passion for medieval social history. His colleagues at Illinois remember especially his keen intellect, elegant taste, literary flair, and quick, sometimes mischievous wit. (He once persuaded some of his students that he followed medieval tradition and trimmed his front lawn with sheep rather than a lawn mower.) Establishing a scholarly reputation as a leading expert on medieval monasticism, Bennett heeded a spiritual call in midlife and became a Benedictine monk and ordained priest at St. Anselm's Abbey in Washington, D.C. He often served Mass at the parish church of his grandparents in Baltimore. Yet Bennett never lost his passion for European and world history, teaching regularly as a visiting professor at Georgetown University. An indefatigable worker with insatiable curiosity, he viewed each new edition as an exciting learning opportunity. At the time of his sudden and unexpected death in February 2005 he was working on a world history of slavery, which grew out of his research and reflected his proud heritage and intensely ethical concerns. A complex and many-sided individual, Bennett was a wonderful conversationalist, an inspiring human being, and the beloved brother and uncle of a large extended family. His sudden passing has been a wrenching loss for all who knew him.

About the Authors

John P. McKay Born in St. Louis, John P. McKay received his B.A. from Wesleyan University (1961), his M.A. from the Fletcher School of Law and Diplomacy (1962), and his Ph.D. from the University of California, Berkeley (1968). He began teaching history at the University of Illinois in 1966 and became a Professor there in 1976. John won the Herbert Baxter Adams Prize for his book *Pioneers for Profit: Foreign Entrepreneurship and Russian Industrialization, 1885–1913* (1970). He has also written *Tramways and Trolleys: The Rise of Urban Mass Transport in Europe* (1976) and has translated Jules Michelet's *The People* (1973). His research has been supported by fellowships from the Ford Foundation, the Guggenheim Foundation, the National Endowment for the Humanities, and IREX. He has written well over a hundred articles, book chapters, and reviews, which have appeared in numerous publications, including *The American Historical Review, Business History Review, The Journal of Economic History,* and *Slavic Review.* He contributed extensively to C. Stewart and P. Fritzsche, eds., *Imagining the Twentieth Century* (1997).

Bennett D. Hill A native of Philadelphia, Bennett D. Hill earned an A.B. from Princeton (1956) and advanced degrees from Harvard (A.M., 1958) and Princeton (Ph.D., 1963). He taught history at the University of Illinois, where he was department chair from 1978 to 1981. He published *English Cistercian Monasteries and Their Patrons in the Twelfth Century* (1968), *Church and State in the Middle Ages* (1970), and articles in *Analecta Cisterciensia, The New Catholic Encyclopaedia, The American Benedictine Review,* and *The Dictionary of the Middle Ages.* His reviews appeared in *The American Historical Review, Speculum, The Historian,* the *Journal of World History,* and *Library Journal.* He was one of the contributing editors to *The Encyclopedia of World History* (2001). He was a Fellow of the American Council of Learned Societies and served on the editorial board of *The American Benedictine Review,* on committees of the National Endowment for the Humanities, and as vice president of the American Catholic Historical Association (1995–1996). A Benedictine monk of St. Anselm's Abbey in Washington, D.C., he was also a Visiting Professor at Georgetown University.

John Buckler Born in Louisville, Kentucky, John Buckler received his Ph.D. from Harvard University in 1973. In 1980 Harvard University Press published his *Theban Hegemony, 371–362 B.C.* He published *Philip II and the Sacred War* (Leiden, 1989) and also edited *BOIOTIKA: Vorträge vom 5. Internationalen Böotien-Kolloquium* (Munich, 1989). In 2003 he published *Aegean Greece in the Fourth Century B.C.* In the following year appeared his editions of W. M. Leake, *Travels in the Morea* (three volumes), and Leake's *Peloponnesiaca.* Cambridge University Press published his *Central Greece and the Politics of Power in the Fourth Century,* edited by Hans Beck, in 2007.

Clare Haru Crowston Born in Cambridge, Massachusetts, and raised in Toronto, Clare Haru Crowston received her B.A. in 1985 from McGill University and her Ph.D. in 1996 from Cornell University. Since 1996, she has taught at the University of Illinois, where she has served as associate chair and Director of Graduate Studies, and is currently Associate Professor of history. She is the author of *Fabricating Women: The Seamstresses of Old Regime France, 1675–1791* (Duke University Press, 2001), which won two awards, the Berkshire Prize and the Hagley Prize. She edited two special issues of the *Journal of Women's History* (vol. 18, nos. 3 and 4) and has published numerous articles and reviews in journals such as *Annales: Histoire, Sciences Sociales, French Historical Studies, Gender and History,* and the *Journal of Economic History.* Her research has been supported with grants from the National Endowment for the Humanities, the Mellon Foundation, and the Bourse Châteaubriand of the French government. She is a past president of the Society for French Historical Studies and a former chair of the Pinkney Prize Committee.

Merry E. Wiesner-Hanks Having grown up in Minneapolis, Merry E. Wiesner-Hanks received her B.A. from Grinnell College in 1973 (as well as an honorary doctorate some years later), and her Ph.D. from the University of Wisconsin–Madison in 1979. She taught first at Augustana College in Illinois, and since 1985 at the University of Wisconsin–Milwaukee, where she is currently UWM Distinguished Professor in the department of history. She is the co-editor of the *Sixteenth Century Journal* and the author or editor of nineteen books and many articles that have appeared in English, German, Italian, Spanish, and Chinese. These include *Early Modern Europe, 1450–1789* (Cambridge, 2006), *Women and Gender in Early Modern Europe* (Cambridge, 3d ed., 2008), and *Gender in History* (Blackwell, 2001). She currently serves as the Chief Reader for Advanced Placement World History and has also written a number of source books for use in the college classroom, including *Discovering the Western Past* (Houghton Mifflin, 6th ed., 2007) and *Discovering the Global Past* (Houghton Mifflin, 3d ed., 2006), and a book for young adults, *An Age of Voyages, 1350–1600* (Oxford, 2005).

Brief Contents

Contents

Chapter 17

Absolutism in Central and Eastern Europe to 1740   559

Chapter 18

Toward a New Worldview, 1540–1789   589

Chapter 19

The Expansion of Europe in the Eighteenth Century   621

Chapter 20
The Changing Life of the People   653

Chapter 21
The Revolution in Politics, 1775–1815   683

Chapter 22
The Revolution in Energy and Industry, ca 1780–1860   717

Chapter 23

Ideologies and Upheavals, 1815–1850   **747**

Chapter 24

Life in the Emerging Urban Society in the
Nineteenth Century   **779**

Chapter 30
Cold War Conflicts and Social Transformations, 1945–1985 981

Chapter 31
Revolution, Rebuilding, and New Challenges: 1985 to the Present 1019

Maps

Listening to the Past

Preface

A History of Western Society grew out of the authors' desire to infuse new life into the study of Western Civilization. We knew that historians were using imaginative questions and innovative research to open up vast new areas of historical interest and knowledge. We also recognized that these advances had dramatically affected the subject of European economic, intellectual, and, especially, social history, while new research and fresh interpretations were also revitalizing the study of the traditional mainstream of political, diplomatic, and religious developments. Despite history's vitality as a discipline, however, it seemed to us at the time that both the broad public and the intelligentsia were generally losing interest in the past. That, fortunately for us all, has not proven the case.

It was our conviction, based on considerable experience introducing large numbers of students to the broad sweep of Western Civilization, that a book in which social history was the core element could excite readers and inspire a renewed interest in history. Our strategy was thus twofold. First, we incorporated recent research by social historians as we sought to re-create the life of ordinary people in appealing human terms. At the same time, we were determined to give great economic, political, cultural, and intellectual developments the attention they unquestionably deserve. We wanted to give individual readers and instructors a balanced, integrated perspective so that they could pursue—on their own or in the classroom—those themes and questions that they found particularly exciting and significant. In an effort to realize fully the potential of our fresh yet balanced approach, we made many changes, large and small, in the editions that followed.

Changes in the Ninth Edition

In preparing the Ninth Edition we have worked hard to keep our book up-to-date by including as much valuable and relevant new scholarship as possible. We have also strengthened our distinctive yet balanced approach to a wide range of topics. In addition, we have revised the layout of the chapters somewhat to foreground the historical questions posed and answered in each chapter, and added a new map feature. This edition includes the best of previous editions, while blending in the most important recent findings.

Conceptual and Content Revisions

Several main lines of revision have guided our many changes. In particular, we have approached the history of the West as part of the history of the world and have devoted more space to Europe's interactions with the rest of the world. This has meant that some parts of the book have been completely reconceptualized and reorganized, as have many of the sections within chapters. Chapter 15 is now entirely devoted to European exploration, discovery, and conquest and also includes coverage of world contacts before Columbus. Chapter 7 includes fuller discussion of Central Asian steppe peoples; Chapter 19 includes discussion of European trade with Asia; and Chapter 20 incorporates extended coverage of the impact of colonial products, including sugar, tea, coffee, and tobacco. Chapter 21 has considerable new material on the Haitian revolution; Chapter 29 includes more on World War II outside of Europe; and Chapter 30 has more on decolonization in the Middle East and Africa.

A second major change is updated discussion of gender throughout the text. The development of women's and gender history has been a central part of the expansion of historical knowledge over the last several decades, and this edition includes even fuller discussion of the role of gender in shaping human experience than did previous editions. Some of this new material focuses on women, including expanded discussion of women in medieval monasticism (Chapter 10), women's role in the court culture of early modern Europe (Chapter 16), and women's work in the Industrial Revolution (Chapter 22). Some new text focuses explicitly on norms and patterns of masculinity, including those of classical Athens and Sparta (Chapter 3) and medieval knightly culture (Chapter 10). Other sections ask readers to consider the ways in which gender is related to other social hierarchies, such as social status and race (Chapters 1, 13, and 30), or ways in which religious or intellectual concepts are gendered (Chapters 2 and 16). New scholarship on gender has meant revisions in other sections as well, including discussion of the Roman family, the Reformation, the witch-hunts, the scientific revolution, nineteenth-century cities, and cold war Europe. The discussion of gender is accompanied by updates to the material on sexuality in many chapters, as this is a field of scholarship growing very rapidly.

These two major lines of revision are accompanied by continued enhancement of content that began in earlier editions. The social history focus that has been the core element of this book since its first edition continues, with more material on Roman family life (Chapter 5), popular religious practices (Chapters 10, 11, and 20), and the consumer revolution (Chapter 20), to cite just a few examples. In addition to more material on Europe in a global perspective, we have continued to incorporate more discussion of groups and regions that are frequently shortchanged in the general histories of Europe and Western Civilization. This expanded scope reflects the renewed awareness within the profession of Europe's enormous historical diversity, as well as the efforts of contemporary Europeans to understand the ambivalent and contested meanings of their national, regional, ethnic, and pan-European identities. Examples of this enlarged scope include more discussion of the Celts and Huns (Chapter 7), more on the Vikings and Magyars in eastern Europe (Chapter 8), and more material on Scandinavia in several chapters. Chapter 10 has been reconceptualized from a unit that focuses solely on Christians to one that explores Muslim and Jewish as well as Christian popular religion, and it includes discussions of similarities and differences among these three groups. The history of Jews in Europe is incorporated into a number of chapters as well. Several chapters examine notions of race during times of significant cultural change, including the Renaissance (Chapter 13), the first wave of colonization (Chapter 15), the Enlightenment (Chapter 18), and nineteenth-century urban society (Chapter 24).

An important part of this continued broader focus is material on Islam. Chapter 8 now begins with the development of Islam and includes comprehensive discussion of Muslim Spain. Chapter 9 maintains the discussion of the Arab influence in medieval Sicily highlighted in previous editions. Chapters 17, 25, and 27 all include significant new material on the Ottoman Empire. Several of the new features focus on Muslims living in Europe, as well as issues involving Christian-Muslim relations.

We believe that including examples of problems of historical interpretations in our text helps our readers develop the critical-thinking skills that are among the most precious benefits of studying history. Examples of this more open-ended, interpretative approach include a discussion of the importance of the Lost Gospels (Chapter 6), disagreements about the pathology of the Black Death (Chapter 12), debates about the impact of Enlightenment thought (Chapter 18), and renewed debate on personal and collective responsibility for the Holocaust (Chapter 29).

Concern with terminology is key to new ways in which history is being studied, researched, and presented, and among the historiographical issues we present are some that ask readers to consider the implications of words they (and historians) use regularly without thinking much about them. This includes a consideration of what we mean by "the West" (Chapter 1), discussion of the terms "Middle Ages" (Chapter 8), "Renaissance," and "modern" (Chapter 13), and disputes about who was and was not part of "the nation" (Chapter 25) or included in understandings of "Europe" (Chapter 31).

This edition includes several major changes in the organization of chapters. Chapter 7 now focuses explicitly on late antiquity, taking into account the exciting new scholarship on this period of transition. Chapter 9 brings together material on political developments in the High Middle Ages previously in several chapters, and Chapter 11 focuses on medieval urban life and culture. Chapter 14 now includes material on the Reformations, religious wars, and witch-hunts, while, as noted above, Chapter 15 now focuses on exploration and overseas expansion.

New Pedagogical Features

To help focus and guide the reader, we pose specific historical questions keyed to the main chapter headings at the beginning of each chapter. These questions are then answered in the course of each chapter and repeated in an end-of-chapter summary that concisely reiterates the chapter's findings. For this edition, many of the questions have been reframed, and the chapter summaries rewritten, to maximize the usefulness of this popular pedagogical device. Dates have been added to most chapter titles.

This edition also adds a new feature, "Mapping the Past." Historians have long relied on maps to help explain the stories that they tell, but we have found that students often do not pay as much attention to the maps as they should. Thus in the new "Mapping the Past" feature, one map in each chapter includes questions for discussion. Some of these questions refer only to a single map, while others encourage students to compare different maps in order to trace processes over time.

Distinctive Features

In addition to the new "Mapping the Past" feature, this edition continues to include distinctive features from earlier editions that guide the reader in the process of historical understanding.

Individuals in Society

Included in each chapter is the feature "Individuals in Society," which offers a brief study of a woman, man, or group, informing us about the societies in which they lived. Each study or biographical sketch has been carefully integrated into the body of the text. The "Individuals in Society" feature grew out of our long-standing focus on people's lives and the varieties of historical experience, and we believe that readers will empathize with these human beings as they themselves seek to define their own identities. The spotlighting of individuals, both famous and obscure, perpetuates the greater attention to cultural and intellectual developments that we used to invigorate our social history in earlier editions, and it reflects changing interests within the historical profession as well as the development of "micro-history."

The range of men and women we consider is broad. For this edition, and sometimes at readers' suggestion, we have dropped some individuals and replaced them with others who add their own contributions to history. Chapter 4 now focuses on the Greek mathematician Archimedes and the practical application of science. Chapter 10 looks at the German abbess and mystic Hildegard of Bingen and Chapter 11 at the Italian merchant Francesco Datini. In keeping with this edition's increasing attention to individuals from outside western Europe who had an impact on European developments, Chapter 17 looks at Hürrem, first the concubine and then the wife of Suleiman the Magnificent, and Chapter 21 at Toussaint L'Ouverture, leader of the revolution in the French colony of Saint-Domingue. Chapter 23 focuses on the French historian Jules Michelet, who viewed nationalism as a means of lessening social tensions, and Chapter 30 on Margaret Thatcher, the first woman to become prime minister in Britain. Chapter 31 focuses on Tariq Ramadan, the controversial European-Muslim intellectual. In addition to these new individuals, in some cases, such as Nefertiti (Chapter 1), Theodora (Chapter 7), and Leonardo da Vinci (Chapter 13), we have kept the same individuals, but completely rewritten the feature to bring it in line with current scholarship.

Listening to the Past

A two-page feature called "Listening to the Past" extends and illuminates a major historical issue considered in each of the text's chapters through the presentation of a source or small group of sources. In the new edition we have reviewed our selections and made judicious substitutions. Chapter 5 now focuses on a complex magic charm used during the Roman Empire and perhaps earlier to attract a lover. Chapter 11 again takes up the theme of love, exploring the courtly love tradition in medieval literature. Chapter 20 focuses on Louis Sebastien Mercier's comments on everyday life in eighteenth-century Paris, and Chapter 23 on the reflections of a Czech historian writing during the revolution of 1848. Chapter 27 features Arab protests regarding the establishment of the League of Nations mandates in the former Ottoman Empire and the establishment of a Jewish homeland in Palestine. Chapter 31 examines riots in the suburbs of Paris by French people of Arab descent in late 2005. As in the "Individuals in Society" feature, in addition to these brand-new sources, sources that appeared in previous editions have often been contextualized in new ways reflective of current scholarship.

Each primary source opens with a problem-setting introduction and closes with "Questions for Analysis" that invite students to evaluate the evidence as historians would. Drawn from a range of writings addressing a variety of social, cultural, political, and intellectual issues, these sources promote active involvement and critical interpretation. Selected for their interest and importance and carefully fitted into their historical context, these sources do indeed allow the student to "listen to the past" and to observe how history has been shaped by individual men and women, some of them great aristocrats, others ordinary folk.

Images in Society

This edition continues to include the photo essay "Images in Society." The complete text now contains eight essays, each consisting of a short narrative with questions, accompanied by several pictures. The goal of the feature is to encourage students to think critically: to view and compare visual illustrations and draw conclusions about the societies and cultures that produced those objects. Thus, in Chapter 1 appears the discovery of the "Iceman," the frozen remains of an unknown herdsman. "The Roman Villa at Chedworth" in Britain mirrors Roman provincial culture (Chapter 6). The essay "From Romanesque to Gothic" treats the architectural shift in medieval church building and aims to show how the Gothic cathedral reflected the ideals and values of medieval society (Chapter 11). "Art in the Reformation" (Chapter 14) examines both the Protestant and Catholic views of religious art. Chapter 17 presents the way monarchs displayed their authority visually in "Absolutist Palace Building." Moving to modern times, the focus in Chapter 19 changes to "London: The Remaking of a Great City," which depicts how Londoners rebuilt their city after a great catastrophe. "Class and Gender Boundaries in Women's Fashion, 1850–1914" studies women's clothing in relationship to women's evolving position in society and gender relations (Chapter 24). "Pablo Picasso and Modern Art" looks at some of Picasso's greatest paintings to gain insight into his principles and the modernist revolution in art (Chapter 28).

Additional Features

The illustrative component of our work has been carefully revised. We have added many new illustrations to our extensive art program, which includes more than four hundred color reproductions, letting great art and important events come alive. As in earlier editions, all illustrations have been carefully selected to complement the text, and all carry informative captions, based on thorough research, that enhance their value and have been revised for the current edition. Artwork remains an integral part of our book; the past can speak in pictures as well as in words. The use of full color serves to clarify the maps and graphs and to enrich the textual material. The maps and map captions have been updated to correlate directly to the text, and new maps, as well as the "Mapping the Past" feature, have been added.

Each chapter includes a chronology feature that lists major developments in the period discussed in the chapter. In addition, topic-specific timelines appear at key points throughout the book. Once again we provide a unified timeline at the end of the text. Comprehensive and easy to locate, this useful timeline allows students to compare developments over the centuries.

A list of Key Terms concludes each chapter. These terms are highlighted in boldface in the text. The student may use these terms to test his or her understanding of the chapter's material.

In addition to posing chapter-opening questions and presenting more problems in historical interpretation, we have quoted extensively from a wide variety of primary sources in the narrative, demonstrating in our use of these quotations how historians evaluate evidence. Thus primary sources are examined as an integral part of the narrative as well as presented in extended form in the "Listening to the Past" chapter feature. We believe that such an extensive program of both integrated and separate primary source excerpts will help readers learn to interpret and think critically.

Each chapter concludes with a carefully selected list of suggestions for further reading, revised and updated to keep them current with the vast amount of new work being done in many fields. These bibliographies are shorter than those in previous editions, as readers may now find more extensive suggestions for further reading on the website **college.hmco.com/history/west/mckay/western_society/9e/student_home.html**.

Throughout the text, icons direct students to online interactive maps and primary sources corresponding to discussions in the text and to the student and instructor websites.

Flexible Format

Western Civilization courses differ widely in chronological structure from one campus to another. To accommodate the various divisions of historical time into intervals for a two-quarter, three-quarter, or two-semester period, *A History of Western Society* is published in four versions, three of which embrace the complete work:

- One-volume hardcover edition
- Two-volume paperback: *Volume I: From Antiquity to the Enlightenment* (Chapters 1–17); *Volume II: From Absolutism to the Present* (Chapters 16–31)
- Three-volume paperback: *Volume A: From Antiquity to 1500* (Chapters 1–13); *Volume B: From the Renaissance to 1815* (Chapters 12–21); *Volume C: From the Revolutionary Era to the Present* (Chapters 21–31)
- *Since 1300* (Chapters 12–31), paperback for courses on Europe since the Renaissance

Note that overlapping chapters in both the two- and the three-volume sets permit still wider flexibility in matching the appropriate volume with the opening and closing dates of a course term.

Ancillaries

A wide array of supplements accompany this text to help students better master the material and to help instructors in teaching from the book:

- Student Website
- Instructor Website
- Online Instructor's Resource Manual
- HM Testing CD-ROM (powered by Diploma)
- Online Study Guide (powered by eCommerce)
- PowerPoint maps, images, and lecture outlines
- PowerPoint questions for personal response systems
- Blackboard™ and WebCT™ course cartridges
- Eduspace™ (powered by Blackboard™)
- Interactive ebook
- HistoryFinder

The *Student Website,* prepared by Leslie Kauffman, is a companion website for students that includes a wide range of material correlated to each book chapter such as learning objectives, chapter outlines, pre-class quizzes, interactive flashcards, chronological ordering exercises, primary sources, interactive map exercises, and ACE self-tests. Students can also find general text resources such as an online glossary, audio mp3 files of chapter summaries, and material on how to study more effectively. Throughout the text, icons direct students to relevant exercises and self-testing material located on the student website. Access the student website for this text by visiting **college.hmco.com/history/west/mckay/western_society/9e/student_home.html**.

The *Instructor Website* is a companion website for instructors. It features all of the material on the student website plus additional password-protected resources that help instructors teach the course, such as an electronic version of the *Instructor's Resource Manual* and *PowerPoint* slides. Access the instructor website for this text by visiting **college.hmco.com/history/west/mckay/western_society/9e/instructor_home.html**.

The *Instructor's Resource Manual,* prepared by John Reisbord, contains instructional objectives, chapter outlines, lecture suggestions, guidelines for using primary sources, classroom activities, map activities, audiovisual bibliographies, Internet resources, and suggested readings.

HM Testing (powered by *Diploma*) offers instructors a flexible and powerful tool for test generation and test management. Now supported by the Brownstone Research Group's market-leading *Diploma* software, this new version of *HM Testing* significantly improves on functionality and ease of use by offering all the tools needed to create, author, deliver, and customize multiple types of tests. *Diploma* is currently in use at thousands of college and university campuses throughout the United States and Canada. The *HM Testing* content for this text was developed by John Reisbord and offers key term identification, essay questions (with guidelines for how to effectively write the essay), multiple-choice questions (with page references to the correct responses), and map questions that refer to maps in the text, as well as a final exam.

The *Online Study Guide* (powered by *eCommerce*) offers students additional materials to aid their study and mastery of the text. The *Study Guide* content was developed by Carla Falkner of Northeast Mississippi Community College and offers learning objectives, chapter key points, review questions, major political ideas exercises, issues for essay and discussion, geography questions, map feature questions, and primary source analysis.

We are pleased to offer a collection of Western Civilization *PowerPoint* lecture outlines, maps, and images for use in classroom presentations. Detailed lecture outlines correspond to the book's chapters and make it easier for instructors to cover the major topics in class. The art collection includes all of the photos and maps in the text, as well as numerous other images from our Western Civilization titles. *PowerPoint* questions and answers for use with personal response system software are also offered to adopters free of charge.

A variety of assignable homework and testing material has been developed to work with the *Blackboard™* and *WebCT™* course management systems, as well as with *Eduspace™*: Houghton Mifflin's Online Learning Tool (powered by *Blackboard™*). *Eduspace™* is a web-based online learning environment that provides instructors with a gradebook and communication capabilities, such as synchronous and asynchronous chats and announcement postings. It offers access to assignments such as over 650 gradable homework exercises, writing assignments, interactive maps with questions, primary sources, discussion questions for online discussion boards, and tests, which all come ready to use. Instructors can choose to use the content as is, modify it, or even add their own. *Eduspace™* also contains an interactive ebook, which contains in-text links to interactive maps, primary sources, and audio pronunciation files, as well as review and self-testing material for students.

HistoryFinder, a new Houghton Mifflin technology initiative, helps instructors create rich and exciting classroom presentations. This online tool offers thousands of online resources, including art, photographs, maps, primary sources, multimedia content, Associated Press interactive modules, and ready-made *PowerPoint* slides. *HistoryFinder*'s assets can easily be searched by keyword, or browsed from pull-down menus of topic, media type, or by textbook. Instructors can then browse, preview, and download resources straight from the website.

Acknowledgments

It is a pleasure to thank the many instructors who read and critiqued the manuscript through its development:

Hugh Agnew
George Washington University

Melanie Bailey
Centenary College of Louisiana

Rachael Ball
Ohio State University

Eugene Boia
Cleveland State University

Robert Brown
State University of New York, Finger Lakes Community College

Richard Eichman
Sauk Valley Community College

David Fisher
Texas Technical University

Wayne Hanley
West Chester University of Pennsylvania

Michael Leggiere
Louisiana State University, Shreveport

John Mauer
Tri-County Technical College

Nick Miller
Boise State University

Wyatt Moulds
Jones County Junior College

Elsa Rapp
Montgomery County Community College

Anne Rodrick
Wofford College

Sonia Sorrell
Pepperdine University

Lee Shai Weissbach
University of Louisville

Special thanks also go to Dr. Todd A. Beach, Advanced Placement History teacher at Eastview High School in Apple Valley, Minnesota, for his work on the DBQ appendix of the Advanced Placement Edition of this text.

It is also a pleasure to thank our many editors at Houghton Mifflin for their efforts over many years. To Christina Horn, who guided production, and to Tonya Lobato and Melissa Mashburn, our development editors, we express our special appreciation. And we thank Carole Frohlich for her contributions in photo research and selection.

Many of our colleagues at the University of Illinois and the University of Wisconsin–Milwaukee continue to provide information and stimulation, often without even knowing it. We thank them for it. John Buckler thanks Professor Jack Cargill for his advice on topics in Chapter 2. He also wishes to thank Professor Nicholas Yalouris, former General Inspector of Antiquities, for his kind permission to publish the mosaic from Elis, Greece, in Chapter 3. He is likewise grateful to Dr. Amy C. Smith, Curator of the Ure Museum of Archaeology of the University of Reading, for her permission to publish the vase on page 64. Sincerest thanks go also to Professor Paul Cartledge of Clare College, Cambridge University, for his kind permission to publish his photograph of the statue of Leonidas in Chapter 3. John McKay expresses his deep appreciation to Jo Ann McKay for her sharp-eyed editorial support and unfailing encouragement. For their invaluable comments and suggestions, Clare Crowston thanks the following individuals: Martin Bruegel, Antoinette Burton, Don Crummey, Max Edelson, Tara Fallon, Masumi Iriye, Craig Koslofsky, Janine Lanza, John Lynn, M. J. Maynes, Kathryn Oberdeck, Dana Rabin, and John Randolph. Merry Wiesner-Hanks would like to thank the many students over the years with whom she has used earlier editions of this book. Their reactions and opinions helped shape her revisions to this edition, and she hopes it remains worthy of the ultimate praise that they bestowed on it, that it's "not boring like most textbooks." She would, as always, also like to thank her husband, Neil, without whom work on this project would not be possible.

Each of us has benefited from the criticism of his or her coauthors, although each of us assumes responsibility for what he or she has written. John Buckler has written the first six chapters; Bennett Hill continued the narrative through Chapter 16; and John McKay has written Chapters 17 through 31. Beginning with this edition, Merry Wiesner-Hanks assumed primary responsibility for Chapters 7 through 14 and Clare Crowston assumed primary responsibility for Chapters 15 through 21. Finally, we continue to welcome the many comments and suggestions that have come from our readers, for they have helped us greatly in this ongoing endeavor.

J. P. M.   B. D. H.   J. B.   C. H. C.   M. E. W.

A History of Western Society

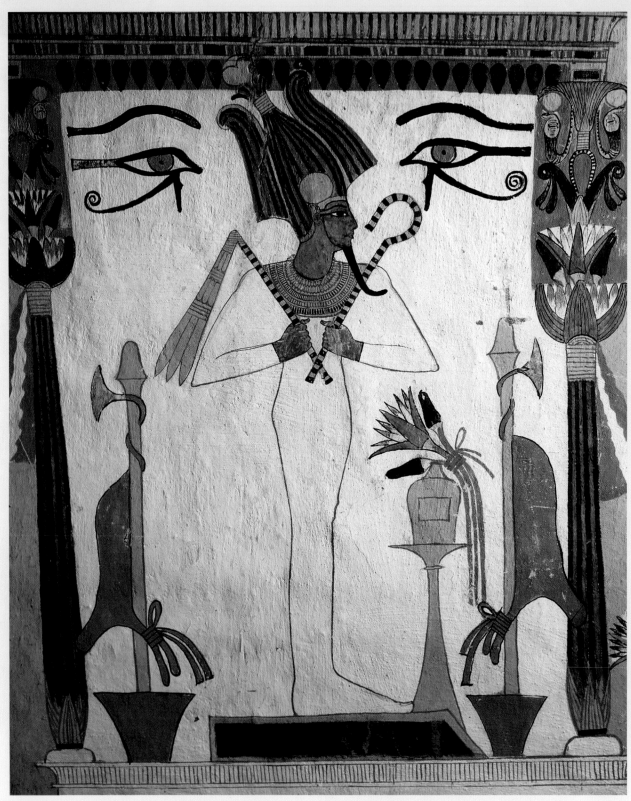

Osiris. Egyptian lord of life and death, powerful and serene, here depicted in his full regalia.
(G. Dagli-Orti/The Art Archive)

ORIGINS,
CA 400,000–1100 B.C.

The civilization and cultures of the modern Western world, like great rivers, have many sources. These sources have flowed from many places and directions. Peoples in western Europe developed numerous communities uniquely their own but also sharing some common features. They mastered such diverse subjects as astronomy, mathematics, geometry, trigonometry, engineering, religious practices, and social organization. Yet the earliest of these peoples did not record their learning and lore in systems of writing. Their lives and customs are consequently largely lost to us.

Other early peoples confronted many of the same basic challenges as those in Europe. They also made progress, but they took the important step of recording their experiences in writing. The most enduring innovations occurred in the ancient Near East, a region that includes the lands bordering the Mediterranean's eastern shore, the Arabian peninsula, parts of northeastern Africa, and perhaps above all Mesopotamia, the area of modern Iraq. Fundamental to the development of Western civilization and culture was the invention of writing by the Sumerians, which allowed knowledge of the past to be preserved. It also facilitated the spread and accumulation of learning, science, and literature. Ancient Near Eastern civilizations also produced the first written law codes, as well as religious concepts that still permeate daily life.

But how do we know and understand these things? Before embarking on the study of history, it is necessary to ask, "What is it?" Only then can the peoples and events of tens of thousands of years be placed into a coherent whole.

Understanding Western History

Most human groups have left some record of themselves. Sometimes they left artifacts, at other times pictures or signs, and at still other times written documents. In many of these records, groups set out distinctions between themselves and others. Sometimes these distinctions are between

Online Study Center

This icon will direct you to interactive activities and study materials on the website **college.hmco.com/pic/mckaywest9e**

small groups such as neighboring tribes, sometimes be-tween countries, and sometimes between vast parts of the world. One of the most enduring of the latter is the idea of "the West" and "the East."

• *What factors are key to understanding the meaning of "the West" and its history?*

Describing the West

What do we mean by "the West"? Everyone has an an-swer, but these answers vary widely. Some may point to geography, others to culture and traditions, and still oth-ers to economic or political systems. Many of these an-swers look to the present rather than to the past, but the West as a concept has a very long history.

Ideas about the West and the distinction between West and East derived originally from the ancient Greeks. Greek civilization grew up in the shadow of earlier civi-lizations to the south and east of Greece, especially Egypt and Mesopotamia. Greeks defined themselves in relation to these more advanced cultures, which they saw as "Eastern." Later Europeans divided certain regions of the world into the "Near East" and the "Far East." Greeks were also the first to use the word *Europe* for a geo-graphic area, taking the word from the name of a minor goddess. They set Europe in opposition to "Asia" (who was also a minor goddess), by which they meant both what we now call Asia and what we call Africa.

The Greeks passed this conceptualization on to the Romans, who saw themselves clearly as the West. For some Romans, Greece remained part of the West, while other Romans came to view Greek traditions as vaguely "eastern." To Romans, the East was more sophisticated and more advanced, but also decadent and somewhat im-moral. Roman value judgments shape preconceptions, stereotypes, and views of differences between the West and the East—what were also called the "Occident" and the "Orient"—to this day. We can see them reflected in comments about the "mysterious East" and "oriental ways of thinking."

Greco-Roman ideas about the West—as about so much else—were passed on to people who lived in western and northern Europe, who saw themselves as the inheritors of this classical tradition and thus as the West. When these Europeans established colonies outside of Europe begin-ning in the late fifteenth century, they regarded what they were doing as taking Western culture with them, even though many aspects of Western culture, such as Christianity, had actually originated in what Europeans by that point regarded as the East. With colonization,

Western came to mean those cultures that included sig-nificant numbers of people of European ancestry, no matter where on the globe they were located.

In the early twentieth century educators and other leaders in the United States became worried that many people, especially young people, were becoming cut off from European intellectual and cultural traditions. They encouraged the establishment of college and university courses focusing on "Western civilization," the first of which was taught at Columbia University in 1919. The course was intended to broaden students' knowledge about the Western world as the United States emerged from its isolation to become a world leader after World War I. In designing the course, faculty included cultures that as far back as the ancient Greeks had been consid-ered Eastern, such as Egypt and Mesopotamia, describ-ing them as the "cradles of Western civilization." This conceptualization and the course spread to other colleges and universities, evolving into what became known as the introductory Western civilization course, the staple of historical instruction for generations of college students in North America.

After World War II divisions between the West and the East changed again. Now there was a new division be-tween East and West within Europe, with Western com-ing to imply a capitalist economy and Eastern part of the Communist Eastern bloc. Japan became Western, and some Greek-speaking areas Eastern. The collapse of com-munism in the Soviet Union and eastern Europe in the 1980s brought yet another refiguring, with much of east-ern Europe joining the European Union, originally a Western organization.

At the beginning of the twenty-first century, Western still suggests a capitalist economy, but it also has certain cultural connotations, such as individualism and compe-tition, which some see as negative and others as positive. Islamic radicals often describe their aims as an end to Western cultural, economic, and political influence, though Islam itself is generally described, along with Ju-daism and Christianity, as a Western monotheistic reli-gion. Thus, throughout its long history, the meaning of "the West" has shifted, but in every era it has meant more than a geographical location.

What Is History, and Why?

The term *history* comes from the Greek word *historie,* coined by Herodotus in the fifth century B.C. For him it meant the record of his investigations and inquiries into the past, which he published for future generations. Since his initial venture, history has remained the effort to reconstruct the past to discover what people thought, what they did, and how their beliefs and actions continue to influence human life. To appreciate the past fully, we must put it into perspective so that we can understand the factors that have helped shape us as individuals, the society in which we live, and the nature of other people's societies. Why else should we study civilizations as separated from ours through time, distance, and culture as classical Greece, medieval Germany, and modern Russia? Although most of the people involved in these epochs are long dead, what they did has touched everyone alive today.

To answer the questions mentioned above, historians examine a variety of evidence. They usually begin with primary sources, firsthand accounts by people who lived through the events, people in the best position to know what happened, who was responsible for it, why it happened, and what it meant. Individuals left numerous narratives and many other types of literary documents recording their experiences; the human tendency to keep the past alive produces a huge collection of writings. In addition to detailed narratives, there are chronicles, in which people noted events in chronological order (therefore the name) and sometimes offered brief explanations of what occurred. A unique literary source for the record of antiquity is papyrology, the study of documents written on manuscripts made from papyrus, a plant that grows abundantly in Egypt. Ancient peoples ranging from inhabitants of the Old Kingdom of Egypt to those living during the Roman period recorded not only literature but also deeds, contracts, and descriptions of local customs. In the medieval period scribes produced thousands of documents giving detailed accounts of agricultural life on manors—how they were run, what the local customs were, and how society actually functioned. These scribes, generally Christian monks, also left records of religious thinking and political affairs. Whether written thousands of years ago or reported in the morning newspapers, these records constitute the primary sources upon which history is built.

Inscriptions are another literary source of information about the past. An inscription is anything written on imperishable material such as stone. Societies have often carved their messages in stone for several important reasons. First, any literate person could understand them. They also served as public records erected in open places for all to see. Documents ranging from ancient treaties that have survived the ravages of time, to religious proclamations of faith and honorific decrees issued during the medieval period, to the Vietnam memorial in Washington can all be considered inscriptions. Even the

Chronology

3200 B.C.	Development of wheeled transport and invention of cuneiform writing
ca 3200–2200 B.C.	Sumerian and Akkadian domination in Mesopotamia
ca 3100 B.C.	Invention of Egyptian hieroglyphic writing
3100–ca 1333 B.C.	Evolution of Egyptian polytheism and belief in personal immortality
3000–1000 B.C.	Origins and development of anthropomorphic religion in Mesopotamia
ca 2700–1000 B.C.	Arrival of Indo-European peoples in western Asia and Europe
ca 2660–1640 B.C.	Old and Middle Kingdoms in Egypt
ca 2600–1200 B.C.	Expansion of Mesopotamian trade with neighbors
ca 2000–1595 B.C.	Babylonian empire in Mesopotamia
ca 1790 B.C.	*Epic of Gilgamesh* and Hammurabi's law code
ca 1600–1200 B.C.	Hittite power in Anatolia
ca 1570–1075 B.C.	New Kingdom in Egypt
ca 1400 B.C.	Development of Phoenician alphabet
ca 1300–1100 B.C.	Increased use of iron in western Asia

simple dog tag worn by a member of our armed forces is a historical inscription. Coins, too, often bear inscriptions. During the Roman Empire the emperors recorded their regnal dates on their currency, thus giving a public record of their reign. In the United States today, many recent quarters proclaim when various states entered the Union, some pertinent symbol, and the date of issue. No matter what their form, these are all written records.

Further evidence of the importance of literary sources, especially in the contemporary world, comes from official statistics covering almost everything from the annual number of deaths in automobile accidents to the daily results of the stock market. Even e-mail ensures the quick and wide dispersal of information throughout the world.

All these written materials provide historians with intriguing raw resources.

Historians also receive help from nonliterary sources such as archaeology. Excavations of various sites have revealed much information from all periods that is not present in the written record. So-called museum archaeologists make sense of what field archaeologists have found. New explorations of long lost sites have in many cases literally uncovered the physical remains of earlier cultures. Archaeology has thus proven invaluable in providing a unique, visible picture of how people actually lived, and comparisons of these findings document how cultures developed. Many travelers today walk the streets of Ephesus, where Paul the Apostle preached. Current excavations at Old Sarum in England vividly reveal how its prehistoric society gave way to the new Christianity: the old pagan mound still rises above the newly excavated early but sophisticated Christian cathedral. In the United States itself archaeology has shed light on the first years of European habitation in New York City and on the lives of Native Americans in the West.

In the face of this remarkable body of literary and nonliterary evidence, historians must try to distinguish the accurate from the false or unreliable. They do so by focusing on the earliest information first. They compare various versions of particular events or large trends with one another. Some people who have left evidence of the past were more intelligent or better informed than others, and their testimony is preferred by historians and indeed strengthened by other writers who independently reported the same things. When two or more dependable sources record the same thing in the same way, historians conclude that they present an accurate account of events.

Once historians decide which sources are reliable, they use this information to establish facts or to explain the meaning of their findings. Their conclusions, when published, are considered secondary sources, scholarly interpretations of what they and others discovered. For instance, a scholar who finds an undiscovered manuscript reads it to understand its contribution to existing historical knowledge. The next question becomes how to fit it into what is already known. The problem then becomes whether the manuscript is accurate and whether it agrees with known sources. If it does, it strengthens their value. If, however, it does not, scholars must reopen the whole question of what actually happened. In short, history must be rethought on the basis of every new piece of evidence.

Understanding of the past does not necessarily come easily—that is one of the joys and frustrations of history. Unlike chemists, historians cannot reproduce experiments under controlled conditions. No two historical events are precisely alike. People cannot be put into test tubes, and they are not as predictable as atoms or hydrocarbons. History is about people, the most complex organisms on this planet. To complicate matters, for many epochs of history only the broad outlines are known, so interpretation is especially difficult. For example, historians know that the Hittite Empire collapsed at the height of its power, but interpretations of the causes of the catastrophe are still speculative. At the other end of the spectrum, some developments are so vast and complex that historians must master mountains of data before they can even begin to interpret developments properly. Events as diverse as the end of the Western Roman Empire, the origins of the Industrial Revolution, and the causes of the French Revolution are very complicated because so many people brought so many different forces to bear for so many reasons. In such cases, there is never one simple explanation that will satisfy everyone.

Still another matter complicates an accurate understanding of the past: the attempt to understand history is uniquely human. Interpretations of the past sometimes change because people's points of view change in the course of life. The values and attitudes of one generation may not be shared by another. Despite such differences in interpretation, the efforts of historians to examine and appreciate the past can give them a perspective that is valuable to the present. It is through analysis and interpretation that historians come to appreciate not only the past but also its relation to life today.

An example of this process comes from examining what the concepts "Western civilization" and "the West" mean. Interpretations of them have changed over time and space. The Greeks, for instance, defined the West as themselves; lands and peoples to the west of them were either barbarians or unknown. The Romans likewise thought of themselves as Western and considered their neighbors in modern France, Greece, and Germany as outsiders until they adopted Greco-Roman culture. During the Middle Ages Europeans spread their civilization into eastern Europe, while the Byzantines spread classical and medieval culture into Russia. This intermingling changed the concept of the West. Social practices and traditional Mediterranean ideas resulted in a civilization that could reasonably be called European.

In the early modern period, during the age of exploration, Europeans discovered the New World, the Americas, and ventured farther into the Pacific. By geographical expansion and emigration they gradually so Europeanized the peoples there that they also entered the intellectual world of the West. West met East in social, economic, intellectual, and cultural contexts. During the nineteenth and twentieth centuries, modern technology significantly reinforced earlier Western values of individualism and private enterprise. The Chinese and Japanese willingly adopted certain aspects of Western culture, such as commercial connections and Western-style armed forces, and some learned Western languages. Yet they also retained much of their own culture. Today people the world over use computers, cellular telephones, and e-mail—all Western inventions. Therefore, the West is obviously as much a cultural concept as it is a physical place on the map. Local differences remain, but the influence of the West has far outstripped geography. Although no one should say that Western civilization has conquered the world, it is safe to say that no other culture has done as much to shape global life.

From Caves to Towns

- *How did early peoples socially develop from living in caves to creating more stable and sophisticated towns?*

Virtually every day brings startling news about the path of human evolution. We now know that by about 400,000 B.C. early peoples were making primitive stone tools, which has led historians to refer to this time as the Paleolithic period. During this period, which lasted until about 7000 B.C., people survived as nomadic gatherers and hunters, usually living in caves or temporary shelters. (See the feature "Images in Society: The Iceman.") Although they accomplished striking achievements, they contributed little to our understanding of history. They properly belong to the realm of anthropology, which studies prehistoric peoples. A reasonable dividing line between anthropology and history is the **Neolithic period,** usually dated between 7000 and 3000 B.C. The term *Neolithic* stems from the new stone tools that came into use at that time. The ways in which peoples used these tools led to fundamental changes in civilization. With them Neolithic men and women built a life primarily and permanently based on agriculture and animal husbandry. They thereby broke with previous nomadic practices.

Sustained agriculture made possible a stable and secure life. Neolithic farmers developed the primary economic activity of the ancient world and one still vital today. With this settled routine came the evolution of towns and eventually of cities. Neolithic farmers usually raised more food than they could consume, so their surpluses permitted larger, healthier populations. Population growth in turn created an even greater reliance on settled farming, as only systematic agriculture could sustain the in-creased numbers of people. Since surpluses of food could also be bartered for other commodities, the Neolithic era witnessed the beginnings of the large-scale exchange of goods. Neolithic farmers also improved their tools and agricultural techniques. They domesticated bigger, stronger animals to work for them, invented the plow, and developed new mutations of seeds. By 3000 B.C. they had invented the wheel. Agricultural surpluses also made possible the division of labor. It freed some people to become artisans who made tools, pottery vessels, woven baskets, clothing, and jewelry. In short, these advances resulted in a wealthier, more comfortable, and more complex life.

These developments generally led to the further evolution of towns and a whole new way of life. People not necessarily related to one another created rudimentary governments that transcended the family. These governments, led by a recognized central authority, made decisions that channeled the shared wisdom, physical energy, and resources of the whole population toward a common goal. These societies made their decisions according to custom, the generally accepted norms of traditional conduct. Here was the beginning of law. Towns also meant life in individual houses or groups of them, which led to greater personal independence. Growing wealth and the need for communal cooperation prompted people to erect public buildings and religious monuments. These groups also protected their possessions and themselves by raising walls.

Many scholars consider walled towns the basic feature of Neolithic society. Yet numerous examples prove that some Neolithic towns existed without stone or mud-brick walls. For instance, at Stonehenge in England the natives erected wooden palisades for safety. At Unteruhldingen in Germany the community established its unwalled town just offshore on a lake. They let nature defend them. The most concentrated collection of walled towns is found in Mesopotamia. This fact presents a historical problem. Since generations of archaeologists and historians have concentrated their attention on this region, they have considered it typical. Yet they have failed to properly appreciate circumstances elsewhere. The fundamental points about this period are that these men and women created stable communities based on agriculture. They defended their towns in various ways by common consent and effort. This organized communal effort is far more important than the types of defenses they built.

The simplest way to support these conclusions is to examine briefly Stonehenge now and Mesopotamia afterward, each in its own unique context. A mute but engaging glimpse of a particular Neolithic society can

Images in Society

The Iceman

On September 19, 1991, two German vacationers climbing in the Italian Alps came upon one of the most remarkable finds in European history: a corpse lying face-down and covered in ice (Image 1). They had stumbled on a mystery that still intrigues archaeologists and many others in the scientific world. After chiseling the body out of the ice, various specialists examined the man. Having died 5,300 years ago, he is the earliest and best-preserved corpse from the Neolithic period (Image 2).

The skin of most corpses found in glaciers appears white and waxy, but the skin of the Iceman, as he is generally known, was brown and dry. Forces of nature had so desiccated the body that it became mummified: the body, including the internal organs, was perfectly preserved. The Iceman's less perishable possessions also survived, so scientists were able to examine him almost as though he had died recently.

The Iceman was quite fit, was between twenty-five and thirty-five years of age, and stood about five feet two inches tall. The bluish tinge of his teeth showed that he had enjoyed a diet of milled grain, perhaps

millet—and also showed that he came from an environment where crops were grown. He wore an unlined robe of animal skins that he had stitched together with careful needlework, using thread made of grass, which he probably had made for himself. Over his robe he wore a cape of grass, very much like capes worn by shepherds in this region as late as the early twentieth century (even as late as the Second World War German soldiers stuffed straw into their boots to withstand the fierce Russian cold). The Iceman also wore a furry cap.

The equipment discovered with the Iceman demonstrates his mastery of several technologies. He carried a hefty copper ax (a sign of stoneworking), but he seems to have relied chiefly on archery. In his quiver were numerous wooden arrow shafts and two finished arrows, all indicating a great deal of knowledge and ingenuity (Image 3). The arrows had flint heads (another sign of stoneworking), and feathers were attached with a resin-like glue to the ends of the shafts. These simple facts convey much information about the technological knowledge of this mysterious

Image 1 The Discovery of the Iceman *(Paul Hanny)*

Image 2 The Face of the Iceman *(Keystone Press Agency Ltd./Rex Features)*

Image 3 The Iceman's Quiver *(S.N.S./Sipa Press)*

Image 4 X-ray of the Iceman's Shoulder *(South Tyrol Museum of Archaeology/AP/Wide World Photos)*

man. He knew how to work stone, he knew the value of feathers to direct the arrows, and he was fully aware of the basics of ballistics. He chose for his bow the wood of the yew, some of the best wood in central Europe. Yet yew trees do not grow everywhere, so the use of yew wood proves that the Iceman had thoroughly explored his environment. He carried his necessary supplies in a primitive rucksack that he had made.

One last mystery surrounds the Iceman. When his body was first discovered, scholars assumed that he was a hapless traveler overtaken by a fierce snowstorm. But a recent autopsy found an arrowhead lodged under his left shoulder (Image 4). The Iceman was not alone on his last day. Someone accompanied him, someone who shot him from below and behind. The Iceman is the victim in the first murder mystery of Western history.

Given this information, can you picture the circumstances of the Iceman's discovery (Image 1)? What was he doing there? From Image 2 can you imagine how nature preserved his remains? From the picture of his arrows (Image 3) can you conclude anything about the Iceman's self-reliance? From Image 4 comes the evidence for the cause of his death. Does it necessarily prove that Neolithic society was as violent as ours?

Online Study Center **Improve Your Grade**
Going Beyond Images in Society

readily be seen today in industrial England. Between 4700 and 2000 B.C. arose the Stonehenge people, named after the famous stone circle on Salisbury Plain. Though named after a single spot, this culture spread throughout Great Britain, Ireland, and Brittany in France. Circles like Stonehenge sometimes contained the houses of permanent settlers. Some were fortified enclosures in which the inhabitants established safe havens for themselves. Both were proto-urban centers. Some of these sites have yielded burial remains. Others were dedicated to religious rituals. They provided magical, not military, protection. They all served diverse social functions, another testimony to Neolithic creativity. Stonehenge and neighboring sites reveal the existence of prosperous, well-organized, and centrally led communities. They also provide evidence for cooperation among similarly constituted societies. None of them individually could have built the circle. By pooling their resources, human and material, they raised it. Thus Stonehenge itself testifies to contact and cohesion among stable groups that cooperated toward a common goal. These factors alone prove the widening horizon of these Neolithic peoples.

Stonehenge offers another insight into this Neolithic culture. It indicates an intellectual world that encompassed astronomy, the environment, and religion. The circle is oriented toward the midwinter sunset and the midsummer sunrise. Stonehenge thus marked the clock-like celestial change of the seasons. This silent evidence proves the existence of a society prosperous enough to endure over long periods during which lore about heaven and earth could be preserved and passed along to successive generations. It also demonstrates that these communities considered themselves members of a wider world that they amiably shared with the deities of nature and the broader universe. Even the magnificent Stonehenge, however, cannot lead to history. The Stonehenge people achieved wonders, but they lacked the literacy to spread their legacy to others beyond their own culture. That breakthrough came in Mesopotamia.

Mesopotamian Civilization

The origins of Western civilization are generally traced to an area that is today not seen as part of the West: Mesopotamia, the Greek name for the land between the Euphrates and Tigris Rivers. There the arid climate confronted the peoples with the hard problem of farming with scant water supplies. Farmers learned to irrigate their land and later to drain it to prevent the buildup of salt in the soil. **Irrigation** on a large scale, like building stone circles in western Europe, demanded organized group effort. That in turn underscored the need for strong central authority to direct it. This corporate spirit led to governments in which individuals subordinated some of their particular concerns to broader interests. These factors made urban life possible in a demanding environment. By about 3000 B.C. the Sumerians, whose

Stonehenge Seen in regal isolation, Stonehenge sits among the stars and in April 1997 was along the path of the comet Hale-Bopp. Long before Druids existed, a Neolithic society laboriously built this circle to mark the passing of the seasons. *(Jim Burgess)*

Mapping the Past

MAP 1.1 Spread of Cultures in the Ancient Near East   This map depicts the area of ancient Mesopotamia and Egypt, a region often called the "cradle of civilization." Map 1.3 on page 26 shows the balance of power that later extended far beyond the regions depicted in Map 1.1. **①** Does this expansion indicate why Mesopotamia and Egypt earned the title of "cradle"? **②** What geographical features of this region naturally suggest the direction in which civilization spread? **③** Why did the first cultures of Mesopotamia spread farther than the culture of Egypt?

Online Study Center   **Improve Your Grade** Interactive Map:
Spread of Cultures in the Ancient Near East

origins are mysterious, established a number of cities in the southernmost part of Mesopotamia, which became known as Sumer. The Sumerians soon turned the region into what generations have called the "cradle of civilization" (see Map 1.1). Some might argue that this phrase should be honorably retired, for civilization was advancing by various degrees from England to Mesopotamia. No one, however, can deny that the fundamental innovation of the Sumerians was the creation of writing, which helped unify this society culturally and opened it to the broader world that we still share today.

• *How did the people in Mesopotamia master their environment, invent writing to record their experiences and thoughts, and create a permanent and vibrant civilization?*

The Invention of Writing and the First Schools

The origins of writing probably go back to the ninth millennium B.C., when Near Eastern peoples used clay tokens as counters for record keeping. By the fourth millennium people had realized that drawing pictures of the tokens on clay was simpler than making tokens. This breakthrough in turn suggested that more information could be conveyed by adding pictures of still other objects. The result was a complex system of pictographs, in which each sign pictured an object. These pictographs were the forerunners of a Sumerian form of writing known as **cuneiform,** from the Latin term for "wedge-shaped," used to describe the strokes of the stylus.

	MEANING	PICTOGRAPH	IDEOGRAM	PHONETIC SIGN
A	Star			
B	Woman			
C	Mountain			
D	Slave woman			
E	Water In			

FIGURE 1.1 Sumerian Writing *(Source: Excerpted from S. N. Kramer,* The Sumerians: Their History, Culture and Character, *University of Chicago Press, Chicago, 1963. Copyright © 1963 by The University of Chicago Press. Reprinted by permission.)*

How did this pictographic system work, and how did it evolve into cuneiform writing? At first, if a scribe wanted to indicate a star, he simply drew a picture of it (line A of Figure 1.1) on a wet clay tablet, which became rock-hard when baked. Anyone looking at the picture would know what it meant and would think of the word for star. This complicated and laborious system had serious limitations. It could not represent abstract ideas or combinations of ideas. For instance, how could it depict a slave woman?

The solution appeared when the scribe discovered that signs could be combined to express meaning. To refer to a slave woman the scribe used the sign for woman (line B) and the sign for mountain (line C)—literally, "mountain woman" (line D). Because the Sumerians regularly obtained their slave women from the mountains, this combination of signs was easily understandable.

The next step was to simplify the system. Instead of drawing pictures, the scribe made conventionalized signs that were generally understood to represent ideas. Thus the signs became *ideograms:* they symbolized ideas. The sign for star could also be used to indicate heaven, sky, or even god.

The real breakthrough came when the scribe learned to use signs to represent sounds. For instance, the scribe

drew two parallel wavy lines to indicate the word *a* or "water" (line E). Besides water, the word *a* in Sumerian also meant "in." The word *in* expresses a relationship that is very difficult to represent pictorially. Instead of trying to invent a sign to mean "in," some clever scribe used the sign for water because the two words sounded alike. This phonetic use of signs made possible the combining of signs to convey abstract ideas.

The Sumerian system of writing was so complicated that only professional scribes mastered it, and even they had to study it for many years. By 2500 B.C. scribal schools flourished throughout Sumer. Most students came from wealthy families and were male. Each school had a master, teachers, and monitors. Discipline was strict, and students were caned for sloppy work and misbehavior. One graduate of a scribal school had few fond memories of the joy of learning:

My headmaster read my tablet, said:
"There is something missing," caned me.
. . . .
The fellow in charge of silence said:
"Why did you talk without permission," caned me.
The fellow in charge of the assembly said:
"Why did you stand at ease without permission," caned me.[1]

The Sumerian system of schooling set the educational standards for Mesopotamian culture, and the Akkadians and, later, the Babylonians adopted its practices and techniques. Mesopotamian education always had a practical side because of the economic and administrative importance of scribes. Most scribes took administrative positions in the temple or palace, where they kept records of business transactions, accounts, and inventories. But scribal schools did not limit their curriculum to business affairs. They were also centers of culture and scholarship. Topics of study included mathematics, botany, and linguistics. Advanced students copied and studied the classics of Sumerian literature. Talented students and learned scribes wrote compositions of their own. As a result, many literary, mathematical, and religious texts survive today, giving a full picture of Mesopotamian intellectual and spiritual life.

Mesopotamian Thought and Religion

The Mesopotamians made significant and sophisticated advances in mathematics using a numerical system based on units of sixty, ten, and six. They developed the concept of place value—that the value of a number depends on where it stands in relation to other numbers. The

Mesopotamians did not consider mathematics a purely theoretical science. The building of cities, palaces, temples, and canals demanded practical knowledge of geometry and trigonometry.

Mesopotamian medicine was a combination of magic, prescriptions, and surgery. Mesopotamians believed that demons and evil spirits caused sickness and that magic spells could drive them out. Or, they believed, the physician could force the demon out by giving the patient a foul-tasting prescription. As medical knowledge grew, some prescriptions were found to work and thus were true medicines. In this slow but empirical fashion medicine grew from superstition to an early form of rational treatment.

Mesopotamian thought had a profound impact in theology and religion. The Sumerians originated many beliefs, and their successors added to them. The Mesopotamians believed that many gods run the world, but they did not consider all gods and goddesses equal. Some deities had very important jobs, taking care of music, law,

sex, and victory, while others had lesser tasks, overseeing leatherworking and basketweaving. The god in charge of metalworking was hardly the equal of the god of wisdom.

Mesopotamian gods lived their lives much as human beings lived theirs. The gods were anthropomorphic, or human in form. Unlike men and women, they were powerful and immortal and could make themselves invisible. Otherwise, Mesopotamian gods and goddesses were very human: they celebrated with food and drink, and they raised families. They enjoyed their own "Garden of Eden," a green and fertile place. They could be irritable, vindictive, and irresponsible.

The Mesopotamians did not worship their deities because the gods were benevolent. Human beings were too insignificant to pass judgment on the conduct of the gods, and the gods were too superior to honor human morals. Rather, the Mesopotamians worshiped the gods because they were mighty. Likewise, it was not the place of men and women to understand the gods. The Sumerian equivalent to the biblical Job once complained to his god:

Ziggurat The ziggurat is a stepped tower that dominated the landscape of the Sumerian city. Surrounded by a walled enclosure, it stood as a monument to the gods. Monumental stairs led to the top, where sacrifices were offered for the welfare of the community. *(Charles & Josette Lemars/Corbis)*

The man of deceit has conspired against me,
And you, my god, do not thwart him,
You carry off my understanding.[2]

The motives of the gods were not always clear. In times of affliction one could only offer sacrifices to appease them.

The Mesopotamians had many myths to account for the creation of the universe. According to one Sumerian myth (echoed in Genesis, the first book of the Bible), only the primeval sea existed at first. The sea produced heaven and earth, which were united. Heaven and earth gave birth to Enlil, who separated them and made possible the creation of the other gods. Babylonian beliefs were similar. In the beginning was the primeval sea, the goddess Tiamat, who gave birth to the gods. When Tiamat tried to destroy the gods, Marduk, the chief god of the Babylonians, proceeded to kill her and divide her body and thus created the sky and earth. These myths are the earliest known attempts to answer the question, "How did it all begin?" The Mesopotamians obviously thought about these matters, as about the gods, in human terms. They never organized their beliefs into a philosophy, but their myths offered understandable explanations of natural phenomena. The myths were emotionally satisfying, and that was their greatest appeal.

Online Study Center **Improve Your Grade**
Primary Source: A Mesopotamian Creation Myth: Earth, Gods, and Humans

In addition to myths, the Sumerians produced the first epic poem, the *Epic of Gilgamesh,* which evolved as a reworking of at least five earlier myths. An epic poem is a narration of the achievements, labors, and sometimes the failures of heroes that embodies a people's or a nation's conception of its own past. Historians can use epic poems to learn about various aspects of a society, and to that extent epics can be used as historical sources. The Sumerian epic recounts the wanderings of Gilgamesh—the semihistorical king of Uruk—and his companion Enkidu, their fatal meeting with the goddess Ishtar, after which Enkidu dies, and Gilgamesh's subsequent search for eternal life. During his search Gilgamesh learns that life after death is so dreary that he returns to Uruk, where he becomes a good king and ends his life happily. The *Epic of Gilgamesh* is not only an excellent piece of literature but also an intellectual triumph. It shows the Sumerians grappling with such enduring questions as life and death, humankind and deity, and immortality. Despite its great antiquity, it addresses questions of importance to people today. (See the feature "Listening to the Past: A Quest for Immortality" on pages 32–33.)

Sumerian Social and Gender Divisions

Their harsh environment fostered a grim, even pessimistic, spirit among the Mesopotamians. The Sumerians sought to please and calm the gods, especially the patron deity of the city. Encouraged and directed by the traditional priesthood, which was dedicated to understanding the ways of the gods, the people erected shrines in the center of each city and then built their houses around them. The best way to honor the gods was to make the shrine as grand and as impressive as possible, for gods who had a splendid temple might think twice about sending floods to destroy the city.

Sumerian society was a complex arrangement of freedom and dependence, and its members were divided into four categories: nobles, free clients of the nobility, commoners, and slaves. **Nobles** consisted of the king and his family, the chief priests, and high palace officials. Generally, the king rose to power as a war leader, elected by the citizenry, who established a regular army, trained it, and led it into battle. The might of the king and the frequency of warfare quickly made him the supreme figure in the city, and kingship soon became hereditary. The symbol of royal status was the palace, which rivaled the temple in grandeur.

The king and the lesser nobility held extensive tracts of land that were, like the estates of the temple, worked by slaves and clients. **Clients** were free men and women who were dependent on the nobility. In return for their labor, the clients received small plots of land to work for themselves. Although this arrangement assured the clients of a livelihood, the land they worked remained the possession of the nobility or the temple. Thus not only did the nobility control most—and doubtless the best—land, they also commanded the obedience of a huge segment of society. They were the dominant force in Mesopotamian society.

Commoners were free. They were independent of the nobility; however, they could not rival the nobility in social status and political power. Commoners belonged to large families that owned land in their own right. Commoners could sell their land, if the family approved, but even the king could not legally take their land without their approval. Male commoners had a voice in the political affairs of the city and full protection under the law.

Until comparatively recent times, slavery has been a fact of life throughout the history of Western society. Some Sumerian slaves were foreigners and prisoners of war. Some were criminals who had lost their freedom as punishment for their crimes. Still others served as slaves to repay debts. These were more fortunate than the others, because the law required that they be freed after three years. But all slaves were subject to whatever treatment their owners might mete out. They could be beaten and even branded. Yet they were not considered dumb beasts. Slaves engaged in trade and made profits. Indeed, many slaves were able to buy their freedom. They could borrow money and received at least some legal protection.

Each of these social categories included both men and women, but their experiences were not the same, for Sumerian society made clear distinctions based on gender. Sumerian society—and all Western societies that followed, until very recently—was **patriarchal,** that is, most power was held by older adult men, especially those from the elite groups. Scholars debate the origins of patriarchy, for a hierarchy based on gender was already in place by the time the first written records appear. It may have been linked to private ownership of property and plow agriculture, which significantly increased the food supply, but also significantly increased the resources needed to produce that food. Men generally carried out the plowing and care for animals, which led to boys' being favored over girls for the work they could do for their parents while young and the support they could provide in their parents' old age. Boys became the normal inheritors of family land. Women could sometimes inherit if there were no sons in a family, but they did not gain the political rights that came with land ownership for men.

The states that developed in the ancient Middle East, beginning with Sumer, further heightened gender distinctions. They depended on taxes and tribute as well as slave labor for their support, so their rulers were very interested in maintaining population levels. All these states were dominated by hereditary aristocracies, whose members became concerned with maintaining the distinction between themselves and the majority of the population, and by male property owners who wanted to be sure the children their wives bore were theirs. These concerns led to attempts to control women's reproduction through laws governing sexual relations and, more importantly, through marriage norms and practices that set up a very unequal relationship between spouses. In most states, laws were passed mandating that women be virgins on marriage and imposing strict punishment for a married woman's adultery; sexual relations outside of marriage on the part of husbands were not considered adultery. Concern with family honor thus became linked to women's sexuality in a way that it was not for men; men's honor revolved around their work activities and, for more prominent families, around their performance of public duties, including keeping written records, in the expanding government bureaucracies. These economic and political developments were accompanied and supported by cultural norms and religious concepts that heightened gender distinctions. In some places heavenly hierarchies came to reflect those on earth, with the gods arranged in a hierarchy dominated by a single male god, who was viewed as the primary creator of life. Because other hierarchies such as those of hereditary aristocracy privileged the women connected to powerful or wealthy men, women did not see themselves as part of a coherent group and often supported the institutions and intellectual structures that subordinated them.

The Spread of Mesopotamian Culture

The Sumerians established the basic social, economic, and intellectual patterns of Mesopotamia, but the Semites played a large part in spreading Sumerian culture far beyond the boundaries of Mesopotamia. The interaction of the Sumerians and Semites, in fact, gives one of the very first glimpses of a phenomenon that can still be seen today. History provides abundant evidence of peoples of different origins coming together, usually on the borders of an established culture. The result was usually cultural change, outweighing any hostility, for each side learned from the other. The outcome in these instances was the evolution of a new culture that consisted of two or more old parts. Although the older culture almost invariably looked on the newcomers as inferior, the new just as invariably contributed something valuable to the old. So it was in 2331 B.C. The Semitic chieftain Sargon conquered Sumer and created a new empire. The symbol of his triumph was a new capital, the city of Akkad. Sargon, the first "world conqueror," led his armies to the Mediterranean Sea. Although his empire lasted only a few generations, it spread Mesopotamian culture throughout the Fertile Crescent, the belt of rich farmland that extends from Mesopotamia in the east up through Syria in the north and down to Egypt in the west (see Map 1.1).

The question is why Mesopotamian culture had such an immediate and wide appeal. In the first place it was successful and enjoyed the prestige of its success. Newcomers wanted to find a respectable place in this old and venerated culture. It also provided an easy means of communication among people on a broad scale. The Eblaites (a Semitic people) could efficiently deal with the Mesopotamians and others who embraced this culture in ways

Sargon of Akkad This bronze head, with elaborately worked hair and beard, portrays the great conqueror Sargon of Akkad. The eyes were originally inlaid with precious jewels, which have since been gouged out. This head was found in the ruins of the Assyrian capital of Ninevah, where it had been taken as loot. (*Bildarchiv Hansmann/Interfoto*)

that all could understand. Culture ignores borders. Despite local variations, so much common ground existed that similar political and economic institutions, exchange of ideas and religious beliefs, methods of writing, and a shared etiquette served as links among all who embraced Mesopotamian culture.

● *Once they had put down roots, how did Mesopotamians spread their culture to the broader world?*

The Triumph of Babylon

Although the empire of Sargon was extensive, it was short-lived. The Akkadians, too, failed to solve the problems posed by Mesopotamia's geography and population pattern. It was left to the Babylonians to unite Mesopotamia politically and culturally. The Babylonians were Amorites, a Semitic people who had migrated from Arabia and settled on the site of Babylon along the middle Euphrates, where that river runs close to the Tigris. Babylon enjoyed an excellent geographical position and was ideally suited to be the capital of Mesopotamia. It dominated trade on the Tigris and Euphrates Rivers: all commerce to and from Sumer and Akkad had to pass by its walls. It also looked beyond Mesopotamia. Babylonian merchants followed the Tigris north to Assyria and Anatolia. The Euphrates led merchants to Syria, Palestine, and the Mediterranean. The city grew great because of its commercial importance and soundly based power.

Babylon was also fortunate to have a farseeing and able king, Hammurabi (r. 1792–1750 B.C.). Hammurabi set out to do three things: make Babylon secure, unify Mesopotamia, and win for the Babylonians a place in Mesopotamian civilization. The first two he accomplished by conquering Assyria in the north and Sumer and Akkad in the south. Then he turned to his third goal.

Politically, Hammurabi joined in his kingship the Semitic concept of the tribal chieftain and the Sumerian idea of urban kingship. Culturally, he encouraged the spread of myths that explained how Marduk, the god of Babylon, had been elected king of the gods by the other Mesopotamian deities. Hammurabi's success in making Marduk the god of all Mesopotamians made Babylon the religious center of Mesopotamia. Through Hammurabi's genius the Babylonians made their own contribution to Mesopotamian culture—a culture vibrant enough to maintain its identity while assimilating new influences. Hammurabi's conquests and the activity of Babylonian merchants spread this enriched culture north to Anatolia and west to Syria and Palestine.

Life Under Hammurabi

One of Hammurabi's most memorable accomplishments was the proclamation of a **law code** that offers a wealth of information about daily life in Mesopotamia. Hammurabi's was not the first law code in Mesopotamia; indeed, the earliest goes back to about 2100 B.C. Like earlier lawgivers, Hammurabi proclaimed that he issued his laws on divine authority "to establish law and justice in the language of the land, thereby promoting the welfare of the people." Hammurabi's code inflicted such penalties as mutilation, whipping, and burning. Despite its severity, a spirit of justice and a sense of responsibility pervade the code. Hammurabi genuinely felt that his duty was to govern the Mesopotamians as righteously as possible. He tried to regulate the relations of his people so that they could live together in harmony.

The practical impact of Hammurabi's code is much debated. There is much disagreement about whether it recorded laws already established, promulgated new laws, or simply proclaimed what was just and proper. It is also unknown whether Hammurabi's proclamation, like others before it, was legally binding on the courts. At the very least, Hammurabi pronounced to the world the principles of justice he encouraged, while giving everyone visible evidence of his intentions as ruler of Babylonia.

The Code of Hammurabi has two striking characteristics. First, the law differed according to the social status and gender of the offender. Aristocrats were not punished as harshly as commoners, nor commoners as harshly as slaves. Certain actions that were crimes for women were not crimes for men. Second, the code demanded that the punishment fit the crime. It called for "an eye for an eye, and a tooth for a tooth," at least among equals. However, an aristocrat who destroyed the eye of a commoner or slave could pay a fine instead of losing his own eye. Otherwise, as long as criminal and victim shared the same social status, the victim could demand exact vengeance.

Hammurabi's code began with legal procedure. There were no public prosecutors or district attorneys, so individuals brought their own complaints before the court. Each side had to produce written documents or witnesses to support its case. In cases of murder, the accuser had to prove the defendant guilty; any accuser who failed to do so was put to death. This strict law was designed to prevent people from lodging groundless charges. The Mesopotamians were very worried about witchcraft and sorcery. Anyone accused of witchcraft, even if the charges were not proved, underwent an ordeal by water. The gods themselves would decide the case. The defendant was thrown into the Euphrates, which was considered the instrument of the gods. A defendant who sank was guilty; a defendant who floated was innocent. Another procedural regulation covered the conduct of judges. Once a judge had rendered a verdict, he could not change it. Any judge who did so was fined heavily and deposed. In short, the code tried to guarantee a fair trial and a just verdict.

Consumer protection is not a modern idea; it goes back to Hammurabi's day. Merchants had to guarantee the quality of their goods and services. A boat builder who did sloppy work had to repair the boat at his own expense. A boatman who lost the owner's boat or sank someone else's boat replaced it and its cargo. House builders guaranteed their work with their lives. Careless work could result in the collapse of a house and the death of its inhabitants. If that happened, the builder was put to death. A merchant who tried to increase the interest

Law Code of Hammurabi Hammurabi ordered his code to be inscribed on a stone pillar and set up in public. At the top of the pillar Hammurabi is depicted receiving the scepter of authority from the god Shamash. (*Hirmer Verlag München*)

rate on a loan forfeited the entire amount. Hammurabi's laws tried to ensure that consumers got what they paid for and paid a just price.

Because farming was essential to Mesopotamian life, Hammurabi's code dealt extensively with agriculture. Tenant farming was widespread, and tenants rented land on a yearly basis. Instead of money they paid a portion of their crops as rent. Unless the land was carefully cultivated, it quickly reverted to wasteland. Therefore, tenants faced severe penalties for neglecting the land or not working it at all. Since irrigation was essential to grow crops, tenants had to keep the canals and ditches in good repair. Otherwise the land would be subject to floods and farmers would face crippling losses. Anyone whose neglect of the canals resulted in damaged crops had to bear all the expense of the lost crops. Those tenants who could not pay the costs were forced into slavery.

Hammurabi gave careful attention to marriage and the family. As elsewhere in the Near East, marriage had aspects of a business agreement. The prospective groom or his father and the father of the future bride arranged everything. The groom offered the father a bridal gift, usually money. If the man and his bridal gift were acceptable, the father provided his daughter with a dowry. After marriage the dowry belonged to the woman (although the husband normally administered it) and was a means of protecting her rights and status. Once the two men agreed on financial matters, they drew up a contract; no marriage was considered legal without one. Either party could break off the marriage, but not without paying a stiff penalty. Fathers often contracted marriages while their children were still young. The girl either continued to live in her father's house until she reached maturity or went to live in the house of her father-in-law. During this time she was legally considered a wife. Once she and her husband came of age, they set up their own house.

The wife was expected to be rigorously faithful. The penalty for adultery, defined as sex between a married woman and a man not her husband, was death. According to Hammurabi's code: "If the wife of a man has been caught while lying with another man, they shall bind them and throw them into the water."[3] There was no corresponding law for married men. The husband had the power to spare his wife by obtaining a pardon for her from the king. He could, however, accuse his wife of adultery even if he had not caught her in the act. In such a case she could try to clear herself before the city council that investigated the charge. If she was found innocent, she could take her dowry and leave her husband. If a woman decided to take the direct approach and kill her husband, she was impaled.

The husband had virtually absolute power over his household. He could even sell his wife and children into slavery to pay debts. Sons did not lightly oppose their fathers, and any son who struck his father could have his hand cut off. A father was free to adopt children and include them in his will. Artisans sometimes adopted children to teach them the family trade. Although the father's power was great, he could not disinherit a son without just cause. Cases of disinheritance became matters for the city to decide, and the code ordered the courts to forgive a son for his first offense. Only if a son wronged his father a second time could he be disinherited.

Prostitution, both male and female, was as common in Mesopotamia as it is today. Then as now, prostitution entailed selling sex for money. Though disreputable, it was not illegal in Mesopotamia and was instead taxed. Prostitutes, like Mesopotamians in general, differed in social status. A special type of prostitution, its meaning still disputed, was the "temple prostitute" who performed sexual acts in the temple as part of her sacred duties. Sex was a routine part of her religious life. The money went to the goddess of the temple. Other women lived as courtesans, mistresses who served clients who were their patrons on a regular basis. Courtesans were both sexual partners and social companions to wealthy and powerful men, who generally had wives and children as well. Prostitutes and courtesans differed from concubines, who were simply women who lived with men without marriage. All of them lived under the protection of the law.

Hammurabi's law code took magic as a fact of life. Magic is the invocation of the gods or the powers of the underworld to act to people's advantage. Magic was often associated with religion and medicine. Mesopotamians, like countless others, genuinely believed that supernatural forces could directly and benevolently intervene on their behalf. In devout belief they used chants and incantations to call on higher, unseen powers to bring them happiness.

Law codes, preoccupied as they are with the problems of society, provide a bleak view of things. Other Mesopotamian documents give a happier glimpse of life. Although Hammurabi's code dealt with marriage in a hard-fisted fashion, countless wills and testaments show that husbands habitually left their estates to their wives, who in turn willed the property to their children. Hammurabi's code restricted married women from commercial pursuits, but financial documents prove that many women engaged in business without hindrance. Some carried on the family business, while others became wealthy landowners in their own right.

Marriage was primarily an arrangement between families, but evidence of love has also survived. A Mesopotamian poem tells of two people meeting secretly in the city. Their parting is delightfully romantic:

Come now, set me free, I must go home,
Kuli-Enlil . . . set me free, I must go home.
What can I say to deceive my mother?[4]

Mesopotamians found their lives lightened by holidays and religious festivals. Traveling merchants brought news of the outside world and swapped marvelous tales. Despite their pessimism, the Mesopotamians enjoyed a vibrant and creative culture that left its mark on the entire Near East.

Egypt, the Land of the Pharaohs (3100–1200 B.C.)

The Greek historian and traveler Herodotus in the fifth century B.C. called Egypt the "gift of the Nile." No other single geographical factor had such a fundamental and profound impact on the shaping of Egyptian life, society, and history as the Nile (see Map 1.2). Unlike the rivers of Mesopotamia, it rarely brought death and destruction by devastating entire cities. The river was primarily a creative force. The Egyptians never feared the relatively tame Nile in the way the Mesopotamians feared the Tigris. Instead, they sang its praises:

Hail to thee, O Nile, that issues from the earth and comes to
*   keep Egypt alive! . . .*
He that waters the meadows which Re [Ra] created,
He that makes to drink the desert . . .
He who makes barley and brings emmer [wheat] into
*   being . . .*
He who brings grass into being for the cattle . . .
He who makes every beloved tree to grow . . .
O Nile, verdant art thou, who makest man and cattle to
*   live.*[5]

Online Study Center Improve Your Grade
Primary Source: The Hymn to the Nile

In the mind of the Egyptians, the Nile was the supreme fertilizer and renewer of the land. Each September the Nile floods its valley, transforming it into a huge area of marsh or lagoon. By the end of November the water retreats, leaving behind a thin covering of fertile mud ready to be planted with crops.

The annual flood made the growing of abundant crops almost effortless, especially in southern Egypt. Herodotus, used to the rigors of Greek agriculture, was amazed by the ease with which the Egyptians raised crops:

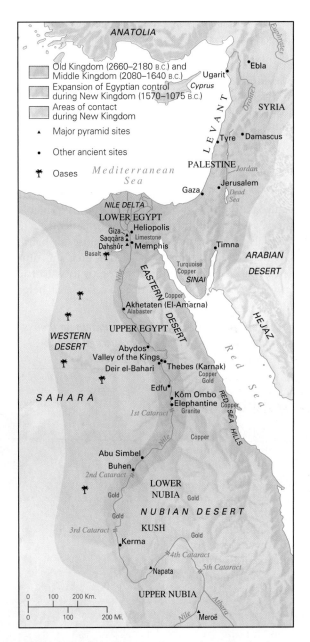

MAP 1.2 Ancient Egypt Geography and natural resources provided Egypt with centuries of peace and abundance.

Online Study Center Improve Your Grade
Interactive Map: Ancient Egypt and the Levant

For indeed without trouble they obtain crops from the land more easily than all other men. . . . They do not labor to dig furrows with the plough or hoe or do the work which other men do to raise grain. But when the river by itself inundates the fields and the water recedes, then each man, having sown his field, sends pigs into it. When the pigs trample down the seed, he waits for the harvest. Then when the pigs thresh the grain, he gets his crop.[6]

The extraordinary fertility of the Nile Valley made it easy to produce an annual agricultural surplus, which in turn sustained a growing and prosperous population. The Nile also unified Egypt. The river was the region's principal highway, promoting easy communication throughout the valley.

Egypt was fortunate in that it was nearly self-sufficient. Besides the fertility of its soil, Egypt possessed enormous quantities of stone, which served as the raw material of architecture and sculpture. Abundant clay was available for pottery, as was gold for jewelry and ornaments. The raw materials that Egypt lacked were close at hand. The Egyptians could obtain copper from Sinai and timber from Lebanon. They had little cause to look to the outside world for their essential needs, a fact that helps explain the insular quality of Egyptian life.

● *What challenges did the Egyptians face in taming their own environment, and how did they so succeed that their culture became basic to Western society?*

of kings. For modern historical purposes, however, it is more useful to divide Egyptian history into periods (see page 21). The political unification of Egypt ushered in the period known as the Old Kingdom (2660–2180 B.C.), an era remarkable for prosperity, artistic flowering, and the evolution of religious beliefs.

In religion, the Egyptians developed complex, often contradictory, ideas of their gods. They were polytheistic in that they worshiped many gods, some mightier than others. Their beliefs were all rooted in the environment and human ecology. The most powerful of these gods was Amon, a primeval sky-god, and Ra, the sun-god. Amon created the entire cosmos by his thoughts. He caused the Nile to make its annual inundations and the northern wind to blow. He brought life to the land and its people, and he sustained both. The Egyptians cherished Amon because he championed fairness and honesty, especially for the common people. The Egyptians called him the "vizier of the humble" and the "voice of the poor." He was also a magician and physician who cured ills, protected people from natural dangers,

The God-King of Egypt

Geographical unity quickly gave rise to political unification of the country under the authority of a king whom the Egyptians called "pharaoh." The precise details of this process have been lost. The Egyptians themselves told of a great king, Menes, who united Upper and Lower Egypt into a single kingdom around 3100 B.C. Thereafter the Egyptians divided their history into dynasties, or families

Ra and Horus The god Ra appears on the left in a form associated with Horus, the falcon-god. The red circle over Ra's head identifies him as the sun-god. In this scene Ra also assumes characteristics of Osiris, god of the underworld. He stands in judgment of the dead woman on the right. She meets the god with respect but without fear, as he will guide her safely to a celestial heaven. (*Egyptian Museum, Cairo*)

and protected travelers. The Egyptians considered Ra the creator of life. He commanded the sky, earth, and underworld. This giver of life could also take it without warning. Ra was associated with the falcon-god Horus, the "lord of the sky," who served as the symbol of divine kingship. Horus united Egypt and bestowed divinity on the pharaoh. The obvious similarities between Amon and Ra eventually led the Egyptians to combine them into one god, **Amon-Ra.** Yet the Egyptians never fashioned a formal theology to resolve these differences. Instead they worshiped these gods as different aspects of the same celestial phenomena.

The Egyptians likewise developed views of an afterlife that reflected the world around them. The dry air of Egypt preserves much that would decay in other climates. Thus there was a sense of permanence about Egypt: the past was never far from the present. The dependable rhythm of the seasons also shaped the fate of the dead. According to the Egyptians, Osiris, a fertility god associated with the Nile, died each year, and each year his wife, Isis, brought him back to life. Isis gave birth to Osiris's son Horus and is frequently shown in paintings and statues holding her infant son. Osiris eventually became king of the dead, and he weighed human beings' hearts to determine whether they had lived justly enough to deserve everlasting life. Osiris's care of the dead was shared by Anubis, the jackal-headed god who annually helped Isis to resuscitate Osiris. Anubis was the god of mummification, so essential to Egyptian funerary rites. The Egyptians preserved these ideas in the ***Book of the Dead,*** which explained that after death the soul left the body to become part of the divine. It entered gladly through the gate of heaven and remained in the presence of Aton (a sun-god) and the stars. Thus the Egyptians did not draw a firm boundary between the human and the divine, and life did not end with death.

Online Study Center **Improve Your Grade**
Primary Source: The Egyptian Book of the Dead's Declaration of Innocence

The focal point of religious and political life in the Old Kingdom was the **pharaoh,** who commanded the wealth, resources, and people of all Egypt. The pharaoh's power was such that the Egyptians considered him to be Horus

Periods of Egyptian History

Period	Dates	Significant Events
Archaic	3100–2660 B.C.	Unification of Egypt
Old Kingdom	2660–2180 B.C.	Construction of the pyramids
First Intermediate	2180–2080 B.C.	Political chaos
Middle Kingdom	2080–1640 B.C.	Recovery and political stability
Second Intermediate	1640–1570 B.C.	Hyksos "invasion"
New Kingdom	1570–1075 B.C.	Creation of an Egyptian empire; Akhenaten's religious policy

in human form, a living god on earth, who became one with Osiris after death. His wife was associated with Isis, for both the queen and the goddess were viewed as protectors. The pharaoh was not simply the mediator between the gods and the Egyptian people. Above all, he was the power that achieved the integration between gods and human beings, between nature and society, that ensured peace and prosperity for the land of the Nile. The pharaoh was thus a guarantee to his people, a pledge that the gods of Egypt (strikingly unlike those of Mesopotamia) cared for their people.

The king's surroundings had to be worthy of a god. Only a magnificent palace was suitable for his home; in fact, the very word *pharaoh* means "great house." Only later, in the Eighteenth Dynasty (see page 24), did it come to mean "king." Just as the pharaoh occupied a great house in life, so he reposed in a great **pyramid** after death. The massive tomb contained all the things needed by the pharaoh in his afterlife. The walls of the burial chamber were inscribed with religious texts and spells relating to the king's journeys after death. Contrary to common belief, no curses for violation of the pyramid have been found. The pyramid also symbolized the king's power and his connection with the sun-god. After burial the entrance was blocked and concealed to ensure the pharaoh's undisturbed peace. To this day the great pyramids at Giza near Cairo bear silent but magnificent testimony to the god-kings of Egypt.

The Pharaoh's People

Because the common folk stood at the bottom of the social and economic scale, they were always at the mercy of grasping officials. The arrival of the tax collector was never a happy occasion. One Egyptian scribe described the worst that could happen:

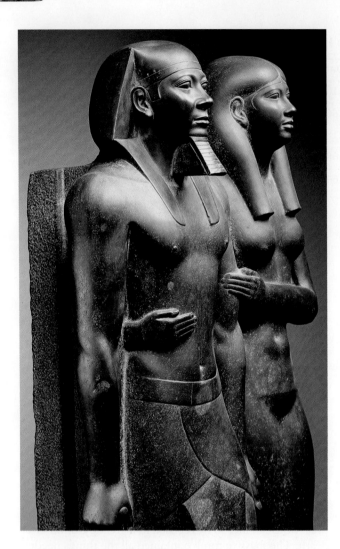

King Menkaure and Queen   The pharaoh and his wife represent all the magnificence, serenity, and grandeur of Egypt. *(Old Kingdom, Dynasty 4, reign of Mycerinus, 2532–2510 B.C.; Greywacke; H × W × D: 54^{11}/$_{16}$ × 22^{3}/$_{8}$ × 21^{5}/$_{16}$ in. (139 × 57 × 54 cm). Harvard University—Museum of Fine Arts Expedition, 11.1738. Museum of Fine Arts, Boston)*

And now the scribe lands on the river-bank and is about to register the harvest-tax. The janitors carry staves and the Nubians rods of palm, and they say, Hand over the corn, though there is none. The cultivator is beaten all over, he is bound and thrown into a well, soused and dipped head downwards. His wife has been bound in his presence and his children are in fetters.[7]

That was an extreme situation. Nonetheless, taxes might amount to 20 percent of the harvest, and tax collection could be brutal.

The regularity of the climate meant that the agricultural year was also routine and dependable. For the Egyptian peasants who formed the bulk of the population, the agricultural year normally began in July, when the mud of the Nile covered the land. The waters receded four months later, and then the land was plowed and sowed. This was a particularly busy time, for the crops had to be planted before the land dried. The next period, from mid-March to July, saw the harvesting of crops. Rural men and women also nurtured a large variety of fruit trees, vegetables, and vines. They tended cattle and poultry, and when time permitted they hunted and fished in the marshlands of the Nile. People could routinely depend on these aspects of life. This very regularity gave a sense of calm and order to Egypt that was not found in Mesopotamia or later in Greece.

Egyptian society seems to have been a curious mixture of freedom and constraint. Slavery did not become widespread until the New Kingdom (1570–1075 B.C.). There was neither a caste system nor a color bar, and humble people could rise to the highest positions if they possessed talent. On the other hand, most ordinary folk were probably little more than serfs who could not easily leave the land of their own free will. Peasants were also subject to forced labor, including work on the pyramids and canals. Young men were drafted into the pharaoh's army, which served both as a fighting force and as a labor corps.

The vision of thousands of people straining to build the pyramids and countless artists adorning the pharaoh's tomb brings to the modern mind a distasteful picture of absolute power. Indeed, the Egyptian view of life and society is alien to those raised with modern concepts of individual freedom and human rights. To ancient Egyptians the pharaoh embodied justice and order—harmony among human beings, nature, and the divine. If the pharaoh was weak or allowed anyone to challenge his unique position, he opened the way to chaos. Twice in Egyptian history the pharaoh failed to maintain rigid centralization. During those two eras, known as the First and Second Intermediate Periods, Egypt was exposed to civil war and invasion. Yet the monarchy survived, and in each period a strong pharaoh arose to crush the rebels or expel the invaders and restore order.

The Hyksos in Egypt (1640–1570 B.C.)

While Egyptian civilization flourished behind its bulwark of sand and sea, momentous changes were taking place in

Pyramids of Giza Giza was the burial place of the pharaohs of the Old Kingdom and of their aristocracy, whose smaller rectangular tombs surround the two foremost pyramids. The small pyramid probably belonged to a pharaoh's wife. *(Jose Fuste Raga/Corbis)*

Egyptian Harvest Scene This cheerful wall painting depicts two aspects of the harvest. Workers at the top right pick bunches of ripe grapes for winemaking. Their colleagues in the center stamp the grapes, and the large pottery jars store the wine. *(Louvre/Réunion des Musées Nationaux/Art Resource, NY)*

the ancient Near East, changes that would leave their mark even on rich, insular Egypt. These changes involved enormous and remarkable movements, especially of peoples who spoke Semitic tongues.

The original home of the Semites was perhaps the Arabian peninsula. Some tribes moved into northern Mesopotamia, others into Syria and Palestine, and still others into Egypt. Shortly after 1800 B.C. people whom the Egyptians called **Hyksos,** which means "Rulers of the Uplands," began to settle in the Nile Delta. The movements of the Hyksos were part of a larger pattern of migration of peoples during this period. The history of Mesopotamia records many such wanderings of people in search of better homes for themselves. Such nomads normally settled in and accommodated themselves with the native cultures. The process was mutual, for each group had something to give to and to learn from the other.

So it was in Egypt, but Egyptian tradition, as later recorded by the priest Manetho in the third century B.C., depicted the coming of the Hyksos as a brutal invasion:

In the reign of Toutimaios—I do not know why—the wind of god blew against us. Unexpectedly from the regions of the east men of obscure race, looking forward confidently to

Shabti Figurines   The Egyptians believed in an afterlife in which earthly work must go on. They made Shabti figurines that could be called magically to life to do that work for them. The figurines fulfilled in death the tasks that ordinary human beings did in life. *(Courtesy of the Trustees of the British Museum)*

victory, invaded our land, and without a battle easily seized it all by sheer force. Having subdued those in authority in the land, they then barbarously burned our cities and razed to the ground the temples of the gods. They fell upon all the natives in an entirely hateful fashion, slaughtering them and leading both their children and wives into slavery. At last they made one of their people king, whose name was Salitis. This man resided at Memphis, leaving in Upper and Lower Egypt tax collectors and garrisons in strategic places.[8]

The Hyksos created a capital city at Avaris, located in the northeastern Nile Delta, but they probably exerted direct rule no farther south.

Although the Egyptians portrayed the Hyksos as a conquering horde, they were probably no more than no-

mads looking for good land. Their entry into the delta was probably gradual and generally peaceful. The Hyksos brought with them the method of making bronze and casting it into tools and weapons that became standard in Egypt. They thereby brought Egypt fully into the **Bronze Age** culture of the Mediterranean world, a culture in which the production and use of bronze implements became basic to society. Bronze tools made farming more efficient than ever before because they were sharper and more durable than the copper tools they replaced. The Hyksos' use of bronze armor and weapons as well as horse-drawn chariots and the composite bow, made of laminated wood and horn and far more powerful than the simple wooden bow, revolutionized Egyptian warfare. However much the Egyptians learned from the Hyksos, Egyptian culture eventually absorbed the newcomers. The Hyksos came to worship Egyptian gods and modeled their monarchy on the pharaonic system.

The New Kingdom: Revival and Empire (1570–1075 B.C.)

Politically, Egypt was only in eclipse. The Egyptian sun shone again when a remarkable line of kings, the pharaohs of the Eighteenth Dynasty, arose to challenge the Hyksos. These pharaohs pushed the Hyksos out of the delta, subdued Nubia in the south, and conquered Palestine and parts of Syria in the northeast. In this way, Egyptian warrior-pharaohs inaugurated the New Kingdom—a period in Egyptian history characterized by enormous wealth and conscious imperialism. During this period, probably for the first time, widespread slavery became a feature of Egyptian life. The pharaoh's armies returned home leading hordes of slaves who constituted a new labor force for imperial building projects.

The kings of the Eighteenth Dynasty created the first Egyptian empire. They ruled Palestine and Syria through their officers and incorporated the neighboring region of Nubia into the kingdom of Egypt. Egyptian religion and customs flourished in Nubia, making a huge impact on African culture there and in neighboring areas. The warrior-kings celebrated their success with monuments on a scale unparalleled since the pharaohs of the Old Kingdom had built the pyramids. Even today the colossal granite statues of these pharaohs and the rich tomb objects of Tutankhamon ("King Tut") testify to the might and splendor of the New Kingdom.

Tutankhamon as Pharaoh   This painted casket depicts the pharaoh as the defender of the kingdom repulsing its invaders. Tutankhamon rides into battle under the signs of the sun-disk and the vulture-goddess, indicating that he and Egypt enjoy the protection of the gods. *(Egyptian Museum, Cairo)*

One of the most extraordinary of this unusual line of kings was Akhenaten (r. 1367–1350 B.C.), a pharaoh more concerned with religion than with conquest. Nefertiti, his wife and queen, encouraged his religious bent. (See the feature "Individuals in Society: Nefertiti, the 'Perfect Woman.'") The precise nature of Akhenaten's religious beliefs remains debatable. The problem began during his own lifetime. His religion was often unpopular among the people and the traditional priesthood, and its practice declined in the later years of his reign. After his death, it was condemned and denounced; consequently, not much is known about it. Most historians, however, agree that Akhenaten and Nefertiti were monotheists; that is, they believed that the sun-god Aton, whom they worshiped, was universal, the only god. They considered all other Egyptian gods and goddesses frauds and disregarded their worship. Yet their belief suffered from an obvious flaw. The pharaoh himself was considered the son of god, and monotheism obviously cannot have two gods. What Akhenaten meant by **monotheism** is that only Aton among the traditional Egyptian deities was god.

Akhenaten's monotheism, imposed from above, failed to find a place among the people. The prime reason for Akhenaten's failure is that his god had no connection with the past of the Egyptian people, who trusted the old gods and felt comfortable praying to them. Average Egyptians were no doubt distressed and disheartened when their familiar gods were outlawed, for those gods were the heavenly powers that had made Egypt powerful and unique. The fanaticism and persecution that accompanied the new monotheism were in complete defiance of the Egyptian tradition of tolerant **polytheism,** or worship of several gods. Thus, when Akhenaten died, his religion died with him.

The Hittites and the End of an Era (ca 1640–1100 B.C.)

Like the Mesopotamians and the Egyptians before them, the Hittites introduced a new element into the development of the ancient Near East. The Hittites were the first Indo-Europeans to become broadly important throughout the region. The term **Indo-European** refers to a large family of languages that includes English, most of the languages of modern Europe, including Greek and Latin, and languages as far afield as Persian and Sanskrit, spoken in ancient Turkey and India. During the eighteenth and nineteenth centuries European scholars learned that peoples who spoke related languages had

spread as far west as Ireland and as far east as Central Asia. Archaeologists were subsequently able to assign rough dates to these migrations and to put them into their historical context. As a result, historians learned that in the course of their experiences in their new world, these peoples made a singular place for themselves. They also left a lasting imprint on the Near East before the empires of the whole region suffered the shock of new peoples and widespread disruption.

- *How did the Hittites rise to power, and how did they and other Near East peoples survive the collapse of the great empires?*

The Coming of the Hittites (ca 1640–1200 B.C.)

The rise of the Hittites to prominence in Anatolia is reasonably clear. During the nineteenth century B.C. the

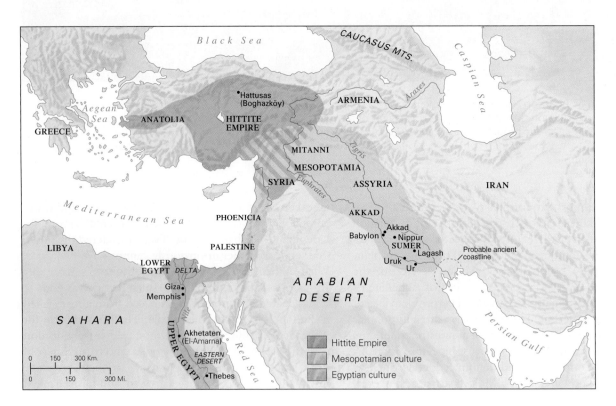

MAP 1.3 Balance of Power in the Near East   This map shows the regions controlled by the Hittites and Egyptians at the height of their power. The striped area represents the part of Mesopotamia conquered by the Hittites during their expansion eastward.

Online Study Center   **Improve Your Grade** Interactive Map: Balance of Power in the Near East

Individuals in Society

Nefertiti, the "Perfect Woman"

Egyptians understood the pharaoh to be the living embodiment of the god Horus, the source of law and morality, and the mediator between gods and humans. His connection with the divine stretched to members of his family, so that his siblings and children were also viewed as in some ways divine. Because of this, a pharaoh often took his sister or half-sister as one of his wives. This concentrated divine blood set the pharaonic family apart from those of other Egyptians (who did not marry close relatives) and allowed the pharaohs to imitate the gods, who in Egyptian mythology often married their siblings. A pharaoh chose one of his wives to be the "Great Royal Wife," or principal queen. Often this was a relative, though sometimes it was one of the foreign princesses who married pharaohs to establish political alliances.

The familial connection with the divine allowed a handful of women to rule in their own right in Egypt's long history. We know the names of four female pharaohs, of whom the most famous was Hatshepsut (r. 1479–1458 B.C.). She was the sister and wife of Thutmose II and, after he died, served as regent for her young stepson Thutmose III, who was actually the son of another woman. Hatshepsut sent trading expeditions and sponsored artists and architects, ushering in a period of artistic creativity and economic prosperity. She built one of the world's great buildings, an elaborate terraced temple at Deir el Bahri, which eventually served as her tomb. Hatshepsut's status as a powerful female ruler was difficult for Egyptians to conceptualize, and she is often depicted in male dress or with a false beard, thus looking more like the male rulers who were the norm. After her death, Thutmose III tried to destroy all evidence that she had ever ruled, smashing statues and scratching her name off inscriptions, perhaps because of personal animosity and perhaps because he wanted to erase the fact that a woman had once been pharaoh. Only within the last decades have historians and archaeologists begun to (literally) piece together her story.

Though female pharaohs were very rare, many royal women had power through their position as "Great Royal Wives." The most famous of these was Nefertiti, the wife of Akhenaten. Her name means "the perfect (or beautiful) woman has come," and inscriptions also give her many other titles. Nefertiti used her position to spread the new religion of the sun-god Aton. Together she and Akhenaten built a new palace at Akhetaten, the present Amarna, away from the old centers of power. There they developed the cult of Aton to the exclusion of the traditional deities. Nearly the only literary survival of their religious belief is the "Hymn to Aton," which declares Aton to be the only god. It describes Nefertiti as "the great royal consort whom he! Akhenaten! Loves, the mistress of the Two Lands! Upper and Lower Egypt!"

Nefertiti, queen of Egypt. (Bildarchiv Preussischer Kulturbesitz/ Art Resource, NY)

Nefertiti is often shown the same size as her husband, and in some inscriptions she is performing religious rituals that would normally have been done only by the pharaoh. The exact details of her power are hard to determine, however. An older theory held that her husband removed her from power, though there is also speculation that she may have ruled secretly in her own right after his death. Her tomb has long since disappeared, though in 2003 an enormous controversy developed over her possible remains. There is no controversy that the bust shown above, now in a Berlin museum, represents Nefertiti, nor that it has become an icon of female beauty since it was first discovered in the early twentieth century.

Questions for Analysis

1. Why might it have been difficult for Egyptians to accept a female ruler?
2. What opportunities do hereditary monarchies such as that of ancient Egypt provide for women? How does this fit with gender hierarchies in which men are understood as superior?

Online Study Center **Improve Your Grade**
Going Beyond Individuals in Society

native kingdoms in the area engaged in suicidal warfare that left most of Anatolia's once-flourishing towns in ashes and rubble. In this climate of exhaustion the Hittite king Hattusilis I built a hill citadel at Hattusas, the modern Boghazköy, from which he led his Hittites against neighboring kingdoms (see Map 1.3). Hattusilis's grandson and successor, Mursilis I (ca 1595 B.C.), extended the Hittite conquests as far as Babylon. Upon his return home, the victorious Mursilis was assassinated by members of his own family, an act that plunged the kingdom into confusion and opened the door to foreign invasion. Mursilis's career is representative of the success and weakness of the Hittites. They were extremely vulnerable to attack by vigilant and tenacious enemies. Yet once they were united behind a strong king, the Hittites were a power to be reckoned with.

The Hittites, like the Egyptians of the New Kingdom, produced an energetic and able line of kings who built a powerful empire. Perhaps their major contribution was the introduction of iron into war and agriculture in the form of weapons and tools. Around 1300 B.C. the Hittites stopped the Egyptian army of Rameses II at the Battle of Kadesh in Syria. Having fought each other to a standstill, the Hittites and Egyptians first made peace, then an alliance. Alliance was followed by friendship, and friendship by active cooperation. The two greatest powers of the early Near East tried to make war between them impossible.

They next included the Babylonians in their diplomacy. All three empires developed an official etiquette in which they treated one another as "brothers," using this gendered familial term to indicate their connection. They made alliances for offensive and defensive protection and swore to uphold one another's authority. These contacts facilitated the exchange of ideas throughout the Near East. Furthermore, the Hittites passed much knowledge

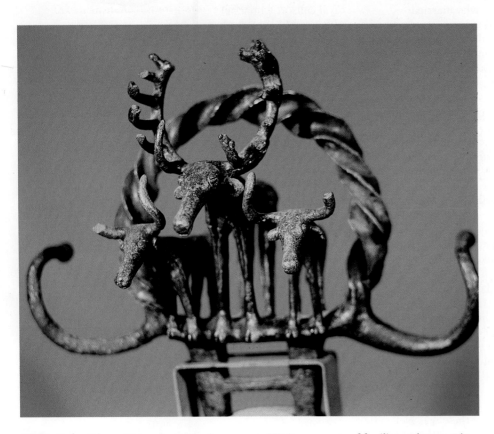

Hittite Solar Disc   This cult standard represents Hittite concepts of fertility and prosperity. The circle surrounding the animals is the sun, beneath which stands a stag flanked by two bulls. Stylized bull's horns spread from the base of the disc. The symbol is also one of might and protection from outside harm. (*Museum of Anatolian Civilizations, Ankara*)

and lore from the Near East to the newly arrived Greeks in Europe. The details of Hittite contact with the Greeks are unknown, but enough literary themes and physical objects exist to prove the connection.

The Fall of Empires and the Survival of Cultures (ca 1200 B.C.)

As seen, the Battle of Kadesh ushered in a welcome period of peace and stability in the Near East that lasted until the thirteenth century B.C. Then, however, foreign invaders destroyed both the Hittite and the Egyptian empires. The most famous of these marauders, called the **Sea Peoples** by the Egyptians, launched a series of stunning attacks that brought down the Hittites and drove the Egyptians back to the Nile Delta. Yet the Sea Peoples and other dimly known peoples did no serious damage to the social and cultural advances made by their predecessors.

The basic social, economic, and cultural patterns of the Near East not only survived the onslaught, but also maintained their hold on the entire area. They filled an aching void in the lives of both disrupted peoples and newcomers, a pattern already seen many times before. Yet it is a mistake to think that the Egyptian and Hittite civilizations survived to face a cultural vacuum.

The Egyptians took the lead in the recovery by establishing commercial contact with their new neighbors. With the exchange of goods went ideas. Both sides shared practical concepts of shipbuilding, metal technology, and methods of trade that allowed merchants safely and efficiently to transact business over long distances. They all—old-timers and newcomers—began to establish and recognize recently created borders, which helped define them geographically and politically. One of the most striking and enduring of these developments was the cultural exchange among them.

When the worst was over, the Egyptians made contact with the Semitic peoples of Palestine and Syria whom they found living in small walled towns. Farther north in the land soon to be named Phoenicia, they also encountered a people who combined sophisticated seafaring with urban life.

The situation in northern Syria reflected life in the south. Small cities in all these places were mercantile centers rich not only in manufactured goods but also in agricultural produce, textiles, and metals. The cities flourished under royal families that shared power and dealt jointly in foreign affairs. These northerners relied heavily on their Mesopotamian heritage. While adopting Babylonian writing to communicate with their more distant neighbors to the east, they also adapted it to write their own north Semitic language. Their texts provide a wealth of information about their life. At the same time they welcomed the knowledge of Mesopotamian literature, mathematics, and culture. They worshiped both their own and Mesopotamian deities. Yet the cultural exchange remained a mixture of adoption, adaptation, contrast, and finally balance, as the two cultures came to understand and appreciate each other.

Southern Anatolia presented a similar picture. Settlements there consisted of trading colonies and small agricultural communities. Thousands of cuneiform tablets testify to commercial and cultural exchanges with Mesopotamia. Here also the Hittite heritage sturdily lived on, especially in politics and social relations. In Anatolia kingship and temple were closely allied, but the government was not a **theocracy** (rule by a priestly order). A city assembly of adult free men worked together under the king, and a prince administered the cities. Thus some men who were not members of the elite had a voice in their political and social affairs. The world of these people rested on a mixture of the Hittite past and their own native achievements. This combination enabled them to create an environment uniquely their own.

A pattern emerged in Palestine, Syria, and Anatolia. In these areas native cultures established themselves during the prehistoric period. Upon coming into contact with the Egyptian and Mesopotamian civilizations, they adopted many aspects of these cultures, adapting them to their own traditional customs. Yet they also contributed to the advance of Egyptian and Mesopotamian cultures by introducing new technologies and religious ideas. The result was the emergence of a huge group of communities stretching from Egypt in the south to Anatolia in the north and from the Levant in the west to Mesopotamia in the east. Each enjoyed its own individual character, while at the same time sharing many common features with its neighbors.

Chapter Summary

- *What factors are key to understanding the meaning of "the West" and its history?*
- *How did early peoples socially develop from living in caves to creating more stable and sophisticated towns?*
- *How did the people in Mesopotamia master their environment, invent writing to record their experiences and thoughts, and create a permanent and vibrant civilization?*
- *Once they had put down roots, how did Mesopotamians spread their culture to the broader world?*
- *What challenges did the Egyptians face in taming their own environment, and how did they so succeed that their culture became basic to Western society?*
- *How did the Hittites rise to power, and how did they and other Near East peoples survive the collapse of the great empires?*

Even before studying the history of Western people, historians had to decide what they meant by "the West": what made it integral while distinct from other cultures. An associated challenge was to determine what history was and how to write it. They accomplished both tasks by taking hard looks at themselves and their achievements. They decided what was important enough to record. Having done that, they created a reliable yardstick for understanding how the West differed from other cultures.

The peoples in Mesopotamia first took up this challenge by inventing writing, initially for financial records and then to record their experiences and thoughts about politics and religion. These written records indicate that their society was marked by social and gender hierarchies. The Mesopotamians advanced politically, all the while spreading their influence farther afield. Finally, the Babylonians, a new people, blended their culture with the older Mesopotamian civilization, thereby permanently furthering developments in the Near East and subsequently the broader world.

Around the same time, different peoples in Egypt confronted and triumphed over different challenges to create a new society that was distinctly their own. They developed their own government and formed a society so stable that they successfully absorbed newcomers and formed the second major cultural influence of the early West.

Finally, the Hittites, an Indo-European people, entered the Near East from the north. Distant ancestors of the modern folk of Europe and the Americas, the Hittites brought new organizational skills and methods of social and political organization. They thereby added a new and valuable ingredient to this already culturally rich area. Near East peoples received hard knocks from hostile invaders beginning around the thirteenth century B.C., but key social, economic, and cultural patterns survived to enrich future generations.

Key Terms

Neolithic period	pharaoh
irrigation	pyramid
cuneiform	Hyksos
nobles	Bronze Age
clients	monotheism
patriarchal	polytheism
law code	Indo-European
Amon-Ra	Sea Peoples
Book of the Dead	theocracy

Online Study Center **Improve Your Grade** Flashcards

Suggested Reading

Brosius, Maria. *The Persians: An Introduction.* 2006. Covers all of Persian history from the beginnings to Alexander the Great.

Burl, Aubery. *The Stonehenge People.* 1987. An examination of the people and their monuments by the leading expert on the topic.

David, A. Rosalie. *Pyramid Builders of Ancient Egypt,* 2d ed. 1996. Studies the lives of the people who actually labored to build the pyramids for their pharaohs.

Harding, A. F. *European Societies in the Bronze Age.* 2000. A comprehensive survey of developments in Europe.

King, Helen. *Health in Antiquity.* 2005. Traces the significance of good health throughout the ancient world, rather than concentrating only on disease and its treatment.

Kuhrt, Amelie. *The Ancient Near East,* 2 vols. 1995. A broad-ranging work that covers the region from the earliest time to Alexander's conquest.

Kyle, Donald G. *Sport and Spectacle in the Ancient World.* 2006. Analyzes the history of sport and spectacle in the ancient world from the ancient Near East to the Roman Empire, using archaeological and art historical evidence to examine many aspects of sporting activities.

Leick, Gwendolyn. *The Babylonians.* 2002. Provides an introduction to all aspects of Babylonian life and culture.

McDowell, A. G. *Village Life in Ancient Egypt: Laundry Lists and Love Songs.* 1999. A readable study of the basic social and economic factors of the entire period.

Rice, Michael. *Egypt's Making: The Origins of Ancient Egypt.* 2004. Treats the prehistory and earliest history of Egypt.

Robins, Gay. *Women in Ancient Egypt.* 1993. Provides a solid overview of women's lives.

Schmandt-Besserat, Denise. *Before Writing.* 1992. A two-volume work on the origins of writing in Mesopotamia.

Silverman, David P. *Ancient Egypt.* 1997. Gives a good general account of the region.

Notes

1. Quoted in S. N. Kramer, *The Sumerians* (Chicago: University of Chicago Press, 1963), p. 238. John Buckler is the translator of all uncited quotations from a foreign language in Chapters 1–6.
2. J. B. Pritchard, ed., *Ancient Near Eastern Texts,* 3d ed. (Princeton, N.J.: Princeton University Press, 1969), p. 590. Hereafter called ANET.
3. Ibid., p. 171.
4. Kramer, p. 251.
5. ANET, p. 372.
6. Herodotus, *The Histories* 2.14.
7. Quoted in A. H. Gardiner, "Ramesside Texts Relating to the Taxation and Transport of Corn," *Journal of Egyptian Archaeology* 27 (1941): 19–20.
8. Manetho, *History of Egypt,* frag. 42.75–77.

Listening to the Past

A Quest for Immortality

The human desire to escape the grip of death, to achieve immortality, is one of the oldest wishes of all peoples. The Sumerian Epic of Gilgamesh *is the earliest recorded treatment of this topic. The oldest elements of the epic go back at least to the third millennium* B.C. *According to tradition, Gilgamesh was a king of Uruk whom the Sumerians, Babylonians, and Assyrians considered a hero-king and a god. In the story Gilgamesh and his friend Enkidu set out to attain immortality and join the ranks of the gods. They attempt to do so by performing wondrous feats against fearsome agents of the gods, who are determined to thwart them.*

During their quest Enkidu dies. Gilgamesh, more determined than ever to become immortal, begins seeking anyone who might tell him how to do so. His journey involves the effort not only to escape from death but also to reach an understanding of the meaning of life.

The passage begins with Enkidu speaking of a dream that foretells his own death.

Listen, my friend [Gilgamesh], this is the dream I dreamed last night. The heavens roared, and earth rumbled back an answer; between them I stood before an awful being, the sombre-faced man-bird; he had directed on me his purpose. His was a vampire face, his foot was a lion's foot, his hand was an eagle's talon. He fell on me and his claws were in my hair, he held me fast and I smothered; then he transformed me so that my arms became wings covered with feathers. He turned his stare towards me, and he led me away to the palace of Irkalla, the Queen of Darkness [the goddess of the underworld; in other words, an agent of death], to the house from which none who enters ever returns, down the road from which there is no coming back.

At this point Enkidu dies, whereupon Gilgamesh sets off on his quest for the secret of immortality. During his travels he meets with Siduri, the wise and good-natured goddess of wine, who gives him the following advice.

Gilgamesh, where are you hurrying to? You will never find that life for which you are looking. When the gods created man they allotted to him death, but life they retained in their own keeping. As for you, Gilgamesh, fill your belly with good things; day and night, night and day, dance and be merry, feast and rejoice. Let your clothes be fresh, bathe yourself in water, cherish the little child that holds your hand, and make your wife happy in your embrace; for this too is the lot of man.

Ignoring Siduri's advice, Gilgamesh continues his journey, until he finds Utnapishtim. Meeting Utnapishtim is especially important because, like Gilgamesh, he was once a mortal, but the gods so favored him that they put him in an eternal paradise. Gilgamesh puts to Utnapishtim the question that is the reason for his quest.

Oh, father Utnapishtim, you who have entered the assembly of the gods, I wish to question you concerning the living and the dead, how shall I find the life for which I am searching?

Utnapishtim said, "There is no permanence. Do we build a house to stand forever, do we seal a contract to hold for all time? Do brothers divide an inheritance to keep forever, does the flood-time of rivers endure? . . . What is there between the master and the servant when both have fulfilled their doom? When the Anunnaki [the gods of the underworld], the judges, come together, and Mammetun [the goddess of fate] the mother of destinies, together they decree the fates of men. Life and death they allot but the day of death they do not disclose.

Then Gilgamesh said to Utnapishtim the Faraway, "I look at you now, Utnapishtim, and your appearance is no different from mine; there is nothing strange in your features. I thought I should find you like a hero prepared for battle, but you lie here taking your ease on your back. Tell me truly, how was it that you came to enter the company of the gods and to possess everlasting life?" Utnapishtim said to Gilgamesh, "I shall reveal to you a mystery, I shall tell you a secret of the gods."

Utnapishtim then tells Gilgamesh of a time when the great god Enlil had become angered with the Sumerians and encouraged the other gods to wipe out humanity. The god Ea, however, warned Utnapishtim about the gods' decision to send a great flood to destroy the Sumerians. He commanded Utnapishtim to build a boat big enough to hold his family, various artisans, and all animals in order to survive the flood that was to come. Although Enlil was infuriated by the Sumerians' survival, Ea rebuked him. Then Enlil relented and blessed Utnapishtim with eternal paradise. After telling the story, Utnapishtim foretells Gilgamesh's fate.

Utnapishtim said, ". . . The destiny was fulfilled which the father of the gods, Enlil of the mountain, had decreed for Gilgamesh: In netherearth the darkness will show him a light: of mankind, all that are known, none will leave a monument for generations to compare with his. The heroes, the wise men, like the new moon have their waxing and waning. Men will say, Who has ever ruled with might and power like his? As in the dark month, the month of shadows, so without him there is no light. O Gilgamesh, this was the meaning of your dream [of immortality]. You were given the kingship, such was your destiny, everlasting life was not your destiny. Because of this do not be sad at heart, do not be grieved or oppressed; he [Enlil] has given you power to bind and to loose, to be the darkness and the light of mankind. He has given unexampled supremacy over the people, victory in battle from which no fugitive returns, in forays and assaults from which there is no going back. But do not abuse this power, deal justly with your servants in the palace, deal justly before the face of the Sun."

Gilgamesh, from decorative panel of a lyre unearthed at Ur. (*The University Museum, University of Pennsylvania, neg. T4-108*)

Questions for Analysis

1. What does the *Epic of Gilgamesh* reveal about Sumerian attitudes toward the gods and human beings?

2. At the end of his quest, did Gilgamesh achieve immortality? If so, what was the nature of that immortality?

3. What does the epic tell us about Sumerian views of the nature of human life? Where do human beings fit into the cosmic world?

Source: The Epic of Gilgamesh, translated by N. K. Sanders. Penguin Classics 1960, Second revised edition, 1972, pp. 91–119. Copyright © N. K. Sanders, 1960, 1964, 1972. Reproduced by permission of Penguin Books Ltd.

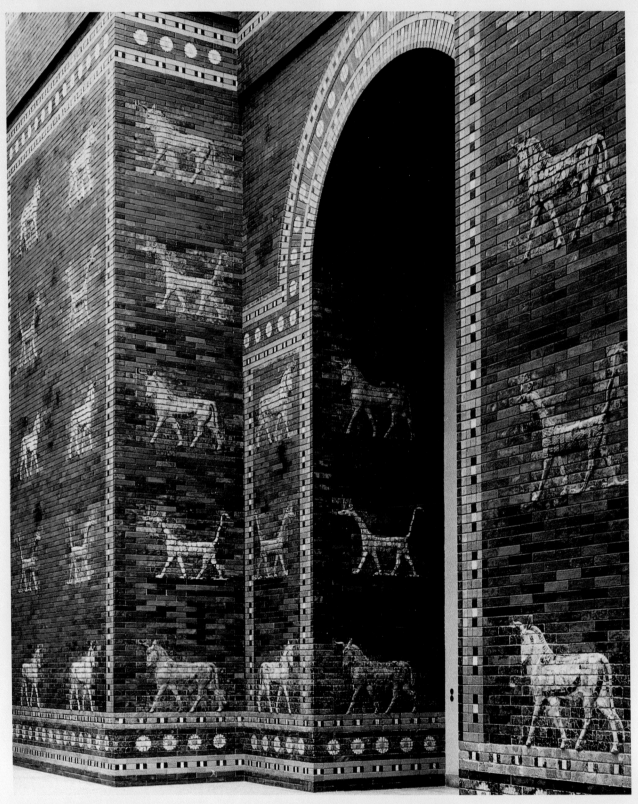

Reconstruction of the "Ishtar Gate," Babylon, early sixth century B.C. Located in the Berlin Museum. *(Bildarchiv Preussischer Kulturbesitz/Art Resource, NY)*

chapter preview

Disruption and Diffusion
• *How did Egypt pass on its heritage to its African neighbors and how did new cultures develop?*

The Children of Israel
• *How did the Hebrew state evolve, and what was daily life like in Hebrew society? What forces helped shape Hebrew religious thought, still influential in today's world?*

Assyria, the Military Monarchy
• *What enabled the Assyrians to overrun their neighbors, and how did their cruelty finally cause their undoing?*

The Empire of the Persian Kings
• *How did Iranian nomads build the Persian Empire, and what sort of life did their policies create for the Near East?*

SMALL KINGDOMS AND MIGHTY EMPIRES IN THE NEAR EAST,
CA 1100–513 B.C.

The migratory invasions that brought down the Hittites and stunned the Egyptians in the late thirteenth century B.C. ushered in an era of confusion and weakness. Although much was lost in the chaos, the old cultures of the ancient Near East survived to nurture new societies. In the absence of powerful empires, the Phoenicians, Hebrews, and many other peoples carved out small independent kingdoms until the Near East was a patchwork of them. During this period Hebrew culture and religion evolved under the influence of urbanism, kings, and prophets.

In the ninth century B.C. this jumble of small states gave way to an empire that for the first time embraced the entire Near East. Yet the very ferocity of the Assyrian Empire led to its downfall only two hundred years later. In 550 B.C. the Persians and Medes, who had migrated into Iran, created a "world empire" stretching from Anatolia in the west to the Indus Valley in the east. For over two hundred years the Persians gave the ancient Near East peace and stability.

Disruption and Diffusion

If the fall of empires was a time of massive political disruption, it also ushered in a period of cultural diffusion, an expansion of what had already blossomed in the broad region. Even though empires expired, many small kingdoms survived, along with a largely shared culture. These small states and local societies had learned much from the great powers, but they nonetheless retained their own lore and native traditions, which they passed on to their neighbors, thus diffusing a Near Eastern culture that was slowly becoming common in nature. The best-known examples can be found along the coast of the eastern Mediterranean, where various peoples—some of them newcomers such as the Philistines—created homes and petty kingdoms in Phoenicia and Palestine (see Map 2.1).

• *How did Egypt pass on its heritage to its African neighbors and how did new cultures develop?*

Online Study Center

This icon will direct you to interactive activities and study materials on the website **college.hmco.com/pic/mckaywest9e**

MAP 2.1 Small Kingdoms of the Near East This map illustrates the political fragmentation of the Near East after the great wave of invasions that occurred during the thirteenth century B.C.

Online Study Center **Improve Your Grade**
Interactive Map: Small Kingdoms of the Near East

The End of Egyptian Power

The invasions of the Sea Peoples brought the great days of Egyptian power to an end. The long wars against invaders weakened and impoverished Egypt, causing political upheaval and economic chaos. One scribe left behind a somber portrait of stunned and leaderless Egypt:

The land of Egypt was abandoned and every man was a law to himself. During many years there was no leader who could speak for others. Central government lapsed, small officials and headmen took over the whole land. Any man, great or small, might kill his neighbor. In the distress and vacuum that followed . . . men banded together to plunder one another. They treated the gods no better than men, and cut off the temple revenues.[1]

No longer able to dream of foreign conquests, Egypt looked to its own security from foreign invasion. Egyptians suffered four hundred years of political fragmentation, a new dark age known to Egyptian specialists as the Third Intermediate Period (eleventh–seventh centuries B.C.). (See the feature "Individuals in Society: Wen-Amon.")

In southern Egypt, meanwhile, the pharaoh's decline opened the way to the energetic Nubians, who extended their authority northward throughout the Nile Valley. Since the imperial days of the Eighteenth Dynasty (see pages 24–26), the Nubians, too, had adopted many features of Egyptian culture. Now Nubian kings and aristo-

Egyptian Plowing Despite Egyptian political defeat, ordinary life went on as usual. Here a farmer and his pair of oxen still plow the field as before. His wife follows behind sowing seeds, preparing for the new harvest. *(Deir el-Medina, Thebes/The Bridgeman Art Library)*

crats embraced Egyptian culture wholesale. Thus the Nubians and the Libyans repeated an old Near Eastern phenomenon: new peoples conquered old centers of political and military power but were assimilated into the older culture.

The reunification of Egypt occurred late and unexpectedly. With Egypt distracted and disorganized by foreign invasions, an independent African state, the kingdom of Kush, grew up in the region of modern Sudan with its capital at Nepata. Like the Libyans, the Kushites worshiped Egyptian gods and used Egyptian hieroglyphs. In the eighth century B.C. their king, Piankhy, swept through the entire Nile Valley from Nepata in the south to the delta in the north. United once again, Egypt enjoyed a brief period of peace during which Egyptians continued to assimilate their conquerors. Nonetheless, reunification of the realm did not lead to a new Egyptian empire.

Yet Egypt's legacy to its African neighbors remained vibrant and rich. By trading and exploring southward along the coast of the Red Sea, the Egyptians introduced

Chronology

ca 1100–653 B.C.	Third Intermediate Period in Egypt
ca 1100–400 B.C.	Era of the prophets in Israel
ca 1025–925 B.C.	United Hebrew kingdom
950–730 B.C.	Movement of new peoples into Egypt
ca 950–500 B.C.	Beginning of the Hebrew Bible
ca 900–612 B.C.	Assyrian Empire
ca 900–550 B.C.	Phoenician seafaring and trading in the Mediterranean
ca 710–550 B.C.	Creation of the Persian Empire
ca 600–500 B.C.	Spread of Zoroastrianism
586–538 B.C.	Babylonian Captivity of the Hebrews
ca 550–513 B.C.	Expansion of Persian trade from western Asia to India

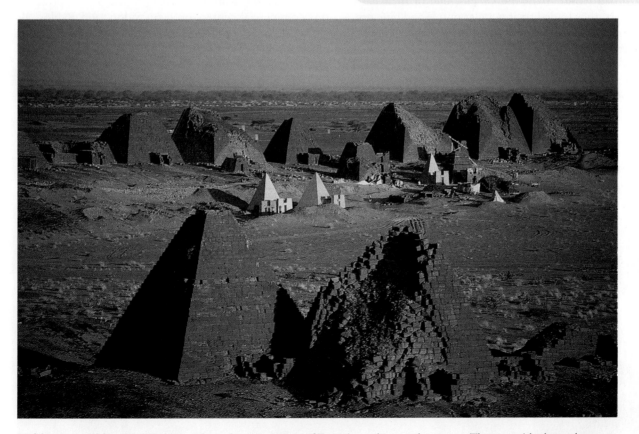

Nubian Pyramids The Nubians adopted many aspects of Egyptian culture and customs. The pyramids shown here are not as magnificent as their Egyptian predecessors, but they served the same purpose of honoring the dead king. Their core was constructed of bricks, which were then covered with stone blocks. At the doors of the pyramids stood monumental gates to the interiors of the tombs. *(Michael Yamashita)*

their goods and ideas as far south as the land of Punt, probably a region on the Somali coast. Egypt was the primary civilizing force in Nubia, which became another version of the pharaoh's realm, complete with royal pyramids and Egyptian deities. Egyptian religion penetrated as far south as Ethiopia.

The Rise of Phoenicia

One of the sturdy peoples who rose to prominence were the Phoenicians, Semitic-speakers who had long inhabited several cities along the coast of modern Lebanon. Although they had lived during the great days of the Hittites and Egyptians, in this period the Phoenicians came into their own. Fully independent, they put their freedom to excellent use. Unlike the Philistine newcomers, who turned from seafaring to farming, the Phoenicians took to the sea. They were master shipbuilders, their stout ships able to face the hardships of the Mediterranean. They became the seaborne merchants of their broad world. With the Greeks, one of their early customers, they traded their popular purple and blue textiles, from which originated their Greek name, Phoenicians, meaning **"Purple People."**

The growing success of the Phoenicians, combined with peace in the Near East, brought them prosperity. In addition to textiles and purple dye, they began to manufacture goods for export, such as metal tools, weapons, and cooking ware. They also expanded their trade to Egypt, where they mingled with other local traders. Egypt, however, simply opened still wider horizons. They struck out along the coast of North Africa to establish new markets in places where they encountered little competition. This route soon took them to Carthage, meaning "New City" in Phoenician, which prospered to become the leading city in the western Mediterranean. Although the Phoenicians did not found colonies, as did the later Greeks (see page 66), they planted trading posts and small farming communities along the coast. From them they shared the vital culture of the more developed Near East with less urbanized peoples. Yet they did not impose their culture, preferring instead to let the natives adopt whatever they found desirable. In this peaceful fashion the Phoenicians spread their trade and something of their customs. But they did so as merchants, not missionaries. Their trade routes eventually took them to the far western Mediterranean and beyond to the Atlantic Ocean.

Phoenician culture was urban, based on the prosperous commercial centers of Tyre, Sidon, and Byblos, all cities still thriving today. The Phoenicians' overwhelming cultural achievement was the development of an alphabet (see Figure 2.1): they, unlike other literate peoples, used one letter to designate one sound, a system that vastly simplified writing and reading. The Greeks modified this alphabet and then used it to write their own language.

Phoenician Ships   These small ships seem too frail to breast the waves. Yet Phoenician mariners routinely sailed them, loaded with their cargoes, to the far ports of the Mediterranean. *(British Museum/Michael Holford)*

Individuals in Society

Wen-Amon

Surprising as it may sound, the life of a bureaucrat is not always easy. Wen-Amon, an official of the temple of Amon-Ra at Karnak in Egypt, learned that on an authorized mission to Phoenicia. He left his own narrative of his travels, which date to sometime in the eleventh century B.C. Egypt, the shattered kingdom, could no longer exert the authority that it had enjoyed under the pharaohs of the New Kingdom. Despite this political disruption, Egyptian officials continued to expect the traditional respect of the people whom they called "Asiatics." These Asiatics, however, had begun to doubt the power of Egypt and expressed their independence by openly opposing its authority.

Wen-Amon personally experienced this changed atmosphere when he was sent to Byblos in Phoenicia to obtain lumber for Amon-Ra's ceremonial barge. Wen-Amon's detailed account of his experiences comes in the form of an official report to the chief priest of the temple.

Entrusted with ample funds in silver to pay for the lumber, Wen-Amon set out on his voyage. He docked at Dor, in modern Israel, which was independent of the pharaoh, but the local prince received him graciously. While his ship was at anchor, one of Wen-Amon's own sailors vanished with the silver. Wen-Amon immediately reported the robbery to the prince and demanded that he investigate the theft. Wen-Amon pointed out that the silver belonged to Amon-Ra and the great men of Egypt. The prince flatly told Wen-Amon that he did not care whether Wen-Amon and the others were important men. He pointed out that an Egyptian, one of Wen-Amon's own men, had stolen the silver. It was not the prince's problem. No earlier Asian prince would have dared speak to a high Egyptian official in such terms.

Although rebuffed, Wen-Amon found a ship from Byblos and robbed it of an equivalent amount of silver. When he left Dor and entered the harbor of Byblos, the prince there, who had learned of the theft, ordered him to leave. For twenty-nine days there was an impasse. Each day that Wen-Amon remained, the prince told him to get out, but respect both for the great days of Egypt and for Amon-Ra kept the prince from laying hands on Wen-Amon. Finally, the prince sent for Wen-Amon and asked for his papers. A heated argument ensued, with the prince shouting, "I am not your servant. I am not the servant of him who sent you either." Then he asked Wen-Amon what silly voyage he was

making. By this time the Egyptian was greatly annoyed, and he reminded the prince of the greatness of Amon-Ra. He flatly stated that unless the prince honored the great god, he and his land would have neither health nor prosperity. When the two calmed down, the prince agreed to send the timber to Egypt.

After the timber was loaded aboard his ship, Wen-Amon saw eleven enemy ships entering the harbor. They anchored, and those in charge reported to the prince of Byblos that they had come for the Egyptians. He refused to hand them over, saying that he would never arrest a messenger of Amon-Ra. He agreed, however, to send Wen-Amon away first and allow the enemy ships to pursue the Egyptians. Stormy seas blew the Egyptian ship into Hittite territory. When Wen-Amon landed there, Queen Heteb granted him protection and asylum.

The papyrus breaks off at this point, but it is obvious that Wen-Amon weathered his various storms to return safely to Egypt. The document illustrates the presumption of power by Wen-Amon and his bluster at the lack of respect shown him. It also shows how Egypt's neighbors no longer feared Egyptian power. Finally, it illustrates the impact of Egyptian culture and religion on the peoples living along the coast of the Levant. Although Egyptian political power was in eclipse, its cultural legacy endured.

The essentials of Egyptian writing: a sheet of papyrus, a stylus or pen, an ink well.
(Réunion des Musées Nationaux/Art Resource, NY)

Questions for Analysis

1. What do Wen-Amon's experiences tell us about political conditions in the eastern Mediterranean?
2. Since Wen-Amon could no longer depend on the majesty of Egypt for respect, how did he fulfill his duty?

Online Study Center   **Improve Your Grade**
Going Beyond Individuals in Society

HIEROGLYPHIC	REPRESENTS	UGARITIC	PHOENICIAN	GREEK	ROMAN
	Throw stick	T		Γ	G
	Man with raised arms			E	E
	Basket with handle			K	K
	Water			M	M
	Snake			N	N
	Eye		O	O	O
	Mouth		?	Π	P
	Head		9	P	R
	Pool with lotus flowers		W	Σ	S
	House		9	B	B
	Ox-head		K	A	A

FIGURE 2.1 Origins of the Alphabet   List of Roman, hieroglyphic, Ugaritic, Phoenician, and Greek sign forms. *(Source: A. B. Knapp,* The History and Culture of Ancient Western Asia and Egypt, *Dorsey Press, Chicago, 1988, p. 191. Reprinted by permission of Wadsworth, a division of Thomson Learning, www.thomsonrights.com)*

The Children of Israel

The fall of the Hittite Empire and Egypt's collapse created a vacuum of power in the western Near East that allowed for the rise of numerous small states. South of Phoenicia arose a small kingdom, the land of the ancient Jews or Hebrews. It is difficult to say precisely who the Hebrews were and what brought them to this area, because virtually the only source for much of their history is the Bible, which is essentially a religious document. Even though it contains much historical material, it also contains many Hebrew myths and legends. Moreover, it was compiled at different times, with the earliest parts dating to between about 950 and 800 B.C.

Earlier Mesopotamian and Egyptian sources refer to people called the **Hapiru,** which seems to mean homeless, independent **nomads.** These nomads led roaming lives, always in search of pasturage for their flocks. According to Hebrew tradition, the followers of Abraham migrated from Mesopotamia, but Egyptian documents record Hapiru already in Syria and Palestine in the second millennium B.C. The Hebrews were probably a part of them. Together with other seminomadic peoples, they

probably migrated into the Nile Delta seeking good land. According to the Bible the Egyptians enslaved them. One group, however, under the leadership of Moses, perhaps a semimythical figure, left Egypt in what the Hebrews remembered as the Exodus. From Egypt they wandered in the Sinai Peninsula until they settled in Palestine in the thirteenth century B.C.

In Palestine the Hebrews encountered the Philistines; the Amorites, relatives of Hammurabi's Babylonians; and the Semitic-speaking Canaanites. Despite numerous wars, contact between the Hebrews and their new neighbors was not always hostile. The Hebrews freely mingled with the Canaanites, and some went so far as to worship **Baal,** an ancient Semitic fertility god represented as a golden calf. Archaeological research supports the biblical account of these developments. In 1990 an expedition sponsored by Harvard University discovered a statue of a golden calf in its excavations of Ashkelon in modern Israel. Despite the anger expressed in the Bible over Hebrew worship of Baal, there is nothing surprising about the phenomenon. Once again, newcomers adapted themselves to the culture of an older, well-established people.

The greatest danger to the Hebrews came from the Philistines, whose superior technology and military organization at first made them invincible. In Saul (ca 1000 B.C.), a farmer of the tribe of Benjamin, the Hebrews found a champion and a spirited leader. In the biblical account Saul carried the war to the Philistines, often without success. Yet in the meantime he established a monarchy over the twelve Hebrew tribes.

Saul's work was carried on by David of Bethlehem, who in his youth had followed Saul into battle against the Philistines. Through courage and cunning, David pushed back the Philistines and waged war against his other neighbors. To give his kingdom a capital, he captured the city of Jerusalem, which he enlarged, fortified, and made the religious and political center of his realm. David's military successes won the Hebrews unprecedented security, and his forty-year reign was a period of vitality and political consolidation. His work in consolidating the monarchy and enlarging the kingdom paved the way for his son Solomon.

Solomon (ca 965–925 B.C.) applied his energies to creating a nation out of a collection of tribes ruled by a king. He divided the kingdom into twelve territorial districts, cutting across the old tribal borders. To bring his kingdom up to the level of its more sophisticated neighbors, he set about a building program to make Israel a respectable Near Eastern state. Work was begun on a magnificent temple in Jerusalem and on cities, palaces, fortresses, and roads. Solomon dedicated the temple in grand style and made it the home of the Ark of the Covenant, the cherished chest that contained the holiest of Hebrew religious articles. The temple in Jerusalem was intended to be the religious heart of the kingdom and the symbol of Hebrew unity. Solomon turned a rude kingdom into a state with broad commercial horizons and greater knowledge of the outside world. At his death, the Hebrews broke into two political halves (see Map 2.1). The northern part of the kingdom of David and Solomon became Israel, with its capital at Samaria. The southern half was Judah, and Jerusalem remained its center. With polit-

ical division went a religious rift: Israel, the northern kingdom, established rival sanctuaries for gods other than Yahweh. The Hebrew nation was divided, but at least it was divided into two far more sophisticated political units than before the time of Solomon. Nonetheless, war soon broke out between them, as recorded in the Bible. Unexpected and independent evidence of this warfare came to light in August 1993, when an Israeli archaeologist found an inscription that refers to the "House of David," the royal line of Israel. The stone celebrates an Israelite victory from the early ninth century B.C. This discovery is the first mention of King David's royal family outside the Bible and helps confirm the biblical account of the fighting between the two kingdoms.

Eventually, the northern kingdom of Israel was wiped out by the Assyrians, but the southern kingdom of Judah survived numerous calamities until the Babylonians crushed it in 587 B.C. The survivors were sent into exile in Babylonia, a period commonly known as the **Babylonian Captivity.** In 538 B.C. the Persians, under their king Cyrus the Great, permitted some forty thousand exiles to return to Jerusalem. During and especially after the

The Golden Calf According to the Hebrew Bible, Moses descended from Mount Sinai, where he had received the Ten Commandments, to find the Hebrews worshiping a golden calf, which was against Yahweh's laws. In July 1990 an American archaeological team found this model of a gilded calf inside a pot. The figurine, which dates to about 1550 B.C., is strong evidence for the existence of the cult represented by the calf in Palestine. (*Courtesy of the Leon Levy Expedition to Ashkelon. Photo: Carl Andrews*)

Babylonian Captivity, the exiles redefined their beliefs and practices and thus established what they believed was the law of Yahweh. Those who lived by these precepts can be called *Jews*.

- *How did the Hebrew state evolve, and what was daily life like in Hebrew society? What forces helped shape Hebrew religious thought, still influential in today's world?*

The Evolution of Jewish Religion

Hand in hand with their political evolution from fierce nomads to urban dwellers, the Hebrews were evolving spiritual ideas that still permeate Western society. Their chief literary product, the Hebrew Bible, has fundamentally influenced both Christianity and Islam and still exerts a compelling force on the modern world.

Online Study Center **Improve Your Grade**
Primary Source: "In the Beginning . . .": The Hebrews Explain Creation

Fundamental to an understanding of the Jewish religion is the concept of the **Covenant,** a formal agreement between Yahweh and the Hebrew people. According to the Bible, the god **Yahweh,** who in medieval Latin became "Jehovah," appeared to Moses on Mount Sinai. There Yahweh made a covenant with the Hebrews that was in fact a contract: if the Hebrews worshiped Yahweh as their only god, he would consider them his chosen people and protect them from their enemies. The Hebrews believed that Yahweh had led them out of bondage in Egypt and had helped them conquer their new land, the Promised Land. In return, the Hebrews worshiped Yahweh alone and obeyed his Ten Commandments, an ethical code of conduct revealed to them by Moses.

Online Study Center **Improve Your Grade**
Primary Source: Moses Descends Mount Sinai with the Ten Commandments

Unlike Akhenaten's monotheism, Hebrew monotheism became the religion of a whole people, deeply felt and cherished. Some might fall away from Yahweh's worship, and various holy men had to exhort the Hebrews to honor the Covenant, but on the whole the people clung to Yahweh. Yet the Hebrews did not consider it their duty to spread the belief in the one god, as later Christians did. As the chosen people, their chief duty was to maintain the worship of Yahweh as he demanded. That worship was embodied in the Ten Commandments, which forbade the Hebrews to steal, murder, lie, or commit adultery. The Covenant was a constant force in He-

brew life. (See the feature "Listening to the Past: The Covenant Between Yahweh and the Hebrews" on pages 54–55.)

From the Ten Commandments evolved Hebrew law, a code of law and custom originating with Moses and built on by priests and prophets. The earliest part of this code, the **Torah** or Mosaic law, was often as harsh as Hammurabi's code, which had a powerful impact on it. Later tradition, largely the work of prophets who lived from the eleventh to the fifth centuries B.C., put more emphasis on righteousness than on retribution.

The uniqueness of the Hebrews' religion can be seen by comparing the essence of Hebrew monotheism with the religious outlook of the Mesopotamians. Whereas the Mesopotamians considered their gods capricious, the Hebrews knew what Yahweh expected. The Hebrews believed that their god would protect them and make them prosper if they obeyed his commandments. Their devotion to Yahweh also influenced their attitude toward magic. The Jews strenuously condemned everyone and everything connected with invoking the intervention of forces from the other world. They felt that magicians, witches, astrologers, and soothsayers harmfully and wrongly usurped powers that properly belonged to Yahweh. The Mesopotamians, however, accepted magic as a natural part of their religious life. The Mesopotamians thought human beings insignificant compared to the gods, so insignificant that the gods might even be indifferent to them. The Hebrews, too, considered themselves puny in comparison with Yahweh. Yet they were Yahweh's chosen people, whom he had promised never to abandon. Finally, though the Mesopotamians believed that the gods generally preferred good to evil, their religion did not demand ethical conduct. The Hebrews could please their god only by living up to high moral standards as well as worshiping him.

Yahweh is a single god, not surrounded by lesser gods and goddesses; there is thus no female divinity in Judaism, though occasionally aspects of God are described in feminine terms, such as Sophia, the wisdom of God. Though Yahweh is conceptualized as masculine, he did not have sexual relations as Mesopotamian, Egyptian, and Greek male deities did, so that his masculinity was spiritualized, and human sexual relations were a source of ritual impurity. Despite this, sex itself was basically good because it was part of Yahweh's creation, and the bearing of children was seen in some ways as a religious function. In the codes of conduct written down in the Hebrew Bible—which Christians adopted and later termed the "Old Testament" to parallel specific Christian writings termed the "New Testament"—sex between a married woman and a man not her husband was termed an "abomination," as were incest and sex between men. Men were free to have sexual relations with concubines, servants, and slaves, along with their wives. The possibility of divorce was also gender-specific: a man could divorce his wife unilaterally (though community norms frowned on divorce for frivolous reasons), but a wife could not divorce her husband, even for desertion. In general Judaism frowned on celibacy—"chastity" is defined in Jewish law as refraining from illicit sexual activities, not from sex itself—and almost all major Jewish thinkers and rabbis were married.

Religious leaders were important in Judaism, but not as important as the written texts they interpreted; these texts came to be regarded as the word of Yahweh and thus had a status other writings did not. The most important task for observant Jews was studying religious texts, an activity limited to men until the twentieth century. Women were obliged to provide for men's physical needs so that they could study, which often meant that Jewish women were more active economically than their contemporaries of other religions. Women's religious rituals tended to center on the home, while men's centered on the temple. The reverence for a particular text or group of texts was passed down from Judaism to the other Western monotheistic religions that grew from it, Christianity and Islam, which gave (and continue to give) the statements about gender in these texts particular power.

Family Life in Israel

The nomadic Hebrews first entered modern Palestine as tribes, numerous families who thought of themselves as all related to one another. At first, good farmland, pastureland, and water spots were held in common by the tribe. Common use of land was—and still is—characteristic of nomadic peoples. Typically each family or group of families in the tribe drew lots every year to determine who worked which fields. But as formerly nomadic peoples turned increasingly to settled agriculture, communal use of land gave way to family ownership. In this respect the experience of the ancient Hebrews seems typical of that of many early peoples. Slowly the shift from nomad to farmer affected far more than just how people fed themselves. Family relationships reflected evolving circumstances. With the transition to settled agriculture, the tribe gradually became less important than the extended family. As in Mesopotamia, land was handed down within families, generally from father to son.

The development of urban life among the Jews created new economic opportunities, especially in crafts and trades. People specialized in certain occupations, such as milling flour, baking bread, making pottery, weaving, and carpentry. All these crafts were family trades. Sons worked with their father, daughters with their mother. If the business prospered, the family might be assisted by a few paid workers or slaves. The practitioners of a craft usually lived in a particular section of town, a custom still prevalent in the Middle East today. Commerce and trade developed later than crafts. Trade with neighboring countries was handled by foreigners, usually Phoenicians. Jews dealt mainly in local trade, and in most instances craftsmen and farmers sold directly to their customers.

These social and economic developments also left their mark on daily life by prompting the compilation of two significant works, the Torah and the Talmud. The Torah is basically the Mosaic law, or the first five books of the Bible. The Talmud is a later work composed during the period between the Roman destruction of the second temple in A.D. 70 and the Arab conquest of A.D. 636. The **Talmud** records civil and ceremonial law and Jewish legend. The dietary rules of the Jews provide an excellent example of both the relationship between the Torah and the Talmud and their effect on ordinary life and culture. According to the Torah, people were not to eat meat that they found in the field. This very sensible prohibition protected them from eating dangerous food. Yet if meat from the countryside could not be eaten, some rules were needed for meat in the city. The solution found in the Talmud was a set of regulations for the proper way to conduct ritual slaughter and to prepare food. Together these two works regulated and codified Jewish dietary customs.

Assyria, the Military Monarchy

Small kingdoms like those of the Phoenicians and the Hebrews could exist only in the absence of a major power. The beginning of the ninth century B.C. saw the rise of such a power: the Assyrians of northern Mesopotamia, whose chief capital was at Nineveh on the Tigris River. The Assyrians were a Semitic-speaking people heavily influenced, like so many other peoples of the Near East, by the Mesopotamian culture of Babylon to the south. They were also one of the most warlike peoples in history, largely because throughout their history they were threatened by neighboring folk. Living in an open, exposed land, the Assyrians experienced frequent and devastating attacks by the wild, war-loving tribes to their north and east and by the Babylonians to the south. The constant threat to survival experienced by the

Assyrians promoted political cohesion and military might. Yet they were also a mercantile people who had long pursued commerce with both the Babylonians in the south and other peoples in the north.

• *What enabled the Assyrians to overrun their neighbors, and how did their cruelty finally cause their undoing?*

The Power of Assyria

For over two hundred years the Assyrians labored to dominate the Near East. In 859 B.C. the new Assyrian king, Shalmaneser, unleashed the first of a long series of attacks on the peoples of Syria and Palestine. Year after relentless year, Assyrian armies hammered at the peoples of the West. These ominous events inaugurated two turbulent centuries marked by Assyrian military campaigns, constant efforts by Syria and the two Jewish kingdoms to maintain or recover their independence, and eventual Assyrian conquest of Babylonia and northern Egypt. In addition, periodic political instability occurred in Assyria itself, which prompted stirrings of freedom throughout the Near East.

Under the Assyrian kings Tiglath-pileser III (774–727 B.C.) and Sargon II (r. 721–705 B.C.), both mighty warriors, the Near East trembled as never before under the

blows of Assyrian armies. The Assyrians stepped up their attacks on Anatolia, Syria, and Palestine. The kingdom of Israel and many other states fell; others, like the kingdom of Judah, became subservient to the warriors from the Tigris. In 717 to 716 B.C., Sargon led his army in a sweeping attack along the Philistine coast, where he defeated the pharaoh. Sargon also lashed out at Assyria's traditional enemies to the north and then turned south against a renewed threat in Babylonia. By means of almost constant warfare, Tiglath-pileser and Sargon carved out an Assyrian empire that stretched from east and north of the Tigris River to central Egypt (see Map 2.2). Revolt against the Assyrians inevitably promised the rebels bloody battles and cruel sieges.

Though atrocity and terrorism struck unspeakable fear into Assyria's subjects, Assyria's success was actually due to sophisticated, farsighted, and effective military organization. By Sargon's time the Assyrians had invented the mightiest military machine the ancient Near East had ever seen. The mainstay of the Assyrian army was the infantryman armed with spear and sword and protected by helmet and armor. The Assyrian army also featured archers, some on foot, others on horseback, still others in chariots—the latter ready to wield lances once they had expended their supply of arrows. Some infantry archers wore heavy armor. These soldiers served as a primitive

Surrender of the Jews
The Jewish king Jahu finally surrendered to the Assyrians. Here his envoy kneels before the Assyrian king Shalmaneser III in total defeat. Although the Assyrian king treated Jahu well, his people were led off into slavery. *(British Museum/Michael Holford)*

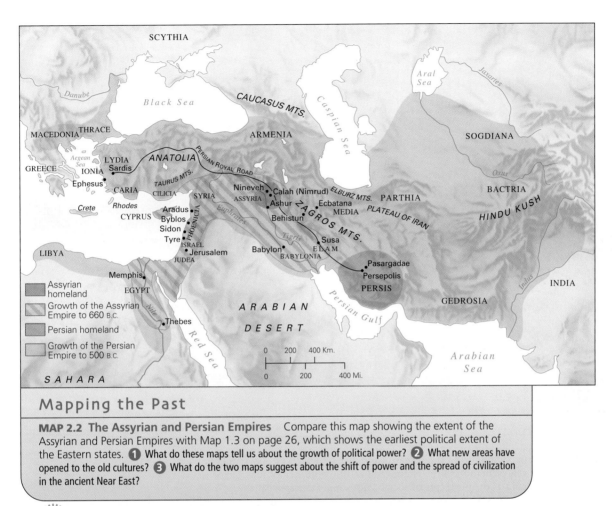

Mapping the Past

MAP 2.2 The Assyrian and Persian Empires   Compare this map showing the extent of the Assyrian and Persian Empires with Map 1.3 on page 26, which shows the earliest political extent of the Eastern states. ❶ What do these maps tell us about the growth of political power? ❷ What new areas have opened to the old cultures? ❸ What do the two maps suggest about the shift of power and the spread of civilization in the ancient Near East?

Online Study Center   **Improve Your Grade** Interactive Map: Assyrian and Persian Empires

field artillery, whose job was to sweep the enemy's walls of defenders so that others could storm the defenses. Slingers also served as artillery in pitched battles. For mobility on the battlefield, the Assyrians organized a corps of chariots.

Assyrian military genius was remarkable for the development of a wide variety of siege machinery and techniques, including excavation to undermine city walls and battering rams to knock down walls and gates. Never before in the Near East had anyone applied such technical knowledge to warfare. The Assyrians even invented the concept of a corps of engineers, who bridged rivers with pontoons or provided soldiers with inflatable skins for swimming. And the Assyrians knew how to coordinate their efforts, both in open battle and

in siege warfare. King Sennacherib's account of his siege of Jerusalem in 701 B.C. is a vivid portrait of the Assyrian war machine:

As to Hezekiah, the Jew, he did not submit to my yoke, I laid siege to 46 of his strong cities, walled forts and to the countless small villages in their vicinity, and conquered them by means of well-stamped earth-ramps, and battering rams brought thus near to the walls combined with the attack by foot soldiers, using mines, breaches as well as sapper work. . . . Himself I made prisoner in Jerusalem, his royal residence, like a bird in a cage. I surrounded him with earthwork in order to molest those who were leaving his city's gate.[2]

Royal Lion Hunt This wall painting from the seventh century B.C. depicts an Assyrian king frightening a lion, a typical representation of the energy and artistic brilliance of Assyrian artists. The lion hunt signified the king as the protector of society, not simply as a sportsman. *(Louvre/Réunion des Musées Nationaux/Art Resource, NY)*

Online Study Center **Improve Your Grade**
Primary Source: Jerusalem Besieged: The Assyrian King Sennacherib's Account of Events

The Jews recorded this same incident, and historians find it interesting to see how two different peoples interpreted the same event. The Jews ignored political and military events and insisted that the siege of Jerusalem resulted from Hezekiah's disbelief that Yahweh could repel the Assyrian invasion. For the Assyrians the conquest was proof of their military superiority. For the Jews it stood as a symbol of the fate of those who mistrusted their god.

Assyrian Rule and Culture

Not only did the Assyrians know how to win battles, but they also knew how to use their victories. As early as the reign of Tiglath-pileser III, the Assyrian kings began to organize their conquered territories into an empire. The lands closest to Assyria became provinces governed by Assyrian officials. Kingdoms beyond the provinces were not annexed but became dependent states that followed Assyria's lead. The Assyrian king chose their rulers either by regulating the succession of native kings or by supporting native kings who appealed to him. Against more distant states the Assyrian kings waged frequent war in order to conquer them outright or make the dependent states secure.

In the seventh century B.C. Assyrian power seemed firmly established. Yet the downfall of Assyria was swift and complete. Babylon finally won its independence in 626 B.C. and joined forces with a newly aggressive people, the Medes, an Indo-European-speaking folk from Iran. Together the Babylonians and the Medes destroyed the Assyrian Empire in 612 B.C., paving the way for the rise of the Persians. The Hebrew prophet Nahum spoke for many when he asked: "Nineveh is laid waste: who will bemoan her?"[3] Their cities destroyed and their power shattered, the Assyrians disappeared from history, remembered only as a cruel people of the Old Testament who oppressed the Hebrews. Two hundred years later, when the Greek adventurer and historian Xenophon passed by the ruins of Nineveh, he marveled at the extent of the former city but knew nothing of the Assyrians. The glory of their empire was forgotten.

Yet modern archaeology has brought the Assyrians out of obscurity. In 1839 the intrepid English archaeologist and traveler A. H. Layard began the most noteworthy excavations of Nineveh, then a mound of debris beside the Tigris. His findings electrified the world. Layard's workers unearthed masterpieces, including monumental sculpted figures—huge winged bulls, human-headed lions, and sphinxes—as well as brilliantly sculpted friezes. Equally valuable were the numerous Assyrian cuneiform documents, which ranged from royal accounts of mighty military campaigns to simple letters by common people.

Among the most renowned of Layard's finds were the Assyrian palace reliefs, whose number has been increased by the discoveries of twentieth-century archaeologists. Assyrian kings delighted in scenes of war, which their artists depicted in graphic detail. By the time of Ashurbanipal (r. 668–633 B.C.), Assyrian artists had hit on the idea of portraying a series of episodes—in fact, a visual narrative of events that had actually taken place. Scene followed scene in a continuous frieze, so that the viewer could follow the progress of a military campaign from the time the army marched out until the enemy was conquered.

Assyrian art fared better than Assyrian military power. The techniques of Assyrian artists influenced the Persians, who adapted them to gentler scenes. In fact, many Assyrian innovations, military and political as well as artistic, were taken over wholesale by the Persians. Although the memory of Assyria was hateful throughout the Near East, the fruits of Assyrian organizational genius helped enable the Persians to bring peace and stability to the same regions where Assyrian armies had spread terror.

The Empire of the Persian Kings

Like the Hittites before them, the Iranians were Indo-Europeans from central Europe and southern Russia. They migrated into the land to which they have given their name, the area between the Caspian Sea and the Persian Gulf. Like the Hittites, they then fell under the spell of the more sophisticated cultures of their Mesopotamian neighbors. Yet the Iranians went on to create one of the greatest empires of antiquity, one that encompassed scores of peoples and cultures. The Persians, the most important of the Iranian peoples, had a farsighted conception of empire. Though as conquerors they willingly used force to accomplish their ends, they normally preferred to depend on diplomacy to rule. They usually respected their subjects and allowed them to practice their native customs and religions. Thus the Persians gave the Near East both political unity and cultural diversity. Never before had Near Eastern people viewed empire in such intelligent and humane terms.

● *How did Iranian nomads build the Persian Empire, and what sort of life did their policies create for the Near East?*

The Land of the Medes and Persians

Persia—the modern country of Iran—is a stark land of towering mountains and flaming deserts with a broad central plateau in the heart of the country (see Map 2.2). Between the Tigris-Euphrates Valley in the west and the Indus Valley in the east rises an immense plateau that cuts the interior from the sea. Iran's geographical position and topography explain its traditional role as the highway between East and West. Throughout history wild, nomadic tribes migrating from the broad steppes of Russia and Central Asia have streamed into Iran. Confronting the uncrossable salt deserts, most of them have turned either eastward or westward, moving until reaching the advanced and wealthy urban centers of Mesopotamia and India. Where cities emerged along the natural lines of east-west communications, Iran became the area in which nomads met urban dwellers, an area of unique significance for the civilizations of both East and West.

The Iranians entered this land around 1000 B.C. as part of the vast movement of Indo-European-speaking peoples whose wanderings took them from Europe to India (see page 26). These Iranians were nomads who migrated with their flocks and herds. They were also horse breeders, and the horse gave them a decisive military advantage over the prehistoric peoples of Iran. These centuries of immigration saw constant cultural interchange between conquering newcomers and conquered natives.

Two groups of Iranians gradually began coalescing into larger units. The Persians settled in Persia, the modern region of Fars in southern Iran. Their kinsmen, the Medes, occupied Media in the north, with their capital at Ecbatana, the modern Hamadan. Even though they were distracted by grave pressure from their neighbors, the

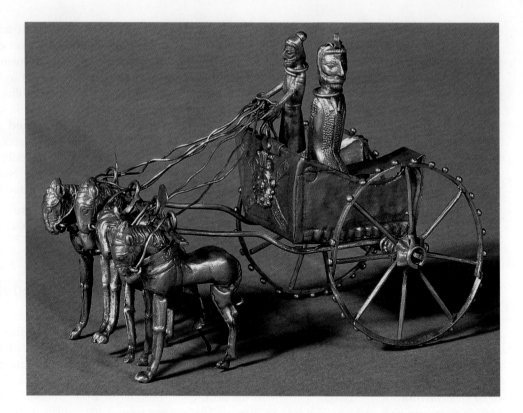

Persian Charioteers
Here are two Persians riding in a chariot pulled by four horses. The chariot is simple in construction but elegant in ornamentation. The harness of the horses is worked in elaborate and accurate detail. This chariot was used for ceremonial purposes, not for warfare. *(Courtesy of the Trustees of the British Museum)*

Medes united under one king around 710 B.C. They next extended their control over the Persians to the south. In 612 B.C. they joined the Babylonians to overthrow the Assyrian Empire. With the rise of the Medes, the balance of power in the Near East shifted for the first time east of Mesopotamia.

The Rise of the Persian Empire (550–540 B.C.)

In 550 B.C. Cyrus the Great (r. 559–530 B.C.), king of the Persians and one of the most remarkable statesmen of antiquity, conquered the Medes as the first step in the creation of one of the greatest empires of the ancient world. He also thought of Iran as a state, a concept that has survived to play its part in the contemporary world. Furthermore, Cyrus held an enlightened view of empire. He appreciated the value of the many far older, more advanced, and more sophisticated civilizations of his new realm. He nurtured and protected them so that conquered peoples continued to enjoy their institutions, religions, languages, and ways of life. His Persian Empire became a political organization sheltering many different civilizations. Consequently, the Persians gave the ancient

Near East more than two hundred years of peace, prosperity, and security.

Having united Iran, Cyrus set out to secure it from hostile neighbors. Turning west, he swept into Anatolia, easily overthrowing the young kingdom of Lydia. Its king Croesus, not only proverbial for his wealth, was also in close touch with the Greeks. Also to his west was Babylonia, enjoying a new period of power after the fall of the Assyrians. To the southwest lay Egypt, still weak and vulnerable. Turning to the east, Cyrus confronted the challenge of tough, mobile nomads capable of massive and destructive incursions deep into Iranian territory.

In a series of major campaigns, Cyrus won control of the west. His defeat of Croesus and his Lydians held lasting significance for Western civilization in that his march took him to the eastern Mediterranean. In the westernmost part of modern Turkey he encountered the Greeks, whose destiny would become deeply entwined with that of the Persians. More immediately important at the time, Cyrus the conqueror demonstrated to the world unmistakable signs of his benevolence. He spared the life of Croesus to serve him as friend and adviser. He allowed the Greeks to live according to their customs, thus making it possible for Greek culture to spread farther inland to the east. Cyrus's humanity likewise extended to the

Jews, whom he found enslaved in Babylonia. He sent them home, returned their sacred objects to them, and rebuilt the temple of Yahweh in Jerusalem. The thankful Jews considered him the shepherd of Yahweh, the lord's anointed. Cyrus's humane policy created a Persian Empire in which the culture and religions of its members were respected and honored. Seldom have conquerors been as wise, sensitive, and farsighted as Cyrus and his Persians.

Thus Spake Zarathustra

Iranian religion was originally simple. **Ahuramazda,** the chief god, was the creator and benefactor of all living creatures. Mithra, the sun-god, whose cult would later spread throughout the Roman Empire, saw to justice and redemption. As in ancient India, fire was a particularly important god. The sacred fire consumed the blood sacrifices that the early Iranians offered to all their deities. Early Iranian religion remained close to nature, unencumbered by ponderous theological beliefs. A priestly class, the **Magi,** developed among the Medes to officiate at sacrifices, chant prayers to the gods, and tend the sacred flame. In time the Iranians built fire temples for their sacrifices and rites.

Around 600 B.C. the religious thinking of Zarathustra—Zoroaster, as he is better known—breathed new meaning into Iranian religion. Zoroaster preached a novel concept of divinity and human life. Life, he taught, is a constant battleground for the two opposing forces of good and evil. Ahuramazda embodied good and truth but was opposed by Ahriman, a hateful spirit who stood for evil and lies. Ahuramazda and Ahriman were locked together in a cosmic battle for the human race, a battle that stretched over thousands of years.

Zoroaster emphasized the individual's responsibility to choose between good and evil. He taught that people possessed the free will to decide between Ahuramazda and Ahriman and that they must rely on their own conscience to guide them through life. Their decisions were crucial, Zoroaster warned, for there would be a time of reckoning. He promised that Ahuramazda would eventually triumph over evil and lies, and that at death each person would stand before the tribunal of good. Ahuramazda, like the Egyptian god Osiris, would judge whether the dead had lived righteously and on that basis would weigh their lives in the balance. In short, Zoroaster taught the concept of a last judgment at which Ahuramazda would decide each person's eternal fate.

In Zoroaster's thought, the last judgment was linked to the notion of a divine kingdom after death for those who had lived according to good and truth. Liars and the wicked, denied this blessed immortality, would be condemned to eternal pain, darkness, and punishment. Thus

Persian Saddle-Cloth   This elaborately painted piece of leather, dating from the fourth or third century B.C., served a ceremonial rather than a practical function. *(The State Hermitage Museum)*

Funeral Pyre of Croesus
This scene, an excellent example of the precision and charm of ancient Greek vase painting, depicts the Lydian king Croesus on his funeral pyre. He pours a libation to the gods, while his slave lights the fire. Herodotus has a happier ending, when he says that Cyrus the Great set fire to the pyre, but that Apollo sent rain to put it out. *(Louvre/Réunion des Musées Nationaux/Art Resource, NY)*

Zoroaster preached a last judgment that led to a heaven or a hell.

Zoroaster's teachings converted Darius (r. 521–486 B.C.), who did not, however, try to impose it on others. Under the protection of the Persian kings **Zoroastrianism** swept through Iran, winning converts and sinking roots that sustained healthy growth for centuries. Zoroastrianism survived the fall of the Persian Empire to influence liberal Judaism, Christianity, and early Islam, largely because of its belief in a just life on earth and a happy afterlife that satisfied the longings of most people. Good behavior in the world, even though unrecognized at the time, would receive ample reward in the hereafter. Evil, no matter how powerful in life, would be punished after death. In some form or another, Zoroastrian concepts still pervade the major religions of the West and every part of the world touched by Islam.

Persia's World Empire

Cyrus's successors rounded out the Persian conquest of the ancient Near East. King Darius and his son Xerxes (r. 486–464 B.C.) reached the high-water mark when they unsuccessfully tried to conquer Greece. The Persians never won a permanent foothold in Europe. Yet Darius carried Persian arms into India. Around 513 B.C.

western India became the satrapy (or province) of Hindush, which included the valley of the Indus River. Thus within thirty-seven years (550–513 B.C.) the Persians transformed themselves from a subject people to the ruler of an empire that included Anatolia, Egypt, Mesopotamia, Iran, and western India. They had created a **world empire** encompassing all the oldest and most honored kingdoms and peoples of the ancient Near East. Never before had this region been united in one such vast political organization (see Map 2.2).

The Persians knew how to preserve the peace they had won on the battlefield. Unlike the Assyrians, they did not resort to royal terrorism to maintain order. Instead, the Persians built an efficient administrative system to govern the empire. They enforced Persian laws that demanded obedience and loyalty from those governed. At the same time their system honored the customs of those governed. The Persians also protected their subjects from foreign invasion and official corruption.

Persian kings took their responsibilities seriously. They established their capital at Persepolis, "the City of the Persians," near modern Schiras, Iran. These kings received reports from their officials and entertained delegations both from their subjects and from foreign powers. From Persepolis they sent directions to the provinces. To do so they maintained a sophisticated system of roads linking the empire. The main highway, the famous **Royal Road,** spanned some 1,677 miles from the Greek city of Ephesus on the coast of Asia Minor to Susa in western Iran. Other roads branched out to link all parts of the empire from the coast of Asia Minor to the valley of the Indus River. This system of communications enabled Persian kings to keep in intimate touch with their subjects and officials. They were thereby able to make the concepts of right, justice, and good government a practical reality.

The Impact of Zoroastrianism The Persian kings embraced Zoroastrianism as the religion of the realm. This rock carving at Behistun records the bond. King Darius I is seen trampling on one rebel with others behind him. Above is the sign of Ahuramazda, the god of truth and guardian of the Persian king. *(Robert Harding World Imagery)*

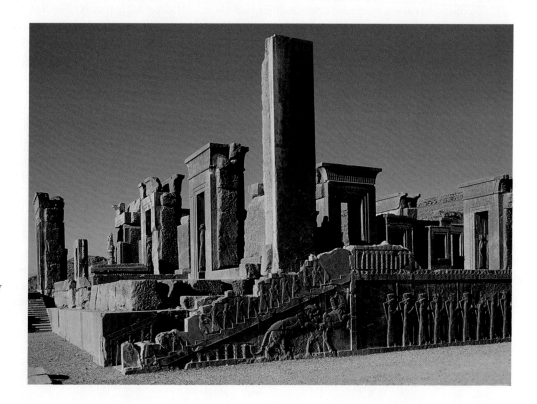

The Royal Palace at Persepolis King Darius began and King Xerxes finished building a grand palace worthy of the glory of the Persian Empire. Pictured here is the monumental audience hall, where the king dealt with ministers of state and foreign envoys. *(George Holton/Photo Researchers)*

Chapter Summary

- *How did Egypt pass on its heritage to its African neighbors and how did new cultures develop?*
- *How did the Hebrew state evolve, and what was daily life like in Hebrew society? What forces helped shape Hebrew religious thought, still influential in today's world?*
- *What enabled the Assyrians to overrun their neighbors, and how did their cruelty finally cause their undoing?*
- *How did Iranian nomads build the Persian Empire, and what sort of life did their policies create for the Near East?*

Online Study Center **ACE the Test**

Key Terms

"Purple People"	Torah
Hapiru	Talmud
nomads	Ahuramazda
Baal	Magi
Babylonian Captivity	Zoroastrianism
Covenant	world empire
Yahweh	Royal Road

Online Study Center **Improve Your Grade** Flashcards

Early civilizations created wealth and stability, but invasions and chaos threatened to destroy it all. Yet both well-established peoples and vigorous newcomers salvaged the best of the past, including many aspects of Egyptian culture. The Phoenicians in particular took advantage of the situation to spread commodities and ideas through trade. Through warfare with their neighbors, the Hebrews created a small kingdom centered on the temple in Jerusalem. Their kingdom was short-lived, but their religious beliefs and written codes of law and custom proved to be long-lasting. Judaism, their monotheistic religion, continues as a vibrant faith today and was an important source for Christianity and Islam.

In this world rose the Assyrians, another Semitic people who had lived on its periphery. They spread their power by brutal conquests. They disrupted life through much of the area, forging an extensive empire ruled by terror. Their enemies finally brought them down, but at least they had provided a modicum of stability to the region.

The Persians assimilated the best of the civilizations that they found around them. Through conquest that was mild compared with that of the Assyrians, they broadened the geographical horizons of the ancient world. Their empire looked west to the Greeks and east to the peoples of the Indus Valley, and they gave the Near East a long period of peace.

Suggested Reading

Alon, Gedaliah. *The Jews in Their Land.* 1989. Covers the Talmudic period.

Boyce, Mary. *Zoroastrianism.* 1979. A sound and readable treatment of the essence of Zoroastrianism.

Edwards, David N. *The Nubian Past.* 2004. Examines the history of Nubia and the Sudan, incorporating archaeological evidence to supplement historical sources.

Frye, Richard N. *History of Ancient Iran.* 1984. A comprehensive survey by one of the leading scholars in the field.

Gates, Charles. *Ancient Cities: The Archaeology of Urban Life in the Ancient Near East and Egypt, Greece, and Rome.* 2003. Provides a survey of ancient life primarily from an archaeological point of view, but one that includes cultural and social interests.

Hoffmeier, James K. *Israel in Egypt: The Evidence for the Authenticity of the Exodus Tradition.* 1997. Discusses evidence for the account in Hebrew Scripture concerning the Exodus.

Markoe, Glenn E. *The Phoenicians.* 2000. A fresh investigation of the Phoenicians at home and abroad in the western Mediterranean over their long history, with many illustrations.

Meyers, Carol. *Discovering Eve: Ancient Israelite Women in Context*. 1988. Examines the roles of Israelite women.

Morkot, Robert G. *The Black Pharaohs: Egypt's Nubian Rulers*. 2000. Examines the growth of the Kushite kingdom and its rule over pharaonic Egypt in the eighth century B.C.

Niditch, Susan. *Ancient Israelite Religion*. 1997. A brief but broad interpretation of Jewish religious developments.

Pastor, Jack. *Land and Economy in Ancient Palestine*. 1997. Discusses the basics of economic life of the period.

Redford, Donald B. *Egypt, Canaan, and Israel in Ancient Times*. 1992. Presents a study of the political, cultural, and religious relationships among the peoples of Egypt, Assyria, and the Near East during thousands of years of history.

Saggs, H. W. F. *Everyday Life in Babylonia and Assyria,* rev. ed. 1987. Offers a general and well-illustrated survey of Mesopotamian history from 3000 to 300 B.C.

Notes

1. James H. Breasted, *Ancient Records of Egypt,* vol. 4 (Chicago: University of Chicago Press, 1907), para. 398.
2. J. B. Pritchard, ed., *Ancient Near Eastern Texts,* 3d ed. (Princeton, N.J.: Princeton University Press, 1969), p. 288.
3. Nahum 3:7.

Listening to the Past

The Covenant Between Yahweh and the Hebrews

These passages from the Hebrew Bible address two themes important to Hebraic thinking. The first is the meaning of kingship; the second is the nature of the Covenant between the Hebrews and the Lord, Yahweh. The selection also raises the difficult question of how much of the Hebrew Bible can be accepted historically. As we discussed in this chapter, the Hebrew Bible is not a document that we may accept as literal truth, but it does tell us a great deal about the people who created it. From the following passages we may discern what the Hebrews thought about their own past and religion.

The background of the excerpt is a political crisis that has some archaeological support. The war with the Philistines put a huge strain on Hebrew society. The passage below describes an incident when Nahash, the king of the Ammonites, threatens to destroy the Hebrews. New and effective political and military leadership was needed to meet the situation. The elders of the tribes had previously chosen judges to lead the community only in times of crisis. The Hebrews, however, demanded that a kingship be established, even though Yahweh was their king. They turned to Samuel, the last of the judges, who anointed Saul as the first Hebrew king. In this excerpt Samuel reviews the political, military, and religious situation confronting the Hebrews, reminding them of their obligation to honor the Covenant and expressing hesitation in naming a king.

Then Nahash the Ammonite came up and encamped against Jabeshgilead: and all the men of Jabesh said unto Nahash, Make a covenant with us, and we will serve thee. And Nahash the Ammonite answered them, On this condition will I make a covenant with you, that I may thrust out all your right eyes, and lay it for a reproach upon all Israel. And the elders of Jabesh said unto him, Give us seven days' respite, that we may send messengers unto all the coasts of Israel: and then, if there be no man to save us, we will come out to thee.

Then came the messengers to Gibeah of Saul, and told the tidings in the ears of the people: and all the people lifted up their voices, and wept. And, behold, Saul came after the herd out of the field; and Saul said, What aileth the people that they weep? And they told him the tidings of the men of Jabesh. And the Spirit of God came upon Saul when he heard those tidings, and his anger was kindled greatly. And he took a yoke of oxen, and hewed them in pieces, and sent them throughout all the coasts of Israel by the hands of messengers, saying, Whosoever cometh not forth after Saul and after Samuel, so shall it be done unto his oxen. And the fear of the Lord fell on the people, and they came out with one consent. And when he numbered them in Bezek, the children of Israel were three hundred thousand, and the men of Judah thirty thousand. And they said unto the messengers that came, Thus shall ye say unto the men of Jabeshgilead, To morrow, by that time the sun be hot, ye shall have help. And the messengers came and shewed it to the men of Jabesh; and they were glad. Therefore the men of Jabesh said, To morrow we will come out unto you, and ye shall do with us all that seemeth good unto you. And it was so on the morrow, that Saul put the people in three companies; and they came into the midst of the host in the morning watch, and slew the Ammonites until the heat of the day: and it came to pass, that they which remained were scattered, so that two of them were not left together.

And the people said unto Samuel, Who is he that said, Shall Saul reign over us? bring the men, that we may put them to death. And Saul said, There shall not a man be put to death this day: for to day the Lord hath wrought salvation in Israel. Then said Samuel to the people, Come, and let us go to Gilgal, and renew the kingdom there. And all the people went to Gilgal; and there they made Saul king before the Lord in Gilgal; and there they sacrificed sacrifices of peace offerings before the Lord; and there Saul and all the men of Israel rejoiced greatly.

And Samuel said unto all Israel, Behold, I have hearkened unto your voice in all that you said to me, and have made a king over you. And now, behold, the king walks before you; and I am old and gray-headed; and behold, my sons are with you: and I have walked before you from my childhood until this day. Behold, here I am: witness against me before the Lord, and before his anointed: whose ox have I taken? or whose ass have I taken? or whom have I defrauded? whom have I oppressed? or of whose hand have I received any bribe to blind my eyes with it? and I will restore it to you.

And they said, You have not defrauded us, nor oppressed us, neither have you taken anything from any man's hand. And he said to them, the Lord is witness against you, and his anointed is witness this day, that you have not found anything in my hand. And they answered, he is witness. And Samuel said unto the people, It is the Lord that advanced Moses and Aaron, and that brought your fathers up out of the land of Egypt. Now therefore stand still, that I may reason with you before the Lord of all the righteous acts of the Lord, which he did to you and your fathers.

At this point Samuel reminds the Hebrews of their Covenant with Yahweh. He lists the times when they had broken that Covenant, the times when they had served other gods. He also reminds them of Yahweh's punishment for their backsliding. He tells them frankly that they are wrong to demand a king to rule over them, for Yahweh was their lord, god, and king. Nonetheless, Samuel gives way to their demands.

Now therefore behold the king whom you have chosen, and whom you have desired! and behold, the Lord has set a king over you. If you will fear the Lord, and serve him, and obey his voice, and not rebel against the commandment of the Lord, then shall both you and also the king who reigns over you continue following the Lord your God: But if you will not obey the voice of the Lord, but rebel against the commandment of the Lord, then shall the hand of the Lord be against you, as it was against your fathers. Now therefore stand and see this great thing, which the Lord will do before your eyes. Is it not wheat harvest today? I will call to the Lord, and he shall send thunder and rain; that you may perceive and see that your

Ark of the Covenant, depicted in a relief from Capernaum Synagogue, second century A.D. *(Ancient Art & Architecture Collection)*

wickedness is great, which you have done in the sight of the Lord, in asking you a king. So Samuel called to the Lord; and the Lord sent thunder and rain that day: and all the people greatly feared the Lord and Samuel. And all the people said to Samuel, pray for your servants to the Lord your God, so that we will not die: for we have added to all of our sins this evil, to ask us for a king. And Samuel said to the people, Fear not: you have done all this wickedness; yet turn not aside from following the Lord, but serve the Lord with all your heart; And do not turn aside; for then should you go after vain things, which cannot profit nor deliver; for they are vain. For the Lord will not forsake his people for his great name's sake: because it pleases the Lord to make you his people. Moreover, as for me, God forbid that I should sin against the Lord in ceasing to pray for you: but I will teach you the good and the right way: Only fear the Lord, and serve him in truth with all your heart: for consider how great things he has done for you. But if you shall still act wickedly, you will be consumed, both you and your king.

Questions for Analysis

1. How did Samuel explain his anointment of a king?

2. What was Samuel's attitude toward kingship?

3. What were the duties of the Hebrews toward Yahweh?

4. Might those duties conflict with those toward the secular king? If so, in what ways, and how might the Hebrews avoid the conflict?

Source: 1 Samuel 11:1–15; 12:1–7, 13–25. Abridged and adapted from *The Holy Bible,* King James Version.

Dionysos at sea. Dionysos here symbolizes the Greek sense of exploration, independence, and love of life. *(Bildarchiv Preussischer Kulturbesitz/Art Resource, NY)*

CLASSICAL GREECE,
CA 1650–338 B.C.

chapter preview

Hellas: The Land
• *When the Greeks arrived in Hellas, how did they adapt themselves to their new landscape?*

The Polis
• *After the Greeks had established the polis in which they lived their political and social lives, how did they shape it into its several historical forms?*

The Archaic Age (800–500 B.C.)
• *What major developments mark the Archaic Greek period in terms of spread of culture and the growth of cities?*

The Classical Period (500–338 B.C.)
• *How did the Greeks develop their literature, philosophy, religion, and art, and how did war affect this intellectual and social process?*

The Final Act (404–338 B.C.)
• *How did the Greek city-states meet political and military challenges, and how did Macedonia become dominant?*

The rocky peninsula of Greece was the home of the civilization that fundamentally shaped Western civilization. The Greeks were the first to explore most of the questions that continue to concern Western thinkers to this day. Going beyond mythmaking and religion, the Greeks strove to understand, in logical, rational terms, both the universe and the position of men and women in it. The result was the birth of philosophy and science—subjects that were as important to most Greek thinkers as religion. The Greeks speculated on human beings and society and created the very concept of politics.

While the scribes of the ancient Near East produced king lists, the Greeks invented history to record and understand how people and states functioned in time and space. In poetry the Greeks spoke as individuals. In drama they dealt with the grandeur and weakness of humanity and with the demands of society on the individual. The greatest monuments of the Greeks were not temples, statues, or tombs, but profound thoughts set down in terms as fresh and immediate today as they were some 2,400 years ago.

The history of the Greeks is divided into two broad periods: the Hellenic period (the subject of this chapter), roughly the time between the arrival of the Greeks (approximately 2000 B.C.) and the victory over Greece in 338 B.C. by Philip of Macedon; and the Hellenistic period (the subject of Chapter 4), the age beginning with the remarkable reign of Philip's son, Alexander the Great (336–323 B.C.) and ending with the Roman conquest of the Hellenistic East (200–146 B.C.).

Hellas: The Land

Hellas, as the Greeks still call their land, encompassed the Aegean Sea as well as the Greek peninsula (see Map 3.1). Mountains divide the land, leaving few plains and rivers that are generally no more than creeks, most of which go dry in the summer. Greece is, however, blessed with good harbors, the most important of which look to the east. The islands of the

Online Study Center

This icon will direct you to interactive activities and study materials on the website **college.hmco.com/pic/mckaywest9e**

MAP 3.1 Ancient Greece   In antiquity, the home of the Greeks included the islands of the
Aegean and the western shore of Turkey as well as the Greek peninsula itself.

Online Study Center   Improve Your Grade Interactive Map: Ancient Greece

Aegean serve as steppingstones to Asia Minor, usually defined as the region from the modern Turkish coast to the Euphrates River. Thus Greece proper and the **Aegean basin** formed an intimate realm for a common Greek culture. The major regions of Greece were Thessaly and Boeotia in the north and center, lands marked by fertile plains and small rivers that flowed even in summer. Good and abundant land provided the wealth to maintain a strong population capable of fielding good cavalry and infantry. Immediately to the south of Boeotia is Attica, an area of thin soil but home to the olive and the vine. Its harbors looked to the Aegean, which invited its inhabitants, the Athenians, to concentrate on maritime commerce. Still farther south in the Peloponnesus the land is a patchwork of high mountains and small plains. These geographical features divided the area into several regions, of which the most important were Argos in the northeast, Arcadia in the center, and Laconia and Messenia in the south. The geographical fragmentation of Greece encouraged political fragmentation. Furthermore, communications were extraordinarily poor. Rocky tracks were far more common than roads, which were seldom paved. These conditions prohibited the growth of a great empire like those of the Near East.

• *When the Greeks arrived in Hellas, how did they adapt themselves to their new landscape?*

Chronology

ca 1650–1000 B.C.   Arrival of the Mycenaean Greeks in Europe

ca 1100–800 B.C.   Evolution of the polis; Greek migrations within the Aegean basin; poems of Homer and Hesiod

ca 800–500 B.C.   Rise of Sparta and Athens; flowering of lyric poetry

776 B.C.   Founding of the Olympic games

ca 750–550 B.C.   Greek colonization of the Mediterranean

ca 700–500 B.C.   Concentration of landed wealth

ca 640 B.C.   Use of coinage in western Asia

ca 525–362 B.C.   Birth and development of tragedy, historical writing, and philosophy; spread of monumental architecture

499–479 B.C.   Persian wars

431–404 B.C.   Peloponnesian War

404–338 B.C.   Spartan and Theban hegemonies; success of Philip of Macedon

The Minoans and Mycenaeans (ca 2000–ca 1100 B.C.)

The origins of Greek civilization are complicated, obscure, and diverse. Neolithic peoples had already built prosperous communities in the Aegean, but not until about 2000 B.C. did they establish firm contact with one another. By then artisans had discovered how to make bronze, which gave these Stone Age groups more efficient tools and weapons. With the adoption of metallurgy came even greater prosperity. The Aegean is a relatively small sea, and land is seldom far off. Some Cretan farmers and fishermen began to trade their surpluses with their neighbors. The central position of Crete in the eastern Mediterranean made it a crucial link in this trade. The Cretans voyaged to Egypt, Asia Minor, other islands, and mainland Greece. They thereby played a vital part in creating an Aegean economy that brought them all into close contact. These favorable circumstances produced the flourishing and vibrant **Minoan** culture on Crete, named after the mythical King Minos.

As seen earlier, only literacy can lead to history. Although the Minoans created a script now called Linear A, very little of it can be read with any certainty. Thus it cannot serve as a historical source. Instead, archaeology and art offer some glimpses of life on the island. The symbol of Minoan culture was the palace and its outlying buildings. About 1650 B.C. Crete was dotted with them, such as those at Mallia on the northern coast and Kato Zakro on the eastern tip of the island. Towering above all others in importance was the palace at Cnossus. It was the political and economic center of its society, but its relations with the other palaces are still disputed. Each palace was the political and economic center of its society. Few specifics are known about Minoan life except that at its head stood a king and his nobles, who governed the lives of their farmers, sailors, shepherds, and artisans. Minoan society, at Cnossus and elsewhere, was wealthy and, to judge by the absence of fortifications on the island, relatively peaceful. Minoan artistic remains, including frescoes and figurines, show women as well as men leading

Mycenaean Lion Hunt
The Mycenaeans were a robust, warlike people who enjoyed the thrill and the danger of hunting. This scene on the blade of a dagger depicts hunters armed with spears and protected by shields defending themselves against charging lions. *(National Archaeological Museum/ Archaeological Receipts Fund)*

religious activities, watching entertainment, and engaging in athletic competitions such as leaping over a bull. We do not know if these represent daily life or mythological scenes, but many scholars see gender norms in Crete as less restrictive for women and more egalitarian than elsewhere in the ancient world.

This pleasant situation continued until the arrival of Greek-speaking peoples in the Balkans around 2000 B.C. They came gradually as individual groups who spoke various dialects of the same language. Study of these dialects, aided by archaeology, gives a reasonable idea of how the immigrants spread. The three main groups were the Aeolians, who settled in Thessaly and Boeotia. Others speaking Ionian made their homes in Attica and Euboea, but they claimed that they were indigenous. A later group whose tongue was Dorian occupied Argos, Laconia (the home of the Spartans), and Messenia. Despite these dialects, the Greeks considered themselves a distinct and related folk. By about 1650 B.C. one group had founded a powerful kingdom at Mycenae, while others spread elsewhere in Greece. They merged with native inhabitants, and from that union emerged the society that modern scholars call **Mycenaean,** after the most famous site of this new culture.

Under these conditions of foreign contact and local growth, early Mycenaean Greeks raised other palaces and established cities at Thebes, Athens, Tiryns, Pylos, and elsewhere. As in Crete, the political unit was the kingdom. The king and his warrior aristocracy stood at the top of society. The seat and symbol of the king's power and wealth was his palace, which was also the economic center of the kingdom. Within its walls royal artisans fashioned jewelry and rich ornaments, made and decorated fine pottery, forged weapons, prepared hides and wool for clothing, and manufactured the other goods needed by the king and his retainers. Palace scribes kept records in Greek with a script known as **Linear B,** which was derived from Minoan Linear A. The scribes kept account of taxes and drew up inventories of the king's possessions. From the palace, as at Cnossus, the Mycenaean king directed the lives of his subjects. Little is known of the king's subjects except that they were the artisans, traders, and farmers of Mycenaean society. The Mycenaean economy was marked by an extensive division of labor, all tightly controlled from the palace. At the bottom of the social scale were male and female slaves, who were normally owned by the king and aristocrats but who also worked for ordinary people.

The Linear B tablets also held a surprise for those interested in Greek religion. Some of them recorded offerings to deities such as Zeus, Apollo, and Athena, the traditional Olympian gods. As late as 1995 Greek archaeologists in Thebes discovered over two hundred new Linear B tablets that are as yet unpublished. These tablets, as well as those already known, prove that the Greeks brought their traditional deities with them on their journey to Greece.

Contacts between the Minoans and Mycenaeans were originally peaceful, and Minoan culture flooded the Greek mainland. But around 1450 B.C. the Mycenaeans attacked Crete, destroying many Minoan palaces and taking possession of the grand palace at Cnossus. For about the next fifty years, the Mycenaeans ruled much of the island until a further wave of violence left Cnossus in ashes.

Whatever the explanation of these events, Mycenaean kingdoms in Greece benefited from the fall of Cnossus and the collapse of its trade. Mycenaean commerce quickly expanded throughout the Aegean, reaching as far abroad as Anatolia, Cyprus, and Egypt. Throughout central and southern Greece, Mycenaean culture flourished as never before. Palaces became grander, and citadels were often protected by mammoth stone walls. Prosperity, however, did not bring peace, and between 1300 and 1000 B.C. kingdom after kingdom suffered attack and destruction. Some modern scholars have attributed these events to the Sea Peoples, who wreaked such havoc in the eastern Mediterranean (see page 29). The best argument for absolving them from blame lies in the lack of any alien artifacts in Greece and the Aegean. If invaders, they proved remarkably tidy. Although later Greeks accused the Dorians of overthrowing the Mycenaean kingdoms, these centers undoubtedly fell because of mutual discord, just as their descendants would commit political suicide in the Peloponnesian War (see pages 73–74).

The fall of the Mycenaean kingdoms ushered in a period of such poverty, disruption, and backwardness that historians usually call it the "Dark Age" of Greece (ca 1100–800 B.C.). Even literacy, which was not widespread in any case, was a casualty of the chaos. Nonetheless, the Greeks survived the storm to preserve their culture and civilization. Greece remained Greek; nothing essential was swept away. Greek religious cults remained vital to the people, and basic elements of social organization continued to function effectively. It was a time of change and challenge, but not of utter collapse.

This period also saw a development of enormous importance for the course of Western civilization. The disruption of Mycenaean societies caused the widespread and prolonged movement of Greek peoples. They dispersed beyond mainland Greece farther south to Crete and in greater strength across the Aegean to the shores of Asia Minor. They arrived during a time when traditional states and empires had collapsed. Economic hardship was common, and various groups wandered for years. Yet by the end of the Dark Age, the Greeks had spread their culture throughout the Aegean basin.

Homer, Hesiod, Gods, and Heroes (1100–800 B.C.)

The Greeks, unlike the Hebrews, had no sacred book that chronicled their past. Instead they had Homer's *Iliad* and *Odyssey* to describe a time when gods still walked the earth. And they learned the origin and descent of the gods from the *Theogony*, an epic poem by Hesiod. Instead of authentic history, the poems of Homer and Hesiod offered the Greeks an ideal past, a largely legendary Heroic Age. These literary works deserve reading for their own sakes, but they are not reliable historical documents. Nor were they meant to be. In terms of pure history they contain scraps of information about the Bronze Age, much about the early Dark Age, and some about

the poets' own era. Chronologically, then, the Heroic Age falls mainly in the period between the collapse of the Mycenaean world and the rebirth of literacy.

The *Iliad* recounts an expedition of Mycenaeans, whom Homer called "Achaeans," to besiege the city of Troy in Asia Minor. The war was begun, as Homer tells it, by a Trojan prince's abduction of the beautiful wife of a Mycenaean king. The heart of the *Iliad*, however, concerns the quarrel between Agamemnon, the king of Mycenae, and Achilles, the tragic hero of the poem, and how their quarrel brought suffering to the Achaeans. Only when Achilles put away his anger and pride did he consent to come forward and face and kill the Trojan hero Hector. The *Odyssey*, probably composed later than the *Iliad*, narrates the adventures of Odysseus, one of the Achaean heroes who fought at Troy, during his voyage home from the fighting.

Online Study Center **Improve Your Grade**
Primary Source: Odysseus Is Rescued by the Princess Nausicaa

The splendor of these poems does not lie in their plots, although the *Odyssey* is a marvelous adventure story. Rather, both poems portray engaging but often flawed characters who are larger than life and yet typically human. Homer was also strikingly successful in depicting the great gods, who generally sit on Mount Olympus and watch the fighting at Troy like spectators at a baseball game, although they sometimes participate in the action. Homer's deities are reminiscent of Mesopotamian gods and goddesses. Hardly a decorous lot, the Olympians are raucous, petty, deceitful, and splendid. In short, they are human.

Homer at times portrayed the gods in a serious vein, but he never treated them in a systematic fashion, as did Hesiod, who lived somewhat later than Homer. Hesiod's epic poem the *Theogony* traces the descent of Zeus. Hesiod was influenced by Mesopotamian myths, which the Hittites had adopted and spread to the Aegean. Like the Hebrews, Hesiod envisaged his cosmogony—his account of the way the universe developed—in moral and gendered terms. Originally the primary deity was an earth goddess, Gaia, but through a series of incestuous relationships and generational conflicts, Zeus emerged triumphant. He established a moral order with himself at the head, ending the chaotic female-dominated system. In *Theogony* and others of his works, Hesiod attributes all human problems to the first woman, Pandora, whose curiosity led her to open the container in which pain, war, and other evils had been enclosed.

Polis of Argos   This view of modern Argos remarkably illustrates the structure of an ancient polis. Atop the hill in the background are the remains of the ancient acropolis. At its foot to the right are foundations of ancient public and private buildings, spreading beyond which are modern houses, situated where ancient houses were located. The trees and cut grain in the foreground were also major features of the *chora,* the agricultural basis of the polis. *(John Buckler)*

 # The Polis

After the upheavals that ended the Mycenaean period and the slow recovery of prosperity during the Dark Age, the Greeks developed their basic political and institutional unit, the **polis.** The term *polis* is generally interpreted as "city-state," one of the worst possible translations of a word that is basically untranslatable. Despite its defects, however, *city-state* is at least a term generally understood and accepted. Two problems arise in an attempt to understand the polis. The first is how it developed, and the second is what it was. Even the Greeks took the polis for granted. Although they remembered a time when kings ruled over many parts of Greece, they did not know how the polis evolved from those legendary kingdoms. In his *Politics* (1.1.9) Aristotle describes the growth of the polis in terms that are as biological as they are political. For example, he states that "man is by nature a being of the polis." He means that people developed the polis as naturally as plants and animals themselves develop. The biological analogy is wrong, but the concept of political evolution is largely correct.

● *After the Greeks had established the polis in which they lived their political and social lives, how did they shape it into its several historical forms?*

Origins of the Polis

Recent archaeological expeditions and careful study have done much to clarify the origins of the polis. Even during the late Mycenaean period, towns had grown up around palaces. These towns and even smaller villages performed basically local functions. The first was to administer the ordinary political affairs of the community. The village also served a religious purpose in that no matter how small, each had its local cult to its own deity. The exchange of daily goods made these towns and villages economically important, if only on a small scale. These settlements also developed a social system that was particularly their own. They likewise had their own views of the social worth and status of their inhabitants and the nature of their public responsibilities. In short, they relied on custom and mutual agreement to direct their ordinary affairs.

The coming of the Dorians did not significantly change this political evolution, but it had two effects. In some cases it disrupted the task of rebuilding and consolidating some of these developing communities. The Dorians at times carved out territory for themselves at the expense of the natives, but they also assimilated the culture around them. This process actually strengthened the sense of identity among the local people. The situation could have been cataclysmic, but for the most part it was not. The native inhabitants acknowledged their differences with the newcomers. They maintained their traditional religion, albeit sometimes in altered form, but they also accepted the religious validity of new cults. In addition, they looked upon the Dorians as fellow Greeks. Recent archaeological and historical studies reveal a picture of continuity and assimilation.

When fully developed, each polis normally shared a surprisingly large number of features with other poleis. Physically a polis was a society of people who lived in a city *(asty)* and cultivated the surrounding countryside *(chora)*. The city's water supply came from public fountains, springs, and cisterns. By the fifth century B.C. the city was generally surrounded by a wall. The city contained a point, usually elevated, called the **acropolis** and a public square or marketplace called the *agora*. On the acropolis, which in the early period was a place of refuge, stood the temples, altars, public monuments, and various dedications to the gods of the polis. The agora was originally the place where the warrior assembly met, but it became the political center of the polis. In the agora were porticoes, shops, and public buildings and courts.

City and Chora

Until quite recently most scholars have concentrated their attention on the city. The city provides a wealth of evidence on urban planning and daily life, and often yields public documents that illustrate the actual functioning of the polis. Nevertheless, the countryside was vital to the city and to the polis in general for a variety of reasons. Previous pictures of life there depict a scene that is dull and backward: not much happening in the country. Reality was very different. The traditional view overlooks the vitality and the basic importance of the village. The essential significance of the land is that it fed the city. Agriculture in most Greek communities indeed proved basic and far more important than local trade and urban economic dealings. Life in the polis demanded the integration of the chora and the city.

Since the Neolithic period, agriculture had provided the basis for Greek society. Farmers learned how to tame and nurture wild strains of trees and other plants. They discovered the value of irrigation to intensify their agricultural yields. The agricultural significance of the farmers on the chora and the regularity of the seasons bred a stable society. While mostly content to leave daily politics to the men of the city, male farmers made their opinions known to their fellow citizens. Although they spent most of their days tending their fields and remained the economic basis of the polis, they never ignored the larger political issues confronting their community.

A previously unappreciated aspect of the countryside was its religious significance. Today people normally think first of the great religious festivals celebrated in the city. Although they were indeed important, most Greek religious practices were rooted in the country. The sanctuaries there were a reflection of the cults of the deities that nurtured the polis. The sanctuaries themselves and the religious rites connected with them were means of appealing to the gods to protect the crops, animals, and

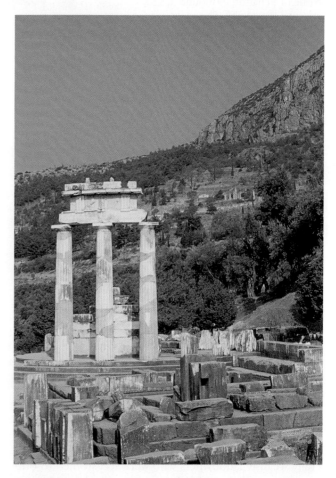

The Delphic Oracle The Marmaria, the sanctuary of Athena, is seen here against the backdrop of the mountains that surround the sanctuary of Apollo. Around the oracle clustered many temples to various deities, shrines, and other sacred buildings, all of them in a remote mountainous area especially chosen by Apollo to be his home and the place where he answered the supplications of the faithful. *(John Buckler)*

Early Greek Warfare Before the hoplites became the backbone of the army, wealthy warriors rode into battle in a chariot, dismounted, and engaged the enemy. This scene, almost a photograph, shows on the left the warrior protecting the chariot before it returns to the rear. The painter has caught the lead horses already beginning the turn. *(Courtesy of the Ure Museum of Greek Archaeology, University of Reading)*

people who depended on the earth for survival. The sanctuaries and other religious sites on the borders of the polis linked country and city dwellers in one religious unit. They also served as sources of identification of the polis in that sacred buildings, shrines, and altars were the physical symbols of a particular people, no matter where in the polis they lived. The religious dedications in them were the possessions not only of the gods but also of the polis itself. The permanent dedications made to the gods reflected the power and prestige of the polis.

The average polis did not have a standing army. Instead it relied on its citizens for protection. Very rich citizens often served as cavalry, which was, however, never as important as the heavily armed infantry, or **hoplites.** These were the backbone of the army. They wore metal helmets and body armor, carried heavy, round shields, and armed themselves with spears and swords. They provided their own equipment and were basically amateurs. In the classical period (ca 500–338 B.C.) they were generally wealthy landowners who were accustomed to outdoor labor. When in battle, they stood in several dense lines in which cohesion and order became as valuable as courage. This effort also gave them a sense of comradeship and pride, creating a sense of masculinity that was linked to military service. Poor men made up the lightly armed infantry. Usually wielding only a javelin or two each, they used their mobility in rough areas to harass hoplites. In some instances the citizens of a polis hired

mercenaries to fight their battles. Mercenaries were expensive, untrustworthy, and willing to defect to a higher bidder. Even worse, they sometimes seized control over the polis that had hired them.

Regardless of its size or wealth, the polis was fundamental to Greek life. The polis was far more than a political institution. Above all it was a community of citizens whose customs were at the same time the laws of the polis. Even though the physical, religious, and political form of the polis varied from place to place, it was the very badge of Greekness.

Governing Structures

Greek city-states had several different types of government. **Monarchy,** rule by a king, was surprisingly not one of them. Although prevalent during the Mycenaean period, it afterwards declined. While Sparta boasted of two kings, they were only part of a more broadly based constitution. During fully developed historical times Greek states were either democracies or oligarchies. Sporadic periods of violent political and social upheaval often led to a third type of government—tyranny. **Tyranny** was rule by one man who had seized power by unconstitutional means, generally by using his wealth to win a political following that toppled the existing legal government.

Only democracy and oligarchy played lasting, broad roles in Greek political life, and these two forms flourished across Greece well into later years. **Democracy,** the power of the people, meant that all citizens, without respect to birth or wealth, administered the workings of government. Although Athens is easily the most famous of the Greek democracies, it was not alone. The people of Argos in the Peloponnesus independently governed their powerful city by a democracy quite similar to the Athenian one. So too with Corcyra, the great city that governed the island also named Corcyra, the modern Corfu. These democracies generally established friendly relations with one another, sharing many basic features while developing their own particular forms of popular rule.

Yet Greek democracy did not really live up to its name. In reality, Greek democracy meant the rule of citizens, not "the people" as a whole, and citizenship was drastically limited. In Athens and in other democracies, only free adult men who had lived in the polis a long time were citizens. Women, foreigners, slaves, and others had no rights. The 10 to 20 percent of the population who were citizens theoretically shared equally in the determination of policy and the administration of government. Moreover, they generally did so in practice. Along with military service, citizenship provided men with an opportunity to bond with one another, and it became an important component in Greek ideas of masculinity.

Most Greek states actually preferred oligarchy to democracy as their favorite form of government. **Oligarchy,** which literally means "the rule of the few," was government by a small group of wealthy citizens who were not necessarily aristocratic by birth. Oligarchy generally gave its whole population—leaders and people alike—stable government and freedom to prosper. Men could advance politically by earning enough wealth to qualify for full citizenship. Full citizenship meant the right to vote for officials and to hold office. The roll of oligarchic cities includes many of the most illustrious of the Greek states. A well-known example is Corinth, where landowners, merchants, artisans, and working people stood solidly behind a government that prospered for well over 350 years. At Corinth the wealthy governed according to the ideal called **isonomia,** meaning "equality shared under the law." Although the wealthy governed the city, they officially endorsed social mobility for capable men and application of the law equally to everyone. Corinthian oligarchs also listened to the will of the citizens, a major factor in their long success.

Several other oligarchies likewise deserve notice. Two were located in Arcadia: Mantinea in the north and Tegea in the south. These two city-states depended on agriculture for their prosperity, not on commerce as did Corinth. They too found in oligarchy the key to prosper-

ity and the means to create stable governments. They too allowed all citizens the opportunity to gain the wealth needed to join the governing class and to rise socially. Easily the most influential oligarchic state was Thebes in the region of Boeotia. It too depended on agriculture for its wealth. It was only one of the oligarchic cities in the area, but it was certainly the most powerful. Stable at home, Thebes united these other oligarchies to form the first effective federal government of city-states in Greece, the "Boeotian Confederacy." Thebes and the other oligarchies were responsible for the creation of federalism as a valid, working political principle of government. **Federalism** in Greece meant a system of government in which individual city-states joined to create one general government. This federalism is actually the same principle of the United States of America, which is a federal government of individual states joined together for the common good. The Boeotian Confederacy of oligarchic city-states proved to be so successful that elsewhere in Greece other states followed its example. It proved to be particularly popular and widespread later in the Hellenistic period (see page 98).

During the classical period, however, despite the allure of federalism, the citizens of the vast majority of city-states were determined to remain free and autonomous. The very integration of the polis proved to be one of its basic weaknesses. The political result, as earlier in Sumer, was almost constant warfare. The polis could dominate, but unlike earlier and later empires, it could not incorporate.

The Archaic Age (800–500 B.C.)

Generally known as Archaic primarily because of its art and literature, this period can be seen as a time when the Greeks recovered from the downfall of the Mycenaean kingdoms and continued the advances made during the Dark Age. These years ushered in one of the most vibrant periods of Greek history, an era of extraordinary expansion geographically, artistically, and politically. Greeks ventured as far east as the Black Sea and as far west as Spain (see Map 3.2). With the rebirth of literacy, this period also witnessed a tremendous literary flowering as poets broke away from the heroic tradition and wrote about their own lives. Politically these were the years when Sparta and Athens—the two poles of the Greek experience—rose to prominence.

• *What major developments mark the Archaic Greek period in terms of spread of culture and the growth of cities?*

Overseas Expansion

During the years 1100–800 B.C. the Greeks not only re-covered from the breakdown of the Mycenaean world but also grew in wealth and numbers. This new prosperity brought new problems. The increase in population meant that many families had very little land or none at all. Land hunger and the resulting social and political tensions drove many Greek men and women to seek new homes outside of Greece. Other factors, largely intangible, played their part as well: the desire for a new start, a love of excitement and adventure, and natural curiosity about what lay beyond the horizon.

From about 750 to 550 B.C., Greeks from the mainland and Asia Minor traveled throughout the Mediterranean and even into the Atlantic Ocean in their quest for new land. They sailed in the greatest numbers to Sicily and southern Italy, where there was ample space for expansion. They also sailed farther west to Sardinia, southern France and Spain, and even the Canary Islands. In Sicily they found the Sicels, who had already adopted many Carthaginian customs, including a nascent urban culture. Fiercely independent, they greeted the coming of the Greeks just as they had the arrival of the Carthaginians. They welcomed Greek culture but not Greek demands for their land. Nonetheless, the two peoples made a somewhat uneasy accommodation, and there was some intermarriage among them. There was enough land in Sicily for Greeks and Sicels alike, so both flourished, albeit not always peacefully.

In southern Italy the Greeks encountered a number of Indo-European peoples. They were for the most part rural and enjoyed few material comforts. Some of their villages were evolving into towns, but in the mountains looser tribal units prevailed. They both welcomed Greek culture, and the Greeks found it easy to establish prosperous cities without facing significant local hostility.

Some adventurous Greeks sailed to Sardinia and the southern coast of modern France. In Sardinia they established outposts that were originally trading stations, meant primarily for bartering with the natives. Commerce was so successful that some Greeks established perma-

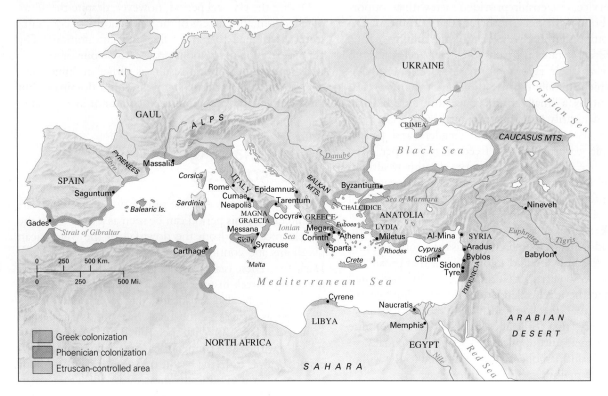

MAP 3.2 Colonization of the Mediterranean   Though the Greeks and Phoenicians colonized the Mediterranean basin at about the same time, the Greeks spread much farther.

Online Study Center   **Improve Your Grade** Interactive Map: Phoenician and Greek Colonization nent towns there. Greek influence, in terms of physical remains and the ideas that they reflect, was far stronger on the island than was recognized even a few years ago. From these new outposts Greek influence extended to southern France. The modern city of Marseilles began as a Greek colony and later sent settlers to southern Spain.

Colonization changed the entire Greek world, both at home and abroad. In economic terms the expansion of the Greeks created a much larger market for agricultural and manufactured goods. From the east, especially from the northern coast of the Black Sea, came wheat in a volume beyond the capacity of Greek soil. In return flowed Greek wine and olive oil, which could not be produced in the harsher climate of the north. Greek-manufactured goods, notably rich jewelry and fine pottery, circulated from southern Russia to Spain. During this same period the Greeks adopted the custom of minting coins, which they apparently imported from Lydia. At first coinage was of little economic importance, and only later did it replace the common practice of barter. In the barter system one person simply exchanges one good for another without the use of money. Each person decides the value of the goods traded. Even today, especially in the backcountry of Greece, a surprisingly large number of economic transactions are done by barter. Thus Greek culture and economics, fertilized by the influences of other societies, spread throughout the Mediterranean basin.

Colonization presented the polis with a huge challenge, for it required organization and planning on an unprecedented scale. The colonizing city, called the *metropolis,* or mother city, first decided where to establish the colony, how to transport colonists to the site, and who would sail. Then the metropolis collected and stored the supplies that the colonists would need both to feed themselves and to plant their first crop. The metropolis also had to provide adequate shipping for the voyage. All preparations ready, a leader, called an **oikist,** ordered the colonists to sail. The oikist was then in full command of the band until the colony was established in its new site and capable of running its own affairs. A significant aspect of colonizing ventures was that male colonists were considered political equals and were expected to have a voice in the new colony.

Once the colonists landed, the oikist laid out the new polis, selected the sites of temples and public buildings, and established the government. Then he surrendered power to the new leaders. The colony was thereafter independent of the metropolis. For the Greeks, colonization had two important aspects. First, it demanded that the polis assume a much greater public function than

ever before, thus strengthening the city-state's institutional position. Second, colonization spread the polis and its values far beyond the shores of Greece. Even more important, colonization on this scale had a profound impact on the course of Western civilization. It meant that the prevailing culture of the Mediterranean basin would be Greek, the heritage to which Rome would later fall heir.

The Growth of Sparta

During the Archaic period the Spartans expanded the boundaries of their polis and made it the leading power in Greece. Like other Greeks, the Spartans faced the problems of overpopulation and land hunger. Unlike other Greeks, the Spartans solved these problems by conquest, not by colonization. To gain more land, the Spartans set out in about 735 B.C. to conquer Messenia, a rich, fertile region in the southwestern Peloponnesus. This conflict, the First Messenian War, lasted for twenty years and ended in a Spartan triumph. The Spartans appropriated Messenian land and turned the Messenians into *helots,* or state serfs.

In about 650 B.C. Spartan exploitation and oppression of the Messenian helots led to a helot revolt so massive and stubborn that it became known as the Second Messenian War. The Spartan poet Tyrtaeus, a contemporary of these events, vividly portrays the ferocity of the fighting:

For it is a shameful thing indeed
When with the foremost fighters
An elder falling in front of the young men
Lies outstretched,
Having white hair and grey beard,
Breathing forth his stout soul in the dust,
Holding in his hands his genitals
stained with blood.[1]

Confronted with such horrors, Spartan enthusiasm for the war waned. Finally, after some thirty years of fighting, the Spartans put down the revolt. Nevertheless, the political and social strain it caused led to a transformation of the Spartan polis.

It took the full might of the Spartan people, aristocrat and commoner alike, to win the Second Messenian War. After the victory non-noblemen, who had done much of the fighting, demanded rights equal to those of the nobility. They had taken their place in the battle line next to their aristocratic neighbors but lacked the social prestige and political rights of their noble companions. The agitation of these non-nobles disrupted society until the aristocrats agreed to remodel the state.

Periods of Greek History

Period	Significant Events	Major Writers
Bronze Age 2000–1100 B.C.	Arrival of the Greeks in Greece Rise and fall of the Mycenaean kingdoms	
Dark Age 1100–800 B.C.	Greek migrations within the Aegean basin Social and political recovery Evolution of the polis Rebirth of literacy	Homer Hesiod
Archaic Age 800–500 B.C.	Rise of Sparta and Athens Colonization of the Mediterranean basin Flowering of lyric poetry Development of philosophy and science in Ionia	Archilochus Sappho Tyrtaeus Solon Anaximander Heraclitus
Classical Period 500–338 B.C.	Persian wars Growth of the Athenian Empire Peloponnesian War Rise of drama and historical writing Flowering of Greek philosophy Spartan and Theban hegemonies Conquest of Greece by Philip of Macedon	Herodotus Thucydides Aeschylus Sophocles Euripides Aristophanes Plato Aristotle

The "Lycurgan regimen," as the reforms were called after a legendary lawgiver, was a new political, economic, and social system. Political distinctions among Spartan men were eliminated, and all citizens became legally equal. Actual governance of the polis was in the hands of two kings who were primarily military leaders. The kings and twenty-eight elders made up a council that deliberated on foreign and domestic matters and prepared legislation for the assembly, which consisted of all Spartan citizens. The real executive power of the polis was in the hands of five *ephors,* or overseers, elected from and by all the citizens. In effect, the Lycurgan regimen did nothing more than broaden the aristocracy, while at the same time setting limits on its size. Social mobility was for the most part abolished, and instead an aristocratic warrior class governed the polis.

To provide for their economic needs, the Spartans divided the land of Messenia among all citizens. Helots worked the land, raised the crops, provided the Spartans with their living, and occasionally served in the army. The Spartans kept the helots in line by means of systematic terrorism, hoping to beat them down and keep them quiet. Spartan citizens were supposed to devote their time exclusively to military training.

In the Lycurgan system every citizen owed primary allegiance to Sparta. Suppression of the individual together with emphasis on military prowess led to a barracks state. Family life itself was sacrificed to the polis. Once Spartan boys reached the age of seven, they were enrolled in separate companies with other boys their age. They lived in this **homosocial** (same-sex) setting for most of their lives. They slept outside on reed mats and underwent rugged physical and military training until age twenty-four, when they became frontline soldiers. For the rest of their lives, Spartan men kept themselves prepared for combat. Their military training never ceased, and the older men were expected to be models of endurance, frugality, and sturdiness to the younger men. In battle Spartans were supposed to stand and die rather than retreat. An anecdote frequently repeated about one Spartan mother sums up Spartan military values. As her son was setting off to battle, the mother handed him his shield and advised him to come back either victorious, carrying the shield, or dead, being carried on it. In the Lycurgan regimen, Spartan men were expected to train vigorously, disdain luxury and wealth, do with little, and like it.

In this militaristic atmosphere, citizen women were remarkably free. As in all classical cultures, there was an emphasis on childbearing, but the Spartan leadership viewed maternal health as important for the bearing of healthy, strong children and thus encouraged women to participate in athletics and to eat well. With men in military service most of their lives, citizen women owned property and ran the household; they were not physically restricted or secluded. Marriage often began with a trial marriage period to make sure the couple could have children, with divorce and remarriage the normal course if they were unsuccessful. Men saw their wives only rarely when they sneaked out of camp, and their most meaningful relations were same-sex ones. Spartan military leaders viewed such relationships as militarily advantageous, judging that men would fight more fiercely in defense of close comrades and lovers. Close links among men thus contributed to Spartan dedication to the state and understanding of civic virtue, which were admired throughout the Greek world.

The Evolution of Athens

Like Sparta, Athens faced pressing social and economic problems during the Archaic period, but the Athenian response was far different from that of the Spartans. Instead of creating an oligarchy, the Athenians extended to all citizens the right and duty of governing the polis. Indeed, the Athenian democracy was one of the most thoroughgoing in Greece.

The late seventh century B.C. was for Athens a time of turmoil, the causes of which are virtually unknown. In 621 B.C. Draco, an Athenian aristocrat, doubtless under pressure from the peasants, published the first law code of the Athenian polis. His code was thought harsh, but it nonetheless embodied the ideal that the law belonged to the citizens. Nevertheless, peasant unrest continued.

By the early sixth century B.C. social and economic conditions led to another explosive situation. The aristocracy still governed Athens oppressively. The aristocrats owned the best land, met in an assembly to govern the polis, and interpreted the law. Noble landowners were forcing small farmers into economic dependence. Many families were sold into slavery; others were exiled and their land was pledged to the rich. Poor farmers who had borrowed from their wealthy neighbors had to put up their land as collateral. If a farmer was unable to repay the loan, his creditor put a stone on the borrower's field to signify his indebtedness and thereafter took one-sixth of the annual yield until the debt was paid. If the farmer had to borrow again, he pledged himself and sometimes his family. If he was again unable to repay the loan, he became the slave of his creditor. Because the harvests of the poor farmer were generally small, he could usually raise enough crops to live on but not enough to repay his loan.

In many other city-states, conditions like those in Athens led to the rise of tyrants. One person who recognized these problems clearly was Solon, himself an aristocrat and poet, and a man opposed to tyrants. He was also the one man in Athens who enjoyed the respect of both aristocrats and peasants. Like Hesiod, Solon used his poetry to condemn the aristocrats for their greed and dishonesty. Solon recited his poems in the Athenian agora, where anyone there could hear his relentless call for justice and fairness. The aristocrats realized that Solon was no crazed revolutionary, and the common people trusted him. Around 594 B.C. the nobles elected him *archon,* chief magistrate of the Athenian polis, and gave him extraordinary power to reform the state.

Solon immediately freed all people enslaved for debt, recalled all exiles, canceled all debts on land, and made enslavement for debt illegal. He also divided society into four legal groups on the basis of wealth. In the most influential group were the wealthiest citizens, but even the poorest and least powerful men enjoyed certain rights. Solon allowed them into the old aristocratic assembly, where they could take part in the election of magistrates.

In all his work, Solon gave thought to the rights of the poor as well as the rich. He gave common men a place in government and a voice in the political affairs of Athens. Although Solon's reforms solved some immediate problems, they did not bring peace to Athens. Some aristocrats attempted to make themselves tyrants, while others banded together to oppose them. In 546 B.C. Pisistratus, an exiled aristocrat, returned to Athens, defeated his opponents, and became tyrant. Pisistratus reduced the power of the aristocracy while supporting the common people. Under his rule Athens prospered, and his building program began to transform the city into one of the splendors of Greece. His reign as tyrant promoted the growth of democratic ideas by arousing rudimentary feelings of equality in many Athenian men.

Athenian acceptance of tyranny did not long outlive Pisistratus, for his son Hippias ruled harshly, committing excesses that led to his overthrow. After a brief period of turmoil between factions of the nobility, Cleisthenes, a wealthy and prominent aristocrat, emerged triumphant in 508 B.C., largely because he won the support of lower-status men. Cleisthenes reorganized the state completely but presented every innovation to the assembly for discussion and ratification. All Athenian citizens had a voice in Cleisthenes' work.

Cleisthenes created the **deme,** a local unit, to serve as the basis of his political system. Citizenship was tightly linked to the deme, for each deme kept the roll of those men within its jurisdiction who were admitted to citizenship.

Cleisthenes also created ten new tribes as administrative units. All the demes were grouped in tribes, which thus formed the link between the demes and the central government. The central government included an assembly of all citizens and a new council of five hundred members. Cleisthenes is often credited with the institution of *ostracism,* a vote of the Athenian citizens by which the man receiving the most votes went into exile. The goal of ostracism was to rid the state peacefully of a difficult or potentially dangerous politician.

The democracy functioned on the idea that all full citizens, the *demos,* were sovereign. Yet not all citizens could take time from work to participate in government. Therefore, they delegated their power to other citizens by creating various offices meant to run the democracy. The most prestigious of them was the board of ten archons, who were charged with handling legal and military matters. Six of them oversaw the Athenian legal system. They presided over courts, fixed dates for trials, and ensured that the laws of Athens were consistent. They were all elected for one year. After leaving office they entered the *Areopagus,* a select council of ex-archons who handled cases involving homicide, wounding, and arson.

Legislation was in the hands of two bodies, the **boule,** or council, composed of five hundred members, and the **ecclesia,** the assembly of all citizens. The boule, separate from the Areopagus, was perhaps the major institution of the democracy. By supervising the various committees of government and proposing bills to the assembly, it guided Athenian political life. It received foreign envoys and forwarded treaties to the assembly for ratification. It oversaw the granting of state contracts and was responsible for receiving many revenues. It held the democracy together. Nonetheless, the assembly had the final word. Open to all male citizens over eighteen years of age, it met at a specific place to vote on matters presented to it. The assembly could either accept, amend, or reject bills put before it. Every member could express his opinion on any subject on the agenda, and a simple majority vote was needed to pass or reject a bill.

Athenian democracy was to prove an inspiring ideal in Western civilization. It demonstrated that a large group of people, not just a few, could efficiently run the affairs of state. By heeding the opinions, suggestions, and wisdom of all its citizens, the polis enjoyed the maximum amount of good counsel. Because all citizens could speak their minds, they did not have to resort to rebellion or conspiracy to express their desires. Like all democracies in ancient Greece, however, Athenian democracy was

limited. Slaves, women, recent migrants, and foreigners could not be citizens; their opinions about political issues were not taken into account or recorded.

The Classical Period (500–338 B.C.)

In the years 500 to 338 B.C., Greek civilization reached its highest peak in politics, thought, and art. In this period the Greeks beat back the armies of the Persian Empire. Then, turning their spears against one another, they destroyed their own political system in a century of warfare. Some thoughtful Greeks felt prompted to record and analyze these momentous events. Herodotus (ca 485–425 B.C.), from Asia Minor, traveled the Greek world to piece together the course of the Persian wars. Although he consulted documents when he could find them, he relied largely on the memories of the participants. Not only is he the "father of history," he is also the first oral historian. Next came Thucydides (ca 460–ca 399 B.C.), whose account of the Peloponnesian War remains a classic of Western literature. Unlike Herodotus, he was often a participant in the events that he described.

This era also saw the flowering of philosophy, as thinkers in Ionia and on the Greek mainland began to ponder the nature and meaning of the universe and human experience; they used their intellects to explain the world around them and to determine humanity's place in it. The Greeks invented drama, and the Athenian tragedians Aeschylus, Sophocles, and Euripides explored themes that still inspire audiences today. Greek architects reached the zenith of their art and created buildings whose very ruins still inspire awe. Because Greek intellectual and artistic efforts attained their fullest and finest expression in these years, this age is called the "classical period." Few periods in the history of Western society can match it in sheer dynamism and achievement.

● *How did the Greeks develop their literature, philosophy, religion, and art, and how did war affect this intellectual and social process?*

The Persian Wars (499–479 B.C.)

One of the hallmarks of the classical period was warfare. In 499 B.C. the Ionian Greeks, with the feeble help of Athens, rebelled against the Persian Empire. In 490 B.C. the Persians struck back at Athens but were beaten off at the Battle of Marathon, a small plain in Attica (see Map

Mapping the Past

MAP 3.3 The Peloponnesian War This map shows the alignment of states during the Peloponnesian War, while Map 3.5 on page 87 shows interstate rivalry in the fourth century B.C.—two very disruptive periods in Greek history. ❶ What does Map 3.3 tell us about the balance of power during the Peloponnesian War? Which states led the others? ❷ Does Map 3.5 show the same situation? Are the leading states in Map 3.3 still the leaders in Map 3.5, or has power shifted elsewhere? What does Map 3.5 tell us about the growing political disintegration of Greece?

3.3). This victory taught the Greeks that they could defeat the Persians and successfully defend their homeland. It prompted the Persians to try again. In 480 B.C. the Persian king Xerxes led a mighty invasion force into Greece. In the face of this emergency, many of the Greeks united and pooled their resources to resist the invaders. The Spartans provided the overall leadership and commanded the Greek armies. The Athenians, led by the wily Themistocles, provided the heart of the naval forces.

The first confrontations between the Persians and the Greeks occurred at the pass of Thermopylae and in the waters off Artemisium, the northern tip of Euboea. At Thermopylae the Greek hoplites, heavily armed foot soldiers, showed their mettle. Before the fighting began, a report came in that when the Persian archers shot their bows the arrows darkened the sky. One gruff Spartan replied merely, "Fine, then we'll fight in the shade." The Greeks at Thermopylae fought heroically, but the Persians took the position. In 480 B.C. the Greek fleet, inspired by the energetic Themistocles, met the Persian armada at Salamis, an island just south of Athens. Though outnumbered by the Persians, the Greek navy won an overwhelming victory. The remnants of the Persian fleet retired, and with them went all hope of Persian victory. In the following year, a coalition of Greek forces, commanded by the Spartan Pausanias with assistance from the Athenian Aristides, smashed the last Persian army at Plataea, a small polis in Boeotia. Greece remained free.

The significance of these Greek victories is nearly incalculable. By defeating the Persians, the Greeks ensured that they would not be taken over by a monarchy, which they increasingly viewed as un-Greek. The Persian king symbolized lack of freedom and submission to one man. Monarchy had become a threat to the concept of individual Greek freedom. The decisive victories meant that Greek political forms and intellectual concepts would be handed down to later societies.

Growth of the Athenian Empire (478–431 B.C.)

For the Greeks, who had just won the Persian wars, that conflict was a beginning, not an end. Before them was a novel situation: the defeat of the Persians had created a power vacuum in the Aegean. The state with the strongest navy could turn the Aegean into its lake. In 478 B.C., to take advantage of this situation, the Athenians and their allies, again led by Aristides, formed the **Delian League,** a grand naval alliance aimed at liberating Ionia from Persian rule. The league took its name from the small island of Delos, on which stood a religious center sacred to all parties. The Delian League was intended as a free alliance under the leadership of Athens. Athenians provided most of the warships and crews and determined how many ships or how much money each member of the league should contribute to the allied effort.

The Athenians, supported by the Delian League and led by the young aristocrat Cimon, carried the war against Persia. But Athenian success had a sinister side. While the Athenians drove the Persians out of the Aegean, they also became increasingly imperialistic, even to the point of turning the Delian League into an Athenian empire. Athens began reducing its allies to the status of subjects. The Athenians sternly put down dissident or rebellious governments, replacing them with trustworthy puppets. Tribute was often collected by force, and the Athenians placed the economic resources of the Delian League under tighter and tighter control. Athenian ideas of freedom and democracy did not extend to the citizens of other cities.

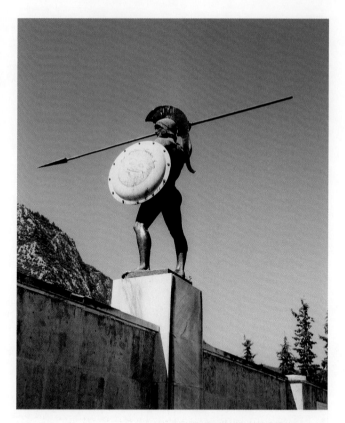

Leonidas at Thermopylae This heroic statue symbolizes the sacrifice of King Leonidas at the battle. Together with his Spartans, the Thespians, and the Thebans, he heroically died to stop the Persians at the pass of Thermopylae. *(Professor Paul Cartledge)*

Athens justified its conduct by its successful leadership. In about 467 B.C. Cimon defeated a new and huge Persian force at the Battle of the Eurymedon River in Asia Minor, once again removing the shadow of Persia from the Aegean. But as the threat from Persia waned and the Athenians treated their allies more harshly, major allies such as Thasos revolted (ca 465 B.C.), requiring the Delian League to use its forces against its own members. The expansion of Athenian power and the aggressiveness of Athenian rule also alarmed Sparta and its allies. While relations between Athens and Sparta cooled, Pericles (ca 494–429 B.C.) became the leading statesman in Athens. Like the democracy he led, Pericles, an aristocrat of solid intellectual ability, was aggressive and imperialistic. At last, in 459 B.C. Sparta and Athens went to war over conflicts between Athens and some of Sparta's allies. Though the Athenians conquered Boeotia, Megara, and Aegina in the early stages of the war, they met defeat in Egypt and later in Boeotia. The war ended in 445 B.C. with no serious damage to either side and nothing settled. But this war divided the Greek world between the two great powers.

During the 440s and 430s Athens continued its severe policies toward its subject allies and came into conflict with Corinth, one of Sparta's leading supporters (see Map 3.3). In 433 B.C. Athens sided with Corcyra against Corinth in a dispute between the two. Together with the Corcyraean fleet, an Athenian squadron defeated the Corinthian navy in open combat. The next year Corinth and Athens collided again, this time over the Corinthian colony of Potidaea, in a conflict the Athenians also won. In this climate of anger and escalation, Pericles took the next step. To punish Megara for alleged sacrilege, Pericles in 432 B.C. persuaded the Athenians to pass a law, the Megarian Decree, that excluded Megarians from trading with Athens and its empire. In response the Spartans convened a meeting of their allies, whose complaints of Athenian aggression ended with a demand that Athens be stopped. Reluctantly the Spartans agreed to declare war. The real reason for war, according to the Athenian historian Thucydides, was very simple: "The truest explanation, though the one least mentioned, was the great growth of Athenian power and the fear it caused the Lacedaemonians [Spartans], which drove them to war."[2]

The Peloponnesian War (431–404 B.C.)

At the outbreak of this conflict, the Peloponnesian War, the Spartan ambassador Melesippus warned the Athenians: "This day will be the beginning of great evil for the Greeks." Few men have ever prophesied more accurately. The Peloponnesian War lasted a generation and brought in its wake fearful plagues, famine, civil wars, widespread destruction, and huge loss of life.

After a Theban attack on the nearby polis of Plataea, the Peloponnesian War began in earnest. In the next seven years, the army of Sparta and its Peloponnesian allies invaded Attica five times. The Athenians stood behind their walls, but in 430 B.C. the cramped conditions nurtured a dreadful plague, which killed huge numbers, eventually claiming Pericles himself. (See the feature "Listening to the Past: The Great Plague at Athens, 430 B.C." on pages 92–93.) The death of Pericles opened the door to a new breed of politicians, men who were rash, ambitious, and more dedicated to themselves than to Athens. One such was Cleon, a very daring and in some ways a very capable man. To divert the constant Spartan invasions of Attica, Cleon proposed a counterattack at Pylos, a rocky peninsula in Messenia immediately

opposite the Spartan-occupied island of Sphacteria. Spartan forces were defeated, yet the outcome failed to bring peace. Instead, the energetic Spartan commander Brasidas widened the war in 424 B.C. by capturing Amphipolis on the northern coast of the Aegean, one of Athens's most valuable subject states. Two years later, both Cleon and Brasidas were killed in a battle to recapture the city. Recognizing that ten years of war had resulted only in death, destruction, and stalemate, Sparta and Athens concluded the Peace of Nicias in 421 B.C.

The Peace of Nicias resulted in a cold war. But even cold war can bring horror and misery. Such was the case when in 416 B.C. the Athenians sent a fleet to the neutral island of Melos with an ultimatum: the Melians could surrender or perish. The motives of the Athenians were frankly and brutally imperialistic. The Melians resisted. The Athenians conquered them, killed the men of military age, and sold the women and children into slavery.

The cold war grew hotter, thanks to the ambitions of Alcibiades (ca 450–404 B.C.), an aristocrat, a kinsman of Pericles, and a student of the philosopher Socrates. A shameless opportunist, Alcibiades widened the war to further his own career and to increase the power of Athens. He convinced the Athenians to attack Syracuse, the leading polis in Sicily. His only valid reason lay in the argument that such an operation would cut the grain supply from Sicily to the Peloponnesus. The undertaking was vast, requiring an enormous fleet and thousands of sailors and soldiers. Trouble began at the outset. Alcibiades' political enemies indicted him, whereupon he fled to Sparta rather than stand trial. Meanwhile, in 414 B.C. the Athenians laid siege to Syracuse. The Syracusans fought back bravely, and even a huge Athenian relief force failed to conquer the city. Finally, in 413 B.C. the Syracusans counterattacked, completely crushing the Athenians. Thucydides wrote the epitaph for the Athenians: "infantry, fleet, and everything else were utterly destroyed, and out of many few returned home."[3]

The disaster in Sicily ushered in the final phase of the war, which was marked by three major developments: the renewal of war between Athens and Sparta, Persia's intervention in the war, and the revolt of many Athenian subjects. The year 413 B.C. saw Sparta's declaration of war against Athens and widespread revolt within the Athenian Empire. Yet Sparta still lacked a navy, the only instrument that could take advantage of the unrest of Athens's subjects, most of whom lived either on islands or in Ionia. The sly Alcibiades, now working for Sparta, provided a solution: he engineered an alliance between Sparta and Persia. The Persians agreed to build a fleet for Sparta. In return, the Spartans promised to give Ionia back to Persia. Now equipped with a fleet, the Spartans challenged the Athenians in the Aegean, the result being a long roll of inconclusive naval battles.

The strain of war prompted the Athenians in 407 B.C. to recall Alcibiades from exile. He cheerfully double-crossed the Spartans and Persians, but even he could not restore Athenian fortunes. In 405 B.C. Athens met its match in the Spartan commander Lysander, a man whose grasp of strategy, politics, and diplomacy easily rivaled Alcibiades'. Lysander destroyed the last Athenian fleet at the Battle of Aegospotami, after which the Spartans blockaded Athens until it was starved into submission. After twenty-seven years the Peloponnesian War was over, and the evils prophesied by the Spartan ambassador Melesippus in 431 B.C. had come true.

Athenian Arts in the Age of Pericles

In the last half of the fifth century B.C., Pericles turned Athens into the showplace of Greece. He appropriated Delian League funds to pay for a huge building program, planning temples and other buildings to honor Athena, the patron goddess of the city, and to display to all Greeks the glory of the Athenian polis. Pericles also pointed out that his program would employ many Athenians and bring economic prosperity to the city.

Thus began the undertaking that turned the Acropolis into a monument for all time. Construction of the Parthenon began in 447 B.C., followed by the Propylaea, the temple of Athena Nike (Athena the Victorious), and the Erechtheum (see Map 3.4). Even the pollution of modern Athens, although it is destroying the ancient buildings, cannot rob them of their splendor and charm.

The planning of the architects and the skill of the workmen who erected these buildings were both very sophisticated. Visitors approaching the Acropolis first see the Propylaea, the ceremonial gateway, a building of complicated layout and grand design whose Doric columns seem to hold up the sky. On the right is the small temple of Athena Nike, whose dimensions harmonize with those of the Propylaea. The temple was built to commemorate the victory over the Persians, and the

The Acropolis of Athens These buildings embody the noblest spirit of Greek architecture. From the entrance visitors walk through the Propylaea and its pillars. Ahead opens the grand view of the Parthenon, still noble in ruins. To the left stands the Erechtheum, the whole a monument to Athens itself. *(Courtesy, Sotiris Toumbis Editions)*

MAP 3.4 Ancient Athens By modern standards, the city of Athens was hardly more than a town, not much larger in size than one square mile. Yet this small area reflects the concentration of ancient Greek life in the polis.

Ionic frieze above its columns depicts the struggle between the Greeks and the Persians. Here for all the world to see is a tribute to Athenian and Greek valor—and a reminder of Athens's part in the victory.

To the left of the visitors, as they pass through the Propylaea, stands the Erechtheum, an Ionic temple that housed several ancient shrines. On its southern side is the famous Portico of the Caryatids, a porch whose roof is supported by statues of Athenian maidens. The graceful Ionic columns of the Erechtheum provide a delicate relief from the prevailing Doric order of the massive Propylaea and Parthenon.

As visitors walk on, they obtain a full view of the Parthenon, thought by many to be the perfect Doric temple. The Parthenon is the chief monument to Athena and her city. The sculptures that adorn the temple portray the greatness of Athens and its goddess. The figures on the eastern pediment depict Athena's birth, those on the west the victory of Athena over the god Poseidon in their struggle for the possession of Attica. Inside the Parthenon stood a huge statue of Athena, the masterpiece of the great sculptor Phidias.

In many ways the Athenian Acropolis is the epitome of Greek art and its spirit. Although the buildings were dedicated to the gods and most of the sculptures portray gods, these works nonetheless express the Greek fascination with the human and the rational. Greek deities were anthropomorphic, and Greek artists portrayed them as human beings. While honoring the gods, Greek artists were thus celebrating human beings. In the Parthenon sculptures it is visually impossible to distinguish the men and women from the gods and goddesses. The Acropolis also exhibits the rational side of Greek art. Greek artists portrayed action in a balanced, restrained, and sometimes even serene fashion, capturing the noblest aspects of human beings: their reason, dignity, and promise.

Other aspects of Athenian cultural life were as rooted in the life of the polis as were the architecture and sculpture of the Acropolis. The development of drama was tied to the religious festivals of the city. The polis sponsored the production of plays and required that wealthy citizens pay the expenses of their production. At the beginning of the year, dramatists submitted their plays to the archon. He chose those he considered best and assigned a theatrical troupe to each playwright. Although most Athenian drama has perished, enough has survived to prove that the archons had superb taste. Many plays were highly controversial, but the archons neither suppressed nor censored them.

Mosaic of the Muses   Not found in a great or famous urban center, this mosaic nonetheless testifies to the wide dissemination of culture and art throughout Greece. The figures of the mosaic represent the nine Muses, goddesses of the arts. The lyre of Apollo occupies the center, and Clio, the goddess of history, is represented by the scroll in the upper right of the lyre. (*Professor Nicolas Yalouris, Former General Inspector of Antiquities, Athens*)

The Athenian dramatists were the first artists in Western society to examine such basic questions as the rights of the individual, the demands of society on the individual, and the nature of good and evil. Conflict is a constant element in Athenian drama. The dramatists used their art to portray, understand, and resolve life's basic conflicts.

Aeschylus (525–456 B.C.), the first of the great Athenian dramatists, was also the first to express the agony of the individual caught in conflict. In his trilogy of plays, *The Oresteia,* Aeschylus deals with the themes of betrayal, murder, and reconciliation, urging that reason and justice be applied to reconcile fundamental conflicts. The final play concludes with a prayer that civil dissension never be allowed to destroy the city and that the life of the city be one of harmony and grace.

Sophocles (496–406 B.C.) also dealt with matters personal and political. In *Antigone* he highlights conflicts between divine and human law and comments on the gender order in Greek society. Antigone defies Creon, her uncle and king, to follow divinely established rules and bury her brother against his decree. Creon rages that she is not above the laws he has established, and that if he does not punish her she will be more man than he is. Antigone escapes her punishment by committing suicide.

Sophocles' masterpieces have inspired generations of playwrights. Perhaps his most famous plays are *Oedipus the King* and its sequel, *Oedipus at Colonus. Oedipus the King* is the ironic story of a man doomed by the gods to kill his father and marry his mother. Try as he might to avoid his fate, Oedipus's every action brings him closer to its fulfillment. When at last he realizes that he has carried out the decree of the gods, Oedipus blinds himself and flees into exile. In *Oedipus at Colonus* Sophocles dramatizes the last days of the broken king, whose patient suffering and uncomplaining piety win him an exalted position. In the end the gods honor him for his virtue. The interpretation of these two plays has been hotly debated, but Sophocles seems to be saying that human beings should obey the will of the gods, even without fully understanding it, for the gods stand for justice and order.

Euripides (ca 480–406 B.C.), the last of the three great Greek tragic dramatists, also explored the theme of personal conflict within the polis and sounded the depths of the individual. With Euripides drama entered a new, and in many ways more personal, phase. To him the gods were far less important than human beings. The essence of Euripides' tragedy is the flawed character—men and women who bring disaster on themselves and their loved ones because their passions overwhelm reason. Although Euripides' plays were less popular in his lifetime than were those of Aeschylus and Sophocles, Euripides was a dramatist of genius whose work later had a significant impact on Roman drama.

Writers of comedy treated the affairs of the polis bawdily and often coarsely. Even so, their plays also were performed at religious festivals. The comic playwrights dealt primarily with the political affairs of the polis and the conduct of its leading politicians. Best known are the comedies of Aristophanes (ca 445–386 B.C.), an ardent lover of his city and a merciless critic of cranks and quacks. He lampooned eminent generals, at times depicting them as morons. He commented snidely on Pericles, poked fun at Socrates, and hooted at Euripides. Like Aeschylus, Sophocles, and Euripides, Aristophanes used his art to dramatize his ideas on the right conduct of the citizen and the value of the polis.

Online Study Center **Improve Your Grade**
Primary Source: Socrates Has His Great Mind in the Clouds

Despite the undeniable achievements of the Athenians, many modern historians have exaggerated their importance. They have created the notion of Athenocentricism, the mistaken opinion that Athens stood solely at the center of classical Greek life. This idea fails to do justice to the other Greeks who also shaped society, culture, and history. Athenocentricism actually distorts and denies the richness of the Greek experience. Greece, like the United States, profited by incorporating many different ideas into one enduring culture.

Daily Life in Periclean Athens

In sharp contrast with the rich intellectual and cultural life of Periclean Athens stands the simplicity of its material life. The Athenians—and in this respect they were typical of Greeks in general—lived very happily with comparatively few material possessions. In the first place, there were very few material goods to own. The thousands of machines, tools, and gadgets considered essential for modern life had no counterparts in Athenian life.

The Athenian house was rather simple. Whether large or small, the typical house consisted of a series of rooms built around a central courtyard, with doors opening onto the courtyard. Many houses had bedrooms on an upper floor. Artisans often set aside a room to use as a shop or work area. Larger houses often had a room at the front where the men of the family ate and entertained guests, and a *gynaikon* (women's quarter) at the back where women worked, ate, and slept. Other rooms included the kitchen and bathroom. By modern standards there was not much furniture. In the men's dining room were couches, a sideboard, and small tables. Cups and other pottery were often hung from pegs on the wall.

In the courtyard were the well, a small altar, and a washbasin. If the family lived in the country, the stalls of the animals faced the courtyard. Country dwellers kept oxen for plowing, pigs for slaughtering, sheep for wool, goats for cheese, and mules and donkeys for transportation. Even in the city chickens and perhaps a goat or two roamed the courtyard together with dogs and cats.

Cooking, done over a hearth in the house, provided welcome warmth in the winter. Baking and roasting were done in ovens. Food consisted primarily of various grains, especially wheat and barley, as well as lentils, olives, figs, and grapes. Garlic and onion were popular garnishes, and wine was always on hand. These foods were stored at home in large jars; with them the Greek family sometimes ate fish, chicken, and vegetables. Women ground wheat into flour, baked it into bread, and on special occasions made honey or sesame cakes. The Greeks used olive oil for cooking, as families still do in modern Greece; they also used it as an unguent and as lamp fuel.

By American standards, the Greeks did not eat much meat. On special occasions, such as important religious festivals, the family ate the animal sacrificed to the god and gave the god the exquisite delicacy of the thighbone wrapped in fat. The only Greeks who consistently ate meat were the Spartan warriors. They received a small portion of meat each day, together with the infamous Spartan black broth, a ghastly concoction of pork cooked in blood, vinegar, and salt. One Greek, after tasting the broth, commented that he could easily understand why the Spartans were so willing to die.

In the city a man might support himself as a craftsman—a potter, bronzesmith, sailmaker, or tanner—or he could contract with the polis to work on public buildings, such as the Parthenon and Erechtheum. Certain crafts, including spinning and weaving, were generally done by women. Men and women without skills worked as paid laborers but competed with slaves for work. Slaves were usually foreigners and often barbarians. By "barbarians" the Greeks meant people whose native language was not Greek. Citizens, slaves, and barbarians were paid the same amount for their work.

Slavery was commonplace in Greece, as it was throughout the ancient world. In its essentials Greek slavery resembled Mesopotamian slavery. Slaves received some protection under the law and could buy their freedom. On the other hand, masters could mistreat or neglect their slaves, although killing them was illegal. Most slaves in Athens served as domestics and performed light labor around the house. Nurses for children, teachers of reading and writing, and guardians for young men were often slaves. The lives of these slaves were much like those of their owners. Other slaves were skilled workers who could be found working on public buildings or in small workshops.

Woman Grinding Grain   Here a woman takes the grain raised on the family farm and grinds it by hand in a mill. She needed few tools to turn the grain into flour. *(National Archaeological Museum, Athens/Archaeological Receipts Fund)*

The importance of slavery in Athens must not be exaggerated. Athenians did not own huge gangs of slaves as did Roman owners of large estates. Slave labor competed with free labor and kept wages down, but it never replaced the free labor that was the mainstay of the Athenian economy.

Most Athenians supported themselves by agriculture, but unless the family was fortunate enough to possess holdings in a plain more fertile than most of the land, they found it difficult to reap a good crop from the soil. Many people must have consumed nearly everything they raised. Attic farmers were free and, though hardly prosperous, by no means destitute. They could usually expect yields of five bushels of wheat and ten of barley per acre for every bushel of grain sown. A bad harvest meant a lean year. In many places rural families grew more barley than wheat because of the nature of the soil. Wherever possible they also cultivated vines and olive trees.

Gender and Sexuality

The social condition of Athenian women has been the subject of much debate. One of the difficulties is the fragmentary nature of the evidence. Women appear frequently in literature and art, often in idealized roles, but seldom in historical contexts of a wider and more realistic nature. This is due in part to the fact that most Greek historians of the time recounted primarily the political, diplomatic, and military events of the day, events in which women seldom played a notable part. Yet that does not mean that women were totally invisible in the life of the polis. It indicates instead that ancient sources provide only a glimpse of how women affected the society in which they lived. Athenian men believed that men and women should be segregated and that women should not appear in public, but the reality was less limiting than the ideal.

The status of a free woman of the citizen class was strictly protected by law. Only her children, not those of foreigners or slaves, could be citizens. She was in charge of the household and the family's possessions, yet the law protected her primarily to protect her husband's interests. Raping a free woman was a lesser crime than seducing her, because seduction involved the winning of her affections. This law was concerned not with the husband's feelings but with ensuring that he need not doubt the legitimacy of his children.

Women in Athens and elsewhere in Greece received a certain amount of social and legal protection from their dowries. Upon marriage, the bride's father gave the couple a gift of land or money, which the husband administered. However, it was never his; and in the rare cases of divorce, it returned to the wife's domain. The same is often true in Greece today among the upper class.

A citizen woman's main functions were to bear and raise children. Childbirth could be dangerous for both mother and infant, so pregnant women often made sacrifices or visited temples to ask help from the gods. Demeter and Artemis were particularly favored. In practical terms, citizen women relied on their friends, relatives, and midwives to assist in the delivery. Greek physicians did not concern themselves with obstetrical care.

Citizen women never appeared in court or in the public political assemblies that were the heart of Athenian democracy, though they did attend public festivals, ceremonies, and funerals. They took part in annual processions to honor the goddess Athena and in harvest festivals honoring the goddess Demeter, who protected the city's crops. In a few cases, women were priestesses in the cults of various goddesses. Priestesses prayed in public on behalf of the city and, like priests, were paid for their services. The most prominent priestess was at Delphi, near Athens, where the god Apollo was understood to give messages about the future. The priestess at the oracle at Delphi interpreted these prophecies, and people came from all over Greece and beyond to hear them.

The demands of survival required some ordinary women to work in honest, if somewhat humble, jobs. Chief among them were such ordinary occupations as shopkeepers, which obviously included a public economic importance. Though the reality was more complicated than the ideal, prosperous and respectable citizen women did spend much of their time in the house. We know the names of no female poets, artists, or philosophers from classical Athens. If women wrote anything, it has not survived, as it was not considered worthy of note.

The sources surviving from ancient Athens provide a great deal of information about attitudes toward sexuality among the educated male elite. Plato and Aristotle, the two most important philosophers of ancient Athens, were both suspicious of the power of sexual passion, warning that it distracted men from reason and the search for knowledge. Both men praised a love that was intellectualized and nonsexual, the type of attachment we still term "platonic." (Neither Plato nor Aristotle was concerned about what sex does to women except as this affects men.) Plato developed a dualistic view of both humans and the world, arguing that the unseen realm of ideas was far superior to the visible material world, and that the human mind or soul was trapped in a material body. This mind-body split was a gendered concept, with men associated more with the mind and women with the body. Women's bodies were also viewed as more influenced by their sexual and reproductive organs than were men's; Plato described the womb as an

"animal" that wandered freely around the body, causing physical and mental problems. (This is why the words *hysteria* and *hysterectomy* both have the same Greek root.)

The mind-body split did not originate with Plato, but his acceptance and elaboration of it helped make this concept an important part of Western philosophy from that time on, and led some groups (though not Plato) to reject sexual activity completely. In Aristotle the mind-body split is reflected in the process of procreation (what he termed "generation"), with the male providing the "active principle" and the female simply the "material."

In classical Athens, part of an adolescent citizen's training in adulthood was supposed to entail a hierarchical sexual and tutorial relationship with an older man, who most likely was married and may have had other female sexual partners as well. These relationships between adolescents and men were often celebrated in literature and art, in part because Athenians regarded perfection as possible only in the male. The perfect body was that of the young male, and perfect love was that between an adolescent and an older man, not that between a man and an imperfect woman. This love was supposed to

Greek Courtship Here two young lovers embrace. With one arm around his girl and the other holding a wine vessel, the boy draws his girl nearer. With a smile she seems more interested in her music, for with her right thumb she turns the boy down. *(Erich Lessing/Art Resource, NY)*

Mosaic Portrait of Sappho   The Greek letters in the upper left corner identify this idealized portrait as that of Sappho. The mosaic, which was found in Sparta, dates to the Roman Empire and testifies to Sappho's popularity in antiquity. *(Museum of Sparta/Archaeological Receipts Fund)*

become intellectualized and "platonic" once the adolescent became an adult.

How often actual sexual relations between men or between men and women approached the ideal in Athens is very difficult to say, as most of our sources are prescriptive, idealized, or fictional. (This is also true for the tiny number of sources that refer to female-female sexual desire, the most famous of which are the poems of Sappho, a female poet who lived on the island of Lesbos in the sixth century B.C. Sappho and her home island were later associated with female homosexuality, but we do not know how much her poetry reflected her life.) We know that female and male prostitution was legal and common, and that female prostitutes were divided into well-educated and beautiful **hetairai** and the lower-class, ordinary prostitutes the Greeks called **pornoi.** (See the feature "Individuals in Society: Aspasia.") We also know that most Athenians married and had children, for they saw the continuation of the family line as essential. Sex-

ual desire and procreation were both important aspects of life, but they were not necessarily linked for ancient Greeks.

Greek Religion

Greek religion is extremely difficult for modern people to understand, largely because of the great differences between Greek and modern cultures. In the first place, it is not even easy to talk about "Greek religion," since the Greeks had no uniform faith or creed. Although the Greeks usually worshiped the same deities—Zeus, Hera, Apollo, Athena, and others—the cults of these gods and goddesses varied from polis to polis. The Greeks had no sacred books such as the Bible, and Greek religion was often a matter more of ritual than of belief. Nor did cults impose an ethical code of conduct. Greeks did not have to follow any particular rule of life, practice certain virtues, or even live decent lives in order to participate. Unlike the Egyptians and Hebrews, the Greeks lacked a priesthood as the modern world understands the term. In Greece priests and priestesses existed to care for temples and sacred property and to conduct the proper rituals, but not to make religious rules or doctrines, much less to enforce them. In short, there existed in Greece no central ecclesiastical authority and no organized creed.

Although temples to the gods were common, they were unlike modern churches or synagogues in that they were not normally places where a congregation met to worship as a spiritual community. Instead, the individual Greek man or woman either visited the temple occasionally on matters of private concern or walked in a procession to a particular temple to celebrate a particular festival. In Greek religion the altar, which stood outside the temple, was important; when the Greeks sought the favor of the gods, they offered them sacrifices. Greek religious observances were generally cheerful. Festivals and sacrifices were frequently times for people to meet together socially, times of high spirits and conviviality rather than of pious gloom. By offering the gods parts of the sacrifice while consuming the rest themselves, worshipers forged a bond with the gods. Some deities were particularly worshiped by men and some by women.

The most important members of the Greek pantheon were Zeus, the king of the gods, and his consort, Hera.

Individuals in Society

Aspasia

If it is necessary for me indeed to speak of female virtues, to those of you who have now become widows, I shall explain the entire situation briefly. It is in your hands whether you will not fall below your nature. The greatest glory to you is to be least talked about by men, either for excellence or blame" (Thucydides 2.46). These words were reportedly uttered by Pericles to the widows at a public funeral honoring those killed during the first year of the Peloponnesian War. Whether Pericles actually said the words is for the most part irrelevant. Their significance is in their expression of Athenian gender ideals. Pericles had just finished a long speech praising the dead soldiers as ideal men, then added this brief comment about women. While men's actions should be noted and recorded, he said, women's should be ignored, for their "greatest glory" was oblivion.

This ideal became the reality for most Athenian women, whose names and actions never became part of "history." It was not true, however, for the woman Pericles himself may have cared the most about—Aspasia.

Aspasia was born in the Greek city of Miletus and came to Athens in about 445 B.C. She is easily one of the most intriguing women in ancient history. Little is known about her life, but she played a role in Athenian society that was far more renowned than, and far different from, that allegedly proposed for Athenian women by Pericles.

Once in Athens, Aspasia may have become a *hetaira,* which literally means "companion." The duties of a hetaira varied. She accompanied men at dinners and drinking parties, where their wives would not have been welcome, and also served as a sexual partner. The major attractions of a successful hetaira included beauty, intelligent conversation, and proper etiquette. In return she was paid for her services. No contemporary sources specifically say that Aspasia was a hetaira, but she may have been.

Contemporary sources do make clear that Aspasia enjoyed a rare opportunity for a woman to influence the men who shaped the political life of Athens. The Roman biographer Plutarch reports that she enjoyed the company of the most famous men in Athens. Their conversation included philosophy, and in one of the philosopher Plato's dialogues Socrates claims that she taught him the art of public speaking. The story is

probably not true, but it points to her public reputation.

Aspasia was introduced to Pericles, who was either already divorced from his wife or divorced her soon afterward. Because Aspasia was not an Athenian citizen, she and Pericles could not marry, but they did have a son, also named Pericles. When Pericles' sons by his wife died in an epidemic, Pericles pressured the Athenian citizenship to let his son by Aspasia become a citizen. Sons of noncitizen women were normally barred from citizenship (a law Pericles himself had introduced), but the law was waived in this case.

Idealized portrait of Aspasia.
(Alinari/Art Resource, NY)

Pericles was powerful enough to get his way, though he could not halt criticism and ridicule. Not only had he let himself get attached to a foreign woman, but he was more devoted to her than Athenians felt was appropriate for an adult man. Even Athens's greatest statesman was expected to follow the proper gender order in his personal relationships.

Pericles died shortly after his son became a citizen, and Aspasia disappears from the historical record. We can celebrate her achievements, but we do not know what motivated her. A funeral speech attributed to her is included in one of Plato's dialogues, but whether these were her actual words we will never know.

Questions for Analysis

1. How did Aspasia's position as a foreigner in Athens shape her opportunities?
2. In what ways does her story support and in what ways does it contradict the general picture of gender roles in Athenian society?

Online Study Center **Improve Your Grade**
Going Beyond Individuals in Society

Although they were the mightiest and most honored of the deities who lived on Mount Olympus, their divine children were closer to ordinary people. Apollo was especially popular. He represented the epitome of youth, beauty, benevolence, and athletic skill. He was also the god of music and culture and in many ways symbolized the best of Greek culture. His sister Athena, who patronized women's crafts such as weaving, was also a warrior-goddess and had been born from the head of Zeus without a mother. Best known for her cult at Athens, to which she gave her name, she was highly revered throughout Greece, even in Sparta, which eventually became a fierce enemy of Athens. Artemis was Apollo's elder sister. A virgin and a huntress, she oversaw women's passage from virginity to marriage. Paradoxically, though a huntress, she also protected wildlife. There was something wild and free about her. Other divinities watched over every aspect of human life.

The Greeks also honored some heroes. A hero was born of a union of a god or goddess and a mortal and was an intermediate between the divine and the human. A hero displayed his divine origins by performing deeds beyond the ability of human beings. Herakles (or Hercules) was easily the greatest of them. He successfully fulfilled twelve labors, all of which pitted him against mythical opponents or tasks. Like other heroes, he protected mortals from supernatural dangers and provided an ideal of vigorous masculinity.

Besides the Olympian gods, each polis had its own minor deities, each with his or her own local cult. In many instances Greek religion involved the official gods and goddesses of the polis and their cults. The polis administered the cults and festivals, and all were expected to participate in this civic religion, regardless of whether they even believed in the deities being worshiped. Participating unbelievers, who seem to have been a small minority,

Temple at Bassae   The temple at Bassae stands in wild splendor in the mountains of Arcadia. It is an almost perfect Dorian temple, with its massive columns surrounding the *cella,* the inner room that contained the statue of Apollo. In such elevated, lonely places many Greeks felt that they entered a region dear to the gods. *(John Buckler)*

Sacrificial Scene   Much of Greek religion was simple and festive, as this scene demonstrates. The participants include women and boys dressed in their finest clothes and crowned with garlands. Musicians add to the festivities. Only the sheep will not enjoy the ceremony. *(National Archaeological Museum, Athens/Archaeological Receipts Fund)*

were not considered hypocrites. Rather, they were seen as patriotic, loyal citizens who in honoring the gods also honored the polis. If this attitude seems contradictory, an analogy may help. Before baseball games Americans stand at the playing of the national anthem, whether they are Democrats, Republicans, or neither and whether they agree or disagree with the policies of the current administration. They honor their nation as represented by its flag in somewhat the same way an ancient Greek honored the polis and demonstrated solidarity with it by participating in the state cults.

Some Greeks turned to mystery religions like those of the Eleusinian mysteries in Attica and of Trophonios in Boeotia. These mystery religions in some ways foreshadowed aspects of early Christian practices by their rites of initiation, their acceptance of certain doctrines, and generally their promise of life after death. The basic concept of these cults was to unite individuals in an exclusive religious society with particular deities. Those who joined went through a period of preparation in which they learned the essential beliefs of the cult and its necessary rituals. Once they had successfully undergone initiation,

they were forbidden to reveal the secrets of the cult. Consequently, modern scholars know comparatively little about their tenets.

Much religion was local and indeed domestic. Each village possessed its own cults and rituals, and individual families honored various deities privately in their homes. These native rites often remained unknown far beyond their own communities. Women may have played an important part in these celebrations, which in general included all elements of society, slaves included. Many people also believed that magic rituals and spells were effective and sought the assistance of individuals reputed to have special knowledge or powers to cure disease, drive away ghosts, bring good weather, or influence the action of others.

Though Greek religion in general was individual or related to the polis, the Greeks also shared some Pan-Hellenic festivals, the chief of which were held at Olympia in honor of Zeus and at Delphi in honor of Apollo. The festivities at Olympia included the famous games, athletic contests that have inspired the modern Olympic games. Held every four years, these games were for the glory of

A Greek God Few pieces of Greek art better illustrate the conception of the gods as greatly superior forms of human beings than this magnificent statue, over six feet ten inches in height. Here the god, who may be either Poseidon or Zeus, is portrayed as powerful and perfect but human in form. *(National Archaeological Museum, Athens/Archaeological Receipts Fund)*

Zeus. They attracted visitors from all over the Greek world and lasted well into Christian times. The Pythian games at Delphi were also held every four years, but these contests differed from the Olympic games by including musical and literary contests. Both the Olympic and the Pythian games were unifying factors in Greek life, bringing Greeks together culturally as well as religiously.

The Flowering of Philosophy

The myths and epics of the Mesopotamians are ample testimony that speculation about the origin of the universe and of humans did not begin with the Greeks. The signal achievement of the Greeks was the willingness of some to treat these questions in rational rather than mythological terms. Although Greek philosophy did not fully flower until the classical period, Ionian thinkers had already begun in the Archaic period to ask what the universe was made of. These men are called the Pre-Socratics, for their work preceded the philosophical revolution begun by the Athenian Socrates. Though they were keen observers, the Pre-Socratics rarely undertook deliberate experimentation. Instead, they took individual facts and wove them into general theories. Despite appearances, they believed, the universe was actually simple and subject to natural laws. Drawing on their observations, they speculated about the basic building blocks of the universe.

Online Study Center **Improve Your Grade**
Primary Source: The Greeks Seek Answers:
The Pre-Socratic Philosophers

The first of the Pre-Socratics, Thales (ca 600 B.C.), learned mathematics and astronomy from the Babylonians and geometry from the Egyptians. Yet there was an immense and fundamental difference between Near Eastern thought and the philosophy of Thales. The Near Eastern peoples considered such events as eclipses to be evil omens. Thales viewed them as natural phenomena that could be explained in natural terms. In short, he asked why things happened. He believed the basic element of the universe to be water. Although he was wrong, the way in which he had asked the question was momentous: it was the beginning of the scientific method.

Thales' follower Anaximander (d. ca 547 B.C.) continued his work. Anaximander was the first of the Pre-Socratics to use general concepts, which are essential to abstract thought. He theorized that the basic element of the universe is the "boundless" or "endless"—something infinite and indestructible. In his view the earth floats in a void, held in balance by its distance from everything else in the universe. Heraclitus (ca 500 B.C.), however, declared the primal element to be fire. He also declared that the world had neither beginning nor end. Although the universe was eternal, it changed constantly. An outgrowth of this line of speculation was the theory of Democritus (b. ca 460 B.C.) that the universe was made up of invisible, indestructible atoms. The culmination of Pre-Socratic thought was the theory that four simple substances made up the universe: fire, air, earth, and water.

With this impressive heritage behind them, the philosophers of the classical period ventured into new areas of speculation. This development was partly due to the work of Hippocrates (second quarter of the fifth century B.C.), the father of medicine. Like Thales, Hippocrates sought natural explanations for phenomena. Basing his opinions on empirical knowledge, not on religion or magic, he taught that natural means could be employed to fight disease. The human body, he declared, contained four humors, or fluids: blood, phlegm, black bile, and yellow bile. In a healthy body the four humors were in perfect balance; too much or too little of any particular humor caused illness. But Hippocrates broke away from the mainstream of Ionian speculation by declaring that medicine was a separate craft that had its own set of principles.

The distinction between natural science and philosophy on which Hippocrates insisted was also promoted by the Sophists, who traveled the Greek world teaching young men. Despite differences of opinion on philosophical matters, the Sophists all agreed that human beings were the proper subject of study. They also believed that excellence could be taught, and they used philosophy and rhetoric to prepare young men for life in the polis. The Sophists put great emphasis on logic and the meanings of words. They criticized traditional beliefs, religion, rituals, and myths and even questioned the laws of the polis. In essence, they argued that nothing is absolute, that everything is relative. Hence more traditional Greeks considered them wanton and harmful, men who were interested in "making the worse seem the better cause."

One of those who was thought to be a Sophist was Socrates (ca 470–399 B.C.). He was not strictly a Sophist, because he never formally taught or collected fees from anyone. He nonetheless shared the Sophists' belief that human beings and their environment were the essential subjects of philosophical inquiry. Like the Sophists, Socrates thought that excellence could be learned and passed on to others. His approach when posing ethical questions and defining concepts was to start with a general topic or problem and to narrow the matter to its essentials. He did so by continuous questioning, a running dialogue. Never did he lecture. Socrates thought that by constantly pursuing excellence, an essential part of which

was knowledge, human beings could approach the supreme good and thus find true happiness. Yet in 399 B.C. Socrates was brought to trial, convicted, and executed on charges of corrupting the youth of the city and introducing new gods.

Socrates' student Plato (427–347 B.C.) carried on his master's search for truth. Unlike Socrates, however, Plato founded a philosophical school, the Academy. He spent his entire life trying to determine the ideal polis. This ideal state could exist only when its citizens were well educated. From education came the possibility of determining an all-comprising unity of virtues that would lead to an intelligent, moral, and ethical life. He further concluded that only divine providence could guide people to virtue. In his opinion, divine providence was one intelligible and individualistic being. In short, he equated god with the concept of good. Plato's tool was mathematics as the servant of education. Although human life is transitory, ideas are permanent. If people could master the essential ideas, guided by mathematics, their souls would become immortal. It was the highest duty of true statesmen to educate their people to reach this higher good.

Plato developed the theory that all visible, tangible things are unreal and temporary, copies of "forms" or "ideas" that are constant and indestructible. Only the mind, not the senses, can perceive eternal forms. In Plato's view the highest form is the idea of good. He discussed these ideas in *The Republic* and *The Laws*. His perfect polis was utopian and could exist only if its rulers were philosophers. Despite his efforts, Plato ultimately failed to realize his utopia, but at least he introduced the concept of trying to shape an ideal society.

Aristotle (384–322 B.C.) carried on the philosophical tradition of Socrates and Plato. Aristotle tried to understand the changes of nature—what caused them and where they led. He also attempted to bridge the gap between abstract truth and concrete perception. He argued that the universe is finite, spherical, and eternal. In the process, he discussed an immaterial being that is his conception of a god that neither created the universe nor guided it. He discussed these ideas in two masterful works, *Physics* and *Metaphysics*, in which he combined empiricism, or observation, and speculative method. He postulated the four principles of matter, form, movement, and goal. Although Aristotle considered nature impersonal, he also concluded that it had its own purpose.

For Aristotle, nature's primary purpose and aim was perfection, and Aristotle termed anything less than

Statue of Eirene   The Athenians erected this statue of Eirene (Peace) holding Ploutos (Wealth) in her left arm. Athens had seen only war for some fifty-six years, and the statue celebrated the Common Peace of 375 B.C. The bitter irony of this poignant scene is that the treaty lasted scarcely a year. *(Glyptothek, Munich/Studio Koppermann)*

perfect "monstrous." Women, in his opinion, were imperfect men, the result of something wrong with the conception that created them—their parents were too young or too old, or too diverse in age, or one of them was not healthy. Because nature always aimed at perfection, woman was thus "a deformity, but one which occurs in the ordinary course of nature."[4] Aristotle was not sure exactly why imperfect men were required in the natural scheme of things, but he decided that it must be because they performed a function necessary for men. His fundamental question about women was "What are women *for?*" whereas about men it was "What *is* man?" Aristotle did view the household and women's role within it as important, but because he regarded women as fundamentally intellectually inferior, he saw their primary function as procreation, not companionship. The philosopher Plato agreed. As we saw above, he viewed the best love and friendship as that between men, and he commented in one of his dialogues that originally all humans had been male, but some had been reborn as women when they proved to be cowardly and wicked. In his most important work, the *Republic,* Plato does include women among the group of people who governed the rest, but because he also abolishes the family for this group, these are women who have rejected or escaped the traditional female role and have become more like men.

Online Study Center   **Improve Your Grade**
   Primary Source: Plato on the Equality of Women
   in His Republic

Athenian philosophers thus reflected their own society in their thought, but they also called for a broader examination of the universe and the place of humans in it than had earlier thinkers. Both the breadth of their vision and its limitations are important legacies to Western civilization.

The Final Act (404–338 B.C.)

The turbulent period from 404 to 338 B.C. is sometimes mistakenly seen as a period of failure and decline. It was instead a vibrant era in which Plato and Aristotle thought and wrote, one in which literature, oratory, and historical writing flourished. The architects of the fourth century B.C. designed and built some of the finest buildings of the classical period, and engineering made great strides. If the fourth century was a period of decline, this was so only in politics. The Peloponnesian War and its aftermath proved that the polis had reached the limits of its success

MAP 3.5 Greece in 362 B.C. The fourth century B.C. witnessed the rapid growth of Greek federalism as states sought allies to gain security from rival powers.

as an effective political institution. The attempts of various city-states to dominate the others led only to incessant warfare. The polis system was committing suicide.

The Greeks of the fourth century B.C. experimented seriously with two political concepts in the hope of preventing war. First was the **Common Peace,** the idea that the states of Greece, whether large or small, should live together in peace and freedom, each enjoying its own laws and customs. In 386 B.C. this concept was a vital part of a peace treaty with the Persian Empire, in which the Greeks and Persians pledged themselves to live in harmony.

Federalism, the second concept to become prominent, already had a long history in some parts of Greece (see page 65). Strictly speaking, the new impetus toward federalism was intended more to gain security through numbers than to prevent war. Greek leagues had usually grown up in regions where geography shaped a well-defined area and where people shared a broad kinship. By banding together, the people of these leagues could mar-

shal their resources, both human and material, to defend themselves from outside interference. In the fourth century B.C. at least ten other federations of states either came into being or were revitalized (see Map 3.5). Federalism never led to a United States of Greece, but the concept held great importance not only for fourth-century Greeks but also for the Hellenistic period and beyond. In 1787, when the Founding Fathers met in Philadelphia to frame the Constitution of the United States, they studied Greek federalism very seriously in the hope that the Greek past could help guide the American future.

• *How did the Greek city-states meet political and military challenges, and how did Macedonia become dominant?*

The Struggle for Hegemony

If neither the Common Peace nor federalism put an end to interstate rivalry, the main reason was the stubborn desire of the principal states to dominate the others. The chief states—Sparta, Athens, and Thebes—each tried to create a **hegemony,** that is, a political ascendancy over other states, even though they sometimes paid lip service to the ideals of the Common Peace. In every instance, the ambition, jealousy, pride, and fear of the major powers doomed the effort to achieve genuine peace. In short, each major power wanted to be the leader, or *hegemon,* and refused to bow to the others that aspired to the same position.

When the Spartan commander Lysander defeated Athens in 404 B.C., the Spartans used their victory to build an empire instead of ensuring the freedom of all Greeks. Their decision quickly brought the Spartans into conflict with Persia, which now demanded the return of Ionia to its control (see page 70), and also with their own allies. The Spartan king Agesilaos, an impetuous man of mediocre ability, waged a fruitless war against the Persians in Ionia. From 400 to 386 B.C. that war eventually engulfed Greece itself. After years of stalemate the Spartans made peace with Persia and their Greek enemies. The result was the first formal Common Peace, the King's Peace of 386 B.C., which cost Sparta its empire but not its position of ascendancy in Greece.

Not content with Sparta's hegemony of Greece, Agesilaos betrayed the very concept of the Common Peace to punish cities that had opposed Sparta during the war. He treacherously ordered Thebes to be seized and even condoned an unwarranted and unsuccessful attack on Athens. Agesilaos had gone too far. Even though it appeared that his naked use of force had made Sparta supreme in Greece, his imperialism was soon to lead to Sparta's downfall at the hands of the Thebans, the very people whom he sought to tyrannize.

The first sign of Spartan failure came in 378 B.C. after an unprovoked attack on Athens. The enraged Athenians created the Second Athenian Confederacy, a federation of states to guarantee the Greeks their rights under the Common Peace (see Map 3.5). Thebes joined Athens, and the two fought Sparta until 371 B.C. Owing to its growing fear of Theban might, Athens made a separate peace with Sparta. Left alone, Thebes defended itself until later that year, when the brilliant Theban general Epaminondas routed the Spartan army on the small plain of Leuctra.

The defeat of the once-invincible Spartans stunned the Greeks, who wondered how Thebes would use its victory. Epaminondas, also a gifted statesman, immediately grappled with the problem of how to translate military success into political reality. First, in a series of invasions

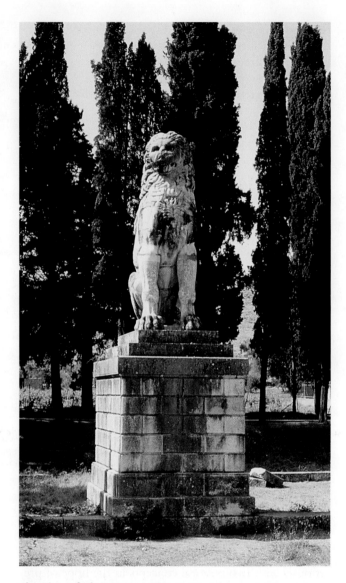

The Lion of Chaeronea This stylized lion marks the mass grave of nearly three hundred elite Theban soldiers who valiantly died fighting the Macedonians at the Battle of Chaeronea. After the battle, when Philip II viewed the bodies of these brave troops, he said: "May those who suppose that these men did or suffered anything dishonorable perish wretchedly." *(Caroline Buckler)*

he eliminated Sparta as a major power and liberated Messenia. He concluded alliances with many Peloponnesian states but made no effort to dominate them. Steadfastly refusing to create a Theban empire, he instead sponsored federalism in Greece. He also threw his support behind the Common Peace. Although he made Thebes the leader of Greece from 371 to 362 B.C., other city-states and leagues were bound to Thebes only by voluntary alliances. By his insistence on the liberty of the Greeks, Epaminondas, more than any other person in Greek history, successfully blended the three concepts of hegemony, federalism, and the Common Peace. His premature death at the Battle of Mantinea in 362 B.C. put an end to his efforts, but not to these three political ideals. The question was whether anyone or any state could realize them all.

Philip and the Macedonian Ascendancy

While the Greek states exhausted one another in endless conflicts, a new and unlikely power rose in the north. In 359 B.C. Philip II, one of the most remarkable men in history, became king of Macedonia. Macedonia was by nature potentially strong. The land, extensive and generally fertile, bordered on the east by the Aegean Sea, nurtured a numerous and hardy population. Yet Macedonia was often distracted by foreign opportunists, the Athenians among them, and divided by internal dissension. Nevertheless, under a strong king Macedonia was a power to be reckoned with. Although the Greeks considered the Macedonians backward, Philip was a brilliant, cultured, and sometimes charming man. As a youth he spent several years in Thebes, when Epaminondas was at the height of his power. In Thebes Philip learned about Greek politics and observed the military innovations of Epaminondas. He also fully understood the strengths and needs of the Macedonians, whose devotion he won virtually on the day that he ascended the throne.

The young Philip, already a master of diplomacy and warfare, quickly saw Athens as the principal threat to Macedonia. Once he had secured the borders of Macedonia against barbarian invaders, he launched a series of military operations in the northwestern Aegean. Not only did he win rich territory, but he also slowly pushed the Athenians out of the region. Yet the Greeks themselves opened to him the road to ultimate victory in Greece. The opportunity came from still another internecine Greek conflict, the Sacred War of 356 to 346 B.C. The war broke out when the Phocians seized and plundered the sanctuary of Apollo at Delphi. Their sacrilege was openly condoned by Athens and Sparta. When the Thebans and other Greeks failed to liberate Delphi, they invited Philip to intervene. He quickly crushed the Phocians in 346 B.C. and intimidated Athens and Sparta. Athens immediately made peace with him, and he returned to his ambitions in the northern Aegean.

One man in Athens, the orator and politician Demosthenes, concluded that Philip wanted not peace but the rule of all of Greece. He accused Philip of a war of aggression, against which he warned his countrymen and the rest of Greece. Conventional wisdom holds that Demosthenes was right, but careful examination of the treaty and subsequent events prove that Athens, not Philip, broke the peace. Others also saw Philip as a threat. A comic playwright used graveyard humor to depict one of Philip's ambassadors warning the Athenians:

Do you know that your battle will be with men
Who dine on sharpened swords,
And gulp burning firebrands for wine?
Then immediately after dinner the slave
Brings us dessert—Cretan arrows
Or pieces of broken spears.
We have shields and breastplates for
Cushions and at our feet slings and arrows,
And we are crowned with catapults.[5]

These dire predictions and the progress of Philip's military operations at last had their effect. Demosthenes persuaded the Athenians to make an alliance with Thebes, which also saw the Macedonian threat. In 338 B.C. the armies of Thebes and Athens met Philip's veterans at the Boeotian city of Chaeronea. There on one summer's day Philip's army won a hard-fought victory that gave him command of Greece and put an end to classical Greek freedom. Because the Greeks could not put aside their quarrels, they fell to an invader. Yet Philip was wise enough to retain much of what the fourth-century Greeks had achieved. Not opposed to the concepts of peace and federalism, he sponsored a new Common Peace in which all of Greece, except Sparta, was united in one political body under his leadership. Philip thus used the concepts of hegemony, the Common Peace, and federalism as tools of Macedonian domination. The ironic result was the end of the age of classical Greece.

Chapter Summary

- *When the Greeks arrived in Hellas, how did they adapt themselves to their new landscape?*
- *After the Greeks had established the polis in which they lived their political and social lives, how did they shape it into its several historical forms?*
- *What major developments mark the Archaic Greek period in terms of spread of culture and the growth of cities?*
- *How did the Greeks develop their literature, philosophy, religion, and art, and how did war affect this intellectual and social process?*
- *How did the Greek city-states meet political and military challenges, and how did Macedonia become dominant?*

The Greeks entered a land of mountains and small plains, which led them to establish small communities. Sometimes these small communities were joined together in kingdoms, most prominently the Minoan kingdom on the island of Crete and the Mycenaean kingdom on the mainland. Minoans and Mycenaeans used written records, and the fall of these kingdoms led writing to disappear for centuries, a period known as the Greek Dark Age (1100–800 B.C.).

Even though kingdoms collapsed, Greek culture continued to spread, and more independent communities were formed. Such a community, called a polis, developed social and political institutions. Some were democracies, in which government was shared among all citizens, which meant adult free men. Other Greeks established smaller governing bodies of citizens, called oligarchs, who directed the political affairs of all.

During the Archaic Age (800–500 B.C.) Greeks colonized much of the Mediterranean, establishing cities in Asia Minor, southern Italy, Sicily, and southern France. This brought them into contact with many other peoples, and also spread Greek culture widely. During this period Sparta and Athens became the most important polises.

Sparta and Athens joined together to fight the Persian Empire, but later turned against one another in the Peloponnesian War (431–404 B.C.). During this time of

warfare, Athenian leaders turned their city into an architectural showplace, supporting the creation of buildings and statues that are still prized. Playwrights presented tragedies and comedies that dealt with basic issues of life. Life for the men in Athens who were citizens revolved around public political assemblies, while for women it revolved around the household, for Athenian thinkers regarded women as inferior and did not think they should have a public role. Both women and men took part in ceremonies honoring gods and goddesses, though some men, most prominently the philosophers Plato and Aristotle, developed ideas about the universe and the place of humans in it that did not involve the gods.

The Greeks destroyed a good deal of their flourishing world in a series of wars. Despite their political advances, they never really learned how to routinely live peacefully with one another. Their disunity allowed for the rise of Macedonia under the leadership of King Philip II, a brilliant military leader.

Key Terms

Aegean basin	federalism
Minoan	oikist
Mycenaean	homosocial
Linear B	deme
polis	boule
acropolis	ecclesia
hoplites	Delian League
monarchy	hetairai
tyranny	pornoi
democracy	Common Peace
oligarchy	hegemony
isonomia	

Online Study Center   **Improve Your Grade** Flashcards

Suggested Reading

Blundell, Sue. *Women in Ancient Greece.* 1995. An accessible overview of the lives of Greek women.

Boardman, John. *The Greeks Overseas.* 2001. Provides a masterful examination of Greek expansion into the Mediterranean.

Buckler, John. *Aegean Greece in the Fourth Century B.C.* 2003. Treats in detail the history of this very influential century.

Burford, Alison. *Land and Labor in the Greek World.* 1993. Covers the entire topic of agriculture, from tools to practices of land use.

Burkert, Walter. *Greek Religion.* 1987. The authoritative study of ancient religious beliefs, with much material from the sources.

Cartledge, Paul. *The Spartans: The World of the Warrior Heroes of Ancient Greece.* 2002. Tells the story of the rise and fall of Sparta in a lively book designed for a general audience, and assesses the Spartans' legacy to Western culture.

Cohen, David. *Law, Sexuality, and Society: The Enforcement of Morals in Classical Athens.* 1992. Examines the social and legal context of adultery, same-sex relations, and other types of sexual conduct.

Fisher, N. R. E. *Slavery in Ancient Greece.* 1993. A brief analysis of the wide variety of situations faced by Greek slaves.

Gotshalk, R. R. *Homer and Hesiod, Myth and Philosophy.* 2000. Provides a good account of these authors' poetry and their purpose.

Hansen, Mogens Herman. *Polis: An Introduction to the Ancient Greek City-State.* 2006. A thorough introduction to the development and organization of Greek city-states, including famous examples such as Athens and Sparta and lesser-known ones.

Patterson, Cynthia B. *The Family in Greek History.* 2001. Treats the public and private relations of the family, which were interconnected.

Roberts, Jennifer Tolbert. *Athens on Trial: The Antidemocratic Tradition in Western Thought.* 1996. Discusses the antidemocratic tradition in Western thought from its origin in reactions to Athenian democracy to the present.

Thomas, Carol G. *Myth Becomes History.* 1993. An excellent treatment of early Greece and modern historical attitudes toward it.

Winkler, John J. *The Constraints of Desire.* 1989. Examines the anthropology of sex and gender in ancient Greece.

Notes

John Buckler is the translator of all uncited quotations from a foreign language in Chapters 1–6.
1. J. M. Edmonds, *Greek Elegy and Iambus* (Cambridge, Mass.: Harvard University Press, 1931), I.70, frag. 10.
2. Thucydides, *History of the Peloponnesian War* 1.23.
3. Ibid., 7.87.6.
4. Aristotle, *Generation of Animals,* trans. A. L. Peck. Loeb Classics (Cambridge, Mass.: Harvard University Press, 1943), IV, vi, 460.
5. J. M. Edmonds, *The Fragments of Attic Comedy* (Leiden: E. J. Brill, 1971), 2.366–369, Mnesimachos frag. 7.

Listening to the Past

The Great Plague at Athens, 430 B.C.

In 430 B.C. many of the people of Attica sought refuge in Athens to escape the Spartan invasion. The overcrowding of people, the lack of proper sanitation, and the scarcity of clean water exposed the huddled population to virulent disease. Under these conditions, a severe plague attacked the crowded masses. The great historian Thucydides lived in Athens at the time and contracted the disease himself. He was one of the fortunate people who survived the ordeal. For most people, however, the disease proved fatal. Thucydides left a vivid description of the nature of the plague and of people's reaction to it.

People in perfect health suddenly began to have burning feelings in the head; their eyes became red and inflamed; inside their mouths there was bleeding from the throat and tongue, and the breath became unnatural and unpleasant. The next symptoms were sneezing and hoarseness of voice, and before long the pain settled on the chest and was accompanied by coughing. Next the stomach was affected with stomach-aches and with vomitings of every kind of bile that has been given a name by the medical profession, all this being accompanied by great pain and difficulty. In most cases there were attacks of ineffectual retching, producing violent spasms; this sometimes ended with this stage of the disease, but sometimes continued long afterwards. Externally the body was not very hot to the touch, nor was there any pallor: the skin was rather reddish and livid, breaking out into small pustules and ulcers. But inside there was a feeling of burning, so that people could not bear the touch even of the lightest linen clothing, but wanted to be completely naked, and indeed most of all would have liked to plunge into cold water. Many of the sick who were uncared for actually did so, plunging into the water-tanks in an effort to relieve a thirst which was unquenchable; for it was just the same with them whether they drank much or little. Then all the time they were

afflicted with insomnia and the desperate feeling of not being able to keep still.

In the period when the disease was at its height, the body, so far from wasting away, showed surprising powers of resistance to all the agony, so that there was still some strength left on the seventh or eighth day, which was the time when, in most cases, death came from the internal fever. But if people survived this critical period, then the disease descended to the bowels, producing violent ulceration and uncontrollable diarrhoea, so that most of them died later as a result of the weakness caused by this. For the disease, first settling in the head, went on to affect every part of the body in turn, and even when people escaped its worst effects, it still left its traces on them by fastening upon the extremities of the body. It affected the genitals, the fingers, and the toes, and many of those who recovered lost the use of these members; some, too, went blind. There were some also who, when they first began to get better, suffered from a total loss of memory, not knowing who they were themselves and being unable to recognize their friends.

Words indeed fail one when one tries to give a general picture of this disease; and as for the suffering of individuals, they seemed almost beyond the capacity of human nature to endure. Here in particular is a point where the plague showed itself to be something quite different from ordinary diseases: though there were many dead bodies lying about unburied, the birds and animals that eat human flesh either did not come near them or, if they did taste the flesh, died of it afterwards. Evidence for this may be found in the fact that there was a complete disappearance of all birds of prey: they were not to be seen either around the bodies or anywhere else. But dogs, being domestic animals, provided the best opportunity of observing this effect of the plague.

These, then, were the general features of the disease, though I have omitted all kinds of peculiarities which occurred in various individual cases. Meanwhile, during all this time there was no serious outbreak of any of the usual kinds of illness; if any such cases did occur, they ended in the plague. Some died in neglect, some in spite of every possible care being taken of them. As for a recognized method of treatment, it would be true to say that no such thing existed; what did good in some cases did harm in others. Those with naturally strong constitutions were no better able than the weak to resist the disease, which carried away all alike, even those who were treated and dieted with the greatest care. The most terrible thing of all was the despair into which people fell when they realized that they had caught the plague. Terrible, too, was the sight of people dying like sheep through having caught the disease as a result of nursing others. This indeed caused more deaths than anything else. For when people were afraid to visit the sick, then they died with no one to look after them. Indeed, there were many houses in which all the inhabitants perished through lack of attention. When, on the other hand, they did visit the sick, they lost their own lives, and this was particularly true of those who made it a point of honor to act properly. Such people felt ashamed to think of their own safety and went into their friends' houses at times when even the members of the household were so overwhelmed by the weight of their calamities that they had actually given up the usual practice of making laments for the dead. Yet still the ones who felt most pity for the sick and the dying were those who had had the plague themselves and had recovered from it. They knew what it was like and at the same time felt themselves to be safe, for no one caught the disease twice, or, if he did, the second attack was never fatal. . . .

A factor that made matters much worse than they were already was the removal of people from the country into the city, and this particularly affected the newcomers. There were no houses for them, and, living as they did during the hot season in badly ventilated huts, they died like flies. The bodies of the dying were heaped one on top of the other, and half-dead creatures could be seen staggering about in the streets or flocking around the fountains in their desire for water.

The catastrophe was so overwhelming that people, not knowing what would happen next to them, became indifferent to every rule of religion

Coin depicting the god Asclepius, represented by a snake, putting an end to urban plague. (*Bibliothèque nationale de France*)

and law. Athens owed to the plague the beginnings of a state of unprecedented lawlessness. People now began openly to venture on acts of self-indulgence which before then they used to keep in the dark. Thus they resolved to spend their money quickly and to spend it on pleasure, since money and life alike seemed equally ephemeral. As for what is called honor, no one showed himself willing to abide by its laws, so doubtful was it whether one would survive to enjoy the name for it. It was generally agreed that what was both honorable and valuable was the pleasure of the moment and everything that might conceivably contribute to that pleasure. No fear of god or law of man had a restraining influence. As for the gods, it seemed to be the same thing whether one worshiped them or not, when one saw the good and the bad dying indiscriminately. As for offenses against human law, no one expected to be punished. Instead, everyone felt that already a far heavier sentence had been passed on him and was hanging over him, and that before the time for its execution arrived, it was only natural to get some pleasure out of life.

This, then, was the calamity that fell upon Athens, and the times were hard indeed, with people dying inside the city and the land outside being laid waste.

Questions for Analysis

1. What does this account of the plague say about human nature when put in an extreme crisis?

2. Does popular religion offer any solace during such a catastrophe?

3. How did public laws and customs cope with such a disaster?

Source: R. Warner, trans., *Thucydides, History of the Peloponnesian War* (Penguin Classics, 1954), pp. 152–156. Translation copyright © Rex Warner, 1954. Introduction and Appendices copyright © M. I. Finley, 1972. Reproduced by permission of Penguin Books Ltd.

Tetrapylon of Aphrodisias. This monumental gate celebrates the beautiful and rich city of Aphrodisias in modern Turkey. *(John Buckler)*

THE HELLENISTIC WORLD, 336–146 B.C.

chapter preview

Alexander and the Great Crusade

• *Why did Alexander launch his massive attack on the Persian Empire? Did he have a pressing reason to take such a huge risk?*

Alexander's Legacy

• *What was Alexander's legacy to the Hellenistic world, and what did it mean to Greeks and Easterners alike? What were its effects on this new world?*

The Spread of Hellenism

• *How far did Hellenism spread, and what effect did it have on both Greeks and those unfamiliar with Greek culture?*

The Economic Scope of the Hellenistic World

• *What economic effect did Alexander's opening of the East have on Greeks and Easterners? Did close economic contact bring them together in any significant way?*

Hellenistic Intellectual Advances

• *How did Hellenistic scientific, philosophical, medical, and religious advances affect the lives of men and women in this period?*

Two years after his conquest of Greece, Philip II of Macedon fell victim to an assassin's dagger. Philip's twenty-year-old son, historically known as Alexander the Great (r. 336–323 B.C.), assumed the Macedonian throne. This young man, one of the most remarkable personalities of Western civilization, was to have a profound impact on history. By overthrowing the Persian Empire and by spreading *Hellenism*—Greek culture, language, thought, and way of life—as far as India, Alexander was instrumental in creating a new era, traditionally called **Hellenistic** to distinguish it from the Hellenic. As a result of Alexander's exploits, the individualistic and energetic culture of the Greeks came into intimate contact with the venerable older cultures of the Near East.

Alexander and the Great Crusade

• *Why did Alexander launch his massive attack on the Persian Empire? Did he have a pressing reason to take such a huge risk?*

In 336 B.C. Alexander inherited not only Philip's crown but also his policies. After his victory at Chaeronea, Philip had organized the states of Greece into a huge league under his leadership and announced to the Greeks his plan to lead them and his Macedonians against the Persian Empire. Fully intending to carry out Philip's designs, Alexander proclaimed to the Greek world that the invasion of Persia was to be a great crusade, a mighty act of revenge for the Persian invasion of Greece in 480 B.C. It would also be the means by which Alexander would create an empire of his own in the East.

Despite his youth, Alexander was well prepared to lead the attack. Philip had groomed his son to become king and had given him the best education possible. In 334 B.C. Alexander led an army of Macedonians and Greeks into Asia Minor. With him went a staff of philosophers and poets, scientists whose job it was to map the country and study strange animals and plants, and the historian Callisthenes, who was to write an

Online Study Center

This icon will direct you to interactive activities and study materials on the website **college.hmco.com/pic/mckaywest9e**

MAP 4.1 Alexander's Conquests   This map shows the course of Alexander's invasion of the Persian Empire and the speed of his progress. More important than the great success of his military campaigns was his founding of Hellenistic cities in the East.

Online Study Center **Improve Your Grade** Interactive Map:
Conquests of Alexander the Great

account of the campaign. Alexander intended not only a military campaign but also an expedition of discovery.

In the next three years Alexander won three major battles at the Granicus River, Issus, and Gaugamela. As Map 4.1 shows, these battle sites stand almost as road signs marking his march to the East. When Alexander reached Egypt, he quickly seized the land, honored the priestly class, and was proclaimed pharaoh, the legitimate ruler of the country. He next marched to the oasis of Siwah, west of the Nile Valley, to consult the famous oracle of Zeus-Amon. No one will ever know what the priest told him, but henceforth Alexander considered himself the son of Zeus. Next he marched into western Asia, where at Gaugamela he defeated the Persian army. After this victory the principal Persian capital of Persepolis easily fell

to him. There he performed a symbolic act of retribution by burning the buildings of Xerxes, the invader of Greece. In 330 B.C. he took Ecbatana, the last Persian capital, and pursued the Persian king to his death.

The Persian Empire had fallen, and the war of revenge was over, but Alexander had no intention of stopping. He dismissed his Greek troops but permitted many of them to serve on as mercenaries. Alexander then began his personal odyssey. With his Macedonian soldiers and Greek mercenaries, he set out to conquer the rest of Asia. He plunged deeper into the East, into lands completely unknown to the Greek world. It took his soldiers four additional years to conquer Bactria and the easternmost parts of the now-defunct Persian Empire, but still Alexander was determined to continue his march.

In 326 B.C. Alexander crossed the Indus River and entered India. There, too, he saw hard fighting, and finally at the Hyphasis River his troops refused to go farther. Alexander was enraged by the mutiny, for he believed he was near the end of the world. Nonetheless, the army stood firm, and Alexander relented. Still eager to explore the limits of the world, Alexander turned south to the Arabian Sea. Though the tribes in the area did not oppose him, he waged a bloody, ruthless, and unnecessary war against them. After reaching the Arabian Sea and turning west, he led his army through the grim Gedrosian Desert. The army suffered fearfully, and many soldiers died along the way; nonetheless, in 324 B.C. Alexander reached his camp at Susa. The great crusade was over, and Alexander himself died the next year in Babylon.

Alexander's Legacy

Alexander so quickly became a legend during his lifetime that he still seems superhuman. That alone makes a reasoned interpretation of him very difficult. Some historians have seen him as a high-minded philosopher, and none can deny that he possessed genuine intellectual gifts. Others, however, have portrayed him as a bloody-minded autocrat, more interested in his own ambition than in any philosophical concept of the common good. Alexander is the perfect example of the need for the historian to interpret the known facts carefully.

Alexander at the Battle of Issus   At left, Alexander the Great, bareheaded and wearing a breastplate, charges King Darius, who is standing in a chariot. The moment marks the turning point of the battle, as Darius turns to flee from the attack. (*National Museum, Naples/Alinari/Art Resource, NY*)

Online Study Center **Improve Your Grade**
Primary Source: Alexander the Great Remembered: Visions of Divinity

The historical record shows that Alexander in a drunken brawl murdered the friend who had saved his life at the Battle of the Granicus River. Alexander also used his power to have several other trusted officials, who had done nothing to offend him, assassinated. Other uglier and grimmer facts argue against the view that Alexander was a humane and tolerant man. In eastern Iran and India he savagely and unnecessarily slaughtered peoples whose only crime was their desire to be left in peace.

The only rationale to support those who see Alexander as a philosopher-king comes from a banquet held in 324 B.C. at the end of his career of carnage. This event is very important for a variety of reasons. It came immediately on the heels of a major Macedonian mutiny. The veteran and otherwise loyal Macedonians resented Alexander's new policy of giving high offices to Persians, people whom they had conquered after great suffering. Alexander realized that his Macedonians were too few to administer his new empire and that he needed the ability and experience of the Persians. As a gesture of reconciliation and to end the mutiny, Alexander named the entire Macedonian army his kinsmen and held a vast banquet to heal wounds. He reserved the place of honor for the Macedonians, giving the Persians and others positions of lesser status. At the banquet Alexander offered a public prayer for harmony and partnership between the Macedonians and the Persians, and this prayer has been interpreted as an expression of deep philosophical views. (See the feature "Listening to the Past: Alexander and the Brotherhood of Man" on pages 120–121.) But far from representing an ideal desire for the brotherhood of man, the gesture was a blatant call for Macedonians and Persians to form a superior union for the purpose of ruling his new empire. The concepts of universal harmony and the brotherhood of man became common during the Hellenistic period, but they were the creations of talented philosophers, not the battle-hardened king of Macedonia.

Alexander was instrumental in changing the face of politics in the eastern Mediterranean. His campaign swept away the Persian Empire, which had ruled the East for over two hundred years. In its place he established a Macedonian monarchy.

More important in the long run was his founding of new cities and military colonies, which scattered Greeks and Macedonians throughout the East. Thus the practical result of Alexander's campaign was to open the East to the tide of Hellenism.

● *What was Alexander's legacy to the Hellenistic world, and what did it mean to Greeks and Easterners alike? What were its effects on this new world?*

The Political Legacy

In 323 B.C. Alexander the Great died at the age of thirty-two. The main question at his death was whether his vast empire could be held together. A major part of his legacy is what he had not done. Although he fathered a successor while in Bactria, his son was an infant at Alexander's death. The child was too young to assume the duties of kingship and was cruelly murdered. That meant that Alexander's empire was a prize for the taking by the strongest of his generals. Within a week of Alexander's death a round of fighting began that was to continue for forty years. No single Macedonian general was able to replace Alexander as emperor of his entire domain. In effect, the strongest divided it among themselves. By 263 B.C. three officers had split the empire into large monarchies (see Map 4.2). Antigonus Gonatas became king of Macedonia and established the Antigonid dynasty, which ruled until the Roman conquest in 168 B.C. Ptolemy, son of Lagus, made himself king of Egypt, and his descendants, the Ptolemies, assumed the powers and position of pharaohs. Seleucus, founder of the Seleucid dynasty, carved out a kingdom that stretched from the coast of Asia Minor to India. In 263 B.C. Eumenes, the Greek ruler of Pergamum, a city in western Asia Minor, won his independence from the Seleucids and created the Pergamene monarchy. Though the Seleucid kings soon lost control of their easternmost provinces, Greek influence in this area did not wane. In modern Turkestan and Afghanistan another line of Greek kings established the kingdom of Bactria and even managed to spread their power and culture into northern India.

The political face of Greece itself changed during the Hellenistic period. The day of the polis was over; in its place rose leagues of city-states. The two most powerful and extensive were the Aetolian League in western and central Greece and the Achaean League in the Peloponnesus. Once-powerful city-states like Athens and Sparta sank to the level of third-rate powers.

The political history of the Hellenistic period was dominated by the great monarchies and the Greek leagues. The political fragmentation and incessant warfare that

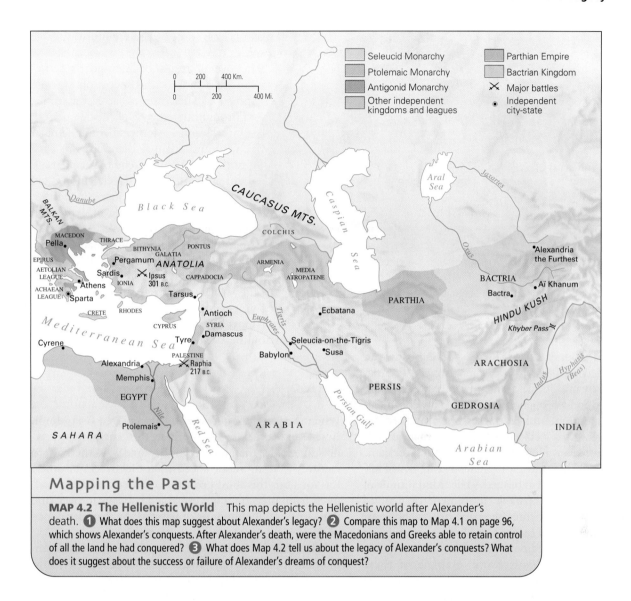

Mapping the Past

MAP 4.2 The Hellenistic World This map depicts the Hellenistic world after Alexander's death. **1** What does this map suggest about Alexander's legacy? **2** Compare this map to Map 4.1 on page 96, which shows Alexander's conquests. After Alexander's death, were the Macedonians and Greeks able to retain control of all the land he had conquered? **3** What does Map 4.2 tell us about the legacy of Alexander's conquests? What does it suggest about the success or failure of Alexander's dreams of conquest?

marked the Hellenic period continued on an even wider and larger scale during the Hellenistic period. Never did the Hellenistic world achieve political stability or lasting peace. Hellenistic kings never forgot the vision of Alexander's empire, spanning Europe and Asia, secure under the rule of one man. Try though they did, they were never able to re-create it. In this respect Alexander's legacy fell not to his generals but to the Romans of a later era.

The Cultural Legacy

As Alexander waded ever deeper into the East, distance alone presented him with a serious problem: how was he to retain contact with the Greek world behind him?

Communications were vital, for he drew supplies and re-inforcements from Greece and Macedonia. Alexander had to be sure that he was never cut off and stranded far from the Mediterranean world. His solution was to plant cities and military colonies in strategic places. In these settlements Alexander left Greek mercenaries and Macedonian veterans who were no longer up to active campaigning. Besides keeping the road open to the West, these settlements served the purpose of dominating the countryside around them.

Their military significance apart, Alexander's cities and colonies became powerful instruments in the spread of Hellenism throughout the East. The Roman biographer Plutarch described Alexander's achievement in glowing

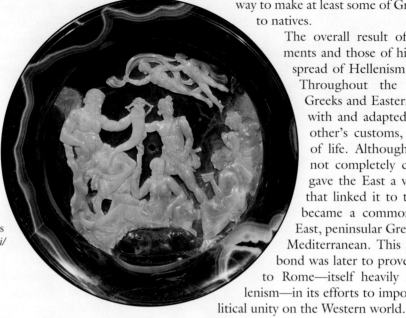

Tazza Farnese This exquisite detail of a cameo bowl from Hellenistic Egypt dates from about 125 B.C. The figure on the left represents the Nile pouring out the horn of plenty. The other figures represent the deities who gave Egypt its great riches. *(G. Dagli-Orti/ The Art Archive)*

terms: "Having founded over 70 cities among barbarian peoples and having planted Greek magistracies in Asia, Alexander overcame its wild and savage way of life."[1] Alexander had indeed opened the East to an enormous wave of immigration, and his successors continued his policy by inviting Greek colonists to settle in their realms. For seventy-five years after Alexander's death, Greek immigrants poured into the East. At least 250 new Hellenistic colonies were established. The Mediterranean world had seen no comparable movement of peoples since the days of Archilochus (see page 66), when wave after wave of Greeks had turned the Mediterranean basin into a Greek-speaking region.

One concrete and almost exotic example of these trends comes from the newly discovered Hellenistic city of Ay Khanoum. Situated on the borders of Russia and Afghanistan and not far from China, the city was predominately Greek. It had the typical Greek trappings of a gymnasium, various temples, and administration buildings. It was not, however, purely Greek. It also contained a temple and artistic remains that prove that the Greeks and the natives had already embraced aspects of each other's religions. One of the most curious discoveries was a long inscription written in Greek verse by Clearchus, a pupil of Aristotle. The inscription, carved in stone, was set up in a public place for all to see. Clearchus had simply copied the precepts of famous Greeks. The inscription was philosophy for the common people, a contribution to popular culture. It provided the Greeks with a link to their faraway homeland. It was also an easy

way to make at least some of Greek culture available to natives.

The overall result of Alexander's settlements and those of his successors was the spread of Hellenism as far east as India. Throughout the Hellenistic period, Greeks and Easterners became familiar with and adapted themselves to each other's customs, religions, and ways of life. Although Greek culture did not completely conquer the East, it gave the East a vehicle of expression that linked it to the West. Hellenism became a common bond among the East, peninsular Greece, and the western Mediterranean. This pre-existing cultural bond was later to prove supremely valuable to Rome—itself heavily influenced by Hellenism—in its efforts to impose a comparable political unity on the Western world.

The Spread of Hellenism

When the Greeks and Macedonians entered Asia Minor, Egypt, and the more remote East, they encountered civilizations older than their own. In some ways the Eastern cultures were more advanced than the Greek, in others less so. Thus this third great tide of Greek migration differed from preceding waves, which had spread over land that was uninhabited or inhabited by less-developed peoples.

What did the Hellenistic monarchies offer Greek immigrants politically and materially? More broadly, how did Hellenism and the cultures of the East affect one another? What did the meeting of East and West entail for the history of the world?

● *How far did Hellenism spread, and what effect did it have on both Greeks and those unfamiliar with Greek culture?*

Cities and Kingdoms

One of the major developments of these new kingdoms was the resurgence of monarchy, which had many repercussions. For most Greeks, monarchs were something out of the heroic past, something found in Homer's *Iliad* but not in daily life. Furthermore, most Hellenistic kingdoms embraced numerous different peoples who had little in common. Hellenistic kings thus needed a new political concept to unite them. One solution was the creation of a ruler cult that linked the king's authority with that of the gods. Thus, royal power had divine approval and was meant to create a political and religious bond between the kings and their subjects. These deified kings were not considered gods as mighty as Zeus or Apollo, and the new ruler cults probably made little religious impact on those ruled. Nonetheless, the ruler cult was an easily understandable symbol of unity within the kingdom.

Hellenistic kingship was hereditary, which gave women who were members of royal families more power than any women in democracies, in which citizenship was limited to men. Wives of kings and queen mothers had influence over their husbands and sons, and a few women ruled in their own right when there was no male heir.

Although Alexander's generals created huge kingdoms, the concept of monarchy, even when combined with the ruler cult, never replaced the ideal of the polis. Consequently, the monarchies never won the deep emotional loyalty that Greeks had once felt for the polis. Hellenistic kings needed large numbers of Greeks to run their kingdoms. Otherwise royal business would grind to a halt, and the conquerors would soon be swallowed up

by the far more numerous conquered population. Obviously, then, the kings had to encourage Greeks to immigrate and build new homes. The Hellenistic kings thus confronted the problem of making life in the new monarchies resemble the traditional Greek way of life. Since Greek civilization was urban, the kings continued Alexander's policy of establishing cities throughout their kingdoms in order to entice Greeks to immigrate. Yet the creation of these cities posed a serious political problem that the Hellenistic kings failed to solve.

To the Greeks civilized life was unthinkable without the polis, which was far more than a mere city. The Greek polis was by definition **sovereign**—an independent, autonomous state run by its citizens, free of any outside power or restraint. Hellenistic kings, however, refused to grant sovereignty to their cities. In effect, these kings willingly built cities but refused to build a polis.

Hellenistic monarchs gave their cities all the external trappings of a polis. Each had an assembly of citizens, a council to prepare legislation, and a board of magistrates to conduct the city's political business. Yet, however similar to the Greek polis they appeared, these cities could not engage in diplomatic dealings, make treaties, pursue their own foreign policy, or wage their own wars. None could govern its own affairs without interference from

The Main Street of Pergamum No matter where in old Greece they had come from, all Greeks would immediately feel at home walking along this main street in Pergamum. They would all see familiar sights. To the left is the top of the theater where they could watch the plays of the great dramatists, climb farther to the temple, and admire the fortifications on the right. *(Faith Cimok, Turkey)*

Theater of Stratos Excavation of this theater in Stratos, a major city in northwestern Greece, began only in 1994. Not a city in the mainstream of Greek affairs, Stratos nevertheless shared the love and appreciation of the arts that stamped all of Greek culture. Even in its partially excavated state, the theater boasts the remains of a stone building in the foreground, the orchestra, and behind it the seats. Beyond its many architectural refinements, the theater is of interest because most Greek plays were staged in small theaters such as this. *(John Buckler)*

the king, who, even if he stood in the background, was the real sovereign. In the eyes of the king the cities were important parts of the kingdom, but the welfare of the whole kingdom came first. The cities had to follow royal orders, and the king often placed his own officials in the cities to see that his decrees were followed.

A new Hellenistic city differed from a Greek polis in other ways as well. The Greek polis had one body of law and one set of customs. In the Hellenistic city Greeks represented an elite citizen class. Natives and non-Greek foreigners who lived in Hellenistic cities usually possessed lesser rights than Greeks and often had their own laws. In some instances this disparity spurred natives to assimilate Greek culture in order to rise politically and socially. The Hellenistic city was not homogeneous and could not spark the intensity of feeling that marked the polis.

An excellent example of this process comes from the city of Pergamum in northwestern Anatolia. Previously an important strategic site, its new Greek rulers turned it into a magnificent city complete with all the typical buildings of the polis. They built the usual government buildings, gymnasia, and baths. They founded a library second only to that in Alexandria. They erected temples to the traditional deities, but they also built an imposing temple to the Egyptian gods. Furthermore, Jews established a synagogue in the city. Especially in the agora Greeks and indigenous people met to conduct business and to learn about each other. Greeks felt as though they were at home, and the evolving culture mixed Greek and local elements.

The old Greek cities of Asia Minor actually, if unintentionally, aided this development by maintaining and spreading traditions that went back for centuries. They served as models for the new foundations by providing a rich legacy of culture and tradition. They shone with such physical beauty in buildings and arts that through their very charm they made Hellenism attractive. They also represented a gracious style of civilized life. In their very combination of refinement, sophistication, and elegance they inspired imitation of the best in Greek culture. All new cities saw in them a link between the past and the blossoming future.

In many respects the Hellenistic city resembled a modern city. It was a cultural center with theaters, temples, and libraries. It was a seat of learning, home of poets, writers, teachers, and artists. It was a place where people could find amusement. The Hellenistic city was also an economic center that provided a ready market for grain and produce raised in the surrounding countryside. The city was an emporium, scene of trade and manufacturing. In short, the Hellenistic city offered cultural and economic opportunities but did not foster a sense of united, integrated enterprise.

There were no constitutional links between city and king. The city was simply his possession. Hellenistic kings tried to make the kingdom the political focus of citizens' allegiance. If the king could secure the frontiers of his kingdom, he could give it a geographical identity. He could then hope that his subjects would direct their primary loyalty to the kingdom rather than to a particular city. However, the kings' efforts to fix their borders led only to sustained warfare. Boundaries were determined by military power, and rule by force became the chief political principle of the Hellenistic world.

Though Hellenistic kings never built a true polis, that does not mean that their urban policy failed. Rather, the Hellenistic city was to remain the basic social and political unit throughout the Hellenistic world until the sixth century A.D. Cities were the chief agents of Hellenization, and their influence spread far beyond their walls. These cities formed a broader cultural network in which Greek language, customs, and values flourished. Roman rule in the Hellenistic world would later be based on this urban culture, which facilitated the rise and spread of Christianity. In broad terms, Hellenistic cities were remarkably successful.

Men and Women in Hellenistic Monarchies

If the Hellenistic kings failed to satisfy the Greeks' political yearnings, they nonetheless succeeded in giving them unequaled economic and social opportunities. The ruling dynasties of the Hellenistic world were Macedonian, and Greeks filled all important political, military, and diplomatic positions. They constituted an upper class that sustained Hellenism in the barbarian East. Besides building Greek cities, Hellenistic kings offered Greeks land and money as lures to further immigration.

The opening of the East offered ambitious Greeks opportunities for well-paying jobs and economic success. The Hellenistic monarchy, unlike the Greek polis, did not depend solely on its citizens to fulfill its political needs. Talented Greek men could expect to rise quickly in the government bureaucracy. Appointed by the king, these administrators did not have to stand for election each year, as had many officials of a Greek polis. Since they held their jobs year after year, they had ample time to evolve new administrative techniques. Naturally, they became more efficient than the amateur officials common in Hellenic Greek city-states. The needs of the Hellenistic monarchy and the opportunities it offered thus gave rise to a professional corps of Greek administrators.

Greeks and Macedonians also found ready employment in the armies and navies of the Hellenistic monarchies. Alexander had proved the Greco-Macedonian style of warfare to be far superior to that of other peoples, and Alexander's successors, themselves

Marital Advice This small terra-cotta sculpture is generally seen as a mother advising her daughter, a new bride. Such intimate scenes of ordinary people were popular in the Hellenistic world, in contrast to the idealized statues of gods and goddesses of the classical period. *(British Museum/Michael Holford)*

experienced officers, realized the importance of trained Greek and Macedonian soldiers. Moreover, Hellenistic kings were extremely reluctant to arm the native populations or to allow them to serve in the army, fearing military rebellions among their conquered subjects. The result was the emergence of professional armies and navies consisting entirely of Greeks and Macedonians.

Greeks were able to dominate other professions as well. The kingdoms and cities recruited Greek writers and artists to create Greek literature, art, and culture on Asian soil. Architects, engineers, and skilled craftsmen found their services in great demand because of the building policies of the Hellenistic monarchs. If Hellenistic kingdoms were to have Greek cities, those cities needed Greek buildings—temples, porticoes, gymnasia, theaters, fountains, and houses. Architects and engineers were sometimes commissioned to design and build whole cities, which they laid out in checkerboard fashion and filled with typical Greek buildings. An enormous wave of construction took place during the Hellenistic period.

The Great Altar of Pergamum   A new Hellenistic city needed splendid art and architecture to prove its worth in Greek eyes. The king of Pergamum ordered the construction of this monumental altar, now in Berlin. The scenes depict the mythical victory of the Greek gods over the Giants, who symbolize barbarism. The altar served the propaganda purpose of celebrating the victory of Hellenism over the East. (*Bildarchiv Preussischer Kulturbesitz/Art Resource, NY*)

Increased physical and social mobility benefited some women as well as men. More women learned to read than before, and they engaged in occupations in which literacy was beneficial, including care of the sick. During the Hellenistic period some women took part in commercial transactions. They still lived under legal handicaps; in Egypt, for example, a Greek woman needed a male guardian to buy, sell, or lease land, to borrow money, and to represent her in other transactions. Yet often such a guardian was present only to fulfill the letter of the law. The woman was the real agent and handled the business being transacted.

Online Study Center **Improve Your Grade**
Primary Source: Gender in the Hellenistic Age: A Woman of Intellectual Merit

Because real power in the Hellenistic world was held by monarchs, the political benefits of citizenship were much less than they had been in the classical period. The diminished importance of citizenship meant that it was awarded more easily. Even women sometimes received honorary citizenship from foreign cities because of aid given in times of crisis. Few women achieved these honors, however, and those who did were from the upper classes.

Despite the opportunities they offered, the Hellenistic monarchies were hampered by their artificial origins. Their failure to win the political loyalty of their Greek subjects and their policy of wooing Greeks with lucrative positions encouraged a feeling of uprootedness and self-serving individualism among Greek immigrants. Once a Greek man had left home to take service with, for instance, the army or the bureaucracy of the Ptolemies, he had no incentive beyond his pay and the comforts of life

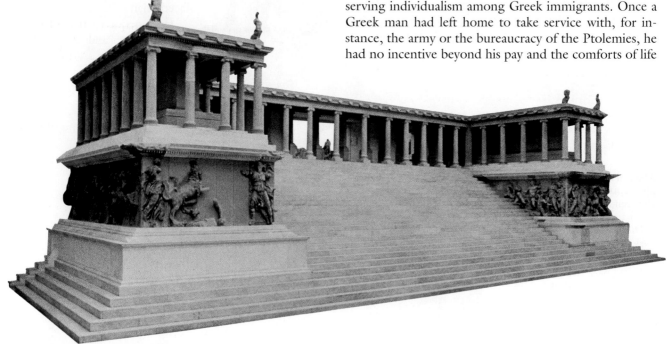

in Egypt to keep him there. If the Seleucid king offered him more money or a promotion, he might well accept it and take his talents to Asia Minor. Why not? In the realm of the Seleucids he, a Greek, would find the same sort of life and environment that the kingdom of the Ptolemies had provided him. Thus professional Greek soldiers and administrators were very mobile and apt to look to their own interests, not their kingdom's.

One result of these developments was that the nature of warfare changed. Except in the areas of Greece and to some extent Macedonia, Hellenistic soldiers were professionals. Unlike the citizen hoplites of classical Greece, these men were regular soldiers capable of intricate maneuvers. Hellenistic kings paid them well, often giving them land as an incentive to remain loyal. Only in Macedonia among the kingdoms was there a national army that was devoted to its land, homes, and monarchy. The loyalty, skill, and bravery of Macedonian soldiers made them the most formidable in the Hellenistic world.

As long as Greeks continued to replenish their professional ranks, the kingdoms remained strong. In the process they drew an immense amount of talent from the Greek peninsula, draining the vitality of the Greek homeland. However, the Hellenistic monarchies could not keep recruiting Greeks forever, in spite of their wealth and willingness to spend lavishly. In time the huge surge of immigration slowed greatly. Even then the Hellenistic monarchs were reluctant to recruit Easterners to fill posts normally held by Greeks. The result was at first the stagnation of the Hellenistic world and finally, after 202 B.C., its collapse in the face of the young and vigorous Roman republic.

Greeks and Easterners

Because they understood themselves to be "the West," Greeks generally referred to Egypt and what we now call the Near East collectively as "the East." Many historians have continued that usage, seeing the Hellenistic period as a time when Greek and "Eastern" cultures blended to some degree. Eastern civilizations were older than Greek, and the Greeks were a minority outside of Greece. Hellenistic monarchies were remarkably successful in at least partially Hellenizing Easterners and spreading a uniform culture throughout the East, a culture to which Rome eventually fell heir. The prevailing institutions, laws, and language of the East became Greek. Indeed, the Near East had seen nothing comparable since the days when Mesopotamian culture had spread throughout the area.

Yet the spread of Greek culture was wider than it was deep. At best it was a veneer, thicker in some places than

Cultural Blending Ptolemy V, a Macedonian by birth and the Hellenistic king of Egypt, dedicated this stone to the Egyptian sacred bull of the Egyptian god Ptah. Nothing here is Greek or Macedonian, a sign that the conquered had, in some religious and ceremonial ways, won over their conquerors. *(Egyptian Museum, Cairo)*

in others. Hellenistic kingdoms were never entirely unified in language, customs, and thought. Greek culture took firmest hold along the shores of the Mediterranean, but farther east, in Persia and Bactria, it was less strong. The principal reason for this curious phenomenon is that Greek culture generally did not extend far beyond the reaches of the cities. Many urban residents adopted the aspects of Hellenism that they found useful, but others in the countryside generally did not embrace it wholly.

The Ptolemies in Egypt provide an excellent example of this situation. They made little effort to spread Greek culture, and unlike other Hellenistic kings they were not city builders. Indeed, they founded only the city of Ptolemais near Thebes. At first the native Egyptian population, the descendants of the pharaoh's people, retained their traditional language, outlook, religion, and way of life. Initially untouched by Hellenism, the natives continued to be the foundation of the state: they fed it by their labor in the fields and financed its operations with their taxes.

Under the pharaohs talented Egyptians had been able to rise to high office, but during the third century B.C. the Ptolemies cut off this avenue of advancement. Instead of converting the natives to Hellenism, the Ptolemies tied them to the land even more tightly, making it nearly impossible for them to leave their villages. The bureaucracy of the Ptolemies was ruthlessly efficient, and the native population was viciously and cruelly exploited. Even in times of hardship the king's taxes came first, although payment might mean starvation for the natives. Their desperation was summed up by one Egyptian, who scrawled the warning: "We are worn out; we will run away."[2] To many Egyptians revolt or a life of brigandage was certainly preferable to working the land under the harsh Ptolemies.

Throughout the third century B.C. the Greek upper class in Egypt had little to do with the native population. Many Greek bureaucrats established homes in Alexandria and Ptolemais, where they managed finances, served as magistrates, and administered the law. Other Greeks settled in military colonies and supplied the monarchy with fighting men. But in the second century B.C. Greeks and native Egyptians began to intermarry and mingle their cultures. The language of the native population influenced Greek, and many Greeks adopted the Egyptian religion and ways of life. Simultaneously, natives adopted Greek customs and language and began to play a role in the administration of the kingdom and even to serve in the army. While many Greeks and Egyptians remained aloof from each other, the overall result was the evolution of a widespread Greco-Egyptian culture.

Meanwhile the Seleucid kings established many cities and military colonies in western Asia Minor and along the banks of the Tigris and Euphrates Rivers in order to nurture a vigorous and large Greek population. Especially important to the Seleucids were the military colonies, for they needed Greeks to defend the kingdom. The Seleucids had no elaborate plan for Hellenizing the native population, but the arrival of so many Greeks was bound to have an impact. Seleucid military colonies were generally founded near native villages, thus exposing rural residents to all aspects of Greek life. Many Easterners found Greek political and cultural forms attractive and imitated them. In Asia Minor and Syria, for instance, numerous native villages and towns developed along Greek lines,

and some of them became Hellenized cities. Farther east, the Greek kings who replaced the Seleucids in the third century B.C. spread Greek culture to their neighbors, even into the Indian subcontinent.

For non-Greeks the prime advantage of Greek culture was its very pervasiveness. The Greek language became the common speech of Egypt and the Near East. A common dialect called **koine** even influenced the speech of peninsular Greece itself. Greek became the speech of the royal court, bureaucracy, and army. It was also the speech of commerce: anyone who wanted to compete in business had to learn it. As early as the third century B.C. some Greek cities were giving citizenship to Hellenized natives.

The vast majority of Hellenized Easterners, however, took only the externals of Greek culture while retaining the essentials of their own ways of life. Though Greeks and Easterners adapted to each other's ways, there was never a true fusion of cultures. Nonetheless, each found useful things in the civilization of the other, and the two fertilized each other. This fertilization, this mingling of Greek and Eastern elements, is what makes Hellenistic culture unique and distinctive.

Hellenism and the Jews

A prime illustration of cultural mingling is the impact of Greek culture on the Jews. At first, Jews in Hellenistic cities were treated as resident aliens. As they grew more numerous, they received permission to form a political corporation, a **politeuma,** which gave them a great deal of autonomy. The Jewish politeuma, like the Hellenistic city, obeyed the king's commands, but there was virtually no royal interference with the Jewish religion. Indeed, the Greeks were always reluctant to tamper with anyone's religion. Antiochus III (ca 242–187 B.C.), for instance, recognized that most Jews had become loyal subjects, and he treated them with great kindness and dignity. In his efforts to solidify his empire he endorsed their religious customs and ensured their political rights. He went so far as to deny any uninvited foreigner permission to enter the temple at Jerusalem. As a result, Hellenism and Judaism usually met on friendly terms. Only the Seleucid king Antiochus Epiphanes (175–ca 164 B.C.) tried to suppress the Jewish religion in Judaea. He did so not because he hated the Jews (who were a small part of his kingdom), but because he was trying to unify his realm culturally to meet the threat of Rome. To the Jews he extended the same policy that he applied to all subjects. Apart from this instance, Hellenistic Jews suffered no official religious persecution. Some Jews were given the right to become full citizens of Hellenistic cities, but few exercised that right. Citizenship would have allowed them to vote in the assembly and serve as magistrates, but it would also have obliged them to worship the gods of the city—a practice few Jews chose to follow.

Jews living in Hellenistic cities often embraced a good deal of Hellenism. So many Jews learned Greek, especially in Alexandria, that the Old Testament was translated into Greek and services in the synagogue came to be conducted in Greek. Jews often took Greek names, used Greek political forms, adopted Greek practice by forming their own trade associations, put inscriptions on graves as the Greeks did, and much else. Yet no matter how much of Greek culture or its externals Jews borrowed, they normally remained attached to their religion.

The Economic Scope of the Hellenistic World

Alexander's conquest of the Persian Empire not only changed the political face of the ancient world but also brought the East fully into the sphere of Greek economics. Yet the Hellenistic period did not see a revolution in the way people lived and worked. The material demands of Hellenistic society remained as simple as those of Athenian society in the fifth century B.C. Clothes and furniture were essentially unchanged, as were household goods, tools, and jewelry. The real achievement of Alexander and his successors was linking East and West in a broad commercial network. The spread of Greeks throughout the Near East and Egypt created new markets and stimulated trade. The economic unity of the Hellenistic world, like its cultural bonds, would later prove valuable to the Romans.

• *What economic effect did Alexander's opening of the East have on Greeks and Easterners? Did close economic contact bring them together in any significant way?*

Commerce

Alexander's conquest of the Persian Empire had immediate effects on trade. In the Persian capitals Alexander had found vast sums of gold, silver, and other treasure. This wealth financed the creation of new cities, the building of roads, and the development of harbors. Most of the great monarchies coined their money on the Attic standard, which meant that much of the money used in Hellenistic kingdoms had the same value. Traders were less in need of moneychangers than in the days when each major power

coined money on a different standard. As a result of Alexander's conquests, geographical knowledge of the East increased dramatically, making the East far better known to the Greeks than previously. The Greeks spread their law and methods of transacting business. Whole new fields lay open to Greek merchants, who eagerly took advantage of the new opportunities. Commerce itself was a leading area where Greeks and non-Greeks met on grounds of common interest. In bazaars, ports, and trading centers Greeks learned of Eastern customs and traditions while spreading knowledge of their own culture.

The Seleucid and Ptolemaic dynasties traded as far afield as India, Arabia, and sub-Saharan Africa. Overland trade with India and Arabia was conducted by caravan and was largely in the hands of Easterners. The caravan trade never dealt in bulk items or essential commodities; only luxury goods could be transported in this very expensive fashion. Once the goods reached the Hellenistic monarchies, Greek merchants took a hand in the trade.

Essential to the caravan trade from the Mediterranean to Afghanistan and India were the northern route to Dura on the Euphrates River and the southern route through Arabia. The desert of Arabia may seem at first unlikely and inhospitable terrain for a line of commerce, but to the east of it lies the plateau of Iran, from which trade routes stretched to the south and still farther east to China. Commerce from the East arrived at Egypt and the excellent harbors of Palestine, Phoenicia, and Syria. From these ports goods flowed to Greece, Italy, and Spain. The backbone of this caravan trade was the camel—shaggy, ill-tempered, but durable. Only its mother could consider it beautiful, but the camel is a splendid beast of burden, and few other animals could have endured the harsh heat and aridity of the caravan routes.

Over the caravan routes traveled luxury goods that were light, rare, and expensive. In time these luxury items became more of a necessity than a luxury. In part this development was the result of an increased volume of trade. In the prosperity of the period more people could afford to buy gold, silver, ivory, precious stones, spices, and a host of other easily transportable goods. Perhaps the most prominent goods in terms of volume were tea and silk. Indeed, the trade in silk later gave the major route the name the **Great Silk Road,** for not only was this route prominent in antiquity, but it also was used in early modern times. In return the Greeks and Macedonians sent east manufactured goods, especially metal weapons, cloth, wine, and olive oil. Although these caravan routes can trace their origins to earlier times, they became far more prominent in the Hellenistic period.

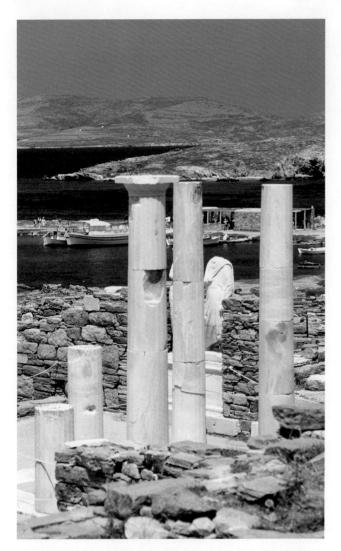

Harbor and Warehouse at Delos During the Hellenistic period Delos became a thriving trading center. From Delos cargoes were shipped to virtually every part of the Mediterranean. *(Rolf Richardson/age fotostock/superstock)*

The commercial contacts brought people together, even if sometimes indirectly. The merchants and the caravan cities were links in a chain that reached from the Mediterranean Sea at least to Afghanistan and Iran. Ideas passed along these routes as easily as, and probably more comfortably than, gold and ivory.

The Ptolemies discovered how to use monsoon winds to establish direct contact with India. One hardy merchant has left a firsthand account of sailing this important maritime route:

Hippalos, the pilot, observing the position of the ports and the conditions of the sea, first discovered how to sail across the ocean. Concerning the winds of the ocean in this region, when with us the Etesian winds begin, in India a wind between southwest and south, named for Hippalos, sets in from the open sea. From then until now some mariners set forth from Kanes and some from the Cape of Spices. Those sailing to Dimurikes [in southern India] throw the bow of the ship farther out to sea. Those bound for Barygaza and the realm of the Sakas [in northern India] hold to the land no more than three days; and if the wind remains favorable, they hold the same course through the outer sea, and they sail along past the previously mentioned gulfs.[3]

Although this sea route never replaced overland caravan traffic, it kept direct relations between East and West alive, stimulating the exchange of ideas as well as goods.

More economically important than this exotic trade were commercial dealings in essential commodities like raw materials, grain, and industrial products. The Hellenistic monarchies usually raised enough grain for their own needs as well as a surplus for export. For the cities of Greece and the Aegean this trade in grain was essential, because many of them could not grow enough. Fortunately for them, abundant wheat supplies were available nearby in Egypt and in the Crimea in southern Russia.

Most trade in bulk commodities was seaborne, and the Hellenistic merchant ship was the workhorse of the day. The merchant ship had a broad beam and relied on sails for propulsion. It was far more seaworthy than the contemporary warship, which was long, narrow, and built for speed. A small crew of experienced sailors could handle the merchant vessel easily. Maritime trade provided opportunities for workers in other industries and trades: sailors, shipbuilders, dockworkers, accountants, teamsters, and pirates. Piracy was always a factor in the Hellenistic world and remained so until Rome extended its power throughout the East.

The Greek cities paid for their grain by exporting olive oil and wine. When agriculture and oil production developed in Syria, Greek products began to encounter com-

Business customs developed and became standardized, so that merchants from different nationalities communicated in a way understandable to all of them.

The durability and economic importance of the caravan routes are amply demonstrated by the fact that the death of Alexander, the ensuing wars of his successors, and the triumph of the Parthians in Iran had little effect on the trade. Numerous mercantile cities grew up along these distant tracks, places where native cultures combined with both Greco-Macedonian and Eastern cultures to create local but nonetheless cosmopolitan societies.

petition from the Seleucid monarchy. Later in the Hellenistic period, Greek oil and wine found a lucrative market in Italy. Another significant commodity was fish, which for export was either salted, pickled, or dried. This trade was doubly important because fish provided poor people with an essential element of their diet. Salt too was often imported, and there was some very slight trade in salted meat, which was a luxury item. Far more important was the trade in honey, dried fruit, nuts, and vegetables. Of raw materials, wood was high in demand, but little trade occurred in manufactured goods.

Slaves were a staple of Hellenistic trade. The wars provided prisoners for the slave market; to a lesser extent, so did kidnapping and capture by pirates. The number of slaves involved cannot be estimated, but there is no doubt that slavery flourished. Both old Greek states and new Hellenistic kingdoms were ready slave markets, as was Rome when it emerged triumphant from the Second Punic War (see pages 141–142).

Throughout the Mediterranean world slaves were almost always in demand. Only the Ptolemies discouraged both the trade and slavery itself, and they did so only for economic reasons. Their system had no room for slaves, who would only have competed with free labor. Otherwise slave labor was to be found in the cities and temples of the Hellenistic world, in the factories and fields, and in the homes of wealthier people. In Italy and some parts of the East, slaves performed manual labor for large estates and worked the mines. They were vitally important to the Hellenistic economy.

Industry

Although demand for goods increased during the Hellenistic period, no new techniques of production appear to have developed. The discoveries of Hellenistic mathematicians and thinkers failed to produce any significant corresponding technological development. Manual labor, not machinery, continued to turn out the raw materials and few manufactured goods the Hellenistic world used. Human labor was so cheap and so abundant that kings had no incentive to encourage the invention and manufacture of laborsaving machinery.

The Ptolemies ran their gold mines along the same harsh lines. One historian gives a grim picture of the miners' lives:

The kings of Egypt condemn [to the mines] those found guilty of wrong-doing and those taken prisoner in war, those who were victims of false accusations and were put into jail because of royal anger. . . . The condemned—and they are

very many—all of them are put in chains, and they work persistently and continually, both by day and throughout the night, getting no rest, and carefully cut off from escape.[4]

The Ptolemies even condemned women and children to work in the mines. All of them—men, women, and boys—worked until they died.

Apart from gold and silver, which were used primarily for coins and jewelry, iron was the most important metal and saw the most varied use. Even so, the method of its production never became very sophisticated. The Hellenistic Greeks did manage to produce a low-grade steel by adding carbon to iron.

Pottery remained an important commodity, and most of it was made locally. The pottery used in the kitchen, the coarse ware, did not change at all. Fancier pots and bowls, decorated with a shiny black glaze, came into use during the Hellenistic period. This ware originated in Athens, but potters in other places began to imitate its style, heavily cutting into the Athenian market. In the second century B.C. a red-glazed ware, often called Samian, burst on the market and soon dominated it. Athens still held its own, however, in the production of fine pottery. Despite the change in pottery styles, the method of production of all pottery, whether plain or fine, remained essentially unchanged.

Agriculture

Hellenistic kings paid special attention to agriculture. Much of their revenue was derived from the produce of royal land, rents paid by the tenants of royal land, and taxation of agricultural land. Some Hellenistic kings even sought out and supported agricultural experts. The Ptolemies, for instance, sponsored experiments on seed grain, selecting seeds that seemed hardy and productive and trying to improve their characteristics. Indeed, the Ptolemies made the greatest strides in agriculture, and the reason for their success was largely political. Egypt had a strong tradition of central authority dating back to the pharaohs, which the Ptolemies inherited and tightened. They could decree what crops Egyptian farmers would plant and what animals would be raised, and they had the power to carry out their commands. The Ptolemies recognized the need for well-planned and constant irrigation, and much native labor went into the digging and maintenance of canals and ditches. The Ptolemies also reclaimed a great deal of land from the desert, including the Fayum, a dried lake bed near the Nile.

The centralized authority of the Ptolemies explains how agricultural advances occurred at the local level in

Egypt. But such progress was not possible in any other Hellenistic monarchy. Despite royal interest in agriculture and a more studied approach to it in the Hellenistic period, there is no evidence that agricultural productivity increased. Whether Hellenistic agricultural methods had any influence on Eastern practices is unknown.

Hellenistic Intellectual Advances

Although it was once fashionable to criticize the intellectual achievements of the Hellenistic period in contrast to those of the classical period, the critics themselves deserve the criticism. The peoples of the Hellenistic era took the ideas and ideals of the classical Greeks and advanced them to new heights. Their achievements created the intellectual and religious atmosphere that deeply influenced Roman thinking and eventually the religious thought of liberal Judaism and early Christianity. Far from being stagnant, this was a period of vigorous growth. Its achievements included new religious ideas, startling innovations in philosophy, and remarkable advances in science and medicine.

• *How did Hellenistic scientific, philosophical, medical, and religious advances affect the lives of men and women in this period?*

Religion in the Hellenistic World

In religion the most significant new ideas were developed outside of Greece. At first the Hellenistic period saw the spread of Greek religious cults throughout the Near East and Egypt. When Hellenistic kings founded cities, they also built temples and established new cults and priesthoods for the old Olympian gods. The new cults enjoyed the prestige of being the religion of the conquerors, and they were supported by public money. The most attractive aspects of the Greek cults, at least to the Greeks, were their rituals and festivities, as they were at least familiar. Greek cults sponsored literary, musical, and athletic contests, which were staged in beautiful surroundings among impressive Greek buildings. In short, the cults offered bright and lively entertainment, both intellectual and physical. They fostered Greek culture and traditional sports and thus were a splendid means of displaying Greek civilization outside of Greece.

Despite various advantages, Greek cults suffered from some severe shortcomings. They were primarily concerned with ritual. Participation in the civic cults did not even require belief (see pages 82–83). On the whole, the civic cults neither appealed to religious emotions nor embraced matters such as sin and redemption. Although the new civic cults were lavish in pomp and display, they could not satisfy deep religious feelings or spiritual yearnings.

Greeks increasingly sought solace from other sources. Educated and thoughtful people turned to philosophy as a guide to life, while others turned to superstition, magic, or astrology. Still others might shrug and speak of **Tyche,** which meant "Fate" or "Chance" or "Doom"—a capricious and sometimes malevolent force.

Hellenistic kings made no effort to spread Greek religion among their Eastern subjects. The Greeks always considered religion a matter best left to the individual. Greek cults were attractive only to those socially aspiring individuals who adopted Greek culture for personal advancement. Otherwise Easterners were little affected by Greek religion. Nor did native religions suffer from the arrival of the Greeks. Some Hellenistic kings limited the power of native priesthoods, but they also subsidized some indigenous cults with public money. Alexander the

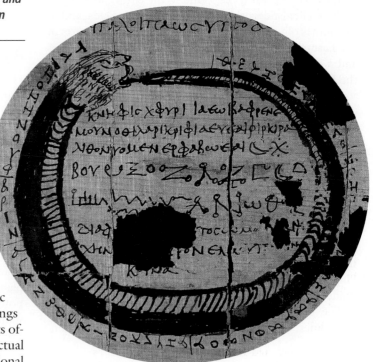

Hellenistic Magic This magical text, written in Greek and Egyptian, displays a snake surrounding the magical incantation. The text is intentionally obscure. *(British Library)*

Hellenistic Mystery Cult   The scene depicts part of the ritual of initiation into the cult of Dionysus. The young woman here has just completed the ritual. She now dances in joy as the official with the sacred staff looks on. *(Scala/Art Resource, NY)*

Great actually reinstated several cults that the Persians had suppressed.

Beginning in the second century B.C., some individuals were increasingly attracted to new **mystery religions,** so called because they featured a body of ritual not to be divulged to anyone not initiated into the cult. These new mystery cults incorporated aspects of both Greek and Eastern religions and had broad appeal for people who yearned for personal immortality. Since the Greeks were already familiar with old mystery cults, such as the Eleusinian mysteries in Attica, the new cults did not strike them as alien or barbarian. Familiar, too, was the concept of preparation for an initiation. Devotees of the Eleusinian mysteries and other such cults had to prepare themselves mentally and physically before entering the gods' presence. Thus the mystery cults fit well with Greek usage.

The new religions enjoyed one tremendous advantage over the old Greek mystery cults. Whereas old Greek mysteries were tied to particular places, such as Eleusis, the new religions spread throughout the Hellenistic world. People did not have to undertake long and expensive pilgrimages just to become members of the religion. In that sense the mystery religions came to the

people, for temples of the new deities sprang up wherever Greeks lived.

The mystery religions all claimed to save their adherents from the worst that fate could do and promised life for the soul after death. They all had a single concept in common: the belief that by the rites of initiation devotees became united with a god, usually male, who had himself died and risen from the dead. The sacrifice of the god and his victory over death saved the devotee from eternal death. Similarly, all mystery religions demanded a period of preparation in which the convert strove to become holy, that is, to live by the religion's precepts. Once aspirants had prepared themselves, they went through an initiation in which they learned the secrets of the religion. The initiation was usually a ritual of great emotional intensity, symbolizing the entry into a new life.

The mystery religions that took the Hellenistic world by storm were the Egyptian cults of Serapis and Isis. Serapis, who was invented by King Ptolemy, combined elements of the Egyptian god Osiris with aspects of the Greek gods Zeus, Pluto (the prince of the underworld), and Asclepius. Serapis was believed to be the judge of souls, who rewarded virtuous and righteous people with eternal life. Like Asclepius, he was a god of healing. Serapis became an international god, and many Hellenistic Greeks thought of him as Zeus. Associated with Isis and Serapis was Anubis, the old Egyptian god who, like Charon in the Greek pantheon, guided the souls of initiates to the realm of eternal life.

The cult of Isis enjoyed even wider appeal than that of Serapis. Isis, wife of Osiris, claimed to have conquered Tyche and promised to save any mortal who came to her. She became the most important goddess of the Hellenistic world, and her worship was very popular among women. Her priests claimed that she had bestowed on humanity the gift of civilization and founded law and literature. She was the goddess of marriage, conception, and childbirth, and like Serapis she promised to save the souls of her believers.

Mystery religions took care of the big things in life, but many people resorted to ordinary magic for daily matters. When a cat walked across their path, they stopped until someone else had passed by them. Or they could throw three rocks across the road. A snake in the house presented a complex problem. If only an ordinary snake, people immediately invoked the god Sabazios, who was associated with the afterlife. They were on safer ground if the snake was red. They then established a shrine on the spot. People often purified their houses to protect them from Hecate, a sinister goddess associated with magic and witchcraft. People could even resurrect the dead by commanding, "I adjure you, life spirit walking in the air: enter this body, inspire it, empower it, resurrect it by the power of the eternal god, and make it walk about in this place: for I am he who acts through the power of Thayth, the holy god."[5] Many people had dreams that only seers and augurs could interpret. Today psychiatrists do the same thing for exorbitant fees. Some of these practices are familiar today because some old fears are still alive.

Philosophy and the People

Philosophy during the Hellenic period was the exclusive province of the wealthy, for only they had leisure enough to pursue philosophical studies. During the Hellenistic period, however, philosophy reached out to touch the lives of more men and women than ever before. The reasons for this development were several. Since the ideal of the polis had declined, politics no longer offered people an intellectual outlet. Moreover, much of Hellenistic life, especially in the new cities of the East, seemed unstable and without venerable traditions. Greeks were far more mobile than they had ever been before, but their very mobility left them feeling uprooted. Many people in search of something permanent, something unchanging in a changing world, turned to philosophy. Another reason for the increased influence of philosophy was the decline of traditional religion and a growing belief in Tyche. To protect against the worst that Tyche could do, many Greeks looked to philosophy.

Philosophers themselves became much more numerous, and several new schools of philosophical thought emerged. In spite of their many differences, the major branches of philosophy agreed on the necessity of making people self-sufficient. They all recognized the need to equip men and women to deal successfully with Tyche. The major schools of Hellenistic philosophy all taught that people could be truly happy only when they had turned their backs on the world and focused full attention on one enduring thing. They differed chiefly on what that enduring thing was.

Two significant philosophies caught the minds and hearts of contemporary Greeks and some Easterners, as well as some later Romans. The first was **Epicureanism,** a practical philosophy of serenity in an often tumultuous world. Epicurus (340–270 B.C.) founded this school of philosophy based on scientific theories. Accepting Democritus's idea that the universe is composed of indestructible particles, Epicurus put forward a naturalistic theory of the universe. Although he did not deny the existence of the gods, he taught that they had no effect on human life. The essence of Epicurus's belief was that the principal good of human life is pleasure, which he defined as the absence of pain. He was not advocating drunken revels or sexual dissipation, which he thought actually caused pain. Instead, Epicurus concluded that any violent emotion is undesirable and advocated mild self-discipline. Even poverty he considered good, as long as people had enough food, clothing, and shelter. Epicurus also taught that individuals can most easily attain peace and serenity by ignoring the outside world and looking into their personal feelings and reactions. Thus Epicureanism led to quietism.

Epicureanism taught its followers to ignore politics and issues, for politics led to tumult, which would disturb the soul. Although the Epicureans thought that the state originated through a social contract among individuals, they did not care about the political structure of the state. They were content to live in a democracy, oligarchy, monarchy, or any other form of government, and they never speculated about the ideal state. Their ideals stood outside all political forms.

Tyche This statue depicts Tyche as the bringer of bounty to people. Some Hellenistic Greeks worshiped Tyche in the hope that she would be kind to them. Philosophers tried to free people from her whimsies. Others tried to placate her. *(Faith Cimok, Turkey)*

Online Study Center **Improve Your Grade**
Primary Source: A Materialistic Ethic: The Principal Doctrines of Epicureanism

Opposed to the passivity of the Epicureans, Zeno (335–262 B.C.), a philosopher from Citium in Cyprus, advanced a different concept of human beings and the universe. Zeno first came to Athens to form his own school, the Stoa, named after the building where he preferred to teach. **Stoicism** became the most popular Hellenistic philosophy and the one that later captured the mind of Rome. Zeno and his followers considered nature an expression of divine will; in their view, people could be happy only when living in accordance with nature. They stressed the unity of man and the universe, stating that all men were brothers and were obliged to help one another. Stoicism's science was derived from Heraclitus, but its broad and warm humanity was the work of Zeno and his followers.

Unlike the Epicureans, the Stoics taught that people should participate in politics and worldly affairs. Yet this idea never led to the belief that individuals should try to change the order of things. Time and again the Stoics used the image of an actor in a play: the Stoic plays an assigned part but never tries to change the play. To the Stoics the important question was not whether they achieved anything, but whether they lived virtuous lives. In that way they could triumph over Tyche, for Tyche could destroy achievements but not the nobility of their lives.

Though the Stoics evolved the concept of a world order, they thought of it strictly in terms of the individual. Like the Epicureans, they were indifferent to specific political forms. They believed that people should do their duty to the state in which they found themselves. The universal state they preached about was ethical, not political. The Stoics' most significant practical achievement was the creation of the concept of **natural law.** The Stoics concluded that as all men were brothers, partook of divine reason, and were in harmony with the universe, one law—a part of the natural order of life—governed them all.

The Stoic concept of a universal state governed by natural law is one of the finest heirlooms the Hellenistic world passed on to Rome. The Stoic concept of natural law, of one law for all people, became a valuable tool when the Romans began to deal with many different peoples with different laws. The ideal of the universal state gave the Romans a rationale for extending their empire to the farthest reaches of the world. The duty of individuals to their fellows served the citizens of the Roman Empire as the philosophical justification for doing their duty. In this respect, too, the real fruit of Hellenism was to ripen only under the cultivation of Rome.

Hellenistic Science

The area in which Hellenistic culture achieved its greatest triumphs was science. The most notable of the Hellenistic astronomers was Aristarchus of Samos (ca 310–230 B.C.), who was educated in Aristotle's school. Aristarchus concluded that the sun is far larger than the earth and that the stars are enormously distant from the earth. He argued against Aristotle's view that the earth was the center of the universe. Instead, Aristarchus propounded the **heliocentric theory**—that the earth and planets revolve around the sun. His work is all the more impressive because he lacked even a rudimentary telescope. Aristarchus had only the human eye and brain, but they were more than enough.

Unfortunately, Aristarchus's theories did not persuade the ancient world. In the second century A.D. Claudius Ptolemy, a mathematician and astronomer in Alexandria, accepted Aristotle's theory of the earth as the center of the universe, and this view prevailed for fourteen hundred years. Aristarchus's heliocentric theory lay dormant until resurrected in the sixteenth century by the brilliant Polish astronomer Nicolaus Copernicus.

In geometry Hellenistic thinkers discovered little that was new, but Euclid (ca 300 B.C.), a mathematician who lived in Alexandria, compiled a valuable textbook of existing knowledge. His book *The Elements of Geometry* has exerted immense influence on Western civilization, for it rapidly became the standard introduction to geometry. Generations of students, from the Hellenistic period to the present, have learned the essentials of geometry from it.

The greatest thinker of the Hellenistic period was Archimedes (ca 287–212 B.C.), a native of Syracuse. (See the feature "Individuals in Society: Archimedes and the Practical Application of Science.") As both a theoretical and a practical scientist, he was far more interested in pure mathematics than in useful inventions. His mathematical research, covering many fields, was his greatest contribution to Western thought. In his book *On Plane Equilibriums* Archimedes dealt for the first time with the basic principles of mechanics, including the principle of the lever. He once said that if he were given a lever and a suitable place to stand, he could move the world. With his treatise *On Floating Bodies* he founded the science of hydrostatics. He concluded that whenever a solid floats in a liquid, the weight of the solid is equal to the weight of the liquid displaced. He made his discovery when he

stepped into a bath. He noticed that the weight of his body displaced a volume of water equal to it. He immediately ran outside shouting, "Eureka, eureka" (I have found it, I have found it).[6]

Archimedes was willing to share his work with others, among them Eratosthenes (285–ca 204 B.C.), a man of almost universal interests. From his native Cyrene in North Africa, Eratosthenes traveled to Athens, where he studied philosophy and mathematics. He refused to join any of the philosophical schools, for he was interested in too many things to follow any particular dogma. Around 245 B.C. King Ptolemy invited Eratosthenes to Alexandria. The Ptolemies had done much to make Alexandria an intellectual, cultural, and scientific center. Eratosthenes came to Alexandria to become librarian of the royal library, a position of great prestige. The library was a huge collection of Greek writings, including such classic works as the poems of Homer, the histories of Herodotus and Thucydides, and the philosophical works of Plato and Aristotle. The library became one of the foremost intellectual centers of the ancient world. Eratosthenes had the honor of becoming its head. While there he continued his mathematical work and by letter struck up a friendship with Archimedes.

Unlike Archimedes, Eratosthenes did not devote his life entirely to mathematics, although he never lost interest in it. He used mathematics to further the geographical studies for which he is most famous. He calculated the circumference of the earth geometrically, estimating it as about 24,675 miles. He was not wrong by much: the earth is actually 24,860 miles in circumference. Eratosthenes also concluded that the earth was a spherical globe, that the landmass was roughly four-sided, and that the land was surrounded by ocean. He discussed the shapes and sizes of land and ocean and the irregularities of the earth's surface. He drew a map of the earth and used his own system of explaining the divisions of the earth's landmass.

Online Study Center **Improve Your Grade**
Primary Source: The Genius of Hellenistic Science: Eratosthenes Computes the Earth's Circumference

Using geographical information gained by Alexander the Great's scientists, Eratosthenes tried to fit the East into Greek geographical knowledge. Although for some reason he ignored the western Mediterranean and Europe, he declared that a ship could sail from Spain either around Africa to India or directly westward to India. Not until the great days of Western exploration did sailors such as Vasco da Gama and Magellan actually prove Eratosthenes' theories. Like Eratosthenes, other Greek ge-

Individuals in Society

Archimedes and the Practical Application of Science

Throughout the ages generals have besieged cities to force them to surrender. Sieges were particularly hard and violent, bringing misery to soldiers and civilians alike. Between 213 and 211 B.C. the Roman general Marcellus laid close siege to the strongly walled city of Syracuse, the home of Archimedes. Not a soldier, Archimedes was the greatest scientist of his age. He towered above all others in abstract thought. The Roman siege challenged him to a practical response. Hiero, king of Syracuse and friend of Archimedes, turned to him for help.

The king persuaded Archimedes to prepare for him offensive and defensive engines to be used in every kind of warfare. These he had never used himself, because he spent the greater part of his life in freedom from war and amid the festal rites of peace. But at the present time his apparatus stood the Syracusans in good stead, and, with the apparatus, its fabricator. When, therefore, the Romans assaulted them by sea and land, the Syracusans were stricken dumb with terror. They thought that nothing could withstand so furious an onset by such forces.

Archimedes, however, began to ply his engines, and shot against the land forces of the attackers all sorts of missiles and immense masses of stones, which came down with incredible din and speed. Nothing whatever could ward off their weight, but they knocked down in heaps those who stood in their way, and threw their ranks into confusion. At the same time huge beams were suddenly projected over the ships from the walls, which sank some of them with great weights plunging down from on high. Others were seized at the prow by iron claws, or beaks like the beaks of cranes, drawn straight up into the air, and then plunged stern first into the depths, or were turned round and round by means of enginery within the city, and dashed upon the steep cliffs that jutted out beneath the wall of the city, with great destruction of the fighting men on board, who perished in the wrecks. Frequently, too, a ship would be lifted out of the water into mid-air, whirled here and there as it hung there, a dreadful spectacle, until its crew had been thrown out and hurled in all directions. Then it would fall empty upon the walls, or slip away from the clutch that had held it. As for the engine that Marcellus was bringing up on the bridge of ships, and which was called "sambuca" [large mechanically operated scaling ladders carried on ships]. While it was still some distance off in its approach to the wall, a stone of 500 pounds' weight was discharged at it, then a second and a third. Some of them, falling upon it with great noise and surge of wave, crushed the foundation of the engine, shattered its framework, and dislodged it from the platform, so that Marcellus, in perplexity, ordered his ships to sail back as fast as they could and his land forces to retire. . . .

Many of their ships, too, were dashed together, and they could not retaliate in any way upon their foes. For Archimedes had built most of his engines close behind the wall, and the Romans seemed to be fighting against the gods, now that countless mischiefs were poured out upon them from an invisible source.

At last the Romans became so fearful that whenever they saw a bit of rope or a stick of timber projecting a little over the wall. "There it is," they shouted, "Archimedes is training some engine upon us." They then turned their backs and fled. Seeing this, Marcellus desisted from all the fighting and assault, and thenceforth depended on a long siege.

For all his genius, Archimedes did not survive the siege. His deeds of war done, he returned to his thinking and his mathematical problems, even with the siege still in the background. When Syracuse was betrayed to the Romans, soldiers streamed in, spreading slaughter and destruction throughout the city. A Roman soldier came upon Archimedes in his study and killed him outright, thus ending the life of one of the world's greatest thinkers.

Archimedes' mill. A slave turns a large cylinder fitted with blades to form a screw that draws water from a well.
(Courtesy, Soprintendenza Archeologica di Pompei. Photograph by Penelope M. Allison)

Questions for Analysis

1. How did Archimedes' engines repulse the Roman attacks?
2. What effect did his weapons have on the Roman attackers?
3. What is the irony of Archimedes' death?

Source: Reprinted by permission of the publishers and the Trustees of the Loeb Classical Library™ from *Plutarch: Volume V,* Loeb Classical Library™ Volume 87, trans. Bernadotte Perrin (Cambridge, Mass.: Harvard University Press), 1917. The Loeb Classical Library™ is a registered trademark of the President and Fellows of Harvard College.

Online Study Center **Improve Your Grade**
Going Beyond Individuals in Society

Catapult This model shows a catapult as its crew would have seen it in action. The arrow was loaded on the long horizontal beam, its point fitting into the housing. There the torsion spring under great pressure released the arrow at the target, which could be some 400 yards away. *(Courtesy, Noel Kavan)*

ographers also turned their attention southward to Africa. During this period the people of the Mediterranean learned of the climate and customs of Ethiopia and gleaned some scant information about equatorial Africa.

For all of its speculation, Hellenistic science made an inestimable, if grim, contribution to practical life. The Greeks and Macedonians applied theories of mechanics to build siege machines, thus revolutionizing the art of warfare. In short, they invented the first effective artillery in Western history. Fully realizing the practical possibilities of these new machines, Philip of Macedonia introduced them to the broader world. The catapult became the first and most widely used artillery piece. The earliest catapults could shoot only large arrows and small stones. By the time Alexander the Great besieged Tyre in 332 B.C., his catapults threw stones big enough to knock down city walls. Generals soon realized that they could also hurl burning bundles over the walls to start fires in the city. To approach enemy town walls safely, engineers built siege towers, large wooden structures that served as artillery platforms, and put them on wheels so that soldiers could roll them up to the wall. Once there archers stationed on top of them swept the enemy's ramparts

with arrows, while other soldiers manning catapults added missile fire. Once the walls were cleared, soldiers from the towers swept over the enemy's ramparts and into the city. To aid the siege towers, generals added battering rams that consisted of long, stout shafts housed in reinforced shells. Inside the shell the crew pushed the ram up to the wall and then heaved the shaft against the wall. Rams proved even more effective than catapults in bringing down large portions of walls.

Right from the beginning Macedonian kings showed the way in the practical use of all these machines. There is no better example than Philip II's attack on Perinthos in 340 B.C.:

Philip launched a siege of Perinthos, advancing engines to the city and assaulting the walls in relays day after day. He built towers 120 feet tall that rose far above the towers of Perinthos. From their superior height he kept wearing down the besieged. He mined under the wall and also rocked it with battering-rams until he threw down a large section of it. The Perinthians fought stoutly and threw up a second wall. Philip rained down great destruction through his many and various arrow-shooting catapults. . . . Philip continually battered the walls with his rams and made breaches in them. With his arrow-firing catapults clearing the ramparts of defenders, he sent his soldiers in through the breaches in tight formation. He attacked with scaling-ladders the parts of the walls that had been cleared.[7]

For the Perinthians this grim story had a happy ending when their allies arrived to lift the siege. Hellenistic generals built larger, more complex, and more effective machines until no city was safe from them.

If these new engines made waging war more efficient, they also added to the misery of the people. War was no longer confined to the battlefield and fought between soldiers. Now the populations of whole cities feared for their lives. Survival of such a siege as that of Perinthos led to terror for the survivors. Many were killed in the slaughter and rape that generally came with the taking of the city. The survivors were often sold into slavery. War had come to embrace the whole population. Ironically, Hellenistic science, dedicated to improving human life, succeeded in making it more dangerous and horrible.

Despite its undeniable brilliance, Hellenistic science suffered from a remarkable weakness almost impossible for practical-minded Americans to understand. With the exception of artillery and a few other inventions, the Hellenistic people seldom turned discoveries to practical use. They generally preferred abundant slave labor to laborsaving machines. For them technology was a road not taken.

Hellenistic Medicine

The study of medicine flourished during the Hellenistic period, and Hellenistic physicians carried the work of Hippocrates into new areas. Herophilus, who lived in the first half of the third century B.C., worked at Alexandria and studied the writings of Hippocrates. He accepted Hippocrates' theory of the four humors and approached the study of medicine in a systematic, scientific fashion: he dissected dead bodies and measured what he observed. He discovered the nervous system and concluded that two types of nerves, motor and sensory, existed.

Herophilus also studied the brain, which he considered the center of intelligence, and discerned the cerebrum and cerebellum. His other work dealt with the liver, lungs, and uterus. His younger contemporary Erasistratus also conducted research on the brain and nervous system and improved on Herophilus's work. Erasistratus too followed in the tradition of Hippocrates and preferred to let the body heal itself by means of diet and air.

Both Herophilus and Erasistratus were members of the **Dogmatic school** of medicine at Alexandria. In this school speculation played an important part in research. So, too, did the study of anatomy. To learn more about human anatomy, Herophilus and Erasistratus dissected corpses and even vivisected criminals whom King Ptolemy contributed for the purpose. The practice of vivisection seems to have been short-lived, although dissection continued. Better knowledge of anatomy led to improvements in surgery. These advances enabled the Dogmatists to invent new surgical instruments and techniques.

In about 280 B.C. Philinus and Serapion, pupils of Herophilus, led a reaction against the Dogmatists. Believing that the Dogmatists had become too speculative, they founded the **Empiric school** of medicine at Alexandria. Claiming that the Dogmatists' emphasis on anatomy and physiology was misplaced, they concentrated instead on the observation and cure of illnesses. They also laid heavier stress on the use of drugs and medicine to treat illnesses. Heraclides of Tarentum (perhaps first century B.C.) carried on the Empiric tradition and dedicated himself to observation and use of medicines. He discovered the benefits of opium and worked with other drugs that relieved pain. He also steadfastly rejected the relevance of magic to drugs and medicines.

The Hellenistic world was also plagued by people who claimed to cure illnesses through incantations and magic. Their potions included such concoctions as blood from the ear of an ass mixed with water to cure fever, or the liver of a cat killed when the moon was waning and

An Unsuccessful Delivery   This funeral stele depicts a mother who has perhaps lost her own life as well as her baby's. Childbirth was the leading cause of death for adult women in antiquity, though funeral stele showing this are quite rare. Another of the few that do show death in childbirth bears the heartbreaking words attributed to the mother by her grieving family: "All my labor could not bring the child forth; he lies in my womb, among the dead." (*National Archaeological Museum, Athens/Archaeological Receipts Fund*)

preserved in salt. Broken bones could be cured by applying the ashes of a pig's jawbone to the break. The dung of a goat mixed with old wine was good for healing broken ribs. One charlatan claimed that he could cure epilepsy by making the patient drink spring water, drawn at night, from the skull of a man who had been killed but not cremated. These quacks even claimed that they could cure mental illness. The treatment for a person suffering from melancholy was calf dung boiled in wine. No doubt the patient became too sick to be depressed.

Quacks who prescribed such treatments were very popular but did untold harm to the sick and injured. They and greedy physicians also damaged the reputation of dedicated doctors who honestly and intelligently tried to heal and alleviate pain. The medical abuses that arose in the Hellenistic period were so flagrant that the Romans, who later entered the Hellenistic world, developed an intense dislike and distrust of physicians. The Romans considered the study of Hellenistic medicine beneath the dignity of a Roman, and even as late as the time of the Roman Empire, few Romans undertook the study of Greek medicine. Nonetheless, the work of men like Herophilus and Serapion made valuable contributions to the knowledge of medicine, and the fruits of their work were preserved and handed on to the West.

Chapter Summary

Online Study Center **ACE the Test**

- *Why did Alexander launch his massive attack on the Persian Empire? Did he have a pressing reason to take such a huge risk?*
- *What was Alexander's legacy to the Hellenistic world, and what did it mean to Greeks and Easterners alike? What were its effects on this new world?*
- *How far did Hellenism spread, and what effect did it have on both Greeks and those unfamiliar with Greek culture?*
- *What economic effect did Alexander's opening of the East have on Greeks and Easterners? Did close economic contact bring them together in any significant way?*
- *How did Hellenistic scientific, philosophical, medical, and religious advances affect the lives of men and women in this period?*

Although Alexander may not originally have intended to march all the way to the Indus Valley, he gained so much territory that he saw every reason to continue as far as possible. It was an almost foolhardy adventure, but it permanently changed the face of world history.

Alexander's legacy proved of essential importance to the future of the West. He brought the vital civilization of the Greeks into intimate contact with the older cultures of the East. He added enormously to Western knowledge of the culturally rich East. Neither he nor anyone else during these years brought unity to the East and West, but he at least guaranteed that they would henceforth live productive lives in the same world.

Most enduring of all, Alexander's work and that of his successors spread Hellenism far beyond its native soil. Even though it was superficial in some areas, it provided a common means of communication and shared values. The ideals and ideas of the West spread and blended with Eastern ideas and customs to create a whole new environment.

For ordinary men and women, the greatest practical boon of the Hellenistic adventure was economic. Trade connected the world on a routine basis. Economics brought people together just as surely as it brought them goods. By the end of the Hellenistic period, the ancient world had become far broader and more economically intricate than ever before.

Hellenistic achievements included intellectual advances as well as trade connections. Mystery religions, such as the worship of the goddess Isis, provided many people with answers to their questions about the meaning of life, while others turned to practical philosophies such as Stoicism for ethical guidance. Mathematicians and scientists developed theoretical knowledge and applied this to practical problems in geography, mechanics, and weaponry. Physicians also approached medicine in a systematic fashion, though many people relied on magic and folk cures for treatment of illness.

Key Terms

Hellenistic
sovereign
koine
politeuma
Great Silk Road
Tyche
mystery religions

Epicureanism
Stoicism
natural law
heliocentric theory
Dogmatic school
Empiric school

Online Study Center **Improve Your Grade** Flashcards

Suggested Reading

Bosworth, A. B. *Conquest and Empire: The Reign of Alexander the Great.* 1988. Sets Alexander's career in a broad context.

Bowman, Alan K. *Egypt After the Pharaohs.* 1986. A readable account of the impact of the Greeks and Macedonians on Egyptian society.

Burkert, Walter. *Ancient Mystery Cults.* 1987. A brief comparative study of the rituals, membership, and organization of secret mystery cults of the ancient world, written by the foremost historian of Greek religion.

Cartledge, Paul. *Alexander the Great.* 2004. The story of Alexander's life and rise to power and of the impact of his conquests, by the chair of the classics department at Cambridge University.

Cohen, Getzel M. *The Hellenistic Settlements in Europe, the Islands, and Asia Minor.* 1996. A welcome contribution to the understanding of the impact of the Greeks on the world around them.

Lloyd, G. E. R. *Greek Science After Aristotle.* 1963. A good survey of Hellenistic science.

McKechnie, Paul. *Outsiders in the Greek Cities of the Fourth Century.* 1989. Provides an interesting study of the social dislocation of the Greeks in the time of Philip II and Alexander the Great.

Pomeroy, Sarah B. *Women in Hellenistic Egypt.* 1984. Studies women in the kingdom from which the most ancient evidence has survived.

Samuel, Alan E. *The Promise of the West.* 1988. Studies the connections among Greek, Roman, and Jewish culture and thought and their significance for Western history.

Sharples, R. W. *Stoics, Epicureans, Sceptics.* 1996. Provides a good synthesis of these three major branches of Hellenistic philosophy.

Shipley, Graham. *The Greek World After Alexander, 323–30 B.C.* 2000. A very thorough discussion of political, socioeconomic, intellectual, and cultural developments.

Vatai, F. L. *Intellectuals in Politics in the Greek World from Early Times to the Hellenistic Age.* 1984. A general treatment of the role of the intellectual in the classical and Hellenistic worlds.

Wallbank, F. W. *The Hellenistic World,* rev. ed. 1993. Examines political events, social systems, literature, science, and new religious movements.

Notes

1. Plutarch, *Moralia* 328E.
2. Quoted in W. W. Tarn and G. T. Griffith, *Hellenistic Civilizations,* 3d ed. (Cleveland and New York: Meridian Books, 1961), p. 199.
3. *Periplous of the Erythraian Sea* 57.
4. Diodorus 3.12.2–3.
5. G. Luck, *Arcana Mundi* (Baltimore: Johns Hopkins University Press, 2006), no. 23, p. 137.
6. Vitruvius, *On Architecture* 9 Preface, 10.
7. Diodorus 16.74.2.

Listening to the Past

Alexander and the Brotherhood of Man

One historical problem challenged historians throughout the twentieth century and has yet to be solved to everyone's satisfaction. After returning to Opis, north of Babylon in modern Iraq, Alexander found himself confronted with a huge and unexpected mutiny by his Macedonian veterans. He held a banquet to pacify them, and he included in the festivities some Persians and other Asian followers, some nine thousand in all. During the festivities he offered a public prayer for harmony and partnership in rule between the Macedonians and Persians. Many modern scholars have interpreted this prayer as an expression of his desire to establish a "brotherhood of man." The following passage provides the evidence for this view. From it all readers can determine for themselves whether Alexander attempted to introduce a new philosophical ideal or whether he harbored his own political motives for political cooperation.

8. When [Alexander] arrived at Opis, he collected the Macedonians and announced that he intended to discharge from the army those who were useless for military service either from age or from being maimed in the limbs; and he said he would send them back to their own abodes. He also promised to give those who went back as much extra reward as would make them special objects of envy to those at home and arouse in the other Macedonians the wish to share similar dangers and labours. Alexander said this, no doubt, for the purpose of pleasing the Macedonians; but on the contrary they were, not without reason, offended by the speech which he delivered, thinking that now they were despised by him and deemed to be quite useless for military service. Indeed, throughout the whole of this expedition they had been offended at many other things; for his adoption of the Persian dress, thereby exhibiting his contempt for their opinion often caused them grief, as did also his accoutring the foreign soldiers called Epigoni in the Macedonian style,

and the mixing of the alien horsemen among the ranks of the Companions. Therefore they could not remain silent and control themselves, but urged him to dismiss all of them from his army; and they advised him to prosecute the war in company with his father, deriding Ammon by this remark. When Alexander heard this . . . , he ordered the most conspicuous of the men who had tried to stir up the multitude to sedition to be arrested. He himself pointed out with his hand to the shield-bearing guards those whom they were to arrest, to the number of thirteen; and he ordered these to be led away to execution. When the rest, stricken with terror, became silent, he mounted the platform again, and spoke as follows:

9. "The speech which I am about to deliver will not be for the purpose of checking your start homeward, for, so far as I am concerned, you may depart wherever you wish; but for the purpose of making you understand when you take yourselves off, what kind of men you have been to us who have conferred such benefits upon you. . . .

10. . . . Most of you have golden crowns, the eternal memorials of your valour and of the honour you receive from me. Whoever has been killed has met with a glorious end and has been honoured with a splendid burial. Brazen statues of most of the slain have been erected at home, and their parents are held in honour, being released from all public service and from taxation. But no one of you has ever been killed in flight under my leadership. And now I was intending to send back those of you who are unfit for service, objects of envy to those at home; but since you all wish to depart, depart all of you! Go back and report at home that your king Alexander, the conqueror of the Persians, Medes, Bactrians, and Sacians; the man who has subjugated the Uxians, Arachotians, and Drangians; who has also acquired the rule of the Parthians, Chorasmians, and Hyrcanians, as far as the Caspian Sea . . . —report that when you

returned to Susa you deserted him and went away, handing him over to the protection of conquered foreigners. Perhaps this report of yours will be both glorious to you in the eyes of men and devout I ween in the eyes of the gods. Depart!"

11. Having thus spoken, he leaped down quickly from the platform, and entered the palace, where he paid no attention to the decoration of his person, nor was any of his Companions admitted to see him. Not even on the morrow was any one of them admitted to an audience; but on the third day he summoned the select Persians within, and among them he distributed the commands of the brigades, and made the rule that only those whom he proclaimed his kinsmen should have the honour of saluting him with a kiss. But the Macedonians who heard the speech were thoroughly astonished at the moment, and remained there in silence near the platform; nor when he retired did any of them accompany the king, except his personal Companions and the confidential body-guards. Though they remained most of them had nothing to do or say; and yet they were unwilling to retire. But when the news was reported to them . . . they were no longer able to restrain themselves; but running in a body to the palace, they cast their weapons there in front of the gates as signs of supplication to the king. Standing in front of the gates, they shouted, beseeching to be allowed to enter, and saying that they were willing to surrender the men who had been the instigators of the disturbance on that occasion, and those who had begun the clamour. They also declared they would not retire from the gates either day or night, unless Alexander would take some pity upon them. When he was informed of this, he came out without delay; and seeing them lying on the ground in humble guise, and hearing most of them lamenting with loud voice, tears began to flow also from his own eyes. He made an effort to say something to them, but they continued their importunate entreaties. At length one of them, Callines by name, a man conspicuous both for his age and because he was a captain of the Companion cavalry, spoke as follows, "O king, what grieves the Macedonians is that you have already made some of the Persians kinsmen to yourself, and that Persians are called Alexander's kinsmen, and have the honour of saluting you with a kiss; whereas none of the Macedonians have as yet enjoyed this honour." Then Alexander, interrupting him, said, "But all

This gilded case for a bow and arrows indicates that Alexander's success came at the price of blood. These vigorous scenes portray more military conflict than philosophical compassion. *(Archaeological Museum Salonica/Dagli-Orti/The Art Archive)*

of you without exception I consider my kinsmen, and so from this time I shall call you." When he had said this, Callines advanced and saluted him with a kiss, and so did all those who wished to salute him. Then they took up their weapons and returned to the camp, shouting and singing a song of thanksgiving. After this Alexander offered sacrifice to the gods to whom it was his custom to sacrifice, and gave a public banquet, over which he himself presided, with the Macedonians sitting around him; and next to them the Persians; after whom came the men of the other nations, preferred in honour for their personal rank or for some meritorious action. The king and his guests drew wine from the same bowl and poured out the same libations, both the Grecian prophets and the Magians commencing the ceremony. He prayed for other blessings, and especially that harmony and community of rule might exist between the Macedonians and Persians.

Questions for Analysis

1. What was the purpose of the banquet at Opis?

2. Were all of the guests treated equally?

3. What did Alexander gain from bringing together the Macedonians and Persians?

Source: Arrian, *Anabasis of Alexander* 7.8.1–11.9 in F. R. B. Goldophin, ed., *The Greek Historians,* vol. 2. Copyright 1942 and renewed 1970 by Random House, Inc. Used by permission of Random House, Inc.

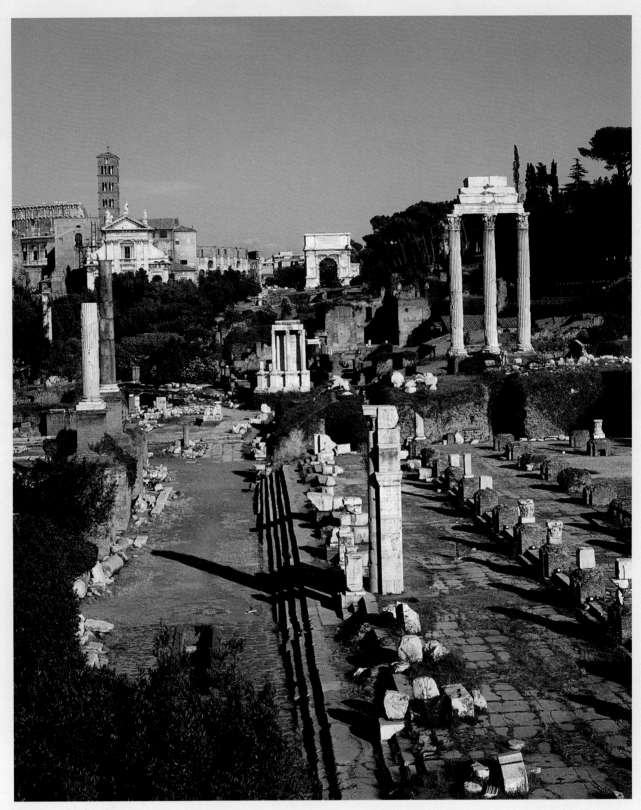

The Roman Forum. *(Josephine Powell)*

5

THE RISE OF ROME, CA 750–44 B.C.

chapter preview

The Land and Its Early Settlers
• *How did the land help shape Roman developments?*

The Roman Republic
• *What was the nature of the Roman republic?*

Roman Expansion
• *How did the Romans expand farther into Italy?*

Old Values and Greek Culture
• *What values did the Romans embrace because of their expansion?*

The Late Republic (133–31 B.C.)
• *What were the main problems and achievements of the late republic?*

Who is so thoughtless and lazy that he does not want to know in what way and with what kind of government the Romans in less than 53 years conquered nearly the entire inhabited world and brought it under their rule—an achievement previously unheard of?"[1] This question was first asked by Polybius, a Greek historian who lived in the second century B.C. With keen awareness Polybius realized that the Romans were achieving something unique in world history.

What was that achievement? Was it simply the creation of a huge empire? Hardly. The Persians had done the same thing. For that matter, Alexander the Great had conquered vast territories in a shorter time. Was it the creation of a superior culture? Even the Romans admitted that in matters of art, literature, philosophy, and culture they learned from the Greeks. Rome's achievement lay in the ability of the Romans not only to conquer peoples but to incorporate them into the Roman system. Rome succeeded where the Greek polis had failed. Unlike the Greeks, who refused to share citizenship, the Romans extended their citizenship first to the Italians and later to the peoples of the provinces. With that citizenship went Roman government and law. Rome created a world state that embraced the entire Mediterranean area and extended northward.

Nor was Rome's achievement limited to the ancient world. Rome's law, language, and administrative practices shaped later developments in Europe and beyond. London, Paris, Vienna, and many other modern European cities began as Roman colonies or military camps. When the Founding Fathers created the American republic, they looked to Rome as a model. On the darker side, Napoleon and Mussolini paid their own tribute to Rome by aping its forms. Whether Founding Father or modern autocrat, all were acknowledging admiration for the Roman achievement.

Roman history is usually divided into two periods: the republic, the age in which Rome grew from a small city-state to ruler of an empire, and the empire, the period when the republican constitution gave way to constitutional monarchy.

Online Study Center

This icon will direct you to interactive activities and study materials on the website **college.hmco.com/pic/mckaywest9e**

The Land and Its Early Settlers

While the Greeks pursued their destiny in the East, other peoples in western Europe developed their own individual societies. The most historically important of them were the Etruscans and Romans who entered the peninsula of Italy and came into contact with the older cultures of the Mediterranean. The Etruscans were the first significant newcomers; their arrival can reasonably be dated to about 750 B.C. Italy gave them a genial homeland. Shaped like a boot, with the island of Sicily at its toe, Italy occupies the center of the Mediterranean basin. As Map 5.1 shows, the two geographical features of Italy and Sicily thrust southward toward the North African coast, thereby dividing the Mediterranean into two basins.

● *How did the land help shape Roman developments?*

The Etruscans and the Roman Settlement of Italy (ca 750–509 B.C.)

The Etruscans remain a mysterious people, still surrounded by numerous uncertainties. They did, however, develop the land by establishing permanent settlements that evolved into the first Italian cities. In political organization they resembled the Greek city-states, each governing itself while maintaining contact with its neighbors. The wealth of these cities, along with their political and military institutions, enabled them to form a loosely organized league of cities whose domination extended as far north as the Po Valley and as far south as Latium and Campania (see Map 5.1). Their influence spread over the surrounding countryside, which they regularly cultivated. Having established a strong agricultural base, they mined the rich mineral resources of the land. Secure in their new home, they looked out to the wider world, especially to the East. The Mediterranean has always been a highway, and one of its major routes led to Greece. From an early period the Etruscans began to trade natural products, especially iron, in return for Greek luxury goods. They thereby built a rich cultural life that became the foundation of civilization throughout Italy. In the process they touched a small collection of villages subsequently called Rome.

The Romans, to whom the Etruscans introduced the broader world, had settled in Italy by the eighth century B.C. According to one legend of the founding of Rome, Romulus and Remus founded the city in 753 B.C. Romulus built his home on the Palatine Hill, while Remus chose the Aventine (see inset of Map 5.1). They built Rome's first walls, which were inviolable, reflecting the Etruscan concept of the **pomerium,** a sacred boundary intended to keep out anything evil or unclean. Under Etruscan influence the Romans prospered, spreading over all of Rome's seven hills.

The Etruscans soon drew the fledgling Rome into their orbit. From 753 to 509 B.C. a line of Etruscan kings ruled the city and introduced many customs. The Ro-

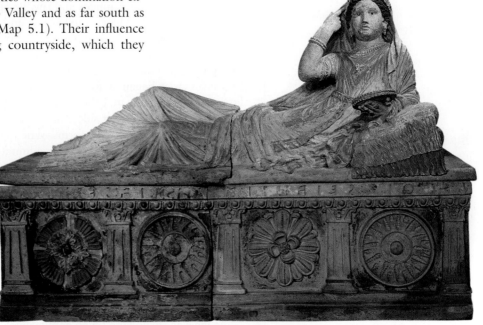

Sarcophagus of Lartie Seianti
The woman portrayed on this lavish sarcophagus is the noble Etruscan Lartie Seianti. Although the sarcophagus is her place of burial, she is portrayed as in life, comfortable and at rest. The influence of Greek art on Etruscan is apparent in almost every feature of the sarcophagus. *(Archaeological Museum, Florence/Nimatallah/Art Resource, NY)*

mans adopted the Etruscan alphabet, which the Etruscans themselves had adopted from the Greeks. The Romans later handed on this alphabet to medieval Europe and thence to the modern Western world. The Romans also adopted symbols of political authority from the Etruscans. The symbol of the Etruscan king's right to execute or scourge his subjects was a bundle of rods and an ax, called in Latin the **fasces,** which the king's retainer carried before him on official occasions. When the Romans expelled the Etruscan kings, they created special attendants called "lictors" to carry the fasces before their new magistrates, the consuls. Even the **toga,** the white woolen robe worn by citizens, came from the Etruscans. In engineering and architecture the Romans adopted the vault and the arch from the Etruscans. Above all, it was thanks to the Etruscans that the Romans truly became urban dwellers.

Under the Etruscans Rome enjoyed contacts with the larger Mediterranean world, while the city continued to grow. In the years 575 to 550 B.C. temples and public buildings began to grace the city. The Capitoline Hill became its religious center when the temple of Jupiter Optimus Maximus (Jupiter the Best and Greatest) was built there. The **Forum** ceased to be a cemetery and began its history as a public meeting place, a development parallel to that of the Greek agora. Trade in metalwork became common, and wealthier Romans began to import large numbers of fine Greek vases. The Etruscans had found Rome a collection of villages and made it a city.

The Roman Conquest of Italy (509–290 B.C.)

Roman expansion was hardly accidental. The Romans had to master themselves before they could rule others. Above all, that meant that they must build a political system that both governed the citizenry and directed its energy in public affairs. The Romans faced a political and social challenge in these years, the meeting of which permitted them effectively to rule themselves and eventually others.

Early Roman history is an uneven mixture of fact and legend. Roman traditions often contain an important kernel of truth, but that does not make them history. In many cases they are significant because they illustrate the ethics, morals, and ideals that Roman society considered valuable.

Several of Rome's founding legends involve sexual violence, and gender norms were deeply embedded in Roman ideals. In the story of Romulus and Remus,

Chronology	
750–133 B.C.	Traditional founding of Rome; evolution of the Roman state
750–31 B.C.	Beginning of the economic growth of Rome
509–290 B.C.	Roman conquest of Italy
499–186 B.C.	Introduction of Greek deities
ca 494–287 B.C.	Struggle of the Orders
264–133 B.C.	Punic Wars and the conquest of the East
262 B.C.	Growth of large estates
239–159 B.C.	Rise of Latin literature
88–31 B.C.	Civil war
86–35 B.C.	Birth of historical and political writing

Romulus appealed to other rulers to send women to Rome to marry young Roman men. When the Sabines refused, young Roman men abducted Sabine women, raped them while their families watched, and then married them. Later the Sabine women protected their children in a war between the Sabines and the Romans, which led to a truce. There is no evidence that what became known as the "rape of the Sabine women" actually happened, but the story was frequently retold as history. Roman historians used it to highlight the centrality of marriage and legitimate birth to Roman citizenship and the way Romans integrated non-Romans into their culture; they did not emphasize the fact that this happened through rape.

Another of Rome's founding myths told the story of Tarquin, an Etruscan king, and Lucretia. During a military campaign Tarquin's men took bets on who had the most virtuous wife. Only Lucretia, the wife of Tarquin's cousin, was at home virtuously spinning wool (the other women were out with friends), and Tarquin's son decided to seduce her. She refused; he threatened to kill her, and he raped her; then she denounced him to her husband. Lucretia killed herself at the shame of the rape, which led the Roman populace to rise up against the Etruscans and found the republic, which tradition held was in 509 B.C. Like the story of the Sabine women, there is no clear evidence that these events actually happened, but the legends clearly link women's sexual honor with the Roman state. Lucretia became the symbol of virtuous Roman

Rome

FIELD OF MARS

QUIRINAL HILL

VIMINAL HILL

CAPITOLINE MT.

Tiber

JANICULUM

Senate House

Forum

Regia

Temple of Jupiter

ESQUILINE MT.

PALATINE MT.

CAELIAN MT.

Circus Maximus

AVENTINE MT.

ALPS

APENNINES

Po

Arno

UMBRIA

PICENUM

ETRURIA

Tiber

SABINI

AEQUI

VESTINI

Veii

Rome

SAMNIUM

LATIUM

APULIA

CAMPANIA

Adriatic Sea

CORSICA

SARDINIA

CALABRIA

Tarentum

LUCANIA

Tyrrhenian Sea

BRUTTIUM

Messana

Mediterranean Sea

SICILY

Syracuse

Carthage

Cape Bon

NORTH AFRICA

— Roman boundary before the Punic Wars

— Roman boundary before Augustus

— Roman internal regional divisions

— Major road

0   50   100 Km.

0   50   100 Mi.

MAP 5.1 Italy and the City of Rome   The geographical configuration of the Italian peninsula shows how Rome stood astride north-south communication routes and how the state that united Italy stood poised to move into Sicily and northern Africa.

womanhood, and her suicide was portrayed in statues and paintings throughout Rome's long history, and again in the Renaissance two thousand years later.

Online Study Center **Improve Your Grade**
Primary Source: The Power of Myth: Livy and the Rape of Lucretia

The republic was actually founded in the years after 509 B.C., when the Romans fought numerous wars with their neighbors on the Italian peninsula. They became soldiers, and the grim fighting bred tenacity, a prominent Roman trait. At an early date the Romans also learned the value of alliances and how to provide leadership for their allies. Alliances with the Latin towns around them provided them with a large reservoir of manpower. These alliances involved the Romans in still other wars and took them farther afield in the Italian peninsula.

The growth of Roman power was slow but steady. Not until roughly a century after the founding of the republic did the Romans drive the Etruscans entirely out of Latium. Around 390 B.C. the Romans suffered a major setback when a new people, the Celts—or **Gauls,** as the Romans called them—swept aside a Roman army and sacked Rome. More intent on loot than on land, they agreed to abandon Rome in return for a thousand pounds of gold.

From 390 to 290 B.C. the Romans rebuilt their city and recouped their losses. They also reorganized their army to create the mobile legion, a flexible unit capable of fighting on either broken or open terrain. The Romans finally brought Latium and their Latin allies fully under their control and conquered Etruria (see Map 5.1). In 343 B.C. they grappled with the

Samnites in a series of bitter wars for the possession of Campania and southern Italy. The Samnites were a formidable enemy and inflicted serious losses on the Romans. But the superior organization, institutions, and manpower of the Romans won out in the end. Although Rome had yet to subdue the whole peninsula, for the first time in history the city stood unchallenged in Italy.

The Romans spread their culture by sharing their religious cults, mythology, and drama. They, like other pagans, liberally shared their religious beliefs with others, which in turn furthered the Romanization of Italy.

Roman religion opened a unique way to the appreciation of Roman law. Seen at its ideal, religion was virtually inseparable from law. Yet the spread of Roman culture was not part of a planned ideological onslaught by the Romans. Nor was it very different from the ways in which the Romans extended their political, military, and legal systems. Even so, the process eventually created a common ground for all the peoples living in Italy and made Italy Roman. In later years the Romans continued this process until all these influences spread throughout the Mediterranean basin.

Rome's success in diplomacy and politics was as important as its military victories. With many of their oldest allies, such as the Latin cities, the Romans shared full Roman citizenship. In other instances they granted citizenship without the **franchise** (*civitas sine suffragio*). Allies

Guard Dog The doorway of the house opened directly onto the street. This entrance is protected by a dog who is always on guard. The notice warns "CAVE CANEM" (beware of the dog). (*Robert Frerck/Odyssey/Chicago*)

who held this status enjoyed all the rights of Roman citizenship except that they could not vote or hold Roman offices. They were subject to Roman taxes and calls for military service but ran their own local affairs. The Latin allies were able to acquire full Roman citizenship by moving to Rome. A perhaps humble but very efficient means of keeping the Romans and their colonies together were the Roman roads, many of which were in use as late as the medieval period. These roads provided an easy route of communication between the capital and outlying areas, allowed for the quick movement of armies, and offered an efficient means of trade. They were the tangible sinews of unity.

By their willingness to extend their citizenship, the Romans took Italy into partnership. Here the political genius of Rome triumphed where Greece had failed. Rome proved itself superior to the Greek polis because it both conquered and shared the fruits of conquest with the conquered. Rome could consolidate where Greece could only dominate. The unwillingness of the Greek polis to share its citizenship condemned it to a limited horizon. Not so with Rome. The extension of Roman citizenship strengthened the state, gave it additional manpower and wealth, and laid the foundation of the Roman Empire.

The Roman Republic

The Roman republic consisted of its constitution and the people who made it. The Romans' first problem was to create the political institutions needed to govern effectively an ever-expanding and influential state. The second was the sharing of the obligations and privileges that came with that effort. The Romans did not expect these challenges, but they struggled hard to meet them. In the process they fashioned both a state and a society. If the effort was demanding, the Romans confronted it so successfully that the Roman republic became one of the preeminent institutions of the ancient world—one still admired today.

● *What was the nature of the Roman republic?*

The Roman State

The Romans summed up their political existence in a single phrase: *senatus populusque Romanum,* "the Roman senate and people." These words were a statement and a proclamation. The Romans often abbreviated this concept as "SPQR." The letters epitomized the Roman people, their state, and their way of life. SPQR became a shorthand way of saying "Rome," just as "U.S.A." says "the United States of America." The real genius of the Romans lay in the fields of politics and law. Unlike the Greeks, they did not often speculate on the ideal state or on political forms. Instead, they realistically met actual challenges and created institutions, magistracies, and legal concepts to deal with practical problems. Change was consequently commonplace in Roman political life, and the constitution of 509 B.C. was far simpler than that of 27 B.C. Moreover, the Roman constitution, unlike the American, was not a single written document. Rather, it was a set of traditional beliefs, customs, and laws.

In the early republic social divisions determined the shape of politics. Political power was in the hands of the aristocracy—the **patricians,** who were wealthy landowners. Patrician families formed clans, as did aristocrats in early Greece. Patrician men dominated the affairs of state, provided military leadership in time of war, and monopolized knowledge of law and legal procedure. The common people of Rome, the **plebeians,** had few of the patricians' advantages. Some plebeians formed their own clans and rivaled the patricians in wealth. Many plebeian merchants increased their wealth in the course of Roman expansion, but most plebeians were poor. They were the artisans, small farmers, and landless urban dwellers. The plebeians, rich and poor alike, were free citizens with a voice in politics. Nonetheless, they were overshadowed by the patricians.

Perhaps the greatest institution of the republic was the **senate,** which had originated under the Etruscans as a council of noble elders who advised the king. During the republic the senate advised the consuls and other magistrates. Because the senate sat year after year, while magistrates changed annually, it provided stability and continuity. It also served as a reservoir of experience and knowledge. Technically, the senate could not pass legislation; it could only offer its advice. But increasingly, because of the senate's prestige, its advice came to have the force of law.

The Romans created several assemblies through which men elected magistrates and passed legislation. The earliest was the *comitia curiata,* which had religious, political, and military functions. According to Roman tradition, King Servius Tullius (578–535 B.C.), who reorganized the state into 193 *centuries* for military purposes, created the *comitia centuriata* as a political body to decide Roman policy. The comitia centuriata voted in centuries, which in this instance means political blocs. The patricians possessed the majority of centuries because they shouldered most of the burden of defense. Thus they could easily

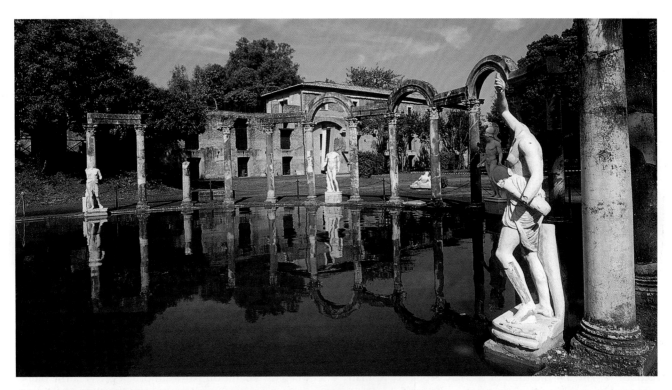

Canopus, Hadrian's Villa This view of Hadrian's villa embodies sublime and serene beauty. The columns and statues lend dignity, and the pond suggests rest. In the background a spacious house offers a retreat from the cares of imperial duties. *(Mark Edward Smith/TIPS Images)*

outvote the plebeians. In 471 B.C. plebeian men won the right to meet in an assembly of their own, the *concilium plebis,* and to pass ordinances. In 287 B.C. the bills passed in the concilium plebis were recognized as binding on the entire population.

The chief magistrates of the republic were the two consuls, elected for one-year terms. At first the consulship was open only to patrician men. The consuls commanded the army in battle, administered state business, convened the comitia centuriata, and supervised financial affairs. In effect, they and the senate ran the state. The consuls appointed *quaestors* to assist them in their duties, and in 421 B.C. the quaestorship became an elective office open to plebeian men. The quaestors took charge of the public treasury and prosecuted criminals in the popular courts.

In 366 B.C. the Romans created a new office, that of **praetor,** and in 227 B.C. the number of praetors was increased to four. When the consuls were away from Rome, the praetors could act in their place. The praetors dealt primarily with the administration of justice. When he took office, a praetor issued a proclamation declaring the principles by which he would interpret the law. These proclamations became very important because they usually covered areas where the law was vague and thus helped clarify the law.

Other officials included the powerful *censors,* created in 443 B.C., who had many responsibilities, the most important being supervision of public morals, the power to determine who lawfully could sit in the senate, the registration of citizens, and the leasing of public contracts. Later officials were the *aediles,* four in number, who supervised the streets and markets and presided over public festivals.

After the age of overseas conquest, the Romans divided the Mediterranean area into provinces governed by ex-consuls and ex-praetors. Because of their experience in Roman politics, they were well suited to administer the affairs of the provincials and to fit Roman law and custom into new contexts.

One of the most important achievements of the Romans was their development of law. Roman law began as a set of rules that regulated the lives and relations of citizens. This civil law, or **ius civile,** consisted of statutes, customs, and forms of procedure. Roman assemblies added to the body of law, and praetors interpreted it. The spirit of the law aimed at protecting the property, lives, and reputations of citizens, redressing wrongs, and giving satisfaction to victims of injustice.

As the Romans came into more frequent contact with foreigners, they had to devise laws to deal with disputes between Romans and foreigners and between foreigners under Roman jurisdiction. In these instances, where there was no precedent to guide the Romans, the legal decisions of the praetors proved of immense importance. The praetors adopted aspects of other legal systems and resorted to the law of equity—what they thought was right and just to all parties. Free, in effect, to determine law, the praetors enjoyed a great deal of flexibility. This situation illustrates the practicality and the genius of the Romans. By addressing specific, actual circumstances the praetors developed a body of law, the *ius gentium,* "the law of peoples," that applied to Romans and foreigners and that laid the foundation for a universal conception of law. By the time of the late republic, Roman jurists were reaching decisions on the basis of the Stoic concept of **ius naturale,** "natural law," a universal law that could be applied to all societies.

Social Conflicts in Rome

Another important aspect of early Roman history was a great social conflict, usually known as the **Struggle of the Orders,** that developed between patricians and plebeians. The plebeians wanted real political representation and safeguards against patrician domination. The plebeians' efforts to obtain recognition of their rights is the crux of the Struggle of the Orders.

Rome's early wars gave the plebeians the leverage they needed: Rome's survival depended on the army, and the army needed the plebeians. The first showdown between plebeians and patricians came, according to tradition, in 494 B.C. To force the patricians to grant concessions, the plebeians seceded from the state; they literally walked out of Rome and refused to serve in the army. The plebeians' general strike worked. Because of it the patricians made important concessions. One of these was social. In 445 B.C. the patricians passed a law, the *lex Canuleia,* which for the first time allowed patricians and plebeians to marry one another. Furthermore, the patricians recognized the right of plebeians to elect their own officials, the **tribunes.** The tribunes in turn had the right to pro-

tect the plebeians from the arbitrary conduct of patrician magistrates. The tribunes brought plebeian grievances to the senate for resolution. The plebeians were not bent on undermining the state. Rather, they used their gains only to win full equality under the law.

The law itself was the plebeians' primary target. Only the patricians knew what the law was, and only they could argue cases in court. All too often they had used the law for their own benefit. The plebeians wanted the law codified and published. The result of their agitation was the Law of the Twelve Tables, so called because the laws, which covered civil and criminal matters, were inscribed on twelve large bronze plaques. Later still, the plebeians forced the patricians to publish legal procedures as well. The plebeians had broken the patricians' legal monopoly and henceforth enjoyed full protection under the law.

The decisive plebeian victory came with the passage of the Licinian-Sextian rogations (or laws) in 367 B.C. Licinius and Sextus were plebeian tribunes who led a ten-year fight for further reform. Rich plebeians, such as Licinius and Sextus themselves, joined the poor to mount a sweeping assault on patrician privilege. Wealthy plebeians wanted the opportunity to provide political leadership for the state. They demanded that the patricians allow them access to all the magistracies of the state. If they could hold the consulship, they could also sit in the senate and advise the senate on policy. The two tribunes won approval from the senate for a law that stipulated that one of the two annual consuls must be a plebeian. Though decisive, the Licinian-Sextian rogations did not automatically end the Struggle of the Orders. That happened only in 287 B.C. with the passage of a law, the *lex Hortensia,* that gave the resolutions of the concilium plebis the force of law for patricians and plebeians alike.

The results of the compromise between the patricians and the plebeians were far-reaching. They secured economic reform and defined the access of all citizens to public land. The principal result was the definition of political leadership. Plebeians could now hold the consulship, which brought with it the consular title, places of honor in the senate, and such cosmetic privileges as wearing the purple toga, the symbol of aristocracy. Far more important, the compromise established a new nobility shared by the plebeians and the patricians. They were both groups of wealthy aristocrats who had simply agreed to share the great offices of power within the republic. This would lead not to major political reform but to an extension of aristocratic rule. Nevertheless, the patricians were wise enough to give the plebeians wider political rights than they had previously enjoyed. The compromise was typically Roman.

The Struggle of the Orders resulted in a Rome stronger and better united than before. It could have led to anarchy, but again certain Roman traits triumphed. The values fostered by their social structure predisposed the Romans to compromise, especially in the face of common danger. Resistance and confrontation in Rome never exploded into class warfare. Instead, both sides resorted to compromises to hammer out a realistic solution. Important, too, were Roman patience, tenacity, and a healthy sense of the practical. These qualities enabled both sides to keep working until they had resolved the crisis. The Struggle of the Orders ended in 287 B.C. with a new concept of Roman citizenship. All male citizens shared equally under the law. Theoretically, all men could aspire to the highest political offices.

The Struggle of the Orders made all male citizens equal before the law, but a man's independence was limited by the power that the male head of the family, termed the **paterfamilias,** had over him. This was also true for all women, who even as adults were always under the legal guardianship of some man. The paterfamilias was the oldest dominant male of the family. He held nearly absolute power over the lives of his wife and children as long as he lived. He could legally kill his wife for adultery or divorce her at will. He could kill his children or sell them into slavery. He could force the children to marry against their will. Until the paterfamilias died, his sons could not legally own property. At his death the wife and children of the paterfamilias inherited his property.

Along with his biological kin, the paterfamilias also had authority over slaves, servants, adopted children, and others who lived in his household. In poor families this group might be very small, but among the wealthy it could include hundreds of slaves and servants.

Roman Expansion

Once the Romans had settled their internal affairs, they were free to turn their attention to the larger world around them. As seen earlier, they had already come to terms with the Italic peoples in Latium. Only later did Rome achieve primacy over its Latin allies, partly because of successful diplomacy and partly because of overwhelming military power. In 282 B.C. Rome expanded even farther in Italy and extended its power across the sea to Sicily, Corsica, and Sardinia.

- *How did the Romans expand farther into Italy?*

Italy Becomes Roman

In only twenty years, from 282 to 262 B.C., the Romans dramatically built on their earlier successes. Just as they had spread their religion through cult, mythology, and drama, now they expanded politically throughout Italy. Their energy was remarkable, and the results they achieved were not always due to warfare. They established a string of colonies throughout Italy, some of them populated by Romans and others by Latins. The genius of the Romans lay in bringing these various peoples into one political system. First the Romans divided the Italians into two broad classes. Those living closest to Rome were incorporated into the Roman state. They enjoyed the full franchise and citizenship that the Romans themselves possessed. The other class comprised those Italians who lived farther afield. They were bound by treaty with the Romans and were considered allies. Although they received lesser rights of active citizenship, the allies retained their right of local self-government. The link between the allies and Rome was as much social as political, as both were ruled by aristocrats.

These contacts—social, political, and legal—with their neighbors led the Romans to a better acquaintance with the heritage, customs, and laws of their fellow Italians. Rome and the rest of Italy began to share similar views of their common welfare. By including others in the Roman political and social system, Rome was making Italy Roman.

Overseas Conquest (282–146 B.C.)

In 282 B.C., when the Romans had reached southern Italy, they embarked upon a series of wars that left them the rulers of the Mediterranean world. The nature of these wars demands attention. Unlike their attitude toward the Italians or even the Etruscans, the Romans felt that they were dealing with foreigners, people not akin to them. They were also moving into areas largely unfamiliar to them. These wars became fiercer and were fought on a larger scale than those in Italy. Yet there was nothing ideological about them. Unlike Napoleon or Hitler, the Romans did not map out grandiose strategies for world conquest. They had no idea of what lay before them. If they could have looked into the future, they would have stood amazed. In many instances the Romans did not even initiate action; they simply responded to situations as they arose. Nineteenth-century Englishmen were fond of saying, "We got our empire in a fit of absence of mind." The Romans could not go quite that far. Though they sometimes declared war reluctantly, they nonetheless felt the need to dominate, to eliminate any state that could threaten them.

The Samnite wars had drawn the Romans into the political world of southern Italy. In 282 B.C., alarmed by the powerful newcomer, the Greek city of Tarentum in southern Italy called for help from Pyrrhus, king of Epirus in western Greece. A relative of Alexander the Great and an excellent general, Pyrrhus won two furious battles but suffered heavy casualties—thus the phrase **Pyrrhic victory** for a victory involving severe losses. Roman bravery and tenacity led him to comment: "If we win one more battle with the Romans, we'll be completely washed up." Against Pyrrhus's army the Romans threw new legions, and in the end manpower proved decisive. In 275 B.C. the Romans drove Pyrrhus from Italy and extended their sway over southern Italy. Once they did, the island of Sicily became a key for them to block Carthaginian expansion northward.

The Punic Wars and Beyond (264–133 B.C.)

By 264 B.C. Carthage (see Map 5.2) was the unrivaled power of the western Mediterranean. Since the second half of the eighth century B.C., it had built its wealth on trade in tin and precious metals. It commanded one of the best harbors on the northern African coast and was supported by a fertile hinterland. The Carthaginians were for the most part merchants, not soldiers, and they made contributions to geographical knowledge by exploring as far west as the Atlantic coasts of northern Africa and Spain. They soon dominated the commerce of the western Mediterranean. By the fourth century B.C. they were fully integrated into the Hellenistic economy, which now spread from Gibraltar to the Parthian empire.

Commercial ambitions led to political conflict. Expansion led to war with the Etruscans and Greeks, but the Carthaginians won control of parts of Sardinia, Spain, and Sicily. At the end of a long string of wars, the Carthaginians held control of only the western tip of Sicily but retained considerable influence farther to the west. In fact, the Carthaginians had created and defended a mercantile empire that stretched from western Sicily to beyond Gibraltar.

This in essence is the background of the **First Punic War** between Rome and Carthage, two powers expanding into the same area. The First Punic War lasted for twenty-three years (264–241 B.C.). The Romans quickly learned that they could not conquer Sicily unless they controlled the sea. Although they lacked a fleet and hated the sea as fervently as cats hate water, with grim resolution the Romans built a navy. They fought seven major naval battles with the Carthaginians, won six, and finally wore them down. In 241 B.C. the Romans took possession of Sicily, which became their first real province. Once again Rome's resources, manpower, and determination proved decisive.

The peace treaty between the two powers brought no peace, in part because in 238 B.C. the Romans took advantage of Carthaginian weakness to seize Sardinia and Corsica. Although unable to resist, many Carthaginians concluded that genuine peace between Carthage and Rome was impossible. One such man was Hamilcar Barca, a Carthaginian commander who had come close to victory in Sicily. The only way Carthage could recoup its fortune was by success in Spain, where the Carthaginians already enjoyed a firm foothold. In 237 B.C. Hamilcar led an army to Spain in order to turn it into Carthaginian territory. With him he took his nineteen-year-old son, Hannibal, but not before he had led Hannibal to an altar and made him swear

Triumphal Column of Caius Duilius
This curious monument celebrates Rome's first naval victory in the First Punic War. In the battle Caius Duilius destroyed fifty Carthaginian ships. He then celebrated his success by erecting this column that portrays the prows of the enemy ships projecting from the column. (*Alinari/Art Resource, NY*)

ever to be an enemy to Rome. In the following years Hamilcar and his son-in-law Hasdrubal subjugated much of southern Spain and in the process rebuilt Carthaginian power. Rome responded in two ways: first, the Romans made a treaty with Hasdrubal in which the Ebro River formed the boundary between Carthaginian and Roman interests, and second, the Romans began to extend their own influence in Spain.

In 221 B.C. the young Hannibal became Carthaginian commander in Spain, and soon Roman and Carthaginian policies clashed at the city of Saguntum. When Hannibal laid siege to Saguntum, which lay within the sphere of Carthaginian interest, the Romans declared war, claiming that Carthage had attacked a friendly city. So began the Second Punic War, one of the most desperate wars ever fought by Rome. In 218 B.C. Hannibal struck first by marching more than a thousand miles over the Alps into Italy. Once there, he defeated one Roman army at the Battle of Trebia and later another at the Battle of Lake Trasimene in 217 B.C. In the following year, Hannibal won his greatest victory at the Battle of Cannae, in which he inflicted some forty thousand casualties on the Romans. He then spread devastation throughout Italy, and a number of cities in central and southern Italy rebelled against Rome. Syracuse, Rome's ally during the First Punic War, also went over to the Carthaginians. Yet Hannibal failed to crush Rome's iron circle of Latium, Etruria, and Samnium. The wisdom of Rome's political policy of extending rights and citizenship to its allies showed itself in these dark hours. And Rome fought back.

In 210 B.C. Rome found its answer to Hannibal in the young commander Scipio, later better known as Scipio Africanus. Scipio copied Hannibal's methods of mobile warfare, streamlining the legions by making their components capable of independent action and introducing new weapons. In the following years, Scipio operated in Spain, which in 207 B.C. he wrested from the Carthaginians. Also in 207 B.C. the Romans sealed Hannibal's fate in Italy. At the Battle of Metaurus, the Romans destroyed a major Carthaginian army coming to reinforce Hannibal. With Hannibal now bottled up in southern Italy, Scipio in 204 B.C. struck directly at Carthage itself. A Roman fleet landed his legions in North Africa, which prompted the Carthaginians to recall Hannibal from Italy to defend the homeland.

In 202 B.C., near the town of Zama (see Map 5.2), Scipio defeated Hannibal in one of the world's truly decisive battles. Scipio's victory meant that the world of the western Mediterranean would henceforth be Roman. Roman language, law, and culture, fertilized by Greek influences, would in time permeate this entire region. The victory at Zama meant that Rome's heritage would be passed on to the Western world.

The **Second Punic War** contained the seeds of still other wars. Unabated fear of Carthage led to the Third Punic War, a needless, unjust, and savage conflict that ended in 146 B.C. when Scipio Aemilianus, grandson of Scipio Africanus, destroyed the old hated rival. As the Roman conqueror watched the death pangs of that great city, he turned to his friend Polybius with the words: "I fear and foresee that someday someone will give the same order about my fatherland." It would, however, be centuries before an invader would stand before the gates of Rome.

During the war with Hannibal, the Romans had invaded Spain, a peninsula rich in material resources and the home of fierce warriors. When the Roman legions tried to reduce the Spanish tribes, they met with bloody and determined resistance. Not until 133 B.C., after years of brutal and ruthless warfare, did Scipio Aemilianus finally conquer Spain.

Rome Turns East (211–133 B.C.)

During the dark days of the Second Punic War, King Philip V of Macedonia made an alliance with Hannibal against Rome. Despite the mortal struggle in the West, the Romans found the strength to turn eastward to settle accounts. Their first significant victory came over the Macedonians in 197 B.C. The Roman general Titus Flamininus demanded that the Macedonians agree to give full liberty to the Greeks. Two years later he defeated the Spartans. In 189 B.C. the Seleucid kingdom fell to the Romans, but decisive victory came in 146 B.C., when the Romans conquered the Achaean League, sacked Corinth, and finally defeated Macedonia, which they made a Roman province. In 133 B.C. Attalus III, the last king of Pergamum, bequeathed his kingdom to the Romans. The Ptolemies of Egypt meekly obeyed Roman wishes.

The Romans had used the discord and disunity of the Hellenistic world to divide and conquer it. Once they had done so, they faced the formidable challenge of governing it without further warfare, which they met by establishing the first Roman provinces in the East. They ultimately succeeded in fusing the honored culture and civilization of the Hellenistic world, with its blend of Greek and Eastern cultures, with the new and vibrant Roman civilization. (See the feature "Listening to the Past: A Magic Charm" on pages 148–149.) As seen earlier, Greek cultural influence had already fertilized Roman life, but now Rome began to create the political and

Mapping the Past

MAP 5.2 Roman Expansion During the Republic   Previous maps have shown that the Greeks and Macedonians concentrated their energies on opening the East. This map indicates that Rome for the first time looked to the West. **❶** What does
this say about the expansion of Roman power in the Mediterranean? **❷** What does this foreshadow for the subsequent development of Europe?

administrative machinery to hold the Mediterranean together under a mutually shared cultural and political system. The Romans, nonetheless, were as usual practical as well as somewhat altruistic. They declared that the Mediterranean had become *mare nostrum,* "our sea."

Old Values and Greek Culture

Rome had conquered the Mediterranean world, but some Romans considered that victory a misfortune. The historian Sallust (86–34 B.C.), writing from hindsight, complained that the acquisition of an empire was the beginning of Rome's troubles:

But when through labor and justice our Republic grew powerful, great kings defeated in war, fierce nations and mighty peoples subdued by force, when Carthage the rival of the Roman people was wiped out root and branch, all the seas and lands lay open, then fortune began to be harsh and to throw everything into confusion. The Romans had easily borne labor, danger, uncertainty, and hardship. To them leisure, riches—otherwise desirable—proved to be burdens and torments. So at first money, then desire for power grew great. These things were a sort of cause of all evils.[2]

Sallust was not alone in his feelings. At the time some senators had opposed the destruction of Carthage on the grounds that fear of their old rival would keep the Romans in check. In the second century B.C. the Romans learned that they could not return to what they fondly considered a simple life. They were world rulers. The responsibilities they faced were complex and awesome. They had to change their institutions, social patterns, and way of thinking to meet the new era. They were in fact building the foundations of a great imperial system. It was a daunting challenge, and there were failures along the way. Roman generals and politicians would destroy each other. Even the republican constitution would eventually be discarded. But in the end Rome triumphed here just as it had on the battlefield, for out of the turmoil would come the *pax Romana*—"Roman peace."

How did the Romans of the day meet these challenges? How did they lead their lives and cope with these momentous changes? Obviously there are as many answers to these questions as there were Romans. Yet two men represent the major trends of the second century B.C. Cato the Elder shared the mentality of those who longed for the good old days and idealized the traditional agrarian way of life. Scipio Aemilianus led those who embraced the new urban life, with its eager acceptance of Greek culture. Forty-nine years older than Scipio, Cato was a product of an earlier generation, one that confronted a rapidly changing world. Cato and Scipio were both aristocrats, and neither of them was typical, even of the aristocracy. But they do exemplify opposing sets of attitudes that marked Roman society and politics in the age of conquest.

• *What values did the Romans embrace because of their expansion?*

Cato and the Traditional Ideal

Marcus Cato (234–149 B.C.) was born a plebeian, but his talent and energy carried him to Rome's highest offices. He created an image of himself as the bearer of "traditional" Roman virtues, perhaps to offset his rather humble origins. His description of his life is thus partly invented, but some details probably reflect the way many Romans actually lived.

Like most Romans, Cato and his family began the day early in the morning. The Romans divided the period of daylight into twelve hours and the darkness into another twelve. The day might begin as early as half past four in summer, as late as half past seven in winter. Because Mediterranean summers are invariably hot, people liked to take every advantage of the cool mornings. Cato and his family, like modern Italians, ordinarily started the morning with a light breakfast, usually nothing more than some bread and cheese. After breakfast the family went about its work.

Because of his political aspirations, Cato often used the mornings to plead law cases. He walked to the marketplace of the nearby town and defended anyone who wished his help. He received no fees for these services but did put his neighbors in his debt. In matters of law and politics Roman custom was very strong. It demanded that Cato's clients give him their political support or their votes in repayment whenever he asked for them. These clients knew and accepted their obligations to Cato for his help. The notion of clientage was a particularly Roman social and political custom: free men entrusted their lives to a more powerful man, and in exchange they gained from their patron some social entertainment and his protection. Custom, not law, governed this relationship. In return for his generosity toward his clients, the patron expected their support in public life and private matters. The bond thus proved reciprocal. Clientage helped men of lower social status to advance themselves and to advance the careers of their patrons.

Cato was married—though he never mentions the name of his wife—as were almost all Roman citizens. Grooms were generally somewhat older than their brides, who often married in their early teens. There were two types of marriage in Rome, one of which put the woman under control of her husband's family (marriage *cum manu*) and one of which kept her under her father's control (marriage *sine manu*). Each had advantages and disadvantages for women.

Women could inherit property under Roman law, though they generally received a smaller portion of any family inheritance than their brothers did. Women's inheritance usually came as a dowry on marriage. In the earliest Roman marriage laws, men could divorce their wives without any grounds while women could not divorce their husbands, but by the time of Cato these laws had changed, and both men and women could initiate divorce. Women appear to have gained greater control over their dowries, perhaps in response to the fact that Rome's military conquests meant that many husbands were away for long periods of time and women needed some say over family finances.

Both Romans and Greeks felt that children should be raised in the lap of their mother, a woman who kept her house in good order and personally saw to the welfare of her children. In wealthy homes during the period, the matron had begun to employ a slave as a wet nurse. According to Cato, his wife refused to delegate her maternal duties. Like most ordinary Roman women, she nursed her son herself and bathed and swaddled him daily.

Until the age of seven, children were under their mother's care. During this time the matron began to educate her daughters in the management of the household.

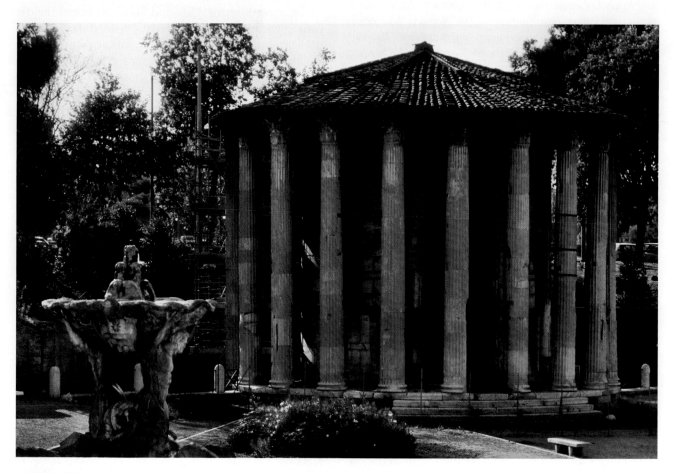

Temple of Mater Matuta   This round temple was dedicated to Mater Matuta, a very old Roman mother goddess. Its shape and architectural ornamentation indicate Hellenistic influence. *(Vanni/Art Resource, NY)*

After the age of seven, sons—and in many wealthy households daughters too—began to receive formal education. Formal education for wealthy children was generally in the hands of tutors, who were often Greek slaves, for parents wanted their children to learn Greek literature and philosophy. By the late republic, there were also a few schools. Most children learned skills from their own parents or through apprenticeships with artisans; slave boys and girls were occasionally formally apprenticed in trades such as leatherwork, weaving, or metalsmithing.

In the country Romans like Cato continued to take their main meal at midday. This meal included either coarse bread made from the entire husk of wheat or porridge made with milk or water; it also included turnips, cabbage, olives, and beans. With the midday meal the family drank ordinary wine mixed with water. Afterward any Roman who could took a nap. This was especially true in the summer, when the Mediterranean heat can be fierce. Slaves, artisans, and hired laborers, however, continued their work. In the evening Romans ate a light meal and went to bed at nightfall.

The agricultural year followed the sun and the stars—the farmer's calendar. Like Hesiod in Boeotia, the Roman farmer looked to the sky to determine when to plant, weed, shear sheep, and perform other chores. Spring was the season for plowing. Roman farmers plowed their land at least twice and preferably three times. The third plowing was to cover the sown seed in ridges and to use the furrows to drain off excess water. Farmers used oxen and donkeys to pull the plow, collecting the dung of the animals for fertilizer. Besides spreading manure, some farmers fertilized their fields by planting lupines and beans; when they began to pod, the farmers plowed them under. The main money crops, at least for rich soils, were wheat and flax. Forage crops included clover, vetch, and alfalfa. Prosperous farmers like Cato raised olive trees chiefly for the oil. They also raised grapevines for the production of wine. Cato and his neighbors harvested their cereal crops in summer and their grapes in autumn. Harvests varied depending on the soil, but farmers could usually expect yields of 5½ bushels of wheat or 10½ bushels of barley per acre.

An influx of slaves resulted from Rome's wars and conquests. The Roman attitude toward slaves and slavery had little in common with modern views. To the Romans slavery was a misfortune that befell some people, but it did not entail any racial theories. Races were not enslaved because the Romans thought them inferior. The black African slave was treated no worse—and no better—than the Spaniard. Indeed, some slaves were valued because of their physical distinctiveness: black Africans and blond Germans were particular favorites. For the talented slave the Romans always held out the hope of eventual freedom. **Manumission**—the freeing of individual slaves by their masters—became so common that it was limited by law. Not even Christians questioned the institution of slavery. It was just a fact of life.

Online Study Center **Improve Your Grade**
Primary Source: The Process of Freedom:
   Manumissions of Hellenistic Slaves

For Cato and most other Romans, religion played an important part in life. Originally the Romans thought of the gods as invisible, shapeless natural forces. Only through Etruscan and Greek influence did Roman deities take on human form. Jupiter, the sky-god, and his wife Juno became equivalent to the Greek Zeus and Hera. Mars was the god of war but also guaranteed the fertility of the farm and protected it from danger. The gods of the Romans were not loving and personal. They were stern, powerful, and aloof. But as long as the Romans honored the cults of their gods, they could expect divine favor. The shrine of the goddess Vesta, for example, was tended by six *vestal virgins* chosen from patrician families. Roman military losses were sometimes blamed on inattention by the vestal virgins, another link between female honor and the Roman state.

Along with the great gods the Romans believed in spirits who haunted fields, forests, crossroads, and even the home itself. Some of these deities were hostile; only magic could ward them off. The spirits of the dead, like ghosts in modern horror films, frequented places where they had lived. They too had to be placated but were ordinarily benign. As the poet Ovid (43 B.C.–A.D. 17) put it:

The spirits of the dead ask for little.
They are more grateful for piety than for an expensive gift—
Not greedy are the gods who haunt the Styx below.
A rooftile covered with a sacrificial crown,
Scattered kernels, a few grains of salt,
Bread dipped in wine, and loose violets—
These are enough.
Put them in a potsherd and leave them in the middle of the road.[3]

A good deal of Roman religion consisted of rituals such as those Ovid describes. These practices lived on long after the Romans had lost interest in the great gods. Even Christianity could not entirely wipe them out. Instead, Christianity was to incorporate many of these rituals into its own style of worship.

Scipio Aemilianus: Greek Culture and Urban Life

The old-fashioned ideals that Cato represented came into conflict with a new spirit of wealth and leisure. The conquest of the Mediterranean world and the spoils of war made Rome a great city. Roman life, especially in the cities, was changing and becoming less austere. The spoils of war went to build baths, theaters, and other places of amusement. Romans and Italian townspeople began to spend more of their time in leisure pursuits. Simultaneously, the new responsibilities of governing the world produced in Rome a sophisticated society. Romans developed new tastes and a liking for Greek culture and literature. They began to learn the Greek language. It became common for an educated Roman to speak both Latin and Greek. Hellenism dominated the cultural life of Rome. Even die-hards like Cato found a knowledge of Greek essential for political and diplomatic affairs. The poet Horace (64–8 B.C.) summed it up well: "Captive Greece captured her rough conqueror and introduced the arts into rustic Latium."

One of the most avid devotees of Hellenism and the new was Scipio Aemilianus, the destroyer of Carthage. Scipio realized that broad and worldly views had to replace the old Roman narrowness. The new situation called for new ways. Rome was no longer a small city on the Tiber; it was the capital of the world, and Romans had to adapt themselves to that fact. Scipio was ready to become an innovator in both politics and culture. He broke with the past in the conduct of his political career, choosing a more personal style of politics, one that reflected his own views and looked unflinchingly at the broader problems that the success of Rome brought to its people. He embraced Hellenism wholeheartedly. Perhaps more than anyone else of his day, Scipio represented the new Roman—imperial, cultured, and independent.

In his education and interests, too, Scipio broke with the past. As a boy he had received the traditional Roman training, learning to read and write Latin and becoming acquainted with the law. He mastered the fundamentals of rhetoric and learned how to throw the javelin, fight in armor, and ride a horse. But later Scipio also learned Greek and be-

came a fervent Hellenist. As a young man he formed a lasting friendship with the historian Polybius, who actively encouraged him in his study of Greek culture and in his intellectual pursuits. In later life Scipio's love of Greek learning, rhetoric, and philosophy became legendary. Scipio also promoted the spread of Hellenism in Roman society. He became the center of the Scipionic Circle, a small group of Greek and Roman artists, philosophers, historians, and poets. Conservatives like Cato tried to stem the rising tide of Hellenism, but men like Scipio carried the day and helped make the heritage of Greece an abiding factor in Roman life.

The new Hellenism profoundly stimulated the growth and development of Roman art and literature. The Roman conquest of the Hellenistic East resulted in wholesale confiscation of Greek paintings and sculpture to grace Roman temples, public buildings, and private homes. Roman artists copied many aspects of Greek art, but their emphasis on realistic portraiture carried on a native tradition.

Fabius Pictor (second half of the third century B.C.), a senator, wrote the first *History of Rome* in Greek. Other Romans translated Greek classics into Latin. Still others, such as the poet Ennius (239–169 B.C.), the father of

African Acrobat Conquest and prosperity brought exotic pleasure to Rome. Every feature of this sculpture is exotic. The young African woman and her daring gymnastic pose would catch anyone's attention. And to add to the spice of her act, she performs using a live crocodile as her platform. Americans would have loved it. (*Courtesy of the Trustees of the British Museum*)

Roman Table Manners   This mosaic is a floor that can never be swept clean. It whimsically suggests what a dining room floor looked like after a lavish dinner and also tells something about the menu: a chicken head, a wishbone, and remains of various seafood, vegetables, and fruit are easily recognizable. *(Museo Gregoriano Profano, Vatican Museums/Scala/Art Resource, NY)*

Latin poetry, studied Greek philosophy, wrote comedies in Latin, and adapted many of Euripides' tragedies for the Roman stage. Plautus (ca 254–184 B.C.) specialized in rough humor. He too decked out Greek plays in Roman dress but was no mere imitator. The Roman dramatist Terence (ca 195–159 B.C.), a member of the Scipionic Circle, wrote comedies of refinement and grace that owed their essentials to Greek models. His plays lacked the energy and the slapstick of Plautus's rowdy plays. All early Roman literature was derived from the Greeks, but it managed in time to speak in its own voice and to flourish because it had something of its own to say.

The conquest of the Mediterranean world brought the Romans leisure, and Hellenism influenced how they spent their free time. Many rich urban dwellers changed their eating habits by consuming elaborate meals of exotic dishes. A whole suckling pig stuffed with sausages was a favorite treat, and a lucky guest might even dine on peacocks, ostriches, and rare fish, all washed down with vintage wines.

During the second century B.C. the Greek custom of bathing also became a Roman passion and an important part of the day. In the early republic Romans had bathed infrequently, especially in the winter. Now large buildings containing pools and exercise rooms went up in great numbers, and the baths became an essential part of the Roman city. They became even more elaborate several centuries later. Architects built intricate systems of aqueducts to supply the bathing establishments with water. Conservatives railed at this Greek custom, calling it a waste of time and an encouragement to idleness. They were correct in that bathing establishments were more than just places to take a bath. They included gymnasia, where men exercised and played ball. Women had opportunities to bathe, generally in separate facilities or at separate times. The baths contained hot-air rooms to induce a good sweat and pools of hot and cold water to finish the actual bathing. They also contained snack bars and halls, where people chatted and read, and even libraries and lecture halls. The baths were socially important

Dressing of the Bride   Preparing for the wedding was an occasion for fun and ceremony. On the night before the event, the bride tried on her wedding dress for a favorable omen. The next morning her mother fastidiously dressed her or supervised a maid to do so. Last, the bride was crowned with a veil of flowers she had picked herself. *(Vatican Museums/Scala/Art Resource, NY)*

places where men and women went to see and be seen. Social climbers tried to talk to the right people and wangle invitations to dinner; politicians took advantage of the occasion to discuss the affairs of the day; marriages were negotiated by wealthy fathers. Prostitutes added to the attraction of many baths. These women were often slaves or members of the lower classes, who could also be found in brothels and inns. Actresses and entertainers likewise sometimes turned to prostitution as an easy way to increase their earnings, and baths provided good places to work. Despite the protests of conservatives and moralists, the baths at least furnished people—rich and poor—with places for clean and healthy relaxation.

Online Study Center **Improve Your Grade**
   Primary Source: Public Space in an Urban Setting:
   The Sounds of a Roman Bath

Did Hellenism and new social customs corrupt the Romans? Perhaps the best answer is this: the Roman state and the empire it ruled continued to exist for six more centuries. Rome did not collapse; the state continued to prosper. The golden age of literature was still before it. The high tide of its prosperity still lay in the future. The Romans did not like change but took it in stride. That was part of their practical turn of mind and their strength.

The Late Republic (133–31 B.C.)

The wars of conquest created serious problems for the Romans, some of the most pressing of which were political. The republican constitution had suited the needs of a simple city-state but was inadequate to meet the requirements of Rome's new position in international affairs (see Map 5.2). Sweeping changes and reforms were necessary to make it serve the demands of a state holding vast territory. A system of provincial administration had to be established. Officials had to be appointed to govern the provinces and administer the law. These officials and administrative organs had to find places in the constitution. Armies had to be provided for defense, and a system of tax collection had to be created.

Other political problems were equally serious. During the wars Roman generals commanded huge numbers of troops for long periods of time. These men of great power and prestige were on the point of becoming too mighty for the state to control. Although Rome's Italian allies had borne much of the burden of the fighting, they received fewer rewards than did Roman officers and soldiers. Italians began to agitate for full Roman citizenship, including the right to vote.

• *What were the main problems and achievements of the late republic?*

Unrest in Rome and Italy

There were serious economic problems, too. Hannibal's operations and the warfare in Italy had left the countryside a shambles. The movements of numerous armies had disrupted agriculture. The prolonged fighting had also drawn untold numbers of Roman and Italian men away from their farms for long periods. The families of these soldiers could not keep the land under full cultivation. The people who defended Rome and conquered the world for Rome became impoverished for having done their duty.

These problems, complex and explosive, largely account for the turmoil of the closing years of the republic. The late republic was one of the most dramatic eras in Roman history. It produced some of Rome's most famous figures: the Gracchi, Marius, Sulla, Cicero, Pompey, and Julius Caesar, among others. In one way or another, each of these men attempted to solve Rome's problems. Yet they were also striving for the glory and honor that were the supreme goals of the senatorial aristocracy. Personal ambition often clashed with patriotism to create political tension throughout the period.

When the legionaries returned to their farms in Italy, they encountered an appalling situation. All too often their farms looked like the farms of people they had conquered. Two courses of action were open to them. They could rebuild as their forefathers had done, or they could take advantage of an alternative not open to their ancestors and sell their holdings. The wars of conquest had made some men astoundingly rich. These men wanted to invest their wealth in land. They bought up small farms to create huge estates, which the Romans called **latifundia**.

The purchase offers of the rich landowners appealed to the veterans for a variety of reasons. Many veterans had seen service in the East, where they had tasted the rich city life of the Hellenistic states. They were reluctant to return home and settle down to a dull life on the farm. Often their farms were so badly damaged that rebuilding hardly seemed worthwhile. Besides, it was hard to make big profits from small farms. Nor could the veterans supplement their income by working on the latifundia. Although the owners of the latifundia occasionally hired free men as day laborers, they preferred to use slaves. Slaves could not strike or be drafted into the army. Confronted by these conditions, veterans and their families opted to sell their land. They took what they could get for their broken farms and tried their luck elsewhere.

Most veterans migrated to the cities, especially to Rome. Although some found work, most did not. Industry and small manufacturing were generally in the hands of slaves. Even when work was available, slave labor kept the wages of free men low. Instead of a new start, veterans and their families encountered slum conditions that matched those of many modern American cities.

This trend held ominous consequences for the strength of Rome's armies. The Romans had always believed that only landowners should serve in the army, for only they had something to fight for. Landless men, even if they were Romans and lived in Rome, could not be conscripted into the army. These landless men may have been veterans of major battles and numerous campaigns; they may have won distinction on the battlefield. But once they sold their land, they became ineligible for further military service. A large pool of experienced manpower was going to waste. The landless ex-legionaries wanted a new start, and they were willing to support any leader who would provide it.

One man who recognized the plight of Rome's peasant farmers and urban poor was an aristocrat, Tiberius Gracchus (163–133 B.C.). Appalled by what he saw, Tiberius warned his countrymen that the legionaries were losing their land while fighting Rome's wars:

The wild beasts that roam over Italy have every one of them a cave or lair to lurk in. But the men who fight and die for Italy enjoy the common air and light, indeed, but nothing else. Houseless and homeless they wander about with their wives and children. And it is with lying lips that their generals exhort the soldiers in their battles to defend sepulchres and shrines from the enemy, for not a man of them has an hereditary altar, not one of all these many Romans an ancestral tomb, but they fight and die to support others in luxury, and though they are styled masters of the world, they have not a single clod of earth that is their own.[4]

Until his death Tiberius Gracchus sought a solution to the problems of the veterans and the urban poor.

After his election as tribune of the people in 133 B.C., Tiberius proposed that public land be given to the poor in small lots. Although his reform enjoyed the support of some very distinguished and popular aristocrats, he immediately ran into trouble for a number of reasons. First, his reform bill angered many wealthy aristocrats who had usurped large tracts of public land for their own use. They had no desire to give any of it back, so they bitterly resisted Tiberius's efforts. This was to be expected, yet he unquestionably made additional problems for himself. He introduced his land bill in the concilium plebis without consulting the senate. When King Attalus III left the kingdom of Pergamum to the Romans in his will, Tiberius had the money appropriated to finance his reforms—another slap at the senate. As tribune he acted

Pompeii The eruption of Mt. Vesuvius that buried this Italian city in A.D. 79 preserved a singular view of Roman life. The huge temple of Jupiter in the near foreground dominated the city. Other temples and sacred places surround it. Next to it lie the marketplace and various public buildings. *(Guido Alberto Rossi/Altitude)*

totally within his rights. Yet the way in which he proceeded was unprecedented. Many powerful Romans became suspicious of Tiberius's growing influence with the people, some even thinking that he aimed at tyranny. Others opposed him because of his unparalleled methods. After all, there were proper ways to do things in Rome, and he had not followed them. As a result, violence broke out when a large body of senators, led by the *pontifex maximus* (the chief priest), killed Tiberius in cold blood. It was a black day in Roman history. The very people who directed the affairs of state and administered the law had taken the law into their own hands. The death of Tiberius was the beginning of an era of political violence. In the end that violence would bring down the republic.

Although Tiberius was dead, his land bill became law. Furthermore, Tiberius's brother Gaius Gracchus (153–121 B.C.) took up the cause of reform. Gaius was a veteran soldier with an enviable record, but this fiery orator made his mark in the political arena. Gaius also became tribune and demanded even more extensive reform than

had his brother. To help the urban poor Gaius pushed legislation to provide them with cheap grain for bread. He defended his brother's land law and suggested other measures for helping the landless. He proposed that Rome send many of its poor and propertyless people out to form colonies in southern Italy. The poor would have a new start and lead productive lives. The city would immediately benefit because excess, nonproductive families would leave for new opportunities abroad. Rome would be less crowded, sordid, and dangerous.

Gaius went a step further and urged that all Italians be granted full rights of Roman citizenship. This measure provoked a storm of opposition, and it was not passed in Gaius's lifetime. Yet in the long run he proved wiser than his opponents. In 91 B.C. many Italians revolted against Rome over the issue of full citizenship, thus triggering the Social War, so named from the Latin word *socium*, or "ally." After a brief but hard-fought war (91–88 B.C.), the senate gave Roman citizenship to all Italians. Had the senate listened to Gaius earlier, it could have prevented a great deal of bloodshed. Yet Gaius himself was also at fault. Like his brother Tiberius, Gaius aroused a great deal of personal and factional opposition. To many he seemed too radical and too hasty to change things. Many political opponents considered him belligerent and headstrong. When Gaius failed in 121 B.C. to win the tribunate for the third time, he feared for his life. In desperation he armed his staunchest supporters, whereupon the senate ordered the consul Opimius to restore order. He did so by having Gaius killed, along with three thousand of Gaius's supporters who opposed the senate's order. Once again the cause of reform had met with violence.

The death of Gaius brought little peace, and trouble came from two sources: the outbreak of new wars in the Mediterranean basin and further political unrest in Rome. In 112 B.C. Rome declared war against the rebellious Jugurtha, king of Numidia in North Africa. Numidia had been one of Rome's **client kingdoms,** kingdoms still ruled by their own kings but subject to Rome. These kingdoms entered into a political relationship with Rome that was usually friendly but was not a relationship between equals: Rome always remained the senior partner. The kingdoms followed Rome's lead in foreign affairs but conducted their own internal business according to their own laws and customs. Client kingdoms generally lay on the outskirts of Roman control, which gave them an additional measure of local control. The benefits of these relations were mutual, for the client kingdoms enjoyed the protection of Rome while defending Rome's borders. In time many of these states became provinces of the Roman Empire.

Meanwhile, the Roman legions made little headway against Jugurtha until 107 B.C., when Gaius Marius, an Italian *new man* (a politician not from the traditional Roman aristocracy), became consul. Marius's values were those of the military camp. A man of fierce vigor and courage, Marius saw the army as the tool of his ambition. He took the unusual but not wholly unprecedented step of recruiting an army by permitting landless men to serve in the legions. Marius thus tapped Rome's vast reservoir of idle manpower. His volunteer army was a professional force, not a body of draftees. In 106 B.C. Marius and his new army handily defeated Jugurtha.

An unexpected war broke out in the following year when two German peoples, the Cimbri and Teutones, moved into Gaul and later into northern Italy. After the Germans had defeated Roman armies sent to repel them, Marius was again elected consul, even though he was legally ineligible. From 104 to 100 B.C. Marius annually held the consulship. Despite the military necessity, Marius's many consulships meant that a Roman commander repeatedly held unprecedented military power in his hands. This would later translate into a political problem that the Roman republic never solved.

Before engaging the Cimbri and Teutones, Marius reformed the Roman army. There was, however, a disturbing side to his reforms, one that would henceforth haunt the republic. To encourage enlistments, Marius promised land to his volunteers after the war. Poor and landless veterans flocked to him, and together they conquered the Germans by 101 B.C. When Marius proposed a bill to grant land to his veterans, the senate refused to act, in effect turning its back on the soldiers of Rome. It was a disastrous mistake. Henceforth the legionaries expected the commanders—not the senate or the state—to protect their interests. Through Marius's reforms the Roman army became a professional force, but it owed little allegiance to the state. By failing to reward the loyalty of Rome's troops, the senate set the stage for military rebellion and political anarchy.

The Social War brought Marius into conflict with Sulla, who was consul in 88 B.C. First Marius and later Sulla defeated the Italian rebels. In the final stages of the war, while putting down the last of the rebels, Sulla was deposed from his consulship because of factional chaos in Rome. He immediately marched on Rome and restored order, but it was an ominous sign of the deterioration of Roman politics and political ideals. With some semblance of order restored, Sulla in 88 B.C. led an army to the East, where King Mithridates of Pontus in Asia Minor challenged Roman rule. In Sulla's absence, rioting and political violence again exploded in Rome. Marius and his supporters marched on Rome and launched a reign of terror.

Although Marius died peacefully in 86 B.C., his supporters continued to hold Rome. Once Sulla had defeated Mithridates, he once again, this time in 82 B.C., marched on Rome. After a brief but intense civil war, Sulla entered Rome and ordered a ruthless butchery of his opponents. He also proclaimed himself dictator. He launched many political and judicial reforms, including strengthening the senate while weakening the tribunate, increasing the number of magistrates in order to administer Rome's provinces better, and restoring the courts.

In 79 B.C. Sulla voluntarily abdicated his dictatorship and permitted the republican constitution to function normally once again. Yet his dictatorship cast a long shadow over the late republic. Sulla the political reformer proved far less influential than Sulla the successful general and dictator. Civil war was to be the constant lot of Rome for the next fifty years, until the republican constitution gave way to the empire of Augustus in 27 B.C. The history of the late republic is the story of the power struggles of some of Rome's most famous figures: Julius

Caesar and Pompey, Augustus and Marc Antony. One figure who stands apart is Cicero (106–43 B.C.), a practical politician whose greatest legacy to the Roman world and to Western civilization is his mass of political and oratorical writings. Yet Cicero commanded no legions, and only legions commanded respect.

Civil War

In the late republic many other Romans were grappling with the simple and inescapable fact that their old city-state constitution was unequal to the demands of overseas possessions and the governing of provinces. (See the feature "Individuals in Society: Quintus Sertorius.") Thus even Sulla's efforts to put the constitution back together proved hollow. Once the senate and other institutions of the Roman state had failed to come to grips with the needs of empire, once the authorities had lost control of their own generals and soldiers, and once the armies put their faith in commanders instead of in Rome, the republic was doomed.

Sulla's real political heirs were Pompey and Julius Caesar, with at least Caesar realizing that the days of the old republican constitution were numbered. Pompey, a man of boundless ambition, began his career as one of Sulla's lieutenants. After his army put down a rebellion in Spain, he himself threatened to rebel unless the senate allowed him to run for consul. He and another ambitious politician, Crassus, pooled political resources, and both won the consulship. They dominated Roman politics until the rise of Julius Caesar, who became consul in 59 B.C. Together the three concluded a political alliance, the **First Triumvirate,** in which they agreed to advance one another's interests.

The man who cast the longest shadow over these troubled years was Julius Caesar (100–44 B.C.). More than a mere soldier, Caesar was a cultivated man. Born of a noble family, he received an excellent education, which he furthered by studying in Greece with some of the most eminent teachers of the day. He had serious intellectual interests, and his literary ability was immense. Caesar was a superb orator, and his affable personality and wit made him popular. He was also a shrewd politician of unbridled ambition. Since military service was an effective steppingstone to politics, Caesar launched his military career in Spain, where his courage won the respect and affection of his troops. Personally brave and tireless, Caesar was a military genius who

knew how to win battles and turn victories into permanent gains.

Online Study Center **Improve Your Grade**
Primary Source: A Man of Unlimited Ambition: Julius Caesar

In 58 B.C. Caesar became governor of Cisalpine Gaul, or modern northern Italy. By 50 B.C. he had conquered all of Gaul, or modern France. Caesar's account of his operations, his *Commentaries* on the Gallic wars, became a classic in Western literature and most schoolchildren's introduction to Latin. By 49 B.C. the First Triumvirate had fallen apart. Crassus had died in battle, and Caesar and Pompey, each suspecting the other of treachery, came to blows. The result was a long and bloody civil war that raged from Spain across northern Africa to Egypt.

Online Study Center **Improve Your Grade**
Primary Source: The Tyrant Is Dead! But . . . : Cicero Offers Faint Praise for Antony

Egypt was ruled by a Greek dynasty that had been in power for centuries, and right at this point was also in the middle of a battle over who would be the supreme ruler. This fight was not between two generals, but between brother and sister, Ptolemy XIII and Cleopatra VII (69–30 B.C.). Cleopatra first allied herself with Pompey but then switched her alliance to Caesar. The two became lovers as well as allies, and she bore him a son. She returned to Rome with Caesar, but was hated by the Roman people as a symbol of the immoral East and a threat to what were viewed as traditional Roman values.

Although Pompey enjoyed the official support of the Roman government, Caesar finally defeated Pompey's forces in 45 B.C. He had overthrown the republic and made himself dictator.

Julius Caesar was not merely another victorious general. Politically brilliant, he was determined to make basic reforms, even at the expense of the old constitution. He took the first long step to break down the barriers

Julius Caesar In this bust, the sculptor portrays Caesar as a man of power and intensity. It is a study of determination and an excellent example of Roman portraiture. (*Museo Archeologico Nazionale Naples/Scala/Art Resource, NY*)

Individuals in Society

Quintus Sertorius

Quintus Sertorius, son of a prominent Italian family, stands as a prime example of the transition of the Roman republic from local power to master of the Mediterranean world. Born not in Rome itself but in nearby Nurisa (modern Norcia) in 126 B.C., he became a Roman citizen. Like many of his contemporaries, he rose to high office and took part in the political and military upheavals of the day. He became a rebel against Rome and helped shape the new Mediterranean community.

Sertorius launched his public career in Rome, where he mastered Roman law and became a gifted military officer. When two barbarian tribes invaded Gaul in 105 B.C., he fought so effectively that his ability and valor brought him to the attention of senior Roman military commanders. These events honed his martial skills and acquainted him with the new peoples gradually entering western Europe.

Sertorius's success in Gaul led him in 97 B.C. to higher command in Spain. From that time until his death, his destiny and Spain's would be intertwined. He, like Marius, Sulla, and other notable men, was swept up in this vast and chaotic episode in republican history. He chose the wrong side and upon defeat fled to Spain, where he worked to establish his own independent authority.

A surprising accident put another tool of authority into Sertorius's hands. As the story goes, one of his soldiers, while hunting, encountered a white fawn. Instead of killing the doe, he presented it to Sertorius, who made a pet of it. Sertorius declared that the animal was the gift of Diana, whose attributes included the gifts of wisdom and prophecy. The superstitious Spaniards, who had long believed in Diana's cult of the stag, believed that Diana had blessed Sertorius. This divine endorsement made him seem more Spanish and enhanced his authority among the Spaniards.

The Roman civil war soon reached Spain. Sertorius's reputation and exploits persuaded many Spaniards to invite him to lead them against the Romans. He agreed, even though he always remained a Roman at heart. He began to organize these supporters along Roman military lines. He taught them Roman principles of military command and tactics so that they could meet the greatly feared Roman army in successful, organized bodies.

These things done, Sertorius led the Spaniards against the Romans. Instead of meeting the Roman legions face-to-face, he resorted to ambushes, flanking movements, and quick marches to isolate the enemy. He also struck at Roman supply lines. His success prompted many Romans to switch sides. Even some senators left Rome to join him. Welcoming them with honor, he got them involved in the civil government that he introduced. Sertorius modeled his Spanish state along Roman civil lines but under his leadership. Spain had never seen so many military, cultural, and civil developments in such a short time.

This statue of Quintus Sertorius still bears testimony to Rome's respect for his efforts to unite Romans and Spaniards.
(Courtesy, Luca Bonacina)

Many Greeks and Romans joined Sertorius because of his success and generosity. This flattering response seemed to bolster his plans but led to his failure and death. The Romans to whom he had bestowed a home began to insult, punish, and abuse the Spaniards while doing everything possible to thwart Sertorius's plans. Then they rebelled against him, hoping either to topple him and reign in his place or to return the province to Roman rule. Finally, with a treachery that matched that of the conspirators against Caesar, some Romans who were still considered loyal assassinated Sertorius at a banquet in 73 B.C. Roman generals from the East easily took control of Spain and ultimately reaped Sertorius's harvest.

Death and defeat did not erase Sertorius's achievements in Spain. He above any of his predecessors introduced the region to Greco-Roman culture. He gave the land and its peoples a civil government that united them. He turned their tribal hordes into an army along Roman lines. He paved the way for peaceful Spanish inclusion into the quickly evolving Roman Empire.

Questions for Analysis

1. How did Sertorius create a state in Spain?
2. What was his legacy to Spain, Rome, and Western civilization in general?

Online Study Center **Improve Your Grade**
Going Beyond Individuals in Society

between Italy and the provinces, extending citizenship to many of the provincials who had supported him. Caesar also took measures to cope with Rome's burgeoning population. By Caesar's day perhaps 750,000 people lived in Rome. Caesar drew up plans to send his veterans and some 80,000 of the poor and unemployed to colonies throughout the Mediterranean. He founded at least twenty colonies, most of which were located in Gaul, Spain, and North Africa. These colonies were important agents in spreading Roman culture in the western Mediterranean. A Roman empire composed of citizens, not subjects, was the result.

In 44 B.C. a group of conspirators assassinated Caesar and set off another round of civil war. Caesar had named his eighteen-year-old grandnephew, Octavian—or Augustus, as he is better known to history—as his heir. Augustus joined forces with two of Caesar's lieutenants, Marc Antony and Lepidus, in a pact known as the Second Triumvirate, and together they hunted down and defeated Caesar's murderers. In the process, however, Augustus and Antony came into conflict.

In 41 B.C. Antony met Cleopatra, who had gone back to Egypt after Julius Caesar's assassination. Though Antony was already married to Augustus's sister Octavia, he became Cleopatra's lover. Augustus and other Roman leaders described Antony as a romantic and foolish captive of the seductive Cleopatra, particularly after Antony repudiated Octavia, married Cleopatra, and changed his will to favor his children by Cleopatra. Roman sources are viciously hostile to Cleopatra, and she became the model of the *femme fatale* whose sexual attraction led men to their doom. Romans turned against Antony as a traitor and a weakling, and in 31 B.C. Augustus defeated the army and navy of Cleopatra and Antony at the Battle of Actium in Greece. The two committed suicide, an incident that has been the subject of countless paintings and many movies. This victory put an end to an age of civil war that had lasted since the days of Sulla.

Chapter Summary

Online Study Center **ACE the Test**

- *How did the land help shape Roman developments?*
- *What was the nature of the Roman republic?*
- *How did the Romans expand farther into Italy?*
- *What values did the Romans embrace because of their expansion?*
- *What were the main problems and achievements of the late republic?*

The land of Italy proved kinder to the Romans and their neighbors than did the peninsula of Hellas to the Greeks. The newcomers settled comfortably on the seven hills of Rome by the banks of the Tiber River. They came into contact with the Etruscans, who had settled in Italy before their arrival. Separate villages soon merged into one city, creating a single community. Under the governance of the more politically and socially advanced Etruscans, the Romans fully entered the wider world around them.

Once established, the Romans created an advanced and flexible political constitution of their own. Their society fell into two principal groups: the aristocratic patricians who led the community and the commoners who made up the rest of the citizenry and filled the ranks of the army. Though often at odds, these two basic social groups learned how to live and work together, and thus created a powerful, unified state.

From these beginnings the Romans spread their power and influence through the rest of Italy. Beginning as conquerors, the Romans learned to use alliances and political agreements to unite their efforts with those of other Italian communities to create a common policy. They put this association on a formal political basis to create a government shared by Romans and non-Romans. Looking beyond Italy, the Romans fought three hard wars with the Carthaginians, their Punic neighbors in North Africa. In the process they included the Greeks of southern Italy in their growing empire. As these wars spread to western Europe, the Romans won control of Spain and Gaul, modern France. Further warfare next took them eastward into the Hellenistic world. Conquest followed conquest to create the nucleus of the Roman Empire.

These tumultuous events fundamentally reshaped Roman society. Though some Romans longed for what they saw as simpler times, many were dazzled by Hellenistic sophistication and ways of life. They learned to appreciate the arts and intellectual pursuits of the older Greek and Eastern cultures. They joined fully the broad cultural world of the Mediterranean, all the while making their own contribution.

Yet in some ways the Romans had moved too far and too fast from their small beginnings. Their empire had become too big for them to manage easily. Their constitution and political institutions could no longer adequately cope with the burdens and pressures that imperial life brought. After a series of bloody civil wars, the general Octavian, soon to be more generally known as Augustus, restored order and forever changed the nature of Roman life and government.

Key Terms

pomerium	Struggle of the
fasces	Orders
toga	tribunes
Forum	paterfamilias
Gauls	Pyrrhic victory
franchise	First Punic War
patricians	Second Punic War
plebeians	manumission
senate	latifundia
praetor	client kingdoms
ius civile (civil law)	First Triumvirate
ius naturale (natural law)	

Online Study Center **Improve Your Grade** Flashcards

Suggested Reading

Bauman, Richard A. *Women and Politics in Ancient Rome.* 1992. Explores the influential role of Roman women in business, government, law, and public affairs.

Bradley, Keith R. *Slavery and Rebellion in the Roman World.* 1989. Analyzes slave revolts.

Dixon, Suzanne. *The Roman Family.* 1992. Focuses on legal and cultural changes in the Roman family and how these affected family members.

Gardner, Jane F. *Being a Roman Citizen.* 1993. A broad work that includes material on ex-slaves, the lower classes, and much else.

Gelzer, Mattias. *Caesar, Politician and Statesman*, English trans. 1968. Remains the best study of Caesar and his times, with much material from original sources.

Gruen, Erich S. *Culture and National Identity in Republican Rome.* 1992. Explores the effects of the introduction of Greek ideas, literature, and learning into central aspects of Roman life.

Gruen, Erich S. *The Last Generation of the Roman Republic.* 1974. Explores the political history of the last republic.

Haynes, Sibylle. *Etruscan Civilization: A Cultural History.* 2000. A wonderfully illustrated history of the Etruscans.

Kallet-Marx, Robert. *Hegemony to Empire.* 1995. Examines how Rome's power in the eastern Mediterranean became established between 148 and 62 B.C.

Kamm, Antony. *Julius Caesar.* 2006. An excellent brief biography designed for students that deals with his life as a politician, orator, and writer.

Lazenby, J. F. *Hannibal's War: A Military History of the Second Punic War.* 1998. An account of the conflict.

Scullard, H. H. *A History of the Roman World, 753–146 B.C.*, 4th ed. 1993. A broad account of Roman history.

Smith, Christopher J. *Early Rome and Latium: Economy and Society, c. 1000 to 500 B.C.* 1996. Examines early Roman expansion on the Italian peninsula.

Turcan, Robert. *The Gods of Ancient Rome: Religion in Everyday Life from Archaic to Imperial Times.* 2000. Examines the meaning of the gods to the Romans and the rituals associated with their worship, including family and state religions; written for students and general readers.

Williams, Craig A. *Roman Homosexuality: Ideologies of Masculinity in Classical Antiquity.* 1999. Examines ways in which Roman ideals of masculinity were linked with the sexual experiences of men in both literature and society.

Notes

1. Polybius, *The Histories* 1.1.5. John Buckler is the translator of all uncited quotations from a foreign language in Chapters 1–6.
2. Sallust, *War with Catiline* 10.1–3.
3. Ovid, *Fasti* 2.535–539.
4. Plutarch, *Life of Tiberius Gracchus* 9.5–6.

Listening to the Past

A Magic Charm

The pursuit of love is one of the oldest histories in the world. It also takes many shapes, some of them rather complicated. Not everything is as simple as boy meets girl, as this love charm demonstrates.

The following magical text comes from a papyrus found in Egypt and now housed in Paris. It dates from the period of the Roman Empire, but parts of it go back for centuries, which testifies to the popularity of these rituals. Here the lovelorn applicant is instructed to take the following steps in a rigorously prescribed order. By turning to magic he plans to win the heart of his beloved. Although the incantations sound like gibberish, the gods of the underworld understand them. The ritual not only has power over the daemons, or lesser spirits of the underworld, and over the spirits of the dead, but also can direct the actions of the living. The incantations are vital because they allow the human petitioner to contact these gods directly. In this case the applicant seeks the love of his desired whether or not she desires him in return. Similar love charms designed for women to attract men and for both men and women to attract members of the same sex have also been discovered.

Take wax [or clay] from a potter's wheel and form two figures, one male and one female. Make the male one look like Ares in arms, holding a sword in his left hand and pointing it at her right collarbone. Her arms must be (tied) behind her back, and she must kneel. Fasten the magical substance on her head or neck. On the figure of the woman you want to attract write as follows. On the head: ISEE IAO ITHI OUNE BRIDO LOTHION NEBOUTOSOUALETH. On the right ear: OUER MECHAN. On the left: LIBABA OIMATHOTHO. On the face: AMOUNABREO. On the right eye: ORORMOTHIO AETH. On the other: CHOBOUE. On the right shoulder: ADETA MEROU. On the right arm: ENE PSA ENESGAPH. On the other: MELCHIOU

MELCHIEDA. On the hands: MELCHAMELCHOU AEL. On the breast write the name, on her mother's side, of the woman you want to attract. On the heart: BALAMIN THOOUTH. Under the abdomen: AOBES AOBAR. On her sexual organs: BLICHIANEOI OUOIA. On her buttocks: PISSADARA. On the sole of the right foot: ELO. On the other: ELOAIOE. Take thirteen bronze needles and stick one in the brain and say: "I am piercing your brain, NN." Stick two in the ears, two in the eyes, one in the mouth, two in the midriff, one in the hands, two in the genital organs, two in the soles, saying each time: "I am piercing such and such a member of NN, so that she may remember me, NN alone." Take a lead tablet and write on it the same formula and recite it. Tie the lead leaf [i.e., the lead tablet] to the two creatures with thread from the loom after making three hundred sixty-five knots, saying, as you have learned: "Abrasax, hold her fast." As the sun is setting, you must place it near the tomb of a person who has died an untimely or a violent death, along with the flowers of the season.

The formula to be written and recited: "I am handing over this binding spell to you, gods of the underworld, HYESEMIGADON and KORE PERSEPHONE ERESCHIGAL and ADONIS, the BARBARITHA, chthonic HERMES THOOUTH PHOKENTAZEPSEU AERCHTHATOUMI SONKTAI KALBANACHAMRE and to mighty ANUBIS PSIRINTH who has the keys to the realm of Hades, to gods and daemons of the underworld, to men and women who have died before their time, to young men and women, from year to year, from month to month, from day to day, from hour to hour. I adjure all the daemons in this place to assist this daemon. Arouse yourself for me, whoever you are, male or female, and enter every place, every neighborhood, every house, and attract and bind,

Amulet of Abrasax, the demon with the head of a cock, the body of a Roman soldier, feet of snakes, and whip in the right hand. This amulet protected against other demons. (*Kelsey Museum of Archaeology, University of Michigan, KM 26054*)

attract NN, daughter of NN, whose magical substance you have. Make NN, daughter of NN be in love with me. Let her not have sexual intercourse with another man, . . . let her not have pleasure with another man, only with me, NN, so that she, NN, is unable to drink or eat, to love, to be strong, to be healthy, to enjoy sleep, NN without me, NN, because I adjure you by the fearful, the awesome name, the name at whose sound the earth will open, the name at whose terrifying sound the daemon will panic, the name at whose sound rivers and rocks will explode. I adjure you, daemon-dead [i.e., the spirit of a dead person], male or female, in the name of BARBARITHA CHENMBRA and in the name of ABRAT ABRASAX SESENGEN BARPHARANGES and in the name of MARMAREOTH MARMARAUOTH MARMARAOTH MARECHTHANA AMARZA MARIBEOTH. Listen to my commands and to the names. Just arouse yourself from the repose that holds you, whoever you are, male or female, and enter every place, every neighborhood, every house, and bring her, NN, to me, and keep her from eating and drinking, and let her, NN, not enjoy the attempt of any other man, not even that of her own man, only my own, NN. Yes, drag her, NN, by her hair, by her heart, by her soul to me, NN, every hour of life [or: eternity], night and day, until she comes to me, NN, and let her, NN, remain inseparable from me. Do this, bind her for all the time of my life and force her, NN, to be my, NN, servant, and let her not flutter away from me for even one hour of life [or: eternity]. If you accomplish this for me, I will let you rest at once. For I am BARBAR ADONAI who hides the stars, who governs with his bright splendor the heaven; [I am] the lord of the world, ATHTHOUIN IATHOUIN SELBIOUOTH AOTH SARBA THIOUTH IATHRIERATH ADONAI LA ROURA BIA BI BIOTHE ATHOTH SABAOTH

EA NIAPHA AMARACHTHI SATAMA ZAUATHTHERE SERPHO IALADA IALE SBESI IATHTHA MARADTHA ACHIL THTHEE CHOOO OE EACHO KANSAOSA ALKMOURI THYR OSO MAI. Attract her, bind her, NN, make her love me, desire me, yearn for me, NN, (add the usual), because I adjure you, daemon-dead, in the name of the terrible, the great IAEO BAPH RENEMOUN OTHI LARIKRIPHIA EYEAI PHIRKIRALITHON YOMEN ER PHABOEA, to bring her, NN, to me.

Questions for Analysis

1. How does this magical charm invoke the help of the gods?

2. Does the woman he seeks favor him, or is she reluctant?

3. Is the charm to entice love or to force submission?

Source: G. Luck, *Magic and the Occult in the Greek and Roman Worlds: A Collection of Ancient Texts*, pp. 129–131. © 2006 The Johns Hopkins University Press. Reprinted with permission of The Johns Hopkins University Press.

149

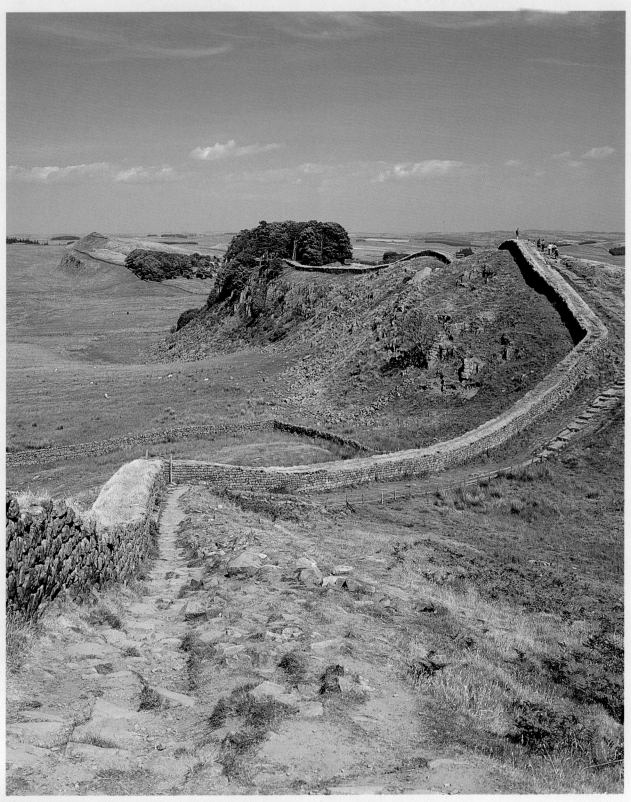

Hadrian's Wall. *(D. J. Ball/Tony Stone Images/Getty Images)*

THE PAX ROMANA, 31 B.C.–A.D. 450

Had the Romans conquered the entire Mediterranean world only to turn it into their battlefield? Would they, like the Greeks before them, become their own worst enemies, destroying one another and wasting their strength until they perished? At Julius Caesar's death in 44 B.C., it must have seemed so to many. Yet finally, in 31 B.C., Augustus restored peace to a tortured world, and with peace came prosperity, new hope, and a new vision of Rome's destiny. The Roman poet Virgil expressed this vision most nobly:

You, Roman, remember—these are your arts:
To rule nations, and to impose the ways of peace,
To spare the humble and to war down the proud.[1]

In place of the republic, Augustus established what can be called a constitutional monarchy. He attempted to achieve lasting cooperation in government and balance among the people, magistrates, senate, and army. His efforts were not always successful. His settlement of Roman affairs did not permanently end civil war. Yet he carried on Caesar's work. It was Augustus who created the structure that the modern world calls the "Roman Empire." He did his work so well and his successors so capably added to it that Rome realized Virgil's hope. For the first and second centuries A.D., the lot of the Mediterranean world was the Roman peace—the **pax Romana,** a period of security, order, harmony, flourishing culture, and expanding economy. It was a period that saw the wilds of Gaul, Spain, Germany, eastern Europe, and western Africa introduced to Greco-Roman culture. By the third century A.D., Rome and its culture had left an indelible mark on the ages to come.

Augustus's Settlement (31 B.C.–A.D. 14)

When Augustus put an end to the civil wars that had raged since 88 B.C., he faced monumental problems of reconstruction. Sole ruler of the entire Mediterranean world as no Roman had ever been before, he had a rare opportunity to shape the future. But how?

Online Study Center

This icon will direct you to interactive activities and study materials on the website **college.hmco.com/pic/mckaywest9e**

Augustus could easily have declared himself dictator, as Caesar had, but the thought was repugnant to him. Augustus was neither an autocrat nor a revolutionary. His solution, as he put it, was to restore the republic. But was that possible? Some eighteen years of anarchy and civil war had shattered the republican constitution. In stark reality, by Augustus's day no one alive had even lived under the ancestral constitution. The events of the middle republic, the aftermath of the Punic Wars, and the upheavals of the civil wars had dramatically and irreversibly changed it. Nor could it be rebuilt. Augustus recognized these problems but did not let them stop him. From 29 to 23 B.C. he toiled to heal Rome's wounds. The first problem facing him was to rebuild the constitution and the organs of government. Next he had to demobilize much of the army yet maintain enough soldiers in the provinces of the empire to meet the danger of barbarians at Rome's European frontiers. Augustus was highly successful in meeting these challenges. His gift of peace to a war-torn world sowed the seeds of a literary flowering that produced some of the finest fruits of the Roman mind.

● *How did Augustus restore stability; what political and military changes did he institute; and how did he spread Roman influence to northern and western Europe?*

The Principate and the Restored Republic

Augustus claimed that in restoring constitutional government he was also restoring the republic. Typically Roman, he preferred not to create anything new; he intended instead to modify republican forms and offices to meet new circumstances. Augustus planned for the senate to take on a serious burden of duty and responsibility. He expected it to administer some of the provinces, continue to be the chief deliberative body of the state, and act as a court of law. Yet he did not give the senate enough power to become his partner in government. As a result, the senate could not live up to the responsibilities that Augustus assigned. Many of its prerogatives shifted to Augustus and his successors by default.

Augustus's own position in the restored republic was something of an anomaly. He could not simply surrender the reins of power, for someone else would only have seized them. But how was he to fit into a republican constitution? Again Augustus had his own answer. He became *princeps civitatis,* "First Citizen of the State." This prestigious title carried no power; it indicated only that

Augustus was the most distinguished of all Roman citizens. In effect, it designated Augustus as the first among equals, a little "more equal" than anyone else in the state. Clearly, much of the *principate,* as the period of First Citizen is known, was a legal fiction. Yet that need not imply that Augustus, like a modern dictator, tried to clothe himself with constitutional legitimacy. In an inscription known as *Res Gestae* (The Deeds of Augustus), Augustus described his constitutional position:

In my sixth and seventh consulships [28–27 B.C.], I had ended the civil war, having obtained through universal consent total control of affairs. I transferred the Republic from my power to the authority of the Roman people and the senate. . . . After that time I stood before all in rank, but I had power no greater than those who were my colleagues in any magistracy.[2]

Augustus as Imperator   Here Augustus, dressed in breastplate and uniform, emphasizes the imperial majesty of Rome and his role as *imperator.* The figures on his breastplate represent the restoration of peace, one of Augustus's greatest accomplishments and certainly one that he frequently stressed. *(Erich Lessing/Art Resource, NY)*

What is to be made of Augustus's constitutional settlement? Despite his claims to the contrary, Augustus had not restored the republic. Augustus had created a **constitutional monarchy,** something completely new in Roman history. The title **princeps,** First Citizen, came to mean in Rome, as it does today, "prince" in the sense of a sovereign ruler.

Online Study Center **Improve Your Grade**
Primary Source: The Res Gestae of Augustus Caesar: Propaganda in the First Century A.D.

Augustus was not exactly being a hypocrite, but he carefully kept his real military power in the background. As consul he had no more constitutional and legal power than his fellow consul. Yet in addition to the consulship Augustus had many other magistracies, which his fellow consul did not. Constitutionally, his ascendancy within the state stemmed from the number of magistracies he held and the power granted him by the senate. At first he held the consulship annually; then the senate voted him proconsular power on a regular basis. The senate also voted him *tribunicia potestas*—the "full power of the tribunes." Tribunician power gave Augustus the right to call the senate into session, present legislation to the people, and defend their rights. He held either high office or the powers of chief magistrate year in and year out. No other magistrate could do the same. In 12 B.C. he became *pontifex maximus,* the chief priest of the state. By assuming this position of great honor, Augustus also became chief religious official. Without specifically saying so, he had created the office of emperor, which included many traditional powers separated from their traditional offices.

The main source of Augustus's power was his position as commander of the Roman army. His title **imperator,** with which Rome customarily honored a general after a major victory, came to mean "emperor" in the modern sense of the term. Augustus governed the provinces where troops were needed for defense. The frontiers were his special concern. There Roman legionaries held the German barbarians at arm's length. The frontiers were also areas where fighting could be expected to break out. Augustus made sure that Rome went to war only at his command. He controlled deployment of the Roman army and paid its wages. He granted it bonuses and gave veterans retirement benefits. Thus he avoided the problems with the army that the old senate had created for itself. Augustus never shared control of the army, and no Roman found it easy to defy him militarily.

Augustus made a momentous change in the army by making it a permanent, professional force. This was

Chronology

27 B.C.–A.D. 68	Julio-Claudian emperors; expansion into northern and western Europe; growth and stability of trade in the empire
17 B.C.–A.D. 17	Flowering of Latin literature
ca 3 B.C.–A.D. 29	Life of Jesus
ca A.D. 30–312	Spread of Christianity
A.D. 41–54	Creation of the imperial bureaucracy
A.D. 60–120	Composition of the New Testament
A.D. 69–96	Consolidation of the European frontiers
A.D. 70–ca 118	"Silver age" of Latin literature
A.D. 96–180	"Golden age" of prosperity and huge expansion of trade
A.D. 96–180	"Five good emperors"; increasing barbarian menace on the frontiers
A.D. 193–284	Military monarchy; extension of citizenship to all free men
A.D. 278–337	Steady spread of administration, government, and law from Britain to Syria
A.D. 284–337	Inflation and decline of trade and industry; transition to the Middle Ages in the West and the Byzantine Empire in the East
A.D. 337	Baptism of Constantine

Rome's first standing army. Soldiers received regular and standard training under career officers who advanced in rank according to experience, ability, valor, and length of service. Legions were transferred from place to place, as the need arose. They had no regular barracks. In later years of the empire soldiers could live with their families in the camps themselves. By making the army professional, Augustus forged a reliable tool for the defense of the empire. The army could also act against the central authority, much as Marius's army had earlier. Yet the mere fact that men could make a career of the army meant that it became a recognized institution of government and that its soldiers had the opportunity to achieve a military effectiveness superior to that of most of its enemies.

The very size of the army was a special problem for Augustus. Rome's legions numbered thousands of men, far more than were necessary to maintain peace. What was

Augustus to do with so many soldiers? This sort of problem had constantly plagued the late republic, whose leaders never found a solution. Augustus gave his own answer in the *Res Gestae:* "I founded colonies of soldiers in Africa, Sicily, Macedonia, Spain, Achaea, Gaul, and Pisidia. Moreover, Italy has 28 colonies under my auspices."[3] At least forty new colonies arose, most of them in the western Mediterranean. Augustus's veterans took abroad with them their Latin language and culture. His colonies, like Julius Caesar's, were a significant tool in the spread of Roman culture throughout the West.

Roman colonies were very different from earlier Greek colonies. Greek colonies were independent. Once founded, they went their own way. Roman colonies were part of a system—the Roman Empire—that linked East with West in a mighty political, social, and economic network. The glory of the Roman Empire was its great success in uniting the Mediterranean world and spreading Greco-Roman culture throughout it. Roman colonies played a crucial part in that process, and Augustus deservedly boasted of the colonies he founded.

Augustus, however, also failed to solve a momentous problem. He never found a way to institutionalize his position with the army. The ties between the princeps and the army were always personal. The army was loyal to the princeps but not necessarily to the state. The Augustan principate worked well at first, but by the third century A.D. the army would make and break emperors at will. Nonetheless, it is a measure of Augustus's success that his settlement survived as long and as well as it did.

Augustus's Administration of the Provinces

In the areas under his immediate jurisdiction, Augustus put provincial administration on an ordered basis and improved its functioning. Believing that the cities of the empire should look after their own affairs, he encouraged local self-government and urbanism. Augustus respected local customs and ordered his governors to do the same.

As a spiritual bond between the provinces and Rome, Augustus encouraged the cult of Roma, goddess and guardian of the state. In the Hellenistic East, where king-worship was an established custom, the cult of *Roma et Augustus* grew and spread rapidly. Augustus then introduced it in the West. By the time of his death in A.D. 14, nearly every province in the empire could boast an altar or a shrine to *Roma et Augustus*. In the West it was not the person of the emperor who was worshiped but his *genius*—his guardian spirit. In praying for the good health and welfare of the emperor, Romans and provincials were praying for the empire itself. The cult became a symbol of Roman unity.

Roman Expansion into Northern and Western Europe

For the history of Western civilization, one of the most momentous aspects of Augustus's reign was Roman expansion into the wilderness of northern and western Europe (see Map 6.1). In this respect Augustus was following in Julius Caesar's footsteps. Carrying on Caesar's work, Augustus pushed Rome's frontier into the region of modern Germany.

Augustus began his work in the west and north by completing the conquest of Spain. In Gaul, apart from minor campaigns, most of his work was peaceful. He founded twelve new towns, and the Roman road system linked new settlements with one another and with Italy. But the German frontier, along the Rhine River, was the scene of hard fighting. In 12 B.C. Augustus ordered a major invasion of Germany beyond the Rhine. Roman legions advanced to the Elbe River, and a Roman fleet explored the North Sea and Jutland. The area north of the Main River and west of the Elbe was on the point of becoming Roman. But in A.D. 9 Augustus's general Varus lost some twenty thousand troops at the Battle of the Teutoburger Forest. Thereafter the Rhine remained the Roman frontier.

Meanwhile more successful generals extended the Roman standards as far as the Danube. Roman legions penetrated the area of modern Austria, southern Bavaria, and western Hungary. The regions of modern Serbia, Bulgaria, and Romania fell. Within this area the legionaries built fortified camps. Roads linked these camps with one another, and settlements grew up around the camps. Traders began to frequent the frontier and to traffic with the barbarians. Thus Roman culture—the rough-and-ready kind found in military camps—gradually spread into the northern wilderness.

Although this process is most clearly seen in the provincial towns and cities, people in the countryside likewise adopted the aspects of Roman culture that appealed to them. Roman culture was adaptable and convenient, and the Romans did not force it on others. All over the empire native peoples adopted those aspects that fit in with their own ways of life. That much said, ambitious people throughout the empire knew that the surest path to political advancement lay in embracing Roman civilization and culture.

Boscoreale Cup The central scene lavishly depicted on the side of a silver cup shows Augustus seated in majesty. In his right hand he holds an orb that represents his position as master of the world. The scroll in his left hand symbolizes his authority as lawgiver. On his right is a group of divinities who support his efforts, on his left a group of barbarians who have submitted to Rome. (© *Musée du Louvre*)

One excellent example of this process comes from the modern French city of Lyons. The site was originally the capital of a native tribe, and after his conquest of Gaul, Caesar made it a Roman military settlement. Augustus took an important step toward Romanization and conciliation in 12 B.C., when he made it a political and religious center, with responsibilities for administering the area and for honoring the gods of the Romans and Gauls. Physical symbols of this fusion of two cultures can still be seen today. For instance, the extensive remains of the amphitheater and other buildings at Lyons testify to the fact that the Gallo-Roman city was prosperous enough to afford expensive Roman buildings and the style of life that they represented. Second, the buildings show that the local population appreciated Roman culture and did not find it alien. At Lyons, as at many other of these new cities, there emerged a culture that was both Roman and native. Many such towns were soon granted Roman citizenship for their embrace of Roman culture and government and their importance to the Roman economy. (See the feature "Listening to the Past: Rome Extends Its Citizenship" on pages 186–187.)

Although Lyons is typical of the success of Romanization in new areas, the arrival of the Romans often provoked resistance from tribes of peoples who were not

Greco-Roman and who simply wanted to be left alone. Romans generally referred to such people as **barbarians,** a word derived from a Greek word for those who did not speak Greek. In other cases the prosperity and wealth of the new Roman towns lured barbarians eager for plunder. The Romans maintained peaceful relations with the barbarians whenever possible, but Roman legions remained on the frontier to repel hostile barbarians. The result was the evolution of a consistent, systematic frontier policy.

Literary Flowering and Social Changes

The Augustan settlement's gift of peace inspired a literary flowering unparalleled in Roman history. With good reason this period is known as the golden age of Latin literature. Augustus and many of his friends actively encouraged poets and writers. Horace, one of Rome's finest poets, offered his own opinion of Augustus and his era:

With Caesar [Augustus] the guardian of the state
Not civil rage nor violence shall drive out peace,
Nor wrath which forges swords
And turns unhappy cities against each other.[4]

These lines are not empty flattery, despite Augustus's support of many contemporary Latin writers. To a generation that had known only vicious civil war, Augustus's settlement was an unbelievable blessing.

The tone and ideal of Roman literature, like that of the Greeks, was humanistic and worldly. Roman poets and prose writers celebrated the dignity of humanity and the range of its accomplishments. They stressed the physical and emotional joys of a comfortable, peaceful life. Their works were highly polished, elegant in style, and intellectual in conception. Roman poets referred to the gods often and treated mythological themes, but always the core of their work was human, not divine.

Virgil (70–19 B.C.), Rome's greatest poet, celebrated the new age in the *Georgics,* a poetic work on agriculture in four books. Virgil delighted in his own farm, and his poems sing of the pleasures of peaceful farm life. The poet also tells how to keep bees, grow grapes and olives,

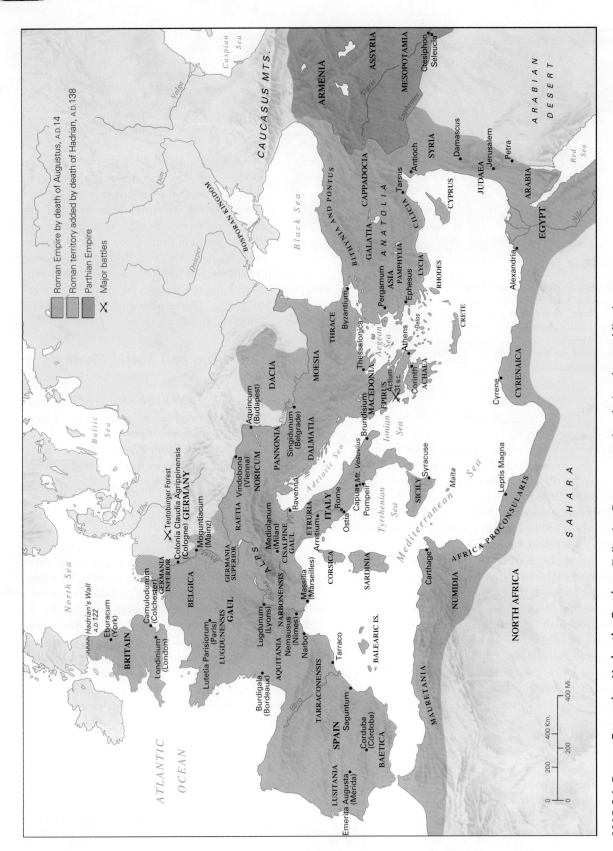

MAP 6.1 Roman Expansion Under the Empire Following Roman expansion during the republic, Augustus added vast tracts of Europe to the Roman Empire, which the emperor Hadrian later enlarged by assuming control over parts of central Europe, the Near East, and North Africa.

Map legend:

Roman Empire by death of Augustus, A.D. 14

Roman territory added by death of Hadrian, A.D. 138

Parthian Empire

X Major battles

plow, and manage a farm. Throughout the *Georgics* Virgil writes about things he himself has seen, rather than drawing from the writings of others. Virgil could be vivid and graphic as well as pastoral. Even a small event could be a drama for him. The death of a bull while plowing is hardly epic material, yet Virgil captures the sadness of the event in the image of the farmer unyoking the remaining animal:

Look, the bull, shining under the rough plough,
falls to the ground
and vomits from his mouth blood mixed with foam,
and releases his dying groan.
Sadly moves the ploughman, unharnessing the
young steer grieving for the death of his brother
and leaves in the middle of the job
the plough stuck fast.[5]

Virgil's poetry is robust yet graceful. A sensitive man who delighted in simple things, Virgil left in his *Georgics* a charming picture of life in the Italian countryside during a period of peace.

Virgil's masterpiece is the *Aeneid,* an epic poem that is the Latin equivalent of the Greek *Iliad* and *Odyssey.* In the *Aeneid* Virgil expressed his admiration for Augustus's work by celebrating the shining ideal of a world blessed by the pax Romana. Virgil's account of the founding of Rome and the early years of the city gave final form to the legend of Aeneas, a Trojan hero who escaped to Italy at the fall of Troy. The legend of Aeneas was a third story about the founding of Rome, along with those of Romulus and the rape of Lucretia (see page 125). This one was also gendered. As Virgil told it, Aeneas became the lover of Dido, the widowed queen of Carthage, but left her because his destiny called him to found Rome. She committed suicide, and their relationship eventually became the cause of the Punic Wars. In leaving Dido, an "Eastern" queen, Aeneas put the good of the state ahead of marriage or pleasure; the parallels between this story and the real events involving Antony and Cleopatra were not lost on Virgil's audience. Virgil believed passionately in Rome's greatness, and he portrayed Rome as the protector of the good and noble against the forces of darkness and disruption, symbolized in part by a foreign queen. This fit well with Augustus's aims; he had encouraged Virgil to write the *Aeneid* and made sure it was published immediately after Virgil died.

Ara Pacis This scene from the Ara Pacis, the Altar of Peace erected in Rome by Augustus, celebrates Augustus's restoration of peace and imperial family values. On this side, Mother Earth is depicted with twin babies on her lap, framed by nymphs representing land and sea. The sheep and the cow are both agricultural and sacrificial animals. Other sides of the altar show Romulus and Remus (another set of twins) and Augustus and his wife Livia in traditional Roman clothing. *(Scala/Art Resource, NY)*

The poet Ovid shared Virgil's views of the simple pleasures of life and also celebrated the popular culture of the day. In his *Fasti* (ca A.D. 8) he takes a personal approach to discuss and explain the ordinary festivals of the Roman year, festivals that most Romans took for granted. Without his work, the modern world would be much the poorer in its knowledge of the popular religion of imperial Rome. For instance, he tells his readers that on a journey to Rome he encountered a white-robed crowd in the middle of the road. A priest and farmers were performing an annual festival ritual. Ovid stopped to ask the priest what was happening. The priest explained that they were sacrificing to Mildew, not a farmer's favorite goddess. By burning the offerings the priest and his friends asked the goddess to be so content with them that she would not attack the crops. He further asked her not to attack the farmers' tools but to be satisfied with swords and other weapons of iron. He reminded her that "there is no need for them; the world lives in peace."[6] In his poetry Ovid, like Virgil, celebrates the pax Romana, while giving a rare glimpse of ordinary Roman life.

In its own way Livy's history of Rome, titled simply *Ab Urbe Condita* (From the Founding of the City), is the prose counterpart of the *Aeneid*. Livy (59 B.C.–A.D. 17) received training in Greek and Latin literature, rhetoric, and philosophy. He even urged the future emperor Claudius to write history. Livy loved and admired the heroes and great deeds of the republic, but he was also a friend of Augustus and a supporter of the principate. He especially approved of Augustus's efforts to restore what he saw as republican virtues. Livy's history began with the legend of Aeneas and ended with the reign of Augustus. His theme of the republic's greatness fitted admirably with Augustus's program of restoring the republic. Livy's history was colossal, consisting of 142 books, and only a quarter of it still exists. Livy was a sensitive writer and something of a moralist. Like Thucydides, he felt that history should be applied to the present. His history later became one of Rome's legacies to the modern world. During the Renaissance *Ab Urbe Condita* found a warm admirer in the poet Petrarch and left its mark on Machiavelli, who read it avidly.

The poet Horace (65–8 B.C.) rose from humble beginnings to friendship with Augustus. The son of an ex-slave and tax collector, Horace nonetheless received an excellent education. He loved Greek literature and finished his education in Athens. After Augustus's victory he returned to Rome and became Virgil's friend. Horace happily turned his pen to celebrating Rome and Augustus.

Concern with morality and with what were perceived as traditional Roman virtues was a matter not just for literature in Augustan Rome, but also for law. Augustus promoted marriage and childbearing through legal changes that released free women and freedwomen (female slaves who had been freed) from male guardianship if they had given birth to a certain number of children. Men and women who were unmarried or had no children were restricted in the inheritance of property. Adultery, defined as sex with a married woman or a woman under male guardianship, was made a crime, not simply the private family matter it had been. In imperial propaganda, Augustus had his own family depicted as a model of traditional morality, with his wife Livia at his side dressed in conservative and somewhat old-fashioned clothing rather than the more daring Greek styles that wealthy women were actually wearing in Rome at the time.

Same-sex relationships were denounced as part of the immorality of the late republic and as nonprocreative. Same-sex relationships among men in Rome had followed a pattern similar to that of Greece: often between an older man and a younger, or between men who were different in social status, such as a slave and his owner. We do not know very much about same-sex relationships among women in Rome, though court gossip and criticism of powerful women, including the wives of Augustus's successors, sometimes included charges of such relationships, along with charges of heterosexual promiscuity and other sexual slander.

The solidity of Augustus's work became obvious at his death in A.D. 14. Since the principate was not technically an office, Augustus could not legally hand it to a successor. Augustus recognized this problem and long before his death had found a way to solve it. He shared his consular and tribunician powers with his adopted son, Tiberius, thus grooming him for the principate. In his will Augustus left most of his vast fortune to Tiberius, and the senate formally requested Tiberius to assume the burdens of the principate. Formalities apart, Augustus had succeeded in creating a dynasty.

Online Study Center **Improve Your Grade**
Primary Source: A Critical Assessment of the Reign of Augustus Caesar

The Coming of Christianity

During the reign of the emperor Tiberius (A.D. 14–37), perhaps in A.D. 29, Pontius Pilate, prefect of Judaea, the Roman province created out of the Jewish kingdom of Judah, condemned Jesus of Nazareth to death. At the time a minor event, this has become one of the best-known moments in history. How did these two men come to their historic meeting? The question is not idle, nor the answer simple. The Hellenistic world and Rome were as important as Judaism to Christianity. As seen in Chapter 4, the Hellenistic Greeks provided the entire East with a common language, widely shared literary forms, and a pervasive culture that had for years embraced Judaea. Rome contributed political administration to Hellenistic culture. The mixture was not always harmonious. Some Jews embraced aspects of Greco-Roman culture, while others shunned it. It was a situation common to other parts of the Roman Empire, where people addressed these novel developments in their own ways. In Judaea, Roman rule aroused hatred and unrest among some Jews. This climate of hostility affected the lives of all who lived there. It formed the backdrop of Jesus' life, and it had a fundamental impact on his ministry. These factors also ultimately paved the way for Christianity to spread far from its native land to the broader world of the Roman Empire. Without an understanding of this age of anxiety in Judaea, one cannot fully appreciate Jesus and his followers.

- *Why did Christianity, originally a minor local religion, sweep across the Roman world to change it fundamentally?*

Unrest in Judaea

The entry of Rome into Jewish affairs was anything but peaceful. The civil wars that destroyed the republic wasted the prosperity of Judaea and the entire eastern Mediterranean world. Jewish leaders took sides in the fighting, and Judaea suffered its share of ravages and military confiscations. The Roman senate and Augustus backed one leader, Herod (r. 37–4 B.C.) and appointed him king of Judaea. King Herod gave Judaea prosperity and security, but the Jews hated his acceptance of Greek culture. He was also a bloodthirsty prince who murdered his own wife and sons. At his death the Jews in Judaea broke out in revolt. For the next ten years Herod's successor waged almost constant war against the rebels. Added to the horrors of civil war were years of crop failure, which caused famine and plague. Men calling themselves prophets proclaimed the end of the world and the coming of the **Messiah,** the savior of Israel.

At length the Romans intervened to restore order. Augustus put Judaea under the charge of a prefect answerable directly to the emperor. Religious matters and local affairs became the responsibility of the *Sanhedrin,* the highest Jewish judicial body. Although many prefects tried to perform their duties scrupulously and conscientiously, many others were rapacious and indifferent to Jewish culture. Often acting from fear rather than cruelty, some prefects fiercely stamped out any signs of popular discontent. Pontius Pilate, prefect from A.D. 26 to 36, is typical of such incompetent officials. Especially hated were the Roman tax collectors, called "publicans," many of whom pitilessly gouged the Jews. In Christian writings, "publicans and sinners" became a common negative phrase. Clashes between Roman troops and Jewish guerrillas inflamed the anger of both sides.

Among the Jews two movements spread. First was the rise of the Zealots, extremists who worked and fought to rid Judaea of the Romans. Resolute in their worship of Yahweh, they refused to pay any but the tax levied by the Jewish temple. Their battles with the Roman legionaries were marked by savagery on both sides. As usual the innocent caught in the middle suffered grievously. As Roman policy grew tougher, even moderate Jews began to hate the conquerors. Judaea came more and more to resemble a tinderbox, ready to burst into flames at a single spark.

The second movement was the growth of militant **apocalypticism**—the belief that the coming of the Messiah was near. This belief was an old one among the Jews. But by the first century A.D. it had become more widespread and fervent than ever before. Apocalyptic predictions appeared in many texts, including the anonymous Apocalypse of Baruch, which foretold the destruction of the Roman Empire. First would come a period of great tribulation, misery, and injustice. At the worst of the suffering, the Messiah would appear. The Messiah would destroy the Roman legions and all the kingdoms that had ruled Israel. Then the Messiah would inaugurate a period of happiness and plenty for the Jews.

This was no abstract notion among the Jews. As the ravages of war became widespread and conditions worsened, more and more people prophesied the imminent coming of the Messiah. According to Christian Scripture, one such was John the Baptist, "the voice of one crying in the wilderness, Prepare ye the way of the lord."[7] Many Jews did just that. The sect described in the Dead Sea Scrolls readied itself for the end of the world. Its members were probably Essenes, an ascetic group whose social organization closely resembled that of early Christians. Members of this group shared possessions, precisely as John the Baptist urged people to do. Yet this sect, unlike the Christians, also made military preparations for the day of the Messiah.

Jewish religious aspirations were only one part of the story. What can be said of the pagan world of Rome and its empire, into which Christianity was shortly to be born? To answer that question one must first explore the spiritual environment of the pagans, many of whom would soon be caught up in the new Christian religion. The term **pagans** refers to all those who believed in the Greco-Roman gods. Paganism at the time of Jesus' birth can be broadly divided into three spheres: the official state religion of Rome, the traditional Roman cults of hearth and countryside, and the new mystery religions that flowed from the Hellenistic East. The official state religion and its cults honored the traditional deities: Jupiter, Juno, Mars, Vesta, and such newcomers as Isis (see page 111). This very formal religion was conducted on an official level by socially prominent state priests and priestesses. The state cults were a bond between the gods and the people, a religious contract to ensure the well-being of Rome. Most Romans felt that the official cults must be maintained for the welfare of the state, and Augustus was careful to link them to him. After all, observance of the traditional official religion had brought Rome victory, empire, security, and wealth.

For emotional and spiritual satisfaction, many Romans also observed cults of home and countryside. These traditional cults brought the Romans back in touch with nature and with something elemental to Roman life. Particularly popular was the rustic shrine—often a small building or a sacred tree in an enclosure—to honor the native spirit of the locality. Though familiar and simple, even this traditional religion was not enough for many. They wanted something more personal and immediate. Many common people believed in a supernatural world seen dimly through dreams, magic, miracles, and spells. They wanted some sort of revelation about this supernatural world and security in it after death. Some people turned to astrology in the belief that they could read their destiny in the stars.

Many men and women in the Roman Empire found spiritual security and an emotional outlet in the various Hellenistic mystery cults. For example, the cult of Bacchus was marked by wine drinking and often by drunken frenzy. The cult of the Great Mother, Cybele, was celebrated with emotional and even overwrought processions, and it offered its worshipers the promise of immortality. The cult of Isis also involved emotional public rituals and became so popular that Augustus banned it as an un-Roman political threat. The appeal of the mystery religions was not simply that they provided emotional release. They gave their adherents what neither the traditional cults nor philosophy could—above all, security. Yet the mystery religions were by nature exclusive, and none was truly international, open to everyone.

The Life and Teachings of Jesus

Into this climate of Roman religious yearning, political severity, fanatical Zealotry, and Messianic hope came Jesus of Nazareth (ca 3 B.C.–A.D. 29). He was raised in Galilee, stronghold of the Zealots. A typically Jewish town, Galilee had come under Roman political rule and with it Hellenism and Roman culture. Yet in Jesus' day both remained a veneer, deeper among those who had political and business dealings with the Greeks and Romans than among ordinary folk. Although most people spoke Aramaic, some Jews knew Latin and Greek, which they used for official purposes. In all, they knew the Hebrew Bible far better than Virgil's *Aeneid*. Through Galilee passed major trade routes, which means that it was hardly a backwater or isolated area. Ideas moved as easily as merchandise along these routes.

Much contemporary scholarship has attempted to understand who Jesus was and what he meant by his teachings. Views vary widely. Some see him as a visionary and a teacher, others as a magician and a prophet, and still others as a rebel and a revolutionary. The search for the historical Jesus is complicated by many factors. One is the difference between history and faith. History relies on proof for its conclusions; faith depends on belief. Thus whether Jesus is divine or not is not an issue to be decided by historians. Their role is to understand him in his religious, cultural, social, and historical context.

To sort out the various and often conflicting interpretations, historians must begin with the sources. The principal evidence for the life and deeds of Jesus are the four Gospels of the New Testament. These Gospels—the word means "good news"—are neither biographies of Jesus nor histories of his life. They are records of his teachings and religious doctrines with certain details of his life. The aim was to build a community of faith that believed that Jesus represented the culmination of the Messianic tradition. The earliest Gospels were written some seventy-five years after his death, and modern biblical scholars have used literary analysis to detect a num-

ber of discrepancies among the four. For that matter, so did ancient writers, both pagan and Christian. These discrepancies did not come from authors' having had different memories of the events of Jesus' life and mission. Instead, the writers all gave their own theological interpretations of them.

The four Gospels that are now in Christian Scripture are called "canonical," a word that means "authentic." They were the most widely circulating accounts of Jesus' teachings in the first centuries after his life, and by the fourth century officials in the Christian church decided that they, along with other types of writing such as letters and prophecies, would form Christian Scripture.

They were not the only records of Jesus' teachings, however, and in recent decades other early texts have been retrieved from the deserts of the Middle East after centuries of burial. They are also termed "Gospels," but they include teachings that differ from those in the canonical Gospels. For example, in the canonical Gospels twelve of Jesus' followers have a special status as "apostles." All are male, and one, Peter, appears as especially prominent. In one of the recently discovered Gospels, by contrast, Jesus reveals special teachings to one of his female followers, Mary Magdalene, which annoys Peter and the other men in Jesus' circle. The newest of the recently discovered Gospels is also one of the most surprising. In 2006 a small group of scholars published a papyrus document containing the Gospel of Judas Iscariot, the apostle who in the canonical Gospels betrayed Jesus. It depicts Judas not only as Jesus' most beloved disciple but also as the only one to whom he revealed his destiny. At Jesus' bidding, Judas must betray him so that Jesus can escape the prison of his mortal body. The often contradictory accounts in the various Gospels indicate that early Christians had a diversity of beliefs about Jesus' nature and purpose. Only slowly, as the Christian church became an institution, were lines drawn more clearly between what was considered correct teaching and what was considered incorrect, or **heresy.**

Despite this diversity, there were certain things about Jesus' teachings that almost all the sources agree on: he preached of a heavenly kingdom, one of eternal happiness in a life after death. His teachings were essentially Jewish. His orthodoxy enabled him to preach in the synagogue and the temple. His major deviation from orthodoxy was his insistence that he taught in his own name, not in the name of Yahweh. Was he then the Messiah? A small band of followers thought so, and Jesus claimed that he was. Yet Jesus had his own conception of the Messiah. Unlike the Messiah of the Apocalypse of

Pontius Pilate and Jesus This Byzantine mosaic from Ravenna illustrates a dramatic moment in Jesus' trial and crucifixion. Jesus stands accused before Pilate, but Pilate symbolically washes his hands of the whole affair. *(Scala/Art Resource, NY)*

Baruch, Jesus would not destroy the Roman Empire. He told his disciples flatly that they were to "render unto Caesar the things that are Caesar's." Jesus would establish a spiritual kingdom, not an earthly one. He told his disciples that his kingdom was "not of this world."

Online Study Center **Improve Your Grade**
Primary Source: The Gospel According to Matthew: The Sermon on the Mount

Of Jesus' life and teachings the prefect Pontius Pilate knew little and cared even less. All that concerned him was the maintenance of peace and order. The crowds following Jesus at the time of the Passover, a highly emotional time in the Jewish year, alarmed Pilate, who faced a volatile situation. Some Jews believed that Jesus was the long-awaited Messiah. Others were disappointed because

he refused to preach rebellion against Rome. Still others who hated and feared Jesus wanted to be rid of him. The last thing Pilate wanted was a riot on his hands. To avert riot and bloodshed, Pilate condemned Jesus to death. According to Christian Scripture, after being scourged, he was hung from a cross until he died in the sight of family, friends, enemies, and the merely curious.

Once Pilate's soldiers had carried out the sentence, the entire matter seemed to be closed. Yet on the third day after Jesus' crucifixion, an odd rumor began to circulate in Jerusalem. Some of Jesus' followers were saying he had risen from the dead, while others accused them of having stolen his body. For the earliest Christians and for generations to come, the resurrection of Jesus became a central element of faith—and more than that, a promise: Jesus had triumphed over death, and his resurrection promised all Christians immortality. In Jerusalem, meanwhile, the tumult subsided. Jesus' followers lived quietly and peacefully, unmolested by Roman or Jew. Pilate had no quarrel with them, and Judaism already had many minor sects.

The Spread of Christianity

The memory of Jesus and his teachings sturdily survived. Believers in his divinity met in small assemblies or congregations, often in one another's homes, to discuss the meaning of Jesus' message. These meetings always took place outside the synagogue. They included such orthodox Jews as the Pharisees. These earliest Christians were clearly defining their faith to fit the life of Jesus into an orthodox Jewish context. Only later did these congregations evolve into what can be called a church with a formal organization and set of beliefs. One of the first significant events occurred in Jerusalem on the Jewish festival of Pentecost, when Jesus' followers assembled. They were joined by Jews from many parts of the world, including some from as far away as Parthia to the east, Crete to the west, Rome, and Ethiopia. These early followers were Hellenized Jews, many of them rich merchants. They were in an excellent position to spread the word throughout the known world.

The catalyst in the spread of Jesus' teachings and the formation of the Christian church was Paul of Tarsus, a Hellenized Jew who was comfortable in both the Roman and Jewish worlds. He had begun by persecuting the new sect, but on the road to Damascus he was converted to belief in Jesus. He was the single most important figure responsible for changing Christianity from a Jewish sect into a separate religion. Paul was familiar with Greek philosophy, and he had actually discussed the tenets of the new religion with Epicurean and Stoic philosophers in Athens. Indeed, one of his seminal ideas may have stemmed from the Stoic concept of the unity of mankind. He proclaimed that the mission of Christianity was "to make one of all the folk of men."[8] His vision was to include all the kindred of the earth. That concept meant that he urged the Jews to include non-Jews in the faith. He was the first to voice a universal message of Christianity.

Paul's vision proved both bold and successful. When he traveled abroad, he first met with the leaders of the local synagogue before going out among the people. He applied himself especially to the Greco-Romans, whom he did not consider common or unclean because they were not Jews. He even said that there was no difference between Jews and **Gentiles** (non-Jews), which in orthodox Jewish thought was not only revolutionary but also heresy. Paul found a ready audience among the Gentiles, who converted to the new religion with surprising enthusiasm. Paul's approach succeeded beyond expectation.

Many early Christian converts were women, who seem to have come particularly from the Greco-Roman middle classes. Paul greeted male and female converts by name in his letters, and noted that women provided financial support for his activities. Missionaries and others spreading the Christian message worked through families and friendship networks. The growing Christian communities in various cities of the Roman Empire had different ideas about many things, including the proper gender roles for believers. Some communities favored giving women a larger role, while others were more restrictive (see page 175).

Christianity might have remained just another sect had it not reached Rome, the capital of the Western world. Contrary to modern notions, the early Christians were generally tolerated. Paganism had room for many religions. Rome proved to be a dramatic step in the spread of Christianity for different reasons. First, Jesus had told his followers to spread his word throughout the world, thus making his teachings universal. The pagan Romans also considered their secular empire universal, and early Christians there combined the two concepts of **universalism.** Secular Rome provided another advantage to Christianity. If all roads led to Rome, they also led outward to the provinces of central and western Europe. The very stability and extent of the Roman Empire enabled early Christians easily to spread their faith. Paul himself said of the Christians in Rome (1 Romans 8): "First I thank my God through Jesus Christ for you all, that your faith is spoken of throughout the whole world." The **catacombs** just outside of Rome testify to the vitality of the new religion and pagan toleration of it. Although many people today think of the catacombs as secret meeting places of oppressed Christians, they were actually huge public underground cemeteries along the famous Via Appia, one of Rome's proudest lanes.

The catacombs and other archaeological sites provide a concrete idea of how Christianity spread in the West. At first pagan and Christian artistic motifs were common, and in some cases pagan influence proved stronger than Christian. Later tombs, however, were decorated more with biblical scenes. The catacombs eventually became the honored resting places of the early popes and sites of pilgrimage. Although at first the religious community in Rome was a very important one among many, in the

The Catacombs of Rome The early Christians used underground crypts and rock chambers to bury their dead. The bodies were placed in these galleries and then sealed up. The catacombs became places of pilgrimage, and in this way the dead continued to be united with the living. *(Catacombe di Priscilla, Rome/Scala/Art Resource, NY)*

course of time it would become the center of Western Christendom. From Rome Christianity spread southward to Africa and northward into Europe and across the Channel to Britain.

The Appeal of Christianity

Christianity appealed to common people and to the poor. Its communal celebration of the Lord's Supper gave men and women a sense of belonging. Christianity also offered its adherents the promise of salvation. Christians believed that Jesus on the cross had defeated evil and that he would reward his followers with eternal life after death. Christianity also offered the possibility of forgiveness. Human nature was weak, and even the best Christians would fall into sin. But Jesus loved sinners and forgave those who repented. In its doctrine of salvation

and forgiveness alone, Christianity had a powerful ability to give solace and strength to believers.

Christianity was attractive to many because it gave the Roman world a cause. Instead of passivity, Christianity stressed the ideal of striving for a goal. Every Christian, no matter how poor or humble, supposedly worked to realize the triumph of Christianity on earth. This was God's will, a sacred duty for every Christian. By spreading the word of Christ, Christians played their part in God's plan. No matter how small, the part each Christian played was important. Since this duty was God's will, Christians believed that the goal would be achieved. The Christian was not discouraged by temporary setbacks, believing Christianity to be invincible.

Christianity gave its devotees a sense of community. No Christian was alone. All members of the Christian community strove toward the same goal of fulfilling God's plan. Each individual community was in turn a member of a greater community. And that community, according to Christian Scripture, was indestructible, for Jesus had promised, "upon this rock I will build my church; and the gates of hell shall not prevail against it."[9]

Augustus's Successors

Augustus's success in creating solid political institutions was tested by the dynasty he created, the Julio-Claudians, who schemed against one another trying to win and hold power. This situation allowed a military commander, Vespasian, to claim the throne and establish a new dynasty. Vespasian's dynasty was followed by a series of emperors who were successful militarily and politically.

• *How did Augustus's successors build on his foundation to enhance Roman power and stability?*

The Julio-Claudians and the Flavians (27 B.C.–A.D. 96)

For fifty years after Augustus's death the dynasty that he established—known as the **Julio-Claudians** because they were all members of the Julian and Claudian clans—provided the emperors of Rome. Some of the Julio-Claudians, such as Tiberius and Claudius, were sound rulers and able administrators. Others, including Caligula and Nero, were weak and frivolous men who exercised their power stupidly. Although their enemies later accused them of outrages such as murder and incest, the Julio-Claudians gave the empire a broad and welcome period of peace and prosperity.

One of the most momentous achievements of the Julio-Claudians was Claudius's creation of an imperial bureaucracy composed of professional administrators. Even the most energetic emperor could not run the empire alone. The numerous duties and immense responsibilities of the emperor prompted Claudius to delegate power. He began by giving the freedmen of his household official duties, especially in finances. It was a simple, workable system. Claudius knew his ex-slaves well and could discipline them at will. The effect of Claudius's innovations was to enable the emperor to rule the empire more easily and efficiently.

One of the worst defects of Augustus's settlement—the army's ability to interfere in politics—became obvious during the Julio-Claudian period. Augustus had created a special standing force, the Praetorian Guard, as an imperial bodyguard. In A.D. 41 one of the Praetorians

murdered Caligula while others hailed Claudius as the emperor. Under the threat of violence, the senate ratified the Praetorians' choice. It was a story repeated frequently. During the first three centuries of the empire, the Praetorian Guard all too often murdered emperors they were supposed to protect and saluted emperors of their own choosing.

Claudius was murdered by his fourth wife to allow her son by a previous marriage, Nero, to become emperor. In A.D. 68 Nero's inept rule led to military rebellion and his death, thus opening the way to widespread disruption. In A.D. 69, the "Year of the Four Emperors," four men claimed the position of emperor. Roman armies in Gaul, on the Rhine, and in the East marched on Rome to make their commanders emperor. The man who emerged triumphant was Vespasian, commander of the eastern armies, who entered Rome in 70 and restored order. Nonetheless, the Year of the Four Emperors proved that the Augustan settlement had failed to end civil war.

Not a brilliant politician, Vespasian did not institute sweeping reforms, as had Augustus, or solve the problem of the army in politics. To prevent usurpers from claiming the throne, Vespasian designated his sons Titus and Domitian as his successors. By establishing the Flavian dynasty (named after his clan), Vespasian turned the principate into an open and admitted monarchy. He also expanded the emperor's power by increasing the size of the budding bureaucracy Claudius had created.

One of Vespasian's first tasks was to suppress rebellions that had erupted at the end of Nero's reign. The most famous had taken place in Judaea, which still seethed long after Jesus' crucifixion. Long-standing popular unrest and atrocities committed by Jews and Romans alike sparked a massive revolt in A.D. 66. Four years later a Roman army reconquered Judaea and reduced Jerusalem by siege. The Jewish survivors were enslaved, and their state was destroyed. The mismanagement of Judaea was one of the few—and worst—failures of the Roman imperial administration.

The Flavians carried on Augustus's work on the frontiers. Domitian, the last of the Flavians, won additional territory in Germany and consolidated it in two new provinces. He defeated barbarian tribes on the Danube frontier and strengthened that area as well. Even so, Domitian was one of the most hated of Roman emperors because of his cruelty, and he fell victim to an assassin's dagger. Nevertheless, the Flavians had given the Roman world peace and had kept the legions in line. Their work paved the way for the era of the "five good emperors," the golden age of the empire.

The Age of the "Five Good Emperors" (A.D. 96–180)

The Flavians gave way to a remarkable line of emperors, generally known as the **five good emperors,** who ruled the empire wisely, fairly, and humanely. They created an almost unparalleled period of prosperity and peace. Their generally victorious wars were confined to the frontiers, and even the serenity of Augustus's day seemed to pale in comparison. These emperors were among the noblest, most dedicated, and ablest men in Roman history. Yet fundamental political and military changes had taken place since the time of Augustus's rule.

Augustus had claimed that his influence arose from the collection of offices the senate had bestowed on him. However, there was in law no such office as emperor. Augustus was merely the First Citizen. Under the Flavians the principate became a full-blown monarchy, and by the time of the Antonines the principate was an office with definite rights, powers, and prerogatives. In the years between Augustus and the Antonines, the emperor had become an indispensable part of the imperial machinery. In short, without the emperor the empire would quickly fall to pieces. Augustus had been monarch in fact but not in theory; during their reigns, the Antonines were monarchs in both.

The five good emperors were not power-hungry autocrats. The concentration of power was the result of empire. The easiest and most efficient way to run the Roman Empire was to invest the emperor with vast powers. Furthermore, Roman emperors on the whole proved to be effective rulers and administrators. As capable and efficient emperors took on new tasks and functions, the emperor's hand was felt in more areas of life and government. Increasingly the emperors became the source of all authority and guidance in the empire. The five good emperors were benevolent and exercised their power intelligently, but they were absolute kings all the same. Lesser men would later throw off the façade of constitutionality and use this same power in a despotic fashion.

Typical of the five good emperors is the career of Hadrian, who became emperor in A.D. 117. He was born in Spain, a fact that illustrates the importance of the provinces in Roman politics. Hadrian received his education at Rome and became an ardent admirer of Greek culture. He caught the attention of his elder cousin Trajan, the future emperor, who started him on a military career. At age nineteen Hadrian served on the Danube frontier, where he learned the details of how the Roman army lived and fought and saw for himself the problems

The Emperor Marcus Aurelius This equestrian statue, with the emperor greeting his people, represents both the majesty and the peaceful intentions of this emperor and philosopher—one of the five good emperors. Equestrian statues present an image of idealized masculinity, but most portray their subjects as fierce and warlike, not with a hand raised in peace as Marcus Aurelius's hand is here. *(Tibor Bognar/Alamy)*

of defending the frontiers. When Trajan became emperor in A.D. 98, Hadrian was given important positions in which he learned how to defend and run the empire. At Trajan's death in 117 Hadrian assumed power.

Roman government had changed since Augustus's day. One of the most significant changes was the enormous growth of the imperial bureaucracy created by Claudius. Hadrian reformed this system by putting the bureaucracy on an organized, official basis. He established imperial administrative departments to handle the

MAP 6.2 Roman Britain Though the modern state of Great Britain plays a major role in international affairs, it was a peripheral part of the Roman Empire, a valuable area but nonetheless definitely on the frontier.

work formerly done by imperial freedmen. Hadrian also separated civil service from military service. Men with little talent or taste for the army could instead serve the state as administrators. Hadrian's bureaucracy demanded professionalism from its members. Administrators made a career of the civil service. These innovations made for more efficient running of the empire and increased the authority of the emperor—the ruling power of the bureaucracy.

The Roman army had also changed since Augustus's time. The Roman legion had once been a mobile unit, but its duties under the empire no longer called for mobility. The successors of Augustus generally called a halt to further conquests. The army was expected to defend what had already been won. Under the Flavian emperors (A.D. 69–96) the frontiers became firmly fixed, except for a brief period under Trajan, who attempted to expand the empire. Forts and watch stations guarded the borders. Behind the forts the Romans built a system of roads that allowed the forts to be quickly supplied and reinforced in times of trouble. The army had evolved into a garrison force, with legions guarding specific areas for long periods.

The personnel of the legions was changing, too. Italy could no longer supply all the recruits needed for the army. Increasingly only the officers came from Italy and from the more Romanized provinces. The legionaries were mostly drawn from the less civilized provinces, especially the ones closest to the frontiers. A major trend was already obvious in Hadrian's day: fewer and fewer Roman soldiers were really Roman. In the third century A.D. the barbarization of the army would result in an army indifferent to Rome and its traditions. In the age of the five good emperors, however, the army was still a source of economic stability and a Romanizing agent (see Map 6.2). Men from the provinces and even barbarians joined the army to learn a trade and to gain Roman citizenship. Even so, the signs were ominous. Veterans from Julius Caesar's campaigns would hardly have recognized Hadrian's troops as Roman legionaries. (See the feature "Individuals in Society: Bithus, a Typical Roman Soldier.")

Life in the "Golden Age"

Many people, both ancient and modern, have considered these years one of the happiest epochs in Western history. But popular accounts have also portrayed Rome as already decadent by the time of the five good emperors. If Rome was decadent, who kept the empire running? For that matter, can life in Rome itself be taken as representative of life in other parts of the empire? Rome was unique and must be seen as such. Surely Rome no more resembled a provincial city like Cologne than New York could possibly resemble Watseka, Illinois. Only when the uniqueness of Rome is understood in its own right can one turn to the provinces to obtain a full and reasonable picture of the empire under the Antonines.

• *What was life like in the city of Rome in the "golden age," and what was it like in the provinces?*

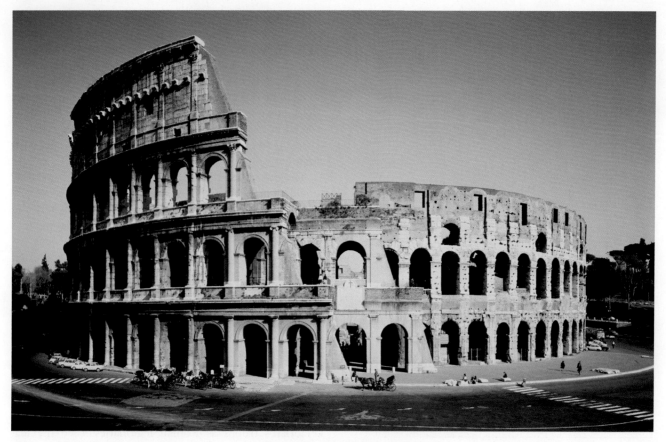

The Coliseum This splendid building was the site of some of Rome's bloodiest games. In it thousands of spectators viewed gladiatorial games between men, sometimes women, and animals. Yet it stands as a monument to the Roman sense of beauty and architectural skill. *(Scala/Art Resource, NY)*

Imperial Rome

Rome was truly an extraordinary city, especially by ancient standards. It was also enormous, with a population somewhere between 500,000 and 750,000. Although it could boast of stately palaces, noble buildings, and beautiful residential areas, most people lived in jerrybuilt apartment houses. They worked at a variety of productive and service jobs. Fire and crime were perennial problems, even after Augustus created fire and urban police forces. Streets were narrow and drainage was inadequate. During the republic sanitation had been a common problem. Numerous inscriptions record prohibitions against dumping human refuse and even cadavers on the grounds of sanctuaries and cemeteries. Under the empire this situation improved. By comparison with medieval and early modern European cities, Rome was a healthy enough place to live.

Rome was such a huge city that the surrounding countryside could not feed it. Because of the danger of starvation, the emperor, following republican practice, provided the citizen population with free grain for bread and, later, oil and wine. By feeding the citizenry the emperor prevented bread riots caused by shortages and high prices. For the rest of the urban population who did not enjoy the rights of citizenship, the emperor provided grain at low prices. This measure was designed to prevent speculators from forcing up grain prices in times of crisis. By maintaining the grain supply the emperor kept the favor of the people and ensured that Rome's poor and idle did not starve.

The emperor and other wealthy citizens also entertained the Roman populace, often at vast expense. The most popular forms of public entertainment were gladiatorial contests and chariot racing. Gladiatorial fighting was originally an Etruscan funerary custom, a blood sacri-

Individuals in Society

Bithus, a Typical Roman Soldier

Few people think of soldiers as missionaries of culture, but they often are. The culture that they spread is seldom of high intellectual or artistic merit, but they expose others to their own traditions, habits, and ways of thinking. A simple modern example may suffice. In World War II American GIs in Italy taught children there how to play baseball. From their very presence the young Americans taught their Italian friends many other things about the United States and themselves learned a great deal about Italian life and values. Even today a stranger can wander around an Italian town and see the results of this meeting of two cultures.

The same was true of the armies of the Roman Empire. The empire was so vast even by modern standards that soldiers were recruited from all parts of it to serve in distant places. A soldier from Syria might find himself keeping watch on Hadrian's Wall in Britain. He brought with him the ideas and habits of his birthplace and soon realized that others lived life differently. Yet they all lived in the same empire. Despite their ethnic differences, they were united by many commonly shared beliefs and opinions. Although the Roman Empire never became totally Romanized, soldiers, like officials and merchants, played their part in disseminating Roman ideas of government, religion, and way of life.

One such person was the infantryman Bithus, who was born in Thrace, the modern region of northeastern Greece. His career was eventful but not particularly distinguished. He is, however, typical of many others who served in the legions. Bithus's military life took him far from his native Thrace. His career started with basic training during which he learned to march and to use standard weapons.

His training over, Bithus was sent to Syria, where he spent most of his career. There he met others from as far west as Gaul and Spain, from West Africa, and from the modern Middle East. This experience gave him an idea of the size of the empire. It also taught him about life in other areas. Unlike many other cohorts that were shifted periodically, his saw service in one theater. While in the army, he raised a family, much like soldiers today. The children of soldiers like Bithus often themselves joined the army, which thereby became a fruitful source of its own recruitment. After twenty-five years of duty, Bithus received his reward on November 7, 88. Upon mustering out of the army he received the grant of Roman citizenship for himself and his family.

Idealized statue of a Roman soldier.
(Deutsches Archaeologisches Institut, Rome)

In his civilian life the veteran enjoyed a social status that granted him honor and privileges accorded only to Romans. From his military records there is no reason to conclude that Bithus had even seen Rome, but because of his service to it, he became as much a Roman as anyone born near the Tiber.

The example of Bithus is important because it is typical of thousands of others who voluntarily supported the empire. In the process they learned about the nature of the empire and something about how it worked. They also exchanged experiences with other soldiers and the local population that helped shape a sense that the empire was a human as well as a political unit.

Questions for Analysis

1. What did Bithus gain from his twenty-five years of service in the Roman army?
2. What effect did soldiers such as Bithus have on the various parts of the Roman Empire where they served, both in their way of seeing new cultures and in their way of sharing new experiences?

Source: Corpus Inscriptionum Latinarum, vol. 16 (Berlin: G. Reimer, 1882), no. 35.

Online Study Center   **Improve Your Grade**
Going Beyond Individuals in Society

Gladiatorial Games Though hardly games, the contests were vastly popular among the Romans. Gladiators were usually slaves, but successful ones could gain their freedom. The fighting was hard but fair, and the gladiators shown here look equally matched. *(Interphoto Press)*

fice for the dead. Even a humane man like Hadrian staged extravagant contests. In A.D. 126 he sponsored six days of such combats, during which 1,835 pairs of gladiators dueled, usually with swords and shields. Many **gladiators** were criminals, some of whom were sentenced to be slaughtered in the arena. These convicts were given no defensive weapons and stood little real chance of survival. Other criminals were sentenced to fight in the arena as fully armed gladiators. Some gladiators were the slaves of gladiatorial trainers; others were prisoners of war. Still others were free men who volunteered for the arena. Even women at times engaged in gladiatorial combat. What drove these men and women? Some obviously had no other choice. For a criminal condemned to die, the arena was preferable to the imperial mines, where convicts worked digging ore and died under wretched conditions. At least in the arena the gladiator might fight well enough to win freedom. Others no doubt fought for the love of danger or for fame. Some Romans protested gladiatorial fighting, but the emperors recognized the political value of such spectacles, and most Romans appear to have enjoyed them. Christian authors generally opposed gladiatorial and animal combat, but this did not lead to immediate bans.

The Romans were even more addicted to chariot racing than to gladiatorial shows. Under the empire four permanent teams competed against one another. Each had its own color—red, white, green, or blue. Some Romans claimed that people cared more about their favorite team than about the race itself. Two-horse and four-horse chariots ran a course of seven laps, about five miles. A successful driver could be the hero of the hour. One charioteer, Gaius Appuleius Diocles, raced for twenty-four years. During that time he drove 4,257 starts and won 1,462 of them. His admirers honored him with an inscription that proclaimed him champion of all charioteers.

Roman spectacles such as gladiator fights and chariot racing are fascinating subjects for movies and computer games, but they were not everyday activities for Romans. As is evident on tombstone inscriptions, ordinary Romans were proud of their work and accomplishments and affectionate toward their families and friends. They were eager to be remembered after death for these things, not for bloody entertainments.

Rome and the Provinces

The question of how much Roman civilization influenced life in the **provinces** is impossible to answer, but enough evidence survives to indicate a complex development. The problem, as usual, depends primarily on the surviving sources. The rural population throughout the empire left few records, yet the inscriptions that remain point to a melding of cultures. A growing number of inscriptions prove that indigenous peoples and newcomers alike learned at least a smattering of Latin in the West and Greek in the East. They used the official imperial languages largely for legal and state religious purposes. Moreover, knowledge of them enhanced the social and political status of their speakers. They were no longer outsiders. Language provided these people with the tool to take their place in the actual running of the empire. They became bilingual—they spoke their native language and either Latin or Greek. The provincial peoples of the Roman Empire were not linguists, but those in the West were unintentionally creating the Romance family of languages, which includes Spanish, Italian, French, Portuguese, and Romanian. This process was at first more urban than rural, but the importance of cities and towns to the life of the wider countryside ensured that its effects spread far afield. Rather than think in terms of one language and culture dominating another, it is far more accurate to observe the evolution of a new culture, with each existing culture fertilizing others.

A brief survey of the provinces proves the point. For instance, in Gaul country people retained their ancestral

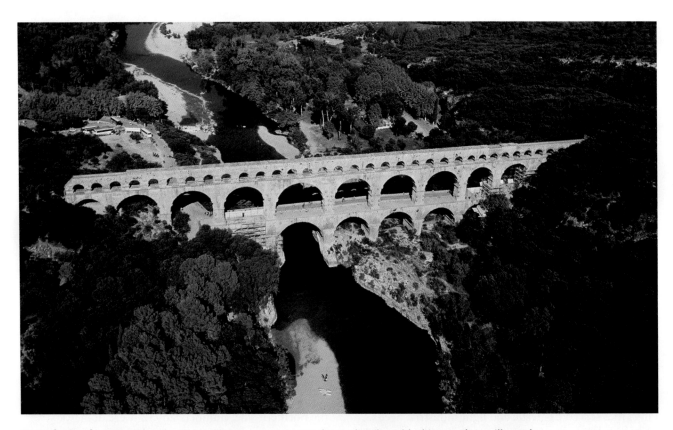

Pont du Gard Long after the Roman Empire gave way to the medieval world, this aqueduct still stands in France, where until recently it still carried water to Nîmes. The aqueduct is not only a splendid feat of Roman engineering but also a work of art. *(Yann Arthus-Bertrand/Altitude)*

gods, and there was not much difference in many parts of the province between the original Celtic villages and their Roman successors. Along the Rhine River, Romans provided the capital for commerce, agricultural development of the land, and large-scale building. Roman merchants also became early bankers, who loaned money to the natives and often brought them under financial control. The native inhabitants formed the labor force. They normally lived in villages and huts near the villas of successful merchants, whose wives brought Roman household items and clothing. Although Roman ideas spread and there was a good deal of cultural blending, native customs and religions continued to thrive. The Romans also learned about and began to respect native gods. Worship of them became popular among the Romans and the Greeks, which encouraged local peoples to preserve their religions.

Roman soldiers had originally been prohibited from marrying, though they often formed permanent relationships with local women. In the late second century

the emperor permitted them to marry, and mixed-ethnicity couples became common in border areas. Because military units were moved as needed, women often ended up far from their homelands with their soldier-husbands.

The situation on the eastern bank of the Rhine was also typical of life on the borders, but it demonstrates the rawer features of frontier life. To this troubled land the Romans brought peace and stability, first by building forts and roads and then by opening the rivers to navigation. Around the forts grew native villages, and peace encouraged more intensive cultivation of the soil. The region became more prosperous than ever before, and prosperity attracted Roman settlers. Roman veterans mingled with the Celtic population and sometimes married into Celtic families. The **villa,** a country estate, not the city, was the primary unit of organized political life. This pattern of life differed from that of the Mediterranean, but it prefigured that of the early Middle Ages. The same was true in Britain, where the normal social

Images in Society

The Roman Villa at Chedworth

On the European borders of the Roman Empire, the villa was often as important as the town. Indeed, villas sometimes assumed many of the functions of towns. They were economic and social centers from which landlords directed the life of the surrounding countryside. The villa at Chedworth in Roman Britain provides an excellent example of them. The ordinary villa included a large courtyard with barns, gardens, storehouses, and buildings for processing agricultural products and manufacturing goods. The villa also included the comfortable living quarters of the owner and his family. These structures included the usual bedrooms and baths. A small temple or shrine often provided a center for religious devotions. Quarters for servants and slaves were nearby but set apart from the great houses. Equally important were the other buildings that served domestic and light industrial needs. The villa, then, was essentially a small, self-contained community. Yet it was not necessarily isolated. The villa at Chedworth was connected by roads and rivers to other similar neighboring villas. The whole picture depicts a society that, though rural, was nonetheless cultured, comfortable, and in touch with the wider world. A good analogy is the American southern plantation before the Civil War. Like many of these villas, Chedworth survived the demise of the Roman Empire. They all remained to play a crucial role in preserving Greco-Roman civilization in northern Europe.

What did a Roman villa look like, and how can archaeological remains define and explain its functioning? Since few ancient structures remain intact, many must obviously be reconstructed from excavations. Image 1 is the archaeological ground plan of Chedworth. At first it seems to show only a series of foundations. Yet a closer look reveals its design. The large buildings marked 3, 5a, and 5 are the remains of the manorial houses. Rooms 10 through 25a are the bath structures. Number 17 is a small temple. Buildings on the northern side, numbers 26–32, were domestic quarters.

Two questions immediately arise. How do we know what these buildings looked like, and how do we know how they functioned? By analyzing the physical remains and the building techniques of the site, ar-

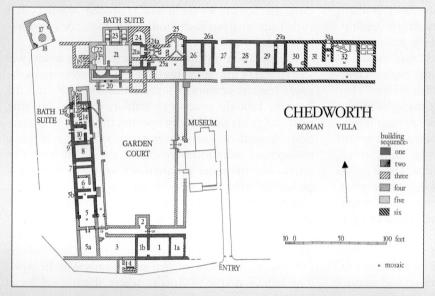

Image 1 Ground Plan of the Roman Villa at Chedworth (*From R. Goodburn, The Roman Villa, Chedworth. Reproduced with permission.*)

Image 2 Archaeological Reconstruction of the Villa *(Courtesy, Professor Albert Schachter)*

Image 3 Aerial View of Chedworth *(Courtesy of West Air Photography)*

Image 4 A View of the Site Today *(John Buckler)*

chaeologists and architects have made a patient reconstruction of the entire villa (see Image 2). Artifacts found in the structures reveal their functions. The most obvious example is the elaborate bath complex of numbers 19–25a. Image 3 gives an aerial view of the villa, and Image 4 provides an excellent cameo of the western wing of the villa.

From this information can you determine from the ground plan (Image 1) and the reconstruction (Image 2) what the villa actually looked like? From Image 3, an aerial view of Chedworth, together with Images 1 and 2, can you locate the landlord's houses, the temple, and the domestic buildings? Now using these three images, can you identify the buildings in Image 4? Lastly, from this material can you imagine the functions of the villa in its environmental and cultural context?

Online Study Center **Improve Your Grade**
Going Beyond Images in Society

Roman History After Augustus

Period	Important Emperors	Significant Events
Julio-Claudians 27 B.C.–A.D. 68	Augustus, 27 B.C.–A.D. 14 Tiberius, 14–37 Caligula, 37–41 Claudius, 41–54 Nero, 54–68	Augustan settlement Beginning of the principate Birth and death of Jesus Expansion into northern and western Europe Creation of the imperial bureaucracy
Year of the Four Emperors 69	Nero Galba Otho Vitellius	Civil war Major breakdown of the concept of the principate
Flavians 69–96	Vespasian, 69–79 Titus, 79–81 Domitian, 81–96	Growing trend toward the concept of monarchy Defense and further consolidation of the European frontiers
Antonines 96–180	Nerva, 96–98 Trajan, 98–117 Hadrian, 117–138 Antoninus Pius, 138–161 Marcus Aurelius, 161–180 Commodus, 180–192	The "golden age"—the era of the "five good emperors" Economic prosperity Trade and growth of cities in northern Europe Beginning of barbarian menace on the frontiers
Severi 193–235	Septimius Severus, 193–211 Caracalla, 198–217 Elagabalus, 218–222 Severus Alexander, 222–235	Military monarchy All free men within the empire given Roman citizenship
"Barracks Emperors" 235–284	Twenty-two emperors in forty-nine years	Civil war Breakdown of the empire Barbarian invasions Severe economic decline
Tetrarchy 284–337	Diocletian, 284–305 Constantine, 306–337	Political recovery Autocracy Legalization of Christianity Transition to the Middle Ages in the West Birth of the Byzantine Empire in the East

and economic structures were farms and agricultural villages. (See the feature "Images in Society: The Roman Villa at Chedworth" on pages 172–173.) Very few cities were to be found, and many native Britons were largely unacquainted with Greco-Roman culture. In Britain, as elsewhere, the Romans made local tribal leaders into their clients, though these relationships were not always amicable. In 47, for example, Boudicca, the queen of one tribe, led an army attacking Roman London.

Across eastern Europe the pattern was much the same. In the Alpine provinces north of Italy, Romans and native Celts came into contact in the cities, but native cultures flourished in the countryside. In Illyria and Dalmatia, the regions of modern Albania and the former Yugoslavia, the native population never widely embraced either Roman culture or urban life. Similarly, the Roman soldiers who increasingly settled parts of these lands made little effort to Romanize the natives, and there was less intermarriage than in Celtic areas. To a certain extent, however, Romanization occurred simply because these peoples lived in such close proximity.

The same situation existed in Asia Minor and elsewhere. In contrast with northern Europe, Asia Minor had long enjoyed the peace and stability of Roman rule. The lives of urban men and women reflected that benefit. A quiet corner of the empire, the small province of

Pamphylia in modern Turkey, gives an excellent idea of this life. The well-preserved ruins of the ancient city of Aspendos, still there today, give a full picture of a comfortable and thriving people. The city sits among fertile fields ideally suited for agriculture. The resources of the land provided raw materials for industry and trade. The Eurymedon River flowing next to the city served as an avenue to the outside world. Manufactured goods and raw materials passed along it to keep it in touch with the rest of the empire and brought in immigrants from elsewhere. For the people of Aspendos the city itself was the focus of life. There the men handled their political affairs in the council house (*bouleuterion*), and men and women frequented the ample marketplace for their ordinary needs. Temples and later a Christian basilica gave them ornate buildings in which to worship or just to think about spiritual matters. Their cultural life was surprisingly bright for an area that now seems so remote from the rest of the world. In their magnificent theater men and women enjoyed the great plays of the past and those popular in their own day. The city also offered many other places to relax. Absent was a place for gladiatorial games. That too was typical of the eastern Roman Empire, where gladiatorial contests were far less popular than horse racing.

This comfortable life also gave the Aspendians an excellent setting to pursue studies such as philosophy, literature, and history. More than just places to live, cities like Aspendos were centers of the intellectual and cultural life that spread abroad. The people here, like those elsewhere in the empire, kept fully in touch with the great thoughts and events of the day. Taken together, cities like Aspendos in the East, those along the Rhine in the West, and the many others throughout the empire united in a vibrant economic and cultural life that spanned the entire Mediterranean (see Map 6.3). They also passed it along as a rich heritage to later peoples in Europe.

Obviously the Romans went to no great lengths to spread their culture. Their chief aim was political stability, which they maintained through alliances as well as the suppression of any rebellions. As long as the empire prospered and the revenues reached the imperial coffers, the Romans were willing to live and let live. As a result, Europe fully entered into the economic and cultural life of the Mediterranean world.

The age of the five good emperors was generally one of peace, progress, and prosperity. The work of the Romans in northern and western Europe was a permanent contribution to the history of Western society. This period was also one of consolidation. Roads and secure sea-lanes linked the empire in one vast web, with men and women traveling and migrating more often than they had in earlier eras. The empire had become a commonwealth of cities, and urban life was its hallmark.

Rome in Disarray and Recovery (A.D. 177–450)

The long years of peace and prosperity abruptly gave way to a convulsed period of domestic upheaval and foreign invasion. The last of the five good emperors was followed by a long series of able but ambitious military commanders who used their legions to make themselves emperors. Law yielded to the sword. Yet even during the worst of this ordeal, many people clung to the old Roman ideals. Only the political mechanisms of the empire, its sturdy civil service and its ordinary lower officials, protected by loyal soldiers, staved off internal collapse and foreign invasion. Not until the coming of Diocletian did one man triumph over all his rivals to end the long period of strife. In 284 he reconstructed the empire and restored Roman life to peace and security.

Once Diocletian had ended the period of turmoil, succeeding emperors confronted the work of repairing the damage. Restoring the Roman Empire was the daunting challenge to the emperor Constantine (r. 306–337). While the price was high, he achieved success. Yet the Roman world, like Humpty Dumpty, could not quite be put back together again.

• *What factors led Rome into political and economic chaos, and how and to what extent did it recover?*

Civil Wars and Foreign Invasions in the Third Century

After the death of Marcus Aurelius, the last of the five good emperors, misrule by his successors led to a long and intense spasm of fighting. More than twenty different emperors ascended the throne in the forty-nine years between 235 and 284. Many rebels, loyal generals and their soldiers, and innocent civilians died in the conflagration. At various times parts of the empire were lost to mutinous generals, one of whom—Postumus—set up his own empire in Gaul for about ten years (259–269). Yet other men, like the iron-willed Aurelian (270–275), dedicated their energies to restoring order. So many military commanders ruled that the middle of the third century has become known as the age of the **barracks emperors.**

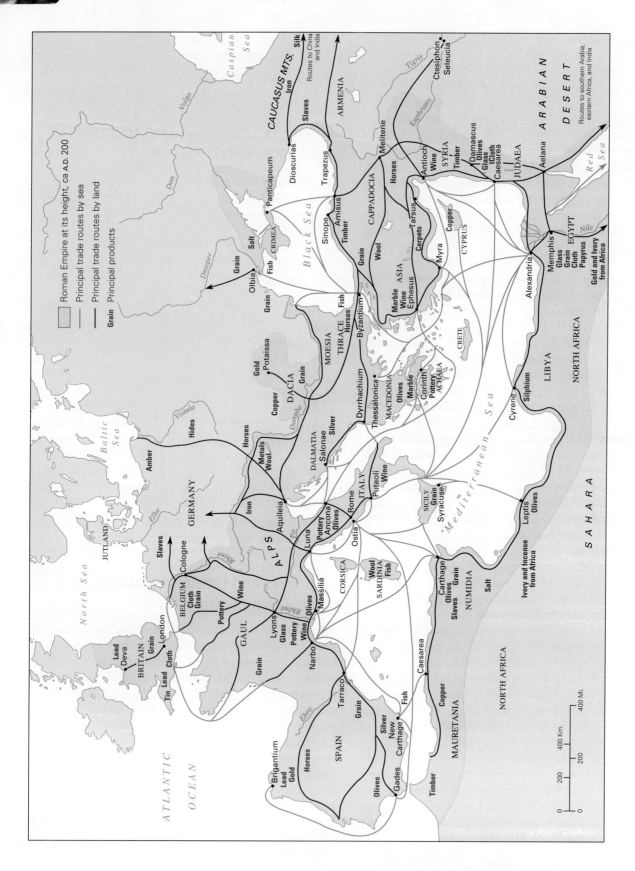

The Augustan principate had become a military monarchy, and that monarchy was nakedly autocratic.

While the empire seemed intent on committing suicide, barbarians on the frontiers took full advantage of the chaos to overrun vast areas. When they reached the Rhine and the Danube, they often found gaping holes in the Roman defenses. During much of the third century bands of Goths devastated the Balkans as far south as Greece and down into Asia Minor. The Alamanni, a Germanic people, swept across the Danube. At one point they reached Milan in Italy before being beaten back. Meanwhile, the Franks, still another Germanic folk, hit the Rhine frontier. Once loose, they invaded eastern and central Gaul and northeastern Spain. Saxons from Scandinavia sailed into the English Channel in search of loot. In the east the Sasanids overran Mesopotamia. If the army had guarded the borders instead of creating and destroying emperors, none of these onslaughts would have been successful. At the very least, the barracks emperors managed to stave off total ruin at the hands of the barbarians.

Turmoil in Farm and Village Life

This chaos also disrupted areas elsewhere in the empire, even when the local people remained distant from barbarian invaders. These convulsions gave rise to local lawlessness in which ordinary men and women suffered dreadfully. Renegade soldiers and corrupt imperial officials together with many greedy local agents preyed on local people. In many places in the countryside, farmers appealed to the government to protect them so that they could cultivate the land. Others encountered officials who requisitioned their livestock and compelled them to do forced labor. Facing ruin, many rural families deserted the land and simply fled. Although many of those in authority were unsympathetic and even violent to villagers, many others tried justly and fairly to maintain order. They did what they could to ensure justice to all under their authority. Yet even the best of them also suffered. If they could not meet their tax quotas, they paid the deficits from their own pockets. They too were being impoverished. Because the local officials were themselves being so hard-pressed, they squeezed what they needed from rural families. By the end of the third century the entire empire tottered on the brink of ruin.

Reconstruction Under Diocletian and Constantine (A.D. 284–337)

At the close of the third century A.D. the emperor Diocletian (r. 284–305) put an end to the period of turmoil. Repairing the damage done in the third century was the major work of the emperor Constantine (r. 306–337) in the fourth. But the price was high.

Under Diocletian, Augustus's polite fiction of the emperor as first among equals gave way to the emperor as absolute autocrat. The princeps became *dominus*—"lord." The emperor claimed that he was "the elect of god"—that he ruled because of divine favor. Constantine even claimed to be the equal of Jesus' first twelve followers. To underline the emperor's exalted position, Diocletian and Constantine adopted the gaudy court ceremonies and trappings of the Persian Empire. People entering the emperor's presence prostrated themselves before him and kissed the hem of his robes. Constantine went so far as to import Persian eunuchs to run the palace. The Roman emperor had become an Eastern monarch.

No mere soldier, but rather an adroit administrator, Diocletian gave serious thought to the empire's ailments. He recognized that the empire and its difficulties had become too great for one man to handle. To solve these problems, Diocletian divided the empire into a western and an eastern half (see Map 6.4). Diocletian assumed direct control of the eastern part; he gave the rule of the western part to a colleague, along with the title **augustus,** which had become synonymous with emperor. Diocletian and his fellow augustus further delegated power by appointing two men to assist them. Each man was given the title of *caesar* to indicate his exalted rank. Although this system is known as the **Tetrarchy** because four men ruled the empire, Diocletian was clearly the senior partner and final source of authority.

Mapping the Past

MAP 6.3 The Economic Aspect of the Pax Romana
This map gives a good idea of trade routes and the economic expansion of the Roman Empire at its height. Map 11.2 on page 340 is a similar map that shows trade in roughly the same area nearly a millennium later. Examine both maps and answer the following questions: ❶ To what extent did Roman trade routes influence later European trade routes? ❷ What similarities and differences do you see in trade in the Mediterranean during these two periods?

Online Study Center **Improve Your Grade** Interactive Map: Economic Aspect of Pax Romana

MAP 6.4 The Roman World Divided Under Diocletian, the Roman Empire was first divided into a western and an eastern half, a development that foreshadowed the medieval division between the Latin West and the Byzantine East.

Online Study Center **Improve Your Grade** Interactive Map: Roman World Divided

Diocletian's Tetrarchy The emperor Diocletian's attempt to reform the Roman Empire by dividing rule among four men is represented in this piece of sculpture. Here the four tetrarchs demonstrate their solidarity by clasping one another on the shoulder. Nonetheless each man has his other hand on his sword—a gesture that proved prophetic when Diocletian's reign ended and another struggle for power began. *(Alinari/Art Resource, NY)*

Each half of the empire was further split into two prefectures, each governed by a prefect responsible to an augustus. Diocletian reduced the power of the old provincial governors by dividing provinces into smaller units. He organized the prefectures into small administrative units called **dioceses,** which were in turn subdivided into small provinces. Provincial governors were also deprived of their military power, leaving them only civil and administrative duties.

Diocletian's political reforms were a momentous step. The Tetrarchy soon failed, but Diocletian's division of the empire into two parts became permanent. Constantine and later emperors tried hard but unsuccessfully to keep the empire together. Throughout the fourth century A.D. the eastern and the western sections drifted apart. In later centuries the western part witnessed the fall of Roman government and the rise of barbarian kingdoms, while the eastern empire evolved into the majestic Byzantine Empire.

The most serious immediate matters confronting Diocletian and Constantine were economic, social, and religious. They needed additional revenues to support the army and the imperial court. Yet the wars and the barbarian invasions had caused widespread destruction and poverty. The fighting had struck a serious blow to Roman agriculture, which the emperors tried to revive. Christianity had become too strong either to ignore or to crush. The responses to these problems by Diocletian, Constantine, and their successors helped create economic and social patterns that influenced later developments.

Inflation and Taxes

The barracks emperors had dealt with economic hardship by depreciating the currency, cutting the silver content of coins until money was virtually worthless. As a result, the entire monetary system fell into ruin. In Egypt governors had to order bankers to accept imperial money. The immediate result was crippling inflation throughout the empire.

The empire was less capable of recovery than in earlier times. Wars and invasions had disrupted normal commerce and the means of production. Mines were exhausted in the attempt to supply much-needed ores, especially gold and silver. The turmoil had hit the cities especially hard. Markets were disrupted, and travel became dangerous. Merchant and artisan families rapidly left devastated regions. The prosperous industry and commerce of Gaul and the Rhineland declined markedly. Those who owed their prosperity to commerce and the needs of urban life likewise suffered. Cities were no longer places where trade and industry thrived. The devastation of the countryside increased the difficulty of feeding and supplying the cities. The destruction was so extensive that many wondered whether the ravages could be repaired at all.

The response of Diocletian and Constantine to these problems was marked by compulsion, rigidity, and loss of individual freedom. Diocletian's attempt to curb inflation illustrates the methods of absolute monarchy. In a move unprecedented in Roman history, he issued an

Arch of Constantine Though standing in stately surroundings, Constantine's arch is decorated with art plundered from the arches of Trajan and Marcus Aurelius. He robbed them rather than decorate his own with the inferior work of his own day. *(Michael Reed, photographer/ www.mike-reed.com)*

edict that fixed maximum prices and wages throughout the empire.

The emperors dealt with the tax system just as strictly and inflexibly. As in the past, local officials bore the responsibility of collecting imperial taxes. Constantine made these officials into a hereditary class; son followed father whether he wanted to or not. In this period of severe depression many localities could not pay their taxes. In such cases these local officials had to make up the difference from their own funds. This system soon wiped out a whole class of moderately wealthy people. It was a bad policy for everyone involved.

With the monetary system in ruins, most imperial taxes became payable in kind—that is, in goods or produce instead of money. The major drawback of payment in kind is its demands on transportation. Goods have to be moved from where they are grown or manufactured to where they are needed. Accordingly, the emperors locked into their occupations all those involved in the growing, preparation, and transportation of food and essential commodities. A baker or shipper could not go into any other business, and his son took up the trade at his death. The late Roman Empire had a place for everyone, and everyone had a place.

The Decline of Small Farms

Because of worsening conditions during the third century A.D., many free tenant farmers and their families were killed, fled the land to escape the barbarians, or abandoned farms ravaged in the fighting. Consequently, large tracts of land lay deserted. Great landlords with ample resources began at once to reclaim as much of this land as they could. The huge estates that resulted, called villas, were self-sufficient. Because they often produced more than they consumed, they successfully competed with the declining cities by selling their surplus in the countryside. They became islands of stability in an unsettled world.

While the villas were growing, rural residents who remained on the land barely held their own. They were too poor and powerless to stand against the tide of chaos. They were exposed to the raids of barbarians or brigands and to the tyranny of imperial officials. For relief they turned to the great landlords. After all, the landowners were men of considerable resources, lords in their own right. They were wealthy and had many people working their land. They were independent and capable of defending themselves. If need be, they could—and at times did—field a small force of their own. Already influential, the landowning class united in protest against the demands of imperial officials.

In return for the protection and security landlords could offer, the small landholders gave over their lands. Free men and their families became clients of the landlords and lost much of their freedom. To guarantee a steady supply of labor, the landlords bound them to the soil. They could no longer decide to move elsewhere. Henceforth they and their families worked their patrons' land, not their own. Free men and women were becoming what would later be called serfs.

The Acceptance of Christianity

In religious affairs Constantine took the decisive step of recognizing Christianity as a legitimate religion. No longer would Christians suffer persecution for their beliefs as they occasionally had earlier. Constantine himself died a Christian in 337. Why had the pagans persecuted Christians in the first place? Polytheism is by nature tolerant of new gods and accommodating in religious matters. Why was Christianity singled out for violence? Such questions as these are still matters of scholarly debate to which some broad answers can be given.

A splendid approach to these problems has come from the eminent Italian scholar Marta Sordi.[10] Confronting a very complicated topic, she distinguishes among many different phases in the relationship between Christianity and official Roman acceptance of it. The Christians exaggerated the degree of pagan hostility to them, and most of the gory stories about the martyrs are fictitious. There were indeed some cases of pagan persecution of the Christians, but with few exceptions they were local and sporadic in nature. Even Nero's notorious persecution was temporary and was limited to Rome. No constant persecution of Christians occurred. Instead, pagans and Christians alike enjoyed long periods of tolerance and even friendship. Nonetheless, some pagans thought that Christians were atheists because they scorned the traditional pagan gods. Christians in fact either denied the existence of pagan gods or called them evil spirits. They went so far as to urge people not to worship pagan gods. In turn pagans, who believed in their gods as fervently as the Christians theirs, feared that the gods would withdraw their favor from the Roman Empire because of Christian blasphemy.

At first many pagans genuinely misunderstood Christian practices and rites. Even educated and cultured people like the historian Tacitus opposed Christianity because they saw it as a bizarre new sect. Tacitus believed that Christians hated the whole human race. As a rule early Christians kept to themselves. Romans distrusted and feared their exclusiveness, which seemed unsociable and even subversive. They thought that such secret rites as the Lord's Supper, at which Christians said that they ate and drank the body and blood of Jesus, were acts of cannibalism. Pagans also thought that Christians indulged in immoral and indecent rituals. They considered Christianity one of the worst of the mystery cults, for one of the hallmarks of many of those cults was rituals many Romans found unacceptable.

Another source of misunderstanding was that the pagans did not demand that Christians *believe* in pagan gods. Official Roman religion was never a matter of belief or ethics but of publicly celebrated rituals linked to the good of the state. All the pagans expected was performance of a ritual sacrifice as a demonstration of patriotism and loyalty. Those Christians who sacrificed went free, no matter what they personally believed.

As time went on, pagan hostility decreased. Pagans realized that Christians were not working to overthrow the state and that Jesus was no rival of Caesar. The emperor Trajan forbade his governors to hunt down Christians. Trajan admitted that he thought Christianity an abomination, but he preferred to leave Christians in peace.

The stress of the third century, however, seemed to some emperors the punishment of the gods. What else could account for such anarchy? With the empire threatened on every side, a few emperors thought that one way to appease the gods was by offering them the proper sacrifices. Such sacrifices would be a sign of loyalty to the empire, a show of Roman solidarity and religious piety. Consequently, a new wave of persecutions began out of desperation. Although the Christians depicted the emperor Diocletian as a fiend, he persecuted them in the hope that the gods would restore their blessings on Rome. Yet even these persecutions were never very widespread or long-lived; most pagans were not greatly sympathetic to the new round of persecutions. By the late third century, pagans had become used to Christianity. Constantine's acceptance of Christianity can be seen as the pagans' alliance with the strongest god of them all. Pagan and Christian alike must have been relieved when Constantine legalized the Christian religion.

Online Study Center **Improve Your Grade**
Primary Source: In Hoc Signo Vinces (By This Sign, Conquer): The Conversion of Constantine

In time the Christian triumph would be complete. In 380 the emperor Theodosius made Christianity the official religion of the Roman Empire. At that point

Martyrion at Aphrodisias   This trefoil building in Asia Minor is probably the remains of a *martyrion,* or martyrium, a church dedicated to a martyr. Martyrs were people killed for their belief in Jesus' divinity. There were not as many martyrs as Christians claimed, but the Christians considered them all heroes. This church probably honors a martyr now unidentified. *(M. Ali Dogenci, Turkey)*

Christians began to persecute the pagans for their beliefs. History had come full circle.

The Construction of Constantinople

The triumph of Christianity was not the only event that made Constantine's reign a turning point in Roman history. Constantine took the bold step of building a new capital for the empire. Constantinople, the New Rome, was constructed on the site of Byzantium, an old Greek city on the Bosporus. Throughout the third century emperors had found Rome and the West hard to defend. The eastern part of the empire was more easily defensible and escaped the worst of the barbarian devastation. It was wealthy and its urban life still vibrant. Moreover Christianity was more widespread in the East than in the West, and the city of Constantinople was intended to be a Christian center.

From the Classical World to Late Antiquity

Constantine had restored order, but what kind of order? Was it possible for one man to reconstruct the whole Roman Empire, indeed all of the ancient world? The answer is obviously no. Much was gone forever. Much still survived, but even more was still changing. The Roman god Janus well symbolizes this period. Janus's two faces looked both ways, in this case to the past and the future, for indeed the West was entering a vast new phase in its development. As usual in the case of major historical developments, an understanding of this whole epoch provides controversy, speculation, and new interpretations. One of the most dramatic questions is whether the Roman Empire even actually fell. Nearly all historians today agree that history, like a river, constantly flows and that all divisions of time are artificial. Historians now realize that the fourth century, which used to be seen as one of the central turning points in history, saw continuity along with change.

A great deal of the past lived on through these years of change. People still lived under the authority of the emperors and the guidance of Roman law. Essential ideas such as the value of individuals and their responsibilities to the state remained strong. In both halves of the empire, culture continued relatively unchanged. Greco-Roman architecture and art still adorned the land, not yet in the splendid and inspiring ruins that we see today, but vigorously alive. People communicated with one another as usual, in Latin throughout the West and Greek in the East, and those who could read still read the great creations of literature in these languages. The past was still the present.

Yet the gentle breeze of change also blew. Government had evolved from the SPQR of the past to the Christian monarchy of the new age. Whereas in the past the pagan gods had overseen the welfare of the state, now the Christian God with the earthly aid of the emperor and church officials protected the realm. The law of the church had increasingly mingled with that of the Caesars to govern life. The empire itself split from the unified principate of Augustus to two tenuously linked empires dividing the Western world. That in the West became the home of barbarians who absorbed much of the prevailing Roman culture while altering it with their own ideas, customs, and even languages. They were building a different world on classical foundations.

Paganism and the old gods faded into the background as Christianity came to prevail. Religion too brought its innovations. People struggled to understand Jesus' message to them. They disagreed over it, with some claiming to stand for the truth while branding those who disagreed as heretics. Christianity introduced a contest for people's souls in a way that paganism had never done. Greek philosophy, with its logic and amiable controversy, was replaced by theology, as thinkers tried earnestly to understand God and then teach others the meaning of his message. Christianity brought to religion a violence generally absent from paganism.

Through all these changes the lives of ordinary men and women did not change dramatically. They farmed, worked in cities, and hoped for the best for their families. They took new ideas, blended them with old, and created new cultural forms and ways of meeting life's challenges. The fourth century was a period of transition. The many forms that shaped it gave rise to a vibrant intellectual, spiritual, and political life that forever changed the face of Western civilization.

Chapter Summary

Online Study Center **ACE the Test**

- *How did Augustus restore stability; what political and military changes did he institute; and how did he spread Roman influence to northern and western Europe?*
- *Why did Christianity, originally a minor local religion, sweep across the Roman world to change it fundamentally?*
- *How did Augustus's successors build on his foundation to enhance Roman power and stability?*
- *What was life like in the city of Rome in the "golden age," and what was it like in the provinces?*
- *What factors led Rome into political and economic chaos, and how and to what extent did it recover?*

Once Augustus had restored order, he made it endure by remodeling the Roman government. The old constitution of the city-state gave way to the government of an empire. Although Augustus tried to save as much of the old as possible, he necessarily created a virtually new and much expanded system of rule. Furthermore, he made it endure.

As life settled down under this calming order, a small event with universal repercussions occurred in remote and insignificant Judaea. There a young Jew named Jesus taught a new religion promising salvation to all who embraced it. Some Jewish leaders opposed his teachings and persuaded Roman officials to execute him. Yet this new religion did not die with him. Instead it spread across the East, then to Rome, and by the end of the period throughout the empire.

Augustus's success in creating solid political institutions was tested by the dynasty he created, the Julio-Claudians. The fifty years during which they ruled Rome saw emperors and empresses trying to win and hold power through multiple political marriages, murder, and other tactics. In A.D. 70, Vespasian, a military commander, established a new dynasty, the Flavians, who restored some stability in Rome and expanded the empire. The Flavians were followed by a series of effective emperors, later called the "five good emperors," who created a more effective bureaucracy and larger army to govern the huge Roman Empire.

For many Romans these were rich and happy years. Much of the population enjoyed sufficient leisure time, which many spent pursuing literature and art. Others preferred watching spectacular games including gladiatorial contests and horse races. In the ever-expanding provinces, Roman and native cultures combined, and products and peoples moved easily across huge areas.

The good times fell into disarray when a series of weak, but rapacious, emperors fought all opponents for the throne. Civil war, chaos, and economic depression resulted. To worsen matters, barbarians on the frontiers took advantage of these internal troubles to invade, plunder, and destroy. These factors brought Rome near collapse. With the end apparently at hand, two stern and gifted emperors, Diocletian and Constantine, restored order and breathed fresh life into the economic and social order. By the end of this period, Christianity had made such gains that it was recognized as the official religion of the empire. By the end of Constantine's reign the Roman Empire was politically divided and religiously changing. Still, many aspects of Greco-Roman culture remained strong.

Key Terms

pax Romana	universalism
constitutional	catacombs
monarchy	Julio-Claudians
princeps	five good emperors
imperator	gladiators
barbarians	provinces
Messiah	villa
apocalypticism	barracks emperors
pagans	augustus
heresy	Tetrarchy
Gentiles	dioceses

Online Study Center **Improve Your Grade** Flashcards

Suggested Reading

Bradley, K. R. *Slaves and Masters in the Roman Empire: A Study of Social Control.* 1988. A brief book that examines how the institution of slavery was maintained over time and how the lives of slaves in the Roman world were controlled by their masters.

Burns, Thomas S. *Rome and the Barbarians, 100 B.C.–A.D. 400.* 2003. Analyzes the impact that the Romans had on the barbarians and that the barbarians had on the Romans.

Cunliffe, Barry. *Greeks, Romans and Barbarians.* 1988. Uses archaeological and literary evidence to discuss the introduction of Greco-Roman culture into western Europe.

D'Ambra, Eve. *Roman Women.* 2006. Examines women's lives in all social ranks, using material sources as well as written works.

Ehrman, Bard D. *Lost Scriptures: Books That Did Not Make It into the New Testament.* 2003. One of a series of books by this author designed for general readers that explore the diversity in early Christianity.

Esler, Philip F. *The Early Christian World.* 2004. An enormous collection by experts in the field that covers all aspects of the development of early Christianity.

Fredriksen, Paula. *From Jesus to Christ*, 2d ed. 2000. Studies the ways in which early Christians transformed the Jesus in the New Testament into the Christ of Christian tradition.

Goldsworthy, Adrian. *Roman Warfare.* 2000. Provides a concise treatment of warfare from republican to imperial times.

Goodman, Martin. *The Roman World, 44 B.C.–A.D. 180.* 1997. A good general treatment of the empire.

Greene, Kevin. *The Archaeology of the Roman Economy.* 1986. Offers an intriguing way to picture the Roman economy through physical remains.

MacMullen, Ramsay. *Christianizing the Roman Empire.* 1986. A thorough discussion by one of the leading scholars in the field.

MacMullen, Ramsay. *Roman Social Relations, 50 B.C. to A.D. 284.* 1981. Examines changes and continuities in social relations.

Noy, David. *Foreigners at Rome.* 2000. Studies the mingling of visitors and natives in the city and how tourists and locals affected each other's lives.

Shotter, David. *Augustus Caesar.* 1991. A brief study designed for students that examines the political, social, and cultural impact of the emperor's work.

Syme, Ronald. *The Augustan Aristocracy.* 1985. Studies the new order that Augustus created to help him administer the empire.

Notes

1. Virgil, *Aeneid* 6.851–853. John Buckler is the translator of all uncited quotations from a foreign language in Chapters 1–6.
2. Augustus, *Res Gestae* 6.34.
3. Ibid., 5.28.
4. Horace, *Odes* 4.15.
5. Virgil, *Georgics* 3.515–519.
6. Ovid, *Fasti* 4.925.
7. Matthew 3:3.
8. Acts 17:26.
9. Matthew 16:18.
10. See Marta Sordi, *The Christians and the Roman Empire* (London: Croom Helm, 1986).

Rome Extends Its Citizenship

One of the most dramatic achievements of the pax Romana was the extension of citizenship throughout the Roman Empire. Citizenship gave people advantages in judicial procedures, property transmission, and commercial relations. Male citizens could vote, and both female and male citizens passed citizenship on to their children. By granting citizenship to most people in the empire, the Roman government in effect took them into partnership.

Yet various emperors went even further by viewing Rome not only as a territorial but also as a political concept. In their eyes Rome was a place and an idea. Not every Roman agreed with these cosmopolitan views. The emperor Claudius (r. 41–54) took the first major step in this direction by allowing Romanized Gauls to sit in the senate. He was roundly criticized by some Romans, but in the damaged stone inscription that follows, he presents his own defense.

Surely both my great-uncle, the deified Augustus, and my uncle, Tiberius Caesar, were following a new practice when they desired that all the flower of the colonies and the municipalities every-where—that is, the better class and the wealthy men—should sit in this senate house. You ask me: Is not an Italian senator preferable to a provincial? I shall reveal to you in detail my views on this matter when I come to obtain approval for this part of my censorship [a magistracy that determined who was eligible for citizenship and public offices]. But I think that not even provincials ought to be excluded, provided that they can add distinction to this senate house.

Look at that most distinguished and most flourishing colony of Vienna [the modern Vienne in France], how long a time already it is that it has furnished senators to this house! From that colony comes that ornament of the equestrian order—and there are few to equal him—Lucius

Vestinus, whom I cherish most intimately and whom at this very time I employ in my affairs. And it is my desire that his children may enjoy the first step in the priesthoods, so as to advance afterwards, as they grow older, to further honors in their rank. . . . I can say the same of his brother, who because of this wretched and most shameful circumstance cannot be a useful senator for you.

The time has now come, Tiberius Caesar Germanicus [Claudius himself], now that you have reached the farthest boundaries of Narbonese Gaul, for you to unveil to the members of the senate the import of your address. All these distinguished youths whom I gaze upon will no more give us cause for regret if they become senators than does my friend Persicus, a man of most noble ancestry, have cause for regret when he reads among the portraits of his ancestors the name Allobrogicus. But if you agree that these things are so, what more do you want, when I point out to you this single fact, that the territory beyond the boundaries of Narbonese Gaul already sends you senators, since we have men of our order from Lyons and have no cause for regret. It is indeed with hesitation, members of the senate, that I have gone outside the borders of the provinces with which you are accustomed and familiar, but I must now plead openly the cause of Gallia Comata [a region in modern France]. And if anyone, in this connection, has in mind that these people engaged the deified Julius in war for ten years, let him set against that the unshakable loyalty and obedience of a hundred years, tested to the full in many of our crises. When my father Drusus was subduing Germany, it was they who by their tranquility afforded him a safe and securely peaceful rear, even at a time when he had been summoned away to the war from the task of organizing the census which was still new and unaccustomed to the Gauls. How difficult such an operation is for us at this precise moment we are learning all too well from experience, even though the survey is aimed at nothing more than an official record of our resources. [The rest of the inscription is lost.]

Only later, in A.D. 212, did the emperor Caracalla (198–217) extend Roman citizenship to all freeborn men with the exception of those called dediticii, *whose identity remains a source of controversy. Caracalla claimed that he made this proclamation because the gods had saved him from a plot on his life. Some modern scholars, however, have suggested that he wanted more citizens to tax. Whatever the truth, Caracalla continued the work of Augustus (27 B.C.–A.D. 14) and Claudius. The Romans succeeded where the Greeks had failed: they built an empire of citizens. The following is a damaged copy of Caracalla's edict.*

The Emperor Caesar Marcus Aurelius Serverus Antoninus Augustus [Caracalla] declares: . . . I may show my gratitude to the immortal gods for preserving me in such [circumstances?]. Therefore I consider that in this way I can . . . rend proper service to their majesty . . . by bringing with me to the worship [?] of the gods all who enter into the number of my people. Accordingly, I grant Roman citizenship to all aliens, throughout the world, with no one remaining outside the citizen bodies except the *dediticii*. For it is proper that the multitude should not only help carry [?] all the burdens but should also now be included in my victory.

Citizenship was often granted to soldiers who had fought in the Roman army. The usual reasons were conspicuous bravery or wounds suffered in the course of duty. The emperor Trajan (98–117) made such a grant of citizenship in 106 to British soldiers who had served in the campaign in Dacia, a southern region of the former Yugoslavia. These men were also honored for their valor with an early discharge.

The Emperor Trajan . . . has granted Roman citizenship before completion of military service to the infantrymen and cavalrymen whose

Provocatio, the right of appeal, was considered a fundamental element of Roman citizenship. *(Courtesy of the Trustees of the British Museum)*

names appear below, serving in the First British Thousand-Man Ulpian Decorated Loyal Fortunate Cohort composed of Roman citizens, which is on duty in Dacia under Decimus Terentius Scaurianus, for having dutifully and faithfully discharged the Dacian campaign.

Questions for Analysis

1. What was the basic justification underlying Claudius's decision to allow Gallic nobles to sit in the senate? Did he see them as debasing the quality of the senate?

2. What do his words tell us about the changing nature of the Roman Empire?

3. What was the significance of Caracalla's extension of Roman citizenship to all freeborn men?

4. Notice that Trajan linked citizenship with military service. Can you think of modern parallels?

Source: Slightly adapted and abbreviated from N. Lewis and M. Reinhold, *Roman Civilization,* 2 vols. Copyright © 1966 by Columbia University Press, New York. Reprinted with permission of the publisher.

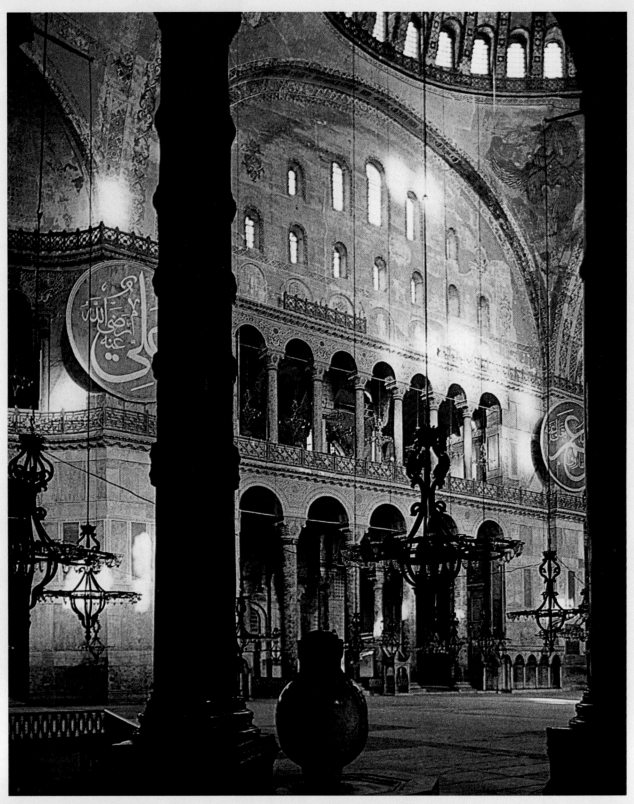

Hagia Sophia ("Holy Wisdom"), built by the emperor Justinian in the sixth century, was the largest Christian cathedral in the world for a thousand years. After Constantinople was conquered by the Ottoman Turks in 1453, it became a mosque, and today is a museum. *(Sadea Editore)*

LATE ANTIQUITY, 350–600

T he Roman Empire, with its powerful—and sometimes bizarre— leaders, magnificent buildings, luxurious clothing, and bloody amusements, has long fascinated people. Politicians and historians have closely studied the reasons for its successes and have even more closely analyzed the weaknesses that led to its eventual collapse. From the third century onward, the Western Roman Empire slowly disintegrated. The last Roman emperor in the West, Romulus Augustus, was deposed by the Ostrogothic chieftain Odoacer in 476, but much of the empire had already come under the rule of various barbarian tribes well before this. Scholars have long seen this era as one of the great turning points in Western history, a time when the ancient world was transformed into the very different medieval world. During the last several decades, however, focus has shifted to continuities as well as changes, and what is now usually termed "late antiquity" has been recognized as a period of creativity and adaptation, not simply of decline and fall.

The two main agents of continuity were the Eastern Roman (or Byzantine) Empire and the Christian church. The Byzantine Empire lasted until 1453, a thousand years longer than the Western Roman Empire, and preserved and transmitted much of ancient law, philosophy, and institutions. Missionaries and church officials spread Christianity within and far beyond the borders of the Roman Empire, transforming a small sect into the most important and wealthiest institution in Europe. The main agents of change in late antiquity were the barbarian groups migrating into the Roman Empire. They brought different social, political, and economic structures with them, but as they encountered Roman culture and became Christian, their own ways of doing things were also transformed.

The Byzantine Empire

Constantine had tried to maintain the unity of the Roman Empire, but during the fifth and sixth centuries the Western and Eastern halves drifted apart. From Constantinople, Eastern Roman emperors worked to

Online Study Center

This icon will direct you to interactive activities and study materials on the website **college.hmco.com/pic/mckaywest9e**

MAP 7.1 The Byzantine Empire, ca 600 The strategic position of Constantinople on the waterway between the Black Sea and the Mediterranean was clear to Constantine when he chose the city as the capital of the Eastern Roman Empire, and it was also clear to later rulers and military leaders. Byzantine territories in Italy were acquired in Emperor Justinian's sixth-century wars and were held for several centuries.

Online Study Center **Improve Your Grade** Interactive Map: Byzantine Empire, ca 600

hold the empire together and to reconquer at least some of the West from barbarian tribes. Justinian (r. 527–565) waged long and hard-fought wars against the Ostrogoths and temporarily regained Italy and North Africa, but his conquests had disastrous consequences. Justinian's wars exhausted the resources of the state, destroyed Italy's economy, and killed a large part of Italy's population. The wars also paved the way for the easy conquest of Italy by another Germanic tribe, the Lombards, shortly after Justinian's death. In the late sixth century, the territory of the Western Roman Empire came once again under Germanic sway.

However, the Roman Empire continued in the East. The Eastern Roman or Byzantine Empire (see Map 7.1) preserved the forms, institutions, and traditions of the old Roman Empire, and its people even called themselves Romans. Byzantine emperors traced their lines back past Constantine to Augustus. The senate that sat in Constantinople carried on the traditions and preserved the glory of the old Roman senate. The army that defended the empire was the direct descendant of the old Roman legions. Even the chariot factions of the Roman Empire lived on under the Byzantines, who cheered their favorites as enthusiastically as had the Romans of Hadrian's day. The Byzantine Empire maintained a high standard of living, and for centuries the Greeks were the most civilized people in the Western world. Most important, however, is the role of Byzantium as preserver of the wisdom of the ancient world. Byzantium protected the intellectual heritage of Greco-Roman civilization and then passed it on to the rest of Europe.

● *How was the Byzantine Empire able to survive for so long, and what were its most important achievements?*

Sources of Byzantine Strength

While the Western parts of the Roman Empire gradually succumbed to Germanic invaders, the Eastern Roman or Byzantine Empire survived Germanic, Persian, and Arab attacks. In 540 the Huns and Bulgars crossed the Danube and raided the Balkans as far south as the Isthmus of Corinth. In 559 a force of Huns and Slavs reached the gates of Constantinople. In 583 the Avars, a mounted Mongol people who had swept across Russia and southeastern Europe, seized Byzantine forts along the Danube and reached the walls of Constantinople. Between 572 and 630 the Sasanid Persians posed a formidable threat, and the Greeks were repeatedly at war with them. Beginning in 632 the Arabs pressured the Greek empire (see Chapter 8).

Why didn't one or a combination of these enemies capture Constantinople as the Germans had taken Rome? The answer lies in strong military leadership and even more in the city's location and its excellent fortifications. Under the skillful leadership of General Priskos (d. 612), Byzantine armies inflicted a severe defeat on the Avars in 601. Then, after a long war, the emperor Heraclius I (r. 610–641), helped by dynastic disputes among the Persians and Muslim pressures on them, crushed the Persians at Nineveh in Iraq. Massive triple walls, built by Constantine and Theodosius II (408–450) and kept in good repair, protected Constantinople from sea invasion. Within the walls huge cisterns provided water, and vast gardens and grazing areas supplied vegetables and meat. Such strong fortifications and provisions meant that, if attacked by sea, the defending people could hold out far longer than the besieging army. Attacking Constantinople by land posed greater geographical and logistical problems than a seventh- or eighth-century government could solve. The site was not absolutely impregnable—as the Venetians demonstrated in 1204 and the Ottoman Turks in 1453 (see pages 284 and 580)—but it was almost so. For centuries, the Byzantine Empire served as a bulwark for the West, protecting it against invasions from the East.

The Law Code of Justinian

One of the most splendid achievements of the Byzantine emperors was the preservation of Roman law for the medieval and modern worlds. Roman law had developed from many sources—decisions by judges, edicts of the emperors, legislation passed by the senate, and the opinions of jurists expert in the theory and practice of law. By the fourth century, it had become a huge, bewildering mass,

Chronology

312	Constantine legalizes Christianity in Roman Empire
340–419	Life of Saint Jerome; creation of the Vulgate
354–430	Life of Saint Augustine
380	Theodosius makes Christianity official religion of Roman Empire
385–461	Life of Saint Patrick
481–511	Reign of Clovis
527–565	Reign of Justinian
529	*The Rule of Saint Benedict*
542–560	"Justinian plague"

and its sheer bulk made it almost unusable. Some laws were outdated; some repeated or contradicted others.

Sweeping and systematic codification took place under the emperor Justinian. He appointed a committee of eminent jurists to sort through and organize the laws. The result was the *Code,* which distilled the legal genius of the Romans into a coherent whole, eliminated outmoded laws and contradictions, and clarified the law itself. Not content with the *Code,* Justinian set about bringing order to the equally huge body of Roman *jurisprudence,* the science or philosophy of law.

During the second and third centuries, the foremost Roman jurists had expressed varied learned opinions on complex legal problems. To harmonize this body of knowledge, Justinian directed his jurists to clear up disputed points and to issue definitive rulings. Accordingly, in 533 his lawyers published the *Digest,* which codified Roman legal thought. Finally, Justinian's lawyers compiled a handbook of civil law, the *Institutes.* These three works—the *Code,* the *Digest,* and the *Institutes*—are the backbone of the *corpus juris civilis,* the "body of civil law," which is the foundation of law for nearly every modern European nation.

Online Study Center **Improve Your Grade**
Primary Source: The Corpus Juris Civilis of Justinian Addresses the Problem of Adultery

The following excerpts on marriage and adultery from the corpus juris civilis provide valuable information on gender relations in Roman and Byzantine law:

Justinian and His Attendants   This mosaic detail is composed of thousands of tiny cubes of colored glass or stone called *tessarae*, which are set in plaster against a blazing golden background. Some attempt has been made at naturalistic portraiture. *(Scala/Art Resource, NY)*

—Roman citizens unite in legal marriage when they are joined according to the precepts of the law, and males have attained the age of puberty and the females are capable of childbirth . . . [they must] if the latter have also the consent of the relatives under whose authority they may be, for this should be obtained and both civil and natural law require that it should be secured.

—The lex Julia ["Julian law," dating from 18 B.C.] declares that wives have no right to bring criminal accusations for adultery against their husbands, even though they may desire to complain of the violation of the marriage vow, for while the law grants this privilege to men it does not concede it to women.[1]

Byzantine Intellectual Life

The Byzantines prized education; because of them many masterpieces of ancient Greek literature have survived to

influence the intellectual life of the modern world. The literature of the Byzantine Empire was predominately Greek, although Latin was long spoken by top politicians, scholars, and lawyers. Indeed, Justinian's *Code* was first written in Latin. Among the large reading public, history was a favorite subject. Generations of Byzantines read the historical works of Herodotus, Thucydides, and others. Some Byzantine historians abbreviated long histories, such as those of Polybius, while others wrote detailed narratives of their own days.

The most remarkable Byzantine historian was Procopius (ca 500–ca 562), who left a rousing account praising Justinian's reconquest of North Africa and Italy. Proof that the wit and venom of ancient writers such as Archilochus and Aristophanes lived on in the Byzantine era can be found in Procopius's *Secret History*, a vicious and uproarious attack on Justinian and his wife, the empress Theodora. (See the feature "Individuals in Society:

Individuals in Society

Theodora of Constantinople

The most powerful woman in Byzantine history was the daughter of a bear trainer for the circus. Theodora (ca 497–548) grew up in what her contemporaries regarded as an undignified and morally suspect atmosphere, and she worked as a dancer and burlesque actress, both dishonorable occupations in the Roman world. Despite her background, she caught the eye of Justinian, who was then a military leader and whose uncle (and adoptive father) Justin had himself risen from obscurity to become the emperor of the Byzantine Empire. Under Justinian's influence, Justin changed the law to allow an actress who had left her disreputable life to marry whom she liked, and Justinian and Theodora married in 525. When Justinian was proclaimed co-emperor with his uncle Justin on April 1, 527, Theodora received the rare title of *augusta*, empress. Thereafter her name was linked with Justinian's in the exercise of imperial power.

Most of our knowledge of Theodora's early life comes from the *Secret History*, a tell-all description of the vices of Justinian and his court, written by Procopius (ca 550), who was the official court historian and thus spent his days praising those same people. In the *Secret History*, he portrays Theodora and Justinian as demonic, greedy, and vicious, killing courtiers to steal their property. In scene after detailed scene, Procopius portrays Theodora as particularly evil, sexually insatiable, depraved, and cruel, a temptress who used sorcery to attract men, including the hapless Justinian.

In one of his official histories, *The History of the Wars of Justinian*, Procopius presents a very different Theodora. Riots between the supporters of two teams in chariot races—who formed associations somewhat like street gangs and somewhat like political parties—had turned deadly, and Justinian wavered in his handling of the perpetrators. Both sides turned against the emperor, besieging the palace while Justinian was inside it. Shouting N-I-K-A (Victory), the rioters swept through the city, burning and looting, and destroyed half of Constantinople. Justinian's counselors urged flight, but, according to Procopius, Theodora rose and declared:

For one who has reigned, it is intolerable to be an exile. . . . If you wish, O Emperor, to save yourself, there is no difficulty: we have ample funds and there are the ships. Yet reflect whether, when you have once escaped to a place of security, you will not prefer death to safety. I agree with an old saying that the purple [that is, the color worn only by emperors] is a fair winding sheet to be buried in].

Justinian rallied, had the rioters driven into the hippodrome, and ordered between thirty and thirty-five thousand men and women executed. The revolt was crushed and Justinian's authority restored, an outcome approved by Procopius.

Other sources describe or suggest Theodora's influence on imperial policy. Justinian passed a number of laws that improved the legal status of women, such as allowing women to own property the same way that men could and to be guardians over their own children. Justinian is reputed to have consulted her every day about all aspects of state policy, including religious policy regarding the doctrinal disputes that continued throughout his reign.

Theodora's influence over her husband and her power in the Byzantine state continued until she died, perhaps of cancer, twenty years before Justinian. Her influence may have even continued after death, for Justinian continued to pass reforms favoring women and, at the end of his life, accepted her interpretation of Christian doctrine. Institutions that she established, including hospitals, orphanages, houses for the rehabilitation of prostitutes, and churches, continued to be reminders of her charity and piety.

Theodora has been viewed as a symbol of the manipulation of beauty and cleverness to attain position and power, and also as a strong and capable co-ruler who held the empire together during riots, revolts, and deadly epidemics. Just as Procopius expressed both views, the debate has continued to today among writers of science fiction and fantasy as well as biographers and historians.

The empress Theodora shown with the halo—symbolic of power in Eastern art. (Scala/Art Resource, NY)

Questions for Analysis

1. How would you assess the complex legacy of Theodora?
2. Since the public and private views of Procopius are so different regarding the empress, should he be trusted at all as a historical source?

Online Study Center **Improve Your Grade**
Going Beyond Individuals in Society

Theodora of Constantinople.") Witness Procopius's description of Justinian's character:

For he was at once villainous and amenable; as people say colloquially, a moron. He was never truthful with anyone, but always guileful in what he said and did, yet easily hoodwinked by any who wanted to deceive him. His nature was an unnatural mixture of folly and wickedness.[2]

How much of this is true and how much the hostility of a sanctimonious hypocrite relishing the gossip he spreads, we will never know. Certainly *The Secret History* is robust reading.

Byzantine Science and Medicine

Although the Byzantines discovered little that was new in mathematics and geometry, they passed Greco-Roman learning on to the Arabs, who assimilated it and made remarkable advances with it. The Byzantines were equally uncreative in astronomy and natural science, but they faithfully learned what the ancients had to teach. Only when science could be put to military use did they make advances. For example, the best-known Byzantine scientific discovery was chemical—"Greek fire" or "liquid fire," an explosive compound of crude oil mixed with resin and sulfur that was heated and propelled by a pump through a bronze tube. As the liquid jet left the tube, it was ignited—somewhat like a modern flamethrower. Greek fire saved Constantinople from Arab assault in 678. In mechanics the Byzantines continued the work of Hellenistic and Roman inventors of artillery and siege machinery. Just as Archimedes had devised machines to stop the Romans, so Byzantine scientists improved and modified devices for defending their empire.

The Byzantines devoted a great deal of attention to medicine, and the general level of medical competence was far higher in the Byzantine Empire than in western Europe.

The Byzantines assimilated the discoveries of Hellenic and Hellenistic medicine but added very few of their own. The basis of their medical theory was Hippocrates' concept of the four humors (see page 85). Byzantine physicians emphasized the importance of diet and rest and relied heavily on herbal medicines. Perhaps their most dangerous practice was excessive use of bleeding and burning, which often further weakened already feeble patients.

Greek medical science could not cope with the terrible disease, often called the "Justinian plague," that swept through the Byzantine Empire, Italy, southern France, Iberia, and the Rhine Valley between 542 and about 560. Probably originating in northwestern India and carried to the Mediterranean region by ships, the disease was similar to modern forms of the bubonic plague. Characterized by high fever, chills, delirium, and enlarged lymph nodes (the buboes that gave bubonic plague its name), or by inflammation of the lungs that caused hemorrhages of black blood, the Justinian plague carried off tens of thousands of people. The epidemic had profound political as well as social consequences. It weakened Justinian's military resources, thus hampering his efforts to restore unity to the Mediterranean world.

Anicia Juliana (462?–528?) The daughter of a Byzantine emperor and a great benefactor of the church and the arts, Anicia Juliana commissioned a manuscript of the works of the physician Dioscorides (fl. first century) on herbal medicines, which remained the standard reference work on the subject for centuries. She is shown here seated between two Virtues, Magnanimity and Patience. *(Austrian National Library Picture Archive)*

By the ninth or tenth century, most major Greek cities had hospitals for the care of the sick. The hospital operated by the Pantokrator monastery in Constantinople possessed fifty beds divided into five wards for different illnesses. Hospital staff included a specialist in the functions and diseases of the eye, a surgeon who performed hernia repairs, two general practitioners, two surgeons who worked an outpatient clinic, a female medical practitioner who handled diseases of women, and an attendant responsible for keeping instruments clean. The imperial Byzantine government bore the costs of this and other hospitals.

The Growth of the Christian Church

As the Western Roman Empire disintegrated in the fourth and fifth centuries, the Christian church survived and grew, becoming the most important institution in Europe. The able administrators and highly creative thinkers of the church developed permanent institutions and complex philosophical concepts.

• *What factors enabled the Christian church to expand and thrive?*

The Idea of a Church

Scriptural scholars tell us that the earliest use of the word *church* in the New Testament appears in Saint Paul's Letter to the Christians of Thessalonica in northern Greece, written about A.D. 51. *Church* means assembly or congregation (in Greek, *ekklesia*); by *ekklesia* Paul meant the local community of Christian believers. In Paul's later letters the word refers to the entire Mediterranean-wide assembly of Jesus' followers. After the legalization of Christianity by the emperor Constantine (see page 181) and the growth of institutional offices and officials, the word *church* was sometimes applied to those officials—much as we use the terms *the college* or *the university* when referring to academic administrators.

In early Christian communities the local people elected their leaders, or bishops. Bishops were men with reputations for having special spiritual charisma or with acknowledged administrative ability, learning, or preaching skills. Bishops were responsible for the community's goods and oversaw the distribution of those goods to the poor. They also were responsible for maintaining orthodox (established or correct) doctrine within the community and for preaching. Bishops alone could confirm believers in their faith and ordain men as priests.

The bishops of Rome used the text known as the Petrine Doctrine (see page 198) to support their assertions of authority over the bishops in the church. Thus the popes maintained that they represented "the church." The word *church,* therefore, has several connotations. Although modern Catholic theology frequently defines the church as "the people of God" and identifies it with local and international Christian communities, in the Middle Ages the institutional and monarchical interpretations tended to be stressed.

The Church and the Roman Emperors

The church benefited considerably from the emperors' support. In return, the emperors expected the support of the Christian church in maintaining order and unity. Constantine had legalized the practice of Christianity in the empire in 312 and encouraged it throughout his reign. He freed the clergy from imperial taxation. At churchmen's request, he helped settle theological disputes and thus preserved doctrinal unity within the church. Constantine generously endowed the building of Christian churches, and one of his gifts—the Lateran Palace in Rome—remained the official residence of the popes until the fourteenth century. Constantine also declared Sunday a public holiday, a day of rest for the service of God. Because of its favored position in the empire, Christianity slowly became the leading religion (see Map 7.2).

In 380 the emperor Theodosius made Christianity the official religion of the empire. Theodosius stripped Roman pagan temples of statues, made the practice of the old Roman state religion a treasonable offense, and persecuted Christians who dissented from orthodox doctrine. Most significant, he allowed the church to establish its own courts and to use its own body of law, called "canon law." These courts, not the Roman government, had jurisdiction over the clergy and ecclesiastical disputes. At the death of Theodosius, the Christian church was considerably independent of the Roman state. The foundation for later growth in church power had been laid.

What was to be the church's relationship to secular powers? How was the Christian to render unto Caesar the things that were Caesar's while returning to God what was due to God? This problem had troubled the earliest disciples of Christ. The toleration of Christianity and the coming to power of Christian emperors in the fourth century did not make it any easier.

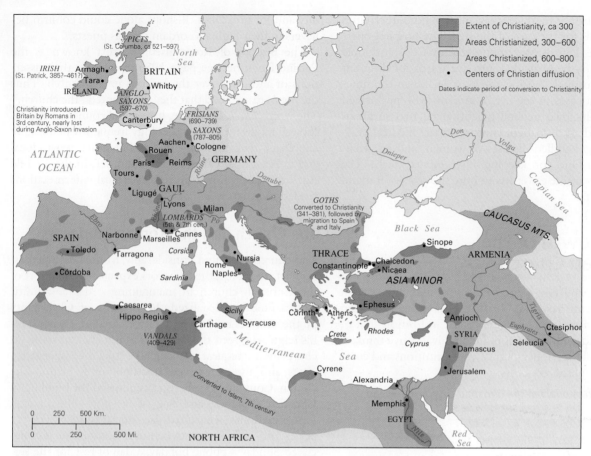

MAP 7.2 The Spread of Christianity Originating in Judaea, the southern part of modern Israel and Jordan, Christianity first spread throughout the Roman world and then beyond it in all directions.

Online Study Center **Improve Your Grade** Interactive Map: Spread of Christianity

In the fourth century, theological disputes frequently and sharply divided the Christian community. Some disagreements had to do with the nature of Christ. For example, **Arianism,** which originated with Arius (ca 250–336), a priest of Alexandria, denied that Christ was divine and co-eternal with God the Father—two propositions of orthodox Christian belief. Arius held that God the Father was by definition uncreated and unchangeable. Jesus, however, was born of Mary, grew in wisdom, and suffered punishment and death. Therefore, Arius reasoned, Jesus the Son must be less or inferior to the Unbegotten Father, who was incapable of suffering and did not die. Jesus was created by the will of the Father and thus was not co-eternal with the Father. Orthodox theologians branded Arius's position a heresy—the denial of a basic doctrine of faith.

Arianism enjoyed such popularity and provoked such controversy that Constantine, to whom religious disagreement meant civil disorder, interceded. He summoned church leaders to a council in Nicaea in Asia Minor and presided over it personally. The council produced the Nicene Creed, which defined the orthodox position that Christ is "eternally begotten of the Father" and of the same substance as the Father. Arius and those who refused to accept the creed were banished, the first case of civil punishment for heresy. This participation of the emperor in a theological dispute within the church paved the way for later emperors to do the same.

So active was the emperor Theodosius in church matters that he was eventually at loggerheads with Bishop Ambrose of Milan (339–397). Theodosius ordered Ambrose to hand over his cathedral church to the emperor.

Ambrose's response had important consequences for the future:

At length came the command, "Deliver up the Basilica"; I reply, "It is not lawful for us to deliver it up, nor for your Majesty to receive it. By no law can you violate the house of a private man, and do you think that the house of God may be taken away? . . . But do not burden your conscience with the thought that you have any right as Emperor over sacred things. . . . It is written, God's to God and Caesar's to Caesar. The palace is the Emperor's, the churches are the Bishop's. To you is committed jurisdiction over public, not over sacred buildings."[3]

Ambrose's statement was to serve as the cornerstone of the Christian theory of civil-ecclesiastical relations for centuries. Ambrose insisted that the church was independent of the state's jurisdiction and that, in matters relating to the faith or the church, the bishops were to be the judges of emperors, not the other way around. In a Christian society harmony and peace depended on agreement between the bishop and the secular ruler. But if disagreement developed, the church was ultimately the superior power because the church was responsible for the salvation of all (including the emperor). In a letter to the emperor Anastasius I, Pope Gelasius I (492–496) put this idea another way, stating that both the civil and the religious authorities were created by God and were essential to a well-ordered Christian society. Each was supreme in its own domain—the church in the spiritual, the civil in the secular—and cooperation in building a Christian society was their mutual responsibility. In later centuries, theologians, canonists, and propagandists repeatedly cited Ambrose's and Gelasius's position as the basis of relations between the two powers.

Online Study Center **Improve Your Grade**
Primary Source: An Emperor Brought to Heel: Saint Ambrose and Emperor Theodosius

Later Byzantine emperors continued the pattern of active involvement in church affairs. They appointed the highest officials of the church hierarchy; the emperors or their representatives presided at ecumenical councils; and the emperors controlled some of the material resources of the church—land, rents, and dependent peasantry. On the other hand, the emperors performed few liturgical functions and rarely tried to impose their views in theological disputes. Greek churchmen vigorously defended the church's independence; some even asserted the superiority of the bishop's authority over the emperor; and the church possessed such enormous economic wealth and influence over the population that it could block

government decisions. The **Orthodox church,** the name generally given to the Eastern Christian church, was less independent of secular control than the Western Christian church, but it was not simply a branch of the Byzantine state.

The steady separation of the Byzantine East and the Germanic West rests partly on the ways Christianity and classical culture were received in the two parts of the Roman Empire. In the West, Christians initially constituted a small, alien minority within the broad Roman culture; they kept apart from the rest of society. In Byzantium, by contrast, most Greeks were Christian. *Apologists,* or defenders, of Christianity insisted on harmony between Christianity and classical culture: they used Greek philosophy to buttress Christian tenets. In late antiquity the two parts of the Christian church were not completely separate, however. Most church theology in the West came from the East. Until the eighth century, the popes, who were often selected by the clergy of Rome, continued to send announcements of their elections to the emperors at Constantinople—a sign that the Roman popes long thought of themselves as bishops of the Roman Empire.

Bishops and the Pope

The early Christian church benefited from the brilliant administrative abilities of some church leaders and from identification of the authority and dignity of the bishop of Rome with the imperial traditions of the city. With the empire in decay, educated people joined and worked for the church in the belief that it was the one institution able to provide leadership. Bishop Ambrose, for example, the son of the Roman prefect of Gaul, was a trained lawyer and the governor of a province. He is typical of the Roman aristocrats who held high public office, were converted to Christianity, and subsequently became bishops. Such men later provided social continuity from Roman to Germanic rule. As bishop of Milan, Ambrose himself exercised responsibility in the temporal as well as the ecclesiastical affairs of northern Italy.

During the reign of Diocletian (284–305), the Roman Empire had been divided for administrative purposes into geographical units called dioceses. Gradually the church made use of this organizational structure. Christian bishops established their headquarters, or sees, in the urban centers of the old Roman dioceses. A bishop's jurisdiction extended throughout the diocese. The center of his authority was his cathedral (from the Latin *cathedra,* meaning "chair"). Thus, church leaders capitalized on the Roman imperial method of organization and adapted it to ecclesiastical purposes.

The bishops of Rome—known as "popes," from the Latin word *papa,* meaning "father"—claimed to speak and act as the source of unity for all Christians. They based their claim to be the successors of Saint Peter and heirs to his authority as chief of the apostles on Jesus' words:

You are Peter, and on this rock I will build my church, and the jaws of death shall not prevail against it. I will entrust to you the keys of the kingdom of heaven. Whatever you declare bound on earth shall be bound in heaven; whatever you declare loosed on earth shall be loosed in heaven.[4]

Theologians call this statement the **Petrine Doctrine.**

After the removal of the capital and the emperor to Constantinople (see page 182), the bishop of Rome exercised considerable influence in the West because he had no real competitor there. The bishops of Rome stressed that Rome had been the capital of a worldwide empire and emphasized the special importance of Rome in the framework of that empire. Successive bishops of Rome reminded Christians in other parts of the world that Rome was the burial place of Saint Peter and Saint Paul. Moreover, according to tradition, Saint Peter, the chief of Christ's first twelve followers, had lived and had been executed in Rome. No other city in the world could make such claims. Hence the bishop of Rome was called "Patriarch of the West." In the East, the bishops of Antioch, Alexandria, Jerusalem, and Constantinople, because of the special dignity of their sees, also gained the title of patriarch. Their jurisdictions extended over lands adjoining their sees; they consecrated bishops, investigated heresy, and heard judicial appeals.

In the fifth century the bishops of Rome began to stress their supremacy over other Christian communities and to urge other churches to appeal to Rome for the resolution of disputed doctrinal issues. Thus Pope Innocent I (401–417) wrote to the bishops of Africa:

We approve your action in following the principle that nothing which was done even in the most remote and distant provinces should be taken as finally settled unless it came to the notice of this See, that any just pronouncement might be confirmed by all the authority of this See.[5]

The prestige of Rome and of the church as a whole was also enhanced by the courage and leadership of the Roman bishops. As described in Chapter 6 (see page 183), church officials played important roles in addressing civil problems previously handled by Roman imperial authorities. The fact that it was Christian leaders, rather than imperial administrators, who responded to dire urban needs could not help but increase the prestige and influence of the church.

Although Popes Innocent I and Leo I (440–461) strongly asserted the primacy of the Roman papacy, local Christian communities and their leaders often exercised authority over their churches. Particular social and political situations determined the actual power of the bishop of Rome in a given circumstance. The importance of arguments for the Roman primacy rests in the fact that they served as precedents for later appeals.

The Development of Christian Monasticism

Christianity began and spread as a city religion. Since the first century, however, some especially pious Christians had felt that the only alternative to the decadence of urban life was complete separation from the world. All-consuming pursuit of material things, gross sexual promiscuity, and general political corruption disgusted them. They believed that the Christian life as set forth in the Gospel could not be lived in the midst of such immorality. They rejected the values of Roman society and were the first real nonconformists in the church.

The fourth century witnessed a significant change in the relationship of Christianity and the broader society. Until Constantine's legalization of Christianity, Christians were a persecuted minority. People were tortured and killed for their faith. Christians greatly revered these martyrs, the men and women who, like Jesus, suffered and died for their faith. When Christianity was legalized and the persecutions ended, a new problem arose. Whereas Christians had been a suffering minority, now they came to be identified with the state: non-Christians could not advance in the imperial service. And if Christianity had triumphed, so too had "the world," since secular attitudes and values pervaded the church. The church of martyrs no longer existed. Some scholars believe that the monasteries provided a way of life for those Christians who wanted to make a total response to Christ's teachings; the monks became the new martyrs. Saint Anthony of Egypt (251?–356), the earliest monk for whom there is concrete evidence and the man later considered the father of monasticism, went to Alexandria during the last persecution in the hope of gaining martyrdom. Christians believed that monks, like the martyrs before them, could speak to God and that their prayers had special influence.

Monasticism began in Egypt in the third century. At first individuals and small groups withdrew from cities and organized society to seek God through prayer in desert or mountain caves and shelters. Gradually large colonies of monks gathered in the deserts of Upper Egypt. These monks were called hermits, from the Greek word *eremos,* meaning "desert." Many devout women also were attracted to this **eremitical** life. We have no way of knowing how many hermits there were in the fourth and fifth centuries because their conscious aim was a hidden life known only to God. Although monks and nuns led isolated lives and the monastic movement represented the antithesis of the ancient ideal of an urban social existence, ordinary people soon recognized the monks and nuns as holy people and sought them as spiritual guides.

Some church leaders did not approve of eremitical life, however. Hermits sometimes claimed to have mystical experiences, direct communications with God. If hermits could communicate directly with the Lord, what need had they for the priest and the institutional church? Saint Basil (329?–379), the scholarly bishop of Caesarea in Cappadocia in Asia Minor, opposed the eremitical life on other grounds: the impossibility of material self-sufficiency; the danger of excessive concern with the self; and the fact that the eremitical life did not provide the opportunity for the exercise of charity, the first virtue of any Christian. The Egyptian ascetic Pachomius (290–346?) had organized communities of men and women at his coenobitic (communal) monastery at Tabennisi on the Upper Nile, drawing thousands of recruits. Saint Basil and the church hierarchy encouraged **coenobitic monasticism,** communal living in monasteries. Communal living, they felt, provided an environment for training the aspirant in the virtues of charity, poverty, and freedom from self-deception.

Western and Eastern Monasticism

In the fourth, fifth, and sixth centuries, information about Egyptian monasticism came to the West, and both men and women sought the monastic life. When monasticism spread to western Europe, several factors worked against the continuation of the eremitical form. The harsh weather of northern Europe that lasted for many months of the year discouraged isolated living. In the dense forests, wild animals and wandering Germanic tribes presented obvious dangers. Thus most of the monasticism that developed in Gaul, Italy, Spain, England, and Ireland was coenobitic.

In 529 Benedict of Nursia (480–543), who had experimented with both the eremitical and the communal forms of monastic life, wrote a brief set of regulations for the monks who had gathered around him at Monte Cassino between Rome and Naples. Benedict's guide for monastic life proved more adaptable than and slowly replaced all others. *The Rule of Saint Benedict* came to influence all forms of organized religious life in the Roman church. Men and women who lived in monastic houses all followed sets of rules, first those of Benedict and later those written by other individuals, and because of this came to be called **regular clergy,** from the Latin word *regulus* (rule). Priests and bishops who staffed churches in which people worshiped and who were not cut off from the world were called **secular clergy.** (According to official church doctrine, women are not members of the clergy, but this distinction was not clear to most medieval people.)

Saint Benedict conceived of his *Rule* as a simple code for ordinary men. It outlined a monastic life of regularity, discipline, and moderation in an atmosphere of silence. Each monk had ample food and adequate sleep. The monk spent part of each day in formal prayer, which Benedict called the *Opus Dei* (Work of God) and Christians later termed the divine office, the public prayer of the church. This consisted of chanting psalms and other prayers from the Bible in that part of the monastery church called the "choir." The rest of the day was passed in manual labor, study, and private prayer.

Online Study Center **Improve Your Grade**
Primary Source: The Rule of Saint Benedict: Work and Pray

Why did the Benedictine form of monasticism eventually replace other forms of Western monasticism? The answer lies partly in its spirit of flexibility and moderation and partly in the balanced life it provided. Early Benedictine monks and nuns spent part of the day in prayer, part in study or some other form of intellectual activity, and part in manual labor. The monastic life as conceived by Saint Benedict struck a balance between asceticism and activity. It thus provided opportunities for men of entirely different abilities and talents—from mechanics to gardeners to literary scholars. The Benedictine form of religious life also proved congenial to women. Five miles from Monte Cassino at Plombariola, Benedict's twin sister Scholastica (480–543) adapted the *Rule* for the use of her community of nuns. The adoption of Benedict's *Rule* by houses of women paralleled that in houses of men.

Benedictine monasticism also succeeded partly because it was so materially successful. In the seventh and eighth centuries monasteries pushed back forests and wastelands, drained swamps, and experimented with crop rotation. Benedictine houses made a significant contribution to the agricultural development of Europe. The communal nature of their organization, whereby property was held in common and profits were pooled and reinvested, made this contribution possible.

Finally, monasteries conducted schools for local young people. Some learned about prescriptions and herbal remedies and went on to provide medical treatment in their localities. A few copied manuscripts and wrote books. Local and royal governments drew on the services of the literate men and able administrators the monasteries produced. This was not what Saint Benedict had intended, but perhaps the effectiveness of the institution he designed made it inevitable.

Monasticism in the Greek Orthodox world differed in fundamental ways from the monasticism that evolved in western Europe. First, while *The Rule of Saint Benedict* gradually became the universal guide for all western European monasteries, each individual house in the Byzantine world developed its own *typikon,* or set of rules for organization and behavior. The *typika* contain regulations about novitiate, diet, clothing, liturgical functions, commemorative services for benefactors, and the election of officials, such as the *hegoumenos,* or superior of the house. Second, education never became a central feature of the Greek houses. Monks and nuns had to be literate to perform the services of the choir, but no monastery assumed responsibility for the general training of the local young.

There were also similarities between Western and Eastern monasticism. As in the West, Eastern monasteries became wealthy, with fields, pastures, livestock, and buildings. Since bishops and patriarchs of the Greek church were recruited only from the monasteries, Greek houses also exercised cultural influence.

Christian Ideas and Practices

The growth of Christianity was not simply a matter of institutions such as the papacy and monasteries, but also of ideas. Christian beliefs and practices changed as different groups of people accepted Christianity and as the political and social context changed.

• *How did Christian ideas and practices respond to changing political and social circumstances in the Roman Empire?*

Saint Benedict Holding his *Rule* in his left hand, the seated and cowled patriarch of Western monasticism blesses a monk with his right hand. His monastery, Monte Cassino, is in the background. (*Biblioteca Apostolica Vaticana*)

Christianity and Classical Culture

Christians were initially a tiny marginal group, but Christianity eventually became the official religion of the Roman Empire. As this happened, Christian leaders and thinkers, especially those who were highly educated, gradually came to terms with classical culture. Elements of Greek and Roman philosophy and of various pre-Christian religious beliefs were incorporated into Christian teachings.

Christians in the first and second centuries believed that the end of the world was near. They expected to witness the return of Christ, and therefore they considered knowledge useless and learning a waste of time. The important duty of the Christian was to prepare for the Second Coming of the Lord. Good Christians who sought the Kingdom of Heaven through the imitation of Christ believed that they had to disassociate themselves from the "filth" that Roman culture embodied.

As Saint Paul wrote, "The wisdom of the world is foolishness, we preach Christ crucified." Tertullian (ca 160–220), an influential African church father and writer, condemned all secular literature as foolishness in the eyes of God. He called Greek philosophers such as Aristotle "hucksters of eloquence" and compared them to "animals of self-glorification." "What has Athens to do with Jerusalem," he demanded, "the Academy with the Church? We have no need for curiosity since Jesus Christ, nor for inquiry since the gospel." Tertullian insisted that Christians would find all the wisdom they needed in the Bible.

On the other hand, Christianity encouraged adjustment to the ideas and institutions of the Roman world. Some biblical texts urged Christians to accept the existing social, economic, and political establishment. Specifically addressing Christians living among non-Christians in the hostile environment of Rome, the author of the First Letter of Peter had written about the obligations of Christians:

Always behave honorably among pagans, so that they can see your good works for themselves and, when the day of reckoning comes, give thanks to God for the things which now make them denounce you as criminals. . . .

For the sake of the Lord, accept the authority of every social institution: the emperor, as the supreme authority, and the governors as commissioned by him to punish criminals and praise good citizenship. God wants you to be good citizens. . . . Have respect for everyone and love for your community; fear God and honour the emperor.[6]

Even had early Christians wanted to give up Greco-Roman ideas and patterns of thought, they would have had great difficulty doing so. Therefore, they had to adapt their Roman education to their Christian beliefs. Saint Paul himself believed that there was a good deal of truth in pagan thought, as long as it was correctly interpreted and understood.

The result was a compromise. Christians gradually came to terms with Greco-Roman culture. Saint Jerome (340–419), a distinguished theologian and linguist, remains famous for his translation of the Old and New Testaments from Hebrew and Greek into vernacular Latin. Called the "Vulgate," his edition of the Bible served as the official translation until the sixteenth century, and scholars rely on it even today. Familiar with the writings of classical authors, Saint Jerome also believed that Christians should study the best of ancient thought because it would direct their minds to God. He maintained that the best ancient literature should be interpreted in light of the Christian faith.

Christian Notions of Gender and Sexuality

Christian attitudes toward gender and sexuality illustrate the ways early Christians adopted the views of their contemporary world. In his plan of salvation, Jesus, whom Christians accept as the Messiah, considered women the equal of men. He attributed no disreputable qualities to women and did not refer to them as inferior creatures. On the contrary, women were among his earliest and most faithful converts. He discussed his mission with them (John 4:21–25), and the first persons to whom he revealed himself after his resurrection were women (Matthew 28:9–10).

Women took an active role in the spread of Christianity, preaching, acting as missionaries, being martyred alongside men, and perhaps even baptizing believers. Early Christians expected Jesus to return to earth very soon and taught that people should concentrate on this Second Coming. Because of this, marriage and normal family life should be abandoned, and Christians should depend on their new spiritual family of co-believers. Early Christians often met in people's homes and called one another brother and sister, a metaphorical use of family terms that was new to the Roman Empire in which Christianity developed. Some women embraced the ideal of virginity and either singly or in monastic communities declared themselves "virgins in the service of Christ." All this made Christianity seem dangerous to many Romans, especially when becoming Christian actually led some young people to avoid marriage, which was viewed by Romans as the foundation of society and the proper patriarchal order.

Not all Christian teachings about gender were radical, however. Many early followers of Jesus, particularly the Apostle Paul, whose letters make up a major part of the New Testament, had ambivalent ideas about women's proper role in the church, and in the first century A.D. they began to place restrictions on female believers. Paul and later writers forbade women to preach, and women were gradually excluded from holding official positions in Christianity other than in women's monasteries. Women in monasteries were to be considered not virgins who had chosen to serve Christ, but rather "brides of

The Marys at Jesus' Tomb This late-fourth-century ivory panel tells the story of Mary Magdalene and another Mary who went to Jesus' tomb to anoint the body (Matthew 28:1–7). At the top guards collapse when an angel descends from Heaven, and at the bottom the Marys listen to the angel telling them that Jesus had risen. Immediately after this, in Matthew's Gospel, Jesus appears to the women. Here the artist uses Roman artistic styles to convey Christian subject matter, an example of the assimilation of classical form and Christian teaching. *(Castello Sforzesco/Scala/Art Resource, NY)*

Christ," that is, in a dependent relationship with a man. Both Jewish and classical Mediterranean culture viewed female subordination as natural and proper, so in limiting the activities of female believers Christianity was following well-established patterns, just as it patterned its official hierarchy after that of the Roman Empire.

Christian teachings about sexuality also built on classical culture. Many early church leaders, who are often called the church fathers, renounced marriage and sought to live chaste lives not only because they expected the Second Coming imminently, but also because they accepted the hostility toward the body that derived from certain strains of Hellenistic philosophy. Just as spirit was superior to matter, the mind was superior to the body. The church fathers acknowledged that God had established marriage for the generation of children, but they believed it to be a concession to weak souls who could not bear celibacy. Though God had clearly sanctioned marriage, celibacy was the highest good. This emphasis on self-denial led to a strong streak of misogyny (hatred of women) in their writings, for they saw women and female sexuality as the chief obstacles to their preferred existence. They also saw intercourse as little more than animal lust, the triumph of the inferior body over the superior mind. Same-sex relations—which were generally acceptable in the Greco-Roman world, especially if they were between socially unequal individuals—were evil, though only slightly worse than other types of sexual relations because they could not lead to procreation. The church fathers' misogyny and hostility toward sexuality had a greater influence on the formation of later attitudes than did the relatively egalitarian actions and words of Jesus.

Saint Augustine on Human Nature, Will, and Sin

The most influential church father in the West was Saint Augustine of Hippo (354–430). Saint Augustine was born into an urban family in what is now Algeria in North Africa. His father, a minor civil servant, was a pagan; his mother, Monica, a devout Christian. Because his family was poor, the only avenue to success in a highly competitive world was a classical education.

Augustine's mother believed that a good classical education, although pagan, would make her son a better Christian, so the child received his basic education in the local school. At the age of seventeen, Augustine went to nearby Carthage to continue his education. There he experimented with several philosophies and Christian groups whose ideas differed from those of most church authorities. As was normal for young Roman men, he began relations with a concubine, who later had a son. In 383 he traveled to Rome, where he endured not only illness but also disappointment in his teaching: his students fled when their bills were due.

Augustine then took a teaching position in Milan, where he had frequent conversations with Bishop Ambrose. Through these, and through insights gained from reading Saint Paul's Letter to the Romans, Augustine became a Christian, receiving Christian baptism from Ambrose, who also baptized his son. Augustine returned to Africa, where his mother and son soon died, and later became bishop of the seacoast city of Hippo Regius. He was a renowned preacher to Christians there, a vigorous defender of orthodox Christianity, and the author of more than ninety-three books and treatises.

Augustine's autobiography, *The Confessions,* is a literary masterpiece and one of the most influential books in the history of Europe. Written in the rhetorical style and language of late Roman antiquity, it marks the synthesis of Greco-Roman forms and Christian thought. *The Confessions* describes Augustine's moral struggle, the conflict between his spiritual and intellectual aspirations and his sensual and material self. Many Greek and Roman philosophers had taught that knowledge and virtue are the same: a person who knows what is right will do what is right. Augustine rejected this idea. He believed that a person may know what is right but fail to act righteously because of the innate weakness of the human will. People do not always act on the basis of rational knowledge. For example, Augustine regarded a life of chastity as the best possible life even before he became a Christian. As he notes in *The Confessions,* as a young man he prayed to God for "chastity and continency" and added "but not yet." His education had not made his will strong enough to avoid lust or any other evil; that would come only through God's power and grace.

Augustine's ideas on sin, grace, and redemption became the foundation of all subsequent Western Christian theology, Protestant as well as Catholic. He wrote that the basic or dynamic force in any individual is the will, which he defined as "the power of the soul to hold on to or to obtain an object without constraint." The end or goal of the will determines the moral character of the individual. When Adam ate the fruit forbidden by God in the Garden of Eden (Genesis 3:6), he committed the "original sin" and corrupted the will. Adam's sin was not simply his own, but was passed on to all later humans through sexual intercourse; even infants were tainted. Original sin thus became a common social stain, in Augustine's opinion, transmitted by concupiscence, or sexual desire. Coitus

was theoretically good since it was created by God, but it had been corrupted by sin, so every act of intercourse was evil and every child was conceived through a sinful act. By viewing sexual desire as the result of disobedience to divine instructions by Adam and Eve, Augustine linked sexuality even more clearly with sin than had earlier church fathers. Because Adam disobeyed God and fell, all human beings have an innate tendency to sin: their will is weak. But according to Augustine, God restores the strength of the will through grace, which is transmitted in certain rituals that the church defined as **sacraments.** Grace results from God's decisions, not from any merit on the part of the individual.

The initial sacrament in any individual's life was baptism, and, because of his ideas about original sin, Augustine became a firm supporter of infant baptism instead of the then more commonly practiced adult baptism. Augustine held that babies who died before being baptized could not enter Heaven and that they spent eternity in Hell; this harsh view was moderated by later Catholic theologians who posited the notion of "limbo," a place where unbaptized babies remained until the Second Coming of Jesus. The fate of unbaptized babies remained a topic of debate among Catholic and later Protestant theologians for centuries. (In 2006 a papal commission recommended that Pope Benedict XVI abolish the concept of limbo and affirm that unbaptized babies go straight to Heaven. Though the pope himself had earlier noted that limbo was "only a theological hypothesis," he decided to delay making a definitive decision to abolish it.)

Augustine also argued against the Donatist heretical movement promoted by the North African bishop of Carthage, Donatus (313–347). Donatism denied the value of sacraments administered by priests or bishops who had denied their faith under persecution or had committed grave sins. For the Donatists the holiness of the minister was as important as the sacred rites he performed. Donatists viewed the true church, therefore, as a small spiritual elite that was an alternative to society. Augustine responded that, through God's action, the rites of the church have an objective and permanent validity regardless of the priest's spiritual condition. The notion of the church as a special spiritual elite recurred many times in the Middle Ages. Each time it was branded a heresy, and Augustine's arguments were marshaled against it.

When the Visigothic chieftain Alaric conquered Rome in 410, horrified pagans blamed the disaster on the Christians. In response, Augustine wrote *City of God.* This profoundly original work contrasts Christianity with the secular society in which it existed. Filled with references to ancient history and mythology, it remained for centuries

Heaven in Augustine's *City of God* Heavenly Jerusalem, from a twelfth-century Czech illuminated manuscript of Augustine's *City of God.* Augustine's writings were copied and recopied for many centuries in all parts of Europe, and they remained extremely influential. In this copy, the Czech king Wenzeslas and his grandmother are portrayed in the lower right corner; they probably paid for the manuscript. *(Erich Lessing/Art Resource, NY)*

the standard statement of the Christian philosophy of history.

According to Augustine, history is the account of God acting in time. Human history reveals that there are two kinds of people: those who live the life of the flesh in the City of Babylon and those who live the life of the spirit in the City of God. The former will endure eternal hellfire; the latter will enjoy eternal bliss.

Augustine maintained that states came into existence as the result of Adam's fall and people's inclination to sin. The state is a necessary evil, but it can work for the good by providing the peace, justice, and order that Christians need in order to pursue their pilgrimage to the City of God. The particular form of government—whether

monarchy, aristocracy, or democracy—is basically irrelevant. Any civil government that fails to provide justice is no more than a band of gangsters.

Although the state results from moral lapse—from sin—neither is the church (the Christian community) entirely free from sin. The church is certainly not equivalent to the City of God. But the church, which is concerned with salvation, is responsible for everyone, including Christian rulers. Churches later used Augustine's theory to defend their belief in the ultimate superiority of the spiritual power over the temporal. This remained the dominant political theory until the late thirteenth century.

Online Study Center **Improve Your Grade**
Primary Source: Saint Augustine Denounces Paganism and Urges Romans to Enter the City of God

Christian Missionaries and Conversion

The word *catholic* derives from a Greek word meaning "general," "universal," or "worldwide." Christ had said that his teaching was for all peoples, and Christians sought to make their faith catholic—that is, believed everywhere. This could be accomplished only through missionary activity. As Saint Paul had written to the Christian community at Colossae in Asia Minor, "there is no room for distinction between Greek and Jew, between the circumcised or the uncircumcised, or between barbarian or Scythian, slave and free man. There is only Christ; he is everything and he is in everything."[7] Paul urged Christians to bring the "good news" of Christ to all peoples. The Mediterranean served as the highway over which Christianity spread to the cities of the Roman Empire. From there missionaries took Christian teachings to the countryside, and then to areas beyond the borders of the empire.

● *What techniques did missionaries develop to convert barbarian peoples to Christianity?*

Missionaries on the Continent

During the Roman occupation, Christian communities were scattered throughout Gaul and Britain. The effective beginnings of Christianity in Gaul can be traced to Saint Martin of Tours (ca 316–397), a Roman soldier who, after giving away half his cloak to a naked beggar, had a vision of Christ and was baptized. Martin founded the monastery of Ligugé, the first in Gaul, which became a center for the evangelization of the country districts. In 372 he became bishop of Tours and introduced a rudimentary parish system. The Christianization of rural areas followed a different pattern from that of the cities.

Religion was not a private or individual matter; it was a social affair; and the religion of the chieftain or king determined the religion of the people. Thus missionaries concentrated their initial efforts not on the people, but on kings or tribal chieftains. According to custom, kings negotiated with all foreign powers, including the gods. Because Christian missionaries represented a "foreign" power (the Christian God), the king dealt with them. Germanic kings accepted Christianity because they believed that the Christian God was more powerful than pagan gods and that the Christian God would deliver victory in battle, or because Christianity taught obedience to (kingly) authority, or because Christian priests possessed knowledge and a charisma that could be associated with kingly power. Kings who converted, such as Ethelbert of Kent and the Frankish chieftain Clovis, sometimes had Christian wives. Conversion may also have indicated that barbarian kings wanted to enjoy the cultural advantages that Christianity brought, such as literate assistants and an ideological basis for their rule.

In eastern Europe, missionaries traveled far beyond the boundaries of the Byzantine Empire. In 863 the emperor Michael III sent the brothers Cyril (826–869) and Methodius (815–885) to preach Christianity in Moravia (the region of modern central Czech Republic). Other missionaries succeeded in converting the Russians in the tenth century. Cyril invented a Slavic alphabet using Greek characters, and this script (called the "Cyrillic alphabet") is still in use today. Cyrillic script made possible the birth of Russian literature. Similarly, Byzantine art and architecture became the basis and inspiration of Russian forms. The Byzantines were so successful that the Russians claimed to be the successors of the Byzantine Empire. For a time Moscow was even known as the "Third Rome" (the second Rome being Constantinople).

Christianity in the British Isles

Tradition identifies the conversion of Ireland with Saint Patrick (ca 385–461). Born in western England to a Christian family of Roman citizenship, Patrick was captured and enslaved by Irish raiders and taken to Ireland, where he worked as a herdsman for six years. He escaped and returned to England, where a vision urged him to Christianize Ireland. In preparation, Patrick studied in Gaul and was consecrated a bishop in 432. He returned to Ireland, where he converted the Irish tribe by tribe, first baptizing the king. In 445, with the approval of Pope Leo I, Patrick established his see in Armagh. The ecclesiastical organization that Patrick set up, however, differed from church structure on the continent in a fundamental way: Armagh was a monastery, and the monastery, rather than the diocese, served as the center of ecclesiastical organization. Local tribes and the monastery were interdependent, with the tribe supporting the monastery economically and the monastery providing religious and educational services for the tribe. By the time of Patrick's death, the majority of the Irish people had received Christian baptism. In his missionary work, Patrick had the strong support of Bridget of Kildare (ca 450–ca 528), daughter of a wealthy chieftain and his concubine. Bridget defied parental pressure to marry and became a nun. She and the other nuns at Kildare instructed relatives and friends in basic Christian doctrine, made religious vestments for churches, copied books, taught

Ardagh Silver Chalice This chalice, crafted about A.D. 800 and used for wine in Christian ceremonies, formed part of the treasure of Ardagh Cathedral in County Limerick, Ireland. Made of several types of metal, it is decorated with Celtic patterns in the same way that Irish manuscripts from this era are. Christianity was widespread in Ireland long before anywhere else in northern Europe, and Celtic traditions and practices differed significantly from those of Rome. *(National Museum of Ireland)*

children, and above all set a religious example by their lives of prayer. In Ireland and later in continental Europe, women shared in the process of conversion.

A strong missionary fervor characterized Irish Christianity. Perhaps the best representative of Irish-Celtic zeal was Saint Columba (ca 521–597), who established the monastery of Iona on an island in the Inner Hebrides off the west coast of Scotland (see Map 7.4 on page 214). Iona served as a base for converting the pagan Picts of Scotland. Columba's proselytizing efforts won him the title "Apostle of Scotland," and his disciples carried the Christian Gospel to the European continent.

The Christianization of the English really began in 597, when Pope Gregory I (590–604) sent a delegation of monks under the Roman Augustine to Britain. Augustine's approach, like Patrick's, was to concentrate on converting the king. When he succeeded in converting Ethelbert, king of Kent, the baptism of Ethelbert's people took place as a matter of course. Augustine established his headquarters, or see, at Canterbury, the capital of Kent.

In the course of the seventh century, two Christian forces competed for the conversion of the pagan Anglo-Saxons: Roman-oriented missionaries traveling north from Canterbury, and Celtic monks from Ireland and northwestern Britain. Monasteries were established at Iona, Lindisfarne, Jarrow, and Whitby.

The Roman and Celtic church organization, types of monastic life, and methods of arriving at the date of the central feast of the Christian calendar, Easter, differed completely. Through the influence of King Oswiu of Northumbria and the energetic abbess Hilda of Whitby, the Synod (ecclesiastical council) held at Whitby in 664 opted to follow the Roman practices. The conversion of the English and the close attachment of the English church to Rome had far-reaching consequences because Britain later served as a base for the Christianization of the continent (see Map 7.2).

Conversion and Assimilation

Between the fifth and tenth centuries, the great majority of peoples living on the European continent and the nearby islands were baptized as Christians. When a ruler marched his people to the waters of baptism, though, the work of Christianization had only begun. Baptism meant either sprinkling the head or immersing the body in water. Conversion meant awareness and acceptance of the beliefs of Christianity, including those that seemed strange or radical, such as "love your enemies" or "do good to those that hate you."

How did missionaries and priests get masses of pagan and illiterate peoples to understand and live by Christian ideals and teachings? They did so through preaching, assimilation, and the penitential system. Preaching aimed at instruction and edification. Instruction presented the basic teachings of Christianity. Edification was intended to strengthen the newly baptized in their faith through stories about the lives of Christ and the saints. But deeply ingrained pagan customs and practices could not be stamped out by words alone or even by imperial edicts. Christian missionaries often pursued a policy of assimilation, easing the conversion of pagan men and women by stressing similarities between their customs and beliefs and those of Christianity. In the same way that classically trained scholars such as Jerome and Augustine blended Greco-Roman and Christian ideas, missionaries and converts mixed pagan ideas and practices with Christian ones. Bogs and lakes sacred to Germanic gods became associated with saints, as did various aspects of ordinary life, such as traveling, planting crops, and worrying about a sick child. Aspects of existing midwinter celebrations, which often centered on the return of the sun as the days became longer, were incorporated into celebrations of Christmas. Spring rituals involving eggs and rabbits (both symbols of fertility) were added to Easter.

A letter from Pope Gregory I beautifully illustrates this policy. Sent to Augustine of Canterbury in Britain in 601, it expresses the pope's intention that pagan buildings and practices be given a Christian significance:

Therefore, when by God's help you reach our most reverent brother, Bishop Augustine, we wish you to inform him that we have been giving careful thought to the affairs of the English, and have come to the conclusion that the temples of the idols among that people should on no account be destroyed. The idols are to be destroyed, but the temples themselves are to be aspersed with holy water, altars set up in them, and relics deposited there. For if these temples are well-built, they must be purified from the worship of demons and dedicated to the service of the true God. In this way we hope that the people, seeing that their temples are not destroyed, may abandon their error and, flocking more readily to their accustomed resorts, may come to know and adore the true God.[8]

The way that assimilation works is perhaps best appreciated through the example of Saint Valentine's Day. There were two Romans named Valentine. Both were Christian priests, and both were martyred for their beliefs in the third century, around the middle of February. (Nothing in the lives of the two Christian martyrs connects them with lovers or the exchange of messages and gifts. That practice began in the later Middle Ages.) Since about order to receive God's forgiveness. In the early church, "confession" meant that the sinner publicly acknowledged charges laid against him or her and publicly carried out the penitential works prescribed by the priest or bishop. For example, the adulterer might have to stand outside the church before services wearing a sign naming his or her sin and asking the prayers of everyone who entered.

Beginning in the late sixth century, however, Irish and English missionaries brought the more private penitential system to continental Europe. **Penitentials** were manuals for the examination of conscience. The penitent knelt individually before the priest, who questioned the penitent about the sins he or she might have committed. A penance such as fasting on bread and water for a period of time or saying specific prayers was imposed as medicine for the soul. The penitential system made sin and forgiveness an individual rather than a community matter and encouraged the private examination of conscience, particularly because penitentials advised priests to ask about people's thoughts and desires as well as about their actions.

Most religious observances continued to be community matters, however, as they had been in the ancient world. People joined with family members, friends, and neighbors to attend baptisms and funerals, presided over by a priest. They prayed to saints or to the Virgin Mary to intercede with God, or they simply asked the saints for protection and blessing. The entire village participated in processions marking saints' days or points in the agricultural year, often carrying images of saints or their **relics**— bones, articles of clothing, or other objects associated with the life of a saint—around the houses and fields.

Migrating Peoples

The migration of peoples from one area to another has been a dominant and continuing feature of Western history. Mass movements of Europeans occurred in the fourth through sixth centuries, in the ninth and tenth centuries, and in the twelfth and thirteenth centuries. From the sixteenth century to the present, such movements have been almost continuous, involving not just the European continent but the entire world. The causes of early migrations varied and are not thoroughly understood by scholars. But there is no question that the migrations profoundly affected both the regions to which peoples moved and the ones they left behind.

• *How did the migration of barbarian groups such as the Celtic and Germanic tribes shape political structures and notions of ethnic identity?*

Pope Gregory I and Scribes One of the four "Doctors" (or Learned Fathers) of the Latin church, Gregory (590–604) is shown on the cover of this tenth-century ivory book writing at his desk while the Holy Spirit, in the form of a dove, whispers in his ear. Below, scribes copy Gregory's works. *(Kunsthistorisches Museum, Vienna/Art Resource, NY)*

150 B.C. the Romans had celebrated the festival of Lupercalia, at which they asked the gods for fertility for themselves, their fields, and their flocks. This celebration occurred in mid-February, shortly before the Roman New Year and the arrival of spring. Thus the early church "converted" the old festival of Lupercalia into Saint Valentine's Day. The fourteenth of February was still celebrated as a festival, but it had taken on a Christian meaning.

A process with an equally profound, if gradual, impact on the conversion of the pagan masses was the rite of reconciliation in which the sinner revealed his or her sins in

Procession to a New Church   In this sixth-century ivory carving, two men in a wagon, accompanied by a procession of people holding candles, carry a relic casket to a church under construction. Workers are putting tiles on the church roof. New churches often received holy items when they were dedicated, and processions were common ways in which people expressed community devotion. *(Amt fuer kirchliche Denmalpflege. Foto: Ann Muenchow)*

The Idea of the Barbarian

In surveying the world around them, the ancient Greeks often conceptualized things in dichotomies, or sets of opposites: light and dark, hot and cold, wet and dry, mind and body, male and female, and so on. One of their key dichotomies was Greek and non-Greek, and the Greeks coined the word *barbaros* for those whose native language was not Greek, because they seemed to the Greeks to be speaking nonsense syllables—bar, bar, bar. ("Bar-bar" is the Greek equivalent to "blah-blah" or "yada-yada.") Barbaros originally meant someone who did not speak Greek, but gradually it also implied that the people were unruly, savage, and more primitive than people in the advanced civilization of Greece. The word brought this meaning with it when it came into Latin and other European languages, and the Romans referred to those who lived beyond the northeastern boundary of Roman territory as **barbarians.**

The modern study of ethnography (writing about the formation of ethnic groups) involves the systematic recording of the major characteristics of different human cultures. Scholars today identify three models of ethnic formation among the peoples who came in contact with the Romans and whom the Romans called barbarians.

First, there were Germanic peoples, whose identity was shaped by a militarily successful or "royal" family. For example, the Salian Franks, Lombards, and Goths attracted and controlled followers from other peoples by getting them to adhere to the cultural traditions of the leading family. Followers assimilated the "kernel family's" legendary traditions and myths, which traced their origins to a family or individual of divine ancestry. The kernel family led these followers from their original territory, won significant victories over other peoples, and settled someplace within the Roman world. In the fifth century these groups formed large political units, and their rulers began to issue law codes regulating interpersonal relations for members of the group.

A second model of ethnic formation derives from Central Asian steppe peoples such as the Huns, Avars, and Alans. These were polyethnic seminomadic and sedentary groups led by small bodies of steppe commanders. (The term *steppe* refers to the vast semiarid plain in Russian Siberia.) These peoples constituted large confederations whose success depended on constant expansion by military victory or the use of terror. Defeat in battle or the death of a leader could lead to the disintegration of the confederation, and the confederations did not develop written law codes in this era.

The Slavs of eastern Europe represent a third model of barbarian ethnic formation. They were loosely organized bands of peoples who lacked centralized leadership and intermingled with other groups as they migrated. No group records from this period survive, so the only information about the Slavs comes from outsiders. The sense of a "Slavic" identity, or of an identity that was, for example, Polish or Russian or Serbian, was the product of a later period.

One fundamental trait characterizes all barbarian peoples: the formation of the ethnic groups did not represent a single historical event. Rather, the formation was a continuous and changing process extending over long periods of time.

Migrating groups that the Romans labeled barbarians had pressed along the Rhine-Danube frontier of the Roman Empire since about A.D. 150 (see page 155). In the third and fourth centuries, increasing pressures on the frontiers from the east and north placed greater demands on military manpower, which plague and a declining birthrate had reduced. Therefore, Roman generals recruited barbarians to fill the ranks. They bribed Germanic chiefs with treaties and gold and Germanic masses with grain. By the late third century a large percentage of military recruits were Germanic.

Several types of barbarian peoples entered the empire and became affiliated with Roman government. The *laeti,* refugees or prisoners of war, and their families were settled in areas of Gaul and Italy under the supervision of Roman prefects and landowners. Generally isolated from the local Roman population, the laeti farmed regions depopulated by plague. The men had to serve in the Roman army. Free barbarian units called **foederati,** stationed near major provincial cities, represented a second type of affiliated barbarian group. Research has suggested that rather than giving them land, the Romans assigned the foederati shares of the tax revenues from the region.[9] Living in close proximity to Roman communities, the foederati quickly assimilated into Roman culture. In fact, in the fourth century, some rose to the highest ranks of the army and moved in the most cultured and aristocratic circles.

Celts, Germans, and Huns

As Julius Caesar advanced through Gaul between 58 and 50 B.C. (see page 144), the largest barbarian groups he encountered were Celts (whom the Romans called Gauls) and Germans. Modern historians have tended to use the terms *German* and *Celt* in a racial sense, but recent research stresses that *Celt* and *German* are linguistic terms, a Celt being a person who spoke a Celtic language, an ancestor of the modern Gaelic or Breton language, and a German one who spoke a Germanic language, an ancestor of modern German, Dutch, Danish, Swedish, or Norwegian.

Celts and Germans were similar to one another in many ways. In the first century A.D., the Celts lived east of the Rhine River in an area bounded by the Main Valley and extending westward to the Somme River. Germans were more numerous along the North and Baltic Seas. Both Germans and Celts used wheeled plows and a three-field system of crop rotation. Before the introduction of Christianity, both Celtic and Germanic peoples were polytheistic, with hundreds of gods and goddesses with specialized functions whose celebrations were often linked to points in the yearly agricultural cycle. Worship was often outdoors at sacred springs, groves, or lakes.

The Celts had developed iron manufacturing, using shaft furnaces as sophisticated as those of the Romans to produce iron swords and spears. Celtic priests, called druids, had legal and educational as well as religious functions, orally passing down laws and traditions from generation to generation. Bards singing poems and ballads also passed down stories of heroes and gods, which, were written down much later. Celtic peoples conquered by the Romans often assimilated to Roman ways, adapting the Latin language and other aspects of Roman culture. By the fourth century A.D., under pressure from Germanic groups, the Celts had moved westward, settling in Brittany (modern northwestern France) and throughout the British Isles (England, Wales, Scotland, and Ireland). The Picts of Scotland as well as the Welsh, Britons, and Irish were peoples of Celtic descent (see Map 7.3).

The migrations of the Germanic peoples were important in the political and social transformations of late antiquity. Many modern scholars have tried to explain who the Germans were and why they migrated. The present consensus, based on the study of linguistic and archaeological evidence, is that there were not one but rather many Germanic peoples with very different cultural traditions. The largest Germanic tribe, the Goths, was a polyethnic group consisting of perhaps fifteen thousand to twenty thousand warriors, which with women and children amounted to one hundred thousand people. The tribe was supplemented by slaves, *coloni,* peoples who, because of their desperate situation under Roman rule, joined the Goths during their migrations.[10]

Combined with linguistic data, archaeological remains—bone fossils, cooking utensils, jewelry, weapons of war, and other artifacts—suggest three broad groupings of Germanic peoples. One group lived along the North and Baltic Seas in the regions of present-day northern Germany, southern Sweden, and Denmark. A second band inhabited the area between the Elbe and Oder Rivers. A third group lived along the Rhine and Weser Rivers, closest to the Roman frontier. Although these groupings sometimes showed cultural affiliation, they were very fluid and did not possess political, social, or ethnic solidarity.

Why did the Germans migrate? Like the Celts, in part they were pushed by groups living farther eastward, especially by the Huns from Central Asia in the fourth and fifth centuries. In part, they were searching for more regular supplies of food, better farmland, and a warmer climate. Conflicts within and among Germanic groups also led to war and disruption, which motivated groups to move. Franks fought Alemanni in Gaul; Visigoths fought Vandals in the Iberian Peninsula and across North Africa; and Angles and Saxons fought Celtic-speaking Britons in England.

All these factors can be seen in the movement of the Visigoths, one of the Germanic tribes, from an area north of the Black Sea southeastward into the Roman Empire. Pressured by defeat in battle, starvation, and the movement of the Huns, the Visigoths petitioned the emperor Valens to admit them to the empire. Seeing in the hordes of warriors the solution to his manpower problem, Valens agreed. Once the Visigoths were inside the empire, Roman authorities exploited their hunger by forcing them to sell their own people as slaves in exchange for dog flesh: "the going rate was one dog for one Goth." Still, the Visigoths sought peace. Fritigern offered himself as a friend and ally of Rome in exchange for the province of Thrace—land, crops, and livestock. With a Roman army of between thirty thousand and forty thousand men against about ten thousand Goths, Valens did not take the offer seriously, and his council voted for battle. When the two armies met on August 9, 378, near Adrianople, the Visigoths slashed down the Roman army, including thirty-five high-ranking officers and the emperor Valens himself. But the Goths had neither the equipment nor the tactical skill to take the city of Adrianople. The Battle of Adrianople created no notable change in the military or political history of the Roman Empire.

As the Visigoths migrated into Thrace and the Balkans, however, they forced the Romans to change imperial policy toward the barbarians. That policy alternated between official recognition by treaty and enmity. Alaric I's invasion of Italy and sack of Rome in 410 represents the culmination of hostility between the Visigoths and the

Vandal Landowner In this mosaic, a Vandal landowner rides out from his Roman-style house. His clothing—Roman short tunic, cloak, and sandals—reflects the way some Celtic and Germanic tribes accepted Roman lifestyles, though his beard is more typical of barbarian men's fashion. (*Courtesy of the Trustees of the British Museum*)

Mapping the Past

MAP 7.3 The Barbarian Migrations   This map shows the migrations of various barbarian groups in late antiquity and can be used to answer the following questions: ❶ The map has no political boundaries. What does this suggest about the impact of barbarian migrations on political structures? ❷ Human migration is caused by a combination of push factors—circumstances that lead people to leave a place—and pull factors—things that attract people to a new location. Based on the information in this and earlier chapters, what push and pull factors might have shaped the migration patterns you see on the map? ❸ The movements of barbarian peoples used to be labeled "invasions" and are now usually described as "migrations." How do the dates on the map support the newer understanding of these movements?

Romans. The Goths burned and looted the city for three days, which caused many Romans to wonder whether God had deserted them. This led the imperial government to pull its troops from the British Isles and many areas north of the Alps, leaving these northern areas more vulnerable and open to migrating groups. A year later Alaric died, and his successor led his people into southwestern Gaul.[11] Establishing their headquarters at Toulouse, they exercised a weak domination over Spain until a Muslim victory at Guadalete in 711 ended Visigothic rule.

One significant factor in Germanic migration was pressure from nomadic steppe peoples from Central Asia. This included the Alans, Avars, Bulgars, Khazars, and most prominently the Huns, who attacked the Black Sea area and the Eastern Roman Empire beginning in the fourth century. Under the leadership of their warrior-king Attila, the Huns swept into central Europe in 451, attacking Roman settlements in the Balkans and Germanic settlements along the Danube and Rhine Rivers. Several Germanic groups allied with them, as did the sister of the Roman emperor, and a huge army took the city of Metz, now in eastern France. After Attila turned his army southward and crossed the Alps into Italy, a papal delegation, including Pope Leo I himself, asked him not to attack Rome. Though papal diplomacy was later credited with stopping the advance of the Huns, a plague that spread among Hunnic troops and their dwindling food supplies were probably much more important. The Huns retreated from Italy, and within a year Attila was dead. Later leaders were not as effective, and the Huns were never again an important factor in European history. Their conquests had slowed down the movements of various Germanic groups, however, allowing barbarian peoples to absorb more of Roman culture as they picked the Western Roman Empire apart.

Germanic Kingdoms

Between 450 and 565, the Germans established a number of kingdoms, but none other than the Frankish kingdom lasted very long. The Germanic kingdoms did not have definite geographical boundaries, and their locations are approximate. The Vandals, whose destructive ways are commemorated in the word *vandal,* settled in North Africa. In northern and western Europe in the sixth century, the Burgundians ruled over lands roughly circumscribed by the old Roman army camps at Lyons, Besançon, Geneva, and Autun.

In northern Italy the Ostrogothic king Theodoric (r. 471–526) established his residence at Ravenna and gradually won control of all Italy, Sicily, and the territory north and east of the upper Adriatic. Although attached to the customs of his people, Theodoric pursued a policy of assimilation between Germans and Romans. He maintained close relations with the emperor at Constantinople and attracted able scholars such as Cassiodorus to his administration. Theodoric's accomplishments were significant, but his administration fell apart after his death.

The kingdom established by the Franks in the sixth century, in spite of later civil wars, proved to be the most powerful and enduring of all the barbarian kingdoms. The Franks were a confederation of peoples who originated in the marshy lowlands north and east of the northernmost part of the Rhine frontier of the Roman Empire. They spoke a Germanic language. In the fourth and fifth centuries, they settled within the empire and allied with the Romans, some attaining high military and civil positions. In the sixth century one group, the Salian Franks, issued a law code called the **Salic Law,** the earliest description of Germanic customs. Chlodio (fifth century) is the first member of the Frankish dynasty for

whom evidence survives. According to legend, Chlodio's wife went swimming, encountered a sea monster, and conceived Merowig. The Franks believed that Merowig, a man of supernatural origins, founded their ruling dynasty, which was thus called **Merovingian.**

The reign of Clovis (ca 481–511) marks the decisive period in the development of the Franks as a unified people. Through military campaigns, Clovis acquired the central provinces of Roman Gaul. The next two centuries witnessed the steady assimilation of Franks and Gallo-Romans, as many Franks adopted the Latin language and Roman ways, and Gallo-Romans copied Frankish customs and Frankish personal names. These centuries also saw Frankish acquisition of the Burgundian kingdom and of territory held by the Goths in Provence.[12]

Many writers have debated the issue of Clovis's conversion from Arian to Roman Christianity. His near-contemporary, Gregory, bishop of Tours, attributed Clovis's conversion to the influence of his Catholic wife, Chlotilde. Another contemporary writer holds that Clovis prayed to the Christian god in his war with the Alamanni (ca 496); in thanksgiving for his victory, he accepted baptism. A third contemporary witness believed that the conversion was "the personal choice of an intelligent monarch." One student of the Franks argues that Clovis was baptized in 508 (not in 496, as has been traditionally believed), at the time he was at war in southwestern Gaul with the Visigothic king Alaric II, and that there was propaganda value to be gained by appearing as the defender of Catholicism against Arianism.[13] Certainly, conversion brought Clovis the crucial support of the papacy and of the bishops of Gaul. (See the feature "Listening to the Past: The Conversion of Clovis" on pages 220–221.)

Anglo-Saxon England

The island of Britain was populated by various Celtic-speaking tribes when it was conquered by Rome during the reign of Claudius. During the first four centuries of the Christian era, it shared fully in the life of the Roman Empire. Towns were planned in the Roman fashion, with temples, public baths, theaters, and amphitheaters. In the countryside large manors controlled the surrounding lands. Roman merchants brought Eastern luxury goods and Eastern religions—including Christianity—into Britain. The Romans suppressed the Celtic chieftains, and a military aristocracy governed. In the course of the second and third centuries, many Celts assimilated to Roman culture, becoming Roman citizens and joining the Roman army.

In 407 the emperor Honorius (r. 395–423), faced with the Visigothic army attacking Rome under Alaric, withdrew imperial troops from Britain. The Picts from Scotland and the Scots from Ireland invaded British Celtic territory. According to the eighth-century historian Bede (see page 245), the Celtic king Vortigern invited the Saxons from Denmark to help him against his rivals in Britain. Saxons and other Germanic tribes from modern-day Norway, Sweden, and Denmark turned from assistance to conquest, attacking in a hit-and-run fashion. Their goal was plunder, and at first their invasions led to no permanent settlements. As more Germanic peoples arrived, however, they took over the best lands and eventually conquered most of Britain. Some Britons fled to Wales and the westernmost parts of England, north toward Scotland, and across the English Channel to Brittany. Others remained and eventually intermarried with Germanic peoples.

Historians have labeled the period 500 to 1066, the year of the Norman Conquest, "Anglo-Saxon," after the two largest Germanic tribes, the Angles and the Saxons. The Germanic tribes destroyed Roman culture in Britain. Christianity disappeared; large urban buildings were allowed to fall apart; and tribal custom superseded Roman law.

The Anglo-Saxon invasion gave rise to a rich body of Celtic mythology, particularly legends about King Arthur, who first appeared in Welsh poetry in the sixth century and later in histories, epics, and saints' lives. In the twelfth century, stories about Arthur were included in Geoffrey of Monmouth's very popular *History of the Kings of Britain,* a fictional account of British history that was regarded as fact for centuries. The legends were also spread by traveling poets and minstrels, and they gradually evolved into an elaborate story. According to these texts, when Arthur, the illegitimate son of the king of Britain, successfully drew a sword from a stone, Merlin, the court magician, revealed Arthur's royal parentage. Arthur won recognition as king, and the mysterious Lady of the Lake gave him the invincible sword Excalibur. He fought many battles and went on many quests, including a search for the Holy Grail, the cup supposedly used by Jesus at the Last Supper, which was said to have miraculous powers. Arthur held his court at Camelot, where his knights were seated at the Round Table (to avoid quarrels over precedence). Those knights—including Sir Tristan, Sir Lancelot, Sir Galahad, and Sir Percival (Parsifal)—and Arthur's wife Guinevere, whose ill-fated romance with Sir Lancelot led to the end of the Arthurian kingdom, played a large role in later medieval literature, and their stories were told again and again. In their earliest form as Welsh poems, the Arthurian legends may represent Celtic hostility to Anglo-Saxon invaders, but they later came to be more important as representations of the ideal of medieval knightly chivalry and as great stories whose retelling has continued to the present.

Whether Arthur had any basis in historical reality is hotly debated, with some scholars arguing that he was based on myths about deities, while others assert that he might have been based on one or another Romanized Celtic leader, a warrior rather than a king. Most scholars see him as a composite figure who evolved over the centuries as different stories were told about him and his associates.

The beginnings of the Germanic kingdoms in Britain are nearly as obscure as Arthur, but scholars suspect that they came into being in the seventh and eighth centuries. The scholar Bede described seven kingdoms: the Saxon kingdoms of the East Saxons (Essex), South Saxons (Sussex), and West Saxons (Wessex); the Jutish kingdom of Kent; and the kingdoms of the Angles, Mercians, and Northumbrians (see Map 7.4). The names imply that these peoples thought of themselves in tribal rather than geographical terms. Because of Bede's categorization, scholars often refer to the Heptarchy, or seven kingdoms, of Anglo-Saxon Britain. The suggestion of total Anglo-Saxon domination, however, is not entirely accurate. Germanic tribes never subdued Scotland, where the Picts remained strong, or Wales, where Celtic-speaking Welsh and Britons continued to put up stubborn resistance.

Thus Anglo-Saxon England was divided along ethnic and political lines. The Germanic kingdoms in the south, east, and center were opposed by the Britons in the west, who wanted to get rid of the invaders. The Anglo-Saxon kingdoms also fought among themselves, causing boundaries to shift constantly. Finally, in the ninth century, under pressure from the Danish, or Viking, invasions, the Celtic Britons and the Germanic Anglo-Saxons were molded together under the leadership of King Alfred of Wessex (r. 871–899).

Barbarian Society

Germanic and Celtic society had originated in the northern parts of central and western Europe and the southern regions of Scandinavia during the Iron Age (800–500 B.C.). After Germanic kingdoms replaced the Roman Empire as the primary political structure throughout much of Europe, barbarian customs and traditions formed the basis of European society for centuries.

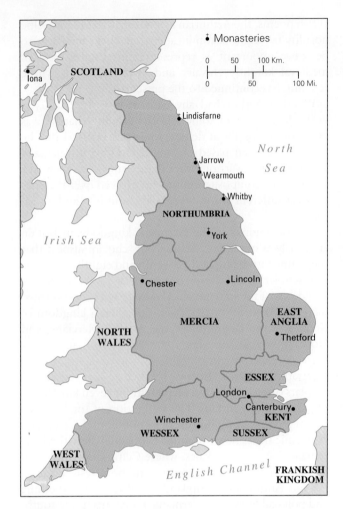

MAP 7.4 Anglo-Saxon England The seven kingdoms of the Heptarchy—Northumbria, Mercia, East Anglia, Essex, Kent, Sussex, and Wessex—dominated but did not subsume Britain. Scotland remained a Pict stronghold, while the Celts resisted invasion of their native Wales by Germanic tribes.

Scholars have long understood the importance of barbarian society, but they have been hampered in investigating it because most Germanic and Celtic groups did not write and thus kept no written records before their conversion to Christianity. The earliest information about them comes from *Germania,* a description of Germanic laws and customs written by the Roman politician and historian Tacitus (ca 56–ca 117). Tacitus, who had never traveled in areas with a significant Germanic population, took his information from earlier writers who had, and perhaps from soldiers or merchants who had gone beyond the borders of the Roman Empire. Thus his descriptions are secondhand at best and were also shaped by his purpose in writing, for he thought that his fellow Romans had grown corrupt and immoral, and he saw the Germans as simpler and braver. Other Roman authors also had particular points of view when describing barbarian society, so their writings must be combined with archaeological evidence and other types of sources to gain a more accurate picture. These newer sources, from Scandinavia and the British Isles, include inscriptions carved in stone, bone, and wood and written in the **runic alphabet.** The oldest comes from shortly after the time of Tacitus. Early runic inscriptions are usually short and are limited to names, but later runes describe the actions of kings and other powerful individuals. A few with very ordinary purposes, such as letters and greetings, have been unearthed in Norway, and scholars can use them to find information about a wide range of activities.

Online Study Center **Improve Your Grade**
Primary Source: Noble Savages: Rome Encounters the Germans

● *What patterns of social, political, and economic life characterized barbarian society?*

Kinship, Custom, and Class

Barbarians generally had no notion of the state as we use the term today; they thought in social, not political, terms. The basic social unit was the tribe, a group whose members believed that they were all descended from a common ancestor. Blood united them; kinship protected them. Law was custom—unwritten, preserved in the minds of the elders of the tribe, and handed down by word of mouth from generation to generation. Every tribe had its customs, and every member of the tribe knew what they were. Members were subject to their tribe's customary laws wherever they went, and friendly tribes respected one another's laws.

Barbarian tribes were led by tribal chieftains, who are often called kings, though this implies broader power than they actually had. The chief was the member recognized as the strongest and bravest in battle and was elected from among the male members of the strongest family. He led the tribe in war, settled disputes among its members, conducted negotiations with outside powers, and offered sacrifices to the gods. The period of migrations and conquests of the Western Roman Empire witnessed the strengthening of kingship among tribes.

Closely associated with the king in some southern tribes was the **comitatus,** or "war band." Writing at the end of the first century, Tacitus described the war band as

Runic Inscriptions An eighth-century chest made of whalebone depicting warriors, other human figures, and a horse, with a border of runic letters. This chest tells a story in both pictures and words. The runes are one of the varieties from the British Isles, from a time and place in which the Latin alphabet was known as well. Runes and Latin letters were used side-by-side in some parts of northern Europe for centuries. *(Erich Lessing/Art Resource, NY)*

the bravest young men in the tribe. They swore loyalty to the chief, fought with him in battle, and were not supposed to leave the battlefield without him; to do so implied cowardice, disloyalty, and social disgrace. A social egalitarianism existed among members of the war band. The comitatus had importance for the later development of feudalism.

During the migrations of the third and fourth centuries, however, and as a result of constant warfare, the war band was transformed into a system of stratified ranks. Among the Ostrogoths, for example, a warrior nobility and several other nobilities evolved. Contact with the Romans, who produced such goods as armbands for trade with the barbarians, stimulated demand for armbands. Thus armbands, especially the gold ones reserved for the "royal families," promoted the development of hierarchical ranks within war bands. During the Ostrogothic conquest of Italy under Theodoric, warrior-nobles also sought to acquire land as both a mark of prestige and a means to power. As land and wealth came into the hands of a small elite class, social inequalities emerged and gradually grew stronger.[14] These inequalities help explain the origins of the European noble class (see pages 313–314).

Law

Early barbarian tribes had no written laws, but beginning in the late sixth century some tribal chieftains began to collect, write, and publish lists of their customs. They were encouraged to do so because the Christian missionaries who were slowly converting the barbarians to Christianity wanted to know the tribal customs. Churchmen wanted to read about barbarian ways in order to assimilate the tribes to Christianity. Augustine of Canterbury, for example, persuaded King Ethelbert of Kent to have his folk laws written down; these *Dooms of Ethelbert* date from between 601 and 604, roughly five years after Augustine's arrival in Britain. Moreover, by the sixth century many barbarian kings needed regulations for the Romans under their jurisdiction as well as for their own people.

According to the code of the Salian Franks, every person had a particular monetary value to the tribe. This value was called the **wergeld,** which literally means "man-money" or "money to buy off the spear." Men of fighting age had the highest wergeld, then women of childbearing age, children, and finally the aged. Everyone's value reflected his or her potential military worthiness. If a person accused of a crime agreed to pay the wergeld and if the victim and his or her family accepted the payment, there was peace (hence the expression "money to buy off the spear"). If the accused refused to pay the wergeld or if the victim's family refused to accept it, a blood feud ensued. Individuals depended on their kin for protection, and kinship served as a force of social control.

Historians and sociologists have difficulty interpreting the early law codes, partly because they are patchwork affairs studded with additions made in later centuries. Yet much historical information can be gleaned from these codes. For example, the Salic Law (see page 212) of the Salian Franks offers a general picture of Frankish life and problems in the early Middle Ages and is typical of the law codes of other tribes, such as the Visigoths, Burgundians, Lombards, and Anglo-Saxons.

The Salic Law lists the monetary fines to be paid to the victim or the family for such injuries as theft, rape, assault, arson, and murder:

If any person strike another on the head so that the brain appears, and the three bones which lie above the brain shall project, he shall be sentenced to 1200 denars, which make 300 shillings. . . .

If any one have killed a free woman after she has begun bearing children, he shall be sentenced to 2400 denars, which make 600 shillings. . . .

If any one shall have drawn a harrow through another's harvest after it has sprouted, or shall have gone through it with a wagon where there was no road, he shall be sentenced to 120 denars, which make 30 shillings.[15]

This is not a systematic statement of a body of law, but rather a list of fines for particular offenses. Germanic law aimed at the prevention or reduction of violence. It was not concerned with abstract justice.

Some codes had specific clauses that protected the virtue of women. For example, the Salic Law of the Franks fined a man the large amount of 15 solidi (from *solidus,* a coin originally minted by Constantine and later the basis of much European currency, such as the English shilling) if he pressed the hand of a woman, and 35 if he touched her above the elbow. The very high fine of 600 solidi for the murder of a woman of childbearing years—the same value attached to military officers of the king, to priests, and to boys preparing to become warriors—suggests the importance of women in Frankish society, at least for their childbearing capacity.

At first, Romans had been subject to Roman law and Germans to Germanic custom. As German kings accepted Christianity and as Romans and barbarians increasingly intermarried, the distinction between the two laws blurred and, in the course of the seventh and eighth centuries, disappeared. The result would be the new feudal law, to which all who lived in certain areas were subject.

Social and Economic Structures

Barbarian groups usually resided in small villages, and climate and geography determined the basic patterns of agricultural and pastoral life. Many tribes lived in small settlements on the edges of clearings where they raised barley, wheat, oats, peas, and beans. They tilled their fields with simple wooden scratch plows and harvested their grains with small iron sickles. The kernels of grain were eaten as porridge, ground up for flour, or fermented into strong, thick beer; the vast majority of people's caloric intake came from grain in some form.

Information about the gender division of labor is difficult to find, but based on later practices men probably cared for larger animals, such as cattle, while women took care of poultry. Women also had responsibility for spinning the thread that went into the manufacture of clothing and all textiles. Both sexes performed the heavy work of raising, grinding, and preserving cereals.

Within the small villages, there were great differences in wealth and status. Free men and their families constituted the largest class. The number of cattle a man possessed indicated his wealth and determined his social status. "Cattle were so much the quintessential indicator of wealth in traditional society that the modern English term 'fee' (meaning cost of goods or services), which developed from the medieval term 'fief,' had its origin in the Germanic term *fihu* . . . , meaning cattle, chattels, and hence, in general, wealth."[16] Free men also shared in tribal warfare. Slaves (prisoners of war) worked as farm laborers, herdsmen, and household servants.

Did the barbarians produce goods for trade and exchange? Ironworking represented the most advanced craft; much of northern Europe had iron deposits, and the dense forests provided wood for charcoal. Most villages had an oven and smiths who produced agricultural tools and instruments of war—one-edged swords, arrowheads, and shields. In the first two centuries A.D., the quantity and quality of Germanic goods increased dramatically, and the first steel swords were superior to the weapons of Roman troops. These goods were produced for war and for the subsistence economy, not for trade. Goods were also used for gift giving, a major social custom. Gift giving conferred status on the giver, who, in giving, showed his higher (economic) status, cemented friendship, and placed the receiver in his debt.[17] Goods that could not be produced in the village were acquired by raiding and warfare rather than by commercial exchanges. Raids between tribes brought the victors booty; the cattle and slaves captured were traded or given as gifts. Warfare determined the economy and the individual's status within barbarian society.

Barbarian tribes were understood as made up of kin groups, and those kin groups were made up of families, the basic social unit in barbarian society. Families were responsible for the debts and actions of their members and for keeping the peace in general. Barbarian law codes set strict rules of inheritance based on position in the family and often set aside a portion of land that could not be sold or given away by any family member.

Germanic society was patriarchal: within each household the father had authority over his wife, children, and slaves. Some wealthy and powerful men had more than one wife, a pattern that continued even after they became Christian, but polygamy was not widespread among ordinary people. A woman was considered to be under the legal guardianship of a man, and she had fewer rights to own property than did Roman women in the late empire. However, once they were widowed (and there must have

been many widows in such a violent, warring society), women sometimes assumed their husbands' rights over family property and held the guardianship of their children. Just as did classically trained scholars such as Augustine, Germanic religious writers and prelates doubted the spiritual equality of women. For those writers, women demonstrated their spiritual worth by converting their husbands, raising pious children, endowing churches and monasteries, and dispensing charity to the poor.

Women found outlets for their talents in monasteries and convents as writers, copyists, artists, embroiderers, teachers, and estate managers. Some houses of religious women, such as Mauberge in northern Francia under Abbess Aldegund (ca 661), produced important scholarship. The dowry required for entrance to a convent restricted admission as full sisters to upper-class women, but poorer women were taken in as lay sisters. Many women viewed the convent as a place of refuge from family pressures or tribal violence. The sixth-century queen Radegund, for example, was forced to marry Chlotar I, the murderer of several of her relatives. Radegund later escaped her polygamous union and lived out her life in a convent.

Chapter Summary

Online Study Center **ACE the Test**

- *How was the Byzantine Empire able to survive for so long, and what were its most important achievements?*
- *What factors enabled the Christian church to expand and thrive?*
- *How did Christian ideas and practices respond to changing political and social circumstances in the Roman Empire?*
- *What techniques did missionaries develop to convert barbarian peoples to Christianity?*
- *How did the migration of barbarian groups such as the Celtic and Germanic tribes shape political structures and notions of ethnic identity?*
- *What patterns of social, political, and economic life characterized barbarian society?*

Late antiquity was a period of rupture and transformation, but also of continuities and assimilation. Migrating barbarian groups broke the Western Roman Empire apart, creating much smaller states and more localized economies. As they encountered Roman culture and became Christian, their own ways of doing things were transformed, and the result was a blend of barbarian and Roman culture. In eastern Europe, the Byzantine Empire thrived throughout late antiquity, maintaining Roman traditions. Throughout Europe, leaders in the Christian church energetically developed more complex ideas and stronger institutional structures, transforming Christianity into the most powerful agent in the making of Europe.

In the east, the Byzantine Empire withstood attacks from Germanic tribes and steppe peoples and remained a state until 1453, a thousand years longer than the

Western Roman Empire. Byzantium preserved the philosophical and scientific texts of the ancient world—which later formed the basis for study in science and medicine in both Europe and the Arabic world—and produced a great synthesis of Roman law, the Justinian *Code,* which shapes legal structures in much of Europe and former European colonies to this day.

Christianity gained the support of the fourth-century emperors and gradually adopted the Roman system of hierarchical organization. The church possessed able administrators and leaders whose skills were tested in the chaotic environment of the end of the Roman Empire in the West. Bishops expanded their activities, and in the fifth century the bishops of Rome began to stress their supremacy over other Christian communities. Monasteries offered opportunities for individuals to develop deeper spiritual devotion and also provided a model of Christian living, a pattern of agricultural development, and a place for education and learning.

Christian thinkers reinterpreted the classics in a Christian sense, incorporating elements of Greek and Roman philosophy and of various pagan religious groups into Christian teachings. Prime among these were certain aspects of Greco-Roman notions of gender and sexuality. Most Christian thinkers accepted Greco-Roman ideas that men were superior to women, though they viewed sexuality and the body with greater suspicion than had ancient pagans and developed a strong sense that chastity and an ascetic life were superior to marriage and family life. Of these early thinkers, Augustine of Hippo was the most influential. His ideas about sin, free will, sexuality, and the role of government shaped western European thought from the fifth century on.

Christianity had a dynamic missionary policy, and the church slowly succeeded in assimilating—that is, adapting—barbarian peoples to Christian teaching. Christian missionaries preached the Gospel to Germanic, Celtic, and Slavic peoples, instructed them in the basic tenets of the Christian faith, and used penitentials to give them a sense of expected behavior. Christianity refashioned the Germanic and classical legacies, creating new rituals and practices that were meaningful to people.

The migration of barbarian groups into Europe from the east affected both the regions to which peoples moved and the ones they left behind. Migrations were caused by many factors, including food shortages, disputes among groups, and pressure from outside, and they sometimes involved military actions, though not always. Barbarians are often divided into large linguistic groups, such as the Celtic and Germanic tribes, with ties to other tribes based on kinship and military alliances, not on loyalty to a particular government. Most barbarian states were weak and short-lived, though that of the Salian Franks was relatively more unified and powerful. Germanic-speaking Angles and Saxons invaded Celtic-speaking England and established a group of small kingdoms that slowly became more unified.

Though barbarian states were generally feeble politically, barbarian customs and traditions formed the basis of European society for centuries. Barbarian law codes, written down for the first time in the sixth century, set out social and gender distinctions and held the family responsible for the actions of an individual. Most people lived in family groups in villages, where men, women, and children shared in the agricultural labor that sustained society. Christianity and the barbarian states absorbed many aspects of Roman culture, and the Byzantine Empire continued to thrive, but western Europe was very different in 600 from how it had been in 350.

Key Terms

Arianism	penitentials
Orthodox church	relics
Petrine Doctrine	barbarians
eremitical	foederati
coenobitic	Salic Law
monasticism	Merovingian
regular clergy	runic alphabet
secular clergy	comitatus
sacraments	wergeld

Online Study Center **Improve Your Grade** Flashcards

Suggested Reading

Brown, Peter. *Augustine of Hippo,* rev. ed. 2000. The best biography of Saint Augustine, which treats him as a symbol of change.

Brown, Peter. *The Body and Society: Men, Women, and Sexual Renunciation in Early Christianity.* 1988. Explores early Christian attitudes on sexuality and how they replaced Roman ones.

Brown, Peter. *The World of Late Antiquity,* A.D. 150–750, rev. ed. 1989. A lavishly illustrated survey that stresses social and cultural change and has clearly written introductions to the entire period.

Burns, Thomas S. *Rome and the Barbarians, 100 B.C.–400 A.D.* 2003. Argues that Germanic and Roman culture assimilated more than they conflicted.

Cameron, Averil. *The Mediterranean World in Late Antiquity, AD 395–600.* 1993. Focuses especially on political and economic changes.

Clark, Gilian. *Women in Late Antiquity: Pagan and Christian Lifestyles.* 1994. Explores law, marriage, and religious life.

Dunn, Marilyn. *The Emergence of Monasticism: From the Desert Fathers to the Early Middle Ages.* 2003. Focuses on the beginnings of monasticism.

Evans, James Allan. *The Empress Theodora: Partner of Justinian.* 2003. Provides a brief, yet balanced and thorough treatment of the empress's life.

Fletcher, Richard. *The Barbarian Conversion: From Paganism to Christianity.* 1998. A superbly written analysis of conversion to Christianity.

Herrin, Judith. *The Formation of Christendom.* 1987. The best synthesis of the development of the Christian church from the third to the ninth centuries.

Macmullen, Ramsey. *Christianity and Paganism in the Fourth to Eighth Centuries.* 1998. Explores the influences of Christianity and paganism on each other.

Norwich, John Julius. *Byzantium: The Early Centuries.* 1989. An elegantly written brief survey.

Pelikan, Jaroslav. *The Excellent Empire: The Fall of Rome and the Triumph of the Church.* 1987. Describes how interpretations of the fall of Rome have influenced our understanding of Western culture.

Todd, Malcolm. *The Early Germans,* 2d ed. 2004. Uses archaeological and literary sources to analyze Germanic social structure, customs, and religion and to suggest implications for an understanding of migration and ethnicity.

Wells, Peter S. *The Barbarians Speak: How the Conquered Peoples Shaped Roman Europe.* 1999. Presents extensive evidence of Celtic and Germanic social and technical development.

Notes

1. Quoted in J. B. Bury, *History of the Latter Roman Empire,* vol. 1 (New York: Dover, 1958), pp. 233–234.
2. R. Atwater, trans., *Procopius: The Secret History* (Ann Arbor: University of Michigan Press, 1963), bk. 8.
3. R. C. Petry, ed., *A History of Christianity: Readings in the History of Early and Medieval Christianity* (Englewood Cliffs, N.J.: Prentice Hall, 1962), p. 70.
4. Matthew 16:18–19.
5. H. Bettenson, ed., *Documents of the Christian Church* (Oxford: Oxford University Press, 1947), p. 113.
6. Peter 2:11–20.
7. Colossians 3:9–11.
8. L. Sherley-Price, trans., *Bede: A History of the English Church and People* (Baltimore: Penguin Books, 1962), pp. 86–87.
9. See W. Goffart, *Barbarians and Romans: The Techniques of Accommodation* (Princeton, N.J.: Princeton University Press, 1980), chap. 3 and esp. Conclusion, pp. 211–230.
10. H. Wolfram, *History of the Goths* (Berkeley: University of California Press, 1988), pp. 6–10.
11. Ibid., pp. 125–131.
12. E. James, *The Franks* (New York: Basil Blackwell, 1988), pp. 3, 7–10, 58.
13. I. Wood, *The Merovingian Kingdoms, 450–751* (New York: Longman, 1994), pp. 41–45.
14. P. J. Geary, *Before France and Germany: The Creation and Transformation of the Merovingian World* (New York: Oxford University Press, 1988), pp. 108–112.
15. E. F. Henderson, ed., *Select Historical Documents of the Middle Ages* (London: G. Bell & Sons, 1912), pp. 176–189.
16. Geary, *Before France and Germany,* p. 46.
17. Ibid., p. 50.

The Conversion of Clovis

Modern Christian doctrine holds that conversion is a process, the gradual turning toward Jesus and the teachings of the Christian Gospels. But in the early medieval world, conversion was perceived more as a one-time event determined by the tribal chieftain. If he accepted baptism, the mass conversion of his people followed. This selection about the Frankish king Clovis is from The History of the Franks *by Gregory, bishop of Tours (ca 504–594), written about a century after the events it describes.*

The first child which Clotild bore for Clovis was a son. She wanted to have her baby baptized, and she kept urging her husband to agree to this. "The gods whom you worship are no good," she would say. "They haven't even been able to help themselves, let alone others. . . . Take your Saturn, for example, who ran away from his own son to avoid being exiled from his kingdom, or so they say; and Jupiter, that obscene perpetrator of all sorts of mucky deeds, who couldn't keep his hands off other men, who had his fun with all his female relatives and couldn't even refrain from intercourse with his own sister. . . .

"You ought instead to worship Him who created at a word and out of nothing heaven, and earth, the sea and all that therein is, who made the sun to shine, who lit the sky with stars, who peopled the water with fish, the earth with beasts, the sky with flying creatures, by whose hand the race of man was made, by whose gift all creation is constrained to serve in deference and devotion the man He made." However often the Queen said this, the King came no nearer to belief. . . .

The Queen, who was true to her faith, brought her son to be baptized. . . . The child was baptized; he was given the name Ingomer; but no sooner had he received baptism than he died in his white robes. Clovis was extremely angry. He began immediately to reproach his Queen. "If he had been dedicated in the name of my gods," he said, "he would have lived without question; but now that he has been baptized in the name of your God he has not been able to live a single day!"

"I give thanks to Almighty God," replied Clotild, "the Creator of all things who has not found me completely unworthy, for He has deigned to welcome into his Kingdom a child conceived in my womb. . . ."

Some time later Clotild bore a second son. He was baptized Chlodomer. He began to ail and Clovis said, "What else do you expect? It will happen to him as it happened to his brother: no sooner is he baptized in the name of your Christ than he will die!" Clotild prayed to the Lord and at His commands the baby recovered.

Queen Clotild continued to pray that her husband might recognize the true God and give up his idol-worship. Nothing could persuade him to accept Christianity. Finally war broke out against the Alamanni and in this conflict he was forced by necessity to accept what he had refused of his own free will. It so turned out that when the two armies met on the battlefield there was a great slaughter and the troops of Clovis were rapidly being annihilated. He raised his eyes to Heaven when he saw this, felt compunction in his heart and was moved to tears. "Jesus Christ," he said, "you who Clotild maintains to be the Son of the living God, you who deign to give help to those in travail and victory to those who trust in you, in faith I beg the glory of your help. If you will give me victory over my enemies, and if I may have evidence to that miraculous power which the people dedicated to your name say that they have experienced, then I will believe in you and I will be baptized in your name. I have called upon my own gods, but, as I see only too

Ninth-century ivory carving showing Clovis being baptized by Saint Remi. *(Musée Condé, Chantilly/Laurie Platt Winfrey, Inc.)*

clearly, they have no intention of helping me. I therefore cannot believe that they possess any power for they do not come to the assistance of those who trust them. I now call upon you. I want to believe in you, but I must first be saved from my enemies." Even as he said this the Alamanni turned their backs and began to run away. As soon as they saw that their King was killed, they submitted to Clovis. "We beg you," they said, "to put an end to this slaughter. We are prepared to obey you." Clovis stopped the war. He made a speech in which he called for peace. Then he went home. He told the Queen how he had won a victory by calling on the name of Christ. This happened in the fifteenth year of his reign (496).

The Queen then ordered Saint Remigius, Bishop of the town of Rheims, to be summoned in secret. She begged him to impart the word of salvation to the King. The Bishop asked Clovis to meet him in private and began to urge him to believe in the true God, Maker of Heaven and earth, and to forsake his idols, which were powerless to help him or anyone else. The King replied: "I have listened to you willingly, holy father. There remains one obstacle. The people under my command will not agree to forsake their gods. I will go and put to them what you have just said to me." He arranged a meeting with his people, but God in his power had preceded him, and before he could say a word all those present shouted in unison: "We will give up worshipping our mortal gods, pious King, and we are prepared to follow the immortal God about whom Remigius preaches." This news was reported to the Bishop. He was greatly pleased and he ordered the baptismal pool to be made ready. . . . The baptistry was prepared, sticks of incense gave off clouds of perfume, sweet-smelling candles gleamed bright and the holy place of baptism was filled with divine fragrance. God filled the hearts of all present with such grace that they imagined themselves to have been transported to some perfumed paradise. King Clovis asked that he might be baptized first by the Bishop. Like some new Constantine he stepped forward to the baptismal pool, ready to wash away the sores of his old leprosy and to be cleansed in flowing water from the sordid stains which he had borne so long.

King Clovis confessed his belief in God Almighty, three in one. He was baptized in the name of the Father, the Son and the Holy Ghost, and marked in holy chrism [an anointing oil] with the sign of the Cross of Christ. More than three thousand of his army were baptized at the same time.

Questions for Analysis

1. Who took the initiative in urging Clovis's conversion? What can we deduce from that?

2. According to this account, why did Clovis ultimately accept Christianity?

3. For the Salian Franks, what was the best proof of divine power?

4. On the basis of this selection, do you consider *The History of the Franks* reliable history? Why?

Sources: L. Thorpe, trans., *The History of the Franks by Gregory of Tours* (Harmondsworth, England: Penguin, 1974), p. 159; P. J. Geary, ed., *Readings in Medieval History* (Peterborough, Ontario: Broadview Press, 1991), pp. 165–166.

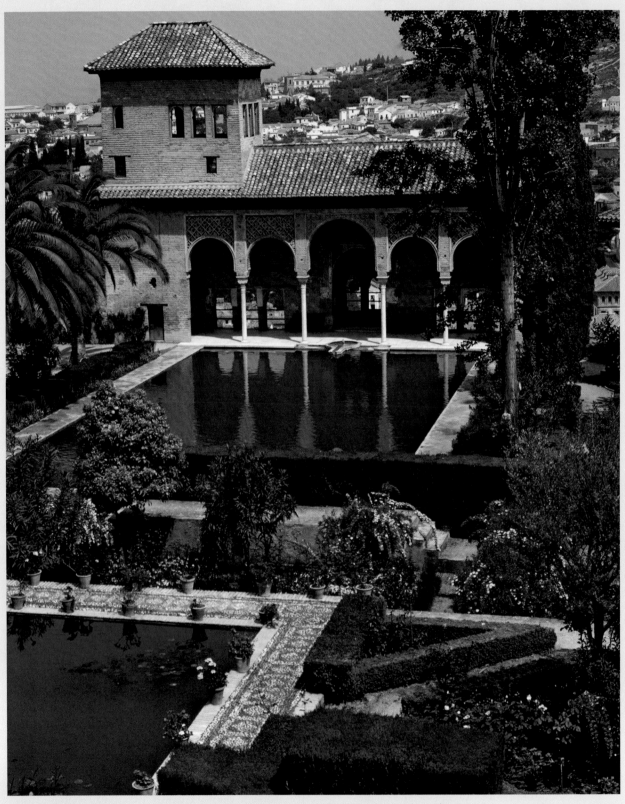

Garden built by Muslim rulers in Seville, Spain. Tranquil gardens such as this one represented paradise in Islamic culture, perhaps because of the religion's desert origins. *(Ric Ergenbright/Corbis)*

EUROPE IN THE EARLY MIDDLE AGES, 600–1000

In the fifteenth century writers and scholars in the growing cities of northern Italy began to think that they were living in a new era, one in which the glories of ancient Greece and Rome were being reborn. What separated their own time from classical antiquity, in their opinion, was a long period of darkness, to which a seventeenth-century professor gave the name "Middle Ages" (*Medium Aevum* in Latin). In this conceptualization, Western history was divided into three periods—ancient, medieval (a word derived from the Latin), and modern.

This three-part schema is still the primary way of organizing Western history. Exactly what marked the dividing lines between these periods was not very clear, however. For a long time the end of the Roman Empire in the West in 476 was seen as the division between the classical period and the Middle Ages, but as we saw in the last chapter, more recent historians have emphasized continuities as well as changes in the fifth and sixth centuries. The transition from ancient to medieval was a slow process, not a single event. The agents in this process included not only the Germanic tribes whose migrations broke the Roman Empire apart but also the new religion of Islam, Slavic and steppe peoples in eastern Europe, and Christian officials and missionaries. The period from the end of antiquity to about 1000, conventionally known as the "Early Middle Ages," was a time of disorder and destruction, but also of the creation of a new type of society. People at the time did not know that they were living in an era that would later be labeled "middle" or sometimes even "dark," and we can wonder whether they would have shared this somewhat negative view of their own times.

The Spread of Islam

In the seventh century A.D. two empires dominated the area today called the Middle East: the Byzantine-Greek-Christian empire and the Sasanian-Persian-Zoroastrian empire. The Arabian peninsula lay between the two. The Sasanian dynasty, which descended from Persian-speaking people of present-day southern Iran, maintained political control over very diverse

Online Study Center

This icon will direct you to interactive activities and study materials on the website **college.hmco.com/pic/mckaywest9e**

peoples through government officials and by requiring loyalty to the ancient religion of Iraq, Zoroastrianism (see pages 49–50). The Sasanian capital of Ctesiphon in what is now central Iraq had become a center of Jewish religious learning and a refuge for pagan philosophers and medical scientists from the Greek cities after Justinian forbade the teaching of pagan philosophy and law in 529. The cosmopolitan culture thus created became the source of much classical Greek philosophical and medical knowledge that later came to the European world in Arabic translations.

Around 610 in the commercial city of Mecca in what is now Saudi Arabia, a merchant called Muhammad began to have religious visions. By the time he died in 632, all Arabia had accepted his creed. A century later his followers controlled Syria, Palestine, Egypt, North Africa, Spain, and part of France. This Arabic expansion profoundly affected the development of Western civilization as well as the history of Africa and Asia.

• *How did the spread of Islam shape European history in this era?*

The Arabs

In Muhammad's time Arabia was inhabited by various tribes, most of them Bedouins. These nomadic peoples grazed goats and sheep on the sparse patches of grass that dotted the vast semiarid peninsula. Other Arabs lived in the southern valleys and coastal towns along the Red Sea in Yemen, Mecca, Medina, and the northwestern region called "Hejaz." The Hejazi led a more sophisticated life and supported themselves by agriculture and trade. Their caravan routes crisscrossed Arabia and carried goods to Byzantium, Persia, and Syria. The Hejazi had wide commercial dealings but avoided cultural contacts with their Jewish, Christian, and Persian neighbors. The wealth produced by their business transactions led to luxurious and extravagant living in the towns.

Although the nomadic Bedouins condemned the urbanized lifestyle of the Hejazi as immoral and corrupt, Arabs of both types respected one another's local tribal customs. They had no political unity beyond their tribal bonds. Custom demanded the rigid observance of family obligations and the performance of religious rituals. Custom insisted that an Arab be proud, generous, and swift to take revenge. Custom required courage in public and avoidance of behavior that could bring social disgrace.

Although the various tribes differed markedly, they had certain religious rules in common. For example, all Arabs kept three months of the year as sacred; during

that time fighting stopped so that everyone could attend holy ceremonies in peace. The city of Mecca was the religious center of the Arab world, and fighting was never tolerated there. All Arabs prayed at the Kaaba, the sanctuary in Mecca. Within the Kaaba was a sacred black stone that Arabs revered because they believed it had fallen from heaven.

What eventually molded the diverse Arab tribes into a powerful political and social unity was the religion based on the teachings of Muhammad.

The Prophet Muhammad

Except for a few vague remarks in the **Qur'an,** the sacred book of Islam, Muhammad (ca 571–632) left no account of his life. Arab tradition accepts some of the sacred legends that developed about him as historically true, but those legends were not written down until about a century after his death. (Similarly, the earliest accounts of the life of Jesus, the Christian Gospels, were not written until forty to sixty years after his death.) Orphaned at the age of six, Muhammad was brought up by his grandfather. When he was a young man, he became a merchant in the caravan trade. Later he entered the service of a wealthy widow, and their subsequent marriage brought him financial independence. The Qur'an reveals him to be an extremely devout man, ascetic, self-disciplined, and literate, but not educated.

Since childhood Muhammad had been subject to seizures during which he lost consciousness and had visions. After 610 these visions apparently became more frequent. Unsure for a time about what he should do, Muhammad discovered his mission after a vision in which the angel Gabriel instructed him to preach. Muhammad described his visions in a stylized and often rhyming prose and used this literary medium as his *Qur'an,* or "prayer recitation."

Muhammad's revelations were written down by his followers during his lifetime and organized into chapters shortly after his death. In 651 Muhammad's third successor as religious leader, Othman, arranged to have an official version published. The Qur'an is regarded by Muslims as the direct words of God to his Prophet Muhammad and is therefore especially revered. (These revelations were in Arabic. When Muslims use translations in other languages, they do so alongside the original Arabic.) At the same time, other sayings and accounts of Muhammad, which gave advice on matters that went beyond the Qur'an, were collected into books termed *hadith.* Muslim tradition (*Sunna*) consists of both the Qur'an and the hadith.

Muhammad's visions ordered him to preach a message of a single God and to become God's Prophet, which he began to do in his hometown of Mecca. He gathered followers slowly but also provoked a great deal of resistance, and in 622 he migrated with his followers to Medina, an event termed the *hijra* that marks the beginning of the Muslim calendar. At Medina Muhammad was much more successful, gaining converts and working out the basic principles of the faith. In 630 Muhammad returned to Mecca at the head of a large army, and by his death in 632 he had unified most of the Arabian peninsula into a religious/political community (termed the *umma*) of *Muslims*, a word meaning those who comply with God's will. (The first umma was formed by the Charter of Medina in 622 and included the local Jewish community, which established a precedent for the later protection of Jews under Islam.) The religion itself came to be called **Islam,** which means "submission to God." The Kaaba was rededicated as a Muslim holy place, and Mecca became the most holy city in Islam. According to Muslim tradition, the Kaaba predates the creation of the world and represents the earthly counterpart of God's heavenly throne, to which "pilgrims come dishevelled and dusty on every kind of camel."[1]

The Teachings of Islam

Muhammad's religion eventually attracted great numbers of people, partly because of the straightforward nature of its doctrines. The strictly monotheistic theology outlined in the Qur'an has only a few central tenets. Allah, the Arabic word for God, is all-powerful and all-knowing. Muhammad, Allah's prophet, preached his word and carried his message. Muhammad described himself as the successor both of the Jewish patriarch Abraham and of Christ, and he claimed that his teachings replaced theirs. He invited and won converts from Judaism and Christianity.

Because Allah is all-powerful, believers must submit themselves to him. All Muslims have the obligation of the *jihad* (literally "self-exertion") to strive or struggle to lead a virtuous life and to spread God's rule and law. In some cases striving was individual against sin; in others it was social and communal and could involve armed conflict, though this was not an essential part of jihad. The Islamic belief of "striving in the path of God" is closely related to the central feature of Muslim doctrine, the coming Day of Judgment. Muslims need not be concerned about *when* judgment will occur, but they must believe with absolute and total conviction that the Day of Judgment *will* come. Consequently, all of a Muslim's

Chronology

ca 571–632	Life of the Prophet Muhammad
700	Lindisfarne Gospel produced in Northumbria
711–720	Muslim conquest of Spain
ca 720	Venerable Bede writes *Ecclesiastical History of the English People*
760s–840s	Carolingian Renaissance
768–814	Reign of Charlemagne
800–900	Free peasants in western Europe increasingly tied to the land as serfs
820	Muslim mathematician al-Khwarizmi writes first treatise on algebra
843	Treaty of Verdun divides Carolingian kingdom
850–1000	Most extensive Viking raids
ca 900	Establishment of Kievan Rus
950	Muslim Córdoba is Europe's largest and most prosperous city
1001	Establishment of kingdom of Hungary

thoughts and actions should be oriented toward the Last Judgment and the rewards of Heaven. The Muslim vision of paradise features lush green gardens surrounded by refreshing streams. There the saved, clothed in rich silks, lounge on brocade couches, nibbling ripe fruits, sipping delicious beverages, and enjoying the companionship of physically attractive people.

Online Study Center **Improve Your Grade**
Primary Source: The Qur'an: Call for Jihad

To merit the rewards of Heaven, a person must follow the strict code of moral behavior that Muhammad prescribed. The Muslim must recite a profession of faith in God and in Muhammad as God's prophet: "There is no god but God and Muhammad is his prophet." The believer must pray five times a day, fast and pray during the sacred month of Ramadan, and contribute alms to the poor and needy. If possible, the believer must make a pilgrimage to Mecca once during his or her lifetime. According to the Muslim *shari'a,* or sacred law, these five practices—the profession of faith, prayer, fasting, giving alms to the poor, and pilgrimage to Mecca—constitute the **Five Pillars of Islam.**

Muhammad and the Earlier Prophets   Muhammad, with his head surrounded by fire representing religious fervor, leads Abraham, Moses, and Jesus in prayer. Islamic tradition holds that Judaism, Christianity, and Islam all derive from the pure religion of Abraham, but humankind has strayed from that faith. Therefore, Muhammad, as "the seal (last) of the prophets," had to transmit God's revelations to humankind. *(Bibliothèque nationale de France)*

The Qur'an forbids alcoholic beverages and gambling. It condemns business *usury*—that is, lending money at interest rates or taking advantage of market demand for products by charging high prices for them. A number of foods, such as pork, are also forbidden, a dietary regulation adopted from the Mosaic law of the Hebrews.

By earlier Arab standards, the Qur'an sets forth an austere sexual morality. Muslim jurisprudence condemned licentious behavior on the part of men as well as women, which enhanced the status of women in Muslim society. So, too, did Muhammad's opposition to female infanticide. About marriage, illicit intercourse, and inheritance, the Qur'an states:

[Of] women who seem good in your eyes, marry but two, three, or four; and if ye still fear that ye shall not act equitably then only one. . . . The whore and the fornicator: whip each of them a hundred times. . . .

The fornicator shall not marry other than a whore; and the whore shall not marry other than a fornicator. . . .

Men who die and leave wives behind shall bequeath to them a year's maintenance.

And your wives shall have a fourth part of what you leave, if you have no issue [offspring]; but if you have issue, then they shall have an eighth part. . . .

With regard to your children, God commands you to give the male the portion of two females.

Polygyny, the practice of men having more than one wife, was common in Arab society before Muhammad, though for economic reasons the custom was limited to the well-to-do. Nevertheless, some commentators hold that in limiting the number of wives to four—or even one if the man could not treat all fairly—Muhammad was being revolutionary.

Westerners tend to think polygyny degrading to women, but in a military society where there were apt to be many widows, polygyny provided women with a measure of security. With respect to matters of property, Muslim women were more emancipated than Western women. For example, a Muslim woman retained complete jurisdiction over one-third of her property when she married and could dispose of it in any way she wished. Women in most European countries and the United States did not gain these rights until the nineteenth century.[2]

The Muslim who faithfully observed the laws of the Qur'an could hope for salvation. According to the Qur'an, salvation is by God's grace and choice alone. Because God is all-knowing and all-powerful, he knows from the moment of a person's conception whether that person will be saved. Although later Muslim scholars have held a number of positions on the topic of predestination, ranging from complete fatalism to a strong belief in human free will, Muhammad maintained that predestination gave believers the will and courage to try to achieve the impossible. Devout Muslims came to believe that the performance of the faith's basic rules would automatically gain them salvation. Moreover, the believer who suffered and died for his faith in battle was immediately ensured the rewards of the Muslim heaven.

What did early Muslims think of Jesus? Jesus is mentioned in ninety-three verses of the Qur'an, which affirms that he was born of Mary the Virgin. He is described as a righteous prophet who performed miracles and continued the work of Abraham and Moses, and he was a sign of the coming Day of Judgment. But Muslims held that Jesus was an apostle only, not God, and that people (that is, Christians) who called Jesus divine committed blasphemy (showing contempt for God). Muslims esteemed the Judeo-Christian Scriptures as part of God's revelation, although they believed that Christian communities had corrupted the Scriptures and that the Qur'an superseded them. The Christian doctrine of the Trinity—that there is one God in three persons (Father, Son, and Holy Spirit)—posed a powerful obstacle to Muslim-Christian understanding because of Islam's total and uncompromising monotheism.[3]

There are many similarities among Islam, Christianity, and Judaism. All three religions are monotheistic; all worship the same God. Like Jews, Muslims customarily worship together at sundown on Fridays, and no assembly or organized church is essential. Muslims call Jews and Christians *dhimmis,* or "protected people," because they were people of the book, the Hebrew Scriptures.

Expansion and Schism

Islam transcended the geographical and public aspects of the Arabic tribal religion represented by Bedouin and Hejazi societies (see page 224). Every Muslim hoped to achieve salvation by following the requirements of Islam. For the believer, the petty disputes and conflicts of tribal society paled before the simple teachings of Allah. On this basis, Muhammad united the nomads of the desert and the merchants of the cities. The doctrines of Islam, instead of the ties of local custom, bound all Arabs.

By the time Muhammad died in 632, he had welded together all the Bedouin tribes. The crescent of Islam, the Muslim symbol, prevailed throughout the Arabian peninsula. During the next century one rich province of the old Roman Empire after another came under Muslim domination—first Syria, then Egypt, and then all of North Africa (see Map 8.1). Long and bitter wars (572–591, 606–630) between the Byzantine and Persian Empires left both so weak and exhausted that they easily fell to Muslim attack. The government headquarters of this vast new empire was established at Damascus in Syria by the ruling Umayyad family. By the early tenth century a Muslim proverb spoke of the Mediterranean Sea as a Muslim lake, though the Greeks at Constantinople contested that notion. From the Arabian peninsula, Muslims carried their faith deep into Africa and across Asia all the way to India.

Despite the clarity and unifying force of Muslim doctrine, a schism soon developed within the Islamic faith. Neither the Qur'an nor the hadith gave clear guidance about how successors to Muhammad were to be chosen, but a group of Muhammad's closest followers elected Abu Bakr, who was a close friend of the Prophet's and a member of a small tribe affiliated to the Prophet's tribe, as **caliph,** a word meaning "successor." This election set a precedent for the ratification of the subsequent patriarchal caliphs, though it was unsuccessfully opposed militarily by other Arab tribes.

A more serious opposition developed later among supporters of the fourth caliph, Ali. Ali claimed the caliphate because of his blood ties with Muhammad—he was Muhammad's cousin and son-in-law—and because the Prophet had designated him as *imam,* or leader. Ali was assassinated shortly after becoming caliph, and his supporters began to assert that he should rightly have been the first caliph and that all subsequent caliphs were usurpers. These supporters of Ali—termed *Shi'ites* or *Shi'a* from Arabic terms meaning "supporters" or "partisans" of Ali—saw Ali and subsequent imams as the divinely

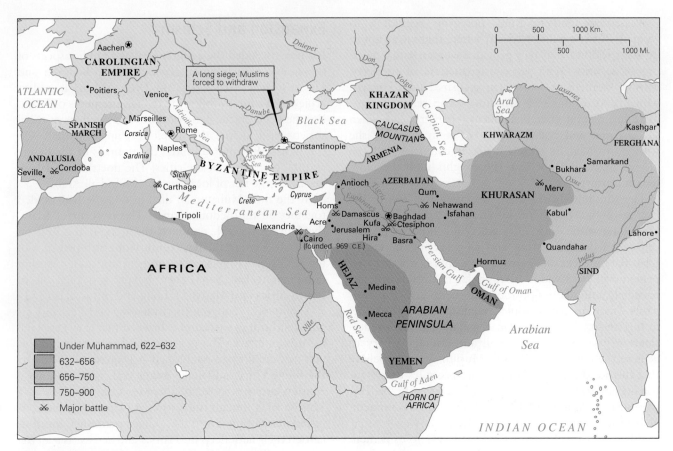

MAP 8.1 The Islamic World, ca 900   The rapid expansion of Islam in a relatively short span of time testifies to the Arabs' superior fighting skills, religious zeal, and economic organization as well as to their enemies' weakness.

Online Study Center   **Improve Your Grade** Interactive Map: The Expansion of Islam to 732

inspired leaders of the community. The larger body of Muslims who accepted the first elections—termed *Sunnis,* a word derived from *Sunna,* the traditional beliefs and practices of the community—saw the caliphs as political leaders. Since Islam did not have an organized church and priesthood, the caliphs had an additional function of safeguarding and enforcing the religious law (shari'a) with the advice of scholars (*ulama*), particularly the jurists, judges, and scholastics who were knowledgeable about the Qur'an and hadith. Over the centuries, many different kinds of Shi'ites appeared, and enmity between Sunni and Shi'a Muslims sometimes erupted into violence.

Muslim Spain

In Europe, Muslim political and cultural influence was felt most strongly in the Iberian Peninsula. In 711 a Muslim force crossed the Strait of Gibraltar and easily defeated the weak Visigothic kingdom. A few Christian princes supported by the Frankish rulers held out in northern mountain fortresses, but the Muslims took over most of Spain. A member of the Umayyad dynasty, Abd al-Rahman (r. 756–788), established a kingdom in Spain with its capital at Córdoba.

Throughout the Islamic world, Muslims used the term **al-Andalus** to describe the part of the Iberian Peninsula under Muslim control. The name al-Andalus probably derives from the Arabic for "land of the Vandals," the Germanic people who swept across Spain in the fifth century. In the eighth century al-Andalus included the entire peninsula from Gibraltar in the south to the Cantabrian Mountains in the north (see Map 8.1). Today we often use the word *Andalusia* to refer especially to southern Spain, but eighth-century Christians throughout Europe called the peninsula "Moorish Spain" because the people who invaded and conquered it were Moors—Berbers from northwest Africa. The ethnic term *Moorish* can be misleading, however, because the peninsula was home to sizable numbers of Jews and Christians as well as (Muslim) Moors. In business transactions and in much of daily life, all peoples used the Arabic language. With Muslims, Christians, and Jews trading with and learning from one another and occasionally intermarrying, Moorish Spain and Norman Sicily (see Chapter 9) were the only distinctly pluralistic societies in medieval Europe.

Harvesting Dates This detail from an ivory casket given to a Córdoban prince reflects the importance of fruit cultivation in the Muslim-inspired agricultural expansion in southern Europe in the ninth and tenth centuries. (*Louvre/Réunion des Musées Nationaux/Art Resource, NY*)

Between roughly the eighth and twelfth centuries, Muslims, Christians, and Jews lived close together in Andalusia, and some scholars believe that the early part of this period was an era of remarkable interfaith harmony. Jews in Muslim Spain were generally treated well, and Córdoba became a center of Jewish as well as Muslim learning. Many Christians adopted Arabic patterns of speech and dress, gave up the practice of eating pork, and developed a special appreciation for Arabic music and poetry. Some Christian women of elite status chose the Muslim practice of veiling their faces in public. Records describe Muslim and Christian youths joining in celebrations and merrymaking. These assimilated Christians, called Mozarabs, did not attach much importance to the doctrinal differences between the two religions.

Al-Andalus can be analyzed from several perspectives. From the sophisticated centers of Muslim culture in Baghdad, Damascus, and Cairo (founded 969), al-Andalus seemed a provincial backwater, a frontier outpost with little significance in the wide context of Islamic civilization. "Northern barbarians," on the other hand—the Muslim name for European peoples—acknowledged the splendor of Spanish culture. For example, the Saxon nun and writer Hroswita of Gandersheim called the city of

Córdoba "the ornament of the world." With a population of about half a million; with well-paved and well-lighted streets and an abundance of fresh water; with 1,000 mosques, 900 public baths, 213,177 houses for ordinary people, and 60,000 mansions for officials and the wealthy; with 80,455 shops and 13,000 weavers producing silks, woolens, and brocades; with 27 free schools and a library containing 400,000 volumes (the largest library in northern Europe, at the Benedictine abbey of St. Gall in Switzerland, had 600 books), Córdoba was indeed an ornament, and the Western world had no comparable urban center.

In Spain, as elsewhere in the Arab world, the Muslims had an enormous impact on agricultural development. They began the cultivation of rice, sugar cane, citrus fruits, dates, figs, eggplants, carrots, and, after the eleventh century, cotton. These crops, together with new methods of field irrigation, provided the urban population with food products unknown in the rest of Europe.

About 950 Caliph Abd al-Rahman III (912–961) of the Umayyad dynasty of Córdoba ruled most of the Iberian Peninsula from the Mediterranean in the south to the Ebro River in the north. Christian Spain consisted of the tiny kingdoms of Castile, León, Catalonia, Aragon, Navarre, and Portugal. Civil wars among al-Rahman's descendents weakened the caliphate, and the small northern Christian kingdoms expanded southward.

Science and Medicine

The Islamic world, both in Spain and elsewhere, profoundly shaped Christian European culture. Toledo, for example, became an important center of learning through which Arab intellectual achievements entered and influenced western Europe. Arabic knowledge of science and mathematics, derived from the Chinese, Greeks, and Hindus, was highly sophisticated. The Muslim mathematician al-Khwarizmi (d. 830) wrote the important treatise *Algebra,* the first work in which the word *algebra* is used mathematically. Al-Khwarizmi adopted the Hindu system of numbers (1, 2, 3, 4), used it in his *Algebra,* and applied mathematics to problems of physics and astronomy. Scholars at Baghdad translated Euclid's *Elements,* the basic text for plane and solid geometry. Muslims also instructed Westerners in the use of the zero, which permitted the execution of complicated problems of multiplication and long division. Use of the zero represented an enormous advance over clumsy Roman numerals. (Since our system of numbers is actually Hindu in origin, the term *Arabic numerals,* coined about 1847, is a misnomer.)

Middle Eastern Arabs translated and codified the scientific and philosophical learning of Greek and Persian antiquity. In the ninth and tenth centuries that knowledge was brought to Spain, where between 1150 and 1250 it was translated into Latin. Europeans' knowledge of Aristotle changed the entire direction of European philosophy and theology (see page 85). Isaac Newton's discoveries in mathematics in the seventeenth century rested on ancient Greek theories translated in Spain.

In the transmission of Greek learning, one Muslim technological accomplishment played a most significant role—paper. Second-century Chinese initially used rags to make paper, but they soon shifted to woody fibers from such plants as hemp, jute, and bamboo. The Chinese invented paper not for writing but for wrapping goods. Merchants and Buddhist missionaries carried the skills of papermaking to Samarkand in Central Asia (see Map 8.1). After Arab armies overran Central Asia in the eighth century, Muslim papermakers improved on Chinese techniques: Muslims beat the fibers of rags and then used starch to fill the pores in the surfaces of the sheets. They carried this new method to Baghdad in Iraq, Damascus in Syria, Cairo in Egypt, and the Maghrib (North Africa), from which it entered Spain. Even before the invention of printing (see page 418), papermaking had a revolutionary impact on the collection and diffusion of knowledge and thus on the transformation of society.[4]

Muslim medical knowledge far surpassed that of the West. By the ninth century Arab physicians had translated most of the treatises of Hippocrates. The Baghdad physician al-Razi (865–925) produced an encyclopedic treatise on medicine that was translated into Latin and circulated widely in the West. Al-Razi was the first physician to make the clinical distinction between measles and smallpox. The great surgeon of Córdoba, al-Zahrawi (d. 1013), produced an important work in which he discussed the cauterization of wounds (searing with a branding iron) and the crushing of stones in the bladder. Arabic science reached its peak in the physician, philologist, philosopher, poet, and scientist ibn-Sina of Bukhara (980–1037), known in the West as Avicenna. His *al-Qanun* codified all Greco-Arabic medical thought, described the contagious nature of tuberculosis and the spreading of diseases, and listed 760 pharmaceutical drugs.

Unfortunately, many of these treatises came to the West as translations from Greek to Arabic and then to Latin and inevitably lost a great deal in translation. Nevertheless, in the ninth and tenth centuries Arabic knowledge and experience in anatomy and pharmaceutical prescriptions much enriched Western knowledge.

Muslim-Christian Relations

Beyond Andalusian Spain, mutual animosity restricted contact between Muslims and Christians. The Muslim expansion into Christian Europe in the eighth and ninth centuries left a legacy of bitter hostility. Christians felt threatened by a faith that acknowledged God as creator of the universe but denied the doctrine of the Trinity and that accepted Jesus as a prophet but denied his divinity. Europeans' perception of Islam as a menace helped inspire the Crusades of the eleventh through thirteenth centuries (see pages 279–286).

By the thirteenth century Western literature sometimes displayed a sympathetic view of Islam. The Bavarian knight Wolfram von Eschenbach's *Parzival* and the Englishman William Langland's *Piers the Plowman*—two poems that survive in scores of manuscripts, suggesting that they circulated widely—reveal some broad-mindedness and tolerance toward Muslims. Some travelers in the Middle East were impressed by the kindness and generosity of Muslims and with the strictness and devotion with which Muslims observed their faith.[5]

More frequently, however, Christian literature portrayed Muslims as the most dreadful of Europe's enemies, guilty of every kind of crime. In his *Inferno* the great Florentine poet Dante placed the Muslim philosophers Avicenna and Averroes with other virtuous "heathens," among them Socrates and Aristotle, in the first circle of Hell, where they endured only moderate punishment. Muhammad, however, Dante consigned to the ninth circle, near Satan himself, where he was condemned as a spreader of discord and scandal.

Muslim views of Christians were also mixed, but here disinterest may have been more common than hostility. Muslim historical writing reflects strong knowledge of European geography but shows an almost total lack of interest in European languages, life, and culture. Muslims had a strong aversion to travel in Europe. Medieval Europe had no resident Muslim communities where a traveler could find the mosques, foods, or other things desirable for the Muslim way of life. When compelled to make diplomatic or business contacts, Muslims preferred to send Jewish or Christian intermediaries. Commercially, from the Muslim perspective, Europe had very little to offer apart from woolens from the Frisian Islands in the North Sea, which the Muslims admired, and some slaves from central and southeastern Europe.

In their understanding of the nature and purpose of the state, Muslims and Christians revealed an important similarity and a very real difference. Just as for Christians the state existed to provide the peace, order, and justice wherein the Christian could pursue his or her pilgrimage to the City of God (see page 203), so for Muslims the function of the Islamic state was "to assure that all Muslims could lead a life in keeping with the mandates of the Qur'an and discharge their obligations to Allah."[6] Thus both peoples viewed the state from a theological perspective. In the central Middle Ages European rulers reinvigorated the concept of the state, in part by defining it as an organized territory with definite geographical boundaries recognized by other states. Muslims, however, did not conceive of their states as territorial entities limited by distinct boundaries. Medieval Muslim geographers paid little attention to, or entirely ignored, territorial boundaries. Rather, what distinguished one region from another was whether most inhabitants were Muslims or nonbelievers. Territories in which the preponderance of the people were Muslims belonged to the *Dar-al-Islam,* the House of Islam; regions in which most were Christians or of some other non-Muslim faith constituted the *Dar-al-Harb,* the House of War.

Animosity between Muslims and Christians increasingly shaped relations between the two groups in Spain.

Shroud Fragment Rich and powerful people were often buried in precious fabrics. This Islamic silk cloth brocaded with gold thread was produced in Almería, a Muslim city in southern Spain, around 1100. It bears a false Arabic inscription for commercial purposes: "This was made in Baghdad, may God protect it." Made for a Christian bishop, the shroud is a fine example of cross-cultural influences. *(Silk and metallic yarns; compound weave; L × W: 16⅞ × 19¹¹⁄₁₆ in. [43 × 50 cm.]. Museum of Fine Arts, Boston, Ellen Page Hall Fund, 33.371)*

Muslim teachers feared that close contact between the two peoples would lead to Muslim contamination and become a threat to the Islamic faith. Christian bishops worried that a knowledge of Islam would lead to ignorance of essential Christian doctrines. Both Muslim scholars and Christian theologians argued that assimilation such as that of the Mozarabs was wrong.

Thus, beginning in the late tenth century, Muslim regulations increasingly defined what Christians and Muslims could do. A Christian, however much assimilated, remained an **infidel**. An infidel was an unbeliever, and the word carried a pejorative or disparaging connotation. Mozarabs had to live in special sections of cities; could not learn the Qur'an, employ Muslim workers or servants, build new churches, or ring church bells; and had to be buried in their own cemeteries. Such restrictions were enhanced in the twelfth century when al-Andalus was taken over by the Almohad dynasty, an extremist group from Morocco that outlawed Judaism and Christianity. When Christian forces conquered Muslim territory in subsequent centuries, Christian rulers regarded their Muslim and Jewish subjects as infidels and enacted similar restrictive measures.

The Frankish Kingdom

Several centuries before the Muslim conquest of Spain, the Frankish king Clovis converted to Roman Christianity and established a large kingdom in what had been Roman Gaul (see page 212). Though at the time the Frankish kingdom was established it was simply one barbarian kingdom among many, it became the most important state in Europe, expanding to become an empire. Rulers after Clovis used a variety of tactics to enhance their authority and create a stable system.

● *How did Frankish rulers govern their kingdoms?*

The Merovingians

The initial success of the Frankish king Clovis rested on three major developments: Clovis's series of military victories over other Germanic tribes; his acquisition of the wealthy provinces of Roman Gaul with their administrative machinery intact; and, after his conversion to orthodox Christianity, the ideological support of the Roman papacy and of the bishops of Gaul. By selecting Paris—the legendary scene of the martyrdom of Saint Denis, believed to be a disciple of Saint Paul—as his capital, Clovis identified himself with the cult of Saint Denis and used it to strengthen his rule. The Frankish kingdom under Clovis included much of what is now France and a large section of southwestern Germany.

Clovis established the Merovingian dynasty, named after a mythical founder Merowig. Before he died, Clovis arranged for his kingdom to be divided among his four sons, not according to strict acreage but in portions yielding roughly equal revenues. Historians have long described Merovingian Gaul in the sixth and seventh centuries as wracked by civil wars, chronic violence, and political instability as Clovis's descendants fought among themselves. So brutal and destructive were these wars and so violent the ordinary conditions of life that the term *Dark Ages* came to designate the entire Merovingian period. Recent research has presented a more complex picture. The civil wars were indeed destructive, but they "did not pose a threat to the survival of the kingdom. In a sense, they were a unifying part of the structure of the Frankish state in the sixth century and for most of the seventh."[7]

What caused the civil wars? First, the death or even reported death of a king triggered crisis and war. Lacking a clear principle of succession, any male of Merovingian blood could claim the throne, and there were often many possibilities within the Merovingian family. A prince-claimant had to prove himself worthy on the battlefield. Second, the desire for new lands provoked conflict. Royal officials and warriors had similar desires for new estates, and they sold their support to the prince who would promise them more lands. Royal armies also wanted war because war meant booty and plunder. No one disputed the Merovingian family's right to rule: it alone possessed the blood and charisma. The issue was which member. Thus the royal family and the royal court served as the focus around which conflicts arose, and in this sense the civil wars actually held the kingdom together.

Merovingian politics provided royal women with opportunities, and some queens not only influenced but occasionally also dominated events. The theoretical status of a princess or queen rested on her diplomatic importance, with her marriage sealing or divorce breaking an alliance; on her personal relationship with her husband and her ability to give him sons and heirs; on her role as the mother and guardian of princes who had not reached legal adulthood; and on her control of the royal treasury. For example, when King Chilperic I (561–584) was murdered, his wife Fredegunda controlled a large state treasury. The historian Fredegar alleges that Queen Brunhilda (d. 613), wife of King Sigebert of the East Frankish kingdom, killed twelve kings in pursuit of her political goals, including Sigebert, some of her grandchildren, and their offspring. When her sister Galswintha was found strangled to death in bed shortly after her marriage to Chilperic, ruler of the West Frankish kingdom, Brunhilda suspected that Chilperic had murdered her so that he could marry his then mistress, Fredegunda. Brunhilda instigated war between the two kingdoms. After 592 she was the real power behind her sons' and grandsons' shaky thrones, and she also ruled Burgundy, which her maneuvers had united to the East Frankish kingdom. Contemporaries may have exaggerated Brunhilda's murders, but her career reflects both the domestic violence of the Merovingian royal family and the fierce determination of some queens to exercise power.

Merovingian Army   This sixth- or seventh-century ivory depicts a nobleman in civilian dress followed by seven warriors. Note that the mounted men do not have stirrups and that they seem to have fought with spears and bows and arrows. The power of the Frankish aristocracy rested on such private armies. *(Landesmuseum, Trier)*

Merovingian Government

How did Merovingian rulers govern? What were their sources of income? How did they communicate with their peoples? While local administration probably varied somewhat according to regional tradition, the **civitas**—the city and surrounding territory—served as the basis of the administrative system in the Frankish kingdom. A **comites**—senior official or royal companion, later called a count—presided over the civitas. He collected royal revenue, heard lawsuits, enforced justice, and raised troops. To receive his tax revenues, a Frankish king had to be sure of the comites's loyalty. Rebellion led to confiscation of the comites's lands.

A ruler's general sources of income were revenues from the royal estates, which were especially large in the north; the right to hospitality when he visited an area (with wives, children, servants, court officials, and several hundred warriors, plus all their horses, hospitality could be a severe drain on the resources of a region); the conquest and confiscation of new lands, which replenished lands given as monastic or religious endowments; and the "gifts" of subject peoples, such as plunder and tribute paid by peoples east of the Rhine River. Specific income derived from a land tax paid by all free landowners, which was originally collected by the Romans and continued by the Franks. In the course of the seventh century, the value of this tax declined as all Franks gradually gained immunity from it. In fact, the term **Frank** began to be associated with freedom from taxation, which may have been an incentive for Gallo-Romans to shift their ethnic allegiance to the Franks. Fines imposed for criminal offenses and tolls and customs duties on roads, bridges, and waterways (and the goods transported over them) also yielded income. As with the Romans, the minting of coins was a royal monopoly, with drastic penalties for counterfeiting. For all this the comites had responsibility.

Merovingian, Carolingian (see page 234), and later medieval rulers led peripatetic lives, traveling constantly to check up on local administrators and peoples. Merovingian kings also relied on the comites and bishops to gather and send local information to them. Gallo-Roman by descent, bishops and comites were usually native to the regions they administered and knew their areas well. Frankish royal administration involved a third official, the *dux* (duke). He was a military leader, commanding troops in the territory of several civitas, and thus responsible for all defensive and offensive strategies. Kings seem to have appointed only Franks to this position.

Clovis and his descendants in the sixth and seventh centuries also issued **capitularies,** administrative and legislative orders divided into *capitula,* chapters or articles. These laws attempted to regulate a variety of matters: for example, protecting priests, monks, nuns, and church property from violence; defining ownership and inheritance; and punishing drunkenness, robbery, arson, rape, and murder. Apart from the violent and crime-ridden realities of Merovingian society, capitularies show the strong influence of Roman law. They also reveal Merovingian kings trying to maintain law and order, holding courts, and being actively involved in exercising judicial authority.

The court or household of Merovingian kings also included scribes who kept records, legal officials who advised the king on matters of law, and treasury agents responsible for aspects of royal finance. These officials could all read and write Latin. Over them all presided the mayor of the palace, the most important secular figure after the king in the kingdom. Usually a leader of one of the great aristocratic families, the mayor governed the palace and the kingdom in the king's absence.

Kings also consulted regularly with the leaders of the aristocracy. This class represented a fusion of Franks and the old Gallo-Roman leadership. Its members possessed landed wealth—villas over which they exercised lordship, dispensing local customary, not royal, law—and they often had rich and lavish lifestyles. When they were with the king, they constituted the royal court, those around the king at a given time. If the king consulted them and they were in agreement, there was peace. Failure to consult could mean resentment and the potential for civil war.

The Rise of the Carolingians

From this aristocracy there gradually emerged in the eighth century one family that replaced the Merovingian dynasty. The emergence of the Carolingians—whose name comes from the Latin *Carolus,* or Charles—rests on several factors. First, beginning with Pippin I (d. 640), the head of the family acquired and held onto the powerful position of mayor of the palace. Pippin I served as head of the Frankish bureaucracy, governed in the king's absence, and, after the king, was the most important figure in the Frankish kingdom. Second, a series of advantageous marriage alliances brought the family estates and influence in different parts of the Frankish world. Thus Pippin II (d. 714), through his first marriage, won influence in the territory around Echternach (modern Luxembourg) and, by his second wife, estates in the Meuse Valley. The landed wealth and treasure acquired by Pippin II, his son Charles Martel (r. 714–741), and Pippin III (r. 751–768) formed the basis of Carolingian power. Although Pippin II and Charles Martel possessed more lands than any other single aristocratic family, and al-

though they held the positions of mayor of the palace and duke, their ultimate supremacy was by no means certain. Other dukes rallied to the support of the Merovingians, and Pippin devoted much energy to fighting these magnates. Only his victory over them and King Theuderich at Tertry in 687 ensured his dominance. Such victories gave the family a reputation for military strength.

Charles Martel's successful wars against the Saxons, Frisians, Alamanni, and Bavarians further enhanced the family's prestige. In 732 Charles Martel defeated a Muslim force near Poitiers in central France. Muslims and Christians have interpreted the battle differently. To the Muslims it was a minor skirmish won by the Franks because of Muslim difficulties in maintaining supply lines over long distances and the distraction of ethnic conflicts and unrest in Islamic Spain. For Christians the Frankish victory was one of the great battles of history, halting Muslim expansion in Europe. Charles Martel and later Carolingians used it to enhance their reputation, portraying themselves as defenders of Christendom against the Muslims.

The Battle of Poitiers helped the Carolingians acquire the support of the church, perhaps their most important asset. Irish, Frankish, and Anglo-Saxon missionaries, of whom the Englishman Boniface (680–754) is the most famous, preached Christianity to pagan peoples and worked to reorganize the Frankish church. Boniface ordered the oak of Thor, a tree near the village of Fritzlar in central Germany sacred to many pagans, cut down and used the wood to build a church. When the god Thor did not respond by killing him with his lightning bolts, Boniface won many converts. With close ties to the Roman papacy, Boniface participated in establishing the abbey of Fulda and the archdiocese of Mainz, held church councils, and promoted *The Rule of Saint Benedict* in all monasteries. (Boniface was not successful in the latter. Many monasteries preferred to be guided by several monastic directives.) The Carolingian mayors of the palace, Charles Martel and Pippin III, fully supported this evangelizing activity, as missionaries also preached obedience to secular authorities as a religious duty.

Online Study Center **Improve Your Grade**
Primary Source: St. Boniface Destroys the Oak of Thor

As mayor of the palace, Charles Martel had exercised the power of king of the Franks. His son Pippin III aspired to the title as well. Against the background of collaboration between missionaries and the Frankish mayors, Pippin sent delegates to ask Pope Zacharias whether the man who held the power should also have the title of king. Pippin's ambassadors reached Rome at a diplomat-

Saint Boniface The upper panel of this piece from an early-eleventh-century Fulda Mass book shows the great missionary to Germany baptizing, apparently by full immersion. The lower panel shows his death scene, with the saint protecting himself with a Gospel book. The fluttering robes are similar to those in earlier Anglo-Saxon books, probably modeled on illustrations in books that Boniface brought to Fulda Abbey from England. *(Stadtsbibliothek Bamberg, Ms. Lit. I, fol. 126v)*

Zacharias "by virtue of his apostolic authority commanded that Pippin should be made king."[8] Chilperic, the last Merovingian ruler, was consigned to a monastery. An assembly of Frankish magnates elected Pippin king, and he was anointed by Boniface at Soissons. When, in 754, Lombard expansion again threatened the papacy, Pope Stephen II journeyed to the Frankish kingdom seeking help. On this occasion, he personally anointed Pippin and gave him the title "Patrician of the Romans." Pippin promised restitution of the papal lands.

Thus an important alliance had been struck between the papacy and the Frankish monarchs. On a successful campaign in Italy in 756, Pippin made a large donation to the papacy. The gift consisted of estates in central Italy that technically belonged to the Byzantine emperor. Because of his **anointment,** Pippin's kingship took on a special spiritual and moral character. Before Pippin only priests and bishops had received anointment. Pippin became the first to be anointed with the sacred oils and acknowledged as *rex et sacerdos* (king and priest). Anointment, rather than royal blood, set the Christian king apart. By having himself anointed, Pippin cleverly eliminated possible threats to the Frankish throne coming from other claimants, and the pope promised him support in the future. When Pippin died, his son Charles succeeded him.

The Empire of Charlemagne

Charles the Great (r. 768–814), generally known by the French version of his name, Charlemagne, built on the military and diplomatic foundations of his ancestors and on the administrative machinery of the Merovingian kings. He expanded the Frankish kingdom into what is now Germany and Italy and, late in his long reign, was crowned emperor by the pope.

• *What accounts for Charlemagne's political and diplomatic successes?*

Charlemagne's Personal Qualities and Marriage Strategies

Charlemagne's secretary and biographer Einhard wrote a lengthy idealization of this warrior-ruler. It has serious flaws, partly because it is modeled directly on the Roman author Suetonius's *Life of the Emperor Augustus.* Still, it is the earliest medieval biography of a layman, and historians consider it generally accurate:

ically opportune moment. In the eighth century the Lombards severely threatened the papacy, which, being subject to the Byzantine emperor, looked to Constantinople for support. But Byzantium, pressured from the outside by attacks from the Arabs and the Avars and wracked internally by the dispute over the veneration of icons, known as iconoclasm, was in no position to send help. Pope Zacharias therefore shifted his allegiance from the Greeks to the Franks and told Pippin that "it was better to call him king who had the royal power 'in order to prevent provoking civil war in Francia'" and that

Charles was large and strong, and of lofty stature, though not disproportionately tall . . . the upper part of his head was round, his eyes very large and animated, nose a little long, hair fair, and face laughing and merry. Thus his appearance was always stately and dignified . . . although his neck was thick and somewhat short, and his belly rather prominent; but the symmetry of the rest of his body concealed these defects. His gait was firm, his whole carriage manly and his voice clear, but not so strong as his size led one to expect. His health was excellent, except during the four years preceding his death. . . .

In accordance with the national custom, he took frequent exercise on horseback and in the chase. . . . He . . . often practiced swimming, in which he was such an adept that none could surpass him. . . . He used not only to invite his sons to his bath, but his nobles and friends.[9]

Though crude and brutal, Charlemagne was a man of enormous intelligence. He appreciated good literature, such as Saint Augustine's *City of God,* and Einhard considered him an unusually effective speaker. Recent scholarship disputes Einhard's claim that Charlemagne could not write.

Online Study Center **Improve Your Grade**
Primary Source: The Life of Charlemagne: The Emperor Himself

The security and continuation of his dynasty and the need for diplomatic alliances governed Charlemagne's complicated marriage pattern. The high rate of infant mortality required many sons. Married first to the daughter of Desiderius, king of the Lom-

Reliquary Bust of Charlemagne
This splendid twelfth-century gothic idealization portrays the emperor of legend and myth rather than the squat, potbellied ruler described by his contemporary Einhard. The jeweled helmet or crown is symbolic of Charlemagne's role as defender of church and people. *(Photo: Ann Münchow, © Domkapitel Aachen)*

bards, Charlemagne divorced her either because she failed to produce a child within a year or for diplomatic reasons. His second wife, Hildegard, produced nine children in twelve years. When she died, Charlemagne married Fastrada, daughter of an East Frankish count whose support he needed in his campaign against the Saxons. Charlemagne had a total of four legal wives and six concubines, and even after the age of sixty-five he continued to sire children. Though three sons reached adulthood, only one outlived him. Four surviving grandsons ensured perpetuation of the family.

Territorial Expansion

Continuing the expansionist policies of his ancestors, Charlemagne fought more than fifty campaigns and became the greatest warrior of the early Middle Ages. He subdued all of the north of modern France. In the south the lords of the mountainous ranges of Aquitaine fought off his efforts at total conquest. The Muslims in northeastern Spain were checked by the establishment of strongly fortified areas known as *marches*.

Charlemagne's greatest successes were in today's Germany. In the course of a thirty-year war against the Saxons, he added most of the northwestern German tribes to the Frankish kingdom. Because of their repeated rebellions, Charlemagne ordered, according to Einhard, more than four thousand Saxons slaughtered in one day.

He also achieved spectacular results in the south. In 773 to 774 the Lombards in northern Italy again threatened the papacy. Charlemagne marched south, overran fortresses at Pavia and Spoleto, and incorporated Lombardy into the Frankish kingdom. To his title king of the Franks he added king of the Lombards. Charlemagne also ended Bavarian independence and defeated the nomadic Avars, opening the Danubian plain for later settlement. He successfully fought the Byzantine Empire for Venetia (excluding the city of Venice itself), Istria, and Dalmatia and temporarily annexed those areas to his kingdom.

Charlemagne also tried to occupy Basque territory in northwestern Spain. When his long siege of Saragossa proved unsuccessful and the Saxons on his

Frankish Kingdom, 768
Areas conquered by Charlemagne
Tributary peoples
Byzantine territories

MAP 8.2 Charlemagne's Conquests Though Charlemagne's hold on much of his territory was relatively weak, the size of his empire was not equaled again until the nineteenth-century conquests of Napoleon. (*Source: Some data from Michael McCormick,* Origins of the European Economy: Communications and Commerce, A.D. 300–900 *[Cambridge: Cambridge University Press, 2001], p. 762.)*

Online Study Center **Improve Your Grade** Interactive Map: The Carolinglan World

northeastern borders rebelled, Charlemagne decided to withdraw, but the Basques annihilated his rear guard, which was led by Count Roland, at Roncesvalles (778) near Pamplona in the Pyrenees. This attack represented Charlemagne's only defeat, and he forbade people to talk about it. However, the expedition inspired the great medieval epic *The Song of Roland*. Based on legend and written about 1100 at the beginning of the European crusading movement, the poem portrays Roland as the ideal chivalric knight and Charlemagne as exercising a sacred kind of kingship. Although many of the epic's details differ from the historical evidence, *The Song of Roland* is important because it reveals the popular image of Charlemagne in later centuries.

By around 805 the Frankish kingdom included all of northwestern Europe except Scandinavia (see Map 8.2). Not since the third century A.D. had any ruler controlled so much of the Western world.

The Government of the Carolingian Empire

Charlemagne ruled a vast rural world dotted with isolated estates and small villages and characterized by constant warfare. According to the chroniclers of the time, only seven years between 714 and 814 were peaceful. Charlemagne's empire was not a state as people today understand that term; it was a collection of peoples and tribes. Apart from a small class of warrior-aristocrats and clergy and a tiny minority of Jews, almost everyone engaged in agriculture. Towns served as the headquarters of bishops, as ecclesiastical centers. The Carolingians inherited the office and the administrative machinery of the Merovingian kings and the functions of the mayor of the palace. The Carolingians relied heavily on the personality and energy of the monarchs. The scholar-adviser Alcuin (see page 247) wrote that "a king should be strong against his enemies, humble to Christians, feared by pagans, loved by the poor and judicious in counsel and maintaining justice."[10] Charlemagne worked to realize that ideal. By military expeditions that brought wealth—lands, booty, slaves, and tribute—and by peaceful travel, personal appearances, and the sheer force of his personality, Charlemagne sought to awe newly conquered peoples and rebellious domestic enemies with his fierce presence and terrible justice. By confiscating the estates of great territorial magnates, he acquired lands and goods with which to gain the support of lesser lords, further expanding the territory under his control.

The political power of the Carolingians rested on the cooperation of the dominant social class, the Frankish aristocracy. By the seventh century, through mutual cooperation and frequent marriage alliances, these families exercised great power that did not derive from the Merovingian kings. The Carolingians themselves had emerged from this aristocracy, and the military and political success that Carolingians such as Pippin II achieved depended on the support of the nobility. The lands and booty with which Charles Martel and Charlemagne rewarded their followers in these families enabled the nobles to improve their economic position, but it was only with noble help that the Carolingians were able to wage wars of expansion and suppress rebellions. In short, Carolingian success was a matter of reciprocal help and reward.[11]

For administrative purposes, Charlemagne divided his entire kingdom into *counties* based closely on the old Merovingian civitas (see page 233). Each of the approximately six hundred counties was governed by a count (or in his absence by a viscount) who published royal orders, held courts and resolved legal cases, collected taxes and tolls, raised troops for the army, and supervised maintenance of roads and bridges. Counts were at first sent out from the royal court; later a person native to the region was appointed. As a link between local authorities and the central government, Charlemagne appointed officials called **missi dominici,** "agents of the lord king." The empire was divided into visitorial districts. Each year beginning in 802, two missi (singular: *missus*), usually a count and a bishop or abbot, visited assigned districts. They held courts; investigated the district's judicial, financial, and clerical activities; and organized commissions to regulate crime, moral conduct, the clergy, education, the poor, and many other matters. The missi checked up on the counts. In the marches, especially in unstable or threatened areas such as along the Spanish and Danish frontiers, officials called *margraves* had extensive powers to govern.

A modern state has institutions of government, such as a civil service, courts of law, financial agencies for collecting and apportioning taxes, and police and military powers with which to maintain order internally and defend against foreign attack. These did not exist in Charlemagne's empire. Instead, society was held together by dependent relationships cemented by oaths promising faith and loyalty.

Although the empire lacked viable institutions, some Carolingians involved in governing did have vigorous political ideas. The abbots and bishops who served as Charlemagne's advisers worked out what was for their time a sophisticated political ideology. They wrote that a ruler may hold power from God but is responsible to the law. Just as all subjects of the empire were required to obey him, he too was obliged to respect the law. They envisioned a unified Christian society presided over by a king who was responsible for maintaining peace, law, and order and doing justice, without which neither the ruler nor the kingdom had any justification. These views derived largely from Saint Augustine's theories of kingship. Inevitably, they could not be realized in an illiterate preindustrial society. But they were the seeds from which medieval and even modern ideas of government were to develop.

The Imperial Coronation of Charlemagne

In autumn of the year 800, Charlemagne paid a momentous visit to Rome. Einhard gives this account of what happened:

His last journey there [to Rome] was due to another factor, namely that the Romans, having inflicted many injuries on Pope Leo—plucking out his eyes and tearing out his tongue, he had been compelled to beg the assistance of the king. Accordingly, coming to Rome in order that he might set in order those things which had exceedingly disturbed the condition of the Church, he remained there the whole winter. It was at the time that he accepted the name of Emperor and Augustus. At first he was so much opposed to this that he insisted that although that day was a great [Christian] feast, he would not have entered the Church if he had known beforehand the pope's intention. But he bore very patiently the jealousy of the Roman Emperors [that is, the Byzantine rulers] who were indignant when he received these titles. He overcame their arrogant haughtiness with magnanimity.[12]

For centuries scholars have debated the significance of the imperial coronation of Charlemagne. Did Charlemagne plan the ceremony in Saint Peter's on Christmas Day, or did he merely accept the title of emperor? What did he have to gain from it? If, as Einhard implies, the coronation displeased Charlemagne, did that displeasure rest on Pope Leo's role in the ceremony, which, on the principle that he who gives can also take away, placed the pope in a higher position than the emperor? Did Pope Leo arrange the coronation in order to identify the Frankish monarchy with the papacy and papal policy?

Though final answers will probably never be found, several things seem certain. First, Charlemagne gained the imperial title of Holy Roman emperor and considered himself a Christian king ruling a Christian people. His motto, *Renovatio romani imperi* (Revival of the Roman Empire), suggested a revival of the Western empire in the terms of Augustinian political philosophy. Charlemagne was consciously perpetuating old Roman imperial notions while at the same time identifying with the new Rome of the Christian church. Charlemagne and his government represented a combination of Frankish practices and Christian ideals, two basic elements of medieval European society. Second, later German rulers were eager to gain the imperial title and to associate themselves with the legends of Charlemagne and ancient Rome. They wanted to use the ideology of imperial Rome to strengthen their positions. Finally, ecclesiastical authorities continually cited the event as proof that the dignity of the imperial crown could be granted only by the pope.

When Charlemagne went to Rome in 800, Pope Leo III showed him signs of respect due only to the emperor. The Carolingian family thus received official recognition from the leading spiritual power in Europe, and the papacy gained a military protector. From Baghdad, Harun al Rashid, caliph of the Abbasid Empire (786–809), congratulated the Frankish ruler with the gift of an elephant. It was named Abu'l Abbas after the founder of the Abbasid dynasty and may have served as a symbol of the diplomatic link between the Muslim world and Christian Europe. Having plodded its way to Charlemagne's court at Aachen, the elephant survived for nine years, and its death was considered important enough to be mentioned in the Frankish *Royal Annals* for the year 810.

Though the Muslim caliph recognized Charlemagne as a fellow sovereign, the Greeks regarded the papal acts as rebellious and Charlemagne as a usurper. The imperial coronation thus marks a decisive break between Rome and Constantinople. The coronation of Charlemagne, whether planned by the Carolingian court or by the papacy, was to have a profound effect on the course of German history and on the later history of Europe.

Decentralization and "Feudalism"

Charlemagne left his vast empire to his sole surviving son, Louis the Pious (r. 814–840), who attempted to keep the empire intact. This proved to be impossible. Members of the nobility engaged in plots and open warfare against the emperor, often allying themselves with one of Louis's three sons. (See the feature "Individuals in Society: Ebo of Reims.") In 843, shortly after Louis's death, those sons agreed to the **Treaty of Verdun,** which divided the empire into three parts: Charles the Bald received the western part, Lothar the middle and the title of emperor, and Louis the eastern part, from which he acquired the title "the German" (see Map 8.3). Though of course no one knew it at the time, this treaty set the pattern for political boundaries in Europe that has been maintained until today. Other than brief periods under Napoleon and Hitler, Europe would never again see as large a unified state as it had under Charlemagne, which is one reason he has become an important symbol of European unity in the twenty-first century.

The large-scale division of Charlemagne's empire was accompanied by a decentralization of power at the local level. Nobles increased their authority in their own territories and built up groups of military followers who were primarily loyal to them, not to some distant king or emperor. The nobles had different amounts of power and wealth. The most powerful were those able to gain the allegiance of others, often symbolized in an oath-swearing ceremony of homage and fealty that grew out of earlier Germanic oaths of loyalty. In this ceremony, a fighter swore his loyalty as a **vassal**—from a Celtic term meaning "servant"—to the more powerful individual, who be-

MAP 8.3 Division of the Carolingian Empire, 843 The Treaty of Verdun (843), which divided the empire among Charlemagne's grandsons, is frequently taken as the start of the separate development of Germany, France, and Italy. The "middle kingdom" of Lothar, however, lacking defensive borders and any political or linguistic unity, quickly broke up into numerous small territories.

came his lord. In return for the vassal's loyalty, aid, and military assistance, the lord promised him protection and material support, which might be a place in his household but was more likely land of his own, called a **fief** (*feudum* in Latin, from which the term **feudalism** was later coined to describe this political system). The fief theoretically still belonged to the lord, and the vassal only had the use of it. Families living on the fief produced the food and other goods necessary to maintain the warrior, and the fief might contain forests, churches, and towns.

The feudal system was thus based on personal ties of loyalty cemented by grants of land, and people had no sense of allegiance to an abstract state or governmental system. In some parts of Europe, such as Ireland and the Baltic area, warrior-aristocrats or clan chieftains who controlled relatively small regions were the ultimate political authorities; they generally did not grant fiefs to secure loyalty but relied on strictly personal ties. Thus the word *feudal* does not properly apply to these areas.

Homage and Fealty In this manuscript illumination, a vassal kneels before the lord, places his clasped hands between those of the lord, and declares, "I become your man." Although the rite of entering a feudal relationship varied widely across Europe and sometimes was entirely verbal, we have a few illustrations of it. Sometimes the lord handed over a clump of earth, representing the fief, and the ceremony concluded with a kiss, symbolizing peace between them. *(Austrian National Library Picture Archive, Cod. VinDOB, 2262, fol. 174 [E8.037])*

Some historians argue, in fact, that the word *feudalism* should not be used at all, as it was unknown in the Middle Ages. In addition, the system that would later be called feudalism changed considerably in form and pattern between the ninth and fifteenth centuries, and differed from place to place. The feudalism of England in 1100, for example, differed greatly from that of France, scarcely fifty miles away, at the same time. The problem is that no one has come up with a better term for this loose arrangement of personal and property ties.

Whether one chooses to use the word *feudalism* or not, this system functioned as a way to organize political authority, particularly because vassals also owed obligations other than military service to the lord. They served as advisers and judges at the lord's court, provided lodging for the lord when he was traveling through their fief, gave

him gifts at important family events, such as marriages or the births of children, and might contribute ransom money if the lord was captured.

Along with granting fiefs for military service, lords rewarded officials in the Christian church with fiefs for spiritual services or promises of allegiance. In addition, the church held pieces of land on its own and granted fiefs in return for promises of assistance from knightly vassals. Abbots and abbesses of monasteries, bishops, and archbishops were either lords or vassals in many feudal arrangements.

Women other than abbesses were generally not granted fiefs, but in most parts of Europe they could inherit them if their fathers had no sons. (Because women could hold fiefs, the word *lord* does not always mean a man in the feudal context; it simply means the person or institution that holds the rights of lordship.) Occasionally, women did go through services swearing homage and fealty and swore to send fighters when the lord demanded them. More commonly, women acted as their husbands' surrogates when the men were away, defending the territory from attack and carrying out his administrative duties.

Though historians debate this, fiefs appear to have been granted extensively first by Charles Martel and then by his successors, including Charlemagne and his grandsons. These fiefs went particularly to their most powerful nobles, who often took the title of count. While countships were not hereditary in the eighth century, they tended to remain within the same family. In the ninth century regional concentrations of power depended on family connections and political influence at the king's court. The weakening of the Carolingian Empire, however, served to increase the power of regional authorities. Civil wars weakened the power and prestige of kings because there was little they could do about domestic violence. Likewise, the great invasions of the ninth century, especially the Viking invasions (see page 230), weakened royal authority. The West Frankish kings could do little to halt the invaders, and the aristocracy had to assume responsibility for defense. Common people turned for protection to the strongest local power, the counts, whom they considered their rightful rulers. Thus, in the ninth and tenth centuries great aristocratic families increased their authority in the regions of their vested

Individuals
in Society

Ebo of Reims

The term *social mobility* came into broad use only in the twentieth century, but what it signifies—having the opportunity for an upward shift in status within society—is probably as old as organized society itself. "In all ages, service to the state and to men of power has raised some individuals and has enabled them to share in the social prestige that attaches to power."* In the Christian Middle Ages the Catholic Church provided the widest path for social advancement, and the archbishop symbolized political as well as religious prestige. Ebo of Reims (ca 775–851) represents one such individual.

Ebo's father was a serf freed by Charlemagne; his mother, Himiltruda, was the nurse of Louis the Pious. Ebo's mother probably launched his career, for Ebo was brought up with Louis at the "palace school" at Aachen, where nobles and others were trained for administrative and judicial service to the emperor. A bond was forged between Ebo and Louis. When Louis became king of Aquitaine, he made Ebo his librarian; when Louis succeeded as emperor in 814, he secured for Ebo the important archiepiscopal see of Reims.

Ebo proved himself a very competent administrator. He began construction of a new cathedral, gaining imperial permission to use the city walls as building blocks. Ebo organized the cathedral chapter—the local clergy who handled routine business of the diocese under the bishop. He reformed the monasteries in his see, ending the diverse forms of religious life by enforcing *The Rule of Saint Benedict* in all houses. Ebo also patronized learning and the arts. He supported the production of manuscripts and the school long associated with the cathedral, and he commissioned the production of a book that bears his name, the *Ebo Gospels*.

Ebo served the emperor as *missus* in his province, where he worked to extend royal authority. Archbishop Ebo served both church and state when, acting on behalf of Pope Pascal I and Louis the Pious, he led a mission to King Harold of Denmark, whose goal was the conversion of the Danes to Christianity and peaceful relations with the Franks. When Harold and a large Danish entourage visited Louis in 826, the Danes were baptized, and Harold became Louis's vassal.

In 830 Louis was past fifty, an old man by contemporary standards. Louis had three adult sons. Adult sons often posed a test of medieval kingship. Sons wanted power on their own, resented paternal control, and often rebelled. In 833 Archbishop Ebo served as counselor to the sons of Louis the Pious in their plot to remove Louis and replace him with Lothar. Ebo headed a commission of bishops that drew up charges against the emperor, accusing him of failing in his imperial responsibilities, promoting discord among the Frankish people, and tolerating his (second) wife Judith's adultery, thereby bringing moral scandal to the kingdom. Louis was forced to renounce the throne and to do public penance. The charges proved false, and within months Louis regained his throne. A church council deposed Ebo, consigning him to a monastery. When Louis the Pious died, Lothar restored Ebo to Reims, but the pope refused to approve the appointment. Then a dispute with Lothar led Ebo to seek the support of Louis the German, who made him bishop of Hildesheim. Ebo died at Hildesheim.

Emperor Louis the Pious confers with bishops and lay magnates. (Bibliothèque nationale de France)

Why did Ebo betray his boyhood friend and great benefactor? Was he resentful about some real or perceived slight and did he desire revenge? Was he willing to listen to dangerous advice? Did he wish to show himself the equal of any magnate who opposed the emperor? The *Annals of St.-Bertin*, the chief source of information about these events, describes Ebo as ungrateful, disobedient, disloyal, and cruel. What do you think?

Questions for Analysis

1. How does the career of Ebo of Reims illustrate social mobility?
2. What do Ebo's church appointments tell us about the Frankish state? What secular functions did bishops perform?

*K. Bosl, "On Social Mobility in Medieval Society," in *Early Medieval Society*, ed. S. L. Thrupp (New York: Appleton-Century-Crofts, 1967).

Sources: R. McKitterick, *The Frankish Kingdoms Under the Carolingians* (New York: Longman, 1983); J. L. Nelson, *Politics and Ritual in Early Medieval Europe* (London: Ronceverte, 1986).

Online Study Center **Improve Your Grade**
Going Beyond Individuals in Society

Ox Team Plowing   From an eleventh-century calendar showing manorial occupations for each month, this illustration for January—the time for sowing winter wheat—shows two pairs of oxen pulling a wheeled plow, which was designed for deeper tillage. One man directs the oxen, a second prods the animals, and a third drops seeds in the ground. *(British Library Cott. Tib. B.V. 3, Min. Pt 1)*

interests. They built private castles for defense and to live in, and they governed virtually independent territories in which distant and weak kings could not interfere. Though they might officially be vassals of that king, they sometimes divided their territory into smaller parts and granted these segments to their own vassals.

Throughout western Europe, counts or earls exercised the most effective political power at the local level: they raised armies of fighting men, held courts that dispensed some form of law, coined money used in commercial transactions, and conducted relations with outside or foreign powers. Modern political scientists call these the powers of a sovereign or independent state. In the early Middle Ages local counts or earls administered these powers, and for their own personal benefit.

Feudalism actually existed at two social levels: the highest level consisted of royal officials, such as counts, who ruled great feudal principalities, while armed retainers who became knights formed a lower level, holding fiefs that may have been no larger than a small village with its surrounding land. In fact, some knights were landless and lived in the household of a king, count, or other high feudal lord. A wide and deep gap in social standing and political function separated these levels. (See the feature "Listening to the Past: Feudal Homage and Fealty" on pages 256–257.)

Manorialism, Serfdom, and the Slave Trade

Though *feudalism* is sometimes used to describe the entire social and political system of medieval Europe, the vast majority of people were not involved in the feudal system at all. They lived in family groups in villages or small towns and made their living predominantly by raising crops and animals. The village and the land surrounding it were called a *manor*, from the Latin word for "dwelling" or "homestead." Some fiefs might include only one manor, while great lords or kings might have hundreds of manors under their direct control. Residents of manors provided work for their lord in exchange for protection, a system that was later referred to as **manorialism.** Free peasants surrendered themselves and their lands to the lord's jurisdiction. The land was given back, but the peasants became tied to the land by various kinds of payments and services. Like feudalism, manorialism involved an exchange. Because the economic power of the warring class rested on landed estates worked by peasants, feudalism and manorialism were inextricably linked.

In France, England, Germany, and Italy, local custom determined precisely what services villagers would provide to their lord, but certain practices became common

Balkan Neck Shackle (tenth century) The slave trader restrained the captive by slipping the chain through the loops in the neck collar (*top*), fastening it securely, and then attaching the chain to the captive's limbs. Similar devices for controlling slaves while allowing them to walk were later used in other parts of the world. (*Courtesy of the National Museum of History, Soa*)

everywhere. The peasant was obliged to give the lord a percentage of the annual harvest, usually in produce, sometimes in cash. The peasant paid a fee to marry someone from outside the lord's estate. To inherit property, the peasant paid a fine, often the best beast the person owned. Above all, the peasant became part of the lord's permanent labor force. With vast stretches of uncultivated virgin land and a tiny labor population, lords encouraged population growth and immigration. The most profitable form of capital was not land but laborers.

In entering into a relationship with a feudal lord, free farmers lost status. Their position became servile, and they became **serfs.** That is, they were bound to the land and could not leave it without the lord's permission. Serfdom was not the same as slavery in that lords did not own the person of the serf, but serfs were subject to the jurisdiction of the lord's court in any dispute over property and in any case of suspected criminal behavior.

The transition from freedom to serfdom was slow; its speed was closely related to the degree of political order in a given region. In the late eighth century there were still many free peasants. And within the legal category of serfdom there were many economic levels, ranging from the highly prosperous to the desperately poor. Nevertheless, a social and legal revolution was taking place. By the year 800 perhaps 60 percent of the population of western Europe—completely free a century before—had been reduced to serfdom. The ninth-century Viking assaults on Europe, discussed below, created extremely unstable conditions and individual insecurity, leading to additional loss of personal freedom.

Though serfdom was not slavery, the Carolingian trade in actual slaves was extensive, generally involving persons captured in war. Merchants in early medieval towns exchanged slaves for the luxury goods their noble and clerical customers desired, most of which came into Europe from the East. The Muslim conquest of Spain produced thousands of prisoner-slaves, as did Charlemagne's long wars against the Lombards, Avars, Saxons, and other groups. When Frankish conquests declined in the tenth century, merchants obtained people on the empire's eastern border who spoke Slavic languages, the origin of our word *slave*. Slaves sold across the Mediterranean fetched three or four times the amounts brought within the Carolingian Empire, so most slaves were sold to Muslims. For Europeans and Arabs alike, selling captives and other slaves was standard procedure. Christian moralists sometimes complained about the sale of Christians to non-Christians, but they did not object to slavery itself.

In general, the Carolingian period witnessed moderate population growth, as indicated by the steady reduction of forests and wasteland. The highest aristocrats and church officials lived well, with fine clothing and at least a few rooms heated by firewood. Male nobles hunted and managed their estates, while female nobles generally oversaw the education of their children and sometimes inherited and controlled land on their own. Craftsmen and craftswomen on manorial estates manufactured textiles, weapons, glass, and pottery, primarily for local consumption. Sometimes abbeys and manors served as markets; goods were shipped away to towns and fairs for sale; and a good deal of interregional commerce existed.

In the towns, which were generally small, artisans and merchants produced and traded luxury goods for noble and clerical patrons. The modest economic expansion benefited townspeople and nobles, but it did not alter the lives of most people very much.

Early Medieval Culture and Society

It is perhaps ironic that Charlemagne's most enduring legacy was the stimulus he gave to scholarship and learning. Barely literate himself, preoccupied with the control of vast territories, much more a warrior than an intellectual, he nevertheless set in motion a cultural revival that had widespread and long-lasting consequences.

- *What were the significant intellectual and cultural changes in Charlemagne's era?*

Scholarship and Religious Life in Northumbria

The revival of learning associated with Charlemagne and his court at Aachen drew its greatest inspiration from seventh- and eighth-century intellectual developments in the Anglo-Saxon kingdom of Northumbria, situated at the northernmost tip of the old Roman world. Despite the victory of the Roman forms of Christian liturgy at the Synod of Whitby in 664 (see page 206), Irish-Celtic culture permeated the Roman church in Britain and resulted in a flowering of artistic and scholarly activity. Northumbrian creativity owes a great deal to the intellectual curiosity and collecting zeal of Saint Benet Biscop (ca 628–689). The manuscripts and other treasures he brought back from Italy formed the library on which much later study rested.

Nuns and Learning   In this tenth-century manuscript, the scholar Saint Aldhelm offers his book *In Praise of Holy Virgins* to a group of nuns, one of whom already holds a book. Early medieval nuns and monks spent much of their time copying manuscripts, preserving much of the learning of the classical world as well as Christian texts. (*His Grace the Archbishop of Canterbury and the Trustees of Lambeth Palace Library. MS 200, fol. 68v*)

Northumbrian monasteries produced scores of books: *missals* (used for the celebration of the Mass), *psalters* (which contained the 150 psalms and other prayers used by the monks in their devotions), commentaries on the Scriptures, illuminated manuscripts, law codes, and collections of letters and sermons. The finest product of Northumbrian art is probably the Gospel book produced at Lindisfarne around 700. The incredible expense involved in the publication of such a book—for vellum (calfskin or lambskin specially prepared for writing), coloring, and gold leaf—represents in part an aristocratic display of wealth. The script, *uncial,* is a Celtic version of contemporary Greek and Roman handwriting. The illustrations have a strong Eastern quality, combining the abstract, nonrepresentational style of the Christian Middle East and the narrative (storytelling) approach of classical Roman art. Likewise, the use of geometrical decorative designs shows the influence of Syrian art. Many scribes, artists, and illuminators must have participated in the book's preparation.

In Gaul and Anglo-Saxon England, women shared with men the work of evangelization and the new Christian learning. Kings and nobles, seeking suitable occupations for daughters who did not or would not marry, founded monasteries for nuns, some of which were double monasteries. A **double monastery** housed men and women in two adjoining establishments and was governed by one superior, an *abbess*. Nuns looked after the children given to the monastery as *oblates* (offerings), the elderly who retired at the monastery, and travelers who needed hospitality. Monks provided protection, since an isolated house of women invited attack in a violent age. Monks also did the heavy work on the land.

Perhaps the most famous abbess of the Anglo-Saxon period was Saint Hilda (d. 680). A noblewoman of considerable learning and administrative ability, she ruled the double monastery of Whitby on the Northumbrian coast, advised kings and princes, hosted the famous synod of 664, and encouraged scholars and poets. Five monks from Whitby later became bishops. Several generations after Hilda, Saint Boniface (see page 234) wrote many letters pleading for copies of books to Whitby and other houses of nuns; these letters attest to the nuns' intellectual reputations.[13]

The finest representative of Northumbrian, and indeed all Anglo-Saxon, scholarship is the Venerable Bede (ca 673–735). When he was seven his parents gave him as an oblate to Benet Biscop's monastery at Wearmouth. Later he was sent to the new monastery at Jarrow five miles away. Surrounded by the books Benet Biscop had brought from Italy, Bede spent the rest of his life there.

King Edwin of Northumbria's Palace Complex This modern illustration reveals a large barnlike structure protected by wooden defenses along sloped terraces. Edwin reigned from 616 to 632. (© *English Heritage, NMR*)

Modern scholars praise Bede for his *Ecclesiastical History of the English People* (ca 720), the chief source of information about early Britain. Bede searched far and wide for his information, discussed the validity of his evidence, compared various sources, and exercised rare critical judgment. For these reasons, he has been called "the first scientific intellect among the Germanic peoples of Europe."[14]

Bede popularized the system of dating events from the birth of Christ, rather than from the foundation of the city of Rome, as the Romans had done, or from the regnal years of kings, as the Germans did. He introduced the term *anno Domini,* "in the year of the Lord," abbreviated A.D. He fitted the entire history of the world into this new dating method. (The reverse dating system of B.C., "before Christ," does not seem to have been widely used before 1700.) Saint Boniface introduced this system of

Saint Luke from the Ada Gospels (late eighth to early ninth century)   In this lavishly illuminated painting from a manuscript of the four Gospels of the New Testament, a statuesque Saint Luke sits enthroned, his clothing falling in distinct folds reminiscent of Byzantine art. He is surrounded by an elaborate architectural framework, and above him is a winged ox, the symbol of Luke in early Christian art. The Ada school of painting was attached to the court of Charlemagne and gets its name from Ada, a sister of Charlemagne who commissioned some of the school's work. *(Municipal Library, Trier, HS 22 fol. 85r)*

reckoning time throughout the Frankish empire of Charlemagne.

Is Bede representative of early medieval monasticism? Aside from brief visits to Lindisfarne and York, Bede passed his long and uneventful life in the quiet of his monastery. Using the two hundred to three hundred volumes on early Christian thought that Benet Biscop had brought back from Rome, Bede made that scholarship accessible to his barbarian present. His commentaries on sections of the biblical books of Genesis, Exodus,

Samuel, Kings, Acts, and Revelation survive in hundreds of manuscripts, indicating that they were widely studied throughout the Middle Ages. Although the monk-scholar is a fixture in the modern popular imagination, most monks spent their lives in more active work in fields and farms or in management and administration. In neither the pattern of his life nor his considerable pedagogical achievement can the "Venerable" Bede (the adjective means "marked by holiness in life") be called typical.

At about the time the monks at Lindisfarne were producing their Gospel book and Bede was writing his *History* at Jarrow, another Northumbrian monk was at work on a nonreligious epic poem that provides considerable information about the society that produced it. In contrast to the works of Bede, which were written in Latin, the poem *Beowulf* was written in the vernacular Anglo-Saxon. Although *Beowulf* is the only native English heroic epic, all the events of the tale take place in Denmark and Sweden, suggesting the close relationship between England and the continent in the eighth century. Scholars have hailed *Beowulf* as a masterpiece of Western literature.

Had they remained entirely insular, Northumbrian cultural achievements would have been of slight significance. But an Englishman from Northumbria played a decisive role in the transmission of English learning to the Carolingian Empire and continental Europe.

The Carolingian Renaissance

In Roman Gaul through the fifth century, the general culture rested on an education that stressed grammar; the works of the Greco-Roman orators, poets, dramatists, and historians; and the legal and medical treatises of the Roman world. Beginning in the seventh and eighth centuries, a new cultural tradition common to Gaul, Italy, the British Isles, and to some extent Spain emerged. This culture was based primarily on Christian sources. Scholars have called this new Christian and ecclesiastical culture, and the educational foundation on which it was based, the "Carolingian Renaissance," because Charlemagne was its major patron.

In a letter addressed to the abbot of Fulda, with copies sent to every monastery and bishopric in his kingdom, Charlemagne directed that the monasteries "should cultivate learning and educate the monks and secular clergy so that they might have a better understanding of the Christian writings." Likewise, in a "General Admonition" to all the leading clergy, he urged the establishment of cathedral and monastic schools where boys might learn to read and to pray properly. Thus the main purpose of this rebirth of learning was to promote an understanding of the Scriptures and of Christian writers and to instruct people to pray and praise God in the correct manner.

At his court at Aachen, Charlemagne assembled learned men from all over Europe. The most important scholar and the leader of the palace school was the Northumbrian Alcuin (ca 735–804). From 781 until his death, Alcuin was the emperor's chief adviser on religious and educational matters. An unusually prolific writer, he prepared some of the emperor's official documents and wrote many moral *exempla,* or "models," that set high standards for royal behavior and constitute a treatise on kingship. Alcuin's letters to Charlemagne set forth political theories on the authority, power, and responsibilities of a Christian ruler.

Aside from Alcuin's literary efforts, what did the scholars at Charlemagne's court do? They copied books and manuscripts and built up libraries. They used the beautifully clear handwriting known as "caroline minuscule," from which modern Roman type is derived. (This script is called **minuscule** because unlike the Merovingian majuscule, which had letters of equal size, minuscule had both uppercase and lowercase letters.) Caroline minuscule improved the legibility of texts and meant that a

sheet of vellum could contain more words and thus be used more efficiently. With the materials at hand, many more manuscripts could be copied. Book production on this scale represents a major manifestation of the revival of learning. Caroline minuscule illustrates the way a seemingly small technological change has broad cultural consequences.

Although scholars worked with Latin, exchanged books between monasteries, and generally collaborated in book production, the common people spoke local or vernacular languages. The Bretons, for example, retained their local dialect, and the Saxons and Bavarians could not understand each other. Some scholars believe that Latin words and phrases gradually penetrated the various vernacular languages, facilitating communication among diverse peoples.

Once basic literacy was established, monastic and other scholars went on to more difficult work. By the middle years of the ninth century, there was a great outpouring of more sophisticated books. Ecclesiastical writers imbued with the legal ideas of ancient Rome and the theocratic ideals of Saint Augustine instructed the semibarbaric rulers of the West. And it is no accident that medical study in the West began at Salerno in southern Italy in the late ninth century, *after* the Carolingian Renaissance.

Organ Music from the Utrecht Psalter The most famous of all Carolingian manuscripts, the Utrecht Psalter (ca 825–850), contains the Old Testament book of Psalms illustrated with ink drawings. Here an illustration for Psalm 150—"Praise him with blast of trumpet, praise him with strings and pipe"—shows the organ that Louis the Pious built for the palace chapel at Aachen. In the Carolingian period, books played a large role in the spread of Christianity and in the promotion of learning. *(University Library, Utrecht)*

Alcuin completed the work of his countryman Boniface—the Christianization of northern Europe. Latin Christian attitudes penetrated deeply into the consciousness of European peoples. By the tenth century the patterns of thought and the lifestyles of educated western Europeans were those of Rome and Latin Christianity.

Health and Medical Care in the Early Middle Ages

A surprising amount of information is known about medical treatment in the early Middle Ages. Medical practice consisted primarily of drug and prescription therapy. Through the monks' efforts and the recovery of Greek and Arabic manuscripts, a large body of the ancients' prescriptions was preserved and passed on. Balsam was recommended for coughs. For asthma an ointment combining chicken, wormwood, laurel berries, and oil of roses was to be rubbed on the chest. The scores of prescriptions to rid the body of lice, fleas, and other filth reflect frightful standards of personal hygiene. The large number of prescriptions for eye troubles suggests that they too must have been common.

Poor diet caused frequent stomach disorders and related ailments such as dysentery, constipation, and diarrhea. For poor circulation a potion of meadow wort, oak rind, and lustmock was recommended. Pregnancy and childbirth posed grave threats of infection for both mother and child. Infants and children were especially susceptible to a range of illnesses, and about half of the children born died before age five, though parents tried to protect them with prayers, amulets worn around the neck, and various herbal mixtures.

All wounds and open injuries invited infection, and infection invited gangrene. Several remedies were known for wounds. Physicians appreciated the antiseptic properties of honey, and prescriptions recommended that wounds be cleaned with it. When an area or a limb had become gangrenous, the physician was instructed to cut above the diseased flesh in order to hasten a cure. The juice of white poppy plants—the source of heroin—could be added to wine and drunk as an anesthetic. Egg whites, which have a soothing effect, were prescribed for burns.

The spread of Christianity in the Carolingian era had a beneficial effect on medical knowledge and treatment. Several of the church fathers expressed serious interest in medicine. The church was deeply concerned about human suffering, whether physical or mental. Christian teaching vigorously supported concern for the poor, sick, downtrodden, and miserable. Churchmen taught that, while all knowledge came from God, He had supplied it so that people could use it for their own benefit.

The foundation of a school at Salerno in southern Italy sometime in the ninth century gave a tremendous impetus to medical study by laypeople. The school's location attracted Arabic, Greek, and Jewish physicians from all over the Mediterranean region. Students flocked there from northern Europe. The Jewish physician Shabbathai Ben Abraham (931–982) left pharmacological notes that were widely studied in later centuries.

Physicians were few in the early Middle Ages, and only the rich could afford them. Local folk medicine practiced by nonprofessionals provided such help as other people could get. Apparently most illnesses simply took their course, and death came early. A forty-year-old was considered old. People's vulnerability to ailments for which there were no probable cures contributed to a fatalistic acceptance of death at an early age.

Invasions and Migrations

After the Treaty of Verdun (843), continental Europe was fractured politically. All three kingdoms controlled by the sons of Louis the Pious (see Map 8.3) were torn by domestic dissension and disorder. The frontier and coastal defenses erected by Charlemagne and maintained by Louis the Pious were neglected. No European political power was strong enough to put up effective resistance to external attacks. Three groups attacked Europe: Vikings from Scandinavia, representing the final wave of Germanic migrants; Muslims from the Mediterranean; and Magyars forced westward by other peoples (see Map 8.4).

- *What effects did the assaults and migrations of the Vikings, Magyars, and Muslims have on the rest of Europe?*

Vikings in Western Europe

From the moors of Scotland to the mountains of Sicily, there arose in the ninth century the prayer, "Save us, O God, from the violence of the Northmen." The Northmen, also known as Vikings, were Germanic peoples from Norway, Sweden, and Denmark who had remained beyond the sway of the Christianizing and civilizing influences of the Carolingian Empire. Some scholars believe that the name *Viking* derives from the old Norse

Monasteries
← Vikings
← Magyars
← Muslims

0   200   400 Km.
0   200   400 Mi.

Mapping the Past

MAP 8.4 Invasions and Migrations of the Ninth Century This map shows the Viking, Magyar, and Arab invasions and migrations in the ninth century. Compare it with Map 7.3 (page 211) on the barbarian migrations of late antiquity to answer the following questions: ❶ What similarities do you see in the patterns of migration in these two periods? What significant differences? ❷ How is Viking expertise in shipbuilding and sailing reflected on this map? Based on the information in Map 7.3, what would you assume about the maritime skills of earlier Germanic tribes?

word *vik,* meaning "creek." A Viking, then, was a pirate who waited in a creek or bay to attack passing vessels.

The Vikings were superb seamen. Their boats, built using advanced methods, gave them great speed and maneuverability. Propelled either by oars or by sails, deckless, and about sixty-five feet long, a Viking ship could carry between forty and sixty men—enough to harass an isolated monastery or village. These ships, navigated by thoroughly experienced and utterly fearless sailors, moved through the most complicated rivers, estuaries, and waterways in Europe. The Carolingian Empire, with no navy and no notion of the importance of sea power, was helpless. The Vikings moved swiftly, attacked, and escaped to return again.

Scholars disagree about the reasons for Viking attacks and migrations. Recent research asserts that a very unstable Danish kingship and disputes over the succession led to civil war and disorder, which drove warriors abroad in search of booty and supporters. Other writers insist that the Vikings were looking for trade and new commercial contacts. In that case, there were no better targets for plunder than the mercantile centers of Francia and Frisia.

Viking attacks were savage. The Vikings burned, looted, and did extensive short-term property damage, but there is little evidence that they caused long-term destruction—perhaps because, arriving in small bands, they lacked the manpower to do so. They seized magnates and high churchmen and held them for ransom; they also demanded tribute from kings. In 844–845 Charles the Bald had to raise seven thousand pounds of silver, and across the English Channel Anglo-Saxon rulers collected a land tax, the Danegeld, to buy off the Vikings. The Vikings exploited conflicts among the Carolingians, as in 841 when they sailed up the Seine and sacked Rouen, knowing that Charles the Bald had crushed a revolt of nobles there just a few weeks earlier and that the region was vulnerable. The Carolingians also manipulated the Vikings; Lothar used his Viking ally Harald against his brothers in Frisia. In the Seine and Loire Valleys the frequent presence of Viking war bands seems to have had economic consequences, stimulating the production of food and wine and possibly the manufacture (for sale) of weapons and the breeding of horses.

In the early tenth century Danish Vikings besieged Paris with fleets of more than a hundred highly maneuverable ships, and the Frankish king Charles the Simple bought them off with a large part of northern France. The Vikings established the province of "Northmanland," or Normandy as it was later known, intermarrying with the local population and creating a distinctive Norman culture. From there they sailed around Spain and

Animal Headpost from Viking Ship Skilled woodcarvers produced ornamental headposts for ships, sledges, wagons, and bedsteads. The fearsome quality of many carvings suggests that they were intended to ward off evil spirits and to terrify. (© *University Museum of Cultural Heritage, Oslo. Photographer: Eirik Irgens Johnsen*)

into the Mediterranean, eventually conquering Sicily from the Muslim Arabs in 1060–1090, while other Normans crossed the English Channel, defeating Anglo-Saxon forces in 1066.

Between 876 and 954 Viking control extended from Dublin across the Irish Sea to Britain, across northern Britain between the Dee and the Solway Rivers, and then across the North Sea to the Vikings' Scandinavian homelands. Norwegian Vikings moved farther west than any Europeans had before, establishing permanent settlements on Iceland and short-lived settlements in Greenland and Newfoundland in what is now Canada.

In their initial attacks on isolated settlements, the Vikings put many people to the sword. From the British Isles and territories along the Baltic Sea, they took *thralls* (slaves) for the markets of Magdeburg on the Elbe River and Regensburg in Bavaria on the Danube, for the fairs of Lyons on the Rhône River, and to supply the huge demand for slaves in the Muslim world. The slave trade represented an important part of Viking commerce. The Icelander Hoskuld Dala-Kolsson of Laxardal paid three marks of silver, three times the price of a common concubine, for a pretty Irish girl; she was one of twelve offered by a Viking trader. No wonder many communities bought peace by paying tribute.

Along with destruction, the Vikings made positive contributions to the areas they settled. They carried their unrivaled knowledge of shipbuilding and seamanship everywhere. The northeastern and central parts of England where the Vikings settled became known as the *Danelaw* because Danish, not English, law and customs prevailed there. Scholars believe that some legal institutions, such as the ancestor of the modern grand jury, originated in the Danelaw. York in northern England, once a Roman army camp and then an Anglo-Saxon town, became a thriving center of Viking trade with Scandinavia. At Dublin on the east coast of Ireland, Viking ironworkers, steelworkers, and comb makers established a center for trade with the Hebrides, Iceland, and Norway. The Irish cities of Limerick, Cork, Wexford, and Waterford trace their origins to Viking trading centers.

Slavs and Vikings in Eastern Europe

In antiquity the Slavs lived in central Europe, farming with iron technology, building fortified towns, and worshiping a variety of deities. With the start of the mass migrations of the late Roman Empire, the Slavs moved in different directions and split into what later historians identified as three groups. The group labeled the West Slavs included the Poles, Czechs, Slovaks, and Wends. The South Slavs, comprising peoples who became the Serbs, Croats, Slovenes, Macedonians, and Bosnians, migrated southward into the Balkans and eventually achieved a relatively high degree of political development. In the seventh century Slavic peoples created the state of Moravia along the banks of the Danube River. Rulers of Moravia first sent for Orthodox Christian missionaries from the Byzantine Empire, but in the tenth century they decided to ally themselves with the Roman church. Most of the other West and South Slavs also slowly became Roman Christian. The pattern was similar to that of the Germanic tribes: first the ruler was baptized, and then missionaries preached, built churches, and spread Christian teachings among the common people. The ruler of Poland was able to convince the pope to establish an independent archbishopric there in 1000, the beginning of a long-lasting connection between Poland and the Roman church. In the Balkans the Serbs accepted Orthodox Christianity, while the Croats became Roman Christian, a division that has had a long impact; it was one of the factors in the civil war in this area in the late twentieth century. The Bulgars also became Orthodox Christian and in the early tenth century

built a strong state that attacked Constantinople a number of times.

Between the fifth and ninth centuries, the eastern Slavs, from whom the Ukrainians, Russians, and White Russians descend, moved into the vast and practically uninhabited area of present-day European Russia and Ukraine. This enormous area consisted of an immense virgin forest to the north, where most of the eastern Slavs settled, and an endless prairie grassland to the south. Probably organized as tribal communities, the eastern Slavs, like many North American pioneers much later, lived off the great abundance of wild game and crude "slash and burn" agriculture. After clearing a piece of the forest to build log cabins, they burned the stumps and brush. The ashes left a rich deposit of potash and lime, and the land produced several good crops before it was exhausted. The people then moved on to another untouched area and repeated the process.

In the ninth century the Vikings appeared in the lands of the eastern Slavs. Called "Varangians" in the old Russian chronicles, the Vikings were interested primarily in international trade, and the opportunities were good. Moving up and down the rivers, they soon linked Scandinavia and northern Europe to the Black Sea and to the Byzantine Empire with its capital at Constantinople. They raided and looted the cities along the Caspian Sea several times in the tenth century, taking booty and slaves. They built a few strategic forts along the rivers, from which they raided the neighboring Slavic tribes and collected tribute, especially in the form of slaves. As in the west, raids for plunder gradually turned into trading missions, and the Vikings established settlements, intermarried, and assimilated with Slavic peoples.

In order to increase and protect their international commerce, the Vikings declared themselves the rulers of the eastern Slavs. According to tradition, the semi-legendary chieftain Ruirik founded a princely dynasty about 860. In any event, the Varangian ruler Oleg (r. 878–912) established his residence at Kiev in modern-day Ukraine. He and his successors ruled over a loosely united confederation of Slavic territories known as Rus with its capital at Kiev until 1054. (The word *Russia* comes from *Rus*, though the origins of *Rus* are hotly debated, with some historians linking it with Swedish words and others with Slavic words.) The Viking prince and his clansmen quickly became assimilated into the Slavic population, taking local wives and emerging as the noble class.

Assimilation was accelerated by the conversion of the Vikings and local Slavs to Eastern Orthodox Christianity by missionaries of the Byzantine Empire. The written language of these missionaries, an early form of Slavic now known as Old Church Slavonic, was subsequently used in all religious and nonreligious documents in **Kievan Rus.** Thus the rapidly Slavified Vikings left two important legacies for the future: they created a loose unification of Slavic territories under a single ruling prince and a single ruling dynasty, and they imposed a basic religious unity by accepting Orthodox Christianity, as opposed to Roman Catholicism, for themselves and the eastern Slavs.

Online Study Center **Improve Your Grade**
Primary Source: Religious Competition in Kievan Rus

Even at its height under Great Prince Iaroslav the Wise (r. 1019–1054), the unity of Kievan Rus was extremely tenuous. Trade, not government, was the main concern of the rulers. Moreover, the Slavified Vikings failed to find a way of peacefully transferring power from one generation to the next. In medieval western Europe, this fundamental problem of government was increasingly resolved by resorting to the principle of primogeniture: the king's eldest son received the Crown as his rightful inheritance when his father died. Civil war was thus averted; order was preserved. In early Rus, however, there were apparently no fixed rules, and much strife accompanied each succession.

Possibly to avoid such chaos, Great Prince Iaroslav, before his death in 1054, divided Kievan Rus among his five sons, who in turn divided their properties when they died. Between 1054 and 1237, Kievan Rus disintegrated into more and more competing units, each ruled by a prince claiming to be a descendant of Ruirik. Even when only one prince claimed to be the great prince, the whole situation was unsettled.

The princes divided their land like private property because they thought of it as private property. A given prince owned a certain number of farms or landed estates and had them worked directly by his people, mainly slaves, called *kholops* in Russian. Outside of these estates, which constituted the princely domain, the prince exercised only limited authority in his principality. Excluding the clergy, two kinds of people lived there: the noble boyars and the commoner peasants.

The **boyars** were descendants of the original Viking warriors, and they also held their lands as free and clear private property. Although the boyars normally fought in princely armies, the customary law declared that they could serve any prince they wished. The ordinary peasants were also truly free. They could move at will wherever opportunities were greatest. In the touching phrase of the times, theirs was "a clean road, without bound-

aries."[15] In short, fragmented princely power, private property, and personal freedom all went together.

Magyars and Muslims

Along with Vikings from the north, nomadic central European steppe peoples known as Magyars moved westward in Europe in the late ninth century, crossing the Danube, attacking villages, gaining wealth, taking captives, and forcing leaders to pay tribute in an effort to prevent looting and destruction. Small groups of Magyars riding swift horses raided as far west as Spain and the Atlantic coast. They subdued northern Italy, compelled Bavaria and Saxony to pay tribute, and even penetrated into the Rhineland and Burgundy. Because of their skill with horses and their eastern origins, the Magyars were often identified with the earlier Huns by those they conquered, though they are probably unrelated ethnically. This identification may be the origin of the word *Hungarian*, though the word may also derive from a Turkish word for arrows bound together.

Magyar forces were defeated by a combined army of Frankish and other Germanic troops at the Battle of Lechfeld near Augsburg in southern Germany in 955, and the Magyars settled in the area that is now Hungary in eastern Europe. Much as Clovis had centuries earlier, their ruler Géza (r. 970–997), who had been a pagan, decided to become a Roman Christian. This gave him the support of the papacy and offered prospects for alliances with other Roman Christian rulers against the Byzantine Empire, Hungary's southern neighbor. Géza's son Stephen I (r. 997–1038) was officially crowned the king of Hungary by a papal representative on Christmas Day of 1001. He supported the building of churches and monasteries, built up royal power, and encouraged the use of Latin and the Roman alphabet. Hungary's alliance with the papacy shaped the later history of eastern Europe just as Charlemagne's alliance with the papacy shaped western European history. The Hungarians adopted settled agriculture, wrote law codes, and built towns, and Hungary became an important crossroads of trade for German and Muslim merchants.

The ninth century also saw invasions into western Europe from the south. Muslim fleets had attacked Sicily, which was part of the Byzantine Empire, beginning in the seventh century, and by the end of the ninth century they controlled most of the island. The Muslims drove northward and sacked Rome in 846. Expert seamen, they sailed around the Iberian Peninsula, braved the notoriously dangerous shoals and winds of the Atlantic coast, and captured towns along the Adriatic coast almost all the way to Venice. They attacked Mediterranean settlements along the coast of Provence and advanced on land as far as the Alps. In the tenth century Frankish, papal, and Byzantine forces were able to retake much territory, though the Muslims continued to hold Sicily. Under their rule, agricultural innovations from elsewhere in the Muslim world led to new crops such as cotton and sugar, and fortified cities became centers of Muslim learning. Disputes among the Muslim rulers on the island led one faction to ask the Normans for assistance, and between 1060 and 1090 the Normans gradually conquered the whole island.

What was the effect of these invasions on the structure of European society? From the perspective of those living in what had been Charlemagne's empire, Viking, Magyar, and Muslim attacks accelerated the fragmentation of political power. Lords capable of rallying fighting men,

supporting them, and putting up resistance to the invaders did so. They also assumed political power in their territories. Weak and defenseless people sought the protection of local strongmen, and free peasants sank to the level of serfs. This period is thus often seen as one of terror and chaos.

People in other parts of Europe might have had a different opinion, however. In Muslim Spain, scholars worked in thriving cities, and new crops enhanced ordinary people's lives. In eastern Europe, states such as Moravia and Hungary became strong kingdoms. A Viking point of view might be the most positive, for by 1100 descendants of the Vikings not only ruled their homelands in Denmark, Norway, and Sweden, but also ruled Normandy, England, Sicily, Iceland, and Kievan Rus, with an outpost in Greenland and occasional voyages to North America.

Chapter Summary

Online Study Center   **ACE the Test**

- *How did the spread of Islam shape European history in this era?*
- *How did Frankish rulers govern their kingdoms?*
- *What accounts for Charlemagne's political and diplomatic successes?*
- *What were the significant intellectual and cultural changes in Charlemagne's era?*
- *What effects did the assaults and migrations of the Vikings, Magyars, and Muslims have on the rest of Europe?*

In the seventh century the diverse Arab tribes were transformed into a powerful political and social force by the teachings of the Prophet Muhammad. They conquered much of the Middle East and North Africa, and in the eighth century they crossed into Europe, eventually gaining control of most of the Iberian Peninsula. Muslim-controlled Spain, known as al-Andalus, was the most advanced society in Europe in terms of agriculture, sci-

ence, and medicine. Some Christian residents assimilated to Muslim practices, but hostility between the two groups was also evident as each increasingly regarded members of the other as infidels.

In western Europe, Frankish rulers of the Merovingian dynasty built on the foundations established by Clovis in the fifth century, dividing their territories into regions and sending out royal officials, later called counts, to administer the regions. Their authority was frequently challenged by civil wars and rebellions by nobles. One of these nobles, Charles Martel, held the important position of mayor of the palace, and in the eighth century he took power and established a new dynasty, the Carolingians. The Carolingians used both military victories and strategic marriage alliances to enhance their authority.

Carolingian government reached the peak of its development under Charles Martel's grandson, Charlemagne. Building on the military and diplomatic foundations of his ancestors, Charlemagne waged constant warfare to expand his kingdom, eventually coming to control most of central and western continental Europe except Muslim

Spain. Christian missionary activity among the Germanic peoples continued, and strong ties were forged with the Roman papacy, which eventually resulted in Charlemagne's coronation as emperor. After his death his empire was divided between his grandsons in the Treaty of Verdun (843). This division of Charlemagne's empire was accompanied by a decentralization of power at the local level, and a new political form involving mutual obligations, later called "feudalism," developed. The power of the local nobles in the feudal structure rested on landed estates worked by peasants in another system of mutual obligation termed "manorialism." An overwhelmingly agricultural economy supplied food for local needs, but there was some interregional trade in glass, pottery, and woolens and a sizable long-distance trade in slaves.

Charlemagne's support of education and learning proved his most enduring legacy. The revival of learning associated with Charlemagne and his court at Aachen, sometimes styled the "Carolingian Renaissance," drew its greatest inspiration from seventh- and eighth-century intellectual developments in the Anglo-Saxon kingdom of Northumbria in northern England. Here women and men in monasteries produced beautiful illustrated texts, and the Venerable Bede popularized the Christian dating system now in use in most of the world. Monks and nuns in many parts of Europe also copied medical texts, and some Greek and Arabic medical knowledge filtered into Western Latin culture, though much was lost.

After the Treaty of Verdun, continental Europe was fractured politically, with no European political power strong enough to put up effective resistance to external attack. Vikings from Scandinavia carried out raids for plunder along the coasts and rivers of western Europe and traveled as far as Iceland, Greenland, and North America. Eventually they settled in England and France, where they established the state of Normandy. In eastern Europe Vikings traded down the rivers as far as Constantinople and formed the state of Kievan Rus, assimilating to Slavic culture and converting to the Orthodox religion. Like the Vikings, the Magyars initially invaded Europe for plunder and then established a permanent state; their ruler Stephen I was crowned as king by a papal representative two hundred years after Charlemagne's coronation. Thus, in both western and eastern Europe, civil rulers and church leaders supported each other's goals and utilized each other's prestige and power, though their alliances and disputes had little effect on the daily lives of most people in early medieval Europe.

Key Terms

Qur'an	missi dominici
Islam	Treaty of Verdun
Five Pillars of Islam	vassal
caliph	fief
al-Andalus	feudalism
infidel	manorialism
civitas	serfs
comites	double monastery
Frank	minuscule
capitularies	Kievan Rus
anointment	boyars

Online Study Center   **Improve Your Grade** Flashcards

Suggested Reading

Ahmed, Leila. *Women and Gender in Islam: Historical Roots of a Modern Debate.* 1992. The starting point for all research on Islam and gender.

Barbero, Allesandro. *Charlemagne: Father of a Continent.* 2004. A wonderful biography of Charlemagne and study of the times in which he lived that argues for the complexity of his legacy.

Barford, P. M. *The Early Slavs: Culture and Society in Early Medieval Eastern Europe.* 2001. An excellent survey of developments in much of eastern Europe.

Bitel, Lisa. *Women in Early Medieval Europe, 400–1100.* 2002. Uses literary works and archaeological evidence as well as more traditional types of sources to trace all aspects of women's lives: social, intellectual, political, economic.

Duby, Georges. *The Early Growth of the European Economy: Warriors and Peasants from the Seventh to the Twelfth Century.* 1978. Relates economic behavior to other aspects of human experience in a thoroughly readable style.

Esposito, John L. *Islam: The Straight Path,* updated ed. 2004. An informed and balanced work based on the best modern scholarship and original sources.

Fletcher, Richard. *The Cross and the Crescent: Christianity and Islam from Muhammad to the Reformation.* 2003. A highly readable introduction to the intricate and controversial relationships between Christianity and Islam down to the sixteenth century.

Glick, Thomas F. *Islamic and Christian Spain in the Early Middle Ages.* 1979. A good introduction to cultural and political developments and interactions.

James, Edward. *The Origins of France: From Clovis to the Capetians, 500–1000,* 2d ed. 2006. A solid introductory survey of early French history with an emphasis on family relationships.

Lings, Martin. *Muhammad: His Life Based on the Earliest Sources.* 1987. A clearly written narrative of the life of the Prophet Muhammad and the foundation of Islam based exclusively on eighth- and ninth-century Arabic sources.

Reynolds, Susan. *Fiefs and Vassals: The Medieval Evidence Reconsidered.* 1996. A comprehensive challenge to traditional conceptions of feudalism, the fief, and vassalage that is leading to a rethinking of medieval political relationships.

Riche, Pierre. *Daily Life in the World of Charlemagne.* Trans. JoAnn McNamara. 1978. A detailed study of many facets of Carolingian society.

Sawyer, Peter, ed. *The Oxford Illustrated History of the Vikings.* 1997. A sound account of the Vikings by an international team of scholars.

Verhulst, Adriaan. *The Carolingian Economy.* 2002. A brief survey of all aspects of the economy, including agrarian production, crafts, and commerce, designed for students.

Wood, Ian. *The Merovingian Kingdoms, 450–751.* 1994. The best general treatment of the Merovingians.

Notes

1. F. E. Peters, *A Reader on Classical Islam* (Princeton, N.J.: Princeton University Press, 1994), pp. 208–209.
2. J. O'Faolain and L. Martines, eds., *Not in God's Image: Women in History from the Greeks to the Victorians* (New York: Harper & Row, 1973), pp. 108–114.
3. See Jane I. Smith, "Islam and Christendom: Historical, Cultural, and Religious Interaction from the Seventh to the Fifteenth Centuries," in *The Oxford History of Islam,* ed. John L. Esposito (New York: Oxford University Press, 1999), pp. 317–321.
4. J. M. Bloom, *Paper Before Print: The History and Impact of Paper in the Islamic World* (New Haven: Yale University Press, 2001), pp. 9–10, 17, 45, 85–89.
5. JoAnn Hoeppner Moran Cruz, "Western Views of Islam in Medieval Europe," in *Perceptions of Islam,* ed. D. Blanks and M. Frassetto (New York: St. Martin's Press, 1999), pp. 55–81.
6. See R. W. Brauer, *Boundaries and Frontiers in Medieval Muslim Geography* (Philadelphia: American Philosophical Society, 1995), p. 41.
7. I. Wood, *The Merovingian Kingdoms, 450–751* (New York: Longman, 1994), p. 101.
8. Quoted in R. McKitterick, *The Frankish Kingdoms Under the Carolingians, 751–987* (New York: Longman, 1983), p. 34.
9. Einhard, *The Life of Charlemagne,* with a foreword by S. Painter (Ann Arbor: University of Michigan Press, 1960), pp. 50–51.
10. Quoted in McKitterick, p. 77.
11. See K. F. Werner, "Important Noble Families in the Kingdom of Charlemagne," in *The Medieval Nobility: Studies on the Ruling Class of France and Germany from the Sixth to the Twelfth Century,* ed. and trans. T. Reuter (New York: North-Holland, 1978), pp. 174–184.
12. Quoted in B. D. Hill, ed., *Church and State in the Middle Ages* (New York: John Wiley & Sons, 1970), pp. 46–47.
13. J. Nicholson, "Feminae Glorisae: Women in the Age of Bede," in *Medieval Women,* ed. D. Baker (Oxford: Basil Blackwell, 1978), pp. 15–31, esp. p. 19; and C. Fell, *Women in Anglo-Saxon England and the Impact of 1066* (Bloomington: Indiana University Press, 1984), p. 109.
14. R. W. Southern, *Medieval Humanism and Other Studies* (Oxford: Basil Blackwell, 1970), p. 3.
15. Quoted in R. Pipes, *Russia Under the Old Regime* (New York: Charles Scribner's Sons, 1974), p. 48.

Listening to the Past

Feudal Homage and Fealty

Feudalism provided social and political order held together by bonds of kinship, homage, and fealty and by grants of benefices—lands or estates given by king, lay lord, or ecclesiastical officer (bishop or abbot) to another member of the nobility or to a knight. In return for the benefice, or fief, the recipient became the vassal of the lord and agreed to perform certain services, usually military ones. Feudalism developed in the ninth century during the disintegration of the Carolingian Empire because rulers needed fighting men and officials. In a society that lacked an adequate government bureaucracy, a sophisticated method of taxation, or even the beginnings of national consciousness, personal ties provided some degree of cohesiveness.

In the first document, a charter dated 876, the emperor Charles the Bald (r. 843–877), Charlemagne's grandson, grants a benefice. In the second document, dated 1127, the Flemish notary Galbert of Bruges describes homage and fealty before Count Charles the Good of Flanders (r. 1119–1127). The ceremony consists of three parts: the act of homage; the oath of fealty, intended to reinforce the act; and the investiture (apparently with property). Because all three parts are present, historians consider this evidence of a fully mature feudal system.

In the name of the holy and undivided Trinity. Charles by the mercy of Almighty God august emperor . . . let it be known to all the faithful of the holy church of God and to our now, present and to come, that one of our faithful subjects, by name of Hildebertus, has approached our throne and has beseeched our serenity that through this command of our authority we grant to him for all the days of his life and to his son after him, in right of usufruct and benefice, certain estates which are . . . called Cavaliacus, in the county of Limoges. Giving assent to his prayers for reason of his meritorious service, we have ordered this charter to be written, through which we grant to him the estates already mentioned, in all their entirety, with lands, vineyards, forests, meadows, pastures, and with the men living upon them, so that, without causing any damage through exchanges or diminishing or lessening the land, he for all the days of his life and his son after him, as we have said, may hold and possess them in right of benefice and usufruct. . . .

Done of the sixteenth kalends of August [July 15th] the thirty-seventh year of the reign of Charles most glorious emperor in France . . . at Ponthion in the palace of the emperor. In the name of God, happily. Amen.

On Thursday, the seventh of the ides of April [April 7, 1127], acts of homage were again made to the count, which were brought to a conclusion through this method of giving faith and assurance. First, they performed homage in this fashion: the count inquired if [the prospective vassal] wished completely to become his man. He replied, "I do wish it," and with his hands joined and covered by the hands of the count, the two were united by a kiss. Second, he who had done the homage gave faith to the representative of the count in these words: "I promise in my faith that I shall henceforth be faithful to Count William, and I shall fully observe the homage owed him against all men, in good faith and without deceit." Third, he took an oath on the relics of the saints. Then the count, with the rod which he had in his right hand, gave investiture to all those who by this promise had given assurance and due homage to the count, and had taken the oath.

256

The hand of God blesses Charles the Bald as he receives the Bible, symbolic of his connection with Israelite kings David and Solomon. (*Bibliothèque nationale de France*)

Questions for Analysis

1. Why was the charter drawn up? Why did Charles grant the benefice?

2. Who were the "men living on it," and what economic functions did they perform?

3. What did the joined hands of the prospective vassal and the kiss symbolize?

4. In the oath of fealty, what was meant by the phrase "in my faith"? Why did the vassal swear on relics of the saints? What were these, and why were they used?

5. What does this ceremony tell us about the society that used it?

Source: The History of Feudalism by David Herlihy, ed. Copyright © 1970 by David Herlihy. Reprinted by permission of HarperCollins Publishers, Inc.

257

In this thirteenth-century manuscript, knights of King Henry II stab Archbishop Thomas Becket in 1170 in Canterbury Cathedral, a dramatic example of church-state conflict. Becket was soon made a saint, and the spot where the murder occurred became a pilgrimage site; it is still a top tourist destination. *(HIP/Art Resource, NY)*

chapter
9

chapter preview

Political Revival
- *How did medieval rulers create larger and more stable territories?*

Finance
- *What types of institutions did medieval rulers develop to provide their realms with sufficient taxes and other income?*

Law and Justice
- *How did the administration of law contribute to the development of national states?*

The Papacy
- *How did the papacy attempt to reform the church, and what was the response from other powerful rulers?*

The Crusades
- *How did the motives, course, and consequences of the Crusades reflect and shape developments in Europe?*

The Expansion of Christianity
- *What were the effects of the expansion of Christianity into northern and eastern Europe?*

STATE AND CHURCH IN THE HIGH MIDDLE AGES, 1000–1300

Beginning in the last half of the tenth century, the invasions that had enhanced European fragmentation gradually ended, and domestic disorder slowly subsided. Feudal rulers began to develop new institutions of government that enabled them to assert their power over lesser lords and the general population. Centralized states slowly crystallized, first in western Europe, and then in eastern and northern Europe as well. At the same time, energetic popes built their power within the Western Christian church and asserted their superiority over kings and emperors. A papal call to retake the holy city of Jerusalem led to nearly two centuries of warfare between Christians and Muslims. Christian warriors, clergy, and settlers moved out in all directions from western and central Europe, so that through conquest and colonization border regions were gradually incorporated into a more uniform European culture.

Political Revival

The eleventh century witnessed the beginnings of new political stability. Rulers in France, England, and Germany worked to reduce private warfare and civil anarchy. Domestic disorder subsided, and external invasions from the Vikings, Muslims, and Magyars (see page 248) gradually declined. In some parts of Europe, lords in control of large territories began to manipulate feudal institutions to build up their power even further, becoming kings over growing and slowly centralizing states.

- *How did medieval rulers create larger and more stable territories?*

Medieval Origins of the Modern State

Rome's great legacy to Western civilization had been the concepts of the state and the law, but for almost five hundred years after the disintegration of the Roman Empire in the West, the state as a reality did not exist. Political authority was completely decentralized. Power was spread among

Online Study Center

This icon will direct you to interactive activities and study materials on the website **college.hmco.com/pic/mckaywest9e**

many lords who gave their localities such protection and security as their strength allowed. The fiefdoms, kingdoms, and territories that covered the continent of early medieval Europe did not have the characteristics or provide the services of a modern state. They did not have jurisdiction over many people, and their laws affected a relative few. There existed many, frequently overlapping layers of authority—earls, counts, barons, knights—between a king and the ordinary people.

In these circumstances, medieval rulers had common goals. The rulers of England, France, and Germany wanted to strengthen and extend royal authority in their territories. They wanted to establish an effective means of communication with all peoples in order to increase public order. They wanted more revenue and efficient bureaucracies. The solutions they found to these problems laid the foundations for modern national states.

The modern state is an organized territory with definite geographical boundaries that are recognized by other states. It has a body of law and institutions of government. The modern national state counts on the loyalty of its citizens, or at least of a majority of them. In return it provides order so that citizens can go about their daily work and other activities. It protects its citizens and their property. The state tries to prevent violence and to apprehend and punish those who commit it. It supplies a currency or medium of exchange that permits financial and commercial transactions. It conducts relations with foreign governments. To accomplish these minimal functions, the state must have officials, bureaucracies, laws, courts of law, soldiers, information, and money. By the twelfth century medieval kingdoms and some lesser lordships possessed these attributes, at least to the extent that most modern states have them.

England

Before the Viking invasions, England had never been united under a single ruler. The victory of the remarkable Alfred, king of the West Saxons (or Wessex), over Guthrun the Dane, a Viking leader, at Edington in 878

The Bayeux Tapestry William's conquest of England was recorded in thread on a narrative embroidery panel measuring 231 feet by 19 inches. In this scene, two nobles and a bishop acclaim Harold Godwinson as king of England. The nobles hold a sword, symbol of military power, and the bishop holds a stole, symbol of clerical power. Harold himself holds a scepter and an orb, both symbols of royal power. The embroidery provides an important historical source for the clothing, armor, and lifestyles of the Norman and Anglo-Saxon warrior class. It eventually ended up in Bayeux in northern France, where it is displayed in a museum today and is incorrectly called a "tapestry," which is a different kind of needlework. *(Tapisserie de Bayeux et avec autorisation spéciale de la Ville de Bayeux)*

inaugurated a great political revival. Alfred and his immediate successors built a system of local defenses and slowly extended royal rule beyond Wessex to other Anglo-Saxon peoples until one law, royal law, took precedence over local custom. England was divided into local units called "shires," or counties, each under the jurisdiction of a shire-reeve (a word that soon evolved into "sheriff") appointed by the king. Sheriffs were unpaid officials from well-off families responsible for collecting taxes, catching and trying criminals, and raising infantry.

This unity did not prevent England from being conquered by the Vikings. In 1013 the Danish ruler Swen Forkbeard invaded England. His son Canute completed the subjugation of the island. King of England (1016–1035) and after 1030 king of Norway as well, Canute made England the center of his empire. He promoted a policy of assimilation and reconciliation between Anglo-Saxons and Vikings. King Edward the Confessor (r. 1042–1066), the son of an Anglo-Saxon father and a Norman mother who had taken Canute as her second husband, personified this assimilation. When Edward died childless, there were a number of claimants to the throne—the Anglo-Saxon noble Harold Godwinson (ca 1022–1066), who had been crowned by English nobles; the Norwegian king Harald III (r. 1045–1066), grandson of Canute; and Duke William of Normandy, who was the illegitimate son of Edward's cousin. Duke William was the descendant of Danish Vikings who had been given territory in northern France as a fief in the tenth century. He united his own vassals against external enemies and began to exert tighter control over them. He required them to personally swear homage, set up specific quotas of knights from every piece of land he distributed, and forbade them to fight with each other or build their own castles.

In 1066 William invaded England with his Norman vassals, met the exhausted forces of Harold, who had just defeated the Norwegians and had marched hundreds of miles to meet the Normans. William defeated them and later became known as William the Conqueror. He further solidified royal power on both sides of the English Channel, limiting the power of both his noble vassals and church officials and transforming the feudal system into a unified monarchy. In England William preserved the Anglo-Saxon institution of having sheriffs represent the king at the local level, but he replaced Anglo-Saxon sheriffs with Normans. He also retained another Anglo-Saxon device, the *writ*. This brief administrative order, written in the Anglo-Saxon vernacular by a government clerk, was the means by which the central government communicated with people at the local level.

Chronology

936–973	Reign of Otto I in Germany
1059	Lateran Council restricts election of the pope to the College of Cardinals
1066	Norman conquest of England
1073–1085	Pontificate of Gregory VII
1095–1291	Crusades
1154–1189	Reign of Henry II of England; revision of legal procedure; beginnings of common law
1162	Thomas Becket named archbishop of Canterbury
1180–1223	Reign of Philip II (Philip Augustus) in France
1198–1216	Innocent III; height of the medieval papacy
1215	Magna Carta
1230s	Papacy creates the Inquisition
1236	Ferdinand of Castile and León captures Córdoba
1290	Jews expelled from England
1306	Jews expelled from France
1397	Queen Margrete establishes Union of Kalmar

William retained Anglo-Saxon institutions that served his purposes and also introduced a major innovation, the Norman inquest. At his Christmas court in 1085, William discussed the state of the kingdom with his vassals and decided to conduct a systematic investigation of the entire country. The survey was to be made by means of *inquests,* or general inquiries, held throughout England. William wanted to determine how much wealth there was in his new kingdom, who held what land, and what land had been disputed among his vassals since the Conquest of 1066. Groups of royal officials were sent to every part of the country. In every village and farm, the priest and six local people were put under oath to answer the questions of the king's commissioners truthfully. In the words of a contemporary chronicler:

He sent his men over all England into every shire and had them find out how many hundred hides there were in the shire [a hide was a measure of land large enough to support

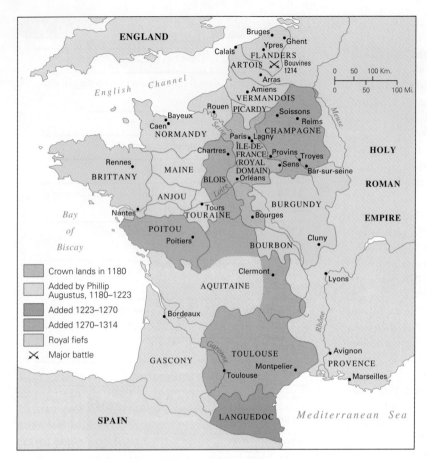

MAP 9.1 The Growth of the Kingdom of France   Some scholars believe that Philip II received the title "Augustus" (from a Latin word meaning "to increase") because he vastly expanded the territories of the kingdom of France. The province of Toulouse in the south became part of France as a result of the crusade against the Albigensians (see page 284).

one family], or what land and cattle the king himself had, or what dues he ought to have in twelve months from the shire. Also . . . what or how much everybody had who was occupying land in England, in land or cattle, and how much money it was worth. So very narrowly did he have it investigated, that there was no single hide nor yard of land, nor indeed . . . one ox nor one cow nor one pig was there left out, and not put down in his record: and all these records were brought to him afterwards.[1]

The resulting record, called **Domesday Book** from the Anglo-Saxon word *doom,* meaning "judgment," still survives. It is an invaluable source of social and economic information about medieval England.

Online Study Center **Improve Your Grade**
   Primary Source: William the Conqueror and
   Domesday Book: A Contemporary Description

   The Conqueror's scribes compiled *Domesday Book* in less than a year. It provided William and his descendants with information vital for the exploitation and govern-

ment of the country. Knowing the amount of wealth every area possessed, the king could tax accordingly. Knowing the amount of land his vassals had, he could allot knight service fairly. The inclusion of material covering England helped English kings regard their country as one unit.

In 1128 William's granddaughter Matilda was married to Geoffrey of Anjou. Their son, who became Henry II of England and inaugurated the Angevin (from Anjou, his father's county) dynasty, inherited the French provinces of Normandy, Anjou, Maine, and Touraine in northwestern France. When Henry married the great heiress Eleanor of Aquitaine in 1152, he claimed lordship over Aquitaine, Poitou, and Gascony in southwestern France (see Map 9.1). Each of these provinces was separate and was only loosely linked to the others by dynastic law and personal oaths. The histories of England and France in the High Middle Ages were closely intertwined, however, leading to disputes and conflicts down to the fifteenth century.

France

France also became increasingly unified in this era. Following the death of the last Carolingian ruler in 987, an assembly of nobles selected Hugh Capet, head of a powerful clan in the West Frankish kingdom, as his successor. Soon after his own coronation, Hugh crowned his son Robert to ensure the succession and prevent disputes after his death and to weaken the feudal principle of elective kingship. The Capetian kings (so called from the *cope,* or cloak, Hugh wore as abbot of Saint-Denis) subsequently saved France from further division, but this was hardly apparent in 987. Compared with the duke of Normandy, the first rulers of the **Capetian dynasty** were weak. By hanging on to what they had, however, they laid the foundation for later political stability.

This stability came slowly. In the early twelfth century France still consisted of a number of virtually independent provinces. Each was governed by a local ruler; each had its own laws, customs, coinage, and dialect. Unlike the king of England, the king of France had jurisdiction over a very small area. Chroniclers called King Louis VI (r. 1108–1137) *roi de Saint-Denis,* king of Saint-Denis, because the territory he controlled was limited to Paris and the Saint-Denis area surrounding the city (see Map 9.1). This region, called the *Île-de-France,* or royal domain, became the nucleus of the French state. The clear goal of the medieval French king was to increase the royal domain and extend his authority.

The term *Saint-Denis* had political and religious charisma, which the Crown exploited. Following the precedent of the Frankish chieftain Clovis (see page 212), Louis VI and his Capetian successors supported and identified with the cult of Saint Denis, a deeply revered saint whom the French believed protected the country from danger. Under the saint's banner, the *oriflamme,* French kings fought their battles and claimed their victories. The oriflamme rested in the abbey of Saint-Denis, which served as the burial place of the French kings. The Capetian kings identified themselves with the cult of Saint Denis in order to tap popular devotion to him and tie that devotion and loyalty to the monarchy.

The work of unifying France began under Louis VI's grandson Philip II (r. 1180–1223). Rigord, Philip's biographer, gave him the title "Augustus" (from a Latin word meaning "to increase") because he vastly enlarged the territory of the kingdom of France. When King John of England, who was Philip's vassal for the rich province of Normandy, defaulted on his feudal obligation to come to the French court, Philip declared Normandy forfeit to the French crown. He enforced his declaration militarily, and in 1204 Normandy fell to the French. He gained other northern provinces as well, and by the end of his reign Philip was effectively master of northern France.

In the thirteenth century Philip Augustus's descendants acquired important holdings in the south. By the end of the thirteenth century most of the provinces of modern France had been added to the royal domain through diplomacy, marriage, war, and inheritance. The king of France was stronger than any group of nobles who might try to challenge his authority.

Philip Augustus devised a method of governing the provinces and providing for communication between the central government in Paris and local communities. Philip decided that each province would retain its own institutions and laws. But royal agents, called **baillis** in the north and **seneschals** in the south, were sent from Paris into the provinces as the king's official representatives with authority to act for him. Often middle-class lawyers, these men possessed full judicial, financial, and military jurisdiction in their districts. The baillis and seneschals were appointed by, paid by, and responsible to the king. Unlike the English sheriffs, they were never natives of the provinces to which they were assigned, and they could not own land there. This policy reflected the fundamental principle of French administration that royal interests superseded local interests.

Central Europe

In the middle of Europe, the German king Otto I (r. 936–973) defeated many other lords to build up his power. To do this, Otto relied on the church, getting financial support and the bulk of his army from ecclesiastical lands. Otto asserted the right to control ecclesiastical appointments. Before receiving religious consecration and being invested with the staff and ring symbolic of their offices, bishops and abbots had to perform feudal homage for the lands that accompanied the church office. This practice, later known as "lay investiture," created a grave crisis in the eleventh century, as we will see later in this chapter.

Some of our knowledge of Otto derives from *The Deeds of Otto,* a history of his reign in heroic verse written by a nun, Hroswita of Gandersheim (ca 935–ca 1003). A learned poet, she also produced six verse plays, and she is considered the first dramatist writing in Europe after the fall of the Roman Empire.

In 955 Otto I inflicted a crushing defeat on the Magyars in the Battle of Lechfeld (see page 252), which made Otto a great hero to the Germans. He used this victory to have himself crowned emperor in 962 by the pope in

Christ Enthroned with Saints and the Emperor Otto I (tenth century) Between 933 and 973 Emperor Otto I founded the church of Saint Mauritius in Magdeburg. As a memorial to the event, Otto commissioned the production of this ivory plaque showing Christ accepting a model of the church from the emperor. Ivory was a favorite medium of Ottonian artists, and squat figures in a simple geometrical pattern characterize their work. *(The Metropolitan Museum of Art, Bequest of George Blumenthal, 1941 [41.100.157]. Photograph © 1986 The Metropolitan Museum of Art)*

Aachen, which had been the capital of the Carolingian Empire. He chose this site to symbolize his intention to continue the tradition of Charlemagne and to demonstrate papal support for his rule. It was not exactly clear what Otto was the emperor *of*, however, though by the eleventh century people were increasingly using the term **Holy Roman Empire** to refer to a loose confederation of principalities, duchies, cities, bishoprics, and other types of regional governments stretching from Denmark to Rome and from Burgundy to Poland.

In this large area of central Europe, unified nation-states did not develop until the nineteenth century. The Holy Roman emperors shared power with princes, dukes, archbishops, counts, bishops, abbots, and cities. The office of emperor remained an elected one, though the

electors included only seven men—four secular rulers of large territories within the empire and three archbishops.

Between 1000 and 1300, regionally based princely authorities emerged in the larger states in the empire as dynasties that had a strong sense of local identity and traced their descent through the paternal line. Newly constructed stone castles bearing the family name symbolized the dynasty's power and served as the center of its lands and rights—that is, of its *Landesherrschaft,* or territorial lordship.

Through most of the first half of the twelfth century, civil war wracked Germany. When Conrad III died in 1152, the resulting anarchy was so terrible that the electors decided that the only alternative to continued chaos was the selection of a strong ruler. They chose Frederick Barbarossa of the house of Hohenstaufen.

Frederick Barbarossa (r. 1152–1190) tried valiantly to bring peace to the empire, using his family duchy of Swabia in southwestern Germany as a power base (see Map 9.2). Like William the Conqueror in England and Philip in France, Frederick required vassals to take an oath of allegiance to him as emperor and appointed officials to exercise full imperial authority over local communities. He forbade private warfare, establishing **Landfrieden,** sworn peace associations with the princes of various regions. These peace associations had the judicial authority to punish breaches of the peace and criminals. Penalties for serious crimes, such as incendiary conduct during a conflict, increased from maiming to execution. Barbarossa and later rulers traveled continually and extensively, and the royal court could mete out justice anywhere. In general, however, legal jurisdiction in the Holy Roman Empire was in the hands of local counts, dukes, margraves, and bishops.

Frederick Barbarossa surrounded himself with men trained in Roman law (see page 273), and he used Roman law to justify his assertion of imperial rights over the towns of northern Italy. Between 1154 and 1188 Frederick made six expeditions into Italy. His scorched-earth policy was successful at first, making for significant conquests in the north. The brutality of his methods, however, provoked revolts, and the Italian cities formed an alliance with the papacy. In 1176 Frederick suffered a defeat at Legnano (see Map 9.2). This battle marked the first time a feudal cavalry of armed knights was decisively defeated by bourgeois infantrymen. Frederick was forced to recognize the municipal autonomy of the northern Italian cities. The northern and southern parts of the Holy Roman Empire remained separate and, unlike England and France, did not become unified states until the

Castile, in the north-central part of the peninsula, became the strongest of the growing Christian kingdoms, and Aragon, in the northeast, the second most powerful. In 1085 King Alfonso VI of Castile and León captured Toledo on the Tagus River in central Spain, center of the old Visigothic kingdom. He immediately named Bernard, a monk of Cluny in Burgundy, as archbishop of Toledo. Alfonso, who had married a Frenchwoman, invited French knights to settle in the *meseta,* the central plateau of Spain, a region well suited for sheep farming, viticulture, and cereal agriculture.

The Almoravid dynasty, which ruled much of northwestern Africa, briefly reunified the Muslim state in the late eleventh century, but the Almoravids were themselves conquered by forces of the Almohad dynasty. Alfonso VIII (1158–1214), aided by the kings of Aragon, Navarre, and Portugal, crushed the Almohad-led Muslims at Las Navas de Tolosa in 1212, accelerating the Christian push southward. The kings of Castile, Aragon, and several smaller states established representative assemblies (the *cortes*), which were structured with separate meetings for the clergy, nobility, and urban dwellers. James the Conqueror of Aragon (r. 1213–1276) captured Valencia on the Mediterranean coast in 1233, immediately turning the chief mosque into a cathedral.

In 1236 Ferdinand of Castile and León captured the great Muslim industrial and intellectual center of Córdoba in the heart of Andalusia. The city's mosque became a Christian cathedral, and the city itself served thereafter as the main military base against Granada. When Seville fell to Ferdinand's Castilians in 1248 after a long siege, Christians controlled the entire Iberian Peninsula, save for the small state of Granada (see Map 9.3).

Once in Seville, Ferdinand's heart "was full of joy at the great reward God had given him for his labours. . . . His mother (wanted) to revive the archiepiscopal see which had of old been abandoned, despoiled (by the Muslims) . . . and a worthy foundation was established in honor of Saint Mary."[2] Ferdinand's mother thus inspired the use of the chief mosque as the diocesan cathedral. Just as the Muslims had used the sites of ancient pagan shrines for the erection of their mosques when they

MAP 9.2 The Holy Roman Empire and the Kingdom of Sicily, ca 1200 Frederick Barbarossa greatly expanded the size of the Holy Roman Empire, but it remained a loose collection of various types of governments. The kingdom of Sicily included mainland areas as well as the island in 1200, with an ethnically mixed population ruled by Norman kings.

nineteenth century, when a new wave of centralization led to the formation of Germany and Italy.

The Iberian Peninsula

In the eleventh century divisions and civil war in the caliphate of Córdoba allowed Christian armies to conquer an increasingly large part of the Iberian Peninsula.

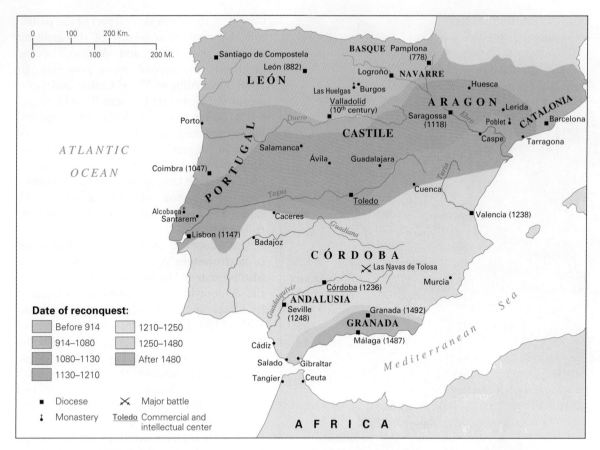

MAP 9.3 The Reconquista   The Christian conquest of Muslim Spain was followed by ecclesiastical reorganization, with the establishment of dioceses, monasteries, and the Latin liturgy, which gradually tied the peninsula to the heartland of Christian Europe and to the Roman papacy. *(Source: Adapted from David Nicholas, The Evolution of the Medieval World. Copyright © 1992. Reprinted by permission of Pearson Education Limited.)*

Online Study Center   **Improve Your Grade** Interactive Map: Christian Reconquista of Muslim Spain

conquered Spain in the eighth century, so Christians followed suit, and many other mosques throughout Spain were also turned into churches. Since religious buildings serve as windows into the broader culture, with valuable social, intellectual, and economic information, scholars in many fields have deplored this assimilation of mosques to Christian religious use, as it involved the destruction of Muslim art.

Muslim Spain had had more cities than any other country in Europe, and Christian Spain became highly urbanized. Victorious Christian rulers expelled the Muslims and recruited immigrants from France and elsewhere in Iberia. One example was the town of Logroño. King Alfonso VI decreed

that a town should be established there, assembling from all parts of the world burgesses of many different trades . . . Gaston, Bretons, English, Burgundians, Normans, Toulousains, Provençals and Lombards, and many other traders of various nations and foreign tongues; and thus he populated a town of no mean size.[3]

The thirteenth century thus witnessed a huge migration of peoples from the north to the depopulated cities of the central and southern parts of the peninsula.

Fourteenth-century clerical propagandists called the movement to expel the Muslims the **reconquista** (reconquest)—a sacred and patriotic crusade to wrest the country from "alien" Muslim hands. This religious myth

Almohad Banner   This finely worked embroidered banner is typical of Muslim style; it incorporates Arabic lettering on the edges and includes no representation of the human form. The Almohads were a strict Muslim dynasty from North Africa that had ruled about half of Spain in the twelfth century. In 1212 King Alfonso VIII of Castile won a decisive victory over Almohad forces at Las Navas de Tolosa, and Christian holdings in Spain increased. *(Institut Amatller d'Art Hispanic)*

became part of Spanish political culture and of the national psychology. As a consequence of the reconquista, the Spanish and Portuguese learned how to administer vast tracts of newly acquired territory. When, in the sixteenth and seventeenth centuries, they gained overseas empires in the Americas, Africa, and Asia, medieval models guided them. The precedents of medieval Spain were imposed on colonial Mexico, Brazil, Peru, Angola, and the Philippines.

 Finance

As medieval rulers expanded their territories and extended their authority, they developed institutions to rule more effectively, including an enlarged bureaucracy of officials and larger armies. Officials and armies cost money, and rulers in various countries developed slightly different ways of acquiring more revenue and handling financial matters, some more successful than others.

• *What types of institutions did medieval rulers develop to provide their realms with sufficient taxes and other income?*

England

In England, William the Conqueror's son Henry I (r. 1100–1135) established a bureau of finance called the **Exchequer** (for the checkered cloth at which his officials collected and audited royal accounts), which became the first institution of the government bureaucracy of England. Henry's income came from a variety of sources: from taxes paid by peasants living on the king's estates; from the *Danegeld,* an old tax originally levied to pay tribute to the Danes; from the *dona,* an annual gift from the

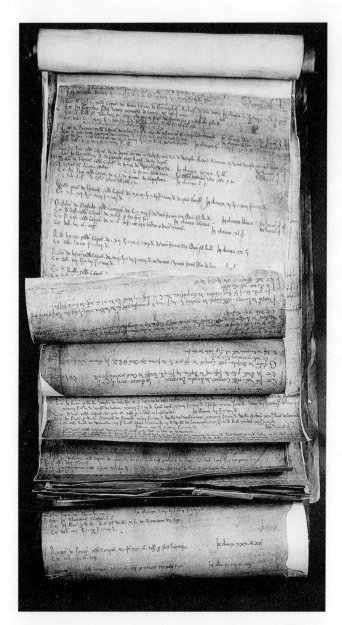

The Pipe Rolls Twice yearly English medieval sheriffs appeared before the Barons of the Exchequer to account for the monies they had collected from the royal estates and from fines for civil and criminal offenses. Clerks recorded these revenues and royal expenditures on the pipe rolls, whose name derives from the pipelike form of the rolled parchments. A roll exists for 1129–1130, then continuously from 1156 to 1832, representing the largest series of English public records. *(Crown copyright material in the Public Record Office is reproduced by permission of the Controller of the Britannic Majesty's Stationery Office [E40 1/1565])*

church; from money paid to the Crown for settling disputes; and from fines paid by people found guilty of crimes. Henry also received income because of his position as a feudal lord. If, for example, one of his vassals died and the son wished to inherit the father's properties, the heir had to pay Henry a tax called **relief.** From the knights Henry took **scutage,** money paid in lieu of the performance of military service. With the scutage collected, Henry could hire mercenary troops. The sheriff in each county was responsible for collecting all these sums and paying them to the king's Exchequer twice a year. Henry, like other medieval kings, made no distinction between his private income and state revenues, though the officials of the Exchequer began to keep careful records of the monies paid into and out of the royal treasury.

France

The development of royal financial agencies in most continental countries lagged behind the English Exchequer. Twelfth-century French rulers derived their income from their royal estates in the Île-de-France. As Philip Augustus and his successors added provinces to the royal domain, the need for money became increasingly acute. Philip made the baillis and seneschals responsible for collecting taxes in their districts. This income came primarily from fines and confiscations imposed by the courts.

In the thirteenth century French rulers acquired some income from the church and some from people living in the towns. Townspeople paid **tallage** or the **taille**—a tax arbitrarily laid by the king. In all parts of the country, feudal vassals owed military service to the king when he called for it. Louis IX converted this military obligation into a cash payment, called "host tallage," and thus increased his revenues. Moreover, pervasive anti-Semitism allowed Philip Augustus, Louis VIII, and Louis IX to tax their Jewish subjects mercilessly.

Medieval people believed that a good king lived on the income of his own land and taxed only in time of a grave emergency—that is, a just war. Because the church, and not the state, performed what we call social services—such as education and care of the sick, the aged, and orphaned children—there was no ordinary need for the government to tax. Taxation meant war financing. The French monarchy could not continually justify taxing the people on the grounds of the needs of war. Thus the French kings were slow to develop an efficient bureau of finance. French provincial laws and institutions—in contrast to England's early unification—also retarded the growth of a central financial agency. Not until the fourteenth century, as a result of the Hundred Years' War, did a state financial bureau emerge—the Chamber of Accounts.

Sicily

The one secular government other than England that developed a financial bureaucracy was the kingdom of Sicily. Sicily is a good example of how a strong government could be built on a feudal base by determined rulers. The Sicilian administration came to have a significant Muslim component.

Like England, Sicily had come under Norman domination. Between 1061 and 1091 a bold Norman knight, Roger de Hauteville, and a small band of mercenaries defeated the Muslims and Greeks who controlled the island. Roger then governed a heterogeneous population of Sicilians, Italians, Greeks, Jews, Arabs, and Normans. Like William the Conqueror in England, he introduced Norman institutions in Sicily and made them work as a means of government. Roger distributed scattered fiefs to his followers so no vassal would have a centralized power base. He took an inquest of royal property and rights and forbade private warfare.

To these Norman practices, Roger fused Arabic and Greek governmental devices. For example, he retained the Kalbid Muslims' (previous rulers over Sicily) main financial agency, the **diwān,** a sophisticated bureau for record keeping and administration.

Under his son and heir, Count Roger II (r. 1130–1154), the process of state building continued. Roger II developed diplomatic ties with the Fatimid rulers of Egypt, exchanging letters, gifts, and embassies with the caliph al-Hafid. Because Sicilians and Muslims usually could not read each other's languages, the diwān kept official documents in Greek, Latin, and Arabic. It supervised the royal estates in Sicily, collected revenues, managed the state monopoly of the sale of salt and lumber, and registered all income to the treasury. With revenues derived from those products, Roger hired mercenaries. He encouraged appeals from local courts to his court because such appeals implied respect for the royal court.

Arabic influence in Sicily is also evident in the public presentation, or image, of the king. Following Islamic custom, Roger II became less visible, deliberately secluding himself in his palace at Palermo. On special occasions, he rode out in elegant finery surrounded by retinues of guards, household retainers, and "lords of the diwān," thereby ceremonially displaying himself. Some Christian critics considered this practice evidence of the tyranny of the Norman kings, but an Arabic courtier praised

Roger II because "he followed the way of Muslim rulers. . . . He broke with the custom of the Franks who are not acquainted with such things. . . . He treated the Muslims with respect, took them as his companions, and kept the Franks off (protected) them."[4] In the multicultural society of medieval Sicily, Muslims and Greeks, as well as Normans, staffed the army, the judiciary, and the diwān. Roger's relative seclusion did not keep him from expanding his territory, and in 1137 his forces took the city of Naples and much of the surrounding territory in southern Italy. The entire area came to be known as the kingdom of Sicily (or sometimes the kingdom of the Two Sicilies), and was often caught up in conflicts between the pope, the Holy Roman emperor, and the kings of France and Spain over control of Italy.

Frederick II

Frederick II (r. 1212–1250), grandson of Roger II of Sicily through his mother and grandson of Frederick Barbarossa of Germany through his father, was crowned king of the Germans at Aachen (1216) and Holy Roman emperor at Rome (1220). He concentrated his attention on Sicily. Frederick banned private warfare and placed all castles and towers under royal administration. He also replaced town officials with royal governors and subordinated feudal and ecclesiastical courts to the king's courts. Royal control of the nobility, of the towns, and of the judicial system added up to great centralization, which required a professional bureaucracy and sound state financing.

In 1224 Frederick founded the University of Naples to train officials for his bureaucracy. University-educated administrators and lawyers emphasized the stiff principles of Roman law, such as the maxim of the Justinian *Code* that "what pleases the prince has the force of law." Frederick's financial experts regulated agriculture, public works, and even business. Frederick secured the tacit consent of his people to regular taxation. This was a noteworthy achievement when most people believed that taxes should be levied only in time of grave emergency. Frederick defined emergency broadly. For much of his reign he was involved in a bitter dispute with the papacy, and he used this as a reason to levy taxes. Moreover, he continued the use of Muslim institutions such as the diwān, and he tried to administer justice fairly to all his subjects, declaring, "We cannot in the least permit Jews and Saracens (Muslims) to be defrauded of the power of our protection and to be deprived of all other help, just because the difference of their religious practices makes

Palatine Chapel at Palermo (1132–1140) Muslim crafts-men from Egypt painted the wooden ceiling of the royal chapel for King Roger of Sicily. This section shows the diverse peoples—Jews, Christians, Muslims—who lived in Palermo. *(Burgerbibliothek Bern Cod. 120 II, fol. 98r)*

them hateful to Christians,"[5] implying a degree of toler-ation exceedingly rare at the time.

Frederick's contemporaries called him the "Wonder of the World." He certainly transformed the kingdom of Sicily. But Sicily required constant attention, and Freder-ick's absences on crusade and on campaigns in mainland Italy took their toll. Shortly after he died, the unsuper-vised bureaucracy fell to pieces. The pope, as feudal over-lord of Sicily, called in a French prince to rule.

Frederick showed little interest in the northern part of the Holy Roman Empire. He concentrated his attention on Sicily rather than on the historic Hohenstaufen stronghold of Swabia. When he visited the German parts of the empire in the expectation of securing support for his Italian policy, he made sweeping concessions to the princes, bishops, duchies, and free cities. He exempted German churchmen and lay princes from taxation and from the jurisdiction of imperial authorities. These moves weakened imperial authority, and in the later Mid-dle Ages lay and ecclesiastical princes held sway in the Holy Roman Empire.

Law and Justice

In the early Middle Ages society perceived of major crimes as acts against an individual, and a major crime was settled when the accused made a cash payment to the victim or his or her kindred. In the High Middle Ages suspects were pursued and punished for acting against the *public* interest. Throughout Europe, however, the form and application of laws depended on local and provincial custom and practice. In the twelfth and thir-teenth centuries the law was a hodgepodge of Germanic customs, feudal rights, and provincial practices. Kings in France and England wanted to blend these elements into a uniform system of rules acceptable and applicable to all their peoples. Legal developments in continental coun-tries like France were strongly influenced by Roman law, while England slowly built up a unique unwritten com-mon law.

● *How did the administration of law contribute to the development of national states?*

France and the Holy Roman Empire

The French king Louis IX (r. 1226–1270) was famous in his time for his concern for justice. Each French province, even after being made part of the kingdom of France, retained its unique laws and procedures, but Louis IX created a royal judicial system. He established the Parlement of Paris, a kind of supreme court that wel-comed appeals from local administrators and from the courts of feudal lords throughout France. By the very act of appealing the decisions of feudal courts to the Par-lement of Paris, French people in far-flung provinces were recognizing the superiority of royal justice.

Louis sent royal judges to all parts of the country to check up on the work of the baillis and seneschals and to hear complaints of injustice. He was the first French monarch to publish laws for the entire kingdom. The Parlement of Paris registered (or announced) these laws, which forbade private warfare, judicial duels, gambling, blaspheming, and prostitution. Louis sought to identify justice with the kingship, and gradually royal justice touched all parts of the kingdom.

In the Holy Roman Empire, justice was administered at two levels. The manorial or seigneurial court, presided over by the lay or ecclesiastical lord, dealt with such matters as damage to crops and fields, trespass, boundary disputes, and debt—common conflicts at a time when princes were expanding their colonial jurisdictions over forestland and wasteland and receiving thousands of new settlers. Dukes, counts, margraves, bishops, and abbots possessed an authority called **Landgericht,** or regional magistracies. With this power, the lord's agents, or representatives, dispensed justice in serious criminal cases involving theft, arson, assault with a weapon, rape, and homicide. Regional magistrates held powers of high justice, that is, the right to execute a criminal; the imposition of the death penalty by hanging was the distinctive feature of this court.

Henry II and Thomas Becket

Under Henry II (r. 1154–1189) England developed and extended a **common law,** a law that originated in, and was applied by, the king's court and that in the next two or three centuries became common to the entire country. England was unusual in developing one system of royal courts and one secular law. Henry I had occasionally sent out **circuit judges** (royal officials who traveled a given circuit or district) to hear civil and criminal cases. Every year royal judges left London and set up court in the counties. Wherever the king's judges sat, there sat the king's court.

Henry also improved procedure in criminal justice. In 1166 he instructed the sheriffs to summon local juries to conduct inquests and draw up lists of known or suspected criminals. These lists, or indictments, sworn to by the juries, were to be presented to the royal judges when they arrived in the community. This accusing jury is the ancestor of the modern grand jury. Judges determined guilt or innocence in a number of ways. They heard testimony, sought witnesses, and read written evidence. If these were lacking and if a suspect had a bad public reputation, he or she might be submitted to trial by ordeal. An accused person could be tried by fire or water. In the latter case, the accused was tied hand and foot and dropped in a lake or river. People believed that water was

The Customs of Aragon This illumination, imitating the style of Parisian court art, shows King James of Aragon (r. 1213–1276) presiding over a law court. King James—called "the Conqueror" because of his victories over Catalonia, Valencia, and Majorca—ordered several codifications of law. The most important of these, the Customs of Aragon (1247), drew on Roman canonical practice for legal procedures. (*Initial N: King James I of Aragon Overseeing Court of Law Vidal Mayor, 83.MQ.165, fol. 72v. © The J. Paul Getty Museum, Los Angeles*)

a pure substance and would reject anything foul or unclean. Thus a person who sank was considered innocent; a person who floated was found guilty. Trial by ordeal was a ritual that appealed to the supernatural for judgment. God determined guilt or innocence, and thus a priest had to be present to bless the water.

Henry II disliked ordeal, and it was used less during his reign than it was on the continent. Gradually, in the course of the thirteenth century, the king's judges adopted the practice of calling on twelve people (other than the accusing jury) to consider the question of innocence or guilt. This became the jury of trial, but it was very slowly accepted because medieval people had more confidence in the judgment of God than in the judgment of twelve ordinary people.

One aspect of Henry's judicial reforms encountered stiff resistance from an unexpected source: the friend and former chief adviser whom Henry had made archbishop of Canterbury—Thomas Becket. Henry selected Becket as archbishop in 1162 because he believed he could depend on Becket's support. But when Henry wanted to bring all persons in the kingdom under the jurisdiction of the royal courts, Becket's opposition led to a dramatic conflict between temporal and spiritual powers.

In the 1160s many literate people accused of crimes claimed "benefit of clergy" even though they were not clerics and often had no intention of being ordained. An accused person proved he was a cleric by his ability to read. (Later, university students and merchants—who had to keep records—could claim it.) After the courts established the practice of opening the Bible to the Fiftieth Psalm and asking the accused to read, they found that criminals had memorized the passage. Benefit of clergy gave the accused the right to be tried in church courts, which meted out mild punishments. A person found guilty in the king's court might suffer mutilation—loss of a hand or foot or castration—or even death. Ecclesiastical punishments tended to be an obligation to say certain prayers or to make a pilgrimage.

In 1164 Henry II insisted that everyone, including clerics, be subject to the royal courts. Becket vigorously protested that church law required clerics to be subject to church courts. When Becket proceeded to excommunicate one of the king's vassals, the issue became more complicated. Because no one was supposed to have any contact with an excommunicated person, it appeared that the church could arbitrarily deprive the king of necessary military forces. The disagreement between Henry II and Becket dragged on for years. The king grew increasingly bitter that his appointment of Becket had proved to be such a mistake. Late in December 1170, in a fit of rage, Henry expressed the wish that Becket be destroyed. Four knights took the king at his word. They rode to Canterbury Cathedral and, as the archbishop was leaving evening services, slashed off the crown of his head and scattered his brains on the pavement.

What Thomas Becket could not achieve in life, he gained in death. The assassination of an archbishop turned public opinion in England and throughout western Europe against the king. Miracles were recorded at Becket's tomb; Becket was made a saint; and in a short time Canterbury Cathedral became a major pilgrimage and tourist site. Henry had to back down. He did public penance for the murder and gave up his attempts to bring clerics under the authority of the royal court.

King John and Magna Carta

Henry II's sons Richard I, known as Lion-Hearted (r. 1189–1199), and John (r. 1199–1216) lacked their father's interest in the work of government. Richard looked on England as a source of revenue for his military enterprises. Soon after his accession, he departed on crusade to the Holy Land. During his reign he spent only six months in England, and the government was run by ministers trained under Henry II.

John's basic problems were financial. King John inherited a heavy debt from his father and brother. The country had paid dearly for Richard's crusading zeal. While returning from the Holy Land, Richard had been captured, and England had paid an enormous ransom—much of it in wool, England's primary export—to secure his release. Further, during the entire period of 1180–1220, England experienced severe inflation, which drove prices up. In 1204 John lost the rich province of Normandy to Philip Augustus of France and then spent the rest of his reign trying to get it back. John took scutage, and each time increased the amount due. He forced widows to pay exorbitant fines to avoid unwanted marriages. He sold young girls who were his feudal wards to the highest bidder. These actions antagonized the nobility.

John also alienated the church and the English townspeople. He rejected the pope's nominee to be archbishop of Canterbury. And he infuriated the burghers of the towns by extorting money from them and threatening to revoke their charters of self-government.

All the money John raised did not bring him success. In July 1214 John's coalition of Flemish, German, and English cavalry suffered a severe defeat at the hands of Philip Augustus of France at Bouvines in Flanders. This battle ended English hopes for the recovery of territories from France and also strengthened the barons' opposition to John. His ineptitude as a soldier in a society that idealized military glory was the final straw. Rebellion begun by northern barons eventually grew to involve many members of the English nobility, including the archbishop of Canterbury and the earl of Pembroke, the leading ecclesiastical and lay peers. After lengthy negotiations, John met the barons in 1215 at Runnymede, a meadow along the Thames River. There he was forced to approve and to attach his seal to the peace treaty called **Magna Carta,** "Magna" (great or large) because it was so long and detailed.

For contemporaries, Magna Carta was intended to redress the grievances that particular groups—the barons, the clergy, the merchants of London—had against King John. Charters were not unusual: many kings and lords at the time issued them and then sometimes revoked them, as John did almost immediately. This revocation was largely ignored, however, and every English king un-

Thieves Plunder Saint Edmund's Chapel This eleventh-century painting shows thieves searching for jewelry and rich burial fabrics and even pulling the iron nails out of the wooden structure. They are also trying to dig up the coffin of Saint Edmund, the king of East Anglia (r. 841–869), who was defeated in battle and executed by Danish invaders and whose bones could be sold as relics. Crime and violence preoccupied secular and religious authorities alike. *(Pierpont Morgan Library/ Art Resource, NY)*

til 1485 reissued Magna Carta as evidence of his promise to observe the law. Thus this charter alone acquired enduring importance. It came to signify the principle that everyone, including the king and the government, must obey the law.

Online Study Center **Improve Your Grade**
Primary Source: Magna Carta: The Great Charter of Liberties

Although legal scholars coined the phrase "rule of law" only in the late nineteenth century, in the later Mid-dle Ages references to Magna Carta underlined the old Augustinian theory that a government, to be legitimate, must promote law, order, and justice. As the royal justice Henry of Bracton (d. 1268) put it, the English shall be *"Non sub homine sed sub Deo et lege"* (Not under man but under God and the law), a maxim that today appears over the entrance to Harvard Law School. Thus an English king may not disregard or arbitrarily suspend the law to suit his convenience. Drawn up initially to protect baronial interests, Magna Carta was used in later centuries to protect the interests of widows, orphans, townspeople, freemen, and the church. For example, Chapter 39 states, "No freeman shall be captured or imprisoned or disseised (dispossessed) or outlawed or exiled or in any way destroyed, nor will we go against him or send against him, except by the lawful judgment of his peers or by the law of the land." This statement contains the germ of the idea of "due process of law," meaning that a person has the right to be heard and defended in court and is entitled to the protection of the law. Because later generations referred to Magna Carta as a written statement of English liberties, it gradually came to have an almost sacred importance as a guarantee of law and justice.

In the thirteenth century the judicial precedents set under Henry II slowly evolved into permanent institutions. The king's judges asserted the royal authority and applied the same principles everywhere in the country. English people found the king's justice more rational and evenhanded than the justice meted out in the baronial courts. Respect for the king's law and courts promoted loyalty to the Crown. By the time of Henry's great-grandson Edward I (r. 1272–1307), one law, the common law, operated all over England.

Common Law and Roman Law

In the later Middle Ages the English common law developed features that differed strikingly from the system of Roman law operative in continental Europe. The common law relied on **precedent**: a decision in an important case served as an authority for deciding similar cases. By contrast, continental judges, trained in Roman law, used the fixed legal maxims of the Justinian *Code* (see page 191) to decide their cases. Thus the common-law system evolved according to the changing experience of the people, while the Roman-law tradition tended toward a more rigid or static approach. In countries influenced by the common law, such as Canada and the United States, the court is open to the public; in countries with Roman-law traditions, such as France and the Latin American nations, courts need not be public. Under the common law, people accused in criminal cases have the right to access to the evidence against them; under the other system, they do not. The common law urges judges to be impartial; in the Roman-law system, judges interfere freely in activities in their courtrooms. Finally, whereas torture is foreign to the common-law tradition, it was once widely used in the Roman legal system as a method of securing evidence or proof.

The extension of law and justice led to a phenomenal amount of legal codification all over Europe. For example, the English judge Henry of Bracton wrote *Treatise on the Laws and Customs of England*. Legal texts and encyclopedias exalted royal authority, consolidated royal power, and emphasized political and social uniformity.

The Peace of God

Along with the courts, the church also worked to promote peace. Petty crimes proved most destructive of order and stability. Attacks on churches for the ceremonial vessels and sacred objects; assaults on traveling priests, monks, and merchants for the money or goods they might be carrying; seizure of peasants' livestock and extortion through threats of burning their crops and homes; and kidnapping rustics and holding them for ransom—these kinds of violent acts were endemic across western Europe. The church had always preached peace; in the late tenth and early eleventh centuries it began to do something about it.

At a series of church councils (assemblies of bishops and abbots) in central France, where the violence was the worst, the bishops took action. Councils formed peace associations—groups of men in particular districts who assessed themselves and used the money to provide armed protection against thuggish lords. The councils also published decrees forbidding attacks on peasants, clerics, and merchants and prohibiting the destruction of crops and unfortified places under penalty of total exclusion from the Christian community. These measures had some success in reducing the violence of minor feudal lords, but not in stopping great barons from private warfare.

Another ecclesiastical effort, the Truce of God, had less impact. In this movement churchmen tried to reduce the amount of warfare by limiting the number of days on which fighting was permitted. Sundays, special feast days, and the seasons of Lent and Advent were to be free of fighting. If all the forbidden days had been observed, fighting would have been permissible only eighty days of

the year. Nobles and kings did not take the Truce of God very seriously, however, and it remained simply an ideal.

The Papacy

Kings and emperors were not the only rulers consolidating their power in the High Middle Ages. During the ninth and tenth centuries the church came under the control of kings and feudal lords, who chose priests and bishops in their territories, granting them fiefs and expecting loyalty and service in return. Popes were chosen by wealthy Roman families from among their members, and after gaining the papal office they paid more attention to their family political fortunes than to the institutional or spiritual health of the church. Church offices from village priest to pope were sources of income as well as positions of authority. They brought with them the right to collect taxes and fees and often the profits from land under the officeholder's control. They were thus sometimes sold outright—a practice called **simony,** after Simon Magus, a wealthy man mentioned in the New Testament who wanted to buy his way into Heaven. Not surprisingly, clergy at all levels who had bought their positions or had been granted them for political reasons provided little spiritual guidance, and their personal lives were rarely models of high moral standards.

Under the leadership of a series of reforming popes in the eleventh century, the church tried to correct some of these problems, though reforms were not always welcome.

• *How did the papacy attempt to reform the church, and what was the response from other powerful rulers?*

The Gregorian Reforms

The papal reform movement of the eleventh century is frequently called the Gregorian reform movement, after Pope Gregory VII (1073–1085), its most prominent advocate. Serious efforts at reform actually began somewhat earlier, under Pope Leo IX (1049–1054).

During the ninth and tenth centuries the papacy provided little leadership to the Christian peoples of western Europe. Factions in Rome sought to control the papacy for their own material gain. Popes were appointed to advance the political ambitions of their families—the great aristocratic families of the city—and not because of special spiritual qualifications. A combination of political machinations and sexual immorality damaged the pa-

Emperor Otto III Handing a Staff to Archbishop Adalbert of Prague (tenth century) The staff, or crozier, symbolized a bishop's spiritual authority. Receiving the staff from the emperor gave the appearance that the bishop gained his spiritual rights from the secular power. Pope Gregory VII vigorously objected to this practice. *(Bildarchiv Marburg/Art Resource, NY)*

pacy's moral prestige. For example, Pope John XII (955–963) was appointed pope by his powerful father when he was only eighteen, and lacking interest in spiritual matters he concentrated on expanding papal territories.

At the local parish level, there were many married priests. Taking Christ as the model for the priestly life, the Roman church had always encouraged clerical celibacy, and celibacy had been an obligation for ordination since the fourth century. But in the tenth and eleventh centuries probably a majority of European priests were married or living with women, and in some cases they were handing down church positions and property to their children.

Leo and his successors believed that lay control was largely responsible for the church's problems, so they proclaimed the church independent from secular rulers. At a church council held in the ancient church of Saint John Lateran in 1059, representatives decided on a new method of electing the pope that would remove the influence of Roman aristocratic factions and make papal elections independent of imperial influences. Since the

eighth century the priests of the major churches in and around Rome had constituted a special group, called a "college," that advised the pope when he summoned them to meetings. These chief priests were called "cardinals," from the Latin *cardo,* meaning "hinge." The cardinals were the hinges on which the church turned. The Lateran Council of 1059 decreed that the authority and power to elect the pope rested solely in this **college of cardinals.** The college retains that power today. In the Middle Ages the college of cardinals numbered around twenty-five or thirty, most of them from Italy. In 1586 the figure was set at seventy, though today it is much larger, with cardinals from around the world. (At the death of Pope John Paul II in 2005, there were 183 cardinals, 117 of whom were under age eighty and so could vote for the next pope; this age limit on voting was set in 1975.) When the office of pope was vacant, the cardinals were responsible for governing the church.

While reform began long before Gregory's pontificate and continued after it, Gregory VII was the first pope to emphasize the *political* authority of the papacy. His belief that kings had failed to promote reform in the church prompted him to claim an active role in the politics of Western Christendom. He believed that the pope, as the successor of Saint Peter, was the vicar of God on earth and that papal orders were the orders of God. Gregory was particularly opposed to **lay investiture**—the selection and appointment of church officials by secular authority, often symbolized by laymen giving bishops and abbots their symbols of office, such as a staff and ring. In February 1075 Pope Gregory held a council at Rome that decreed that clerics who accepted investiture from laymen were to be deposed, and laymen who invested clerics were to be *excommunicated* (cut off from the sacraments and all Christian worship).

The church's penalty of **excommunication** relied for its effectiveness on public opinion. Gregory believed that the strong support he enjoyed for his *moral* reforms would carry over to his political ones; he thought that excommunication would compel rulers to abide by his changes. Immediately, however, Henry IV in the empire, William the Conqueror in England (see page 261), and Philip I in France protested.

Why did the issue of lay investiture provoke the wrath of kings? Any institution or organization needs a bureaucracy or administration to function. In the late eleventh century virtually the only people who could read and write were monks and priests. Therefore, kings appointed monks and clerics as their administrators, and they felt that it was perfectly appropriate to choose the men they wished. Because these men were also church officials, rulers used the income from church offices, bishoprics, and abbacies to provide their incomes. From the perspective of a king or emperor, this practice had the merit of financial prudence and had long stood the test of time. Gregory VII's condemnation of lay investiture, which denounced lay appointments and using church income to support royal officials, seemed revolutionary.

The struggle against lay investiture had the effect of emphasizing the distinction between priests and laypeople. For many centuries most monks had not been priests, but in the twelfth century increasing numbers of monks were ordained priests. Women could not be ordained, however. Thus the Gregorian reform movement, in building a strict hierarchical church structure and in subjecting all houses of monks and nuns to the bishop's authority, gave female monasticism a secondary status. Church councils in the eleventh and twelfth centuries forbade monks and nuns to sing church services together and ordered priests to limit their visits to convents,

heightening the sense that contact with nuns should be viewed with suspicion and avoided when possible. Church reformers put a greater emphasis on clerical celibacy and chastity. As part of these measures, in 1298 in the papal decree *Periculoso* Pope Boniface VIII ordered all female religious to be strictly **cloistered,** that is, that the nuns remain permanently inside the walls of the convent and that visits with those from outside the house, including family members, be limited. *Periculoso* was not enforced everywhere, but it did mean that convents became more cut off from medieval society. People also gave more donations to male monastic houses where monks who had been ordained as priests could say memorial masses, and fewer to women's houses, many of which became impoverished.

Emperor Versus Pope

The strongest reaction to Gregory's moves came from the Holy Roman Empire. The emperor Henry IV had supported the moral aspects of church reform within the empire, but, like most rulers, he selected and invested most high church officials. In two basic ways, however, the relationship of the emperors to the papacy differed from that of other monarchs: the pope crowned the emperor, and both the empire and the Papal States claimed northern Italy. Since the time of Charlemagne (see page 235), the emperor had controlled some territory and bishops in Italy.

An increasingly bitter exchange of letters between emperor and pope ensued. Gregory accused Henry of lack of respect for the papacy and insisted that disobedience to the pope was disobedience to God. Henry protested in a now-famous letter beginning "Henry King not by usurpation, but by the pious ordination of God, to Hildebrand, now not Pope, but false monk." Henry went on to argue that Gregory's type of reform undermined royal authority and that the pope "was determined to rob me of my soul and my kingdom or die in the attempt."[6]

Online Study Center **Improve Your Grade**
Primary Source: The Investiture Controversy Begins: Mutual Recriminations

Within the empire, those who had the most to gain from the dispute quickly took advantage of it. In January 1076 many of the German bishops who had been invested by Henry withdrew their allegiance from the pope. Gregory replied by excommunicating them and suspending Henry from the emperorship. The lay nobility delighted in the bind the emperor had been put in: with Henry IV excommunicated and cast outside the Christian fold, they did not have to obey him and could advance their own interests. Powerful nobles invited the pope to come to Germany to settle their dispute with Henry. Gregory hastened to support them. The Christmas season of 1076 witnessed an ironic situation in Germany: the clergy supported the emperor, while the great nobility favored the pope.

Henry outwitted the pope. Crossing the Alps in January 1077, he approached the castle of Countess Matilda of Tuscany, where the pope was staying. According to legend, Henry stood for three days in the snow seeking forgiveness. As a priest, Pope Gregory was obliged to grant absolution and to readmit the emperor to the Christian community. Some historians claim that this marked the peak of papal power because the most powerful ruler in Europe, the emperor, had bowed before the pope. Actually, Henry scored a temporary victory. When the sentence of excommunication was lifted, Henry regained the emperorship and authority over his rebellious subjects. But in the long run, in Germany and elsewhere, secular rulers were reluctant to pose a serious challenge to the papacy for the next two hundred years.

In Germany the controversy over lay investiture and the position of the king in Christian society continued. In 1080 Gregory VII again excommunicated and deposed the emperor. In return, Henry invaded Italy, captured Rome, and controlled the city when Gregory died in 1085. But Henry won no lasting victory. Gregory's successors encouraged Henry's sons to revolt against their father. With lay investiture the ostensible issue, the conflict between the papacy and the successors of Henry IV continued into the twelfth century.

Finally, in 1122 at a conference held at Worms, the issue was settled by compromise. Bishops were to be chosen according to canon law—that is, by the clergy—in the presence of the emperor or his delegate. The emperor surrendered the right of investing bishops with the ring and staff. But since lay rulers were permitted to be present at ecclesiastical elections and to accept or refuse feudal homage from the new prelates, they still possessed an effective veto over ecclesiastical appointments. Papal power was enhanced, but neither side won a clear victory.

The long controversy had tremendous social and political consequences in Germany. For half a century, between 1075 and 1125, civil war was chronic in the empire. The lengthy struggle between papacy and emperor allowed emerging noble dynasties to enhance their position. To control their lands, the great lords built cas-

Countess Matilda A staunch supporter of the reforming ideals of the papacy, Countess Matilda (ca 1046–1115) planned this dramatic meeting at her castle at Canossa in the Apennines. The arrangement of the figures—King Henry kneeling, Abbot Hugh of Cluny lecturing, and Matilda persuading—suggests contemporary understanding of the scene in which Henry received absolution. Matilda's vast estates in northern Italy and her political contacts in Rome made her a person of considerable influence in the late eleventh century. *(Biblioteca Apostolica Vaticana)*

tles, symbolizing their increased power and growing independence. (In no European country do more castles survive today.) The castles were both military strongholds and centers of administration for the surrounding territories. The German high aristocracy subordinated the knights, enhanced restrictions on peasants, and compelled Henry IV and Henry V to surrender certain rights and privileges. When the papal-imperial conflict ended in 1122, the nobility held the balance of power in Germany, and later German kings, such as Frederick Barbarossa (see page 264), would fail in their efforts to strengthen the monarchy against the princely families.

For these reasons, particularism, localism, and feudal independence characterized the Holy Roman Empire in the High Middle Ages. The investiture controversy had a catastrophic effect there.

The Papal Curia

In the late eleventh century and throughout the twelfth, the papacy pressed Gregory's campaign for reform of the church. The popes held a series of councils that met in the papal palace of the Lateran in Rome and that ratified the decisions made at the meeting in Worms ending lay investiture, ordered bishops to live less extravagantly, and passed other measures designed to make procedures more uniform. These Lateran councils passed a series of measures against clerical marriage and concubinage, ordering married priests to give up their wives and children or face dismissal. Most apparently obeyed, though we have little information on what happened to these families.

Pope Urban II laid the foundations for the papal monarchy by reorganizing the central government of the Roman church, the papal writing office (the chancery), and papal finances. He recognized the college of cardinals as a definite consultative body. These agencies, together with the papal chapel, constituted the papal court, or **curia Romana (Roman curia)**—the papacy's administrative bureaucracy and its court of law. The papal curia, although not fully developed until the mid-twelfth century, was the first well-organized institution of monarchical authority in medieval Europe.

The Roman curia had its greatest impact as a court of law. As the highest ecclesiastical tribunal, it formulated church law, termed **canon law,** for all of Christendom. The curia sent legates to hold councils in various parts of Europe. Councils published decrees and sought to enforce the law. When individuals in any part of Christian Europe felt they were being denied justice in their local church courts, they could appeal to Rome. In the High Middle Ages, slowly but surely, the papal curia developed into the court of final appeal for all of Christian Europe.

What kinds of appeals came to the Roman curia? The majority of cases related to disputes over church property or ecclesiastical elections and above all to questions of marriage and annulment. Since the fourth century Christian values had influenced the administration of the law, and bishops frequently sat in courts that heard marriage cases. Beginning in the tenth and eleventh centuries church officials began to claim that they had exclusive jurisdiction over marriage. Appeals to an ecclesiastical tribunal, rather than to a civil court, or appeals from a civil court to a church court implied the acceptance of the latter's jurisdiction. Moreover, most of the popes in the twelfth and thirteenth centuries were canon lawyers who pressed the authority of church courts.

Innocent III and His Successors

The most famous of the lawyer-popes was Innocent III (1198–1216), who became the most powerful pope in history. During his pontificate the church in Rome declared itself to be supreme, united and "catholic" (worldwide), responsible for the earthly well-being and eternal salvation of all citizens of Christendom. Innocent pushed the kings of France, Portugal, and England to do his will, compelling King Philip Augustus of France to take back his wife, Ingeborg of Denmark. He forced King John of England to accept as archbishop of Canterbury a man John did not want.

Innocent called the fourth Lateran Council in 1215, which affirmed the idea that ordained priests had the power to transform bread and wine during church ceremonies into the body and blood of Christ (a change termed "transubstantiation"). This power was possessed by no other group in society, not even kings. According to papal doctrine, priests now had the power to mediate for everyone with God, which set the spiritual hierarchy of the church above the secular hierarchies of kings and other rulers. The council also affirmed that Christians should confess their sins to a priest at least once a year and ordered Jews and Muslims to wear special clothing that set them apart from Christians.

By the early thirteenth century papal efforts at reform begun more than a century earlier had attained phenomenal success. Yet the seeds of future difficulties were being planted. As the volume of appeals to Rome multiplied, so did the size of the papal bureaucracy. As the number of lawyers increased, so did concern for legal niceties and technicalities, fees, and church offices. Nevertheless, the power of the curia continued to grow, as did its bureaucracy.

Thirteenth-century popes devoted their attention to the bureaucracy and to their conflicts with the German emperor Frederick II. Some, like Gregory IX (1227–1241), abused their prerogatives to such an extent that their moral impact was seriously weakened. Even worse, Innocent IV (1243–1254) used secular weapons, including military force, to maintain his leadership. These popes badly damaged papal prestige and influence. By the early fourteenth century the seeds of disorder would grow into a vast and sprawling tree, and once again cries for reform would be heard.

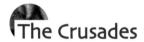

The Crusades

The Crusades of the eleventh and twelfth centuries were the most obvious manifestation of the papal claim to the leadership of Christian society. The **Crusades** were wars sponsored by the papacy for the recovery of the holy city of Jerusalem from the Muslims. The enormous popular response to papal calls for crusading reveals the influence of the reformed papacy. The Crusades also reflect the church's new understanding of the noble warrior class, for whom war against the church's enemies was understood as a religious duty. The word *crusade* was not actually used at the time and did not appear in English until the late sixteenth century. It means literally "taking the cross," from the cross that soldiers sewed on their garments as a Christian symbol. At the time people going off to fight simply said they were taking "the way of the cross" or "the road to Jerusalem."

Though the reconquista in Spain (see page 266) did not directly inspire the Crusades to the Middle East, the pope did sponsor groups of soldiers in this campaign as well as in the Norman campaign against the Muslims in Sicily. In both campaigns Pope Gregory VII asserted that any land conquered from the Muslims belonged to the papacy because it had been a territory held by "infidels," the word meaning unbeliever that Christians and Muslims both used to describe the other. Thus these earlier wars set a pattern for the centuries-long Crusades.

- *How did the motives, course, and consequences of the Crusades reflect and shape developments in Europe?*

Background

The Roman papacy had been involved in the bitter struggle over church reform and lay investiture with the German emperors. If the pope could muster a large army against the enemies of Christianity, his claim to be leader of Christian society in the West would be strengthened. Moreover, in 1054 a serious theological disagreement had split the Greek church of Byzantium and the Roman church of the West. The pope and the patriarch of Constantinople excommunicated each other and declared the beliefs of the other to be "anathema," that is, totally unacceptable for Christians. The pope believed that a crusade would lead to strong Roman influence in Greek territories and eventually the reunion of the two churches.

In 1071 Turkish soldiers defeated a Greek army at Manzikert in eastern Anatolia and occupied much of Asia Minor (see Map 9.4). The emperor at Constantinople appealed to the West for support. Shortly afterward the holy city of Jerusalem fell to the Turks. Pilgrimages to holy places in the Middle East became very dangerous, and the papacy claimed to be outraged that the holy city was in the hands of unbelievers. Since the Muslims had held Palestine since the eighth century, the papacy actually feared that the Seljuk Turks would be less accommodating to Christian pilgrims than the Muslim rulers had been.

In 1095 Pope Urban II journeyed to Clermont in France and on November 27 called for a great Christian holy war against the infidels. Urban's appeal at Clermont represents his policy of *rapprochement,* or reconciliation, with Byzantium, with church union his ultimate goal. (Mutual ill will, quarrels, and the plundering of Byzantine property by undisciplined Westerners were to frustrate this hope.) He urged Christian knights who had been fighting one another to direct their energies against the true enemies of God, the Muslims. Urban proclaimed an **indulgence,** or remission of the temporal penalties imposed by the church for sin, to those who would fight for and regain the holy city of Jerusalem.

Online Study Center **Improve Your Grade**
Primary Source: Call for Crusade: Urban II at the Council of Clermont

Godfrey of Bouillon, Raymond of Toulouse, and other great lords from northern France immediately had the cross of the Crusader sewn on their tunics. Encouraged by popular preachers such as Peter the Hermit and by papal legates in Germany, Italy, and England, thousands of people of all classes joined the crusade. Although most of the Crusaders were French, pilgrims from many regions streamed southward from the Rhineland, through Germany and the Balkans. Of all of the developments of the High Middle Ages, none better reveals Europeans' religious and emotional fervor and the influence of the reformed papacy than the extraordinary outpouring of support for the First Crusade. (See the feature "Listening to the Past: An Arab View of the Crusades" on pages 292–293.)

Motives and Course of the Crusades

Religious convictions inspired many Crusaders, but for the curious and the adventurous the Crusades offered foreign travel and excitement. It provided kings, who were trying to establish order and build states, with the perfect opportunity to get rid of troublemaking knights. It gave land-hungry younger sons a chance to acquire

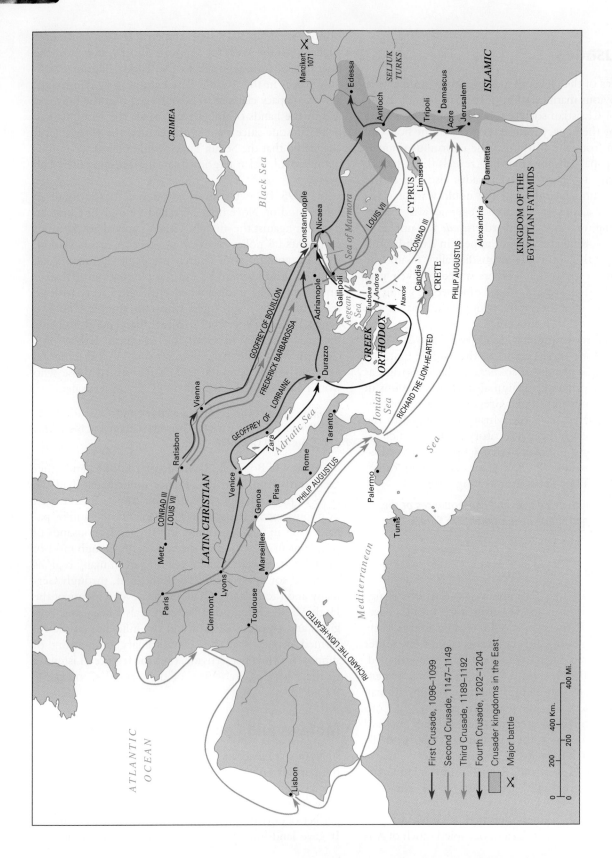

ATLANTIC
OCEAN

Black Sea

CRIMEA

Sea of Marmora

SELJUK
TURKS

Manzikert
1071

Edessa

Antioch

ISLAMIC

Tripoli
Damascus
Acre
Jerusalem

Constantinople

Nicaea

LOUIS VII

CYPRUS
Limasol

CONRAD III

Damietta

Adrianople

GODFREY OF BOUILLON

FREDERICK BARBAROSSA

Gallipoli

Aegean
Sea

Euboea
Andros

Naxos

Candia
CRETE

Alexandria

KINGDOM OF THE
EGYPTIAN FATIMIDS

Vienna

GEOFFREY OF LORRAINE

Durazzo

GREEK
ORTHODOX

RICHARD THE LION-HEARTED

PHILIP AUGUSTUS

Ratisbon

CONRAD III
LOUIS VII

Metz

LATIN CHRISTIAN

Venice

Zara

Adriatic Sea

Rome

Taranto

Ionian
Sea

Paris

Clermont
Lyons

Toulouse

Marseilles

Genoa
Pisa

PHILIP AUGUSTUS

Palermo

Tunis

Mediterranean

Sea

RICHARD THE LION-HEARTED

Lisbon

First Crusade, 1096–1099
Second Crusade, 1147–1149
Third Crusade, 1189–1192
Fourth Crusade, 1202–1204
Crusader kingdoms in the East
Major battle

0   200   400 Km.

0   200   400 Mi.

fiefs in the Middle East. Even some members of the middle class who stayed at home profited from the Crusades. Nobles often had to borrow money from the burghers to pay for their expeditions, and they put up part of their land as security. If a noble did not return home or could not pay the interest on the loan, the middle-class creditor took over the land.

The Crusades also brought latent Christian prejudice against the Jews to the surface. Between the sixth and tenth centuries descendants of **Sephardic** (from the modern Hebrew word *Separaddi*, meaning "Spanish" or "Portuguese") **Jews** had settled along the trade routes of western Europe; northern European Jews, those living north of the Alps, later came to be called **Ashkenazi.** In the eleventh century Jews played a major role in the international trade between the Muslim Middle East and the West. Jews also lent money to peasants, townspeople, and nobles. When the First Crusade was launched, many poor knights had to borrow from Jews to equip themselves for the expedition. Debt bred resentment. (See the feature "Individuals in Society: The Jews of Speyer: A Collective Biography.")

The First Crusade was successful, mostly because of the dynamic enthusiasm of the participants. The Crusaders had little more than religious zeal. They knew nothing about the geography or climate of the Middle East. Although there were several counts with military experience among the host, the Crusaders could never agree on a leader, and the entire expedition was marked by disputes among the great lords. Lines of supply were never set up. Starvation and disease wracked the army, and the Turks slaughtered hundreds of noncombatants. Nevertheless, convinced that "God wills it," the war cry of the Crusaders, the army pressed on, defeating the Turks in several land battles and besieging a few larger towns. Finally in 1099, after they had been on their way for three years, they reached Jerusalem, and after a month-long siege they got inside the city, where they slaugh-

tered the Muslim defenders. Fulcher of Chartres, a chaplain on the First Crusade, commented, "If you had been there your feet would have been stained to the ankles in the blood of the slain. What shall I say? None of them were left alive. Neither women nor children were spared."[7]

With Jerusalem taken, many Crusaders regarded their mission accomplished, and they set off for home again. Only the appearance of Egyptian troops convinced them that they needed to stay, and slowly institutions were set up to rule territories and the Muslim population. Four small "Crusader states"—Jerusalem, Edessa, Tripoli, and Antioch—were established; castles and fortified towns were built to defend against Muslim reconquest (see Map 9.4). Reinforcements arrived in the form of pilgrims and fighters from Europe, so that there was constant coming and going by land and more often by sea after the Crusaders conquered port cities such as Acre. Between 1096 and 1270 the crusading ideal was expressed in eight papally approved expeditions to the East, though none after the First Crusade accomplished very much. Despite this lack of success, for roughly two hundred years members of noble families in Europe went nearly every generation.

Women from all walks of life participated in the Crusades. Because of the chroniclers' belief that the *fragilitas sexus* ("weaker sex") was unfit for arms and the chroniclers' aristocratic bias, we know more about royal and noble women than about others. After her husband King Fulk died, Queen Melisande ruled the Latin kingdom of Jerusalem. When King Louis IX of France was captured on the Seventh Crusade (1248–1254), his wife Queen Marguerite negotiated the surrender of the Egyptian city of Damietta to the Muslims. In war zones some women concealed their sex by donning chain mail and helmets and fought with the knights.

Much of medieval warfare consisted of the besieging of towns and castles. Help could not enter; nor could anyone leave. The larger the number of besiegers, the greater was the chance the fortification would fall. Women swelled the numbers of besiegers. Women assisted in filling the moats surrounding fortified places with earth so that ladders and war engines could be brought close. More typically, women provided water to fighting men, a service not to be underestimated in the hot, dry climate of the Middle East. They worked as washerwomen, foraged for food, and provided sexual services. There were many more European men than women, however, so there was a fair amount of intermarriage or at least intergroup sexual relations between Christian men and Muslim women.

Mapping the Past

MAP 9.4 The Routes of the Crusades This map shows the many different routes that Western Christians took over the centuries to reach Jerusalem. Use it and the information in the text to answer the following questions: **1** How were the results of the various Crusades shaped by the routes that the Crusaders took? **2** How did the routes offer opportunities for profit for Venetian and other Italian merchants? **3** Why might the Byzantines have worried about Crusaders even before the Fourth Crusade?

Online Study Center **Improve Your Grade** Interactive Map: Routes of the Crusades

The Capture of Jerusalem in 1099 As engines hurl stones to breach the walls, Crusaders enter on scaling ladders. Scenes from Christ's passion in the top half of the piece identify the city as Jerusalem. *(Bibliothéque nationale de France)*

The Muslim states in the Middle East were politically fragmented when the Crusaders first came, and it took about a century for them to reorganize. They did so dramatically under Saladin (Salah al-Din), who unified Egypt and Syria, and in 1187 the Muslims retook Jerusalem. Christians immediately attempted to take it back in what was later called the Third Crusade (1189–1192). Frederick Barbarossa of the Holy Roman Empire, Richard the Lion-Hearted of England, and Philip Augustus of France participated, and the Third Crusade was better financed than previous ones. But disputes among the leaders and strategic problems prevented any lasting results. The Crusaders were not successful in retaking Jerusalem, but they did keep their hold on port towns, and Saladin allowed pilgrims safe passage to Jerusalem. He also made an agreement with Christian rulers for keeping the peace. From that point on, the Crusader states were more important economically than politically or religiously, giving Italian and French merchants direct access to Eastern products such as perfumes and silk.

Individuals in Society

The Jews of Speyer: A Collective Biography

In the winter of 1095–1096 news of Pope Urban II's call for a crusade spread. In spring 1096 the Jews of northern France, fearing that a crusade would arouse anti-Semitic hostility, sent a circular letter to the Rhineland's Jewish community seeking its prayers. Jewish leaders in Mainz responded, "All the (Jewish) communities have decreed a fast. . . . May God save us and save you from all distress and hardship. We are deeply fearful for you. We, however, have less reason to fear (for ourselves), for we have heard not even a rumor of the crusade."* Ironically, French Jewry survived almost unscathed, while the Rhenish Jewry suffered frightfully.

Beginning in the late tenth century Jews trickled into Speyer—partly through Jewish perception of opportunity and partly because of the direct invitation of the bishop of Speyer. The bishop's charter meant that Jews could openly practice their religion, could not be assaulted, and could buy and sell goods. But they could not proselytize their faith, as Christians could. Jews also extended credit on a small scale and, in an expanding economy with many coins circulating, determined the relative value of currencies. Unlike their Christian counterparts, many Jewish women were literate and acted as moneylenders. Jews also worked as skilled masons, carpenters, and jewelers. As the bishop had promised, the Jews of Speyer lived apart from Christians in a walled enclave where they exercised autonomy: they maintained law and order, raised taxes, and provided religious, social, and educational services for their community. (This organization lasted in Germany until the nineteenth century.) Jewish immigration to Speyer accelerated; everyday relations between Jews and Christians were peaceful.

But Christians resented Jews as newcomers, outsiders, and aliens; for enjoying the special protection of the bishop; and for providing economic competition. Anti-Semitic ideology had received enormous impetus from the virulent anti-Semitic writings of Christian apologists in the first six centuries A.D. Jews, they argued, were *deicides* (Christ killers); worse, Jews could understand the truth of Christianity but deliberately rejected it; thus they were inhuman. By the late eleventh century anti-Semitism was an old and deeply rooted element in Western society.

Late in April 1096 Emich of Leisingen, a petty lord from the Rhineland who had the reputation of being a lawless thug, approached Speyer with a large band of Crusaders. Joined by a mob of burghers, they planned to surprise the Jews in their synagogue on Saturday morning, May 3, but the Jews prayed early and left before the attackers arrived. Furious, the mob randomly murdered eleven Jews. The bishop took the entire Jewish community into his castle, arrested some of the burghers, and cut off their hands. News of these events raced up the Rhine to Worms, creating confusion in the Jewish community. Some took refuge with Christian friends; others sought the bishop's protection.

An engraving (18th century) of the mass suicide of the Jews of Worms in 1096, when they were overwhelmed by Crusaders (with shields).
(Bildarchiv Preussischer Kulturbesitz/Art Resource, NY)

A combination of Crusaders and burghers killed a large number of Jews, looted and burned synagogues, and desecrated the Torah (see page 43) and other books. Proceeding on to the old and prosperous city of Mainz, Crusaders continued attacking Jews. Facing overwhelming odds, eleven hundred Jews killed their families and themselves. Crusaders and burghers vented their hatred by inflicting barbaric tortures on the wounded and dying. The Jews were never passive; everywhere they resisted. If the Crusades had begun as opposition to Islam, after 1096 that hostility extended to all those who Christians saw as enemies of society, including heretics, Jews, and lepers. But Jews continued to move to the Rhineland and to make important economic and intellectual contributions. Crusader-burgher attacks served as harbingers of events to come in the later Middle Ages and well into modern times.

Questions for Analysis

1. How do you explain Christian attacks on the Jews of Speyer? Were they defenses of faith?
2. What is meant by the phrase "dehumanization of the enemy"? Can you give other examples?

*Quoted in R. Chazan, *In the Year 1096: The First Crusade and the Jews* (Philadelphia: Jewish Publication Society, 1996), p. 28.

Online Study Center   Improve Your Grade
Going Beyond Individuals in Society

In 1202 Innocent III sent out preachers who called on Christian knights to retake Jerusalem. Those who responded—in what would become the Fourth Crusade—decided that going by sea would be better than going by land, and they stopped in Constantinople for supplies. The supplies never materialized, and in 1204 the Crusaders decided to capture and sack Constantinople instead, destroying its magnificent library and shipping gold, silver, and relics home. The Byzantine Empire, as a political unit, never recovered from this destruction. Although the Crusader Baldwin IX of Flanders was chosen emperor, the empire splintered into three parts and soon consisted of little more than the city of Constantinople. Moreover, the assault by one Christian people on another—even though one of the goals of the Crusades was reunion of the Greek and Latin churches—made the split between the churches permanent. It also helped discredit the entire crusading movement and obviously had no effect on Muslim successes.

In 1208, in one of the most memorable episodes, two expeditions of children set out on a crusade to the Holy Land. One contingent turned back; the other was captured and sold into slavery. A seventh crusade in 1248, led by King Louis of France, tried to come in through Egypt. Louis also sent monks to the court of the Mongols in Central Asia, who were at this point led by Genghis Khan, to make a treaty that would encircle the Muslims. The monks were unsuccessful, but they brought back geographical knowledge of Asia and the peoples they had encountered.

In the late thirteenth century Turkish armies gradually conquered all other Muslim rules and then turned against the Crusader states. In 1291 their last stronghold, the port of Acre, fell in a battle that was just as bloody as the first battle for Jerusalem two centuries earlier. Knights then needed a new battlefield for military actions, which some found in Spain, where the rulers of Aragon and Castile continued fighting Muslims until 1492.

Crusades Within Europe

Crusades were also mounted against groups within Europe that were perceived as threats. In 1208 Pope Innocent III proclaimed a crusade against a group in southern France known either as the Cathars (from the Greek *katharos,* meaning "pure") or as the **Albigensians** (from the town of Albi in southern France). The Albigensians asserted that the material world was created not by the good God of the New Testament, but by a different evil God of the Old Testament. The good God had created spiritual things, and the evil God or the Devil had created

material things; in this dualistic understanding, the soul was good and the body evil. Forces of good and evil battled constantly, and leading a perfect life meant being stripped of all physical and material things. To free oneself from the power of evil, a person had to lead a life of extreme asceticism. Albigensians were divided into the "perfect," who followed the principles strictly, and the "believers," who led ordinary lives until their deaths, when they repented and were saved. They used the teachings of Jesus about the evils of material goods to call for the church to give up its property, rejected the authority of the pope and the sacraments of the church, and began setting up their own bishoprics.

The Albigensians won many adherents in southern France. Faced with widespread defection, Pope Innocent III proclaimed a crusade against them. Fearing that religious division would lead to civil disorder, the French monarchy joined the crusade against the Albigensians. Under Count Simon de Montfort, a northern French noble who had been part of the disastrous Fourth Crusade in Constantinople, the French inflicted a savage defeat on the Albigensians in 1213. After more years of fighting, the leaders agreed to terms of peace, which left the French monarchy the primary beneficiary. The county of Toulouse in southern France, which had supported the Albigensians, passed to the authority of the French crown.

The end of the war did not mean an end to Albigensianism, but the papacy decided that education and investigations would be more effective ways to combat heresy than military campaigns. The pope founded the University of Toulouse, which he hoped would promote knowledge and combat ignorance, error, and incorrect belief. In the 1230s and 1240s the papacy established the papal **Inquisition,** sending out inquisitors with the power to seek out suspected heretics, question them in private without revealing who had denounced them, and sentence them to punishments ranging from penance to life imprisonment. Heretics who did not repent were handed over to the secular government to be burned, and their property was confiscated. These measures were very successful, and the last Albigensian leaders were burned in the 1320s, though their beliefs did not die out completely.

Fearful of encirclement by imperial territories, the popes also promoted crusades against Emperor Frederick II in 1227 and 1239. This use of force backfired, damaging papal credibility as the sponsor of peace.

Along with the papal Inquisition, the Crusades also inspired the establishment of new religious orders. For example, the Knights Templars, founded in 1118 with the strong backing of Saint Bernard of Clairvaux (see page 319), combined the monastic ideals of obedience and self-denial with the crusading practice of military aggression. Another order, the Teutonic Knights, waged wars against the pagan Prussians in the Baltic region. After 1230, and from a base in Poland, they established a new territory, Christian Prussia, and gradually the entire eastern shore of the Baltic came under their hegemony. Military orders served to unify Christian Europe.

Consequences of the Crusades

The Crusades provided the means for what one scholar has called "the aristocratic diaspora," the movement of knights from their homes in France to areas then on the frontiers of Christian Europe.[8] Wars of foreign conquest had occurred before the Crusades, as the Norman Conquest of England in 1066 illustrates (see page 261), but for many knights migration began with the taking of the cross. Restless, ambitious knights, many of them younger sons with no prospects, left on crusade to the Holy Land, and some of them were able to carve out lordships in Palestine, Syria, and Greece. Along the Syrian and Palestinian coasts, the Crusaders set up a string of feudal states that managed to survive for about two centuries before the Muslims reconquered them; many of the castles they built still stand today.

The Crusades introduced some Europeans to Eastern luxury goods, but their immediate cultural impact on the West remains debatable. Strong economic and intellectual ties with the East had already been developed by the late eleventh century. The Crusades did provide great commercial profits for Italian merchants, who profited from outfitting military expeditions, the opening of new trade routes, and the establishment of trading communities in the Crusader states. After those kingdoms collapsed, Muslim rulers still encouraged trade with European businessmen. Commerce with the West benefited both Muslims and Europeans, and it continued to flourish.

The Crusades proved to be a disaster for Jewish-Christian relations. The experience of the Rhenish Jews during the First Crusade (see page 283) was not unusual; later Crusades brought similar violence. Hostility between Christians and Jews increased, enhanced by Christian merchants' and financiers' resentment of Jewish business competition and by accusations that Jews engaged in the ritual murder of Christians to use their blood in religious rituals. These accusations, termed the "blood libel," were condemned by Christian rulers and higher church officials, but were often spread through sermons preached by local priests. They also charged

Jews with being "Christ killers" and of using the communion host for diabolical counter-rituals. Jews were accused of killing a Christian child and using his blood in Passover *matzot* (the unleavened bread eaten during the eight-day Passover festival) in Norwich in England in 1144, with similar accusations occurring in other cities in England, France, Germany, and Spain over the next several centuries. Such accusations led to the killing of Jewish families and sometimes entire Jewish communities, sometimes by burning people alive in the synagogue or Jewish section of town.

Legal restrictions on Jews gradually increased. The Third Lateran Council in 1179 forbade Jews to have Christian servants or employees and forbade Christians to live in Jewish parts of town, and the Fourth Lateran Council in 1215 forbade Jews to hold public office, appear in public on Christian holy days, or appear in Christian parts of town without a badge marking them as Jews. Jews were prohibited from engaging in any trade with Christians except money-lending—which only fueled popular resentment—and in 1275 King Edward I of England prohibited that as well. In 1290 he expelled the Jews from England in return for a large parliamentary grant; it would be four centuries before they would be allowed back in. King Philip the Fair of France followed Edward's example in 1306, and many Jews went to the area of southern France known as Provence, which was not yet part of the French kingdom. In July 1315 the king's need for revenue led him to readmit the Jews to France in return for a huge lump sum and for an annual financial subsidy. The returnees faced new economic pressures as well as old hostilities, however. In the thirteenth century Jews in Aragon and Castile came under increasing pressure to convert, and in the 1260s the harsh anti-Jewish measures of the Fourth Lateran Council were included in a new Castilian law code, the *Siete Partidas*.

The Crusades also left an inheritance of deep bitterness in Christian-Muslim relations. Each side dehumanized the other, viewing those who followed the other religion as unbelievers. Whereas Europeans perceived the Crusades as sacred religious movements, Muslims saw them as expansionist and imperialistic. Even today some Muslims see the conflict between Arab and Jew as just another manifestation of the medieval Crusades and view the leaders of the state of Israel as new Crusaders or as tools of Western imperialism.

The European Crusades had a profound effect in shaping the very identity of the West. They represent the first great colonizing movement beyond the geographical boundaries of the European continent. The ideal of a sacred mission to conquer or convert Muslim peoples entered Europeans' consciousness and became a continuing goal. When in 1492 Christopher Columbus sailed west, hoping to reach India, he used the language of the Crusades in his diaries, which show that he was preoccupied with the conquest of Jerusalem (see Chapter 15). Columbus wanted to establish a Christian base in India from which a new crusade against Islam could be launched.

The Crusades testify to the religious enthusiasm of the High Middle Ages, but Steven Runciman, a distinguished scholar of the Crusades, concludes in his three-volume history:

The triumphs of the Crusades were the triumphs of faith. . . . In the long sequence of interaction and fusion between orient and occident out of which our civilization has grown, the Crusades were a tragic and destructive episode. . . . High ideals were besmirched by cruelty and greed, enterprise and endurance by a blind and narrow self-righteousness; and the Holy War itself was nothing more than a long act of intolerance in the name of God, which is the sin against the Holy Ghost.[9]

The Expansion of Christianity

The Crusades had a profound impact on both Europe and the Middle East, but they were not the only example of Christian expansion in the High Middle Ages. As we saw earlier (page 266), Christian kingdoms were established in the Iberian Peninsula through the *reconquista,* and Muslim holdings were reduced to the small state of Granada in the south. The reconquista brought the establishment of a Roman ecclesiastical structure, and by the end of the thirteenth century Spain had fifty-one bishoprics. These bishoprics, along with new monasteries, aided the growth of Christian culture. Both also enhanced royal power, for church officials provided financial, political, and ideological support for the monarchs who had endowed their institutions.

The pattern in Spain was replicated in northern and eastern Europe in the centuries after the millennial year 1000. People and ideas moved from western France and western Germany into Ireland, Scandinavia, the Baltic lands, and eastern Europe, with significant cultural consequences for those territories. Wars of expansion, the establishment of new Christian bishoprics, and the vast migration of colonists, together with the papal emphasis on a unified Christian world, brought about the gradual Christianization of a larger area (see Map 9.5).

- *What were the effects of the expansion of Christianity into northern and eastern Europe?*

MAP 9.5 Christianization of the Baltic Region   Dioceses and monasteries served as the means by which pagan Baltic peoples were Christianized and brought into the framework of Latin Christian culture. (*Source: Some data from R. Bartlett,* The Making of Europe: Conquest, Colonization and Cultural Change, 950–1350 *[Princeton, N.J.: Princeton University Press, 1993], pp. 16 and 259)*

Northern Europe

In 1177 John de Courcy, a Norman with small estates in Somerset (southwestern England), crossed the Irish Sea with his army and raided Ulcad in the province of Ulster. John easily defeated the local ruler, Rory MacDunlevy, seized the town of Downpatrick, and with this foothold built himself a sizable lordship. Other Anglo-Norman settlers followed. Ireland had been Christian since the days of Saint Patrick (see page 205), but John de

Courcy's intervention led to the remodeling of the Irish church from a monastic structure to an episcopal one with defined territorial dioceses. The Anglo-Norman invasion also meant the introduction of the fief, feudal cavalry, and Anglo-Norman landlords, as well as the beginnings of chartered towns on an English pattern. Similarly, Anglo-Norman, Anglo-French, and Flemish knights poured into Scotland in the twelfth century, bringing the fief and the language of feudalism. In 1286 the descendants of twelfth-century colonists held five of the thirteen Scottish earldoms. Scottish feudalism closely resembled that of western France, and immigrant knights transformed Scottish society.

Latin Christian influences entered the Scandinavian and Baltic regions primarily through the erection of dioceses. As an easily identifiable religious figure, as judge, and as the only person who could ordain priests, the bishop was the essential instrument in the spread of Christianity. Otto I (see page 263) established the first Scandinavian sees—Schleswig, Ribe, and Århus in Denmark—between 948 and 965. In 1060 a network of eight bishoprics was organized, and in 1103–1104 the Danish kingdom received its first archbishopric, Lund, in Scania (now part of Sweden). In Norway Christianity spread in coastal areas beginning in the tenth century, and King Olaf II (r. 1015–1028) brought in clergy and bishops from England and Germany to establish the church more firmly. From Norway Christianity spread to Iceland. In all of these areas, royal power advanced institutional Christianity; the traditional Norse religions practiced by the Vikings were outlawed and their adherents sometimes executed.

Christianity progressed more slowly in Sweden and Finland, in part because royal power was weaker. In the 1060s, however, six dioceses were set up in Sweden, and in 1164 Uppsala in Sweden, long a center of the pagan cults of Thor and Odin, became a Catholic archdiocese. Sweden took over much of modern-day Finland in the thirteenth century, and Swedish-speaking settlers moved into islands and coastal areas. Christian missionaries preached, baptized, and built churches, working among both the Swedish-speaking and Finnish-speaking populations, though pagan and Christian practices existed side-by-side for centuries. The Sami people of the far north in Scandinavia (formerly known as Lapps), who lived by fishing, hunting, and herding reindeer, remained pagan until the eighteenth century.

Centralized monarchy came to Scandinavia somewhat later than it did to western Europe. There was little feudalism in the classic sense of fiefs and oaths of loyalty, and during the High Middle Ages higher nobles frequently came into conflict with monarchs. In 1397 Queen Margrete I (1353–1412) united the crowns of Denmark, Sweden-Finland, and Norway in the **Union of Kalmar.** She built up royal power and worked toward creating a stronger state, checking the power of the nobility and creating a stronger financial base for the monarchy. The union gradually disintegrated in the fifteenth century, though Denmark continued to rule Norway until 1814.

Eastern Europe

In the lands between the Oder River in the east and the Elbe and Saale Rivers in the west lived the Wends, a West Slavic people, and their linguistic cousins, the Balts, the ancestors of Lithuanians, Latvians, Livonians, and Estonians. These peoples remained pagan in spite of extensive Christian missionary activity. Nevertheless, Otto I established a string of dioceses along his northern and eastern frontiers to pacify newly conquered Slavic lands and to Christianize. Among these were the archdiocese of Magdeburg, intended for "all the people of the Slavs beyond the Elbe and Saale, lately converted and to be converted to God,"[10] and the dioceses of Brandenburg, Schwerin, and Lübeck, all filled with German bishops. Repeated Slavic revolts, illustrating ethnic opposition to German lords and German bishops, indicate that the new faith did not easily penetrate the Baltic region. Only the ruthless tactics of Albert the Bear (d. 1170) pacified the region and forced the incorporation of the eastern and northern bishoprics into the structure of the Western Christian church.

A member of the Saxon nobility with experience in border warfare against the Slavs, Albert the Bear reconquered the town of Brandenburg on June 11, 1157. With this base, and to support his **Ostiedlung** (orientation to the east), Albert proclaimed a German crusade against the Slavs. He invited Dutch, Flemish, and German knights from the Rhineland to colonize conquered territories. To keep the region as far as the Oder pacified, he built castles manned by these newly recruited knights. Slav revolts were ruthlessly crushed.

Along with German knights, German (or Roman) ecclesiastical influences entered other parts of eastern Europe in the tenth and eleventh centuries. Prague in Bohemia became a bishopric in 973; from Prague missionaries set out to convert the Poles. The first diocese in Poland, Poznan, was erected in 968. Likewise, Esztergom in Hungary became a diocese in 1001, and during the eleventh century Hungarian rulers established new ecclesiastical centers along the Danube and eastward into Transylvania (modern central Romania).

Saint Hedwig of Bavaria (1174–1243) Hedwig was married to Henry, duke of Saxony, by whom she had seven children and from whom she suffered great abuse. She ruled Silesia (today partly in the Czech Republic, partly in Poland) when her husband was away at war; conducted diplomatic negotiations; and founded monasteries, including Trebnitz, the first Cistercian house for women. Hedwig and her niece, Saint Elizabeth of Hungary (1207–1231), illustrate the powerful influence of women in the spread of Christianity in central and eastern Europe. In a manuscript commissioned by her fourteenth-century descendants (shown in small-scale donor portraits), Hedwig carries a book, a rosary, and a tiny statue of the Virgin Mary, references to her devout character. *(The John Paul Getty Museum, Los Angeles, Court Atelier of Duke Ludwig I of Liegnitz and Brieg [illuminator], Vita beatae Hedwigis, 1353. Tempera colors, colored washes and ink bound between wood boards covered with red-stained pigskin, 34.1 × 24.8 cm)*

In the twelfth and thirteenth centuries tens of thousands of German settlers poured into eastern Europe, including Silesia, Mecklenburg, Bohemia, Poland, Hungary, and Transylvania. Towns there contained the residence of the military leader of the region, the duke, and his servants and knights. The Christian baptism of Duke Mieszko (d. 992) and his court in 966 at Gniezno led to the construction of a cathedral, the arrival of churchmen, and the building of churches and monasteries for monks and nuns. All these people represented a demand for goods and services. Centers such as Gniezno, Cracow, Wroclaw, and Plock attracted craftsmen and merchant immigrants seeking business opportunities.

With urbanization came Germanization. Duke Boleslaw's charter for his new city of Cracow in Poland stated that "the city of Cracow was converted to German law and the site of the market, the houses and the courtyards was changed by the duke's officials."[11] Boleslaw specifically excluded Polish peasants from becoming burgesses because he feared the depopulation of his estates. New immigrants were German in descent, name, language, and law. Towns such as Cracow and Riga engaged in long-distance trade and gradually grew into large urban centers, and there were also hundreds of small market towns populated by German immigrants.

Christendom

Christianity began as a small group within Judaism during a time of religious questioning, and it spread to non-Jews along the trade routes of the Roman Empire during the first several centuries A.D. Christians were persecuted sporadically by Roman authorities, but most of the time they were not, and the religion spread. In the fourth century the emperor Constantine recognized Christianity as a legitimate religion and hoped that it might be useful in keeping the Roman Empire intact; he called church councils and shaped their decisions about theological and institutional matters. In 380 the emperor Theodosius made Christianity the official religion of the Roman Empire by forbidding pagan worship.

Through the actions of Constantine and Theodosius, Christianity became in some ways a state as well as a religion. Early medieval writers began to use the word **Christendom** to refer to this realm of Christianity. Sometimes notions of Christendom were linked directly to specific states, such as Charlemagne's empire or the Holy Roman Empire. More often Christendom was quite vague, a sort of loose sense of the body of all people who were Christian. When the pope called for crusades, for example, he spoke not only of the retaking of Jerusalem, but also of the defense of Christendom. When missionaries, officials, and soldiers took Christianity into the Iberian Peninsula, Scandinavia, or the Baltic region, they understood what they were doing as the expansion of Christendom.

From the point of view of popes such as Gregory VII and Innocent III, Christendom was a unified hierarchy with the papacy at the top. They pushed for uniformity of religious worship and campaigned continually for the same pattern of religious service, the Roman liturgy in Latin, in all countries and places. They forbade vernacular Christian rituals or those that differed in their pattern of worship, and in this they were successful. In 1081 Gregory wrote triumphantly to King Alfonso VI of Castile and León: "Most dearly beloved, know that one thing pleases us greatly . . . namely, that in the churches of your realm, you have caused the order of the Mother of all, the holy Roman church, to be received and celebrated in the ancient way."[12] Under Innocent (see page 278) papal directives and papal legates flowed to all parts of Europe; twelve hundred prelates obediently came to

Rome from the borderlands as well as the heartland for the Fourth Lateran Council of 1215; and the same religious service was celebrated everywhere.

As we have seen in this chapter, however, not everyone had the same view. Kings and emperors may have accepted the Roman liturgy in the areas under their control, but they had their own ideas of the way power should operate in Christendom, even if this brought them into conflict with the papacy. This did not mean that they had any less loyalty to Christendom as a concept, however, but simply a different idea about how it should be structured and who could best defend it. The battles in the High Middle Ages between popes and kings and between Christians and Muslims were signs of how deeply religion had replaced tribal, political, and ethnic structures as the essence of Western culture. Christian Europeans identified themselves first and foremost as citizens of Christendom or even described themselves as belonging to "the Christian race."[13] Whether Europeans were Christian in their observance of the Gospels remains another matter.

Chapter Summary

Online Study Center **ACE the Test**

- *How did medieval rulers create larger and more stable territories?*
- *What types of institutions did medieval rulers develop to provide their realms with sufficient taxes and other income?*
- *How did the administration of law contribute to the development of national states?*
- *How did the papacy attempt to reform the church, and what was the response from other powerful rulers?*
- *How did the motives, course, and consequences of the Crusades reflect and shape developments in Europe?*
- *What were the effects of the expansion of Christianity into northern and eastern Europe?*

The end of the great invasions signaled the beginning of profound changes in European society. As domestic disorder slowly subsided, feudal rulers began to develop new institutions of government that enabled them to assert their power over lesser lords and the general population. Centralized states slowly crystallized, first in England and France, where rulers such as William the Conqueror and Philip Augustus manipulated feudal institutions to build up their power. In central Europe the German king Otto had himself declared emperor and tried to follow a similar path, but unified nation-states did not develop until the nineteenth century. Emperors instead shared power with princes, dukes, archbishops, counts, bishops, abbots, and cities. In the Iberian Peninsula Christian rulers of small states slowly expanded their territories, taking over land from Muslim rulers in the reconquista.

As medieval rulers expanded territories and extended authority, they required more officials, larger armies, and more money with which to pay for them. They developed different sorts of financial institutions to provide taxes and other income. The most effective financial bureaucracies were those developed in England, including a bureau of finance called the Exchequer, and in Sicily, where Norman rulers retained the main financial agency that had been created by their Muslim predecessors. By contrast, the rulers of France and other continental states continued to rely primarily on the income from their own lands to support their military endeavors.

In the twelfth and thirteenth centuries rulers in Europe sought to transform a hodgepodge of oral and written customs and rules into a uniform system of laws acceptable and applicable to all their peoples. In England such changes caused conflict with church officials, personified in the dispute between King Henry II and Thomas Becket, the archbishop of Canterbury. Fiscal and legal measures by Henry's son John led to opposition from the high nobles of England, who forced him to sign Magna Carta agreeing to promise to observe the law. Magna Carta had little immediate impact, but it came to signify the principle that everyone, including the king and the government, must obey the law. Legal developments in continental countries like France were strongly influenced by Roman law, while England slowly built up a unique unwritten common law.

At the same time that kings were creating more centralized realms, energetic popes built up their power within the Western Christian church and asserted their superiority over kings and emperors. The Gregorian reform movement led to a grave conflict with kings over lay investiture. The papacy achieved a technical success on the religious issue, but in Germany the greatly increased power of the nobility, at the expense of the emperor, represents the significant social consequence. Having put its own house in order, the Roman papacy built the first strong government bureaucracy in the twelfth and thirteenth centuries. In the High Middle Ages, the church exercised general leadership of European society.

A papal call to retake the holy city of Jerusalem led to the Crusades, nearly two centuries of warfare between Christians and Muslims. The enormous popular response to papal calls for crusading reveals the influence of the reformed papacy and a new sense that war against the church's enemies was a duty of nobles. The Crusades were initially successful, and small Christian states were established in the Middle East. These did not last very long, however, and other effects of the Crusades were disastrous. Jewish communities in Europe were regularly attacked; relations between the Western and Eastern Christian churches were poisoned by the Crusaders' attack on Constantinople; and Christian-Muslim relations became more uniformly hostile than they had been earlier.

These centuries also saw the penetration of Latin Christian culture into northern and eastern Europe. Christian warriors, clergy, and settlers moved out in all directions from western and central Europe, bringing the gradual Christianization of a larger area through conquest and colonization. The movement of people was particularly evident in eastern Europe, where German-speaking settlers moved into areas populated by Slavs, establishing towns and bishoprics. Both the Crusades in the Middle East and the expansion of Christianity in Iberia, Scandinavia, and the Baltic region created a stronger sense of loyalty to Christendom among many people living in Europe.

Key Terms

Domesday Book	college of cardinals
Capetian dynasty	lay investiture
baillis/seneschals	excommunication
Holy Roman Empire	cloistered
Landfrieden	curia Romana
reconquista	(Roman curia)
Exchequer	canon law
relief	Crusades
scutage	indulgence
tallage/taille	Sephardic Jews
diwān	Ashkenazi
Landgericht	Albigensians
common law	Inquisition
circuit judges	Union of Kalmar
Magna Carta	Ostiedlung
precedent	Christendom
simony	

Online Study Center **Improve Your Grade** Flashcards

Suggested Reading

Abulafia, David. *Frederick II: A Medieval Emperor.* 1992. A beautifully written biography that sets Frederick's life in a broad context.

Bartlett, Robert. *England Under the Norman and Angevin Kings, 1075–1225.* 2000. An excellent synthesis of social, cultural, and political history in highly readable prose.

Bartlett, Robert. *The Making of Europe: Colonization and Cultural Change, 950–1350.* 1993. A broad survey of many of the developments traced in this chapter.

Chazan, Robert. *In the Year 1096: The First Crusade and the Jews.* 1996. A thorough discussion of the Rhineland Jews and many issues related to the Jews and the Crusades.

Edgington, Susan B., and Sarah Lambert, eds. *Gendering the Crusades.* 2002. Contains articles that look at the roles of men and women.

Fletcher, Richard. *The Quest for El Cid.* 1990. Provides an excellent introduction to Spanish social and political conditions through a study of Rodrigo Dias, the eleventh-century soldier of fortune who became the Spanish national hero.

Holt, J. C. *Magna Carta,* 2d ed. 1992. The authoritative study of Magna Carta.

Johns, Jeremy. *Arabic Administration in Norman Sicily.* 2002. A comprehensive account of Arabic influences on the politics of Norman Sicily.

Lowney, Chris. *A Vanished World: Medieval Spain's Golden Age of Enlightenment.* 2006. Explores the complex interactions among Jews, Muslims, and Christians in the era of practical coexistence, and traces growing intolerance.

Madden, Thomas. *The New Concise History of the Crusades.* 2005. A highly readable brief survey by the preeminent American scholar of the Crusades.

O'Shea, Stephen. *The Perfect Heresy: The Revolutionary Life and Death of the Medieval Cathars.* 2000. A stimulating journalistic account of this Christian heresy.

Prestwich, Michael. *Armies and Warfare in the Middle Ages: The English Experience.* 1996. An exciting and readable survey of many aspects of English warfare.

Tellenbach, Gerd. *The Church in Western Europe from the Tenth to the Twelfth Century.* 1993. A very good survey by an expert on the investiture controversy.

Tyerman, Christopher. *Fighting for Christendom: Holy War and the Crusades.* 2005. Assesses the impact of the Crusades on modern times.

Notes

1. D. C. Douglas and G. E. Greenaway, eds., *English Historical Documents,* vol. 2 (London: Eyre & Spottiswoode, 1961), p. 853.
2. Bartlett, *The Making of Europe: Conquest, Colonization and Cultural Change, 950–1350* (Princeton, N.J.: Princeton University Press, 1993), p. 13.
3. Ibid., p. 178.
4. J. Johns, *Arabic Administration in Norman Sicily: The Royal Diwān* (New York: Cambridge University Press, 2002), p. 289.
5. Ibid., p. 293.
6. I. S. Robinson, *The Papacy, 1073–1198: Continuity and Innovation* (New York: Cambridge University Press, 1990), p. 403.
7. Fulcher of Chartres, *A History of the Expedition to Jerusalem, 1095–1127,* trans. Frances Rita Ryan and ed. Harold S. Fink (Knoxville: University of Tennessee Press, 1969), p. 121.
8. Bartlett, *The Making of Europe,* p. 24.
9. S. Runciman, *A History of the Crusades,* vol. 3: *The Kingdom of Acre* (Cambridge: Cambridge University Press, 1955), p. 480.
10. Bartlett, *The Making of Europe,* p. 8.
11. Quoted in ibid., pp. 179–180.
12. Quoted in ibid., p. 249.
13. Ibid., pp. 250–255.

An Arab View of the Crusades

The Crusades helped shape the understanding that Arabs and Europeans had of each other and all subsequent relations between the Christian West and the Arab world. To medieval Christians the Crusades were papally approved military expeditions for the recovery of holy places in Palestine; to the Arabs these campaigns were "Frankish wars" or "Frankish invasions" for the acquisition of territory.

Early in the thirteenth century Ibn Al-Athir (1160–1223), a native of Mosul, an important economic and cultural center in northern Mesopotamia (modern Iraq), wrote a history of the First Crusade. He relied on Arab sources for the events he described. Here is his account of the Crusaders' capture of Antioch.

The power of the Franks first became apparent when in the year 478/1085–86* they invaded the territories of Islam and took Toledo and other parts of Andalusia. Then in 484/1091 they attacked and conquered the island of Sicily and turned their attention to the African coast. Certain of their conquests there were won back again but they had other successes, as you will see.

In 490/1097 the Franks attacked Syria. This is how it all began: Baldwin, their King, a kinsman of Roger the Frank who had conquered Sicily, assembled a great army and sent word to Roger saying: "I have assembled a great army and now I am on my way to you, to use your bases for my conquest of the African coast. Thus you and I shall become neighbors."

Roger called together his companions and consulted them about these proposals. "This will be a fine thing for them and for us!" they declared, "for by this means these lands will be converted to the Faith!" At this Roger raised one leg and farted loudly, and swore that it was of more use than their advice. "Why?" "Because if this army comes here it will need quantities of provisions and fleets of ships to transport it to Africa, as well as

reinforcements from my own troops. Then, if the Franks succeed in conquering this territory they will take it over and will need provisioning from Sicily. This will cost me my annual profit from the harvest. If they fail they will return here and be an embarrassment to me here in my own domain." . . .

He summoned Baldwin's messenger and said to him: "If you have decided to make war on the Muslims your best course will be to free Jerusalem from their rule and thereby win great honor. I am bound by certain promises and treaties of allegiance with the ruler of Africa." So the Franks made ready to set out to attack Syria.

Another story is that the Fatimids of Egypt were afraid when they saw the Seljuqids extending their empire through Syria as far as Gaza, until they reached the Egyptian border and Atsiz invaded Egypt itself. They therefore sent to invite the Franks to invade Syria and so protect Egypt from the Muslims.† But God knows best.

When the Franks decided to attack Syria they marched east to Constantinople, so that they could cross the straits and advance into Muslim territory by the easier, land route. When they reached Constantinople, the Emperor of the East refused them permission to pass through his domains. He said: "Unless you first promise me Antioch, I shall not allow you to cross into the Muslim empire." His real intention was to incite them to attack the Muslims, for he was convinced that the Turks, whose invincible control over Asia Minor he had observed, would exterminate every one of them. They accepted his conditions and in 490/1097 they crossed the Bosphorus at Constantinople. . . . They . . . reached Antioch, which they besieged.

When Yaghi Siyan, the ruler of Antioch, heard of their approach, he was not sure how the Christian people of the city would react, so he made

Miniature showing heavily armored knights fighting Muslims. *(Bibliothéque nationale de France)*

the Muslims go outside the city on their own to dig trenches, and the next day sent the Christians out alone to continue the task. When they were ready to return home at the end of the day he refused to allow them. "Antioch is yours," he said, "but you will have to leave it to me until I see what happens between us and the Franks." "Who will protect our children and our wives?" they said. "I shall look after them for you." So they resigned themselves to their fate, and lived in the Frankish camp for nine months, while the city was under siege.

Yaghi Siyan showed unparalleled courage and wisdom, strength and judgment. If all the Franks who died had survived they would have overrun all the lands of Islam. He protected the families of the Christians in Antioch and would not allow a hair of their heads to be touched.

After the siege had been going on for a long time the Franks made a deal with . . . a cuirass-maker called Ruzbih whom they bribed with a fortune in money and lands. He worked in the tower that stood over the riverbed, where the river flowed out of the city into the valley. The Franks sealed their pact with the cuirass-maker, God damn him! and made their way to the watergate. They opened it and entered the city. Another gang of them climbed the tower with their ropes. At dawn, when more than 500 of them were in the city and the defenders were worn out after the night watch, they sounded their trumpets. . . . Panic seized Yaghi Siyan and he opened the city gates and fled in terror, with an escort of thirty pages. His army commander arrived, but when he discovered on enquiry that Yaghi Siyan had fled, he made his escape by

another gate. This was of great help to the Franks, for if he had stood firm for an hour, they would have been wiped out. They entered the city by the gates and sacked it, slaughtering all the Muslims they found there. This happened in jumada I (491/April/May 1098). . . .

It was the discord between the Muslim princes . . . that enabled the Franks to overrun the country.

Questions for Analysis

1. From the Arab perspective, when did the Crusades begin?

2. How did Ibn Al-Athir explain the Crusaders' expedition to Syria?

3. Why did Antioch fall to the Crusaders?

4. The use of dialogue in historical narrative is a very old device dating from the Greek historian Thucydides (fifth century B.C.). Assess the value of Ibn Al-Athir's dialogues for the modern historian.

Sources: P. J. Geary, ed., *Readings in Medieval History* (Peterborough, Ontario: Broadview Press, 1991), pp. 443–444; E. J. Costello, trans., *Arab Historians of the Crusades* (Berkeley and Los Angeles: University of California Press, 1969).

*Muslims traditionally date events from Muhammad's *hegira*, or emigration, to Medina, which occurred in 622 according to the Christian calendar.

†Although Muslims, Fatimids were related doctrinally to the Shi'ites, and the dominant Sunni Muslims considered the Fatimids heretics.

In these scenes from a German manuscript, *Speculum Virginum*, ca 1190, the artist shows men, women, and children harvesting, raking, sowing, and digging. All residents in a village engaged in agricultural tasks. *(Rheinisches Landesmuseum, Bonn)*

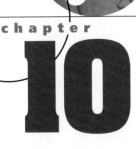

THE CHANGING LIFE OF THE PEOPLE IN THE HIGH MIDDLE AGES

In one of the writings produced at the court of the late-ninth-century Anglo-Saxon king Alfred, Christian society is described as composed of those who pray, those who fight, and those who work. This image of society as divided into three **orders** gained wide circulation in the High Middle Ages. Those who used this model argued that the relationship among the three orders was beneficial rather than exploitative: peasants toiled for the other two orders, but in return they received the prayers of the monks and the physical protection of the nobles. This schema was especially popular among people who were worried about changes they saw around them, and they asserted that the three orders had been established by God. Every person had been assigned a specific social place, in their opinion, and that was the way it should remain.

Enormous social divisions certainly existed in medieval Europe, but they were not as simple or static as the tripartite model suggested or as its advocates hoped. Among the nobility and the peasantry, there were great differences in wealth and status and considerable social mobility. The model does not take townspeople and the emerging commercial classes (see pages 331–345) into consideration. It completely excludes those who were not Christian, such as Jews, Muslims, and pagans. Those who used the model, generally bishops and other church officials, ignored the fact that each of these groups was made up of both women and men; they spoke only of warriors, monks, and farmers. Despite—or perhaps because of—these limitations, the model of the three orders was a powerful mental construct. We can use it to organize our investigation of life in the High Middle Ages, though we can broaden our categories to include groups and issues that medieval authors did not.

Village Life

The evolution of localized feudal systems into more centralized states traced in the last chapter had relatively little impact on the daily lives of most people in Europe except when they involved warfare. In theory

Online Study Center
This icon will direct you to interactive activities and study materials on the website **college.hmco.com/pic/mckaywest9e**

only nobles fought, but in reality fighting often destroyed the houses, barns, and fields of ordinary people, who might also be killed either directly or as a result of the famine, disease, and devastation that often accompanied war. During times of war, people might use a local castle as a place of refuge, taking their children and animals to seek shelter within its outer walls, but most of the time they viewed castles at a distance, working and living without paying much attention to political developments concerning nobles and kings.

This lack of attention went in the other direction as well. Since villagers did not perform what were considered "noble" deeds, the aristocratic monks and clerics who wrote the records that serve as historical sources did not spend time or precious writing materials on them. When common people were mentioned, it was usually with contempt or in terms of the services and obligations they owed. Usually—but not always. In the early twelfth century Honorius, a monk and teacher at the monastery of Autun, wrote: "What do you say about the agricultural classes? Most of them will be saved because they live simply and feed God's people by means of their sweat."[1]

• *What was life like for the rural common people of medieval Europe?*

Slavery, Serfdom, and Upward Mobility

Rural common people are often lumped together and called "peasants," but it is important to remember that their conditions varied widely across Europe. Geographical and climatic features as well as human initiative and local custom determined the particular quality of rural life. The problems that faced the farmer in Yorkshire, England, where the soil was rocky and the climate rainy, were very different from those of the Italian peasant in the sun-drenched Po Valley.

Medieval theologians lumped everyone who worked the land into the category of "those who work," but in fact there were many levels of peasants, ranging from complete slaves to free and very rich farmers. The High Middle Ages was a period of considerable fluidity with significant social mobility.

Slaves were found in western Europe in the High Middle Ages, but in steadily declining numbers. The word *slave* derives from *Slav*, which attests to the widespread trade in men and women from the Slavic areas in the early Middle Ages. Around the year 1200 aristocratic and upper-middle-class households in Provence, Catalonia, Italy, and Germany had a few slaves—Slavs from the

The Three Orders of Society (fourteenth century) This book illustration shows the most common image of medieval society: those who fight, those who pray, and those who work. The group of clergy shown here includes a veiled nun; nuns were technically not members of the clergy, but most people considered them as such. (*Bibiothèque royale, Brussels*)

Baltic, Syrians, and blacks from sub-Saharan Africa. Recent research has also demonstrated the persistence of **ancillae,** female chattel slaves whose lifelong legal servitude passed to their descendants, in Scandinavia, the Balkans, Sicily, and Italian cities well into the sixteenth century.

Most rural people in western Europe in the High Middle Ages were serfs rather than slaves, though the distinction between slave and serf was not always clear. Both lacked freedom—the power to do as they wished—and both were subject to the arbitrary will of one person, the lord. Unlike a slave, however, a serf could not be bought and sold like an animal or an inanimate object.

People's legal status was based on memory and traditions, not on written documents. The serf was required to perform labor services on the lord's land, usually three days a week except during the planting or harvest seasons, when it was more. Serfs frequently had to pay arbitrary levies. When a man married, he had to pay his lord a fee. When he died, his son or heir had to pay an inheritance tax to inherit his parcels of land. The precise amounts of tax paid to the lord on these important occasions depended on local custom and tradition. A free person had to pay rent to the lord but could move and live as he or she wished.

Serfs were tied to the land, and serfdom was a hereditary condition. A person born a serf was likely to die a serf, though many serfs did secure their freedom. About 1187 Glanvill, an official of King Henry II and an expert on English law, described how **villeins** (literally, "inhabitants of small villages")—as English serfs were called—could be made free:

A person of villein status can be made free in several ways. For example, his lord, wishing him to achieve freedom from the villeinage by which he is subject to him, may quit-claim [release] him from himself and his heirs; or he may give or sell him to another with intent to free him. It should be noted, however, that no person of villein status can seek his freedom with his own money, for in such a case he could, according to the law and custom of the realm, be recalled to villeinage by his lord, because all the chattels of a villein are deemed to such an extent the property of his lord that he cannot redeem himself from villeinage with his own money, as against his lord. If, however, a third party provides the money and buys the villein in order to free him, then he can maintain himself for ever in a state of freedom as against his lord who sold him. . . . If any villein stays peaceably for a year and a day in a privileged town and is admitted as a citizen into their commune, that is to say, their gild, he is thereby freed from villeinage.[2]

Chronology

909	Abbey of Cluny established
1050–1300	Steady rise in population
ca 1075–ca 1140	Life of Orderic Vitalis
1080–1180	Period of milder climate
1098–1179	Life of Hildegard of Bingen
Early 1100s	Production of iron increases greatly
1100–1200	Rapid expansion of the Cistercian Order
1200	Notion of chivalry begins to develop
1215	Fourth Lateran Council accepts seven sacraments

Thus serfs could not buy freedom with their own money, since technically all "chattels"—that is, all goods (including money)—belonged to the lord. But they could give money to a third party, who could use it to buy their freedom. Many energetic and hard-working serfs acquired their freedom through this method of **manumission** in the High Middle Ages. More than anything else, the economic revival that began in the eleventh century (see pages 331–345) advanced the cause of individual liberty. The revival saw the rise of towns, increased land productivity, the growth of long-distance trade, and the development of a money economy. With the advent of a money economy, serfs could save money and, through a third-person intermediary, use it to buy their freedom.

Another opportunity for increased personal freedom, or at least for a reduction in traditional manorial obligations and dues, was provided by the reclamation of wasteland and forestland in the eleventh and twelfth centuries. Lords organized groups of villagers to cut down forests or fill in swamps and marshes between villages to make more land available for farming. In some parts of Europe, this process of filling up empty space between existing villages was also accompanied by moving into new areas. In areas bordering the North Sea, walls and dikes were built slightly out in the water, then the water was pumped out, more soil added, and new land created behind the dikes. The thirteenth century witnessed German peasant migrations into Brandenburg, Pomerania, Prussia, and the Baltic States, with Germans establishing new villages between existing Slavic villages or pushing the Slavs eastward. In the Iberian Peninsula, Christian villagers followed after the Christian armies that were slowly reducing the area under Muslim control. In Scandinavia, farms were established in areas that had previously been used to harvest furs or lumber.

This type of agricultural advancement frequently improved the peasants' social and legal condition. A serf could clear a patch of fen or forestland, make it productive, and, through prudent saving, buy more land and eventually purchase freedom. In the thirteenth century there were many free tenants on the lands of the bishop of Ely in eastern England; these tenants had moved into the area in the twelfth century and drained the fens. Likewise, settlers on the lowlands of the abbey of Bourbourg in Flanders, who had erected dikes and extended the arable lands, possessed hereditary tenures by 1159. They secured personal liberty and owed their overlord only small payments.

In the thirteenth century the noble class frequently needed money to finance crusading, building, or other projects. For example, in 1240 when Geoffrey de Montigny became abbot of Saint-Pierre-le-Vif in the Séenonais region of France, he found the abbey church in disrepair. Geoffrey also discovered that the descendants of families who had once owed the abbey servile obligations now refused to recognize their bondage. Some of these peasants had grown wealthy. When the abbot determined to reclaim these peasants in order to get revenues to rebuild his church, a legal struggle ensued. In 1257 a compromise was worked out whereby Geoffrey manumitted 366 persons, who in turn agreed to pay him five hundred pounds a year over a twelve-year period.

Peasants who remained in the villages of their birth often benefited because landlords, threatened with the loss of serfs, relaxed ancient obligations and duties. While it would be unwise to exaggerate the social impact of the settling of new territories, frontier lands in the Middle Ages did provide opportunities for upward mobility.

The Manor

In the High Middle Ages most European peasants, free and unfree, lived in family groups in small villages. As we saw in Chapter 8 (page 242), the village and the land surrounding it were called a manor and were controlled by a noble or a church official such as a bishop, abbot, or abbess.

The manor was the basic unit of medieval rural organization and the center of rural life. All other generalizations about manors and manorial life have to be limited by variations in the quality of the soil, local climatic conditions, and methods of cultivation. Manors varied from several thousand to as few as 120 acres. Recent evidence suggests that a manor might include several villages, a village whose produce was divided among several lords, or an isolated homestead.

The arable land of the manor was divided into two sections. The *demesne,* or home farm, was cultivated for the lord. The other part was held by the peasantry. Usually the peasants' portion was larger and was held on condition that they cultivate the lord's demesne. All the arable land, both the lord's and the peasants', was divided into strips that were scattered throughout the manor. If one strip yielded little, other strips (with better soil) might be more bountiful. All peasants cooperated in the cultivation of the land, working it as a group. This meant that all shared in any disaster as well as in any large harvest.

Most parts of Europe depended on grain-based agriculture, with a gender division of labor typical of that in grain-growing societies. Men were responsible for clearing new land, plowing, and the care of large animals, and women were responsible for the care of small animals, spinning, and food preparation. Both sexes harvested and planted, though often there were gender-specific tasks within each of these major undertakings. Women and men worked in the vineyards and in the harvest and preparation of crops needed by the textile industry—flax and plants used for dyeing cloth, such as madder (which produces shades of red) and woad (which yields blue dye). Along coastal areas people depended on fishing for much of their food, either eating the fish or trading them for grain and other agricultural products with those living farther inland. In fishing communities small houses and small family groups again predominated, with wives and daughters drying and salting fish for later use, while husbands and brothers went out in boats.

In western and central Europe, villages were generally made up of small houses for individual families, with one married couple, their children (including stepchildren), and perhaps one or two other relatives—a grandmother, a cousin whose parents had died, an unmarried sister or brother of one of the spouses. The household thus contained primarily a **nuclear family,** and some households contained only an unmarried person, a widow, or several unmarried people living together. Villages themselves were also *nucleated*—that is, the houses were clumped together, with the fields stretching out beyond the group of houses. In southern and eastern Europe, though nuclear families and single-person households were not unknown, extended families were more likely to live in the same household or very near to one another than in northern Europe. Father and son, or two married brothers, might share a house with the families of both, forming what demographers call a **stem** or **complex household.**

A manor usually held pasture or meadowland for the grazing of cattle, sheep, and sometimes goats. Often the manor had some forestland as well. Forests were the source of wood for building and for fuel, resin for lighting, ash for candles, ash and lime for fertilizers and all sorts of sterilizing products, and bark for the manufacture of rope. From the forests came wood for the construction of barrels, vats, and all sorts of storage containers. Last but hardly least, the forests were used for feeding pigs, cattle, and domestic animals on nuts, roots, and wild berries. If the manor was intersected by a river, it had a welcome source of fish and eels.

Lords generally appointed officials—termed **bailiffs** in England—from outside the village to oversee the legal and business operations of their manors, collect taxes and fees, and handle disputes. At regular intervals, the lords or their officials also held manorial courts, which handled legal matters such as fights, assaults or robberies, litigation between villagers, and infractions of laws or customs regarding the fields, roads, or public places. The manorial courts relied more on the collective memory of village traditions and customs than on written laws, so that groups of responsible adult men, sometimes called **jurors,** were often asked to decide issues, such as who had the rights to a certain piece of land, by simply talking among themselves or to others who might know. Because of this, jurors were chosen from among those most likely to know the facts of the case—the opposite of modern jury selection. Both plaintiff and defendant often brought in others who would swear to their view of the case or their good character. Punishments were generally fines or occasionally banishment; imprisonment and corporal punishments were rare. (Serious criminal cases were not handled by the manorial courts but rather by a royal or other higher-level court.)

The medieval village had no police as we know them, so villagers who saw a crime or infraction were expected to chase the perpetrator and yell to others to join in what was termed *raising the hue and cry.* Villages in many parts of Europe also developed institutions of self-government to handle issues such as crop rotation, and they chose additional officials such as constables and ale-tasters without the lord's interference. We do not know how these officials were chosen or elected in many cases, but we do know that they were always adult men and were generally heads of households. Women had no official voice in running the village, nor did slaves or servants (female or male), who often worked for and lived with wealthier vil-

Boarstall Manor, Buckinghamshire In 1440 Edmund Rede, lord of this estate, had a map made showing his ancestor receiving the title from King Edward I (*lower field*). Note the manor house, church, and peasants' cottages along the central road. In the common fields, divided by hedges, peasants cultivated on a three-year rotation cycle: winter wheat, spring oats, a year fallow. Peasants' pigs grazed freely in the woods, indicated by trees. We don't know whether peasants were allowed to hunt the deer. (*Buckinghamshire Record Office, Aylesbury*)

lage families. Women did buy, sell, and hold land independently and, especially as widows, headed households; when they did they were required to pay all rents and taxes. In areas of Europe where men were gone fishing or foresting for long periods of time, or where men left seasonally or more permanently in search of work elsewhere, women made decisions about the way village affairs were to be run, though they did not set up formal institutions to do this.

Manors do not represent the only form of medieval rural economy. In Frisia, in parts of Germany, and in much of southern France, free independent farmers held **allodial land**—that is, land that they owned outright, free of rents and services. These farms tended to be small and were surrounded by large estates that gradually swallowed them up. In Scandinavia the soil was so poor and the climate so harsh that people tended to live on widely scattered farms rather than in villages, but they still lived in relatively small family groups.

Agricultural Methods

The fields of the village were farmed in what historians term the **open-field system,** a pattern that differs sharply from modern farming practices. In the open-field system, the arable land of a manor was divided into two or three fields without hedges or fences to mark the individual holdings of the lord, serfs, and freemen. The village as a whole decided what would be planted in each field, rotating the crops according to tradition and need. Some fields would be planted in crops such as wheat, rye, peas, or barley for human consumption, some in oats or other crops for both animals and humans, and some would be left unworked or *fallow* to allow the soil to rejuvenate. The exact pattern of this rotation varied from location to location, but in most areas with open-field agriculture the holdings farmed by any one family did not consist of a whole field but instead of strips in many fields.

Farmers knew the value of animal fertilizers such as chicken and sheep manure. Because cattle were fed on the common pasture and were rarely stabled, gathering their manure was laborious and time-consuming. Nevertheless, whenever possible, animal manure was gathered and thinly spread. So also was house garbage—eggshells, fruit cores, onion skins—that had disintegrated in a compost heap.

Local needs, the fertility of the soil, and dietary customs determined what was planted and the method of crop rotation. Where one or several manors belonged to a great aristocratic establishment, such as the abbey of Cluny, which needed large quantities of oats for horses, more of the arable land would be planted in oats than in other cereals. The milder climate of the Mediterranean area allowed for more frequent planting and a greater range of agricultural products; families tended to farm individual square plots rather than long strips. Milder climate also meant that more work (and play) could take place outdoors, which may have somewhat alleviated crowding in households with many family members. Throughout Europe, living space—especially living space

close enough to a fire to feel some warmth in cold weather—was cramped, dark, smoky, and smelly, with animals and people both sharing tight quarters, sometimes with each other. Nobles in castles had more total space, of course, but in many parts of Europe they too huddled around fires during much of the year.

During the tenth and eleventh centuries peasants and nobles may have moved away from their fires somewhat, for Europe experienced a significant warming trend. Meteorologists believe that a slow but steady retreat of polar ice occurred between the ninth and eleventh centuries. The century between 1080 and 1180 witnessed exceptionally clement weather in England, France, and Germany, with mild winters and dry summers. Increased agricultural output had a profound impact on society: it improved Europeans' health, commerce, industry, and general lifestyle. A better diet had an enormous impact on women's lives: it meant increased body fat, which increased fertility; also, more iron in the diet meant that women were less anemic and less subject to opportunistic diseases. Some researchers believe that it was in the High Middle Ages that Western women began to outlive men. Improved opportunities also encouraged people to marry somewhat earlier, which meant larger families and further population growth. Demographers often figure that in an era before reliable artificial means of contraception, but in which women nursed their own children (which inhibits fertility), every three years earlier that people married brought on average one more child.

Agricultural Improvements

The tenth and eleventh centuries also witnessed a remarkable spurt in mechanization, especially in the use of energy. Water mills were one important part of this. In the ancient world, slaves ground the grain for bread; as slavery was replaced by serfdom, grinding became a woman's task. When water mills were introduced into an area, women turned to other tasks, such as raising animals, working in gardens or vineyards, raising and preparing flax to make linen, or spinning yarn for cloth. A water mill unearthed near Monte Cassino in Italy could grind about 1.5 tons of grain in ten hours, a quantity that would formerly have required the exertions of forty people. Both lords and villagers recognized the advantages of water-powered mills, and the increase in the number of mills along streams, under bridges, and even floating in the middle of rivers was spectacular. By the mid-ninth century, on the lands of the abbey of Saint-Germaine-des-Prés near Paris, there were 59 water mills. Succeeding generations saw a continued increase. Thus,

Windmill The mill was constructed on a pivot so that it could turn in the direction of the wind. Used primarily to grind grain, as shown here with a man carrying a sack of grain to be ground into flour, windmills were also used to process cloth, brew beer, drive saws, and provide power for iron forges. *(Bodleian Library, Oxford, MS Bodl 264, fol. 81R)*

on the Robec River near Rouen, there were 2 mills in the tenth century, 4 in the eleventh, 10 in the thirteenth, and 12 in the fourteenth. William the Conqueror ordered mills counted along with other agricultural items in the *Domesday Book,* and his assessors recorded 5,624.

Besides grinding wheat or other grains to produce flour, water mills became essential in *fulling,* the process of scouring, cleansing, and thickening cloth. No longer did men or women trample cloth in a trough; instead wooden hammers were raised and dropped on the cloth by means of a revolving drum connected to the spindle of a water wheel. Water mills revolutionized grinding and fulling by using natural, rather than human, energy. The expansion of cloth production in medieval Europe rested on a base of water power. Water-powered grain mills freed women to spin—the bottleneck in cloth production, as each weaver needed at least six spinners to supply yarn—and enabled women and men to full cloth at a much faster rate.

Successful at adapting waterpower to human needs, medieval engineers soon harnessed wind power. They replaced the wheels driven by water with sails. But while water always flows in the same direction, wind can blow from many directions. Windmill engineers solved this problem very ingeniously by mounting the framed wooden body, which contained the machinery and carried the sails, on a massive upright post free to turn in the wind. After 1180 the construction of windmills accelerated. Many were erected in the flat areas of northern Europe, including Holland, that lacked fast-flowing streams.

In the early twelfth century the production of iron increased greatly. Iron was first used in agriculture for plowshares (the part of the plow that cuts the furrow and grinds up the earth), and then for pitchforks, spades, and axes. Harrows—cultivating instruments with heavy teeth that broke up and smoothed the soil—began to have iron instead of wooden teeth.

Plows and harrows were increasingly drawn by horses. The development of the padded horse collar that rested on the horse's shoulders and was attached to the load by shafts led to dramatic improvements. The horse collar meant that the animal could put its entire weight into the task of pulling. The use of horses, rather than oxen, spread in the twelfth century because horses' greater speed brought greater efficiency to farming and reduced the amount of human labor involved. The quality of the soil and the level of rainfall in the area seem to have determined whether peasants shifted from ox teams to horses. Horses worked best on light, dry, and easily tilled soil, but they had difficulties plowing through clay soils and in places where heavy moisture caused earth to cling to the plow. Oxen, on the other hand, worked well on heavy, muddy, or clay soil, but they slipped and suffered hoof damage on dry, stony land. Thus, in England horses were employed in the light soils of Norfolk on the northeastern coast and on the stony lands of Yorkshire, while oxen remained common in the Midlands until the late sixteenth century. At the same time, horses were an enormous investment, perhaps comparable to a modern tractor. They had to be shod (another indication of increased iron production), and the oats they ate were costly.

The thirteenth century witnessed a tremendous spurt in the use of horses to haul carts to market. Consequently, goods reached market faster, and the number of markets to which the peasant had access increased. Peasants not only sold products, but also bought them as their opportunities for spending on at least a few nonagricultural goods multiplied.

Agricultural yields varied widely from place to place and from year to year. Even with good iron tools, horsepower, and careful use of seed and fertilizer, medieval peasants were at the mercy of the weather. Even today too much or too little rain can cause terrible financial loss and extreme hardship. Medieval families were far more vulnerable. Townspeople were wholly dependent on the surrounding countryside for food, which could not be shipped over long distances. A poor harvest meant that both townspeople and rural people suffered.

By twenty-first-century standards, medieval agricultural yields were very low, but there was striking improvement over time. Between the ninth and early thirteenth centuries, yields of cereals appear to have approximately doubled, and on the best-managed estates the farmer harvested 5 bushels of grain for every bushel of seed planted. (A modern Illinois farmer expects to get 40 bushels of soybeans, 150 bushels of corn, and 50 bushels of wheat for every bushel of seed planted.) Grain yields were probably greatest on large manorial estates, where there was more professional management, and may have hit 12 or 15 to 1 in good years. As low as that may seem by current standards, it marked a rise in productivity equal to that of the years just before the start of the great agricultural revolution of the eighteenth century.

Households, Work, and Food

Life for most people in medieval Europe meant country life. A person's horizons were largely restricted to the manor on which he or she was born. True, peasants who colonized such sparsely settled regions as eastern Germany must have traveled long distances. But most people rarely traveled more than twenty-five miles beyond their villages. Everyone's world was small, narrow, and provincial in the original sense of the word: limited by the boundaries of the province. This way of life did not have entirely unfortunate results. People had a strong sense of family and the certainty of its support and help in time of trouble. Men and women knew what their life's work would be—the same as their mother's or father's. They had a sense of place, and pride in that place was reflected in adornment of the village church. Religion and the village gave people a sense of identity, rootedness, and security, which some commentators argue has been lost in modern, urban, industrialized society.

Life on the manor may have been stable, but it was dull. Medieval men and women often sought escape in heavy drinking. English judicial records of the thirteenth century reveal a surprisingly large number of "accidental" deaths. Strong, robust, commonsensical people do not ordinarily fall on their knives and stab themselves, or slip out of boats and drown, or get lost in the woods on a winter's night, or fall from horses and get trampled. The victims were probably drunk. Many of these accidents occurred, as the court records say, "coming from an ale." Brawls and violent fights were frequent at taverns.

The size and quality of peasants' houses varied according to their relative prosperity, and that prosperity usually depended on the amount of land held. Poorer peasants lived in windowless cottages built of wood and clay or wattle (poles interwoven with branches or reeds) and thatched with straw. These cottages consisted of one large room that served as the kitchen and living quarters for all. The house had an earthen floor and a fireplace. The lack of windows meant that the room was very sooty. A trestle table, several stools, one or two beds, and a chest for storing clothes constituted the furniture. A shed attached to the house provided storage for tools and shelter for animals. Prosperous peasants added rooms and furniture as they could be afforded, and some wealthy peasants in the early fourteenth century had two-story houses with separate bedrooms for parents and children.

Every house had a small garden and an outbuilding. Onions, garlic, turnips, and carrots were grown and stored through the winter in the main room of the dwelling or in the shed attached to it. Cabbage was raised almost everywhere and, after being shredded, salted, and packed in vats of hot water, was turned into kraut. Peasants ate vegetables not because they appreciated their importance for good health but because there was usually little else available. Preserving and storing foods were the basic responsibility of the women and children.

Medieval households were not self-sufficient, but bought cloth, metal, leather goods, and even some food from village market stalls. They also bought ale, the universal drink of the common people in northern Europe. By modern American standards, the rate of consumption was heroic. Each monk of Abingdon Abbey in twelfth-century England was allotted three gallons a day, and a man working in the fields for ten hours probably drank much more.[3] Women dominated in the production of ale for the community market. This industry required an initial investment in large vessels and knowledge of the correct proportions of barley, water, yeast, and hops. Women found brewing hard and dangerous work: it involved carrying twelve-gallon vats of hot liquid. Records of the English coroners' courts reveal that 5 percent of women who died accidentally did so in brewing accidents, by falling into the vats of boiling liquid.[4]

The mainstay of the diet for peasants everywhere—and for all other classes—was bread. It was a hard, black substance made of barley, millet, and oats, rarely of expensive wheat flour. Bread might be baked at home, but most households did not have ovens, which were expensive to build and posed a fire danger. Thus bread was baked in communal ovens or purchased from households that specialized in bread-baking.

The diet of people living in an area with access to a river, lake, or stream would be supplemented with fish, which could be preserved by salting. People living close to the sea could gather shellfish such as oysters, mussels, and whelks. Many places had severe laws against hunting and trapping in the forests. Deer, wild boars, and other game were strictly reserved for the king and nobility. These laws were flagrantly violated, however, and stolen rabbits and wild game often found their way to peasants' tables. In places like the Bavarian Alps of southern Germany, where hundreds of sheep grazed on the mountainsides, or at Cheddar in southwestern England, cheese was a staple.

Lists of peasant obligations and services to the lord, such as the following from Battle Abbey, commonly included the payment of chickens and eggs: "John of Coyworth holds a house and thirty acres of land, and owes yearly 2 p at Easter and Michaelmas; and he owes a cock and two hens at Christmas, of the value of 4 d."[5] Chickens and eggs must have been highly valued in the prudently managed household. Animals were too valuable to be used for food on a regular basis. The weaker animals were often slaughtered in the fall so that they did not need to be fed through the winter, and their meat was

Man Stomping on Grapes Before the invention of the winepress in 1526, grapes were crushed by human power—people treading on them in barrels. The French province of Poitou, the region of Bordeaux, and the Rhine and Moselle Valleys supplied wine to an expanding European market. The staple drinks for peasants and monks were ale, beer, and cider; wine was considered an aristocratic drink. *(Glasgow University Library, Department of Special Collections, Ms Hunter 229)*

salted and was eaten only on great feast days such as Christmas and Easter. Some scholars believe that, by the mid-thirteenth century, there was an increase in the consumption of meat generally. If so, this improvement in diet is further evidence of an improved standard of living.

Then as now, farmers ate their main meal around noon. This was often soup—a thick *potage* of boiled cabbage, onions, turnips, and peas seasoned with a bone or perhaps a sliver of meat. The evening meal, taken at sunset, consisted of leftovers from the noon meal, perhaps with bread, cheese, milk, or ale.

Once children were able to walk, they helped their parents in the hundreds of chores that had to be done. Small children were set to collecting eggs, if the family had chickens, or gathering twigs and sticks for firewood. As

Baking Bread   Bread and beer or ale were the main manorial products for local consumption. While women dominated the making of ale and beer, men and women cooperated in the making and baking of bread—the staple of the diet. Most people did not have ovens in their own homes because of the danger of fire, but instead used the communal manorial oven, which, like a modern pizza oven, could bake several loaves at once. *(Bibliothèque nationale de France)*

they grew older, children had more responsible tasks, such as weeding the family's vegetable garden, milking the cows, shearing the sheep, cutting wood for fires, and helping with the planting or harvesting.

Health Care

Scholars are only beginning to explore questions of medieval health care, and there are still many aspects of public health that we know little about. The steady rise in population between the mid-eleventh and fourteenth centuries, usually attributed to warmer climate, increased food supply, and a reduction of violence with growing political stability, may also be ascribed partly to better health care. A recent study of skeletal remains in the village of Brandes in Burgundy showed that peasants enjoyed very good health: they were well built and had excellent teeth, and their bones revealed no signs of chronic disease. Obviously we cannot generalize about the health of all people on the basis of evidence from one village, but such research indicates that medieval adults were tough.

What care existed for the sick? As in the past, the sick everywhere depended above all on the private nursing care of relatives and friends. Beginning in the twelfth century in the British Isles, however, the royal family, the clergy, noble men and women, and newly rich merchants also established institutions to care for the sick or for those who for some reason could not take care of themselves. Within city walls they built hospitals, which were not hospitals in the modern sense, but rather places where those with chronic diseases that were not contagious, poor expectant mothers, the handicapped, people recovering from injuries, foundling children, and mentally retarded or psychologically disturbed children or adults went for care. Outside city walls they built leprosariums or small hospices for people with leprosy and other contagious diseases. Such institutions might be staffed by members of religious orders, people who had less formally devoted themselves to lives of service, laymen and laywomen who were paid for their work, or a combination of the three. In the thirteenth century there were at least 113 hospitals in England with possibly as many as 3,494 beds, or one bed for every 600 to 1,000 persons. (In 1982 the ratio in England was 1 bed for every 108 persons.)

The organization of hospitals followed the structure and routine of monastic communities. Patients were segregated according to sex, wore a common uniform, and were required to keep periods of silence and to attend devotions in the hospital chapel. In the twelfth century medical personnel at hospitals were trained on the job, but by the thirteenth century some had been trained in faculties of medicine at Europe's new universities (see page 345). There were few university-trained physicians, however—one document lists ninety physicians (*medicus*) in all of England for a population of perhaps 2 million people—and day-to-day hospital care was in the hands of people whose medical training was more practical than theoretical. We have no information about rates of recovery, so we cannot judge whether those who were treated by university-trained physicians did better than other patients. University training was completely theoretical, so the food, warm bed, and nursing care provided by hospitals may have made more of a difference than the occasional doctor visit.

Outside of hospitals, university-trained physicians were a luxury only the wealthy could afford. For externally visible ailments, such as wounds, skin diseases, or broken bones, people turned to barber-surgeons who were trained in an apprenticeship system. Barber-surgeons also carried out bloodletting, using leeches or nicking a vein with a small knife to draw out blood, the most common course of treatment for many internal illnesses or as a health maintenance measure. Barber-surgeons, as their name suggests, also cut hair, for scissors were a relatively rare household item. (The barber pole, with red and blue stripes of blood running down the armlike pole, reflects this dual role; it would have been one of many markers of occupation people would have seen outside houses as they walked through the streets of a medieval town.) For other internal ailments people used apothecaries—also trained through an apprenticeship system—to suggest and mix drugs, which combined herbs, salts, metals, and more fanciful ingredients such as "dragon's blood."

People also relied on men and women who had no official training at all, but learned healing techniques from their parents or other older people. Such healers gained a reputation as "cunning men" or "wise women" through the results (or the assumed results) of their treatments, which were often mixtures of herbal remedies, sayings, specific foods, prayers, amulets, and ritual healing activities. Such combinations were also what people prescribed for themselves, for most treatment of illness was handled by home remedies handed down orally or perhaps through a cherished handwritten family herbal, cookbook, or household guide. Highly learned clergy frowned on such treatments, as they bordered on, or indeed actually included, the magical and perhaps implied doubts of God's ability to heal. Many clergy were active participants in them, however, blessing objects to be used in healing rituals or placing them under the altar cloth during the Mass.

Childbirth and Child Abandonment

The most dangerous period of life for any person, peasant or noble, was infancy and early childhood. In normal years perhaps as many as one-third of all children died before age five, and in years with plagues, droughts, or famines this share climbed to more than half. Children often died from accidents as well as from malnutrition and illness, wandering into cooking fires, drowning in potholes in the road, or getting in the way of horses or cattle. Reaching adulthood meant that people had survived the most dangerous part of their lives, and many lived well into their fifties and sixties.

Childbirth was dangerous for mothers as well as for infants. Though mortality statistics are difficult to determine, every woman would have known someone who died in childbirth, and most would have seen such a death. Women developed prayers, rituals, and special sayings to ensure safe and speedy childbirth. Village women helped their friends, relatives, sisters, and daughters through childbirth, and women who were more capable acquired specialized midwifery skills. In larger towns and cities, such women gradually developed into professional midwives who were paid for their services and who trained younger women as apprentices, just as barber-surgeons and apothecaries trained their male apprentices. For most women, however, childbirth was handled by female friends and family, not by professionals.

The abandonment of infant children seems to have been the most favored form of family limitation and was widely practiced throughout the Middle Ages. Parents or guardians left children somewhere, sold them, or legally gave authority to some other person or institution. Why did parents do this? What became of the children? What attitudes did medieval society have toward this practice?

Poverty or local natural disaster led some parents to abandon their children because they could not support them. Before the eleventh century food was so scarce that few parents could feed themselves, let alone children. Thus Saint Patrick wrote that in times of famine, fathers would sell their sons and daughters so that the children could be fed. Parents sometimes gave children away because they were illegitimate or the result of incestuous unions. An eighth-century penitential collection describes the proper treatment for a woman who exposes her unwanted child—that is, leaves it in the open to die—because she has been raped by an enemy or is unable to nourish it. She is not to be blamed, but she should do penance.[6]

Sometimes parents believed that someone of greater means or status might find the child and bring it up in

Monastic Entrance In a world with few career opportunities for "superfluous children," monasteries served a valuable social function. Because a dowry was expected, monastic life was generally limited to the children of the affluent. Here a father—advising his son to be obedient and holding a bag of money for the monastery—hands his son over to the abbot. The boy does not look enthusiastic. *(The J. Paul Getty Museum, Los Angeles. Unknown illuminator, Initial Q: An Abbot Receiving a Child Decretum, ca 1170–1180 [83.MQ.163.fol.63])*

better circumstances than the natal parents could provide. Disappointment in the sex of the child or its physical weakness or deformity might have also led parents to abandon it. Among Christians, superfluous children could be given to monasteries as **oblates**. The word *oblate* derives from the Latin *oblatio,* meaning "offering." Boys and girls were given to monasteries or convents as permanent gifts. By the seventh century church councils and civil codes had defined the practice: "Parents of any social status could donate a child, of either sex, at least up to the age of ten." Contemporaries considered oblation a religious act, since the child was offered to God often in recompense for parental sin. But oblation also served social and economic functions. The monastery nurtured and educated the child in a familial atmosphere, and it provided career opportunities for the mature monk or nun whatever his or her origins. Oblation has justifiably been described as "in many ways the most humane form of abandonment ever devised in the West."[7]

Recent research suggests that abandonment was very common among the poor until about the year 1000. The next two hundred years, which saw great agricultural change and relative prosperity, witnessed a low point in the abandonment of poor children. On the other hand, in the twelfth and thirteenth centuries the incidence of

noble parents giving their younger sons and daughters to religious houses increased dramatically; nobles wanted to preserve their estates intact for their eldest sons. Consequently, oblates composed a high percentage of monastic populations. At Winchester in England, for example, 85 percent of the new monks between 1030 and 1070 were oblates. In the early thirteenth century the bishop of Paris observed that children were "cast into the cloister by parents and relatives just as if they were kittens or piglets whom their mothers could not nourish; so that they may die to the world not spiritually but . . . civilly, that is—so that they may be deprived of their hereditary position and that it may devolve on those who remain in the world." The abandonment of children remained socially acceptable. Ecclesiastical and civil authorities never legislated against it.[8]

Popular Religion

Apart from the land, the weather, and local legal and social conditions, religion had the greatest impact on the daily lives of ordinary people in the High Middle Ages. Religious practices varied widely from country to country and even from province to province. But nowhere was religion a one-hour-a-week affair. Most people in medieval Europe were Christian, but there were small Jewish communities scattered in many parts of Europe and Muslims in the Iberian Peninsula, Sicily, other Mediterranean islands, and southeastern Europe.

● *How did religious practices and attitudes permeate everyday life?*

Village Churches and Christian Symbols

For Christians the village church was the center of community life—social, political, and economic as well as religious—with the parish priest in charge of a host of activities. Although church law placed the priest under the bishop's authority, the manorial lord appointed him and financed such education in Latin, Scripture, and liturgy as he might receive. Parish priests were peasants and often were poor. They received a tithe of produce from their parishioners, and depending on the spiritual quality of their lives they enjoyed status and prestige. Since they often worked in the fields with the people, they understood the people's labor, needs, and frustrations. The parish priest was also responsible for the upkeep of the village church and for taking the lead in providing local poor relief.

According to official church doctrine, the center of the Christian religious life was the Mass, the re-enactment of Christ's sacrifice on the cross. Every Sunday and on holy days, the villagers stood at Mass or squatted on the floor (there were no chairs), breaking the painful routine of work. The feasts that accompanied baptisms, weddings, funerals, and other celebrations were commonly held in the churchyard. Medieval drama originated in the church. Mystery plays, based on biblical episodes, were performed first in the sanctuary, then on the church porch, which was often in front of the west door, and then at stations around the town.

From the church porch the priest read orders and messages from royal and ecclesiastical authorities to his parishioners. Royal judges traveling on circuit opened their courts on the church porch. The west front of the church, with its scenes of the Last Judgment, was the background against which the justices disposed of civil and criminal cases. In busy mercantile centers such as London, business agreements and commercial exchanges were made in the aisles of the church itself, as at Saint Paul's.

Popular religion consisted largely of rituals heavy with symbolism. Before slicing a loaf of bread, the pious woman tapped the sign of the cross on it with her knife. Before planting, the village priest customarily went out and sprinkled the fields with water, symbolizing refreshment and life. Everyone participated in village processions. The entire calendar was designed with reference to Christmas, Easter, and Pentecost, events in the life of Jesus and his disciples. The varying colors of the vestments the priests wore at Mass gave villagers a sense of the changing seasons of the church's liturgical year. The signs and symbols of Christianity were visible everywhere.

Saints and Sacraments

Along with days marking events in the life of Jesus, the Christian calendar was filled with saints' days. **Saints** were individuals who had lived particularly holy lives and were honored locally or more widely for their connection with the divine. The saints had once lived on earth and thus could well understand human problems. They could be helpful intercessors with Christ or God the Father. In the church women and men prayed to the saints; the stone in the church altar contained **relics** of the saints— bones, articles of clothing, the saint's tears, saliva, even the dust from the saint's tomb. These relics often belonged to a local saint to whom the church itself had been dedicated.

The cult of the saints had begun in the East, spread in the early Middle Ages, and gained enormous popularity in the West in the eleventh and twelfth centuries. People believed that the saints possessed supernatural powers that enabled them to perform miracles, and the saint became the special property of the locality in which his or her relics rested. Thus, to secure the saint's support and to guarantee the region's prosperity, a busy traffic in relics developed. The understanding that existed between the saint and the peasants rested on the customary medieval relationship of mutual fidelity and aid: in return for the saint's healing and support, peasants would offer the saint prayers, loyalty, and gifts at the shrine or church under his or her patronage. (See the feature "Listening to the Past: The Pilgrim's Guide to Santiago de Compostela" on pages 328–329.)

In the later Middle Ages popular hagiographies (biographies of saints based on myths, legends, and popular stories) attributed specialized functions to the saints. Saint Elmo (ca 300), who supposedly had preached unharmed during a thunder and lightning storm, became the patron of sailors. Saint Agatha (third century), whose breasts were torn with shears because she rejected the attentions of a powerful suitor, became the patron of wet nurses, women with breast difficulties, and bell ringers (because of the resemblance of breasts to bells). Saint Jude the Apostle, whom no one invoked because his name resembled that of Jesus' betrayer, Judas, became the patron of lost causes. Saint Gertrude was reputed to guard houses against the entry of mice.

How were saints chosen, and what was the official church position on them? What had been their social background when alive? Since the early days of Christianity, individuals whose exemplary virtue was proved by miracles at their tombs had been venerated by laypeople. Although, as part of the general centralization of papal power in the twelfth and thirteenth centuries, the Roman authorities insisted that they had the exclusive right to examine the lives and activities of candidates for sainthood in a formal "trial," popular opinion still continued to declare people saints. Between 1185 and 1431 only seventy official investigations were held at Rome, but hundreds of new persons across Europe were venerated as saints. Church officials and educated clergy evaluated candidates according to the "heroic virtue" of their lives, but laypeople judged solely by the saint's miracles. Some clergy preached against the veneration of relics and called it idolatry, but their appeals had little effect.

Current research suggests that a connection exists between the models of holiness and the character of the social structure in different parts of Europe. Northern and southern Europeans chose saints of different social backgrounds or classes. In Italy and Mediterranean lands saints tended to be non-aristocrats, whereas in France and Germany primarily men and women of the nobility became saints. The cult of the saints, which developed in a rural and uneducated environment, represents a central feature of popular culture in the Middle Ages.

Along with the veneration of saints, a new religious understanding developed in the High Middle Ages. Twelfth-century theologians expanded on Saint Augustine's understanding of **sacraments**—outward and visible signs regarded as instituted by Christ to give grace—and created an entire sacramental system. Only a priest could dispense a sacrament (except when someone was in danger of death), and the list of seven sacraments, originally compiled by Peter Lombard, was formally accepted by the Fourth Lateran Council in 1215.

Baptism is the rite by which a person enters the Christian community. This is signified by sprinkling the person with holy water or fully immersing him or her in water. If the person has reached the age of reason (seven), a profession of faith and repentance for previous sins are required. *Penance* (from the Latin *poena,* meaning "punishment") is the rite by which, through oral confession to a priest, sins committed after baptism are forgiven. The penitent often has to perform some act as compensation, such as paying for stolen goods or apologizing for sins against charity. **Eucharist** is the name given to the central ceremony of Christian worship (also called the Mass, the Lord's Supper, and Holy Communion) as well as to the bread and wine consecrated by the priest and consumed by believers. In *confirmation,* a person becomes a full member of the Christian community through the laying on of the bishop's hands and his anointment of the candidate's forehead with oil. *Matrimony* as a sacrament derives from Jesus' presence at the marriage feast of Cana, the first public appearance of his ministry, which medieval theologians interpreted as proof of his wish to bless marriages. In the eleventh century the church claimed exclusive jurisdiction over marriage, and civil au-

The Eucharist The Fourth Lateran Council of 1215 encouraged all Christians to receive the Eucharist at least once a year after confession and penance. Here a priest places the consecrated bread, called a *host,* on people's tongues. (*Biblioteca Apostolica Vaticana*)

thorities acquiesced. *Orders* is the rite by which men, through the laying on of the bishop's hands and his anointment of the candidates' hands, become ordained as priests. Last, *extreme unction* or *anointment of the sick* is usually administered when a person is gravely ill and in danger of death.

Medieval Christians believed that these seven sacraments brought grace, the divine assistance or help needed to lead a good Christian life and to merit salvation. Sermons and homilies taught that at the center of the sacramental system stood the Eucharist, the small piece of bread that through the words of priestly consecration at the Mass became the living body of Christ and, when worthily consumed, became a channel of Christ's grace. The ritual of consecration, repeated at every altar of Christendom, became a unifying symbol in a complex world. The sacramental system, however, did not replace strong devotion to the saints.

Beliefs

Was popular religion largely a matter of rituals and ceremonies? What did people actually *believe?* It is difficult to say, partly because medieval peasants left few written records of their thoughts, and partly because in every age there is often great disparity between what people profess to believe and their conduct or the ways they act on their beliefs.

Peasants had a strong sense of the presence of God. They believed that God rewarded the virtuous with peace, health, and material prosperity and punished sinners with disease, poor harvests, and war. Sin was caused by the Devil, who lurked everywhere and constantly incited people to evil deeds and sin, especially sins of the flesh. Sin frequently took place in the dark. Thus evil and the Devil were connected in the peasant's mind with darkness or blackness. In some medieval literature, the Devil is portrayed as black, an identification that has had a profound and sorry impact on Western racial attitudes.

In the eleventh century theologians began to emphasize Mary's spiritual motherhood of all Christians. The huge outpouring of popular devotions to Mary concentrated on her special relationship to Christ as all-powerful intercessor with him. The most famous prayer, "Salve Regina," perfectly expresses medieval people's confidence in Mary, their advocate with Christ:

Hail, holy Queen, Mother of Mercy! Our life, our sweetness, and our hope. To thee we cry, poor banished children of Eve; to thee we send up our sighs, mourning and weeping in this valley of tears. Turn, then, most gracious advocate, thy merciful eyes upon us; and after this our exile show us the blessed fruit of thy womb, Jesus. O merciful, O loving, O sweet Virgin Mary!

The Mass was in Latin, but the priest delivered sermons on the Gospel in the vernacular. Anyway, he was supposed to. An almost universal criticism of parish priests in the twelfth and thirteenth centuries was that they were incapable of explaining basic Christian teachings to their parishioners. The growth of the universities (see page 347) did not improve the situation because few diocesan clerics attended them, and those who did and won degrees secured administrative positions with prelates or lay governments. The only parish priest to be canonized as a saint in the entire Middle Ages, the Breton lawyer and priest Saint Yves (d. 1303), had resigned a position as a diocesan judge to serve rural parishioners. At the trial for his canonization, laypeople stressed that not only had he led a simple and frugal life but he also had put his forensic skills to the service of preaching the Christian Gospels. He represents a great exception to the prevailing inability of medieval parish clergy to preach in a rural milieu. Parish priests celebrated the liturgy and administered the sacraments, but they had other short-

comings. A thirteenth-century Alsatian chronicler said that the peasants of the region did not complain that their pastors had concubines because that made them less fearful for the virtue of their daughters.[9]

Nevertheless, people grasped the meaning of biblical stories and church doctrines from the paintings on the church walls or, in wealthy parishes, the scenes in stained-glass windows. Illiterate and uneducated, they certainly could not reason out the increasingly sophisticated propositions of clever theologians. Still, Scriptural references and proverbs dotted everyone's language. The English *goodbye,* the French *adieu,* and the Spanish *adios* all derive from words meaning "God be with you." Christianity was the foundation of the common people's culture for most Europeans.

Muslims and Jews

The interpenetration of Christian ceremonies and daily life for most Europeans meant that those who did not participate or who had different religious rituals were clearly marked as outsiders. This included Muslims in the Iberian Peninsula, where Christian rulers were establishing kingdoms in territory won through the reconquista (see pages 265–267). Islam was outlawed in their territories, and some of the Muslims left Spain, leaving room for new settlers from elsewhere in Christian Europe. Other Muslims converted, becoming **conversos** or what were in Spain called "New Christians." In more isolated villages, people simply continued their Muslim rituals and practices, including abstaining from pork, reciting verses from the Qur'an, praying at specified times of the day, and observing Muslim holy days, though they might hide this from the local priest or visiting church or government officials. As in Christianity and in other Muslim areas around the world, they often venerated the tombs of individuals regarded as saints, asking them for assistance and praying for blessings.

Islam was geographically limited in medieval Europe, but by the late tenth century Jews could be found in many areas, often brought in as clients of rulers because of their skills as merchants. There were Jewish communities in Italian cities and in the cities along the Rhine such as Cologne, Worms, Speyer, and Mainz. Jews migrated from there to England and France, where they generally lived in the growing towns, often separate from the larger Christian community. Jewish dietary laws require meat to be handled in a specific way, so Jews had their own butchers; there were Jewish artisans in many other trades as well, though Jews were forbidden to join Christian guilds. Jews held weekly religious services on

Saturday, the Sabbath holy day of rest, and celebrated an annual cycle of holidays, including the High Holidays of Rosh Hashanah and Yom Kippur in the fall and Passover in the spring. Each of these holidays involved special prayers, services, and often foods, and many of them commemorated specific events from Jewish history, including various times that they had been rescued from captivity.

The Crusades brought violence against Jews in many cities (see pages 281–283), and restrictions on Jews increased in much of Europe. Christian officials meeting in the Third and Fourth Lateran Councils limited Jewish-Christian relations and required Jews to wear badges of identification. In the late thirteenth century Jews were expelled from England and in the early fourteenth century from France. Many of them went to Muslim and Christian areas of the Iberian Peninsula, where the rulers of both faiths initially welcomed them, though restrictions and violence gradually became more common there as well. Jews continued to live in the independent cities of the Holy Roman Empire and Italy, and some migrated eastward into new towns that were being established in Slavic areas.

Religion and the Cycle of Life

Increasing suspicion and hostility marked relations between religious groups throughout the Middle Ages, but there were also important similarities in the ways Christians, Jews, and Muslims in Europe understood and experienced their religions. In all three traditions, every major life transition was marked by a ceremony that included religious elements. Christian weddings might be held in the village church or at the church door, though among well-to-do families the wedding was held in the house of the bride or bridegroom. A priest's blessing was often sought, though it was not essential to the marriage, for Christian doctrine defined marriage as an agreement between a man and a woman. As long as consent was given freely, the spouses were old enough to know what they were doing, and the agreement was made in words of present tense (that is, not promising to marry some time in the future), the marriage was theologically valid. Exchanging rings and a kiss solemnized this contract between the spouses. Muslim weddings were also finalized by a contract between the bride and groom and were often overseen by a wedding official, though any man with knowledge of Islamic principles could officiate. Jewish weddings were guided by statements in Talmudic law that weddings were complete when the bride had entered the "chuppah," which medieval Jewish authorities

interpreted to mean a room in the groom's house. (By the sixteenth century the chuppah was often a cloth canopy held by four tall posts, a practice that continues in Jewish wedding ceremonies today.) Among wealthy families, this room might be decorated for the occasion with tapestries and flowers.

A wedding generally meant a party of some sort, with food, music, dancing, and lots of drinking. It often included rituals that symbolized the proper hierarchical relations between the spouses—such as placing the husband's shoe on the bedstead over the couple, symbolizing his authority—or that worked to ensure the couple's fertility—such as untying all the knots in the household, for tying knots was one way that people reputed to have magical powers bound up the reproductive power of a man. All this came together in what was often the final event of a wedding, the priest blessing the couple in their marriage bed, often with family and friends standing around or banging on pans, yelling, or otherwise making as much noise as possible. The friends and family members had generally been part of the discussions, negotiations, and activities leading up to the marriage; marriage united two families and was far too important to leave up to two young people alone. Among serfs the lord's permission was often required, with a special fee paid to obtain this. (This permission did *not* include the right to deflower the bride; the idea that lords had the "right of first night," the *jus primae noctis,* had a particularly long life, but there is no evidence of its existence in any legal sources.)

The involvement of family and friends in choosing one's spouse might lead to conflict, but more often the wishes of the young people and their parents, kin, and community were quite similar; all hoped for marriages that provided economic security, honorable standing, and a good number of healthy children. The best marriages offered companionship, emotional support, and even love, but these were understood to grow out of the marriage, not necessarily precede it. Jewish authorities described the best marriages as predestined in heaven and allowed divorce for truly bad matches that clearly did not reflect such heavenly matching. Although earlier Jewish customs had given the right to divorce only to men, by the medieval period German Jewish courts allowed women to petition for divorce as well and held that they could not be divorced without their consent. Among Christians, marriage was increasingly regarded as officially indissoluble, though wealthy people could generally obtain annulment in return for payment to a church official, while poorer folk could use abandonment or simply moving apart as a last resort. Breaking up a

Foolish Maidens on a Wedding Door of the Cathedral in Strasbourg (thirteenth century) Medieval cathedrals sometimes had a side door depicting a biblical story of ten young women who went to meet a bridegroom. Five of them were wise and took extra oil for their lamps, and five were foolish and did not (Matthew 25:1–13). In the story, which is a parable about always being prepared for the end of the world, the foolish maidens were out of oil when the bridegroom arrived and missed the wedding feast. The "maidens' door" became a popular site for weddings, which were held right in front of it. *(Erich Lessing/Art Resource, NY)*

marriage meant breaking up the basic production and consumption unit, however, which was a very serious matter, so marital dissolution by any means other than the death of one spouse was rare.

Children and Religion

Most brides hoped to be pregnant soon after their weddings, and if the rituals during the weddings had not been effective in bringing this about, there were other avenues to try. Christian women hoping for children said special prayers to the Virgin Mary or her mother Anne; wore amulets of amber, bone, or mistletoe thought to increase fertility; repeated charms and verses they had learned from other women; or, in desperate cases, went on pilgrimages to make special supplications. Muslim and Jewish women wore small cases with sacred verses or

asked for blessings from religious leaders. Women continued these prayers and rituals through pregnancy and childbirth, often combining religious traditions with folk beliefs handed down orally. Women in southern France, for example, offered prayers for easy childbirth and healthy children to Saint Guinefort, a greyhound who had been mistakenly killed by his owner after saving the owner's child from a poisonous snake. The fact that Guinefort was a dog meant he could never become an official saint, but women saw him as a powerful and martyred protector of children.

Judaism, Christianity, and Islam all required women to remain separate from the community after childbirth and often had special ceremonies welcoming them back once this period was over. Muslim women were prohibited from touching the Qur'an, entering a mosque, or engaging in religious fasts for forty days, after which their relatives brought special clothes and gifts for the child. Six weeks after giving birth, a Jewish woman underwent a ritual bath of purification, called a *mikvah,* in a special room or building in the Jewish part of town. By the Middle Ages the Virgin Mary's purification bath after the birth of Jesus had become a Christian holiday called Candlemas celebrated on February 2. A Christian woman also went through a ritual of thanksgiving and purification, called *churching,* six weeks after giving birth. During churching the mother went to church with the women who had assisted in the birth; in English these women were known as her "god-siblings," a word that became shortened to "gossip." The new mother made an offering of money or perhaps yarn she had spun and was blessed by the priest. This ritual varied from parish to parish, but it often included a prayer such as "Almighty and everlasting God, who has freed this woman from the danger of bearing a child, consider her to be strengthened from every pollution of the flesh so that with a clean heart and pure mind she may deserve to enter into the bosom of our mother, the church, and make her devoted to Your service."[10]

Religious ceremonies also welcomed children into the community. Among Christian families, infants were baptized quickly after they were born, for without baptism they could not enter Heaven. Thus midwives who delivered children who looked especially weak and sickly often baptized them in an emergency service. Mothers whose children had died before they could be baptized sometimes carried them many miles to special chapels where the priest was thought to have powers of revitalization; he blew "life" back into the children just long enough for baptism, and then the children were buried. (These chapels became surrounded by graveyards with hundreds of infant bodies; from those bodies archaeologists can tell that the children had sometimes been dead for weeks before they were buried.) In normal baptisms, the women who had assisted the mother in the birth often carried the baby to church, where carefully chosen godparents vowed their support. Godparents were often close friends or relatives, but parents might also choose prominent villagers or even the local lord in the hope that he might later look favorably on the child and provide for it in some way. When a child was baptized, a few grains of salt were dropped on its tongue. Salt had been the symbol of purity, strength, and incorruptibility for the ancient Hebrews, and the Romans had used it in their sacrifices. It was used in Christian baptism to drive away demons and to strengthen the infant in its new faith.

Within Judaism, a boy was circumcised and given his name in a ceremony when he was in his eighth day of life. This *brit milah,* or "covenant of circumcision," was viewed as a reminder of the covenant between God and Abraham described in Hebrew Scripture. There was no corresponding ceremony for girls, who were generally named during the first regular worship service after their birth. (Within the last several decades, Jews in many parts of the world have developed a naming ceremony for girls called *simhat bat.*) Muslims also circumcised boys in a special ritual, though the timing varied from a few days after birth to adolescence. Circumcision is not mentioned in the Qur'an, but Muhammad was understood to have been circumcised, so the practice was part of following his example. For both Jews and Muslims, circumcision was often accompanied by a family celebration or, in the case of wealthy families, a lavish feast; for sons of rulers, circumcision celebrations could be public occasions and go on for many days.

Death and the Afterlife

Death was similarly marked by religious ceremonies. Christians called for a priest when they thought the hour of death was near. The priest brought a number of objects and substances regarded as having power over death and the sin related to it: holy water to be sprinkled on and around the dying person; holy oil for anointing him or her; a censer with incense to be waved around; the priest's stole for the dying person to touch; a crucifix with an image of the dying Christ to remind him or her of Christ's own agony and death; lighted candles to drive back the darkness both figuratively and literally, which was often placed in the person's hand as he or she was just about to take a last breath (or "give up the ghost" as

the phrase still goes); and the communion host consecrated by the priest during the sacrament of extreme unction and then consumed by the dying person.

Once the person had died, the body was washed— usually by female family members or women who made their living this way—and was put in special clothing or a sack of plain cloth and buried within a day or two. Family and friends joined in a funeral procession, again with candles, holy water, incense, and a crucifix and marked by the ringing of church bells; sometimes extra women were hired so that the mourning and wailing were especially loud. The procession carried the body into the church, where there were psalms, prayers, and a funeral Mass, and then to a consecrated space for burial, the wealthy sometimes inside the church—in the walls, un-

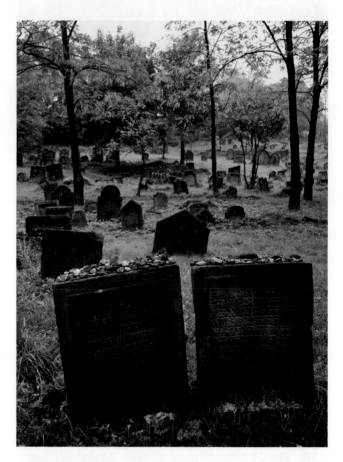

Jewish Cemetery Tomb in Worms of a thirteenth-century German Jewish rabbi who was imprisoned by the emperor and died in prison. Jewish and Christian cemeteries were separated in medieval Europe, with Christian cemeteries generally next to churches and Jewish ones often outside town walls. *(Erich Lessing/Art Resource, NY)*

der the floor, or under the building itself in a crypt—but most often in the churchyard or a cemetery close by. Individual graves did not have permanent markers, and as churchyards were used for over hundreds of years they became full of skeletal remains. When gravediggers dug a hole for the newest body, they often moved the bones they encountered to a special small building, called a charnel house or an ossuary, where they were available for public view. Standing at the graveside, the priest asked for God's grace on the soul of the deceased and also asked that soul to "rest in peace."

This final request was made not only for the benefit of the dead, but also for that of the living. The souls of the dead were widely believed to return to earth: mothers who had died in childbed seeking to take their children with them; executed criminals seeking revenge on those who had brought them to justice (for this reason they were buried at crossroads, permanently under the sign of the cross, or under the gallows itself); everyday people seeking help from surviving family members in achieving their final salvation. Priests were hired to say memorial masses on anniversaries of family deaths, especially one week, one month, and one year afterward; large churches had a number of side altars so that many masses could be going on at one time.

Learned theologians sometimes denied that souls actually returned, and during the twelfth century they increasingly emphasized the idea of **purgatory,** a place where souls on their way to Heaven went after death to make amends for their earthly sins. (Those on their way to Hell went straight there.) Souls safely in purgatory did not wander the earth, but they could still benefit from earthly activities; memorial masses, prayers, and donations made in their names could shorten their time in purgatory and hasten their way to Heaven. So could **indulgences,** documents bearing the pope's name that released the souls from purgatory. (Indulgences, it was believed, also relieved the living of penalties imposed by the priest in confession for serious sins.) Indulgences could be secured for a small fee, and people came to believe that indulgences and pilgrimages to the shrines of saints could ensure a place in Heaven for their deceased relatives (and also, perhaps, for themselves). Thus the bodies of the dead on earth and their souls in purgatory both required things from the living, for death did not sever family obligations and connections.

The living also had obligations to the dead among Muslims and Jews. In both groups, deceased people were to be buried quickly, and special prayers were to be said by mourners and family members. Muslim funeral prac-

tices involved washing the body, covering it completely with a cloth, and carrying it to the burial ground by foot in a funeral procession; all Muslim men who saw a procession were to join it. Muslims said prayers and fasted on behalf of the dead and maintained a brief period of official mourning. The Qur'an promises an eternal paradise with flowing rivers to "those who believe and do good deeds" (Qur'an, 4:57) and a hell of eternal torment to those who do not.

Jewish funerals also involved prayers and readings from Scripture, with the body covered and treated respectfully. After a death, family members observed specified periods of mourning during which the normal activities of daily life were curtailed. Every day for eleven months after a death and every year after that on the anniversary of the death, a son of the deceased was to recite Kaddish, a special prayer of praise and glorification of God. Judaism emphasized this life more than an afterlife, so beliefs about what happens to the soul after death were more varied; the very righteous might go directly to a place of spiritual reward, but most souls went first to a place of punishment and purification generally referred to as *Gehinnom.* After a period that did not exceed twelve months, the soul ascended to the world to come. Those who were completely wicked during their lifetimes might simply go out of existence or continue in an eternal state of remorse.

Nobles

The **nobility,** though a small fraction of the total population, strongly influenced all aspects of medieval culture—political, economic, religious, educational, and artistic. Despite political, scientific, and industrial revolutions, the nobility continued to hold real political and social power in Europe down to the nineteenth century. In order to account for this continuing influence, it is important to understand the development of the nobility in the High Middle Ages.

• *How were the lives of nobles different from the lives of common people?*

Origins and Status of the Nobility

In the early Middle Ages noble status was limited to very few families in Europe. Nobles were generally descended from officials at the Carolingian court and leading families among Germanic tribes. They held large tracts of land, often acquired as fiefs, and had authority over those who lived on this land.

Beginning in the eleventh century trained combatants who fought from horseback also began to claim noble status. They referred to themselves in Latin as *miles* and in French as *chevaliers,* both of which translate as "knights." Knights had military obligations to higher nobles or kings; through military valor, a fortunate marriage, or outstanding service to king or lord, poor knights could and did achieve positions in the upper nobility. Even those who did not climb that high took over fiefs and castles, gained income from lands, and asserted legal control over peasants. The noble class grew larger and more diverse, ranging from poor knights who held tiny pieces of land (or sometimes none at all) to dukes and counts with vast territories.

Members of the nobility enjoyed special legal status. They were free personally, with immunity from almost all outside authorities. Nobles were limited only by military obligation to king, duke, or prince, but they had certain rights and responsibilities. Noblemen raised troops and commanded them in the field and held courts that dispensed a sort of justice. Nobles sometimes coined money for use within their territories. They were the political, military, and judicial authorities over the people who settled on their lands, made political decisions affecting them, resolved disputes among them, and protected them in time of attack. Noble privileges were heritable, perpetuated by blood and not by wealth alone. In most places, for a son or daughter to be considered a noble, both parents had to be noble. Women who were not noble could not usually enter the nobility through marriage, though evidence from Germany shows that some women were ennobled because they had married nobles.

Originally, most knights focused solely on military skills, but gradually a different ideal of knighthood emerged, usually termed **chivalry.** Chivalry was a code of conduct originally devised by the clergy to transform the crude and brutal behavior of the knightly class. It may have originated in oaths administered to Crusaders in which fighting was declared to have a sacred purpose and knights vowed loyalty to the church as well as to their lords. Other qualities gradually became part of chivalry: bravery, generosity, honor, graciousness, mercy, and eventually gallantry toward women. The chivalric ideal—and it was an ideal, not a standard pattern of behavior—created a new standard of masculinity for nobles, in which loyalty and honor remained the most important qualities, but graceful dancing and intelligent conversation were not considered unmanly.

Saint Maurice Certain individuals were held up to young men as models of ideal chivalry. Some of these were real people, such as King Richard the Lion-Hearted, and some were literary creations, such as Sir Lancelot in the stories of King Arthur. Still others were somewhere in between—that is, individuals who were probably real but whose lives were embellished with many stories. One of these was Saint Maurice (d. 287), a soldier apparently executed by the Romans for refusing to renounce his Christian faith. He first emerges in the Carolingian period, and later he was held up as a model knight and declared a patron of the Holy Roman Empire and protector of the imperial (German) army in wars against the pagan Slavs. His image was used on coins, and his cult was promoted by the archbishops of Magdeburg, who moved his relics to their cathedral. Until 1240 he was portrayed as a white man, but after that he was usually represented as a black man, as in this sandstone statue from Magdeburg Cathedral (ca 1250). We have no idea why this change happened. Who commissioned this statue? Who carved it? Did an actual person serve as the model, and if so what was he doing in Magdeburg? *(Image of the Black Project, Harvard University/ Hickey-Robertson, Houston)*

Childhood

For children of aristocratic birth, the years from infancy to around the age of seven or eight were primarily years of play. Infants had rattles, as the twelfth-century monk Guibert of Nogent reports, and young children had special toys. Of course, then as now, children would play with anything handy—balls, rings, pretty stones, horns, small household objects. Gerald of Wales, who later became a courtier of King Henry II, describes how as a child he built monasteries and churches in the sand while his brothers were making castles and palaces. Vincent of Beauvais, who composed a great encyclopedia around 1250, recommended that children be bathed twice a day, fed well, and given ample playtime.

Guibert of Nogent speaks in several places in his autobiography of "the tender years of childhood"—the years from six to twelve. Describing the severity of the tutor whom his mother assigned to him, Guibert wrote:

Placed under him, I was taught with such purity and checked with such honesty from the vices which commonly spring up in youth that I was kept from ordinary games and never allowed to leave my master's company, or to eat anywhere else than at home . . . ; in everything I had to show self-control. . . . While others of my age wandered everywhere at will and were unchecked in the indulgence of such inclinations as were natural at their age, I, hedged in with constant restraints and dressed in my clerical garb, would sit and look at the troops of players like a beast awaiting sacrifice.[11]

Guibert's mother had intended him for the church. Other boys and girls had much more playtime and freedom.

At about the age of seven, a boy of the noble class who was not intended for the church was placed in the household of one of his father's friends or relatives. There he became a servant to the lord and received formal training in arms. He was expected to serve the lord at the table, to assist him as a private valet when called on to do so, and, as he gained experience, to care for the lord's horses and equipment. The boy might have a great deal of work to do, depending on the size of the household and the personality of the lord. The work children did, medieval people believed, gave them experience and preparation for later life.

Training was in the arts of war. The boy learned to ride and to manage a horse. He had to acquire skill in wielding a sword, which sometimes weighed as much as twenty-five pounds. He had to be able to hurl a lance, shoot with a bow and arrow, and care for armor and other equipment. Increasingly, in the eleventh and twelfth centuries, noble youths learned to read and write some Latin. Still, on thousands of charters from that period, nobles signed with a cross (+) or some other mark. Literacy among the nobility became more common in the thirteenth century. Formal training was concluded around the age of twenty-one with the ceremony of knighthood. The custom of knighting, though never universal, seems to have been widespread in France and England but not in Germany.

Noble girls were also trained in preparation for their future tasks. They were often taught to read the local language and perhaps some Latin and to write and do enough arithmetic to keep household accounts. They also learned music, dancing, and embroidery and how to ride and hunt, both common noble pursuits. Much of this took place in the girl's own home, but, like boys, noble girls were often sent to the homes of relatives or higher nobles to act as servants or ladies in waiting. While her brothers cared for armor and horses, a noble girl looked after clothing and household goods and learned how to run a household. She often learned from experience that she could expect to spend weeks, months, or even years running a castle and a manor on her own while her future husband was away fighting.

Youth and Marriage

The ceremony of knighthood was one of the most important in a man's life, but knighthood did not necessarily mean adulthood, power, and responsibility. Sons were completely dependent on their fathers for support. A young man remained a youth until he was in a financial position to marry—that is, until his father died. That might not happen until he was in his late thirties, and marriage at forty was not uncommon. A famous English soldier of fortune, William Marshal, had to wait until he was forty-five to take a wife. One factor—the inheritance of land and the division of properties—determined the lifestyles of the aristocratic nobility. The result was tension, frustration, and sometimes violence.

Once knighted, the young man traveled for two to three years. His father selected a group of friends to accompany, guide, and protect him. The band's chief pursuit was fighting. They meddled in local conflicts, sometimes departed on crusade, hunted, and did the tournament circuit. The **tournament,** in which a number of men competed from horseback (in contrast to the **joust,** which involved only two competitors), gave the young knight experience in pitched battle. Since the horses and equipment of the vanquished were forfeited to the victors, the knight could also gain a reputation and a profit. Young knights took great delight in spending money on horses, armor, gambling, drinking, and women. Everywhere they went, they stirred up trouble, for chivalric ideals of honorable valor and gallant masculinity rarely served as a check on actual behavior. It is no wonder that kings supported the Crusades to rid their countries of the violence caused by bands of footloose young knights.

Parents often wanted to settle daughters' futures as soon as possible. Men tended to prefer young brides. A woman in her late twenties or thirties would have fewer years of married fertility, limiting the number of children she could produce and thus threatening the family's continuation. Therefore, aristocratic girls in the High Middle Ages were married at around the age of sixteen, often to much older men. This marriage pattern reduced the "market value" of young women, as there were more of them than there were older men, and it contributed to a rise in the dowries that young women presented to their husbands on marriage. In the early Middle Ages the custom was for the groom to present a dowry to the bride and her family, but by the late twelfth century the proc-

ess was reversed. Thereafter, the sizes of dowries offered by brides and their families rose higher and higher. Families engaged in complicated marriage strategies to balance the money they paid out to marry off daughters with the money they received in marrying off sons.

Within noble families and medieval society as a whole, paternal control of the family property and wealth led to serious difficulties. Because marriage was long delayed for men and remarriage was common, a considerable age difference often existed between husbands and wives and between fathers and sons. Because of this generation gap, fathers were often distant figures, and disputes between generations were common as older men held on to property and power.

Disputes between brothers were also common. Early medieval societies had had different sorts of inheritance patterns: sometimes property was divided among sons; sometimes it passed to the youngest son and sometimes to the oldest, a system termed **primogeniture.** (Daughters were almost always excluded from inheriting family land, though they received cash and goods as their inheritance, often as dowries on marriage.) Division of property was certainly fairest, but this caused family holdings to become smaller over generations, and increasingly families adopted primogeniture. This made oldest sons wealthier and more powerful than their younger brothers. This difference was further enhanced by the marriage market, for an oldest son could attract a wife with a large dowry, which further increased his wealth. Opportunities for younger sons in the marriage market were sometimes so dismal that they were sent to careers in the church or simply forbidden to marry. Such a situation did not encourage affection among siblings, and the resentments of younger sons sometimes boiled over into violence.

When society included so many married young women and unmarried young men, sexual tensions also arose. The young male noble, unable to marry for a long time, could satisfy his lust with peasant girls or prostitutes. But what was a young woman unhappily married to a much older man to do? Medieval literature is filled with stories of young bachelors in love with young married women and of cuckolded husbands who are not able to see what is going on in their households. Scholars disagree, however, about whether this reflected social realities or was simply wishful thinking.

Power and Responsibility

A male member of the nobility became an adult when he came into the possession of his property. He then ac-

Elephant Ivory Mirror Case The mirror case, forerunner of the modern woman's compact, protected a polished metal disk used by wealthy ladies as a looking glass. In this mid-fourteenth-century case, the French artist created a chivalric hunting scene. An aristocratic couple on horseback, holding falcons and accompanied by attendants, is portrayed in a forested landscape that is held in an eight-lobed frame with lions around the disk. Amazingly, the diameter of the case is less than four inches. Elephant ivory came from sub-Saharan Africa via the Mediterranean trade. *(The Metropolitan Museum of Art, Gift of George M. Blumenthal, 1941 [41.100.160]. Photograph © The Metropolitan Museum of Art)*

quired vast authority over lands and people. With it went responsibility. In the words of Honorius of Autun:

Soldiers: You are the arm of the Church, because you should defend it against its enemies. Your duty is to aid the oppressed, to restrain yourself from rapine and fornication, to repress those who impugn the Church with evil acts, and to resist those who are rebels against priests. Performing such a service, you will obtain the most splendid of benefices from the greatest of Kings.[12]

Nobles rarely lived up to this ideal, and there are countless examples of nobles attacking the church. In the early thirteenth century Peter of Dreux, count of Brittany, spent so much of his time attacking the church that he was known as the "Scourge of the Clergy."

The nobles' conception of rewards and gratification did not involve the kind of postponement envisioned by the clergy. They wanted rewards immediately. Since by definition a military class is devoted to war, those rewards came through the pursuit of arms. When nobles were not involved in local squabbles with neighbors—usually disputes over property or over real or imagined slights—they participated in tournaments designed to show off their masculinity to an audience.

Complete jurisdiction over properties allowed the noble, at long last, to gratify his desire for display and lavish living. Since his status in medieval society depended on the size of his household, he would be eager to increase the number of household retainers. The elegance of his clothes, the variety and richness of his table, the number of horses and followers, the freedom with which he spent money—all were public indications of his social standing. To maintain this lifestyle, nobles often borrowed from financiers or wealthy monasteries.

At the same time, nobles had a great deal of work to do. The responsibilities of a nobleman in the High Middle Ages depended on the size and extent of his estates, the number of dependents, and his position in his territory relative to others of his class and to the king. As a vassal, he was required to fight for his lord or for the king when called on to do so. By the mid-twelfth century this service was limited to forty days a year in most parts of western Europe. The noble was obliged to attend his lord's court on important occasions when the lord wanted to put on great displays, such as at Easter, Pentecost, and Christmas. When the lord knighted his eldest son or married off his eldest daughter, he called his vassals to his court. The vassals were expected to attend and to present a contribution known as a "gracious aid."

Until the late thirteenth century, when royal authority intervened, a noble in France or England had great power over the knights and peasants on his estates. He maintained order among them and dispensed justice to them. Holding the manorial court, which punished criminal acts and settled disputes, was one of his gravest obligations. The quality of justice varied widely: some lords were vicious tyrants who exploited and persecuted their peasants; others were reasonable and evenhanded. In any case, the quality of life on the manor and its productivity were related in no small way to the temperament and decency of the lord—and his lady.

Women played a large and important role in the functioning of the estate. They were responsible for the practical management of the household's "inner economy"—cooking, brewing, spinning, weaving, caring for yard animals. The lifestyle of medieval warrior-nobles required constant travel, both for purposes of war and for the supervision of distant properties. When the lord was away for long periods, the women frequently managed the herds, barns, granaries, and outlying fields as well. When her husband went to the Holy Land between 1060 and 1080, the lady Hersendis was the sole manager of her family's properties in northern France.

Nor were women's activities confined to managing households and estates in their husbands' absence. Medieval warfare was largely a matter of brief skirmishes, and few men were killed in any single encounter. But altogether the number slain ran high, and there were many widows. Aristocratic widows frequently controlled family properties and fortunes and exercised great authority; in Spain, France, and Germany they bought, sold, and otherwise transferred property. Gertrude, labeled "Saxony's almighty widow" by the chronicler Ekkehard of Aura, took a leading role in conspiracies against the emperor Henry V. And Eilika Billung, widow of Count Otto of Ballenstedt, built a castle at Burgwerben on the Saale River and, as advocate of the monastery of Goseck, removed one abbot and selected his successor.

Throughout the High Middle Ages, fighting remained the dominant feature of the noble lifestyle. The church's preaching and condemnations reduced but did not stop violence. Lateness of inheritance, together with the military ethos of their culture, encouraged petty warfare and disorder. The nobility thus represented a constant source of trouble for the monarchy. In the thirteenth century kings drew on the support of the middle classes to build the administrative machinery that gradually laid the foundations of strong royal government. The Crusades relieved the rulers of France, England, and the German Empire of some of their most dangerous elements. Complete royal control of the nobility, however, came only in modern times.

Monasteries and Convents

Peasants and nobles were not the only important groups in medieval society. In intellectual models and social reality, Christian religious personnel were an influential third group. Priests, bishops, monks, and nuns played significant intellectual, spiritual, social, and economic roles both as individuals and as members of institutions. In the previous chapter we traced the evolution of the papacy and the church hierarchy in the High Middle Ages; here we focus on monks, nuns, and others who lived in religious houses.

In the fifth century Saints Benedict and Scholastica had written rules (*regulus* in Latin) for the men and women living in monasteries and convents (see page 199), who were known as regular clergy. In the early Middle Ages many houses followed the Benedictine *Rule,* while others developed their own patterns. In the High Middle Ages this diversity became more formalized, and **religious orders,** groups of monastic houses following a particular rule, were established. Historians term the foundation, strengthening, and reform of religious orders in the High Middle Ages the "monastic revival." They link it with the simultaneous expansion of papal power (see pages 275–278), because many of the same individuals were important in both.

Medieval people believed that monks and nuns performed an important social service, prayer. In the Middle Ages prayer was looked on as a vital service, as crucial as the labor of peasants and the military might of nobles. Just as the knights protected and defended society with the sword and the peasants provided sustenance through their toil, so the monks and nuns worked to secure God's blessing for society with their prayers and chants.

• *What roles did the men and women affiliated with religious orders play in medieval society?*

Monastic Revival

In the early Middle Ages the best Benedictine monasteries had been citadels of good monastic observance and centers of learning, copying and preserving manuscripts, maintaining schools, and setting high standards of monastic observance. Charlemagne had encouraged and supported these monastic activities, and the collapse of the Carolingian Empire had disastrous effects.

The Viking, Magyar, and Muslim invaders attacked and ransacked many monasteries across Europe. Some communities fled and dispersed. In the period of political disorder that followed the disintegration of the Carolingian Empire, many religious houses fell under the control and domination of local lords. Powerful laymen appointed themselves or their relatives as abbots, took the lands and goods of monasteries, and spent monastic revenues. The level of spiritual observance and intellectual activity in monasteries and convents declined.

Since the time of Charlemagne, secular powers had selected church officials and compelled them to become their vassals. Abbots, bishops, and archbishops thus had military responsibilities that required them to fight with their lords, or at least to send contingents of soldiers when called on to do so. Church law forbade clerics to shed blood, but many prelates found the excitement of battle too great to resist. In the ninth century Abbot Lupus of Ferrieres wrote his friend Abbot Odo of Corbie:

I am often most anxious about you, recalling your habit of heedlessly throwing yourself, all unarmed, into the thick of battle whenever your youthful energy is overcome with the greedy desire to conquer. . . . I, as you know, have never learned how to strike an enemy or to avoid his blows. Nor do I know how to execute all the other obligations of military service on foot or horseback.[13]

Lupus preferred the quiet of his scriptorium to the noise of the battlefield.

In the twelfth and thirteenth centuries ecclesiastical barons owed heavy contingents of knight service; some prelates actually fought with the king. For example, in twelfth-century England the abbot of Peterborough owed the king the service of sixty knights, the abbot of Bury Saint Edmunds forty knights, and the archbishop of Canterbury the huge service of five hundred knights. As feudal lords, ecclesiastical officials also had judicial authority over knights and peasants on their lands. For some prelates the conflict between their religious duties on the one hand and their judicial and military obligations on the other posed a serious dilemma.

In 909 William the Pious, duke of Aquitaine, established the abbey of Cluny near Macon in Burgundy. (Because monasteries and convents were headed by an abbot or abbess, both are sometimes referred to as "abbeys.") In his charter of endowment, Duke William declared that Cluny was to enjoy complete independence from all feudal (or secular) and episcopal lordships. The new monastery was to be subordinate only to the authority of Saints Peter and Paul as represented by the pope. The duke then renounced his own possession of and influence over Cluny.

Online Study Center **Improve Your Grade**
Primary Source: The Foundation of Cluny

This monastery and its foundation charter came to exert vast religious influence. The first two abbots of Cluny, Berno (910–927) and Odo (927–942), followed the Benedictine *Rule* closely and set very high standards of religious behavior. Cluny gradually came to stand for clerical celibacy and the suppression of simony (the sale of church offices). In the eleventh century Cluny was fortunate in having a series of highly able abbots who ruled for a long time. These abbots paid careful attention to sound economic management. In a disorderly world, Cluny gradually came to represent religious and political stability. Therefore, laypersons placed lands under its custody and monastic priories (a priory is a religious house, usually smaller in number than an abbey, governed by a prior or prioress) under its jurisdiction for reform. Benefactors wanted to be associated with Cluniac piety, and monasteries under Cluny's jurisdiction enjoyed special protection, at least theoretically, from violence. In this way, hundreds of monasteries, primarily in France and Spain, came under Cluny's authority.

Some scholars believe that the monastic revival spreading from Cluny influenced reform of the Roman papacy and eventually of the entire Christian church. Certainly Abbot Odilo of Cluny (994–1048) was a close friend of the German emperor Henry III, who promoted reform throughout the empire. Pope Gregory VII, who carried the ideals of reform to extreme lengths (see pages 274–275), had spent some time at Cluny. And the man who consolidated the reform movement and strengthened the medieval papal monarchy, Pope Urban II (1088–1099), had been a monk and prior at Cluny. The precise degree of Cluny's impact on the reform movement cannot be measured, but the broad goals of the Cluniac movement and those of the Roman papacy were the same.

Deeply impressed laypeople showered gifts on monasteries with good reputations, such as Cluny and its many daughter houses. But as the monasteries became richer, the lifestyle of the monks grew increasingly luxurious. Monastic observance and spiritual fervor declined. Soon fresh demands for reform were heard, and the result was the founding of new religious orders in the late eleventh and early twelfth centuries.

The Cistercians, because of their phenomenal expansion and the great economic, political, and spiritual influence they exerted, are the best representatives of the new reforming spirit. In 1098 a group of monks left the rich abbey of Molesmes in Burgundy and founded a new house in the swampy forest of Cîteaux. They planned to avoid all involvement with secular feudal society. They decided to accept only uncultivated lands far from regular habitation. They intended to refuse all gifts of mills,

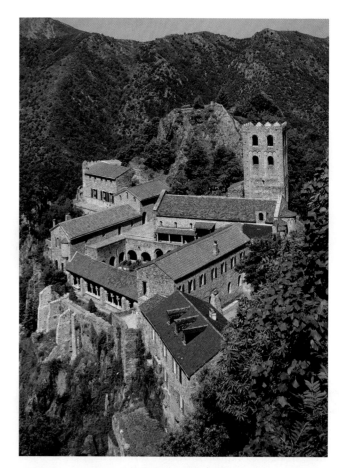

Monastery of Saint Martin de Canigou The Benedictine monastery of Saint Martin de Canigou was constructed in 1009 in the eastern Pyrenees by a nobleman from one of the small Christian kingdoms in northern Spain. Like hundreds of other monasteries, it came under the influence of the abbey of Cluny. With its thick walls and strategic position, it served as a Christian defensive fortress against the Muslims in battles of the reconquista. *(Editions Gaud)*

serfs, tithes, and ovens—the traditional manorial sources of income. The early Cistercians (the word is derived from *Cîteaux*) determined to avoid elaborate liturgy and ceremony and to keep their chant simple. Finally, they refused to allow the presence of powerful laypeople in their monasteries because such influence was usually harmful to careful observance.

The first monks at Cîteaux experienced sickness, a dearth of recruits, and terrible privations. But their obvious sincerity and high ideals eventually attracted attention. In 1112 a twenty-three-year-old nobleman called Bernard joined the community at Cîteaux, together with some of his brothers and other noblemen. Three years later Bernard was appointed founding abbot of Clairvaux in Champagne. From this position he conducted a vast correspondence, attacked the theological views of Peter Abelard (see page 347), intervened in the disputed papal election of 1130, drafted a constitution for the Knights Templars, and preached the Second Crusade. This reforming movement gained impetus. Cîteaux founded 525 new monasteries in the course of the twelfth century, and its influence on European society was profound. In England Saint Gilbert (1085?–1189) organized a community of nuns at Sempringham that followed the more rigorous Cistercian rule "as far as the weakness of their sex allowed," as Gilbert put it. This convent established several daughter houses, and Gilbert asked the Cistercians to take them all on as official female branches. They refused, saying that they did not want the burden of overseeing women, setting a pattern for other men's religious orders.

Unavoidably, however, Cistercian success brought wealth, and wealth brought power. By the later twelfth century economic prosperity and political power had begun to compromise the original Cistercian ideals.

Recruitment of Monks and Nuns

Toward the end of his *Ecclesiastical History,* when he was well into his sixties, Orderic Vitalis (ca 1075–ca 1140), a monk of the Norman abbey of Saint Evroul, interrupted his narrative to explain movingly how he happened to become a monk:

And so, O glorious God, you didst inspire my father Odeleric to renounce me utterly and submit me in all things to thy governance. So, weeping, he gave me, a weeping child, into the care of the monk Reginald, and sent me away into exile for love of thee, and never saw me again. And I, a mere boy, did not presume to oppose my father's wishes, but obeyed him in all things, for he promised me for his part that if I became a monk I should taste of the joys of Heaven with the Innocents after my death. . . . And so, a boy of ten, I crossed the English channel and came into Normandy as an exile, unknown to all, knowing no one. . . . But thou didst suffer me through thy grace to find nothing but kindness among strangers. I was received as an oblate in the abbey of St. Evroul by the venerable abbot Mainier in the eleventh year of my life. . . . The name of Vitalis was given me in place of my English name, which sounded harsh to the Normans.[14]

Orderic Vitalis was one of the leading scholars of his time. As such, he is not a representative figure or even a typical monk. In one respect, however, Orderic was quite representative of the monks of the High Middle Ages: although he had no doubt that God wanted him to be a monk, the decision was actually made by his parents, who gave him to a monastery as a child oblate. Orderic was the son of Odeleric, a Norman priest of the household of Earl Roger of Montgomery and (after the Conquest of 1066) Shrewsbury, and an Englishwoman. The law requiring a celibate priesthood was not yet operative in England, but qualms of conscience may have led Odeleric to place his son in a Norman monastery.

Medieval monasteries were religious institutions whose organization and structure fulfilled the social needs of the feudal nobility. The monasteries provided noble children with both an honorable and aristocratic life and opportunities for ecclesiastical careers. Some men did become monks as adults, apparently for a wide variety of reasons: belief in a direct call from God, disgust with the materialism and violence of the secular world, the encouragement and inspiration of others, economic failure or lack of opportunity, poverty, sickness, fear of Hell. However, until about the early thirteenth century most men who became monks seem to have been given as child oblates by their parents (see page 306).

In the thirteenth century more monks were recruited from the middle class, that is, from small landholders or traders in the district near the abbey. As medieval society changed economically and as European society ever so slowly developed middle-class traits, the monasteries almost inevitably drew their manpower, when they were able, from the middle classes. Until that time they were preserves of the aristocratic nobility.

Throughout the Middle Ages social class also defined the kinds of religious life open to women. Kings and nobles usually established convents for their daughters, sisters, aunts, or aging mothers. Entrance was restricted to women of the founder's class. Like monks, many nuns came into the convent as children, and very often sisters, cousins, aunts, and nieces could all be found in the same place. Thus, though nuns were to some degree cut off from their families because they were cloistered, family relationships were maintained within the convent.

The founder's endowment and support greatly influenced the later social, economic, and political status of the convent. Social and religious bonds between benefactors and communities of nuns frequently continued over many generations. A few convents received large endowments and could accept many women. Amesbury Priory in Wiltshire, England, for example, received a handsome endowment from King Henry II in 1177, and his successors Henry III and Edward I also made lavish gifts. In 1256 Amesbury supported a prioress and 76 nuns, 7 priests, and 16 lay brothers. It owned 200 oxen, 23 horses, 7 cows, 4 calves, 300 pigs, and 4,800 sheep.

The convent raised one hundred pounds in annual rents and forty pounds from the wool clip, very large sums at the time. The entrance of such highborn ladies as the dowager queen Eleanor (widow of Henry III), Edward I's daughter Mary, and his niece Isabella of Lancaster stimulated the gift of additional lands and privileges. By 1317 Amesbury had 177 nuns. Most houses of women, however, possessed limited resources and remained small in numbers.

Life in Convents and Monasteries

Within convents the office of **abbess** or **prioress,** the house's superior, customarily went to a nun of considerable social standing. Thus William the Conqueror's daughter Cecelia became abbess of her mother's foundation, Holy Trinity Abbey in Caen, and Henry II's daughter became abbess of Barking. Since an abbess or prioress had responsibility for governing her community and for representing it in any business with the outside world, she was a woman of local power and importance. Sometimes her position brought national prominence. In 1306 Edward I of England summoned several abbesses to Parliament; he wanted their financial support for the expenses connected with knighting his eldest son.

The office of abbess was the most powerful position a woman could hold in medieval society (see the feature "Individuals in Society: Hildegard of Bingen"). Abbesses were part of the feudal structure in the same way that bishops and abbots were, with manors under their financial and legal control. They appointed tax collectors, bailiffs, judges, and often priests in the territory under their control; some abbesses in the Holy Roman Empire even had the right to name bishops and send representatives to the imperial diets. Abbesses also opened and supported hospitals, orphanages, and schools; they hired builders, sculptors, and painters to construct and decorate residences and churches.

Both convents and monasteries generally owned land, and the administration of an abbey's estates and properties consumed considerable time. The operation of a large establishment, such as Cluny in Burgundy or Bury Saint Edmunds in England, which by 1150 had several hundred monks, involved planning, prudence, and wise management. The usual method of economic organization was the manor. Many monastic manors were small enough and close enough to the abbey to be supervised directly by the abbot or abbess. But if a monastery held and farmed vast estates, the properties were divided into administrative units, and supervisory responsibilities were divided.

Monasteries for men were headed by an **abbot** or **prior,** who was generally a member of a noble family, often a younger brother in a family with several sons. The main body of monks, known as *choir monks,* were aristocrats and did not till the land themselves. In each house one monk, the *cellarer,* or general financial manager, was responsible for supervising the peasants or lay brothers who did the agricultural labor. **Lay brothers** were generally peasants and had simpler religious and intellectual obligations than did the choir monks. The cellarer had to see to it that the estates of the monastery produced enough income to cover its expenses. In women's houses one of the nuns was generally chosen as cellarer and was in charge of **lay sisters** who did the actual physical work. Another monk or nun, the *almoner,* was responsible for feeding and caring for the poor of the neighborhood. At the French abbey of Saint-Requier in the eleventh century, 110 persons were fed every day. At Corbie fifty loaves of bread were distributed daily to the poor. The *novice master* or *novice mistress* was responsible for the training of recruits, instructing them in the *Rule,* the chant, the Scriptures, and the history and traditions of the house. The efficient operation of a monastic house also required the services of cooks, laundresses, gardeners, seamstresses, mechanics, blacksmiths, pharmacists, and others whose essential work has left, unfortunately, no written trace.

The pattern of life within individual monasteries varied widely from house to house and from region to region. One central activity, however, was performed everywhere. Daily life centered on the *liturgy* or *Divine Office,* psalms and other prayers prescribed by Saint Benedict, which monks and nuns prayed seven times a day and once during the night. Prayers were offered for peace, rain, good harvests, the civil authorities, the monks' families, and their benefactors. Monastic patrons in turn lavished gifts on the monasteries, which often became very wealthy.

Everything connected with prayer was understood as praise of God, so abbeys spent a large percentage of their income on splendid objects to enhance the liturgy. They sought to accumulate sacred vessels of embossed silver and gold and altar cloths of the finest silks, velvets, and embroideries. Containers of sweet-smelling incense brought at great expense from Asia were used at the altars. Every monastery tried to acquire the relics of its patron saint, which necessitated the production of a beautiful reliquary to house them. The pages of Gospel books were richly decorated with gold leaf, and the books' bindings were ornamented and bejeweled. In some abbeys monks and nuns spent much of their time copying books and manuscripts and then *illuminating*

Beekeeping at Monte Cassino
In this painting, lay brothers and peasants gather honey for the Benedictine monastery of Monte Cassino in Italy. Monasteries were important producers of agricultural products as well as spiritual services. Because of the scarcity and expense of sugar, honey was the usual sweetener for pastries and liquids throughout the Middle Ages. This illustrator had clearly never seen the process, for medieval beekeepers used veils, nets, and gloves to keep from getting stung, just as modern beekeepers do. *(Biblioteca Apostolica Vaticana)*

them, decorating them with human and animal figures or elaborate designs, often painted in bright colors or gold. The liturgy, then, inspired a great deal of art, and monasteries and convents became the crucibles of art in Western Christendom.

A few monasteries and convents became centers of learning where talented residents wrote their own works as well as copying those of others. Hroswitha of Gandersheim (930 or 940?–1002), for example, a German nun, wrote poems, epics, and plays in Latin that praised virgin martyrs, many of them including humorous scenes as well as grisly executions. In the twelfth and thirteenth centuries many monks gained considerable reputations for their knowledge and experience in the practice of both the canon law of the church and the civil law of their countries. For example, the Norman monk Lanfranc, because of his legal knowledge and administrative ability, became the chief adviser of William the Conqueror as archbishop of Canterbury.

Monks and nuns also performed social services. Monasteries often ran schools that gave primary education to young boys, while convents took in girls. Abbeys like Saint Albans, situated north of London on a busy thoroughfare, served as hotels and resting places for travelers. Monasteries frequently operated "hospitals" and lepro-

saria, which provided care and attention to the sick, the aged, and the afflicted—primitive care, it is true, but often all that was available. In short, monasteries and convents performed a variety of social services in an age when there was no "state" and no conception of social welfare as a public responsibility.

Economic Activities and Difficulties

The religious houses of medieval Europe usually took full advantage of the resources and opportunities their locations offered. For example, the raising of horses could produce income in a world that depended on horses for travel and warfare. Some monasteries, such as the Cistercian abbey of Jervaulx in Yorkshire, became famous for and quite wealthy from their production of prime breeds. In the eleventh and twelfth centuries, a period of considerable monastic expansion, large tracts of swamp, fen, forest, and wasteland were brought under cultivation— principally by the Cistercians (see Map 10.1).

The Cistercians, whose rules insisted that they accept lands far from human habitation and forbade them to be involved in the traditional feudal-manorial structure, were ideally suited to the agricultural needs and trends of their times. In the Low Countries (present-day Holland,

Individuals in Society

Hildegard of Bingen

The tenth child of a lesser noble family, Hildegard (1098–1179) was given as an oblate to an abbey in the Rhineland when she was eight years old; there she learned Latin and received a good education. She spent most of her life in various women's religious communities, two of which she founded herself. When she was a child, she began having mystical visions, often of light in the sky, but told few people about them. In middle age, however, her visions became more dramatic: "And it came to pass . . . when I was 42 years and 7 months old, that the heavens were opened and a blinding light of exceptional brilliance flowed through my entire brain. And so it kindled my whole heart and breast like a flame, not burning but warming . . . and suddenly I understood of the meaning of expositions of the books."* She wanted the church to approve of her visions and wrote first to Saint Bernard of Clairvaux, who answered her briefly and dismissively, and then to Pope Eugenius, who encouraged her to write them down. Her first work was *Scivias* (Know the Ways of the Lord), a record of her mystical visions that incorporates vast theological learning.

Obviously possessed of leadership and administrative talents, Hildegard left her abbey in 1147 to found the convent of Rupertsberg near Bingen. There she produced *Physica* (On the Physical Elements) and *Causa et Curae* (Causes and Cures), scientific works on the curative properties of natural elements, poems, a mystery play, and several more works of mysticism. She carried on a huge correspondence with scholars, prelates, and ordinary people. When she was over fifty she left her community to preach to audiences of clergy and laity, and she was the only woman of her time whose opinions on religious matters were considered authoritative by the church.

Hildegard's visions have been explored by theologians and also by neurologists, who judge that they may have originated in migraine headaches, as she reports many of the same phenomena that migraine sufferers do: auras of light around objects, areas of blindness, feelings of intense doubt and intense euphoria. The interpretations that she develops come from her theological insight and learning, however, not ill-

In one of her visions, Hildegard saw the metaphorical figure Synagogue as a very tall woman who holds in her arms Moses with the stone tablets of the Ten Commandments. (Rheinische Bildarchiv, Koln)

ness. That same insight also emerges in her music, which is what she is best known for today. Eighty of her compositions survive—a huge number for a medieval composer—most of them written to be sung by the nuns in her convent, so they have strong lines for female voices. Many of her songs and chants have been recorded recently by various artists and are available on compact disc, as downloads, and on several websites.

Questions for Analysis

1. Why do you think Hildegard might have kept her visions secret? Why do you think she sought church approval for them?
2. In what ways might Hildegard's vision of Synagogue have been shaped by her own experiences? How does this vision compare with other ideas about the Jews that you have read about in this chapter?

*From *Scivias*, trans. Mother Columba Hart and Jane Bishop, *The Classics of Western Spirituality* (New York/Mahwah: Paulist Press, 1990).

Online Study Center **Improve Your Grade**
Going Beyond Individuals in Society

Monk and Nun in Stocks   Many monasteries and convents were centers of learning and piety, but others were not, and monks and nuns were frequently criticized for immorality, luxurious living, and inattention to their vows. Such criticism was expressed in plays and songs and also in pictures. This painting shows a monk and nun in stocks, heavy wooden frames with holes for restraining the ankles and sometimes the wrists, used as punishment. A person confined in stocks endured great physical discomfort as well as the shame of public disgrace. The painting is most likely not a realistic scene, but rather part of a satirical criticism of monastic life. *(British Library Roy. 10. f. IV. 187)*

Belgium, and French Flanders), they built dikes to hold back the sea, and the reclaimed land was put to the production of cereals. In the eastern parts of Germany—Silesia, Mecklenburg, and Pomerania—they took the lead in draining swamps and cultivating wasteland. As a result of their efforts, the rich, rolling land of French Burgundy was turned into lush vineyards. In northern and central England, the rocky soil and damp downs of Lincolnshire, poorly suited to agriculture, were turned into sheep runs. By the third quarter of the twelfth century, the Cistercians were raising sheep and playing a large role in the production of England's most important crop, wool.

Some monasteries got involved in iron and lead mining. In 1291 the Cistercian abbey of Furness operated at least forty forges. The German abbeys of Königsbronn, Waldsassen, and Saabergen also mined iron in the thirteenth century. The monks entered this industry first to fill their own needs, but in an expanding economy they soon discovered a large market. Iron had hundreds of uses. Nails, hammers, plows, armor, spears, axes, stirrups, horseshoes, and many weapons of war were made from this basic metal. Lead also had a great variety of uses. It could be used for roofing; as an alloy for strengthening silver coinage; for framing pane-glass windows in parish, monastery, and cathedral churches; and even for lavatory drainpipes.

Some monasteries lent their surplus revenues to the local nobility and peasantry. In the twelfth century the abbey of Savigny in Normandy, for example, acted as a banking house, providing loans at interest to noble families of Normandy and Brittany. Although church law opposed usury, or lending at interest, monasteries and convents did so anyway, becoming important providers of credit in the medieval economy.

Despite their many economic activities, monasteries' income did not always meet their expenses. Cluny is a good example. Life at Cluny was lavish and extravagant. The monks dined on rich food and wore habits of the best cloth available. Cluny's abbots and priors traveled with sizable retinues. They worked to make the liturgy ever more magnificent, spending large sums on elaborate vestments and jeweled vessels. Revenue came from the hundreds of monasteries scattered across France, Italy, Spain, and England that Cluny had reformed in the eleventh century. Novices were expected to make gifts of land or cash when they entered Cluny. For reasons of security, knights departing on crusade often placed their estates under Cluny's authority. Still this income was not enough. Cluny had two basic alternatives—cut costs or borrow money—and the abbots chose the latter, leading the monastery into debt. By the early thirteenth century other small and great monasteries were facing comparable financial difficulties.

Mother house: Citeaux

First four daughter houses

Other daughter houses

Present-day boundaries

Main areas of Cistercian commercial production

Cereals

Wine

Wool and cloth

Mining

Horse breeding

Source: Lekai, Louis J. *The Cistercians; Ideals and Reality.* The Kent State University Press (1977).

0 150 300 Km.
0 150 300 Mi.

Mapping the Past

MAP 10.1 Cistercian Expansion The rapid expansion of the Cistercian order in the twelfth century reflects the spiritual piety of the age and its enormous economic vitality. Use the map and the information in your text to answer the following questions: ❶ What economic activities were especially developed by the Cistercians? How did these influence medieval economic development? ❷ The Cistercians originally intended to live far from existing towns and villages and to not be involved in traditional feudal-manorial society. Does this map suggest they were successful in their aims? (To answer this, you may also want to look at the maps in Chapter 11.)

The agricultural recession of the fourteenth century (see pages 371–372) forced the lay nobility to reduce their endowment of monasteries. This development, combined with internal mismanagement, compelled many houses to restrict the number of recruits so that they could live within their incomes. Since the nobility continued to send their children to monasteries, there was no shortage of applicants for the limited number of places. Widespread relaxation in the observance of the Benedictine *Rule* and the weakening of community life, however, meant that the atmosphere in many monasteries resembled that of a comfortable and secure rooming house rather than an austere religious establishment.

Chapter Summary

- *What was life like for the rural common people of medieval Europe?*
- *How did religious practices and attitudes permeate everyday life?*
- *How were the lives of nobles different from the lives of common people?*
- *What roles did the men and women affiliated with religious orders play in medieval society?*

Generalizations about peasant life in the High Middle Ages must always be qualified according to manorial customs, the weather and geography, and the personalities of local lords. Everywhere, however, the performance of agricultural services and the payment of rents preoccupied peasants, with men, women, and children all working the land. Though peasants led hard lives, the reclamation of wastelands and forestlands, migration to frontier territory, or manumission offered means of social mobility. The warmer climate of the High Middle Ages and technological improvements such as water mills and horse-drawn plows increased the available food supply, though the mainstay of the peasant diet was still coarse bread. Death in childbirth of both infant and mother was a common occurrence, though there were some improvements in health care through the opening of hospitals.

Religion provided strong emotional and spiritual solace for the majority of Europeans who were Christians as well as for Muslims and Jews. Within Christianity, the village church was the center of community life, where people attended services, honored the saints, and experienced the sacraments. People also carried out rituals full of religious meaning in their daily lives, and every major life transition—childbirth, weddings, death—was marked by a ceremony that included religious elements. This was true for Muslims and Jews as well as Christians, but the centrality of Christian ceremonies for most people meant that Muslims and Jews were increasingly marked as outsiders, and Christian persecution of Jews increased in the late eleventh century.

Nobles were a tiny fraction of the total population, but they exerted great power over all aspects of life. Aristocratic values and attitudes, often described as chivalry, shaded all aspects of medieval culture. By 1100 the knightly class was united in its ability to fight on horseback, its insistence that each member was descended from a valorous ancestor, its privileges, and its position at the top of the social hierarchy. Noble children were trained for their later roles in life, with boys trained for war and girls for marriage and running estates. Noblemen often devoted considerable time to fighting, and intergenerational squabbles were common. Yet noblemen, and sometimes noblewomen, also had heavy judicial, political, and economic responsibilities.

Monks and nuns exercised a profound influence on medieval society. In their prayers, monks and nuns battled for the Lord, just as the chivalrous knights did on the battlefield. In their chants and rich ceremonials and in their architecture and literary productions, monasteries and convents inspired Christian peoples. In the tenth century, under the leadership of the abbey of Cluny, many monasteries shook off the dominance of local lords and became independent institutions. Cluny's success led people to donate land and goods, and it became wealthier, leading those who sought a more rigorous life to found a new religious order, the Cistercians. Monks and nuns were generally members of the upper classes and spent much of their days in group prayer and other religious activities, while lay brothers and sisters worked the lands owned by the monastery. Monasteries were an important part of the economy of medieval Europe, though sometimes they lived beyond their means, which was also true of nobles and people who lived in Europe's growing towns.

Key Terms

orders	Eucharist
ancillae	conversos
villeins	purgatory
manumission	indulgences
nuclear family	nobility
stem/complex household	chivalry
bailiffs	tournament
jurors	joust
allodial land	primogeniture
open-field system	religious orders
oblates	abbess/prioress
saints	abbot/prior
relics	lay brothers/ lay sisters
sacraments	

Suggested Reading

Bennett, Judith M. *A Medieval Life: Cecelia Penifader of Brigstock, c. 1297–1344.* 1998. An excellent brief introduction to all aspects of village life from the perspective of one woman; designed for students.

Brooke, Rosalind, and Christopher Brooke. *Popular Religion in the Middle Ages.* 1984. A readable synthesis of material on the beliefs and practices of ordinary Christians.

Duby, Georges. *The Chivalrous Society.* Trans. C. Postan. 1977. A classic study of the three orders as a model of medieval society.

Glick, Leonard B. *Abraham's Heirs: Jews and Christians in Medieval Europe.* 1999. Provides information on many aspects of Jewish life and Jewish-Christian relations.

Hanawalt, Barbara A. *The Ties That Bound: Peasant Families in Medieval England.* 1986. A very readable study of gender and family relations in the countryside.

Herlihy, David. *Medieval Households.* 1985. Treats marriage patterns, family size, sexual relations, and emotional life.

Kaeuper, Richard W. *Chivalry and Violence in Medieval Europe.* 2006. Examines the role chivalry played in promoting violent disorder.

Karras, Ruth M. *From Boys to Men: Formations of Masculinity in Late Medieval Europe.* 2002. Explores the way boys of different social groups were trained in what it meant to be a man; designed for students.

Kealey, Edward J. *Medieval Medicus: A Social History of Anglo-Norman Medicine.* 1981. An excellent analysis of all aspects of medical care.

Keen, Maurice. *Chivalry.* 1984. The classic study of chivalry as an ideal.

Lawrence, C. H. *Medieval Monasticism: Forms of Religious Life in Western Europe in the Middle Ages.* 1988. Provides a solid introduction to monastic life as it was practiced.

Newman, Barbara. *Voice of the Living Light: Hildegard of Bingen and Her World.* 1998. A book designed for general readers that places the medieval mystic within her social, intellectual, and political contexts.

Rubin, Miri. *Gentile Tales: The Narrative Assault on Late Medieval Jews.* 2004. Explores the way that stories that were spread about Jews contributed to violence against them.

Shahar, Shulamit. *The Fourth Estate: A History of Women in the Middle Ages.* 2d ed. 2003. Analyzes attitudes toward women and provides information on the lives of women in many situations, including nuns, peasants, noblewomen, and townswomen, in western Europe between the twelfth and the fifteenth centuries.

Webb, Diana. *Medieval European Pilgrimage, c. 700–c. 1500.* 2002. Examines the role of pilgrimage in Christianity.

Notes

1. Honorius of Autun, "Elucidarium sive Dialogus de Summa Totius Christianae Theologiae," in *Patrologia Latina,* ed. J. P. Migne (Paris: Garnier Brothers, 1854), vol. 172, col. 1149.
2. Glanvill, "De Legibus Angliae," bk. 5, chap. 5, in *Social Life in Britain from the Conquest to the Reformation,* ed. G. G. Coulton (London: Cambridge University Press, 1956), pp. 338–339.
3. On this quantity and medieval measurements, see D. Knowles, "The Measures of Monastic Beverages," in *The Monastic Order in England* (Cambridge: Cambridge University Press, 1962), p. 717.
4. Ibid., p. 149.
5. S. R. Scargill-Bird, ed., *Custumals of Battle Abbey in the Reigns of Edward I and Edward II* (London: Camden Society, 1887), pp. 213–219.
6. Ibid., pp. 214, 223.
7. Ibid., pp. 238–239.
8. Ibid., pp. 297, 299, and Conclusion.
9. A. Vauchez, *The Laity in the Middle Ages: Religious Beliefs and Devotional Practices,* ed. D. E. Bornstein, trans. M. J. Schneider (Notre Dame, Ind.: University of Notre Dame Press, 1993), pp. 99–102.
10. Translated and quoted in Susan C. Karant-Nunn, *The Reformation of Ritual: An Interpretation of Early Modern Germany* (London: Routledge, 1997), p. 77.
11. J. F. Benton, ed. and trans., *Self and Society in Medieval France: The Memoirs of Abbot Guibert of Nogent* (New York: Harper & Row, 1970), p. 46.
12. Honorius of Autun, "Elucidarium sive Dialogus," vol. 172, col. 1148.
13. Quoted in P. Riche, *Daily Life in the World of Charlemagne,* trans. JoAnn McNamara (Philadelphia: University of Pennsylvania Press, 1978), p. 86.
14. M. Chibnall, ed. and trans., *The Ecclesiastical History of Ordericus Vitalis* (Oxford: Oxford University Press, 1972), 2.xiii.

The Pilgrim's Guide to Santiago de Compostela

Making pilgrimages to the shrines of holy persons is a common practice in many religions. A pilgrimage to Mecca, for example, is obligatory for all Muslims (see page 225). Many Christian shrines contained a body understood to be that of a saint or objects that had been in physical contact with the saint; thus believers perceived shrines as places where Heaven and earth met. A visit to a shrine and veneration of the saint's relics, Christians believed, would lead to the saint's intercession with God. After Jerusalem and Rome, the shrine of Saint James (Sant'Iago in Spanish) at Compostela in the Iberian Peninsula became the most famous in the Christian world. Santiago de Compostela was situated in the kingdom of Navarre, a small state in the Pyrenees Mountains between (French) Gascony and (Spanish) Léon.

The apostle James, a fisherman like his brother, the apostle John (Matthew 4:21), is said to have carried Christianity to Spain, then returned to Palestine where he was beheaded, the first apostle martyred (Acts 12:1–2). Somehow James's bones were miraculously taken back to Compostela, where they were later discovered, and a series of churches were built on the site. In 1075 Alfonso VI of Castile, one of the most important leaders of the reconquista, began construction of a huge shrine-cathedral at the site of his tomb. In the 1300s James himself was linked to the reconquista, as church and state officials pushed the legend that James had begun the expulsion of Muslims from Spain. The fact that the Prophet Muhammad, the founder of Islam, lived six centuries after James did not bother those telling the story, and images of "St. James the Moor-slayer" became common.

Pilgrims streamed to the site from all over Europe, particularly as roads were improved and hostels and inns opened along the routes. Once at the shrine, pilgrims were expected to make contributions as large as their means allowed, lest the saint be offended and retaliate with some sort of affliction.

Pilgrims' donations financed the superb Romanesque sculpture at Santiago. In the twelfth century an unknown French author gathered many of the pilgrims' experiences, along with accounts of the life and martyrdom of St. James and the miracles attributed to him after his death. He put these together in a sort of guidebook, which was frequently recopied for interested readers. This Pilgrim's Guide *describes the scene at the cathedral itself and also details the characteristics of people one would meet on the way.*

The church, however, was begun in the year 1116 of the Spanish era [A.D. 1078]. . . .

From the time when it was begun up to the present day, this church is renewed by the light of the miracles of the blessed James. In it, indeed, health is given to the sick, sight restored to the blind, the tongue of the mute is loosened, hearing is given to the deaf, soundness of limb is granted to cripples, the possessed are delivered, and what is more, the prayers of the faithful are heard, their vows are accepted, the bonds of sin are broken, heaven is opened to those who knock, consolation is given to the grieving, and all the people of foreign nations, flocking from all parts of the world, come together here in crowds bearing with them gifts of praise to the Lord. . . .

After this valley is found the land of Navarre, which abounds in bread and wine, milk and cattle. The Navarrese and Basques are held to be exactly alike in their food, their clothing and their language, but the Basques are held to be of whiter complexion than the Navarrese. The Navarrese wear short black garments extending just down to the knee, like the Scots, and they wear sandals which they call *lavarcas* made of raw hide with the hair on and are bound around the foot with thongs, covering only the soles of the feet and leaving the upper foot bare. In truth, they wear black woollen hooded and fringed capes, reaching

Pilgrim's badge from Santiago de Compostela. Enterprising smiths began making metal badges for pilgrims to buy as proof of their journey and evidence of their piety. The scallop shell became particularly associated with Saint James and eventually with pilgrimages in general. Pilgrims who had visited many shrines would clink from the badges worn on their hats or capes, sometimes becoming objects of satire just as tourists laden with souvenirs are today. *(Institut Amatller d'Art Hispanic)*

Pilgrims' routes: monasteries in Cluny, Vézelay, Saint-Gilles, and Moissac served as inns for pilgrims.

to their elbows, which they call *saias*. These people, in truth, are repulsively dressed, and they eat and drink repulsively. For in fact all those who dwell in the household of a Navarrese, servant as well as master, maid as well as mistress, are accustomed to eat all their food mixed together from one pot, not with spoons but with their own hands, and they drink with one cup. If you saw them eat you would think them dogs or pigs. If you heard them speak, you would be reminded of the barking of dogs. For their speech is utterly barbarous. . . .

This is a barbarous race unlike all other races in customs and in character, full of malice, swarthy in color, evil of face, depraved, perverse, perfidious, empty of faith and corrupt, libidinous, drunken, experienced in all violence, ferocious and wild, dishonest and reprobate, impious and harsh, cruel and contentious, unversed in anything good, well-trained in all vices and iniquities, like the Geats and Saracens in malice. . . .

However, they are considered good on the battlefield, bad at assaulting fortresses, regular in giving tithes, accustomed to making offerings for altars. For, each day, when the Navarrese goes to church, he makes God an offering of bread or wine or wheat or some other substance. . . .

Then comes Galicia . . . this is wooded and has rivers and is well-provided with meadows and excellent orchards, with equally good fruits and very clear springs; there are few cities, towns or cornfields. It is short of wheaten bread and wine, bountiful in rye bread and cider, well-stocked with cattle and horses, milk and honey, ocean fish both gigantic and small, and wealthy in gold, silver, fabrics, and furs of forest animals and other riches, as well as Saracen treasures. The Galicians, in truth, more than all the other uncultivated Spanish peoples, are those who most closely resemble our French race by their manners, but they are alleged to be irascible and very litigious. . . .

Questions for Analysis

1. What sorts of miracles does the author describe as happening at the church?

2. How would you evaluate the author's opinion of the people of Navarre? of Galicia? How do these people compare with his own countrymen, the French?

3. How would you compare his description of the miracles with the descriptions of the people? Which descriptions seem to be more vivid and detailed? Why?

4. Pilgrimages were in many ways the precursors of modern tourism. How would you compare the two in terms of economic effects and the expectations of the travelers?

Source: The Pilgrim's Guide to Santiago de Compostela, critical edition and annotated translation by Paula Gerson, Jeanne Krochalis, Annie Shaver-Crandell, and Alison Stones. Copyright © 1997. Reprinted by permission of the authors. Data for map from Jonathan Sumption, *Pilgrimage: An Image of Medieval Religion* (Totowa, N.J.: Rowman and Littlefield, 1975).

329

This manuscript illumination shows a street scene of a medieval town, with a barber, cloth merchants, and an apothecary all offering their wares and services on the ground floor of their household-workshops. *(Snark/Art Resource, NY)*

THE CREATIVITY AND CHALLENGES OF MEDIEVAL CITIES

chapter preview

Towns and Economic Revival
• *How did medieval cities originate, and what impact did they have on the economy and on culture?*

Medieval Universities
• *How did universities evolve, and what needs of medieval society did they serve?*

Vernacular Culture
• *What do oral traditions and vernacular literature reveal about medieval culture?*

Architecture and Art
• *How did cathedrals express the ideals, attitudes, and interests of medieval people?*

Cities and the Church
• *Why did towns become the center of religious heresy, and what was the church's response?*

The High Middle Ages witnessed some of the most remarkable achievements in the entire history of Western society. Europeans displayed tremendous creativity and vitality in many facets of culture. Relative security and an increasing food supply allowed for the growth and development of towns and a revival of long-distance trade. The university, a new—and very long-lasting—type of educational institution came into being, providing advanced training in theology, medicine, and law. Traditions and values were spread orally through stories and songs, some of which were written down as part of the development of vernacular literature. Gothic cathedrals manifested medieval people's deep Christian faith and their pride in their own cities, though the cities were also home to heretical movements that challenged church power.

Towns and Economic Revival

The rise of towns and the growth of a new business and commercial class was a central part of Europe's recovery after the disorders of the tenth century. The growth of towns was made possible by some of the changes we have already traced: a rise in population; increased agricultural output, which provided an adequate food supply for new town dwellers; and a minimum of peace and political stability, which allowed merchants to transport and sell goods. The development of towns was to lay the foundations for Europe's transformation, centuries later, from a rural agricultural society into an urban industrial society—a change with global implications. In their backgrounds and abilities, townspeople represented diversity and change. Their occupations and their preoccupations were different from those of the feudal nobility and the laboring peasantry.

• *How did medieval cities originate, and what impact did they have on the economy and on culture?*

Online Study Center

This icon will direct you to interactive activities and study materials on the website **college.hmco.com/pic/mckaywest9e**

The Rise of Towns

Early medieval society was agricultural and rural. The emergence of a new class that was neither of these constituted a social revolution. Most of the members of the new class—artisans and merchants—came from the peasantry. The landless younger sons of large families were driven away by land shortage. Some were forced by war and famine to seek new possibilities. As in central Europe and Spain after the reconquista (see page 266), others were immigrants colonizing newly conquered lands. And some were unusually enterprising and adventurous, curious, and willing to take a chance.

Medieval towns began in many different ways. Some were fortifications erected during the ninth-century Viking invasions. Such towns were at first places of defense into which farmers from the surrounding countryside moved when their area was attacked. Later, merchants were attracted to the fortifications because they had something to sell and wanted to be where the customers were. They settled just outside the walls, in the *faubourgs* or *suburbs*—both of which mean "outside" or "in the shelter of the walls." Other towns grew up around great cathedrals and monasteries. Cathedrals such as Notre Dame in Paris conducted schools that drew students from far and wide. Consequently, traders and merchants settled near religious establishments to cater to the residents' economic needs. Concentrations of people accumulated, and towns came into being.

Few towns of the tenth and eleventh centuries were "new" in the sense that American towns and cities, carved out of forest and wilderness, were new in the seventeenth and eighteenth centuries. Some medieval towns that had become flourishing centers of trade by the mid-twelfth century had originally been Roman army camps. York in northern England, Bordeaux in west-central France, and Cologne in west-central Germany are good examples of ancient towns that underwent revitalization in the eleventh century. Some Italian seaport cities, such as Venice, Pisa, and Genoa, had been centers of shipping and commerce in earlier times; trade with Constantinople and the East had never stopped entirely. The restoration of order and political stability promoted rebirth and new development.

Whether evolving from a newly fortified place or an old Roman army camp, from a cathedral site, a river junction, or a place where several overland routes met, medieval towns had a few common characteristics. Walls

Carcassonne This town in Languedoc (southern France) originated in pre-Roman times. Its thick double walls provide an excellent example of the fortified medieval town. *(Guido Alberto Rossi/TIPS Images)*

enclosed the town. (The terms *burgher* and *bourgeois* derive from the Old English and Old German words *burg, burgh, borg,* and *borough* for "a walled or fortified place." Thus a burgher or bourgeois was originally a person who lived or worked inside the walls.) The town had a marketplace. It often had a mint for the coining of money and a court to settle disputes.

In each town, many people inhabited a small, cramped area. As population increased, towns rebuilt their walls, expanding the living space to accommodate growing numbers. Through an archaeological investigation of the amount of land gradually enclosed by walls, historians have extrapolated rough estimates of medieval towns' populations. For example, the walled area of the German city of Cologne equaled 100 hectares in the tenth century (1 hectare = 2.471 acres), about 320 hectares in the twelfth, and 397 hectares in the fourteenth century. In the late twelfth century Cologne's population was at least 32,000; in the mid-fourteenth century it was perhaps 40,000. The concentration of the textile industry in the Low Countries brought into being the most populous cluster of cities in western Europe: Ghent with about 56,000 people, Bruges with 27,000, Tournai and Brussels with perhaps 20,000 each. Venice, Florence, and Paris, each with about 110,000 people, and Milan with possibly 200,000 led all Europe in population (see Map 11.1).

Town Liberties and Merchant Guilds

In the words of the Greek poet Alcaeus, "Not houses finely roofed or well built walls, nor canals or dockyards make a city, but men able to use their opportunity."[1] People and opportunity is fundamentally what medieval towns meant—concentrations of people and varieties of chances. No matter where groups of traders congregated, they settled on someone's land and had to secure permission to live and trade from king or count, abbot or bishop. Aristocratic nobles, bishops, abbesses, and abbots soon realized that profits and benefits flowed to them and their territories from the markets set up on their land.

The history of towns in the eleventh through thirteenth centuries consists largely of merchants' efforts to acquire liberties. In the Middle Ages *liberties* meant special privileges. **Town liberties** included the privilege of living and trading on the lord's land. The most important privilege a medieval townsperson could gain was personal freedom. It gradually developed that an individual who lived in a town for a year and a day, and was accepted by the townspeople, was free of servile obligations and status. More than anything else, perhaps, the liberty

Chronology

1100–1200	Merchant guilds founded in many cities
1143	Founding of Lübeck, first city in the Hanseatic League
1180–1270	Height of construction of cathedrals in France
1200–1300	Craft guilds founded in many cities
ca 1200	Founding of first universities
1216	Papal recognition of Dominican order
1221	Papal recognition of Franciscan order
1225–1274	Life of Thomas Aquinas; *Summa Theologica*
1233	Papacy creates new ecclesiastical court, the Inquisition
1302	Pope Boniface VIII declares all Christians subject to the pope in *Unam Sanctam*

of personal freedom that came with residence in a town contributed to the emancipation of the serfs in the High Middle Ages. Liberty meant citizenship, and citizenship in a town implied the right to buy and sell goods there. Unlike foreigners and outsiders, the full citizen did not have to pay taxes and tolls in the market. Obviously, this increased profits.

In the twelfth and thirteenth centuries towns slowly gained legal and political rights. Since the tenth century some English boroughs had held courts with jurisdiction over members of the town in civil and criminal matters. In the twelfth century such English towns as London and Norwich developed courts that applied a special kind of law called "law merchant." It dealt with commercial transactions, debt, bankruptcy, proof of sales, and contracts. Gradually towns across Europe acquired the right to hold municipal courts that alone could judge members of the town. In effect, this right gave them judicial independence.

Merchants used their power and wealth to control urban life as well as to win independence from feudal lords. They joined together to form a **merchant guild** that prohibited nonmembers from trading in the town, and they often made up the earliest town government, serving as mayors and members of the city council, so that a town's economic policies were determined by its merchants' self-interest.

- ● Over 80,000
- ◉ Over 40,000
- • Over 20,000
- ○ Over 10,000
- ◦ Marketing center, under 10,000
- ── Boundary of the Holy Roman Empire

0   150   300 Km.
0   150   300 Mi.

Mapping the Past

MAP 11.1 Population of European Urban Areas, ca Late Thirteenth Century The development of towns and the reinvigoration of trade were directly related in medieval Europe. Using all three maps in this chapter and the information in your text, answer the following questions: ❶ What part of Europe had the highest density of towns? Why? ❷ Which towns were the largest and most important centers of long-distance trade? ❸ What role did textile and other sorts of manufacturing play in the growth of towns? ❹ Does the development of towns seem more closely related to that of universities, monastery schools, or cathedral schools? Why?

By the late eleventh century, especially in the towns of the Low Countries and northern Italy, the leaders of the merchant guilds were rich and powerful. They constituted an oligarchy in their towns, controlling economic life and bargaining with kings and lords for political independence. Full rights of self-government included the right to hold a town court, the right to select the mayor and other municipal officials, and the right to tax residents.

A charter that King Henry II of England granted to the merchants of Lincoln around 1157 nicely illustrates the town's rights. The quoted passages clearly suggest that the merchant guild had been the governing body in the city for almost a century and that anyone who lived in Lincoln for a year and a day was considered free:

Henry, by the grace of God, etc.... Know that I have granted to my citizens of Lincoln all their liberties and cus-

toms and laws which they had in the time of Edward [King Edward the Confessor] and William and Henry, kings of England. And I have granted them their gild-merchant, comprising men of the city and other merchants of the shire, as well and freely as they had it in the time of our aforesaid predecessors. . . . And all the men who live within the four divisions of the city and attend the market, shall stand in relation to gelds [taxes] and customs and the assizes [ordinances or laws] of the city as well as ever they stood in the time of Edward, William and Henry, kings of England. I also confirm to them that if anyone has lived in Lincoln for a year and a day without dispute from any claimant, and has paid the city taxes, and if the citizens can show by the laws and customs of the city that the claimant has remained in England during that period and has made no claim, then let the defendant remain in peace in my city of Lincoln as my citizen, without [having to defend his] right.[2]

Kings and lords were reluctant to grant towns self-government, fearing loss of authority and revenue if they gave the merchant guilds full independence. When burghers bargained for a town's political independence, however, they offered sizable amounts of ready cash and sometimes promised payments for years to come. Consequently, feudal lords ultimately agreed to self-government.

Craft Guilds

Though the initial impetus in the establishment of a town generally came from trade and commerce, towns quickly became centers of production as well. Peasants left their villages—either with their lord's approval or without it—and moved to towns, providing both workers and mouths to feed. Some of them began to specialize in certain types of food and clothing production: some made and sold bread, and others bought cloth and sewed it into clothing. Others purchased and butchered cattle, and then sold the meat to people who made small meat pies and the leather to those who made shoes or bags. Merchants often imported raw materials such as iron or silver, which they sold to people who made armaments and tableware. Wealthy merchants then bought these products for their own use, or they exported the finished products to other areas; certain cities became known for their fine fabrics, their reliable arms and armor, or their elegant gold and silver work.

Like merchants, producers recognized that organizing would bring benefits, and beginning in the twelfth century in many cities they developed **craft guilds** that regulated most aspects of production. They set quality standards for their particular product, and they regulated the size of workshops, the training period, and the conduct of members. In most cities individual guilds, such as those of shoemakers or blacksmiths, achieved a monopoly in the production of one particular product, forbidding nonmembers to work. The craft guild then chose some of its members to act as inspectors and set up a court to hear disputes between members, though the city court remained the final arbiter, particularly in cases involving conflict between merchants and artisans or between members of craft guilds and those who were not members.

Each guild set the pattern by which members were trained. A person who wanted to become a shoemaker, for instance, spent four to seven years as an apprentice, then at least that long as a journeyman, working in the shop of a master dyer, after which the person could theoretically make a "masterpiece." If the masterpiece—in the case of a shoemaker, of course, the masterpiece was a pair of shoes—was approved by the other master shoemakers and if they thought the market in their town was large enough to support another shoemaker, the person could then become a master and start a shop. Though the time required as an apprentice and as a journeyman varied slightly from guild to guild, all guilds followed this same three-stage process. The apprentices and journeymen generally lived with the master and his family and were often forbidden to marry. Conversely, many guilds required that masters be married, as they realized that a wife was absolutely essential to the running of the shop and household and also felt that married men were likely to be more stable and dependable. Guilds limited the amount of raw materials each master could have and the size of the workshop, thus assuring each master that his household-workshop would be able to support itself.

The master's wife assisted in running the shop, often selling the goods her husband had produced. Their children, both male and female, also worked alongside the apprentices and journeymen. The sons were sometimes formally apprenticed, but the daughters were generally not because many guilds limited formal membership to males. Most guilds did allow a master's widow to continue operating a shop for a set period of time after her husband's death, for they recognized that she had the necessary skills and experience. Such widows paid all guild dues, but they were not considered full members and could not vote or hold office in the guilds. The fact that women were not formally guild members did not mean that they did not work in guild shops, however, for alongside the master's wife and daughters female domestic servants often performed the lesser-skilled tasks. In addition, there were a few all-female guilds in several

Spanish Apothecary   Town life meant variety—of peoples and products. Within the town walls, a Spanish pharmacist, seated outside his shop, describes the merits of his goods to a crowd of Christians and Muslims. *(From the* Cantigas *of Alfonso X, ca 1283. El Escorial/Laurie Platt Winfrey, Inc.)*

European cities, particularly in Cologne and Paris, in which girls were formally apprenticed in the same way boys were in regular craft guilds.

Both craft and merchant guilds were not only economic organizations, but also systems of social support. Though they were harsh against outsiders, they were protective and supportive of their members. They took care of elderly masters who could no longer work, and they often supported masters' widows and orphans. They maintained an altar at a city church and provided for the funerals of members and baptisms of their children. Guild members marched together in city parades and re-

inforced their feelings of solidarity with one another by special ceremonies and distinctive dress. Merchant guilds in some parts of Europe, such as the Hansa cities of Hamburg, Lübeck, and Bremen, had special buildings for celebrations and ceremonies.

City Life

Walls surrounded almost all medieval towns and cities. Gates pierced the walls, and visitors waited at the gates to gain entrance to the town. When the gates were opened early in the morning, guards inspected the quantity and quality of the goods brought in and collected the customary taxes. Part of the taxes went to the lord on whose land the town stood, and part to the town council for civic purposes. Constant repair of the walls was usually the town's greatest expense. Many of these walls have been demolished in more recent times to make way for further urban expansion, though some of them still stand. For medieval people, walled cities stood as visible markers of the growing wealth and prominence of merchants and other townspeople within a political and social structure still dominated by the hereditary nobility.

Peasants coming from the countryside and merchants traveling from afar set up their carts as stalls just inside the gates of city walls. The result was that the road nearest the gate was the widest thoroughfare. It was the ideal place for a market because everyone coming in or going out used it. Most streets in a medieval town were marketplaces as much as passages for transit. At the city's main marketplace, poor people selling soap, candles, wooden dishes, and similar cheap products stood next to farmers from the surrounding countryside with eggs, chickens, or vegetables, people selling firewood or mushrooms they had gathered, and pawnbrokers selling used clothing and household goods. Because there was no way to preserve food easily, people—usually female family members or servants—had to shop every day, and the market was where they met their neighbors, exchanged information, and talked over recent events.

In some respects the entire city was a marketplace. The place where a product was made and sold was also typically the merchant's residence. Usually the ground floor was the scene of production. A window or door opened onto the street and displayed the finished product so passersby could look in and see the goods being produced. The merchant's family lived above the business on the second or third floor. As the business and the family expanded, the merchant built additional stories on top of the house.

Second and third stories were built jutting out over the ground floor and thus over the street. Since the streets were narrow to begin with, houses lacked fresh air and light. Initially, houses were made of wood and thatched with straw. Fire was a constant danger; because houses were built so close to one another, fires spread rapidly. Municipal governments consequently urged construction in stone or brick.

Most medieval cities developed with little town planning. As the population increased, space became more and more limited. Air and water pollution presented serious problems. Many families raised pigs for household consumption in sties next to the house. Horses and oxen, the chief means of transportation and power, dropped tons of dung on the streets every year. It was universal practice in the early towns to dump household waste, both animal and human, into the road in front of one's house. The stench must have been abominable. In 1298 the burgesses of the town of Boutham in Yorkshire, England, received the following order (one long, vivid sentence):

To the bailiffs of the abbot of St. Mary's York, at Boutham. Whereas it is sufficiently evident that the pavement of the said town of Boutham is so very greatly broken up . . . , and in addition the air is so corrupted and infected by the pigsties situated in the king's highways and in the lanes of that town and by the swine feeding and frequently wandering about . . . and by dung and dunghills and many other foul things placed in the streets and lanes, that great repugnance overtakes the king's ministers staying in that town and also others there dwelling and passing through, the advantage of more wholesome air is impeded, the state of men is grievously injured, and other unbearable inconveniences . . . , to the nuisance of the king's ministers aforesaid and of others there dwelling . . . : the king, being unwilling longer to tolerate such great and unbearable defects there, orders the bailiffs to cause the pavement to be suitably repaired within their liberty before All Saints next, and to cause the pigsties, aforesaid streets and lanes to be cleansed from all dung . . . and to cause them to be kept thus cleansed hereafter.[3]

A great deal of traffic passed through Boutham in 1298 because of the movement of English troops to battlefronts in Scotland. Conditions there were probably not typical. Still, this document suggests that space, air pollution, and sanitation problems bedeviled urban people in medieval times, as they do today.

People of all sorts, from beggars to fabulously wealthy merchants, regularly rubbed shoulders in the narrow streets and alleys of crowded medieval cities. This interaction did not mean that people were unaware of social differences, however, for clothing was a clear marker of social standing and sometimes of occupation. Monks, nuns, and friars wore black, white, or grey woolen clothing that marked them as members of a particular religious order, while priests and bishops wore layers of specialized clothing, especially when they were officiating at religious services. Military men and servants who lived in noble households wore dress with distinctive colors known as **livery.** Wealthier urban residents wore bright colors, imported silk or fine woolen fabrics, and fancy headgear, while poorer ones wore darker clothing made of rough linen or linen and wool blends. When universities developed in European cities, students wore clothing and headgear that marked their status. University graduates—lawyers, physicians, and university professors—often wore dark robes, trimmed with fur if they could afford it; the dark robes with long hanging sleeves worn by those obtaining master's degrees and the robes with bands of velvet worn by those obtaining doctoral degrees in contemporary academic ceremonies are descended from this medieval dress.

In the later Middle Ages many cities attempted to make clothing distinctions a matter of law as well as of habit. They passed **sumptuary laws** that regulated the value of clothing and jewelry that people of different social groups could wear; only members of high social groups could wear velvet, satin, pearls, or fur, for example, or have clothing embroidered with gold thread or dyed in colors that were especially expensive to produce, such as the purple dye that came from mollusk shells. Along with enforcing social differences, sumptuary laws also attempted to impose moral standards by prohibiting plunging necklines on women or doublets that were too short on men and to protect local industries by restricting the use of imported fabrics or other materials. Some of these laws marked certain individuals as members of groups not fully acceptable in urban society—prostitutes might be required to wear red or yellow bands on their clothes that were supposed to represent the flames of Hell, and Jews to wear yellow circles or stars to distinguish them from their Christian neighbors. (Many Jewish communities also developed their own sumptuary laws prohibiting extravagant or ostentatious dress.) In some cities, sumptuary laws were expanded to include restrictions on expenditures for parties and family celebrations, again set by social class. Weddings for members of the nobility or the urban elite could include imported wine, fancy food, musicians, and hundreds of guests, while those for the children of artisans could serve only local beer to several dozen guests.

Online Study Center **Improve Your Grade**
Primary Source: A Sumptuary Law: Restrictions on Dress

Servants and the Poor

Many urban households hired domestic servants, with a less wealthy household employing one woman who assisted in all aspects of running the household and a wealthier one employing a large staff of male and female servants with specific duties. When there was only one servant, she generally lived and ate with the family, for there was rarely enough space for separate quarters. Even

in wealthier households that had many rooms, servants were rarely separated from their employers the way they would be in the nineteenth century, but instead lived on intimate terms with them. In Italian cities, household servants included slaves, usually young women brought in from areas outside of western Christianity, such as the Balkans. (Like Islam, Christianity favored slaves who were not believers.)

Along with permanent servants, many households hired additional workers to do specific tasks—laundering clothing and household linens, caring for children or invalids, repairing houses and walls, and carrying messages or packages around the city or the surrounding countryside. In contrast to rural peasants, who raised most of their own food, urban workers bought all their food, so they felt any increase in the price of ale or bread immediately. Their wages were generally low, and children from such families sought work at very young ages.

In cities with extensive cloth production, such as Florence or the towns of Flanders, the urban poor included workers who were hired for their labor only by cloth merchants. Such workers did not own the raw materials or the finished product the way guild masters did, but were paid by the piece for the work they did. Producing cloth was a multistage process: sheep were sheared and the wool was sorted and washed; the wool was carded and spun into thread; thread was prepared and then woven into cloth; cloth was fulled (see page 301), dyed, cleaned, stretched, and brushed. If prices dipped, merchants simply did not pay workers, who were left with thread or unfinished cloth that they technically did not own and who had no wages with which to buy food.

The possibilities for legitimate employment were often very limited, and illegal activities offered another way for people to support themselves. They stole merchandise from houses, wagons, and storage facilities, fencing it to local pawnbrokers or taking it to the next town to sell. They stole goods or money directly from people, cutting the strings of their bags or purses. They sold sex for money—what later came to be called prostitution—standing on street corners or moving into houses that by the fifteenth century became official city brothels (see page 394). They made and sold mixtures of herbs and drugs offering to heal all sorts of ailments, perhaps combining this with a puppet show, trained animals, magic tricks, or music to draw customers. Or they did all these things, and also worked as laundresses, day laborers, porters, peddlers, or street vendors when they could. They might also combine these activities with begging, for cities drew in those who were physically incapable of working but whose families could not care for or support them, including orphans, blind people, and the elderly.

The Revival of Long-Distance Trade

The growth of towns went hand in hand with a remarkable revival of trade as artisans and craftsmen manufactured goods for local and foreign consumption (see Map 11.2). Most trade centered in towns and was controlled by professional traders. Long-distance trade was risky and required large investments of capital. Shipwrecks were common. Pirates infested the sea-lanes, and robbers and thieves roamed virtually all of the land routes. Since the risks were so great, merchants preferred to share them. A group of people would thus pool their capital to finance an expedition to a distant place. When the ship or caravan returned and the goods brought back were sold, the investors would share the profits. If disaster struck the caravan, an investor's loss was limited to the amount of that individual's investment.

What goods were exchanged? What towns took the lead in medieval "international" trade? In the late eleventh century the Italian cities, especially Venice, led the West in trade in general and completely dominated trade with the East. Ships carried salt from the Venetian lagoon, pepper and other spices from North Africa, and silks and purple textiles from the East to northern and western Europe. In the thirteenth century Venetian caravans brought slaves from the Crimea and Chinese silks from Mongolia to the West. Lombard and Tuscan merchants exchanged those goods at the town markets and regional fairs of France, Flanders, and England. (Fairs were periodic gatherings that attracted buyers, sellers, and goods from all over Europe.) The towns of Bruges, Ghent, and Ypres in Flanders built up a vast industry in the manufacture of cloth. Italian merchants exchanged their products for Flemish tapestries, fine broadcloth, and various other textiles.

Two circumstances help explain the lead Venice and the Flemish towns gained in long-distance trade. Both enjoyed a high degree of peace and political stability. Geographical factors were equally, if not more, important. Venice was ideally located at the northwestern end of the Adriatic Sea, with easy access to the transalpine land routes as well as the Adriatic and Mediterranean sea-lanes. The markets of North Africa, Byzantium, and Russia and the great fairs of Ghent in Flanders and Champagne in France provided commercial opportunities that Venice quickly seized. The geographical situation of Flanders also offered unusual possibilities: just across the Channel from England, Flanders had easy ac-

cess to English wool. Indeed, Flanders and England developed a very close economic relationship.

Sheep had been raised for their wool in England since Roman times. Beginning in the early twelfth century, but especially after the arrival of Cistercian monks around 1130, the size of the English flocks doubled and then tripled. Scholars have estimated that, by the end of the twelfth century, roughly 6 million sheep grazed on the English moors and downs. They produced fifty thousand sacks of wool a year.[4] Originally, a "sack" of wool was the burden one packhorse could carry, an amount eventually fixed at 364 pounds; fifty thousand sacks, then, represented huge production.

Wool was the cornerstone of the English medieval economy. Population growth in the twelfth century and the success of the Flemish and Italian textile industries created foreign demand for English wool. The production of English wool stimulated Flemish manufacturing, and the expansion of the Flemish cloth industry in turn spurred the production of English wool. The availability of raw wool also encouraged the development of domestic cloth manufacture in England. The towns of Lincoln, York, Leicester, Northampton, Winchester, and Exeter became important cloth-producing towns. The port cities of London, Hull, Boston, and Bristol thrived on the wool trade. In the thirteenth century commercial families in these towns grew fabulously rich.

Business Procedures

From the late eleventh through the thirteenth centuries, a steadily expanding volume of international trade was a sign of the great economic surge, but it was not the only one. Beginning in the 1160s the opening of new silver mines in Germany, Bohemia, northern Italy, northern France, and western England led to the minting and circulation of vast quantities of silver coins. The widespread use of cash brought about an enormous quantitative change in the volume of international trade. Demand for sugar (to replace honey), pepper, cloves, and Asian spices to season a bland diet; for fine wines from the Rhineland, Burgundy, and Bordeaux; for luxury woolens from Flanders and Tuscany; for furs from Ireland and Russia; for brocades and tapestries from Flanders and silks from Constantinople and even China; for household furnishings such as silver plate—not to mention the desire for products associated with a military aristocracy such as swords and armor—surged markedly.

Business procedures changed radically. The individual traveling merchant who alone handled virtually all aspects of exchange evolved into an operation involving

MAP 11.2 Trade and Manufacturing in Medieval Europe   Note the overland and ocean lines of trade and the sources of silver, iron, copper, lead, paper, wool, carpets and rugs, and slaves.

Online Study Center   **Improve Your Grade** Interactive Map: Trade and Manufacturing in Medieval Europe

Legend (Map key):
- Textile and manufacturing areas
- Northern sea routes
- Venetian sea routes
- Genoese sea routes
- Overland routes

Seas and regions: ATLANTIC OCEAN, North Sea, Baltic Sea, Mediterranean Sea, Black Sea, Adriatic Sea, Aegean Sea, Sea of Azov, Bay of Biscay, Ireland, Gotland, Corsica, Sardinia, Sicily, Balearic Is., Crete, Cyprus, Rhodes

Place names and goods:
Bergen (Fish, Pitch), Oslo, Stockholm (Copper), Furs, Honey, Flax, Novgorod, Flax, Hemp, Wax, Reval, Riga, Flax, Pitch, Fish, Kiev, Rostov, Fish, Slave market, Slaves, Caffa, Slave market, Sinope, Trebizond, Sivas, Black Sea

Copenhagen, Königsberg, Warsaw, Cracow, Silver, Iron, Pest, Wheat, Skins+hides, Belgrade, Horses, Silver, Danzig, Grain, Breslau, Tar, Pitch, Horses

Edinburgh, Carlisle, York, Wool, Durham, Chester, Bristol, Lead, Tin, Iron, Southampton, Calais, London, Iron, Bruges, Brussels, Amsterdam, Bremen, Hamburg, Lübeck, Fish, Grain, Flax, Hemp, Fish

Frankfurt, Magdeburg, Leipzig, Salt, Nuremberg, Silver, Paper, Augsburg, Salt, Prague, Vienna, Wine, Budapest, Mfd. wares, Iron, Copper, Cologne, Iron, Paper, Paris, Orléans, Wheat, Strasbourg, Basel, Geneva, Wine, Salt, Lyons, Mfd. wares, Avignon, Marseilles, Wine, Mfd. wares

Milan, Glass, Venice, Bologna, Artwares, Florence, Rome, Wine, Naples, Timber, Pitch, Silver, Ragusa, Slaves, Taranto, Olives, Messina, Sicily, Palermo, Olives, Wine, Syracuse, Tunis, Slave market, Olives, Tripoli, Fish, Gold, Slaves

Rennes, Nantes, Rouen, Flax, Wine, Salt, Fish, Tours, Limoges, Wine, Clermont, Bordeaux, Bayonne, Toulouse, Iron, Wool, Leon, Wool, Santiago, Fruits+foodstuffs, Wine, Toledo, Metalwares, Leather, Paper, Horses, Córdoba, Copper, Olives, Granada, Almeira, Olives, Barcelona, Fruits+foodstuffs, Valencia, Cartagena, Iron, Balearic Is.

Lisbon, Gold, Slaves, Cork, Seville, Cotton, Silk, Ceuta, Slave market, Gold, Slaves, Algiers, Slave market, Olives, Skins+hides, Dates, Slaves, Gold, Wool

Constantinople, Slave market, Olives, Wine, Raisins, Currants, Smyrna, Fruits+foodstuffs, Opium, Ankara, Cotton, Fruits+foodstuffs, Carpets+rugs, Antioch, Tripoli, Iron, Glassware, Damascus, Precious woods, Beirut, Sidon, Tyre, Horses, Jerusalem, Silk, Paper, Cairo, Indigo, Cotton, Alexandria, Slave market, Cotton, Fish, Wool

Scale: 0   200   400 Mi. / 0   200   400 Km.

three separate types of merchants: the sedentary merchant who ran the "home office," financing and organizing the firm's entire export-import trade; the carriers who transported goods by land and sea; and the company agents resident in cities abroad who, on the advice of the home office, looked after sales and procurements. Commercial correspondence, unnecessary when one businessperson oversaw everything and made direct bargains with buyers and sellers, proliferated. Regular courier service among commercial cities began. Commercial accounting became more complex when firms had to deal with shareholders, manufacturers, customers, branch offices, employees, and competing firms. Tolls on roads became high enough to finance what has been called a "road revolution," involving new surfaces, bridges, new passes through the Alps, and new inns and hospices for travelers. The growth of mutual confidence among merchants facilitated the growth of sales on credit.

In all these transformations, merchants of the Italian cities led the way. (See the feature "Individuals in Society: Francesco Datini.") They formalized their agreements with new types of contracts, including permanent partnerships termed *compagnie* (literally "bread together," that is, sharing bread, and the root of the English word *company*). Many of these compagnie began as agreements between brothers or other relatives and in-laws, but quickly grew to include people who were not family members. In addition, they began to involve individuals—including a few women—who invested only their money, leaving the actual running of the business to the active partners.

The ventures of the German Hanseatic League also illustrate these new business procedures. The **Hanseatic League** was a mercantile association of towns. Though scholars trace the league's origin to the foundation of the city of Lübeck in 1143, the mutual protection treaty later signed by Lübeck and Hamburg marks the league's actual expansion. Lübeck and Hamburg wanted mutual security, exclusive trading rights, and, where possible, a monopoly. During the next century, perhaps two hundred cities from Holland to Poland, including Cologne, Brunswick, Dortmund, Danzig, and Riga, joined the league, but Lübeck always remained the dominant member. From the thirteenth to the sixteenth centuries, the Hanseatic League controlled trade along the axis of Novgorod-Reval-Lübeck-Hamburg-Bruges-London, that is, the trade of northern Europe (see Map 11.2). In the fourteenth century the Hanseatics branched out into southern Germany and Italy by land and into French, Spanish, and Portuguese ports by sea.

Across regular, well-defined trade routes along the Baltic and North Seas, the ships of league cities carried furs, wax, copper, fish, grain, timber, and wine. These goods were exchanged for finished products, mainly cloth and salt, from western cities. At cities such as Bruges and London, Hanseatic merchants secured special trading concessions exempting them from all tolls and allowing them to trade at local fairs. Hanseatic merchants established foreign trading centers, called "factories," the most famous of which was the London Steelyard, a walled community with warehouses, offices, a church, and residential quarters for company representatives. By the late thirteenth century Hanseatic merchants had developed an important business technique, the business register. Merchants publicly recorded their debts and contracts and received a league guarantee for them.

The dramatic increase in trade ran into two serious difficulties in medieval Europe. One was the problem of money. Despite investment in mining operations to increase the production of metals, the amount of gold, silver, and copper available for coins was simply not adequate for the increased flow of commerce. Merchants developed paper letters of exchange, in which coins or goods in one location were exchanged for a sealed letter (much like a modern deposit statement), which could be used in place of metal coinage elsewhere. This made the long, slow, and very dangerous shipment of coins unnecessary. Begun in the late twelfth century, the bill of exchange was the normal method of making commercial payments by the early fourteenth century among the cities of western Europe, and it proved to be a decisive factor in the later development of credit and commerce in northern Europe.

The second problem was a moral and theological one. Church doctrine, relying on Scripture (Leviticus 25:36–37, Psalms 37:26, Luke 11:15), frowned on lending money at interest, termed **usury.** It had developed this doctrine in the early Middle Ages when loans were mainly for consumption, tiding someone over, for instance, until the next harvest. Theologians reasoned that it was wrong for a Christian to take advantage of the bad luck or need of another Christian, so loans should be made *pro amore* (out of love), not with an eye for profit. This restriction on Christians is one reason why Jews were frequently moneylenders in early medieval society; it was one of the few occupations not forbidden them by Christian authorities.

The church's prohibition of usury meant that merchants often felt the need to hide their interest and disguise their profit. Gradually the church relaxed the total

Wismar Founded in 1229 in Mecklenburg on the Baltic Sea, Wismar won full rights of self-government in 1236 from the dukes of Mecklenburg-Pomerania, who resided there. A fishing and shipbuilding center, Wismar became one of the most powerful members of the Hanseatic League. Warehouses lined the shore, while the town's many church steeples dominated the skyline. *(Biblioteca Civica "Angelo Mai," Bergamo)*

prohibition of interest, declaring that some interest was legitimate as a payment for the risk the investor was taking, and that only interest above a certain level would be considered usury. (This definition of usury has continued; modern governments generally set limits on the rate legitimate businesses may charge for loaning money.) The church itself then got into the money-lending business, opening pawnshops in cities and declaring that the shops were benefiting the poor by charging a lower rate of interest than that available from secular moneylenders. In rural areas, Cistercian monasteries loaned money at interest.

The stigma attached to lending money was in many ways attached to all the activities of a medieval merchant. Trade was not like agriculture, mining, or making a product; a merchant simply handled goods produced by someone else. Medieval people were uneasy about persons making a profit merely from the investment of money; the investment of labor, skill, and time warranted a profit, but did the investment of merely money? Merchants themselves shared these ideas to some degree, so they gave generous donations to the church and to charities and agreed, at least in principle, that profit should be limited to what was judged to be fair and just. They also took pains not to flaunt their wealth, but instead to dress and furnish their homes in a way that would convey financial stability rather than flashy extravagance. By the end of the Middle Ages, society had come to accept the role of the merchant somewhat, with preachers in Italian cities comparing merchants to Christ, who had "redeemed" the human race from the snares of the Devil in the same way that merchants redeemed loans and merchandise.

The Commercial Revolution

Changes in business procedures, combined with the growth in trade, led to a transformation of the European

Individuals in Society

Francesco Datini

In 1348, when he was a young teenager, Francesco Datini (1335–1410) lost his father, his mother, a brother, and a sister to the Black Death epidemic that swept through Europe (see pages 374–381). Leaving his hometown of Prato in northern Italy, he apprenticed himself to merchants in nearby Florence for several years to learn accounting and other business skills. At fifteen, he moved to the city of Avignon in southern France. The popes were living in Avignon instead of Rome, and the city offered many opportunities for an energetic and enterprising young man. Datini first became involved in the weapons trade, which offered steady profits, and then handled spices, wool and silk cloth, and jewels. He was very successful, and when he was thirty-one he married the young daughter of another merchant in an elaborate wedding that was the talk of Avignon.

In 1378 the papacy returned to Italy, and Datini soon followed, setting up trading companies in Prato, Pisa, Florence, and eventually other cities as well. He focused on cloth and leather and sought to control the trade in products used for preparation as well, especially the rare dyes that created the brilliant colors favored by wealthy noblemen and townspeople. He eventually had offices all over Europe and became one of the richest men of his day, opening a mercantile bank and a company that produced cloth as well as his many branch offices.

Datini was more successful than most, but what makes him particularly stand out was his record keeping. He kept careful account books and ledgers, all of them headed by the phrase "in the name of God and profit." He wrote to the managers of each of his offices every week, providing them with careful advice and blunt criticism: "You cannot see a crow in a bowl of milk." Taking on the son of a friend as an employee, he wrote to the young man: "Do your duty well, and you will acquire honor and profit, and you can count on me as if I were your own father. But if you do not, then do not count on me; it will be as if I had never known you."

When Datini was away from home, which was often, he wrote to his wife every day, and she sometimes responded in ways that were less deferential than we might expect of a woman who was many years younger. "I think it is not necessary," she wrote at one point "to send me a message every Wednesday to say that you will be here on Sunday, for it seems to me that

on every Friday you change your mind."

Datini's obsessive record-keeping lasted beyond his death, for someone put all of his records—hundreds of ledgers and contracts, eleven thousand business letters, and over a hundred thousand personal letters—in sacks in his opulent house in Prato, where they were found in the nineteenth century. They provide a detailed picture of medieval business practices and also reveal much about Datini as a person. Ambitious, calculating, luxury-loving, and a workaholic, Datini seems similar to a modern CEO. Like many of today's self-made super-rich people, at the end of his life Datini began to think a bit more about God and less about profit. In his will, he set up a foundation for the poor in Prato and a home for orphans in Florence, both of which are still in operation. In 1967 scholars established an institute for economic history in Prato, naming it in Datini's honor; the institute now manages the collection of Datini documents and gathers other relevant materials in its archives.

Statue of Francesco Datini outside the city hall in Prato. (Peter Horree/Alamy)

Questions for Analysis

1. How would you evaluate Datini's motto: as an honest statement of his aims, a hypocritical justification of greed, a blend of both, or something else?
2. Changes in business procedures in the Middle Ages have been described as a "commercial revolution." Do Datini's activities support this assessment? Why?

Source: Iris Origo, *The Merchant of Prato: Francesco di Marco Datini, 1335–1410* (New York: Alfred A. Knopf, Inc., 1957).

***Online Study Center* Improve Your Grade**
Going Beyond Individuals in Society

Mechanical Clock   Slowly falling weights provide the force that pushes the hand on the twenty-four-hour face of this large, public sixteenth-century German clock. The gears also regulated the striking of bells, so that the sound of a machine marked time. *(Bibliothèque royale Albert 1er, Brussels)*

economy often called the **commercial revolution** by historians, who see it as the beginning of the modern capitalist economy. Though you may be most familiar with using *revolution* to describe a violent political rebellion such as the American Revolution or the French Revolution, the word is also used more broadly to describe economic and intellectual changes such as the Industrial Revolution and the scientific revolution. These do not necessarily involve violence and may last much longer than political revolutions. What makes them revolutions is the extent of their effects on society. In calling this transformation the "commercial revolution," historians point not only to an increase in the sheer volume of trade and in the complexity and sophistication of business procedures, but also to the new attitude toward business and making money. Some even detect a "capitalist spirit" in which making a profit is regarded as a good thing in itself, regardless of the uses to which that profit is put.

Part of this capitalist spirit was a new attitude toward time. Country people needed only approximate times—dawn, noon, sunset—for their work. Monasteries needed much more precise times to call monks together for the recitation of the Divine Office. In the early Middle Ages monks used a combination of hourglasses, sundials, and water-clocks to determine the time, and then rang bells by hand. About 1280 new types of mechanical mechanisms seem to have been devised in which weights replaced falling water and bells were rung automatically. Records begin to use the word *clock* (from the Latin word for bell) for these machines, which sometimes figured the movement of astronomical bodies as well as the hours. The merchants who ran city councils quickly saw clocks as both useful and a symbol of their prosperity. Beautiful and elaborate mechanical clocks, usually installed on the cathedral or town church, were in general use in Italy by the 1320s, in Germany by the 1330s, in England by the 1370s, and in France by the 1380s. Buying and selling goods had initiated city people into the practice of quantification, and clocks contributed to the development of a mentality that conceived of the universe in quantitative terms.

Capitalism in the Middle Ages primarily involved trade rather than production, so it is termed **mercantile capitalism.** In a few places, such as Florence, cloth production was organized along capitalist lines, with a cloth merchant owning the raw materials, the finished product, and sometimes the tools, and with workers paid simply for their labor. Most production in the Middle Ages was carried out by craft guilds or by people working on their own, however.

The commercial revolution created a great deal of new wealth, which did not escape the attention of kings and other rulers. Wealth could be taxed, and through taxation kings could create strong and centralized states. In the years to come, alliances with the middle classes enabled kings to defeat feudal powers and aristocratic interests and to build the states that came to be called "modern." The commercial revolution also provided the opportunity for thousands of serfs to improve their social position. The slow but steady transformation of European society from almost completely rural and isolated to relatively more sophisticated constituted the greatest effect of the commercial revolution that began in the eleventh century.

Even so, merchants and business people did not run medieval communities other than in central and northern Italy and in the county of Flanders. Most towns remained small, and urban residents were never more than 10 percent of the population. The castle, the manorial village, and the monastery dominated the landscape. The feudal nobility and churchmen determined the preponderant social attitudes, values, and patterns of thought and behavior. The commercial changes of the eleventh through thirteenth centuries did, however, lay the economic foundations for the development of urban life and culture.

Medieval Universities

Just as the first strong secular states emerged in the thirteenth century, so did the first universities. This was no coincidence. The new bureaucratic states and the church needed educated administrators, and universities were a response to this need. The word *university* derives from the Latin *universitas,* meaning "corporation" or "guild." Medieval universities were educational guilds that produced educated and trained individuals, and they continue to influence institutionalized learning in the Western world.

• *How did universities evolve, and what needs of medieval society did they serve?*

Origins

In the early Middle Ages, outside of the aristocratic court or the monastery, anyone who received an education got it from a priest. Priests instructed the clever boys on the manor in the Latin words of the Mass and taught them the rudiments of reading and writing. Few boys acquired elementary literacy, however, and peasant girls did not obtain even that. The peasant father who wished to send his son to school had to secure the permission of his lord because the result of formal schooling tended to be a career in the church or some trade. If a young man were to pursue either, he would have to leave the manor and gain free status. Because the lord stood to lose the services of educated peasants, he limited the number of serfs sent to school.

Since the time of the Carolingian Empire, monasteries and cathedral schools had offered most of the available formal instruction. The monasteries were geared to religious concerns, and the monastic curriculum consisted of studying the Scriptures and the writings of the church fathers. Monasteries wished to maintain an atmosphere of seclusion and silence and were unwilling to accept large numbers of noisy lay students. In contrast, schools attached to cathedrals and run by the bishop and his clergy were frequently situated in bustling cities, and in the eleventh century in Italian cities like Bologna, wealthy businessmen had established municipal schools. In the course of the twelfth century, cathedral schools in France and municipal schools in Italy developed into educational institutions that attracted students from a wide area (see Map 11.3). These schools were called *studium generale* ("general center of study") or *universitas magistrorum et scholarium* ("universal society of teachers and students"), the origin of the English word *university.* The first European universities appeared in Italy in Bologna and Salerno.

The growth of the University of Bologna coincided with a revival of interest in Roman law during the investiture controversy. The study of Roman law as embodied in the Justinian *Code* had never completely died out in the West, but in the late eleventh century a complete manuscript of the *Code* was discovered in a library in Pisa. This discovery led scholars in nearby Bologna, beginning with Irnerius (ca 1055–ca 1130), to study and teach Roman law intently again. His fame attracted students from all over Europe. Irnerius not only explained the Roman law of the Justinian *Code,* but also applied it to difficult practical situations.

At Salerno in southern Italy interest in medicine had persisted for centuries. Medical practitioners—mostly men, but apparently also a few women—received training first through apprenticeship and then in an organized medical school. Individuals associated with Salerno, such as Constantine the African (fl. 1065–1085)—who was a convert from Islam and later a Benedictine monk—

MAP 11.3 Intellectual Centers of Medieval Europe Universities obviously provided more sophisticated instruction than did monastery and cathedral schools. What other factors distinguished the three kinds of intellectual centers?

Online Study Center **Improve Your Grade** Interactive Map: Intellectual Centers of Medieval Europe

began to translate medical works out of Arabic. These translations included writings by the ancient Greek physicians and Muslim medical writers. Students of medicine poured into Salerno and soon attracted royal attention. In 1140, when King Roger II of Sicily took the practice of medicine under royal control, his ordinance stated:

Who, from now on, wishes to practice medicine, has to present himself before our officials and examiners, in order to pass their judgment. Should he be bold enough to disregard this, he will be punished by imprisonment and confiscation of his entire property. In this way we are taking care that our subjects are not endangered by the inexperience of the physicians.[5]

In the first decades of the twelfth century, students converged on Paris. They crowded into the cathedral school of Notre Dame and spilled over into the area later called the "Latin Quarter"—whose name reflects either the Italian origin of many of the students attracted to Paris by the surge of interest in the classics, logic, and theology, or the Latin language spoken in the area. The cathedral school's international reputation drew scholars from all over Europe to Paris.

Abelard and Heloise

One of the young men drawn to Paris was Peter Abelard (1079–1142), the son of a minor Breton knight. Abelard studied in Paris, quickly absorbed a large amount of material, and set himself up as a teacher. He was fascinated by logic, which he believed could be used to solve most problems. He had a brilliant mind and, though orthodox in his philosophical teaching, appeared to challenge ecclesiastical authorities. His book *Sic et Non* (Yes and No) was a list of apparently contradictory propositions drawn from the Bible and the writings of the church fathers. One such proposition, for example, stated that sin is pleasing to God and is not pleasing to God. Abelard used a method of systematic doubting in his writing and teaching. As he put it in the preface to *Sic et Non,* "By doubting we come to questioning, and by questioning we perceive the truth." While other scholars merely asserted theological principles, Abelard discussed and analyzed them. Through reasoning he even tried to describe the attributes of the three persons of the Trinity, the central mystery of the Christian faith. Abelard was severely censured by a church council, but his cleverness, boldness, and imagination made him a highly popular figure among students.

In a supposedly autobiographical statement, *A History of My Calamities,* Abelard described his academic career and his private life. His reputation for intellectual brilliance drew the attention of one of the cathedral canons, Fulbert, who hired Abelard to tutor his clever niece Heloise. The relationship between teacher and pupil passed beyond the intellectual. Abelard said that he seduced Heloise to learn about sexuality. She became pregnant, and Canon Fulbert pressured the couple to marry. Abelard insisted that the union be kept secret for the sake of his career, an arrangement Heloise much resented. Distrusting Abelard, Canon Fulbert hired men to castrate him. Wounded in spirit as well as body, Abelard persuaded Heloise to enter a convent. He became a monk of Saint-Denis; and their baby, baptized Astrolabe for a recent Muslim navigational invention, was given to her

family for adoption. Heloise secured a copy of Abelard's *History* and took great exception to his statement that their relationship had been based solely on physical desire. She considered her religious life hypocritical. Abelard spent his later years as abbot of an obscure monastery in Brittany, where he wrote Heloise letters of spiritual direction. The two unfortunate lovers were united in death and later buried together in a cemetery in Paris. Some scholars consider *A History of My Calamities* the most famous autobiography of the twelfth century, a fine example of the new self-awareness of the period's rebirth of learning. Other scholars believe the entire *History* a forgery, the source of a romantic legend with no basis in historical fact.[6]

Online Study Center **Improve Your Grade**
Primary Source: Letter to Abelard: "I beseech thee. . . ."

Instruction and Curriculum

The influx of students eager for learning, together with dedicated and imaginative teachers, created the atmosphere in which universities grew. In northern Europe—at Paris and later at Oxford and Cambridge in England—associations or guilds of professors organized universities. They established the curriculum, set the length of time for study, and determined the form and content of examinations. By the end of the fifteenth century there were at least eighty universities in Europe. Some universities also offered younger students training in the liberal arts that could serve as a foundation for more specialized study in all areas.

Students at universities were generally considered to be lower-level members of the clergy—this was termed being in "minor orders"—so that any students accused of legal infractions were tried in church, rather than in city courts. This clerical status, along with widely held ideas about women's lesser intellectual capabilities, meant that university education was restricted to men; even more than feudal armies—which were often accompanied by women who did laundry, found provisions, cooked meals, and engaged in sex for money—universities were all-male communities. The few women trained at Salerno during its early years of development were the last women in Europe to receive formal university training in any subject until the nineteenth century, although a handful of professor's daughters in one or two places were reputed to have listened to lectures from behind a curtain. (Most European universities did not admit or grant degrees to women until after World War I.) Though university classes were not especially expensive,

Law Lecture at Bologna   This beautifully carved marble sculpture, with the fluid drapery characteristic of late Gothic style, suggests the students' intellectual intensity. Medieval students often varied widely in age; here some have moustaches and some look like adolescents. *(Museo Civico, Bologna/Scala/Art Resource, NY)*

the many years that university required meant that the sons of peasants or artisans could rarely attend, unless they could find wealthy patrons who would pay their expenses while they studied. Most students were the sons of urban merchants or lower-level nobles, especially the younger sons who would not inherit family lands.

University faculties grouped themselves according to academic disciplines—law, medicine, arts, theology. The professors (a term first used in the fourteenth century) were known as "schoolmen" or **Scholastics.** They developed a method of thinking, reasoning, and writing in which questions were raised and authorities cited on both sides of the question. The goal of the Scholastic method was to arrive at definitive answers and to provide a rational explanation for what was believed on faith. Schoolmen held that reason and faith constituted two harmonious realms whose truths complemented each other.

The Scholastic approach rested on the recovery of classical philosophical texts. Ancient Greek and Arabic texts had entered Europe in the early twelfth century. Knowledge of Aristotle and other Greek philosophers came to Paris and Oxford by way of Islamic intellectual centers at Baghdad, Córdoba, and Toledo. These texts, which formed the basis of Western philosophical and theological speculation, were not the only Islamic gifts. The major contribution of Arabic culture to the new currents of Western thought rested in the stimulus Arabic philosophers and commentators gave to Europeans' reflection on the Greek texts. For example, in Islam a strong tension exists between faith and reason. Western scholars' understanding of Aristotle's philosophy was closely tied to their discovery of Arabic thought. The tension between reason and faith became a fundamental theme in Christian thought.

Aristotle had stressed the importance of the direct observation of nature, as well as the principles that theory must follow fact and that knowledge of a thing requires an explanation of its causes. The schoolmen reinterpreted Aristotelian texts in a Christian sense. But in their exploration of the natural world, they did not precisely follow Aristotle's axioms. Medieval scientists argued from authority, such as the Bible, the Justinian *Code,* or an ancient scientific treatise, rather than from direct observation and experimentation as modern scientists do. Thus the conclusions of medieval scientists were often wrong. Nevertheless, natural science gradually emerged as a discipline distinct from philosophy, and Scholastics laid the foundations for later scientific work.

Many of the problems that Scholastic philosophers raised dealt with theological issues. For example, they addressed the question that interested all Christians, educated and uneducated: how is a person saved? Saint Augustine's thesis—that, as a result of Adam's fall, human beings have a propensity to sin—had become a central feature of church doctrine. The church taught that it possessed the means to forgive the sinful: grace conveyed through the sacraments. However, although grace provided a predisposition to salvation, the Scholastics held that one must also *decide* to use the grace received. In other words, a person must use his or her will and reason to advance to God.

At all universities the standard method of teaching was the *lecture*—that is, a reading. The professor read a passage from the Bible, the Justinian *Code,* or one of Aristotle's treatises. He then explained and interpreted the passage; his interpretation was called a *gloss.* Texts and glosses were sometimes collected and reproduced as textbooks. For example, the Italian Peter Lombard (d. 1160), a professor at Paris, wrote what became the standard textbook in theology, *Sententiae* (The Sentences), a compilation of basic theological principles.

Because books had to be copied by hand, they were extremely expensive, and few students could afford them. Students therefore depended for study on their own or friends' notes accumulated over a period of years. The choice of subjects was narrow. The syllabus at all universities consisted of a core of ancient texts that all students studied and, if they wanted to get ahead, mastered.

Examinations were given after three, four, or five years of study, when the student applied for a degree. The professors determined the amount of material students had to know for each degree, and students frequently insisted that the professors specify precisely what that material was. Examinations were oral and very difficult. If the candidate passed, he was awarded a license to teach, which was the earliest form of academic degree. Initially these licenses granted the title of *master* or *doctor,* still in use today and both derived from Latin words meaning "teach." Bachelor's degrees came later. Most students, however, did not become teachers. They staffed the expanding diocesan, royal, and papal administrations.

Students did not spend all their time listening to lectures or debating, however. Much information about medieval students concerns what we might call their "extracurricular" activities: university regulations forbade them to throw rocks at professors; sermons talked about students' breaking and entering, raping local women, attacking town residents, or disturbing church services; court records discussed their engaging in drunken brawls and riots or stabbing each other in fights and duels. The money sent by parents or patrons was often not sufficient for all expenses, so students augmented this by begging, thieving, or doing odd jobs. They also delayed finishing their studies because life as a student could be very pleasant, without the responsibilities that came with becoming fully adult. Student life was also described by those who knew it best—students themselves—in poems, usually anonymous, that celebrated the joys of Venus (the goddess of love), Bacchus (the god of wine), and Decius (the god of dice).

Thomas Aquinas and the Teaching of Theology

Thirteenth-century Scholastics devoted an enormous amount of time to collecting and organizing knowledge on all topics. These collections were published as **summa,** or reference books. There were summa on law, philosophy, vegetation, animal life, and theology. Saint Thomas Aquinas (1225–1274), a professor at Paris, produced the most famous collection, the *Summa Theologica,* which deals with a vast number of theological questions.

Online Study Center **Improve Your Grade**
Primary Source: Summa Theologica: On Dispensing the Eucharist

Aquinas drew an important distinction between faith and reason. He maintained that, although reason can demonstrate many basic Christian principles such as the existence of God, other fundamental teachings such as the Trinity and original sin cannot be proved by logic. That reason cannot establish them does not, however, mean they are contrary to reason. Rather, people understand such doctrines through revelation embodied in

Scripture. Scripture cannot contradict reason, nor reason Scripture:

The light of faith that is freely infused into us does not destroy the light of natural knowledge [reason] implanted in us naturally. For although the natural light of the human mind is insufficient to show us these things made manifest by faith, it is nevertheless impossible that these things which the divine principle gives us by faith are contrary to these implanted in us by nature [reason]. Indeed, were that the case, one or the other would have to be false, and, since both are given to us by God, God would have to be the author of untruth, which is impossible. . . . [I]t is impossible that those things which are of philosophy can be contrary to those things which are of faith.[7]

Aquinas also investigated the branch of philosophy called *epistemology,* which is concerned with how a person knows something. Aquinas stated that one knows, first, through sensory perception of the physical world—seeing, hearing, touching, and so on. He maintained that there can be nothing in the mind that is not first in the senses. Second, knowledge comes through reason, the mind exercising its natural abilities. Aquinas stressed the power of human reason to know, even to know God. Proofs of the existence of God exemplify the Scholastic method of knowing.

Aquinas began with the things of the natural world—earth, air, trees, water, birds. Then he inquired about their original source or cause: the mover, creator, planner who started it all. Everything, Aquinas maintained, has an ultimate and essential explanation, a reason for existing. Here he was following Aristotle. Aquinas went further and identified this reason for existing, or first mover, with God. Aquinas and all medieval intellectuals held that the end of faith and reason was the knowledge of and union with God. His work later became the fundamental text of Roman Catholic doctrine.

Teaching the Law

Legal scholars as well as theologians attempted to create an all-inclusive system based on logical principles. Irnerius and other teachers at Bologna taught law not as a group of discrete bits of legislation, but as an organic whole related to the society it regulated. Thus, as social and economic structures changed, law would change with them. Like theology, law was something that was created and developed by the human mind, not an unchanging body of immutable customs, which is how law had generally been viewed in the early Middle Ages.

Jurists educated at Bologna and later at other universities—such as Montpellier in France, where Roman law formed an increasingly large part of the legal curriculum—were hired by rulers to systematize their law codes and write legal treatises. In the 1260s the English jurist Henry Bracton wrote a comprehensive treatise bringing together the laws and customs of England, and King Alfonso X of Castile issued the *Siete Partidas* (Book in Seven Parts) that set out a detailed plan for administering his whole kingdom according to Roman legal principles.

When cities gained their freedom from feudal lords, they had to write city charters and law codes for both civil and criminal matters, which grew longer and longer as new issues arose. These law codes were a combination of earlier Germanic law codes and Roman law, blended together in ways that addressed local needs and fit with local customs. Lawyers served as advisers and consultants for city councils, though they themselves were generally not members of the city government.

Canon law (see page 278) was also shaped by the reinvigoration of Roman law, and canon lawyers in ever greater numbers were hired by church officials or became prominent church officials themselves. In about 1140 the Benedictine monk Gratian put together a collection of nearly 3,800 texts covering all areas of canon law. His collection, known as the *Decretum,* became the standard text on which teachers of canon law lectured and commented. The *Decretum* presented material in dialectical form as a series of questions and answers about practical problems judges and lawyers in church courts might confront, such as issues surrounding marriage or cases involving members of the clergy or university students. Canon lawyers worked with the popes—indeed, some popes were canon lawyers—to make sure that the scope of jurisdiction for those courts continued to expand.

Jewish scholars as well as Christian ones produced elaborate commentaries on law and religious tradition. Medieval universities were closed to Jews, but in some cities in the eleventh century special rabbinic academies opened that concentrated particularly on the study of the Talmud, a compilation of legal arguments, proverbs, sayings, and folklore that had been produced in the fifth century in Babylon (present-day Iraq). The Talmud was written in Aramaic, so that simply learning to read it required years of study, and medieval scholars began to produce commentaries on the Talmud to help facilitate this. The most famous of these was that of Rabbi Solomon bar Isaac, known as Rashi (1040–1105), who lived in Troyes, a city in France. Men seeking to become rabbis—highly respected figures within the Jewish community with authority over economic and social as well as religious matters—spent long periods of time studying the Talmud, which served as the basis for their legal decisions in all areas of life.

Medical Training

Like philosophy and law, medical studies at medieval universities were based on classical ideas, particularly those of Hippocrates and Aristotle (see page 85). For the ancient Greeks, ideas about the human body were very closely linked to philosophy and to ideas about the natural world in general. Prime among these was the notion of the four bodily humors, four fluids—blood, phlegm, black bile, and yellow bile—contained in the body that influenced bodily health. Each individual was thought to have a characteristic temperament or *complexion* determined by the balance of the four humors, in the same way that we might describe a person today as having a "positive outlook" or a "Type-A" personality. These four humors corresponded to four qualities—hot, cold, wet, and dry—and to the four basic elements in the Aristotelian universe—earth, air, fire, and water. The organs were primarily viewed as channels for the humors, rather than as having specific functions. Disease was primarily regarded as an imbalance of bodily humors, which could be diagnosed by taking a patient's pulse or examining his or her urine. Treatment was thus an attempt to bring the humors back into balance, which might be accomplished through diet or drugs—usually mixtures of herbal or mineral substances regarded as therapeutic—or as a direct attempt to rebalance the humors through emetics, purgatives, or bloodletting. The bodily humors were somewhat gender-related—women were regarded as tending toward the cold and wet and men toward the hot and dry—so that therapies were also gender-distinctive. The exact balance of humors was different for each individual, however, and heat could cause one fluid to transform into another.

Heat was also viewed as important in reproduction. The sex of an infant, for example, was believed to be determined largely by the amount of heat present during intercourse and gestation; males resulted when there was the proper amount of heat, which caused their sexual organs to be pushed outside the body, and females when there was too little heat, which caused their sexual organs to remain internal. Men's greater heat continued throughout their lives, causing them to burn up their hair and go bald and to develop broader shoulders and bigger brains (because heat rises and causes things to expand).

Although disagreements existed, the ideas of this medical literature spread throughout Europe from Salerno and became the basis of university medical training. University training gave physicians high social status and

Physician's Diagnosis   University-trained physicians rarely touched patients, but instead diagnosed illness by looking at patients' urine. This illustration appeared in a French translation of *De Proprietatibus Rerum* (The Properties of Things), the first encyclopedia of the Middle Ages, by Bartholomaeus Anglicus (Bartholomew the Englishman). Bartholomaeus was an English Franciscan who taught at the universities of Paris and Magdeburg in Germany. This encyclopedia, which was widely copied and translated into several languages, includes material from Greek, Arabic, and Jewish medical writers. *(Snark/Art Resource, NY)*

allowed them to charge high fees. They were generally hired directly by their patients as they were needed, though some had more permanent positions as members of the household staffs of especially wealthy nobles or rulers or in hospitals such rulers had founded (see pages 304–305). In the fifteenth century city governments sometimes hired official city physicians to advise them on medical matters and give opinions in legal cases on such issues as how long a person had been dead or whether a child had taken a breath before it had died. (The latter emerged in cases of suspected infanticide.)

The influence of learned medical literature did not stop with those who could read Greek and Latin, however, for beginning in the fourteenth century in Europe translations and compilations were made in the vernacular languages. Once the printing press was developed in the mid-fifteenth century, these vernacular medical works, along with Latin and Greek medical works, were frequently printed. It is difficult to gauge how often the treatments they recommend were actually applied, but the ideas they contain were shared by most of the population, from the highly learned to the illiterate, until well into the sixteenth century.

Vernacular Culture

University education was conducted completely in Latin, and all learned philosophical, theological, and medical works were written in Latin as well. So were many works of literature, including poetry, plays, stories, and chronicles, particularly those written by monks and nuns. In contrast to Roman times, however, by the High Middle Ages no one spoke Latin as his or her original mother tongue. The barbarian invasions, the mixture of peoples, and evolution over time had resulted in a variety of local **dialects** that blended words and linguistic forms in various ways. These dialects were specific to one region, and as kings increased the size of their holdings they often ruled people who spoke many different dialects. In the early Middle Ages almost all written works continued to be in Latin, but in the High Middle Ages some authors began to write in their local dialect, that is, in the everyday language of their region, which linguistic historians call the vernacular. This new **vernacular literature** gradually transformed some local dialects into literary languages, such as French, German, Italian, and English, while other dialects remained (and remain to this day) simply means of oral communication. Most people in the High Middle Ages could no more read vernacular literature than they could read Latin, however, so oral trans-

mission continued to be the most important way information was conveyed and traditions passed down.

- *What do oral traditions and vernacular literature reveal about medieval culture?*

Oral Traditions and Entertainment

The treatment of illness was only one of many aspects of life in which traditions were handed down orally. Children heard stories about saints, heroes, and magical creatures from their parents; apprentices and journeymen learned the tasks associated with their craft by watching and listening to their masters; people of all types gathered when wandering preachers gave sermons urging them to live better lives or go on pilgrimages. Much of this oral culture is difficult to recover because it was never written down; writing was for important legal or intellectual matters, done by highly trained scribes on expensive parchment or vellum (stretched goatskin or sheepskin).

By the thirteenth century, however, techniques of making paper from old linen cloth and rags began to spread from Spain, where they had been developed by the Arabs, providing a much cheaper material on which to write. People started to write down things that were more mundane and less serious—personal letters, lists, poems, songs, recipes, rules, instructions—in various vernacular dialects, using spellings that were often personal and idiosyncratic. The writings included fables, legends, stories, and myths that had circulated orally for generations, and slowly a body of written vernacular literature developed. From written vernacular records and from discussions in more learned literature, we can gain some access to medieval popular culture, though its full range cannot be completely reconstructed.

The recreation of all classes reflected the fact that medieval society was organized for war and that violence was common. The aristocracy engaged in tournaments or jousts; archery and wrestling had great popularity among ordinary people. The hangings and mutilations of criminals were exciting and well-attended events, with all the festivity of a university town before a Saturday football game. Chroniclers exulted in describing executions, murders, and massacres. Here a monk gleefully describes the gory execution of William Wallace (ca 1270–1305), the Scottish hero who led a revolt against Edward I of England and retains importance as a symbol of resistance to English rule and of Scottish nationalism:

Wilielmus Waleis, a robber given to sacrilege, arson and homicide . . . was condemned to most cruel but justly de-

Spanish Bullfight In this fourteenth-century painting, spectators goad a bull with whips. The Romans may have introduced bullfighting in Spain, but the Muslims popularized it, and Christians continued the tradition. In its medieval version, bullfighters fought from horseback; bullfighters on foot were added in the eighteenth century. *(From the* Cantigas *of Alfonso X, ca 1283. El Escorial/Laurie Platt Winfrey, Inc.)*

served death. He was drawn through the streets of London at the tails of horses, until he reached a gallows of unusual height, there he was suspended by a halter; but taken down while yet alive, he was mutilated, his bowels torn out and burned in a fire, his head then cut off, his body divided into four, and his quarters transmitted to four principal parts of Scotland.[8]

Games and sports were common forms of entertainment and relaxation. There were games akin to modern football, rugby, and soccer in which balls were kicked and thrown, and other games in which balls were hit by sticks, paddles, and rackets much like modern tennis and field hockey. There were wrestling matches ranging from informal bouts between two individuals to organized team matches between two cities. People played card and board games of all types, with paper providing the material for the cards themselves and for writing down rules. They played with dice carved from stone or bone, or with the knucklebones of animals or wood carved in knucklebone shape, somewhat like modern jacks. They trained dogs to fight each other or put them in an enclosure to

fight a captured bear. In Spain, Muslim knights confronted and killed bulls from horseback as part of religious feast days, developing a highly ritualized ceremony that would later be further adapted by Spain's Christian conquerors. All these sports and games were occasions for wagering and gambling, which preachers sometimes condemned (especially when the games were attached to holiday or saints' day celebrations) but had little power to control.

Religious and family celebrations also meant dancing, which the church also attempted to ban or at least regulate, again with little success. Men and women danced in lines toward a specific object, such as a tree or a maypole, or in circles, groups, or pairs with specific step patterns. They were accompanied by a variety of instruments: reed pipes such as the chalumeau (an ancestor of the clarinet) and shawm; woodwinds such as flutes, panpipes, and recorders; stringed instruments including dulcimers, harps, lyres, lutes, zithers, and mandolins; brass instruments such as horns and trumpets; and percussion instruments like drums and tambourines. Many of these instruments were simple and were made by their players.

If nothing else was available, someone often had a Jew's harp, a tiny iron frame with a vibrating strip of metal, which was held between the teeth and plucked, with the notes changing depending on the shape of the mouth. (The origins of the name "Jew's harp" are very obscure and hotly debated, but it appears to have nothing to do with Jews and may have been invented in many different places.) Musicians playing string or percussion instruments often sang as well, and people sang without instrumental accompaniment on festive occasions or while working.

Drama, derived from the church's liturgy, emerged as a distinct art form during the High Middle Ages. For centuries skits based on Christ's Nativity and Resurrection had been performed in monasteries and cathedrals. Beginning in the thirteenth century plays based on these and other biblical themes and on the lives of the saints were performed in the towns. Students of theater history distinguish three kinds of medieval plays: *mystery* plays financed and performed by "misteries," members of the craft guilds; *miracle* plays acted by amateurs or professional actors, not guild members; and *morality* plays in which the characters personified virtues and vices and the actors represented the struggle between good and evil. Performed first at the cathedral altar, then in the church square, later at stations around the town, and finally in the town marketplace, mystery plays enjoyed great popularity. By combining comical farce based on ordinary life with serious religious scenes, they gave ordinary people an opportunity to identify with religious figures and think about the mysteries of their faith.

Troubadour Poetry

In addition to amateur musicians who played and sang for village dances and peasant weddings, professional musicians and poets performed and composed at the courts of nobles and rulers. In Germany and most of northern Europe, they favored stories and songs recounting the great deeds of warrior heroes, such as the knight Roland who fought against the Muslims and Hildebrand who fought the Huns. These epics, known as *chansons de geste* ("songs of great deeds"), celebrate violence, slaughter, revenge, and physical power. In southern Europe, especially in the area of southern France known as Provence, poets who called themselves **troubadours** wrote and sang lyric verses celebrating love, desire, beauty, and gallantry. (See the feature "Listening to the Past: Courtly Love" on pages 366–367.) The word *troubadour* comes from the Provençal word *trobar,* which in

turn derives from the Arabic *taraba,* meaning "to sing" or "to sing poetry." A troubadour was a poet who wrote lyric verse in Provençal, the regional spoken language of southern France, and sang it at one of the noble courts. Troubadours included a few women, called *trobairitz,* most of whose exact identities are not known.

Troubadour lyric poetry enjoyed the patronage of many of the great lords of southern France, including William IX, duke of Aquitaine, himself a famed author. William's granddaughter, Eleanor of Aquitaine, may have taken troubadour poetry to England when she married Henry II. Since the songs of the troubadours were widely imitated in Italy, England, and Germany, they spurred the development of vernacular literature there. In the thirteenth century, for example, German Minnesängers (love singers) such as Walther von der Wogelweide (1170–1220) wrote stylized verses on a variety of topics in an early version of German.

The romantic motifs of the troubadours also influenced the northern French *trouvères,* who wrote adventure-romances in the form of epic poems in a language we call Old French, the ancestor of modern French. At the court of his patron, Marie of Champagne, Chrétien de Troyes (ca 1135–ca 1190) used the legends of the fifth-century British king Arthur (see page 213) to relate stories of lovers who occasionally lapsed in their purity. Chrétien told the story of the noble Lancelot, whose love for Guinevere, the wife of King Arthur, his lord, became physical as well as spiritual. Their sexual relationship led to everyone's ruin, but it also became the best-known part of the "Arthurian cycle" of stories about the legendary king Arthur and his knights at Camelot. Combining chivalric romance and battle-strewn epic, Chrétien wrote down many of these stories, which remained popular for centuries and were later written down in slightly different forms by other authors. Such poems as *Lancelot, Percival and the Holy Grail,* and *Tristan and Isolde* reveal Chrétien as the most innovative figure in the twelfth-century vernacular literature.

Online Study Center **Improve Your Grade**
Primary Source: The Temptation of Sir Lancelot

Most of the troubadours and trouvères came from and wrote for the aristocratic classes, and their poetry suggests the interests and values of noble culture. Their influence eventually extended to all social groups, however, for people who could not read heard the poems and stories from people who could, so that what had originally come from oral culture was recycled back into it every generation.

Architecture and Art

The development of secular vernacular literature focusing on human concerns did not mean any lessening of the importance of religion in medieval people's lives. As we have seen, religious devotion was expressed through daily rituals, holiday ceremonies, and the creation of new institutions such as universities and religious orders. People also wanted permanent visible representations of their piety, and both church and city leaders wanted physical symbols of their wealth and power. These aims found their outlet in the building of tens of thousands of churches, chapels, abbeys, and, most spectacularly, **cathedrals** in the twelfth and thirteenth centuries. (A cathedral is the church of a bishop and the administrative headquarters of a diocese, a church district headed by a bishop. The word comes from the Greek word *kathedra,* meaning "seat," because the bishop's throne, a symbol of the office, is located in the cathedral.)

It is difficult for people today to appreciate the extraordinary amounts of energy, imagination, and money involved in building cathedrals. Between 1180 and 1270 in France alone, eighty cathedrals, about five hundred abbey churches, and tens of thousands of parish churches were constructed. This construction represents a remarkable investment for a country of scarcely 18 million people. More stone was quarried for churches in medieval France than had been mined in ancient Egypt, where the Great Pyramid alone consumed 40.5 million cubic feet of stone.

• *How did cathedrals express the ideals, attitudes, and interests of medieval people?*

Romanesque Churches and Cathedrals

Most of the churches in the early Middle Ages had been built primarily of wood, which meant they were very susceptible to fire. They were often small, with a flat roof, in a rectangular or slightly cross-shaped form called a *basilica,* based on earlier Roman public buildings. The long part of the cross, called the *nave,* was arranged on an east-west axis, so that as people entered the main central door at the foot of the nave they looked eastward, toward Jerusalem. The altar was at the head of the nave, at the point where the arms of the cross, called the *transept,* intersected it. A small rounded *apse* formed the head of the cross.

With the end of the Viking and Magyar invasions and the increasing political stability of the eleventh century, bishops and abbots supported the construction of larger and more fire-resistant churches made almost completely out of stone. These were based on the basilican style, but their cross shape was made more pronounced by increasing the size of the transept and apse and adding a rectangular section called a *choir* between the apse and the altar. As the size of the church grew horizontally, it also grew vertically, as builders adapted Roman-style rounded barrel vaults made of stone for the ceiling; this use of Roman forms led this style to be labeled **Romanesque.** The nave, apse, and each arm of the transept had its own barrel-vault ceiling, which met in the middle over the altar in what was called a *cross vault.* All of these ceilings were extremely heavy and generated a great deal of downward and outward thrust, so that the walls of the church needed to be very thick and sturdy to support them. Thus windows were small, and Romanesque churches could be dark and gloomy. This was alleviated by painting the ceilings and walls in light, bright colors and by filling the church with sculptures, tapestries, paintings, and gold and silver ornaments, all of which would catch the light. Along with the central altar, the side aisles of the nave often contained altars erected by prominent families, wealthy individuals, or craft guilds, often dedicated to specific saints. Lighted candles or priests and monks saying mass could often be found at these side altars, so that larger churches were rarely completely empty.

The exteriors of Romanesque churches became more elaborate as well, with sculptured figures over each door representing biblical figures, saints, rulers, or scenes from the Bible, and with towers over the church with bells that tolled the hours of services. The scenes over each door were specialized in some churches; scenes representing Heaven and Hell were carved over doors designated for pilgrims to enter, while the story of the wise and foolish maidens was carved over a side door in front of which weddings were held or through which wedding parties entered. In northern Europe, twin bell towers often crowned Romanesque churches, giving them a powerful, fortresslike appearance. Built primarily by monasteries, Romanesque churches reflect the quasi-military, aristocratic, and pre-urban society that built them.

Gothic Cathedrals

The inspiration for a new style of architecture originated in the brain of one monk, Suger, abbot of Saint-Denis (1122–1151). When Suger became abbot, he decided to reconstruct the old Carolingian abbey church at Saint-

From Romanesque to Gothic

The word *church* has several meanings: assembly, congregation, sect. The Greek term from which it is derived means "a thing belonging to the Lord," and this concept was applied to the building where a congregation assembled. In the Middle Ages people understood the church building to be "the house of God and the gate to Heaven"; it served as an image or representation of supernatural reality (Heaven). A church symbolized faith. Christians revealed and exercised faith; they communicated with God through prayer—that is, by raising their minds and hearts to God. The church building seemed the ideal place for prayer: communal prayer built faith, and faith encouraged prayer.

Architecture became the dominant art form of the Middle Ages. Nineteenth-century architectural historians coined the term *Romanesque,* meaning "in the Roman manner," to describe church architecture in most of Europe between the tenth and twelfth centuries. The main features of the Romanesque style—solid walls, rounded arches, and masonry vaults—had been the characteristics of large Roman buildings. With the massive barrel vaulting of the roof, heavy walls were required to carry the weight (see Image 1). Romanesque churches had a massive quality, reflecting the increasing political and economic stability of the period and suggesting that they were places of refuge and security in times of attack. A Romanesque church was a "fortress of God."

Gothic churches, by contrast, were walls of light. Visitors and worshipers approached the west end of the building, noticing the carved statues in the *tympanum* (space above the portal, or door), perhaps awestruck by the lancets and rose window over the portal. Inside, a long row of columns directed their gaze down the *nave* (center aisle), and they proceeded to the *transept* (cross aisle), which separated the sanctuary and the choir (reserved for the clergy) from the body of the church (the laypeople's area). See Image 2. So that the flow of pilgrims would not disturb the clergy in their chants, *ambulatories* (walkways) were constructed around the sanctuary. Off the ambulatories, radiating

Image 1 Saint-Savin-sur-Gartempe (Romanesque), Early Twelfth Century. *(Editions Gaud)*

chapels surrounded the *apse,* the semicircular domed projection at the east end of the building. Apsidal chapels, each dedicated to and containing the relics of a particular saint, were visible from the exterior, as were the *flying buttresses* that supported the outward thrusts of the interior vaults. Above the apse and the west, south, and north portals, circular windows emerged from the radiating stone tracery in the form of roses.

Study the model of Chartres Cathedral (Image 3). Cover it with a piece of paper. In the photo of Notre Dame Cathedral on page 359, identify the following parts of a Gothic church: west portal, nave, transept, ambulatory, apse, pointed arch, flying buttress, spire,

Image 2 Amiens Cathedral, Mid-Thirteenth Century.
(Editions Gaud)

Floor Plan

North portal · Apse · East · Transept · Choir and sanctuary · Ambulatory · Nave · West portal · South portal

Spire · Ribbed vaulting · Rose window · Rose window · Lancets · Tympanum · West portal · South portal · Pointed arch · Flying buttress

Image 3 Elements of a Gothic Church (Chartres Cathedral).

Image 4 Sainte-Chapelle, Paris, Mid-Thirteenth Century. *(Scala/Art Resource, NY)*

lancet, rose window. Explain the function of each feature you identify. How do you account for the fact that some churches were never finished?

Compare the interior of the abbey church of Saint-Savin-sur-Gartempe (Image 1), a Romanesque church built in about 1100 in Poitou, France, and the interior of Amiens Cathedral (Image 2), a Gothic church built from 1220 to 1288. What are the most striking differences? What developments made the changes from Romanesque to Gothic structurally possible?

Architecture reveals the interests and values of a society, its goals and aspirations. What does Sainte-Chapelle (Image 4), built by King Louis IX of France to house relics—the crown of thorns placed on Jesus' head before the Crucifixion, a nail from the Crucifixion, a fragment of Jesus' cross—tell us about the values and aspirations of thirteenth-century French society?

A Gothic church represents more than a house of prayer or worship. Medieval people did not compartmentalize the various aspects of their lives as modern people tend to do. What civic, social, economic, and political functions did a church building serve?

Online Study Center **Improve Your Grade**
Going Beyond Images in Society

Denis. Work began in 1137. On June 11, 1144, King Louis VII and a large crowd of bishops, dignitaries, and common people witnessed the solemn consecration of the first **Gothic** church in France.

The new architectural style actually preceded the modern term for it. The Italian Renaissance art historian Giorgio Vasari (1511–1574) first applied the term *Gothic* to the architectural and artistic style that prevailed in Europe (particularly northern Europe) from the mid-twelfth to the sixteenth centuries. Vasari and other Renaissance artists used *Gothic* as a word of abuse: they condemned medieval architecture as barbaric, implying incorrectly that it was the style of the Gothic tribes who had destroyed the classical architecture of the Roman Empire. (See the feature "Images in Society: From Romanesque to Gothic" on pages 356–357.)

In Gothic churches the solid stone barrel-vaulted roof was replaced by a roof made of stone ribs with plaster in between. This made the ceiling much lighter, so that the side pillars and walls did not need to carry so much weight and solid walls could be replaced by windows, which let in great amounts of light. The ribs were also pointed at the top rather than rounded, which dispersed the thrust of the archway in a new way. In addition to ribs that ran down the walls of the church, additional arched stone supports outside the walls, called *flying buttresses,* carried some of the weight and thrust of the roof, allowing builders to go higher and more open still. Thus, in contrast to solid Romanesque structures, Gothic churches became walls of light in which the eye is led upward by the pointed arches and ribbed vaulting; plain glass windows were replaced by colored stained-glass in elaborate designs, often painted or arranged to show biblical scenes.

Begun in the Île-de-France, Gothic architecture spread throughout France with the expansion of royal power. From France the new style spread to England, Germany, Italy, Spain, and eastern Europe. In those countries, the Gothic style competed with strong indigenous architectural traditions and thus underwent transformations that changed it to fit local usage. French master masons were soon invited to design and supervise the construction of churches in other parts of Europe. For example, William of Sens was commissioned to rebuild Canterbury Cathedral after a disastrous fire in 1174.

Organizing and Building

The bishop and the clergy of the cathedral made the decision to build, but they depended on the support of all social classes. Bishops raised revenue from contributions of people in their dioceses, and the clergy appealed to the king and the nobility. Since Suger deliberately utilized the Gothic style to glorify the French monarchy, it was called "French royal style" from its inception. Thus the French kings were generous patrons of many cathedrals. Louis IX endowed churches in the Île-de-France—most notably, Sainte-Chapelle, a small chapel to house relics. Noble families often gave contributions to have their crests in the stained-glass windows. Above all, the church relied on the help of those with the greatest amount of ready cash, the commercial classes.

Money was not the only need. A great number of artisans had to be assembled: quarrymen, sculptors, stonecutters, masons, mortar makers, carpenters, blacksmiths, glassmakers, roofers. Each master craftsman had apprentices, and unskilled laborers had to be recruited for the heavy work. The construction of a large cathedral was rarely completed in a lifetime; many were never finished at all. Because generation after generation added to the building, many Gothic churches show the architectural influences of two or even three centuries. (These variations in style were one of the aspects of Gothic buildings hated by later Renaissance architects, who regarded unity of style as essential in an attractive building.)

Bishops and abbots sketched out what they wanted and set general guidelines, but they left practical needs and aesthetic considerations to the master mason. He held overall responsibility for supervision of the project. (Medieval chroniclers applied the term *architect* to the abbots and bishops who commissioned the projects or the lay patrons who financed them, not to the draftsmen who designed them.) **Master masons** were paid higher wages than other masons; their contracts usually ran for several years, and great care was taken in their selection. Being neither gentlemen, clerics, nor laborers, master masons fit uneasily into the social hierarchy.

Since cathedrals were symbols of civic pride, towns competed to build the largest and most splendid church. In northern France in the late twelfth and early thirteenth centuries, cathedrals grew progressively taller. In 1163 the citizens of Paris began Notre Dame Cathedral, planning it to reach the height of 114 feet. When reconstruction on Chartres Cathedral was begun in 1194, it was to be 119 feet. The people of Beauvais exceeded everyone: their church, started in 1247, reached 157 feet. Unfortunately, the weight imposed on the vaults was too great, and the building collapsed in 1284. Another part collapsed in 1573, and Beauvais Cathedral was never finished, leaving a transept, choir, and apse with no

Notre Dame Cathedral, Paris (begun 1163), View from the South This view offers a fine example of the twin towers (*left*), the spire, the great rose window over the south portal, and the flying buttresses that support the walls and the vaults. Like hundreds of other churches in medieval Europe, it was dedicated to the Virgin. With a nave rising 226 feet, Notre Dame was the tallest building in Europe. *(David R. Frazier/Photo Researchers)*

nave; these parts contain the highest ceiling of any Gothic cathedral, tall enough to hold a fifteen-story office building. Such a collapse was very rare, however, and many cathedrals well over 100 feet tall were built as each bishop and town sought to outdo the neighbors. Medieval people built cathedrals to glorify God—and if mortals were impressed, all the better.

Cathedrals served secular as well as religious purposes. The sanctuary containing the altar and the bishop's chair belonged to the clergy, but the rest of the church belonged to the people. In addition to marriages, baptisms, and funerals, there were scores of feast days on which the entire town gathered in the cathedral for festivities.

Amiens Cathedral could hold the entire town population. Local guilds met in the cathedrals to arrange business deals and plan recreational events and the support of disabled members. Magistrates and municipal officials held political meetings there. Some towns never built town halls because all civic functions took place in the cathedral. Pilgrims slept there; lovers courted there; traveling actors staged plays there. The cathedral belonged to all.

First and foremost, however, the cathedral was intended to teach the people the doctrines of Christian faith through visual images. Architecture became the servant of theology. The main altar was at the east end, pointing toward Jerusalem. The west front of the cathedral faced

Tree of Jesse In Christian symbolism, a tree stands for either life or death. Glassmakers depicted the ancestors of Christ as a tree's branches, based on the prophecy of Isaiah (11:1–2)—"a shoot shall sprout from the stump of Jesse, and from his roots a bud shall blossom, the spirit of the Lord shall rest upon him"—and the genealogy of Jesus in Matthew (1:1–16). In this stained glass from the west façade of Chartres Cathedral (ca 1150–1170), Jesse, David, and Solomon are shown from bottom to top, with Mary holding the Christ child (unseen) at the top. The glass is set within a rectilinear framework. (© Clive Hicks)

the setting sun, and its wall was usually devoted to the scenes of the Last Judgment. The north side, which received the least sunlight, displayed events from the Old Testament. The south side, washed in warm sunshine for much of the day, depicted scenes from the New Testament. This symbolism implied that the Jewish people of the Old Testament lived in darkness and that the Gospel brought by Christ illuminated the world. Every piece of sculpture, furniture, and stained glass had religious or social significance.

Stained glass beautifully reflects the creative energy of the High Middle Ages. It is both an integral part of Gothic architecture and a distinct form of painting. The ancient Egyptians had invented the process. The designer first sketched a picture on a wooden panel the size of the window opening, noting the colors of each form or shape in the planned composition. Then glass blowers made sheets of colored glass, adding metallic oxides—cobalt for blue, manganese for red or purple, silver for yellow— to a basic mixture of sand and ash or lime, which was fused at a high temperature. From the large sheets of stained glass, artisans cut small pieces and laid them out on the wooden panel. Details were added with an enamel emulsion, and the glass was reheated to fuse the enamel. Last, the designer assembled the pieces and linked them together with narrow strips of lead, called *cames*. The assembled window was then set into an iron frame prepared to fit the window opening.[9] As Gothic churches became more skeletal and had more windows, stained glass replaced manuscript illumination as the leading form of painting.

Contributors to the cathedral and workers left their imprints on it. Stonecutters cut their individual marks in each block of stone, partly so that they would be paid. At Chartres the craft and merchant guilds—drapers, furriers, haberdashers, tanners, butchers, bakers, fishmongers, and wine merchants—donated money and are memorialized in stained-glass windows. Thousands of scenes in the cathedral celebrate nature, country life, and the activities of ordinary people.

Tapestry making also came into its own in the fourteenth century. Heavy woolen tapestries were first made in the monasteries and convents as wall hangings for churches. Because they could be moved and lent an atmosphere of warmth, they replaced mural paintings. Early tapestries depicted religious scenes, but later hangings produced for the knightly class bore secular designs, especially romantic forests and hunting spectacles.

Romanesque and Gothic churches housed relics of Jesus, Mary, or the saints. Abbey and cathedral churches at-

Fifteenth-Century Flemish Tapestry   The weavers of Tournai (in present-day Belgium) spent twenty-five years (1450–1475) producing this magnificent tapestry, which is based on the Old Testament story of Jehu, Jezebel, and the sons of Ahab (2 Kings, 9–10). *(Isabella Stewart Gardner Museum, Boston)*

tracted pilgrims from far and near to pray near the relics, which provided economic opportunities for merchants and innkeepers.

Once at least part of a Gothic cathedral had been built, the building began to be used for religious services. The Mass and other services became increasingly complex to fit with their new surroundings. Originally, services were chanted in unison, termed *plainsong* or *Gregorian chant,* but by the eleventh century additional voices singing on different pitches were added to create *polyphony.* Certain parts of the service were broken off into standalone polyphonic pieces called *motets,* a style that composers soon adapted to secular music as well as ecclesiastical. Church leaders sometimes fumed that motets and polyphony made the text impossible to understand—Pope John XXII called this style an "avalanche of notes" in 1324—but, along with incense, candles, stained-glass windows,

and the building itself, music made any service in a Gothic cathedral a rich experience.

Cities and the Church

The soaring towers of Gothic cathedrals were visible symbols of the Christian faith and civic pride of medieval urban residents, but many city people also felt that the church did not meet their spiritual needs. The bishops, usually drawn from the feudal nobility, did not understand urban culture and were suspicious of it. Christian theology, formulated for an earlier rural age, did not address the problems of the more sophisticated mercantile society. The new monastic orders of the twelfth century, such as the Cistercians, situated in remote, isolated areas had little relevance to the towns. Townspeople wanted a pious clergy capable of preaching the Gospel, and they disapproved of clerical ignorance and luxurious living. Critical of the clergy, neglected, and spiritually unfulfilled, townspeople turned to heretical sects.

• *Why did towns become the center of religious heresy, and what was the church's response?*

Heretical Groups

The term *heresy,* which derives from the Greek *hairesis,* meaning "individual choosing," is older than Christianity. At the end of the fourth century, when Christianity became the official religion of the Roman Empire, religious issues took on a legal dimension. Theologians and kings defined the Roman Empire as a Christian society. Since religion was thought to bind society in a fundamental way, religious unity was essential for social cohesion. A heretic, therefore, threatened not only the religious part of the community, but the community itself. Beginning with Emperor Theodosius in the fourth century (page 195), civil authority could (and did) punish heresy. In the early Middle Ages the term *heresy* came to be applied to the position of a Christian who held to doctrines that the church defined as incorrect.

Ironically, the eleventh-century Gregorian reform movement, which had worked to purify the church of disorder, led to some twelfth- and thirteenth-century heretical movements. Papal efforts to improve the sexual morality of the clergy, for example, had largely succeeded. When Gregory VII forbade married priests to celebrate church ceremonies, he expected public opinion to force priests to put aside their wives and concubines. But Gregory did not foresee the consequences of this order. Laypersons assumed they could, and indeed should, remove priests for any type of immorality or for not living according to standards that the parishioners judged appropriate.

In northern Italian towns, Arnold of Brescia, a vigorous advocate of strict clerical poverty, denounced clerical wealth. In France, Peter Waldo, a rich merchant of Lyons, gave his money to the poor and preached that only prayers, not sacraments, were needed for salvation. The **Waldensians**—as Peter's followers were called—bitterly attacked the sacraments and church hierarchy, and they carried these ideas across Europe. As we saw in Chapter 9, the Albigensians asserted that the material world was evil and that religious leaders should be those who rejected worldly things, not the wealthy bishops or the papacy (see pages 284–285).

The Friars

In its continuing struggle against heresy, the church gained the support of two remarkable men, Saint Dominic and Saint Francis, and of the orders they founded. Born in Castile, the province of Spain famous for its zealous Christianity and militant opposition to Islam, Domingo de Gúzman (1170?–1221) received a sound education and was ordained a priest. In 1206 he accompanied his bishop on a mission to preach to the Albigensian heretics in Languedoc. Although the austere simplicity in which they traveled contrasted favorably with the pomp and display of the papal legate in the area, Dominic's efforts had little practical success. Determined to win the heretics back with ardent preaching, Dominic subsequently returned to France with a few followers. In 1216 the group—officially known as the "Preaching Friars" though often called **Dominicans**—won papal recognition as a new religious order. Their name indicates their goal; they were to preach, and in order to preach effectively, they had to study. Dominic sent his recruits to the universities for training in theology.

Francesco di Bernardone (1181–1226), son of a wealthy cloth merchant from the northern Italian town of Assisi, was an extravagant wastrel until he had a sudden conversion. Directed by a vision to rebuild the dilapidated chapel of Saint Damiano in Assisi, Francis sold some of his father's cloth to finance the reconstruction. His enraged father insisted that he return the money and enlisted the support of the bishop. When the bishop told Francis to obey his father, Francis took off all his clothes and returned them to his father. Thereafter he promised to obey only his Father in Heaven. Francis was particularly inspired by two biblical texts: "If you seek perfection, go, sell your possessions, and give to the poor. You will have treasure in heaven. Afterward, come back and follow me" (Matthew 19:21); and Jesus' advice to his disciples as they went out to preach, "Take nothing for the journey, neither walking staff nor travelling bag, nor bread, nor money" (Luke 9:3). Over the centuries, these words have inspired countless young people. With Francis, however, there was a radical difference: he intended to observe them literally and without compromise. He set out to live and preach the Gospel in absolute poverty.

Francis went to live in a cave near Assisi. His father cut him off from any more family money, but Francis took delight in this situation, saying that he was now married to "Lady Poverty." His asceticism did not emphasize withdrawal from the world, but joyful devotion; in contrast to the Albigensians, who saw the material world as evil, Francis saw all creation as God-given and good. He wrote hymns to natural objects such as "brother moon" and was widely reported to perform miracles involving animals, which is how he has become the patron saint of birdbaths in the contemporary world.

The simplicity, humility, and joyful devotion with which Francis carried out his mission soon attracted companions. Although he resisted pressure to establish an order, his followers became so numerous that he was obliged to develop some formal structure. In 1221 the papacy approved the "Rule of the Little Brothers of Saint Francis," as the **Franciscans** were known.

The new Dominican and Franciscan orders differed significantly from older monastic orders such as the Benedictines and the Cistercians. First, the Dominicans and Franciscans were **friars,** not monks. Their lives and work focused on the cities and university towns, the busy centers of commercial and intellectual life, not the secluded and cloistered world of monks. They did not chant the Divine Office (see page 321), and they thought that *more* contact with ordinary Christians, not less, was a better spiritual path.

Second, the friars stressed apostolic poverty, a life based on the Gospel's teachings, in which they would own no property and depend on Christian people for their material needs. Hence they were called **mendicants** or mendicant orders, that is, begging friars. Benedictine and Cistercian abbeys, on the other hand, held land—not infrequently great tracts of land. The Franciscans originally vowed absolute poverty—Francis wanted them never to have more at one time than they would need in a day—but the order grew so fast that this became impossible to maintain, and Francis's original standards were relaxed.

Finally, the friars usually drew their members largely from the burgher class, from small property owners and shopkeepers. The monastic orders, by contrast, gathered their members (at least until the thirteenth century) overwhelmingly from the nobility.

The friars represented a response to the spiritual and intellectual needs of the thirteenth century. While the Franciscans initially accepted uneducated men, the Dominicans showed a marked preference for university graduates. A more urban and sophisticated society required a highly educated clergy. The Dominicans soon held professorial chairs at leading universities, and they count Thomas Aquinas, probably the greatest medieval philosopher in Europe, as their most famous member. But the Franciscans followed suit at the universities and also produced intellectual leaders. The friars interpreted

Christian doctrine for the new urban classes. By living Christianity as well as by preaching it, they won the respect of the medieval bourgeoisie.

As the orders of friars were being established, women sought to develop similar women's orders devoted to active service out in the world. Clare of Assisi (1193–1253), like Francis the child of a wealthy Italian urban family, refused to marry, sought to live in poverty, and became a follower of Francis, who established a place for her to live in a nearby church. She was joined by other women, and they attempted to establish a rule for life in their community that would follow Francis's ideals of absolute poverty and allow them to serve the poor. Her rule was accepted by the papacy only after many decades, and then only because she agreed that the order, called the **Poor Clares,** would be enclosed.

In the growing cities of Europe, especially in the Netherlands, groups of women seeking to live religious lives came together as what later came to be known as **Beguines.** (The origins of the word are debated.) They lived communally in small houses called beguinages, combining a life of prayer with service to the needy, but took no formal vows. In a few cities these beguinages grew quite large, eventually incorporating churches and other buildings as well as housing for several hundred women. Beguine spirituality emphasized direct personal communication with God, sometimes through mystical experiences, rather than through the intercession of a saint or official church rituals. Many Beguines were also devoted to the church's sacraments, however, especially the Eucharist, and initially some church officials gave guarded approval of the movement. By the fourteenth century, however, they were declared heretical and much of their property was confiscated, for church officials were clearly uncomfortable with women who were neither married nor cloistered nuns.

The Friars and Papal Power

Beginning in 1233 the papacy used the friars to staff its new ecclesiastical court, the Inquisition (see pages 284–285). Popes selected the friars to direct the Inquisition because bishops proved unreliable and because special theological training was needed. *Inquisition* means "investigation," and the Franciscans and Dominicans developed expert methods of rooting out unorthodox thought. Ironically, within a hundred years of Francis's death one of the Inquisition's targets was the Spiritual Franciscans, a breakaway group that wanted to follow

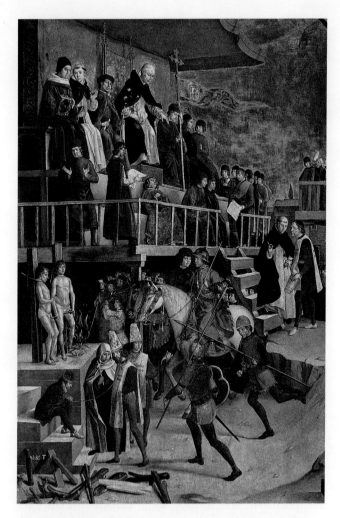

Saint Dominic and the Inquisition   The fifteenth-century court painter to the Spanish rulers Ferdinand and Isabella, Pedro Berruguete here portrays an event from the life of Saint Dominic: Dominic presides at the trial of Count Raymond of Toulouse, who had supported the Albigensian heretics. Raymond, helmeted and on horseback, repented and was pardoned; his companions, who would not repent, were burned. Smoke from the fire has put one of the judges to sleep, and other officials, impervious to the human tragedy, chat among themselves. *(Museo del Prado, Madrid/Institut Amatller d'Art Hispanic)*

Francis's original ideals of poverty and denied the pope's right to countermand that ideal.

Modern Americans consider the procedures of the Inquisition exceedingly unjust, and there was substantial criticism of it in the Middle Ages. The accused did not learn the evidence against them or see their accusers; they

were subjected to lengthy interrogations often designed to trap them; and torture could be used to extract confessions. Medieval people, however, believed that heretics destroyed the souls of their neighbors. By attacking religion, it was also thought, heretics destroyed the very bonds of society. By the mid-thirteenth century secular governments steadily pressed for social conformity, and they had the resources to search out and punish heretics. So successful was the Inquisition as a tool of royal power that within a century heresy had been virtually extinguished.

Popes and kings jointly supported the Inquisition, but in the late thirteenth century the papacy came into a violent dispute with several of Europe's leading rulers. In 1294 King Edward I of England and Philip the Fair of France declared war on each other. To finance this war, both kings laid taxes on the clergy. Kings had been taxing the church for decades. Pope Boniface VIII (1294–1303), arguing from precedent, insisted that kings gain papal consent for taxation of the clergy and forbade churchmen to pay the taxes. But Edward and Philip refused to accept this decree, partly because it hurt royal finances and partly because the papal order threatened royal authority within their countries. Edward immediately denied the clergy the protection of the law, an action that meant its members could be attacked with impunity. Philip halted the shipment of all ecclesiastical revenue to Rome. Boniface had to back down.

Philip the Fair and his ministers continued their attack on all powers in France outside royal authority. Philip arrested a French bishop who was also the papal legate. When Boniface defended the ecclesiastical status and diplomatic immunity of the bishop, Philip declared that the pope was a heretic. The papacy and the French monarchy waged a bitter war of propaganda. Finally, in 1302, in a letter titled **Unam Sanctam** (because its opening sentence spoke of one holy Catholic Church), Boniface insisted that all Christians were subject to the pope. Although the letter made no specific reference to Philip, it held that kings should submit to papal authority. Philip's university-trained advisers responded with an argument drawn from Roman law. They maintained that the king of France was completely sovereign in his kingdom and responsible to God alone. French mercenary troops went to Italy and assaulted and arrested the aged pope at Anagni. Although Boniface was soon freed, he died shortly afterward. The confrontation at Anagni foreshadowed serious difficulties in the Christian church, but religious struggle was only one of the crises that would face Western society in the fourteenth century.

Chapter Summary

Online Study Center   ACE the Test

- *How did medieval cities originate, and what impact did they have on the economy and on culture?*
- *How did universities evolve, and what needs of medieval society did they serve?*
- *What do oral traditions and vernacular literature reveal about medieval culture?*
- *How did cathedrals express the ideals, attitudes, and interests of medieval people?*
- *Why did towns become the center of religious heresy, and what was the church's response?*

Medieval cities—whether beginning around the sites of cathedrals, fortifications, or market towns—recruited people from the countryside with the promise of greater freedom and new possibilities. Cities provided economic opportunity, which, together with the revival of long-distance trade and a new capitalistic spirit, led to greater wealth, a higher standard of living, and upward social mobility for many people. Merchants and artisans formed guilds to protect their means of livelihood. Not everyone in medieval cities shared in the prosperity, however; many residents lived hand-to-mouth on low wages.

The towns that became centers of trade and production in the High Middle Ages developed into cultural and intellectual centers. Trade brought in new ideas as well as merchandise, and in many cities a new type of educational institution—the university—emerged from cathedral and municipal schools. Universities developed theological, legal, and medical courses of study based on classical models and provided trained officials for the new government bureaucracies. University-trained professionals joined merchants and guild masters as well-off members of the urban elite, heading large households staffed with servants and charging high prices for their services.

University education was in Latin and was limited to men, but the High Middle Ages also saw the creation of new types of vernacular literature. Poems, songs, and stories, written down in local dialects, celebrated things of concern to ordinary people. In this, the troubadours of southern France led the way, using Arabic models to create romantic stories of heterosexual love. The ability to read the vernacular was still limited, however, so oral transmission continued as the most important way that information was conveyed and traditions passed down. The oral culture of medieval cities included plays with re-

ligious themes, but also violent entertainments, bawdy songs, and dancing.

Economic growth meant that merchants, nobles, and guild masters had disposable income they could spend on artistic products and more elaborate consumer goods. They supported the building of churches and cathedrals as visible symbols of their Christian faith and their civic pride; cathedrals in particular grew larger and more sumptuous, with high towers, stained-glass windows, and multiple altars. The sturdy Romanesque style was replaced by the soaring Gothic, in which sophisticated building techniques allowed windows to grow ever taller and wider. Cathedrals were places for socializing as well as worship, and increasingly complex music added to the experience.

Town residents demonstrated their deep religious faith in the construction of Gothic cathedrals, but many urban people thought that the church did not fulfill their spiritual needs. They turned instead to heresies, many of which, somewhat ironically, denied the value of material wealth. Combating heresy became a principal task of new types of religious orders, most prominently the Dominicans and Franciscans, who preached, ministered to city dwellers, and also staffed the papal Inquisition, a special court designed to root out heresy. These efforts were largely successful, and the church continued to exercise leadership of Christian society in the High Middle Ages, though the clash between the papacy and the kings of France and England at the end of the thirteenth century seriously challenged papal power.

Key Terms

town liberties	troubadours
merchant guild	cathedrals
craft guilds	Romanesque
livery	Gothic
sumptuary laws	master masons
Hanseatic League	Waldensians
usury	Dominicans
commercial revolution	Franciscans
mercantile capitalism	friars
Scholastics	mendicants
summa	Poor Clares
dialects	Beguines
vernacular literature	*Unam Sanctam*

Online Study Center   Improve Your Grade Flashcards

(continued on page 368)

Listening to the Past

Courtly Love

Whether female or male, the troubadour poets celebrated fin'amor, a Provençal word for the pure or perfect love a knight was supposed to feel for his lady, which has in English come to be called chivalry or "courtly love." In courtly love lyrics, the writer praises his or her love object, idealizing the beloved and promising loyalty and great deeds. Most of these songs are written by, or from the perspective of, a male lover who is socially beneath his female beloved; her higher status makes her unattainable, so the lover's devotion can remain chaste and pure, rewarded by her handkerchief, or perhaps a kiss, but nothing more. The noblemen and noblewomen who listened to these songs viewed such love as ennobling, and some authors even wrote courtly love lyrics directed to the Virgin Mary, the ultimate unattainable woman.

Scholars generally agree that poetry praising perfect love originated in the Muslim culture of the Iberian Peninsula, where heterosexual romantic love had long been the subject of poems and songs. Southern France was a border area where Christian and Muslim cultures mixed; Spanish Muslim poets sang at the courts of Christian nobles, and Provençal poets picked up their romantic themes.

Other aspects of courtly love are hotly debated. Was it simply a literary convention, or did it shape actual behavior? Did it celebrate adultery, or was true courtly love pure (and unrequited)? How should we interpret medieval physicians' reports of people (mostly young men) becoming gravely ill from "lovesickness"; did the doctors really believe in the physical power of love? Were there actually "courts of love" in which women judged lovers based on a system of rules? Did courtly love lead to greater respect for women or toward greater misogyny, as desire for a beloved so often ended in frustration?

It is very difficult to know whether courtly love literature influenced the treatment of real women to any great extent—peasant women were certainly no less in danger of rape from knightly armies in the thirteenth century than they had been in the tenth—but it did introduce an ideal of heterosexual romance into Western literature that had not been there in the classical or early medieval period. People who study contemporary popular culture note how much courtly love ideals still shape romantic conventions. Countless movies, songs, and novels explore love between people of different social groups, though now the love generally remains pure by having either the lover or the beloved tragically die young.

The following poem was written by Arnaut Daniel, a thirteenth-century troubadour praised by writers from Dante in the thirteenth century to Ezra Pound in the twentieth. Not much is known about him, but the songs that have survived capture courtly love conventions perfectly.

I only know the grief that comes to me,
to my love-ridden heart, out of over-loving,
since my will is so firm and whole
that it never parted or grew distant from her
whom I craved at first sight, and afterwards:
and now, in her absence, I tell her burning
   words;
then, when I see her, I don't know, so much I
   have to, what to say.

To the sight of other women I am blind, deaf
   to hearing them
since her only I see, and hear and heed,
and in that I am surely not a false slanderer,
since heart desires her more than mouth may
   say;
wherever I may roam through fields and valleys,
   plains and mountains
I shan't find in a single person all those qualities
which God wanted to select and place in her.

I have been in many a good court,
but here by her I find much more to praise:
measure and wit and other good virtues,
beauty and youth, worthy deeds and fair
   disport;
so well kindness taught and instructed her
that it has rooted every ill manner out of her:
I don't think she lacks anything good.

No joy would be brief or short
coming from her whom I endear to guess [my
      intentions],
otherwise she won't know them from me,
if my heart cannot reveal itself without words,
since even the Rhone [River], when rain swells
      it,
has no such rush that my heart doesn't stir
a stronger one, weary of love, when I behold
      her.

Joy and merriment from another woman seems
      false and ill to me,
since no worthy one can compare with her,
and her company is above the others'.
Ah me, if I don't have her, alas, so badly she has
      taken me!
But this grief is amusement, laughter and joy,
since in thinking of her, of her am I gluttonous
      and greedy:
ah me, God, could I ever enjoy her otherwise!

And never, I swear, I have liked game or ball so
      much,
or anything has given my heart so much joy
as did the one thing that no false slanderer
made public, which is a treasure for me only.
Do I tell too much? Not I, unless she is
      displeased:
beautiful one, by God, speech and voice
I'd lose ere I say something to annoy you.

And I pray my song does not displease you
since, if you like the music and lyrics,
little cares Arnaut whether the unpleasant ones
      like them as well.

*Far fewer poems by female troubadours
(trobairitz) have survived than by male, but those
that have express strong physical and emotional
feelings. The twelfth-century Countess of Dia may
have been the wife of a Provençal nobleman, but
biographies of both troubadours and trobairitz were
often made up later to fit the conventions of courtly
love, so we don't know for sure. We do know that the
words to at least four of her songs have survived, one
of them with the melody, which is very rare.*

I've suffered great distress
From a knight whom I once owned.
Now, for all time, be it known:
I loved him—yes, to excess.
      His jilting I've regretted,
Yet his love I never really returned.
Now for my sin I can only burn:
      Dressed, or in my bed.

O if I had that knight to caress
Naked all night in my arms,
He'd be ravished by the charm

In this fourteenth-century
painting, a lady puts the helmet on
her beloved knight. *(akg-images)*

Of using, for cushion, my breast.
      His love I more deeply prize
Than Floris did Blancheor's
Take that love, my core,
      My sense, my life, my eyes!

Lovely lover, gracious, kind,
When will I overcome your fight?
O if I could lie with you one night!
Feel those loving lips on mine!
      Listen, one thing sets me afire:
Here in my husband's place I want you,
If you'll just keep your promise true:
      Give me everything I desire.

Questions for Analysis

1. Both of these songs focus on a beloved who
   does not return the lover's affection. What
   similarities and differences do you see in them?

2. How does courtly love reinforce other aspects
   of medieval society? Are there aspects of
   medieval society it contradicts?

3. Can you find examples from current popular
   music that parallel the sentiments expressed in
   these two songs?

Source: First poem: Leonardo Malcovati, *Prosody in Eng-
land and Elsewhere: A Comparative Approach* (London:
Gival Press, 2006), and online at http://www.trobar.org/
troubadours/; second poem: quoted in J. J. Wilhelm, ed.,
Lyrics of the Middle Ages: An Anthology (New York: Garland
Publishers, 1993), pp. 83–84.

Suggested Reading

Bruckner, Matilda. *Songs of the Women Troubadours.* 2000. Provides analysis and excerpts of songs.

De Ridder-Symoens, Hilde, ed. *A History of the University in Europe,* vol. 1: *Universities in the Middle Ages.* 1991. Up-to-date interpretations by leading scholars.

Gaunt, Simon, and Sarah Kay, eds. *The Troubadours: An Introduction.* 1999. A collection of essays that trace the development of troubadour song and the reception of troubadour poetry.

Gimpel, Jean. *The Medieval Machine: The Industrial Revolution of the Middle Ages.* 1977. Discusses the mechanical and scientific problems involved in constructing cathedrals and other buildings and the invention of new types of tools.

Lambert, Malcolm. *Medieval Heresy: Popular Movements from the Gregorian Reform to the Reformation,* 3d ed. 2000. Analyzes the development and suppression of heresy over several centuries.

LeGoff, Jacques. *Time, Work, and Culture in the Middle Ages.* 1980. Looks at the broad cultural impact of economic change.

Moore, R. I. *The First European Revolution: 970–1215.* 2000. A bold assessment of the long-term significance of the changes discussed in this chapter.

Moore, R. I. *The Formation of a Persecuting Society.* 1990. Sets the Inquisition and medieval heresy within a broad cultural, social, and political context.

Pirenne, Henri. *Economic and Social History of Medieval Europe.* 1956. Remains a valuable study of the economic revival of Europe by a leading French medievalist.

Radding, Charles M. *The Origins of Medieval Jurisprudence.* 1988. Analyzes legal training and the development of law.

Radding, Charles M., and William W. Clark. *Medieval Architecture, Medieval Learning: Builders and Masters in the Age of Romanesque and Gothic.* 1992. A valuable survey of the evolution of architectural styles and their relation to broader intellectual and cultural developments.

Reynolds, Susan. *An Introduction to the History of English Medieval Towns.* 1982. A good survey of the growth of English towns.

Robertson, D. W., Jr. *Abélard and Héloise.* 1972. A highly readable and commonsensical look at the famous relationship.

Siraisi, Nancy. *Medieval and Early Renaissance Medicine: An Introduction to Knowledge and Practice.* 1990. The best place to start for information about both theory and practice.

Spufford, Peter. *Money and Its Use in Medieval Europe.* 1988. Explores coinage, credit, and other aspects of the monetary economy.

Notes

1. Quoted in R. S. Lopez, "Of Towns and Trade," in *Life and Thought in the Early Middle Ages,* ed. R. S. Hoyt (Minneapolis: University of Minnesota Press, 1967), p. 33.
2. Douglas and Greenaway, *English Historical Documents,* vol. 2, pp. 969–970.
3. H. Rothwell, ed., *English Historical Documents,* vol. 3 (London: Eyre & Spottiswoode, 1975), p. 854.
4. M. M. Postan, *The Medieval Economy and Society: An Economic History of Britain in the Middle Ages* (Baltimore: Penguin Books, 1975), pp. 213–214.
5. Quoted in H. E. Sigerist, *Civilization and Disease* (Chicago: University of Chicago Press, 1943), p. 102.
6. See John F. Benton, "Fraud, Fiction and Borrowing in the Correspondence of Abelard and Heloise," in *Culture, Power and Personality in Medieval France,* ed. T. N. Bisson (London and Rio Grande: The Hambledon Press, 1991), pp. 417–449, esp. pp. 430–443, which convincingly demonstrates that "the most personal parts of the correspondence are not genuine" and that the letters were probably written in the later thirteenth century; and the same scholar's "The Correspondence of Abelard and Heloise," in the same volume, pp. 487–512.
7. Quoted in J. H. Mundy, *Europe in the High Middle Ages, 1150–1309* (New York: Basic Books, 1973), pp. 474–475.
8. A. F. Scott, ed., *Everyone a Witness: The Plantagenet Age* (New York: Thomas Y. Crowell, 1976), p. 263.
9. See "The Technique of Stained Glass Windows," in M. Stokstad, *Art History* (New York: Harry N. Abrams, 1995), p. 559, on which I have leaned.

In this lavishly illustrated French chronicle, Wat Tyler, the leader of the English Peasant's Revolt, is stabbed during a meeting with the king. Tyler died soon afterward, and the revolt was ruthlessly crushed. *(Bibliothèque nationale de France)*

THE CRISIS OF THE LATER MIDDLE AGES, 1300–1450

chapter preview

Prelude to Disaster
• *What were the demographic and economic consequences of climate change?*

The Black Death
• *How did the spread of the plague shape European society?*

The Hundred Years' War
• *What were the causes of the Hundred Years' War, and how did the war affect European politics, economics, and cultural life?*

Challenges to the Church
• *What challenges faced the Christian church in the fourteenth century, and how did church leaders, intellectuals, and ordinary people respond?*

Economic and Social Change
• *How did economic and social tensions contribute to revolts, crime, violence, and a growing sense of ethnic and national distinctions?*

During the later Middle Ages, the last book of the New Testament, the Book of Revelation, inspired thousands of sermons and hundreds of religious tracts. The Book of Revelation deals with visions of the end of the world, with disease, war, famine, and death. It is no wonder this part of the Bible was so popular. Between 1300 and 1450 Europeans experienced a frightful series of shocks: climate change, economic dislocation, plague, war, social upheaval, and increased crime and violence. Death and preoccupation with death make the fourteenth century one of the most wrenching periods of Western civilization. Yet, in spite of the pessimism and crises, important institutions and cultural forms, including representative assemblies and national literatures, emerged. Even institutions that experienced severe crisis, such as the Christian church, saw new types of vitality.

Prelude to Disaster

In the first half of the fourteenth century, Europe experienced a series of climate changes that led to lower levels of food production, which had dramatic and disastrous ripple effects. Political leaders attempted to find solutions, but were unable to deal with the economic and social problems that resulted.

• *What were the demographic and economic consequences of climate change?*

Climate Change and Famine

The period from about 1000 to about 1300 saw warmer than usual climate in Europe, which underlay all the changes and vitality of the High Middle Ages. About 1300 the climate changed, becoming colder and wetter. Historical geographers refer to the period from 1300 to 1450 as a "little ice age," which they can trace through both natural and human records.

Online Study Center

This icon will direct you to interactive activities and study materials on the website **college.hmco.com/pic/mckaywest9e**

Death from Famine   In this fifteenth-century painting, dead bodies lie in the middle of a path, while a funeral procession at the right includes a man with an adult's coffin and a woman with the coffin of an infant under her arm. People did not simply allow the dead to lie in the street in medieval Europe, though during famines and epidemics it was sometimes difficult to maintain normal burial procedures. *(Erich Lessing/Art Resource, NY)*

Evidence from nature emerges through the study of Alpine and polar glaciers, tree rings, and pollen left in bogs. Human-produced sources include written reports of rivers freezing and crops never ripening, as well as archaeological evidence such as the abandoned villages of Greenland, where ice floes cut off contact with the rest of the world and the harshening climate meant that the few hardy crops grown earlier could no longer survive. The Viking colony on Greenland died out completely, though Inuit people who relied on hunting sea mammals continued to live in the far north, as they had before the arrival of Viking colonists.

An unusual number of storms brought torrential rains, ruining the wheat, oat, and hay crops on which people and animals almost everywhere depended. Since long-distance transportation of food was expensive and difficult, most urban areas depended for bread and meat on areas no more than a day's journey away. Poor harvests—and one in four was likely to be poor—led to scarcity and starvation. Almost all of northern Europe suffered a

"Great Famine" in the years 1315–1322, which contemporaries interpreted as a recurrence of the biblical "seven lean years" (Genesis 42). Even in non-famine years, the cost of grain, livestock, and dairy products rose sharply.

Reduced caloric intake meant increased susceptibility to disease, especially for infants, children, and the elderly. Workers on reduced diets had less energy, which in turn meant lower productivity, lower output, and higher grain prices. The Great Famine proved to be a demographic disaster in France; in Burgundy perhaps one-third of the population died. The many religious houses of Flanders experienced a high loss of monks, nuns, and priests. In Scandinavia and the Baltic countries, low cereal harvests, declines in meat and dairy production, economic recessions, and the lack of salt, used for preserving herring, resulted in terrible food shortages.

Hardly had western Europe begun to recover from this disaster when another struck: an epidemic of typhoid fever carried away thousands. In 1316, 10 percent of the population of the city of Ypres may have died between

May and October alone. Then in 1318 disease hit cattle and sheep, drastically reducing the herds and flocks. Another bad harvest in 1321 brought famine and death.

The province of Languedoc in France presents a classic example of agrarian crisis. For more than 150 years Languedoc had enjoyed continual land reclamation, steady agricultural expansion, and enormous population growth. Then the fourteenth century opened with four years of bad harvests. Torrential rains in 1310 ruined the harvest and brought on terrible famine. Harvests failed again in 1322 and 1329. In 1332 desperate peasants survived the winter on raw herbs. In the half century from 1302 to 1348, poor harvests occurred twenty times. These catastrophes had grave social consequences. Poor harvests and famine led to the abandonment of homesteads. In parts of the Low Countries and in the Scottish-English borderlands, entire villages were abandoned. This meant a great increase in the number of vagabonds, what we call "homeless people." In Flanders and East Anglia (eastern England), where aspects of the famine have been carefully analyzed, some peasants were forced to mortgage, sublease, or sell their holdings to get money to buy food. Rich farmers bought out their poorer neighbors. When conditions improved, debtors tried to get their lands back, leading to a very volatile land market. To reduce the labor supply and the mouths to feed in the countryside, young men and women sought work in the towns. Poor harvests probably meant that marriage had to be postponed. Later marriages and the deaths caused by famine and disease meant a reduction in population. Meanwhile, the international character of trade and commerce meant that a disaster in one country had serious implications elsewhere. For example, the infection that attacked English sheep in 1318 caused a sharp decline in wool exports in the following years. Without wool, Flemish weavers could not work, and thousands were laid off. Without woolen cloth, the businesses of Flemish, Hanseatic, and Italian merchants suffered. Unemployment encouraged people to turn to crime.

Government Ineptitude

To none of these problems did governments have effective solutions. The three sons of Philip the Fair who sat on the French throne between 1314 and 1328 condemned speculators, who held stocks of grain back until conditions were desperate and prices high; forbade the sale of grain abroad; and published legislation prohibiting fishing with traps that took large catches. These measures had few positive results. As the subsistence crisis deepened, popular discontent and paranoia increased.

Chronology

1309–1376	Babylonian Captivity; papacy in Avignon
1310–1320	Dante, *Divine Comedy*
1315–1322	Famine in northern Europe
1324	Marsiglio of Padua, *Defensor Pacis*
1337–1453	Hundred Years' War
1348	Black Death arrives in mainland Europe
1358	Jacquerie peasant uprising in France
1378	Ciompi revolt in Florence
1378–1417	Great Schism
1381	Peasants' Revolt in England
1387–1400	Chaucer, *Canterbury Tales*
1415	English smash the French at Agincourt
1429	French victory at Orléans; Charles VII crowned king
1431	Joan of Arc declared a heretic and burned at the stake

Starving people focused their anger on the rich, speculators, and the Jews, who were targeted as creditors fleecing the poor through pawnbroking. (Expelled from France in 1306, Jews were readmitted in 1315 and were granted the privilege of lending at high interest rates.) Rumors spread of a plot by Jews and their agents, the lepers, to kill Christians by poisoning the wells. Based on "evidence" collected by torture, many lepers and Jews were killed, beaten, or hit with heavy fines.

In England Edward I's incompetent son, Edward II (r. 1307–1327), used Parliament to set price controls, first on the sale of livestock after disease and poor lambing had driven prices up, and then on ale, which was made from barley (the severe rains of 1315 had contributed to molds and mildews, sharply reducing the crop). Baronial conflicts and wars with the Scots dominated Edward II's reign. Fearing food riots and violence, Edward condemned speculators, which proved easier than enforcing price controls. He did try to buy grain abroad, but yields in the Baltic were low; the French crown, as we have seen, forbade exports; and the grain shipped from Castile in northern Spain was grabbed by Scottish, English, and rogue Hanseatic pirates on the high seas. Such grain as reached southern English ports was stolen by looters and sold on the black market. The Crown's efforts at famine relief failed.

The Black Death

Royal attempts to provide food from abroad were unsuccessful, but they indicate the extent of long-distance shipping by the beginning of the fourteenth century. In 1291 Genoese sailors had opened the Strait of Gibraltar to Italian shipping by defeating the Moroccans. Then, shortly after 1300, important advances were made in the design of Italian merchant ships. A square rig was added to the mainmast, and ships began to carry three masts instead of just one. Additional sails better utilized wind power to propel the ship. The improved design permitted year-round shipping for the first time, and Venetian and Genoese merchant ships could sail the dangerous Atlantic coast even in the winter months.

Ships continually at sea carried all types of cargo, and they also carried vermin of all types, especially insects and rats, which often harbored disease pathogens. Rats, fleas, and cockroaches could live for months on the cargo carried along the coasts, disembarking at ports with the grain, cloth, or other merchandise. Just as modern air travel has allowed diseases such as AIDS and SARS to spread quickly over very long distances, medieval shipping did the same. The most frightful of these diseases first emerged in western Europe in 1347, carried on Genoese ships, a disease that was later called the **Black Death.**

• *How did the spread of the plague shape European society?*

Pathology

Most historians and almost all microbiologists identify the disease that spread in the fourteenth century as the bubonic plague, caused by the bacillus *Yersinia pestis.* The disease normally afflicts rats. Fleas living on the infected rats drink their blood; the bacteria that cause the plague multiply in the flea's gut; and the flea passes them on to the next rat it bites by throwing up into the bite. Usually the disease is limited to rats and other rodents, but at certain points in history—perhaps when most rats have been killed off—the fleas have jumped from their rodent hosts to humans and other animals. One of these times appears to have been in the Eastern Roman Empire in the sixth century, when a plague killed millions of people. Another was in China and India in the 1890s,

when millions died. Doctors and epidemiologists closely studied this outbreak, identified the bacillus as bubonic plague, and learned about the exact cycle of infection for the first time.

The fourteenth-century outbreak showed many similarities to the nineteenth-century outbreak, but also some differences. There are no reports of massive rat die-offs in fourteenth-century records. The plague was often transmitted directly from one person to another through coughing and sneezing (what epidemiologists term *pneumonic* transmission) as well as through flea bites. The fourteenth-century outbreak spread much faster than the nineteenth-century outbreak and was much more deadly, killing as much as one-third of the population when it first spread to an area. These differences have led some historians to question whether the fourteenth-century disease was actually bubonic plague or whether it was some other disease, perhaps something like the Ebola virus. In the late 1990s French paleomicrobiologists studying the tooth pulp from bodies in two plague cemeteries found DNA from *Y. pestis,* a finding that has been viewed as convincing by most medical historians, though similar studies of English plague cemeteries have not yielded the same results.

These debates fuel continued study of medical aspects of the plague. Some scholars suggest that the type of fleas that normally live on humans might have also been agents in plague transmission in the fourteenth century (which would account for the lack of a rat die-off), or that the fourteenth-century strain of the disease might have been particularly deadly, or that improvements in sanitation and public health by the nineteenth century—even in poor countries such as India—might have limited the mortality rate significantly.

Though there is some disagreement about exactly what kind of disease the plague was, there is no dispute about its dreadful effects on the body. The classic symptom of the bubonic plague was a growth the size of a nut or an apple in the armpit, in the groin, or on the neck. This was the boil, or **bubo,** that gave the disease its name and caused agonizing pain. If the bubo was lanced and the pus thoroughly drained, the victim had a chance of recovery. The next stage was the appearance of black spots or blotches caused by bleeding under the skin. (This syndrome did not give the disease its common name; contemporaries did not call the plague the Black Death. Sometime in the fifteenth century, the Latin phrase *atra mors,* meaning "dreadful death," was translated as "black death," and the phrase stuck.) Finally, the victim began to cough violently and spit blood. This stage, indicating the presence of millions of bacilli in the

mas et preratis nris prire do
nunc yplo tuo que redemisti
sanguine tuo, ypeo ne inet
num nascatus nobis. let.

Procession of Saint Gregory   According to the *Golden Legend,* a thirteenth-century collection of saints' lives, the bubonic plague ravaged Rome when Gregory I was elected pope (590–604). This fourteenth-century painting, produced at a time when plague was again striking Europe, shows Gregory leading a procession around the city as new victims fall (*center*). The artist shows everyone in fourteenth-century clothing and may have seen similar plague processions in his own city. (*Musée Condé, Chantilly/Art Resource, NY*)

bloodstream, signaled the end, and death followed in two or three days.

Spread of the Disease

Plague symptoms were first described in 1331 in southwestern China, part of the Mongol Empire. Plague-infested rats accompanied Mongol armies and merchant caravans carrying silk, spices, and gold across Central Asia in the 1330s. Then they stowed away on ships, carrying the disease to the ports of the Black Sea by the 1340s. Later stories told of more dramatic means of spreading the disease as well, reporting that Mongol armies besieging the city of Kaffa on the shores of the Black Sea catapulted plague-infected corpses over the walls to infect those inside. The city's residents dumped the corpses into the sea as fast as they could, but they were already infected.

In October 1347 Genoese ships brought the plague from Kaffa to Messina, from which it spread across Sicily. Venice and Genoa were hit in January 1348, and from the port of Pisa the disease spread south to Rome and east to Florence and all of Tuscany. By late spring southern Germany was attacked. Frightened French authorities chased a galley bearing the disease away from the port of Marseilles, but not before plague had infected the city, from which it spread to Languedoc and Spain. In June 1348 two ships entered the Bristol Channel and introduced it into England. All Europe felt the scourge of this horrible disease (see Map 12.1).

Although urban authorities from London to Paris to Rome had begun to try to achieve a primitive level of sanitation by the fourteenth century, urban conditions remained ideal for the spread of disease. Narrow streets filled with refuse and human excrement were as much cesspools as thoroughfares. Dead animals and sore-covered

Mapping the Past

MAP 12.1 The Course of the Black Death in Fourteenth-Century Europe   Use the map and the information in the text to answer the following questions: **1** How did the expansion of trade that resulted from the commercial revolution contribute to the spread of the Black Death? **2** When did the plague reach Paris? Why do you think it got to Paris before it spread to the rest of northern France or to southern Germany? **3** Which cities were spared? What might account for this? **4** Which regions were spared? Would the reasons for this be the same as those for cities, or might other causes have been operating in rural areas?

Online Study Center   **Improve Your Grade** Interactive Map: Bubonic Plague and Social Upheaval in Fourteenth-Century Europe

beggars greeted the traveler. Houses whose upper stories projected over the lower ones blocked light and air. And extreme overcrowding was commonplace. When all members of an aristocratic family lived and slept in one room, it should not be surprising that six or eight persons in a middle-class or poor household slept in one bed—if they had one. Closeness, after all, provided warmth. Houses were beginning to be constructed of

brick, but many wood, clay, and mud houses remained. A determined rat had little trouble entering such a house.

Standards of personal hygiene remained frightfully low. True, most large cities had public bathhouses, but we have no way of knowing how frequently ordinary people used them. Lack of personal cleanliness, combined with any number of temporary ailments such as diarrhea and the common cold, weakened the body's resistance to serious disease. Fleas and body lice were universal afflictions: everyone from peasants to archbishops had them. One more bite did not cause much alarm. But if that nibble came from a bacillus-bearing flea, an entire household or area was doomed.

Mortality rates cannot be specified because population figures for the period before the arrival of the plague do not exist for most countries and cities. The largest amount of material survives for England, but it is difficult to use; after enormous scholarly controversy, only educated guesses can be made. Of a total English population of perhaps 4.2 million, probably 1.4 million died of the Black Death in its several visits. Densely populated Italian cities endured incredible losses. Florence lost between one-half and two-thirds of its 1347 population of 85,000 when the plague visited in 1348. The most widely accepted estimate for western Europe is that the plague killed about one-third of the population in the first wave of infection.

Nor did central and eastern Europe escape the ravages of the disease. Moving northward from the Balkans, eastward from France, and southward from the Baltic, the plague swept through the German Empire. In the Rhineland in 1349, Cologne and Mainz endured heavy losses. In 1348 it swept through Bavaria, entered the Moselle Valley, and pushed into northern Germany. One chronicler records that, in the summer and autumn of 1349, between five hundred and six hundred died every day in Vienna. Styria, in what today is central Austria, was very hard hit, with cattle straying unattended in the fields.

As the Black Death took its toll on the German Empire, waves of emigrants fled to Poland, Bohemia, and Hungary. The situation there was better, though disease was not completely absent. The plague seems to have entered Poland through the Baltic seaports and spread from there. Still, population losses were lower than elsewhere in Europe. The plague spread from Poland to Russia, reaching Pskov, Novgorod, and Moscow. No estimates have been made of population losses there or in the Balkans. In Serbia, though, the plague left vast tracts of land unattended, which prompted an increase in Albanian immigration to meet the labor shortage.

Across Europe the Black Death recurred intermittently from the 1360s to 1400. It reappeared with reduced virulence from time to time over the following centuries, making its last appearance in the French port city of Marseilles in 1721. Survivors became more prudent. Because periods of famine had caused malnutrition, making people vulnerable to disease, Europeans controlled population growth so that population did not outstrip food supply. Western Europeans improved navigation techniques and increased long-distance trade, which permitted the importation of grain from sparsely populated Baltic regions. They strictly enforced quarantine measures. They worked on the development of vaccines. But it was only in 1947, six centuries after the arrival of the plague in the West, that the American microbiologist Selman Waksman discovered an effective vaccine, streptomycin. Plague continues to infect rodent and human populations sporadically today.

Care

Fourteenth-century medical literature indicates that physicians could sometimes ease the pain, but they had no cure. Medical doctors observed that crowded cities had high death rates, especially when the weather was warm and moist. We understand that warm, moist conditions make it easier for germs, viruses, and bacteria to grow and spread, but fourteenth-century people—lay, scholarly, and medical—thought in terms of "poisons" in the air or "corrupted air" rather than germs. This "corrupted air" came from swamps, unburied animal or human corpses, too much rain, the position of planets or stars, or perhaps other causes. The poisons caused illness, which doctors thought of as an imbalance in the fluids in the body, especially blood. Certain symptoms of the plague, especially bleeding and vomiting, were believed to be the body's natural reaction to too much fluid. These were often symptoms of other illnesses as well, and doctors frequently prescribed bloodletting, that is, taking blood from the body by applying leeches or making small cuts in veins, as standard treatment.

If the plague came from poisoned air, people reasoned, then strong-smelling herbs or other substances, like rosemary, juniper, or sulfur, held in front of the nose or burned as incense might stop it. Perhaps loud sounds like ringing church bells or firing the newly invented cannon might help. Medicines made from plants that were bumpy or that oozed liquid might work, keeping the more dangerous swelling and oozing of the plague away. Because the plague seemed to strike randomly, perhaps wearing jewelry with random number and letter combinations, or drinking water in which ink used to write these magical combinations had been dissolved, would help. Such letter and number combinations, called *cryptograms,* were especially popular in Muslim areas. They were often the first letters of words in prayers or religious sayings, and they gave people a sense of order when faced with the randomness with which the plague seemed to strike.

The Italian writer Giovanni Boccaccio (1313–1375), describing the course of the disease in Florence in the preface to his book of tales, *The Decameron*, identified what many knew—that the disease passed from person to person:

Moreover, the virulence of the pest was the greater by reason that intercourse was apt to convey it from the sick to the whole, just as fire devours things dry or greasy when they are brought close to it. Nay, the evil went yet further, for not merely by speech or association with the sick was the malady communicated to the healthy with consequent peril of common death, but any that touched the clothes of the sick or aught else that had been touched or used by them, seemed thereby to contract the disease.[1]

Online Study Center **Improve Your Grade**
Primary Source: The Plague Hits Florence

Wealthier people often fled cities for the countryside, though sometimes this simply spread the plague faster. Some cities tried shutting their gates to prevent infected people and animals from coming in, which worked in a few cities. They also walled up houses in which there was plague, trying to isolate those who were still healthy from the sick. When the disease struck the town of Salé in Morocco, Ibu Abu Madyan shut in the members of his household with sufficient food and water and allowed no one to enter or leave until the plague had passed. Abu Madyan was entirely successful.

Along with looking for medical causes and cures, people also searched for scapegoats, and savage cruelty sometimes resulted. Many people believed that the Jews had poisoned the wells of Christian communities and thereby infected the drinking water. This charge led to the murder of thousands of Jews across Europe. According to one chronicler, sixteen thousand were killed at the imperial city of Strasbourg alone in 1349. Though sixteen thousand is probably a typical medieval numerical exaggeration, the horror of the massacre is not lessened. Scholars have yet to explain the economic impact that the loss of so many productive people had on Strasbourg and other cities.

If medical science had no effective treatment, could victims' suffering be eased? Perhaps it could, in hospitals. What was the geographical distribution of hospitals, and, although our estimates of medieval populations remain rough, what was the hospital-to-population ratio? How many patients could a hospital serve? Whereas earlier the feudal lord had made philanthropic foundations, beginning in the thirteenth century individual merchants—out of compassion, generosity, and the custom of giving to

parish collections, and in the belief that the sick would be prayerful intercessors with God for the donors' sins—endowed hospitals. Business people established hospitals in the towns of northern France and Flanders; Milan, Genoa, and Venice were well served, and the thirty hospitals in Florence provided a thousand beds in 1339. Sixty hospitals served Paris in 1328—but probably not enough for its population of two hundred thousand. The many hospitals in the Iberian Peninsula continued the Muslim tradition of care for the poor and ill. Merchants in the larger towns of the German Empire, in Poland, and in Hungary also founded hospitals in the fourteenth century, generally later than those in western Europe. Sailors, long viewed as potential carriers of disease, benefited from hospitals reserved for them; in 1300 the Venetian government paid a surgeon to care for sick sailors. At the time the plague erupted, therefore, most towns and cities had hospital facilities.

When trying to determine the number of people a hospital could accommodate, the modern researcher considers the number of beds, the size of the staff, and the building's physical layout. Since each medieval hospital bed might serve two or more patients, we cannot calculate the number of patients on the basis of the beds alone. We know that rural hospices usually had twelve to fifteen beds, and city hospitals, as at Lisbon, Narbonne, and Genoa, had on average twenty-five to thirty beds, but these figures do not tell us how many patients were accommodated. Only the very rare document listing the number of wrapping sheets and coffins for the dead purchased in a given period provides the modern scholar with information on the number of patients a hospital had. Hospitals could offer only shelter, compassion, and care for the dying.

Many people did not see the plague as a medical issue, but instead interpreted it as the result of something within themselves. God must be punishing them for terrible sins, they thought, so the best remedies were religious ones: asking for forgiveness, praying, trusting in God, making donations to churches, and trying to live better lives. In Muslim areas, religious leaders urged virtuous living in the face of death: give to the poor, reconcile with your enemies, free your slaves, and say a proper goodbye to your friends and family.

Social, Economic, and Cultural Consequences

It is noteworthy that, in an age of mounting criticism of clerical wealth, the behavior of the clergy during the

Patients in a Hospital Ward, Fifteenth Century In many cities hospitals could not cope with the large numbers of plague victims. The practice of putting two or more adults in the same bed, as shown here, contributed to the spread of the disease. At the Hôtel-Dieu in Paris, nurses complained of being forced to put eight to ten children in a single bed in which a patient had recently died. *(Giraudon/The Bridgeman Art Library)*

plague was often exemplary. Priests, monks, and nuns cared for the sick and buried the dead. In places like Venice, from which even physicians fled, priests remained to give what ministrations they could. Consequently, their mortality rate was phenomenally high. The German clergy especially suffered a severe decline in personnel in the years after 1350.

In taking their pastoral responsibilities seriously, some clergy did things that the church in a later age would vigorously condemn. The institutional church has traditionally opposed letting laymen and, especially, laywomen administer the sacraments. But the shortage of priests was so great that in 1349 Ralph, bishop of Bath and Wells in England (1329–1363), advised his people that "if they are on the point of death and cannot secure the services of a priest, then they should make confession to each other, as is permitted in the teaching of the Apostles, whether to a layman or, if no man is present, even to a woman."[2]

Economic historians and demographers sharply dispute the impact of the plague on the economy in the late fourteenth century. The traditional view that the plague had a disastrous effect has been greatly modified. The clearest evidence comes from England, where the agrarian economy showed remarkable resilience. While the severity of the disease varied from region to region, it appears that by about 1375 most landlords enjoyed revenues near those of the pre-plague years. By the early fifteenth century seigneurial prosperity reached a medieval peak. Why? The answer appears to lie in the fact that England and many parts of Europe suffered from overpopulation in the early fourteenth century. Population losses caused by the Black Death led to increased productivity by restoring a more efficient balance between labor, land, and capital.

What impact did visits of the plague have on urban populations? The rich evidence from a census of the city of Florence and its surrounding territory taken between

1427 and 1430 is fascinating. The region had suffered repeated epidemics since 1347. In a total population of 260,000 persons, 15 percent were age sixty or over (a very high proportion), suggesting that the plague took the young rather than the mature. Children and youths up to age nineteen constituted 44 percent of the people. Adults between the ages of twenty and fifty-nine, the most economically productive group, represented 41 percent of Florentine society.

The high mortality rate of craftsmen led Florentine guilds to recruit many new members. For example, between 1328 and 1347 the silk merchants guild accepted 730 members, and between 1408 and 1427 it admitted 784. It appears that economic organizations tried to keep their numbers constant, even though the size of the population and its pool of potential guild members was shrinking. Moreover, in contrast to the pre-1348 period, many new members of the guilds were not related to existing members. Thus the post-plague years represent an age of "new men."

The Black Death brought on a general European inflation. High mortality produced a fall in production, shortages of goods, and a general rise in prices. The shortage of labor and workers' demands for higher wages put guild masters on the defensive. They retaliated with measures such as the Statute of Laborers (1351), an attempt by the English Parliament to freeze the wages of English workers at pre-1347 levels. Such statutes could not be enforced and thus were unsuccessful. The price of wheat in most of Europe increased, as did the costs of meat, sausage, and cheese. This inflation continued to the end of the fourteenth century. But wages in the towns rose faster, and the broad mass of people enjoyed a higher standard of living. Population decline meant a sharp increase in per capita wealth. The greater demand for labor meant greater mobility for peasants in rural areas and for industrial workers in the towns and cities. Labor shortages caused by the Black Death throughout the Mediterranean region, from Constantinople to Spain, presented aggressive businessmen with a golden opportunity, and the price of slaves rose sharply.

Even more significant than the social effects were the psychological consequences. The knowledge that the disease meant almost certain death provoked the most profound pessimism. Imagine an entire society in the grip of the belief that it was at the mercy of a frightful affliction

Flagellants In this manuscript illumination from 1349, shirtless flagellants scourge themselves with whips as they walk through the streets of the Flemish city of Tournai. The text notes that they are asking for God's grace to return to the city after it had been struck with the "most grave" illness. *(HIP/Art Resource, NY)*

about which nothing could be done, a disgusting disease from which family and friends would flee, leaving one to die alone and in agony. It is not surprising that some sought release in wild living, while others turned to the severest forms of asceticism and frenzied religious fervor. Some extremists joined groups of **flagellants,** who whipped and scourged themselves as penance for their and society's sins in the belief that the Black Death was God's punishment for humanity's wickedness. Groups of flagellants traveled from town to town, often provoking hysteria against Jews and growing into unruly mobs. Officials worried that they would provoke violence and riots, and ordered groups of them to disband or forbade them to enter cities.

Plague ripped apart the social fabric. In the thirteenth century, funerals, traditionally occasions for the mutual consolation of the living as much as memorial services for the dead, grew increasingly elaborate, with large corteges and many mourners. In the fourteenth century, public horror at the suffering of the afflicted and at the dead reduced the size of mourning processions and eventually resulted in failure even to perform the customary death rites. Fear of infection led to the dead being buried hastily, sometimes in mass graves.

People often used pilgrimages to holy places as justification for their flight from cities. Suspected of being carriers of plague, travelers, pilgrims, and the homeless aroused deep hostility. All European port cities followed the example of Ragusa (modern Dubrovnik in southwestern Croatia on the Dalmatian coast) and quarantined arriving ships, crews, passengers, and cargoes to determine whether they brought the plague. Deriving from a Venetian word, the English term *quarantine* originally meant forty days' isolation.

Popular endowments of educational institutions multiplied. The years of the Black Death witnessed the foundation of new colleges at old universities, such as Corpus Christi and Clare Colleges at Cambridge and New College at Oxford, and of entirely new universities. The beginnings of Charles University in Prague (1348) and the Universities of Florence (1350), Vienna (1364), Cracow (1364), and Heidelberg (1385) were all associated with the plague: their foundation charters specifically mention the shortage of priests and the decay of learning. Whereas universities such as those at Bologna and Paris had international student bodies, new institutions established in the wake of the Black Death had more national or local constituencies. Thus the international character of medieval culture weakened. The decline of cultural cohesion paved the way for schism in the Catholic Church even before the Reformation.

The literature and art of the fourteenth century reveal a terribly morbid concern with death. One highly popular artistic motif, the Dance of Death, depicted a dancing skeleton leading away a living person.

The Hundred Years' War

The plague ravaged populations in Asia, North Africa, and Europe; in western Europe a long international war added further misery to the frightful disasters of the plague. England and France had engaged in sporadic military hostilities from the time of the Norman Conquest in 1066, and in the middle of the fourteenth century these became more intense. From 1337 to 1453, the two countries intermittently fought one another in what was the longest war in European history, ultimately dubbed the Hundred Years' War though it actually lasted 116 years.

- *What were the causes of the Hundred Years' War, and how did the war affect European politics, economics, and cultural life?*

Causes

The Hundred Years' War had both distant and immediate causes. In 1259 France and England signed the Treaty of Paris, in which the English king agreed to become— for himself and his successors—vassal of the French crown for the duchy of Aquitaine. The English claimed Aquitaine as an ancient inheritance. French policy, however, was strongly expansionist, and the French kings resolved to absorb the duchy into the kingdom of France.

In January 1327 Queen Isabella of England, her lover Mortimer, and a group of barons, having deposed and murdered Isabella's incompetent husband, King Edward II, proclaimed his fifteen-year-old son king as Edward III. Isabella and Mortimer, however, held real power until 1330, when Edward seized the reins of government. In 1328 Charles IV of France, the last surviving son of Philip the Fair, died childless. With him ended the Capetian dynasty. An assembly of French barons, meaning to exclude Isabella—who was Charles's sister and the daughter of Philip the Fair—and her son Edward III from the French throne, proclaimed that "no woman nor her son could succeed to the [French] monarchy." French lawyers defended the position with the claim that the exclusion of women from ruling or passing down the right to rule was part of Salic Law, a sixth-century Germanic law code (see page 216), and that Salic Law itself

English Merchants in Flanders   In this 1387 illustration, an English merchant requests concessions from the count of Flanders to trade English wool at a favorable price. Flanders was officially on the French side during the Hundred Years' War, but Flemish cities depended heavily on English wool for their textile manufacturing. Hence the count of Flanders agreed to the establishment of the Merchant Staple, an English trading company with a monopoly on trade in wool. *(British Library)*

Economic factors involving the wool trade and the control of Flemish towns had served as justifications for war between France and England for centuries. The wool trade between England and Flanders served as the cornerstone of both countries' economies; they were closely interdependent. Flanders was a fief of the French crown, and the Flemish aristocracy was highly sympathetic to the monarchy in Paris. But the wealth of Flemish merchants and cloth manufacturers depended on English wool, and Flemish burghers strongly supported the claims of Edward III. The disruption of commerce with England threatened their prosperity.

The Popular Response

The governments of both England and France manipulated public opinion to support the war. Whatever significance modern scholars ascribe to the economic factor, public opinion in fourteenth-century England held that the war was waged for one reason: to secure for King Edward the French crown he had been unjustly denied.

was part of the fundamental law of France. They used this invented tradition to argue that Edward should be barred from the French throne. (This notion became part of French legal tradition until the end of the monarchy in 1789.) The barons passed the crown to Philip VI of Valois (r. 1328–1350), a nephew of Philip the Fair.

In 1329 Edward III paid homage to Philip VI for Aquitaine. In 1337 Philip, eager to exercise full French jurisdiction in Aquitaine, confiscated the duchy. Edward III interpreted this action as a gross violation of the treaty of 1259 and as a cause for war. Moreover, Edward argued, as the eldest directly surviving male descendant of Philip the Fair, he must assume the title of king of France in order to wield his rightful authority in Aquitaine. In short, Edward rejected the decision of the French barons excluding him from the throne. Edward III's dynastic argument upset the feudal order in France: to increase their independent power, French vassals of Philip VI used the excuse that they had to transfer their loyalty to a more legitimate overlord, Edward III. One reason the war lasted so long was that it became a French civil war, with some French barons supporting English monarchs in order to thwart the centralizing goals of the French crown.

Edward III issued letters to the sheriffs describing the evil deeds of the French in graphic terms and listing royal needs. Kings in both countries instructed the clergy to deliver sermons filled with patriotic sentiment. The royal courts sensationalized the wickedness of the other side and stressed the great fortunes to be made from the war. Philip VI sent agents to warn communities about the dangers of invasion and to stress the French crown's revenue needs to meet the attack.

The royal campaign to rally public opinion was highly successful, at least in the early stage of the war. Edward III gained widespread support in the 1340s and 1350s. The English developed a deep hatred of the French and feared that King Philip intended "to have seized and slaughtered the entire realm of England." When England was successful in the field, pride in the country's military proficiency increased.

Most important of all, the Hundred Years' War was popular because it presented unusual opportunities for wealth and advancement. Poor knights and knights who were unemployed were promised regular wages. Criminals who enlisted were granted pardons. The great nobles expected to be rewarded with estates. Royal exhortations to the troops before battles repeatedly stressed that, if victorious, the men might keep whatever they seized. The French chronicler Jean Froissart wrote that, at the time of Edward III's expedition of 1359, men of all ranks flocked to the English king's banner. Some came to acquire honor, but many came "to loot and pillage the fair and plenteous land of France."[3]

Online Study Center **Improve Your Grade**
Primary Source: Warfare Without Chivalry:
The Sack of Limoges

The Course of the War to 1419

The war was fought almost entirely in France and the Low Countries (see Map 12.2). It consisted mainly of a series of random sieges and cavalry raids. In 1335 the French began supporting Scottish incursions into northern England, ravaging the countryside in Aquitaine, and sacking and burning English coastal towns, such as Southampton. Such tactics lent weight to Edward III's propaganda campaign. In fact, royal propaganda on both sides fostered a kind of early nationalism.

During the war's early stages, England was highly successful. At Crécy in northern France in 1346, English longbowmen scored a great victory over French knights and crossbowmen. Although the aim of the longbow was not very accurate, it allowed for rapid reloading, and an English archer could send off three arrows to the French crossbowman's one. The result was a blinding shower of arrows that unhorsed the French knights and caused mass confusion. The ring of cannon—probably the first use of artillery in the West—created further panic. Thereupon the English horsemen charged and butchered the French.

This was not war according to the chivalric rules that Edward III would have preferred. Nevertheless, his son, Edward the Black Prince, used the same tactics ten years

Siege of the Castle of Mortagne Near Bordeaux (1377)   Medieval warfare usually consisted of small skirmishes and attacks on castles. This miniature shows the French besieging an English-held castle, which held out for six months. Most of the soldiers use longbows, although at the left two men shoot primitive muskets above a pair of cannon. Painted in the late fifteenth century, the scene reflects military technology available at the time it was painted, not the time of the actual siege. (*British Library*)

MAP 12.2 English Holdings in France During the Hundred Years' War The year 1429 marked the greatest extent of English holdings in France.

later to smash the French at Poitiers, where he captured the French king and held him for ransom. Again, at **Agincourt** near Arras in 1415, the chivalric English soldier-king Henry V (r. 1413–1422) gained the field over vastly superior numbers. Henry followed up his triumph at Agincourt with the reconquest of Normandy. By 1419 the English had advanced to the walls of Paris (see Map 12.2). But the French cause was not lost. Though England had scored the initial victories, France won the war.

Joan of Arc and France's Victory

The ultimate French success rests heavily on the actions of an obscure French peasant girl, **Joan of Arc,** whose vision and work revived French fortunes and led to victory. A great deal of pious and popular legend surrounds Joan the Maid because of her peculiar appearance on the scene, her astonishing success, her martyrdom, and her canonization by the Catholic Church. The historical fact is that she saved the French monarchy, which was the embodiment of France.

Born in 1412 to well-to-do peasants in the village of Domrémy in Champagne, Joan of Arc grew up in a religious household. During adolescence she began to hear voices, which she later said belonged to Saint Michael, Saint Catherine, and Saint Margaret. In 1428 these voices spoke to her with great urgency, telling her that the dauphin (the uncrowned King Charles VII) had to be crowned and the English expelled from France. Joan went to the French court, persuaded the king to reject the rumor that he was illegitimate, and secured his support for her relief of the besieged city of Orléans.

The astonishing thing is not that Joan the Maid overcame serious obstacles to see the dauphin, and not even that Charles and his advisers listened to her. What is amazing is the swiftness with which they were convinced. French fortunes had been so low for so long that the court believed that only a miracle could save the country. Because Joan cut her hair short and dressed like a man, she scandalized the court. But hoping she would provide the miracle, Charles allowed her to accompany the army that was preparing to raise the English siege of Orléans.

In the meantime Joan, herself illiterate, dictated this letter calling on the English to withdraw:

King of England . . . , do right in the King of Heaven's sight. Surrender to The Maid *sent hither by God the King of Heaven, the keys of all the good towns you have taken and laid waste in France. She comes in God's name to establish the Blood Royal, ready to make peace if you agree to abandon France and repay what you have taken. And you,*

archers, comrades in arms, gentles and others, who are before the town of Orléans, retire in God's name to your own country.[4]

Joan arrived before Orléans on April 28, 1429. Seventeen years old, she knew little of warfare and believed that if she could keep the French troops from swearing and frequenting brothels, victory would be theirs. On May 8 the English, weakened by disease and lack of supplies, withdrew from Orléans. Ten days later Charles VII was crowned king at Reims. These two events marked the turning point in the war.

Online Study Center **Improve Your Grade**
Primary Source: The Trial of Joan of Arc

Joan's presence at Orléans, her strong belief in her mission, and the fact that she was wounded enhanced her reputation and strengthened the morale of the army. In 1430 England's allies, the Burgundians, captured Joan and sold her to the English. When the English handed her over to the ecclesiastical authorities for trial, the French court did not intervene. While the English wanted Joan eliminated for obvious political reasons, sorcery (witchcraft) was the ostensible charge at her trial. Witch persecution was increasing in the fifteenth century, and Joan's wearing of men's clothes appeared not only aberrant but indicative of contact with the Devil. In 1431 the court condemned her as a heretic—her claim of direct inspiration from God, thereby denying the authority of church officials, constituted heresy—and burned her at the stake in the marketplace at Rouen. A new trial in 1456 rehabilitated her name. In 1920 she was canonized and declared a holy maiden, and today she is revered as the second patron saint of France, along with King Louis IX. The nineteenth-century French historian Jules Michelet extolled Joan of Arc as a symbol of the vitality and strength of the French peasant classes.

The relief of Orléans stimulated French pride and rallied French resources. As the war dragged on, loss of life mounted, and money appeared to be flowing into a bottomless pit, demands for an end increased in England. The clergy and intellectuals pressed for peace. Parliamentary opposition to additional war grants stiffened. Slowly the French reconquered Normandy and, finally, ejected the English from Aquitaine. At the war's end in 1453, only the town of Calais remained in English hands.

Costs and Consequences

In France the English had slaughtered thousands of soldiers and civilians. In the years after the sweep of the

Black Death, this additional killing meant a grave loss of population. The English had laid waste to hundreds of thousands of acres of rich farmland, leaving the rural economy of many parts of France a shambles. The war had disrupted trade and the great fairs, resulting in the drastic reduction of French participation in international commerce. Defeat in battle and heavy taxation contributed to widespread dissatisfaction and aggravated peasant grievances.

In England only the southern coastal ports experienced much destruction, and the demographic effects of the Black Death actually worked to restore the land-labor balance (see page 379). The costs of the war, however, were tremendous. England spent over £5 million on the war effort, a huge sum at the time. Manpower losses had greater social consequences. The knights who ordinarily handled the work of local government as sheriffs, coroners, jurymen, and justices of the peace were abroad, and their absence contributed to the breakdown of order at the local level. The English government attempted to finance the war effort by raising taxes on the wool crop. Because of steadily increasing costs, Flemish and Italian buyers could not afford English wool. Consequently, raw wool exports slumped drastically between 1350 and 1450.

Many men of all social classes had volunteered for service in France in the hope of acquiring booty and becoming rich. The chronicler Walsingham, describing the period of Crécy, wrote: "For the woman was of no account who did not possess something from the spoils of . . . cities overseas in clothing, furs, quilts, and utensils . . . tablecloths and jewels, bowls of murra [semiprecious stone] and silver, linen and linen cloths."[5] Walsingham is referring to 1348, in the first generation of war. As time went on, most fortunes seem to have been squandered as fast as they were made.

If English troops returned with cash, they did not invest it in land. In the fifteenth century returning soldiers were commonly described as beggars and vagabonds, roaming about making mischief. Even the large sums of money received from the ransom of the great—such as the £250,000 paid to Edward III for the freedom of King John of France—and the money paid as indemnities by captured towns and castles did not begin to equal the more than £5 million spent. England suffered a serious net loss.

The war stimulated technological experimentation, especially with artillery. Cannon revolutionized warfare, making the stone castle no longer impregnable. Because only central governments, not private nobles, could afford cannon, they strengthened the military power of national states.

The long war also had a profound impact on the political and cultural lives of the two countries. Most notably, it stimulated the development of the English Parliament. Between 1250 and 1450, **representative assemblies** flourished in many European countries. In the English Parliament, German diets, and Spanish cortes, deliberative practices developed that laid the foundations for the representative institutions of modern liberal-democratic nations. While representative assemblies declined in most countries after the fifteenth century, the English Parliament endured. Edward III's constant need for money to pay for the war compelled him to summon not only the great barons and bishops, but knights of the shires and burgesses from the towns as well. Parliament met in thirty-seven of the fifty years of Edward's reign.[6]

The frequency of the meetings is significant. Representative assemblies were becoming a habit. Knights and wealthy urban residents—or the "Commons," as they came to be called—recognized their mutual interests and began to meet apart from the great lords. The Commons gradually realized that they held the country's purse strings, and a parliamentary statute of 1341 required that all nonfeudal levies have parliamentary approval. By signing the law, Edward III acknowledged that the king of England could not tax without Parliament's consent. During the course of the war, money grants were increasingly tied to royal redress of grievances: to raise money, the government had to correct the wrongs its subjects protested.

In England, theoretical consent to taxation and legislation was given in one assembly for the entire country. France had no such single assembly; instead, there were many regional or provincial assemblies. Why did a national representative assembly fail to develop in France? The initiative for convening assemblies rested with the king, who needed revenue almost as much as the English ruler. But the French monarchy found the idea of representative assemblies thoroughly distasteful. Large gatherings of the nobility potentially or actually threatened the king's power. The advice of a counselor to King Charles VI (r. 1380–1422), "above all things be sure that no great assemblies of nobles or of *communes* take place in your kingdom," was accepted.[7] Charles VII (r. 1422–1461) even threatened to punish those proposing a national assembly.

No one in France wanted a national assembly. Linguistic, geographical, economic, legal, and political differences were very strong. People tended to think of themselves as Breton, Norman, Burgundian, or whatever, rather than French. Through much of the fourteenth and early fifteenth centuries, weak monarchs lacked the power to call a national assembly. Provincial assemblies, highly jealous of their independence, did not want a national assembly. The costs of sending delegates to it would be high, and the result was likely to be increased taxation.

In both countries, however, the war did promote the growth of **nationalism**—the feeling of unity and identity that binds together a people. After victories, each country experienced a surge of pride in its military strength. Just as English patriotism ran strong after Crécy and Poitiers, so French national confidence rose after Orléans. French national feeling demanded the expulsion of the enemy not merely from Normandy and Aquitaine but from all French soil. Perhaps no one expressed this national consciousness better than Joan of Arc when she exulted that the enemy had been "driven out of *France*."

Challenges to the Church

In times of crisis or disaster, people of all faiths have sought the consolation of religion. In the fourteenth century, however, the official Christian church offered little solace. In fact, the leaders of the church added to the sorrow and misery of the times. In response to this lack of leadership, members of the clergy challenged the power of the pope, and laypeople challenged the authority of the church itself. Women and men increasingly relied on direct approaches to God, often through mystical encounters, rather than on the institutional church.

• *What challenges faced the Christian church in the fourteenth century, and how did church leaders, intellectuals, and ordinary people respond?*

The Babylonian Captivity and Great Schism

In order to control the church and its policies, Philip the Fair of France pressured Pope Clement V to settle permanently in Avignon in southeastern France, where the popes already had their summer residence (see Map 11.3 on page 346). Clement, critically ill with cancer, lacked the will to resist Philip. The popes lived in Avignon from 1309 to 1376, a period in church history often called the **Babylonian Captivity** (referring to the seventy years the ancient Hebrews were held captive in Mesopotamian Babylon).

The Babylonian Captivity badly damaged papal prestige. The Avignon papacy reformed its financial administration and centralized its government. But the seven popes at Avignon concentrated on bureaucratic matters to the exclusion of spiritual objectives. Though some of the popes led austere lives, the general atmosphere was one of luxury and extravagance. (See the feature "Individuals in Society: Francesco Datini" in Chapter 11 on page 343.) The leadership of the church was cut off from its historic roots and the source of its ancient authority, the city of Rome. In the absence of the papacy, the Papal States in Italy lacked stability and good government. The economy of Rome had been based on the presence of the papal court and the rich tourist trade the papacy attracted. The Babylonian Captivity left Rome poverty-stricken.

In 1377 Pope Gregory XI brought the papal court back to Rome. Unfortunately, he died shortly after the return. At Gregory's death, Roman citizens demanded an Italian pope who would remain in Rome. Between the time of Gregory's death and the opening of the conclave, great pressure was put on the cardinals to elect an Italian. At the time, none of them protested this pressure, and they chose a distinguished administrator, the archbishop of Bari, Bartolomeo Prignano, who took the name Urban VI.

Urban VI (1378–1389) had excellent intentions for church reform, but he went about this in a tactless and bullheaded manner. He attacked clerical luxury, denouncing individual cardinals by name, and even threatened to excommunicate certain cardinals.

The cardinals slipped away from Rome and met at Anagni. They declared Urban's election invalid because it had come about under threats from the Roman mob, and they asserted that Urban himself was excommunicated. The cardinals then elected Cardinal Robert of Geneva, the cousin of King Charles V of France, as pope. Cardinal Robert took the name Clement VII. There were thus two popes—Urban at Rome and Clement VII (1378–1394), who set himself up at Avignon in opposition to Urban. So began the **Great Schism,** which divided Western Christendom until 1417.

The powers of Europe aligned themselves with Urban or Clement along strictly political lines. France naturally recognized the French pope, Clement. England, France's historic enemy, recognized the Italian pope, Urban. Scotland, whose attacks on England were subsidized by France, followed the French and supported Clement. Aragon, Castile, and Portugal hesitated before deciding for Clement at Avignon. The emperor, who bore ancient hostility to France, recognized Urban. At first the Italian city-states recognized Urban; when he alienated them, they opted for Clement.

John of Spoleto, a professor at the law school at Bologna, eloquently summed up intellectual opinion of the schism, or division: "The longer this schism lasts, the more it appears to be costing, and the more harm it does; scandal, massacres, ruination, agitations, troubles and disturbances."[8] The common people, wracked by inflation, wars, and plague, were thoroughly confused about which pope was legitimate. The schism weakened the religious faith of many Christians and brought church leadership into serious disrepute. The schism also brought to the fore conciliar ideas about church government.

The Conciliar Movement

Theories about the nature of the Christian church and its government originated in the very early church, but the years of the Great Schism witnessed their maturity. **Conciliarists** believed that reform of the church could best be achieved through periodic assemblies, or general councils, representing all the Christian people. While acknowledging that the pope was head of the church, conciliarists held that the pope derived his authority from the entire Christian community, whose well-being he existed to promote. Conciliarists favored a balanced or constitutional form of church government, with papal authority shared with a general council, in contrast to the monarchical one that prevailed.

A half century before the Great Schism, in 1324, Marsiglio of Padua, then rector of the University of Paris, had published *Defensor Pacis* (The Defender of the Peace). Marsiglio argued that the state was the great unifying power in society and that the church was subordinate to the state. He put forth the revolutionary ideas that the church had no inherent jurisdiction and should own no property. Authority in the Christian church, according to Marsiglio, should rest in a general council made up of laymen as well as priests, and the council should be superior to the pope. These ideas directly contradicted the medieval notion of a society governed by the church and the state, with the church supreme. *Defensor Pacis* was condemned by the pope, and Marsiglio was excommunicated.

Even more earthshaking than the theories of Marsiglio of Padua were the ideas of the English scholar and theologian John Wyclif (ca 1330–1384). Wyclif wrote that papal claims of temporal power had no foundation in the Scriptures and that the Scriptures alone should be the standard of Christian belief and practice. He urged the abolition of such practices as the veneration of saints, pilgrimages, pluralism, and absenteeism. Sincere Christians, according to Wyclif, should read the Bible for themselves. In response to that idea, the first English translation of the Bible was produced and circulated. Wyclif's views had broad social and economic significance. He urged that the church be stripped of its property. His idea that every Christian free of mortal sin possessed lordship was seized on by peasants in England during a revolt in 1381 and used to justify their goals.

In advancing these views, Wyclif struck at the roots of medieval church structure. Consequently, he has been hailed as the precursor of the Protestant Reformation of the sixteenth century. Although Wyclif's ideas were vigorously condemned by ecclesiastical authorities, they were widely disseminated by humble clerics and enjoyed great popularity in the early fifteenth century. Wyclif's followers were called "Lollards." The term, which means "mumblers of prayers and psalms," refers to what they criticized. Lollard teaching allowed women to preach. Women, some well educated, played a significant role in the movement. After Anne, sister of Wenceslaus, king of Germany and Bohemia, married Richard II of England, members of her household carried Lollard books back to Bohemia.

In response to continued calls throughout Europe for a council, the two colleges of cardinals—one at Rome, the other at Avignon—summoned a council at Pisa in 1409. That gathering of prelates and theologians deposed both popes and selected another. Neither the Avignon pope nor the Roman pope would resign, however, and the appalling result was the creation of a threefold schism.

Finally, because of the pressure of the German emperor Sigismund, a great council met at the imperial city of Constance (1414–1418). It had three objectives: to end the schism, to reform the church "in head and members" (from top to bottom), and to wipe out heresy. The council condemned the Czech reformer Jan Hus (see the feature "Individuals in Society: Jan Hus"), and he was burned at the stake. The council eventually deposed both the Roman pope and the successor of the pope chosen at Pisa, and it isolated the Avignon antipope. A conclave elected a new leader, the Roman cardinal Colonna, who took the name Martin V (1417–1431).

Martin proceeded to dissolve the council. Nothing was done about reform. The schism was over, and though councils subsequently met at Basel and at Ferrara-Florence, in 1450 the papacy held a jubilee celebrating its triumph over the conciliar movement. In the later fifteenth century the papacy concentrated on Italian problems to the exclusion of universal Christian interests. But the schism and the conciliar movement had exposed the crying need for ecclesiastical reform, thus laying the foundation for the great reform efforts of the sixteenth century.

Spoon with Fox Preaching to Geese (southern Netherlands, ca 1430) Taking as his text a contemporary proverb, "When the fox preaches, beware your geese," the artist shows, in the bowl of a spoon, a fox dressed as a monk or friar, preaching with three dead geese in his hood, while another fox grabs one of the congregation. The preaching fox reads from a scroll bearing the word *pax* (peace), implying the perceived hypocrisy of the clergy. The object suggests the widespread criticism of churchmen in the later Middle Ages. *(Painted enamel and gilding on silver; 17.6 cm [6 ⅞ in]. Museum of Fine Arts, Boston, Helen and Alice Coburn Fund, 51.2472)*

Lay Piety and Mysticism

During the fourteenth and fifteenth centuries the laity began to exercise increasing control over parish affairs. The constant quarrels of the mendicant orders (the Franciscans and Dominicans), the mercenary and grasping attitude of the parish clergy, the scandal of the Great Schism, and a divided Christendom all did much to weaken the spiritual mystique of the clergy in the popular mind. The laity steadily took responsibility for the management of parish lands and secured jurisdiction over the structure of the church building and its vestments, books, and furnishings. Lay Christian men and women often formed **confraternities,** voluntary lay groups organized by occupation, devotional preference, neighborhood, or charitable activity. Confraternities expanded rapidly in larger cities and many villages with the growth of the mendicant orders in the thirteenth century. Some confraternities specialized in praying for souls in purgatory, either for specific individuals or for the anonymous mass of all souls. In England they were generally associated with a parish, so are called parish guilds, parish fraternities, or lights; by the late Middle Ages they held dances, church ales, and collections to raise money to clean and repair church buildings and to supply the church with candles and other liturgical objects. Like craft guilds, most confraternities were groups of men, but separate women's confraternities were formed in some towns, often to oversee the production of vestments, altar cloths, and other items made of fabric.

In Holland, beginning in the late fourteenth century, a group of pious laypeople called the Brethren and Sisters of the Common Life lived in stark simplicity while daily carrying out the Gospel teaching of feeding the hungry, clothing the naked, and visiting the sick. The Brethren also taught in local schools with the goal of preparing devout candidates for the priesthood. They sought to make religion a personal inner experience. The spirituality of the Brethren and Sisters of the Common Life found its finest expression in the classic *The Imitation of Christ* by Thomas à Kempis, which gained wide appeal among laypeople. It urges Christians to take Christ as their model, seek perfection in a simple way of life, and look to the Scriptures for guidance in living a spiritual life. In the mid-fifteenth century the movement had founded houses in the Netherlands, in central Germany, and in the Rhineland.

Online Study Center **Improve Your Grade**
Primary Source: *The Imitation of Christ: On True Charity*

Most of this lay piety centered on prayer, pious actions, and charitable giving, but for some individuals, religious devotion included mystical experiences. Bridget of Sweden (1303–1373) was a noblewoman who journeyed to Rome after her husband's death. She began to see visions and gave advice based on these visions to both laypeople and church officials. Because she could not speak Latin, she dictated her visions in Swedish; these were later translated and eventually published in Latin. At the end of her life, Bridget made a pilgrimage to Jerusalem, where she saw visions of the Virgin Mary, who described to her exactly how she was standing "with my knees bent" when she gave birth to Jesus, and how she "showed to the shepherds the nature and male sex of the child."[9] Bridget's visions convey her deep familiarity with biblical texts taught to her through sermons or stories, as there was no Bible available in Swedish. They also provide evidence of the ways in which laypeople used their own experiences to enhance their religious understanding;

Bridget's own experiences of childbirth shaped the way she viewed the birth of Jesus, and she related to the Virgin Mary in part as one mother to another.

Economic and Social Change

In the fourteenth century economic and political difficulties, disease, and war profoundly affected the lives of European peoples. Decades of slaughter and destruction, punctuated by the decimating visits of the Black Death, made a grave economic situation virtually disastrous. In many parts of France and the Low Countries, fields lay in ruin or untilled for lack of labor power. In England, as taxes increased, criticisms of government policy and mismanagement multiplied. Crime and new forms of business organization aggravated economic troubles, and throughout Europe the frustrations of the common people erupted into widespread revolts.

● *How did economic and social tensions contribute to revolts, crime, violence, and a growing sense of ethnic and national distinctions?*

Peasant Revolts

Nobles, clergy, and city dwellers lived on the produce of peasant labor. Early in the thirteenth century the French preacher Jacques de Vitry asked rhetorically, "How many serfs have killed their lords or burnt their castles?"[10] And in the fourteenth and fifteenth centuries social and economic conditions caused a great increase in peasant uprisings (see Map 12.3). They were very common and provide most of the evidence of peasants' long suffering and exploitation.

We will never be able fully to answer Jacques de Vitry's questions, for peasants were not literate and, apart from their explosive uprisings, left no record of their aspirations. The clerical writers who mentioned the rebellions viewed the peasants with aristocratic disdain and hostility. Recent research provides some insight into **peasant revolts** in Flanders in the 1320s. Long-existing conflicts along the Flemish-French border came to a head at Courtrai in July 1302 when Flemish infantry smashed a French army, killing many knights and nobles (their golden spurs retrieved from the battlefield gave the battle its name, the Battle of the Spurs). The Flemish victory failed to resolve disputes over the French crown's claim to fiscal rights over the county of Flanders. Moreover, the peace agreements imposed heavy indemnities on

Flemish peasants, who in 1323 began to revolt in protest of officials' demands for taxes and of the misappropriation of the money collected. Also, monasteries pressed peasants for fees higher than the customary tithes. In retaliation, peasants subjected castles and aristocratic country houses to arson and pillage. A French army intervened and on August 23, 1328, near the town of Cassel in southwestern Flanders, crushed peasant forces. Savage repression and the confiscation of peasant property followed in the 1330s.

In 1358, when French taxation for the Hundred Years' War fell heavily on the poor, the frustrations of the French peasantry exploded in a massive uprising called the **Jacquerie,** after a mythical agricultural laborer, Jacques Bonhomme (Good Fellow). Two years earlier the English had captured the French king John and many nobles and held them for ransom. The peasants resented paying for their lords' release. Recently hit by plague, experiencing famine in some areas, and harassed by nobles, peasants in Picardy, Champagne, and the Île-de-France erupted in anger and frustration. Crowds swept through the countryside, slashing the throats of nobles, burning their castles, raping their wives and daughters, and killing or maiming their horses and cattle. Peasants blamed the nobility for oppressive taxes, for the criminal brigandage of the countryside, for defeat in war, and for the general misery. Artisans, small merchants, and parish priests joined the peasants. Urban and rural groups committed terrible destruction, and for several weeks the nobles were on the defensive. Then the upper class united to repress the revolt with merciless ferocity. Thousands of the "Jacques," innocent as well as guilty, were cut down. That forcible suppression of social rebellion, without any effort to alleviate its underlying causes, served to drive protest underground.

The Peasants' Revolt in England in 1381 involved thousands of people (see Map 12.3). Its causes were complex and varied from place to place. In general, though, the thirteenth century had witnessed the steady commutation of labor services for cash rents, and the Black Death had drastically cut the labor supply. As a result, peasants demanded higher wages and fewer manorial obligations. The parliamentary Statute of Laborers of 1351 (see page 380) had declared:

Whereas to curb the malice of servants who after the pestilence were idle and unwilling to serve without securing excessive wages, it was recently ordained . . . that such servants, both men and women, shall be bound to serve in return for salaries and wages that were customary . . . five or six years earlier.[11]

Individuals in Society

Jan Hus

In May 1990 the Czech Republic's parliament declared July 6, the date of Jan Hus's execution in 1415, a Czech national holiday. The son of free farmers, Hus (ca 1369–1415) was born in Husinec in southern Bohemia, an area of heavy German settlement, and grew up conscious of the ethnic differences between Czechs and Germans. Most of his professors at Charles University in Prague were Germans. In 1396 he received a master's degree, and just before his ordination as a priest in 1400 he wrote that he would not be a "clerical careerist," implying that ambition for church offices motivated many of his peers.

The young priest lectured at the university and preached at the private Bethlehem Chapel. During his twelve years there Hus preached only in Czech. He denounced superstition, the sale of indulgences, and other abuses, but his remarks were thoroughly orthodox. He attracted attention among artisans and the small Czech middle class, but not Germans. His austere life and lack of ambition enhanced his reputation.

Around 1400, Czech students returning from study at Oxford introduced into Bohemia the reforming ideas of the English theologian John Wyclif. When German professors condemned Wyclif's ideas as heretical, Hus and the Czechs argued "academic freedom," the right to read and teach Wyclif's works regardless of their particular merits. When popular demonstrations against ecclesiastical abuses and German influence at the university erupted, King Vaclav IV (1378–1419) placed control of the university in Czech hands. Hus was elected rector, the top administrative official.

The people of Prague, with perhaps the largest urban population in central Europe, 40 percent of it living below the poverty line and entirely dependent on casual labor, found Hus's denunciations of an overendowed church appealing. Hus considered the issues theological; his listeners saw them as socioeconomic.

Church officials in Prague were split about Hus's ideas, and popular unrest grew. The king forced Hus to leave the city, but he continued to preach and write. He disputed papal authority, denounced abuses, and argued that everyone should receive both bread and wine in the Eucharist. (By this time, in standard Western Christian practice, the laity received only the bread; the priest received the wine *for* the laity, a mark of his distinctiveness.) Hus also defended transubstantiation (see page 449); insisted that church authority rested on Scripture, conscience, and tradition (in contrast to sixteenth-century Protestant reformers, who placed

authority in Scripture alone); and made it clear that he had no intention of leaving the church or inciting a popular movement.

In 1413 the emperor Sigismund urged the calling of a general council to end the schism. Hus was invited, and, given the emperor's safe conduct

The execution of Jan Hus.
(University of Prague/The Art Archive)

(protection from attack or arrest), agreed to go. What he found was an atmosphere of inquisition. The safe conduct was disregarded, and Hus was arrested. Under questioning about his acceptance of Wyclif's ideas, Hus repeatedly replied, "I have not held; I do not hold." Council members were more interested in proving Hus a Wyclite than in his responses. They took away his priesthood, banned his teachings, burned his books, and burned Hus himself at the stake. He then belonged to the ages.

The ages have made good use of him. His death aggravated the divisions between the bishops at Constance and the Czech clerics and people. In September 1415, 452 nobles from all parts of Bohemia signed a letter saying that Hus had been unjustly executed and rejecting council rulings. This event marks the first time that an ecclesiastical decision was publicly defied. Revolution swept through Bohemia, with Hussites—Czech nobles and people—insisting on clerical poverty and both the bread and wine at the Eucharist, and with German citizens remaining loyal to the Roman church. In the sixteenth century reformers hailed Hus as the forerunner of Protestantism. In the eighteenth century Enlightenment philosophes evoked Hus as a defender of freedom of expression. In the nineteenth century central European nationalists used Hus's name to defend national sentiment against Habsburg rule. And in the twentieth century Hus's name was used against German fascist and Russian communist tyranny.

Questions for Analysis

1. Since Jan Hus lived and died insisting that his religious teaching was thoroughly orthodox, why has he been hailed as a reformer?
2. What political and cultural interests did the martyred Hus serve?

Online Study Center **Improve Your Grade**
Going Beyond Individuals in Society

MAP 12.3 Fourteenth-Century Peasant Revolts In the later Middle Ages, peasant and urban uprisings were endemic, as common as factory strikes in the industrial world. The threat of insurrection served to check unlimited exploitation.

Online Study Center **Improve Your Grade**
Interactive Map: Fourteenth-Century Peasant Revolts

But this attempt to freeze wages and social mobility could not be enforced. Some scholars believe that in most places the peasantry was better off in the period 1350 to 1450 than it had been for centuries before or was to be for four centuries after.

Why then was the outburst in England in 1381 so serious? It was provoked by a crisis of rising expectations. The relative prosperity of the laboring classes led to demands that the upper classes were unwilling to grant. Unable to climb higher, the peasants sought release for their economic frustrations in revolt. Economic grievances combined with other factors. The south of England, where the revolt broke out, had been subjected to destructive French raids. The English government did little to protect the south, and villagers grew increasingly

frightened and insecure. Moreover, decades of aristocratic violence against the weak peasantry had bred hostility and bitterness. Social and religious agitation by the popular preacher John Ball fanned the embers of discontent. Ball's famous couplet "When Adam delved and Eve span; Who was then the gentleman?" reflected real revolutionary sentiment.

The straw that broke the camel's back in England was the reimposition of a head tax on all adult males. Despite widespread opposition to the tax in 1380, the royal council ordered the sheriffs to collect it again in 1381 on penalty of a huge fine. Beginning with assaults on the tax collectors, the uprising in England followed a course similar to that of the Jacquerie in France. Castles and manors were sacked. Manorial records were destroyed. Many nobles, including the archbishop of Canterbury, who had ordered the collection of the tax, were murdered.

The center of the revolt lay in the highly populated and economically advanced south and east, but sections of the north and the Midlands also witnessed rebellions. Violence took different forms in different places. Urban discontent merged with rural violence. In English towns where skilled Flemish craftsmen were employed, fear of competition led to their being attacked and murdered. Apprentices and journeymen, frustrated because the highest positions in the guilds were closed to them, rioted.

The boy-king Richard II (r. 1377–1399) met Wat Tyler and other leaders of the revolt, agreed to charters ensuring peasants' freedom, tricked them with false promises, and then crushed the uprising with terrible ferocity. The nobility tried to restore ancient duties of serfdom, but nearly a century of freedom had elapsed, and the commutation of manorial services continued. Rural serfdom disappeared in England by 1550.

Urban Conflicts

In Flanders, France, and England, peasant revolts often blended with conflicts involving workers in cities. Unrest also occurred in other cities. In Florence in 1378 the *ciompi,* the poor propertyless workers, revolted. Serious social trouble occurred in Lübeck, Brunswick, and other German cities. In Spain in 1391 aristocratic attempts to impose new forms of serfdom, combined with demands for tax relief, led to massive working-class and peasant uprisings in Seville and Barcelona.

These revolts often occurred in cities where the conditions of work were changing for many people. In the thirteenth century craft guilds had organized production of most goods, with masters, journeymen, and apprentices working side by side. Beginning in the fourteenth century in a few areas of Europe such as Florence and Flanders, individuals who had made money in trade and banking invested in production. They wanted to make products on a larger scale than guilds would allow, so they hired many households, with each household performing only one step of the process. Craft guilds sometimes protested these changes, but in other cities more enterprising or wealthier masters recognized the benefits of this new system and began to hire other households to work for them. This promoted a greater division within guilds between wealthier masters and the poorer masters and journeymen they hired. Some masters became so wealthy that they no longer had to work in a shop themselves, nor did their wives and family members. Instead of being artisans, they became capitalist investors, though they still generally belonged to the craft guild.

While capitalism provided opportunities for some artisans to become investors and entrepreneurs, especially in cloth production, for many it led to a decrease in income and status. Guilds often responded to competition by limiting membership to existing guild families, which meant that journeymen who were not master's sons or who could not find a master's widow or daughter to marry could never become masters themselves. They remained journeymen their entire lives, losing their sense of solidarity with the masters of their craft and in some cities forming separate journeymen's guilds. These journeymen's guilds tried to prevent anyone who was not a member of the guild from working in any craft shop, enforcing their aims with boycotts, strikes, and riots. Such actions often led cities to prohibit journeymen's guilds, but they were still set up illegally, and their secrecy made them stronger. Journeymen developed elaborate initiation rituals and secret ceremonies to enhance group solidarity, and they carried their organizations with them when they traveled in search of work.

Urban uprisings were most often touched off by economic issues, as low- and middle-class workers deeply resented the widening economic and social gap separating them from mercantile elites, but they were also sparked by issues involving honor, such as employers' requiring workers to do tasks they regarded as beneath them. As their actual status and economic prospects declined and their work became basically wage labor, journeymen and poorer masters emphasized skill and honor as qualities that set them apart from less-skilled workers.

The sense of honor developed by craft and journeymen's guilds was a gendered one. When urban economies were expanding in the High Middle Ages, the master's wife and daughters worked alongside him, and the journeymen and apprentices and female domestic servants also carried out productive tasks. (See the feature "Listening to the Past: Christine de Pizan" on pages 404–405.) Women and girls served as a labor reservoir to be utilized when guild needs required. Masters' widows ran shops after the death of their husbands and were expected to pay all guild fees, though they could not participate in running the guild. This informal participation began to change in the fourteenth century, as guilds increasingly came to view the honor of their work as tied to an all-male workplace. First, masters' widows were limited in the amount of time they could keep operating a shop or were prohibited from hiring journeymen; then female domestic servants were excluded from any productive tasks; then the number of his daughters a master craftsman could employ was limited. The timing of these restrictions varied from craft to craft, town to town, and country to country, but because women's participation in guild shops was generally not guaranteed by guild regulations and because widows had no political voice in running the guilds, women as a group were not able to protect their right to work. A few might be allowed to work, but this was on an individual basis and was viewed as a substitute for charity. The separate journeymen's guilds were even more hostile to women's work and never allowed female members. Their secret rituals offered opportunities for men to bond with one another and to express their resentment of economic change through hostility toward women's work as well as toward merchants' privileges.

Sex in the City

Peasant and urban revolts and riots had clear economic bases, but some historians have suggested that late medieval marital patterns may have also played a role in unrest. At what age did people usually marry? The largest amount of evidence on age at first marriage survives from Italy. For girls, population surveys at Prato place the age at 16.3 years in 1372 and at 21.1 years in 1470. Noble and wealthy urban women in cities elsewhere in Europe also generally married while in their late teens, but peasant and poorer urban women, especially in northwestern Europe—including the British Isles, Scandinavia, France, and Germany—waited until their mid- or late twenties to marry. The northwestern European marriage pattern resulted largely from the idea that couples should be economically independent before they married, so both spouses spent long periods as servants or workers in other households saving money and learning skills, or they waited until their own parents had died and the family property was distributed.

The most unusual feature of this pattern was the late age of marriage for women. Women entered marriage as adults and took charge of running a household immediately. They were thus not as dependent on their husbands or their mothers-in-law as were women who married at younger ages. They had fewer pregnancies than women who married earlier, though not necessarily fewer surviving children.

Men of all social groups were older when they married. An Italian chronicler writing about 1354 says that men did not marry before the age of thirty. At Prato in 1371 the average age of men at first marriage was twenty-four years, very young for Italian men, but these data may signal an attempt to regain population losses due to the recent attack of the plague. In general, men were in their middle or late twenties at first marriage, with wealthier urban merchants often much older. Journeymen and apprentices were often explicitly prohibited from marrying, as were the students at universities, as they were understood to be in "minor orders" and thus like clergy, even if they were not intending on careers in the church.

The prohibitions on marriage for certain groups of men and the late age of marriage for most men meant that cities and villages were filled with large numbers of young adult men with no family responsibilities who often formed the core of riots and unrest. Not surprisingly, this situation also contributed to a steady market for sexual services outside of marriage, what in later centuries was termed *prostitution*. Research on the southern French province of Languedoc in the fourteenth and fifteenth centuries has revealed the establishment of legal houses of prostitution in many cities. Municipal authorities in Toulouse, Montpellier, Albi, and other towns set up houses or red-light districts either outside the city walls or away from respectable neighborhoods. For example, authorities in Montpellier set aside Hot Street for prostitution, required public women to live there, and forbade anyone to molest them. Prostitution thus passed from being a private concern to a social matter requiring public supervision. The towns of Languedoc were not unique. Public authorities in Amiens, Dijon, Paris,

Venice, Genoa, London, Florence, Rome, most of the larger German towns, and the English port of Sandwich set up brothels.

Many cities set down rules for the women and their customers, and they justified the existence of municipal brothels with the comment that such women protected honorable girls and women from the uncontrollable lust of young men, an argument at least as old as Saint Augustine. In a few cities such as Florence, authorities also noted that brothels might keep young men from homosexual relations, another, far worse alternative in their eyes. Visiting brothels was associated with achieving manhood in the eyes of young men, though for the women themselves their activities were work. Indeed, in some cases the women had no choice, for they had been traded to the brothel manager by their parents or other people in payment for debt, or had quickly become indebted to him (or, more rarely, her) for the clothes and other finery regarded as essential to their occupation. Poor women—and men—also sold sex illegally outside of city brothels, combining this with other sorts of part-time work such as laundering or sewing. Prostitution was an urban phenomenon because only populous towns had large numbers of unmarried young men, communities of transient merchants, and a culture accustomed to a cash exchange.

Though selling sex for money was legal in the Middle Ages, the position of women who did so was always marginal. In the late fifteenth century cities began to limit brothel residents' freedom of movement and choice of clothing, requiring them to wear distinctive head coverings or bands on their clothing so that they would not be mistaken for "honorable" women. The cities also began to impose harsher penalties on women who did not live in the designated house or section of town. A few prostitutes did earn enough to donate money to charity or buy property, but most were very poor.

Along with buying sex, young men also took it by force. Unmarried women often found it difficult to avoid sexual contacts. Many of them worked as domestic servants, where their employers or employers' sons or male relatives could easily coerce them, or they worked in proximity to men. Female servants were sent on errands alone or with men or worked by themselves in fields far from other people. Notions of female honor kept upper-class women secluded in their homes, particularly in southern and eastern Europe, but there was little attempt anywhere to keep female servants or day laborers from the risk of seduction or rape. Rape was a capital crime in many parts of Europe, but the actual sentences handed out were more likely to be fines and brief imprisonment,

Prostitute Invites a Traveling Merchant   Poverty drove women into prostitution, which, though denounced by moralists, was accepted as a normal part of the medieval social fabric. In the cities and larger towns where prostitution flourished, public officials passed laws requiring prostitutes to wear a special mark on their clothing, regulated hours of business, forbade women to drag men into their houses, and denied business to women with the "burning sickness," gonorrhea. (*Bodleian Library, MS. Bodl. 264, fol. 245V*)

with the severity of the sentence dependent on the social status of the victim and the perpetrator. According to a study of the legal evidence from Venice in the years 1338 to 1358, rape was not considered a particularly serious crime against either the victim or society. Noble youths committed a higher percentage of rapes than their small numbers in Venetian society would imply. The rape of a young girl of marriageable age or a child under twelve was considered a graver crime than the rape of a married woman. Nevertheless, the punishment for rape of a noble marriageable girl was only a fine or about six months' imprisonment. In an age when theft and robbery could be punished by mutilation and forgery and sodomy by burning, this penalty was mild indeed. When an upper-class youth was convicted of the rape of a non-noble girl, his punishment was even lighter. By contrast, the sexual assault of a noblewoman by a working-class man, which was extraordinarily rare, resulted in severe penalization because the crime had social and political overtones.

According to laws regarding rape in most parts of Europe, the victim had to prove that she had cried out and had attempted to repel the attacker, and she had to bring the charge within a short period of time after the attack had happened. Women bringing rape charges were often more interested in getting their own honorable reputations back than in punishing the perpetrators, and for this reason they sometimes asked the judge to force their rapists to marry them.

Same-sex relations—what in the late nineteenth century would be termed *homosexuality*—were another feature of medieval urban life (and of village life, though there are very few sources relating to sexual relations of any type in the rural context). Same-sex relations were of relatively little concern to church or state authorities in the early Middle Ages, but this attitude changed beginning in the late twelfth century. By 1300 most areas had defined such actions as "crimes against nature," with authorities seeing them as particularly reprehensible because they thought they did not occur anywhere else in creation. Same-sex relations, usually termed *sodomy*, became a capital crime in most of Europe, with adult offenders threatened with execution by fire. The Italian cities of Venice, Florence, and Lucca created special courts to deal with sodomy, which saw thousands of investigations.

How prevalent was homosexuality? This is difficult to answer, even in modern society, but Florence provides a provocative case study. The city of Florence passed legislation against sodomy in 1415 and 1418, and in 1432 it set up a special magistracy, the Office of the Night, to "root out . . . the abominable vice of sodomy." This board of professional men at least forty-five years of age and married was elected annually and charged with pursuing and punishing sodomitical activity between males.[12] The name of the magistracy derived from the nocturnal activities of most male encounters, especially in the spring and summer months and on feast days and

Sundays. Between 1432 and the abolition of the magistracy in 1502, about seventeen thousand men came to its attention, which, even over a seventy-year period, represents a great number in a population of about forty thousand. Moreover, careful statistical analysis of judicial records shows that all classes of society engaged in it—men in the textile trade, in commerce, in education, and in the food industry, especially butchers, as well as construction workers, tavern keepers, artists, and innkeepers. Sodomy was not a marginal practice, which may account for the fact that, despite harsh laws and special courts, actual executions for sodomy were rare in Italy. They were also uncommon in England, where despite harsh laws there were only six trials for sodomy during the entire long reign of Queen Elizabeth I (1564–1603). Trials were more common in the Iberian Peninsula, where those charged with sodomy were sometimes tortured to reveal other names, so that sodomy accusations often occurred in waves.

Almost all cases heard by the Florentine court and courts in other cities involved an adult man and an adolescent boy and ranged from sex exchanged for money or gifts to long-term affectionate relationships. Florentines believed in a generational model in which different roles were appropriate to different stages in life. In a socially and sexually hierarchical world, the boy in the passive role was identified as subordinate, dependent, and mercenary, words usually applied to women. Florentines, however, never described the dominant partner in feminine terms, for he had not compromised his masculine identity or violated a gender ideal; in fact, the adult partner might be married or have female sexual partners as well as male. Only if an adult male assumed the passive role was his masculinity jeopardized. Such cases were extremely rare. Same-sex relations often developed within the context of all-male environments, such as the army, the craft shop, and the artistic workshop, and were part of the collective male experience. Homoerotic relationships played important roles in defining stages of life, expressing distinctions of status, and shaping masculine gender identity.

Same-sex relations involving women almost never came to the attention of legal authorities, so it is difficult to find out much about them. Most commentators about sexual relations were male clergy who viewed sex between women as categorically different than sex between men, if they regarded it as sex at all. Female-female desire is expressed in songs, plays, and stories, as is male-male desire. Such literary sources can be used as evidence of the way people understood same-sex relations, though not how common such relations were.

Same-Sex Relations This illustration, from a thirteenth-century French book of morals, interprets female and male same-sex relations as the work of devils, who hover over the couples. This illustration was painted at the time that religious and political authorities were increasingly criminalizing same-sex relations. (*Austrian National Library, Vienna, Cod. 2554, fol. 2r*)

Fur-Collar Crime

The Hundred Years' War had provided employment and opportunity for thousands of idle and fortune-seeking knights. But during periods of truce and after the war finally ended, many nobles once again had little to do. Inflation hurt them. Although many were living on fixed incomes, their chivalric code demanded lavish generosity and an aristocratic lifestyle. Many nobles turned to crime as a way of raising money. The fourteenth and fifteenth centuries witnessed a great deal of "fur-collar crime," so called for the miniver fur nobles alone were allowed to wear on their collars.

Fur-collar crime rarely involved such felonies as homicide, robbery, rape, and arson. Instead, nobles used their superior social status to rob and extort from the weak and then to corrupt the judicial process. Groups of noble brigands roamed the English countryside stealing from both rich and poor. Sir John de Colseby and Sir William Bussy led a gang of thirty-eight knights who stole goods worth £3,000 in various robberies. Operating like modern urban racketeers, knightly gangs demanded that peasants pay "protection money" or else have their hovels burned and their fields destroyed.

Attacks on the rich often took the form of kidnapping and extortion. Wealthy travelers were seized on the highways and held for ransom. In northern England a gang of gentry led by Sir Gilbert de Middleton abducted Sir Henry Beaumont; his brother, the bishop-elect of Durham; and two Roman cardinals in England on a peacemaking visit. Only after ransom was paid were the victims released.

Fur-collar criminals were terrorists, but like some modern-day white-collar criminals who commit nonviolent crimes, medieval aristocratic criminals got away with their outrages. When accused of wrongdoing, fur-collar criminals intimidated witnesses. They threatened jurors. They used "pull" or cash to bribe judges. As a fourteenth-century English judge wrote to a young nobleman, "For the love of your father I have hindered charges being brought against you and have prevented execution of indictment actually made."[13] Criminal activity by nobles continued decade after decade because governments were too weak to stop it.

The ballads of Robin Hood, a collection of folk legends from late medieval England, describe the adventures of the outlaw hero and his band of followers who lived in Sherwood Forest and attacked and punished those who violated the social system and the law. Most of the villains in these simple tales are fur-collar criminals—grasping landlords, wicked sheriffs such as the famous sheriff of Nottingham, and mercenary churchmen. Robin and his merry men performed a sort of retributive justice. Robin Hood was a popular figure because he symbolized the deep resentment of aristocratic corruption and abuse; he represented the struggle against tyranny and oppression.

Ethnic Tensions and Restrictions

Large numbers of people in the twelfth and thirteenth centuries migrated from one part of Europe to another: the English into Scotland and Ireland; Germans, French, and Flemings into Poland, Bohemia, and Hungary; the French into Spain. The colonization of frontier regions meant that peoples of different ethnic backgrounds lived side by side. Everywhere in Europe, towns recruited people from the countryside (see pages 333). In frontier regions, townspeople were usually long-distance immigrants and, in eastern Europe, Ireland, and Scotland, ethnically different from the surrounding rural population. In eastern Europe, German was the language of the towns; in Irish towns, French, the tongue of Norman or English settlers, predominated.

In the early periods of conquest and colonization, and in all regions with extensive migrations, a legal dualism existed: native peoples remained subject to their traditional laws; newcomers brought and were subject to the laws of the countries from which they came. On the Prussian and Polish frontier, for example, the law was that "men who come there . . . should be judged on account of any crime or contract engaged in there according to Polish custom if they are Poles and according to German custom if they are Germans."[14] Likewise, in Spain Mudéjars, Muslim subjects of Christian kings, received guarantees of separate but equal judicial rights. King Alfonso I of Aragon's charter to the Muslims of Toledo states, "They shall be in lawsuits and pleas under their (Muslim) qadi (judges) . . . as it was in the times of the Moors."[15] Thus conquered peoples, whether Muslims in Spain or minority immigrant groups such as Germans in eastern Europe, had legal protection and lived in their own juridical enclaves. Subject peoples experienced some disabilities, but the broad trend was toward legal pluralism.

The great exception to this broad pattern was Ireland. From the start, the English practiced an extreme form of discrimination toward the native Irish. The English distinguished between the free and the unfree, and the entire Irish population, simply by the fact of Irish birth, was unfree. In 1210 King John declared that "English law and custom be established there (in Ireland)." Accordingly, a legal structure modeled on that of England, with county courts, itinerant justices, and the common law (see pages 271–274), was set up. But the Irish had no access to the common-law courts. In civil (property) disputes, an English defendant need not respond to his Irish plaintiff; no Irish person could make a will. In criminal procedures, the murder of an Irishman was not considered a felony. In 1317–1318 Irish princes sent a Remonstrance to the pope complaining that "any non-Irishman is allowed to bring legal action against an Irishman, but an Irishman . . . except any prelate (bishop or abbot) is barred from every action by that fact alone." An English defendant in the criminal matter would claim "that he is not held to answer . . . since he [the plaintiff] is Irish and not of free blood."[16] Naturally, this emphasis on blood descent provoked bitterness.

Other than in Ireland, although native peoples commonly held humbler positions, both immigrant and native townspeople prospered during the expanding economy of the thirteenth century. When economic recession hit during the fourteenth century, ethnic tensions multiplied.

The later Middle Ages witnessed a movement away from legal pluralism or dualism and toward legal homogeneity and an emphasis on blood descent. Competition for ecclesiastical offices and the cultural divisions between town and country people became arenas for ethnic tension. Since bishoprics and abbacies carried religious authority, spiritual charisma, and often rights of appointment to subordinate positions, they were natural objects of ambition. When prelates of a language or "nationality" different from those of the local people gained church positions, the latter felt a loss of influence. Bishops were supposed to be pastors. Their pastoral work involved preaching, teaching, and comforting, duties that could be performed effectively only when the bishop (or priest) could communicate with the people. Ideally, in a pluralistic society, he should be bilingual; often he was not.

In the late thirteenth century, as waves of Germans migrated into Danzig on the Baltic, into Silesia, and into the Polish countryside and towns, they encountered Jakub Swinka, archbishop of Gniezno (1283–1314), whose jurisdiction included these areas of settlement. The bishop hated Germans and referred to them as "dog heads." His German contemporary, Bishop John of Cracow, detested the Poles, wanted to expel all Polish people, and refused to appoint Poles to any church office. In Ireland, English colonists and the native Irish competed for ecclesiastical offices until 1217, when the English government in London decreed:

Since the election of Irishmen in our land of Ireland has often disturbed the peace of that land, we command you . . . that henceforth you allow no Irishman to be elected . . . or preferred in any cathedral . . . (and) you should seek by all means to procure election and promotion to vacant bishoprics of . . . honest Englishmen.[17]

Although criticized by the pope and not totally enforceable, this law remained in effect in many dioceses for centuries.

Likewise, the arrival of Cistercians and mendicants (Franciscans and Dominicans) from France and Germany in Baltic and Slavic lands provoked ethnic hostilities. Slavic prelates and princes saw the German mendicants as "instruments of cultural colonization," and Slavs were strongly discouraged from becoming friars. In 1333, when John of Drazic, bishop of Prague, founded a friary at Roudnice (Raudnitz), he specified that "we shall admit no one to this convent or monastery of any nation except a Bohemian [Czech], born of two Czech-speaking parents."[18] In the fourteenth-century *Dalimil Chronicle,* a

survey of Bohemian history written in Czech and pervaded with Czech hostility toward Germans, one anti-German prince offered 100 marks of silver "to anyone who brought him one hundred noses cut off from the Germans."[19] Urban residents, who were German, countered with their own restrictions. Cobblers in fourteenth-century Beeskow, a town close to the large Slavic population of Lausitz in Silesia, required that "an apprentice who comes to learn his craft should be brought before the master and guild members. . . . We forbid the sons of barbers, linen workers, shepherds, Slavs." The bakers of the same town decreed: "Whoever wishes to be a member must bring proof to the councillors and guildsmen that he is born of legitimate, upright, German folk. . . . No one of Wendish (Slavic) race may be in the guild."[20]

Ethnic purity can be maintained across generations only by prohibiting marriage among groups, and laws did just this. Intermarriage was forbidden in many places, such as Riga on the Baltic (now the capital of Latvia), where legislation for the bakers guild stipulated that "whoever wishes to have the privilege of membership in our company shall not take as a wife any woman who is ill-famed . . . or non-German; if he does marry such a woman, he must leave the company and office." Not only the guilds but also eligibility for public office depended on ethnic purity, as at the German burgher settlement of Pest in Hungary, where a town judge had to have four German grandparents.

The most extensive attempt to prevent intermarriage and protect ethnic purity is embodied in Ireland's **Statute of Kilkenny** (1366), which states that "there were to be no marriages between those of immigrant and native stock; that the English inhabitants of Ireland must employ the English language and bear English names; that they must ride in the English way (that is, with saddles) and have English apparel; that no Irishmen were to be granted ecclesiastical benefices or admitted to monasteries in the English parts of Ireland."[21] Rulers of the Christian kingdoms of Spain drew up comparable legislation discriminating against the Mudéjars.

Late medieval chroniclers used words such as *gens* (race or clan) and *natio* (species, stock, or kind) to refer to different groups. They held that peoples differed according to language, traditions, customs, and laws. None of these were unchangeable, however, and commentators increasingly also described ethnic differences in terms of "blood"—"German blood," "English blood," and so on—which made ethnicity heritable. Religious beliefs also came to be conceptualized as blood, with people regarded as having Jewish blood, Muslim blood, or Christian blood. The most dramatic expression of this was in Spain, where "purity of the blood"—having no Muslim or Jewish ancestors—became an obsession. Blood was also used as a way to talk about social differences, especially for nobles. Just as Irish and English were prohibited from marrying each other, those of "noble blood" were prohibited from marrying commoners in many parts of Europe. As Europeans increasingly came into contact with people from Africa and Asia, and particularly as they developed colonial empires, these notions of blood also became a way of conceptualizing racial categories (see page 429).

Literacy and Vernacular Literature

The development of ethnic identities had many negative consequences, but a more positive effect was the increasing use of national languages. In the High Middle Ages most official documents and works of literature were written in Latin. Beginning in the fourteenth century, however, national languages—the **vernacular**—came into widespread use not only in verbal communication but in literature as well. Two masterpieces of European culture, Dante's *Divine Comedy* (1310–1320) and Chaucer's *Canterbury Tales* (1387–1400), brilliantly manifest this new national pride.

Dante Alighieri (1265–1321) descended from a landowning family in Florence, where he held several positions in the city government. Dante called his work a "comedy" because he wrote it in Italian and in a different style from the "tragic" Latin; a later generation added the adjective *divine,* referring both to its sacred subject and to Dante's artistry. The *Divine Comedy* is an allegorical trilogy of one hundred cantos (verses), each of whose three equal parts (1 + 33 + 33 + 33) describes one of the realms of the next world: Hell, Purgatory, and Paradise. The Roman poet Virgil, representing reason, leads Dante through Hell, where he observes the torments of the damned and denounces the disorders of his own time, especially ecclesiastical ambition and corruption. Passing up into Purgatory, Virgil shows the poet how souls are purified of their disordered inclinations. From Purgatory, Beatrice, a woman

Opening Page from the *Dalimil Chronicle* This history of Bohemia (now part of the Czech Republic) was the first book to be written in the Czech language, and was an important tool in the creation of a Czech national identity. The section reproduced here includes references to "our people" and "our land." The book remains an important part of Czech identity; in 2005 the National Library of the Czech Republic purchased a fragment of an illustrated fourteenth-century Latin translation for nearly half a million dollars. Similar historical chronicles were written in the vernacular languages of many parts of Europe in the fifteenth century and contributed to a growing sense of ethnic and national distinctions. (*Austrian National Library, Vienna*)

Schoolmaster and Schoolmistress Teaching Ambrosius Holbein, elder brother of the more famous Hans Holbein, produced this signboard for the Swiss educator Myconius; it is an excellent example of what we would call commercial art—art used to advertise, in this case Myconius's profession. The German script above promised that all who enrolled, girls and boys, would learn to read and write. Most schools were for boys only, but a few offered instruction for girls as well. By modern standards the classroom seems bleak: the windows have glass panes but they don't admit much light, and the schoolmaster is prepared to use the sticks if the boy makes a mistake. *(Kunstmuseum Basel/Martin Buhler, photographer)*

Dante once loved and the symbol of divine revelation in the poem, leads him to Paradise. In Paradise, home of the angels and saints, Saint Bernard—representing mystic contemplation—leads Dante to the Virgin Mary. Through her intercession, he at last attains a vision of God.

The *Divine Comedy* portrays contemporary and historical figures, comments on secular and ecclesiastical affairs, and draws on Scholastic philosophy. Within the framework of a symbolic pilgrimage to the City of God, the *Divine Comedy* embodies the psychological tensions of the age. A profoundly Christian poem, it also contains bitter criticism of some church authorities. In its symmetrical structure and use of figures from the ancient world, such as Virgil, the poem perpetuates the classical tradition, but as the first major work of literature in the Italian vernacular, it is distinctly modern.

Geoffrey Chaucer (1342–1400), the son of a London wine merchant, was an official in the administrations of the English kings Edward III and Richard II and wrote poetry as an avocation. Chaucer's *Canterbury Tales* is a collection of stories in lengthy rhymed narrative. On a pilgrimage to the shrine of Saint Thomas Becket at Canterbury (see page 271), thirty people of various social backgrounds tell tales. The Prologue sets the scene and describes the pilgrims, whose characters are further re-

vealed in the story each one tells. For example, the gross Miller tells a vulgar story about a deceived husband; the earthy Wife of Bath, who has buried five husbands, sketches a fable about the selection of a spouse; and the elegant Prioress, who violates her vows by wearing jewelry, delivers a homily on the Virgin. In depicting the interests and behavior of all types of people, Chaucer presents a rich panorama of English social life in the fourteenth century. Like the *Divine Comedy, Canterbury Tales* reflects the cultural tensions of the times. Ostensibly Christian, many of the pilgrims are also materialistic, sensual, and worldly, suggesting the ambivalence of the broader society's concern for the next world and frank enjoyment of this one.

Beginning in the fourteenth century, a variety of evidence attests to the increasing literacy of laypeople. Wills and inventories reveal that many people, not just nobles, possessed books—mainly devotional, but also romances, manuals on manners and etiquette, histories, and sometimes legal and philosophical texts. In England the number of schools in the diocese of York quadrupled between 1350 and 1500. Information from Flemish and German towns is similar: children were sent to schools and were taught the fundamentals of reading, writing, and arithmetic. Laymen increasingly served as managers or stewards of estates and as clerks to guilds and town governments; such positions obviously required that they be able to keep administrative and financial records.

The penetration of laymen into the higher positions of governmental administration, long the preserve of clerics, also illustrates rising lay literacy. For example, in 1400 beneficed clerics held most of the posts in the English Exchequer; by 1430 clerics were the exception. With growing frequency, the upper classes sent their daughters to convent schools, where, in addition to instruction in singing, religion, needlework, deportment, and household management, girls gained the rudiments of reading and sometimes writing. Reading and writing were taught separately, and many young people, especially girls, were taught to read but not to write.

The spread of literacy represents a response to the needs of an increasingly complex society. Trade, commerce, and expanding government bureaucracies required more and more literate people. Late medieval culture remained an oral culture in which most people received information by word of mouth. But by the mid-fifteenth century, even before the printing press was turning out large quantities of reading materials, the evolution toward a literary culture was already perceptible.

Chapter Summary

Online Study Center   ACE the Test

- **What were the demographic and economic consequences of climate change?**
- **How did the spread of the plague shape European society?**
- **What were the causes of the Hundred Years' War, and how did the war affect European politics, economics, and cultural life?**
- **What challenges faced the Christian church in the fourteenth century, and how did church leaders, intellectuals, and ordinary people respond?**
- **How did economic and social tensions contribute to revolts, crime, violence, and a growing sense of ethnic and national distinctions?**

The crises of the fourteenth and fifteenth centuries were acids that burned deeply into the fabric of traditional medieval society. Bad weather brought poor harvests, which contributed to widespread famine and disease and an international economic depression. Political leaders attempted to find solutions, but were unable to deal with the economic and social problems that resulted.

In 1348 a new disease, most likely the bubonic plague, came to mainland Europe, carried from the Black Sea by ships. It spread quickly by land and sea and within two years may have killed as much as one-third of the European population. Contemporary medical explanations for the plague linked it to poisoned air or water, and treatments were ineffective. Many people regarded the plague as a divine punishment and sought remedies in religious practices such as prayer, pilgrimages, or donations to churches. Population losses caused by the Black Death led to inflation but in the long run may have contributed to more opportunities for the peasants and urban workers who survived the disease.

The miseries of the plague were enhanced in England and France by the Hundred Years' War, which was fought intermittently in France from 1337 to 1453. The war began as a dispute over the succession to the French crown, and royal propaganda on both sides fostered a kind of early nationalism. The English won most of the battles and in 1419 advanced to the walls of Paris. The appearance of Joan of Arc rallied the French cause, and French troops eventually pushed English forces out of all of France except the port of Calais. The war served as a catalyst for the development of representative government in England. In France, on the other hand, the war stiffened opposition to national assemblies.

Religious beliefs offered people solace through these difficult times, but the Western Christian church was going through a particularly difficult period in the fourteenth and early fifteenth centuries. The Avignon papacy and the Great Schism weakened the prestige of the church and people's faith in papal authority. The conciliar movement, by denying the church's universal sovereignty, strengthened the claims of secular governments to jurisdiction over all their peoples. As members of the clergy challenged the power of the pope, laypeople challenged the authority of the church itself. Women and men increasingly relied on direct approaches to God, often through mystical encounters, rather than on the institutional church. Some, including John Wyclif and Jan Hus, questioned basic church doctrines.

The plague and the war both led to higher taxes and economic dislocations, which sparked peasant revolts in Flanders, France, and England. Peasant revolts often blended with conflicts involving workers in cities, where working conditions were changing to create a greater gap between wealthy merchant-producers and poor propertyless workers. Unrest in the countryside and cities may have been further exacerbated by marriage patterns that left large numbers of young men unmarried and rootless. The pattern of late marriage for men contributed to a growth in prostitution, which was an accepted feature of medieval urban society. Along with peasant revolts and urban crime and unrest, violence perpetrated by nobles was a common part of late medieval life. The economic and demographic crises of the fourteenth century also contributed to increasing ethnic tensions in the many parts of Europe where migration had brought different population groups together. A growing sense of ethnic and national identity led to restrictions and occasionally to violence, but also to the increasing use of national languages for works of literature. The increasing number of schools that led to the growth of lay literacy represents another positive achievement of the later Middle Ages.

Key Terms

Great Famine	Great Schism
Black Death	conciliarists
bubo	confraternities
flagellants	*The Imitation of*
Agincourt	*Christ*
Joan of Arc	peasant revolts
representative	Jacquerie
assemblies	Statute of Kilkenny
nationalism	vernacular
Babylonian Captivity	

Online Study Center **Improve Your Grade** Flashcards

Suggested Reading

Allmand, Christopher. *The Hundred Years War: England and France at War, ca 1300–1450*, rev. ed. 2005. Designed for students; examines the war from political, military, social, and economic perspectives and compares the way England and France reacted to the conflict.

Boswell, John. *Christianity, Social Tolerance, and Homosexuality: Gay People in Western Europe from the Beginning of the Christian Era to the Fourteenth Century*. 1981. Remains an important broad analysis of attitudes toward same-sex relations throughout the Middle Ages.

Dunn, Alastair. *The Peasants' Revolt: England's Failed Revolution of 1381*. 2004. Offers new interpretations of the causes and consequence of the English Peasants' Revolt.

Dyer, Christopher. *Standards of Living in the Later Middle Ages*. 1989. Examines economic realities and social conditions more generally.

Herlihy, David. *The Black Death and the Transformation of the West*, 2d ed. 1997. A fine treatment of the causes and cultural consequences of the disease that remains the best starting point for study of the great epidemic.

Holt, James Clarke. *Robin Hood*. 1982. A soundly researched and highly readable study of the famous outlaw.

Jordan, William Chester. *The Great Famine: Northern Europe in the Early Fourteenth Century*. 1996. Discusses catastrophic weather, soil exhaustion, and other factors that led to the Great Famine and the impact of the famine on community life.

Karras, Ruth M. *Sexuality in Medieval Europe: Doing onto Others*. 2005. A brief overview designed for undergraduates that incorporates the newest scholarship.

Kieckhefer, Richard. *Unquiet Souls: Fourteenth-Century Saints and Their Religious Milieu*. 1984. Sets the ideas of the mystics in their social and intellectual contexts.

Koch, H. W. *Medieval Warfare*. 1978. A beautifully illustrated book covering strategy, tactics, armaments, and costumes of war.

Lehfeldt, Elizabeth, ed. *The Black Death*. 2005. Includes excerpts from debates about many aspects of the Black Death.

Oakley, Frances. *The Western Church in the Later Middle Ages*. 1979. An excellent broad survey.

Robertson, D. W., Jr. *Chaucer's London*. 1968. Evokes the social setting of *Canterbury Tales* brilliantly.

Swanson, R. N. *Religion and Devotion in Europe, c. 1215–c. 1515.* 2004. Explores many aspects of spirituality.

Tuchman, Barbara. *A Distant Mirror: The Calamitous Fourteenth Century.* 1978. Written for a general audience, this remains a vivid description of this tumultuous time.

Notes

1. J. M. Rigg, trans., *The Decameron of Giovanni Boccaccio* (London: J. M. Dent & Sons, 1903), p. 6.
2. Quoted in D. Herlihy, *The Black Death, and the Transformation of the West* (Cambridge, Mass.: Harvard University Press, 1997), p. 42.
3. Quoted in J. Barnie, *War in Medieval English Society: Social Values and the Hundred Years' War* (Ithaca, N.Y.: Cornell University Press, 1974), p. 34.
4. W. P. Barrett, trans., *The Trial of Jeanne d'Arc* (London: George Routledge, 1931), pp. 165–166.
5. Quoted in Barnie, *War in Medieval English Society,* pp. 36–37.
6. See G. O. Sayles, *The King's Parliament of England* (New York: W. W. Norton, 1974), app., pp. 137–141.
7. Quoted in P. S. Lewis, "The Failure of the Medieval French Estates," *Past and Present* 23 (November 1962): 6.
8. Quoted in J. H. Smith, *The Great Schism, 1378: The Disintegration of the Medieval Papacy* (New York: Weybright & Talley, 1970), p. 15.
9. Quoted in Katharina M. Wilson, ed., *Medieval Women Writers* (Athens: University of Georgia Press, 1984), p. 245.
10. Quoted in M. Bloch, *French Rural History,* trans. J. Sondeimer (Berkeley: University of California Press, 1966), p. 169.
11. C. Stephenson and G. Marcham, eds., *Sources of English Constitutional History,* rev. ed. (New York: Harper & Row, 1972), p. 225.
12. M. Rocke, *Forbidden Friendships: Homosexuality and Male Culture in Renaissance Florence* (New York: Oxford University Press, 1996), p. 45.
13. Quoted in B. A. Hanawalt, "Fur Collar Crime: The Pattern of Crime Among the Fourteenth-Century English Nobility," *Journal of Social History* 8 (Spring 1975): 7.
14. Quoted in R. Bartlett, *The Making of Europe: Conquest, Colonization and Cultural Change, 950–1350* (Princeton, N.J.: Princeton University Press, 1993), p. 205.
15. Quoted ibid., p. 208.
16. Quoted ibid., p. 215.
17. Quoted ibid., p. 224.
18. Quoted ibid., p. 228.
19. Quoted ibid., p. 236.
20. Quoted ibid., p. 238.
21. Quoted ibid., p. 239.

Christine de Pizan

Christine de Pizan (1364?–1430; earlier spelled "Pisan") was the daughter and wife of highly educated men who held positions at the court of the king of France. She was widowed at twenty-five with young children and an elderly mother to support. Christine, who herself had received an excellent education, decided to support her family through writing, an unusual choice for anyone in this era before the printing press and unheard of for a woman. She began to write prose works and poetry, sending them to wealthy individuals in the hope of receiving their support. Her works were well received, and Christine gained commissions to write specific works, including a biography of the French king Charles V, several histories, a long poem celebrating Joan of Arc's victory, and a book of military tactics. She became the first woman in Europe to make her living as a writer.

Among Christine's many works were several in which she considered women's nature and proper role in society, which had been a topic of debate since ancient times. The best known of these was The City of Ladies (1404), in which she ponders why so many men have a negative view of women and provides examples of virtuous women to counter this view. Immediately afterward she wrote The Treasure of the City of Ladies (1405, also called The Book of Three Virtues), which provides moral suggestions and practical advice on behavior and household management for women of all social classes. Most of the book is directed toward princesses and court ladies (who would have been able to read it), but she also includes shorter sections for the wives of merchants and artisans, serving-women, female peasants, and even prostitutes. This is her advice to the wives of artisans, whose husbands were generally members of urban craft guilds, such as blacksmiths, bakers, or shoemakers.

All wives of artisans should be very painstaking and diligent if they wish to have the necessities of life. They should encourage their husbands or their workmen to get to work early in the morning and work until late, for mark our words, there is no trade so good that if you neglect your work you will not have difficulty putting bread on the table. And besides encouraging the others, the wife herself should be involved in the work to the extent that she knows all about it, so that she may know how to oversee his workers if her husband is absent, and to reprove them if they do not do well. She ought to oversee them to keep them from idleness, for through careless workers the master is sometimes ruined. And when customers come to her husband and try to drive a hard bargain, she ought to warn him solicitously to take care that he does not make a bad deal. She should advise him to be chary of giving too much credit if he does not know precisely where and to whom it is going, for in this way many come to poverty, although sometimes the greed to earn more or to accept a tempting proposition makes them do it.

In addition, she ought to keep her husband's love as much as she can, to this end: that he will stay at home more willingly and that he may not have any reason to join the foolish crowds of other young men in taverns and indulge in unnecessary and extravagant expense, as many tradesmen do, especially in Paris. By treating him kindly she should protect him as well as she can from this. It is said that three things drive a man from his home: a quarrelsome wife, a smoking fireplace and a leaking roof. She too ought to stay at home gladly and not go every day traipsing hither and yon gossiping with the neighbours and visiting her chums to find out what everyone is doing. That is done by slovenly housewives roaming about the town in groups. Nor should

Several manuscripts of Christine's works included illustrations showing her writing, which would have increased their appeal to the wealthy individuals who purchased them. *(British Library)*

she go off on these pilgrimages got up for no good reason and involving a lot of needless expense. Furthermore, she ought to remind her husband that they should live so frugally that their expenditure does not exceed their income, so that at the end of the year they do not find themselves in debt.

If she has children, she should have them instructed and taught first at school by educated people so that they may know how better to serve God. Afterwards they may be put to some trade by which they may earn a living, for whoever gives a trade or business training to her child gives a great possession. The children should be kept from wantonness and from voluptuousness above all else, for truly it is something that most shames the children of good towns and is a great sin of mothers and fathers, who ought to be the cause of the virtue and good behavior of their children, but they are sometimes the reason (because of bringing them up to be finicky and indulging them too much) for their wickedness and ruin.

Questions for Analysis

1. How would you describe Christine's view of the ideal artisan's wife?

2. The regulations of craft guilds often required that masters who ran workshops be married. What evidence does Christine's advice provide for why guilds would have stipulated this?

3. How are economic and moral virtues linked for Christine?

Source: Christine de Pisan, *The Treasure of the City of Ladies,* translated with an introduction by Sarah Lawson (Peguin Classics, 1985). This translation copyright © 1985 by Sarah Lawson. Reprinted by permission of Penguin Books Ltd. For more on Christine, see C. C. Willard, *Christine de Pisan: Her Life and Works* (1984), and S. Bell, *The Lost Tapestries of the City of Ladies: Christine de Pizan's Renaissance Legacy* (2004).

Michelangelo's frescoes in the Sistine Chapel in the Vatican, commissioned by the pope. The huge ceiling includes biblical scenes, and the far wall, painted much later, shows a dramatic and violent Last Judgment. *(Vatican Museum)*

chapter

13

chapter preview

Economic and Political Developments

• *What economic and political developments in Italy provided the setting for the Renaissance?*

Intellectual Change

• *What were the key ideas of the Renaissance, and how were they different for men and women and for southern and northern Europeans?*

Art and the Artist

• *How did changes in art both reflect and shape new ideas?*

Social Hierarchies

• *What were the key social hierarchies in Renaissance Europe, and how did ideas about hierarchy shape people's lives?*

Politics and the State in the Renaissance (ca 1450–1521)

• *How did the nation-states of western Europe evolve in this period?*

EUROPEAN SOCIETY IN THE AGE OF THE RENAISSANCE, 1350–1550

While the Four Horsemen of the Apocalypse seemed to be carrying war, plague, famine, and death across northern Europe, a new culture was emerging in southern Europe. The fourteenth century witnessed the beginnings of remarkable changes in many aspects of Italian intellectual, artistic, and cultural life. Artists and writers thought that they were living in a new golden age, but not until the sixteenth century was this change given the label we use today—the **Renaissance,** from the French version of a word meaning "rebirth." That word was first used by the artist and art historian Giorgio Vasari (1511–1574) to describe the art of "rare men of genius" such as his contemporary Michelangelo. Through their works, Vasari judged, the glory of the classical past had been reborn—or perhaps even surpassed—after centuries of darkness. Vasari used *Renaissance* to describe painting, sculpture, and architecture, what he termed the "Major Arts." Gradually, however, the word was used to refer to many aspects of life at this time, first in Italy and then in the rest of Europe. This new attitude had a slow diffusion out of Italy, with the result that the Renaissance "happened" at different times in different parts of Europe: Italian art of the fourteenth through the early sixteenth century is described as "Renaissance," and so is English literature of the late sixteenth century, including Shakespeare's plays and poetry.

About a century after Vasari coined the word *Renaissance*, scholars began to use the words *Middle Ages* to refer to the millennium between the ancient world and the Renaissance. They increasingly saw the cultural and political changes of the Renaissance, along with the religious changes of the Reformation (see Chapter 14) and the European voyages of exploration (see Chapter 15), as ushering in the "modern" world. Since then, some historians have chosen to view the Renaissance as a bridge between the medieval and modern eras because it corresponded chronologically with the late medieval period and because there were many continuities along with the changes. Others have questioned whether the word *Renaissance* should be used at all to describe an era in which many social groups saw decline rather than advance. These debates remind us that these labels—medieval, Renaissance, modern—are

Online Study Center

This icon will direct you to interactive activities and study materials on the website **college.hmco.com/pic/mckaywest9e**

407

intellectual constructs, devised after the fact. They all contain value judgments, just as do other chronological designations, such as the "golden age" of Athens and the "Roaring Twenties."

Economic and Political Developments

The cultural achievements of the Renaissance rest on the economic and political developments of earlier centuries. Economic growth laid the material basis for the Italian Renaissance, and ambitious merchants gained political power to match their economic power. They then used their money and power to buy luxuries and hire talent.

- *What economic and political developments in Italy provided the setting for the Renaissance?*

Commercial Developments

In the great commercial revival of the eleventh century, northern Italian cities led the way. By the middle of the twelfth century Venice, supported by a huge merchant marine, had grown enormously rich through overseas trade. Genoa and Milan also enjoyed the benefits of a large volume of trade with the Middle East and northern Europe. These cities fully exploited their geographical positions as natural crossroads for mercantile exchange between the East and the West. Furthermore, in the early fourteenth century Genoa and Venice made important strides in shipbuilding that for the first time allowed their ships to sail all year long. Advances in ship construction greatly increased the volume of goods that could be transported; improvements in the mechanics of sailing accelerated speed.

Scholars tend to agree that the first artistic and literary manifestations of the Italian Renaissance appeared in Florence, which possessed enormous wealth despite geographical constraints: it was an inland city without easy access to sea transportation. But toward the end of the thirteenth century, Florentine merchants and bankers acquired control of papal banking. From their position as tax collectors for the papacy, Florentine mercantile families began to dominate European banking on both sides of the Alps. These families had offices in Paris, London, Bruges, Barcelona, Marseilles, Tunis and other

North African ports, and, of course, Naples and Rome. The profits from loans, investments, and money exchanges that poured back to Florence were pumped into urban industries. Such profits contributed to the city's economic vitality. Banking families, such as the Medici in Florence, controlled the politics and culture of their cities.

By the first quarter of the fourteenth century, the economic foundations of Florence were so strong that even severe crises could not destroy the city. In 1344 King Edward III of England repudiated his huge debts to Florentine bankers and forced some of them into bankruptcy. Florence suffered frightfully from the Black Death, losing at least half its population. Serious labor unrest, such as the *ciompi* revolts of 1378 (see page 392), shook the political establishment. Nevertheless, the basic Florentine economic structure remained stable. Driving enterprise, technical know-how, and competitive spirit saw Florence through the difficult economic period of the late fourteenth century.

A Bank Scene, Florence *Originally a "bank" was just a counter; moneychangers who sat behind the counter became "bankers," exchanging different currencies and holding deposits for merchants and business people. In this scene from fifteenth-century Florence, the bank is covered with an imported Ottoman geometric rug, one of many imported luxury items handled by Florentine merchants. (Prato, San Francesco/Scala/Art Resource, NY)*

Communes and Republics

The northern Italian cities were **communes,** sworn associations of free men seeking complete political and economic independence from local nobles. The merchant guilds that formed the communes built and maintained the city walls, regulated trade, raised taxes, and kept civil order. In the course of the twelfth century, communes at Milan, Florence, Genoa, Siena, and Pisa fought for and won their independence from surrounding feudal nobles. The nobles, attracted by the opportunities of long-distance and maritime trade, the rising value of urban real estate, the new public offices available in the expanding communes, and the chances for advantageous marriages into rich commercial families, frequently settled in the cities. Marriage vows often sealed business contracts between the rural nobility and wealthy merchants, with the large dowries of brides providing cash for their new husbands' businesses. This merger of the northern Italian feudal nobility and the commercial elite created a powerful **oligarchy,** or small group that ruled a city and its surrounding countryside. The ruling oligarchy in any city was tied together by blood, economic interests, and social connections, but was also often divided by hostilities of kinship groups toward one another. Such hostilities sometimes erupted in violence, and Italian communes were often politically unstable.

Conflict between families within the ruling oligarchy was exacerbated by unrest coming from below. Merchant elites made citizenship in the communes dependent on a property qualification, years of residence within the city, and social connections. Only a tiny percentage of the male population possessed these qualifications and thus could hold office in the commune's political councils. The common people, called the **popolo,** were disenfranchised and heavily taxed, and they bitterly resented their exclusion from power. The popolo wanted places in the communal government and equality of taxation. Throughout most of the thirteenth century, in city after city, the popolo used armed force and violence to take over the city governments. Republican governments—in which political power theoretically resides in the people and is exercised by their chosen representatives—were established in Bologna, Siena, Parma, Florence, Genoa, and other cities. The victory of the popolo proved temporary, however, because they could not establish civil order within their cities. Merchant oligarchies reasserted their power and sometimes brought in powerful military leaders to establish order. These military leaders, called **condottieri** (singular, condottiero), had their own mercenary armies, and in many cities they took over political

power as well. The military leader often invented a long noble lineage to justify his takeover of power, pretending he descended from a Germanic king or Roman leader. There was not much that merchant oligarchies could do to retain their power, and many cities in Italy became **signori,** in which one man ruled and handed down the right to rule to his son. Some signori (the word is plural in Italian and is used for both persons and forms of government) kept the institutions of communal government in place, but these had no actual power.

For the next two centuries the Italian city-states were ruled by signori or by merchant oligarchies. Oligarchic regimes possessed constitutions and often boasted about how much more democratic their form of government was than the government in neighboring signori. In actuality, there wasn't much difference. In oligarchies, a small, restricted class of wealthy merchants exercised the judicial, executive, and legislative functions of government. Thus, in 1422 Venice had a population of eighty-four thousand, but two hundred men held all the power; Florence had about forty thousand people, but only six hundred men were part of the government. Even this number is an illusion, for real power in Florence for most of the fifteenth century was actually held by the Medici family. Oligarchic regimes maintained only a façade of republican government. The Renaissance nostalgia for the Roman form of government, combined with calculating shrewdness, prompted the leaders of Venice, Milan, and Florence to use the old forms.

Chronology

1350–1353	Boccaccio, *The Decameron*
1434–1494	Medici family in power in Florence
1440s	Invention of movable metal type
1469	Marriage of Isabella of Castile and Ferdinand of Aragon
1486	Pico della Mirandola, *On the Dignity of Man*
1494	Invasion of Italy by Charles VIII of France
1508–1512	Michelangelo paints ceiling of Sistine Chapel
1513	Machiavelli, *The Prince*
1516	More, *Utopia*
1528	Castiglione, *The Courtier*

In the fifteenth century the signori in many cities and the most powerful merchant oligarchs in others transformed their households into **courts.** They built magnificent palaces in the centers of cities and required all political business be done there. They hired architects to design and build these palaces, artists to fill them with paintings and sculptures, and musicians and composers to fill them with music. They supported writers and philosophers, flaunting their patronage of learning and the arts. They used ceremonies connected with family births, baptisms, marriages, funerals, or triumphant entrances into the city as occasions for magnificent pageantry and elaborate ritual. Courtly culture afforded signori and oligarchs the opportunity to display and assert their wealth and power. The courts of the rulers of Milan, Florence, and other cities were models for those developed later by rulers of nation-states.

The Balance of Power Among the Italian City-States

Renaissance Italians had a passionate attachment to their individual city-states: political loyalty and feeling centered on the local city. This intensity of local feeling perpetuated the dozens of small states and hindered the development of one unified state.

In the fifteenth century five powers dominated the Italian peninsula: Venice, Milan, Florence, the Papal States, and the kingdom of Naples (see Map 13.1). The rulers of the city-states—whether signori in Milan, patrician elitists in Florence, or oligarchs in Venice—governed as monarchs. They crushed urban revolts, levied taxes, killed their enemies, and used massive building programs to employ, and the arts to overawe, the masses.

Venice, with its enormous trade and vast colonial empire, ranked as an international power. Though Venice had a sophisticated constitution and was a **republic** in name, an oligarchy of merchant aristocrats actually ran the city. Milan was also called a republic, but the condottieri-turned-signori of the Sforza family ruled harshly and dominated the smaller cities of the north. Likewise, in Florence the form of government was republican, with authority vested in several councils of state. In reality, between 1434 and 1494, power in Florence was held by the great Medici banking family. Though not public officers, Cosimo (1434–1464) and Lorenzo (1469–1492) ruled from behind the scenes.

Central Italy consisted mainly of the Papal States, which during the Babylonian Captivity had come under the sway of important Roman families. Pope Alexander VI (1492–1503), aided militarily and politically by his son Cesare Borgia, reasserted papal authority in the papal lands. Cesare Borgia became the hero of Machiavelli's *The Prince* (see page 415) because he began the work of uniting the peninsula by ruthlessly conquering and exacting total obedience from the principalities making up the Papal States.

South of the Papal States was the kingdom of Naples, consisting of virtually all of southern Italy and, at times, Sicily. The kingdom of Naples had long been disputed by the Aragonese and by the French. In 1435 it passed to Aragon.

The major Italian city-states controlled the smaller ones, such as Siena, Mantua, Ferrara, and Modena, and competed furiously among themselves for territory. The large cities used diplomacy, spies, paid informers, and any other available means to get information that could be used to advance their ambitions. While the states of northern Europe were moving toward centralization and consolidation, the world of Italian politics resembled a jungle where the powerful dominated the weak.

In one significant respect, however, the Italian city-states anticipated future relations among competing European states after 1500. Whenever one Italian state appeared to gain a predominant position within the peninsula, other states combined to establish a *balance of power* against the major threat. In the formation of these alliances, Renaissance Italians invented the machinery of modern diplomacy: permanent embassies with resident ambassadors in capitals where political relations and commercial ties needed continual monitoring. The resident ambassador was one of the great achievements of the Italian Renaissance.

At the end of the fifteenth century Venice, Florence, Milan, and the papacy possessed great wealth and represented high cultural achievement. However, their imperialistic ambitions at one another's expense and their resulting inability to form a common alliance against potential foreign enemies made Italy an inviting target for invasion. When Florence and Naples entered into an agreement to acquire Milanese territories, Milan called on France for support.

At Florence the French invasion had been predicted by Dominican friar Girolamo Savonarola (1452–1498). In a number of fiery sermons between 1491 and 1494, Savonarola attacked what he called the paganism and moral vice of the city, the undemocratic government of Lorenzo de' Medici, and the corruption of Pope Alexander VI. For a time Savonarola enjoyed popular support among the ordinary people; he became the religious

MAP 13.1 The Italian City-States, ca 1494 In the fifteenth century the Italian city-states represented great wealth and cultural sophistication. The political divisions of the peninsula invited foreign intervention.

leader of Florence and as such contributed to the fall of the Medici dynasty. Eventually, however, people tired of his moral denunciations, and he was excommunicated by the pope and executed. Savonarola stands as proof that the common people did not share the worldly outlook of the commercial and intellectual elite. His career also illustrates the internal instability of Italian cities such as Florence, an instability that invited foreign invasion.

The invasion of Italy in 1494 by the French king Charles VIII (r. 1483–1498) inaugurated a new period in Italian and European power politics. Italy became the focus of international ambitions and the battleground of foreign armies, particularly those of France and the Holy Roman Empire in a series of conflicts called the Habsburg-Valois Wars (named for the German and French dynasties). The Italian cities suffered severely from

Uccello: Battle of San Romano   Fascinated by perspective—the representation of spatial depth or distance on a flat surface—the Florentine artist Paolo Uccello (1397–1475) celebrated the Florentine victory over Siena (1432) in a painting with three scenes. Though a minor battle, it started Florence on the road to domination over smaller nearby states. The painting hung in Lorenzo de' Medici's bedroom. *(National Gallery, London/Erich Lessing/Art Resource, NY)*

continual warfare, especially in the frightful sack of Rome in 1527 by imperial forces under the emperor Charles V. Thus the failure of the city-states to form some federal system, to consolidate, or at least to establish a common foreign policy led to centuries of subjection by outside invaders. Italy was not to achieve unification until 1870.

Intellectual Change

The Renaissance was characterized by self-conscious awareness among fourteenth- and fifteenth-century Italians that they were living in a new era. The realization that something new and unique was happening first came to men of letters in the fourteenth century, especially to the poet and humanist Francesco Petrarch (1304–1374). Petrarch thought that he was living at the start of a new age, a period of light following a long night of Gothic gloom.

Medieval people had believed that they were continuing the glories that had been ancient Rome and had recognized no cultural division between the world of the emperors and their own times. But for Petrarch, the Germanic migrations had caused a sharp cultural break with the glories of Rome and inaugurated what he called the "Dark Ages." Along with many of his contemporaries, Petrarch believed that he was witnessing a new golden age of intellectual achievement.

● *What were the key ideas of the Renaissance, and how were they different for men and women and for southern and northern Europeans?*

Humanism

Petrarch and other poets, writers, and artists showed a deep interest in the ancient past, in both the physical remains of the Roman Empire and classical Latin texts. The study of Latin classics became known as the *studia humanitates,* usually translated as "liberal studies" or the "liberal arts." Like all programs of study, they contained an implicit philosophy, generally known as **humanism,** a term devised by the Florentine rhetorician and historian Leonardo Bruni (1370–1444). The words *humanism* and *humanist* derive ultimately from the Latin *humanitas,* which the ancient Roman writer Cicero had used to mean the literary culture needed by anyone who would be considered educated and civilized. Humanists studied the Latin classics to learn what they reveal about human nature. Humanism emphasized human beings and their achievements, interests, and capabilities.

Appreciation for the literary culture of the Romans had never died in the West, but medieval writers had studied the ancients in order to come to know God. Medieval scholars had interpreted the classics in a Christian sense and had invested the ancients' poems and histories with Christian meaning.

Renaissance humanists approached the classics differently. Whereas medieval writers looked to the classics to reveal God, Renaissance humanists studied the classics to understand human nature. They viewed humanity from a strongly Christian perspective, however: men (and women, though to a lesser degree) were made in the image and likeness of God. For example, in a remarkable essay, *On the Dignity of Man* (1486), the Florentine writer Giovanni Pico della Mirandola (1463–1494) stressed that man possesses great dignity because he was made as Adam in the image of God before the Fall and as Christ after the Resurrection. According to Pico, man's place in the universe is somewhere between the beasts and the angels, but because of the divine image planted in him, there are no limits to what he can accomplish. Humanists generally rejected classical ideas that were opposed to Christianity, or they sought through reinterpretation an underlying harmony between the pagan and secular and the Christian faith.

Interest in human achievement led humanists to emphasize the importance of the individual. Groups such as families, guilds, and religious organizations continued to provide strong support for the individual and to exercise great social influence. Yet in the Renaissance, intellectuals, unlike their counterparts in the Middle Ages, prized their own uniqueness.

The Renaissance witnessed the emergence of many distinctive personalities who gloried in their individuality; they had enormous confidence in their ability to achieve great things. Leon Battista Alberti (1404–1472), a writer, architect, and mathematician, remarked, "Men can do all things if they will."[1] Florentine goldsmith and

Benvenuto Cellini: Saltcellar of Francis I (ca 1540) In gold and enamel, Cellini depicts the Roman sea god, Neptune (with trident, or three-pronged spear), sitting beside a small boat-shaped container holding salt from the sea. Opposite him, a female figure personifying Earth guards pepper, which derives from a plant. Portrayed on the base are the four seasons and the times of day, symbolizing seasonal festivities and daily meal schedules. Classical figures portrayed with grace, poise, and elegance were common subjects in Renaissance art. *(Kunsthistorisches Museum, Vienna/The Bridgeman Art Library)*

sculptor Benvenuto Cellini (1500–1574) prefaced his *Autobiography* with a declaration:

My cruel fate hath warr'd with me in vain:
Life, glory, worth, and all unmeasur'd skill,
Beauty and grace, themselves in me fulfil
That many I surpass, and to the best attain.[2]

Cellini, certain of his genius, wrote so that the whole world might appreciate it.

This attitude of **individualism** stressed personality, uniqueness, genius, and full development of one's capabilities and talents. Thirst for fame, the quest for glory, a driving ambition, and a burning desire for success drove people such as Alberti and Cellini.

The fourteenth- and fifteenth-century humanists loved the language of the classics and considered it superior to the corrupt Latin of the medieval schoolmen. The leading humanists of the early Renaissance were rhetoricians, seeking effective and eloquent oral and written communication. Literary humanists of the fourteenth century wrote each other highly stylized letters imitating ancient authors, and they held witty philosophical dialogues in conscious imitation of the Platonic Academy of the fourth century B.C. They eventually became concerned about form more than about content, however, and more about the way an idea was expressed than about the significance and validity of the idea.

Education

One of the central preoccupations of the humanists was education and moral behavior. Humanists poured out treatises, often in the form of letters, on the structure and goals of education and the training of rulers. They taught that a life active in the world should be the aim of all educated individuals and that education was not simply for private or religious purposes, but benefited the public good. In one of the earliest systematic programs for the young, Peter Paul Vergerio (1370–1444) wrote Ubertinus, the ruler of Carrara:

For the education of children is a matter of more than private interest; it concerns the State, which indeed regards the right training of the young as, in certain aspects, within its proper sphere. . . .

We call those studies liberal which are worthy of a free man; those studies by which we attain and practice virtue and wisdom; that education which calls forth, trains, and develops those highest gifts of body and mind which ennoble men, and which are rightly judged to rank next in dignity to virtue only.[3]

Part of Vergerio's treatise specifies subjects for the instruction of young men in public life: history teaches virtue by examples from the past, ethics focuses on virtue itself, and rhetoric or public speaking trains for eloquence.

Humanists did not simply talk about education, but also put their ideas into practice. They opened schools and academies in Italian cities and courts in which pupils began with Latin grammar and rhetoric, went on to study Roman history and political philosophy, and then learned Greek in order to study Greek literature and philosophy. These classics, humanists taught, would provide models of how to write clearly, argue effectively, and speak persuasively, important skills for future diplomats, lawyers, military leaders, businessmen, and politicians. Merchants and bankers sent their sons to humanist schools, and ambitious young men from outside Italy flocked to these schools or to schools that opened later in their own cities. Humanist teachers and their ideas spread out from Florence across the Alps and eventually to northern European cities like London and Paris. Gradually humanist education became the basis for intermediate and advanced education for a large share of middle- and upper-class males.

Their emphasis on the public role and reputation of the educated individual made humanists ambivalent in their attitudes about education for women. If the best models of moral behavior and clear thought were to be found in classical authors, why should women be denied access to these? Should the new virtues of self-confidence and individualism be extended to include women? Most humanists thought that a program of study that emphasized eloquence and action was not proper for women, for women were not to engage in public activities. They agreed with Leonard Bruni that "rhetoric in all its forms lies absolutely outside the province of women" and that the "field of religion and morals" should be the primary focus of women's education.[4] The Italian humanist and polymath Leon Battista Alberti (1404–1472), discussing morality in his *On the Family,* stressed that a wife's role should be restricted to the orderliness of the household, food and the serving of meals, the education of children, and the supervision of servants. (Alberti never married, so he never put his ideas into practice in his own household.) Humanists never established schools for girls, though a few women of very high social status did gain a humanist education from private tutors. The ideal Renaissance woman looked a great deal more like her medieval counterpart than did the Renaissance man, leading the historian Joan Kelly to ask, in a now-famous essay, "Did women have a Renaissance?" (Her answer was no.)

No book on education had broader influence than Baldassare Castiglione's *The Courtier* (1528). This treatise sought to train, discipline, and fashion the young man into the courtly ideal, the gentleman. According to Castiglione, who himself was a courtier serving several different rulers, the educated man of the upper class should have a broad background in many academic subjects, and his spiritual and physical as well as intellectual capabilities should be trained. The courtier should have easy familiarity with dance, music, and the arts. Castiglione envisioned a man who could compose a sonnet, wrestle, sing a song and accompany himself on an instrument, ride expertly, solve difficult mathematical problems, and, above all, speak and write eloquently. Castiglione also included discussion of the perfect court lady, who, like the courtier, was to be well-educated and able to play a musical instrument, to paint, and to dance. Physical beauty, delicacy, affability, and modesty were also important qualities for court ladies, however, though these were not expected of gentlemen.

Raphael: Portrait of Castiglione In this portrait by Raphael, the most sought-after portrait painter of the Renaissance, Castiglione is shown dressed exactly as he advised courtiers to dress, in elegant, but subdued, clothing that would enhance the splendor of the court, but never outshine the ruler. *(Scala/Art Resource, NY)*

In the sixteenth and seventeenth centuries, *The Courtier* was translated into every European language and widely read. It influenced the social mores and patterns of conduct of elite groups in Renaissance and early modern Europe. Echoes of its ideal for women have perhaps had an even longer life.

Political Thought

No Renaissance book on any topic has been more widely read and studied in all the centuries since its publication (1513) than the short political treatise **The Prince** by Niccolò Machiavelli (1469–1527). The subject of *The Prince* is political power: how the ruler should gain, maintain, and increase it. Machiavelli implicitly addresses the question of the citizen's relationship to the state. As a good humanist, he explores the problems of human nature and concludes that human beings are selfish and out to advance their own interests. This pessimistic view of humanity led him to maintain that the prince might have to manipulate the people in any way he finds necessary:

For a man who, in all respects, will carry out only his professions of good, will be apt to be ruined amongst so many who are evil. A prince therefore who desires to maintain himself must learn to be not always good, but to be so or not as necessity may require.[5]

The prince should combine the cunning of a fox with the ferocity of a lion to achieve his goals. Asking rhetorically whether it is better for a ruler to be loved or feared, Machiavelli writes, "It will naturally be answered that it would be desirable to be both the one and the other; but as it is difficult to be both at the same time, it is much more safe to be feared than to be loved, when you have to choose between the two."[6]

Online Study Center **Improve Your Grade**
Primary Source: *The Prince:* Power Politics During the Italian Renaissance

Medieval political theory had derived ultimately from Saint Augustine's view that the state arose as a consequence of Adam's fall and people's propensity to sin. The test of good government was whether it provided justice, law, and order. Political theorists and theologians from Alcuin to Marsiglio of Padua had stressed the way government *ought* to be; they had set high moral and Christian standards for the ruler's conduct.

Machiavelli maintained that the ruler should be concerned not with the way things ought to be but with the way things actually are. The sole test of a "good" government is whether it is effective, whether the ruler increases his power. Machiavelli did not advocate amoral behavior, but he believed that political action cannot be restricted by moral considerations. While amoral action might be the most effective approach in a given situation, he did not argue for generally amoral, rather than moral, behavior. Nevertheless, on the basis of a crude interpretation of *The Prince*, the word *Machiavellian* entered the language as a synonym for the politically devious, corrupt, and crafty, indicating actions in which the end justifies the means. The ultimate significance of Machiavelli rests on two ideas: first, that one permanent social order reflecting God's will cannot be established, and second, that politics has its own laws, based on expediency, not morality.

Secular Spirit

Machiavelli's *The Prince* is often seen as a prime example of another aspect of the Renaissance, secularism. **Secularism** involves a basic concern with the material world instead of with the eternal world of spirit. A secular way of thinking tends to find the ultimate explanation of everything and the final end of human beings within the limits of what the senses can discover. Even though medieval business people ruthlessly pursued profits and medieval monks fought fiercely over property, the dominant ideals focused on the otherworldly, on life after death. Renaissance people often had strong and deep spiritual interests, but in their increasingly secular society, attention was concentrated on the here and now. Wealth allowed greater material pleasures, a more comfortable life, and the leisure time to appreciate and patronize the arts. The rich, social-climbing residents of Venice, Florence, Genoa, and Rome came to see life more as an opportunity to be enjoyed than as a painful pilgrimage to the City of God.

In *On Pleasure,* humanist Lorenzo Valla (1406–1457) defends the pleasures of the senses as the highest good. Scholars praise Valla as a father of modern historical criticism. His study *On the False Donation of Constantine* (1444) demonstrates by careful textual examination that an anonymous eighth-century document supposedly giving the papacy jurisdiction over vast territories in western Europe was a forgery. Medieval people had accepted the Donation of Constantine as a reality, and the proof that it was an invention weakened the foundations of papal claims to temporal authority. Lorenzo Valla's work exemplifies the application of critical scholarship to old and almost sacred writings as well as the new secular spirit of the Renaissance.

The tales in *The Decameron* (1350–1353) by the Florentine Giovanni Boccaccio (1313–1375), which describe ambitious merchants, lecherous friars, and cuckolded husbands, portray a frankly acquisitive, sensual, and worldly society. Although Boccaccio's figures were stock literary characters, *The Decameron* contains none of the "contempt of the world" theme so pervasive in medieval literature. Renaissance writers justified the accumulation and enjoyment of wealth with references to ancient authors.

Nor did church leaders do much to combat the new secular spirit. In the fifteenth and early sixteenth centuries, the papal court and the households of the cardinals were just as worldly as those of great urban patricians. Of course, most of the popes and higher church officials had come from the bourgeois aristocracy. Renaissance popes beautified the city of Rome, patronized artists and men of letters, and expended enormous enthusiasm and

huge sums of money. Pope Julius II (1503–1513) tore down the old Saint Peter's Basilica and began work on the present structure in 1506. Michelangelo's dome for Saint Peter's is still considered his greatest work. Papal interests, which were far removed from spiritual concerns, fostered, rather than discouraged, the new worldly attitude.

Despite their interest in secular matters, however, few people (including Machiavelli) questioned the basic tenets of the Christian religion. Italian humanists and their aristocratic patrons were anti-ascetic, but they were not agnostics or skeptics. The thousands of pious paintings, sculptures, processions, and pilgrimages of the Renaissance period prove that strong religious feeling persisted.

Christian Humanism

The blend of religious and secular concerns of the Italian humanists is even more pronounced among humanists from northern Europe. In the last quarter of the fifteenth century, students from the Low Countries, France, Germany, and England flocked to Italy, imbibed the "new learning," and carried it back to their countries. Northern humanists, often called **Christian humanists,** interpreted Italian ideas about and attitudes toward classical antiquity, individualism, and humanism in terms of their own traditions. They developed a program for broad social reform based on Christian ideals.

Christian humanists were interested in an ethical way of life. To achieve it, they believed that the best elements of classical and Christian cultures should be combined. For example, the classical ideals of calmness, stoical patience, and broad-mindedness should be joined in human conduct with the Christian virtues of love, faith, and hope. Northern humanists also stressed the use of reason, rather than acceptance of dogma, as the foundation for an ethical way of life. Like the Italians, they were impatient with Scholastic philosophy. Christian humanists had profound faith in the power of human intellect to bring about moral and institutional reform. They believed that, although human nature had been corrupted by sin, it was fundamentally good and capable of improvement through education.

The Englishman Thomas More (1478–1535) towered above other figures in sixteenth-century English social and intellectual history. Trained as a lawyer, More lived as a student in the London Charterhouse, a Carthusian monastery. He subsequently married and practiced law but became deeply interested in the classics. His household served as a model of warm Christian family life and as a mecca for foreign and English humanists, who were

Bennozzo Gozzoli: Procession of the Magi, 1461 This segment of a huge fresco covering three walls of a chapel in the Medici Palace in Florence shows members of the Medici family and other contemporary individuals in a procession accompanying the biblical three wise men (*magi* in Italian) as they brought gifts to the infant Jesus. The painting was ordered by Cosimo and Piero de' Medici, who had just finished building the family palace in the center of the city. Reflecting the self-confidence of his patrons, Gozzoli places the elderly Cosimo and Piero at the head of the procession, accompanied by their grooms. The group behind them includes Pope Pius II (in the last row in a red hat that ties under the chin) and the artist (in the second to the last row in a red hat with gold lettering). *(Scala/Art Resource, NY)*

particularly impressed with the linguistic skills of More's daughters, whom he had trained in Latin and Greek. In the career pattern of such Italian humanists as Petrarch, More entered government service under Henry VIII and was sent as ambassador to Flanders. There More found the time to write *Utopia* (1516), which presents a revolutionary view of society.

Utopia, which means "nowhere," describes an ideal socialistic community on an island somewhere off the mainland of the New World. All children receive a good education, primarily in the Greco-Roman classics, and learning does not cease with maturity, for the goal of all education is to develop rational faculties. Adults divide their days between manual labor or business pursuits and intellectual activities.

Because profits from business and property are held in common, there is absolute social equality. The Utopians use gold and silver to make chamber pots and to prevent wars by buying off their enemies. By this casual use of precious metals, More meant to suggest that the basic problems in society are caused by greed. Citizens of Utopia lead an ideal, nearly perfect existence because they live by reason; their institutions are perfect. More punned on the word *utopia,* which he termed "a good place. A good place which is no place."

More's ideas were profoundly original in the sixteenth century. Contrary to the long-prevailing view that vice and violence existed because people were basically corrupt, More maintained that acquisitiveness and private property promoted all sorts of vices and civil disorders. Since society protected private property, society's flawed institutions were responsible for corruption and war. According to More, the key to improvement and reform of the individual was reform of the social institutions that molded the individual. Today this view is so much taken for granted that it is difficult to appreciate how radical More's approach was in the sixteenth century.

Online Study Center **Improve Your Grade**
Primary Source: *Utopia:* A Question over Diplomatic Advice

Better known by contemporaries than Thomas More was the Dutch humanist Desiderius Erasmus (1466?–1536) of Rotterdam. Orphaned as a small boy, Erasmus was forced to enter a monastery. Although he hated the monastic life, he developed an excellent knowledge of the Latin language and a deep appreciation for the Latin classics. During a visit to England in 1499, Erasmus met the scholar John Colet, who decisively influenced his life's work: the application of the best humanistic learning to the study and explanation of the Bible. As a mature scholar with an international reputation stretching from Cracow to London, a fame that rested largely on his exceptional knowledge of Greek, Erasmus could boast with truth, "I brought it about that humanism, which among the Italians . . . savored of nothing but pure paganism, began nobly to celebrate Christ."[7]

Erasmus's long list of publications includes *The Education of a Christian Prince* (1504), a book combining idealistic and practical suggestions for the formation of a ruler's character through the careful study of Plutarch, Aristotle, Cicero, and Plato; *The Praise of Folly* (1509), a satire of worldly wisdom and a plea for the simple and spontaneous Christian faith of children; and, most important, a critical edition of the Greek New Testament (1516). In the preface to the New Testament, Erasmus explained the purpose of his great work:

For I utterly dissent from those who are unwilling that the sacred Scriptures should be read by the unlearned translated into their vulgar tongue, as though Christ had taught such subtleties that they can scarcely be understood even by a few theologians. . . . Christ wished his mysteries to be published as openly as possible. I wish that even the weakest woman should read the Gospel—should read the epistles of Paul. And I wish these were translated into all languages, so that they might be read and understood, not only by Scots and Irishmen, but also by Turks and Saracens.[8]

Two fundamental themes run through all of Erasmus's work. First, education is the means to reform, the key to moral and intellectual improvement. The core of education ought to be study of the Bible and the classics. (See the feature "Listening to the Past: An Age of Gold" on pages 442–443.) Second, the essence of Erasmus's thought is, in his own phrase, "the philosophy of Christ." By this Erasmus meant that Christianity is an inner attitude of the heart or spirit. Christianity is not formalism, special ceremonies, or law; Christianity is Christ—his life and what he said and did, not what theologians have written. The Sermon on the Mount, for Erasmus, expresses the heart of the Christian message.

The Printed Word

The fourteenth-century humanist Petrarch and the sixteenth-century humanist Erasmus had similar ideas about many things, but the immediate impact of their ideas was very different because of one thing: the printing press with movable metal type. The ideas of Petrarch were spread the same way that ideas had been for centuries, from person to person by hand copying. The ideas

of Erasmus were spread through print, in which hundreds or thousands of identical copies could be made in a short time. Erasmus actually spent his later years living with printer friends, checking his own and others' work for errors as well as translating and writing. Print shops were gathering places for those interested in new ideas. Though printers were trained through apprenticeships just like blacksmiths or butchers, they had connections to the world of politics, art, and scholarship that other craftsmen did not.

Printing with movable metal type developed in Germany in the middle of the fifteenth century as a combination of existing technologies. Several metal-smiths, most prominently Johan Gutenberg, recognized that the metal stamps used to mark signs on jewelry could be covered with ink and used to mark symbols onto a surface, in the same way that other craftsmen were using carved wood stamps. These craftsmen carved a whole page in wood, inked it, and pressed it on paper, and then assembled the paper into a book called a *block-book*. Block printing had been used in China and Korea since at least the eighth century and had spread to Europe by the thirteenth. The carvings could be used only a few dozen times before they became ink-soaked and unreadable, however; and since each word, phrase, or picture was on a separate block, this method of reproduction was extraordinarily expensive and time-consuming.

Using molds as smiths did for tableware or other metal items, Gutenberg and his assistants made stamps—later called *type*—for every letter of the alphabet and built racks that held the type in rows. This type could be rearranged for every page and so used over and over; it could also be melted down and remade once it became flattened through repeated use. They experimented with different types of ink, settling on a type of artists' ink, and with different types of presses, adapting the presses used to press grapes for wine, stamp patterns on fabric, or make block-books.

Books were printed on paper, and by the middle of the fifteenth century, acquiring paper was no problem. The knowledge of paper manufacture had originated in China, and the Arabs introduced it to the West in the twelfth century. Europeans quickly learned that durable paper was far less expensive than the vellum (calfskin) and parchment (sheepskin) on which medieval scribes had relied for centuries. By the fifteenth century the increase in urban literacy, the development of primary schools, and the opening of more universities had created an expanding market for reading materials of all types (see pages 400–401). When Gutenberg developed what he saw at first as a faster way to copy, professional copyists writing by hand

The Print Shop This sixteenth-century engraving captures the busy world of a print shop: On the left, men set pieces of type, and an individual wearing glasses checks a copy. At the rear, another applies ink to the type, while a man carries in fresh paper on his head. At the right, the master printer operates the press, while a boy removes the printed pages and sets them to dry. The well-dressed figure in the right foreground may be the patron checking to see whether his job is done. *(Giraudon/Art Resource, NY)*

and block-book makers, along with monks and nuns in monasteries, were already churning out reading materials on paper as fast as they could for the growing number of people who could read.

Gutenberg's invention involved no special secret technology or materials, and he was not the only one to recognize the huge market for books. Other craftsmen made their own type, built their own presses, and bought their own paper, setting themselves up in business in the cities of Germany, Switzerland, and the Netherlands, and then in Italy, England, and France. By 1480 about 110 cities in Europe had presses, with Venice employing the most and producing about one-eighth of all printed books in Europe. Printing continued to spread to Spain and Scandinavia, and by 1500, roughly fifty years after the first printed books, more than 200 cities and towns in Europe had presses (see Map 13.2). Historians estimate that somewhere between 8 million and 20 million books were printed in Europe before 1500, many more than the number of books produced in all of Western history up to that point.

The effects of the invention of movable-type printing were not felt overnight. Nevertheless, within a half century of the publication of Gutenberg's Bible of 1456, movable type had brought about radical changes. Printing transformed both the private and the public lives of

Europeans. It gave hundreds or even thousands of people identical books, so that they could more easily discuss the ideas that the books contained with one another in person or through letters. Printed materials reached an invisible public, allowing silent individuals to join causes and groups of individuals widely separated by geography to form a common identity; this new group consciousness could compete with older, localized loyalties.

Government and church leaders both used and worried about printing. They printed laws, declarations of war, battle accounts, and propaganda, and they also attempted to censor books and authors whose ideas they thought were wrong. Officials developed lists of prohibited books and authors, enforcing their prohibitions by confiscating books, arresting printers and booksellers, or destroying the presses of printers who disobeyed. None of this was very effective, and books were printed secretly, with fake title pages, authors, and places of publication, and smuggled all over Europe.

Printing also stimulated the literacy of laypeople and eventually came to have a deep effect on their private lives. Although most of the earliest books and pamphlets dealt with religious subjects, students, merchants, and upper- and middle-class people sought books on all subjects, and printers produced anything that would sell. They produced law codes bound in fancy leather bindings

**Major printing centers
with date of establishment**

- ● 15th century
- ● 16th century
- —— Political boundaries
  in 1490

Mapping the Past

MAP 13.2 The Growth of Printing in Europe The speed with which artisans spread printing technology across Europe provides strong evidence for the existing market in reading material. Presses in the Ottoman Empire were first established by Jewish immigrants who printed works in Hebrew, Greek, and Spanish. Use this map and those in other chapters to answer the following questions: **❶** What part of Europe had the greatest number of printing presses by 1550? Why might this be? **❷** Printing was developed in response to a market for reading materials. Use Maps 11.2 and 11.3 (pages 340 and 346) to help explain why printing spread the way it did. **❸** Many historians also see printing as an important factor in the spread of the Protestant Reformation. Use Map 14.2 (page 468) to test this assertion.

Online Study Center **Improve Your Grade** Interactive Map: The Growth of Printing in matching sets for lawyers; medical manuals and guides to healing herbs for doctors, surgeons, pharmacists, and midwives; grammars and dictionaries for students, often in small sizes with paper covers so that they were cheap and could be carried to class; and books of prayers and sermons for members of the clergy. They printed historical romances, biographies, and how-to manuals, such as cookbooks and books of home remedies. They discovered that illustrations increased a book's sales, so published both history and pornography full of woodcuts and engravings. Single-page broadsides and flysheets allowed great public festivals, religious ceremonies, political events, and "wonders" such as comets or two-headed calves to be experienced vicariously by the stay-at-home. Since books and other printed materials were read aloud to illiterate listeners, print bridged the gap between the written and oral cultures.

Art and the Artist

No feature of the Renaissance evokes greater admiration than its artistic masterpieces. The 1400s (*quattrocento*) and 1500s (*cinquecento*) bore witness to dazzling creativity in painting, architecture, and sculpture. In all the arts, the city of Florence led the way. According to Vasari, the painter Perugino once asked why it was in Florence and not elsewhere that men achieved perfection in the arts. The first answer he received was, "There were so many good critics there, for the air of the city makes men quick and perceptive and impatient of mediocrity."[9] But Florence was not the only artistic center, for Rome and Venice also became important, and northern Europeans perfected their own styles.

- *How did changes in art both reflect and shape new ideas?*

Art and Power

In early Renaissance Italy, art manifested corporate power. Powerful urban groups such as guilds or religious confraternities commissioned works of art. The Florentine cloth merchants, for example, delegated Filippo Brunelleschi to build the magnificent dome on the cathedral of Florence and selected Lorenzo Ghiberti to design the bronze doors of the Baptistery. These works represented the merchants' dominant influence in the community. Corporate patronage was also reflected in the Florentine government's decision to hire Michelangelo to create the

sculpture of David, the great Hebrew hero and king. The subject matter of art through the early fifteenth century, as in the Middle Ages, remained overwhelmingly religious. Religious themes appeared in all media—woodcarvings, painted frescoes, stone sculptures, paintings. As in the Middle Ages, art served an educational purpose. A religious picture or statue was intended to spread a particular doctrine, act as a profession of faith, or recall sinners to a moral way of living.

Increasingly in the later fifteenth century, individuals and oligarchs, rather than corporate groups, sponsored works of art. Patrician merchants and bankers and popes and princes supported the arts as a means of glorifying themselves and their families, becoming artistic **patrons.** Vast sums were spent on family chapels, frescoes, religious panels, and tombs. Writing about 1470, Florentine oligarch Lorenzo de' Medici declared that his family had spent the astronomical sum of 663,755 gold florins for artistic and architectural commissions over the previous thirty-five years. Yet "I think it casts a brilliant light on our estate [public reputation] and it seems to me that the monies were well spent and I am very pleased with this."[10] Powerful men wanted to exalt themselves, their families, and their offices. A magnificent style of living enriched by works of art served to prove the greatness and the power of the despot or oligarch.

In addition to power, art reveals changing patterns of consumption in Renaissance Italy. In the rural world of the Middle Ages, society had been organized for war. Men of wealth spent their money on military gear—swords, armor, horses, crenelated castles, towers, family compounds—all of which represent offensive or defensive warfare. As Italian nobles settled in towns (see page 333), they adjusted to an urban culture. Rather than employing knights for warfare, cities hired mercenaries. Expenditure on military hardware declined. For the rich merchant or the noble recently arrived from the countryside, the urban palace represented the greatest outlay of cash. It was his chief luxury, and although a private dwelling, the palace implied grandeur. Within the palace, the merchant-prince's chamber, or bedroom, where he slept and received his intimate guests, was the most important room. In the fourteenth and fifteenth centuries a large, intricately carved wooden bed, a chest, and perhaps a bench served as its sole decorations. The chest held the master's most precious goods—silver, tapestries, jewelry, clothing. Other rooms, even in palaces of fifteen to twenty rooms, were sparsely furnished. As the fifteenth century advanced and wealth increased, the other rooms were gradually furnished with carved chests, tables,

Botticelli: Primavera, or Spring (ca 1482)   Framed by a grove of orange trees, Venus, goddess of love, is flanked on her left by Flora, goddess of flowers and fertility, and on her right by the Three Graces, goddesses of banquets, dance, and social occasions. Above, Venus's son Cupid, the god of love, shoots darts of desire, while at the far right the wind god Zephyrus chases the nymph Chloris. The entire scene rests on classical mythology, though some art historians claim that Venus is an allegory for the Virgin Mary. Botticelli captured the ideal for female beauty in the Renaissance: slender, with pale skin, a high forehead, red-blond hair, and sloping shoulders. *(Digital image © The Museum of Modern Art/Licensed by Scala/Art Resource, NY)*

benches, chairs, tapestries for the walls, paintings (an innovation), and sculptural decorations, and a private chapel was added. Wealthy individuals and families ordered gold dishes, embroidered tablecloths, and paintings of all sizes as art became a means of displaying wealth. By the late sixteenth century the Strozzi banking family of Florence spent more on household goods than on anything else except food; the value of those furnishings was three times that of their silver and jewelry.

After the palace itself, the private chapel within the palace symbolized the largest expenditure. Equipped with the ecclesiastical furniture—tabernacles, chalices, thuribles, and other liturgical utensils—and decorated with religious scenes, the chapel served as the center of the household's religious life and its cult of remembrance of the dead. In fifteenth-century Florence, only the Medici had a private chapel, but by the late sixteenth century most wealthy Florentine families had private chapels.

Subjects and Style

The content and style of Renaissance art were often different from those of the Middle Ages. The individual portrait emerged as a distinct artistic genre. In the fifteenth century members of the newly rich middle class often had themselves painted in scenes of romantic chivalry or courtly society. Rather than reflecting a spiritual ideal, as medieval painting and sculpture tended to do, Renaissance portraits showed human ideals, often portrayed in a more realistic style. The Florentine painter Giotto (1276–1337) led the way in the use of realism; his treatment of the human body and face replaced the formal stiffness and artificiality that had long characterized representation of the human body. Piero della Francesca (1420–1492) and Andrea Mantegna (1430/31–1506) seem to have pioneered *perspective* in painting, the linear representation of distance and space on a flat surface.

As the fifteenth century advanced, the subject matter of art in Italy became steadily more secular. The study of classical texts brought deeper understanding of ancient ideas. Classical themes and motifs, such as the lives and loves of pagan gods and goddesses, figured increasingly in painting and sculpture. Religious topics, such as the Annunciation of the Virgin and the Nativity, remained popular among both patrons and artists, but frequently the patron had himself and his family portrayed. People were conscious of their physical uniqueness and wanted their individuality immortalized.

The sculptor Donatello (1386–1466) probably exerted the greatest influence of any Florentine artist before Michelangelo. His many statues express an appreciation of the incredible variety of human nature. Whereas medieval artists had depicted the nude human body in a spiritualized and moralizing context only, Donatello revived the classical figure, with its balance and self-awareness. The short-lived Florentine Masaccio (1401–1428), sometimes called the father of modern painting, inspired a new style characterized by great realism, narrative power, and remarkably effective use of light and dark. *The Last Supper* by Leonardo da Vinci (1452–1519), with its stress on the tension between Christ and the disciples, is an incredibly subtle psychological interpretation.

Andrea Mantegna: Adoration of the Magi (ca 1495–1505) Applying his study of ancient Roman relief sculpture, Mantegna painted for the private devotion of the Gonzaga family of Mantua this scene of the three wise men coming to visit the infant Christ. The three wise men, depicted as kings, represent the entire world—that is, the three continents known to medieval Europeans: Europe, Asia, and Africa. They also symbolize the three stages of life: youth, maturity, and old age. Here Melchior, the oldest, his large cranium symbolizing wisdom, personifies Europe. He offers gold in a Chinese porcelain cup from the Ming Dynasty. Balthazar, with an olive complexion and dark beard, stands for Asia and maturity. He presents frankincense in a stunning vessel of Turkish tombac ware. Caspar, representing Africa and youth, gives myrrh in an urn of striped marble. The three wise men were a common subject in Renaissance art (compare the illustration on page 417), as they allowed artists to show exotic figures and sumptuous clothing. (© *The J. Paul Getty Museum, Los Angeles. Mantegna, Andrea,* Adoration of the Magi, *ca 1495–1505, distemper on linen, 54.6 × 70.7 cm [85.PA.417]*)

As humanists looked to the classical past for inspiration in their writing, so did architects in constructing buildings. The Florentine architect Filippo Brunelleschi (1377–1446) designed a new hospital for orphans and foundlings set up by the silk-workers' guild in Florence, in which all proportions—of the windows, height, floor plan, and covered walkway with a series of rounded arches—were carefully thought out to achieve a sense of balance and harmony. Brunelleschi later turned his talents to designing and constructing a dome for the Florence Cathedral, based to some degree on Roman domes, but higher and more graceful.

Art produced in northern Europe in the fourteenth and fifteenth centuries tended to be more religious in orientation than that produced in Italy. Some Flemish painters, notably Rogier van der Weyden (1399/1400–1464) and Jan van Eyck (1366–1441), were considered the artistic equals of Italian painters and were much admired in Italy. Van Eyck, one of the earliest artists to use oil-based paints successfully, shows the Flemish love for detail in paintings such as *Ghent Altarpiece* and the portrait *Giovanni Arnolfini and His Bride;* the effect is great realism and remarkable attention to human personality. Northern architecture was little influenced by the classical revival so obvious in Renaissance Italy.

In the fifteenth century Florence was the center of the new art in Italy, but in the early sixteenth century this shifted to Rome, where wealthy cardinals and popes wanted visual expression of the church's and their own families' power and piety. Michelangelo, a Florentine who had spent his young adulthood at the court of Lorenzo de' Medici, went to Rome about 1500 and began the series of statues, paintings, and architectural projects from which he gained an international reputation: the Pieta, Moses, the redesigning of the Capitoline Hill in central Rome, and, most famously, the ceiling and altar wall of the Sistine Chapel. Pope Julius II, who commissioned the Sistine Chapel, demanded that Michelangelo work as fast as he could and frequently visited the artist at his work with suggestions and criticisms. Michelangelo complained in person and by letter about the pope's meddling, but his reputation did not match the

Rogier van der Weyden: Deposition   Taking as his subject the suffering and death of Jesus, a popular theme of Netherlandish piety, van der Weyden describes (in an inverted T) Christ's descent from the cross, surrounded by nine sorrowing figures. An appreciation of human anatomy, the rich fabrics of the clothes, and the pierced and bloody hands of Jesus were all intended to touch the viewers' emotions. *(Museo del Prado/Scala/Art Resource, NY)*

power of the pope, and he kept working. Raphael Sanzio (1483–1520), another Florentine, got the commission for frescoes in the papal apartments, and in his relatively short life he painted hundreds of portraits and devotional images, becoming the most sought-after artist in Europe. Raphael also oversaw a large workshop with many collaborators and apprentices—who assisted on the less difficult sections of some paintings—and wrote treatises on his philosophy of art in which he emphasized the importance of imitating nature and developing an orderly sequence of design and proportion.

Venice became another artistic center in the sixteenth century. Titian (1490–1576) produced portraits, religious subjects, and mythological scenes, developing techniques of painting in oil without doing elaborate drawings first, which speeded up the process and pleased patrons eager to display their acquisition. Titian and other sixteenth-century painters developed an artistic style known in English as "mannerism" (from *maniera* or "style" in Italian) in which artists sometimes distorted figures, exaggerated musculature, and heightened color to express emotion and drama more intently. (This is the style in which Michelangelo painted the Last Judgment in the Sistine Chapel, shown in the frontispiece to this chapter.) Until the twentieth century, "mannerism" was a negative term; critics and art historians preferred the more naturalistic and elegant style of Botticelli and Raphael, but modern critics and artists have appreciated its sense of movement, vivid colors, and passionate expressions.

Patronage and Creativity

Artists in the Renaissance did not produce unsolicited pictures or statues for the general public, but usually worked on commission from patrons. A patron could be an individual, a group such as a guild, a convent, a ruler, or a city council. Patrons varied in their level of involvement as a work progressed; some simply ordered a specific subject or scene, while others oversaw the work of the artist or architect very closely, suggesting themes and styles and demanding changes while the work was in progress.

The right patrons rewarded certain artists very well. Lorenzo Ghiberti's salary of 200 florins a year compared favorably with that of the head of the city government, who earned 500 florins. Moreover, at a time when a person could live in a princely fashion on 300 ducats a year, Leonardo da Vinci was making 2,000 ducats annually.

Renaissance society respected the distinguished artist. In 1537 the prolific letter writer, humanist, and satirizer of princes Pietro Aretino (1492–1556) wrote to Michelangelo while he was painting *The Last Judgment* behind the altar in the Sistine Chapel:

To the Divine Michelangelo: Sir, just as it is disgraceful and sinful to be unmindful of God so it is reprehensible and dishonourable for any man of discerning judgment not to honour you as a brilliant and venerable artist whom the very stars use as a target at which to shoot the rival arrows of their favour. . . . It is surely my duty to honour you with this salutation, since the world has many kings but only one Michelangelo.[11]

Aretino was not alone in addressing Michelangelo as "divine," for the word was widely applied to him, and to a few other artists as well. (See the feature "Individuals in Society: Leonardo da Vinci.") Vasari described a number of painters, sculptors, and architects, in fact, as "rare men of genius." This adulation of the artist has led many historians to view the Renaissance as the beginning of the concept of the artist as genius. In the Middle Ages people believed that only God created, albeit through individuals; the medieval conception recognized no particular value in artistic originality. Renaissance artists and humanists came to think that a work of art was the deliberate creation of a unique personality who transcended traditions, rules, and theories. A genius had a peculiar gift, which ordinary laws should not inhibit.

Renaissance artists were not only aware of their creative power, but they also boasted about it. Describing his victory over five others, including Brunelleschi, in the competition to design the bronze doors of Florence's Baptistery, Ghiberti exulted, "The palm of victory was conceded to me by all the experts and by all my fellow-competitors. By universal consent and without a single exception the glory was conceded to me."[12] Some medieval painters and sculptors had signed their works; Renaissance artists almost universally did so, and many of them incorporated self-portraits, usually as bystanders, in their paintings.

It is important not to overemphasize the Renaissance notion of genius. As certain artists became popular and well-known, they could assert their own artistic styles and pay less attention to the wishes of patrons, but even major artists like Raphael generally worked according to the patron's specific guidelines. Whether in Italy or northern Europe, most Renaissance artists trained in the workshops of older artists; Botticelli, Raphael, Titian, and at times even Michelangelo were known for their large, well-run, and prolific workshops. Though they might be "men of genius," artists were still expected to

Gentile and Giovanni Bellini: Saint Mark Preaching in Alexandria (1504–1507) The Venetian artists Gentile and Giovanni Bellini combine figures and architecture in this painting of Saint Mark, the patron saint of Venice. Saint Mark (on the platform) is wearing ancient Roman dress. Behind him are male citizens of Venice in sixteenth-century Italian garb. In front of him are Ottoman Muslim men in turbans, Muslim women in veils, and various other figures. The buildings in the background are not those of first-century Alexandria (where Saint Mark is reported to have preached) but of Venice and Constantinople in the sixteenth century. The setting is made even more fanciful with a camel and a giraffe in the background. The painting glorifies cosmopolitan Venice's patron saint, a more important feature for the Venetian patron who ordered it than was historical accuracy. Its clear colors and effective perspective and the individuality of the many faces make this a fine example of Renaissance art. *(Scala/Art Resource, NY)*

be well-trained in proper artistic techniques and stylistic conventions, for the notion that artistic genius could show up in the work of an untrained artist did not emerge until the twentieth century. Beginning artists spent years copying drawings and paintings, learning how to prepare paint and other artistic materials, and, by the sixteenth century, reading books about design and composition. Younger artists gathered together in the evenings for further drawing practice; by the later sixteenth century some of these informal groups had turned into more formal artistic "academies," the first of which was begun in 1563 in Florence by Vasari under the patronage of the Medicis.

As Vasari's phrase indicates, the notion of artistic genius that developed in the Renaissance was gendered. All the most famous and most prolific Renaissance artists were male; there are no female architects whose names are known and only one female sculptor. The types of art in which more women were active, such as textiles, needlework, and painting on porcelain, were not re-

garded as "major arts," but only as "minor" or "decorative" arts. (The division between "major" and "minor" arts begun in the Renaissance continues to influence the way museums and collections are organized today.) Like painting, embroidery changed in the Renaissance to become more classical in its subject matter, naturalistic, and visually complex. Embroiderers were not trained to view their work as products of individual genius, however, so they rarely included their names on their works, and there is no way to discover who they were.

Several women did become well-known as painters in their day. Stylistically, their works are different from one another, but their careers show many similarities. The majority of female painters were the daughters of painters or of minor noblemen with ties to artistic circles. Many were eldest daughters or came from families in which there were no sons, so their fathers took unusual interest in their careers. Many women began their careers before they were twenty and produced far fewer paintings after they married, or stopped painting entirely. Women were

Individuals in Society

Leonardo da Vinci

What makes a genius? An infinite capacity for taking pains? A deep curiosity about an extensive variety of subjects? A divine spark as manifested by talents that far exceed the norm? Or is it just "one percent inspiration and ninety-nine percent perspiration," as Thomas Edison said? To most observers, Leonardo da Vinci was one of the greatest geniuses in the history of the Western world. In fact, Leonardo was one of the individuals that the Renaissance label "genius" was designed to describe: a special kind of human being with exceptional creative powers.

Leonardo (who, despite the title of a recent best-seller, is always called by his first name) was born in Vinci, near Florence, the illegitimate son of Caterina, a local peasant girl, and Ser Piero da Vinci, a notary public. Caterina later married another native of Vinci. When Ser Piero's marriage to Donna Albrussia produced no children, he and his wife took in Leonardo. Ser Piero secured Leonardo's apprenticeship with the painter and sculptor Andrea del Verrocchio in Florence. In 1472, when Leonardo was just twenty years old, he was listed as a master in Florence's "Company of Artists."

Leonardo's most famous portrait, *Mona Lisa*, shows a woman with an enigmatic smile that Giorgio Vasari described as "so pleasing that it seemed divine rather than human." The portrait, probably of the young wife of a rich Florentine merchant (her exact identity is hotly debated), may actually be the best-known painting in the history of art. One of its competitors in that designation would be another work of Leonardo's, *The Last Supper,* which has been called "the most revered painting in the world."

Leonardo's reputation as a genius does not rest simply on his paintings, however, which are actually few in number, but rather on the breadth of his abilities and interests. In these, he is often understood to be the first "Renaissance man," a phrase we still use for a multi-talented individual. He wanted to reproduce what the eye can see, and he drew everything he saw around him, including executed criminals hanging on gallows as well as the beauties of nature. Trying to understand how the human body worked, Leonardo studied live and dead bodies, doing autopsies and dissections to investigate muscles and circulation. He carefully analyzed the effects of light, and he experimented with perspective.

Leonardo used his drawings as the basis for his paintings and also as a tool of scientific investigation.

Leonardo da Vinci, Lady with an Ermine. *The enigmatic smile and smoky quality of this portrait can be found in many of Leonardo's works.*
(Czartoryski Museum, Krakow/The Bridgeman Art Library)

He drew plans for hundreds of inventions, many of which would become reality centuries later, such as the helicopter, tank, machine gun, and parachute. He was hired by one of the powerful new rulers in Italy, Duke Ludovico Sforza of Milan, to design weapons, fortresses, and water systems, as well as to produce works of art. Leonardo left Milan when Sforza was overthrown in war and spent the last years of his life painting, drawing, and designing for the pope and the French king.

Leonardo experimented with new materials for painting and sculpture, some of which worked and some of which did not. The experimental method he used to paint *The Last Supper* caused the picture to deteriorate rapidly, and it began to flake off the wall as soon as it was finished. Leonardo actually regarded it as never quite completed, for he could not find a model for the face of Christ that would evoke the spiritual depth he felt it deserved. His gigantic equestrian statue in honor of Ludovico's father, Duke Francesco Sforza, was never made and the clay model collapsed. He planned to write books on many subjects but never finished any of them, leaving only notebooks. Leonardo once said that "a painter is not admirable unless he is universal." The patrons who supported him—and he was supported very well—perhaps wished that his inspirations would have been a bit less universal in scope, or at least accompanied by more perspiration.

Questions for Analysis

1. In what ways do the notion of a "genius" and of a "Renaissance man" both support and contradict one another? Which better fits Leonardo?
2. Has the idea of artistic genius changed since the Renaissance? How?

Sources: Giorgio Vasari, *Lives of the Artists,* vol. 1, trans. G. Bull (London: Penguin Books, 1965); S. B. Nuland, *Leonardo da Vinci* (New York: Lipper/Viking, 2000).

Online Study Center **Improve Your Grade**
Going Beyond Individuals in Society

Artemisia Gentileschi: Esther Before Ahasuerus (ca 1630)   In this oil painting, Gentileschi shows an Old Testament scene of the Jewish woman Esther who saved her people from being killed by her husband, King Ahasuerus. This deliverance is celebrated in the Jewish holiday of Purim. Both figures are in the elaborate dress worn in Renaissance courts. Typical of a female painter, Artemisia Gentileschi was trained by her father. She mastered the dramatic style favored in the early seventeenth century and became known especially for her portraits of strong biblical and mythological heroines. *(Image copyright © The Metropolitan Museum of Art/Art Resource, NY)*

not allowed to study the male nude, which was viewed as essential if one wanted to paint large history paintings with many figures. Women could also not learn the technique of fresco, in which colors are applied directly to wet plaster walls, because such works had to be done out in public, which was judged inappropriate for women. Joining a group of male artists for informal practice was also seen as improper, and the artistic academies that were established were for men only. Like universities, humanist academies, and most craft guild shops, artistic workshops were male-only settings in which men of different ages came together for training and created bonds of friendship, influence, patronage, and sometimes intimacy.

Women were not alone in being excluded from the institutions of Renaissance culture. Though a few "rare men of genius" such as Leonardo or Michelangelo emerged from artisanal backgrounds, most scholars and artists came from families with at least some money. Renaissance culture did not influence the lives of most people in cities and did not affect life in the villages at all. A small, highly educated minority of literary humanists and artists created the culture of and for an exclusive elite. The Renaissance maintained, or indeed enhanced, a gulf between the learned minority and the uneducated multitude that has survived for many centuries.

Social Hierarchies

The division between educated and uneducated people was only one of many social hierarchies evident in the Renaissance. Every society has social hierarchies; in ancient Rome, for example, there were patricians and plebeians (see page 128). Such hierarchies are to some degree descriptions of social reality, but they are also idealizations—that is, they describe how people *imagined* their society to be, without all the messy reality of social-climbing plebeians or groups that did not fit the standard categories. Social hierarchies in the Renaissance built on those of the Middle Ages but also developed new features that contributed to modern social hierarchies.

● *What were the key social hierarchies in Renaissance Europe, and how did ideas about hierarchy shape people's lives?*

Race

Renaissance ideas about what we would term "race" were closely linked with those about ethnicity and "blood" discussed in Chapter 12 (see page 399). In law codes, histories, and other writings, ethnic and religious groups were referred to as *gens* or *natio*, words generally translated as "people" or "nation": the German nation, the Irish people, the Jewish people, and so on. What exactly *made* them German or Irish or Jewish was viewed as a mixture of language, traditions, and customs, but these were also conceptualized as "blood," and people were described as having French blood or Jewish blood. The word *race* was also used in several European languages in the Renaissance to describe such groupings—the French race, the Spanish race—or other social groups, such as "the race of learned gentlemen" or "the race of mankind." It was also used to refer to family line, kindred, or lineage. With all these words—nation, people, blood, race—people did not clearly distinguish between things that we would regard as biologically heritable, such as hair color, and as socially constructed, such as being well-dressed. (The boundaries between these two are not always clear today, of course, as arguments about certain groups being "naturally" gifted musicians or mathematicians demonstrate.)

The contemporary meaning of *race* as a system dividing people into very large groups by skin color and other physical characteristics originated in the eighteenth century, when European natural scientists sought to develop one single system that would explain human differences. They first differentiated "races" by continent of origin—Americanus, Europaeus, Asiaticus, and Africanus—and then by somewhat different geographical areas. The word *Caucasian* was first used by the German anatomist and naturalist Johann Friedrich Blumenbach (1752–1840) to describe light-skinned people of Europe and western Asia because he thought that the Caucasus Mountains on the border between Russia and Georgia

were most likely their original home. He thought that they were the first humans, and the most attractive. (His judgment about Caucasian attractiveness came through studying a large collection of skulls and measuring all other skulls against one from Georgia that he judged to be "the most beautiful form of the skull.") This meaning of *race* has had a long life, though biologists and anthropologists today do not use it, as it has no scientific meaning or explanatory value. Renaissance people thus did not use *race* the way we do, but they did make distinctions based on skin color. These distinctions were interwoven with ethnic, national, and religious distinctions, and they provide some of the background for later conceptualizations of race.

Ever since the time of the Roman republic, a few black Africans had lived in western Europe. They had come, along with white slaves, as the spoils of war. Even after the collapse of the Roman Empire, Muslim and Christian merchants continued to import them. Unstable political conditions in many parts of Africa enabled enterprising merchants to seize people and sell them into slavery. Local authorities afforded them no protection. Long tradition, moreover, sanctioned the practice of slavery. The evidence of medieval art attests to the continued presence of Africans in Europe throughout the Middle Ages and to Europeans' awareness of them.

Beginning in the fifteenth century sizable numbers of black slaves entered Europe. Portuguese explorers imported perhaps a thousand a year and sold them at the markets of Seville, Barcelona, Marseilles, and Genoa. In the late fifteenth century this flow increased, with thousands of people leaving the West African coast. By 1530 between four thousand and five thousand were being sold to the Portuguese each year. By the mid-sixteenth century blacks, slave and free, constituted about 10 percent of the population of the Portuguese cities of Lisbon and Évora; other cities had smaller percentages. In all, blacks made up roughly 3 percent of the Portuguese population. In the Iberian Peninsula, African slaves intermingled with the people they lived among and sometimes intermarried. Cities such as Lisbon had significant numbers of people of mixed African and European descent.

Although blacks were concentrated in the Iberian Peninsula, there must have been some Africans in northern Europe as well. In the 1580s, for example, Queen Elizabeth I of England complained that there were too many "blackamoores" competing with needy English people for places as domestic servants.[13] Black servants were much sought after; the medieval interest in curiosities, the exotic, and the marvelous continued in the

Carpaccio: Black Laborers on the Venetian Docks (detail) Enslaved and free blacks, besides working as gondoliers on the Venetian canals, served on the docks: here, seven black men careen—clean, caulk, and repair—a ship. Carpaccio's reputation as one of Venice's outstanding painters rests on his eye for details of everyday life. *(Gallerie dell'Accademia, Venice/Scala/Art Resource, NY)*

Renaissance. Italian aristocrats had their portraits painted with their black pageboys to indicate their wealth (see the illustration on page 417, in which Gozzoli's depiction of Cosimo de' Medici shows him with a black groom). Blacks were so greatly in demand at the Renaissance courts of northern Italy, in fact, that the Venetians defied papal threats of excommunication to secure them. In the late fifteenth century Isabella, the wife of Gian Galazzo Sforza, took pride in the fact that she owned ten blacks, seven of them females. A black lady's maid was both a curiosity and a symbol of wealth. In 1491 Isabella of Este, duchess of Mantua, instructed her agent to secure a black girl between four and eight years old, "shapely and as black as possible." The duchess saw the child as a source of entertainment: "We shall make her very happy and shall have great fun with her." She hoped the girl would become "the best buffoon in the world,"[14] as the cruel ancient practice of a noble household's retaining a professional "fool" for the family's amusement persisted through the Renaissance—and down to the twentieth century. Tradition, stretching back at least as far as the thirteenth century, connected blacks with music and dance. In Renaissance Spain and Italy, blacks performed as dancers, as actors and actresses in courtly

dramas, and as musicians, sometimes making up full orchestras.

Africans were not simply amusements at court. Adult black slaves served as maids, valets, and domestic servants in Spanish and Italian cities. The Venetians employed blacks—slave and free—as gondoliers and stevedores on the docks. In Portugal, kings, nobles, laborers, monasteries and convents, and prostitutes owned slaves. Slaves supplemented the labor force in virtually all occupations—as agricultural laborers, as craftsmen, and as seamen on ships going to Lisbon and Africa. Agriculture in Europe did not involve large plantations, so large-scale agricultural slavery did not develop there; African slaves formed the primary workforce on the sugar plantations set up by Europeans on the Atlantic islands in the late fifteenth century, however (see page 505).

Until the voyages down the African coast in the late fifteenth century, Europeans had little concrete knowledge of Africans and their cultures. What Europeans did know was based on biblical accounts. The European attitude toward Africans was ambivalent. On the one hand, Europeans perceived Africa as a remote place, the home of strange people isolated by heresy and Islam from superior European civilization. Africans' contact, even as slaves, with Christian Europeans could only "improve" the blacks. Theologians taught that God was light and linked black skin color with the hostile forces of the underworld: evil, sin, and the Devil. Thus the Devil was commonly represented as a black man in medieval and early Renaissance art (see the illustration on page 396). On the other hand, blackness possessed certain positive qualities. It symbolized the emptiness of worldly goods and the humility of the monastic way of life. Black clothes permitted a conservative and discreet display of wealth. Black vestments and funeral trappings indicated grief, and Christ had said that those who mourn are blessed. Negative preconceptions about blackness largely outweighed positive ones, however, and the expanding slave trade only reinforced these.

Class

Just as *race* did not develop its current meaning until after the Renaissance, neither did *class*. The notion of class—working class, middle class, upper class—was developed by nineteenth-century social theorists, most prominently Karl Marx. Looking at their own industrial societies, they decided that the most basic social division was between men who owned the "means of production," that is, factories and equipment, and those who did not and worked for wages. The former were the "bourgeoisie" (the middle class) and the latter the "proletariat" (the working class). (How women fit into this division was not clear. Married women in the nineteenth century could not own property and had no right to their wages, which belonged to their husbands.) This was a system of social differentiation based primarily on wealth.

By contrast, the medieval system of social differentiation was based on function—or least theoretical function—in society. Medieval Europeans conceptualized society in three basic groups: those who pray, or the clergy; those who fight, or the nobility; and those who work, or everyone else (see page 295). These groups were termed **"orders"** or "estates," and many medieval representative assemblies, including those of France and the Low Countries, were organized into three houses by estate. The society of orders worked fairly well in setting out sociolegal categories for membership in representative bodies. It also highlighted the most important social distinction in both medieval and Renaissance Europe, that between noble and commoner. Status as a noble generally brought freedom from direct taxation and rights of jurisdiction over a piece of property and the people who lived on it.

By the thirteenth century, however, and even more so by the fifteenth, the more fixed and inherited hierarchy of orders was interwoven with a more changeable hierarchy based on wealth, what would later come to be termed "social class." This was particularly true in towns. Most residents of towns were technically members of the "third estate," that is, not nobles or clergy, but they included wealthy merchants who oversaw vast trading empires and lived in splendor that rivaled the richest nobles. As we saw above, in many cities these merchants had gained political power to match their economic might, becoming merchant oligarchs who ruled through city councils.

The development of a hierarchy of wealth did not mean an end to the hierarchy of orders, however. Those in the first estate were far more likely to be wealthy than those in the third, but even if they were poorer, they had higher status. If this had not been the case, wealthy Italian merchants would not have bothered to buy noble titles and country villas as they began doing in the fifteenth century, nor would wealthy English or Spanish merchants have been eager to marry their daughters and sons into often impoverished noble families. The nobility maintained its status in most parts of Europe not by maintaining rigid boundaries, but by taking in and integrating the new social elite of wealth. Wealth allowed some male commoners to buy or gain noble titles and female commoners to marry into noble families.

Along with being tied to the hierarchy of orders, social status was also linked with considerations of honor. Among the nobility, for example, certain weapons and battle tactics were favored because they were viewed as more honorable. Among urban dwellers, certain occupations, such as city executioner or manager of the municipal brothel, might be well paid but were understood to be "dishonorable" and so of low status.

Cities were where the hierarchy of orders met the hierarchy of wealth most dramatically. In many cities, a number of urban merchants and bankers were wealthier than all but the highest level of the nobility. Some of these men climbed into the nobility through marriage, service to a monarch, or purchase of a title. More of them heightened social and political distinctions within cities, trying to set themselves off as a privileged social group. Wealthy merchants often dominated city councils, and they made it increasingly difficult for new residents to become citizens. They passed sumptuary laws, essentially urban dress codes that created easily visible distinctions between social groups (see page 338). Nobles and wealthy urban residents could wear fine silk clothing, jewelry, and bright colors and guild masters and artisans

Italian City Scene In this detail from a fresco of the life of Saint Barbara by the Italian painter Lorenzo Lotto, the artist captures the mixing of social groups in a Renaissance Italian city. The crowd of men in the right foreground surrounding the biblical figures includes wealthy merchants in elaborate hats and colorful coats. Two mercenary soldiers (carrying a sword and a pike), probably in hire to a condottiero, wear short doublets and tight hose stylishly slit to reveal colored undergarments, while boys play with toy weapons at their feet. Clothing like that of the soldiers, which emphasized the masculine form, was frequently the target of sumptuary laws for both its expense and its "indecency." At the left, women sell vegetables and bread, which would have been a common sight at any city marketplace. At the very rear, men judge the female saint, who was thought to have been martyred for her faith in the third century. *(Scala/Art Resource, NY)*

linen garments, while servants were restricted to rough, dark clothes and aprons. Individuals tried to evade these laws by wearing the clothing restricted to the group above them, though there were fines for doing so. Sumptuary laws also regulated spending on celebrations such as weddings or baptisms according to social class, and they were justified as a way to limit frivolous spending on luxuries and promote local production, for many laws restricted the purchase of imported clothing or foodstuffs. Along with setting out a hierarchy of wealth, sumptuary laws marked certain groups as outside the social order: Jews were obliged to wear specific symbols on their clothes or hats of a specific color (often yellow) so that they would be easily recognizable, and prostitutes might also be ordered to sew stripes of yellow or red on their clothing, wear a specific type or color of cloak, or keep their hair uncovered so people would not mistake them for "honorable" women.

Gender

While "race" is an eighteenth-century concept and "class" a nineteenth-century concept, "gender" is a concept that grew out of the women's movement that began in the 1970s. Advocates of women's rights increasingly distinguished between "sex," by which they meant physical and anatomical differences (what are often called "biological differences") and "gender," by which they meant a culturally constructed and historically changing system of differences. The boundaries between "sex" and "gender" are debated (are men "biologically" better at math,

and women "biologically" more peaceful, or do such differences simply come from their upbringing?), and the recently emerged transgender movement has questioned whether a model with two sexes or two genders is adequate. The word *gender* is becoming increasingly common, however, even on government forms.

Renaissance people would have understood the word *gender* to refer to categories of nouns in many European languages, not categories of people, but they would have easily grasped the concept. Toward the end of the fourteenth century, learned men (and a few women) began what was termed the **"debate about women"** (*querelle des femmes*), a debate about women's character and nature that would last for centuries. Misogynist critiques of women from both clerical and secular authors denounced females as devious, domineering, and demanding. In answer, several authors, including Giovanni Boccaccio and Christine de Pizan, compiled long lists of famous and praiseworthy women exemplary for their loyalty, bravery, and morality. (See the feature "Listening to the Past: Christine de Pizan" in Chapter 12 on pages

404–405.) Boccaccio's tribute is somewhat ambiguous, for the highest praise he can bestow on a woman is that she is like a man: "What can we think except that it was an error of nature to give female sex to a body which had been endowed by God with a magnificent virile spirit?"[15] Christine de Pizan and several other writers were interested not only in defending women, but also in exploring the reasons behind women's secondary status—that is, why the great philosophers, statesmen, and poets had generally been men. In this they were anticipating recent discussions about the "social construction of gender" by six hundred years.

Online Study Center **Improve Your Grade**
Primary Source: *The Book of the City of Ladies: Advice for a "Wise Princess"*

Some authors who wrote defenses of women also wrote attacks, or, like Baldassare Castiglione in *The Courtier*, included both sides of the argument in a single work, so that it is difficult to gauge their actual opinions. The debate was clearly more than a literary game among intellectuals, however. With the development of the printing press, popular interest in the debate about women grew, and works were translated, reprinted, and shared around Europe. The debate about women also found visual expression, particularly in single-sheet prints that were hung in taverns or people's homes. Prints that juxtaposed female virtues and vices were very popular, with the virtuous women depicted as those of the classical or biblical past and the vice-ridden dressed in contemporary clothes. The favorite metaphor for the virtuous wife was either the snail or the tortoise, both animals that never leave their "houses" and are totally silent, although such images were never as widespread as those depicting wives beating their husbands or hiding their lovers from them.

Beginning in the sixteenth century, the debate about women also became one about female rulers, sparked primarily by dynastic accidents in many countries, including Spain, England, France, and Scotland, which led to women serving as advisers to child kings or ruling in their own right (see pages 436 and 463). The questions vigorously and at times viciously disputed directly concerned the social construction of gender: could a woman's being born into a royal family and educated to rule allow her to overcome the limitations of her sex? Should it? Or stated another way: which was (or should be) the stronger determinant of character and social role, gender or rank? There were no successful rebellions against female rulers simply because they were women, but in part this was because female rulers, especially Queen Elizabeth I of England, emphasized qualities regarded as masculine—physical bravery, stamina, wisdom, duty—whenever they appeared in public. Machiavelli also linked rule and masculinity, using "effeminate" to describe the worst kind of ruler. (*Effeminate* in the Renaissance carried different connotations than it does today, however; strong heterosexual passion was not a sign of manliness, but could make one "effeminate," that is, dominated by as well as similar to a woman.) Male rulers also made sure that they appeared and were portrayed on horseback with armor, weapons, and other symbols of masculinity. The ideal Renaissance king or courtier may have been able to sing and dance, but he was also careful to have people see him as a warrior.

Renaissance Wedding Chest (Tuscany, late fifteenth century) Well-to-do brides provided huge dowries to their husbands in Renaissance Italy, and grooms often gave smaller gifts in return, such as this wedding chest. Appreciated more for their decorative value than for practical storage purposes, such chests were prominently displayed in people's homes. This 37-inch by 47-inch by 28-inch chest is carved with a scene from classical mythology in which Ceres, the goddess of agriculture, is searching for her daughter Proserpina (also known as Persephone), who has been abducted by Pluto, the god of the underworld. The subject may have been a commentary on Renaissance marriage, in which young women often married much older men and went to live in their houses. (*Philadelphia Museum of Art. Purchased with the Bloomfield Moore Fund and with Museum Funds, 1944 [1944-15-7])*

Ideas about women's and men's proper roles shaped the actions of the most powerful Renaissance monarchs and determined those of ordinary men and women even more forcefully. The dominant notion of the "true" man was that of the married head of household, so men whose class and age would have normally conferred political power but who remained unmarried did not participate on the same level as their married brothers. Unmarried men in Venice, for example, could not be part of the ruling council. Women were also understood as "married or to be married," even if the actual marriage patterns in Europe left many women (and men) unmarried until quite late in life (see page 394). This meant that women's work was not viewed as supporting a family—even if it did—and was valued less than men's. If they worked for wages, and many women did, women earned about half to two-thirds of what men did even for the same work, and they received less food (and much less ale or wine) if wages included food.

The maintenance of appropriate power relationships between men and women, with men dominant and women subordinate, served as a symbol of the proper functioning of society as a whole. Disorder in the proper gender hierarchy was linked with other types of social upheaval and was viewed as the most threatening way in which the world could be turned upside down. Carnival plays, woodcuts, and stories frequently portrayed domineering wives in pants and henpecked husbands washing diapers alongside professors in dunce caps and peasants riding princes. Men and women involved in relationships in which the women were thought to have power—an older woman who married a younger man, or a woman who scolded her husband—were often subjected to public ridicule, with bands of neighbors shouting insults and banging sticks and pans in disapproval. Of all the ways in which Renaissance society was hierarchically arranged—class, age, level of education, rank, race, occupation—gender was regarded as the most "natural" and therefore the most important to defend.

Politics and the State in the Renaissance (ca 1450–1521)

The High Middle Ages had witnessed the origins of many of the basic institutions of the modern state. Sheriffs, inquests, juries, circuit judges, professional bureaucracies, and representative assemblies all trace their origins to the twelfth and thirteenth centuries (see pages 259–273). The linchpin for the development of states, however, was strong monarchy, and during the period of the Hundred Years' War, no ruler in western Europe was able to provide effective leadership. The resurgent power of feudal nobilities weakened the centralizing work begun earlier.

Beginning in the fifteenth century, rulers utilized the aggressive methods implied by Renaissance political ideas to rebuild their governments. First in Italy, then in France, England, and Spain, rulers began the work of reducing violence, curbing unruly nobles, and establishing domestic order. They emphasized royal majesty and royal sovereignty and insisted on the respect and loyalty of all subjects. These monarchs ruthlessly suppressed opposition and rebellion, especially from the nobility. They loved the business of kingship and worked hard at it.

● **How did the nation-states of western Europe evolve in this period?**

France

The Hundred Years' War left France drastically depopulated, commercially ruined, and agriculturally weak. Nonetheless, the ruler whom Joan of Arc had seen crowned at Reims, Charles VII (r. 1422–1461), revived the monarchy and France. He seemed an unlikely person to do so. Frail, indecisive, and burdened with questions about his paternity (his father had been deranged; his mother, notoriously promiscuous), Charles VII nevertheless began France's long recovery.

Charles reconciled the Burgundians and Armagnacs, who had been waging civil war for thirty years. By 1453 French armies had expelled the English from French soil except in Calais. Charles reorganized the royal council, giving increased influence to middle-class men, and strengthened royal finances through such taxes as the **gabelle** (on salt) and the *taille* (land tax). These taxes remained the Crown's chief sources of income until the Revolution of 1789.

By establishing regular companies of cavalry and archers—recruited, paid, and inspected by the state— Charles created the first permanent royal army. In 1438 Charles published the **Pragmatic Sanction of Bourges,** asserting the superiority of a general council over the papacy, giving the French crown major control over the appointment of bishops, and depriving the pope of French ecclesiastical revenues. The Pragmatic Sanction established Gallican (or French) liberties because it affirmed the special rights of the French crown over the French church. Greater control over the church and the army helped consolidate the authority of the French crown.

Charles's son Louis XI (r. 1461–1483), called the "Spider King" because of his treacherous character, was very much a Renaissance prince. Facing the perpetual French problem of reduction of feudal disorder, he saw money as the answer. Louis promoted new industries, such as silk weaving at Lyons and Tours. He welcomed foreign craftsmen and entered into commercial treaties with England, Portugal, and the towns of the Hanseatic League (see page 341). He used the revenues raised through these economic activities and severe taxation to improve the army. With the army, Louis stopped aristocratic brigandage and slowly cut into urban independence.

Luck favored his goal of expanding royal authority and unifying the kingdom. On the timely death of Charles the Bold, duke of Burgundy, in 1477, Louis invaded Burgundy and gained some territories. Three years later, the extinction of the house of Anjou brought Louis the counties of Anjou, Bar, Maine, and Provence.

Two further developments strengthened the French monarchy. The marriage of Louis XII (r. 1498–1515) and Anne of Brittany added the large western duchy of Brittany to the state. Then the French king Francis I and Pope Leo X reached a mutually satisfactory agreement in 1516. The new treaty, the Concordat of Bologna, rescinded the Pragmatic Sanction's assertion of the superiority of a general council over the papacy and approved the pope's right to receive the first year's income of new bishops and abbots. In return, Leo X recognized the French ruler's right to select French bishops and abbots. French kings thereafter effectively controlled the appointment and thus the policies of church officials in the kingdom.

England

English society suffered severely from the disorders of the fifteenth century. The aristocracy dominated the government of Henry IV (r. 1399–1413) and indulged in mischievous violence at the local level. Population, decimated by the Black Death, continued to decline. Between 1455 and 1471 adherents of the ducal houses of York and Lancaster waged civil war, commonly called the **Wars of the Roses** because the symbol of the Yorkists was a white rose and that of the Lancastrians a red one. The chronic disorder hurt trade, agriculture, and domestic industry. Under the pious but mentally disturbed Henry VI (r. 1422–1461), the authority of the monarchy sank lower than it had been in centuries.

The Yorkist Edward IV (r. 1461–1483) began establishing domestic tranquillity. He succeeded in defeating the Lancastrian forces and after 1471 began to reconstruct the monarchy. Edward, his brother Richard III (r. 1483–1485), and Henry VII (r. 1485–1509) of the Welsh house of Tudor worked to restore royal prestige, to crush the power of the nobility, and to establish order and law at the local level. All three rulers used methods that Machiavelli himself would have praised—ruthlessness, efficiency, and secrecy.

The Hundred Years' War had been financed by Parliament. Dominated by baronial factions, Parliament had been the arena in which the nobility exerted its power. As long as the monarchy was dependent on the Lords and the Commons for revenue, the king had to call Parliament. Edward IV and subsequently the Tudors, excepting Henry VIII, conducted foreign policy on the basis of diplomacy, avoiding expensive wars. Thus the English monarchy did not depend on Parliament for money, and the Crown undercut that source of aristocratic influence.

Henry VII did summon several meetings of Parliament in the early years of his reign, primarily to confirm laws, but the center of royal authority was the **royal council,** which governed at the national level. There Henry VII revealed his distrust of the nobility: though not completely excluded, very few great lords were among the king's closest advisers. Regular representatives on the council numbered between twelve and fifteen men, and while many gained high ecclesiastical rank (the means, as it happened, by which the Crown paid them), their origins were in the lesser landowning class, and their education was in law. They were, in a sense, middle class.

The royal council handled any business the king put before it—executive, legislative, and judicial. For example, the council conducted negotiations with foreign governments and secured international recognition of the Tudor dynasty through the marriage in 1501 of Henry VII's eldest son Arthur to Catherine of Aragon, the daughter of Ferdinand and Isabella of Spain. The council dealt with real or potential aristocratic threats through a judicial offshoot, the **court of Star Chamber,** so called because of the stars painted on the ceiling of the room. The court applied principles of Roman law, and its methods were sometimes terrifying: accused persons were not entitled to see evidence against them; sessions were secret; torture could be applied to extract confessions; and juries were not called. These procedures ran directly counter to English common-law precedents, but they effectively reduced aristocratic troublemaking.

Unlike the continental countries of Spain and France, England had no standing army or professional civil service bureaucracy. The Tudors relied on the support of unpaid local officials, the **justices of the peace.** These influential landowners in the shires handled all the work of local government. They apprehended and punished criminals, enforced parliamentary statutes, fixed wages and prices, maintained proper standards of weights and measures, and even checked up on moral behavior.

The Tudors won the support of the influential upper middle class because the Crown linked government policy with the interests of that class. A commercial or agricultural upper class fears and dislikes few things more than disorder and violence. The Tudors promoted peace and social order, and the gentry did not object to arbitrary methods, like those of the court of Star Chamber, because the government had halted the long period of anarchy.

Secretive, cautious, and thrifty, Henry VII rebuilt the monarchy. He encouraged the cloth industry and built up the English merchant marine. English exports of wool and the royal export tax on that wool steadily increased. Henry crushed an invasion from Ireland and secured peace with Scotland through the marriage of his daughter Margaret to the Scottish king. When Henry VII died in 1509, he left a country at peace both domestically and internationally, a substantially augmented treasury, and the dignity and role of the royal majesty much enhanced.

Spain

While England and France laid the foundations of unified nation-states during the Renaissance, Spain remained a conglomerate of independent kingdoms. Castile and León formed a single political organization, but Aragon consisted of the principalities of Aragon, Valencia, Majorca, Sicily, Cardeña, and Naples, each tied to the crown of Aragon in a different way. On the one hand, the legacy of Hispanic, Roman, Visigothic, Jewish, and Muslim peoples made for rich cultural diversity; on the other hand, the Iberian Peninsula lacked a common cultural tradition.

The centuries-long reconquista—the wars of the northern Christian kingdoms to control the entire peninsula (see pages 265–267)—had military and religious objectives: conversion or expulsion of the Muslims and Jews and political control of the south. By the middle of the fifteenth century, the kingdoms of Castile and Aragon dominated the weaker Navarre, Portugal, and Granada, and the Iberian Peninsula, with the exception of Granada, had been won for Christianity. But even the wedding in 1469 of the dynamic and aggressive Isabella of Castile and the crafty and persistent Ferdinand of Aragon did not bring about administrative unity. Rather, their marriage constituted a dynastic union of two royal houses, not the political union of two peoples. Although Ferdinand and Isabella (r. 1474–1516) pursued a common foreign policy, until about 1700 Spain existed as a loose confederation of separate kingdoms (see Map 13.3), each maintaining its own *cortes* (parliament), laws, courts, and systems of coinage and taxation.

To curb the rebellious and warring aristocracy, Ferdinand and Isabella revived an old medieval institution: the **hermandades,** or "brotherhoods," which were popular groups in the towns given authority to act as local police forces and judicial tribunals. The hermandades repressed violence with such savage punishments that by 1498 they could be disbanded.

The decisive step Ferdinand and Isabella took to curb aristocratic power was the restructuring of the royal council. Aristocrats and great territorial magnates were rigorously excluded; thus the influence of the nobility on state policy was greatly reduced. Ferdinand and Isabella intended the council to be the cornerstone of their government system, with full executive, judicial, and legislative powers under the monarchy. The council was also to be responsible for the supervision of local authorities. The king and queen therefore appointed only people of middle-class background to the council. The council and various government boards recruited men trained in Roman law, which exalted the power of the Crown as the embodiment of the state.

In the extension of royal authority and the consolidation of the territories of Spain, the church was the linchpin. If the Spanish crown could select the higher clergy, the monarchy could influence ecclesiastical policy, wealth, and military resources. Through a diplomatic alliance with the Spanish pope Alexander VI, the Spanish monarchs secured the right to appoint bishops in Spain and in the Hispanic territories in America. This power enabled the "Catholic Kings of Spain," a title granted Ferdinand and Isabella by the papacy, to establish, in effect, a national church.

Revenues from ecclesiastical estates provided the means to raise an army to continue the reconquista. The victorious entry of Ferdinand and Isabella into Granada on January 6, 1492, signaled the culmination of eight centuries of Spanish struggle against the Arabs in southern Spain and the conclusion of the reconquista (see Map 9.3 on page 266). Granada in the south was incorporated into the Spanish kingdom, and in 1512 Ferdinand conquered Navarre in the north.

There still remained a sizable and, in the view of the majority of the Spanish people, potentially dangerous minority, the Jews. During the long centuries of the reconquista, Christian kings had renewed Jewish rights and privileges; in fact, Jewish industry, intelligence, and money had supported royal power. While Christians of

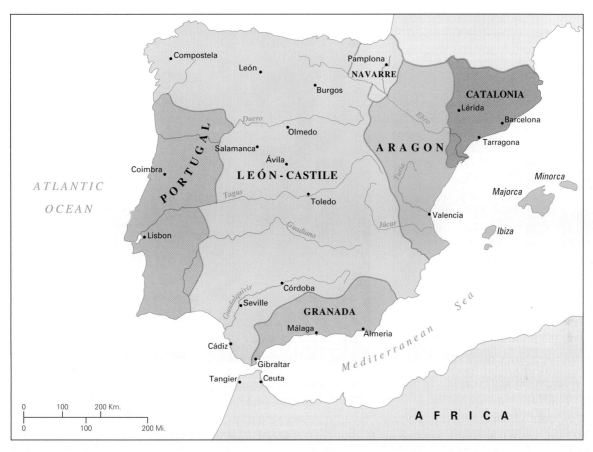

MAP 13.3 Spain in 1492   The marriage of Ferdinand of Aragon and Isabella of Castile in 1469 represented a dynastic union of two houses, not a political union of two peoples. Some principalities, such as León (part of Castile) and Catalonia (part of Aragon), had their own cultures, languages, and legal systems. Barcelona, the port city of Catalonia, controlled a commercial empire throughout the Mediterranean. Most of the people in Granada were Muslims, and Muslims and Jews lived in other areas as well.

all classes borrowed from Jewish moneylenders and while all who could afford them sought Jewish physicians, a strong undercurrent of resentment of Jewish influence and wealth festered. When the kings of France and England had expelled the Jews from their kingdoms (see page 310), many had sought refuge in Spain. In the fourteenth century Jews formed an integral and indispensable part of Spanish life. With vast numbers of Muslims, Jews, and Moorish Christians, medieval Spain represented the most diverse and cosmopolitan country in Europe. Diversity and cosmopolitanism, however, were not medieval social ideals.

Since ancient times, governments had seldom tolerated religious pluralism; religious faiths that differed from the official state religion were considered politically dangerous. But in the fourteenth century anti-Semitism in Spain rose more from popular sentiment than from royal poli-

cies. Rising anti-Semitic feeling was aggravated by fiery anti-Jewish preaching, by economic dislocation, and by the search for a scapegoat during the Black Death. In 1331 a mob attacked the Jewish community of Gerona in Catalonia. In 1355 royal troops massacred Jews in Toledo. On June 4, 1391, inflamed by "religious" preaching, mobs sacked and burned the Jewish community in Seville and compelled the Jews who survived to accept baptism. From Seville anti-Semitic pogroms swept the towns of Valencia, Barcelona, Burgos, Madrid, and Segovia. One scholar estimates that 40 percent of the Jewish population of Spain was killed or forced to convert.[16] Those converted were called *conversos* or **New Christians.**

Conversos were often well-educated and successful. In the administration of Castile, New Christians held the royal secretaryship, controlled the royal treasury, and composed a third of the royal council. In the church,

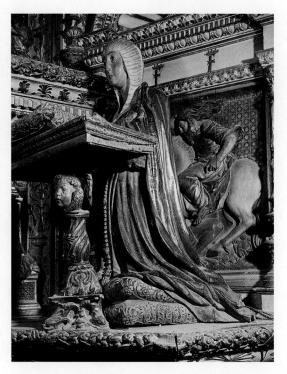

Felipe Bigarny: Ferdinand and Isabella In these wooden sculptures, the Burgundian artist Felipe Bigarny portrays Ferdinand and Isabella as paragons of Christian piety, kneeling at prayer. Ferdinand is shown in armor, a symbol of his military accomplishments and masculinity. Isabella wears a simple white head-covering rather than something more elaborate to indicate her modesty, a key virtue for women, though her actions and writings indicate that she was more determined and forceful than Ferdinand. *(Capilla Real, Granada/Laurie Platt Winfrey, Inc.)*

they held high positions as archbishops, bishops, and abbots. In the administration of the towns, conversos often held the highest public offices; in Toledo they controlled the collection of royal revenues. They included some of the leading merchants and business people. They also served great magnates, and by intermarrying with the nobility they gained political leverage. In the professions of medicine and law, New Christians held the most prominent positions. Numbering perhaps two hundred thousand in a total Spanish population of about 7.5 million, New Christians and Jews exercised influence disproportionate to their numbers.

Such successes bred resentment. Aristocratic grandees resented their financial dependence; the poor hated the converso tax collectors; and churchmen doubted the sincerity of their conversions. Queen Isabella shared these suspicions, and she and Ferdinand sought permission to set up an Inquisition in Spain. Pope Sixtus IV's bull authorizing the Inquisition reached Spain in November 1478, and on September 28, 1480, Ferdinand and Isabella ordered the establishment of tribunals to "search

out and punish converts from Judaism who had transgressed against Christianity by secretly adhering to Jewish beliefs and performing rites of the Jews."[17] Investigations and trials began immediately, as officials of the Inquisition looked for conversos who showed any sign of incomplete conversion, such as not eating pork.

Recent scholarship has carefully analyzed documents of the Inquisition. Most conversos identified themselves as Christians. They insisted that they were happy to be Christians and failed to see why they should be labeled New Christians: many came from families that had received baptism generations before.

In response, officials of the Inquisition developed a new type of anti-Semitism. A person's status as a Jew, they argued, could not be changed by religious conversion, but was in the person's nature as a human being. Judaism was in their blood and was heritable, so Jews could never be true Christians. In what were known as "purity of the blood" laws, having pure Christian blood became a requirement for noble status. Intermarriage between Old and New Christians had been common for centuries, but now many families sought to hide their ancestors. Ideas about Jews developed in Spain were important components in European concepts of race, and discussions of "Jewish blood" later expanded into notions of the "Jewish race."

This new racially based anti-Semitism emerged at the very time a Spanish national feeling was emerging, a national sentiment that looked to the building of a single nation. Whereas earlier anti-Semitism, such as that during the time of the Black Death, alleged Jewish schemes to kill off entire Christian populations—by poisoning the wells, for example, from which Jews derived no profit—fifteenth-century theories held that Jews or New Christians planned to take over all public offices in Spain. Jews, therefore, represented a grave threat to national unity.

Although the Inquisition was a religious institution established to ensure the Catholic faith, it was controlled by the Crown and served primarily as a politically unifying tool. Because the Spanish Inquisition commonly applied torture to extract confessions, first from conversos, then from Muslims, and later from Protestants, it gained a notorious reputation. Thus the word *inquisition,* meaning "any judicial inquiry conducted with ruthless severity," came into the English language. The methods of the Spanish Inquisition were cruel, though not as cruel as the investigative methods of some twentieth-century governments.

Shortly after the conquest of the Moorish stronghold at Granada in 1492, Isabella and Ferdinand issued an edict expelling all practicing Jews from Spain. Of the community of perhaps 200,000 Jews, 150,000 fled. (Efforts were made, through last-minute conversions, to retain good Jewish physicians.) Many Muslims in Granada were forcibly baptized and became another type of New Christian investigated by the Inquisition. Absolute religious orthodoxy and purity of blood ("untainted" by Jews or Muslims) served as the theoretical foundation of the Spanish national state.

The diplomacy of the Catholic rulers of Spain achieved a success they never anticipated. Partly out of hatred for the French and partly out of a desire to gain international recognition for their new dynasty, in 1496 Ferdinand and Isabella married their second daughter Joanna, heiress to Castile, to the archduke Philip, heir through his mother to the Burgundian Netherlands and through his father to the Holy Roman Empire. Philip and Joanna's son, Charles V (r. 1519–1556), thus succeeded to a vast patrimony. When Charles's son Philip II joined Portugal to the Spanish crown in 1580, the Iberian Peninsula was at last politically united. The various kingdoms, however, were administered separately.

Chapter Summary

Online Study Center   ACE the Test

- *What economic and political developments in Italy provided the setting for the Renaissance?*
- *What were the key ideas of the Renaissance, and how were they different for men and women and for southern and northern Europeans?*
- *How did changes in art both reflect and shape new ideas?*
- *What were the key social hierarchies in Renaissance Europe, and how did ideas about hierarchy shape people's lives?*
- *How did the nation-states of western Europe evolve in this period?*

The Italian Renaissance rested on the phenomenal economic growth of the High Middle Ages. In the period from about 1050 to 1300, a new economy emerged based on Venetian and Genoese shipping and long-distance trade and on Florentine banking and cloth manufacture. These commercial activities, combined with the struggle of urban communes for political independence from surrounding feudal lords, led to the appearance of a new ruling group in Italian cities—merchant oligarchs. Unrest in some cities led to their being taken over by single rulers, but however Italian cities were governed, they jockeyed for power with one another and prevented the establishment of a single Italian nation-state.

The Renaissance was characterized by self-conscious awareness among fourteenth- and fifteenth-century Italians, particularly scholars and writers known as humanists, that they were living in a new era. Key to this attitude was a serious interest in the Latin classics, a belief in individual potential, and a more secular attitude toward life. All these are evident in political theory developed in the Renaissance, particularly that of Machiavelli. Humanists opened schools for boys and young men to train them for an active life of public service, but they had doubts about whether humanist education was appropriate for women. As humanism spread to northern Europe, religious concerns became more pronounced, and Christian humanists set out plans for the reform of church and society. Their ideas were spread to a much wider audience than those of early humanists because of the development of the printing press with movable metal type, which revolutionized communication.

Interest in the classical past and in the individual also shaped Renaissance art in terms of style and subject matter. Painting became more naturalistic, and the individual portrait emerged as a distinct artistic genre. Wealthy merchants, cultured rulers, and powerful popes all hired painters, sculptors, and architects to design and ornament public and private buildings. Art in Italy became more secular and classical, while that in northern Europe retained a more religious tone. Artists began to understand themselves as having a special creative genius, though they continued to produce works on order for patrons, who often determined the content and form.

Social hierarchies in the Renaissance built on those of the Middle Ages, but also developed new features that contributed to the modern social hierarchies of race, class, and gender. Black Africans entered Europe in sizable numbers for the first time since the collapse of the Roman Empire, and Europeans fit them into changing understandings of ethnicity and race. The medieval hierarchy of orders based on function in society intermingled with a new hierarchy based on wealth, with new types of elites becoming more powerful. The Renaissance debate about women led many to discuss women's nature and proper role in society, a discussion sharpened by the presence of a number of ruling queens in this era.

With taxes provided by business people, kings in western Europe established greater peace and order, both essential for trade. Feudal monarchies gradually evolved in the direction of nation-states. In Spain, France, and England, rulers also emphasized royal dignity and authority, and they utilized Machiavellian ideas to ensure the preservation and continuation of their governments.

Like the merchant oligarchs and signori of Italian city-states, Renaissance monarchs manipulated culture to enhance their power.

Key Terms

Renaissance	orders
communes	debate about
oligarchy	women
popolo	gabelle
condottieri	Pragmatic Sanction
signori	of Bourges
courts	Wars of the Roses
republic	royal council
humanism	court of Star
individualism	Chamber
The Prince	justices of the
secularism	peace
Christian humanists	hermandades
patrons	New Christians

 Online Study Center **Improve Your Grade** Flashcards

Suggested Reading

Clark, Samuel. *State and Status: The Rise of the State and Aristocratic Power*. 1995. Discusses the relationship between centralizing states and the nobility.

Earle, T. F., and K. J. P. Lowe, eds. *Black Africans in Renaissance Europe*. 2005. Includes essays discussing many aspects of ideas about race and the experience of Africans in Europe.

Eisenstein, Elizabeth. *The Printing Press as an Agent of Change: Communications and Cultural Transformations in Early Modern Europe*. 1979. The definitive study of the impact of printing.

Ertman, Thomas. *The Birth of Leviathan: Building States and Regimes in Medieval and Early Modern Europe*. 1997. A good introduction to the creation of nation-states.

Grafton, Anthony, and Lisa Jardine. *From Humanism to the Humanities: Education and the Liberal Arts in Fifteenth and Sixteenth Century Europe*. 1986. Discusses humanist education and other developments in Renaissance learning.

Hale, J. R. *The Civilization of Europe in the Renaissance.* 1994. A comprehensive treatment of the period, arranged thematically.

Hale, J. R. *Machiavelli and Renaissance Italy.* 1966. A sound short biography.

Harbison, Craig. *The Mirror of the Artist: Northern Renaissance Art in Its Historical Context.* 1995. The best introduction to the art of northern Europe.

Holmes, George, ed. *Art and Politics in Renaissance Italy.* 1993. Treats the art of Florence and Rome against a political background.

Jardine, Lisa. *Worldly Goods: A New History of the Renaissance.* 1998. Discusses changing notions of social status, artistic patronage, and consumer goods.

Lubkin, Gregory. *A Renaissance Court: Milan Under Galeazzo Maria Sforza.* 1994. A wonderful study of one of the most important Renaissance courts.

Man, John. *Gutenberg Revolution: The Story of a Genius and an Invention That Changed the World.* 2002. Presents a rather idealized view of Gutenberg, but has good discussions of his milieu and excellent illustrations.

McConica, James. *Erasmus.* 1991. A sensitive treatment of the leading northern humanist.

Nauert, Charles. *Humanism and the Culture of Renaissance Europe.* 1995. A thorough introduction to humanism throughout Europe.

Netanyahu, Benjamin. *The Origins of the Inquisition in Fifteenth Century Spain.* 1995. An analysis of issues relating to the expulsion of the Jews by the former prime minister of Israel.

Wiesner, Merry E. *Women and Gender in Early Modern Europe*, 2d ed. 2000. Discusses all aspects of women's lives and ideas about gender.

Notes

1. Quoted in J. Burckhardt, *The Civilization of the Renaissance in Italy* (London: Phaidon Books, 1951), p. 89.
2. *Memoirs of Benvenuto Cellini; A Florentine Artist; Written by Himself* (London: J. M. Dent & Sons, 1927), p. 2.
3. Quoted in W. H. Woodward, *Vittorino da Feltre and Other Humanist Educators* (Cambridge: Cambridge University Press, 1897), p. 102.
4. Ibid., p. 127.
5. C. E. Detmold, trans., *The Historical, Political and Diplomatic Writings of Niccolò Machiavelli* (Boston: J. R. Osgood, 1882), pp. 51–52.
6. Ibid., pp. 54–55.
7. Quoted in E. H. Harbison, *The Christian Scholar and His Calling in the Age of the Reformation* (New York: Charles Scribner's Sons, 1956), p. 109.
8. Quoted in F. Seebohm, *The Oxford Reformers* (London: J. M. Dent & Sons, 1867), p. 256.
9. B. Burroughs, ed., *Vasari's Lives of the Artists* (New York: Simon & Schuster, 1946), pp. 164–165.
10. L. Martines, *Power and Imagination: City-States in Renaissance Italy* (New York: Vintage Books, 1980), p. 253.
11. G. Bull, trans., *Aretino: Selected Letters* (Baltimore: Penguin Books, 1976), p. 109.
12. Quoted in P. Murray and L. Murray, *A Dictionary of Art and Artists* (Baltimore: Penguin Books, 1963), p. 125.
13. J. Hale, *The Civilization of Europe in the Renaissance* (New York: Atheneum, 1994), p. 44.
14. Quoted in J. Devisse and M. Mollat, *The Image of the Black in Western Art,* vol. 2, trans. W. G. Ryan (New York: William Morrow, 1979), pt. 2, pp. 187–188.
15. Boccaccio, *Concerning Famous Women,* trans. Guido Guarino (New Brunswick, N.J., Rutgers University Press, 1963), p. 87.
16. See B. F. Reilly, *The Medieval Spains* (New York: Cambridge University Press, 1993), pp. 198–203.
17. B. Netanyahu, *The Origins of the Inquisition in Fifteenth Century Spain* (New York: Random House, 1995), p. 921.

Listening to the Past

An Age of Gold

As the foremost scholar of the early sixteenth century and a writer with international contacts, Desiderius Erasmus (1466?–1536) maintained a vast correspondence. In the letters here, he explains his belief that Europe was entering a golden age. The letters also reflect the spiritual ideals of northern European humanists. Wolfgang Capito (1478?–1541), a German scholar, was professor of theology at the University of Basel. Pope Leo X (1513–1521), second son of Lorenzo de' Medici, extended the hospitality of the papal court to men of letters, sought to rebuild Rome as a Renaissance capital, and pushed the building of the new Saint Peter's Basilica by licensing the sale of indulgences (see page 448).

To Capito

It is no part of my nature, most learned Wolfgang, to be excessively fond of life; whether it is that I have, to my own mind, lived nearly long enough, having entered my fifty-first year, or that I see nothing in this life so splendid or delightful that it should be desired by one who is convinced by the Christian faith that a happier life awaits those who in this world earnestly attach themselves to piety. But at the present moment I could almost wish to be young again, for no other reason but this, that I anticipate the near approach of a golden age, so clearly do we see the minds of princes, as if changed by inspiration, devoting all their energies to the pursuit of peace. The chief movers in this matter are Pope Leo and Francis, King of France.

There is nothing this king does not do or does not suffer in his desire to avert war and consolidate peace . . . and exhibiting in this, as in everything else, a magnanimous and truly royal character. Therefore, when I see that the highest sovereigns of Europe—Francis of France, Charles the King Catholic, Henry of England, and the Emperor Maximilian—have set all their warlike preparations aside and established peace upon solid and, as I trust, adamantine foundations, I am led to a confident hope that not only morality and Christian piety, but also a genuine and purer literature, may come to renewed life or greater splendour; especially as this object is pursued with equal zeal in various regions of the world—at Rome by Pope Leo, in Spain by the Cardinal of Toledo,* in England by Henry, eighth of the name, himself not unskilled in letters, and among ourselves by our young King Charles.† In France, King Francis, who seems as it were born for this object, invites and entices from all countries men that excel in merit or in learning. Among the Germans the same object is pursued by many of their excellent princes and bishops, and especially by Maximilian Caesar,‡ whose old age, weary of so many wars, has determined to seek rest in the employments of peace, a resolution more becoming to his own years, while it is fortunate for the Christian world. To the piety of these princes it is due, that we see everywhere, as if upon a given signal, men of genius are arising and conspiring together to restore the best literature.

Polite letters, which were almost extinct, are now cultivated and embraced by Scots, by Danes, and by Irishmen. Medicine has a host of champions. . . . The Imperial Law is restored at Paris by William Budé, in Germany by Udalric Zasy; and mathematics at Basel by Henry of Glaris. In the theological sphere there was no little to be done, because this science has been hitherto mainly professed by those who are most pertinacious in their abhorrence of the better

---

*Francisco Jiménez de Cisneros (1436–1517), Spanish statesman and adviser to Queen Isabella, who gained renown for his reform of the monasteries and the Spanish church.

† After 1516 king of Spain and much of the Netherlands; after 1519 Holy Roman emperor.

‡ Holy Roman emperor (1493–1519); he was succeeded by his grandson Charles (above).

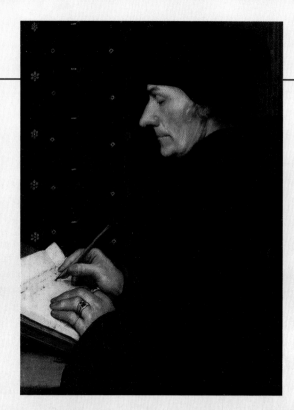

Hans Holbein the Younger, *Erasmus* (ca 1521). Holbein persuaded his close friend Erasmus to sit for this portrait and portrayed him at his characteristic work, writing. *(Louvre/Scala/Art Resource, NY)*

literature,§ and are the more successful in defending their own ignorance as they do it under pretext of piety, the unlearned vulgar being induced to believe that violence is offered to religion if anyone begins an assault upon their barbarism. . . . But even here I am confident of success if the knowledge of the three languages continues to be received in schools, as it has now begun. . . .

The humblest part of the work has naturally fallen to my lot. Whether my contribution has been worth anything I cannot say; . . . although the work was not undertaken by me with any confidence that I could myself teach anything magnificent, but I wanted to construct a road for other persons of higher aims, so that they might be less impeded by pools and stumbling blocks in carrying home those fair and glorious treasures.

Why should I say more? Everything promises me the happiest success. But one doubt still possesses my mind. I am afraid that, under cover of a revival of ancient literature, paganism may attempt to rear its head—as there are some among Christians that acknowledge Christ in name but breathe inwardly a heathen spirit—or, on the other hand, that the restoration of Hebrew learning may give occasion to a revival of Judaism. This would be a plague as much opposed to the doctrine of Christ as anything that could happen. . . . Some books have lately come out with a strong flavour of Judaism. I see how Paul exerted himself to defend Christ against Judaism, and I am aware that some persons are secretly sliding in that direction. . . . So much the more do I wish you to undertake this province; I know that your sincere piety will have regard to nothing but Christ, to whom all your studies are devoted. . . .

To Pope Leo X

While on the one hand, as a private matter, I acknowledge my own felicity in obtaining the approbation not only of the Supreme Pontiff but of Leo, by his own endowments supreme among the supreme, so on the other hand, as a matter of public concern, I congratulate this our age—which bids fair to be an age of gold, if ever such there was—wherein I see, under your happy auspices and by your holy counsels, three of the

chief blessings of humanity are about to be restored to her. I mean, first, that truly Christian piety, which has in many ways fallen into decay; secondly, learning of the best sort, hitherto partly neglected and partly corrupted; and thirdly, the public and lasting concord of Christendom, the source and parent of piety and erudition. These will be the undying trophies of the tenth Leo, which, consecrated to eternal memory by the writings of learned men, will forever render your pontificate and your family‖ illustrious. I pray God that he may be pleased to confirm this purpose in you, and so protract your life, that after the affairs of mankind have been ordered according to your designs, Leo may make a long-delayed return to the skies.

Questions for Analysis

1. What does Erasmus mean by a "golden age"?

2. Do education and learning ensure improvement in the human condition, in his opinion? Do you agree?

3. What would you say are the essential differences between Erasmus's educational goals and those of modern society?

‖The Florentine House of Medici, whose interests Leo X, himself a Medici, was known always to support.

Source: Epistles 522 and 530, from *The Epistles of Erasmus,* trans. F. M. Nichols (London: Longmans, Green & Co., 1901).

§Latin, Greek, and Hebrew.

Giorgio Vasari: *Massacre of Coligny and the Huguenots* (1573). This fresco shows the Saint Bartholomew's Day massacre in Paris, one of many bloody events in the religious wars that accompanied the Reformation. *(Vatican Palace/Scala/Art Resource, NY)*

REFORMATIONS AND RELIGIOUS WARS, 1500–1600

Calls for reform of the Christian church began very early in its history. When Christianity became the official religion of the Roman Empire in the fourth century, many believers thought that the church had abandoned its original mission, and they called for a return to a church that was not linked to the state. Throughout the Middle Ages individuals and groups argued that the church had become too wealthy and powerful and urged monasteries, convents, bishoprics, and the papacy to give up their property and focus on service to the poor. Some asserted that basic teachings of the church were not truly Christian and that changes were needed in theology as well as in institutional structures and practices. The Christian humanists of the late fifteenth and early sixteenth centuries urged reform, primarily through educational and social change.

Sixteenth-century cries for reformation were hardly new. Throughout the centuries, men and women believed that the early Christian church represented a golden age, akin to the golden age of the classical past celebrated by Renaissance humanists. What was new was the breadth of acceptance and the ultimate impact of the calls for reform. In 1500 there was one Christian church in western Europe to which all Christians at least nominally belonged. Fifty years later there were many, a situation that continues today.

Along with the Renaissance, the Reformation is often seen as a key element in the creation of the "modern" world. This radical change contained many elements of continuity, however. Sixteenth-century reformers looked back to the early Christian church for their inspiration, and many of their reforming ideas had been advocated for centuries.

The Early Reformation

Calls for reform in the church came from many quarters in early-sixteenth-century Europe—from educated laypeople such as Christian humanists and urban residents, from villagers and artisans, and from church officials themselves. This dissatisfaction helps explain why the

Online Study Center

This icon will direct you to interactive activities and study materials on the website **college.hmco.com/pic/mckaywest9e**

ideas of an obscure professor from a new and not very prestigious German university found a ready audience. Within a decade of his first publishing his ideas (using the new technology of the printing press), much of central Europe and Scandinavia had broken with the Catholic Church and even more radical concepts of the Christian message were being developed and linked to calls for social change.

- *What were the central ideas of the reformers, and why were they appealing to different social groups?*

The Christian Church in the Early Sixteenth Century

If external religious observances are a measure of depth of heartfelt conviction, Europeans in the early sixteenth century were deeply pious and remained loyal to the Roman Catholic Church. Villagers participated in processions honoring the local saints. Middle-class people made pilgrimages to the great shrines, such as Saint Peter's in Rome. The upper classes continued to remember the church in their wills. People of all social classes devoted an enormous amount of their time and income to religious causes and foundations.

Despite—or perhaps because of—the depth of their piety, many people were also highly critical of the Roman Catholic Church and its clergy. The papal conflict with the German emperor Frederick II in the thirteenth century, followed by the Babylonian Captivity and then the Great Schism, badly damaged the prestige of church leaders. Humanists denounced corruption in the church. In *The Praise of Folly,* Erasmus condemned the superstitions of the parish clergy and the excessive rituals of the monks (see page 325). Many ordinary people agreed. Court records, bishop's visitations of parishes, and even popular songs and printed images show widespread **anticlericalism,** or opposition to the clergy.

Online Study Center **Improve Your Grade**
Primary Source: *The Praise of Folly:* Erasmus on Popular Religious Practice

In the early sixteenth century critics of the church concentrated their attacks on three disorders—clerical immorality, clerical ignorance, and clerical pluralism, with the related problem of absenteeism. Many priests, particularly those ministering to country people, had concubines, and reports of neglect of the rule of celibacy were common. Clerical drunkenness, gambling, and indulgence in fancy dress were also frequent charges. Because

such conduct was completely at odds with the church's rules and moral standards, it scandalized the educated faithful.

The bishops only casually enforced regulations regarding the education of priests. As a result, standards for ordination were shockingly low. Many priests could barely read and write, and critics laughed at illiterate priests mumbling Latin words of the Mass that they could not understand. In northern Europe—in England, for example—recent research shows an improvement in clerical educational standards in the early sixteenth century. Nevertheless, parish priests throughout Europe were not as educated as the educated laity, who condemned the irregularity and poor quality of sermons.

In regard to absenteeism and **pluralism,** many clerics, especially higher ecclesiastics, held several *benefices* (or offices) simultaneously but seldom visited the benefices, let alone performed the spiritual responsibilities those offices entailed. Instead, they collected revenues from all of them and hired a poor priest, paying him just a fraction of the income to fulfill the spiritual duties of a particular local church. Many Italian officials in the papal curia held benefices in England, Spain, and Germany. Revenues from those countries paid the Italian priests' salaries, provoking not only charges of absenteeism but also nationalistic resentment.

There was also local resentment of clerical privileges and immunities. Priests, monks, and nuns were exempt from civic responsibilities, such as defending the city and paying taxes. Yet religious orders frequently held large amounts of urban property, in some cities as much as one-third. City governments were increasingly determined to integrate the clergy into civic life by reducing their privileges and giving them public responsibilities. This brought city leaders into opposition with bishops and the papacy, which for centuries had stressed the independence of the church from lay control and the distinction between members of the clergy and laypeople.

Martin Luther

By itself, widespread criticism of the church did not lead to the dramatic changes of the sixteenth century. Those resulted from the personal religious struggle of a German university professor, Martin Luther (1483–1546), who was also an Augustinian friar. The Augustinian friars were a mendicant order, like the Dominicans and Franciscans, whose members often preached, taught, and assisted the poor. Martin Luther was born at Eisleben in Saxony and was the second son of a copper miner and, later, mine owner. At considerable sacrifice, his father sent him to school and then to the University of Erfurt, where he earned a master's degree with distinction at the young age of twenty-one. Hans Luther intended his son to proceed to the study of law and a legal career, which for centuries had been the steppingstone to public office and material success. Badly frightened during a thunderstorm, however, Martin Luther vowed to become a friar. Much to his father's dismay, he entered the monastery of the Augustinian friars at Erfurt in 1505. Luther was ordained a priest in 1507 and after additional study earned a doctorate of theology. From 1512 until his death in 1546, he served as professor of the Scriptures at the new University of Wittenberg. Luther was deadly serious when he said, years later, "I would not take all the world's goods for my doctorate." His doctorate led to his professorship, and his professorship conferred on him the authority to teach: throughout his life, he frequently cited his professorship as justification for his reforming work.

Martin Luther was a very conscientious friar. His scrupulous observance of the religious routine, frequent confessions, and fasting, however, gave him only temporary relief from anxieties about sin and his ability to meet God's demands. These apprehensions in turn led him to doubt the value of the monastic life itself. Since the medieval church had long held that the monastic life was a sure and certain road to salvation, Luther's confusion and anxieties increased.

Luther's wise and kindly confessor, John Staupitz, directed him to study Saint Paul's letters in the New Testament. Gradually Luther arrived at a new understanding of the Pauline letters and of all Christian doctrine. His understanding is often summarized as "faith alone, grace alone, Scripture alone" (*sola fide, sola gratia, sola Scriptura*). For Christians, salvation and justification come through faith, not good works, though true faith leads to love and to the active expression of faith in helping others. Faith is a free gift of God, not the result of human effort. God's word is revealed only in Scripture, not in the traditions of the church.

At the same time Luther was engaged in scholarly reflections and professorial lecturing, Archbishop Albert of Mainz, who controlled the area in which Wittenberg was located, sought to become the bishop of several other territories as well. He borrowed money from the Fuggers, a wealthy banking family of Augsburg, to pay for the papal dispensation of the rules regarding pluralism. Meanwhile, Pope Leo X, a member of the Medici family, was constructing family chapels and tombs (for which he hired Michelangelo) and continuing the building of St. Peter's Basilica in Rome. He authorized a special St. Pe-

Chronology

1477	Union of Burgundian and Habsburg dynasties
1517	Martin Luther, "Ninety-five Theses on the Power of Indulgences"
1521	Diet of Worms
1521–1559	Habsburg-Valois Wars
1525	Peasants' War in Germany
1526	Turkish victory at Mohács, which allows spread of Protestantism in Hungary
1536	John Calvin, *The Institutes of the Christian Religion*
1540	Papal approval of Society of Jesus (Jesuits)
1542	Sacred Congregation of the Holy Office and Roman Inquisition
1545–1563	Council of Trent
1553–1558	Reign of Mary Tudor and temporary restoration of Catholicism in England
1555	Peace of Augsburg, official recognition of Lutheranism
1558–1603	Reign of Elizabeth and the "Elizabethan Settlement" in England
1559	Treaty of Cateau-Cambrésis
1560–1660	Height of the European witch-hunt
1568–1578	Civil war in the Netherlands
1572	Saint Bartholomew's Day massacre
1598	Edict of Nantes

ter's indulgence and allowed Albert to keep a portion of the revenue collected in the territories over which he was bishop to pay back the Fuggers.

Albert hired a friar from the Dominican order, Johann Tetzel, to run the indulgence sale. Tetzel mounted an advertising blitz. He was a very effective salesman, hawking indulgences—printed on the newly developed printing press—in a way that promised full forgiveness for sins or the end of time in purgatory for one's friends and relatives. One of his slogans—"As soon as coin in coffer rings, the soul from purgatory springs"—brought phenomenal success. Tetzel even drew up a chart with prices for the forgiveness of particular sins.

The Folly of Indulgences In this woodcut from the early Reformation, the church's sale of indulgences is viciously satirized. With one claw in holy water, another resting on the coins paid for indulgences, and a third stretched out for offerings, the church, in the form of a rapacious bird, writes out an indulgence with excrement. The creature's head and gaping mouth represent Hell, with foolish Christians inside, others being cooked in a pot above, and a demon delivering the pope in a three-tiered crown and holding the keys to Heaven, a symbol of papal authority. Illustrations such as this, often printed as single-sheet broadsides and sold very cheaply, clearly conveyed criticism of the church to people who could not read. *(Kunstsammlungen der Veste Coburg)*

What exactly was an **indulgence?** According to Catholic theology, individuals who sin alienate themselves from God. To be reconciled to God, the sinner must confess his or her sins to a priest and do an assigned **penance,** a religious act such as praying or fasting. Sometimes earthly penance is not enough, and beginning in the twelfth century learned theologians increasingly emphasized the idea of **purgatory,** a place where souls on their way to Heaven after death went to make amends for their earthly sins. (Those on their way to Hell went straight there.) When it was first discussed, purgatory was a rather neutral place, unpleasant largely because one was separated from God, but by the fifteenth century it had acquired the fire and brimstone of Hell. Time in purgatory could be shortened by actions of the living, however, such as arranging for memorial masses or saying prayers for the dead.

According to Catholic theology, the church has the authority to grant sinners the remission of the penalties for sin by drawing on what was termed the "treasury of merits." This was a collection of all the virtuous acts that Christ, the apostles, and the saints had done during their lives; their virtue was infinite, and so was the treasury of merit. People thought of it as a sort of strongbox, like those in which merchants carried coins. An indulgence was a piece of parchment (and later paper), signed by the pope or another church official, that substituted a virtuous act from the treasury of merit for penance. The papacy and bishops had given Crusaders such indulgences, and by the later Middle Ages they were offered for making pilgrimages or other pious activities and also sold outright. People widely believed that indulgences secured total remission of penalties for sin and could substitute for both penance and time in purgatory. They ensured swift entry into Heaven and, like prayers for the dead, were effective on behalf of relatives or friends already dead.

Luther was severely troubled that ignorant people believed that they had no further need for repentance once they had purchased indulgences. He wrote a letter to Archbishop Albert on the subject and enclosed in Latin "Ninety-five Theses on the Power of Indulgences." His argument was that indulgences undermined the seriousness of the sacrament of penance, competed with the preaching of the Gospel, and downplayed the importance of charity in Christian life. After Luther's death, biographies reported that the theses were also posted on the door of the church at Wittenberg Castle on October 31, 1517. Such an act would have been very strange—they were in Latin and written for those learned in theology, not for normal churchgoers—but it has become a standard part of Luther lore. In any case, Luther intended the theses for academic debate, but by December 1517 they had been translated into German and were read throughout the Roman Empire.

Online Study Center **Improve Your Grade**
Primary Source: "Ninety-five Theses on the Power and Efficacy of Indulgences"

Luther was ordered to come to Rome, which he was able to avoid because of the political situation in the empire, but he did engage in formal scholarly debate with a representative of the church, Johann Eck, at Leipzig in 1519. He denied both the authority of the pope and the infallibility of a general council. The Council of Constance, he said, had erred when it had condemned Jan Hus (see page 391).

The papacy responded with a letter condemning some of Luther's propositions, ordering that his books be burned, and giving him two months to recant or be excommunicated. Luther retaliated by publicly burning the letter. By January 3, 1521, when the excommunication was supposed to become final, the controversy involved more than theological issues. The papal legate wrote, "All Germany is in revolution. Nine-tenths shout 'Luther' as their war cry; and the other tenth cares nothing about Luther, and cries 'Death to the court of Rome.'"[1]

In this highly charged atmosphere, the twenty-one-year-old emperor Charles V held his first diet (assembly of the Estates of the empire) in the German city of Worms. Charles summoned Luther to appear before the **Diet of Worms.** When ordered to recant, Luther replied in language that rang all over Europe:

Unless I am convinced by the evidence of Scripture or by plain reason—for I do not accept the authority of the Pope or the councils alone, since it is established that they have often erred and contradicted themselves—I am bound by the Scriptures I have cited and my conscience is captive to the Word of God. I cannot and will not recant anything, for it is neither safe nor right to go against conscience. God help me. Amen.[2]

Protestant Thought

As he developed his ideas, Luther gathered followers, who came to be called Protestants. The word **Protestant** derives from the protest drawn up by a small group of reforming German princes at the Diet of Speyer in 1529. The princes "protested" the decisions of the Catholic majority. At first Protestant meant "Lutheran," but with the appearance of many protesting sects, it became a general term applied to all non-Catholic western European Christians.

The most important early reformer other than Luther was the Swiss humanist, priest, and admirer of Erasmus, Ulrich Zwingli (1484–1531). In Zurich, Zwingli announced in 1519 that he would preach not from the church's prescribed readings but, relying on Erasmus's New Testament, go right through the New Testament "from A to Z," that is, from Matthew to Revelation.

Zwingli was convinced that Christian life rested on the Scriptures, which were the pure words of God and the sole basis of religious truth. He went on to attack indulgences, the Mass, the institution of monasticism, and clerical celibacy. In his gradual reform of the church in Zurich, where he remained the rest of his life, he had the strong support of the city authorities, who had long resented the privileges of the clergy.

Luther, Zwingli, and other Protestants agreed on many things. First, how is a person to be saved? Traditional Catholic teaching held that salvation is achieved by both faith and good works. Protestants held that salvation comes by faith alone. Women and men are saved by the arbitrary decision of God, irrespective of good works or the sacraments. God, not people, initiates salvation. (See the feature "Listening to the Past: Martin Luther, *On Christian Liberty*" on pages 480–481.) Second, where does religious authority reside? Christian doctrine had long maintained that authority rests both in the Bible and in the traditional teaching of the church. For Protestants, authority rests in the Word of God as revealed in the Bible alone and as interpreted by an individual's conscience. For a doctrine or issue to be valid, it had to have a scriptural basis. Because of this, most Protestants rejected Catholic teachings about the sacraments (see page 308), holding that only baptism and the Eucharist have scriptural support.

Third, what is the church? Protestants held that the church is a spiritual *priesthood of all believers,* an invisible fellowship not fixed in any place or person, which differed markedly from the Roman Catholic practice of a clerical, hierarchical institution headed by the pope in Rome. Luther re-emphasized the Catholic teaching that the church consists of the entire community of Christian believers. Medieval churchmen, in contrast, had tended to identify the church with the clergy. Fourth, what is the highest form of Christian life? The medieval church had stressed the superiority of the monastic and religious life over the secular. Luther argued that all vocations, whether ecclesiastical or secular, have equal merit and that every person should serve God in his or her individual calling. Celibacy was not superior to marriage, and vows of celibacy went against both human nature and God's commandment.

Protestants did not agree on everything. One important area of dispute was the ritual of the Eucharist (also called communion, or the Lord's Supper). Catholics hold the dogma of **transubstantiation:** by the consecrating words of the priest during the Mass, the bread and wine become the actual body and blood of Christ, who is then fully present in the bread and wine. In opposition,

Lucas Cranach the Elder: The Ten Commandments, 1516   Cranach, who was the court painter for the elector of Saxony from 1505 to 1553, painted this giant illustration of the Ten Commandments (more than 5 feet by 11 feet) for the city hall in Wittenberg just at the point that Luther was beginning to question Catholic doctrine. Cranach became an early supporter of Luther, and many of his later works depict the reformer and his ideas. This close association, and the fact that the painting captures the Protestant emphasis on biblical texts very well, led it to be moved to the Luther House in Wittenberg, the largest museum of the Protestant Reformation in the world. Paintings were used by both Protestants and Catholics to teach religious ideas. *(Lutherhalle, Wittenberg/The Bridgeman Art Library)*

Luther believed that Christ is really present in the consecrated bread and wine, but this is the result of God's mystery, not the actions of a priest. Zwingli understood the Lord's Supper as a *memorial,* in which Christ was present in spirit among the faithful, but not in the bread and wine. The Colloquy of Marburg, summoned in 1529 to unite Protestants, failed to resolve these differences, though Protestants reached agreement on almost everything else.

The Appeal of Protestant Ideas

Every encounter Luther had with ecclesiastical or political authorities attracted attention. Pulpits and printing presses spread his message all over Germany. By the time of his death, people of all social classes had become Lutheran. What was the immense appeal of Luther's religious ideas and those of other Protestants?

Educated people and humanists were much attracted by Luther's words. He advocated a simpler personal religion based on faith, a return to the spirit of the early church, the centrality of the Scriptures in the liturgy and in Christian life, and the abolition of elaborate ceremonies—precisely the reforms the Christian humanists had been calling for. His insistence that everyone should read and reflect on the Scriptures attracted the literate and thoughtful middle classes partly because Luther appealed to their intelligence. This included many priests and monks, who became clergy in the new Protestant churches. There was no official position for women in Protestant churches, but Protestant literature was smuggled into convents. Some nuns (most famously Katharina von Bora, who became Luther's wife) accepted Luther's idea that celibacy was not especially worthy and left their convents, while others remained in their convents but otherwise accepted Protestant teachings.

As we saw above, many townspeople envied the church's wealth, disapproved of the luxurious lifestyle of some churchmen, and resented tithes and ecclesiastical taxation. Protestant doctrines of the priesthood of all believers not only raised the religious status of laypeople, but also provided greater income for city treasuries. After

Zurich became Protestant, the city council taxed the clergy and placed them under the jurisdiction of civil courts.

Hymns, psalms, and Luther's two catechisms (1529), compendiums of basic religious knowledge, show the power of language in spreading the ideals of the Reformation. Such hymns as the famous "A Mighty Fortress Is Our God" (which Luther wrote) expressed deep human feelings, were easily remembered, and imprinted central points of doctrine on the mind. Luther's *Larger Catechism* contained brief sermons on the main articles of faith, whereas the *Shorter Catechism* gave concise explanations of doctrine in question-and-answer form. Both catechisms stressed the importance of the Ten Commandments, the Lord's Prayer, the Apostle's Creed, and the sacraments for the believing Christian. Although originally intended for the instruction of pastors, these catechisms became powerful techniques for the indoctrination of men and women of all ages, especially the young.

Scholars in many disciplines have attributed Luther's fame and success to the invention of the printing press, which rapidly reproduced and made known his ideas. Many printed works included woodcuts and other illustrations, so that even those who could not read could grasp the main ideas. (See the feature "Images in Society: Art in the Reformation" on pages 452–453.) Equally important was Luther's incredible skill with language. Luther's linguistic skill, together with his translation of the New Testament into German in 1523, led to the acceptance of his dialect of German as the standard version of German.

Both Luther and Zwingli recognized that if reforms were going to be permanent, political authorities as well as concerned individuals and religious leaders would have to accept them. Zwingli worked closely with the city council of Zurich, and in other cities and towns of Switzerland and south Germany city councils similarly took the lead. They appointed pastors that they knew had accepted Protestant ideas, required them to swear an oath of loyalty to the council, and oversaw their preaching and teaching.

Luther lived in a territory ruled by a noble—the elector of Saxony—and he also worked closely with political authorities, viewing them as fully justified in asserting control over the church in their territories. Indeed, in his 1520 *Address to the Christian Nobility of the German Nation* he demanded that German rulers reform the papacy and ecclesiastical institutions, and in *On Secular Government* he instructed all Christians to obey their secular rulers, whom he saw as divinely ordained to maintain order. In terms of the process of the Reformation, Luther's hopes were largely fulfilled. Individuals may have been convinced of the truth of Protestant teachings by hearing sermons, listening to hymns, or reading pamphlets, but a territory became Protestant when its ruler, whether a noble or a city council, brought in a reformer or to re-educate the territory's clergy, sponsored public sermons, and confiscated church property. This happened in many of the states of the empire during the 1520s. In every area that became Protestant, there was a slightly differ-ent balance between popular religious ideas and the aims of the political authorities. In some areas certain groups, such as clergy or journeymen, pushed for reforms, while in others the ruler or city council forced religious change on a population that was disinterested or hostile.

The first area outside the empire to officially accept the Reformation was the kingdom of Denmark-Norway under King Christian III (r. 1536–1559). Danish scholars studied at the University of Wittenberg, and Lutheran ideas spread into Denmark very quickly. In the 1530s the king officially broke with the Catholic Church, and most clergy followed. The process went smoothly in Denmark, but in northern Norway and Iceland (which Christian also ruled) there were violent reactions, and Lutheranism was only gradually imposed on a largely unwilling populace. In Sweden, Gustavus Vasa (r. 1523–1560), who came to the throne during a civil war with Denmark, also took over control of church personnel and income, and Protestant ideas spread, though the Swedish church did not officially accept Lutheran theology until later in the century.

The Radical Reformation

Some individuals and groups rejected the idea that church and state needed to be united, and sought to create a voluntary community of believers as they understood it to have existed in New Testament times. In terms of theology and spiritual practices, these individuals and groups varied widely, though they are generally termed "radicals" for their insistence on a more extensive break with the past. Many of them repudiated infant baptism, for they wanted only members who had intentionally chosen to belong. Some adopted the baptism of believers—for which they were given the title of "Anabaptists" or rebaptizers by their enemies—while others saw all outward sacraments or rituals as misguided and concentrated on inner spiritual transformation. Some groups attempted to follow Christ's commandments in the Gospels literally, while others reinterpreted the nature

Images in Society

Art in the Reformation

In the Reformation era, controversy raged over the purpose and function of art. Protestants and Catholics disagreed, and Protestant groups disagreed with one another. The Bible specifically prohibits making images of anything "in the heavens above or the earth below or the waters beneath the earth" (Exodus 20:4–6 and Deuteronomy 5:8–10). Based on this, some Protestant leaders, including Ulrich Zwingli, stressed that "the Word of God" should be the only instrument used in the work of evangelization. Martin Luther disagreed, saying he was not "of the opinion that the Gospel should blight and destroy all the arts." Luther believed that painting and sculpture had value in spreading the Gospel message because "children and simple folk are more apt to retain the divine stories when taught by pictures and parables than merely by words or instruction." Similar debates involved music, with Luther supporting and even writing hymns, and Swiss Protestants removing organs from their churches.

Lucas Cranach the Elder (1472–1553), a close friend of Luther's, is the finest representative of Protestant Reformation artists. He and Luther collaborated on the production of woodcuts and paintings, such as *The Ten Commandments* (see page 450), that spread the new evangelical theology. Each square in Cranach's painting represents one of the Ten Commandments.

Lucas Cranach the Younger (1515–1586) continued his father's work of spreading Luther's message. His woodcut *The True and False Churches* (Image 1) contains blatant and more subtle messages. At the center Luther stands in a pulpit, preaching the word of God from an open Bible. At the right, a flaming open mouth symbolizing the jaws of Hell engulfs the pope, cardinals, and friars, one kind of "false church." The scene at the left actually suggests another kind of "false church," however. Cranach shows a crucified Christ emerging out of the

"lamb of God" on the altar as people are receiving communion. This image represents the Lutheran understanding of the Lord's Supper, in which Christ is really present in the bread and wine, in contrast to other Protestants who saw the ceremony as a memorial (see page 450). The woodcut thus could be understood on different levels by different viewers, which is true of much effective religious art.

For John Calvin, the utter transcendence of God made impossible any attempt to bring God down to human level through visual portraiture; to domesticate or to humanize God would deprive him of his glory. In houses of worship Calvin emphasized the centrality of the divine word, allowing wall inscriptions from the Bible. In later life, Calvin tolerated narrative biblical scenes as long as they did not include pictures of God or Jesus Christ. In the Netherlands, which adopted a Calvinist version of Protestantism, many formerly Catholic churches were stripped of all statues, images, and decoration and were redesigned with a stark, bare simplicity that mirrored the Calvinist ideal. Notice the interior of the church of Saint Bavo in Haarlem (Image 2).

The Catholic Church officially addressed the subject of art at the Council of Trent in December 1563. The church declared that honor and veneration should be given to likenesses of Christ, the Virgin Mary, and the

Image 1 Lucas Cranach the Younger: The True and False Churches
(Staatliche Kunstsammlungen Dresden)

452

Image 2 Church of Saint Bavo, Haarlem *(Pieter Jansz, Saenredam,* S. Bavo in Haarlem. *John G. Johnson Collection, Philadelphia Museum of Art [J 599])*

Image 3 Jesuit Priest Distributing Holy Pictures *(From Pierre Chenu,* The Reformation *[New York: St. Martin's Press, 1986])*

Image 4 Ceiling of the Gesù *(Scala/Art Resource, NY)*

saints; that images would remind people of the saints' virtues, which should be imitated; and that pictorial art would promote piety and the love of God. Examine the painting *Jesuit Priest Distributing Holy Pictures* (Image 3). Such pictures and images of saints were often given to children to help educate them on matters of doctrine. How do these pictures serve the same function as the Protestant *Ten Commandments*?

Both Protestants and Catholics used religious art for propaganda purposes, to oppose religious heterodoxy, and to arouse piety in laypeople. Catholic Reformation art came into full flowering with the style later known as baroque (see page 539). Baroque art originated in Rome and reflected the dynamic and proselytizing spirit of the Counter-Reformation. The church encouraged artists to appeal to the senses, to touch the souls and kindle the faith of ordinary people while proclaiming the power and confidence of the reformed Catholic Church.

In addition to this underlying religious emotionalism, the baroque drew from the Catholic Reformation a sense of drama, motion, and ceaseless striving. The interior of the Jesuit Church of Jesus—the Gesù—combined all these characteristics in its lavish, shimmering, wildly active decorations and frescoes (Image 4). This triumphant, elaborate, and flamboyant church celebrates both the Catholic baroque and Rome as the artistic capital of Europe. How would you compare the Gesù with the Saint Bavo Church (Image 2)?

Online Study Center **Improve Your Grade**
Going Beyond Images in Society

Domestic Scene The Protestant notion that the best form of Christian life was marriage and a family helps explain its appeal to middle-class urban men and women, such as those shown in this domestic scene. The engraving, titled "Concordia" (harmony), includes the biblical inscription of what Jesus called the greatest commandment—"You shall love the Lord your God with all your heart and all your soul and your neighbor as yourself" (Deuteronomy 6; Matthew 22)—on tablets at the back. The father presides as his son says grace; the mother passes bread; the older daughters seem to have begun eating; and small children and animals complete the scene. The large covered bed at the back was both a standard piece of furniture in urban homes and a symbol of proper marital sexual relations. (*Mary Evans Picture Library*)

of Christ. Radicals were often pacifists and refused to hold office or swear oaths, which were required of nearly everyone with any position of authority, including city midwives and toll collectors, as well as anyone involved in court proceedings. Some groups attempted communal ownership of property, living very simply and rejecting anything they thought unbiblical. Different groups blended these practices in different ways and often reacted harshly to a member who deviated, banning the person from the group and requiring other group members—sometimes including the spouse—to shun, or have no contact with, the offending member until he or she changed behavior and asked for forgiveness. Others, however, argued for complete religious toleration and individualism.

Ideas such as absolute pacifism and the distinction between the Christian community and the state brought down on these unfortunate people fanatical hatred and bitter persecution. Protestants and Catholics all saw—quite correctly—the separation of church and state as leading ultimately to the secularization of society. The powerful rulers of Swiss and German society immediately saw the connection between religious heresy and economic dislocation. Civil authorities feared that the com-

bination of religious differences and economic grievances would lead to civil disturbances. In Saxony, in Strasbourg, and in the Swiss cities, radicals were either banished or cruelly executed by burning, beating, or drowning. Their community spirit and the edifying example of their lives, however, contributed to the survival of radical ideas. Later, the Quakers, with their gentle pacifism; the Baptists, with their emphasis on inner spiritual light; the Congregationalists, with their democratic church organization; and in 1787 the authors of the U.S. Constitution, with their opposition to the "establishment of religion" (state churches), would all trace their origins, in part, to the radicals of the sixteenth century.

The German Peasants' War

The radicals represent one way that the ideas of early reformers were pushed farther; as we have seen, many of their ideas had social, economic, and political implications, which is in part why they were seen as so dangerous. Groups that linked Protestant ideas directly to various political and social programs were also threatening. The most far-reaching of these was the German Peasants' War of 1525.

Peasant revolts had erupted in many parts of Europe in the fourteenth and fifteenth centuries (see page 390). In the early sixteenth century the economic condition of the peasantry varied from place to place but was generally worse than it had been in the fifteenth century and was deteriorating. Crop failures in 1523 and 1524 aggravated an explosive situation. In 1525 representatives of the Swabian peasants met at the city of Memmingen and drew up the Twelve Articles expressing their grievances. The Twelve Articles condemned lay and ecclesiastical lords and summarized the agrarian crisis of the early sixteenth century. They complained that nobles had seized village common lands, which traditionally had been used by all; that they had imposed new rents on manorial properties and new services on the peasants working those properties; and that they had forced the poor to pay unjust death duties in the form of the peasants' best horses or cows. Wealthy, socially mobile peasants especially resented these burdens, which they emphasized as new. The peasants believed that their demands conformed to the Scriptures and cited Luther as a theologian who could prove that they did.

Luther wanted to prevent rebellion. Initially he sided with the peasants, and he blasted the lords in his tract *An Admonition to Peace* (1525):

We have no one on earth to thank for this mischievous rebellion, except you lords and princes, especially you blind bishops and mad priests and monks. . . . In your government you do nothing but flay and rob your subjects in order that you may lead a life of splendor and pride, until the poor common folk can bear it no longer.[3]

But, he warned, nothing justified the use of armed force: "The fact that rulers are unjust and wicked does not excuse tumult and rebellion; to punish wickedness does not belong to everybody, but to the worldly rulers who bear the sword." As for biblical support for the peasants' demands, he maintained that Scripture had nothing to do with earthly justice or material gain, a position that Zwingli supported.[4]

Massive revolts first broke out near the Swiss frontier and then swept through Swabia, Thuringia, the Rhineland, and Saxony. The crowds' slogans came directly from Protestant writings. "God's righteousness" and the "Word of God" were invoked in an effort to secure social and economic justice. The peasants who expected Luther's support were soon disillusioned. Freedom for Luther meant independence from the authority of the Roman church; it did *not* mean opposition to legally established secular powers. Firmly convinced that rebellion would hasten the end of civilized society, he wrote the tract *Against the Murderous, Thieving Hordes of the Peasants:* "Let everyone who can smite, slay, and stab [the peasants], secretly and openly, remembering that nothing can be more poisonous, hurtful or devilish than a rebel."[5] The nobility ferociously crushed the revolt. Historians estimate that more than seventy-five thousand peasants were killed in 1525.

The German Peasants' War of 1525 greatly strengthened the authority of lay rulers. Not surprisingly, the Reformation lost much of its popular appeal after 1525, though peasants and urban rebels sometimes found a place for their social and religious ideas in radical groups. Peasants' economic conditions did moderately improve, however. For example, in many parts of Germany, enclosed fields, meadows, and forests were returned to common use.

The Reformation and Marriage

At the same time they were reacting so harshly to radicals and peasants, Luther and Zwingli decided to marry, Luther to a former nun, Katharina von Bora (1499–1532), and Zwingli to a Zurich widow, Anna Reinhart (1491–1538). Both women quickly had several children. Most other Protestant reformers also married, and their wives had to create a new and respectable role for themselves—pastor's wife—to overcome being viewed as simply a new type of priest's concubine. They were living demonstrations of their husband's convictions about the superiority of marriage to celibacy, and they were expected to be models of wifely obedience and Christian charity.

Though they denied that marriage was a sacrament, many Protestant reformers praised marriage in formal treatises, commentaries on the Book of Genesis, household guides, and—most importantly—wedding sermons. They stressed that it had been ordained by God when he presented Eve to Adam, served as a "remedy" for the unavoidable sin of lust, provided a site for the pious rearing of the next generation of God-fearing Christians, and offered husbands and wives companionship and consolation. A proper marriage was one that reflected both the spiritual equality of men and women and the proper social hierarchy of husbandly authority and wifely obedience.

Protestants did not break with medieval scholastic theologians in their idea that women were to be subject to men, a subjection rooted in their original nature and made more pronounced by Eve's primary responsibility for the Fall. Women were advised to be cheerful rather than grudging in their obedience, for in doing so they

Martin Luther and Katharina von Bora, by Lucas Cranach the Elder Cranach painted this double marriage portrait to celebrate Luther's wedding in 1525 to Katharina von Bora, a former nun. The artist was one of the witnesses at the wedding and, in fact, had presented Luther's marriage proposal to Katharina. Using a go-between for proposals was very common, as was having a double wedding portrait painted. This particular couple quickly became a model of the ideal marriage, and many churches wanted their portraits. More than sixty similar paintings, with slight variations, were produced by Cranach's workshop and hung in churches and wealthy homes. *(Uffizi, Florence/Scala/Art Resource, NY)*

demonstrated their willingness to follow God's plan. Men were urged to treat their wives kindly and considerately, but also to enforce their authority, through physical coercion if necessary. Both continental and English marriage manuals use the metaphor of breaking a horse for teaching a wife obedience, though laws did set limits on the husband's power to do so. A few women took Luther's idea about the priesthood of all believers to heart and wrote religious pamphlets and hymns, but no sixteenth-century Protestants officially allowed women to hold positions of religious authority, though monarchs such as Elizabeth I of England and female territorial rulers of the states of the Holy Roman Empire did determine religious policies.

Catholics viewed marriage as a sacramental union that, if validly entered into, could not be dissolved. Protestants saw marriage as a contract in which each partner promised the other support, companionship, and the sharing of mutual goods. Because, in Protestant eyes, marriage was created by God as a remedy for human weakness, marriages in which spouses did not comfort or support one another physically, materially, or emotionally endangered their own souls and the surrounding community. The only solution might be divorce and remarriage, which most Protestants came to allow. Protestant marital courts in Germany, Switzerland, Scandinavia, and later

Scotland and France allowed divorce for adultery and impotence, and sometimes for contracting a contagious disease, "malicious" desertion (meaning intentional desertion, as opposed to unintentional desertion such as extended army service), conviction for a capital crime, or deadly assault. Some of them allowed both parties to marry again, and some only the innocent.

This was a dramatic change in marital law, as Catholic canon law had allowed only separation from bed and board with no remarriage, but it had a less than dramatic impact. Because marriage was the cornerstone of society socially and economically, divorce was a desperate last resort. In many Protestant jurisdictions the annual divorce rate hovered around 0.02 to 0.06 per thousand people. (By contrast, in 2000 the U.S. divorce rate was 4.1 per thousand people.)

Marriage was the proper remedy for lust, and Protestants uniformly condemned prostitution. The licensed brothels that were a common feature of late medieval urban life (see page 394) were closed in Protestant cities, and harsh punishments were set for prostitution. Selling sex was couched in moral rather than economic terms, as simply one type of "whoredom," a term that also included premarital sex, adultery, and other unacceptable sexual activities. Religious reformers such as Luther described women who sold sex in very negative terms and also regarded "whore" as the worst epithet they could hurl at their theological opponents.

Closing the official brothels did not end the exchange of sex for money, of course, but simply reshaped it. Smaller illegal brothels were established, or women moved to areas right outside city walls. Police and other authorities were influenced or bribed to overlook such activities. For Italian city authorities, this fluid situation was more worrisome, and they tended to favor regulation over suppression. They also viewed selling sex as a significant source of municipal income. From 1559 until the mid-eighteenth century in Florence, for example, all women registered as prostitutes were required to contribute an annual tax based on their income, which went to support a convent for women who wished to give up prostitution. Payment of extra taxes would allow a woman to live where she wished in the city and wear any type of clothes she chose, rather than having to follow the sumptuary laws requiring prostitutes to dress a certain way (see page 394).

The Protestant Reformation clearly had a positive impact on marriage, but its impact on women was more mixed. Many nuns had lacked a religious vocation, but convents nevertheless provided women of the upper classes with scope for their literary, artistic, medical, or administrative talents if they could not or would not marry. The Reformation generally brought the closing of monasteries and convents, and marriage became virtually the only occupation for upper-class Protestant women. Women in some convents recognized this and fought the Reformation, or argued that they could still be pious Protestants within convent walls. Most nuns left, however, and we do not know what happened to them. The Protestant emphasis on marriage made unmarried women (and men) suspect, for they did not belong to the type of household regarded as the cornerstone of a proper, godly society.

The Reformation and German Politics

Criticism of the church was widespread in Europe in the early sixteenth century, and calls for reform came from many areas. It was no accident, however, that the reformer whose ideas had the most impact lived in the politically divided Holy Roman Empire. Unlike Spain, France, and England, the Holy Roman Empire lacked a strong central power. The emperor was elected in a process established by the Golden Bull of 1356, a decree issued by the Holy Roman emperor Charles IV (and named after the golden seal attached to it). There were only seven electors—the archbishops of Mainz, Trier, and Cologne, the margrave of Brandenburg, the duke of Saxony, the count palatine of the Rhine, and the king of Bohemia. All these individuals were powerful, but so were many other nobles and church officials who ruled the hundreds of largely independent states in the empire.

Against this background of decentralization and strong local power, Martin Luther had launched a movement to reform the church. Two years after Luther published the Ninety-five Theses, the electors chose as emperor a nineteen-year-old Habsburg prince who ruled as Charles V. The course of the Reformation was shaped by this election and by the political relationships surrounding it.

• *How did the political situation in Germany shape the course of the Reformation?*

The Rise of the Habsburg Dynasty

War and diplomacy were important ways that states increased their power in sixteenth-century Europe, but so was marriage. Because almost all of Europe was ruled by hereditary dynasties—the Papal States and a few cities being the exceptions—claiming and holding resources involved shrewd marital strategies, for it was far cheaper to gain land by inheritance than by war. Royal and noble sons and daughters were important tools of state policy. Even popes and city leaders were often part of such marital strategies; papal nieces, nephews, and sometimes children were coveted marriage partners, as were the wealthy daughters of urban elites. Wealthy urban families, especially in Italy, also transformed themselves into hereditary dynasties through coups and alliances during this period, and they cemented their position through marriages with more established ruling houses.

The benefits of an advantageous marriage, particularly if the wife had no brothers and thus inherited territory, stretched across generations, a process that can be seen most dramatically with the Habsburgs. The Holy Roman emperor Frederick III, a Habsburg who was the ruler of most of Austria, acquired only a small amount of territory—but a great deal of money—with his marriage to Princess Eleonore of Portugal in 1452. He arranged for his son Maximilian to marry Europe's most prominent heiress, Mary of Burgundy, in 1477; she inherited the Netherlands, Luxembourg, and the County of Burgundy in what is now eastern France. Through this union with the rich and powerful duchy of Burgundy, the Austrian house of Habsburg, already the strongest ruling family in the empire, became an international power. The marriage of Maximilian and Mary angered the French, however, who considered Burgundy French territory, and inaugurated centuries of conflict between the Austrian house of Habsburg and the kings of France.

"Other nations wage war; you, happy Austria, marry." Historians dispute the origins of this adage, but no one questions its accuracy, at least in terms of marriage. (The frequency with which the Habsburgs went to war make the saying somewhat ironic.) Maximilian learned the lesson of marital politics well, marrying his son and daughter to the children of Ferdinand and Isabella, the rulers of Spain, much of southern Italy, and eventually the Spanish New World empire. His grandson Charles V (1500–1558) fell heir to a vast conglomeration of territories. Through a series of accidents and unexpected deaths, Charles inherited Spain from his mother, her New World possessions, and the Spanish dominions in Italy, Sicily, and Sardinia. From his father he inherited the Habsburg lands in Austria, southern Germany, the Low Countries, and Franche-Comté in east-central France. Charles would eventually rule about half of Europe.

Charles's inheritance was an incredibly diverse collection of states and peoples, each governed in a different manner and held together only by the person of the emperor (see Map 14.1 on page 460). Charles's Italian adviser, the grand chancellor Gattinara, told the young ruler, "God has set you on the path toward world monarchy." Charles not only believed this but also was convinced that it was his duty to maintain the political and religious unity of Western Christendom.

The Political Impact of the Protestant Reformation

In the sixteenth century the practice of religion remained a public matter. Everyone participated in the religious life of the community, just as almost everyone shared in the local agricultural work. Whatever spiritual convictions individuals held in the privacy of their consciences, the emperor, king, prince, magistrate, or other civil authority determined the official form of religious practice in his (or occasionally her) jurisdiction. Almost everyone believed that the presence of a faith different from that of the majority represented a political threat to the security of the state. Only a tiny minority, and certainly none of the rulers, believed in religious liberty.

Against this background, the religious storm launched by Martin Luther swept across Germany. Anticlericalism blended with hostility to the papacy, which was increasingly seen as Italian rather than international. Papal tax collectors had long been more active in the empire than they were in the more unified nation-states such as France, where royal power restricted them. Luther and other reformers highlighted papal financial exploitation of Germany in their sermons and pamphlets. Though Germany was not a nation, people did have an understanding of being German because of their language and traditions. Luther frequently used the phrase "we Germans" in his attacks on the papacy. Luther's appeal to German patriotism gained him strong support, and national feeling influenced many rulers otherwise confused by or indifferent to the complexities of the religious issues. Some German rulers were sincerely attracted to Lutheran ideas, but material considerations swayed many others to embrace the new faith. The rejection of Roman Catholicism and adoption of Protestantism would mean the legal confiscation of lush farmlands, rich monasteries, and wealthy shrines. A steady stream of duchies, margraviates, free cities, and bishoprics secularized church property, accepted Lutheran theological doctrines, and adopted simpler services conducted in German. Thus many political authorities in the empire used the religious issue to extend their financial and political power and to enhance their independence from the emperor.

Charles V was a vigorous defender of Catholicism, however, so it is not surprising that the Reformation led to religious wars. The first battleground was Switzerland, which was officially part of the Holy Roman Empire, though it was really a loose confederation of thirteen largely autonomous territories called "cantons." Some cantons remained Catholic, and some became Protestant, and in the late 1520s the two sides went to war. Zwingli was killed on the battlefield in 1531, and both sides quickly decided that a treaty was preferable to further fighting. The treaty basically allowed each canton to determine its own religion and ordered each side to give up its foreign alliances, a policy of neutrality that has been characteristic of modern Switzerland.

Trying to halt the spread of religious division, Charles V called an Imperial Diet in 1530, to meet at Augsburg. The Lutherans developed a statement of faith, later called the Augsburg Confession, and the Protestant princes presented this to the emperor. (The Augsburg Confession remained an authoritative statement of belief for many Lutheran churches for centuries.) Charles refused to accept it and ordered all Protestants to return to the Catholic Church and give up any confiscated church property. This threat backfired, and Protestant territories in the empire—mostly north German princes and south German cities—formed a military alliance. The emperor could not respond militarily, as he was in the midst of a

Giorgio Vasari: Fresco of Pope Clement VII and the Emperor Charles V In this double portrait, Vasari uses matching hand gestures to indicate agreement between the pope and the emperor, though the pope's red hat and cape make him the dominant figure. Charles V remained loyal to Catholicism, though the political situation and religious wars in Germany eventually required him to compromise with Protestants. *(Palazzo Vecchio, Florence/Scala/Art Resource, NY)*

series of wars with the French: the Habsburg-Valois Wars, fought in Italy along the eastern and southern borders of France and eventually in Germany. The Turks had also taken much of Hungary and in 1529 were besieging Vienna.

The 1530s and early 1540s saw complicated political maneuvering among many of the powers of Europe. The emperor, the pope, France, England, Protestant and Catholic princes and cities in Germany, Scotland, Sweden, Denmark, and even the Turks made and broke alliances, and the Habsburg-Valois rivalry continued to be played out militarily. Various attempts were made to heal the religious split with a church council, but intransigence on both sides made it increasingly clear that this would not be possible and that war was inevitable. Charles V realized that he was fighting not only for religious unity, but also for a more unified state against territorial rulers who wanted to maintain their independence. He was thus defending both church and empire.

Fighting began in 1546, and initially the emperor was very successful. This success alarmed both France and the pope, however, who did not want Charles to become even more powerful. The pope withdrew papal troops, and the Catholic king of France sent money and troops to the Lutheran princes. Finally, in 1555 Charles agreed to the Peace of Augsburg, which, in accepting the status quo, officially recognized Lutheranism. The political authority in each territory was permitted to decide whether the territory would be Catholic or Lutheran. Most of

northern and central Germany became Lutheran, while the south remained Roman Catholic. There was no freedom of religion, however. Princes or town councils established state churches to which all subjects of the area had to belong. Dissidents had to convert or leave.

Online Study Center **Improve Your Grade**
Primary Source: The Religious Peace of Augsburg

There were limitations and problems in the Peace of Augsburg that would become clear by the late sixteenth century, but it accomplished what its makers hoped it would. It ended religious war in Germany for many decades, and it put political, religious, and economic life clearly in the hands of the territorial rulers. It was immediately evident that this agreement ended Charles V's hope of creating a united empire with a single church. He abdicated in 1556 and moved to a monastery, transferring power over his Spanish and Netherlandish holdings to his son Philip and his imperial power to his brother Ferdinand.

The Spread of the Protestant Reformation

States within the empire and the kingdom of Denmark-Norway were the earliest territories to accept the Protestant Reformation, but by the later 1520s Protestant ideas and dynastic considerations combined to bring religious

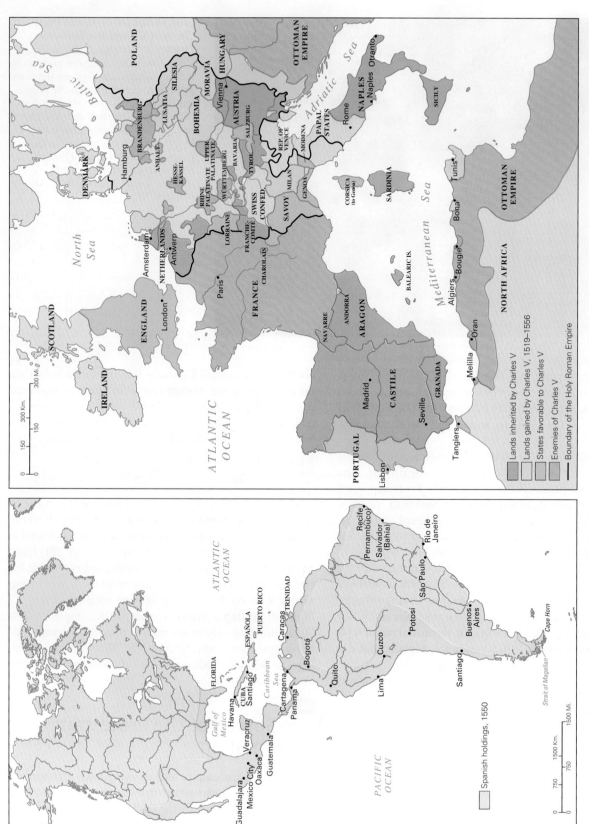

MAP 14.1 The Global Empire of Charles V Charles V exercised theoretical jurisdiction over more European territory than anyone since Charlemagne. He also claimed authority over large parts of North and South America, though actual Spanish control was weak in much of this area.

Online Study Center **Improve Your Grade** Interactive Map: Global Empire of Charles V change to England. Protestant ideas also spread into France and eastern Europe. In all these areas, a second generation of reformers built on Lutheran and Zwinglian ideas to develop their own theology and plans for institutional change. The most important of the second-generation reformers was John Calvin, whose ideas would come to shape Christianity over a much wider area than did Luther's.

• *How did Protestant ideas and institutions spread beyond German-speaking lands?*

The Reformation in England and Ireland

As on the continent, the Reformation in England had economic as well as religious causes. When the personal matter of the divorce of King Henry VIII (r. 1509–1547) became enmeshed with political issues, a complete break with Rome resulted.

Henry was married to Catherine of Aragon, the daughter of Ferdinand and Isabella. Catherine had originally been married to his older brother Arthur, who had died as a youth. Marriage to a brother's widow went against canon law, and Henry had been required to obtain a special papal dispensation to marry Catherine. The marriage was about average for royal marriages—they neither especially hated nor loved one another—but it had produced only one living heir, a daughter, Mary. By 1527 Henry decided that God was showing his displeasure with the marriage by denying him a son, and he appealed to the pope to have the marriage annulled. He was also in love with a court lady-in-waiting, Anne Boleyn, and assumed that she would give him the son he wanted. Normally an annulment would not have been a problem, but the troops of Emperor Charles V were in Rome at that point, and Pope Clement VII was essentially their prisoner. Charles V was the nephew of Catherine of Aragon and thus was vigorously opposed to an annulment, which would have declared his aunt a fornicator and his cousin Mary a bastard. (An annulment declares that there never was a marriage, making children of such a union illegitimate.) The military situation in Rome, added to the fact that an annulment would have called into question the pope's right to grant a dispensation from something proscribed by the Bible, led the pope to stall.

Since Rome appeared to be thwarting Henry's matrimonial plans, he decided to remove the English church from papal jurisdiction. Henry used Parliament to legalize the Reformation in England. The Act in Restraint of Appeals (1533) declared the king to be the supreme sov-

ereign in England and forbade judicial appeals to the papacy, thus establishing the Crown as the highest legal authority in the land. The Supremacy Act (1534) declared the king the supreme head of the Church of England. Both the Act in Restraint of Appeals and the Supremacy Act led to heated debate in the House of Commons. Some opposed the king. John Fisher, the bishop of Rochester, a distinguished scholar and a humanist, lashed the clergy with scorn for its cowardice in abjectly bending to the king's will. Another humanist, Thomas More, resigned the chancellorship: he could not take the oath required by the Supremacy Act because it rejected papal authority and made the king head of the English church. Fisher, More, and other dissenters were beheaded.

When Anne Boleyn failed twice to produce a male child, Henry VIII charged her with adulterous incest and in 1536 had her beheaded. Parliament promptly proclaimed Anne's daughter, the princess Elizabeth, illegitimate and, with the royal succession thoroughly confused, left the throne to whomever Henry chose. His third wife, Jane Seymour, gave Henry the desired son, Edward, but died in childbirth. Henry went on to three more wives. Before he died in 1547, he got Parliament to reverse the decision of 1536, relegitimating Mary and Elizabeth and fixing the succession first in his son and then in his daughters.

Between 1535 and 1539, under the influence of his chief minister, Thomas Cromwell, Henry decided to dissolve the English monasteries because he wanted their wealth. The king ended nine hundred years of English monastic life, dispersing the monks and nuns and confiscating their lands. Hundreds of properties were sold to the middle and upper classes and the proceeds spent on war. The dissolution of the monasteries did not achieve a more equitable distribution of land and wealth. Rather, the redistribution of land strengthened the upper classes and tied them to the Tudor dynasty.

Henry's motives combined personal, political, social, and economic elements. Theologically he retained such traditional Catholic practices and doctrines as confession, clerical celibacy, and transubstantiation. Meanwhile, Protestant literature circulated, and Henry approved the selection of men of Protestant sympathies as tutors for his son.

Did the religious changes accompanying this political upheaval have broad popular support? Some people were certainly dissatisfied with the church in England, but traditional Catholicism exerted an enormously strong and vigorous hold over the imagination and loyalty of the people. The surviving evidence does not allow us to gauge the degree of opposition to (or support for) Henry's

Allegory of the Tudor Dynasty The unknown creator of this work intended to glorify the virtues of the Protestant succession; the painting has no historical reality. Enthroned Henry VIII (r. 1509–1547) hands the sword of justice to his Protestant son Edward VI (r. 1547–1553). The Catholic Queen Mary (r. 1553–1558) and her husband Philip of Spain are followed by Mars, god of war, signifying violence and civil disorder. At right the figures of Peace and Plenty accompany the Protestant Elizabeth I (r. 1558–1603), symbolizing England's happy fate under her rule. *(Yale Center for British Art, Paul Mellon Collection/The Bridgeman Art Library)*

break with Rome. Most clergy and officials accepted Henry's moves, but all did not quietly acquiesce. In 1536 popular opposition in the north to the religious changes led to the Pilgrimage of Grace, a massive multi-class rebellion that proved the largest in English history. The "pilgrims" accepted a truce, but their leaders were arrested, tried, and executed. Recent scholarship points out that people rarely "converted" from Catholicism to Protestantism overnight, particularly where changes were piecemeal and the religious policies of the Crown itself varied, as in England. People responded to an action of the Crown that was played out in their own neighborhood—the closing of a monastery, the ending of Masses for the dead—with a combination of resistance, acceptance, cooperation, and collaboration.

Loyalty to the Catholic Church was particularly strong in Ireland. Ireland had been claimed by English kings since the twelfth century, but in reality the English had

firm control of only the area around Dublin, known as the Pale. In 1536, on orders from London, the Irish parliament, which represented only the English landlords and the people of the Pale, approved the English laws severing the church from Rome. The Church of Ireland was established on the English pattern, and the (English) ruling class adopted the new reformed faith. Most of the Irish people remained Roman Catholic, thus adding religious antagonism to the ethnic hostility that had been a feature of English policy toward Ireland for centuries (see page 397). Irish armed opposition to the Reformation led to harsh repression by the English. Catholic property was confiscated and sold, and the profits were shipped to England. With the Roman church driven underground, Catholic clergy acted as national as well as religious leaders.

The nationalization of the church and the dissolution of the monasteries led to important changes in government administration in both England and Ireland. Vast tracts of formerly monastic land came temporarily under the Crown's jurisdiction, and new bureaucratic machinery had to be developed to manage those properties. Cromwell reformed and centralized the king's household, the council, the secretariats, and the Exchequer. New departments of state were set up. Surplus funds from all departments went into a liquid fund to be applied to areas where there were deficits. This balancing resulted in greater efficiency and economy. Henry VIII's reign saw the growth of the modern centralized bureaucratic state.

In the short reign of Henry's sickly son, Edward VI (r. 1547–1553), strongly Protestant ideas exerted a significant influence on the religious life of the country. Archbishop Thomas Cranmer simplified the liturgy, invited Protestant theologians to England, and prepared the first **Book of Common Prayer** (1549). In stately and dignified English, the *Book of Common Prayer* included, together with the Psalter, the order for all services of the Church of England.

The equally brief reign of Mary Tudor (r. 1553–1558) witnessed a sharp move back to Catholicism. The devoutly Catholic daughter of Catherine of Aragon, Mary rescinded the Reformation legislation of her father's reign and restored Roman Catholicism. Mary's marriage to her cousin Philip of Spain, son of the emperor Charles V, proved highly unpopular in England, and her execution of several hundred Protestants further alienated her subjects. During her reign, many Protestants fled to the continent. Mary's death raised to the throne her sister Elizabeth (r. 1558–1603) and inaugurated the beginnings of religious stability.

Elizabeth had been raised a Protestant, but at the start of her reign sharp differences existed in England. On the one hand, Catholics wanted a Roman Catholic ruler. On the other hand, a vocal number of returning exiles wanted all Catholic elements in the Church of England eliminated. The latter, because they wanted to "purify" the church, were called "Puritans." Probably one of the shrewdest politicians in English history, Elizabeth chose a middle course between Catholic and Puritan extremes. She insisted on dignity in church services and political order in the land. She required her subjects to attend church or risk a fine, but did not care what they actually believed as long as they kept quiet about it. She required officials, clergy, and nobles to swear allegiance to her as the "supreme governor of the Church of England." She initially chose the word *governor* rather than *head* to provide a loophole for English Catholics to remain loyal to her without denying the primacy of the pope. She also realized that *head* might be viewed as inappropriate for a woman, for treatises about the family and proper gender relations always referred to men as the "head."

The parliamentary legislation of the early years of Elizabeth's reign—laws sometimes labeled the **Elizabethan Settlement**—required outward conformity to the Church of England and uniformity in all ceremonies. In 1563 a convocation of bishops approved the Thirty-nine Articles, a summary in thirty-nine short statements of the basic tenets of the Church of England. During Elizabeth's reign, the Anglican church (from the Latin *Ecclesia Anglicana*), as the Church of England was called, moved in a moderately Protestant direction. Services were conducted in English, monasteries were not reestablished, and clergymen were (grudgingly) allowed to marry. But the episcopate was not abolished, and the bishops remained as church officials; apart from language, the services were quite traditional.

Calvinism

In 1509, while Luther was studying for a doctorate at Wittenberg, John Calvin (1509–1564) was born in Noyon in northwestern France. Luther inadvertently launched the Protestant Reformation. Calvin, however, had the greater impact on future generations. His theological writings profoundly influenced the social thought and attitudes of Europeans and English-speaking peoples all over the world, especially in Canada and the United States. Although he had originally intended to have an ecclesiastical career, Calvin studied law, which had a decisive impact on his mind and later thought. In 1533 he experienced a religious crisis, as a result of which he converted to Protestantism.

Convinced that God selects certain people to do his work, Calvin believed that God had specifically called him to reform the church. Accordingly, he accepted an invitation to assist in the reformation of the city of Geneva. There, beginning in 1541, Calvin worked assiduously to establish a Christian society ruled by God through civil magistrates and reformed ministers. Geneva, "a city that was a church," became the model of a Christian community for sixteenth-century Protestant reformers.

To understand Calvin's Geneva, it is necessary to understand Calvin's ideas. These he embodied in **The Institutes of the Christian Religion,** first published in 1536 and definitively issued in 1559. The cornerstone of Calvin's theology was his belief in the absolute sovereignty and omnipotence of God and the total weakness of humanity. Before the infinite power of God, he asserted, men and women are as insignificant as grains of sand.

Calvin did not ascribe free will to human beings because that would detract from the sovereignty of God. Men and women cannot actively work to achieve salvation; rather, God in his infinite wisdom decided at the beginning of time who would be saved and who damned. This viewpoint constitutes the theological principle called **predestination:**

Predestination we call the eternal decree of God, by which he has determined in himself, what he would have become of every individual. . . . For they are not all created with a similar destiny; but eternal life is foreordained for some, and eternal damnation for others. . . . In conformity, therefore, to the clear doctrine of the Scripture, we assert, that by an eternal and immutable counsel, God has once for all determined, both whom he would admit to salvation, and whom he would condemn to destruction. . . . To those whom he devotes to condemnation, the gate of life is closed by a just and irreprehensible, but incomprehensible, judgment. How exceedingly presumptuous it is only to inquire into the causes of the Divine will; which is in fact, and is justly entitled to be, the cause of everything that exists. . . . For the will of God is the highest justice; so that what he wills must be considered just, for this very reason, because he wills it.[6]

Many people consider the doctrine of predestination, which dates back to Saint Augustine and Saint Paul, to be a pessimistic view of the nature of God, who, they feel, revealed himself in the Old and New Testaments as merciful as well as just. But "this terrible decree," as even Calvin called it, did not lead to pessimism or fatalism. Rather, the Calvinist believed in the redemptive work of Christ and was confident that God had elected (saved) him or her. Predestination served as an energizing dynamic, forcing a person to undergo hardships in the constant struggle against evil.

Calvin aroused Genevans to a high standard of morality. He had two remarkable assets: complete mastery of the Scriptures and exceptional eloquence. Through his sermons and a program of religious education, God's laws and man's were enforced in Geneva. Calvin's powerful sermons delivered the Word of God and thereby monopolized the strongest contemporary means of communication: preaching. Through his *Genevan Catechism,* published in 1541, children and adults memorized set questions and answers and acquired a summary of their faith and a guide for daily living. Calvin's sermons and his *Catechism* gave a whole generation of Genevans thorough instruction in the reformed religion.[7]

Young John Calvin Even in youth, Calvin's face showed the strength and determination that were later to characterize his religious zeal. *(Bibliothèque de Genève, Département iconographique)*

In the reformation of the city, the Genevan Consistory also exercised a powerful role. This body consisted of twelve laymen plus the Company of Pastors, of which Calvin was the permanent moderator (presider). The duties of the Consistory were "to keep watch over every man's life [and] to admonish amiably those whom they see leading a disorderly life." Even though Calvin emphasized that the Consistory's activities should be thorough and "its eyes may be everywhere," corrections were considered only "medicine to turn sinners to the Lord."[8]

Although all municipal governments in early modern Europe regulated citizens' conduct, none did so with the severity of Geneva's Consistory under Calvin's leadership. Nor did it make any distinction between what we would consider crimes against society and simple unChristian conduct. Absence from sermons, criticism of ministers, dancing, card playing, family quarrels, and heavy drinking were all investigated and punished by the

Consistory. Serious crimes and heresy were handled by the civil authorities, which, with the Consistory's approval, sometimes used torture to extract confessions. Between 1542 and 1546 alone seventy-six persons were banished from Geneva and fifty-eight executed for heresy, adultery, blasphemy, and witchcraft.

Calvin reserved his harshest condemnation for religious dissenters, declaring them "dogs and swine":

God makes plain that the false prophet is to be stoned without mercy. We are to crush beneath our heel all affections of nature when His honor is concerned. The father should not spare his child, . . . nor husband his own wife or the friend who is dearer to him than life. No human relationship is more than animal unless it be grounded in God.[9]

In the 1550s Spanish humanist Michael Servetus had gained international notoriety for his publications denying the Christian dogma of the Trinity. Servetus had been arrested by the Inquisition but escaped to Geneva, where he was promptly rearrested. At his trial, he not only held to his belief that there is no scriptural basis for the Trinity but also rejected child baptism and insisted that a person under twenty cannot commit a mortal sin. The city fathers considered this last idea dangerous to public morality, "especially in these days when the young are so corrupted." Though Servetus begged that he be punished by banishment, Calvin and the town council maintained that the denial of child baptism and the Trinity amounted to a threat to all society. Servetus was burned at the stake.

Online Study Center **Improve Your Grade**
Primary Source: The Trial of Michael Servetus in Calvin's Geneva

To many sixteenth-century Europeans Calvin's Geneva seemed "the most perfect school of Christ since the days of the Apostles." Religious refugees from France, England, Spain, Scotland, and Italy visited the city. Subsequently, the Reformed church of Calvin served as the model for the Presbyterian church in Scotland, the Huguenot church in France, and the Puritan churches in England and New England.

Calvinism became the compelling force in international Protestantism. The Calvinist ethic of the "calling" dignified all work with a religious aspect. Hard work, well done, was pleasing to God. This doctrine encouraged an aggressive, vigorous activism. These factors, together with the social and economic applications of Calvin's theology, made Calvinism the most dynamic force in sixteenth- and seventeenth-century Protestantism.

The Establishment of the Church of Scotland

Calvinism found a ready audience in Scotland. There as elsewhere, political authority was the decisive influence in reform. The monarchy was weak, and factions of virtually independent nobles competed for power. King James V and his daughter Mary, Queen of Scots (r. 1560–1567), staunch Catholics and close allies of Catholic France, opposed reform. The Scottish nobles supported it. One man, John Knox (1505?–1572), dominated the movement for reform in Scotland.

In 1559 Knox, a dour, single-minded, and fearless man with a reputation as a passionate preacher, set to work reforming the church. He was determined to structure the Scottish church after the model of Geneva, where he had studied and worked with Calvin. In 1560 Knox persuaded the Scottish parliament, which was dominated by reform-minded barons, to enact legislation ending papal authority. The Mass was abolished. Knox then established the Presbyterian Church of Scotland, so named because *presbyters,* or ministers, not bishops, governed it. The Church of Scotland was strictly Calvinist in doctrine, adopted a simple and dignified service of worship, and laid great emphasis on preaching. Knox's *Book of Common Order* (1564) became the liturgical directory for the church. The Presbyterian Church of Scotland was a national, or state, church, and many of its members maintained close relations with English Puritans.

The Reformation in Eastern Europe

While political and economic issues determined the course of the Reformation in western and northern Europe, ethnic factors often proved decisive in eastern Europe. In the later Middle Ages, the migration of diverse peoples into Bohemia, Poland, and Hungary meant that those countries had heterogeneous populations in the sixteenth century. Ethnic background tended to resolve religious matters.

In Bohemia in the fifteenth century, the ethnic grievances of the Czech majority against German economic and ecclesiastical domination (see page 391) fused with Czech resentment at the corruption of the Roman church. By 1500 most Czechs had adopted the ideas of Jan Hus, and the emperor had been forced to recognize a separate Hussite church. Lutheranism spread rapidly among Germans in Bohemia in the 1520s and 1530s; many Germans lived near the border of Luther's Saxony. Moreover, the nobility's identification of Lutheranism with opposition to the Habsburgs contributed, as in Germany, to the growth of Protestantism. The forces of the Catholic Reformation promoted a Catholic spiritual revival in Bohemia, and some areas reconverted. This complicated situation would be one of the causes of the Thirty Years' War (see pages 562–565).

By 1500 Poland and the Grand Duchy of Lithuania were united in a dynastic union. A king, senate, and diet (parliament) governed, but the two territories retained separate officials, judicial systems, armies, and forms of citizenship. In the fifteenth century rulers had granted the Polish *szlachta* (nobility) extensive rights; though hereditary, the monarchy was weak and had to cooperate with the szlachta. The combined realms covered about 440,150 square miles, making Poland-Lithuania the largest European polity. A population of only about 7.5 million people was very thinly scattered over that land.

In comparison with western Europe, Poland-Lithuania was overwhelmingly rural; its largest cities—Gdansk (30,000) and Cracow (15,000)—were very small in population by Italian or French standards. Yet with Germans, Italians, Tartars, and Jews, Poland-Lithuania represented great diversity. Such peoples had come as merchants, invited by medieval rulers because of their wealth or to make agricultural improvements. Each group spoke its native language, though all educated people spoke Latin. In the late fifteenth century Italian Renaissance humanism influenced Polish art, architecture, literature, and historical writing.

Luther's ideas spread first to the German-speaking Baltic towns, then to the University of Cracow, where his works were translated. His ideas met two major obstacles: King Sigismund I (r. 1506–1548) banned Luther's teachings in Poland, and strong anti-German feeling among Poles meant that Lutheranism would have limited success outside Germanized towns.

The Reformed tradition of John Calvin, with its stress on the power of church elders, appealed to the Polish szlachta, however. The fact that Calvinism originated in France, not in Germany, also made it more attractive than Lutheranism. Several Polish magnates, including Jan Laski (1499–1560), converted to Calvinism, and Calvinist nobles dominated the important diet of 1555. But doctrinal differences among Calvinists, Lutherans, and other groups prevented united opposition to Catholicism.

Under Stanislaus Hosius (1505–1579), who attended the Council of Trent, a systematic Counter-Reformation gained momentum. Hosius pressed for reform within the Catholic Church, held provincial synods, and published a comprehensive and clear statement of Roman Catholic faith and morals. The Jesuits (see page 469) complemented his work by establishing schools for the sons of the szlachta. By 1650 the identification of Poland and Roman Catholicism was well established.

Merchants from Poland carried the first news about Martin Luther to Hungary in 1521. Hungarian students flocked to Wittenberg; they became the major agents for the spread of Lutheranism in Hungary, and sympathy for it developed at the royal court at Buda. But concern about "the German heresy" by the Catholic hierarchy and among the magnates found expression in a decree of the Hungarian diet in 1523 that "all Lutherans and those favoring them . . . should have their property confiscated and themselves punished with death as heretics."[10]

A military event on August 26, 1526, had profound consequences for both the Hungarian state and the Protestant Reformation there. On the plain of Mohács in southern Hungary, the Ottoman sultan Suleiman the Magnificent (see page 566) inflicted a crushing defeat on the Hungarians, killing King Louis II, many of the magnates, and more than sixteen thousand ordinary soldiers. Rival factions elected different kings, and the Hungarian kingdom was divided into three parts: the Ottoman Turks absorbed the great plains, including the capital, Buda; the Habsburgs ruled the north and west; and Ottoman-supported Janos Zapolya held eastern Hungary and Transylvania. The Turks were indifferent to the religious conflicts of the infidels.

Mohács led to a great advance of Protestantism. Many Magyar (Hungarian) magnates accepted Lutheranism; Lutheran schools and parishes headed by men educated at Wittenberg multiplied; and peasants welcomed the new faith. In spite of the foundation of Jesuit colleges, in 1585 the papal nuncio noted that 85 percent of the population was Protestant, 10 percent remained Greek Orthodox, and just 5 percent (concentrated in Croatia) stayed Catholic. Hungary seemed lost to Catholicism. Then, in the late seventeenth century, Hungarian nobles' recognition of Habsburg (Catholic) rule and Ottoman Turkish withdrawal in 1699 led to Catholic restoration.

The Catholic Reformation

Between 1517 and 1547 Protestantism made remarkable advances. Nevertheless, the Roman Catholic Church made a significant comeback. After about 1540 no new large areas of Europe, other than the Netherlands, accepted Protestant beliefs (see Map 14.2). Many historians see the developments within the Catholic Church after the Protestant Reformation as two interrelated movements: one a drive for internal reform linked to earlier reform efforts, and the other a Counter-Reformation that opposed Protestants intellectually, politically, militarily, and institutionally. In both movements, the papacy, new religious orders, and the Council of Trent that met from 1545 to 1563 were important agents.

- *How did the Catholic Church respond to the new religious situation?*

The Reformed Papacy

The Renaissance princes who sat on the throne of Saint Peter were not blind to the evils that existed. Modest reform efforts were undertaken, but the idea of reform was closely linked to the idea of a general council representing the entire church. Remembering fifteenth-century conciliar attempts to limit papal authority, early sixteenth-century popes resisted calls for a council. The papal bureaucrats who were the popes' intimates warned the popes against a council, fearing loss of power, revenue, and prestige.

This changed beginning with Pope Paul III (1534–1549), and the papal court became the center of the reform movement rather than its chief opponent. Paul appointed reform-minded cardinals, abbots, and bishops who improved education for the clergy, tried to enforce moral standards among them, and worked on correcting the most glaring abuses. Reform measures that had been suggested since the late Middle Ages, such as prohibiting pluralism and absenteeism, were gradually adopted during the sixteenth century. Paul III and his successors supported the establishment of new religious orders that preached to the common people, the opening of seminaries for training priests, the end of the selling of church offices, and stricter control of clerical life. Their own lives were models of decorum and piety, in contrast to Renaissance popes who had concentrated on building and decorating churches and palaces and on enhancing the power of their own families.

In 1542 Pope Paul III established the Sacred Congregation of the **Holy Office,** with jurisdiction over the Roman Inquisition, a powerful instrument of the Catholic Reformation. The Inquisition was a committee of six cardinals with judicial authority over all Catholics and the power to arrest, imprison, and execute. Under the fervent Cardinal Caraffa, it vigorously attacked heresy.

The Roman Inquisition operated under the principles of Roman law. It accepted hearsay evidence, was not obliged to inform the accused of charges against them, and sometimes applied torture. Echoing one of Calvin's remarks about heresy, Cardinal Caraffa wrote, "No man is to lower himself by showing toleration towards any sort of heretic, least of all a Calvinist."[11] The Holy Office published the *Index of Prohibited Books,* a catalogue of forbidden reading.

Within the Papal States, the Inquisition effectively destroyed heresy (and some heretics). Outside the papal territories, however, its influence was slight. In Venice, a major publishing center, the *Index* had no influence on scholarly research in nonreligious areas such as law, classical literature, and mathematics.

The Council of Trent

Pope Paul III also called an ecumenical council, which met intermittently from 1545 to 1563 at Trent, an imperial city close to Italy. It was called not only to reform the church but also to secure reconciliation with the Protestants. Lutherans and Calvinists were invited to participate, but their insistence that the Scriptures be the sole basis for discussion made reconciliation impossible. International politics repeatedly cast a shadow over the theological debates. Charles V opposed discussions on any matter that might further alienate his Lutheran subjects, fearing the loss of additional imperial territory to Lutheran princes. Meanwhile, the French kings worked against the reconciliation of Roman Catholicism and Lutheranism. As long as religious issues divided the German states, the empire would be weakened, and a weak and divided empire meant a stronger France. Portugal, Poland, Hungary, and Ireland sent representatives, but very few German bishops attended.

In spite of the obstacles, the achievements of the Council of Trent were impressive. The council dealt with both doctrinal and disciplinary matters. It gave equal validity to the Scriptures and to tradition as sources of religious truth and authority. It reaffirmed the seven sacraments and the traditional Catholic teaching on transubstantiation. Thus it rejected Lutheran and Calvinist positions.

The council tackled the problems arising from ancient abuses by strengthening ecclesiastical discipline. Tridentine (from *Tridentum,* the Latin word for Trent) decrees required bishops to reside in their own dioceses, suppressed pluralism and simony, and forbade the sale of indulgences. Clerics who kept concubines were to give them up. The jurisdiction of bishops over all the clergy of their dioceses was made almost absolute, and bishops were ordered to visit every religious house within the diocese at least once every two years. In a highly original decree, the council required every diocese to establish a

Predominant Religion in 1555

- Lutheran
- Calvinist (Reformed)
- Church of England
- Roman Catholic
- Orthodox
- Muslim
- → Spread of Calvinism
- ◂ Huguenot centers

◯ Ottoman Empire, 1566

300 Mi.
150
0
300 Km.
150
0

ATLANTIC
OCEAN

North
Sea

Baltic
Sea

Black
Sea

Adriatic Sea

Mediterranean Sea

IRELAND
Dublin

SCOTLAND
1560
Edinburgh
John Knox,
1505–1572

ENGLAND
1536
Oxford
John Wyclif,
1320–1384
London
Plymouth

Penetration of Calvinism
to England after 1558

NORWAY
1536/1607
Bergen

S W E D E N
Stockholm

Helsinki

Riga

LITHUANIA

Warsaw

PRUSSIA

POLAND

DENMARK
Copenhagen

Hamburg

BRANDENBURG

SAXONY
Wittenberg
Martin Luther
Eisleben,
Birthplace of
Martin Luther,
1483–1546
Erfurt
Leipzig

HOLY ROMAN
EMPIRE

Prague
Jan Hus,
1369–1415

BOHEMIA

MORAVIA

AUSTRIA
Vienna

Buda
Pest
HUNGARY
Belgrade

TRANSYLVANIA

Danube

O T T O M A N
E M P I R E

Münster

Amsterdam
NETHERLANDS
Antwerp
Brussels

Birthplace of
John Calvin,
1509–1564
Noyon

Paris

Rennes

Orléans

FRANCE

Nantes
Edict of Nantes,
1598
La Rochelle

Bordeaux

Toulouse

Marburg
Birthplace of Marburg

Worms
Edict of Worms,
1521

Nuremberg
Augsburg
Munich
Stuttgart
Speyer

Strasbourg

Basel

Zurich
Ulrich Zwingli,
1484–1531

Geneva
John Calvin

Avignon
Marseilles

Milan
Pavia
Genoa

Venice
Trent
Council of Trent,
1545–1563

Florence
Pisa

ITALY
Rome
Roman Inquisition
established, 1542

Naples

Bari

Sicily

Corsica

Sardinia

Barcelona

Balearic Is.

Valencia

Loyola
Birthplace of
Ignatius Loyola,
1491

Madrid

SPAIN

Toledo

Granada

Seville

PORTUGAL

Lisbon

MOROCCO

ALGIERS
OTTOMAN EMPIRE

TUNIS

seminary for the education and training of the clergy; the council even prescribed the curriculum and insisted that preference for admission be given to sons of the poor. Seminary professors were to determine whether candidates for ordination had *vocations,* genuine callings as determined by purity of life, detachment from the broader secular culture, and a steady inclination toward the priesthood. This was a novel idea, since from the time of the early church, parents had determined their sons' (and daughters') religious careers. Finally, great emphasis was laid on preaching and instructing the laity, especially the uneducated.

One decision had especially important social consequences for laypeople. Since the time of the Roman Empire, many couples had treated marriage as a completely personal matter, had exchanged vows privately without witnesses, and had thus formed what were called clandestine (secret) unions. This widespread practice frequently led later to denials by one party, conflicts over property, and disputes in the ecclesiastical courts that had jurisdiction over marriage once it became a sacrament (which occurred in the twelfth century). The Tridentine decree Tametsi (November 1563) stipulated that for a marriage to be valid, consent (the essence of marriage) as given in the vows had to be made publicly before witnesses, one of whom had to be the parish priest. Trent thereby ended secret marriages in Catholic countries. (They remained a problem for civil and church courts in England until the Hardwicke Act of 1753 abolished them.)

The Council of Trent did not meet everyone's expectations. Reconciliation with Protestantism was not achieved, nor was reform brought about immediately. Nevertheless, the Tridentine decrees laid a solid basis for the spiritual renewal of the church and for the enforcement of correction. For four centuries the doctrinal and disciplinary legislation of Trent served as the basis for Roman Catholic faith, organization, and practice.

New Religious Orders

The establishment of new religious orders within the church reveals a central feature of the Catholic Reformation. Most of these new orders developed in response to one crying need: to raise the moral and intellectual level of the clergy and people. (See the feature "Individuals in Society: Teresa of Ávila.") Education was a major goal of the two most famous orders.

The Ursuline order of nuns, founded by Angela Merici (1474–1540), attained enormous prestige for the education of women. The daughter of a country gentleman, Angela Merici worked for many years among the poor, sick, and uneducated around her native Brescia in northern Italy. In 1535 she established the Ursuline order to combat heresy through Christian education. The first women's religious order concentrating exclusively on teaching young girls, the Ursulines sought to re-Christianize society by training future wives and mothers. Because the Council of Trent placed great stress on the *claustration* (strict enclosure) of religious women and called for the end of all active ministries for women, Angela had great difficulty gaining papal approval. Official recognition finally came in 1565, and the Ursulines rapidly spread to France and the New World. Their schools in North America, stretching from Quebec to New Orleans, provided superior education for young women and inculcated the spiritual ideals of the Catholic Reformation.

The Society of Jesus, or **Jesuits,** founded by Ignatius Loyola (1491–1556), a former Spanish soldier, played a powerful international role in resisting the spread of Protestantism, converting Asians and Latin American Indians to Catholicism, and spreading Christian education all over Europe. While recuperating from a severe battle wound in his legs, Loyola studied a life of Christ and other religious books and decided to give up his military career and become a soldier of Christ. During a year spent in seclusion, prayer, and personal mortification, he gained insights that went into his great classic, *Spiritual Exercises* (1548). This work, intended for study during a four-week period of retreat, directed the individual imagination and will to the reform of life and a new spiritual piety.

Mapping the Past

MAP 14.2 Religious Divisions in Europe The Reformations shattered the religious unity of Western Christendom. The situation was even more complicated than a map of this scale can show. Many cities within the Holy Roman Empire, for example, accepted a different faith than the surrounding countryside; Augsburg, Basel, and Strasbourg were all Protestant, though surrounded by territory ruled by Catholic nobles. Use the map and the information in the book to answer the following questions: ❶ Why was the Holy Roman Empire the first arena of religious conflict in sixteenth-century Europe? ❷ Are there similarities in regions where a particular branch of the Christian faith was maintained or took root? ❸ To what degree can nonreligious factors be used as an explanation for the religious divisions in sixteenth-century Europe?

Online Study Center **Improve Your Grade** Interactive Map: Protestant and Catholic Reformations

School of Titian: The Council of Trent Since the early sessions were sparsely attended, this well-attended meeting seems to be a later session or an idealization. The seated figures in the tall white hats are bishops, while the dark-clothed figures around the edges are church lawyers and officials. The guards in the foreground are members of the Swiss guards, founded by Pope Julius II in 1505 to defend the papacy and still serving in that role (and in similar uniforms) today. In the sixteenth century Switzerland was a poor country, as its mountainous terrain was not good for agriculture, and mercenary soldiers were one of its chief "exports." *(Louvre/ Réunion des Musées Nationaux/Art Resource, NY)*

Loyola was a man of considerable personal magnetism. After study at universities in Salamanca and Paris, he gathered a group of six companions and in 1540 secured papal approval of the new Society of Jesus. The first Jesuits, recruited primarily from the wealthy merchant and professional classes, saw the Reformation as a pastoral problem, its causes and cures related not to doctrinal issues but to people's spiritual condition. Reform of the church, as Luther and Calvin understood that term, played no role in the future the Jesuits planned for themselves. Their goal was "to help souls." Loyola also possessed a gift for leadership that consisted in spotting talent and in seeing "how at a given juncture change is more consistent with one's scope than staying the course."[12]

The Society of Jesus developed into a highly centralized, tightly knit organization. Candidates underwent a two-year novitiate, in contrast to the usual one-year probation. In addition to the traditional vows of poverty, chastity, and obedience, professed members vowed "special obedience to the sovereign pontiff regarding missions."[13] Thus as stability—the promise to live his life in the monastery—was what made a monk, so mobility— the commitment to go anywhere for the help of souls— was the defining characteristic of a Jesuit. Flexibility and the willingness to respond to the needs of time and circumstance formed the Jesuit tradition. In this respect, Jesuits were very modern, and they attracted many recruits. They achieved phenomenal success for the papacy and the reformed Catholic Church. Jesuit schools adopted

Individuals in Society

Teresa of Ávila

Seventeenth-century cloisonné enamelwork illustrating Teresa of Ávila's famous vision of an angel piercing her heart.
(By gracious permission of Catherine Hamilton Kappauf)

Her family derived from Toledo, center of the Moorish, Jewish, and Christian cultures in medieval Spain. Her grandfather, Juan Sanchez, made a fortune in the cloth trade. A "New Christian" (see pages 437–439), he was accused of secretly practicing Judaism. Although he endured the humiliation of a public repentance, he moved his family south to Ávila. Beginning again, he recouped his wealth and, aspiring to the prestige of an "Old Christian," bought noble status. Juan's son Alzonzo Sanchez de Cepeda married a woman of thoroughly Christian background, giving his family an aura of impeccable orthodoxy. The third of their nine children, Teresa, became a saint and in 1970 was the first woman declared a Doctor of the Church, a title given to a theologian of outstanding merit.

At age twenty, inspired more by the fear of Hell than the love of God, Teresa (1515–1582) entered the Carmelite Convent of the Incarnation in Ávila. Most of the nuns were daughters of Ávila's leading citizens; they had entered the convent because of a family decision about which daughters would marry and which would become nuns. Their lives were much like those of female family members outside the convent walls, with good food, comfortable surroundings, and frequent visits from family and friends. Teresa was frequently ill, but she lived quietly in the convent for many years. In her late thirties, she began to read devotional literature intensely and had profound mystical experiences—visions and voices in which Christ chastised her for her frivolous life and friends. She described one such experience in 1560:

It pleased the Lord that I should see an angel. . . . Short, and very beautiful, his face was so aflame that he appeared to be one of the highest types of angels. . . . In his hands I saw a long golden spear and at the end of an iron tip I seemed to see a point of fire. With this he seemed to pierce my heart several times so that it penetrated to my entrails. When he drew it out . . . he left me completely afire with the great love of God.*

Teresa responded with a new sense of purpose: although she encountered stiff opposition, she resolved to found a reformed house. Four basic principles were to guide the new convent. First, poverty was to be fully observed, symbolized by the nuns' being barefoot, hence *discalced*. Charity and the nuns' own work must support the community. Second, the convent must keep strict enclosure; the visits of powerful benefactors with material demands were forbidden. Third, Teresa intended an egalitarian atmosphere in which class distinctions were forbidden. She had always rejected the emphasis on "purity of blood," a distinctive and racist feature of Spanish society that was especially out of place in the cloister. All sisters, including those of aristocratic background, must share the manual chores. Finally, like Ignatius Loyola and the Jesuits, Teresa placed great emphasis on obedience, especially to one's confessor.

Between 1562 and Teresa's death in 1582, she founded or reformed fourteen other houses of nuns, traveling widely to do so. Though Teresa did not advocate institutionalized roles for women outside the convent, she did chafe at the restrictions placed on her because of her sex, and she thought of the new religious houses she founded as answers to the Protestant takeover of Catholic churches elsewhere in Europe. From her brother, who had obtained wealth in the Spanish colonies, Teresa learned about conditions in Peru and instructed her nuns "to pray unceasingly for the missionaries working among the heathens." Through prayer, Teresa wrote, her nuns could share in the exciting tasks of evangelization and missionary work otherwise closed to women. Her books, along with her five hundred extant letters, show her as a practical and down-to-earth woman as well as a mystic and a creative theologian.

Questions for Analysis

1. How did sixteenth-century convent life reflect the values of Spanish society?
2. How is the life of Teresa of Ávila typical of developments in the Catholic Reformation? How is her life unusual?

**The Autobiography of St. Teresa of Ávila*, trans. and ed. E. A. Peers (New York: Doubleday, 1960), pp. 273–274.

Online Study Center **Improve Your Grade**
Going Beyond Individuals in Society

Juan de Valdes Leal: Pope Paul III Approves the Jesuit Constitutions This painting by a Spanish artist celebrates the founding of the Jesuits by his fellow countryman Ignatius Loyola. When the Jesuit constitutions were read to him, Paul III supposedly murmured, "There is the finger of God." Judging by other portraits, the depiction of Loyola here is a reasonable likeness, that of the pope an idealization: in 1540 he was a very old man. *(Institut Amatller d'Art Hispanic)*

the modern humanist curricula and methods, and though they first concentrated on the children of the poor, they were soon educating the sons of the nobility. As confessors and spiritual directors to kings, Jesuits exerted great political influence. Operating on the principle that the end sometimes justifies the means, they were not above spying. Indifferent to physical comfort and personal safety, they carried Christianity to India and Japan before 1550 and to Brazil, North America, and the Congo in

the seventeenth century. Within Europe the Jesuits brought southern Germany and much of eastern Europe back to Catholicism.

Religious Violence

In 1559 France and Spain signed the Treaty of Cateau-Cambrésis, which ended the long conflict known as the Habsburg-Valois Wars. Spain was the victor. France, exhausted by the struggle, had to acknowledge Spanish dominance in Italy, where much of the fighting had taken place. The Treaty of Cateau-Cambrésis did not bring peace, however. Instead, over the next century religious differences led to riots, civil wars, and international conflicts. Especially in France and the Netherlands, Protestants and Catholics used violent actions as well as preaching and teaching against each other, for each side regarded the other as a poison in the community that would provoke the wrath of God. Catholics continued to believe that Calvinists and Lutherans could be reconverted; Protestants persisted in thinking that the Roman church should be destroyed. Catholics and Protestants alike feared people of other faiths, who they often saw as agents of Satan. Even more, they feared those who were explicitly identified with Satan: witches living in their midst. The era of religious wars was also the time of the most virulent witch persecutions in European history, as both Protestants and Catholics tried to make their cities and states more godly.

● *What were the causes and consequences of religious violence, including riots, wars, and witch-hunts?*

French Religious Wars

The Habsburg-Valois Wars, waged intermittently through the first half of the sixteenth century, cost more than the French government could afford. In addition to the time-honored practices of increasing taxes and engaging in heavy borrowing, King Francis I (r. 1515–1547) tried two new devices to raise revenue: the sale of public offices and a treaty with the papacy. The former proved to be only a temporary source of money. The offices sold tended to become hereditary within a family, and once a man bought an office he and his heirs were exempt from taxation.

The treaty with the papacy was the Concordat of Bologna (see page 435), in which Francis agreed to recognize the supremacy of the papacy over a universal council. In return, the French crown gained the right to appoint all French bishops and abbots. This understanding gave the monarchy a rich supplement of money and offices and a power over the church that lasted until the Revolution of 1789. The Concordat of Bologna helps explain why France did not later become Protestant: in effect, it established Catholicism as the state religion. Because French rulers possessed control over appointments and had a vested financial interest in Catholicism, they had no need to revolt against Rome.

Luther's tracts first appeared in France in 1518, and his ideas attracted some attention. After the publication of Calvin's *Institutes* in 1536, sizable numbers of French people were attracted to the "reformed religion," as Calvinism was called. Because Calvin wrote in French rather than Latin, his ideas gained wide circulation. Initially, Calvinism drew converts from among reform-minded members of the Catholic clergy, the industrious middle classes, and artisan groups. Most French Calvinists (called **Huguenots**) lived in major cities, such as Paris, Lyons, and Rouen. When Henry II died in 1559, perhaps one-tenth of the population had become Calvinist.

The feebleness of the French monarchy was the seed from which the weeds of civil violence sprang. The three weak sons of Henry II who occupied the throne could not provide the necessary leadership, and they were often dominated by their mother, Catherine de' Medici. The French nobility took advantage of this monarchical weakness. In the second half of the sixteenth century between two-fifths and one-half of the nobility at one time or another became Calvinist. Just as German princes in the Holy Roman Empire had adopted Lutheranism as a means of opposition to Emperor Charles V, so French nobles frequently adopted the reformed religion as a religious cloak for their independence. Armed clashes between Catholic royalist lords and Calvinist antimonarchical lords occurred in many parts of France. Both Calvinists and Catholics believed that the others' books, services, and ministers polluted the community. Preachers incited violence, and ceremonies such as baptisms, marriages, and funerals triggered it.

Protestant teachings called the power of sacred images into question, and mobs in many cities took down and smashed statues, stained-glass windows, and paintings. They ridiculed and tested religious images, throwing them into latrines, using them as cooking fuel or building material, or giving them as toys or masks for children. Though it was often inspired by fiery Protestant sermons, this **iconoclasm** is an example of men and women carrying out the Reformation themselves, rethinking the church's system of meaning and the relationship between the unseen and the seen. Catholic mobs responded by defending images, and crowds on both sides killed their opponents, often in gruesome ways.

A savage Catholic attack on Calvinists in Paris on August 24, 1572 (Saint Bartholomew's Day), followed the usual pattern. The occasion was a religious ceremony, the marriage of the king's sister Margaret of Valois to the Protestant Henry of Navarre, which was intended to help reconcile Catholics and Huguenots. Instead Huguenot wedding guests in Paris were massacred, and other Protestants were slaughtered by mobs. Religious violence spread to the provinces, where thousands were killed. This **Saint Bartholomew's Day massacre** led to a civil war that dragged on for fifteen years. Agriculture in many areas was destroyed; commercial life declined severely; and starvation and death haunted the land.

What ultimately saved France was a small group of moderates of both faiths called **politiques** who believed that only the restoration of strong monarchy could reverse the trend toward collapse. No religious creed was worth the incessant disorder and destruction. Therefore, the politiques favored accepting the Huguenots as an officially recognized and organized pressure group. (But religious toleration, the full acceptance of peoples of different religious persuasions within a pluralistic society, with minorities having the same civil liberties as the majority, developed only in the eighteenth century.) The death of Catherine de' Medici, followed by the assassination of King Henry III, paved the way for the accession of Henry of Navarre (the unfortunate bridegroom of the Saint Bartholomew's Day massacre), a politique who became Henry IV (r. 1589–1610).

Henry knew that the majority of the French were Roman Catholics. Allegedly saying "Paris is worth a Mass," Henry knelt before the archbishop of Bourges and was received into the Roman Catholic Church. Henry's willingness to sacrifice religious principles to political necessity saved France. The **Edict of Nantes,** which Henry published in 1598, granted liberty of conscience and liberty of public worship to Huguenots in 150 fortified towns, such as La Rochelle. The reign of Henry IV and the Edict of Nantes prepared the way for French absolutism in the seventeenth century by helping restore internal peace in France.

The Netherlands Under Charles V

Hostility to a monarch was also part of religious wars in the Netherlands. What began as a movement for the reformation of the church developed into a struggle for Dutch independence.

Emperor Charles V (r. 1519–1556) had inherited the seventeen provinces that compose present-day Belgium and the Netherlands (see page 458). Each of the seventeen provinces of the Netherlands possessed historical liberties: each was self-governing and enjoyed the right to make its own laws and collect its own taxes. In addition to important economic connections, only the recognition of a common ruler in the person of Emperor Charles V united the provinces. The cities of the Netherlands made their living by trade and industry.

In the Low Countries as elsewhere, corruption in the Roman church and the critical spirit of the Renaissance provoked pressure for reform, and Lutheran ideas spread. Charles V had grown up in the Netherlands, however, and he was able to limit their impact. In 1556 Charles V abdicated, dividing his territories between his brother Ferdinand, who received Austria and the Holy Roman Empire, and his son Philip, who inherited Spain, the Low Countries, Milan and the kingdom of Sicily, and the Spanish possessions in the Americas. Philip had grown up in Spain and did not understand the Netherlands.

By the 1560s Protestants in the Netherlands were primarily Calvinists, not Lutherans, and were more militant in their beliefs. Calvinism appealed to the middle classes because of its intellectual seriousness, moral gravity, and emphasis on any form of labor well done. It took deep root among the merchants and financiers in Amsterdam and the northern provinces. Working-class people were also converted. Whereas Lutherans taught respect for the powers that be, Calvinism tended to encourage opposition to "illegal" civil authorities.

In the 1560s Spanish authorities attempted to suppress Calvinist worship and raised taxes, which sparked riots. Thirty churches in Antwerp were sacked and the religious images in them destroyed in a wave of iconoclasm. From Antwerp the destruction spread to Brussels and Ghent and north to the provinces of Holland and Zeeland. From Madrid Philip II sent twenty thousand Spanish troops under the duke of Alva to pacify the Low Countries. Alva interpreted "pacification" to mean the ruthless extermination of religious and political dissidents. On top of the Inquisition, he opened his own tribunal, soon called the "Council of Blood." On March 3, 1568, fifteen hundred men were executed.

For ten years, between 1568 and 1578, civil war raged in the Netherlands between Catholics and Protestants and between the seventeen provinces and Spain. Eventually the ten southern provinces, the Spanish Netherlands (the future Belgium), came under the control of the Spanish Habsburg forces. The seven northern provinces, led by Holland, formed the **Union of Utrecht** and in

MAP 14.3 The Netherlands, 1559–1609 This map shows the division of the seventeen provinces as a result of the religious wars. Some provinces were overwhelmingly agricultural; some were involved in manufacturing; and others were heavily commercial.

1581 declared their independence from Spain. The north was Protestant; the south remained Catholic (see Map 14.3). Philip did not accept this, and war continued, with the Dutch troops gaining victories under the leadership of a local nobleman, William of Nassau, prince of Orange (1533–1584), known as William the Silent. William was shot by a French assassin loyal to Philip (the first known assassination of a political leader by a handgun), and the leaders of the United Provinces looked beyond their borders to other Protestant areas for assistance against the Spanish.

They particularly appealed to the Protestant queen of England, Elizabeth, for assistance. Fearing that the next step would be a Spanish invasion of England, Elizabeth reluctantly sent money and troops. Philip responded by planning and launching an invasion of England, but the Spanish fleet scattered in the English Channel and only half the ships made it back to Spain (see pages 512–513).

Fighting continued off and on in the Netherlands, but the borders set by the Union of Utrecht gradually became permanent, and in 1609 Spain agreed to a truce that recognized the independence of the United Provinces.

The Great European Witch-Hunt

The relationship between the Reformation and the upsurge in trials for witchcraft that occurred at roughly the same time is complex. Increasing persecution for witchcraft actually began before the Reformation in the 1480s, but it became especially common about 1560. Religious reformers' extreme notions of the Devil's powers and the insecurity created by the religious wars contributed to this increase. Both Protestants and Catholics tried and executed witches, with church officials and secular authorities acting together. They regarded both their religious opponents and witches as deluded by the Devil but made a clear distinction between them; heretics might merit burning, but they were only rarely accused of witchcraft. Witches were a special kind of heretic, but their primary crime was a pact with the Devil, not incorrect doctrine.

The heightened sense of God's power and divine wrath in the Reformation era was an important factor in the witch-hunts, but other factors were also significant. One of these was a change in the idea of what a witch was. Nearly all premodern societies believe in witchcraft and make some attempts to control witches, who are understood to be people who use magical forces to do evil deeds. Witches themselves often believe in their own powers, which they can use to earn a living or gain influence over their neighbors. In the later Middle Ages, however, many educated Christian theologians, canon lawyers, and officials added a demonological component to this notion of what a witch was. For them, the essence of witchcraft was making a pact with the Devil that required the witch to do the Devil's bidding. Witches were no longer simply people who used magical power to get what they wanted, but rather people used by the Devil to do what *he* wanted. This demonological or Satanic idea of witchcraft was fleshed out, and witches were thought to engage in wild sexual orgies with the Devil, fly through the night to meetings called sabbats, which parodied the Mass, and steal communion wafers and unbaptized babies to use in their rituals. Some demonological theorists also claimed that witches were organized in an international conspiracy to overthrow Christianity, with a hierarchy similar to the hierarchy of angels and archangels that Christian philosophers had invented. Witchcraft was

Iconoclasm in the Netherlands Calvinist men and women break stained-glass windows, remove statues, and carry off devotional altarpieces. Iconoclasm, or the destruction of religious images, is often described as a "riot," but here the participants seem very purposeful. Calvinist Protestants regarded pictures and statues as sacrilegious and saw removing them as a way to purify the church. *(The Fotomas Index/The Bridgeman Art Library)*

thus spiritualized, and witches became the ultimate heretics, enemies of God.

Trials involving this new notion of witchcraft as diabolical heresy began in Switzerland and southern Germany in the late fifteenth century, became less numerous in the early decades of the Reformation when Protestants and Catholics were busy fighting each other, and then picked up again about 1560. Because so many records have been lost or destroyed, it is difficult to make an estimate for all of Europe, but most scholars agree that during the sixteenth and seventeenth centuries somewhere between 100,000 and 200,000 people were officially tried for witchcraft and between 40,000 and 60,000 were executed.

Though the gender balance varied widely in different parts of Europe, between 75 and 85 percent of those tried and executed were women. Ideas about women, and the roles women actually played in society, were thus important factors shaping the witch-hunts. Some demonologists expressed virulent **misogyny,** or hatred of women, and particularly emphasized women's powerful sexual desire, which could be satisfied only by a demonic lover. Most people viewed women as weaker and so more likely to give in to any kind of offer by the Devil, including better food or nicer clothing. Women were associated with nature, disorder, and the body, all of which were linked with the demonic. Women's actual lack of power in society and gender norms about the use of violence meant that they were more likely to use scolding and cursing to get what they wanted instead of taking people to court or beating them up. Curses were generally expressed (as they often are today) in religious terms; "go to Hell" was calling on the powers of Satan. Women also had more contact with areas of life in which bad things happened unexpectedly, such as preparing food or caring for new mothers, children, and animals.

Learned ideas about the diabolical nature of witchcraft gradually filtered down to common people. Illustrated pamphlets and broadsides portrayed witches riding on pitchforks to sabbats where they engaged in anti-Christian acts such as spitting on the communion host and having sexual relations with demons. Though witch trials were secret, executions were not; they were public spectacles witnessed by huge crowds, with the list of charges read out for all to hear. By the late sixteenth century popular accusations of witchcraft in many parts of Europe involved at least some parts of the demonic conception of witchcraft.

Legal changes also played a role in causing, or at least allowing for, massive witch trials. One of these was a change from an accusatorial legal procedure to an inquisitorial procedure. In the former, a suspect knew the accusers and the charges they had brought, and an accuser could in turn be liable for trial if the charges were not proven; in the latter, legal authorities themselves brought the case. This change made people much more willing to accuse others, for they never had to take personal responsibility for the accusation or face the accused's relatives. Inquisitorial procedure involved intense questioning of the suspect, often with torture; areas in Europe that did not make this change saw very few trials. Torture was also used to get the names of additional suspects, as most lawyers firmly believed that no witch could act alone.

The use of inquisitorial procedure did not always lead to witch-hunts, however. The most famous inquisitions in early modern Europe, those in Spain, Portugal, and Italy, were in fact very lenient in their treatment of people accused of witchcraft: the Inquisition in Spain executed only a handful of witches, the Portuguese Inquisition only one, and the Roman Inquisition none, though in each of these areas there were hundreds of cases. Inquisitors certainly believed in the power of the Devil and were no less misogynist than other judges, but they doubted very much whether the people accused of witchcraft had actually made pacts with the Devil that gave them special powers. They viewed such people not as diabolical Devil-worshipers but as superstitious and ignorant peasants who should be educated rather than executed. Thus most people brought up before the Inquisition for witchcraft were sent home with a warning and a penance.

Most witch trials began with a single accusation in a village or town. Individuals accused someone they knew of using magic to spoil food, make children ill, kill animals, raise a hailstorm, or do other types of harm. Tensions within families, households, and neighborhoods often played a role in these accusations. Women number very prominently among accusers and witnesses as well as among those accused of witchcraft because the actions witches were initially charged with, such as harming children or curdling milk, were generally part of women's sphere. A woman also gained economic and social security by conforming to the standard of the good wife and mother and by confronting women who deviated from it.

Once a charge was made, judges began to question other neighbors and acquaintances, building up a list of suspicious incidents that might have taken place over decades. Historians have pointed out that one of the reasons those accused of witchcraft were often older was that it took years to build up a reputation as a witch. At this point, the suspect was brought in for questioning by legal authorities. Judges and inquisitors sought the exact details of a witch's demonic contacts, including sexual ones. Suspects were generally stripped and shaved in a search for a "witch's mark," or "pricked" to find a spot insensitive to pain, and then tortured.

Detailed records of witch trials survive for many parts of Europe. They have been used by historians to study many aspects of witchcraft, but they cannot directly answer what seems to us an important question: did people really practice witchcraft and think they were witches? They certainly

Hans Baldung Grien: Witches' Sabbat (1510)   In this woodcut, Grien combines learned and popular beliefs about witches: they traveled at night, met at sabbats (or assemblies), feasted on infants (in dish held high), concocted strange potions, and had animal "familiars" that were really demons (here a cat). Grien also highlights the sexual nature of witchcraft by portraying the women naked and showing them with goats, which were common symbols of sexuality. *(Germanisches Nationalmuseum Nürnberg)*

confessed to evil deeds and demonic practices, sometimes without torture, but where would we draw the line between reality and fantasy? Clearly people were not riding through the air on pitchforks, but did they think they did? Did they actually invoke the Devil when they were angry at a neighbor, or was this simply in the mind of their accusers? Trial records cannot tell us, and historians have answered these questions very differently, often using insights from psychoanalysis or the study of more recent victims of torture in their explanations.

Once the initial suspect had been questioned, and particularly if he or she had been tortured, the people who had been implicated were brought in for questioning. This might lead to a small hunt, involving from five to ten victims, and it sometimes grew into a much larger hunt, what historians have called a "witch panic." Panics were most common in the part of Europe that saw the most witch accusations in general—the Holy Roman Empire, Switzerland, and parts of France. Most of this area consisted of very small governmental units, which were jealous of each other and after the Reformation were divided by religion. The rulers of these small territories often felt more threatened than did the monarchs of western Europe, and they saw persecuting witches as a way to demonstrate their piety and concern for order.

Sometimes witch panics were the result of legal authorities' rounding up a group of suspects together. Such panics often occurred after some type of climatic disaster, such as an unusually cold and wet summer, and they came in waves. In large-scale panics a wider variety of suspects were taken in—wealthier people, children, a greater proportion of men. Mass panics tended to end when it became clear to legal authorities, or to the community itself, that the people being questioned or executed were not what they understood witches to be, or that the scope of accusations was beyond belief. Some from their community might be in league with Satan, they thought, but not this type of person and not as many as this.

Similar skepticism led to the gradual end of witch-hunts in Europe. Even in the sixteenth century a few individuals questioned whether witches could ever do harm, make a pact with the Devil, or engage in the wild activities attributed to them. Doubts about whether secret denunciations were valid or torture would ever yield a truthful confession gradually spread among the same type of religious and legal authorities who had so vigorously persecuted witches. Prosecutions for witchcraft became less common and were gradually outlawed. Sporadic trials continued into the eighteenth century, but by then people who thought themselves witches were more likely to be regarded as deluded or mentally defective, meriting pity rather than persecution, even by people who still firmly believed in the Devil. Belief in the power of witches continued among uneducated people, but educated people now sneered at this as superstition. People ceased to bring formal accusations when they knew they would simply be dismissed, and witch trials ended. The last official execution for witchcraft in England was in 1682, though the last one in the Holy Roman Empire was not until 1775.

Chapter Summary

Online Study Center **ACE the Test**

- *What were the central ideas of the reformers, and why were they appealing to different social groups?*
- *How did the political situation in Germany shape the course of the Reformation?*
- *How did Protestant ideas and institutions spread beyond German-speaking lands?*
- *How did the Catholic Church respond to the new religious situation?*
- *What were the causes and consequences of religious violence, including riots, wars, and witch-hunts?*

The Catholic Church in the early sixteenth century had serious problems, and many individuals and groups had long called for reform. This background of discontent helps explain why Martin Luther's ideas found such a ready audience. Luther and other Protestants developed a new understanding of Christian doctrine that emphasized faith, the power of God's grace, and the centrality of the Bible. Protestant ideas were attractive to educated people and urban residents, and they spread rapidly through preaching, hymns, and the printing press. By 1530 many parts of the Holy Roman Empire and Scandinavia had broken with the Catholic Church. Some reformers developed more radical ideas about infant baptism, the ownership of property, and separation between church and state. Both Protestants and Catholics regarded these as dangerous, and radicals were banished or executed. The German Peasants' War, in which Luther's ideas were linked to calls for social and economic reform, was similarly put down harshly. The Protestant reformers did not break with medieval ideas about the proper gender hierarchy, though they did elevate the status of marriage and viewed orderly households as the key building blocks of society.

The progress of the Reformation was shaped by the political situation in the Holy Roman Empire. The Habsburg emperor, Charles V, ruled almost half of Europe along with Spain's overseas colonies. Within the empire his authority was limited, however, and local princes, nobles, and cities actually held most power. This decentral-

ization allowed the Reformation to spread. Charles remained firmly Catholic, and in the 1530s religious wars began in Germany. These were brought to an end with the Peace of Augsburg in 1555, which allowed rulers to choose whether their territory would be Catholic or Lutheran.

In England the political issue of the royal succession triggered the break with Rome, and a Protestant church was established. Protestant ideas also spread into France and eastern Europe. In all these areas, a second generation of reformers built on Lutheran and Zwinglian ideas to develop their own theology and plans for institutional change. The most important of the second-generation reformers was John Calvin, whose ideas would come to shape Christianity over a much wider area than did Luther's.

The Roman Catholic Church responded slowly to the Protestant challenge, but by the 1530s the papacy was leading a movement for reform within the church instead of blocking it. Catholic doctrine was reaffirmed at the Council of Trent, and reform measures such as the opening of seminaries for priests and a ban on holding multiple church offices were introduced. New religious orders such as the Jesuits and the Ursulines spread Catholic ideas through teaching, and in the case of the Jesuits through missionary work.

Religious differences led to riots, civil wars, and international conflicts in the later sixteenth century. In France and the Netherlands, Calvinist Protestants and Catholics used violent actions against one another, and religious differences mixed with political and economic grievances. Long civil wars resulted, which in the case of the Netherlands became an international conflict. War ended in France with the Edict of Nantes in which Protestants were given some civil rights, and in the Netherlands with a division of the country into a Protestant north and Catholic south. The era of religious wars was also the time of the most extensive witch persecutions in European history, as both Protestants and Catholics tried to rid their cities and states of people they regarded as linked to the Devil.

Key Terms

anticlericalism
pluralism
indulgence
penance
purgatory
Diet of Worms
Protestant
transubstantiation
Book of Common Prayer
Elizabethan Settlement
The Institutes of the Christian Religion

predestination
Holy Office
Jesuits
Huguenots
iconoclasm
Saint Bartholomew's Day massacre
politiques
Edict of Nantes
Union of Utrecht
misogyny

Online Study Center **Improve Your Grade** Flashcards

Suggested Reading

Bossy, John. *Christianity in the West, 1500–1700*. 1985. A lively brief overview.

Bouwsma, William J. *John Calvin: A Sixteenth-Century Portrait*. 1988. An authoritative study that situates Calvin within Renaissance culture.

Elton, Geoffrey R. *Reform and Reformation: England, 1509–1558*. 1977. Combines religious, political, and social history.

Holt, Mack P. *The French Wars of Religion, 1562–1629*. 1995. A thorough survey designed for students.

Hsia, R. Po-Chia. *The World of Catholic Renewal, 1540–1770*. 1998. Situates the Catholic Reformation in a global context and provides coverage of colonial Catholicism.

Levack, Brian. *The Witchhunt in Early Modern Europe*, 3d ed. 2007. A good introduction to and helpful bibliographies of the vast literature on witchcraft.

Levi, Anthony. *Renaissance and Reformation: The Intellectual Genesis*. 2002. Surveys the ideas of major Reformation figures against the background of important political issues.

Lindbergh, Carter. *The European Reformations*. 1996. A thorough discussion of the Protestant Reformation and some discussion of Catholic issues.

Monter, William E. *Calvin's Geneva*. 1967. Shows the effect of Calvin's reforms on the social life of the Swiss city.

Oberman, Heiko. *Luther: Man Between God and the Devil*. 1989. Provides a thorough grounding in his thought.

O'Malley, John W. *Trent and All That: Renaming Catholicism in the Early Modern Era*. 2000. Provides an excellent historiographical review of the literature and explains why and how early modern Catholicism influenced early modern European history.

Roper, Lyndal. *The Holy Household: Women and Morals in Reformation Augsburg*. 1991. An important study in local religious history as well as the history of gender and the family.

Shagan, Ethan. *Popular Politics and the English Reformation*. 2003. Analyzes the process of the Reformation in local areas.

Wheatcroft, Andrew. *The Habsburgs: Embodying Empire*. 1995. A solid study of political developments surrounding the Reformation.

Notes

1. Quoted in O. Chadwick, *The Reformation* (Baltimore: Penguin Books, 1976), p. 55.
2. Quoted in E. H. Harbison, *The Age of Reformation* (Ithaca, N.Y.: Cornell University Press, 1963), p. 52.
3. Quoted in S. E. Ozment, *The Age of Reform, 1250–1550: An Intellectual and Religious History of Late Medieval and Reformation Europe* (New Haven, Conn.: Yale University Press, 1980), p. 280.
4. Quoted ibid., p. 281.
5. Quoted ibid., p. 284.
6. J. Allen, trans., *John Calvin: The Institutes of the Christian Religion* (Philadelphia: Westminster Press, 1930), bk. 3, chap. 21, paras. 5, 7.
7. E. W. Monter, *Calvin's Geneva* (New York: John Wiley & Sons, 1967), pp. 98–108.
8. Ibid., p. 137.
9. Quoted in R. H. Bainton, *Women of the Reformation in Germany and Italy* (Minneapolis: Augsburg, 1971), pp. 69–70.
10. Quoted in D. P. Daniel, "Hungary," in *The Oxford Encyclopedia of the Reformation*, vol. 2, ed. H. J. Hillerbrand (New York: Oxford University Press, 1996), p. 273.
11. Quoted in Chadwick, *The Reformation*, p. 270.
12. See J. W. O'Malley, *The First Jesuits* (Cambridge, Mass.: Harvard University Press, 1993), p. 376.
13. Ibid., p. 298.

Martin Luther, *On Christian Liberty*

The idea of liberty or freedom has played a *powerful role in the history of Western society and culture, but the meaning and understanding of liberty has undergone continual change and interpretation. In the Roman world, where slavery was a basic institution, liberty meant the condition of being a free man, independent of obligations to a master. In the Middle Ages possessing liberty meant having special privileges or rights that other persons or institutions did not have. A lord or a monastery, for example, might speak of his or its liberties, and citizens in London were said to possess the "freedom of the city," which allowed them to practice trades and own property without interference. Likewise, the first chapter of Magna Carta (1215), often called the "Charter of Liberties," states: "Holy Church shall be free and have its rights entire and its liberties inviolate," meaning that the English church was independent of the authority of the king.*

The idea of liberty also has a religious dimension, and the reformer Martin Luther formulated a classic interpretation of liberty in his treatise On Christian Liberty (*sometimes translated* On the Freedom of a Christian), *arguably his finest piece. Written in Latin for the pope but translated immediately into German and published widely, it contains the main themes of Luther's theology: the importance of faith, the relationship of Christian faith and good works, the dual nature of human beings, and the fundamental importance of Scripture. Luther writes that Christians were freed from sin and death through Christ, not through their own actions.*

Christian faith has appeared to many an easy thing; nay, not a few even reckon it among the social virtues, as it were; and this they do because they have not made proof of it experimentally, and have never tasted of what efficacy it is. For it is not possible for any man to write well about it, or to understand well what is rightly written, who has not at some time tasted of its spirit, under the pressure of tribulation; while he who has tasted

of it, even to a very small extent, can never write, speak, think, or hear about it sufficiently. . . .

I hope that . . . I have attained some little drop of faith, and that I can speak of this matter, if not with more elegance, certainly with more solidity. . . .

A Christian man is the most free lord of all, and subject to none; a Christian man is the most dutiful servant of all, and subject to everyone.

Although these statements appear contradictory, yet, when they are found to agree together, they will do excellently for my purpose. They are both the statements of Paul himself, who says, "Though I be free from all men, yet have I made myself a servant unto all" (I Cor. 9:19), and "Owe no man anything but to love one another" (Rom. 13:8). Now love is by its own nature dutiful and obedient to the beloved object. Thus even Christ, though Lord of all things, was yet made of a woman; made under the law; at once free and a servant; at once in the form of God and in the form of a servant.

Let us examine the subject on a deeper and less simple principle. Man is composed of a twofold nature, a spiritual and a bodily. As regards the spiritual nature, which they name the soul, he is called the spiritual, inward, new man; as regards the bodily nature, which they name the flesh, he is called the fleshly, outward, old man. The Apostle speaks of this: "Though our outward man perish, yet the inward man is renewed day by day" (II Cor. 4:16). The result of this diversity is that in the Scriptures opposing statements are made concerning the same man, the fact being that in the same man these two men are opposed to one another; the flesh lusting against the spirit, and the spirit against the flesh (Gal. 5:17).

We first approach the subject of the inward man, that we may see by what means a man becomes justified, free, and a true Christian; that is, a spiritual, new, and inward man. It is certain that absolutely none among outward things, under whatever name they may be reckoned, has any influence in producing Christian righteousness or liberty, nor, on the other hand, unrighteousness or slavery. This can be shown by an easy argument.

What can it profit to the soul that the body should be in good condition, free, and full of life, that it should eat, drink, and act according to its pleasure, when even the most impious slaves of every kind of vice are prosperous in these matters? Again, what harm can ill health, bondage, hunger, thirst, or any other outward evil, do to the soul, when even the most pious of men, and the freest in the purity of their conscience, are harassed by these things? Neither of these states of things has to do with the liberty or the slavery of the soul.

And so it will profit nothing that the body should be adorned with sacred vestment, or dwell in holy places, or be occupied in sacred offices, or pray, fast, and abstain from certain meats, or do whatever works can be done through the body and in the body. Something widely different will be necessary for the justification and liberty of the soul, since the things I have spoken of can be done by an impious person, and only hypocrites are produced by devotion to these things. On the other hand, it will not at all injure the soul that the body should be clothed in profane raiment, should dwell in profane places, should eat and drink in the ordinary fashion, should not pray aloud, and should leave undone all the things above mentioned, which may be done by hypocrites.

. . . One thing, and one alone, is necessary for life, justification, and Christian liberty; and that is the most Holy Word of God, the Gospel of Christ, as He says, "I am the resurrection and the life; he that believeth in me shall not die eternally" (John 9:25), and also, "If the Son shall make you free, ye shall be free indeed" (John 8:36), and "Man shall not live by bread alone, but by every word that proceedeth out of the mouth of God" (Matt. 4:4).

Let us therefore hold it for certain and firmly established that the soul can do without everything except the Word of God, without which none at all of its wants is provided for. But, having the Word, it is rich and wants for nothing, since that is the Word of life, of truth, of light, of peace, of justification, of salvation, of joy, of liberty, of wisdom, of virtue, of grace, of glory, and of every good thing. . . .

But you will ask, "What is this Word, and by what means is it to be used, since there are so many words of God?" I answer, "The Apostle Paul (Rom. 1) explains what it is, namely the Gospel of God, concerning His Son, incarnate, suffering, risen, and glorified through the Spirit, the Sanctifier." To preach Christ is to feed the soul, to justify it, to set it free, and to save it, if it believes the preaching. For faith alone, and the efficacious use of the Word of

On effective preaching, especially to the uneducated, Luther urged the minister "to keep it simple for the simple." *(Church of St. Marien, Wittenberg/The Bridgeman Art Library)*

God, bring salvation. "If thou shalt confess with thy mouth the Lord Jesus, and shalt believe in thine heart that God hath raised Him from the dead, thou shalt be saved" (Rom. 9:9); . . . and "The just shall live by faith" (Rom. 1:17). . . .

But this faith cannot consist of all with works; that is, if you imagine that you can be justified by those works, whatever they are, along with it. . . . Therefore, when you begin to believe, you learn at the same time that all that is in you is utterly guilty, sinful, and damnable, according to that saying, "All have sinned, and come short of the glory of God" (Rom. 3:23). . . . When you have learned this, you will know that Christ is necessary for you, since He has suffered and risen again for you, that, believing on Him, you might by this faith become another man, all your sins being remitted, and you being justified by the merits of another, namely Christ alone.

. . . [A]nd since it [faith] alone justifies, it is evident that by no outward work or labour can the inward man be at all justified, made free, and saved; and that no works whatever have any relation to him. . . . Therefore the first care of every Christian ought to be to lay aside all reliance on works, and strengthen his faith alone more and more, and by it grow in knowledge, not of works, but of Christ Jesus, who has suffered and risen again for him, as Peter teaches (I Peter 5).

Questions for Analysis

1. What did Luther mean by liberty?

2. Why, for Luther, was Scripture basic to Christian life?

Source: Luther's Primary Works, ed. H. Wace and C. A. Buchheim (London: Holder and Stoughton, 1896). Reprinted in *The Portable Renaissance Reader,* ed. James Bruce Ross and Mary Martin McLaughlin (New York: Penguin Books, 1981), pp. 721–726.

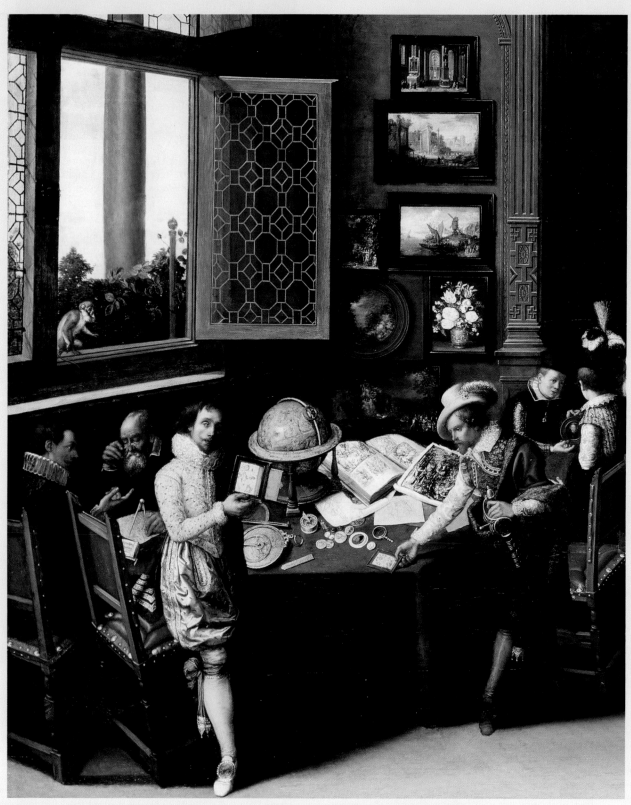

A detail from an early-seventeenth-century Flemish painting depicting maps, illustrated travel books, a globe, a compass, and an astrolabe. *(Reproduced by courtesy of the Trustees, The National Gallery, London)*

chapter

15

chapter preview

World Contacts Before Columbus
• *What was the Afro-Eurasian trading world before Columbus?*

The European Voyages of Discovery
• *How and why did Europeans undertake ambitious voyages of expansion that would usher in a new era of global contact?*

Europe and the World After Columbus
• *What effect did overseas expansion have on the conquered societies, on enslaved Africans, and on world trade?*

Changing Attitudes and Beliefs
• *How did culture and art in this period respond to social and cultural transformation?*

EUROPEAN EXPLORATION AND CONQUEST, 1450–1650

Prior to 1400 Europeans were relatively marginal players in a centuries-old trading system that linked Africa, Asia, and Europe. Elite classes everywhere prized Chinese porcelains and silks, while wealthy members of the Celestial Kingdom, as China called itself, wanted ivory and black slaves from East Africa, and exotic goods and peacocks from India. African people wanted textiles from India and cowrie shells from the Maldive Islands. Europeans craved spices and silks, but they had few desirable goods to offer their trading partners.

Within little more than a century, European nations had embarked on a remarkably ambitious project to dominate this trading system. The European search for Southeast Asian spices led to a new overseas empire in the Indian Ocean and the accidental discovery of the Western Hemisphere. Within a short time, South and North America had joined a worldwide economic and imperial web. The results were trading networks and political empires of truly global proportions. The era of "globalization" had begun.

European states' intrusions into Indian Ocean trade and into new economies in the New World gave them wealth and power. Over time the old Asian-dominated trading world gave way to a new European-dominated one that encompassed the vast territories of the Americas and the Pacific Ocean. Global contacts created new forms of cultural exchange, assimilation, conversion, and resistance. Europeans sought to impose their cultural values on the people they encountered and struggled to comprehend the peoples and societies they found. New forms of racial prejudice emerged in this period, but so did new openness and curiosity about different ways of life. Together with the developments of the Renaissance and the Reformation, the Age of Discovery laid the foundations for the modern world as we know it today.

World Contacts Before Columbus

Columbus did not sail west on a whim. To understand his voyages—and the European explorations that preceded and succeeded them—we must

Online Study Center

This icon will direct you to interactive activities and study materials on the website **college.hmco.com/pic/mckaywest9e**

first understand late medieval trade networks. Historians now recognize important ties between Europe and other parts of the world prior to Columbus's voyages, arguing that a type of "world economy" linked the products and people of Europe, Asia, and Africa in the fifteenth century. The West was not the dominant player in 1492, and the European voyages derived from the possibilities and constraints of this system. The global impact of the discoveries in the New World must be viewed in the context of this world trading system, which it would in turn revolutionize.

● *What was the Afro-Eurasian trading world before Columbus?*

The Trading World of the Indian Ocean

The center of the pre-Columbian world trade network was the Indian Ocean, the globe's third-largest waterway (after the Atlantic and Pacific). To the west its arms reach into the Red and Arabian Seas, through the former to the Mediterranean Sea, and through the latter into the Persian Gulf and southwestern Asia. To the north the Indian Ocean joins the Bay of Bengal; to the east the Pacific; and to the south the west coast of Australia (see Map 15.1). The monsoon winds blow from the west or south between April and August, and from the northwest or northeast between December and March. These seasonal climate patterns determined the rhythms of trade.

The location of the Indian Ocean made it a crossroads for commercial and cultural exchange. Since Han and Roman times, seaborne trade between China (always the biggest market for Southeast Asian goods), India, the Middle East, Africa, and Europe had flowed across the Indian Ocean. From the seventh through the thirteenth centuries, the volume of this trade steadily increased. After a period of decline resulting from the Black Death, demand for Southeast Asian goods accelerated once more in the late fourteenth century.

Merchants congregated in a series of port cities strung around the ocean that harbored a bewildering array of peoples and cultures. The most developed area of this commercial web lay to the east on the South China Sea. In the fifteenth century the port of **Malacca** became a great commercial **entrepôt,** to which goods were shipped for temporary storage while awaiting redistribution to other places. To Malacca came Chinese porcelains, silks, and camphor (used in the manufacture of many medications, including those to reduce fevers); pepper, cloves, nutmeg, and raw materials such as sappanwood and san-

dalwood from the Moluccas; sugar from the Philippines; and Indian printed cotton and woven tapestries, copper weapons, incense, dyes, and opium. Merchants at Malacca stockpiled goods in fortified warehouses while waiting for the next monsoon. With its many mosques and elegant homes, Malacca enjoyed the reputation of being a sophisticated city, full of "music, ballads, and poetry."[1]

Women in Southeast Asia enjoyed relatively high autonomy. Their important role in planting and harvesting rice, the traditional agricultural crop, gave them authority and economic power. In contrast to Europe, the more daughters a Southeast Asian man had, the richer he was. At marriage the groom paid the bride (or sometimes her family) a sum of money, called bride wealth, which remained under her control. This practice was in sharp contrast to the European dowry, which was provided by the wife's family and came under the husband's control. Married couples usually resided in the wife's village and administered property jointly. All children, regardless of gender, inherited equally, and even after Islam took root in parts of the region, the rule that sons receive double the inheritance of daughters was never implemented.

This respect for women's capacity to handle financial affairs carried over to the commercial sphere. Women participated in business as independent entrepreneurs or partners in family businesses, even undertaking long sea voyages to accompany their wares. When Portuguese and Dutch men settled in the region and married local women, their wives continued to play an important role in trade and commerce.

China played a key role in the fifteenth-century revival of Indian Ocean trade. Given its size and its sophisticated artisanal production, China was an economic powerhouse. Historians agree that medieval China had the most advanced economy in the world; one scholar's controversial theory is that its economic superiority to the West continued to 1800.[2]

The Mongol emperors opened the doors of China to the West, encouraging European traders like Marco Polo to do business there. Marco Polo's tales of his travels from 1271 to 1295 and his encounter with the Great Khan fueled Western fantasies about the exotic "Orient." Unbeknownst to the West, the Mongols fell to the new Ming Dynasty in 1368. During the Ming Dynasty (1368–1644), China entered a period of agricultural and commercial expansion, population growth, and urbanization. By the end of the dynasty, the Chinese population had doubled to perhaps 100 million people. The city of Nanjing had one million inhabitants, making it the largest city in the world, while the new capital, Beijing, had more than six hundred thousand inhabitants.

Population growth was one reason for the Chinese desire for more goods. Another was the celebrated naval expeditions led by **Admiral Zheng He.** Between 1405 and 1433 Zheng He led seven voyages to achieve the emperor Yongle's diplomatic, political, geographical, and commercial goals. Yongle wanted to secure China's hegemony over tributary states and form new tribute-paying relations with profitable trade centers. Zheng He's first fleet was composed of 317 ships—including junks, supply ships, water tankers, warships, transports for horses, and patrol boats—carrying twenty-eight thousand sailors and soldiers. Because it bore tons of beautiful porcelains, elegant silks, lacquer ware, and exquisite artifacts to be exchanged for goods abroad, the Chinese called it the "treasure fleet." Sailing as far west as Egypt, the expeditions brought back spices, books, hardwood, and a giraffe from the kingdom of Mali for the imperial zoo. Zheng He may have been appointed commander because as a Muslim he could more easily negotiate with Muslim merchants on the Indian Ocean.

Court conflicts and the need to defend against renewed Mongol encroachment led to the abandonment of the expeditions and shipbuilding after the deaths of Zheng He and the emperor. Despite the Chinese decision not to pursue overseas voyages, trade continued in the South China Sea. A vast immigration of Chinese people to Southeast Asia, sometimes called the Chinese diaspora, followed the expeditions. Immigrants carried with them Chinese culture, including social customs, diet, and practical objects of Chinese technology—calendars, books, scales for weights and measures, and musical instruments.

Another center of trade in the Indian Ocean was India, the crucial link between the Persian Gulf and the Southeast Asian and East Asian trade networks. The subcontinent had ancient links with its neighbors to the northwest: trade between South Asia and Mesopotamia dates back to the origins of civilization. Fashionable women of the Roman Empire were addicted to Indian cotton; and until the decline of Rome exotic animals, ivory, and Chinese silk also made their way to Europe through India. Trade with the Indian Ocean was revived by Arab merchants who circumnavigated India on their way to trade in the South China Sea. The need for stopovers led to the establishment of trading posts at Gujarat and on the Malabar coast, where the cities of Calicut and Quilon became thriving commercial centers.

The inhabitants of India's southeast, Coromandel Coast, traditionally looked east to Southeast Asia, where they had ancient trading and cultural ties. Hinduism and Buddhism arrived in Southeast Asia from India during the Middle Ages, and a brisk trade between Southeast

Chronology

1443	Portuguese establish first African trading post at Arguim
1450–1650	Age of Discovery
1492	Columbus lands on San Salvador
1511	Portuguese capture Malacca from Muslims
1518	Atlantic slave trade begins
1519–1522	Magellan's expedition circumnavigates the world
1520	Spaniards defeat Aztec army
1532	Pizarro arrives in Peru and defeats Inca Empire
1547	Oviedo, *General History of the Indies*
1570–1630	Worldwide commercial boom
1602	Dutch East India Company established

Asian and Coromandel port cities persisted through the early modern period. India itself was an important contributor of goods to the world trading system. Most of the world's pepper was grown in India, and Indian cotton and silk textiles, mainly from the Gujarat region, were also highly prized.

The Indian Ocean trading system was characterized by ancient and active trade conducted from multicultural, cosmopolitan port cities, most of which had some form of autonomous self-government. When the Portuguese arrived, they found a rich commercial world in which mutual self-interest had largely limited violence and attempts to monopolize trade. As one historian stated, "before the arrival of the Portuguese . . . in 1498 there had been no organised attempt by any political power to control the sea-lanes and the long-distance trade of Asia. . . . The Indian Ocean as a whole and its different seas were not dominated by any particular nations or empires."[3]

Africa

Often neglected by historians, Africa played an important role in the world trade system before Columbus. Around 1450 Africa had a few large and developed empires along with hundreds of smaller polities. From 1250 until its defeat by the Ottomans in the sixteenth century, the Mameluke Egyptian empire was one of the most

MAP 15.1 The Afro-Eurasian Trading World Before Columbus   The Indian Ocean was the center of the Afro-Eurasian trading world. After a period of decline following the Black Death and the Mongol invasions, trade revived in the fifteenth century. Muslim merchants dominated trade, linking ports in East Africa and the Red Sea with those in India and the Malay Archipelago. The Chinese Admiral Zheng He's voyages (1405–1433) followed the most important Indian Ocean trade routes, hoping to impose Ming dominance of trade and tribute.   (*Source: Some data from The Times Atlas of World History, 3d ed., page 146.*)

The Port of Banten in Western Java   Influenced by Muslim traders and emerging in the early sixteenth century as a Muslim kingdom, Banten evolved into a thriving entrepôt. The city stood on the trade route to China and, as this Dutch engraving suggests, in the seventeenth century the Dutch East India Company used Banten as an important collection point for spices purchased for sale in Europe. *(Archives Charmet/The Bridgeman Art Library)*

powerful on the continent. Its capital, Cairo, was a center of Islamic learning and religious authority as well as a hub for Indian Ocean trade goods, which the Mamelukes helped to re-orient through the Red Sea. Sharing in the newfound Red Sea prosperity was the African highland state of Ethiopia, which in 1270, saw the rise of a new dynasty claiming descent from the biblical King Solomon and the Queen of Sheba. On the east coast of Africa Swahili-speaking city-states engaged in the Indian Ocean trade, exchanging ivory, rhinoceros horn, tortoise shells, copra, and slaves for textiles, spices, cowrie shells, porcelain, and other goods. The most important cities were Mogadishu, Mombasa, and Kilwa, which had converted to Islam by the eleventh century. Peopled by confident and urbane merchants, they were known for their prosperity and culture.

Another important African contribution to world trade was gold. In the fifteenth century most of the gold that

reached Europe came from Sudan in West Africa and from the Akan peoples living near present-day Ghana. After the introduction of camels around A.D. 300, trade routes crisscrossed the Sahara. In exchange for Saharan salt, Arab and African traders brought gold from the cities of Niani and Timbuktu to be sold in the Mediterranean ports of Fez, Marrakesh, Tunis, and Tripoli. Other trading routes led to the Egyptian cities of Alexandria and Cairo, where the Venetians held commercial privileges.

Nations in the inland savannah that sat astride the north-south caravan routes grew wealthy from this trade. In the mid-thirteenth century Sundiata Keita founded the powerful kingdom of Mali. African merchants carried not only goods, but also ideas, helping spread Islam to West Africa. The celebrated pilgrimage of Keita's successor, **Mansa Musa,** to Mecca in 1324 underscores the links between West Africa and the Muslim world in this period. On his way to Mecca, Musa arrived in Cairo with a caravan that included sixty thousand people and eighty camels, with more than two tons of gold for gifts. Word of this spectacular caravan spread across Europe. The famous Spanish world map of 1375, known as the Catalan atlas, depicts Musa as the king of Africa with scepter in one hand and gold nugget in another. He reportedly even discussed sending vessels to explore the Atlantic Ocean, suggesting that not only Europeans envisaged westward naval exploration.

Mansa Musa used his wealth to invest in new mosques and religious schools, making Timbuktu a renowned center of culture and learning. The Muslim traveler Ibn Battuta visited the city and remarked on the rigorous discipline in its religious schools and also on the "extraordinary" state of affairs between men and women. Not only did families trace descent through the mother's line, but the "women show no bashfulness before men and do not veil themselves, though they are assiduous in attending the prayers."[4] Both husbands and wives, he reported, could have "friends" and "companions" of the opposite sex without provoking dishonor or jealousy. By the time the Portuguese arrived, however, the Malian empire was fading, to be replaced by the Songhay, who themselves fell to Moroccan invasion at the end of the sixteenth century. The Portuguese diversion of gold away from the trans-Sahara routes weakened this area politically and economically, and led to its decline as a center of Islamic scholarship.

Gold was one important object of trade; slaves were another. Slavery was practiced in Africa, as virtually everywhere else in the world, before the arrival of Europeans. Arabic and African merchants crossed the Sahara in both directions with slaves. They took West African slaves to the Mediterranean to be sold in European, Egyptian, or Mideastern markets and also brought eastern Europeans—a major element of European slavery—to West Africa as slaves. In addition, Indian and Arabic merchants traded slaves in the coastal regions of East Africa. European contact would revolutionize the magnitude and character of African slavery (see page 508).

Africa—or legends about Africa—played an important role in Europeans' imagination of the outside world. They long cherished the belief in a Christian nation in Africa ruled by a mythical king, Prester John, thought to be a descendant of one of the three kings who visited Jesus after his birth. In 1165 a letter purportedly written by Prester John to the Byzantine emperor describing the king's vast wealth and the fantastic subjects over whom he ruled appeared in Europe. The letter also promised friendship and solidarity with Christian Europe against Islam. Portuguese explorers carried letters of introduction to Prester John on their voyages along the African coast and were convinced they had found him when, in 1520, a Portuguese embassy reached the Christian Ethiopian court.

The Ottoman and Persian Empires

The Middle East was crucial to the late medieval world trade system, serving as an intermediary for trade from all points of the compass. It was situated at the crossroads between the Baltic States, Central Asia, and Russia to the north; Arabia, Egypt, and East Africa to the south; the Mediterranean, Europe, and West and North Africa to the west; and Southeast and East Asia to the east. In addition to serving as a conduit to trade, the Middle East was an important supplier of goods for foreign exchange, especially silk and cotton.

The most famous trade route leading through the Middle East was the ancient Silk Road that linked the West to the Far East. After its collapse in the aftermath of Mongol rule in the fourteenth century, merchants turned to a northern overland route, which led from the Baltic Sea to Russia, Central Asia, and China. Along this route traveled slaves, fur and timber to the east, and Asian luxury goods to the west. Even more important were the two southern sea routes that brought products from the Indian Ocean trading system. The first came across the Arabian Sea and then up the Red Sea past Aden to Cairo. The second led past Hormuz up the Persian Gulf and on to Baghdad. Standing at the mouths of two seas, Aden and Hormuz had vital economic and strategic importance. From the magnificent capitals of Cairo and Baghdad, goods were sent to bustling trading posts on the eastern Mediterranean coast, such as Alexandria, Damascus, Beirut, and Aleppo.

Two great rival Islamic empires, the Turkish Ottomans and the Persian Safavids, dominated this region. The Ottomans combined excellent military strategy with efficient administration of their conquered territories. Under Sultan Mohammed II (r. 1451–1481), the Ottomans captured **Constantinople** in May 1453, sending shock waves through Europe. Renamed Istanbul, the city became the capital of the Ottoman Empire. With a population of 600,000 to 750,000, it was by far the largest city in Europe and the Middle East and rivaled the great Chinese cities in size.

Online Study Center **Improve Your Grade**
Primary Source: The Fall of Constantinople to the Ottomans: A Lamentation

Having completed the conquest of Anatolia in 1461, the emperor Suleiman I (1494–1566) pressed northwest into the Balkans and by the early sixteenth century controlled the sea trade on the eastern Mediterranean. In 1516 the sultan's forces took Syria and Palestine, followed by Egypt in 1517 and the rest of northern Africa. After defeating the Hungarian king in 1526 and bringing portions of his kingdom into the empire, Suleiman turned to the Habsburg state ruled by Ferdinand I, brother to Habsburg emperor Charles V. In 1529 the Turks besieged the Habsburg capital of Vienna. After a siege of several weeks and high casualties on both sides, the Turks retreated, leaving Vienna as the westward limit of Ottoman expansion into Europe.

Ottoman expansion had political, economic, and religious goals. The Ottomans wished to control the Balkans and the Mediterranean so as to monopolize trade routes with the West and spread Islamic rule. The Balkans themselves were a precious source of timber, dye, and silver. With the defeat of the Mameluke empire, expansion into Egypt gave the Ottomans new access to sources of African gold and control over Red Sea shipping. Similarly, conquest of Baghdad brought control of shipping west out of the Persian Gulf.

Turkish expansion badly frightened Europeans. Ottoman armies seemed nearly invincible and the empire's desire for expansion limitless. In France in the sixteenth century, twice as many books were printed about the Turkish threat as about the American discoveries. The strength of the Ottomans helps explain some of the missionary fervor Christians brought to new territories. It also raised economic concerns. With trade routes to the east in the hands of the Ottomans, Europeans were convinced that they needed new trade routes.

Europeans were not alone in opposing Ottoman ambitions. In the early sixteenth century the Persian Safavid Empire became a powerful Muslim state, reaching its height under Shah Abbas I (r. 1587–1629). Like the Ottomans, the Persians were important intermediary figures in the Afro-Eurasian trading system. Persian merchants could be found throughout this trading world in diaspora communities they formed as far away as the Indian Ocean. Persia was also a major producer and exporter of silk.

The Safavids had complex, often hostile relations with their Ottoman neighbors. Although both were Muslim states, the Ottomans' Sunni faith clashed with the Persians' adherence to Shi'ism. Economically, the two competed for control over trade routes to the east. These conflicts led to the Ottoman-Safavid war of 1615–1618 and to periodic confrontations in the following years.

The Taking of Constantinople by the Turks, April 22, 1453 The Ottoman conquest of the capital of the Byzantine Empire in 1453 sent waves of shock and despair through Europe. Capitalizing on the city's strategic and commercial importance, the Ottomans made it the center of their empire. *(Bibliothèque nationale de France)*

However, the two empires also relied on each other economically; for example, the Ottoman silk industry depended on raw silk imported from Iran.[5]

Despite the fear generated by the Ottomans and the military clashes between Ottoman and European forces, it is important to emphasize that no "iron curtain" separated Christian Europe from the Muslim Middle East. Despite explicit religious laws dividing the world into Muslims and infidels, in practice the Ottoman state tolerated religious differences, protecting Christian and Jewish lives and property. Foreign merchants, travelers, and pilgrims were permitted to enter, and the cities of the empire had established settlements of Christian merchants (see Chapter 17).

It is also important to emphasize the disunities within each world. "Muslims" could be Mameluke Egyptians, Ottomans, Persians, Indians, Africans, or Southeast Asians. In many ways Islam helped foster commerce by offering a common Islamic commercial law and culture; however, there were also many divisions among Muslims. Rivalries among European powers as well as among Muslim states like the Sunni Ottomans and the Shi'ite Persians encouraged a shifting pattern of pragmatic and self-interested alliances that breached the borders supposedly dividing East and West. Eventually the Turks formed a loose alliance with the Portuguese against the Persians, which helped both sides ameliorate their trading positions. For his part, Shah Abbas I sent emissaries to Europe seeking alliances against the Ottomans. He offered trade concessions to the English for their help in eliminating the Portuguese from Hormuz. Before then the Safavids had purchased arms from the Portuguese (acquired from India) to use in combat with the Ottomans.

Genoese and Venetian Middlemen

Europe was the western terminus of the world trading system. Before the Portuguese and Spanish voyages, the Italian city-states of Venice and Genoa controlled the European luxury trade with the East. Centuries-old rivals for this trade, Venice and Genoa both lost importance with the rise of Ottoman power in the eastern Mediterranean and with Portuguese, then Dutch, intrusion into the **spice trade** at its source. After a brilliant period during the late Middle Ages, they entered a long period of decline. However, Italian experience in colonial administration, slaving, and international trade and finance served as crucial models for the Iberian states as they pushed European expansion to new heights. Mariners, merchants, and financiers from Venice and Genoa—most notably Christopher Columbus—played a crucial role in bringing the fruits of this experience to the Iberian Peninsula.

Venice grew in importance with the creation of the Crusader kingdoms, gaining territory and special trading concessions in return for aiding the Crusader armies. The Venetian fleet sacked Constantinople in 1204, placing a new emperor on the throne and gaining exclusive trading rights. When the political situation reversed and they lost those privileges, the Venetians turned their attention south. In 1304 the city established formal relations with the sultan of Mameluke Egypt, opening permanent offices in Cairo, the gateway to trade from India, Southeast Asia, and China.

Venice specialized in expensive luxury goods like spices, silks, and carpets. Venetian traders did not, as later Europeans did, explore new routes to get to the sources of supply of these goods. Instead, they obtained them from middlemen in the eastern Mediterranean and Asia Minor. A little went a long way. Venetians purchased no more than five hundred tons of spices a year around 1400, but with a profit of around 40 percent. The most important by far was pepper, grown in India and Indonesia, which composed 60 percent of the spices they purchased in 1400. In all, one historian has estimated that 70 percent of the Western trade in spices belonged to the Venetians.[6] Other imported goods included grain and sugar from Egypt and silk and cotton from Syria. Venetian merchants redistributed these goods throughout Europe.

Another major element of Venetian trade was slavery. Venetian merchants purchased slaves, many of whom were fellow Christians, in the Balkans. The men went to Egypt for the sultan's army or to work as agricultural laborers on Venetian possessions in the Mediterranean. Young girls, who made up the majority of the trade, were sold in western Mediterranean ports as servants or concubines.

The Venetians exchanged Eastern luxury goods for European products they could trade abroad, including Spanish and English wool, German metal goods, Flemish textiles, and silk cloth made in their own manufactures with imported raw materials. The demand for such goods in the East, however, was low. To make up the difference, the Venetians earned currency in the shipping industry and through trade in firearms and slaves. At least half of what they traded with the East took the form of precious metal, much of it acquired in Egypt and North Africa. When the Portuguese arrived in Asia, they found Venetian coins everywhere.

The spice trade brought riches and power to Venice. After the catastrophe of the Black Death, Venice reached the height of its glory in the 1400s. By 1500 the city's population was 120,000, making it one of the largest in Europe. From its origins as a small fishing village in the sixth century A.D., Venice had created a sizable empire. It controlled an expansive region on the Italian peninsula and had trading posts in North Africa, the Levant, and northern Europe in addition to outright colonies on the west coast of the Adriatic. The islands of Crete and later Cyprus were also controlled by Venice.

Merchant wealth endowed the city with beautiful buildings, art, and a rich and vibrant culture, whose legacy can

Bellini: Procession in the Piazza San Marco   The Piazza San Marco was, and remains, the principal square of Venice. Located on the Grand Canal, it is home to Saint Mark's Basilica and the palace of the doge, the officer elected for life by the city's aristocracy to rule the city. Many Venetian festivals, like this procession recorded in 1496 by the great artist Gentile Bellini, took place in the square. *(Erich Lessing/Art Resource, NY)*

still be appreciated today. The Venetian city-state organized international trade meticulously; its impressive fleet of state-sponsored ships was one of the finest naval forces in Europe.

French invasions in the 1490s distracted and weakened the city, as did the new claims on the spice trade made by the Portuguese in the early 1500s, which the Venetians' Egyptian allies were unable to counter. The Ottoman conquest of Egypt in 1516 raised Venice's hopes briefly. Eager to improve Red Sea trade and to oppose Portuguese attempts to monopolize the spice trade, the Ottomans encouraged traders to bypass Portuguese ports. Spices began to flow again through the Red Sea to Venetian merchants in Cairo. By the 1600s, however, the Dutch had succeeded in monopolizing this trade, ending Venice's centuries-old role as the main European entrepôt for Asian spices. Venice also lost its eastern Mediterranean colonies to Ottoman conquest, leading to a loss of supplies of slaves and other trade goods.

Venice's ancient rival was Genoa. As was the case with Venice, Genoa's fortunes rose with its participation in the Crusades. Having undone Venetian control of Constan-tinople, Genoa dominated the northern route to Asia through the Black Sea. Expansion in the thirteenth and fourteenth centuries took the Genoese as far as Persia and the Far East. In 1291 they sponsored an expedition into the Atlantic in search of "parts of India" by the Vivaldi brothers. The ships were lost, and their exact destination and motivations remain unknown. However, the voyage underlines the long history of Genoese aspirations for Atlantic exploration.

In the fifteenth century Genoa made a bold change of direction. With Venice claiming victory over the spice trade, the Genoese shifted focus from trade to finance and from the Black Sea to the western Mediterranean. Given its location on the northwestern coast of Italy, Genoa had always been active in the western Mediterranean, trading with North African ports, southern France, Spain, and even England and Flanders through the Strait of Gibraltar. When new voyages took place in the western Atlantic, Genoese merchants, navigators, and financiers provided their skills to the Iberian monarchs, whose own subjects had much less commercial experience. The Genoese, for example, ran many of the sugar plantations established on the Atlantic islands colonized by the Portuguese. From their settlement in Seville, Genoese merchants financed Spanish colonization of the New World and conducted profitable trade with its colonies.

The Genoese were also enthusiastic slavers. Like the Venetians, they supplied slaves for agricultural labor on their colonial possessions and as slave soldiers to Mameluke Egypt. Once more, the majority of the slaves were young women sent to serve in southern Europe or Genoa. It was a brutal trade:

In a ship sailing from the Crimea to Chios in 1455 30 per cent of the slaves on board died. Genoese law accepted that a master could beat his slave to death, whilst for the rape of a female the punishment was merely a modest fine combined with the obligation to compensate her owner for the damage to his property.[7]

After the loss of the Black Sea—and thus the source of slaves—to the Ottomans, the Genoese sought new supplies in the West, taking the Guanches (indigenous peoples from the Canary Islands), Muslim prisoners and Jewish refugees from Spain, and by the early 1500s both black and Berber Africans. With the growth of Spanish colonies in the New World, Genoese merchants became important players in the Atlantic slave trade.

The European Voyages of Discovery

As we have seen, Europe was by no means isolated before the voyages of exploration and the "discovery" of the New World; the Europeans were aware of and in contact with the riches of the Indian Ocean trading world. From the time of the Crusades, Italian merchants brought the products of the East to luxury markets in Europe eager for silks, spices, porcelain, and other fine goods. But because they did not produce many products desired by Eastern elites, Europeans were relatively modest players in the Afro-Eurasian trading world. Their limited role was reduced even further in the mid-fourteenth century, when the Black Death, combined with the ravages of the Mongol warlord Tamerlane, led to a collapse in trade routes and commercial markets.

From these lows, however, Europeans would soon undertake new and unprecedented expansion. As population and trade recovered, new European players entered the scene, eager to spread Christianity and to undo Italian dominance of trade with the East. A century after the plague, Iberian explorers began the overseas voyages that helped create the modern world, with staggering conse-

quences for their own continent and the rest of the planet.

● *How and why did Europeans undertake ambitious voyages of expansion that would usher in a new era of global contact?*

Causes of European Expansion

European expansion had multiple causes. By the middle of the fifteenth century, Europe was experiencing a revival of population and economic activity after the lows of the Black Death. While this revival was not sufficient to create population pressure in Europe, it did create new demands for luxury goods from the East and for spices in particular. The fall of Constantinople in 1453 and subsequent Ottoman control of trade routes created obstacles to fulfilling these desires. Europeans needed to find new sources of precious metal to trade with the Ottomans or sources of supply for themselves and thereby eliminate Ottoman interference.

Why were spices so desirable? Introduced into western Europe by the Crusaders in the twelfth century, pepper, nutmeg, ginger, mace, cinnamon, and cloves added flavor and variety to the monotonous diet of Europeans. Spices evoked the scent of the Garden of Eden; they seemed a marvel and a mystery. It is also important to remember that the term *spices* referred not only to flavorings added to food but also to perfumes, medicines, drugs, and dyes. Take, for example, cloves, for which Europeans found many uses. If picked green and sugared, the buds could be transformed into conserve (a kind of jam); if salted and pickled, cloves became a flavoring for vinegar. Cloves sweetened the breath. When added to food or drink, cloves were thought to stimulate the appetite and clear the intestines and bladder. When crushed and powdered, they were a medicine rubbed on the forehead to relieve head colds and applied to the eyes to strengthen vision. Taken with milk, cloves were believed to enhance the pleasures of sexual intercourse.

Apart from a desire for trade goods, religious fervor was another important catalyst for expansion. The passion and energy ignited by the Iberian reconquista encouraged the Portuguese and Spanish to continue the Christian crusade. Just seven months separated Isabella and Ferdinand's entry into Granada on January 2 and Columbus's departure westward on August 3, 1492. Overseas exploration was in some ways a transfer of their religious zeal, enthusiasm for conquest and expansion, and certainty of God's blessing on their ventures from the European continent to new non-Christian territories.

Since organized Muslim polities such as the Ottoman Empire were too strong to defeat, Iberians turned their attention to non-Christian peoples elsewhere.

Combined with eagerness for profits and to spread Christianity was the desire for glory and the urge to chart new waters. Scholars have frequently described the European discoveries as a manifestation of Renaissance curiosity about the physical universe—the desire to know more about the geography and peoples of the world. The detailed journals kept by such voyagers as Christopher Columbus and Antonio Pigafetta (a survivor of Magellan's world circumnavigation) attest to their wonder and fascination with the new peoples and places they visited.

Individual explorers combined these motivations in unique ways. Christopher Columbus was a devout Christian who was increasingly haunted by messianic obsessions in the last years of his life. As Bartholomew Diaz put it, his own motives were "to serve God and His Majesty, to give light to those who were in darkness and to grow rich as all men desire to do." When Vasco da Gama reached the port of Calicut, India, in 1498 and a native asked what the Portuguese wanted, he replied, "Christians and spices."[8] The bluntest of the Spanish conquistadors, Hernando Cortés, announced as he prepared to conquer Mexico, "I have come to win gold, not to plow the fields like a peasant."[9]

Eagerness for exploration could be heightened by a lack of opportunity at home. After the reconquista, enterprising young men of the Spanish upper classes found their economic and political opportunities greatly limited. As a study of the Castilian city of Ciudad Real shows, the ancient aristocracy controlled the best agricultural land and monopolized urban administrative posts. Great merchants and a few nobles (surprisingly, since Spanish law forbade participation by nobles in commercial ventures) dominated the textile and leather-glove manufacturing industries. Consequently, many ambitious men turned to the Americas to seek their fortunes.[10]

Whatever the motivations, the voyages were made possible by the growth of government power. Mariners and explorers did not possess the massive sums needed to explore mysterious oceans and control remote continents. Reassertion of monarchical authority and state centralization in the fifteenth century provided rulers with such resources. In the fifteenth century Isabella and Ferdinand had consolidated their several kingdoms to achieve a more united Spain and had revamped the Spanish bureaucracy. The Spanish monarchy was stronger than before and in a position to support foreign ventures. In Portugal the steadfast financial and moral support of **Prince Henry the Navigator** led to Portugal's phenome-

nal success in the spice trade. Like voyagers, monarchs shared a mix of motivations, from desire to please God to desire to win glory and profit from trade.

For ordinary sailors, life at sea was dangerous, overcrowded, unbearably stench-ridden, filled with hunger, and ill-paid. For months at a time, 100 to 120 people lived and worked in a space of between 150 and 180 square meters, with no available water except a small amount for drinking. Each person had an average of 1.5 meters of space, with more going to officers and wealthy passengers.[11] A lucky sailor would find enough space on deck to unroll his sleeping mat. This is not to mention the horses, cows, pigs, chickens, rats, and lice that accompanied the voyages. As one scholar concluded, "traveling on a ship must have been one of the most uncomfortable and oppressive experiences in the world."[12]

Why did men choose to go to sea? They did so to escape poverty at home, to continue a family trade, to win a few crumbs of the great riches of empire, or to find a better life as illegal immigrants in the colonies. Moreover, many orphans and poor boys were placed on board as young pages and had little say in the decision. Women also paid a price for the voyages of exploration. Left alone for months or years at a time, and frequently widowed, sailors' wives struggled to feed their families. The widow of a sailor lost on Magellan's 1519 voyage had to wait until 1547 to collect her husband's salary from the Crown.[13]

The people who stayed at home had a powerful impact on the process. Court coteries and factions influenced a monarch's decisions and could lavishly reward individuals or cut them out of the spoils of empire. Then there was the public: the small number of people who could read were a rapt audience for tales of fantastic places and unknown peoples. Cosmography, natural history, and geography aroused enormous interest among educated people in the fifteenth and sixteenth centuries. Just as science fiction and speculation about life on other planets excite readers today, quasi-scientific literature about Africa, Asia, and the Americas captured the imaginations of literate Europeans. Gonzalo Fernández de Oviedo's **General History of the Indies** (1547), a detailed eyewitness account of plants, animals, and peoples, was widely read. Indeed, the elite's desire for the exotic goods brought by overseas trade helped propel the whole process of expansion.

Technological Stimuli to Exploration

Technological developments in shipbuilding, weaponry, and navigation provided another impetus for European expansion. Since ancient times, most seagoing vessels had been narrow, open boats called *galleys,* propelled largely by manpower. Slaves or convicts who had been sentenced to the galleys manned the oars of the ships that sailed the Mediterranean, and both cargo ships and warships carried soldiers for defense. Though well suited to the placid and thoroughly explored waters of the Mediterranean, galleys could not withstand the rough winds and uncharted shoals of the Atlantic. The need for sturdier craft, as well as population losses caused by the Black Death, forced the development of a new style of ship that would not require soldiers for defense or much manpower to sail.

In the course of the fifteenth century, the Portuguese developed the **caravel,** a small, light, three-masted sailing ship. Though somewhat slower than the galley, the caravel held more cargo. Its triangular lateen sails and sternpost rudder also made the caravel a much more maneuverable vessel. When fitted with cannon, it could dominate larger vessels, such as the round ships commonly used as merchantmen.

By 1350 *cannon*—iron or bronze guns that fired iron or stone balls—had been fully developed. These pieces of artillery emitted frightening noises and great flashes of fire and could batter down fortresses and even city walls.

Early cannon posed serious technical difficulties. Iron cannon were cheaper than bronze to construct, but they were difficult to cast effectively and were liable to crack and injure artillerymen. Bronze guns, made of copper and tin, were less subject than iron to corrosion, but they were very expensive. All cannon were extraordinarily difficult to move, required considerable time for reloading, and were highly inaccurate. They thus proved inefficient for land warfare. However, they could be used at sea.

Great strides in cartography and navigational aids were also made in this period. Around 1410 Arab scholars reintroduced Europeans to **Ptolemy's *Geography.*** Written in the second century A.D. by a Hellenized Egyptian, the work was a formidable synthesis of the geographical knowledge of the classical world. Its republication provided significant improvements over medieval cartography, showing the world as round and introducing the idea of latitude and longitude to plot position accurately. Ptolemy's work also contained crucial errors. Ignorant of the existence of the Americas, he showed the world as much smaller than it is, so that Asia appeared not very distant from Europe to the west. Based on this work, cartographers fashioned new maps that combined classical knowledge with the latest information from mariners.

Ptolemy's *Geography* The recovery of Ptolemy's *Geography* in the early fifteenth century gave Europeans new access to ancient geographical knowledge. This 1486 world map, based on Ptolemy, is a great advance over medieval maps but contains errors with significant consequences for future exploration. It shows the world watered by a single ocean, with land covering three-quarters of the world's surface and with Europe, Africa, and Asia as the only continents. Africa and Asia are joined, making the Indian Ocean a landlocked sea and rendering the circumnavigation of Africa impossible. The continent of Asia is stretched far to the east, greatly shortening the distance from Europe to Asia. *(Giraudon/Art Resource, NY)*

First the Genoese and Venetians, and then the Portuguese and Spanish, took the lead in these advances.[14]

The magnetic compass enabled sailors to determine their direction and position at sea. The astrolabe, an instrument invented by the ancient Greeks and perfected by Muslim navigators, was used to determine the altitude of the sun and other celestial bodies. It permitted mariners to plot their latitude, or position north or south of the equator.

Many scholars have argued that it was superior European weaponry, shipbuilding, and navigational skill that allowed them to undertake such astonishing voyages and to overcome the resistance of numerically far superior forces. As in the Industrial Revolution, they have argued, the key to European success over others was its openness to new technology and its interest in developing and adopting the most advanced technologies.

These arguments have encountered criticism in recent years. Some scholars have emphasized the extent to which European technology was borrowed from the East. For example, gunpowder, the compass, and the sternpost rudder were all Chinese inventions. The lateen sail, which allowed European ships to tack against the wind, was a product of the Indian Ocean trading world and was brought to the Mediterranean on Arab ships. Navigational aids, such as the astrolabe, were also acquired from others, and advances in cartography drew on the rich tradition of Judeo-Arabic mathematical and astronomical learning in Iberia. This assistance sometimes assumed human form. It was not his own seafaring abilities but assistance from a local guide that helped Vasco da Gama find a sea route from the East African coast to India. In exploring new territories, European sailors thus called on techniques and knowledge developed over centuries in China and the trading world of the Indian Ocean.

Other historians have argued that technological advances were in themselves not that important. Not only were cannon inaccurate and unreliable, but in the tropical conditions of Africa, India, and South America gunpowder got wet and cannon did not fire. Native populations quickly acquired firepower from Europeans who were eager to profit from the weapons trade. These historians have concluded that technological developments arose to meet the needs of exploration, rather than being a necessary precursor to them. To support this case, one scholar points out that the first Portuguese voyages took place in whatever boats were available and with crews unable to make use of a compass or a sea chart. Columbus himself relied on dead reckoning—at which he proved extremely adept—rather than on new navigational devices. As this

Nocturnal An instrument for determining the hour of night at sea by finding the progress of certain stars around the polestar (center aperture). *(National Maritime Museum, London)*

historian concludes, "Neither in Asia nor anywhere else was empire the inevitable corollary of technological superiority."[15]

The Portuguese Overseas Empire

At the end of the fourteenth century Portugal was a small and poor nation on the margins of European life whose principal activities were fishing and subsistence farming. It would have been hard for a European to predict Portugal's phenomenal success overseas in the next two centuries. Yet Portugal had a long history of seafaring and navigation. Blocked from access to western Europe by Spain, the Portuguese turned to the Atlantic and North Africa, whose waters they knew better than almost any other Europeans. Nature favored the Portuguese: winds blowing along their coast offered passage to Africa, its Atlantic islands, and, ultimately, Brazil.

In the early phases of Portuguese exploration, Prince Henry (1394–1460), a younger son of the king, played a leading role. A nineteenth-century scholar dubbed Henry "the Navigator" because of his support for the study of geography and navigation and for the annual expeditions he sponsored down the western coast of Africa. Although he never personally participated in voyages of exploration, Henry's enthusiasm for discovery and his financial support

ARCTIC OCEAN

GREENLAND

Newfoundland
1497

NORTH
AMERICA

Quebec
1608

St. Augustine 1565
San Salvador 1492
NEW
SPAIN
Zacatecas 1492
Mexico City
1519
Guanajuato
Vera Cruz
HONDURAS
Cuba
Jamaica
Cartagena
Panama
Hispaniola 1492
Puerto Rico
Trinidad 1498

SPANISH
MAIN

PACIFIC
OCEAN

Quito
PERU
Lima
1535

Santiago
Buenos Aires
1535

SOUTH
AMERICA

BRAZIL

Potosí

Rio de Janeiro
1516

Cape Horn

Strait of Magellan

1520

PACIFIC
OCEAN

JAPAN
1542

Kyushu

PHILIPPINES

New Guinea

Moluccas
1511

1521

CHINA
Canton
1513
Macao
1557
Malacca
1509
Borneo
Sumatra
Java

ASIA

Bay of
Bengal
Ceylon
1505

INDIA
Goa
1510
Bombay
1507
Calicut
1498

Hormuz
1507

PERSIA

Muscat
Aden 1513

ARABIA

ETHIOPIA

AFRICA

SAHARA

Mombasa
1498

Mozambique

MADAGASCAR
1500

INDIAN
OCEAN

Cape of Good Hope

1522

1519

ATLANTIC
OCEAN

Azores
1493

Canary Is.
1492

Cape Verde Is.
1456

CAPE
VERDE

GUINEA

Timbuktu
Niani
1444

GOLD COAST

Constantinople

Amsterdam
Antwerp
EUROPE
Lisbon
Seville
Ceuta
1415

PACIFIC
OCEAN

Spanish holdings

Portuguese holdings

Magellan and crew
Columbus
Da Gama
Other

3000 Mi.

0   1500   3000 Km.
0   1500   3000 Mi.

ensured that Portugal did not abandon the effort despite early disappointments.

The objectives of Portuguese policy included aristocratic desires for martial glory, the historic Iberian crusade to Christianize Muslims, and the quest to find gold, slaves, an overseas route to the spice markets of India, and the mythical king Prester John. Portugal's conquest of Ceuta, an Arab city in northern Morocco, in 1415 marked the beginning of European exploration and control of overseas territory. In the late 1420s, under Henry's direction, the Portuguese began to settle the Atlantic islands of Madeira (ca 1420) and the Azores (1427). In 1443 the Portuguese founded their first African commercial settlement at Arguim in present-day Mauritania. By the time of Henry's death in 1460, his support for exploration was vindicated by thriving plantations on the Atlantic islands and new access to gold.

Under King John II (r. 1481–1495) the Portuguese established trading posts and forts on the gold-rich Guinea coast and penetrated into the African continent all the way to Timbuktu (see Map 15.2). Portuguese ships transported gold to Lisbon, and by 1500 Portugal controlled the flow of African gold to Europe. The golden century of Portuguese prosperity had begun.

Still the Portuguese pushed farther south down the west coast of Africa. In 1487 Bartholomew Diaz rounded the Cape of Good Hope at the southern tip, but storms and a threatened mutiny forced him to turn back. On a later expedition in 1497 **Vasco da Gama** commanded a fleet of four ships in search of a sea route to the Indian Ocean trade. Da Gama's ships rounded the Cape and sailed up the east coast of Africa. With the help of an Indian guide, da Gama sailed across the Arabian Sea to the port of Calicut in India. Overcoming local hostility, he returned to Lisbon loaded with spices and samples of In-

The Portuguese Fleet Embarked for the Indies   This image shows a Portuguese trading fleet in the late fifteenth century, bound for the riches of the Indies. Between 1500 and 1635, over nine hundred ships sailed from Portugal to ports on the Indian Ocean, in annual fleets composed of five to ten ships. *(British Museum/HarperCollins Publishers/The Art Archive)*

Mapping the Past

MAP 15.2 Overseas Exploration and Conquest, Fifteenth and Sixteenth Centuries   The voyages of discovery marked a dramatic new phase in the centuries-old migrations of European peoples. This map depicts the voyages of Ferdinand Magellan, Christopher Columbus, and Vasco da Gama. ❶ What was the contemporary significance of each of these voyages? ❷ Was the importance of the voyages primarily economic, political, or cultural? ❸ Which voyage had the most impact, and why?

Online Study Center   **Improve Your Grade** Interactive Map: World Exploration, 1492–1535

dian cloth. He had failed to forge any trading alliances with local powers, and Portuguese arrogance ensured the future hostility of Muslim merchants who dominated the trading system. Nonetheless, he had proved the possibility of lucrative trade with the East via the Cape route.

King Manuel (r. 1495–1521) promptly dispatched thirteen ships under the command of Pedro Alvares Cabral, assisted by Diaz, to set up trading posts in India. On April 22, 1500, Cabral's fleet sighted the coast of Brazil in South America and claimed it for the Crown of Portugal. Cabral then proceeded south and east around the Cape of Good Hope and reached India. Half the fleet was lost on the return voyage, but the six spice-laden vessels that dropped anchor in Lisbon harbor in July 1501 more than paid for the entire expedition. Thereafter, a Portuguese convoy set out for passage around the Cape every March. Lisbon became the entrance port for Asian goods into Europe—but this was not accomplished without a fight.

For centuries, port city-states had controlled the rich spice trade of the Indian Ocean, and they did not surrender it willingly. Portuguese commercial activities were accompanied by the destruction or seizure of strategic coastal forts, which later served Portugal as both trading posts and military bases. Alfonso de Albuquerque, whom the Portuguese crown appointed as governor of India (1509–1515), decided that these bases, not inland territories, should control the Indian Ocean. Accordingly, his cannon blasted open the ports of Malacca, Calicut, Ormuz, and Goa, the vital centers of Muslim domination of South Asian trade. This bombardment laid the foundation for Portuguese imperialism in the sixteenth and seventeenth centuries—a strange way to bring Christianity to "those who were in darkness." As one scholar wrote about the opening of China to the West, "while Buddha came to China on white elephants, Christ was borne on cannon balls."[16]

In March 1493, between the voyages of Diaz and da Gama, Spanish ships under a triumphant Genoese mariner named **Christopher Columbus** (1451–1506), in the service of the Spanish crown, entered Lisbon harbor. Spain also had begun the quest for an empire.

The Problem of Christopher Columbus

The year 1992, which marked the quincentenary of Columbus's first voyages to the Americas, spawned an enormous amount of discussion about the significance of his voyages. Journalists, scholars, amateurs, and polemicists debated Columbus's accomplishments and failures. Until the 1980s most writers would have generally agreed with Harvard historian Samuel Eliot Morison in his 1942 biography of the explorer:

The whole history of the Americas stems from the Four Voyages of Columbus; today a score of independent nations and dominions unite in homage to Columbus, the stout-hearted son of Genoa, who carried Christian civilization across the Ocean Sea.[17]

In 1942, the Western Powers believed they were engaged in a life-and-death struggle to defend "Christian civilization" against the evil of fascism.

In contrast to this lavish praise, Columbus has recently been severely criticized. He enslaved and sometimes killed the Indians he encountered. He was a cruel and ineffective governor of Spain's Caribbean colony. Moreover, he did not discover the Americas: Native Americans had occupied the New World for millennia before Columbus, and other Europeans, including the Vikings, had been there before him. Not only did he not discover the continents, but he also misunderstood what he found. Other writers have faulted Columbus as an opportunistic adventurer who originated European exploitation of the non-European world.

Rather than judging Columbus by debates and standards of our time, it is more important to put him into the context of his own time. First, what kind of man was Columbus, and what forces or influences shaped him? Second, in sailing westward from Europe, what were his goals? Third, did he achieve his goals, and what did he make of his discoveries?

Columbus grew up in Genoa and thus drew on the centuries-old tradition of Genoese participation in international trade. In his dream of a westward passage to the Indies, he embodied a long-standing Genoese ambition to circumvent Venetian domination of eastward trade, which was now being claimed by the Portuguese. Columbus was also very knowledgeable about the sea. He had worked as a mapmaker, and he was familiar with such fifteenth-century Portuguese navigational developments as *portolans*—written descriptions of the courses along which ships sailed, showing bays, coves, capes, ports, and the distances between these places—and the use of the magnetic needle as a nautical instrument. As he implied in his *Journal,* he had acquired not only theoretical but also practical experience: "I have spent twenty-three years at sea and have not left it for any length of time worth mentioning, and I have seen everything from east to west [meaning he had been to England] and I have been to Guinea [north and west Africa]."[18] Although some of Columbus's geographical information, such as his measurement of the distance from Portugal to Japan as 2,760 miles when it is actually 12,000, proved inaccurate, his successful thirty-three-day voyage to the Caribbean owed a great deal to his seamanship.

Columbus was also a deeply religious man. He began the *Journal* of his voyage to the Americas in the form of a letter to Ferdinand and Isabella of Spain:

On 2 January in the year 1492, when your Highnesses had concluded their war with the Moors who reigned in Europe, I saw your Highnesses' banners victoriously raised on the towers of the Alhambra, the citadel of the city, and the Moor-

ish king come out of the city gates and kiss the hands of your Highnesses and the prince, My Lord. And later in that same month, on the grounds of information I had given your Highnesses concerning the lands of India . . . your Highnesses decided to send me, Christopher Columbus, to see these parts of India and the princes and peoples of those lands and consider the best means for their conversion.[19]

Columbus had witnessed the Spanish reconquest of Granada and shared fully in the religious and nationalistic fervor surrounding that event. Like the Spanish rulers and most Europeans of his age, Columbus understood Christianity as a missionary religion that should be carried to places and peoples where it did not exist. Although Columbus certainly had material and secular goals, first and foremost, as he wrote in 1498, he believed he was a divine agent: "God made me the messenger of the new heaven and the new earth of which he spoke in the Apocalypse of St. John . . . and he showed me the post where to find it."[20]

What was the object of this first voyage? Columbus gave the answer in the very title of the expedition, "The Enterprise of the Indies." He wanted to find a direct ocean trading route to Asia. Rejected by the Portuguese in 1483 and by Ferdinand and Isabella in 1486, the project finally won the backing of the Spanish monarchy in 1492. The **Santa Fe capitulations** named Columbus viceroy over any territory he might discover and gave him one-tenth of the material rewards of the journey. Inspired by the stories of Marco Polo, Columbus dreamed of reaching the court of the Great Khan (not realizing that the Ming Dynasty had overthrown the Mongols in 1368). Based on Ptolemy's *Geography* and other texts, he expected to pass the islands of Japan and then land on the east coast of China. He carried letters from Ferdinand and Isabella to the khan and an Arabic interpreter, for he assumed that the Great Khan must be in dialogue with Arabic-speaking powers.

How did Columbus interpret what he had found, and in his mind did he achieve what he had set out to do? Columbus's small fleet left the seaport of Palos on August 3 bound for a first stop at the Canary Islands, the westernmost outpost of European civilization. He landed in the Bahamas on October 12, which he christened San Salvador. Columbus believed he had found some small islands off the east coast of Cipangu (Japan). On encountering natives of the islands, he gave them some beads and "many other trifles of small value," pronouncing them delighted with these gifts and eager to trade. In a letter he wrote to Ferdinand and Isabella on his return to Spain, Columbus described the natives as handsome, peaceful, and primitive people whose body painting reminded him of the Canary Islands natives. He concluded that they would make good slaves and could quickly be converted to Christianity. (See the feature "Listening to the Past: Columbus Describes His First Voyage" on pages 518–519.)

Columbus received reassuring reports—via hand gestures and mime—of the presence of gold and of a great king in the vicinity. From San Salvador, Columbus sailed southwest, believing that this course would take him to Japan or the coast of China. He landed on Cuba on October 28. Deciding that he must be on the mainland near the coastal city of Quinsay (Hangzhou), he sent a small embassy inland with letters from Ferdinand and Isabella and instructions to locate the grand city.

The landing party, however, found only sparsely populated villages. In response to this disappointment, Columbus set a course that is still controversial among historians. Instead of continuing north, he turned southwest, apparently giving up on his aim to meet the Great Khan in preference to trying to find gold among the peoples he had discovered. In January, having failed to find the source of gold but having made contact with natives seemingly apt for Christianization and confident of the existence of gold somewhere in the vicinity, he headed back to Spain.

Over the next decades, Columbus's change of course was reconfirmed as the Spanish adopted the model of conquest and colonization they had already introduced in the Canary Islands rather than one of exchange with equals (as envisaged for the Mongol khan). On his second voyage, Columbus forcibly subjugated the island of Hispaniola, enslaved its indigenous peoples, and laid the basis for a system of land grants tied to their labor service. Columbus himself, however, had little interest in or capacity for governing. Revolt soon broke out against him and his brother on Hispaniola. A royal expedition sent to investigate returned the brothers to Spain in chains. Columbus was quickly cleared of wrongdoing, but he did not recover his authority over the territories. Instead, they came under royal control.

Columbus was very much a man of his times. To the end of his life in 1506, he believed that he had found small islands off the coast of Asia. He never realized the scope of his achievement: to have found a vast continent unknown to Europeans, except for a fleeting Viking presence centuries earlier. He could not know that the scale of his discoveries would revolutionize world power, raising issues of trade, settlement, government bureaucracy, and the rights of native and African peoples.

Later Explorers

News of Columbus's first voyage rapidly spread across Europe. On April 1, 1493, a printer in Barcelona published Columbus's letter to Ferdinand and Isabella describing what he had found. By the end of that month the letter had been translated into Latin and published in Rome. Within a year printers in Paris, Basel, Antwerp, and Venice had brought out six more Latin editions, which were soon followed by translations into other European languages. In a 1503 letter Florentine navigator Amerigo Vespucci (1454–1512) wrote about his discoveries on the coast of modern-day Venezuela, stating: "Those new regions which we found and explored with the fleet . . . we may rightly call a New World." This letter, titled *Mundus Novus* (The New World), was the first document to describe America as a continent separate from Asia. In recognition of Amerigo's bold claim, the continent was named for him. (When later cartographers realized that Columbus had made the discovery first, it was too late to change the maps.)

To settle competing claims to the Atlantic discoveries, Spain and Portugal turned to Pope Alexander VI. The **Treaty of Tordesillas** (1494) gave Spain everything to the west of an imaginary line drawn down the Atlantic and Portugal everything to the east. This arbitrary division worked in Portugal's favor when in 1500 an expedition led by Pedro Alvares Cabral landed on the coast of Brazil, which Cabral claimed as Portuguese territory. The country's name derives from the brazilwood trees found there, an important source of red dye (from the word *brasa,* or the reddish color of burning coals).

The search for profits determined the direction of Spanish exploration and expansion into South America. When it became apparent that placer mining (in which ore is separated from soil by panning) in the Caribbean islands was unrewarding and that the Portuguese were reaping enormous riches in Asian trade, new routes to the East and new sources of gold and silver were sought. In 1519 the Spanish ruler Charles V commissioned the Portuguese mariner **Ferdinand Magellan** (1480–1521) to find a direct route to the spices of the Moluccas off the southeast coast of Asia. Magellan sailed southwest across the Atlantic to Brazil, and after a long search along the coast he located the treacherous straits that now bear his name (see Map 15.2). The new ocean he sailed into after a rough passage through the straits seemed so peaceful that Magellan dubbed it the Pacific. He was soon to realize his mistake. His fleet sailed north up the west coast of South America and then headed west into the immense expanse of the Pacific toward the Malay Archipelago. (Some of these islands were conquered in the 1560s and named the "Philippines" for Philip II of Spain.)

Terrible storms, disease, starvation, and violence haunted the expedition. Magellan had set out with a fleet of five ships and around 270 men. Sailors on two of the

World Map of Diogo Ribeiro, 1529 This map integrates the wealth of new information provided by European explorers in the decades after Columbus's 1492 voyage. Working on commission for the Spanish king Charles V, the mapmaker incorporated new details on Africa, South America, India, the Malay Archipelago, and China. Note the inaccuracy in his placement of the Moluccas, or Spice Islands, which are much too far east. This "mistake" was intended to serve Spain's interests in trade negotiations with the Portuguese. (*Biblioteca Apostolica Vaticana*)

ships attempted mutiny on the South American coast; one ship was lost, and another ship deserted and returned to Spain before even traversing the straits. The trip across the Pacific took ninety-eight days, and the men survived on rats and sawdust. Magellan himself was killed in a skirmish in the Philippines. The expedition had enough survivors to man only two ships, and one of them was captured by the Portuguese. One ship with eighteen men returned to Spain from the east by way of the Indian Ocean, the Cape of Good Hope, and the Atlantic in 1522. The voyage had taken almost exactly three years.

Despite the losses, this voyage revolutionized Europeans' understanding of the world by demonstrating the vastness of the Pacific. The earth was clearly much larger than Columbus had believed. The voyage actually made a small profit in spices, but Magellan had proved the westward passage to the Indies to be too long and dangerous for commercial purposes. Turning to its New World colonies, Spain abandoned the attempt to oust Portugal from the Eastern spice trade.

Resounding success in this arena belonged to the Dutch. By the end of the sixteenth century Amsterdam had overtaken Antwerp as the financial capital of Europe. The Dutch had also embarked on foreign exploration and conquest. The Dutch East India Company, founded in 1602, became the major organ of Dutch imperialism and within a few decades expelled the Portuguese from Ceylon and other East Indian islands. By 1650 the Dutch West India Company had successfully intruded on the Spanish possessions in the Americas, in the process gaining control of much of the African and American trade.

English and French explorations lacked the immediate, sensational results of those of the Spanish and Portuguese. In 1497 John Cabot, a Genoese merchant living in London, sailed for Brazil but discovered Newfoundland. The next year he returned and explored the New England coast, perhaps going as far south as Delaware. Since these expeditions found no spices or gold, Henry VII lost interest in exploration. Between 1534 and 1541 Frenchman Jacques Cartier made several voyages and explored the St. Lawrence region of Canada. The first permanent French settlement, at Quebec, was founded in 1608.

New World Conquest

In the West Indies the slow recovery of gold, the shortage of a healthy labor force, and sheer restlessness sped up Spain's search for wealth. In 1519, the year Magellan departed on his worldwide expedition, a brash and determined Spanish adventurer named **Hernando Cortés**

(1485–1547) crossed from Hispaniola to mainland Mexico with six hundred men, seventeen horses, and ten cannon. The conquest of Aztec Mexico had begun.

Cortés landed at Vera Cruz in February 1519. In November he entered **Tenochtitlán** (now Mexico City), capital of the sophisticated Aztec Empire ruled by Montezuma II (r. 1502–1520). Larger than any European city of the time, the capital was the heart of a civilization with advanced mathematics, astronomy, and engineering, with a complex social system, and with oral poetry and historical traditions. In less than two years Cortés had destroyed the monarchy, gained complete control of the capital city, and extended his jurisdiction over much of the Aztec Empire. Why did a strong people defending its own territory succumb to a handful of Spaniards fighting in dangerous and unfamiliar circumstances? Scholars continue to debate this question. The best answer is that, at the time of the Spanish arrival, the Aztec Empire faced internal weaknesses brought on by the resentment of recently subjugated tribes and by the Aztecs' own psychology and attitudes toward war.

Online Study Center **Improve Your Grade**
Primary Source: Cortés on the Aztecs: Two Letters to Charles V

The Spaniards arrived in late summer, when the Aztecs were preoccupied with harvesting their crops and not thinking of war. From the Spaniards' perspective, the timing was ideal. A series of natural phenomena, signs, and portents seemed to augur disaster for the Aztecs. A comet was seen in daytime, and two temples were suddenly destroyed, one by lightning unaccompanied by thunder. These and other apparently inexplicable events had an unnerving and demoralizing effect on the Aztecs.

Even more important was the alienation of newly conquered tribes and the Aztecs' failure to provide an effective military resistance. The Aztec state religion, the sacred cult of Huitzilopochtli, necessitated constant warfare against neighboring peoples to secure captives for religious sacrifice and laborers for agricultural and infrastructural work. When Cortés landed, recently defeated tribes were not yet fully integrated into the empire. Increases in tribute provoked revolt, which led to reconquest, retribution, and demands for higher tribute, which in turn sparked greater resentment and fresh revolt. When the Spaniards appeared, the Totonacs greeted them as liberators, and other subject peoples joined them against the Aztecs.[21]

Montezuma himself refrained from attacking the Spaniards as they advanced toward his capital and welcomed Cortés and his men into Tenochtitlán. Historians have

The Aztec Capital of Tenochtitlán   Occupying a large island, Tenochtitlán was laid out in concentric circles. The administrative and religious buildings were at the heart of the city, which was surrounded by residential quarters. Cortés himself marveled at the city in his letters: "It has four approaches by means of artificial causeways. . . . The city is as large as Seville or Cordoba. . . . There are bridges, very large, strong, and well constructed, so that, over many, ten horsemen can ride abreast. . . . The city has many squares where markets are held. . . . There is one square, twice as large as that of Salamanca, all surrounded by arcades, where there are daily more than sixty thousand souls, buying and selling. In the service and manners of its people, their fashion of living was almost the same as in Spain, with just as much harmony and order." *(The Newberry Library)*

often condemned the Aztec ruler for vacillation and weakness. But he relied on the advice of his state council, itself divided, and on the dubious loyalty of tributary communities. When Cortés—with incredible boldness—took Montezuma hostage, the emperor's influence over his people crumbled.

Forced to leave Tenochtitlán to settle a conflict elsewhere, Cortés placed his lieutenant, Alvarado, in charge. Alvarado's harsh rule drove the Aztecs to revolt, and they almost succeeded in destroying the Spanish garrison. When Cortés returned just in time, the Aztecs allowed his reinforcements to join Alvarado's besieged force. No threatened European or Asian state would have conceived of doing such a thing: dividing an enemy's army and destroying the separate parts was basic to their mili-

tary tactics. But for the Aztecs warfare was a ceremonial act in which "divide and conquer" had no place.

Having allowed the Spanish forces to reunite, the entire population of Tenochtitlán attacked the invaders and killed many Spaniards. In retaliation, the Spaniards executed Montezuma. The Spaniards escaped from the city and inflicted a crushing defeat on the Aztec army at Otumba near Lake Texcoco on July 7, 1520. Aztec weapons proved no match for the terrifyingly noisy and lethal Spanish cannon, muskets, crossbows, and steel swords. After this victory Cortés began the systematic conquest of Mexico.

More amazing than the defeat of the Aztecs was the Spanish victory over the remote Inca Empire perched at 9,800 to 13,000 feet above sea level. Like the Aztecs, the

Incas had created a civilization that rivaled the Europeans in population and complexity. The borders of this vast empire were well fortified and were threatened by no foreign invaders. Like the Romans, the Incas had built an extensive network of roads linking all parts of the empire, which permitted the operation of a highly efficient postal service. The imperial government taxed, fed, and protected its subjects. Grain was plentiful. Apart from an outbreak of smallpox in a distant province—introduced by the Spaniards—no natural disaster upset the general peace. An army of fifty thousand loyal troops stood at the ruler's disposal.

The Incas were totally isolated. They had no contact with other Amerindian cultures and knew nothing of Aztec civilization or its collapse in 1520. Since about 1500 Inca scouts had reported "floating houses" on the seas manned by white men with beards, and tradesmen told of strange large animals with feet of silver (the appearance of horseshoes in the brilliant sunshine). The Spanish told the Incas that they were sent by God—whom Incans may have associated with their creator-god **Virocha**—and the Incas initially believed these claims of good faith.

From 1493 to 1525 the Inca Huayna Capac ruled as a benevolent despot (the word *Inca* refers both to the ruler of the Andeans who lived in the valleys of the Andes in present-day Peru and to the people themselves). His millions of subjects considered him a link between the earth and the sun-god. In 1525 Huascar succeeded his father as Inca and was crowned at Cuzco, the Incas' capital city, with the fringed headband symbolizing his imperial office. However, his rule was threatened by the claims of his half-brother Atauhualpa. Civil war ensued, and Atauhualpa emerged victorious.[22] The five-year struggle may have exhausted him and damaged his judgment.

Francisco Pizarro (ca 1475–1541), a conquistador of modest Spanish origins, landed on the northern coast of Peru on May 13, 1532, the very day Atauhualpa won the decisive battle. The Spaniard soon learned about the war and its outcome. As Pizarro advanced across the steep Andes toward Cuzco, Atauhualpa was proceeding to the capital for his coronation. Like Montezuma in Mexico, Atauhualpa was kept fully informed of the Spaniards' movements, and he stopped at the provincial town of Cajamarca. His plan was to lure the Spaniards into a trap, seize their horses and ablest men for his army, and execute

Doña Marina Translating for Hernando Cortés During His Meeting with Montezuma In April 1519 Doña Marina (or La Malinche as she is known in Mexico) was among twenty women given to the Spanish as slaves. Fluent in Nahuatl and Yucatec Mayan (spoken by a Spanish priest accompanying Cortés), she acted as an interpreter and diplomatic guide for the Spanish. She had a close personal relationship with Cortés and bore his son Don Martín Cortés in 1522. Doña Marina has been seen as a traitor to her people, as a victim of Spanish conquest, and as the founder of the Mexican people. She highlights the complex interaction between native peoples and the Spanish and the particular role women often played as cultural mediators between the two sides. (*American Museum of Natural History, Image VC #31*)

the rest. What had the Inca, surrounded by his thousands of troops, to fear? Atauhualpa thus accepted Pizarro's invitation to meet in the central plaza of Cajamarca with his bodyguards "unarmed so as not to give offense." The Spaniards captured him and collected an enormous ransom in gold. Instead of freeing the new emperor, however, they killed him.

Decades of violence ensued, marked by Incan resistance and internal struggles among Spanish forces for the spoils of empire. By the 1570s the Spanish crown had succeeded in imposing control. With Spanish conquest, a new chapter opened in European relations with the New World.

Europe and the World After Columbus

Europeans had maintained commercial relations with Asia and sub-Saharan Africa since Roman times. In the Carolingian era the slave trade had linked northern Europe and the Islamic Middle East. The High Middle Ages had witnessed a great expansion of trade with Africa and Asia. But with the American discoveries, for the first time commercial and other relations became worldwide, involving all the continents except Australia. European involvement in the Americas led to the acceleration of global contacts. In time, these contacts had a profound influence on European society and culture.

- *What effect did overseas expansion have on the conquered societies, on enslaved Africans, and on world trade?*

Spanish Settlement and Indigenous Population Decline

In the sixteenth century perhaps two hundred thousand Spaniards immigrated to the New World. Mostly soldiers demobilized from the Spanish and Italian campaigns and adventurers and drifters unable to find employment in Spain, they did not come to work. After assisting in the conquest of the Aztecs and the subjugation of the Incas, these drifters wanted to settle down and become a ruling class. They carved out vast estates in temperate grazing areas and imported Spanish sheep, cattle, and horses for the kinds of ranching with which they were familiar. In coastal tropic areas unsuited for grazing the Spanish erected huge sugar plantations. Columbus had introduced sugar into the West Indies; Cortés had introduced

it into Mexico. Sugar was a great luxury in Europe, and demand was high. Around 1550 the discovery of silver at Zacatecas and Guanajuato in Mexico and Potosí in present-day Bolivia stimulated silver rushes. How were the cattle ranches, sugar plantations, and silver mines to be worked? Obviously, by the Amerindians.

The Spanish quickly established the **encomienda system.** The Crown granted the conquerors the right to employ groups of Amerindians as agricultural or mining laborers or as tribute payers. Theoretically, the Spanish were forbidden to enslave the natives; in actuality, the encomiendas were a legalized form of slavery. The European demand for sugar, tobacco, and silver prompted the colonists to exploit the Amerindians mercilessly. Unaccustomed to forced labor, especially in the blistering heat of tropical cane fields or in the dark, dank, and dangerous mines, they died in staggering numbers.

Students of the history of medicine have suggested another crucial explanation for indigenous population losses: disease. Contact with disease builds up bodily resistance; peoples isolated from other societies are not exposed to some diseases and thus do not build resistance. At the beginning of the sixteenth century Amerindians probably had the unfortunate distinction of longer isolation from the rest of humankind than any other people on earth. Crowded concentrations of laborers in the mining camps bred infection, which the miners carried to their home villages. Having little or no resistance to diseases brought from the Old World, the inhabitants of the highlands of Mexico and Peru, especially, fell victim to smallpox, typhus, influenza, and other diseases. According to one expert, smallpox caused "in all likelihood the most severe single loss of aboriginal population that ever occurred."[23] (The old belief that syphilis was a New World disease imported to Europe by Columbus's sailors has been discredited by the discovery of pre-Columbian skeletons in Europe bearing signs of the disease.)

Although disease was the most important cause of indigenous population decline, there were many others. With the native population diverted from traditional agricultural work, cultivation of crops suffered, leading to malnutrition, reduced fertility rates, and starvation. Women forced to work were separated from their infants, leading to high infant mortality rates in a population with no livestock to supply alternatives to breast milk. Malnutrition and hunger in turn reduced resistance to disease.

Many indigenous peoples died through outright violence.[24] According to the Franciscan missionary Bartolomé de Las Casas (1474–1566), the Spanish maliciously murdered thousands:

This infinite multitude of people [the Indians] was . . . without fraud, without subtilty or malice . . . toward the Spaniards whom they serve, patient, meek and peaceful. . . .

To these quiet Lambs . . . came the Spaniards like most c(r)uel Tygres, Wolves and Lions, enrag'd with a sharp and tedious hunger; for these forty years past, minding nothing else but the slaughter of these unfortunate wretches, whom with divers kinds of torments neither seen nor heard of before, they have so cruelly and inhumanely butchered, that of three millions of people which Hispaniola itself did contain, there are left remaining alive scarce three hundred persons.[25]

Las Casas's remarks concentrate on the tropical lowlands, but the death rate in the highlands was also overwhelming.

The Franciscan, Dominican, and Jesuit missionaries who accompanied the conquistadors and settlers played an important role in converting the Amerindians to Christianity, teaching them European methods of agriculture, and inculcating loyalty to the Spanish crown. In terms of numbers of people baptized, missionaries enjoyed phenomenal success, though the depth of the Amerindians' understanding of Christianity remains debatable. Missionaries, especially Las Casas, asserted that the Amerindians had human rights, and through Las Casas's persistent pressure the emperor Charles V abolished the worst abuses of the encomienda system in 1531.

For colonial administrators the main problem posed by the astronomically high death rate was the loss of a subjugated labor force. As early as 1511 King Ferdinand of Spain observed that the Amerindians seemed to be "very frail" and that "one black could do the work of four Indians."[26] Thus was born an absurd myth and the new tragedy of the Atlantic slave trade.

Sugar and Slavery

Throughout the Middle Ages slavery was deeply entrenched in the Mediterranean. The bubonic plague, famines, and other epidemics created a severe shortage of agricultural and domestic workers throughout Europe, encouraging Italian merchants to buy slaves from the Balkans, Thrace, southern Russia, and central Anatolia. During the Renaissance the slave trade represented an important aspect of Italian business enterprise: where profits were high, papal threats of excommunication failed to stop slave traders. The Genoese set up colonial stations in the Crimea and along the Black Sea, and according to an international authority on slavery, these outposts were "virtual laboratories" for the development of slave plantation agriculture in the New World.[27] This form of slavery had nothing to do with race; almost all slaves were white. How, then, did black African slavery enter the European picture and take root in South and then North America?

In 1453 the Ottoman capture of Constantinople halted the flow of white slaves from the Black Sea region and the Balkans. Mediterranean Europe, cut off from its traditional source of slaves, then turned to sub-Saharan Africa, which had a long history of slave trading. The centuries-old trans-Saharan trade was greatly stimulated by the existence of a ready market for slaves in the vineyards and sugar plantations of Sicily and Majorca. (See the feature "Individuals in Society: Juan de Pareja.")

Native to the South Pacific, **sugar** was taken in ancient times to India, where farmers learned to preserve cane juice as granules that could be stored and shipped. From there, sugar traveled to China and the Mediterranean, where islands like Crete, Sicily, and Cyprus had the necessary warm and wet climate. When Genoese and other Italians colonized the Canary Islands and the Portuguese settled on the Madeira Islands, sugar plantations came to the Atlantic. In this stage of European expansion, "the history of slavery became inextricably tied up with the history of sugar."[28] Originally sugar was an expensive luxury that only the very affluent could afford, but population increases and monetary expansion in the fifteenth century led to an increasing demand for it.

Resourceful Italians provided the capital, cane, and technology for sugar cultivation on plantations in southern Portugal, Madeira, and the Canary Islands. Meanwhile, in the period 1490 to 1530, Portuguese traders brought between three hundred and two thousand black slaves to Lisbon each year (see Map 15.3), where they performed most of the manual labor and constituted 10 percent of the city's population. From there slaves were transported to the sugar plantations of Madeira, the Azores, and the Cape Verde Islands. Sugar and the small Atlantic islands gave New World slavery its distinctive shape. Columbus himself, who spent a decade in Madeira, brought sugar plants on his voyages to "the Indies."

Online Study Center **Improve Your Grade**
Primary Source: Fifteenth-Century Slave Trade: The Portuguese in West Africa

As already discussed, European expansion across the Atlantic led to the economic exploitation of the Americas. In the New World, the major problem settlers faced was a shortage of labor. As early as 1495 the Spanish solved the problem by enslaving the native Indians. In

MAP 15.3 Seaborne Trading Empires in the Sixteenth and Seventeenth Centuries By the mid-seventeenth century, trade linked all parts of the world, except for Australia. Notice that trade in slaves was not confined to the Atlantic but involved almost all parts of the world.

Online Study Center **Improve Your Grade** Interactive Map: Worldwide Slave Trade

Individuals in Society

Juan de Pareja

A marginal person is one who lives outside the mainstream of the dominant society, who is not fully assimilated into or accepted by that society. Apart from revealing little known aspects of past cultures, marginalized people teach us much about the values and ideals of the dominant society. Such a person was the Spanish religious and portrait painter Juan de Pareja.

Pareja was born in Antequera, an agricultural region and the old center of Muslim culture near Seville in southern Spain. Of his parents we know nothing. Because a rare surviving document calls him a "mulatto," one of his parents must have been white and the other must have had some African blood. The Spanish word *mulatto* derives from the Arabic *muwallad*, a person of mixed race, and some scholars, using religion to describe ethnic category, speak of Pareja's "Muslim descent." The region from which he came makes that possible, but we do not know whether he actually believed in or practiced Islam.

In 1630 Pareja applied to the mayor of Seville for permission to travel to Madrid to visit his brother and "to perfect his art." The document lists his occupation as "a painter in Seville." Since it mentions no other name, it is reasonable to assume that Pareja arrived in Madrid a free man. Sometime between 1630 and 1648, however, he came into the possession of the artist Diego Velázquez (1599–1660); Pareja became a slave.

In the twelfth century Muslim slaves helped build the cathedral of Saint James at Santiago de Compostela, one of the great shrines of medieval Christendom. During the long wars of the reconquista, Muslims and Christians captured each other in battle and used the defeated as slaves. The fifteenth and sixteenth centuries had seen a steady flow of sub-Saharan Africans into the Iberian Peninsula. Thus early modern Spain was a slaveholding society.

How did Velázquez acquire Pareja? By purchase? As a gift? Had Pareja fallen into debt or committed some crime and thereby lost his freedom? We do not know. Velázquez, the greatest Spanish painter of the seventeenth century, had a large studio with many assistants. Pareja was set to grinding powders to make colors and to preparing canvases. He must have demonstrated ability because, when Velázquez went to Rome in 1648, he chose Pareja to accompany him.

In 1650, as practice for a portrait of Pope Innocent X, Velázquez painted Pareja. That same year, Velázquez signed the document that gave Pareja his freedom, to become effective in 1654. From 1654 until his death Pareja worked in Madrid as an independent painter. Although he received recognition for his work, only one painting survives: *The Calling of Saint Matthew,* signed and dated 1661 (see page 540). Modern art historians dispute its merit. Some believe it shows a forceful baroque energy and considerable originality; others consider it derivative of Velázquez.

Velázquez, Juan de Pareja *(1650).* (The Metropolitan Museum of Art, Fletcher Fund, Rogers Fund, and Bequest of Miss Adelaide Milton de Groot (1876–1967), by exchange, supplemented by gifts from friends of the Museum, 1971. [1971.86]. Photograph © 1986 The Metropolitan Museum of Art)

What does the public career of this seventeenth-century marginal person tell us about the man and his world? After living in Seville and Madrid, he traveled widely, visiting Genoa, Venice, Rome, and Naples. Travel may have broadened him, producing a cosmopolitan man. Pareja's career suggests that a person of talent and ability could rise in Spanish society despite the social and religious barriers that existed at the time. Jonathan Brown, the leading authority on Velázquez, describes Pareja's appearance in Velázquez's portrait as "self-confident." A more enthusiastic student writes, "The Metropolitan is probably the greatest museum in the world . . . and this [Velázquez's portrait of Pareja] is its greatest painting. . . . The man was technically a slave. . . . However, we can see from Velázquez's painting that the two were undeniably equals. That steady look of self-controlled power can even make us wonder which of the two had a higher opinion of himself."

Questions for Analysis

1. Since slavery was an established institution in Spain, speculate on Velázquez's possible reasons for giving Pareja his freedom.
2. What issues of cultural diversity might Pareja have faced in seventeenth-century Spain?

Sources: Jonathan Brown, *Velázquez: Painter and Courtier* (New Haven, Conn.: Yale University Press, 1986); *Grove Dictionary of Art* (New York: Macmillan, 2000); *Sister Wendy Beckett's 1000 Masterpieces* (New York: Dorling Kindersley Inc., 1999).

Online Study Center **Improve Your Grade**
Going Beyond Individuals in Society

A New World Sugar Refinery, Brazil Sugar was the most important and most profitable plantation crop in the New World. This image shows the processing and refinement of sugar on a Brazilian plantation. Sugar cane was grown, harvested, and processed by African slaves who labored under brutal and ruthless conditions to generate enormous profits for plantation owners. *(The Bridgeman Art Library/Getty Images)*

the next two centuries the Portuguese, Dutch, and English followed suit. The horrifyingly rapid decline of the Amerindian population, however, led to the search for new forms of labor.

In Africa, where slavery was entrenched (as it was in the Islamic world, southern Europe, and China), African kings and dealers sold black slaves to European merchants who participated in the transatlantic trade. The Portuguese brought the first slaves to Brazil; by 1600 four thousand were being imported annually. After its founding in 1621, the Dutch West India Company, with the full support of the government of the United Provinces, transported thousands of Africans to Brazil and the Caribbean. In the late seventeenth century, with the chartering of the Royal African Company, the English got involved. Altogether, traders from all these countries brought an estimated ten million African slaves to the Americas from 1650 to 1870.

European sailors found the Atlantic passage cramped and uncomfortable, but conditions for African slaves were lethal. Before 1700, when slavers decided it was better business to improve conditions, some 20 percent of slaves died on the voyage.[29] The most common cause of death was from dysentery induced by poor-quality food and water, intense crowding, and lack of sanitation. Men were often kept in irons during the passage, while women and girls were fair game for sailors. To increase profits, slave traders packed several hundred captives on each ship. One slaver explained that he removed his boots before entering the slave hold because he had to crawl over their packed bodies.[30]

The eighteenth century witnessed the peak of the Atlantic slave trade. In 1790 there were 757,181 blacks in a total U.S. population of 3,929,625. When the first census was taken in Brazil in 1798, blacks numbered about 2 million in a total population of 3.25 million.

The Columbian Exchange

An important historical study asserts that the most significant changes brought about by the Columbian voyages were biosocial. The Age of Discovery led to the migration of peoples, which in turn led to an exchange of fauna and flora—of animals, plants, and disease, a complex process known as the **Columbian Exchange.** Spanish and Portuguese immigrants to the Americas wanted the lifestyle and diet with which they were familiar. Foods that Iberian settlers considered essential—wheat for bread, grapes for wine, olive oil for both culinary and sacramental purposes—were not grown in America. So the migrants sought to turn the New World into the Old: they searched for climatic zones favorable to those crops. Everywhere they settled they raised wheat—in the highlands of Mexico, the Rio de la Plata, New Granada (in northern South America), and Chile. By 1535 Mexico was exporting wheat. Grapes did well in parts of Peru and Chile. It took the Spanish longer to discover areas where suitable soil and adequate rainfall would nourish olive trees, but by the 1560s the coastal valleys of Peru and Chile were dotted with olive groves. Columbus had brought sugar plants on his second voyage; Spaniards also introduced rice and bananas from the Canary Islands, and the Portuguese carried these items to Brazil. All nonindigenous plants and trees had to be brought from Europe, but not all plants arrived intentionally. In clumps of mud on shoes and in the folds of textiles came immigrant grasses such as Kentucky bluegrass, daisies, and the common dandelion.

Apart from wild turkeys and game, Native Americans had no animals for food; apart from alpacas and llamas, they had no animals for travel or to use as beasts of burden. (Human power had moved the huge stones needed to build the monumental Aztec temples.) On his second voyage in 1493 Columbus introduced horses, cattle, sheep, dogs, pigs, chickens, and goats. The multiplication of these animals proved spectacular. By the 1550s, when the Spaniards explored, they brought along herds of swine. The horse enabled the Spanish conquerors and the Amerindians to travel faster and farther and to transport heavy loads.

In return, the Spanish and Portuguese took back to Europe the main American cereal, maize (corn), from Mexico; white potatoes from Peru; and many varieties of beans, squash, pumpkins, avocados, and tomatoes (which Europeans distrusted, fearing that they were sexually stimulating). Maize was the great gift of the Amerindians to all the peoples of the world as food for humans and livestock. Because maize grows in climates too dry for rice and too wet for wheat, gives a high yield per unit of land, and has a short growing season, it proved an especially important crop for Europeans. Initially they looked on the white potato with contempt, but they gradually recognized its nutritional value. Its cultivation slowly spread from west to east—to Ireland, England, and France in the seventeenth century; and to Germany, Poland, Hungary, and Russia in the eighteenth. Ironically, the white potato reached New England from old England in 1718.

Silver and the Economic Effects of Spain's Discoveries

The sixteenth century has often been called Spain's golden century, but silver was far more important than gold. The influence of Spanish armies, Spanish Catholicism, and Spanish wealth was felt all over Europe. This greatness rested largely on the influx of silver from the Americas.

In 1545, at an altitude of fifteen thousand feet where nothing grew because of the cold, and after a two-and-a-half-month journey by pack animal from Lima, Peru, the Spanish discovered an incredible source of silver at Potosí (in present-day Bolivia) in territory conquered from the Inca Empire. The place had no population. By 1600, 160,000 people lived there, making it about the size of the city of London. In the second half of the sixteenth century Potosí yielded perhaps 60 percent of all the silver mined in the world. From Potosí and the mines at Zacatecas and Guanajuato in Mexico, huge quantities of precious metals poured forth. To protect this treasure from French and English pirates, armed convoys transported it to Spain each year. Between 1503 and 1650, 16 million kilograms of silver and 185,000 kilograms of gold entered Seville's port. Spanish predominance, however, proved temporary.

In the sixteenth century Spain experienced a steady population increase, creating a sharp rise in the demand for food and goods. Spanish colonies in the Americas also represented a demand for products. Since Spain had expelled some of its best farmers and businessmen—the Muslims and Jews—in the fifteenth century, the Spanish economy was suffering and could not meet the new demands, and prices rose. Because the cost of manufacturing cloth and other goods increased, Spanish products could not compete with cheaper products made elsewhere in the international market. The textile industry was badly hurt. Prices spiraled upward faster than the government could levy taxes to dampen the economy. (Higher taxes would have cut the public's buying power; with fewer goods sold, prices would have come down.)

Did the flood of silver bullion from America cause the inflation? Prices rose most steeply before 1565, but bullion imports reached their peak between 1580 and 1620. Thus there is no direct correlation between silver imports and the inflation rate. Did the substantial population growth accelerate the inflation rate? It may have done so. After 1600, when population pressure declined, prices gradually stabilized. One fact is certain: the **price revolution** severely strained government budgets. Several times between 1557 and 1647, Spain's King Philip II and his successors repudiated the state debt, thereby undermining confidence in the government and leaving the economy in shambles.

As Philip II paid his armies and foreign debts with silver bullion, Spanish inflation was transmitted to the rest of Europe. Between 1560 and 1600 much of Europe experienced large price increases. Prices doubled and in some cases quadrupled. Spain suffered most severely, but all European countries were affected. Because money bought less, people who lived on fixed incomes, such as the continental nobles, were badly hurt. Those who owed fixed sums of money, such as the middle class, prospered: in a time of rising prices, debts had less value each year. Food costs rose most sharply, and the poor fared worst of all.

In many ways, it was not Spain but China that controlled the world trade in silver. The Chinese demanded silver for its products and for the payment of imperial taxes. China was thus the main buyer of world silver, serving as a "sink" for half the world's production of silver. Just as China was the heart of world trade, so was it, not Europe, the center of the early modern bullion trade. The silver market drove world trade, with the Americas and Japan being mainstays on the supply side and China dominating the demand side.

The Birth of the Global Economy

With the Europeans' discovery of the Americas and their exploration of the Pacific, the entire world was linked for the first time in history by seaborne trade. That trade brought into being three successive commercial empires: the Portuguese, the Spanish, and the Dutch.

In the sixteenth century naval power and shipborne artillery gave Portugal hegemony over the sea route to India. To Lisbon the Portuguese fleet brought spices, which the Portuguese paid for with textiles produced at Gujarat and Coromandel in India and with gold and ivory from East Africa (see Map 15.3). From their fortified bases at Goa on the Arabian Sea and at Malacca on the Malay Peninsula, ships of Malabar teak carried goods to the Portuguese settlement at Macao in the South China Sea. From Macao Portuguese ships loaded with Chinese silks and porcelains sailed to the Japanese port of Nagasaki and to the Philippine port of Manila, where Chinese goods were exchanged for Spanish (that is, Latin

American) silver. Throughout Asia the Portuguese traded in slaves—black Africans, Chinese, and Japanese. The Portuguese exported to India horses from Mesopotamia and copper from Arabia; from India they exported hawks and peacocks for the Chinese and Japanese markets.

Across the Atlantic Portuguese Brazil provided most of the sugar consumed in Europe in the sixteenth and early seventeenth centuries. African slave labor produced the sugar on the plantations of Brazil, and Portuguese merchants controlled both the slave trade between West Africa and Brazil and the commerce in sugar between Brazil and Portugal. The Portuguese were the first worldwide traders, and Portuguese was the language of the Asian maritime trade.

Spanish possessions in the New World constituted basically a land empire, and in the sixteenth century the Spaniards devised a method of governing that empire (see page 538). But across the Pacific the Spaniards also built a seaborne empire centered at Manila in the Philippines, which had been "discovered" by Ferdinand Magellan in 1521. Between 1564 and 1571 the Spanish navigator Miguel Lopez de Legazpi sailed from Mexico and through a swift and almost bloodless conquest took over the Philippine Islands. The city of Manila henceforth served as the transpacific bridge between Spanish America and the extreme Eastern trade.

Chinese silk, sold by the Portuguese in Manila for American silver, was transported to Acapulco in Mexico, and from there it was carried overland to Vera Cruz for re-export to Spain. Because hostile Pacific winds prohibited direct passage from the Philippines to Peru, large shipments of silk also went south from Acapulco to Peru (see Map 15.3). Spanish merchants could never satisfy the European demand for silk, so huge amounts of bullion went from Acapulco to Manila. In 1597, for example, 12 million pesos of silver, almost the total value of the transatlantic trade, crossed the Pacific. After about 1640 the Spanish silk trade declined because it could not compete with Dutch imports.

Stimulated by a large demand for goods in Europe, India, China, and Japan, a worldwide commercial boom occurred from about 1570 to 1630. Many people throughout the world profited: capitalists who advanced money for voyages, captains and crews of ships, and port officials. As spices moved westward or northward, as silks and porcelains moved southward and westward, and as cloth moved eastward and westward, these various goods grew more valuable in the boom of long-distance trade.[31]

In the latter half of the seventeenth century the worldwide Dutch seaborne trade predominated. The Dutch Empire was built on spices. In 1599 a Dutch fleet re-

Chinese Porcelain This porcelain from a seventeenth-century Chinese ship's cargo, recovered from the sea, was intended for European luxury markets. *(Christie's Images)*

crative spice trade. The seaborne empires of Portugal, Spain, and Holland paved the way for the eighteenth-century mercantilist empires of France and Great Britain.

Spain's Global Empire

Spanish expansion into the New World and Asia are even more amazing when considered in light of Spanish expansion within Europe itself. As discussed in Chapter 14, Charles V combined vast and scattered territories across Europe under his rule. From his father's side, he inherited in 1506 the Burgundian lands, which included the Low Countries and Flanders, and in 1519 the Habsburg domains in Austria. As the grandson of Ferdinand and Isabella, in 1516 he became the first monarch to rule a united Spain. In 1530 he capped off this list by being named Holy Roman emperor. Under his reign, Spanish conquistadors brought new territories to Spain's colonial empire. Charles ruled over a vast and multiethnic array of territories (see Map 14.1 on page 460) and thus ruled the first global empire in history.

By 1556 Charles was exhausted by decades of administering this great empire. He had warred with France and the Ottoman Empire throughout his reign. He had also devoted enormous energy to a futile attempt to stamp out the burgeoning Protestant Reformation. (It was he who summoned Martin Luther to the Diet of Worms.) Charles abdicated the Spanish crown and the Netherlands to his son Philip II of Spain and Austria, and other territories in central Europe and the title of Holy Roman emperor to his brother Ferdinand.

Philip inherited his father's overseas Spanish Empire as well as the cascade of silver now flowing from the Americas. In today's world we might view the birth of globalization as a monumental turning point; Philip, however, was more concerned with religious rivalries in Europe. Traditional scholarship has depicted Philip as morose and melancholic, a religious bigot determined to re-impose Roman Catholicism on northern Europe. Recent research portrays him as a more complicated figure. In his youth, "he had visited northern Italy, the Alps, southern Germany, the Rhineland, the Netherlands, parts of France, and southern England."[32] He had walked the streets of Antwerp, Augsburg, Brussels, Cologne, London, and Trent. With the exception of his father, no other European ruler of the time had traveled or seen so much or had accumulated so much political experience in international relations.

turned to Amsterdam carrying 600,000 pounds of pepper and 250,000 pounds of cloves and nutmeg. Those who had invested in the expedition received a 100 percent profit. The voyage led to the establishment in 1602 of the Dutch East India Company, founded with the stated intention of capturing the spice trade from the Portuguese.

The Dutch fleet, sailing from the Cape of Good Hope and avoiding the Portuguese forts in India, steered directly for the Sunda Strait in Indonesia (see Map 15.3). The Dutch wanted direct access to and control of the Indonesian sources of spices. In return for assisting Indonesian princes in local squabbles and disputes with the Portuguese, the Dutch won broad commercial concessions. Through agreements, seizures, and outright war, they gained control of the western access to the Indonesian archipelago. Gradually, they acquired political domination over the archipelago itself. Exchanging European manufactured goods—armor, firearms, linens, and toys—the Dutch soon had a monopoly on the very lucrative

Philip II, ca 1533 This portrait of Philip II as a young man and crown prince of Spain is by the celebrated artist Titian, who was court painter to Philip's father, Charles V. After taking the throne, Philip became another great patron of the artist. *(Scala/Art Resource, NY)*

have been more heretics, and the country would be in a lamentable state like others (the Netherlands) where there is no inquisition as we have in Spain."[33] In this respect, Philip II differed little from the Protestant reformers Luther and Calvin, who initially called for individual liberty of conscience and then insisted on the right of church and civil powers to extirpate heresy within their jurisdictions. Philip was a man of his times, and the times did not favor religious toleration.

With his determination to crush heresy in the Low Countries and with the enormous wealth of American silver enabling him to hire the mercenary armies he needed, why did Philip II have such trouble achieving his goal? Philip was preoccupied with other parts of his vast empire, especially the advance of the Ottoman Turks into the western Mediterranean. This issue—combined with the death of his son and heir Don Carlos and then a revolt of the Moriscos (Muslims) in Granada—made it impossible to concentrate on the Netherlands. At one point in 1566 he complained, "I have so much on my mind that I rarely know what I am doing or saying." Only after Philip learned of the death of Suleiman the Magnificent did he feel able to focus on the Netherlands.[34]

But the Netherlands could not be separated in Philip's mind from what he perceived as the "British problem." In 1586 Mary, Queen of Scots, cousin and heir of Elizabeth of England, became implicated in a plot to assassinate Elizabeth. Hoping to reunite England with Catholic Europe through Mary, Philip gave the conspiracy his full backing. Mary was discovered and beheaded on February 18, 1587. News of her execution reached Philip in mid-April. When Pope Sixtus V (1585–1590) learned of Mary's death on March 24 (the dates suggest the slowness of communication in the late sixteenth century), he promised to pay Philip one million gold ducats the moment Spanish troops landed in England. Conquering England promised the additional benefit of cutting off financial support to the Dutch rebels.

As plans for a naval expedition to attack England proceeded in 1587, two serious difficulties burdened the king. First, he was so badly crippled by gout that he could not sign documents and needed a cane to walk, painfully. Second, official reports indicated that the Ottoman Turks might seize the moment of preoccupation with the Netherlands and England to attack Spain from the Mediterranean. Philip prepared a vast fleet to sail from Lisbon to Flanders, fight off Elizabeth's navy if it attacked, rendezvous with the duke of Parma, commander of Spanish forces in the Netherlands, and escort barges carrying Parma's troops across the English Channel. On May 9, 1588, *la felícissima armada*—"the

After Philip buried his fourth wife, Anna of Austria, to whom he had been deeply devoted, contemporaries noticed a more marked devotion to religion. He relied more and more on God for political help. On the issues of the Inquisition and religious toleration, Philip was completely inflexible. He identified toleration with the growth of heresy, civil disorder, violence, and bloodshed: "Had there been no inquisition (in Spain) there would most fortunate fleet," as it was ironically called in official documents—sailed from Lisbon harbor composed of more than 130 vessels. The **Spanish Armada** met an English fleet in the Channel. The English ships were smaller, faster, and more maneuverable, and many of them had greater firing power than their Spanish counterparts. A combination of storms and squalls, spoiled food and rank water, inadequate Spanish ammunition, and, to a lesser extent, English fire ships that caused the Spanish to scatter gave England the victory. The Armada was defeated before it even reached the Netherlands. On the journey home many Spanish ships went down around Ireland; perhaps 65 managed to reach home ports.

The battle in the Channel has frequently been described as one of the decisive battles in world history. In fact, it had mixed consequences. Spain soon rebuilt its navy, and after 1588 the quality of the Spanish fleet improved. The destruction of the Spanish Armada did not halt the flow of silver from the New World. More silver reached Spain between 1588 and 1603 than in any other fifteen-year period. The war between England and Spain dragged on for years.

The defeat of the Spanish Armada was decisive, however, in the sense that it prevented Philip II from reimposing religious unity on western Europe by force. He did not conquer England, and Elizabeth continued her financial and military support of the Dutch. In the Netherlands neither side gained significant territory. The borders of 1581 tended to become permanent. In 1609 Philip III of Spain (r. 1598–1621) agreed to a truce, in effect recognizing the independence of the United Provinces. In seventeenth-century Spain memory of the loss of the Spanish Armada contributed to a spirit of defeatism. In England the victory contributed to a David and Goliath legend that enhanced English national sentiment.

Changing Attitudes and Beliefs

The age of religious wars and overseas expansion was characterized by an extraordinary degree of intellectual and artistic ferment. This effervescence can be seen in the development of the essay as a distinct literary genre, in other prose, in poetry, in drama, in art, and in music. In many ways, literature, the visual arts, music, and the drama of the period mirrored the social and cultural conditions that gave rise to them. An important theme running through the culture of this time was the encounter with radically new places and peoples.

• *How did culture and art in this period respond to social and cultural transformation?*

New Ideas About Race

Ancient Greeks and Romans were in close contact with Africa and they also practiced slavery, but they did not associate one with the other. Slavery, which was endemic in the ancient world, stemmed from either capture in war or debt. Although generations could be born in captivity, no particular ethnic or racial associations were involved (see page 137). How did slavery come to be so closely associated with race in the Age of Discovery?

Settlers brought to the Americas the racial attitudes they had absorbed in Europe. Their beliefs and attitudes toward Africans derived from Christian theological speculation and Arab ideas. In the sixteenth and seventeenth centuries the English, for example, were extremely curious about Africans' lives and customs, and slavers' accounts were extraordinarily popular. Travel literature depicted Africans as savages because of their eating habits, morals, clothing, and social customs; as barbarians because of their language and methods of war; and as heathens because they were not Christian (nearly the identical language with which the English described the Irish—see page 398). Africans were believed to possess a potent sexuality; African women were considered sexually aggressive, with a "temper hot and lascivious."[35]

"At the time when Columbus sailed to the New World, Islam was the largest world religion, and the only world religion that showed itself capable of expanding rapidly in areas as far apart and as different from each other as Senegal [in northwest Africa], Bosnia [in the Balkans], Java, and the Philippines."[36] Medieval Arabic literature spoke of blacks' physical repulsiveness, mental inferiority, and primitivism. In contrast to civilized peoples from the Mediterranean to China, some Arab writers absurdly claimed, sub-Saharan blacks were the only peoples who had produced no sciences or stable states. Though black kings, the Muslim historian Ibn Khaldun alleged, sold their subjects without even a pretext of crime or war, the victims bore no resentment because they gave no thought to the future and had "by nature few cares and worries; dancing and rhythm are for them inborn."[37]

Medieval Christians and Arabs therefore had similar notions of blacks as primitive people ideally suited to enslavement. The racial biases that the Portuguese, Spanish, Dutch, and English brought to the New World, however, derived primarily from Christian theological speculation. As Europeans turned to Africa for new sources of slaves, they used ideas about Africans' primitiveness and barbarity to defend slavery and even argue that enslavement benefited Africans by bringing the light of Christianity to heathen peoples. Thus, the institution of slavery contributed to the dissemination of more rigid notions of racial inferiority. From rather vague assumptions and prejudices, Europeans developed more elaborate ideological notions of racial superiority and inferiority to safeguard the ever-increasing profits gained from plantation slavery.

Michel de Montaigne and Cultural Curiosity

Racism was not the only possible reaction to the new worlds emerging in the sixteenth century. Decades of religious fanaticism, bringing civil anarchy and war, led both Catholics and Protestants to doubt that any one faith contained absolute truth. Added to these doubts was the discovery of peoples in the New World who had radically different ways of life. These shocks helped produce ideas of **skepticism** and cultural relativism in the sixteenth and seventeenth centuries. Skepticism is a school of thought founded on doubt that total certainty or definitive knowledge is ever attainable. The skeptic is cautious and critical and suspends judgment. Cultural relativism suggests that one culture is not necessarily superior to another, just different. Both notions found expression in the work of Frenchman Michel de Montaigne (1533–1592).

Montaigne descended from a bourgeois family that had made a fortune selling salted herring and wine and in 1477 had purchased the title and property of Montaigne in Gascony. His mother came from a Jewish family that had been forced to flee Spain. Montaigne received a classical education, studied law, and secured a judicial appointment in 1554. He condemned the ancient nobility for being more concerned with war and sports than with the cultivation of the mind.

At the age of thirty-eight Montaigne resigned his judicial post, retired to his estate, and devoted the rest of his life to study, contemplation, and an effort to understand himself. His wealth provided him with the leisure time to do so. A humanist, he believed that the object of life was to "know thyself," for self-knowledge teaches men and women how to live in accordance with nature and God. Montaigne developed a new literary genre, the essay— from the French *essayer,* meaning "to test or try"—to express his thoughts and ideas.

Montaigne's *Essays* provides insight into the mind of a remarkably civilized man. From the ancient authors, especially the Roman Stoic Seneca, Montaigne acquired a sense of calm, patience, tolerance, and broad-mindedness. Mon-

taigne had grown up during the French civil wars, perhaps the worst kind of war. Religious ideology had set family against family, even brother against brother. He wrote:

In this controversy . . . France is at present agitated by civil wars, the best and soundest side is undoubtedly that which maintains both the old religion and the old government of the country. However, among the good men who follow that side . . . we see many whom passion drives outside the bounds of reason, and makes them sometimes adopt unjust, violent, and even reckless courses.[38]

Though he remained a Catholic, Montaigne possessed detachment, independence, openness of mind, and the willingness to look at all sides of a question. As he wrote, "other people's reasons can serve to support me, but seldom to change my course. I listen to them all favorably and decently; but so far as I can remember, I have never up to this moment followed any but my own. I set little value on my own opinion, but I set just as little on those of others."[39]

Montaigne's essay "On Cannibals" reveals the impact of overseas discoveries on one European's consciousness. His tolerant mind rejected the notion that one culture is superior to another:

I long had a man in my house that lived ten or twelve years in the New World, discovered in these latter days, and in that part of it where Villegaignon landed [Brazil]. . . .

I find that there is nothing barbarous and savage in [that] nation, . . . excepting, that every one gives the title of barbarism to everything that is not in use in his own country. As, indeed, we have no other level of truth and reason, than the example and idea of the opinions and customs of the place wherein we live.[40]

Montaigne's rejection of dogmatism, his secularism, and his skepticism thus represented a basic change. In his own time and throughout the seventeenth century, few would have agreed with him. The publication of his ideas, however, anticipated a basic shift in attitudes. Montaigne inaugurated an era of doubt. "Wonder," he said, "is the foundation of all philosophy, research is the means of all learning, and ignorance is the end."[41]

Online Study Center **Improve Your Grade**
Primary Source: Michel de Montaigne on the Fallibility of Human Understanding

Elizabethan and Jacobean Literature

In addition to the essay as a literary genre, the period fostered remarkable creativity in other branches of literature. England, especially in the latter part of Elizabeth's reign and in the first years of her successor, James I (r. 1603–1625), witnessed remarkable literary expression. The terms *Elizabethan* and *Jacobean* (referring to the reign of James) are used to designate the English music, poetry, prose, and drama of this period. The poetry of Sir Philip Sidney (1554–1586), such as *Astrophel* and *Stella,* strongly influenced later poetic writing. *The Faerie Queene* of Edmund Spenser (1552–1599) endures as one of the greatest moral epics in any language. The rare poetic beauty of the plays of Christopher Marlowe (1564–1593), such as *Tamburlaine* and *The Jew of Malta,* paved the way for the work of Shakespeare. Above all, the immortal dramas of William Shakespeare (1564–1616) and the stately prose of the Authorized, or King James, Bible marked the Elizabethan and Jacobean periods as the golden age of English literature.

William Shakespeare, the son of a successful glove manufacturer in Stratford-on-Avon, chose a career on the London stage. By 1592 he had gained recognition as an actor and playwright. He performed in the Lord Chamberlain's Company and became co-owner of the Globe Theatre, which after 1603 presented his plays. Shakespeare's genius lay in the originality of his characterizations, the diversity of his plots, his understanding of human psychology, and his unexcelled gift for language. Shakespeare was a Renaissance man in his deep appreciation of classical culture, individualism, and humanism. Such plays as *Julius Caesar, Pericles,* and *Antony and Cleopatra* deal with classical subjects and figures. Several of his comedies have Italian Renaissance settings. The nine history plays, including *Richard II, Richard III,* and *Henry IV,* enjoyed the greatest popularity among Shakespeare's contemporaries. Written during the decade after the defeat of the Spanish Armada, the history plays express English national consciousness.

Shakespeare's later tragedies, including *Hamlet, Othello,* and *Macbeth,* explore an enormous range of human problems and are open to an almost infinite variety of interpretations. *Othello* portrays an honorable man destroyed by a flaw in his own character and the satanic evil of his supposed friend Iago. *Macbeth*'s central theme is

Titus Andronicus With classical allusions, fifteen murders and executions, a Gothic queen who takes a black lover, and incredible violence, this early Shakespearean tragedy (1594) was a melodramatic thriller that enjoyed enormous popularity with the London audience. Modern critics believe that it foreshadowed *King Lear* with its emphasis on suffering and madness. *(Reproduced by permission of the Marquess of Bath, Longleat House, Warminster, Wilts)*

exorbitant ambition. Shakespeare analyzes the psychology of sin in the figures of Macbeth and Lady Macbeth, whose mutual love under the pressure of ambition leads to their destruction. The central figure in *Hamlet,* a play suffused with individuality, wrestles with moral problems connected with revenge and with the human being's relationship to life and death.

Shakespeare's last play, *The Tempest,* is now viewed by critics as one of his best. The sorcerer-prince Prospero and his daughter Miranda are stranded on an island by Prospero's treacherous brother. There Prospero finds and raises Caliban, whom he instructs in his own language and religion. After Caliban's attempted rape of Miranda, Prospero enslaves him, earning the rage and resentment of his erstwhile pupil. Modern scholars often note the echoes between this play and the realities of imperial conquest and settlement in Shakespeare's day. It is no accident, they argue, that the poet portrayed Caliban as a monstrous, dark-skinned island native whose natural condition is servitude. The author himself borrows words from Montaigne's essay "On Cannibals," suggesting that his portrayal may have implied criticism of superior colonial attitudes rather than an unqualified endorsement.

Another great masterpiece of the Jacobean period was the Authorized Bible. At a theological conference in 1604, a group of Puritans urged James I to support a new translation of the Bible. The king assigned the task to a committee of scholars, and their version was published in 1611. Divided into chapters and verses, the Authorized Version is actually more a revision of earlier Bibles than an original work. Yet it provides a superb expression of the mature English vernacular of the early seventeenth century. Consider Psalm 37:

Fret not thy selfe because of evill doers, neither bee thou envious against the workers of iniquitie.
For they shall soone be cut downe like the grasse; and wither as the greene herbe.
Trust in the Lord, and do good, so shalt thou dwell in the land, and verely thou shalt be fed.

The Authorized Version, so called because it was produced under royal sponsorship (it had no official ecclesiastical endorsement), represented the Anglican and Puritan desire to encourage laypeople to read the Scriptures. It quickly achieved great popularity and displaced all earlier versions. British settlers carried this Bible to the North American colonies, where it became known as the King James Bible. For centuries the King James Bible has had a profound influence on the language and lives of English-speaking peoples.

Chapter Summary

Online Study Center   **ACE the Test**

- **What was the Afro-Eurasian trading world before Columbus?**
- **How and why did Europeans undertake ambitious voyages of expansion that would usher in a new era of global contact?**
- **What effect did overseas expansion have on the conquered societies, on enslaved Africans, and on world trade?**
- **How did culture and art in this period respond to social and cultural transformation?**

Prior to Columbus's voyages, well-developed trade routes linked the peoples and products of Africa, Asia, and Europe. The Indian Ocean was the center of the Afro-Eurasian trade world, ringed by cosmopolitan commercial cities such as Mombasa, Malacca, and Macao. Venetian and Genoese merchants brought sophisticated luxury goods, like silks and spices, into western Europe from the East. Overall, though, Europeans played a minor role in the Afro-Eurasian trading world, since they did not produce many products desired by Eastern elites.

In the sixteenth and seventeenth centuries Europeans gained access to large parts of the globe for the first time. European peoples had the intellectual curiosity, driving ambition, and material incentive to challenge their marginal role in the pre-existing trade world. The revived monarchies of the sixteenth century now possessed sufficient resources to back ambitious seafarers like Christopher Columbus and Vasco da Gama. Exploration and exploitation contributed to a more sophisticated standard of living, in the form of spices and Asian luxury goods, and to a terrible international inflation resulting from the influx of South American silver and gold. Governments, the upper classes, and the peasantry were badly hurt by the resulting inflation. Meanwhile, the middle class of bankers, shippers, financiers, and manufacturers prospered for much of the seventeenth century.

Other consequences of European expansion had global proportions. Indian Ocean trade, long dominated by Muslim merchants operating from autonomous city-ports, increasingly fell under the control of Portuguese merchants sponsored by their Crown. In the New World Europeans discovered territories wholly unknown to them and forcibly established new colonies. The resulting Columbian exchange decimated native populations and fostered exchange of a myriad of plant, animal, and viral species. The slave trade took on new proportions of scale and intensity, as many millions of Africans were transported to labor in horrific conditions in the mines and plantations of the New World.

Cultural attitudes were challenged as well. While most Europeans did not question the superiority of Western traditions and beliefs, new currents of religious skepticism and new ideas about race were harbingers of developments to come. The essays of Montaigne, the plays of Shakespeare, and the King James Bible remain classic achievements of the Western cultural heritage. They both reflected dominant cultural values and projected new ideas into the future.

Key Terms

Malacca	Santa Fe
entrepôt	capitulations
Admiral Zheng He	Treaty of Tordesillas
Mansa Musa	Ferdinand Magellan
Constantinople	Hernando Cortés
spice trade	Tenochtitlán
Prince Henry	Virocha
the Navigator	Francisco Pizarro
General History of	encomienda system
the Indies	sugar
caravel	Columbian
Ptolemy's *Geography*	exchange
Vasco da Gama	price revolution
Christopher	Spanish Armada
Columbus	skepticism

Online Study Center **Improve Your Grade** Flashcards

Suggested Reading

Crosby, Alfred W. *The Columbian Exchange: Biological and Cultural Consequences of 1492*, 30th anniversary ed. 2003. An innovative and highly influential account of the environmental impact of Columbus's voyages.

Davis, David B. *Slavery and Human Progress*. 1984. A moving and authoritative account of New World slavery.

Fernández-Armesto, Felip. *Columbus*. 1992. An excellent biography of Christopher Columbus.

Frederickson, George M. *The Arrogance of Race: Historical Perspectives on Slavery, Racism, and Social Inequality*. 1988. Analyzes the social and economic circumstances associated with the rise of plantation slavery.

Greenblatt, Stephen. *Marvelous Possessions: The Wonder of the New World*. 1991. Describes the cultural impact of New World discoveries on Europeans.

Northrup, David, ed. *The Atlantic Slave Trade*. 1994. Collected essays by leading scholars on many different aspects of the slave trade.

Pérez-Mallaína, Pablo E. *Spain's Men of the Sea: Daily Life on the Indies Fleet in the Sixteenth Century*. 1998. A description of recruitment, daily life, and career paths for ordinary sailors and officers in the Spanish fleet.

Pomeranz, Kenneth, and Steven Topik. *The World That Trade Created: Society, Culture and the World Economy, 1400 to the Present*. 1999. The creation of a world market presented through rich and vivid stories of merchants, miners, slaves, and farmers.

Restall, Matthew. *Seven Myths of Spanish Conquest*. 2003. A re-examination of common ideas about why and how the Spanish conquered native civilizations in the New World.

Scammell, Geoffrey V. *The World Encompassed: The First European Maritime Empires, c. 800–1650*. 1981. A detailed overview of the first European empires, including the Italian city-states, Portugal, and Spain.

Schwarz, Stuart B., ed. *Implicit Understandings: Observing, Reporting and Reflecting on the Encounters Between Europeans and Other Peoples in the Early Modern Era*. 1994. A collection of articles examining the cultural and intellectual impact of encounters between Europeans and non-Europeans during the Age of Discovery.

Subrahamanyam, Sanjay. *The Career and Legend of Vasco da Gama*. 1998. A probing biography that places Vasco da Gama in the context of Portuguese politics and society.

(continued on page 520)

Listening to the Past

Columbus Describes His First Voyage

On his return voyage to Spain in January 1493, Christopher Columbus composed a letter intended for wide circulation and had copies of it sent ahead to Isabella and Ferdinand and others when the ship docked at Lisbon. Because the letter sums up Columbus's understanding of his achievements, it is considered the most important document of his first voyage. Remember that his knowledge of Asia rested heavily on Marco Polo's Travels, published around 1298.

Since I know that you will be pleased at the great success with which the Lord has crowned my voyage, I write to inform you how in thirty-three days I crossed from the Canary Islands to the Indies, with the fleet which our most illustrious sovereigns gave me. I found very many islands with large populations and took possession of them all for their Highnesses; this I did by proclamation and unfurled the royal standard. No opposition was offered.

I named the first island that I found "San Salvador," in honour of our Lord and Saviour who has granted me this miracle. . . . When I reached Cuba, I followed its north coast westwards, and found it so extensive that I thought this must be the mainland, the province of Cathay.* . . . From there I saw another island eighteen leagues eastwards which I then named "Hispaniola."†

Hispaniola is a wonder. The mountains and hills, the plains and meadow lands are both fertile and beautiful. They are most suitable for planting crops and for raising cattle of all kinds, and there are good sites for building towns and villages. The harbours are incredibly fine and there are many great rivers with broad channels and the majority contain gold.‡ The trees, fruits and plants are very different from those of Cuba. In Hispaniola there are many spices and large mines of gold and other metals. . . .§

The inhabitants of this island, and all the rest that I discovered or heard of, go naked, as their mothers bore them, men and women alike. A few of the women, however, cover a single place with a leaf of a plant or piece of cotton which they weave for the purpose. They have no iron or steel or arms and are not capable of using them, not because they are not strong and well built but because they are amazingly timid. All the weapons they have are canes cut at seeding time, at the end of which they fix a sharpened stick, but they have not the courage to make use of these, for very often when I have sent two or three men to a village to have conversation with them a great number of them have come out. But as soon as they saw my men all fled immediately, a father not even waiting for his son. And this is not because we have harmed any of them; on the contrary, wherever I have gone and been able to have conversation with them, I have given them some of the various things I had, a cloth and other articles, and received nothing in exchange. But they have still remained incurably timid. True, when they have been reassured and lost their fear, they are so ingenuous and so liberal with all their possessions that no one who has not seen them would believe it. If one asks for anything they have they never say no. On the

*Cathay is the old name for China. In the log-book and later in this letter Columbus accepts the native story that Cuba is an island that they can circumnavigate in something more than twenty-one days, yet he insists here and later, during the second voyage, that it is in fact part of the Asiatic mainland.
†Hispaniola is the second largest island of the West Indies; Haiti occupies the western third of the island, the Dominican Republic the rest.

‡This did not prove to be true.
§These statements are also inaccurate.

contrary, they offer a share to anyone with demonstrations of heartfelt affection, and they are immediately content with any small thing, valuable or valueless, that is given them. I forbade the men to give them bits of broken crockery, fragments of glass or tags of laces, though if they could get them they fancied them the finest jewels in the world.

I hoped to win them to the love and service of their Highnesses and of the whole Spanish nation and to persuade them to collect and give us of the things which they possessed in abundance and which we needed. They have no religion and are not idolaters; but all believe that power and goodness dwell in the sky and they are firmly convinced that I have come from the sky with these ships and people. In this belief they gave me a good reception everywhere, once they had overcome their fear; and this is not because they are stupid—far from it, they are men of great intelligence, for they navigate all those seas, and give a marvellously good account of everything—but because they have never before seen men clothed or ships like these. . . .

In all these islands the men are seemingly content with one woman, but their chief or king is allowed more than twenty. The women appear to work more than the men and I have not been able to find out if they have private property. As far as I could see whatever a man had was shared among all the rest and this particularly applies to food. . . . In another island, which I am told is larger than Hispaniola, the people have no hair. Here there is a vast quantity of gold, and from here and the other islands I bring Indians as evidence.

In conclusion, to speak only of the results of this very hasty voyage, their Highnesses can see that I will give them as much gold as they require, if they will render me some very slight assistance; also I will give them all the spices and cotton they want. . . . I will also bring them as much aloes as they ask and as many slaves, who will be taken from the idolaters. I believe also that I have found rhubarb and cinnamon and there will be countless other things in addition. . . .

So all Christendom will be delighted that our Redeemer has given victory to our most illustrious King and Queen and their renowned kingdoms, in this great matter. They should hold great celebrations and render solemn thanks to the Holy Trinity with many solemn prayers, for the great triumph which they will have, by the

Christopher Columbus, by Ridolpho Ghirlandio. Friend of Raphael and teacher of Michelangelo, Ghirlandio (1483–1561) enjoyed distinction as a portrait painter, and so we can assume that this is a good likeness of the older Columbus. *(Scala/Art Resource, NY)*

conversion of so many peoples to our holy faith and for the temporal benefits which will follow, for not only Spain, but all Christendom will receive encouragement and profit.

This is a brief account of the facts. Written in the caravel off the Canary Islands.||

15 February 1493

At your orders
THE ADMIRAL

Questions for Analysis

1. How did Columbus explain the success of his voyage?

2. What was Columbus's view of the Native Americans he met?

3. Evaluate his statements that the Caribbean islands possessed gold, cotton, and spices.

4. Why did Columbus cling to the idea that he had reached Asia?

||Actually, Columbus was off Santa Maria in the Azores.

Source: The Four Voyages of Christopher Columbus (Penguin Classics, 1958), pp. 115–123. Copyright © J. M. Cohen, 1958. Reproduced by permission of Penguin Books Ltd.

Notes

1. A. Reid, *Southeast Asia in the Age of Commerce, 1450–1680,*. vol. 2: *Expansion and Crisis* (New Haven, Conn.: Yale University Press, 1993), Chaps. 1 and 2, pp. 1–131.

2. Andre Gunder Frank, *Re-Orient: Global Economy in the Asian Age* (Berkeley: University of California Press, 1998).

3. K. N. Chaudhuri, *Trade and Civilisation in the Indian Ocean: An Economic History from the Rise of Islam to 1750* (Cambridge: Cambridge University Press, 1985), p. 14.

4. Quoted in Erik Gilbert and Jonathan T. Reynolds, *Africa in World History: From Prehistory to the Present* (Upper Saddle River, N.J.: Pearson, 2004), p. 93.

5. Halil Inalcik and Donald Quataert, eds., *An Economic and Social History of the Ottoman Empire, 1300–1914* (Cambridge: Cambridge University Press, 1994), p. 219.

6. G. V. Scammell, *The World Encompassed: The First European Maritime Empires, c. 800–1650* (Berkeley: University of California Press, 1981), pp. 101, 104.

7. Ibid., p. 174.

8. Quoted in C. M. Cipolla, *Guns, Sails, and Empires: Technological Innovation and the Early Phases of European Expansion, 1400–1700* (New York: Minerva Press, 1965), p. 132.

9. Quoted in F. H. Littell, *The Macmillan Atlas: History of Christianity* (New York: Macmillan, 1976), p. 75.

10. See C. R. Phillips, *Ciudad Real, 1500–1750: Growth, Crisis, and Readjustment in the Spanish Economy* (Cambridge, Mass.: Harvard University Press, 1979), pp. 103–104, 115.

11. Pablo E. Pérez-Mallaína, *Spain's Men of the Sea: Daily Life on the Indies Fleet in the Sixteenth Century* (Baltimore: Johns Hopkins University Press, 1998), p. 130.

12. Ibid., p. 133.

13. Ibid., p. 19.

14. Scammell, *The World Encompassed,* p. 207.

15. Ibid., p. 265.

16. Quoted in Cipolla, *Guns, Sails, and Empires,* pp. 115–116.

17. S. E. Morison, *Admiral of the Ocean Sea: A Life of Christopher Columbus* (Boston: Little, Brown, 1942), p. 339.

18. Quoted in F. Maddison, "Tradition and Innovation: Columbus' First Voyage and Portuguese Navigation in the Fifteenth Century," in *Circa 1492: Art in the Age of Exploration,* ed. J. A. Levenson (Washington, D.C.: National Gallery of Art, 1991), p. 69.

19. J. M. Cohen, ed. and trans., *The Four Voyages of Christopher Columbus* (New York: Penguin Books, 1969), p. 37.

20. Quoted in R. L. Kagan, "The Spain of Ferdinand and Isabella," in *Circa 1492: Art in the Age of Exploration,* ed. J. A. Levenson (Washington, D.C.: National Gallery of Art, 1991), p. 60.

21. G. W. Conrad and A. A. Demarest, *Religion and Empire: The Dynamics of Aztec and Inca Expansionism* (New York: Cambridge University Press, 1993), pp. 67–69.

22. Ibid., pp. 135–139.

23. Quoted in Crosby, *The Columbian Exchange: Biological and Cultural Consequences of 1492* (Westport, Conn.: Greenwood, 1972), p. 39.

24. Ibid., pp. 35–59.

25. Quoted in C. Gibson, ed., *The Black Legend: Anti-Spanish Attitudes in the Old World and the New* (New York: Knopf, 1971), pp. 74–75.

26. Quoted in L. B. Rout, Jr., *The African Experience in Spanish America* (New York: Cambridge University Press, 1976), p. 23.

27. C. Verlinden, *The Beginnings of Modern Colonization,* trans. Y. Freccero (Ithaca, N.Y.: Cornell University Press, 1970), pp. 5–6, 80–97.

28. This section leans heavily on D. B. Davis, *Slavery and Human Progress* (New York: Oxford University Press, 1984), pp. 54–62; the quotation is on p. 58.

29. Herbert S. Klein, "Profits and the Causes of Mortality," in David Northrup, ed., *The Atlantic Slave Trade* (Lexington, Mass.: D. C. Heath and Co., 1994), p. 116.

30. Malcolm Cowley and Daniel P. Mannix, "The Middle Passage," in David Northrup, ed., *The Atlantic Slave Trade* (Lexington, Mass.: D. C. Heath and Co., 1994), p. 101.

31. Reid, *Southeast Asia,* vol. 2, pp. 10–26.

32. H. Kamen, *Philip of Spain* (New Haven: Yale University Press, 1997), p. 77.

33. Quoted in ibid., p. 235.

34. Parker, *Grand Strategy of Philip II* (New Haven, Conn.: Yale University Press, 2000), pp. 115–122; the quotation is on p. 119.

35. Quoted in D. P. Mannix, with M. Cowley, *Black Cargoes: A History of the Atlantic Slave Trade* (New York: Viking Press, 1968), p. 19.

36. See P. Brown, "Understanding Islam," *New York Review of Books,* February 22, 1979, pp. 30–33.

37. Quoted in Davis, *Slavery and Human Progress,* pp. 43–44.

38. D. M. Frame, trans., *The Complete Works of Montaigne* (Stanford, Calif.: Stanford University Press, 1958), pp. 175–176.

39. Ibid., p. 618.

40. C. Cotton, trans., *The Essays of Michel de Montaigne* (New York: A. L. Burt, 1893), pp. 207, 210.

41. Ibid., p. 523.

Hyacinthe Rigaud, *Louis XIV, King of France and Navarre* (1701). Louis XIV is surrounded by the symbols of his power: the sword of justice, the scepter of power, and the crown. The vigor and strength of the king's stocking-covered legs contrast with the age and wisdom of his lined face. *(Scala/Art Resource, NY)*

Seventeenth-Century Crisis and Rebuilding

• *What were the common crises and achievements of seventeenth-century states?*

Absolutism in France and Spain

• *To what extent did French and Spanish monarchs succeed in creating absolute monarchies?*

The Culture of Absolutism

• *What cultural forms flourished under absolutist governments?*

Constitutionalism

• *What is constitutionalism, and how did this form of government emerge in England and the Dutch Republic?*

ABSOLUTISM AND CONSTITUTIONALISM IN WESTERN EUROPE, CA 1589–1715

The seventeenth century was a period of crisis and transformation. Agricultural and manufacturing slumps meant that many people struggled to feed themselves and their families. After a long period of growth, population rates stagnated or even fell. Religious and dynastic conflicts led to almost constant war, visiting violence and destruction on ordinary people.

The demands of war reshaped European states. Armies grew larger than they had been since the time of the Roman Empire. To pay for these armies, governments greatly increased taxes. They also created new bureaucracies to collect the taxes and to foster economic activity that might increase state revenue. Despite numerous obstacles, European states succeeded in gathering more power during this period. What one historian described as the long European "struggle for stability" that originated with the Reformation in the early sixteenth century was largely resolved by 1680.[1]

Important differences existed, however, in terms of *which* authority within the state possessed sovereignty—the Crown or privileged groups. Between roughly 1589 and 1715 two basic patterns of government emerged in Europe: absolute monarchy and the constitutional state. Almost all subsequent European governments have been modeled on one of these patterns.

Seventeenth-Century Crisis and Rebuilding

Historians often refer to the seventeenth century as an "age of crisis." After the economic and demographic growth of the sixteenth century, Europe faltered into stagnation and retrenchment. This was partially due to climate changes beyond anyone's control, but it also resulted from the bitterness of religious divides, the increased pressures exerted by governments, and the violence and dislocation of war. Overburdened peasants and city-dwellers took action to defend themselves, sometimes profiting

Online Study Center

This icon will direct you to interactive activities and study materials on the website **college.hmco.com/pic/mckaywest9e**

from elite conflicts to obtain redress of their grievances. In the long run, however, governments proved increasingly able to impose their will on the populace. This period witnessed a spectacular growth in army size as well as new forms of taxation, government bureaucracies, and increased state sovereignty.

• *What were the common crises and achievements of seventeenth-century states?*

Economic and Demographic Crisis

In the seventeenth century the vast majority of western Europeans lived in the countryside. The hub of the rural world was the small peasant village centered on a church and a manor. Life was in many ways circumscribed by the village, although we should not underestimate the mobility induced by war, food shortage, fortune-seeking, and religious pilgrimage.

A small number of peasants in each village owned enough land to feed themselves and the livestock and ploughs necessary to work their land. These independent farmers were leaders of the peasant village. They employed the landless poor, rented out livestock and tools, and served as agents for the noble lord. Below them were small landowners and tenant farmers who did not have enough land to be self-sufficient. These families sold their best produce on the market to earn cash for taxes, rent, and food. At the bottom were the rural proletariat who worked as dependent laborers and servants.

Rich or poor, bread was the primary element of the diet. Ignoring our modern health concerns, the richest ate a white loaf, leaving brown bread to those who could not afford better. Peasants paid stiff fees to the local miller for grinding grain into flour and sometimes to the lord for the right to bake bread in his oven. Bread was most often accompanied with a soup made of roots, herbs, beans, and perhaps a small piece of salt pork. One of the biggest

An English Food Riot Nothing infuriated ordinary women and men more than the idea that merchants and landowners were withholding grain from the market in order to push high prices even higher. In this cartoon an angry crowd hands out rough justice to a rich farmer accused of hoarding. *(Courtesy of the Trustees of the British Museum)*

annual festivals in the rural village was the killing of the family pig. The whole family gathered to help, sharing a rare abundance of meat with neighbors and carefully salting the extra and putting down the lard. In some areas, menstruating women were careful to stay away from the kitchen for fear they might cause the lard to spoil.

Rural society lived on the edge of subsistence. A bad harvest, an illness, or a drop in prices could lead to debt and the loss of one's land. Because of the crude technology and low crop yield, peasants were constantly threatened by scarcity and famine. The fear of hunger marked popular culture, and death was a familiar presence.

The seventeenth century put new stresses on this fragile balance. A colder and wetter climate meant a shorter farming season. Conditions were so bad that scholars refer to this period as a "little ice age." A bad harvest created dearth; a series of bad harvests could lead to famine. Recurrent famines had a significant effect on the population levels of early modern Europe. Using parish registers, historians have traced the correspondence between high prices on the one hand and burials and low birth and marriage rates on the other. Most people did not die of outright starvation, but rather of diseases brought on by malnutrition and exhaustion. Facilitated by the weakened population, outbreaks of bubonic plague continued in Europe until the 1720s.

Industry also suffered. While the evidence does not permit broad generalizations, it appears that the output of woolen textiles, one of the most important European manufactures, declined sharply in the first half of the century. Food prices were high, wages stagnated, and unemployment soared. This economic crisis was not universal: it struck various regions at different times and to different degrees. In the middle decades of the century, Spain, France, Germany, and England all experienced great economic difficulties; but these years were the golden age of the Netherlands.

Peasants and the urban poor were the first to suffer from bad harvests and economic depression. When the price of bread rose beyond their capacity to pay, they frequently took action. In towns they invaded the bakers' shop to seize bread and resell it at a "just price." In rural areas groups of peasants attacked convoys taking grain away to the cities and also redistributed it for what they considered a fair price. Women often took the lead in these actions, since their role as mothers with children to feed gave them some impunity in authorities' eyes. Historians have labeled this vision of a world in which community needs predominate over competition and profit a **moral economy.**

Chronology

1589–1610	Henry IV in France
1598	Edict of Nantes
1602	Dutch East India Company founded
1605–1715	Food riots common across Europe
1635	Birth of French Academy
1640–1680	Golden age of Dutch art (Vermeer, Van Steen, Rembrandt)
1642–1649	English civil war ends with execution of Charles I
1643–1715	Louis XIV in France
1648–1653	The Fronde
1653–1658	Military rule in England under Oliver Cromwell
1659	Treaty of the Pyrenees marks end of Spanish imperial dominance
1660	Restoration of English monarchy under Charles II
1665–1683	Jean-Baptiste Colbert applies mercantilism to France
1685	Edict of Nantes revoked
1688–1689	Glorious Revolution in England
1701–1713	War of the Spanish Succession
1713	Peace of Utrecht

Seventeenth-Century State-Building: Common Obstacles and Achievements

In this context of economic and demographic depression, monarchs began to make new demands on their people. Traditionally, historians have distinguished sharply between the "absolutist" governments of France, Spain, central Europe, and Russia and the constitutionally limited governments of England and the Dutch Republic. Whereas absolutist monarchs gathered all power under their personal control, Dutch and English rulers were obliged to respect laws passed by representative institutions. More recently, historians have emphasized commonalities among these powers. Despite their political differences, absolutist and constitutional monarchs shared common projects of protecting and expanding their frontiers, raising new taxes, and consolidating state control.

Rulers who wished to increase their authority encountered formidable obstacles. Some were purely material. Without paved roads, telephones, or other modern technology, it took weeks to convey orders from the central government to the provinces. States like France and Spain were vast, especially if we take their overseas empires into account. Rulers also suffered from a lack of information about their realms, due to the limited size of their bureaucracies. Without accurate knowledge of the number of inhabitants and the wealth they possessed, it was impossible to police and tax the population effectively. Cultural and linguistic differences presented their own obstacles. Seventeenth-century Basques, Bretons, Languedocians, and Alsatians spoke not French but their own languages. These differences decreased even further their willingness to obey a distant monarch's commands.

A more concrete obstacle was the array of privileged groups who shared in authority and its spoils. The traditional enemy of monarchical power was the nobility. Across Europe, nobles retained great legal, military, political, and financial powers, not to mention the traditional social prestige they commanded. Nobles were not alone in opposing monarchs' new claims. Other competitors included the church, the legislative corps, town councils, guilds, and other bodies that had acquired autonomy over the course of the Middle Ages. In some countries whole provinces held separate privileges and exemptions granted when they entered the kingdom. This special status reinforced local power structures and identities.

A long historical consensus held that absolutist monarchs succeeded in breaking the power of these institutions, with Louis XIV of France serving as the model for absolutist power across Europe. By contrast, mighty kings were humbled in England and the Dutch Republic and were forced to concede political power to elected representatives. Today, historians paint a more nuanced picture of this divide. On the one hand, they emphasize the extent to which absolutist monarchs had to compromise with existing power structures. Louis XIV succeeded because he co-opted and convinced nobles, rather than by crushing their power. On the other hand, historians also recognize that traditional elites retained power in England and the Netherlands. Constitutional limits did not mean democracy, the rule of the people.

If we take a step back from the political differences, we see that these states all succeeded—albeit to varying de-grees—in overcoming the obstacles and achieving new levels of central control. Four achievements stand out in particular: greater taxation, growth in armed forces, larger and more efficient bureaucracies, and the increased ability to compel obedience from their subjects.

Increasing the size and power of the state required new sources of revenue. Medieval kings frequently found temporary financial support through bargains with the nobility: the nobility agreed to an ad hoc grant of money in return for freedom from future taxation. Over the course of the seventeenth century, rulers succeeded in generating new levels of income by either forcing direct taxes ever higher or devising alternative methods of raising money.

Taxation both permitted and required a larger government apparatus. This period witnessed the expansion of government bureaucracies and the creation of administrative techniques to improve communication and efficiency. Bureaucracies were now composed of career officials appointed by and solely accountable to the king. The backgrounds of these civil servants varied. They sometimes came from the middle classes, as in France, the Netherlands, and England. In Spain and eastern Europe, monarchs utilized members of the nobility instead (see Chapter 17).

Over time, government power added up to something close to **sovereignty.** A state may be termed sovereign when it possesses a monopoly over the instruments of justice and the use of force within clearly defined boundaries. In a sovereign state, no system of courts, such as ecclesiastical tribunals, competes with state courts in the dispensation of justice; and private armies, such as those of feudal lords, present no threat to central authority because the state's army is stronger. State law touches all persons in the country. While seventeenth-century states did not acquire total sovereignty, they made important strides toward that goal.

Warfare and the Growth of Army Size

The driving force of seventeenth-century state-building was warfare, characterized by dramatic changes in the size and style of armies. Medieval armies had been raised by feudal lords for particular wars or campaigns, after which the troops were disbanded. In the seventeenth century monarchs took command of recruiting and maintaining armies—in peacetime as well as wartime. Kings deployed their troops both inside and outside the country in the interests of the monarchy. Instead of serving their own interests, army officers were required to be loyal and obedient to the monarchs who commanded them. New techniques for training and deploying soldiers meant a rise in the professional standards of the army.

Along with professionalization came an explosive growth in army size. The French took the lead, with the army growing from roughly 125,000 men in the Thirty Years' War (1630–1648) to 250,000 during the Dutch War (1672–1678) and 340,000 during the War of the League of Augsburg (1688–1697).[2] This growth was caused in part by changes in the style of armies. Mustering a royal army took longer than simply hiring a mercenary band, giving enemies time to form coalitions. The large coalitions Louis XIV confronted required him to fight on multiple fronts with huge armies. In turn, the relative size and wealth of France among European nations allowed Louis to field enormous armies and thereby to pursue the ambitious foreign policies that caused his alarmed neighbors to form coalitions against him.

The death toll was startlingly high for noble officers, who personally led their men in battle. The paramount value of honor for noblemen outshone concerns for safety or material benefit. Nobles had to purchase their positions in the army and supply horses, food, uniforms, and weapons for themselves and their troops. Royal stipends did not begin to cover these expenses, and an officer's position could not be sold if he died in battle. The only legacy an officer's widow received was the debt incurred to fund her husbands' military career. It was not until the 1760s that the French government assumed the costs of equipping troops.

Other European powers were quick to follow the French example. The rise of absolutism in central and eastern Europe was similarly marked by a vast expansion in the size of armies (see Chapter 17). Great Britain followed a similar, albeit distinctive pattern. Instead of building a land army, the British focused on naval forces and eventually built the largest navy in the world.

Many historians believe that the new loyalty, professionalism, and size of the French army is the best case for the success of absolutism under Louis XIV. Whatever his compromises elsewhere, the French monarch had firm control of his armed forces. As in so many other matters, Louis's model was followed across Europe.

Popular Political Action

In the seventeenth century increased pressures of taxation and warfare turned bread riots into armed uprisings. **Popular revolts** were extremely common in England, France, Spain, Portugal, and Italy in the mid-seventeenth century.[3] In 1640 Philip IV of Spain faced revolt in Catalonia, the economic center of his realm. This was the same time he was struggling to put down an uprising in Portugal and the revolt of the northern provinces of the Netherlands. In 1647 the city of Palermo, in Spanish-occupied Sicily, exploded in protest over food shortages caused by a series of bad harvests. Fearing public unrest, the city government subsidized the price of bread, attracting even more starving peasants from the countryside. When Madrid ordered an end to

The Spider and the Fly In reference to the insect symbolism (*upper left*), the caption on the lower left side of this illustration states, "The noble is the spider, the peasant the fly." The other caption (*upper right*) notes, "The more people have, the more they want. The poor man brings everything— wheat, fruit, money, vegetables. The greedy lord sitting there ready to take everything will not even give him the favor of a glance." This satirical print summarizes peasant grievances. (*The New York Public Library/Art Resource, NY*) subsidies, municipal leaders decided to lighten the loaf rather than raise prices. Not fooled by this change, local women led a bread riot, shouting "Long live the king and down with the taxes and the bad government!" The uprising spread to the rest of the island and eventually to Naples on the mainland. Apart from affordable food, rebels demanded the suppression of extraordinary taxes and participation in municipal government. Some dreamed of a republic in which noble tax exemptions would be abolished. Despite initial successes, the revolt lacked unity and strong leadership and could not withstand the forces of aristocratic reaction.[4]

In France urban disorders became so frequent an aspect of the social and political landscape as to be "a distinctive feature of life."[5] Major insurrections occurred at Dijon in 1630 and 1668, at Bordeaux in 1635 and 1675, at Montpellier in 1645, at Lyons in 1667–1668 and 1692, and at Amiens in 1685, 1695, 1704, and 1711. All were characterized by deep popular anger, a vocabulary of violence, and what a recent historian calls "the culture of retribution"—that is, the punishment of royal "outsiders," officials who attempted to announce or collect taxes.[6] These officials were sometimes seized, beaten, and hacked to death. For example, in 1673 Louis XIV's imposition of new taxes on legal transactions, tobacco, and pewter ware provoked an uprising in Bordeaux.

Municipal and royal authorities often struggled to overcome popular revolt. They feared that stern repressive measures, such as sending in troops to fire on crowds, would create martyrs and further inflame the situation, while forcible full-scale military occupation of a city would be very expensive. The limitations of royal authority gave some leverage to rebels. Royal edicts were sometimes suspended, prisoners released, and discussions initiated.

By the end of the seventeenth century, this leverage had largely disappeared. Municipal governments were better integrated into the national structure, and local authorities had prompt military support from the central government. People who publicly opposed royal policies and taxes received swift and severe punishment.[7]

Absolutism in France and Spain

In the Middle Ages jurists held that as a consequence of monarchs' coronation and anointment with sacred oil, they ruled "by the grace of God." Law was given by God; kings discovered or "found" the law and acknowledged that they must respect and obey it. In the absolutist state, kings amplified these claims, asserting that, as they were chosen by God, they were responsible to God alone. They claimed exclusive power to make and enforce laws, denying any other institution or group the authority to check their power.

In 1651 in *Leviathan,* the English philosopher Thomas Hobbes provided a theoretical justification for absolute monarchical authority, arguing that any limits on or divisions of government power would lead only to paralysis or civil war. At the court of Louis XIV the theologian Bossuet proclaimed that the king was the "image" of God on earth and that it was a sacred duty to obey him: "The prince need render account of his acts to no one. . . . Without this absolute authority the king could neither do good nor repress evil. It is necessary that his power be such that no one can hope to escape him, and, finally, the only protection of individuals against the public authority should be their innocence." Historians have been debating since his reign how successfully Louis XIV and other absolutist monarchs realized these claims.

● *To what extent did French and Spanish monarchs succeed in creating absolute monarchies?*

The Foundations of Absolutism: Henry IV, Sully, and Richelieu

Louis XIV's absolutism had long roots. In 1589 his grandfather Henry IV (r. 1589–1610), the founder of the Bourbon dynasty, acquired a devastated country. Civil wars had wracked France since 1561. Catastrophically poor harvests meant that peasants across France lived on the verge of starvation. Commercial activity had fallen to one-third its 1580 level. Nobles, officials, merchants, and peasants wanted peace, order, and stability. "Henri le Grand" (Henry the Great), as the king was called, promised "a chicken in every pot" and inaugurated a remarkable recovery. He was beloved because of the belief that he cared about the people; he was the only king whose statue the Paris crowd did not tear down in the Revolution of 1789.

Aside from a short war in 1601, Henry kept France at peace. Maintaining that "if we are without compassion for the people, they must succumb and we all perish with them," Henry sharply lowered taxes on the overburdened peasants. In compensation for lost revenues, in 1602–1604 he introduced the *paulette,* an annual fee paid by royal officials to guarantee heredity in their offices. (Although effective at the time, the long-term effect of this tax was to reduce royal control over officeholders.)

Along with his able chief minister, the Protestant Maximilien de Béthune, duke of Sully, Henry IV laid the foundations for the growth of state power. He combined the indirect taxes on salt, sales, and transit and leased their collection to financiers. Although the number of taxes declined, revenues increased because of the revival of trade.[8] Henry improved the infrastructure of the country, building new roads and canals and repairing the ravages of years of civil war. In only twelve years he restored public order in France.

As a divinely appointed leader of his people, Henry sought to heal the religious divisions that had torn France apart. In 1598 he issued the **Edict of Nantes** as a compromise between Catholics and Huguenots. The edict allowed Protestants the right to worship in 150 traditionally Protestant towns throughout France; the king gave the towns 180,000 écus to support the maintenance of their military garrisons. This was too much for some devout Catholics. Henry was murdered in 1610 by François Ravaillac, a Catholic zealot, setting off national crisis.

Online Study Center **Improve Your Grade**
Primary Source: Henry IV's Edict of Nantes Grants Limited Toleration to the Huguenots

After the death of Henry IV his wife, the queen-regent Marie de' Medici, headed the government for the child-king Louis XIII (r. 1610–1643). In 1624 Marie de' Medici secured the appointment of Armand Jean du Plessis—Cardinal Richelieu (1585–1642)—to the council of ministers. It was a remarkable appointment. The next year Richelieu became president of the council, and after 1628 he was first minister of the French crown. Richelieu used his strong influence over King Louis XIII to exalt the French monarchy as the embodiment of the French state. One of the greatest servants of that state, Richelieu struggled through the turmoil of the Thirty Years' War to maintain the monarchy's position within Europe and within its own borders.

Richelieu's goal was to subordinate competing groups and institutions to the French monarchy. The nobility constituted the foremost threat. Nobles ran the army, controlled large provinces of France, sat in royal councils, and were immune from direct taxation. Richelieu sought to curb their power. In 1624 he succeeded in reshuffling the royal council, eliminating potential power brokers. Thereafter Richelieu dominated the council in an unprecedented way.

The constructive genius of Cardinal Richelieu is best reflected in the administrative system he established to strengthen royal control. He extended the use of the royal commissioners called **intendants.** France was divided into thirty-two *généralités* (districts), in each of which after 1634 a royal intendant held a commission to perform specific tasks, often financial but also judicial and policing. Intendants painstakingly collected information from local communities for Paris and delivered royal orders from the capital to their districts. Almost always recruited from the newer judicial nobility, the *noblesse de robe* or robe nobility, intendants were appointed directly by the monarch, to whom they were solely responsible. They could not be natives of the districts where they held authority; thus they had no vested interest in their localities. The intendants recruited men for the army, supervised the collection of taxes, presided over the administration of local law, checked up on the local nobility, and regulated economic activities—commerce, trade, the guilds, marketplaces—in their districts. They were to use their power for three related purposes: to inform the central government about their généralités, to enforce royal orders, and to undermine the influence of the regional nobility. As the intendants' power increased under Richelieu, so did the power of the centralized French state.

Under Richelieu the French monarchy also reasserted the principle of one people united by one faith. In 1627 Louis XIII decided to end Protestant military and political independence because, he said, it constituted "a state within a state." According to Louis, Huguenots demanded freedom of conscience but did not allow Catholics to worship in their cities. He interpreted this inequity as *political* disobedience.[9] Attention focused on La Rochelle, fourth largest of the French Atlantic ports and a major commercial center with strong ties to the northern Protestant states of Holland and England. Louis personally supervised the siege of La Rochelle. After the city fell in October 1628, its municipal government was suppressed and its walled fortifications were destroyed. Although Protestants retained the right of public worship, the king reinstated the Catholic liturgy, and Cardinal Richelieu himself celebrated the first Mass. The fall of La Rochelle weakened the influence of aristocratic Huguenots and was one step in the removal of Protestantism as a strong force in French life.

The elimination of potential dissidents at home did not mean hostility to Protestants abroad. Foreign policy under Richelieu aimed primarily at the destruction of the fence of Habsburg territories that surrounded France. Consequently, Richelieu supported the Habsburgs' enemies, including Protestants. In 1631 he signed a treaty with the Lutheran king Gustavus Adolphus promising French support against the Catholic Habsburgs in what has been called the Swedish phase of the Thirty Years' War (see page 562). French influence became an important factor in the political future of the German Empire. Richelieu acquired for France extensive rights in Alsace in the east and Arras in the north.

In building the French state, Richelieu knew that his approach sometimes seemed to contradict traditional Christian teaching. As a priest and bishop, how did he justify his policies? He developed his own *raison d'état* (reason of state): "Where the interests of the state are concerned, God absolves actions which, if privately committed, would be a crime."[10]

Richelieu's successor as chief minister for the boy-king Louis XIV was Cardinal Jules Mazarin (1602–1661). Along with the regent, Queen Mother Anne of Austria, Mazarin continued Richelieu's centralizing policies. His struggle to increase royal revenues to meet the costs of war with Spain led to the uprisings of 1648–1653 known as the **Fronde.** The word *fronde* means "slingshot" or "catapult," and a *frondeur* was originally a street urchin who threw mud at the passing carriages of the rich. The word came to be applied to the many individuals and groups who opposed the policies of the government. The Fronde began among the robe nobility when the judges of the Parisian high law court (the *Parlement*) rejected Anne and Mazarin's proposal to raise new revenues by rescinding judicial salaries. The arrest of several magistrates sparked a popular riot in the capital, whose inhabitants had suffered to meet the costs of war. With the boy-king, Anne of Austria fled the capital for safety. Essentially traditional and conservative, the magistrates agreed to a compromise with the government that largely favored their demands.

The second stage of the Fronde saw the conflict extend to the **noblesse d'épée** or sword nobility, who were also angered by the increasing powers of the central government. The Prince de Condé, one of the highest nobles in France, entered open warfare against the Crown, followed by other nobles and their followers. Popular rebellions led by aristocratic factions broke out in the provinces and spread to Paris.[11] As rebellion continued, civil order broke down completely. In 1651 Anne's regency ended with the declaration of Louis as king in his own right. Much of the rebellion died away, and its leaders came to terms with the government.

The conflicts of the Fronde had significant results for the future. First, it became apparent that compromise between the king and the sword and robe nobility was nec-

essary. Neither side was strong enough to subjugate the other; only violence and disorder could come from a refusal to negotiate. This meant, in some ways, a victory for the forces opposing the king, who were guaranteed the preservation of their traditional privileges. However, the Fronde also quelled—and in some cases killed—the most vociferous opponents of the Crown. The twin evils of noble factionalism and popular riots left the French wishing for peace and for a strong monarch to re-impose order. This was the legacy that Louis XIV inherited when he assumed personal rule in 1661. Humiliated by his flight from Paris, he was determined to avoid any recurrence of rebellion.

Louis XIV and Absolutism

In the reign of Louis XIV (r. 1643–1715), the longest in European history, the French monarchy reached the peak of absolutist development. In the magnificence of his court, in the brilliance of the culture that he presided over and that permeated all of Europe, and in his remarkably long life, the "Sun King" dominated his age.

The boy-king received an education appropriate for his position. He learned to speak Italian and Spanish fluently, spoke and wrote elegant French, and knew some French history and a great deal of European geography. Louis also imbibed the devout Catholicism of his mother, Anne of Austria, and throughout his long life scrupulously performed his religious duties. Religion, Anne, and Mazarin all taught Louis the doctrine of the **divine right of kings:** God had established kings as his rulers on earth, and they were answerable ultimately to God alone. Though kings were divinely anointed and shared in the sacred nature of divinity, they could not simply do as they pleased. They had to obey God's laws and rule for the good of the people.

Louis worked very hard at the business of governing. He ruled his realm through several councils of state, which he personally attended, and through the intendants who acted for the councils in the provinces. A stream of questions and instructions flowed between local districts and Versailles, helping centralize and standardize a hopelessly complex administration. Louis insisted on taking a personal role in many of the decisions issued by the councils.

Councilors of state came from the recently ennobled or the upper middle class. Royal service provided a means of social mobility. These professional bureaucrats served the state in the person of the king, but they did not share power with him. Louis stated that he chose bourgeois officials because he wanted "people to know by the rank of the men who served him that he had no intention of

Rubens: The Death of Henry IV and the Proclamation of the Regency (1622–1625)   In 1622 the regent Marie de' Medici commissioned Peter Paul Rubens to paint a cycle of paintings depicting her life. This one portrays two distinct moments: the assassination of Henry IV (shown on the left ascending to Heaven), and Marie's subsequent proclamation as regent. The queen is seated on a throne in mourning clothes, with the goddess Athena on her right (representing Prudence), a woman in the air holding a rudder (symbolizing regency), and the personification of France kneeling before her offering an orb (symbolizing government). The other twenty-three canvases in the cycle similarly glorify Marie, a tricky undertaking given her unhappy marriage to Henry IV and her tumultuous relationship with her son Louis XIII, who removed her from the regency in 1617. As in this image, Rubens frequently resorted to allegory and classical imagery to elevate the events of Marie's life. *(Réunion des Musées Nationaux/Art Resource, NY)*

sharing power with them."[12] If great ones were the king's advisers, they would seem to share the royal authority; professional administrators from the middle class would not.

Despite increasing financial problems, Louis never called a meeting of the Estates General. The nobility therefore had no means of united expression or action. Nor did Louis have a first minister; he kept himself free from worry about the inordinate power of a Richelieu. Louis also used spying and terror—a secret police force, a system of informers, and the practice of opening private letters—to eliminate potential threats.

Religion was also a tool of national unity under Louis, who continued Richelieu's persecution of Protestants. In 1685 Louis revoked the Edict of Nantes, by which his grandfather Henry IV had granted liberty of conscience to French Huguenots. The new law ordered the destruction of Huguenot churches, the closing of schools, the

Catholic baptism of Huguenots, and the exile of Huguenot pastors who refused to renounce their faith. The result was the departure of some of his most loyal and industrially skilled subjects.

There had been so many mass conversions of Protestants in France that the king's second wife, Madame de Maintenon, could say that "nearly all the Huguenots were converted." Moreover, Richelieu had already deprived French Calvinists of political rights. Why, then, did Louis XIV undertake such an apparently unnecessary, cruel, and self-destructive measure? First, Louis considered religion primarily a political question. Although he was personally tolerant, he hated division within the realm and insisted that religious unity was essential to his royal dignity and to the security of the state. As he put it, his goal was "one king, one law, one faith." Second, while France in the early years of Louis's reign permitted religious liberty, it was not a popular policy. Aristocrats had long petitioned Louis to crack down on Protestants. His decision to do so won him enormous praise: "If the flood of congratulation means anything, it . . . was probably the one act of his reign that, at the time, was popular with the majority of his subjects."[13]

Louis's personal hold on power, his exclusion of great nobles from his councils, and his ruthless pursuit of religious unity persuaded many earlier historians that his reign witnessed the creation of an **absolute monarchy.** Louis supposedly crushed the political pretensions of the nobility, leaving them with social grandeur and court posing but no real power. A later generation of historians has revised that view, showing the multiple constraints on Louis's power and his need to cooperate with the nobles. Louis may have declared his absolute power, but in practice he governed through collaboration with nobles, who maintained tremendous prestige and authority in their ancestral lands. Scholars also underline the traditional nature of Louis's motivations. Like his predecessors, Louis XIV sought to enhance the glory of his dynasty and his country, mostly through war. The creation of a new state apparatus was a means to that goal, not an end in itself.

Financial and Economic Management Under Louis XIV: Colbert

France's ability to build armies and fight wars depended on a strong economy. The king named Jean-Baptiste Colbert (1619–1683), the son of a wealthy merchant-financier of Reims, as controller general of finances. Colbert came to manage the entire royal administration and proved himself a financial genius. His central principle was that the wealth and the economy of France should serve the state. He did not invent the system called "mercantilism," but he rigorously applied it to France.

Mercantilism is a collection of governmental policies for the regulation of economic activities, especially commercial activities, by and for the state. In seventeenth- and eighteenth-century economic theory, a nation's international power was thought to be based on its wealth, specifically its gold supply. Because resources were limited, mercantilist theory held, state intervention was needed to secure the largest part of a limited resource. To accumulate gold, a country always had to sell more goods abroad than it bought. Colbert thus insisted that France should be self-sufficient, able to produce within its borders everything French subjects needed. Consequently, the outflow of gold would be halted; debtor states would pay in bullion; unemployment and poverty would greatly

diminish; and with the wealth of the nation increased, its power and prestige would be enhanced.

Colbert attempted to accomplish self-sufficiency by supporting old industries and creating new ones, especially in textiles, the most important sector of the economy. To ensure high-quality finished products, Colbert reinforced the system of state inspection and regulation and formed guilds in many industries. Colbert encouraged foreign craftsmen to immigrate to France, and he gave them special privileges. He also took measures to bring more female workers into the labor force. To protect French goods, he abolished many domestic tariffs and enacted high foreign tariffs, which prevented foreign products from competing with French ones.

One of Colbert's most ambitious projects was the creation of a merchant marine to transport French goods. He gave bonuses to French shipowners and shipbuilders and established a method of maritime conscription, arsenals, and academies for training sailors. In 1661 France possessed 18 unseaworthy vessels; by 1681 it had 276 frigates, galleys, and ships of the line. In 1664 Colbert founded the Company of the East Indies with (unfulfilled) hopes of competing with the Dutch for Asian trade.

Online Study Center **Improve Your Grade**
Primary Source: Colbert Promotes "The Advantages of Overseas Trade"

Colbert also hoped to make Canada—rich in untapped minerals and some of the best agricultural land in the world—part of a vast French empire. He gathered four thousand peasants from western France and shipped them to Canada, where they peopled the province of Quebec. (In 1608, one year after the English arrived at Jamestown, Virginia, Sully had established the city of Quebec, which became the capital of French Canada.) Subsequently, the Jesuit Jacques Marquette and the merchant Louis Joliet sailed down the Mississippi River and took possession of the land on both sides as far south as present-day Arkansas. In 1684 the French explorer Robert La Salle continued down the Mississippi to its mouth and claimed vast territories and the rich delta for Louis XIV. The area was called, naturally, "Louisiana."

Colbert's most pressing concern was tax collection. Extensive military reform, war, an expanding professional bureaucracy, and the court at Versailles cost a great deal of money. Yet there were many difficulties in raising taxes. English kings relied on one national assembly, Parliament, for consent to taxation for the entire country. The French system was both more complicated and more inequitable. In some provinces, provincial **estates** (representative bodies of clergy, nobles, and commoners) held the authority to negotiate with the Crown over taxes. In provinces without estates, the king held direct control over taxation through his intendants. Throughout France the nobility and clergy enjoyed exemption from the direct property tax, or *taille*; even bourgeois city-dwellers often gained exemption from it. This meant that the tax burden fell most heavily on those with the least wealth. Finally, the practice of subcontracting tax collection to financiers, known as tax-farmers, meant that a good portion of state money fell into private hands.

Despite these difficulties, Colbert managed to raise revenues significantly by cracking down on inefficiencies and corruption. During Colbert's tenure as controller general, Louis was able to pursue his goals without massive tax increases and without creating a stream of new offices. The constant pressure of warfare after Colbert's death, however, undid many of his economic achievements.

Louis XIV's Wars

Louis XIV wrote that "the character of a conqueror is regarded as the noblest and highest of titles." In pursuit of the title of conqueror, he kept France at war for thirty-three of the fifty-four years of his personal rule. In 1666 Louis appointed François le Tellier (later, marquis de Louvois) as secretary of state for war. Under the king's watchful eye, Louvois created a professional army that was modern in the sense that the French state, rather than private nobles, employed the soldiers. Louvois utilized several methods in recruiting troops: dragooning, in which press gangs seized men off the streets; conscription; and, after 1688, lottery. With these techniques, the French army grew to some 340,000 men at its height, enormous by the standards of the day. Louvois also imposed new levels of professionalization. Uniforms and weapons were standardized and a rational system of training and promotion devised. This new military machine gave one state the potential to dominate the affairs of the continent for the first time in European history.

Louis's supreme goal was to expand France to what he considered its "natural" borders and to secure those lands from any threat of outside invasion. A defensive

MAP 16.1 The Acquisitions of Louis XIV, 1668–1713
The desire for dynastic glory and the weakness of his German neighbors encouraged Louis's wars, but his country paid a high price for his acquisitions.

policy in his eyes, it appeared frighteningly aggressive to onlookers. In 1667, using a dynastic excuse, he invaded Flanders, part of the Spanish Netherlands, and Franche-Comté in the east. In consequence, he acquired twelve towns, including the important commercial centers of Lille and Tournai (see Map 16.1). Five years later Louis personally led an army of over one hundred thousand men into Holland, and the Dutch ultimately saved themselves only by opening the dikes and flooding the countryside. The Dutch war lasted six years and eventually involved the Holy Roman Empire and Spain. At the Treaty of Nijmegen (1678), Louis gained additional Flemish towns and all of Franche-Comté. In 1681 Louis seized the city of Strasbourg, and three years later he sent his armies into the province of Lorraine. At that moment the king seemed invincible. In fact, Louis had reached the limit of his expansion. The wars of the 1680s and 1690s brought no additional territories.

Louis understood his wars largely as defensive undertakings, but his enemies naturally viewed French expansion with great alarm. Louis's wars inspired the formation of Europe-wide coalitions against him. As a result, he was obliged to support a huge army in several different theaters of war. This task placed unbearable strains on French resources, especially given the inequitable system of taxation.

Claude Le Peletier, Colbert's successor as minister of finance, resorted to the devaluation of the currency and the old device of selling offices and tax exemptions. Colbert's successors also created new income taxes in 1695 and 1710, which nobles and clergymen had to pay for the first time. In exchange for this money, the king reaffirmed the traditional social hierarchies by granting honors, pensions, and titles to the nobility. Moreover, he did not lessen the burden on commoners, who had to pay the new taxes as well as the old ones.

A series of bad harvests between 1688 and 1694 added social to fiscal catastrophe. The price of wheat skyrocketed. The result was widespread starvation, and in many provinces the death rate rose to several times the normal figure. Parish registers reveal that France buried at least one-tenth of its population in those years, perhaps 2 million in 1693 and 1694 alone. Rising grain prices, new taxes for war, a slump in manufacturing, and the constant nuisance of pillaging troops all meant great suffering for the French people. France wanted peace at any price and won a respite for five years, which was shattered by the War of the Spanish Succession (1701–1713).

In 1700 the childless Spanish king Charles II (r. 1665–1700) died, opening a struggle for control of Spain and its colonies. His will bequeathed the Spanish crown and its empire to Philip of Anjou, Louis XIV's grandson (Louis's wife, Maria-Theresa, had been Charles's sister). This testament violated a prior treaty by which the European powers had agreed to divide the Spanish possessions between the king of France and the Holy Roman emperor, both brothers-in-law of Charles II. Claiming that he was following both Spanish national interests and French dynastic and national interests, Louis broke with the treaty and accepted the will.

In 1701 the English, Dutch, Austrians, and Prussians formed the Grand Alliance against Louis XIV. The allied powers united to prevent France from becoming too strong in Europe and to check France's expanding commercial power in North America, Asia, and Africa. The war dragged on until 1713. The **Peace of Utrecht,** which ended the war, applied the principle of partition. Louis's grandson Philip remained the first Bourbon king of Spain on the understanding that the French and Spanish crowns would never be united. France surrendered Newfoundland, Nova Scotia, and the Hudson Bay territory to England, which also acquired Gibraltar, Minorca, and control of the African slave trade from Spain. The Dutch gained little because Austria received the former Spanish Netherlands (see Map 16.2).

The Peace of Utrecht had important international consequences. It represented the balance-of-power principle in operation, setting limits on the extent to which any one power—in this case, France—could expand. The treaty completed the decline of Spain as a great power. It vastly expanded the British Empire, and it gave European powers experience in international cooperation. The Peace of Utrecht also marked the end of French expansion. Thirty-five years of war had brought rights to all of Alsace and the gain of important cities in the north such as Lille, as well as Strasbourg. But at what price? In 1714 an exhausted France hovered on the brink of bankruptcy. It is no wonder that when Louis XIV died on September 1, 1715, many subjects felt as much relief as they did sorrow.

The Decline of Absolutist Spain in the Seventeenth Century

Spanish absolutism and greatness had preceded those of the French. In the sixteenth century Spain (or, more precisely, the kingdom of Castile) had developed the standard features of absolutist monarchy: a permanent bureaucracy staffed by professionals employed in the various councils of state, a standing army, and national taxes, the *servicios,* which fell most heavily on the poor. France depended on financial and administrative unification within its borders; Spain had developed an international absolutism on the basis of silver bullion from Peru. Spanish gold and silver, armies, and glory had dominated the continent for most of the sixteenth century. In 1580 the Spanish crown annexed Portugal, putting an end to earlier conflicts over the boundaries of their overseas empires.

The Inquisition continued to ensure a dogmatic Catholic orthodoxy in Spain. Converted Jews and Muslims were always under suspicion and subject to imprisonment and even execution. In 1609 Philip III expelled all converted Muslims, known as Moriscos, from Spain. Some three hundred thousand individuals left the country, many going to the Ottoman Empire and North Africa. This measure satisfied the king's Catholic conscience and his fears of potential insurrection, but it was destructive for Spanish society, which lost precious skilled workers and merchants.

Tiepolo: The Triumph of Spain   This painting is from the ceiling of the Royal Palace in Madrid. Arguably the greatest Italian painter of the eighteenth century, Giovanni Tiepolo depicted the Spanish Empire as the self-assured champion of Christian cultural values in Europe and America. *(Palacio Real de Madrid/The Bridgeman Art Library)*

By the early seventeenth century the seeds of disaster were sprouting. By 1715 agricultural crisis and population decline, the loss of artisans and merchants, failure to invest in productive enterprises, and intellectual isolation and psychological malaise all combined to reduce Spain to a second-rate power. The fabulous and seemingly inexhaustible flow of silver from Mexico and Peru, together with the sale of cloth, grain, oil, and wine to the colonies, had greatly enriched Spain. In the early seventeenth century, however, the Dutch and English began to trade with the Spanish colonies, cutting into the revenues that had gone to Spain. Mexico and Peru themselves developed local industries, further lessening their need to buy from Spain. Between 1610 and 1650 Spanish trade with the colonies fell 60 percent. At the same

time, the native Indians and African slaves who toiled in the South American silver mines suffered frightful epidemics of disease. Ultimately, the lodes started to run dry, and the quantity of metal produced steadily declined.

In Madrid, however, royal expenditures constantly exceeded income. To meet mountainous state debt and declining revenues, the Crown repeatedly devalued the coinage and declared bankruptcy. In 1596, 1607, 1627, 1647, and 1680, Spanish kings found no solution to the problem of an empty treasury other than to cancel the national debt. Given the frequency of cancellation, national credit plummeted.

In contrast to the other countries of western Europe, Spain had only a tiny middle class. Public opinion, taking its cue from the aristocracy, condemned moneymaking

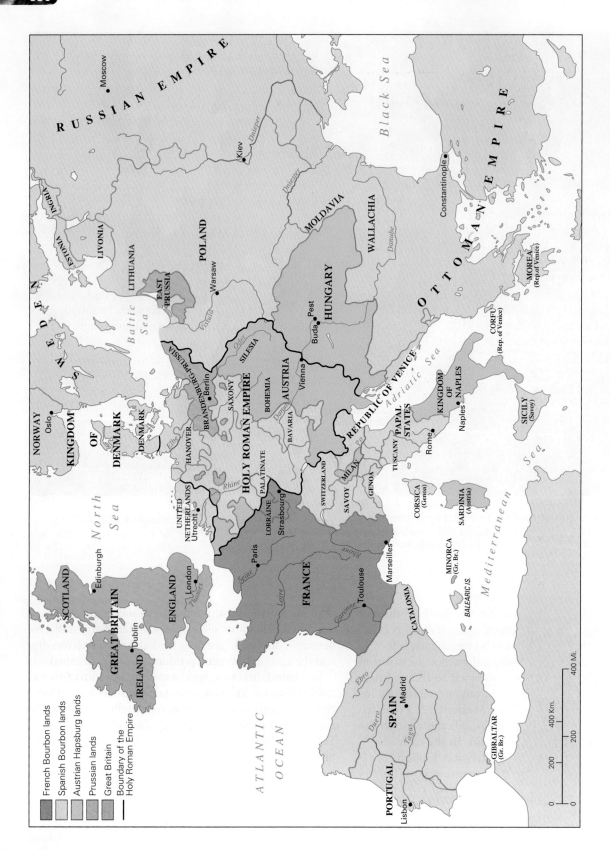

RUSSIAN EMPIRE

Moscow

Kiev

Dnieper

Dniester

MOLDAVIA

WALLACHIA

Danube

Black Sea

OTTOMAN EMPIRE

Constantinople

SWEDEN

INGRIA

ESTONIA

LIVONIA

LITHUANIA

Baltic Sea

POLAND

Warsaw

Vistula

EAST PRUSSIA

HUNGARY

Buda • Pest

Vienna

BRANDENBURG-PRUSSIA

Berlin

SILESIA

Oder

SAXONY

BOHEMIA

AUSTRIA

Danube

HOLY ROMAN EMPIRE

BAVARIA

REPUBLIC OF VENICE

Adriatic Sea

MOREA
(Rep. of Venice)

CORFU
(Rep. of Venice)

NORWAY

Oslo

KINGDOM OF DENMARK

DENMARK

HANOVER

Elbe

UNITED NETHERLANDS

Utrecht

PALATINATE

LORRAINE

Strasbourg

Rhine

SWITZERLAND

SAVOY

MILAN

GENOA

Po

TUSCANY

PAPAL STATES

Rome

KINGDOM OF NAPLES

Naples

SICILY
(Savoy)

Mediterranean Sea

CORSICA
(Genoa)

SARDINIA
(Austria)

North Sea

SCOTLAND

Edinburgh

GREAT BRITAIN

ENGLAND

London

Thames

Dublin

IRELAND

Paris

Seine

Loire

FRANCE

Marseilles

Rhone

Toulouse

Garonne

CATALONIA

MINORCA
(Gr. Br.)

BALEARIC IS.

ATLANTIC OCEAN

Ebro

SPAIN

Madrid

Duero

Tagus

GIBRALTAR
(Gr. Br.)

PORTUGAL

Lisbon

Scale: 0 200 400 Mi.
0 200 400 Km.

Legend:
- French Bourbon lands
- Spanish Bourbon lands
- Austrian Hapsburg lands
- Prussian lands
- Great Britain
- ── Boundary of the Holy Roman Empire

as vulgar and undignified. Those with influence or connections sought titles of nobility and social prestige. Thousands entered economically unproductive professions: there were said to be nine thousand monasteries in the province of Castile alone. The flood of gold and silver had produced severe inflation, pushing the costs of production in the textile industry to the point that Castilian cloth could not compete in colonial and international markets. Many businessmen found so many obstacles in the way of profitable enterprise that they simply gave up.[14]

Spanish aristocrats, attempting to maintain an extravagant lifestyle they could no longer afford, increased the rents on their estates. High rents and heavy taxes in turn drove the peasants from the land. Agricultural production suffered, and peasants departed for the large cities, where they swelled the ranks of unemployed beggars.

Their most Catholic majesties, the kings of Spain, had no solutions to these dire problems. If one can discern personality from pictures, the portraits of Philip III (r. 1598–1622), Philip IV (r. 1622–1665), and Charles II (r. 1665–1700) hanging in the Prado, the Spanish national museum in Madrid, reflect the increasing weakness of the dynasty. Philip III, a pallid, melancholy, and deeply pious man handed the government over to the duke of Lerma, who used it to advance his personal and familial wealth. Philip IV left the management of his several kingdoms to Gaspar de Guzmán, count-duke of Olivares.

Olivares was an able administrator who has often been compared to Richelieu. He did not lack energy and ideas, and he succeeded in devising new sources of revenue.

But he clung to the grandiose belief that the solution to Spain's difficulties rested in a return to the imperial tradition. Unfortunately, the imperial tradition demanded the revival of war with the Dutch at the expiration of a twelve-year truce in 1622 and a long war with France over Mantua (1628–1659). Spain thus became embroiled in the Thirty Years' War. These conflicts, on top of an empty treasury, brought disaster.

In 1640 Spain faced serious revolts in Catalonia and Portugal. The Portuguese succeeded in regaining independence from Habsburg rule under their new king, John IV (r. 1640–1656). In 1643 the French inflicted a crushing defeat on a Spanish army at Rocroi in what is now Belgium. By the Treaty of the Pyrenees of 1659, which ended the French-Spanish conflict, Spain was compelled to surrender extensive territories to France. This treaty marked the decline of Spain as a great power. Spain's long conflict with France ended with the bequeathing of the Spanish crown to a French prince, igniting the War of the Spanish Succession.

Seventeenth-century Spain was the victim of its past. It could not forget the grandeur of the sixteenth century and look to the future. The bureaucratic councils of state continued to function as symbols of the absolute Spanish monarchy. But because those councils were staffed by aristocrats, it was the aristocracy that held real power. Spanish absolutism had been built largely on slave-produced gold and silver. When the supply of bullion decreased, the power and standing of the Spanish state declined.

The most cherished Spanish ideals were military glory and strong Roman Catholic faith. In the seventeenth century Spain lacked the finances and the manpower to fight the expensive wars in which it got involved. Spain also ignored the new mercantile ideas and scientific methods because they came from heretical nations, Holland and England. The incredible wealth of South America destroyed what remained of the Spanish middle class and created contempt for business and manual labor.

The decadence of the Habsburg dynasty and the lack of effective royal councilors also contributed to Spanish failure. Spanish leaders seemed to lack the will to reform. Pessimism and fatalism permeated national life. In the reign of Philip IV, a royal council was appointed to plan the construction of a canal linking the Tagus and Manzanares Rivers in Spain. After interminable debate, the committee decided that "if God had intended the rivers to be navigable, He would have made them so."

In the brilliant novel **Don Quixote,** Spanish writer Miguel de Cervantes (1547–1616) produced one of the

Mapping the Past

MAP 16.2 Europe in 1715 The series of treaties commonly called the Peace of Utrecht (April 1713–November 1715) ended the War of the Spanish Succession and redrew the map of Europe. A French Bourbon king succeeded to the Spanish throne. France surrendered to Austria the Spanish Netherlands (later Belgium), then in French hands, and France recognized the Hohenzollern rulers of Prussia. Spain ceded Gibraltar to Great Britain, for which it has been a strategic naval station ever since. Spain also granted to Britain the *asiento,* the contract for supplying African slaves to America. **❶** Identify the areas on the map that changed hands as a result of the Peace of Utrecht. How did these changes affect the balance of power in Europe? **❷** How and why did so many European countries possess scattered or discontiguous territories? What does this suggest about European politics in this period? **❸** Does this map suggest potential for future conflict?

Peeter Snayers: Spanish Troops (detail) The long wars that Spain fought over Dutch independence, in support of Habsburg interests in Germany, and against France left the country militarily exhausted and financially drained by the mid-1600s. Here Spanish troops—thin, emaciated, and probably unpaid—straggle away from battle. *(Museo Nacional del Prado, Madrid. Photo: José Baztan y Alberto Otero)*

great masterpieces of world literature. *Don Quixote* delineates the whole fabric of sixteenth-century Spanish society. The main character, Don Quixote, lives in a world of dreams, traveling about the countryside seeking military glory. From the title of the book, the English language has borrowed the word *quixotic*. Meaning "idealistic but impractical," the term characterizes seventeenth-century Spain. As a leading scholar has written, "The Spaniard convinced himself that reality was what he felt, believed, imagined. He filled the world with heroic reverberations. Don Quixote was born and grew."[15]

Colonial Administration

Whatever its problems within Europe, Spain continued to rule a vast empire in the Americas. Columbus, Cortés, and Pizarro had claimed the lands they had "discovered" for the Crown of Spain. How were these lands governed? According to the Spanish theory of absolutism, the Crown was entitled to exercise full authority over all im-

perial lands. In the sixteenth century the Crown divided its New World territories into four **viceroyalties,** or administrative divisions: New Spain, which consisted of Mexico, Central America, and present-day California, Arizona, New Mexico, and Texas, with the capital at Mexico City; Peru, originally all the lands in continental South America, later reduced to the territory of modern Peru, Chile, Bolivia, and Ecuador, with the viceregal seat at Lima; New Granada, including present-day Venezuela, Colombia, Panama, and, after 1739, Ecuador, with Bogotá as its administrative center; and La Plata, consisting of Argentina, Uruguay, and Paraguay, with Buenos Aires as the capital.

Within each territory, the viceroy, or imperial governor, exercised broad military and civil authority as the direct representative of the sovereign in Madrid. The viceroy presided over the *audiencia,* a board of twelve to fifteen judges that served as his advisory council and the highest judicial body. The reform-minded Spanish king Charles III (r. 1759–1788) introduced the system of *in-*

tendants, pioneered by the Bourbon kings of France, to the New World territories. These royal officials possessed broad military, administrative, and financial authority within their intendancies and were responsible not to the viceroy but to the monarchy in Madrid.

From the early sixteenth century to the beginning of the nineteenth century, the Spanish monarchy acted on the mercantilist principle that the colonies existed for the financial benefit of the home country. The mining of gold and silver was always the most important industry in the colonies. The Crown claimed the **quinto,** one-fifth of all precious metals mined in South America. Gold and silver yielded the Spanish monarchy 25 percent of its total income. In return, it shipped manufactured goods to the Americas and discouraged the development of native industries.

The Portuguese governed their colony of Brazil in a similar manner. After the union of the Crowns of Portugal and Spain in 1580, Spanish administrative forms were introduced. Local officials called *corregidores* held judicial and military powers. Mercantilist policies placed severe restrictions on Brazilian industries that might compete with those of Portugal. In the seventeenth century the use of black slave labor made possible the cultivation of coffee and cotton, and in the eighteenth century Brazil led the world in the production of sugar. The unique feature of colonial Brazil's culture and society was its thoroughgoing intermixture of Indians, whites, and blacks.

The Culture of Absolutism

Under absolutist monarchs, culture became an instrument of state power. The baroque style in art and music flourished in the context of the Catholic Reformation. Baroque masters like Rubens painted portraits celebrating the glory of European monarchs. The baroque was particularly popular in Spain, Italy, and central Europe. Along with art, architecture became an important tool for absolutist monarchs. Louis XIV made the magnificent palace of Versailles the center of his kingdom, inspiring imitators across Europe (see Chapter 17). Even language reflected the growing power of the Crown. Within France Richelieu established an academy to oversee French literature and language. Outside its borders French became the common language of the European elite.

• **What cultural forms flourished under absolutist governments?**

Baroque Art and Music

Throughout European history, the cultural tastes of one age have often seemed unsatisfactory to the next. So it was with the baroque. The term **baroque** itself may have come from the Portuguese word for an "odd-shaped, imperfect pearl" and was commonly used by late-eighteenth-century art critics as an expression of scorn for what they considered an overblown, unbalanced style. These critics also scorned the Gothic style of medieval cathedrals in favor of a classicism inspired by antiquity and the Renaissance. Specialists now agree that the baroque style marked one of the high points in the history of Western culture.

Rome and the revitalized Catholic Church of the later sixteenth century played an important role in the early development of the baroque. The papacy and the Jesuits encouraged the growth of an intensely emotional, exuberant art. These patrons wanted artists to go beyond the Renaissance focus on pleasing a small, wealthy cultural elite. They wanted artists to appeal to the senses and thereby touch the souls and kindle the faith of ordinary churchgoers while proclaiming the power and confidence of the reformed Catholic Church. In addition to this underlying religious emotionalism, the baroque drew its sense of drama, motion, and ceaseless striving from the Catholic Reformation. The interior of the famous Jesuit Church of Jesus in Rome—the Gesù—combined all these characteristics in its lavish, shimmering, wildly active decorations and frescoes.

Taking definite shape in Italy after 1600, the baroque style in the visual arts developed with exceptional vigor in Catholic countries—in Spain and Latin America, Austria, southern Germany, and Poland. Yet baroque art was more than just "Catholic art" in the seventeenth century and the first half of the eighteenth. True, neither Protestant England nor the Netherlands ever came fully under the spell of the baroque, but neither did Catholic France. And Protestants accounted for some of the finest examples of baroque style, especially in music. The baroque style spread partly because its tension and bombast spoke to an agitated age that was experiencing great violence and controversy in politics and religion.

In painting, the baroque reached maturity early with Peter Paul Rubens (1577–1640), the most outstanding and most representative of baroque painters. Studying in his native Flanders and in Italy, where he was influenced by masters of the High Renaissance such as Michelangelo, Rubens developed his own rich, sensuous, colorful style, which was characterized by animated figures, melodramatic contrasts, and monumental size. Rubens excelled

Juan de Pareja: The Calling of Saint Matthew   Using rich but subdued colors, Pareja depicts the biblical text (Mark 2:13–17), with Jesus in traditional first-century dress and the other figures, arranged around a table covered with an Oriental carpet, in seventeenth-century apparel. Matthew, at Jesus' right hand, seems surprised by the "call." Pareja, following a long tradition, includes himself (*standing, rear center*). *(Museo Nacional del Prado, Madrid/The Bridgeman Art Library)*

in glorifying monarchs such as Queen Mother Marie de' Medici of France (see the painting on page 531). He was also a devout Catholic; nearly half of his pictures treat Christian subjects. Yet one of Rubens's trademarks was fleshy, sensual nudes who populate his canvases as Roman goddesses, water nymphs, and remarkably voluptuous saints and angels.

Rubens was enormously successful. To meet the demand for his work, he established a large studio and hired many assistants to execute his rough sketches and gigantic murals. Sometimes the master artist added only the finishing touches. Rubens's wealth and position—on occasion he was given special diplomatic assignments by the Habsburgs—affirmed that distinguished artists continued to enjoy the high social status they had won in the Renaissance.

In music, the baroque style reached its culmination almost a century later in the dynamic, soaring lines of the endlessly inventive Johann Sebastian Bach (1685–1750).

Organist and choirmaster of several Lutheran churches across Germany, Bach was equally at home writing secular concertos and sublime religious cantatas. Bach's organ music combined the baroque spirit of invention, tension, and emotion in an unforgettable striving toward the infinite. Unlike Rubens, Bach was not fully appreciated in his lifetime, but since the early nineteenth century his reputation has grown steadily.

Court Culture

For much of the seventeenth century, the courts of Europe looked to France, and to the palace of Versailles, for cultural as well as political inspiration. (See the feature "Listening to the Past: The Court at Versailles" on pages 556–557.) Versailles began as a modest hunting lodge. Under Louis XIV's orders, his architects, Le Nôtre and Le Vau, turned what the duke of Saint-Simon called "the most dismal and thankless of sights" into a magnificent palace. Everywhere, the viewer had a sense of grandeur, vastness, and elegance. Enormous staterooms became display galleries for inlaid tables, Italian marble statuary, tapestries woven at the royal factory in Paris, and beautiful furniture. In the gigantic Hall of Mirrors, hundreds of candles illuminated the domed ceiling, where allegorical paintings celebrated the king's victories. The formal gardens celebrated the rationality and order imposed by the Sun King; its classical sculptures depicted Louis as Apollo, king of the gods.

In 1682 Louis formally established his court at Versailles, which became the center of the kingdom: a model of rational order and the perfect symbol of the king's power. The art and architecture of Versailles were tools of Louis's policy, used to overawe his subjects and foreign visitors. The Russian tsar Peter the Great imitated Versailles in the construction of his palace, Peterhof, as did the Prussian emperor Frederick the Great in his palace at Potsdam outside Berlin and the Habsburgs at Schonbrunn outside Vienna. (See the feature "Images in Society: Absolutist Palace Building" on pages 568–569.)

The palace was the summit of political, social, and cultural life. The king required all great nobles to spend at least part of the year in attendance on him at Versailles. Between three thousand and ten thousand people occupied the palace each day. Given the demand for space, even high nobles had to make do with cramped and uncomfortable living quarters. The palace gardens, and the palace itself on some occasions, were open to the public, allowing even local peasants a glimpse of their sovereign. More than a royal residence or administrative center, Versailles was a mirror of French greatness to the world.

Much has been made of the "domestication" of the nobility at Versailles. Elaborate rituals attended every moment of Louis's day, from waking up and dressing in the morning to removing his clothing and retiring at night. Nobles had to follow a tortuous system of court etiquette, and they vied for the honor of serving the monarch, with the highest in rank claiming the privilege to hand the king his shirt. Endless squabbles broke out over what type of chair one could sit on at court and the order in which great nobles entered and were seated in the chapel for Mass.

These rituals were far from meaningless or trivial. The king controlled immense resources and privileges; access to him meant favored treatment for pensions, military and religious posts, honorary titles, and a host of other benefits. Courtiers sought these rewards for themselves and for their family members and followers. As in ancient Rome, patron-client relations—in which a higher-ranked individual protected a lower-ranked one in return for loyalty and services—dominated political life. **Patronage** flowed from the court to the provinces; it was the mechanism through which Louis gained cooperation from social elites.

One family demonstrates the interplay between the state's rationalizing impulses and its reliance on very traditional patterns of nepotism and patronage. Long credited as the "modernizer" of the French army, the minister Louvois acquired his position through family ties, not merit. His father, Michel LeTellier was secretary of war from 1643 to 1677; Louvois succeeded his father in this position from 1677 to his death in 1691 and was succeeded in turn by his own son Barbézieux from 1691 to 1701. The Louvois family not only had powerful connections within the French bureaucracy, but also bought court offices for younger family members to ensure their influence at Versailles.

Although they were denied public offices and posts, women played a central role in the patronage system. At court, the king's wife, mistresses, and other female relatives used their high rank to establish their own patronage relations. They recommended individuals for honors, advocated policy decisions, and brokered alliances between noble factions. Noblewomen played a similar role, bringing their family connections to marriage to form powerful social networks. Onlookers sometimes resented the influence of powerful women at court. The Duke of Saint-Simon said of Madame de Maintenon, Louis XIV's mistress and secret second wife:

The power of Madame de Maintenon was, as may be imagined, immense. She had everybody in her hands, from the highest and most favored ministers to the meanest subject of the realm. Many people have been ruined by her, without having been able to discover the author of the ruin, search as they might.

French Classicism

To this day, culture is a central element of French national pride and identity. French emphasis on culture dates back to Cardinal Richelieu, whose efforts at state centralization embraced cultural activities. In 1635 he gave official recognition to a group of scholars interested in grammar and rhetoric. Thus was born the French Academy. With Richelieu's encouragement, the French Academy began the preparation of a dictionary to standardize the French language; the dictionary was completed in 1694 and has been updated in many successive editions. The Academy survives today as a prestigious society, and retains authority over correct usage in the French language.

Scholars characterize the art and literature of the age of Louis XIV as **French classicism.** By this they mean that the artists and writers of the late seventeenth century imitated the subject matter and style of classical antiquity, that their work resembled that of Renaissance Italy, and that French art possessed the classical qualities of discipline, balance, and restraint. This was a movement away from the perceived excesses of baroque style.

Louis XIV danced gracefully at court ballets in his youth and was an enthusiastic patron of the arts. Music and theater frequently served as backdrops for court ceremonials. Louis favored Jean-Baptiste Lully (1632–1687), whose orchestral works combined lively animation with the restrained austerity typical of French classicism. Lully also composed court ballets, and his operatic productions were a powerful influence throughout Europe. Louis supported François Couperin (1668–1733), whose harpsichord and organ works possessed the regal grandeur the king loved, and Marc-Antoine Charpentier (1634–1704), whose solemn religious music entertained him at meals. Charpentier received a pension for the *Te Deums*, hymns of thanksgiving, he composed to celebrate French military victories.

Louis XIV loved the stage, and in the plays of Molière and Racine his court witnessed the finest achievements in the history of the French theater. When Jean-Baptiste Poquelin (1622–1673), the son of a prosperous tapestry maker, refused to join his father's business and entered the theater, he took the stage name "Molière." As playwright, stage manager, director, and actor, Molière produced comedies that exposed the hypocrisies and follies of society through brilliant caricature. *Tartuffe* satirized the religious hypocrite; *Le Bourgeois Gentilhomme* (The Bourgeois Gentleman) attacked the social parvenu; and *Les Précieuses ridicules* (The Pretentious Young Ladies) mocked the pretensions of the *précieuses*, elite women who ran intellectual salons and wrote and spoke in an elegant and pretentious manner. In structure Molière's plays followed classical models, but they were based on careful social observation. Molière made the bourgeoisie the butt of his ridicule; he stopped short of criticizing the high nobility, reflecting the policy of his royal patron.

Online Study Center **Improve Your Grade**
Primary Source: Molière's Bourgeois Gentlewoman, Mme. Jourdain, Rejects a Noble Son-in-Law

While Molière dissected social mores, his contemporary Jean Racine (1639–1699) based his tragic dramas on Greek and Roman legends. His persistent theme was the conflict of good and evil. Several plays—*Andromaque, Bérénice, Iphigénie,* and *Phèdre*—bear the names of women and deal with the power of female passion. Louis preferred *Mithridate* and *Britannicus* because of the "grandeur" of their themes. For simplicity of language, symmetrical structure, and calm restraint, the plays of Racine represent the finest examples of French classicism. His tragedies and Molière's comedies are still produced today.

With Versailles as the center of European politics, French culture grew in international prestige. Beginning in the reign of Louis XIV, French became the language of polite society and international diplomacy. French also gradually replaced Latin as the language of scholarship and learning. The royal courts of Sweden, Russia, Poland, and Germany all spoke French. In the eighteenth century the great Russian aristocrats were more fluent in French than in Russian. In England the first Hanoverian king, George I, spoke fluent French and only halting English. France inspired a cosmopolitan European culture in the late seventeenth century, which looked to Versailles as its center.

Constitutionalism

While France and later Prussia, Russia, and Austria solved the question of sovereignty with the absolutist state, England and Holland evolved toward the constitutional state. **Constitutionalism** is the limitation of government by law. Constitutionalism also implies a balance between the authority and power of the government, on the one hand, and the rights and liberties of the subjects, on the other.

A nation's constitution may be written or unwritten. It may be embodied in one basic document, occasionally revised by amendment, like the Constitution of the United States. Or it may be only partly formalized and include parliamentary statutes, judicial decisions, and a body of traditional procedures and practices, like the English and Dutch constitutions. Whether written or unwritten, a constitution gets its binding force from the government's acknowledgment that it must respect that constitution—that is, that the state must govern according to the laws. In a constitutional monarchy, a king or queen serves as the head of state and possesses some residual political authority, but the ultimate, or sovereign, power rests in the electorate.

A constitutional government is not the same as a democratic government. In a complete democracy, *all* the people have the right to participate either directly or indirectly (through their elected representatives) in the government of the state. Most men could not vote in Europe until the late nineteenth century, and women gained the franchise only in the twentieth century.

- **What is constitutionalism, and how did this form of government emerge in England and the Dutch Republic?**

Absolutist Claims in England (1603–1649)

In 1588 Queen Elizabeth I of England exercised very great personal power; by 1689 the English monarchy was severely circumscribed. Change in England was anything but orderly. Seventeenth-century England executed one king and experienced a bloody civil war; experimented with military dictatorship, then restored the son of the murdered king; and finally, after a bloodless revolution, established constitutional monarchy. Political stability came only in the 1690s. After such a violent and tumultuous century, how did England produce a constitutional monarchy? What combination of political, socioeconomic, and religious factors brought on a civil war in 1642–1649 and then the constitutional settlement of 1688–1689?

The extraordinary success of Elizabeth I rested on her political shrewdness and flexibility, her careful management of finances, her wise selection of ministers, her clever manipulation of Parliament, and her sense of royal dignity and devotion to hard work. A rare female monarch, Elizabeth imposed her authority in part by refusing to marry. If she had married, proper wifely submission to her husband would have made it difficult to assert royal authority over her subjects. The problem with this strategy was that it left the queen with no immediate heir to continue her legacy.

In 1603 Elizabeth's Scottish cousin James Stuart succeeded her as James I (r. 1603–1625). King James was well educated, learned, and, with thirty-five years' experience as king of Scotland, politically shrewd. But he was not as interested in displaying the majesty of monarchy as Elizabeth had been. Urged to wave at the crowds who waited to greet their new ruler, James complained that he was tired and threatened to drop his breeches "so they can cheer at my arse." The new king failed to live up to the role expected of him in England. Moreover, in contrast to Elizabeth, James was a poor judge of character, and in a society already hostile to the Scots, James's Scottish accent was a disadvantage.[16]

James's greatest problems, however, arose in resistance to his claims for monarchical authority. Like his French counterpart, James was devoted to the theory of the divine right of kings. He expressed his ideas in his essay "The Trew Law of Free Monarchy." According to James

I, a monarch has a divine (or God-given) right to his authority and is responsible only to God. Rebellion is the worst of political crimes. If a king orders something evil, the subject should respond with passive disobedience but should be prepared to accept any penalty for noncompliance. James went so far as to lecture the House of Commons: "There are no privileges and immunities which can stand against a divinely appointed King." This notion, implying total royal jurisdiction over the liberties, persons, and properties of English men and women, formed the basis of the Stuart concept of absolutism. Such a view ran directly counter to the long-standing English idea that a person's property could not be taken away without due process of law. James's expression of such views before the English House of Commons was a grave political mistake.

The House of Commons guarded the state's pocketbook, and James and later Stuart kings badly needed to open that pocketbook. Elizabeth had left James a sizable royal debt. Elizabeth had managed to escape public disapprobation for the debt, but James was left to face the consequences. Elizabeth had also left her Stuart successors a House of Commons that appreciated its own financial strength and intended to use that strength to acquire a greater say in the government of the state. The knights and burgesses who sat at Westminster in the late sixteenth and early seventeenth centuries wanted a voice in royal expenditures, religious reform, and foreign affairs. Essentially, the Commons wanted a measure of sovereignty.

Profound social changes had occurred since the sixteenth century. The English House of Commons during the reigns of James I and his son Charles I (r. 1625–1649) was very different from the assembly Henry VIII had manipulated into passing his Reformation legislation. The dissolution of the monasteries and the sale of monastic land had enriched many people. Enclosure of the common lands and new agricultural techniques had also enriched landowners, while many people invested successfully in commercial ventures, such as the expanding cloth industry. These developments led to a great deal of social mobility. Both in commerce and in agriculture, the English in the late sixteenth and early seventeenth centuries were capitalists, investing their profits to make more money.

The typical pattern was for the commercially successful to set themselves up as country gentry, thus creating an elite group that possessed a far greater proportion of land and of the national wealth in 1640 than had been the case in 1540. Small wonder that in 1640 someone could declare in the House of Commons that "We could buy

Van Dyck: Charles I (ca 1635) Anthony Van Dyck was the greatest of Rubens's many students. In 1633 he became court painter to Charles I. His portrait of Charles just dismounted from a horse emphasizes the aristocratic bearing, elegance, and innate authority of the king. This monarch seemingly needs no pomp or magnificence to display his sovereignty. Van Dyck's success led to innumerable commissions by members of the court and aristocratic society. He had a profound influence on English portraiture and was revered, for example, by Gainsborough. Some scholars believe that this portrait influenced Rigaud's 1701 portrait of Louis XIV (see page 522). *(Scala/Art Resource, NY)*

the House of Lords three times over." Increased wealth had also produced a better-educated and more articulate House of Commons. Many members had acquired at least a smattering of legal knowledge, which they used to search for medieval precedents from which to argue against the king.

In England, unlike France, there was no social stigma attached to paying taxes. Members of the House of Commons were willing to assess and pay taxes provided they had some say in the expenditure of those taxes and

in the formulation of state policies. The Stuart kings, however, considered such ambitions intolerable and a threat to their divine-right prerogative. Consequently, at every Parliament between 1603 and 1640, bitter squabbles erupted between the Crown and the articulate and legally minded Commons. Charles I's attempt to govern without Parliament (1629–1640) and to finance his government by arbitrary nonparliamentary levies, brought the country to a crisis.

Religious Divides

Religious issues also embittered relations between the king and the House of Commons. In the early seventeenth century increasing numbers of English people felt dissatisfied with the Church of England established by Henry VIII and reformed by Elizabeth. Many **Puritans** (see page 463) believed that the Reformation had not gone far enough. They wanted to "purify" the Anglican church of Roman Catholic elements—elaborate vestments and ceremonials, bishops, and even the giving and wearing of wedding rings.

It is difficult to establish what proportion of the English population was Puritan. According to present scholarly consensus, the dominant religious groups in the early seventeenth century were Calvinist; their more zealous members were Puritans. It also seems clear that many English people were attracted by the socioeconomic implications of John Calvin's theology. Calvinism emphasized hard work, sobriety, thrift, competition, and postponement of pleasure, and it tended to link poverty with weakness and moral corruption. These values, which have frequently been called the "Protestant ethic" or "capitalist ethic," fit in precisely with the economic approaches and practices of many successful business people and farmers. While it is hazardous to identify capitalism with Protestantism—there were many successful Catholic capitalists, for example—the "Protestant virtues" represented the prevailing values of members of the House of Commons.

Puritans wanted to abolish bishops in the Church of England, and when James I said, "No bishop, no king," he meant that the bishops were among the chief supporters of the throne. His son Charles I gave the impression of being sympathetic to Roman Catholicism. First, Charles married the French Catholic princess Henrietta Maria, a daughter of Henry IV. Charles also supported the policies of William Laud (1573–1645), archbishop of Canterbury, who tried to impose elaborate ritual on all churches. Laud insisted on complete uniformity of church services and enforced that uniformity through an ecclesiastical court called the "Court of High Commission." People believed that the country was being led back to Roman Catholicism.

In 1637 Laud attempted to impose two new elements on church organization in Scotland: a new prayer book, modeled on the Anglican *Book of Common Prayer,* and bishoprics, which the Presbyterian Scots firmly rejected. The Scots therefore revolted. To finance an army to put down the Scots, King Charles was compelled to summon Parliament in November 1640.

Charles I was an intelligent man, but contemporaries found him deceitful, dishonest, and treacherous. After quarreling with Parliament over his right to collect customs duties on wine and wool and over what the Commons perceived as religious innovations, Charles had dissolved Parliament in 1629. From 1629 to 1640, he ruled without Parliament, financing his government through extraordinary stopgap levies considered illegal by most English people. For example, the king revived a medieval law requiring coastal districts to help pay the cost of ships for defense, but he levied the tax, called "ship money," on inland as well as coastal counties. Most members of Parliament believed that such taxation without consent amounted to despotism. Consequently, they were not willing to trust the king with an army. Moreover, many supported the Scots' resistance to Charles's religious innovations and had little wish for military action against them. Accordingly, this Parliament, called the "Long Parliament" because it sat from 1640 to 1660, enacted legislation that limited the power of the monarch and made arbitrary government impossible.

In 1641 the Commons passed the Triennial Act, which compelled the king to summon Parliament every three years. The Commons impeached Archbishop Laud and abolished the Court of High Commission, then went further and threatened to abolish bishops. King Charles, fearful of a Scottish invasion—the original reason for summoning Parliament—accepted these measures. Understanding and peace were not achieved, however, partly because radical members of the Commons pushed increasingly revolutionary propositions, and partly because Charles maneuvered to rescind those he had already approved.

The next act in the conflict was precipitated by the outbreak of rebellion in Ireland. Ever since Henry II had conquered Ireland in 1171, English governors had mercilessly ruled the land, and English landlords had ruthlessly exploited the Irish people. The English Reformation had made a bad situation worse: because the Irish remained Catholic, religious differences united with economic and political oppression. In 1641 the Catholic gentry led an uprising in response to a feared invasion by anti-Catholic forces of the Long Parliament.

Puritan Occupations These twelve engravings depict typical Puritan occupations and show that the Puritans came primarily from the artisan and lower middle classes. The governing classes and peasants adhered to the traditions of the Church of England. (*Visual Connection Archive*)

Without an army, Charles I could neither come to terms with the Scots nor respond to the Irish rebellion, and the Long Parliament remained unwilling to place an army under a king it did not trust. After a failed attempt to arrest parliamentary leaders, Charles left London for the north of England. There, he recruited an army drawn from the nobility and its cavalry staff, the rural gentry, and mercenaries. The parliamentary army was composed of the militia of the city of London, country squires with business connections, and men with a firm belief in the spiritual duty of serving.

The English civil war (1642–1649) tested whether sovereignty in England was to reside in the king or in Parliament. In 1645 Parliament reorganized its forces into the **New Model Army** under the leadership of Sir Thomas Fairfax and Oliver Cromwell, a member of the House of Commons who had emerged as a military leader during the war. After three years of inconclusive fighting, parliamentary forces finally defeated the king's armies at the Battles of Naseby and Langport in the summer of 1645. To all appearances, the war was over and the parliamentary side had prevailed. The only remaining issue was to obtain formal recognition from Charles on restrictions on royal authority and church reform. Charles, though, refused to concede defeat. Both sides jockeyed for position, waiting for a decisive event. This arrived in the form of the army. In 1647 Cromwell's forces captured the king and dismissed members of the Parliament who opposed his actions. In 1649 the remaining representatives, known as the "Rump Parliament," put Charles on trial for high treason, a severe blow to the theory of divine-right monarchy. Charles was found guilty and beheaded on January 30, 1649, an act that sent shockwaves around Europe.

Puritanical Absolutism in England: Cromwell and the Protectorate

With the execution of Charles, kingship was abolished. A *commonwealth,* or republican government, was proclaimed. Theoretically, legislative power rested in the surviving members of Parliament, and executive power was lodged in a council of state. In fact, the army that had defeated the king controlled the government, and Oliver Cromwell controlled the army. Though called the **Protectorate,** the rule of Cromwell (1653–1658) constituted military dictatorship.

The army prepared a constitution, the Instrument of Government (1653), that invested executive power in a lord protector (Cromwell) and a council of state. The instrument provided for triennial parliaments and gave Par-

Cartoon of 1649: "The Royall Oake of Brittayne" Chopping down this tree signifies the end of royal authority, stability, Magna Carta (see page 272), and the rule of law. As pigs graze (representing the unconcerned common people), being fattened for slaughter, Oliver Cromwell, with his feet in Hell, quotes Scripture. This is a royalist view of the collapse of Charles I's government and the rule of Cromwell. *(Courtesy of the Trustees of the British Museum)*

liament the sole power to raise taxes. But after repeated disputes, Cromwell tore the document up. He continued the standing army and proclaimed quasi-martial law. He divided England into twelve military districts, each governed by a major general. The state rigorously censored the press, forbade sports, and kept the theaters closed in England. On the issue of religion, Cromwell favored some degree of toleration, and the Instrument of Government gave all Christians except Roman Catholics the right to practice their faith. As for Irish Catholicism, Cromwell identified it with sedition and heresy. In September 1649 his army crushed a rebellion at Drogheda and massacred the garrison. Another massacre followed in October. These brutal acts left a legacy of Irish hatred for England that has not yet subsided. Cromwell defended his actions by claiming to have acted only against soldiers in arms and said that a strong deterrent would prevent future bloodshed. After Cromwell's departure for England, the atrocities worsened. Sir William Petty, who served the English government in Ireland, estimated that over six hundred thousand people, or one-third of Ireland's population, died or were exiled as a result of the civil wars. The English banned Catholicism in Ireland, executed priests, and confiscated land from Catholics for English and Scottish settlers.

In England, Cromwell's regulation of the nation's economy had features typical of seventeenth-century absolutism. The lord protector's policies were mercantilist, similar to those Colbert established in France. Cromwell enforced a Navigation Act (1651), requiring that English goods be transported on English ships. The Navigation Act was a great boost to the development of an English merchant marine and brought about a short but successful war with the commercially threatened Dutch. Cromwell also welcomed the immigration of Jews because of their skills, and they began to return to England after four centuries of absence.

Military government collapsed when Cromwell died in 1658 and his ineffectual son succeeded him. Fed up with military rule, the English longed for a return to civilian government, restoration of the common law, and social stability. Government by military dictatorship was an experiment that the English never forgot or repeated. By 1660 they were ready to restore the monarchy.

The Restoration of the English Monarchy

The Restoration of 1660 re-established the monarchy in the person of Charles II (r. 1660–1685), eldest son of Charles I, who returned from exile on the continent to take the throne. At the same time, both houses of Parliament were restored, together with the established Anglican church, the courts of law, and the system of local government through justices of the peace. The Restoration failed to resolve two serious problems, however. What was to be the attitude of the state toward Puritans, Catholics, and dissenters from the established church? And what was to be the relationship between the king and Parliament?

About the first of these issues, Charles II, an easygoing and sensual man, was basically indifferent. He was not interested in doctrinal issues. Members of Parliament were, and they enacted a body of laws that sought to compel religious uniformity. Those who refused to receive the Eucharist of the Church of England could not vote, hold public office, preach, teach, attend the universities, or even assemble for meetings, according to the **Test Act** of 1673. But these restrictions could not be enforced. When the Quaker William Penn held a meeting of his Friends and was arrested, the jury refused to convict him.

In politics Charles II was determined "not to set out in his travels again," which meant that he intended to get along with Parliament. Generally good rapport existed between the king and the strongly royalist Parliament that had restored him. This rapport was due largely to the king's appointment of a council of five men who served both as his major advisers and as members of Parliament, thus acting as liaison agents between the executive and the legislature. This body—known as the "Cabal" from the names of its five members (Clifford, Arlington, Buckingham, Ashley-Cooper, and Lauderdale)—was an ancestor of the later cabinet system. Although its members sometimes disagreed and intrigued among themselves, it gradually came to be accepted that the Cabal was answerable in Parliament for the decisions of the king. This development gave rise to the concept of ministerial responsibility: royal ministers must answer to the Commons.

Harmony between the Crown and Parliament rested on the understanding that Charles would summon frequent Parliaments and that Parliament would vote him sufficient revenues. But Parliament did not grant him an adequate income. Accordingly, in 1670 Charles entered into a secret agreement with his cousin Louis XIV (Charles's mother Henrietta-Maria was the daughter of Henry IV, Louis' grandfather). The French king would give Charles two hundred thousand pounds annually, and in return Charles would relax the laws against Catholics, gradually re-Catholicize England, support French policy against the Dutch, and convert to Catholicism himself. When the details of this treaty leaked out, a great wave of anti-Catholic fear swept England. This fear was compounded by a crucial fact: with no legitimate heir, Charles would be succeeded by his Catholic brother, James, duke of York. A combination of hatred for French absolutism and hostility to Catholicism produced virtual hysteria. The Commons passed an exclusion bill denying the succession to a Roman Catholic, but Charles quickly dissolved Parliament, and the bill never became law.

When James II (r. 1685–1688) succeeded his brother, the worst English anti-Catholic fears, already aroused by Louis XIV's revocation of the Edict of Nantes, were realized. In violation of the Test Act, James appointed Roman Catholics to positions in the army, the universities, and local government. When these actions were challenged in the courts, the judges, whom James had appointed, decided for the king. The king was suspending the law at will and appeared to be reviving the absolutism of his father and grandfather. He went further. Attempting to broaden his base of support with Protestant dissenters and nonconformists, James issued a declaration of indulgence granting religious freedom to all.

Two events gave the signals for revolution. First, seven bishops of the Church of England petitioned the king that they not be forced to read the declaration of indulgence because of their belief that it was an illegal act. They were imprisoned in the Tower of London but subsequently acquitted amid great public enthusiasm. Second, in June 1688 James's second wife produced a male heir. A Catholic dynasty seemed ensured. The fear of a Roman Catholic monarchy supported by France and ruling outside the law prompted a group of eminent persons to offer the English throne to James's Protestant daughter Mary and her Dutch husband, Prince William of Orange. In December 1688 James II, his queen, and their infant son fled to France and became pensioners of Louis XIV. Early in 1689 William and Mary were crowned king and queen of England.

The Triumph of England's Parliament: Constitutional Monarchy and Cabinet Government

The English call the events of 1688 and 1689 the "Glorious Revolution" because it replaced one king with another with a minimum of bloodshed. It also represented the destruction, once and for all, of the idea of divine-right monarchy. William and Mary accepted the English throne from Parliament and in so doing explicitly recog-

nized the supremacy of Parliament. The revolution of 1688 established the principle that sovereignty, the ultimate power in the state, was divided between king and Parliament and that the king ruled with the consent of the governed.

The men who brought about the revolution quickly framed their intentions in the Bill of Rights, the cornerstone of the modern British constitution. The principles of the Bill of Rights were formulated in direct response to Stuart absolutism. Law was to be made in Parliament; once made, it could not be suspended by the Crown. Parliament had to be called at least once every three years. Both elections to and debate in Parliament were to be free in the sense that the Crown was not to interfere in them (this aspect of the bill was widely disregarded in the eighteenth century). The independence of the judiciary was established. No longer could the Crown get the judicial decisions it wanted by threats of removal. There was to be no standing army in peacetime—a limitation designed to prevent the repetition of Cromwellian military government. The Bill of Rights granted "that the subjects which are Protestants may have arms for their defense suitable to their conditions and as allowed by law,"[17] meaning that Catholics could not possess arms because the Protestant majority feared them. Additional legislation granted freedom of worship to Protestant dissenters and nonconformists and required that the English monarch always be Protestant.

The Glorious Revolution found its best defense in political philosopher John Locke's **Second Treatise of Civil Government** (1690). Locke (1632–1704) maintained that people set up civil governments to protect life, liberty, and property. A government that oversteps its proper function—protecting the natural rights of life, liberty, and property—becomes a tyranny. (By "natural" rights Locke meant rights basic to all men because all have the ability to reason.) Under a tyrannical government, the people have the natural right to rebellion. Such rebellion can be avoided if the government carefully respects the rights of citizens and if people zealously defend their liberty. Arguing for a close relationship between economic and political freedom, Locke linked economic liberty and private property with political freedom. On the basis of this link, he justified limiting the vote to property owners. Locke served as the great spokesman for the liberal English revolution of 1688 and 1689 and for representative government. His idea that there are natural or universal rights equally valid for all peoples and societies was especially popular in colonial America. (Colonists also appreciated his arguments that Native Americans had no property rights since they did not cultivate the land and, by extension, no political rights because they possessed no property.)

Online Study Center **Improve Your Grade**
Primary Source: John Locke's Vindication for the Glorious Revolution: The Social Contract

The events of 1688 and 1689 did not constitute a *democratic* revolution. The revolution placed sovereignty in Parliament, and Parliament represented the upper classes. The great majority of English people acquired no say in their government. The English revolution established a constitutional monarchy; it also inaugurated an age of aristocratic government that lasted at least until 1832 and in many ways until 1928, when women received full voting rights.

The Dutch Republic in the Seventeenth Century

In the late sixteenth century the seven northern provinces of the Netherlands fought for and won their independence from Spain as the Republic of United Provinces of the Netherlands—an independence that was confirmed by the Peace of Westphalia ending the Thirty Years' War in 1648 (see page 563). The seventeenth century witnessed an unparalleled flowering of Dutch scientific, artistic, and literary achievement. In this period, often called the "golden age of the Netherlands," Dutch ideas and attitudes played a profound role in shaping a new and modern worldview. At the same time, the United Provinces was another model of the development of the modern constitutional state.

Within each province, an oligarchy of wealthy merchants called "regents" handled domestic affairs in the local Estates. The provincial Estates held virtually all the power. A federal assembly, or **States General,** handled matters of foreign affairs, such as war. But the States General did not possess sovereign authority; all issues had to be referred back to the local Estates for approval. The States General appointed a representative, the **stadholder,** in each province. As the highest executive there, the stadholder carried out ceremonial functions and was responsible for defense and good order. Maurice and

Jan Steen: The Christening Feast As the mother, surrounded by midwives, rests in bed (*rear left*) and the father proudly displays the swaddled child, thirteen other people, united by gestures and gazes, prepare the celebratory meal. Very prolific, Steen was a master of warm-hearted domestic scenes. In contrast to the order and cleanliness of many seventeenth-century Dutch genre paintings, Steen's more disorderly portrayals gave rise to the epithet "a Jan Steen household," meaning an untidy house. (*Wallace Collection, London/The Bridgeman Art Library*)

Room from Het Scheepje (The Little Ship) A retired sea captain who became a successful brewer in Haarlem owned the house (adjacent to his brewery) that included this room. The brass chandelier, plates, tiles, Turkish rug on the table (probably from Transylvania in the Ottoman Empire), oak mantelpiece, and paneling make this a superb example of a Dutch domestic interior during the golden age. A bed built into the wall paneling was warmed at night by coals in the pan hanging by the fireplace. *(Room from Het Scheepje, Haarlem, The Netherlands, early 17th century. Philadelphia Museum of Art, Gift of Edward W. Bok. 1928-66-1)*

William Louis, the sons of William the Silent, held the office of stadholder in all seven provinces. As members of the House of Orange, they were closely identified with Dutch patriotism. The regents in each province jealously guarded local independence and resisted efforts at centralization. Nevertheless, Holland, which had the largest navy and the most wealth, dominated the republic and the States General. Significantly, the Estates assembled at Holland's capital, The Hague.

The government of the United Provinces had none of the standard categories of seventeenth-century political organization. The Dutch were not monarchical but rather fiercely republican. The government was controlled by wealthy merchants and financiers. Though they were rich, their values were strongly middle class, not aristocratic. The Dutch republic was not a strong federation but a confederation—that is, a weak union of strong provinces. The provinces were a temptation to powerful neighbors, yet the Dutch resisted the long Spanish effort at reconquest and withstood both French and English attacks in the second half of the century.

The political success of the Dutch rested on the phenomenal commercial prosperity of the Netherlands. The moral and ethical bases of that commercial wealth were thrift, frugality, and religious toleration. John Calvin had written, "From where do the merchant's profits come except from his own diligence and industry?" This attitude encouraged a sturdy people who had waged a centuries-old struggle against the sea.

Alone of all European peoples in the seventeenth century, the Dutch practiced religious toleration. Peoples of all faiths were welcome within their borders. Although there is scattered evidence of anti-Semitism, Jews enjoyed a level of acceptance and assimilation in Dutch business and general culture unique in early modern Europe. (See the feature "Individuals in Society: Glückel of Hameln.") For example, Benedict Spinoza (1632–1677), a descendant of Spanish Jews who fled the Inquisition, passed his entire life in Amsterdam, supporting himself as a lens grinder while producing important philosophical treatises. The urbanity of Dutch society allowed a rare degree of religious freedom. As long as business people conducted their religion in private, the government did not interfere with them.

In the Dutch Republic, toleration paid off: it attracted a great deal of foreign capital and investment. Deposits at the Bank of Amsterdam were guaranteed by the city council, and in the middle years of the century the bank became Europe's best source of cheap credit and commercial intelligence and the main clearing-house for bills of exchange. People of all races and creeds traded in Amsterdam, at whose docks on the Amstel River five thousand ships were berthed. Joost van den Vondel, the poet of Dutch imperialism, exulted:

Individuals in Society

Glückel of Hameln

Gentleness and deep mutual devotion seem to pervade Rembrandt's The Jewish Bride. (Rijksmuseum-Stichting Amsterdam)

In 1690 a Jewish widow in the small German town of Hameln* in Lower Saxony sat down to write her autobiography. She wanted to distract her mind from the terrible grief she felt over the death of her husband and to provide her twelve children with a record "so you will know from what sort of people you have sprung, lest today or tomorrow your beloved children or grandchildren came and know naught of their family." Out of her pain and heightened consciousness, Glückel (1646–1724) produced an invaluable source for scholars.

She was born in Hamburg two years before the end of the Thirty Years' War. In 1649 the merchants of Hamburg expelled the Jews, who moved to nearby Altona, then under Danish rule. When the Swedes overran Altona in 1657–1658, the Jews returned to Hamburg "purely at the mercy of the Town Council." Glückel's narrative proceeds against a background of the constant harassment to which Jews were subjected—special papers, permits, bribes—and in Hameln she wrote, "And so it has been to this day and, I fear, will continue in like fashion."

When Glückel was "barely twelve," her father betrothed her to Chayim Hameln. She married at age fourteen. She describes him as "the perfect pattern of the pious Jew," a man who stopped his work every day for study and prayer, fasted, and was scrupulously honest in his business dealings. Only a few years older than Glückel, Chayim earned his living dealing in precious metals and in making small loans on pledges (articles held on security). This work required his constant travel to larger cities, markets, and fairs, often in bad weather, always over dangerous roads. Chayim consulted his wife about all his business dealings. As he lay dying, a friend asked if he had any last wishes. "None," he replied. "My wife knows everything. She shall do as she has always done." For thirty years Glückel had been his friend, full business partner, and wife. They had thirteen children, twelve of whom survived their father, eight then unmarried. As Chayim had foretold, Glückel succeeded in launching the boys in careers and in providing dowries for the girls.

Glückel's world was her family, the Jewish community of Hameln, and the Jewish communities into which her children married. Social and business activities took her to Amsterdam, Baiersdorf, Bamberg, Berlin, Cleves, Danzig, Metz, and Vienna, so her world was not narrow or provincial. She took great pride that Prince Frederick of Cleves, later king of Prussia, danced at the wedding of her eldest daughter. The rising prosperity of Chayim's businesses allowed the couple to maintain up to six servants.

Glückel was deeply religious, and her culture was steeped in Jewish literature, legends, and mystical and secular works. Above all, she relied on the Bible. Her language, heavily sprinkled with scriptural references, testifies to a rare familiarity with the basic book of Western civilization. The Scriptures were her consolation, the source of her great strength in a hostile world.

Students who would learn about business practices, the importance of the dowry in marriage, childbirth, the ceremony of bris, birthrates, family celebrations, and even the meaning of life can gain a good deal from the memoirs of this extraordinary woman who was, in the words of one of her descendants, the poet Heinrich Heine, "the gift of a world to me."

Questions for Analysis

1. Consider the ways in which Glückel of Hameln was both an ordinary and an extraordinary woman of her times. Would you call her a marginal or a central person in her society?
2. How was Glückel's life affected by the broad events and issues of the seventeenth century?

* A town immortalized by the Brothers Grimm. In 1284 the town contracted with the Pied Piper to rid it of rats and mice; he lured them away by playing his flute. When the citizens refused to pay, he charmed away their children in revenge.

Source: The Memoirs of Glückel of Hameln, (New York: Schocken Books, 1977).

Online Study Center **Improve Your Grade**
Going Beyond Individuals in Society

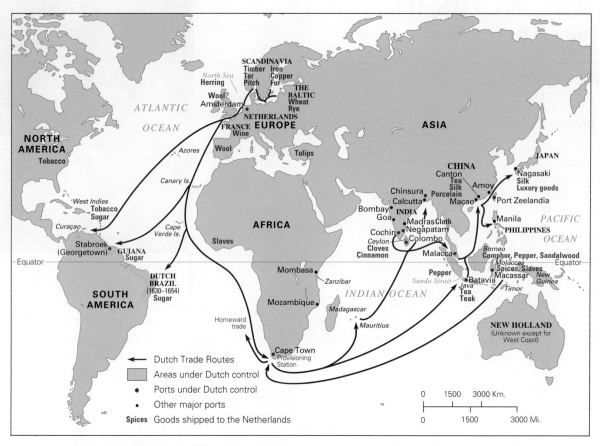

MAP 16.3 Seventeenth-Century Dutch Commerce Dutch wealth rested on commerce, and commerce depended on the huge Dutch merchant marine, manned by perhaps forty-eight thousand sailors. The fleet carried goods from all parts of the globe to the port of Amsterdam.

God, God, the Lord of Amstel cried, hold every conscience
  free;
And Liberty ride, on Holland's tide, with billowing sails
  to sea,
And run our Amstel out and in; let freedom gird the bold,
And merchant in his counting house stand elbow deep
  in gold.[18]

The fishing industry was the original cornerstone of the Dutch economy. For half the year, from June to December, fishing fleets combed the dangerous English coast and the North Sea and raked in tiny herring. Profits from herring stimulated shipbuilding, and even before 1600 the Dutch were offering the lowest shipping rates in Europe. The Dutch merchant marine was the largest in Europe. In 1650 contemporaries estimated that the Dutch had sixteen thousand merchant ships, half the Eu-

ropean total. All the wood for these ships had to be imported: the Dutch bought whole forests from Norway. They also bought entire vineyards from French growers before the grapes were harvested. They controlled the Baltic grain trade, buying entire wheat and rye crops in Poland, east Prussia, and Swedish Pomerania. Because the Dutch dealt in bulk, nobody could undersell them. Foreign merchants coming to Amsterdam could buy anything from precision lenses for the microscope (recently invented by Dutchman Anton van Leeuwenhoek) to muskets for an army of five thousand. Although Dutch cities became famous for their exports—diamonds and linens from Haarlem, pottery from Delft—Dutch wealth depended less on exports than on transport.

In 1602 a group of the regents of Holland formed the **Dutch East India Company,** a joint stock company. The investors each received a percentage of the profits proportional to the amount of money they had put in. Within half a century the Dutch East India Company had cut heavily into Portuguese trading in East Asia. The Dutch seized the Cape of Good Hope, Ceylon, and Malacca and established trading posts in each place. In the 1630s the Dutch East India Company was paying its investors about a 35 percent annual return on their investments. The Dutch West India Company, founded in 1621, traded extensively with Latin America and Africa (see Map 16.3).

Trade and commerce brought the Dutch prodigious wealth. In the seventeenth century the Dutch enjoyed the highest standard of living in Europe, perhaps in the world. Amsterdam and Rotterdam built massive granaries where the surplus of one year could be stored against possible shortages the next. Thus, except in the 1650s, when bad harvests reduced supplies, food prices fluctuated very little. By the standards of Cologne, Paris, or London, salaries were high for all workers—except women, but even women's wages were high when compared with those of women in other parts of Europe. All classes of society, including unskilled laborers, ate well.

The low price of bread meant that, compared to other places in Europe, a higher percentage of the worker's income could be spent on fish, cheese, butter, vegetables, and even meat. A scholar has described the Netherlands as "an island of plenty in a sea of want." Consequently, the Netherlands experienced very few of the food riots that characterized the rest of Europe.[19]

Although the initial purpose of the Dutch East and West India Companies was commercial—the import of spices and silks to Europe—the Dutch found themselves involved in the imperialist exploitation of parts of East Asia and Latin America, with great success. In 1652 the Dutch founded Cape Town on the southern tip of Africa as a fueling station for ships planning to cross the Pacific. But war with France and England in the 1670s hurt the United Provinces. The long War of the Spanish Succession—in which the Dutch prince William of Orange, who was King William III of England, utilized English wealth in the Dutch fight against Louis XIV—was a costly drain on Dutch labor and financial resources. The peace signed in 1713 to end the war marked the beginning of Dutch economic decline.

Chapter Summary

Online Study Center   **ACE the Test**

- *What were the common crises and achievements of seventeenth-century states?*
- *To what extent did French and Spanish monarchs succeed in creating absolute monarchies?*
- *What cultural forms flourished under absolutist governments?*
- *What is constitutionalism, and how did this form of government emerge in England and the Dutch Republic?*

Most parts of Europe experienced the seventeenth century as a period of severe economic, social, and military crisis. Across the continent, rulers faced popular rebellions from their desperate subjects, who were pushed to the brink by poor harvests, high taxes, and decades of war. Many forces, including powerful noblemen, the church, and regional and local loyalties, constrained the state's

authority. Despite these obstacles, most European states emerged from the seventeenth century with increased powers and more centralized control. Whether they ruled through monarchical fiat or parliamentary negotiation, European governments strengthened their bureaucracies, raised more taxes, and significantly expanded their armies.

According to Thomas Hobbes, the central drive in every human is "a perpetual and restless desire of Power, after Power, that ceaseth only in Death." The seventeenth century solved the problem of sovereign power in two fundamental ways: absolutism and constitutionalism. Under Louis XIV France witnessed the high point of absolutist ambition in western Europe. The king saw himself as the representative of God on earth, and it has been said that "to the seventeenth century imagination God was a sort of image of Louis XIV."[20] Under Louis's rule, France developed a centralized bureaucracy, a professional army, and a state-directed economy, all of which he personally supervised.

Despite his claims to absolute power, historians now agree that Louis XIV ruled, in practice, by securing the collaboration of high nobles. In exchange for confirmation of their ancient privileges, the nobles were willing to cooperate with the expansion of state power. This was a common pattern in attempts at absolutism across Europe. In Spain, where monarchs made similar claims to absolute power, the seventeenth century witnessed economic catastrophe and a decline in royal capacities. Spanish rule continued in the colonies and foreshadowed a revival of Spanish fortunes in the eighteenth century.

France's dominant political role in Europe elevated its cultural influence as well. French became the common language of the European elite, as all heads turned to Versailles and the radiant aristocratic culture emanating from it. Within France, the Bourbon monarchy pursued culture as one more aspect of absolutist policy, creating cultural academies, sponsoring playwrights and musicians, and repressing Protestantism with a bloody hand.

As Louis XIV personified absolutist ambitions, so Stuart England exemplified the evolution of the constitutional state. The conflicts between Parliament and the first two Stuart rulers, James I and Charles I, tested where sovereign power would reside. The resulting civil war did not solve the problem. The Instrument of Government provided for a balance of government authority and recognition of popular rights; as such, the Instrument has been called the first modern constitution. Unfortunately, it lacked public support. James II's absolutist tendencies brought on the Glorious Revolution of 1688 and 1689, and the people who made that revolution settled three basic issues: sovereign power was divided between king and Parliament, with Parliament enjoying the greater share; government was to be based on the rule of law; and the liberties of English people were made explicit in written form in the Bill of Rights.

Having won independence from Spain, the United Provinces of the Netherlands provided another model of constitutional government, one dominated by wealthy urban merchants rather than the landed gentry who controlled the English system. The federal constitution of the Netherlands invested power in the Estates General, but diluted their authority by giving veto power to provincial assemblies. Dominated by Holland, the Netherlands provided a shining example of industriousness, prosperity, and relative tolerance for the rest of Europe.

Key Terms

moral economy	viceroyalties
sovereignty	quinto
popular revolts	baroque
Edict of Nantes	patronage
intendants	French classicism
noblesse de robe	constitutionalism
(robe nobility)	Puritans
Fronde	New Model Army
noblesse d'épée	Protectorate
(sword nobility)	Test Act
divine right of kings	*Second Treatise of*
absolute monarchy	*Civil Government*
mercantilism	States General
estates	stadholder
Peace of Utrecht	Dutch East India
Don Quixote	Company

Online Study Center **Improve Your Grade** Flashcards

Suggested Reading

Beik, William. *Urban Protest in Seventeenth-Century France.* 1997. Explores urban violence in France during harsh years of economic and social crisis.

Benedict, Philip, and Myron P. Gutmann, eds. *Early Modern Europe: From Crisis to Stability.* 2005. A helpful introduction to the many facets of the seventeenth-century crisis.

Burke, Peter. *The Fabrication of Louis XIV.* 1992. Explains the use of architecture, art, medals, and other symbols to promote the king's image.

Collins, James B. *The State in Early Modern France.* 1995. A detailed and well-argued survey of French administration from Louis XIII to Louis XVI.

Elliott, John H. *Richelieu and Olivares.* 1984. A comparison of the chief ministers of France and Spain that also reveals differences and similarities in the countries they led.

Gaunt, Peter, ed. *The English Civil War: The Essential Readings.* 2000. A collection showcasing leading historians' interpretations of the civil war.

Hutton, Ronald. *Charles II: King of England, Scotland and Ireland.* 1989. A reliable and highly readable biography of King Charles II.

Israel, Jonathan. *The Dutch Republic: Its Rise, Greatness and Fall, 1477–1806.* 1995. A thorough study of the political history of the republic.

Kettering, Sharon. *Patronage in Sixteenth- and Seventeenth-Century France.* 2002. A collection of essays exploring the role of patronage in politics and noble life, including women's role in patronage networks.

Lynn, John A. *Giant of the Grand Siècle: The French Army, 1610–1715.* 1997. Examines the tremendous growth and professionalization of the French army under Louis XIV.

Pagden, Anthony. *Spanish Imperialism and the Political Imagination.* 1990. Explores Spanish ideas of empire, primarily in Italy and the Americas.

Schama, Simon. *The Embarrassment of Riches: An Interpretation of Dutch Culture in the Golden Age.* 1987. A lengthy but vivid and highly readable account of Dutch culture in the seventeenth century, including a chapter on the mania for speculation on the tulip market.

Te Brake, Wayne. *Shaping History: Ordinary People in European Politics, 1500–1700.* 1998. Examines the political activities of the non-elite in early modern Europe.

Underdown, David. *Revel, Riot, and Rebellion.* 1985. Discusses ordinary people's roles in the English civil war.

Wrightson, Keith. *English Society, 1580–1680.* 1982. Good coverage of English political and social issues of the seventeenth century.

Young, John, ed. *Celtic Dimensions of the British Civil Wars.* 1997. Explores Scotland and Ireland and their involvement in the civil wars in Great Britain.

Notes

1. The classic study Theodore K. Rabb, *The Struggle for Stability in Early Modern Europe* (Oxford: Oxford University Press, 1975).

2. John A. Lynn, "Recalculating French Army Growth," in *The Military Revolution Debate: Readings on the Military Transformation of Early Modern Europe*, ed. Clifford J. Rogers (Boulder, Colo.: Westview Press, 1995), p. 125.

3. G. Parker and L. M. Smith, "Introduction," and N. Steensgaard, "The Seventeenth Century Crisis," in *The General Crisis of the Seventeenth Century*, ed. G. Parker and L. M. Smith (London: Routledge & Kegan Paul, 1985), pp. 1–53, esp. p. 12.

4. H. G. Koenigsberger, "The Revolt of Palermo in 1647," *Cambridge Historical Journal* 8 (1944–1946): 129–144.

5. See W. Beik, *Urban Protest in Seventeenth-Century France: The Culture of Retribution* (New York: Cambridge University Press, 1997), p. 1.

6. Ibid.

7. See ibid., chaps. 1, 2, 3, and 11.

8. Ibid., pp. 22–26.

9. See M. Turchetti, "The Edict of Nantes," in *The Oxford Encyclopedia of the Reformation*, ed. H. J. Hillerbrand, vol. 3 (New York: Oxford University Press, 1996), pp. 126–128.

10. Quoted in J. H. Elliott, *Richelieu and Olivares* (Cambridge: Cambridge University Press, 1984), p. 135; and in W. F. Church, *Richelieu and Reason of State* (Princeton, N.J.: Princeton University Press, 1972), p. 507.

11. James B. Collins, *The State in Early Modern France* (Cambridge: Cambridge University Press, 1995), pp. 65–78.

12. Quoted in J. Wolf, *Louis XIV* (New York: W. W. Norton, 1968), p. 146.

13. Ibid.

14. J. H. Elliott, *Imperial Spain, 1469–1716* (New York: Mentor Books, 1963), pp. 306–308.

15. B. Bennassar, *The Spanish Character: Attitudes and Mentalities from the Sixteenth to the Nineteenth Century*, trans. B. Keen (Berkeley: University of California Press, 1979), p. 125.

16. For a revisionist interpretation, see J. Wormald, "James VI and I: Two Kings or One?" *History* 62 (June 1983): 187–209.

17. C. Stephenson and G. F. Marcham, *Sources of English Constitutional History* (New York: Harper & Row, 1937), p. 601.

18. Quoted in D. Maland, *Europe in the Seventeenth Century* (New York: Macmillan, 1967), pp. 198–199. Copyright © 1967 by A & C Black Ltd.

19. S. Schama, *The Embarrassment of Riches: An Interpretation of Dutch Culture in the Golden Age* (New York: Alfred A. Knopf, 1987), pp. 165–170; quotation is on p. 167.

20. C. J. Friedrich and C. Blitzer, *The Age of Power* (Ithaca, N.Y.: Cornell University Press, 1957), p. 112.

Listening to the Past

The Court at Versailles

Although the duke of Saint-Simon (1675–1755) was a soldier, courtier, and diplomat, his enduring reputation rests on The Memoirs (1788), his eyewitness account of the personality and court of Louis XIV. A nobleman of extremely high status, Saint-Simon resented Louis's high-handed treatment of the ancient nobility and his promotion of newer nobles and the bourgeoisie. The Memoirs, excerpted here, remains a monument of French literature and an indispensable historical source, partly for its portrait of the court at Versailles.

Very early in the reign of Louis XIV the Court was removed from Paris, never to return. The troubles of the minority had given him a dislike to that city; his enforced and surreptitious flight from it still rankled in his memory; he did not consider himself safe there, and thought cabals would be more easily detected if the Court was in the country, where the movements and temporary absences of any of its members would be more easily noticed. . . . No doubt that he was also influenced by the feeling that he would be regarded with greater awe and veneration when no longer exposed every day to the gaze of the multitude.

His love-affair with Mademoiselle de la Vallière, which at first was covered as far as possible with a veil of mystery, was the cause of frequent excursions to Versailles. . . . The visits of Louis XIV becoming more frequent, he enlarged the *château* by degrees till its immense buildings afforded better accommodation for the Court than was to be found at St. Germain, where most of the courtiers had to put up with uncomfortable lodgings in the town. The Court was therefore removed to Versailles in 1682, not long before the Queen's death. The new building contained an infinite number of rooms for courtiers, and the King liked the grant of these rooms to be regarded as a coveted privilege.

He availed himself of the frequent festivities at Versailles, and his excursions to other places, as a means of making the courtiers assiduous in their attendance and anxious to please him; for he nominated beforehand those who were to take part in them, and could thus gratify some and inflict a snub on others. He was conscious that the substantial favours he had to bestow were not nearly sufficient to produce a continual effect; he had therefore to invent imaginary ones, and no one was so clever in devising petty distinctions and preferences which aroused jealousy and emulation. The visits to Marly later on were very useful to him in this way; also those to Trianon [Marly and Trianon were small country houses], where certain ladies, chosen beforehand, were admitted to his table. It was another distinction to hold his candlestick at his *coucher;* as soon as he had finished his prayers he used to name the courtier to whom it was to be handed, always choosing one of the highest rank among those present. . . .

Not only did he expect all persons of distinction to be in continual attendance at Court, but he was quick to notice the absence of those of inferior degree; at his *lever* [formal rising from bed in the morning], his *coucher* [preparations for going to bed], his meals, in the gardens of Versailles (the only place where the courtiers in general were allowed to follow him), he used to cast his eyes to right and left; nothing escaped him, he saw everybody. If any one habitually living at Court absented himself he insisted on knowing the reason; those who came there only for flying visits had also to give a satisfactory explanation; any one who seldom or never appeared there was certain to incur his displeasure. If asked to bestow a favour on such persons he would reply haughtily: "I do not know him"; of such as rarely presented themselves he would say, "He is a man I never see"; and from these judgements there was no appeal.

He always took great pains to find out what was going on in public places, in society, in private houses, even family secrets, and maintained an immense number of spies and tale-bearers. These were of all sorts; some did not know that their reports were carried to him; others did know it; there were others, again, who used to write to him directly, through channels which he prescribed; others who were admitted by the backstairs and saw him in his private room. Many a man in all ranks of life was ruined by these methods, often very unjustly, without ever being able to discover the reason; and when the King had once taken a prejudice against a man, he hardly ever got over it. . . .

No one understood better than Louis XIV the art of enhancing the value of a favour by his manner of bestowing it; he knew how to make the most of a word, a smile, even of a glance. If he addressed any one, were it but to ask a trifling question or make some commonplace remark, all eyes were turned on the person so honored; it was a mark of favour which always gave rise to comment. . . .

He loved splendour, magnificence, and profusion in all things, and encouraged similar tastes in his Court; to spend money freely on equipages [the king's horse carriages] and buildings, on feasting and at cards, was a sure way to gain his favour, perhaps to obtain the honour of a word from him. Motives of policy had something to do with this; by making expensive habits the fashion, and, for people in a certain position, a necessity, he compelled his courtiers to live beyond their income, and gradually reduced them to depend on his bounty for the means of subsistence. This was a plague which, once introduced, became a scourge to the whole country, for it did not take long to spread to Paris, and thence to the armies and the provinces; so that a man of any position is now estimated entirely according to his expenditure on his table and other luxuries. This folly, sustained by pride and ostentation, has already produced widespread confusion; it threatens to end in nothing short of ruin and a general overthrow.

Louis XIV was extremely proud of the gardens at Versailles and personally led ambassadors and other highly ranked visitors on tours of the extensive palace grounds. *(Erich Lessing/Art Resource, NY)*

Questions for Analysis

1. What was the role of etiquette and ceremony at the court of Versailles? How could Louis XIV use them in everyday life at court to influence and control nobles?

2. How important do you think Louis's individual character and personality were to his style of governing? What challenges might this present to his successors?

3. Consider the role of ceremony in some modern governments, such as the U.S. government. How does it compare to Louis XIV's use of ceremony as portrayed by Saint-Simon?

4. Do you think Saint-Simon is an objective and trustworthy recorder of life at court? Why?

Source: F. Arkwright, ed., *The Memoirs of the Duke de Saint-Simon,* vol. 5 (New York: Brentano's, n.d.), pp. 271–274, 276–278.

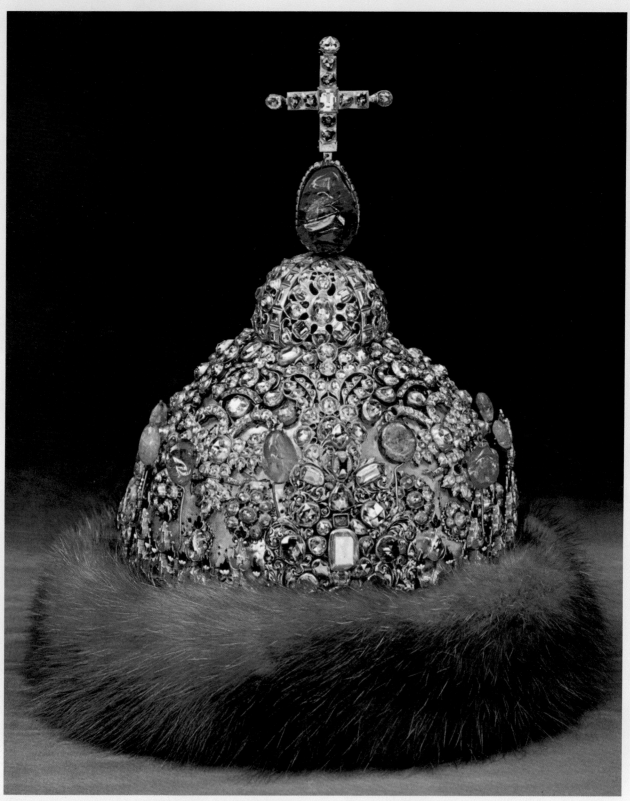

Peter the Great's magnificent new crown, created for his joint coronation in 1682 with his half-brother Ivan. *(State Museum of the Kremlin, Moscow)*

Warfare and Social Change in Central and Eastern Europe

• *What social and economic changes affected central and eastern Europe from 1400 to 1650?*

The Rise of Austria and Prussia

• *How and why did the rulers of Austria and Prussia, each in different political and social environments, manage to build powerful absolute monarchies that proved more durable than that of Louis XIV?*

The Development of Russia and the Ottoman Empire

• *What were the distinctive features of Russian and Ottoman absolutism in this period?*

ABSOLUTISM IN CENTRAL AND EASTERN EUROPE
TO 1740

The crises of the seventeenth century—religious division, economic depression, and war—were not limited to the West. Central and eastern Europe experienced even more catastrophic dislocation, with German lands serving as the battleground of the Thirty Years' War and borders constantly vulnerable to attack from the east. In Prussia and Habsburg Austria absolutist states emerged in the aftermath of this conflict.

Russia and the Ottoman Turks also developed absolutist governments. These empires seemed foreign and exotic to western Europeans, who saw them as the antithesis of their political, religious, and cultural values. To Western eyes, their monarchs respected law—either divine or constitutional—while Eastern despots ruled with an iron fist. The Ottoman Muslim state was home to fanaticism and heresy, and even Russian Orthodoxy had rituals and traditions, if not core beliefs, that differed sharply from either Catholicism or Protestantism. Beneath the surface, however, these Eastern governments shared many similarities with Western ones.

The most successful Eastern empires lasted until 1918, far longer than monarchical rule endured in France, the model of absolutism under Louis XIV. Eastern monarchs had a powerful impact on architecture and the arts, encouraging new monumental construction to reflect their glory. Questions about the relationship between East and West remain potent today, when Turkey's bid for membership in the European Union is controversial both at home and abroad.

Warfare and Social Change in Central and Eastern Europe

When absolute monarchy emerged in the seventeenth century, it built on social and economic foundations laid between roughly 1400 and 1650. In those years the elites of eastern Europe—with the major exception of the Ottoman rulers in the Balkans—rolled back the gains made by the peasantry during the High Middle Ages and re-imposed a harsh serfdom on the rural masses. The nobility also reduced the importance of the

Online Study Center

This icon will direct you to interactive activities and study materials on the website **college.hmco.com/pic/mckaywest9e**

towns and the middle classes. This process differed from developments in western Europe, where peasants won greater freedom and the urban middle class continued its rise. The Thirty Years' War represented the culmination of these changes. Decades of war in central Europe led to depopulation and economic depression, which allowed lords to impose ever-harsher controls on the peasantry.

• *What social and economic changes affected central and eastern Europe from 1400 to 1650?*

Origins of Serfdom

The period from 1050 to 1300 was a time of general economic expansion in eastern Europe characterized by the growth of trade, towns, and population. This meant clearing the forests and colonizing the frontier beyond the Elbe River. Eager to attract settlers to sparsely populated lands, the rulers of eastern Europe offered newcomers economic and legal incentives, providing land on excellent terms and granting greater personal freedom. These benefits were also gradually extended to the local Slavic populations, even those of central Russia. Thus, by 1300 **serfdom** had all but disappeared in eastern Europe. Peasants bargained freely with their landlords and moved about as they pleased. Opportunities and improvements in the East had a positive impact on the West, where the weight of serfdom was also reduced between 1100 and 1300. Thus fundamental social and economic developments moved in tandem across Europe in the High Middle Ages.

After about 1300, however, as Europe's population and economy declined grievously, mostly as a result of the Black Death, East and West parted paths. Across Europe, lords sought to solve their economic problems by more heavily exploiting the peasantry. This reaction generally failed in the West, where by 1500 almost all peasants were free or had their serf obligations greatly reduced. East of the Elbe, however, the landlords won.

Eastern landlords successfully used their political and police power against the peasantry in two ways. First, they restricted or eliminated the peasants' time-honored right of freedom of movement. Thus a peasant could no longer leave the land without his lord's permission, and the lord had no reason to make such concessions. In Prussian territories by 1500 the law required that runaway peasants be hunted down and returned to their lords. Until the mid-fifteenth century, medieval Russian peasants were free to move wherever they wished. Thereafter this freedom was gradually curtailed, so that by 1497 a Russian peasant had the right to move only during a two-week period after the fall harvest. Eastern peasants were losing their status as free and independent men and women.

Second, lords steadily took more of their peasants' land and imposed heavier labor obligations. Instead of being independent farmers paying freely negotiated rents, peasants became forced laborers on the lords' estates. By the early 1500s, lords in many territories could command their peasants to work without pay as many as six days a week.

The gradual erosion of the peasantry's economic position was bound up with manipulation of the legal system. The local lord was also the local prosecutor, judge, and jailer. There were no independent royal officials to provide justice or uphold the common law, allowing lords to rule in their own favor in disputes with peasants.

The Consolidation of Serfdom

Between 1500 and 1650 the social, legal, and economic conditions of peasants in eastern Europe continued to decline, and free peasants became serfs. In Poland nobles gained complete control over their peasants in 1574, after which they could legally inflict the death penalty whenever they wished. In Prussia in 1653 peasants were assumed to be tied to their lords in **hereditary subjugation**—bound to their lords and the land from one generation to the next. In Russia peasants' right to move from an estate was permanently abolished in 1603. In 1649 the tsar lifted the nine-year time limit on the recovery of runaways and eliminated all limits on lords' authority over their peasants. Although political development in the various Eastern states differed, the legal re-establishment of permanent hereditary serfdom was the common fate of Eastern peasants by the mid-seventeenth century.

The consolidation of serfdom accompanied the growth of estate agriculture, particularly in Poland and eastern Germany. In the sixteenth century European economic expansion and population growth resumed after the great declines of the late Middle Ages. Prices for agricultural commodities also rose sharply as gold and silver flowed in from the New World. Thus Polish and German lords had powerful economic incentives to increase the production of their estates. And they did. Lords seized more peasant land for their own estates and then demanded more unpaid labor on those enlarged estates. Though the estates were generally inefficient and technically backward, the great Polish nobles and middle-rank German lords squeezed sizable profits from their impoverished peasants. Surpluses in wheat and timber were sold to foreign merchants, who exported them to the growing cities of the West. Thus the poor East helped feed the wealthier West.

The re-emergence of serfdom in eastern Europe cannot be explained by economic factors alone. Western Europe experienced similar agricultural and population decline in the fourteenth and fifteenth centuries, but its peasants won better rather than harsher conditions. It seems likely that political, rather than economic, factors were crucial. Eastern lords enjoyed much greater political power than did their Western counterparts. In the late Middle Ages central and eastern Europe experienced innumerable wars and general political chaos, which allowed noble landlords to increase their political power. There were, for example, many disputed royal successions, so that weak kings were forced to grant political

Chronology

ca 1400–1650	Re-emergence of serfdom in eastern Europe
1462–1505	Reign of Ivan III in Russia
1533–1584	Reign of Ivan the Terrible in Russia
1620	Habsburgs crush Protestantism in Bohemia
1620–1740	Growth of absolutism in Austria and Prussia
1640–1688	Reign of Frederick William in Prussia
1652	Nikon reforms Russian Orthodox Church
1670–1671	Cossack revolt led by Razin
ca 1680–1750	Construction of palaces by absolutist rulers
1683–1718	Habsburgs defend Vienna, win war with Ottoman Turks
1702	Peter the Great founds St. Petersburg
1713–1740	Growth of Prussian military

Estonia in the 1660s The Estonians were conquered by German military nobility in the Middle Ages and reduced to serfdom. The German-speaking nobles ruled the Estonian peasants with an iron hand, and Peter the Great reaffirmed their domination when Russia annexed Estonia (see Map 17.3 on page 573). *(Mansell Collection/Time Life Pictures/Getty Images)*

favors to win the nobility's support. Thus while strong monarchs and effective central government were rising in Spain, France, and England, kings were generally losing power in the East and could not resist the demands of lords regarding peasants.

Moreover, most Eastern monarchs did not oppose the growth of serfdom. The typical king was only first among noble equals. He, too, wanted to squeeze his peasants. The Western concept of sovereignty, as embodied in a king who protected the interests of all his people, was not well developed in eastern Europe before 1650.

It was not only the peasants who suffered. Also with the approval of kings, landlords systematically undermined the medieval privileges of the towns and the power of the urban classes. Instead of selling products to local merchants, landlords sold directly to foreigners. For example, Dutch ships sailed up the rivers of Poland and eastern Germany to the loading docks of the great estates, completely bypassing the local towns. Moreover, "town air" no longer "made people free," for the Eastern towns had lost their medieval right of refuge and were now compelled to return runaways to their lords. The population of the towns and the importance of the urban middle classes declined greatly.

The Thirty Years' War

The Holy Roman Empire was a confederation of hundreds of principalities, independent cities, duchies, and other polities loosely united under an elected emperor. An uneasy truce had prevailed in the Holy Roman Empire since the Peace of Augsburg of 1555 (see page 459). According to the settlement, the faith of the prince determined the religion of his subjects. Later in the century, however, Catholics grew alarmed because Lutherans, in violation of the Peace of Augsburg, were steadily acquiring German bishoprics. The spread of Calvinism further confused the issue: the Augsburg settlement had pertained only to Lutheranism and Catholicism, so Calvinists ignored it and converted several princes. Also, the militantly active Jesuits had reconverted several Lutheran princes to Catholicism. Lutherans feared that the Augsburg principles would be undermined by Catholic and Calvinist gains. Lutheran princes felt compelled to form the **Protestant Union** (1608), and Catholics retaliated with the Catholic League (1609). Each alliance was determined that the other should make no religious or territorial advance. Dynastic interests were also involved; the Spanish Habsburgs strongly supported the goals of their Austrian relatives—the unity of the empire and the preservation of Catholicism within it.

Violence erupted in 1617 when Ferdinand of Styria, the new Catholic king in Bohemia, closed some Protestant churches. On May 23, 1618, Protestants hurled two of Ferdinand's officials from a castle window in Prague. They fell seventy feet but survived: Catholics claimed that angels had caught them; Protestants said that the officials had fallen on a heap of soft horse manure. Called the "defenestration of Prague," this event marked the beginning of the Thirty Years' War (1618–1648).

The war is traditionally divided into four phases. The first, or Bohemian, phase (1618–1625) was characterized by civil war in Bohemia between the Catholic League, led by Ferdinand, and the Protestant Union, headed by Frederick, the elector of the Palatinate. The Bohemians fought for religious liberty and independence from Habsburg rule. In 1620 Catholic forces defeated Frederick at the Battle of the White Mountain. Ferdinand, who had recently been elected Holy Roman emperor as Ferdinand II, followed up his victories by wiping out Protestantism in Bohemia through forcible conversions and Jesuit missionary work. Within ten years Bohemia was completely Catholic.

The second, or Danish, phase of the war (1625–1629)—so called because of the leadership of the Protestant king Christian IV of Denmark (r. 1588–1648)—

witnessed additional Catholic victories. The Catholic imperial army led by Albert of Wallenstein swept through Silesia, north to the Baltic, and east into Pomerania, scoring smashing victories. Wallenstein, an unscrupulous opportunist who used his vast riches to build an army loyal only to himself, seemed interested more in carving out his own empire than in aiding the Catholic cause. He quarreled with the Catholic League, and soon the Catholic forces were divided. Religion was eclipsed as a basic issue of the war.

Habsburg power peaked in 1629. The emperor issued the Edict of Restitution, whereby all Catholic properties lost to Protestantism since 1552 were restored, and only Catholics and Lutherans were allowed to practice their faiths. When Wallenstein began ruthless enforcement, Protestants throughout Europe feared the collapse of the balance of power in north-central Europe.

The third, or Swedish, phase of the war (1630–1635) began with the arrival in Germany of the Swedish king Gustavus Adolphus (r. 1594–1632). The ablest administrator of his day and a devout Lutheran, he intervened to support the empire's oppressed Protestants. Cardinal Richelieu, chief minister of King Louis XIII of France (r. 1610–1643), subsidized the Swedes, hoping to weaken Habsburg power in Europe. In 1631, with a small but well-disciplined army equipped with superior muskets, Gustavus Adolphus won a brilliant victory at Breitenfeld. Again in 1632 he was victorious at Lützen, though he was fatally wounded in the battle.

The participation of the Swedes in the Thirty Years' War proved decisive for the future of Protestantism and German history. When Gustavus Adolphus landed on German soil, he headed a Baltic empire under Swedish influence. The Swedish victories ended the Habsburg ambition to unite the German states under imperial authority.

Gustavus Adolphus's death in 1632, followed by the Swedes' defeat at the Battle of Nördlingen in 1634, prompted the French to enter the war on the Protestant side, beginning the French, or international, phase of the Thirty Years' War (1635–1648). For almost a century French foreign policy was based on opposition to the Habsburgs because a weak empire enhanced France's international stature. In 1635 Cardinal Richelieu declared war on Spain and again sent financial and military assistance to the Swedes and the German Protestant princes. The war dragged on. The French, Dutch, and Swedes, supported by Scots, Finns, and German mercenaries, burned, looted, and destroyed German agriculture and commerce. The Thirty Years' War lasted so long because neither side had the resources to win a quick, decisive victory. Finally, in October 1648 peace was achieved.

Soldiers Pillage a Farmhouse   Billeting troops among civilian populations caused untold hardships. In this late-seventeenth-century Dutch illustration, brawling soldiers take over a peasant's home, eat his food, steal his possessions, and insult his family. Peasant retaliation sometimes proved swift and bloody. *(Rijksmuseum-Stichting Amsterdam)*

Consequences of the Thirty Years' War

The 1648 **Peace of Westphalia** that ended the Thirty Years' War marked a turning point in European history. Conflicts fought over religious faith ended. The treaties recognized the sovereign, independent authority of more than three hundred German princes (see Map 17.1). Since the time of Holy Roman Emperor Frederick II (1194–1250), Germany had followed a pattern of state-building different from that of France and England: the emperor shared authority with the princes. After the Peace of Westphalia, the emperors' power continued to be severely limited, and the Holy Roman Empire remained a loosely knit federation.

The peace agreement acknowledged the independence of the United Provinces of the Netherlands. France acquired the province of Alsace along with the advantages of the weakened status of the empire. Sweden received a large cash indemnity and jurisdiction over German territories along the Baltic Sea, leaving it as a major threat to the future kingdom of Brandenburg-Prussia. The agreement also denied the papacy the right to participate in central European religious affairs—a restriction symbolizing the reduced political role of the church. In religion, the Peace of Westphalia made the Augsburg agreement of 1555 permanent, with the sole modification that Calvinism, along with Catholicism and Lutheranism, would be a legally permissible creed. The north German states remained Protestant, the south German states Catholic.

The Thirty Years' War was probably the most destructive event for the central European economy and society prior to the twentieth century. Perhaps one-third of urban residents and two-fifths of the rural population died. Entire areas were depopulated by warfare, by the flight of refugees, and by disease. Typhus, dysentery, bubonic plague, and syphilis accompanied the movements of armies.

Because the Thirty Years' War was fought on German soil, the empire experienced untold losses in agricultural land, livestock, trade, and commerce. The trade of south-

MAP 17.1 Europe After the Thirty Years' War Which country emerged from the Thirty Years' War as the strongest European power? What dynastic house was that country's major rival in the early modern period?

Online Study Center **Improve Your Grade** Interactive Map:
Europe During Thirty Years' War

ern cities such as Augsburg, already hard hit by the shift in transportation routes from the Mediterranean to the Atlantic, was virtually destroyed. All of Europe was experiencing severe inflation due to the influx of Spanish silver, but the destruction of land and foodstuffs made the price rise worse in central Europe than anywhere else. Agricultural areas suffered catastrophically. Many small farmers lacked the revenue to rework their holdings and had to become day laborers. In parts of central Europe, especially in areas east of the Elbe River, loss of land contributed to the consolidation of serfdom.[1]

Although the Thirty Years' War contributed to the legal and economic decline of the majority of the population, some people prospered. Nobles and landlords bought the land of failed small farmers, thereby acquiring even greater estates. Northern towns such as Lübeck, Hamburg, and Bremen as well as Essen in the Ruhr area also prospered because of the many refugees they attracted.

The Rise of Austria and Prussia

Serfdom and the Thirty Years' War aided Eastern rulers greatly in their attempts to build absolute monarchies. These rulers not only fought one another but also battled with armies of invaders from Asia. In this atmosphere of continual wartime emergency, monarchs were able to increase the powers of the central state. In exchange for leaving nobles the unchallenged masters of their peasants, the would-be absolutist monarchs of central and eastern Europe gradually gained political power in three key areas. First, they imposed permanent taxes without consent. Second, they maintained permanent standing armies to police the country and fight abroad. Third, they conducted relations with other states as they pleased.

As with all general historical developments, there were important variations on the absolutist theme in eastern Europe. Royal **absolutism** in Prussia was stronger and more effective than in Austria. This would give Prussia a thin edge in the struggle for power in east-central Europe in the eighteenth century. Prussian-style absolutism had great long-term political significance, for it was a rising Prussia that unified the German people in the nineteenth century and imposed on them a militaristic stamp.

• *How and why did the rulers of Austria and Prussia, each in different political and social environments, manage to build powerful absolute monarchies that proved more durable than that of Louis XIV?*

The Austrian Habsburgs

The Austrian Habsburgs controlled a scattered group of territories in central and eastern Europe. By 1618 the Habsburg realm included the German-speaking provinces of Austria, Tyrol, and Styria; the Czech-speaking kingdom of Bohemia; and parts of the kingdom of Hungary. Habsburg lands encompassed different languages, ethnicities, and religious affiliations; some lay within the Holy Roman Empire and some beyond its borders.

Like all of central Europe, the Habsburgs emerged from the Thirty Years' War impoverished and exhausted. Their efforts to destroy Protestantism in the German lands and to turn the weak Holy Roman Empire into a real state had failed. Although the Habsburgs remained the hereditary emperors, real power lay in the hands of a bewildering variety of separate political jurisdictions, including independent cities, small principalities, medium-size states such as Bavaria and Saxony, and some of the territories of Prussia and the Habsburgs.

Defeat in central Europe encouraged the Habsburgs to turn away from a quest for imperial dominance and to focus inward and eastward in an attempt to unify their diverse holdings. An important step in this direction had occurred in Bohemia during the Thirty Years' War. Protestantism had been strong among the Czechs in Bohemia. The lesser Czech nobility was largely Protestant in 1600 and had considerable political power because it dominated the **Bohemian Estates**—the representative body of the different estates, or legal orders. The Habsburgs believed that religious diversity fatally weakened royal power. If they could not impose Catholicism in the empire, at least they could do so in their own domains.

In 1618 the Bohemian Estates rose up in defense of Protestant rights. The Habsburgs crushed the revolt in 1620 at the Battle of the White Mountain. The victorious king, Ferdinand II (r. 1619–1637), drastically reduced the power of the Bohemian Estates. He also confiscated the landholdings of many Protestant nobles and gave them to a few loyal Catholic nobles and to the foreign aristocratic mercenaries who led his armies. After 1650 a large portion of the Bohemian nobility was of recent origin and owed everything to the Habsburgs.

With the help of this new nobility, the Habsburgs established direct rule over Bohemia. The condition of the enserfed peasantry worsened substantially: three days per week of unpaid labor—the *robot*—became the norm, and a quarter of the serfs worked for their lords every day but Sundays and religious holidays. Protestantism was also stamped out. The reorganization of Bohemia was a giant

The Battle of Mohács, 1526 The *Süleymanname* (Book of Suleiman), a biography, contains these fascinating illustrations of the great Ottoman victory at Mohács, which enabled the Turks to add Hungary to their expanding empire. In the right panel, Suleiman in a white turban sits on a black horse surrounded by his personal guard, while his janissary soldiers fire their muskets and cannon at the enemy. In the left panel, the Europeans are in disarray, in contrast to the Turks' discipline and order. *(Topkapi Saray Museum)*

step toward creating absolutist rule. As in France in the same years, the pursuit of religious unity was an essential element of absolutism.

After the Thirty Years' War, Ferdinand III (r. 1637–1657) continued to build state power. He centralized the government in the hereditary German-speaking provinces, which formed the core Habsburg holdings. For the first time, a permanent standing army was ready to put down any internal opposition.

Austrian Rule in Hungary

The Habsburg monarchy then turned toward the plains of Hungary. After the **Battle of Mohács** in 1526, the

kingdom of Hungary was divided between the Ottomans and the Habsburgs. Transylvania in the east became an Ottoman dependent, while the Habsburgs ruled the west and north. In the 1540s the Ottomans organized their Hungarian territories into provinces of the empire. Warfare between the Ottomans and the Habsburgs devastated Hungary during the sixteenth century. Between 1683 and 1699 the Habsburgs pushed the Ottomans from most of Hungary and Transylvania. The recovery of all of the former kingdom of Hungary was completed in 1718.

The Hungarian nobility, despite its reduced strength, effectively thwarted the full development of Habsburg absolutism. Throughout the seventeenth century Hungarian nobles—the most numerous in Europe—rose in revolt against attempts to impose absolute rule. They never triumphed decisively, but neither were they crushed the way the Czech nobility had been in 1620.

The Hungarians resisted because many of them remained Protestants, especially in areas formerly ruled by the Turks. Ottoman rule had been relatively light-handed compared to the harsh reconversion efforts of the Habsburgs. Until the end of the seventeenth century the Ottomans still ruled parts of Hungary, providing a powerful military ally to nobles in areas recovered by the Habsburgs. Finally, the Hungarian nobility, and even part of the peasantry, became attached to a national ideal long before most of the other peoples of eastern Europe. Hungarian nobles were determined to maintain as much independence and local control as possible. In 1703, with the Habsburgs bogged down in the War of the Spanish Succession (see page 534), the Hungarians rose in one last patriotic rebellion under Prince Francis Rákóczy.

Rákóczy and his forces were eventually defeated, but the Habsburgs had to accept a compromise. Charles VI restored many of the traditional privileges of the aristocracy in return for Hungarian acceptance of hereditary Habsburg rule. Thus Hungary, unlike Austria and Bohemia, was never fully integrated into a centralized, absolute Habsburg state.

Despite checks on their ambitions in Hungary, the Habsburgs made significant achievements in state-building by forging consensus with the church and the nobility. A sense of common identity and loyalty to the monarchy grew among elites in Habsburg lands, even to a certain extent in Hungary. The best evidence for this consensus is the spectacular sums approved by the estates for the growth of the army. By the end of the seventeenth century Emperor Leopold commanded a standing army of a hundred thousand men funded by contributions from the provincial estates. German became the language of the common culture and, with ongoing Protestant conversion and emigration, zealous Catholicism also helped fuse a collective identity. Vienna became the political and cultural center of the empire. By 1700 it was a thriving city with a population of one hundred thousand, with its own version of Versailles, the royal palace of Schönbrunn. (See the feature "Images in Society: Absolutist Palace Building" on pages 568–569.)

Empowered by the imperial government, the landed nobility took charge of economic recovery. The nobles increased the burdens of serfdom and profited from the war's population losses to take over vast tracts of land. With technical and commercial innovations, they created a new form of capitalist, market-oriented agriculture, which allowed them to increase their holdings even more at the expense of smaller landowners.

In 1713 Charles VI (r. 1711–1740) proclaimed the so-called **Pragmatic Sanction,** which stated that Habsburg possessions were never to be divided, even if it meant allowing a woman to take the throne. Lacking a male heir, Charles spent much of his reign trying to get this principle accepted within and beyond his realm. His success resulted in the crowning of his daughter Maria Theresa upon Charles's death in 1740.

Prussia in the Seventeenth Century

After 1400 a revitalized landed nobility became the undisputed ruling class in eastern Germany. The Hohenzollern family, which ruled through its senior and junior branches as the imperial electors of Brandenburg and the dukes of Prussia, had little real power. Nothing suggested that this family and its territories would ever play an important role in European or even regional affairs. The **elector of Brandenburg** had the right to help choose the Holy Roman emperor, which bestowed prestige, but the elector had no military strength of his own. Moreover, Brandenburg, the area around Berlin and the elector's power base, was a land-locked combination of sand and swamp (see Map 17.2) that lacked defensible natural frontiers. Contemporaries contemptuously called it the "sand-box of the Holy Roman Empire."[2]

The territory of the elector's cousin, the duke of Prussia, was completely separated from Brandenburg and was part of the kingdom of Poland. By 1600 Prussia's German-speaking peasants had much in common with Polish peasants, for both ethnic groups had seen most of their freedoms reduced or revoked by their noble landlords. (Poland's numerous lesser nobles dominated the Polish state, which was actually a constitutional republic headed by an elected king who had little real power.) In 1618 the junior branch of the Hohenzollern family died out, and Prussia reverted to the elector of Brandenburg.

The elector of Brandenburg was a helpless spectator in the Thirty Years' War, his territories alternately ravaged by Swedish and Habsburg armies. Population fell drastically, and many villages disappeared. Yet this devastation paved the way for Hohenzollern absolutism because foreign armies dramatically weakened the political power of the estates, which helped the very young elector Frederick William (r. 1640–1688), later known as the "Great Elector," to ride roughshod over traditional representative rights and to take a giant step toward royal absolutism. This constitutional struggle was the most crucial in Prussian history until that of the 1860s.

Images in Society

Absolutist Palace Building

By 1700 palace building had become a veritable obsession for the rulers of central and eastern Europe. Their dramatic palaces symbolized the age of absolutist power, just as soaring Gothic cathedrals had expressed the idealized spirit of the High Middle Ages. With its classically harmonious, symmetrical, and geometric design, Versailles, shown in Image 1, served as the model for the wave of palace building that began in the last decade of the seventeenth century.

Located ten miles southwest of Paris, Versailles began as a modest hunting lodge built by Louis XIII in 1623. His son, Louis XIV, loved the site so much that he spent decades enlarging and decorating the original chateau. Between 1668 and 1670, his architect Louis Le Vau enveloped the old building within a much larger second structure that still exists today. In 1682 the new palace became the official residence of the Sun King and his court, although construction continued until 1710, when the royal chapel was completed. At any one time, several thousand people lived in the bustling and crowded palace. The awesome splendor of the eighty-yard Hall of Mirrors, replete with floor-to-ceiling mirrors and ceiling murals illustrating the king's triumphs, contrasted with the strong odors from the courtiers who commonly relieved themselves in discreet corners. Royal palaces like Versailles were intended to overawe the people and proclaim their owners' authority and power.

In 1693 Charles XI of Sweden, having reduced the power of the aristocracy, ordered the construction of his Royal Palace, which dominates the center of Stockholm to this day. Another such palace was Schönbrunn, an enormous Viennese Versailles begun in 1695 by Emperor Leopold to celebrate Austrian military victories and Habsburg might. Image 2 shows architect Joseph Bernhard Fischer von Erlach's ambitious plan for Schönbrunn palace. Erlach's plan emphasizes the palace's vast size and its role as a site for military demonstrations. Ultimately financial constraints resulted in a more modest building.

Petty German princes contributed mightily to the palace-building mania. Frederick the Great of Prussia

noted that every descendant of a princely family "imagines himself to be something like Louis XIV. He builds his Versailles, has his mistresses, and maintains his army."* The elector-archbishop of Mainz, the ruling prince of that city, confessed apologetically that "building is a craze which costs much, but every fool likes his own hat."†

In central and eastern Europe, the favorite noble servants of royalty became extremely rich and powerful, and they too built grandiose palaces in the capital cities. These palaces were in part an extension of the monarch, for they surpassed the buildings of less-favored nobles and showed all the high road to fame and fortune. Take, for example, the palaces of Prince Eugene of Savoy, a French nobleman who became Austria's most famous military hero. It was Eugene who led the Austrian army, smashed the Turks, fought Louis XIV to a standstill, and generally guided the triumph of absolutism in Austria. Rewarded with great wealth by his grateful king, Eugene called on the leading architects of the day, J. B. Fischer von Erlach and

Image 1 Pierre-Denis Martin: View of the Chateau de Versailles, 1722 *(Châteaux de Versailles et de Trianon, Versailles/ Réunion des Musées Nationaux/Art Resource, NY)*

Image 2 Project for the Palace at Schönbrunn (ca 1700) (*Austrian National Library, Vienna*)

Image 4 View of the Petit Parc at Versailles from the Canal (*Bibliothèque nationale de France*)

Image 3 Prince Eugene's Summer Palace, Vienna (*Erich Lessing/Art Resource, NY*)

Johann Lukas von Hildebrandt, to consecrate his glory in stone and fresco. Fischer built Eugene's Winter (or Town) Palace in Vienna, and he and Hildebrandt collaborated on the prince's Summer Palace on the city's outskirts, shown in Image 3. The prince's summer residence featured two baroque gems, the Lower Belvedere and the lovely Upper Belvedere, completed in 1722 and shown here. The building's interior is equally stunning, with crouching giants serving as pillars and a magnificent great staircase.

Palace gardens were an extension of the architecture. The rational orderliness and symmetry of a garden showed that the ruler's force extended even to nature, which offered its subjugated pleasures to the delight of sovereign and courtiers. The terraces and waterworks of these gardens served as showcases for the latest techniques in military and civil engineering. Exotic plants and elaborate designs testified to the sovereign's global trading networks and elevated taste.

The gardens at Versailles, shown in Image 4, exemplify absolutist palace gardens. In the foreground of this image we see a mock naval campaign being enacted on the canal for the edification of courtiers. For diplomatic occasions, Louis XIV himself wrote lengthy guides for viewing the gardens of Versailles. Modern visitors can still follow his itineraries. The themes of the sculptures in the Versailles gardens also hailed Louis's power, with images of Apollo, the sungod, and Neptune, the sea-god, making frequent appearances.

Compare the image of Prince Eugene's summer palace with the plans for Schönbrunn and the palace of Versailles. What did concrete objects and the manipulation of space accomplish for these rulers that mere words could not? What disadvantages might stem from using architecture in this way? Is the use of space and monumental construction still a political tool in today's world?

*Quoted in R. Ergang, *The Potsdam Fuhrer: Frederick William I, Father of Prussian Militarism* (New York: Octagon Books, 1972), p. 13.

†Quoted in J. Summerson, in *The Eighteenth Century: Europe in the Age of Enlightenment,* ed. A. Cobban (New York: McGraw-Hill, 1969), p. 80.

Online Study Center   Improve Your Grade
Going Beyond Images in Society

MAP 17.2 The Growth of Austria and Brandenburg-Prussia to 1748 Austria expanded to the southwest into Hungary and Transylvania at the expense of the Ottoman Empire. It was unable to hold the rich German province of Silesia, however, which was conquered by Brandenburg-Prussia.

When he came to power in 1640, the twenty-year-old Great Elector was determined to unify his three provinces and enlarge them by diplomacy and war. These provinces were Brandenburg; Prussia, inherited in 1618; and scattered holdings along the Rhine, inherited in 1614 (see Map 17.2). Each was inhabited by German-speakers, but each had its own estates. Although the estates had not met regularly during the chaotic Thirty Years' War, taxes could not be levied without their consent. The estates of Brandenburg and Prussia were dominated by the nobility and the landowning classes, known as the **Junkers.** But this was also the case in most European countries that had representative bodies, including the English Parliament before and after the civil war. Had the estates successfully resisted the absolutist demands of the Great Elector, they too might have evolved toward more broadly based constitutionalism.

The struggle between the Great Elector and the provincial estates was long and intense. After the Thirty Years' War, noble representatives zealously reasserted the estates' control over taxes. Yet first in Brandenburg in 1653 and then in Prussia between 1661 and 1663, the Great Elector eventually had his way.

To pay for the permanent standing army he first established in 1660, Frederick William forced the estates to accept the introduction of permanent taxation without consent. The estates' power declined rapidly thereafter, for the Great Elector had both financial independence and superior force. The state's total revenue tripled during his reign, and the size of the army leaped by ten. In 1688 a population of one million was supporting a peacetime standing army of thirty thousand.

Two factors were central to the Great Elector's triumph. First, as in the formation of every absolutist state, war was a decisive factor. The ongoing struggle between Sweden and Poland for control of the Baltic after 1648 and the wars of Louis XIV in western Europe created an atmosphere of permanent crisis. The nomadic Tatars of the Crimea in southern Russia swept through Prussia in the winter of 1656–1657, killing and carrying off thousands as slaves. This invasion softened up the estates and strengthened the urgency of the Great Elector's demands for more military funding.

Second, the nobility proved willing to accept Frederick William's new claims in exchange for reconfirmation of their own privileges. The Junkers had long dominated the government through the estates, but they refused to join representatives of the towns in a common front. Instead, they accepted a compromise with the state whereby the bulk of the new taxes fell on towns and the Junkers received legal confirmation of their authority over the serfs. The elector used naked force to break the liberties of the towns; the main leader of urban opposition in the key city of Königsberg, for example, was arrested and imprisoned for life without trial.

Like Louis XIV, the Great Elector built his absolutist state on collaboration with traditional elites, reaffirming their privileges in return for loyal service and revenue. He also created a larger centralized government bureaucracy to oversee his realm and to collect the new taxes. Pre-existing representative institutions were bypassed. The Diet of Brandenburg did not meet again after 1652. In 1701 the elector's son, Frederick I, received the elevated title of king of Prussia (instead of elector) as a reward for aiding the Holy Roman emperor in the War of the Spanish Succession.

The Consolidation of Prussian Absolutism

Frederick William I, "the Soldiers' King" (r. 1713–1740), completed his grandfather's work. Though crude and ruthless, Frederick William I was the most talented reformer produced by the Hohenzollern family. Under his rule, Prussia built the best army in Europe for its size and transformed into a model military state. It was he who truly established Prussian absolutism and gave it its unique character. In the words of a famous historian of Prussia:

For a whole generation, the Hohenzollern subjects were victimized by a royal bully, imbued with an obsessive bent for military organization and military scales of value. This left a deep mark upon the institutions of Prussiandom and upon the molding of the "Prussian spirit."[3]

Frederick William was intensely attached to military life. He had, for example, an extreme fondness for tall soldiers, whom he credited with superior strength and endurance. Profoundly militaristic in temperament, Frederick William always wore an army uniform, and he lived the highly disciplined life of the professional soldier. He began his work by five or six in the morning; at ten he almost always went to the parade ground to drill or inspect his troops. His love of the army was based on a hard-headed conception of the struggle for power. Years later he summed up his life's philosophy in his instructions to his son: "A formidable army and a war chest large enough to make this army mobile in times of need can create great respect for you in the world, so that you can speak a word like the other powers."[4] This unshakable belief that the welfare of king and state depended on the army above all else reinforced Frederick William's passion for the soldier's life.

The cult of military power provided the rationale for a great expansion of absolutism in Prussia. As the king put it: "I must be served with life and limb, with house and wealth, with honour and conscience, everything must be committed except eternal salvation—that belongs to God, but all else is mine."[5] To achieve these extraordinary demands, Frederick William created a strong centralized bureaucracy and eliminated the last traces of the parliamentary estates and local self-government.

The king's power grab brought him into considerable conflict with the Junkers. In his early years he even threatened to destroy them; yet, in the end, the Prussian nobility was not destroyed but enlisted—into the army. Responding to a combination of threats and opportunities, the Junkers became the officer caste. A new compromise was worked out whereby the proud nobility imperiously commanded the peasantry in the army as well as on the estates.

Penny-pinching and hard-working, Frederick William achieved results. Above all, he built a first-rate army with third-rate resources. The standing army increased from thirty-eight thousand to eighty-three thousand during his reign. Prussia, twelfth in Europe in population, had the fourth largest army by 1740. Moreover, soldier for soldier, the Prussian army was the best in Europe, astonishing foreign observers with its precision, skill, and discipline. For the next two hundred years Prussia and then Prussianized Germany would win many crucial military battles.

Frederick William and his ministers also built an exceptionally honest and conscientious bureaucracy to administer the country and foster economic development. Like the miser he was known to be, the king loved his

A Prussian Giant Grenadier Frederick William I wanted tall, handsome soldiers. He dressed them in tight bright uniforms to distinguish them from the peasant population from which most soldiers came. He also ordered several portraits of his favorites from his court painter, J. C. Merk. Grenadiers wore the miter cap instead of an ordinary hat so that they could hurl their heavy grenades unimpeded by a broad brim. *(The Royal Collection © 2007, Her Majesty Queen Elizabeth II)*

"blue boys" so much that he hated to "spend" them. This most militaristic of kings was, paradoxically, almost always at peace.

Nevertheless, Prussians paid a heavy and lasting price for the obsessions of their royal drillmaster. Civil society became rigid and highly disciplined, and Prussia became the "Sparta of the North"; unquestioning obedience was the highest virtue. As a Prussian minister later summed up, "To keep quiet is the first civic duty."[6] Thus the policies of Frederick William I combined with harsh peasant bondage and Junker tyranny to lay the foundations for a highly militaristic country.

The Development of Russia and the Ottoman Empire

A favorite parlor game of nineteenth-century intellectuals was debating whether Russia was a Western (European) or non-Western (Asian) society. This question was particularly fascinating because it was unanswerable. To this day Russia differs fundamentally from the West in some basic ways, though its history has paralleled that of the West in other aspects.

There was no question in the mind of Europeans, however, that the Ottomans were outsiders. Even absolutist rulers disdained Ottoman sultans as cruel and tyrannical despots. Despite stereotypes, the Ottomans were in many ways more tolerant than the West, providing protection and security to other religions while steadfastly maintaining their Muslim faith. The Ottoman state combined the Byzantine heritage of the territory they conquered with Persian and Arab traditions. Flexibility and openness to other ideas and practices were sources of strength for the empire.

● *What were the distinctive features of Russian and Ottoman absolutism in this period?*

The Mongol Yoke and the Rise of Moscow

The eastern Slavs might have emerged from the Middle Ages weak and politically divided had it not been for the Mongol conquest of the Kievan principality. The Mongols were nomadic tribes from present-day Mongolia who had been temporarily unified in the thirteenth century by Chinggis Khan (1162–1227). In five years his armies subdued all of China. His successors then turned westward, smashing everything in their path and reaching the plains of Hungary before pulling back in 1242. The Mongol army—the Golden Horde—used terror to reduce con-

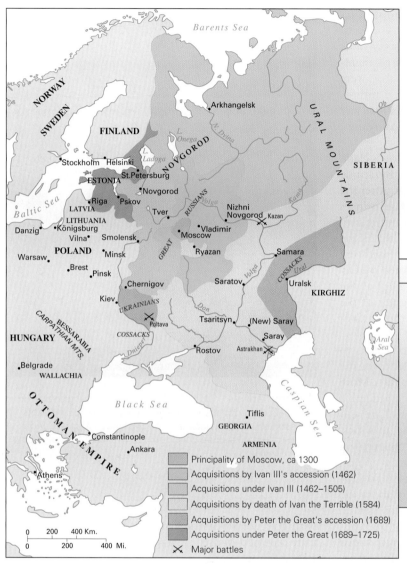

Online Study Center **Improve Your Grade** Interactive Map: Expansion of Russia to 1725

quered peoples to submission. As a show of force, the army would destroy an entire city, slaughtering the whole population before burning the city to the ground.

The Mongols ruled the eastern Slavs for more than two hundred years, the period of the so-called **Mongol Yoke.** They built their capital of Saray on the lower Volga (see Map 17.3) and forced the rival Slavic princes to submit to their rule and to give them tribute and slaves. If conquered peoples rebelled, the Mongols used ruthless violence to re-impose control. The Mongol khan was acknowledged by all the eastern Slavs as the supreme ruler.

Online Study Center **Improve Your Grade**
Primary Source: Russia's Conquest by the Mongols: A Song to Lost Lands

Unification transformed the internal political situation. Although the Mongols conquered, they were quite willing to use local princes as obedient servants and tax collectors. Thus, they did not abolish the title of "great prince," bestowing it instead on the prince who served them best and paid them most handsomely. Beginning with Alexander Nevsky in 1252, the princes of Moscow became particularly adept at serving the Mongols. They loyally put down popular uprisings and collected the khan's taxes. As reward, the princes of Moscow emerged as hereditary great princes. Eventually the Muscovite princes were able to destroy their princely rivals. Ivan III (r. 1462–1505) consolidated power around Moscow and won Novgorod, almost reaching the Baltic Sea (see Map 17.3).

By about 1480 Ivan III felt strong enough to stop acknowledging the khan as his supreme ruler. To legitimize their new authority, the princes of Moscow drew on two sources of authority. First, they declared themselves *autocrats*, meaning that, like the khans, they were the sole source of power. In addition to political authority, Moscow also took over Mongol tribute relations and borrowed institutions like the tax system, postal routes, and the census.

The second source of legitimacy lay in Moscow's claim to the political and religious inheritance of the Byzantine Empire. The title **tsar** is a contraction of *caesar*. After the fall of Constantinople to the Turks in 1453, the princes of Moscow saw themselves as the heirs of both the caesars and Orthodox Christianity, the one true faith. All the other kings of Europe were heretics; only the tsars were rightful and holy rulers. The idea was promoted by Orthodox churchmen, who spoke of "holy Russia" as the "Third Rome." Ivan's marriage to the daughter of the last Byzantine emperor further enhanced the aura of Moscow's imperial inheritance.

Historians long took at face value the tsars' claims to unlimited autocratic power over their people, from the peasants to the highest-ranking nobles or **boyars**. More recently they have begun to emphasize the considerable consensus that existed between the nobility and the self-styled *autocrat*. Along with Mongol tribute relations, Moscow inherited a tradition of ruling in cooperation with local elites. The tsars' success in combining grandiose claims to power with an extremely limited government apparatus is explained through their collaboration with boyars in Moscow and with the provincial gentry. The Russian Orthodox Church helped cement this consensus. Since the national borders of Russia corresponded to the borders of the church, religion was a source of patriotic nationalism and loyalty to the Crown.

The tsars ensured the loyalty of the elite in part by creating new nobles personally loyal to them. These new nobles made up the **service nobility,** whose members held the tsar's land on the explicit condition that they serve in his army.

Tsar and People to 1689

Developments in Russia took a chaotic turn with the reign of Ivan IV (r. 1533–1584), the famous "Ivan the Terrible," who ascended the throne at age three. His mother died, possibly poisoned, when he was eight, leaving Ivan to suffer insults and neglect from the boyars at court. At age sixteen he suddenly pushed aside his hated advisers, and in an awe-inspiring ceremony, complete

Ivan the Terrible Ivan IV, the first to take the title tsar of Russia, executed many Muscovite boyars and their peasants and servants. His ownership of all the land, trade, and industry restricted economic development. *(National Museum, Copenhagen, Denmark)*

with gold coins pouring down on his head, Ivan majestically crowned himself, taking the august title of tsar for the first time.

Selecting the beautiful and kind Anastasia of the Romanov family as his queen, the young tsar soon declared war on the remnants of Mongol power. He defeated the khanates of Kazan and Astrakhan between 1552 and 1556, adding vast new territories to the realm and laying the foundations for the huge, multiethnic Russian empire. In the course of these wars, Ivan virtually abolished the old distinction between hereditary boyar private property and land temporarily granted for service. All nobles, old and new, had to serve the tsar in order to hold land.

In 1557 Ivan turned westward, and for the next twenty-five years he waged an exhausting, unsuccessful war primarily against the large Polish-Lithuanian state. Quarreling with the boyars over the war and suspecting them of a role in the sudden death of his beloved Anastasia in 1560, the increasingly demented Ivan struck down all who stood in his way. A reign of terror ensued in which Ivan jailed and executed anyone he suspected of opposing him. He created a special corps of black-clad soldiers to execute his alleged enemies, along with their families, friends, servants, and peasants. Many victims were intimates of the court from the leading boyar families of Moscow. Their large estates were broken up and reapportioned. Ivan gave about half of the land acquired through such purges to the lower service nobility; the rest he maintained as a personal domain.

Ivan also took strides toward making all commoners servants of the tsar. His endless wars and violent purges depopulated much of central Russia. As the service nobles demanded more from the remaining peasants, growing numbers fled toward wild, recently conquered territories to the east and south. There they formed free groups and outlaw armies known as **Cossacks** and maintained a precarious independence. The solution to the problem of peasant flight was to tie peasants ever more firmly to the land and to the noble landholders, who in turn served the tsar.

Simultaneously, urban traders and artisans were also bound to their towns and jobs so that the tsar could tax them more heavily. Ivan assumed that the tsar owned Russia's trade and industry, just as he owned all the land. The urban classes had no security in their work or property, and even the wealthiest merchants were dependent agents of the tsar. Royal monopolization and service obligations checked the growth of the Russian middle classes and stood in sharp contrast to developments in western Europe, where the middle classes were gaining security in their private property.

As so often in Russia, the death of an iron-fisted tyrant—in this case, Ivan the Terrible in 1584—opened an era of violent struggles for power. Ivan's son, Theodore, died in 1598 without an heir, ushering in the "Time of Troubles" (1598–1613). The close relatives of the deceased tsar intrigued against and murdered one another, alternately fighting and welcoming the invading Swedes

Saint Basil's Cathedral, Moscow With its sloping roofs and colorful onion-shaped domes, Saint Basil's is a striking example of powerful Byzantine influences on Russian culture. According to tradition, an enchanted Ivan the Terrible blinded the cathedral's architects to ensure that they would never duplicate their fantastic achievement, which still dazzles the beholder in today's Red Square. *(George Holton/Photo Researchers)*

and Poles. Cossack bands, led by a former slave named Ivan Bolotnikov, marched northward, rallying peasants and slaughtering nobles and officials. Cossacks and peasants called for the "true tsar," who would restore their freedom of movement, reduce their heavy taxes, and lighten the yoke imposed by the landlords.

This social explosion from below brought the nobles, big and small, to their senses. They put aside their quarrels and finally crushed the Cossack rebellion at the gates of Moscow. In 1613 the nobles elected Ivan the Terrible's sixteen-year-old grandnephew, Michael Romanov, the new hereditary tsar (r. 1613–1645). Michael's election was represented as a restoration of tsarist autocracy. (See the feature "Listening to the Past: A Foreign Traveler in Russia" on pages 586–587.)

Although the new tsar successfully reconsolidated central authority, social and religious uprisings continued through the seventeenth century. In 1652 the patriarch Nikon determined to bring "corrupted" Russian practices of worship into line with the Greek Orthodox model. The self-serving church hierarchy quickly went along, but the intensely religious common people resisted. They saw Nikon as the Antichrist who was stripping them of the only thing they had—the true religion of "holy Russia." Great numbers left the church and formed communities of "Old Believers," who were hunted down and persecuted. As many as twenty thousand people burned themselves alive, singing the "hallelujah" in their chants three times rather than twice, as Nikon had demanded. After the Great Schism, the Russian masses were alienated from the established church, which became dependent on the state for its authority.

The Cossacks revolted once more against a state that was doggedly trying to reduce them to serfdom. Under Stenka Razin they moved up the Volga River in 1670 and 1671, attracting a great army of urban poor and peasants, killing landlords and government officials, and proclaiming freedom from oppression. Eventually this rebellion was defeated.

The normal obstacles to state-building were exacerbated in Russia's case by the huge size of its territory, its thinly spread population, and the economic devastation wrought by the Time of Troubles. Nevertheless, Romanov tsars made several important achievements during the second half of the seventeenth century. After a long war, Russia gained a large mass of Ukraine from weak and decentralized Poland in 1667 (see Map 17.3) and completed the conquest of Siberia by the end of the century. Territorial expansion was accompanied by growth of the bureaucracy and the army. Russian tsars turned to imported foreign experts to help build and reform the Russian army. The great profits from Siberia's natural resources, especially furs, funded the Romanov's bid for great power status.

The Reforms of Peter the Great

Heir to the first efforts at state-building, Peter the Great (r. 1682–1725) embarked on a tremendous campaign to accelerate and complete these processes. A giant for his time, at six feet seven inches, and possessing enormous energy and willpower, Peter was determined to build and improve the army. He was equally determined to continue the tsarist tradition of territorial expansion. After 1689 Peter ruled independently for thirty-six years, only one of which was peaceful.

Fascinated by weapons and foreign technology, the tsar led a group of 250 Russian officials and young nobles on an eighteen-month tour of western European capitals. Traveling unofficially to avoid lengthy diplomatic ceremonies, Peter worked with his hands at various crafts and met with foreign kings and experts. He was particularly impressed with the growing power of the Dutch and the English, and he considered how Russia could profit from their example.

Returning to Russia, Peter entered into a secret alliance with Denmark and Poland to wage a sudden war of aggression against Sweden. Despite the country's small population and limited agricultural resources, Swedish rulers in the seventeenth century had developed a strong absolutist state and had built an excellent standing army. Like other absolutist rulers, Charles XI of Sweden built a beautiful palace in his capital, modeled after Louis XIV's Versailles. Expanding beyond its borders, Sweden held substantial territory in northern Germany, Finland, and Estonia. Yet these possessions were scattered and appeared vulnerable. Above all, Peter and his allies believed that their combined forces could win easy victories because Sweden was in the hands of a new and inexperienced king.

Eighteen-year-old Charles XII (1697–1718) surprised Peter. He defeated Denmark quickly in 1700, then turned on Russia. In a blinding snowstorm, his well-trained professional army attacked and routed unsuspecting Russians besieging the Swedish fortress of Narva on the Baltic coast. Peter and the survivors fled in panic to Moscow. It was, for the Russians, a grim beginning to the long and brutal Great Northern War, which lasted from 1700 to 1721.

Suffering defeat and faced with a military crisis, the energetic Peter responded with a long series of practical but far-reaching measures designed to increase state power,

Gustaf Cederstrom: The Swedish Victory at Narva (1701)   This poignant re-creation focuses on the contrast between the Swedish officers in handsome dress uniforms and the battered Russian soldiers laying down their standards in surrender. Charles XII of Sweden scored brilliant, rapid-fire victories over Denmark, Saxony, and Russia, but he failed to make peace with Peter while he was ahead and eventually lost Sweden's holdings on the Baltic coast. *(The National Museum of Fine Arts, Stockholm)*

strengthen his armies, and gain victory. Tightening up Muscovy's old service system, he required every noble-man, great or small, to serve in the army or in the civil administration—for life. Since a more modern army and government required skilled technicians and experts, Peter created schools and universities to produce them. One of his most hated reforms was requiring a five-year education away from home for every young nobleman. Peter established an interlocking military-civilian bureaucracy with fourteen ranks, and he decreed that all had to start at the bottom and work toward the top. Some people of non-noble origins rose to high positions in this embryonic meritocracy. Drawing on his experience abroad, Peter searched out talented foreigners and

placed them in his service. These measures gradually combined to make the army and government more powerful and efficient.

Peter also greatly increased the service requirements of commoners. In the wake of the Narva disaster, he established a regular standing army of more than two hundred thousand peasant-soldiers commanded by officers from the nobility. In addition, special forces of Cossacks and foreigners numbered more than one hundred thousand. The departure of a drafted peasant boy was celebrated by his family and village almost like a funeral, since the recruit was drafted for life. The peasantry also served with its taxes, which increased threefold during Peter's reign. Serfs were arbitrarily assigned to work in the growing

Peter the Great in 1723 This compelling portrait by Grigory Musikiysky captures the strength and determination of the warrior-tsar after more than three decades of personal rule. In his hand Peter holds the scepter, symbol of royal sovereignty, and across his breastplate is draped an ermine fur, a mark of honor. In the background are the battleships of Russia's new Baltic fleet and the famous St. Peter and St. Paul Fortress that Peter built in St. Petersburg. *(Kremlin Museums, Moscow/The Bridgeman Art Library)*

number of factories and mines. Most of these industrial enterprises were directly or indirectly owned by the state, and they were worked almost exclusively for the military.

The constant warfare of Peter's reign consumed 80 to 85 percent of all revenues and brought only modest territorial expansion. Yet the Great Northern War with Sweden was crowned in the end by Russian victory. Peter's new war machine crushed the smaller army of Sweden in Ukraine at Poltava in 1709, one of the most significant battles in Russian history. The war dragged on until 1721, but Sweden never regained the offensive. Estonia and present-day Latvia (see Map 17.3) came under Russian rule for the first time. Russia became the dominant power on the Baltic Sea and very much a European Great Power. If victory or defeat is the ultimate historical criterion, Peter's reforms were a success.

There were other important consequences of Peter's reign. Because of his feverish desire to use modern technology to strengthen the army, many Westerners and Western ideas flowed into Russia for the first time. For Peter, modernization meant westernization. He thus required nobles to shave their heavy beards and wear Western clothing, previously banned in Russia. He required them to attend parties where young men and women would mix together and freely choose their own spouses. He forced a warrior elite to accept administrative service as an honorable occupation. From these efforts a new class of Western-oriented Russians began to emerge.

Online Study Center **Improve Your Grade**
Primary Source: Peter the Great Imposes Western Styles on the Russians

At the same time, vast numbers of Russians hated Peter's massive changes. For nobles, one of Peter's most detested reforms was the imposition of unigeniture—inheritance of land by one son alone—cutting daughters and other sons from family property. For peasants, the reign of the reforming tsar saw a significant increase in the bonds of serfdom. The gulf between the enserfed peasantry and the educated nobility widened more, even though all were caught up in the demands of the sovereign.

Thus Peter built on the service obligations of old Muscovy. His monarchical absolutism was truly the culmination of the long development of a unique Russian civilization. Yet the creation of a more modern army and state introduced much that was new and Western to Russia. This development paved the way for Russia to move somewhat closer to the European mainstream in its thought and institutions during the Enlightenment, especially under Catherine the Great.

The Growth of St. Petersburg

Nothing exemplifies the scope of Peter's reforms like his creation of St. Petersburg. In 1700, when the Great Northern War began, the city did not exist; there was only a small Swedish fortress on one of the waterlogged islands at the mouth of the Neva River, where it flows into the Baltic Sea. In 1702 Peter the Great's armies seized this desolate outpost. Within a year the reforming tsar decided to build a new city there and to make it, rather than ancient Moscow, his capital.

To secure the Baltic coast, military construction was the main concern for the next eight years. A mighty fortress was built on the newly named Peter Island, and a port and shipyards were built across the river on the mainland as a Russian navy came into being. From the inhospitable northern marshland Peter would create a future metropolis gloriously bearing his name.

After the decisive Russian victory at Poltava in 1709 greatly reduced the threat of Swedish armies, Peter moved into high gear. In one imperious decree after another, he ordered his people to build a city equal to any in the world. Such a city had to be Western and modern, just as Peter's army had to be Western and permanent. From such a "window on Europe," Peter believed, it would be easier to reform the country militarily and administratively.

These general political goals matched Peter's architectural ideas, which had been influenced by his travels in western Europe. First, Peter wanted a comfortable, "modern" city. Modernity meant broad, straight, stone-paved avenues; houses built in a uniform line and not haphazardly set back from the street; large parks; canals for drainage; stone bridges; and street lighting. Second, all buildings had to conform to detailed architectural regulations set down by the government. Finally, each social group—the nobility, the merchants, the artisans, and so on—was to live in a certain section of town. In short, the city and its population were to conform to a carefully defined urban plan.

Peter used the traditional methods of Russian autocracy to build his modern capital. Its creation was just one

St. Petersburg, ca 1760   Rastrelli's remodeled Winter Palace, which housed the royal family until the Russian Revolution of 1917, stands on the left along the Neva River. The Navy Office with its famous golden spire and other government office buildings are nearby and across the river. Russia became a naval power and St. Petersburg a great port. *(Michael Holford)*

of the heavy obligations he dictatorially imposed on all of Russian society. The peasants bore the heaviest burdens. Just as the government drafted peasants for the army, it also drafted twenty-five thousand to forty thousand men each summer to labor in St. Petersburg for three months without pay. Every ten to fifteen peasant households had to furnish one worker each summer and then pay a special tax in order to feed him in St. Petersburg.

Peasants hated this forced labor, and each year one-fourth to one-third of those sent risked brutal punishment to run away. Many peasant construction workers died from hunger, sickness, and accidents. Thus beautiful St. Petersburg was built by the shoveling, carting, and paving of a mass of conscripted serfs.

Peter also drafted more privileged groups to his city. Nobles were summarily ordered to build costly stone houses and palaces in St. Petersburg and to live in them most of the year. The more serfs a noble possessed, the bigger his dwelling had to be. Merchants and artisans were also commanded to settle and build in St. Petersburg. These nobles and merchants were then required to pay for the city's avenues, parks, canals, embankments, and bridges, all of which were costly in money and lives because they were built on a swamp. The building of St. Petersburg was, in truth, an enormous direct tax levied on the wealthy, which in turn forced the peasantry to do most of the work.

By the time of Peter's death in 1725, there were at least six thousand houses and numerous impressive government buildings in St. Petersburg. The city blossomed in the eighteenth century, at least in its wealthy showpiece sections. Peter's youngest daughter, Elizabeth (r. 1741–1762), named as her chief architect Bartolomeo Rastrelli, who came to Russia from Italy as a boy of fifteen in 1715. Combining Italian and Russian traditions into a unique, wildly colorful St. Petersburg style, Rastrelli built many palaces for the nobility and all the larger government buildings erected during Elizabeth's reign. He also rebuilt the Winter Palace as an enormous, aquacolored royal residence, now the Hermitage Museum. All the while St. Petersburg grew rapidly, and its almost three hundred thousand inhabitants in 1782 made it one of the world's largest cities. Peter and his successors created a magnificent royal city from nothing, which unmistakably proclaimed the power of Russia's rulers and the creative potential of the absolutist state.

The Growth of the Ottoman Empire

Most Christian Europeans perceived the Ottomans as the antithesis of their own values and traditions and viewed the empire as driven by an insatiable lust for warfare and conquest. In their view the fall of Constantinople was a catastrophe and the taking of the Balkans a despotic imprisonment of those territories. The Ottoman Empire seemed the epitome of Eastern exoticism, religious fanaticism, and tyranny. From the perspective of the Ottomans, the world looked very different. The siege of Constantinople liberated a glorious city from its long decline under the Byzantines. Rather than being a despoiled captive, the Balkans became a haven for refugees fleeing the growing intolerance of Western Christian powers. The Ottoman Empire provided Jews, Muslims, and even some Christians safety from the Inquisition and religious war: the Iberian powers tried to impose Christianity through conversion or exile, but Islam and Judaism remained part of the conversation of post-Reformation Europe because of the presence of the Ottoman Empire at Europe's gate.

The Ottomans came out of Central Asia as conquering warriors, settled in Anatolia (present-day Turkey), and created one of history's greatest empires (see pages 466 and 566). At their peak in the mid-sixteenth century under Sultan Suleiman the Magnificent (r. 1520–1566), they ruled the most powerful empire in the world. Their possessions stretched from western Persia across North Africa and into the heart of central Europe (see Map 17.4). In 1690 a Turkish visitor to Versailles wrote in his travel diary: "The King of France is the Sultan Suleiman of our time."

Ottoman expansion borrowed from the peoples they conquered. They were heirs to the Byzantine Empire and, through it, of Rome and its vision of universal empire. From the Byzantines, they adopted the tax structure and the use of religion to bind together a diverse empire. From the Persians, the Ottomans borrowed political and financial practices, and from the Arabs, religion and spirituality. This openness and adaptability—missing from most Western accounts of the Ottomans—was largely responsible for the empire's longevity.

When the Ottomans captured Constantinople in 1453, they fulfilled a long-held Islamic dream. They also shattered a bulwark of Christian identity. Founded by the emperor who introduced the Christian church to mighty Rome, for a millennium Constantinople had stood as a symbol of Christianity and its links to imperial power. Though the Byzantine Empire gradually shrank, the city itself had withstood numerous sieges. The loss of Constantinople was not just symbolic but strategic as well. The city stands at the natural gateway between the Black and Mediterranean Seas, between Europe and the Balkans. With the capture of Constantinople—renamed

MAP 17.4 The Ottoman Empire at Its Height, 1566 The Ottomans, like their great rivals the Habsburgs, rose to rule a vast dynastic empire encompassing many different peoples and ethnic groups. The army and the bureaucracy served to unite the disparate territories into a single state under an absolutist ruler.

Istanbul—the Ottomans and Islam occupied a permanent place in the European landscape. By 1600 Istanbul was one of the largest cities in the world, with a population of seven hundred thousand.

Ottoman expansion continued to the south as well. The Ottomans first conquered Syria and Iraq, and in 1517 Sultan Selim I (r. 1512–1520) invaded the Egyptian Mameluke empire and quickly captured Egypt, North Africa, and the Arabian peninsula. His successor, Suleiman the Magnificent, turned north, capturing Bosnia, Croatia, Romania, Ukraine, and part of Hungary at the Battle of Mohács in 1526. For the next hundred and fifty years, the Ottomans ruled the many different

ethnic groups living in southeastern Europe and the eastern Mediterranean. In 1529 their European expansion was halted with a failed siege of the Habsburg capital, Vienna. The Ottoman loss at the Battle of Lepanto in 1571, against the Christian Holy League, confirmed the limits of their ambitions in Europe.

The Ottoman Empire was originally built on a unique model of state and society. There was an almost complete absence of private landed property. Agricultural land was the personal hereditary property of the **sultan,** and peasants paid taxes to use the land. There was therefore no security of landholding and no hereditary nobility, two key features of western European society.

The Ottomans also employed a distinctive form of government administration. The top ranks of the bureaucracy were staffed by the sultan's slave corps. Because Muslim law prohibited enslaving other Muslims, the sultan's agents purchased slaves along the borders of the empire. Within the realm, the sultan levied a "tax" of one thousand to three thousand male children on the conquered Christian populations in the Balkans every year. Young slaves were raised in Turkey as Muslims and were trained to fight and to administer. The most talented rose to the top of the bureaucracy, where they might acquire wealth and power; the less fortunate formed the brave and skillful core of the sultan's army, the janissary corps. Lurid accounts of weeping Christian boys being carried off into Ottoman slavery did much to foster the idea of the brutal, fanatical Turk in the European mind.

After 1453 Istanbul became the capital of the empire and, with the transfer of the caliphate from Cairo, the religious center of Sunni Islam. The "old palace" was for the sultan's female family members, who lived in isolation under the care of eunuchs. The newly constructed Topkapi Palace was where officials worked and young slaves trained for future administrative or military careers. To prevent wives from bringing foreign influence into government—a constant concern in the West—sultans procreated only with their concubines and not with official wives. They also adopted a policy of allowing each concubine to produce only one male heir. At a young age, each son went to govern a province of the empire under his mother's supervision. These practices were intended to stabilize power and prevent a recurrence of the civil wars of the late fourteenth and early fifteenth centuries.

Sultan Suleiman undid these policies when he boldly married his concubine and had several children with her. He established a wing in the Topkapi Palace for his own female family members and his brothers' families. Starting with Suleiman, imperial wives began to take on more power. Marriages were arranged between sultans' daughters and high-ranking servants, creating powerful new members of the imperial household. Over time, the sultan's exclusive authority waned in favor of a more bureaucratic administration. These changes brought the Ottoman court closer to the European model of factionalism, intrigue, and informal female power. (See the feature "Individuals in Society: Hürrem.")

In this period the Ottoman Empire experienced the same economic and social crises that affected the rest of Europe. In the 1580s and 1590s rebellions broke out among many different groups in the vast empire: frustrated students, underpaid janissaries, and ambitious provincial governors. Revolts continued during the sev-

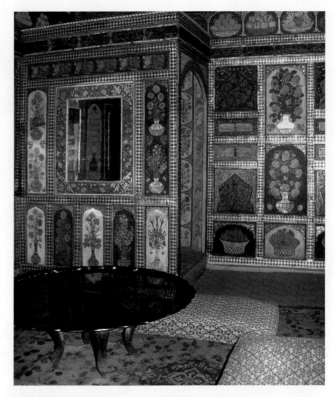

The Sultan's Harem at Topkapi Palace, Istanbul   Sultan Suleiman I created separate quarters at the Topkapi Palace for his wife Hürrem and her ladies-in-waiting. His successors transferred all of their wives, concubines, and female family members to the harem at Topkapi, carefully situated out of sight of the staterooms and courtyards where public affairs took place. The harem was the object of intense curiosity and fascination in the West. (*Vanni/Art Resource, NY*)

enteenth century as the janissaries formed alliances with court factions that resulted in the overthrow or execution of several Ottoman sultans.

In the late seventeenth century the Ottomans succeeded in marshaling their forces for one last attack on the Habsburgs, and a huge Turkish army laid siege to Vienna in 1683. After holding out against great odds for two months, the city was relieved at the last minute by reinforcements, and the Ottomans were forced to retreat. Soon the retreat became a rout. As Russian and Venetian allies attacked on other fronts, the Habsburgs conquered almost all of Hungary and Transylvania by 1699 (see Map 17.4). The Habsburgs completed their victory in 1718, with the Treaty of Passarowitz. These defeats might have led to reform of Ottoman political, military, and economic structures. They did not, and the empire's strength slowly eroded and with it Western fears of the Ottoman threat.

Individuals in Society

Hürrem

In Muslim culture *harem* means a sacred place or a sanctuary, which is forbidden to profane outsiders. The term was applied to the part of the household occupied by women and children and forbidden to men outside the family. The most famous member of the Ottoman sultan's harem was Hürrem, wife of Suleiman the Magnificent.

Hürrem (1505?–1558) came to the harem as a slave-concubine. Like many of the sultan's concubines, Hürrem was of foreign birth. Tradition holds that she was born Aleksandra Lisowska in what was the kingdom of Poland and today is Ukraine. She was captured during a Tatar raid and enslaved. Between 1517 and 1520, when she was about fifteen years old, she entered the imperial harem. Venetian reports insist that she was not outstandingly beautiful but was possessed of wonderful grace, charm, and good humor. These qualities gained her the Turkish nickname Hürrem, or "joyful one." After her arrival in the harem, Hürrem quickly became the imperial favorite.

Suleiman's love for Hürrem led him to break all precedents for the role of a concubine, including the rule that concubines must cease having children once they give birth to a male heir. By 1531 Hürrem had given birth to one daughter and five sons. In 1533 or 1534 Suleiman entered formal marriage with his consort—an unprecedented honor for a concubine. He reportedly gave his exclusive attention to his wife and also defied convention by allowing Hürrem to remain in the palace throughout her life instead of accompanying her son to a provincial governorship as other concubines had done.

Contemporaries were shocked by Hürrem's influence over the sultan and resentful of the apparent role she played in politics and diplomacy. The Venetian ambassador Bassano wrote that "the Janissaries and the entire court hate her and her children likewise, but because the Sultan loves her, no one dares to speak."* She was suspected of using witchcraft to control the sultan and accused of ordering the death of the sultan's first-born son (with another mother) in 1553. These stories were based on court gossip and rumor. The correspondence between Suleiman and Hürrem, unavailable until the nineteenth century, along with Suleiman's own diaries, confirms her status as the sultan's most trusted confidant and adviser. During his frequent absences, the pair exchanged passionate love letters. Hürrem included information about the political situation and warnings about any potential uprisings. She also intervened in affairs between the empire and her former home. She wrote to Polish king Sigismund Augustus and seems to have helped Poland attain its

privileged diplomatic status. She brought a particularly feminine touch to diplomatic relations, sending the Persian shah and the Polish king personally embroidered articles.

Hürrem used her enormous pension to contribute a mosque, two schools, a hospital, a fountain, and two public baths to Istanbul. In Jerusalem, Mecca, and Istanbul, she provided soup kitchens and hospices for pilgrims and the poor. She died in 1558, eight years before her husband. Her son Selim II (r. 1566–1574) inherited the throne.

Hürrem and her ladies in the harem.
(Bibliothèque nationale de France)

Drawing from reports of contemporary Western observers, historians depicted Hürrem as a manipulative and power-hungry social climber. They saw her career as the beginning of a "sultanate of women" in which strong imperial leadership gave way to court intrigue and dissipation. More recent historians have emphasized the intelligence and courage Hürrem demonstrated in navigating the ruthlessly competitive world of the harem.

Hürrem's journey from Ukrainian maiden to harem slave girl to sultan's wife captured enormous public attention. She is the subject of numerous paintings, plays, and novels as well as of an opera, a ballet, and a symphony by the composer Haydn. Interest in and suspicion of Hürrem continues. In 2003 a Turkish miniseries once more depicted her as a scheming intriguer.

Questions for Analysis

1. Compare Hürrem to other powerful early modern women such as Isabella of Castile, Elizabeth I of England, and Catherine de' Medici of France.
2. What can an exceptional woman like Hürrem reveal about the broader political and social world in which she lived?

*Cited in Galina Yermolenko, "Roxolana: The Greatest Empresse of the East," in *The Muslim World* 95 (2005): 2.

Source: Leslie P. Pierce, *The Imperial Harem: Women and Sovereignty in the Ottoman Empire* (New York: Oxford University Press, 1993).

Online Study Center **Improve Your Grade**
Going Beyond Individuals in Society

Religious Diversity in the Ottoman Empire

Despite Western perceptions, the Ottomans were more tolerant of religious differences than were the Europeans. They recognized Christians and Jews as "peoples of the Book" who followed the same biblical tradition as Islam. Building on the practices of the great Middle Eastern empires, the Ottomans divided their subjects into religious communities, and each *millet,* or "nation," enjoyed autonomous self-government under its religious leaders. (The Ottoman Empire recognized Orthodox Christians, Jews, Armenian Christians, and Muslims as distinct millets.) The **millet system** created a powerful bond between the Ottoman ruling class and the different religious leaders, who supported the sultan's rule in return for extensive authority over their own communities. Each millet collected taxes for the state, regulated group behavior, and maintained law courts, schools, synagogues, and hospitals for its people. Individuals outside the ruling elite had status only through their millet membership.

Supported and reassured by religious toleration and cultural autonomy, non-Muslim minorities coexisted and commingled with the Muslim majority. Greek, Jewish, and Armenian merchants moved easily to and from Europe, drawing Ottomans and Europeans closer together despite recurring war and conflict. Armenian merchants excelled as international silk merchants, Jews as textile

manufacturers and financiers, and Greeks as mariners and shipowners, although all three groups participated in all Ottoman occupations in the sixteenth and seventeenth centuries.[7] Religious diversity was mostly a source of strength for the Ottomans, allowing them to integrate many different ethnicities into the empire and to profit from the skills and networks of each group.

Despite its tolerance, the Ottoman Empire was an explicitly Islamic state. Members of the Muslim religious elite were educated at religious schools (*medreses*) attached to mosques. *Muftis* supervised mosques and religious schools and wrote interpretations of Islamic law, and state-appointed *kadis* administered the law. Whereas non-Muslims had their own courts for dealings among themselves, any conflict involving a Muslim was regulated by a kadi in an Islamic court. Wariness of the Islamic courts encouraged non-Muslims to deal with their own as much as possible. However, the Ottomans showed the same openness in law as in empire building. They adopted the most flexible of Muslim law traditions, and they accepted provincial law codes that respected pre-existing local laws. Under Suleiman the Magnificent and his successors, a process of legal centralization began; provincial laws were codified and standardized. The sultan's claim to be caliph—the guide for the community of all Muslims—helped legitimize this process of legal centralization. The legal reforms won Suleiman the title "the Lawgiver" from his subjects.

Chapter Summary

Online Study Center **ACE the Test**

- *What social and economic changes affected central and eastern Europe from 1400 to 1650?*
- *How and why did the rulers of Austria and Prussia, each in different political and social environments, manage to build powerful absolute monarchies that proved more durable than that of Louis XIV?*
- *What were the distinctive features of Russian and Ottoman absolutism in this period?*

From about 1400 to 1650 social and economic developments in eastern Europe diverged from those in western Europe. In the East, after enjoying relative freedom in

the Middle Ages, peasants and townspeople lost freedom and fell under the economic, social, and legal authority of the nobles, who increased their power and prestige.

Within this framework of resurgent serfdom and entrenched nobility, Austrian and Prussian monarchs fashioned absolutist states in the seventeenth and early eighteenth centuries. These monarchs won absolutist control over standing armies, taxation, and representative bodies, but they did not question underlying social and economic relationships. Indeed, they enhanced the privileges of the nobles, who filled enlarged armies and growing state bureaucracies. In exchange for entrenched privileges over their peasants, nobles thus cooperated with the growth of state power.

In Russia the social and economic trends were similar, but the timing of political absolutism was different. Mongol conquest and rule were a crucial experience, and a harsh indigenous tsarist autocracy was firmly in place by the reign of Ivan the Terrible in the sixteenth century. More than a century later Peter the Great succeeded in modernizing Russia's traditional absolutism by reforming the army and the bureaucracy. Farther to the east, the Ottoman sultans developed a distinctive political and economic system in which all land theoretically belonged to the sultan, who was served by a slave corps of administrators and soldiers. The Ottoman Empire was relatively tolerant on religious matters and served as a haven for Jews and other marginalized religious groups.

Triumphant absolutism interacted spectacularly with the arts. Central and eastern European rulers built grandiose palaces, and even whole cities, like St. Petersburg, to glorify their power and majesty.

Key Terms

serfdom	Junkers
hereditary subjugation	Mongol Yoke
Protestant Union	tsar
Peace of Westphalia	boyars
absolutism	service nobility
Bohemian Estates	Cossacks
Battle of Mohács	sultan
Pragmatic Sanction	millet system
elector of Brandenburg	

Online Study Center   **Improve Your Grade** Flashcards

Suggested Reading

Bushkovitch, Paul. *Peter the Great: The Struggle for Power, 1671–1725.* 2001. An outstanding biography of the Russian tsar.

Engel, Barbara A. *Women in Russia, 1700–2000.* 2004. An excellent account of the role of women in Russian society over three centuries.

Goffman, Daniel. *The Ottoman Empire and Early Modern Europe.* 2002. An original and valuable study of Ottoman relations with the European world.

Hagen, William W. *Ordinary Prussians: Brandenburg Junkers and Villagers, 1500–1840.* 2002. Provides a fascinating encounter with the people of a Prussian estate.

Hughes, Lindsey, ed. *Peter the Great and the West: New Perspectives.* 2001. Essays by leading scholars on the reign of Peter the Great and his opening of Russia to the West.

Ingrao, Charles W. *The Habsburg Monarchy, 1618–1815,* 2d ed. 2000. An excellent synthesis of the political and social development of the Habsburg empire in the early modern period.

Kappeler, Adreas. *The Russian Empire: Ethnicity and Nationalism.* 2001. Explains the rise of a multiethnic empire in Russia from the seventeenth century on.

Kollmann, N. Shields. *By Honor Bound: State and Society in Early Modern Russia.* 1999. An excellent study of politics and values among the Russian elite.

Lincoln, W. Bruce. *Sunlight at Midnight: St. Petersburg and the Rise of Modern Russia.* 2001. Captures the spirit of Peter the Great's new northern capital.

McKay, Derek. *The Great Elector: Frederick William of Brandenburg-Prussia.* 2001. Examines the formative years of Prussian power.

Murphey, Rhoads. *Ottoman Warfare, 1500–1700.* 1999. A good introduction to Ottoman military history, including warfare between the Ottomans and European states.

Ogilvie, Sheilagh, and Bob Scribner, eds. *Germany: A New Economic and Social History, 1450–1800,* 2 vols. 1996. A broad overview of life in central Europe in the early modern period.

Parker, Geoffrey. *The Thirty Years War,* 2d ed. 1997. The standard account of the Thirty Years' War.

Quataert, Donald. *The Ottoman Empire, 1700–1922.* 2000. A recent synthesis of Ottoman history by a leading historian.

Riasanovsky, Nicholas V., and Mark Steinberg. *A History of Russia to 1855.* 2004. An excellent starting place for students interested in Russian history.

Notes

1. H. Kamen, "The Economic and Social Consequences of the Thirty Years' War," *Past and Present* 39 (April 1968): 44–61.
2. Quoted in F. L. Carsten, *The Origins of Prussia* (Oxford: Clarendon Press, 1954), p. 175.
3. H. Rosenberg, *Bureaucracy, Aristocracy, and Autocracy: The Prussian Experience, 1660–1815* (Boston: Beacon Press, 1966), p. 38.
4. Ibid., p. 43.
5. Quoted in R. A. Dorwart, *The Administrative Reforms of Frederick William I of Prussia* (Cambridge, Mass.: Harvard University Press, 1953), p. 226.
6. Quoted in Rosenberg, *Bureaucracy, Aristocracy, and Autocracy,* p. 40.
7. D. Goffman, *The Ottoman Empire and Early Modern Europe* (Cambridge: Cambridge University Press, 2002), pp. 9–18, 83–91.

A Foreign Traveler in Russia

Seventeenth-century Russia remained a remote and mysterious land for western and even central Europeans, who had few direct contacts with the tsar's dominion. Developing their ideas of refined society and gradual progress (see Chapter 18), Westerners portrayed eastern Europe as more "barbaric" and less "civilized" than their homelands. Thus they expanded eastern Europe's undeniably harsher social and economic conditions to encompass a very debatable cultural and moral inferiority.

Knowledge of Russia came mainly from occasional travelers who had visited Muscovy and sometimes wrote accounts of what they saw. The most famous of these accounts was by the German Adam Olearius (ca 1599–1671), who was sent to Moscow by the duke of Holstein on three diplomatic missions in the 1630s. These missions ultimately proved unsuccessful, but they provided Olearius with a rich store of information for his Travels in Muscovy, *from which the following excerpts are taken. Published in German in 1647 and soon translated into several languages (but not Russian), Olearius's unflattering but well-informed study played a major role in shaping European ideas about Russia.*

The government of the Russians is what political theorists call a "dominating and despotic monarchy," where the sovereign, that is, the tsar or the grand prince who has obtained the crown by right of succession, rules the entire land alone, and all the people are his subjects, and where the nobles and princes no less than the common folk—townspeople and peasants—are his serfs and slaves, whom he rules and treats as a master treats his servants. . . .

If the Russians be considered in respect to their character, customs, and way of life, they are justly to be counted among the barbarians. . . . The vice of drunkenness is so common in this nation, among people of every station, clergy and laity, high and low, men and women, old and young, that when they are seen now and then lying about in the streets, wallowing in the mud, no attention is paid to it, as something habitual. If a cart driver comes upon such a drunken pig whom he happens to know, he shoves him onto his cart and drives him home, where he is paid his fare. No one ever refuses an opportunity to drink and to get drunk, at any time and in any place, and usually it is done with vodka. . . .

The Russians being naturally tough and born, as it were, for slavery, they must be kept under a harsh and strict yoke and must be driven to do their work with clubs and whips, which they suffer without impatience, because such is their station, and they are accustomed to it. Young and half-grown fellows sometimes come together on certain days and train themselves in fisticuffs, to accustom themselves to receiving blows, and, since habit is second nature, this makes blows given as punishment easier to bear. Each and all, they are slaves and serfs. . . .

Because of slavery and their rough and hard life, the Russians accept war readily and are well suited to it. On certain occasions, if need be, they reveal themselves as courageous and daring soldiers. . . .

Although the Russians, especially the common populace, living as slaves under a harsh yoke, can bear and endure a great deal out of love for their masters, yet if the pressure is beyond measure, then it can be said of them: "Patience, often wounded, finally turned into fury." A dangerous indignation results, turned not so much against their sovereign as against the lower authorities, especially if the people have been much oppressed by them and by their supporters and have not been protected by the higher authorities. And once they are aroused and enraged, it is not easy to appease them. Then, disregarding all dangers that may ensue, they resort to every kind of

The brutality of serfdom is shown in this illustration from Olearius's *Travels in Muscovy*. (*University of Illinois Library, Champaign*)

violence and behave like madmen. . . . They own little; most of them have no feather beds; they lie on cushions, straw, mats, or their clothes; they sleep on benches and, in winter, like the non-Germans [natives] in Livonia, upon the oven, which serves them for cooking and is flat on the top; here husband, wife, children, servants, and maids huddle together. In some houses in the countryside we saw chickens and pigs under the benches and the ovens. . . . Russians are not used to delicate food and dainties; their daily food consists of porridge, turnips, cabbage, and cucumbers, fresh and pickled, and in Moscow mostly of big salt fish which stink badly, because of the thrifty use of salt, yet are eaten with relish. . . .

The Russians can endure extreme heat. In the bathhouse they stretch out on benches and let themselves be beaten and rubbed with bunches of birch twigs and wisps of bast (which I could not stand); and when they are hot and red all over and so exhausted that they can bear it no longer in the bathhouse, men and women rush outdoors naked and pour cold water over their bodies; in winter they even wallow in the snow and rub their skin with it as if it were soap; then they go back into the hot bathhouse. And since bathhouses are usually near rivers and brooks, they can throw themselves straight from the hot into the cold bath. . . .

Generally noble families, even the small nobility, rear their daughters in secluded chambers, keeping them hidden from outsiders; and a bridegroom is not allowed to have a look at his bride until he receives her in the bridal chamber. Therefore some happen to be deceived, being given a misshapen and sickly one instead of a fair one, and sometimes a kinswoman or even a maidservant instead of a daughter; of which there have been examples even among the highborn. No wonder therefore that often they live together like cats and dogs and that wife-beating is so common among Russians. . . .

In the Kremlin and in the city there are a great many churches, chapels, and monasteries, both within and without the city walls, over two thousand in all. This is so because every nobleman who has some fortune has a chapel built for himself, and most of them are of stone. The stone churches are round and vaulted inside. . . . They allow neither organs nor any other musical instruments in their churches, saying: Instruments that have neither souls nor life cannot praise God. . . .

In their churches there hang many bells, sometimes five or six, the largest not over two hundredweights. They ring these bells to summon people to church, and also when the priest during mass raises the chalice. In Moscow, because of the multitude of churches and chapels, there are several thousand bells, which during the divine service create such a clang and din that one unaccustomed to it listens in amazement.

Questions for Analysis

1. In what ways were all social groups in Russia similar, according to Olearius?

2. How did Olearius characterize the Russians in general? What supporting evidence did he offer for his judgment?

3. Does Olearius's account help explain Stenka Razin's rebellion? In what ways?

4. On the basis of these representative passages, why do you think Olearius's book was so popular and influential in central and western Europe?

Source: G. Vernadsky and R. T. Fisher, Jr., eds., *A Source Book for Russian History from Early Times to 1917*, vol. 1 (New Haven: Yale University Press, 1972), pp. 249–251. Copyright © 1972 by Yale University Press. Reprinted by permission of Yale University Press.

Voltaire, the renowned Enlightenment thinker, leans forward on the left to exchange ideas and witty conversation with Frederick the Great, king of Prussia. *(Bildarchiv Preussischer Kulturbesitz/ Art Resource, NY)*

chapter

18

chapter preview

The Scientific Revolution
• *What was revolutionary in new attitudes toward the natural world?*

The Enlightenment
• *How did the new worldview affect the way people thought about society and human relations?*

The Enlightenment and Absolutism
• *What impact did this new way of thinking have on political developments and monarchical absolutism?*

TOWARD A NEW WORLDVIEW, 1540–1789

The intellectual developments of the seventeenth and eighteenth centuries created the modern worldview that the West continues to hold—and debate—to this day. In the seventeenth century fundamentally new ways of understanding the natural world emerged. Those leading the changes saw themselves as philosophers and referred to their field of study as "natural philosophy." In the nineteenth century scholars hailed their achievements as a "scientific revolution" that produced modern science as we know it. The new "science" created in the seventeenth century entailed the search for precise knowledge of the physical world based on the union of experimental observations with sophisticated mathematics. Whereas medieval scholars looked to authoritative texts like the Bible or the classics, seventeenth-century natural philosophers performed experiments and relied on increasingly complex mathematical calculations. The resulting conception of the universe and its laws remained in force until Einstein's discoveries in the first half of the twentieth century.

In the eighteenth century philosophers extended the use of reason from nature to human society. They sought to bring the light of reason to bear on the darkness of prejudice, outmoded traditions, and ignorance. Self-proclaimed members of an "Enlightenment" movement, they wished to bring the same progress to human affairs as their predecessors had brought to the understanding of the natural world. While the scientific revolution ushered in modern science, the Enlightenment created concepts of human rights, equality, progress, universalism, and tolerance that still guide Western societies today.

While many view the scientific revolution and the Enlightenment as bedrocks of the achievement of Western civilization, others have seen a darker side. For these critics, the mastery over nature permitted by the scientific revolution threatens to overwhelm the earth's fragile equilibrium, and the belief in the universal application of "reason" can lead to arrogance and intolerance, particularly intolerance of other people's spiritual values. Such vivid debates about the legacy of these intellectual and cultural developments testify to their continuing importance in today's world.

Online Study Center

This icon will direct you to interactive activities and study materials on the website **college.hmco.com/pic/mckaywest9e**

The Scientific Revolution

The emergence of modern science was a development of tremendous long-term significance. A noted historian has even said that the scientific revolution of the late sixteenth and seventeenth centuries "outshines everything since the rise of Christianity and reduces the Renaissance and Reformation to the rank of mere episodes, mere internal displacements, within the system of medieval Christendom." The scientific revolution was "the real origin both of the modern world and the modern mentality."[1] This statement is an exaggeration, but not much of one. Of all the great civilizations, only that of the West developed modern science. With the scientific revolution Western society began to acquire its most distinctive traits.

- *What was revolutionary in new attitudes toward the natural world?*

Scientific Thought in 1500

Since developments in astronomy and physics were at the heart of the scientific revolution, one must begin with the traditional European conception of the universe. It is important to remember that the practitioners of the scientific revolution did not consider their field *science* but rather **natural philosophy.** Their intention was not to create modern science but to ask fundamental questions about the nature of the universe, its purpose, and how it functioned. They did not set supernatural questions aside, as do modern scientists, but incorporated them in their speculations, which made reference not only to Christian theology but often to magic, alchemy, and astrology as well. The dividing line between matter and spirit, or reason and faith, was much less rigid for participants in the scientific revolution than it is for scientists today.

In the early 1500s natural philosophy was still based primarily on the ideas of Aristotle,

the great Greek philosopher of the fourth century B.C. These ideas had gradually been recovered during the Middle Ages. Medieval theologians such as Thomas Aquinas brought Aristotelian philosophy into harmony with Christian doctrines. According to this revised Aristotelian view, a motionless earth was fixed at the center of the universe. Around it moved ten separate transparent crystal spheres. In the first eight spheres were embedded, in turn, the moon, the sun, the five known planets, and the fixed stars. Then followed two spheres added during the Middle Ages to account for slight changes in the positions of the stars over the centuries. Beyond the tenth sphere was Heaven, with the throne of God and the souls of the saved. Angels kept the spheres moving in perfect circles.

Aristotle's views, suitably revised by medieval philosophers, also dominated thinking about physics and motion on earth. Aristotle had distinguished sharply between the world of the celestial spheres and that of the earth—the sublunar world. The spheres consisted of a perfect, incorruptible "quintessence," or fifth essence. The sublunar world, however, was made up of four imperfect, changeable elements. The "light" elements (air and fire) naturally moved upward, while the "heavy" elements (water and earth) naturally moved downward. These nat-

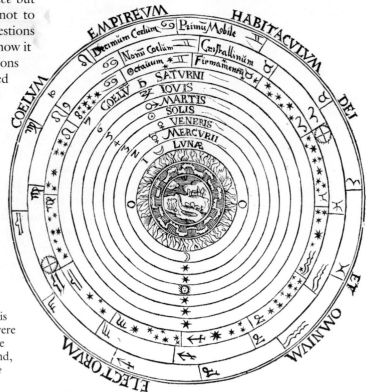

The Aristotelian Universe as Imagined in the Sixteenth Century A round earth is at the center, surrounded by spheres of water, air, and fire. Beyond this small nucleus, the moon, the sun, and the five planets were embedded in their own rotating crystal spheres, with the stars sharing the surface of one enormous sphere. Beyond, the heavens were composed of unchanging ether. (*Image Select/Art Resource, NY*)

ural directions of motion did not always prevail, however, for elements were often mixed together and could be affected by an outside force such as a human being. Aristotle and his followers also believed that a uniform force moved an object at a constant speed and that the object would stop as soon as that force was removed.

Aristotle's ideas about astronomy and physics were accepted with minor revisions for two thousand years, and with good reason. First, they offered an understandable, commonsense explanation for what the eye actually saw. Second, Aristotle's science as interpreted by Christian theologians fit neatly with Christian doctrines. It established a home for God and a place for Christian souls. It put human beings at the center of the universe and made them the critical link in a "great chain of being" that stretched from the throne of God to the most lowly insect on earth. Thus examination of the natural world was primarily a branch of theology, and it reinforced religious thought.

The Copernican Hypothesis

The desire to explain and thereby glorify God's handiwork led to the first great departure from the medieval system. This departure was the work of the Polish clergyman and astronomer Nicolaus Copernicus (1473–1543). As a young man Copernicus studied church law and astronomy in various European universities. He saw how professional astronomers still depended for their most accurate calculations on the second century B.C. work of Ptolemy. Author of a geographical synthesis that profoundly influenced European voyages of exploration (see page 494), Ptolemy was also a great astronomer. His achievement had been to work out complicated rules to explain the minor irregularities in the movement of the planets. These rules enabled stargazers and astrologers to track the planets with greater precision. Many people then (and now) believed that the changing relationships between planets and stars influenced events on earth.

The young Copernicus was uninterested in astrology and felt that Ptolemy's cumbersome and occasionally inaccurate rules detracted from the majesty of a perfect Creator. He preferred an old Greek idea being discussed in Renaissance Italy: that the sun, rather than the earth, was at the center of the universe. Finishing his university studies and returning to a church position in East Prussia, Copernicus worked on his hypothesis from 1506 to 1530. Never questioning the Aristotelian belief in crystal spheres or the idea that circular motion was most perfect and divine, Copernicus theorized that the stars and planets, including the earth, revolved around a fixed sun.

Chronology

ca 1540–1690	Scientific revolution
1543	Copernicus, *On the Revolutions of the Heavenly Spheres*
1564–1642	Life of Galileo
1571–1630	Life of Kepler
1662	Royal Society of London founded
1687	Newton, *Principia* and law of universal gravitation
1690	Locke, *Essay Concerning Human Understanding*
ca 1690–1780	Enlightenment
1694–1778	Life of Voltaire
1700–1789	Growth of book publishing
1720–1780	Rococo style in art and decoration
ca 1740–1780	Salons led by elite women
1740–1786	Reign of Frederick the Great of Prussia
ca 1750–1790	Enlightened absolutists
1751–1765	Diderot and d'Alembert, *Encyclopedia*
1762	Rousseau, *The Social Contract*
1762–1796	Reign of Catherine the Great of Russia
1780–1790	Reign of Joseph II of Austria

Yet Copernicus was a cautious man. Fearing the ridicule of other astronomers, he did not publish his *On the Revolutions of the Heavenly Spheres* until 1543, the year of his death.

The **Copernican hypothesis** had enormous scientific and religious implications, many of which the conservative Copernicus did not anticipate. First, it put the stars at rest, their apparent nightly movement simply a result of the earth's rotation. Thus it destroyed the main reason for believing in crystal spheres capable of moving the stars around the earth. Second, Copernicus's theory suggested a universe of staggering size. If in the course of a year the earth moved around the sun and yet the stars appeared to remain in the same place, then the universe was unthinkably large. Finally, by characterizing the earth as just another planet, Copernicus destroyed the basic idea of Aristotelian physics—that the earthly world was quite different from the heavenly one. Where, then, was the realm of perfection? Where were Heaven and the throne of God?

Online Study Center **Improve Your Grade**
Primary Source: Commentariolus: Copernicus Outlines His Thesis

The Copernican hypothesis brought sharp attacks from religious leaders, especially Protestants. Martin Luther spoke of him as the "new astrologer who wants to prove that the earth moves and goes round. . . . The fool wants to turn the whole art of astronomy upside down." Luther noted that "as the Holy Scripture tells us, so did Joshua bid the sun stand still and not the earth."[2] John Calvin also condemned Copernicus. Catholic reaction was milder at first. The Catholic Church had never held to literal interpretations of the Bible, and not until 1616 did it officially declare the Copernican hypothesis false.

This slow reaction also reflected the slow progress of Copernicus's theory for many years. Other events were almost as influential in creating doubts about traditional astronomical ideas. In 1572 a new star appeared and shone very brightly for almost two years. The new star, which was actually a distant exploding star, made an enormous impression on people. It seemed to contradict the idea that the heavenly spheres were unchanging and therefore perfect. In 1577 a new comet suddenly moved through the sky, cutting a straight path across the supposedly impenetrable crystal spheres. It was time, as a typical scientific writer put it, for "the radical renovation of astronomy."[3]

From Brahe to Galileo

One astronomer who agreed was Tycho Brahe (1546–1601). Born into a prominent Danish noble family, Brahe was tremendously impressed by a partial eclipse of the sun at an early age. Completing his studies abroad and returning to Denmark, he established himself as Europe's leading astronomer with his detailed observations of the new star of 1572. Aided by generous grants from the king of Denmark, Brahe built the most sophisticated observatory of his day. For twenty years he meticulously observed the stars and planets with the naked eye. An imposing man who had lost a piece of his nose in a duel and replaced it with a special bridge of gold and silver alloy, a noble who exploited his peasants arrogantly and approached the heavens humbly, Brahe contributed a great mass of data. His limited understanding of mathematics prevented him, however, from making much sense out of his data. Part Ptolemaic, part Copernican, he

believed that all the planets revolved around the sun and that the entire group of sun and planets revolved in turn around the earth-moon system.

It was left to Brahe's brilliant young assistant, Johannes Kepler (1571–1630), to go much further. Kepler was a medieval figure in many ways. Coming from a minor German noble family and trained for the Lutheran ministry, he long believed that the universe was built on mystical mathematical relationships and a musical harmony of the heavenly bodies. Working and reworking Brahe's mountain of observations in a staggering effort after the Dane's death, this brilliant mathematician eventually went beyond mystical intuitions.

Kepler formulated three famous laws of planetary motion. First, building on Copernican theory, he demonstrated in 1609 that the orbits of the planets around the sun are elliptical rather than circular. Second, he demonstrated that the planets do not move at a uniform speed in their orbits. Third, in 1619 he showed that the time a planet takes to make its complete orbit is precisely related to its distance from the sun. Kepler's contribution was monumental. Whereas Copernicus had speculated, Kepler proved mathematically the precise relations of a sun-centered (solar) system. His work demolished the old system of Aristotle and Ptolemy, and in his third law he came close to formulating the idea of universal gravitation.

While Kepler was unraveling planetary motion, a young Florentine named Galileo Galilei (1564–1642) was challenging all the old ideas about motion. Like so many early scientists, Galileo was a poor nobleman first marked for a religious career. However, he soon became fascinated by mathematics. A brilliant student, in 1589 Galileo became a professor of mathematics at age twenty-five. He proceeded to examine motion and mechanics in a new way. Indeed, his great achievement was the elaboration and consolidation of the **experimental method.** That is, rather than speculate about what might or should happen, Galileo conducted controlled experiments to find out what actually *did* happen. In his famous acceleration experiment, he showed that a uniform force—in this case, gravity—produced a uniform acceleration. Here is how Galileo described his pathbreaking method and conclusion in his *Two New Sciences:*

A piece of wooden moulding . . . was taken; on its edge was cut a channel a little more than one finger in breadth. Having made this groove very straight, smooth and polished, and having lined it with parchment, also as smooth and polished as possible, we rolled along it a hard, smooth and very round bronze ball. . . . Noting . . . the time required to make the descent . . . we now rolled the ball only one-quarter the length of the channel; and having measured the time of its descent, we found it precisely one-half of the former. . . . In such experiments [over many distances], repeated a full hundred times, we always found that the spaces traversed were to each other as the squares of the times, and that this was true for all inclinations of the plane.[4]

With this and other experiments, Galileo formulated the **law of inertia.** Rest was not the natural state of objects. Rather, an object continues in motion forever unless stopped by some external force. Aristotelian physics was in shambles.

In the tradition of Brahe, Galileo also applied the experimental method to astronomy. On hearing details about the invention of the telescope in Holland, Galileo made one for himself and trained it on the heavens. He quickly discovered the first four moons of Jupiter, which clearly suggested that Jupiter could not possibly be embedded in any impenetrable crystal sphere. This discovery provided new evidence for the Copernican theory, in which Galileo already believed. Galileo then pointed his telescope at the moon. He wrote in 1610 in *Siderus Nuncius:*

I feel sure that the moon is not perfectly smooth, free from inequalities, and exactly spherical, as a large school of philosophers considers with regard to the moon and the other heavenly bodies. On the contrary, it is full of inequalities, uneven, full of hollows and protuberances, just like the surface of the earth itself, which is varied. . . . The next object which I have observed is the essence or substance of the Milky Way. By the aid of a telescope anyone may behold this in a manner which so distinctly appeals to the senses that all the disputes which have tormented philosophers through so many ages are exploded by the irrefutable evidence of our eyes, and we are freed from wordy disputes upon the subject. For the galaxy is nothing else but a mass of innumerable stars planted together in clusters.[5]

Reading these famous lines, one feels a crucial corner in Western civilization being turned. The traditional religious worldview, which rested on determining and accepting the proper established authority, was beginning to give way to a new method. This new method of learning and investigating was the greatest accomplishment of the entire scientific revolution, for it proved capable of great extension. A historian investigating documents of

Galileo's Paintings of the Moon When Galileo published the results of his telescopic observations of the moon, he added these paintings to illustrate the marvels he had seen. Galileo made two telescopes, which are shown here. The larger one magnifies fourteen times, the smaller one twenty times. *(Biblioteca Nazionale Centrale, Florence/Art Resource, NY; Museum of Science, Florence/Art Resource, NY)*

the past, for example, is not so different from a Galileo studying stars and rolling balls.

Galileo was employed in Florence by the Medici grand dukes of Tuscany, and his work eventually aroused the ire of some theologians. The issue was presented in 1624 to Pope Urban VIII, who permitted Galileo to write about different possible systems of the world as long as he did not presume to judge which one actually existed. After the publication in Italian of his widely read *Dialogue on the Two Chief Systems of the World* in 1632, which openly lampooned the traditional views of Aristotle and Ptolemy and defended those of Copernicus, Galileo was tried for heresy by the papal Inquisition. Imprisoned and threatened with torture, the aging Galileo recanted, "renouncing and cursing" his Copernican errors.

Newton's Synthesis

The accomplishments of Kepler, Galileo, and other scientists had taken effect by about 1640. The old astronomy and physics were in ruins, and several fundamental breakthroughs had been made. The new findings had not, however, been fused together in a new synthesis, a single explanatory system that would comprehend motion both on earth and in the skies. That synthesis, which prevailed until the twentieth century, was the work of Isaac Newton (1642–1727).

Newton was born into lower English gentry and attended Cambridge University. A genius who spectacularly united the experimental and theoretical-mathematical sides of modern science, Newton was also fascinated by alchemy. He sought the elixir of life and a way to change base metals into gold and silver. Newton was also intensely religious. He was far from being the perfect rationalist so endlessly eulogized by writers in the eighteenth and nineteenth centuries.

Of his intellectual genius and incredible powers of concentration there can be no doubt. Arriving at some of his most basic ideas about physics in 1666 at age twenty-four, but unable to prove these theories mathematically, he attained a professorship and studied optics for many years. In 1684 Newton returned to physics for eighteen extraordinarily intensive months. For weeks on end he seldom left his room except to read his lectures. His meals were sent up, but he usually forgot to eat them, his mind fastened like a vise on the laws of the universe. He opened the third book of his immortal *Mathematical Principles of Natural Philosophy*, published in Latin in 1687 and generally known as the *Principia*, with these lines:

Isaac Newton   This portrait suggests the depth and complexity of the great genius. Is the powerful mind behind those piercing eyes thinking of science or of religion, or perhaps of both? *(Scala/Art Resource, NY)*

In the preceding books I have laid down the principles of philosophy [that is, science]. . . . These principles are the laws of certain motions, and powers or forces, which chiefly have respect to philosophy. . . . It remains that from the same principles I now demonstrate the frame of the System of the World.

Newton made good his grandiose claim. His towering accomplishment was to integrate in a single explanatory system the astronomy of Copernicus, as corrected by Kepler's laws, with the physics of Galileo and his predecessors. Newton did this by means of a set of mathematical laws that explain motion and mechanics. These laws of dynamics are complex, and it took scientists and engineers two hundred years to work out all their implications. Nevertheless, the key feature of the Newtonian synthesis was the **law of universal gravitation.** According to this law, every body in the universe attracts every other body in the universe in a precise mathematical relationship, whereby the force of attraction is proportional to the quantity of matter of the objects and inversely proportional to the square of the distance between them. The whole universe—from Kepler's elliptical orbits to Galileo's rolling balls—was unified in one majestic system.

Causes of the Scientific Revolution

The scientific revolution drew on long-term developments in European culture. The first was the development of the medieval university. By the thirteenth century permanent universities with professors and large student bodies had been established in western Europe to train the lawyers, doctors, and church leaders society required. By 1300 philosophy had taken its place alongside law, medicine, and theology. Medieval philosophers developed a limited but real independence from theologians and a sense of free inquiry. They nobly pursued a body of knowledge and tried to arrange it meaningfully by means of abstract theories.

Within this framework what we now think of as science was able to emerge as a minor but distinct branch of philosophy. In the fourteenth and fifteenth centuries leading universities established new professorships of mathematics, astronomy, and physics (natural philosophy) within their faculties of philosophy. Although the prestige of the new fields was low, critical thinking was now applied to scientific problems by a permanent community of scholars. And an outlet existed for the talents of a Galileo or a Newton: all the great pathfinders either studied or taught at universities.

Second, the Renaissance also stimulated scientific progress. The recovery of the finest works of Greek mathematics—a byproduct of Renaissance humanism's ceaseless search for the knowledge of antiquity—greatly improved European mathematics. The recovery of more texts also showed that classical mathematicians had their differences; Europeans were thus forced to try to resolve these ancient controversies by means of their own efforts. Finally, Renaissance patrons, especially in Italy, often supported scientists as well as artists and writers. Various rulers and wealthy business people funded scientific investigations, as the Medicis of Florence did for Galileo.

The navigational problems of long sea voyages in the age of overseas expansion were a third factor in the scientific revolution. Ship captains on distant shores needed to be able to chart their positions as accurately as possible so that reliable maps could be drawn and the risks of international trade reduced. As early as 1484 the king of Portugal appointed a commission of mathematicians to perfect tables to help seamen find their latitude. This resulted in the first European navigation manual. Navigational problems were also critical in the development of many new scientific instruments, such as the telescope, barometer, thermometer, pendulum clock, microscope, and air pump. Better instruments, which permitted more accurate observations, often led to important new knowledge. Galileo with his telescope was by no means unique.

Better instruments were part of a fourth factor in the scientific revolution: the development of better ways of obtaining knowledge about the world. Two important thinkers, Francis Bacon (1561–1626) and René Descartes (1596–1650), represented key aspects of this improvement in scientific methodology.

The English politician and writer Francis Bacon was the greatest early propagandist for the new experimental method. Rejecting the Aristotelian and medieval method of using speculative reasoning to build general theories, Bacon argued that new knowledge had to be pursued through empirical experimental research. The researcher who wants to learn more about leaves or rocks should not speculate about the subject but should rather collect a multitude of specimens and then compare and analyze them, he said. General principles will then emerge. Bacon's contribution was to formalize the empirical method, which had already been used by Brahe and Galileo, into the general theory of inductive reasoning known as **empiricism.**

Online Study Center **Improve Your Grade**
Primary Source: Francis Bacon Rejects Superstition and Extols the Virtue of Science

The French philosopher René Descartes was a true genius who made his first great discovery in mathematics. As a twenty-three-year-old soldier serving in the Thirty Years' War, he experienced a life-changing intellectual vision on a single night in 1619. Descartes saw that there was a perfect correspondence between geometry and algebra and that geometrical, spatial figures could be expressed as algebraic equations and vice versa. A major step forward in the history of mathematics, Descartes's discovery of analytic geometry provided scientists with an important new tool.

Descartes's greatest achievement was to develop his initial vision into a whole philosophy of knowledge and science. He decided it was necessary to doubt everything that could reasonably be doubted and then, as in geometry, to use deductive reasoning from self-evident principles to ascertain scientific laws. Descartes's reasoning ultimately reduced all substances to "matter" and

The Observatory at Nuremberg   The quest for scientific knowledge in the seventeenth century was already an expensive undertaking that required teamwork and government support, as this encyclopedic illustration suggests. Nuremberg was a historic center of commerce and culture in southern Germany, and its observatory played a pioneering role in early astronomical advances. *(Kunstsammlungen der Veste Coburg)*

"mind"—that is, to the physical and the spiritual. His view of the world as consisting of two fundamental entities is known as **Cartesian dualism.** Descartes was a profoundly original and extremely influential thinker.

Bacon's inductive experimentalism and Descartes's deductive, mathematical reasoning are combined in the modern scientific method, which began to crystallize in the late seventeenth century. Neither man's extreme approach was sufficient by itself. Bacon's inability to appreciate the importance of mathematics and his obsession with practical results clearly showed the limitations of antitheoretical empiricism. Likewise, some of Descartes's positions—he believed, for example, that it was possible to deduce the whole science of medicine from first principles—demonstrated the inadequacy of rigid, dogmatic rationalism. Thus the modern scientific method has joined precise observations and experimentalism with the search for general laws that may be expressed in rigorously logical, mathematical language.

Finally, there is the question of the role of religion in the development of science. Just as some historians have argued that Protestantism led to the rise of capitalism, others have concluded that Protestantism was a fundamental factor in the rise of modern science. Protestantism, particularly in its Calvinist varieties, supposedly made scientific inquiry a question of individual conscience and not of religious doctrine. The Catholic Church, in contrast, supposedly suppressed scientific theories that conflicted with its teachings and thus discouraged scientific progress. The truth is more complicated. *All* Western religious authorities—Catholic, Protestant, and Jewish—opposed the Copernican system to a greater or lesser extent until about 1630, by which time the scientific revolution was definitely in progress. The Catholic Church was initially less hostile than Protestant and Jewish religious leaders, and Italian scientists played a crucial role in scientific progress right up to the trial of Galileo in 1633. Thereafter, the Counter-Reformation church became more hostile to science, a change that helped account for the decline of science in Italy (but not in Catholic France) after 1640. At the same time, Protestant countries such as the Netherlands and Denmark became quite "pro-science," especially countries that lacked a strong religious authority capable of imposing religious orthodoxy on scientific questions.

This was certainly the case with Protestant England after 1630. English religious conflicts became so intense that the authorities could not impose religious unity on anything, including science. Significantly, the forerunners of the Royal Society agreed to discuss only "neutral" scientific questions so as not to come to blows over closely related religious and political disputes. The work of Bacon's many followers during Oliver Cromwell's commonwealth helped solidify the neutrality and independence of science. Bacon advocated the experimental approach precisely because it was open-minded and independent of preconceived religious and philosophical ideas. Neutral and useful, science became an accepted part of life and developed rapidly in England after about 1640.

Science and Society

The rise of modern science had many consequences, some of which are still unfolding. First, it went hand in hand with the rise of a new and expanding social group—the international **scientific community.** Members of this community were linked together by common interests and shared values as well as by journals and the learned scientific societies founded in many countries in the later seventeenth and eighteenth centuries. Expansion of knowledge was the primary goal of this community, and scientists' material and psychological rewards depended on their success in this endeavor. Thus science became competitive, and even more scientific advance was inevitable. Second, as governments intervened to support and sometimes direct research, the new scientific community became closely tied to the state and its agendas. National academies of science were created under state sponsorship in London in 1662, Paris in 1666, Berlin in 1700, and later across Europe.

Third, the scientific revolution introduced not only new knowledge about nature but also a new and revolutionary way of obtaining such knowledge—the modern scientific method. In addition to being both theoretical and experimental, this method was highly critical. It refused to base its conclusions on tradition and established sources, on ancient authorities and sacred texts. This critical attitude to established authority would inspire thinkers to question traditions in other domains as well.

Some things did not change in the scientific revolution. New "rational" methods for approaching nature did not question traditional inequalities between the sexes—and may have worsened them in some ways. When Renaissance courts served as centers of learning, talented noblewomen could find niches in study and research. The rise of a professional scientific community raised barriers for women because the new academies that furnished professional credentials did not accept female members. (This continued for a long time. Marie Curie, the first person to win two Nobel prizes, was rejected by the French Academy of Science in 1911 because she was a woman.[6])

There were, however, a number of noteworthy exceptions. In Italy, universities and academies did offer posts to women, attracting some foreigners spurned by their own countries. In addition, some sectors of accomplishment were more accessible to women, with fine arts being the most important. Women excelled as makers of wax anatomical models and as botanical and zoological illustrators. Because the new scientific method relied on precise observation, illustration became a highly valued skill. Women were also very much involved in informal scientific communities, attending salons, participating in scientific experiments, and writing learned treatises. Some female intellectuals were recognized as full-fledged members of the philosophical dialogue. In England, Margaret Cavendish, Anne Conway, and Mary Astell all con-

Metamorphoses of the Caterpillar and Moth Maria Sibylla Merian (1647–1717), the stepdaughter of a Dutch painter, became a celebrated scientific illustrator in her own right. Her finely observed pictures of insects in the South American colony of Surinam introduced many new species, shown in their various stages of development. For Merian, science was intimately tied with art: she not only painted but also bred caterpillars and performed experiments on them. Her two-year stay in Surinam, accompanied by a teenage daughter, was a daring feat for a seventeenth-century woman. *(Bildarchiv Preussischer Kulturbesitz/Art Resource, NY)*

tributed to debates about Descartes's mind-body dualism, among other issues. Descartes himself conducted an intellectual correspondence with the princess Elizabeth of Bohemia, of whom he stated: "I attach more weight to her judgement than to those messieurs the Doctors, who take for a rule of truth the opinions of Aristotle rather than the evidence of reason."[7]

If women themselves played a limited role in scientific discovery, scholars have recently emphasized the importance of representations of femininity and masculinity in the scientific revolution. Nature was often depicted as a female, whose veil of secrecy needed to be stripped away and penetrated by male experts. In the same time period, the Americas were similarly depicted as a female terrain whose potentially fertile lands needed to be controlled and impregnated by male colonists.

The scientific revolution had few consequences for economic life and the living standards of the masses until the late eighteenth century. True, improvements in the techniques of navigation facilitated overseas trade and helped enrich states and merchant companies. But science had relatively few practical economic applications. Thus the scientific revolution of the seventeenth century was first and foremost an intellectual revolution. For more than a hundred years its greatest impact was on how people thought and believed.

The Enlightenment

The scientific revolution was the single most important factor in the creation of the new worldview of the eighteenth-century **Enlightenment.** This worldview, which has played a large role in shaping the modern mind, grew out of a rich mix of diverse and often conflicting ideas. For the talented (and not-so-talented) writers who espoused them, these ideas competed vigorously for the attention of a growing public of well-educated but fickle readers, who remained a minority of the population. Despite the diversity, three central concepts stand at the core of Enlightenment thinking. The most important and original idea was that the methods of natural science could and should be used to examine and understand all aspects of life. This was what intellectuals meant by *reason,* a favorite word of Enlightenment thinkers. Nothing was to be accepted on faith. Everything was to be submitted to **rationalism,** a secular, critical way of thinking. A second important Enlightenment concept was that the scientific method was capable of discovering the laws of human society as well as those of nature. Thus was social science born. Its birth led to the third key idea, that of

progress. Armed with the proper method of discovering the laws of human existence, Enlightenment thinkers believed that it was at least possible for human beings to create better societies and better people. Their belief was strengthened by some modest improvements in economic and social life during the eighteenth century.

• *How did the new worldview affect the way people thought about society and human relations?*

The Emergence of the Enlightenment

Loosely united by certain key ideas, the European Enlightenment was a broad intellectual and cultural movement that gained strength gradually and did not reach its maturity until about 1750. Yet it was the generation that came of age between the publication of Newton's *Principia* in 1687 and the death of Louis XIV in 1715 that tied the crucial knot between the scientific revolution and a new outlook on life. Talented writers of that generation popularized hard-to-understand scientific achievements for the educated elite.

The most famous and influential popularizer was a versatile French man of letters, Bernard de Fontenelle (1657–1757), who set out to make science witty and entertaining—as easy to read as a novel—for a broad nonscientific audience. This was a tall order, but Fontenelle largely succeeded. His most famous work, *Conversations on the Plurality of Worlds* (1686), begins with two elegant figures walking in the gathering shadows of a large park. One is a woman, a sophisticated aristocrat, and the other is her friend, perhaps even her lover. They gaze at the stars, and their talk turns to a passionate discussion of . . . astronomy! The man confides that "each star may well be a different world," then gently stresses how error is giving way to truth. At one point he explains:

There came on the scene . . . one Copernicus, who made short work of all those various circles, all those solid skies, which the ancients had pictured to themselves. . . . Fired with the noble zeal of a true astronomer, he took the earth and spun it very far away from the center of the universe, where it had been installed, and in that center he put the sun, which had a far better title to the honor.[8]

Rather than despair at this dismissal of traditional understanding, Fontenelle's lady rejoices in the knowledge that the human mind is capable of making great progress.

This concept of progress was essentially a creation of the later seventeenth century. Medieval and Reformation thinkers had been concerned primarily with sin and salvation. The humanists of the Renaissance had emphasized worldly matters, but they had looked backward. They had believed it might be possible to equal the magnificent accomplishments of the ancients, but they did not ask for more. Fontenelle and like-minded writers had come to believe that, at least in science and mathematics, their era had gone far beyond antiquity. Progress, at least intellectual progress, was very possible.

Fontenelle and other writers of his generation were also instrumental in bringing science into conflict with religion. This was a major innovation because many seventeenth-century scientists, both Catholic and Protestant, did not draw antireligious implications from their scientific findings and believed that their work exalted God. The greatest scientist of them all, Isaac Newton, was a devout, if unorthodox, Christian who saw all his studies as directed toward explaining God's message. Fontenelle, in contrast, was skeptical about absolute truth and cynical about the claims of organized religion. Since such unorthodox views could not be stated openly in an absolute monarchy like Louis XIV's France, Fontenelle made his point through subtle editorializing about science. His depiction of the cautious Copernicus as a self-conscious revolutionary was typical. In *Eulogies of Scientists,* Fontenelle exploited with endless variations the fundamental theme of rational, progressive scientists versus prejudiced, reactionary priests.

The progressive and antireligious implications that writers such as Fontenelle drew from the scientific revolution reflected a very real crisis in European thought at the end of the seventeenth century. This crisis had its roots in several intellectual uncertainties and dissatisfactions, of which the demolition of Aristotelian-medieval science was only one.

A second uncertainty involved the whole question of religious truth. The destructive wars of religion that culminated in the Thirty Years' War (1618–1648) had been fought, in part, because religious freedom was an intolerable idea in Europe in the early seventeenth century. Both Catholics and Protestants had believed that religious truth was absolute and therefore worth fighting and dying for. Most Catholics and Protestants also believed that a strong state required unity in religious faith. Yet the disastrous results of the many attempts to impose such religious unity, such as Louis XIV's brutal expulsion of the French Huguenots in 1685, led some people to ask whether ideological conformity in religious matters was really necessary. Others skeptically asked if religious truth could ever be known with absolute certainty and concluded that it could not.

The most famous of these skeptics was Pierre Bayle (1647–1706), a French Huguenot who despised Louis

Popularizing Science   The frontispiece illustration of Fontenelle's *Conversations on the Plurality of Worlds* invites the reader to share the pleasures of astronomy with an elegant lady and an entertaining teacher. The drawing shows the planets revolving around the sun. *(By permission of the Syndics of Cambridge University Library)*

XIV and found refuge in the Netherlands. A teacher by profession and a crusading journalist by inclination, Bayle took full advantage of the toleration and intellectual freedom of his adopted land. He critically examined the religious beliefs and persecutions of the past in his *Historical and Critical Dictionary,* written in French and published in the Netherlands in 1697. Demonstrating that human beliefs had been extremely varied and very often mistaken, Bayle concluded that nothing can ever be known beyond all doubt. In religion as in philosophy, humanity's best hope was open-minded toleration. Bayle's **skepticism** was very influential. Reprinted frequently in the Netherlands and in England, his four-volume *Dictionary* was found in more private libraries of eighteenth-century France than was any other book.

The rapidly growing travel literature on non-European lands and cultures was a third cause of uncertainty. In the wake of the great discoveries, Europeans were learning that the peoples of China, India, Africa, and the Americas all had their own very different beliefs and customs. Europeans shaved their faces and let their hair grow. Turks shaved their heads and let their beards grow. In Europe a man bowed before a woman to show respect. In Siam a man turned his back on a woman when he met her because it was disrespectful to look directly at her. Countless similar examples discussed in the travel accounts helped change the perspective of educated Europeans. They began to look at truth and morality in relative, rather than absolute, terms. If anything was possible, who could say what was right or wrong?

A fourth cause and manifestation of European intellectual turmoil was John Locke's epoch-making *Essay Concerning Human Understanding.* Published in 1690—the same year Locke published his famous *Second Treatise of Civil Government* (see page 548)—Locke's essay brilliantly set forth a new theory about how human beings learn and form their ideas. In doing so, he rejected the prevailing view of Descartes, who had held that all people are born with certain basic ideas and ways of thinking. Locke insisted that all ideas are derived from experience. The human mind at birth is like a blank tablet, or **tabula rasa,** on which the environment writes the individual's understanding and beliefs. Human development is therefore determined by education and social institutions, for good or for evil. Locke's *Essay Concerning Human Understanding* passed through many editions and translations. Along with Newton's *Principia,* it was one of the dominant intellectual inspirations of the Enlightenment.

The Philosophes and the Public

By the time Louis XIV died in 1715, many of the ideas that would soon coalesce into the new worldview had been assembled. Yet Christian Europe was still strongly attached to its traditional beliefs, as witnessed by the powerful revival of religious orthodoxy in the first half of the eighteenth century (see pages 672–673). By the outbreak of the American Revolution in 1775, however, a large portion of western Europe's educated elite had embraced many of the new ideas. This acceptance was the work of one of history's most influential groups of intellectuals, the **philosophes.** It was the philosophes who

proudly proclaimed that they, at long last, were bringing the light of knowledge to their ignorant fellow creatures in an Age of Enlightenment.

Philosophe is the French word for "philosopher," and it was in France that the Enlightenment reached its highest development. There were at least three reasons for this. First, French was the international language of the educated classes in the eighteenth century, and the education of the rich and the powerful across Europe often lay in the hands of French tutors espousing Enlightenment ideas. France's cultural leadership was reinforced by the fact that it was still the wealthiest and most populous country in Europe.

Second, after the death of Louis XIV, French absolutism and religious orthodoxy remained strong, but not too strong. Critical books were often banned by the censors, and their authors were sometimes jailed or exiled—but they were not tortured or burned. Intellectual radicals battled against powerful opposition in France, but they did not face the overwhelming restraints generally found in eastern and east-central Europe.

Third, the French philosophes were indeed philosophers, asking fundamental philosophical questions about the meaning of life, God, human nature, good and evil, and cause and effect. But in the tradition of Bayle and Fontenelle, they were not content with abstract arguments or ivory-tower speculations. They were determined to reach and influence all the French (and European) economic and social elites, many of which were joined together in the eighteenth-century concept of the "republic of letters," an imaginary, transnational realm constituted by all members of the educated or enlightened public.

Suspicious of the people but intensely committed to reason, reform, and slow, difficult progress, the great philosophes and their imitators were not free to write as they wished, since it was illegal in France to openly criticize either church or state. Their most radical works had to circulate in manuscript form. Knowing that direct attacks would probably be banned or burned, the philosophes wrote novels and plays, histories and philosophies, dictionaries and encyclopedias, all filled with satire and double meanings to spread their message to the public. One of the greatest philosophes, the baron de Montesquieu (1689–1755), brilliantly pioneered this approach in *The Persian Letters,* an extremely influential social satire published in 1721. This work consisted of amusing letters supposedly written by two Persian travelers, Usbek and Rica, who see European customs in unique ways and thereby allow Montesquieu to cleverly criticize existing practices and beliefs.

Like many Enlightenment philosophes, Montesquieu saw relations between men and women as particularly representative of overall social and political systems. He used the oppression of women in the Persian harem, described in letters from Usbek's wives, to symbolize Eastern political tyranny. At the end of the book, the rebellion of Usbek's harem against the cruel eunuchs he left in charge of them demonstrates that despotism must ultimately fail. Montesquieu also uses the Persians' observations of habitual infidelity among French wives and the strength of female power behind the throne to poke fun at European social and political customs. As Rica remarks:

The thing is that, for every man who has any post at court, in Paris, or in the country, there is a woman through whose hands pass all the favours and sometimes the injustices that he does. These women are all in touch with one another, and compose a sort of commonwealth whose members are always busy giving each other mutual help and support.

Montesquieu was exaggerating, but he echoed other critics of the informal power women gained in an absolutist system, where royal mistresses and female courtiers could have more access to the king than government ministers.

Having gained fame by using wit as a weapon against cruelty and superstition, Montesquieu settled down on his family estate to study history and politics. His interest was partly personal, for, like many members of the French robe nobility, he was disturbed by the growth in royal absolutism under Louis XIV. But Montesquieu was also inspired by the example of the physical sciences, and he set out to apply the critical method to the problem of government in *The Spirit of Laws* (1748). The result was a complex comparative study of republics, monarchies, and despotisms—a great pioneering inquiry in the emerging social sciences.

Showing that forms of government were shaped by history, geography, and customs, Montesquieu focused on the conditions that would promote liberty and prevent tyranny. He argued that despotism could be avoided if there was a **separation of powers,** with political power divided and shared by a variety of classes and legal estates holding unequal rights and privileges. A strong, independent upper class was especially important, according to Montesquieu, because in order to prevent the abuse of power "it is necessary that by the arrangement of things, power checks power." Admiring greatly the English balance of power among the king, the houses of Parliament, and the independent courts, Montesquieu believed that in France the thirteen high courts—the *parlements*—were

frontline defenders of liberty against royal despotism. Apprehensive about the uneducated poor, Montesquieu was clearly no democrat, but his theory of separation of powers had a great impact on France's wealthy, well-educated elite. The constitutions of the young United States in 1789 and of France in 1791 were based in large part on this theory.

Online Study Center **Improve Your Grade**
Primary Source: Montesquieu Identifies the Necessity for the Separation of Governmental Powers

The most famous and in many ways most representative philosophe was François Marie Arouet, who was known by the pen name Voltaire (1694–1778). In his long career, this son of a comfortable middle-class family wrote more than seventy witty volumes, hobnobbed with kings and queens, and died a millionaire because of shrewd business speculations. His early career, however, was turbulent. In 1717 Voltaire was imprisoned for eleven months in the Bastille in Paris for insulting the regent of France. In 1726 a barb from his sharp tongue led a great French nobleman to have him beaten and arrested. This experience made a deep impression on Voltaire. All his life he struggled against legal injustice and unequal treatment before the law. Released from prison after promising to leave the country, Voltaire lived in England for three years and came to share Montesquieu's enthusiasm for English institutions.

Returning to France and soon threatened again with prison in Paris, Voltaire had the great fortune of meeting Gabrielle-Emilie Le Tonnelier de Breteuil, marquise du Châtelet (1706–1749), an intellectually gifted woman from the high aristocracy with a passion for science. Inviting Voltaire to live in her country house at Cirey in Lorraine and becoming his long-time companion (under the eyes of her tolerant husband), Madame du Châtelet studied physics and mathematics and published scientific articles and translations.

Perhaps the finest representative of a small number of elite Frenchwomen and their intellectual accomplishments during the Enlightenment, Madame du Châtelet suffered nonetheless because of her gender. Excluded on principle from the Royal Academy of Sciences, she depended on private tutors for instruction and became uncertain of her ability to make important scientific discoveries. Madame du Châtelet therefore concentrated on spreading the ideas of others, and her translation with an accompanying commentary of Newton's *Principia* into French for the first (and only) time was her greatest work. But she, who had patiently explained Newton's

Madame du Châtelet The marquise du Châtelet was fascinated by the new world system of Isaac Newton. She helped spread Newton's ideas in France by translating his *Principia* and by influencing Voltaire, her companion for fifteen years until her death. *(Giraudon/Art Resource, NY)*

complex mathematical proofs to Europe's foremost philosophe, had no doubt that women's limited scientific contributions in the past were due to limited and unequal education. She once wrote that if she were a ruler, "I would reform an abuse which cuts off, so to speak, half the human race. I would make women participate in all the rights of humankind, and above all in those of the intellect."[9]

While living at Cirey, Voltaire wrote various works praising England and popularizing English scientific progress. Newton, he wrote, was history's greatest man, for he had used his genius for the benefit of humanity. "It is," wrote Voltaire, "the man who sways our minds by the prevalence of reason and the native force of truth, not they who reduce mankind to a state of slavery by force and downright violence . . . that claims our reverence and admiration."[10] In the true style of the Enlightenment, Voltaire mixed the glorification of science and reason with an appeal for better individuals and institutions.

Yet like almost all of the philosophes, Voltaire was a reformer, not a revolutionary, in social and political matters. He was eventually appointed royal historian in 1743, and his *Age of Louis XIV* portrayed Louis as the dignified leader of his age. Voltaire also began a long correspondence with Frederick the Great and, after the death of his beloved Emilie, accepted Frederick's invitation to come brighten up the Prussian court in Berlin. The two men later quarreled, but Voltaire always admired Frederick as a free thinker and an enlightened monarch.

Unlike Montesquieu, Voltaire pessimistically concluded that the best one could hope for in the way of government was a good monarch, since human beings "are very rarely worthy to govern themselves." Nor did he believe in social and economic equality in human affairs. The idea of making servants equal to their masters was "absurd and impossible." The only realizable equality, Voltaire thought, was that "by which the citizen only depends on the laws which protect the freedom of the feeble against the ambitions of the strong."[11]

Voltaire's philosophical and religious positions were much more radical. In the tradition of Bayle, his voluminous writings challenged, often indirectly, the Catholic Church and Christian theology at almost every point. Though he was considered by many devout Christians to be a shallow blasphemer, Voltaire's religious views were ambiguous and quite typical of the complex attitudes toward religion held by Enlightenment thinkers. Voltaire clearly believed in God, but his was a distant, deistic God, the great Clockmaker who built an orderly universe and then stepped aside and let it run. Above all, Voltaire and most of the philosophes hated all forms of religious intolerance, which they believed often led to fanaticism and savage, inhuman action. Simple piety and human kindness—as embodied in Christ's great commandments to "love God and your neighbor as yourself"—were religion enough, as may be seen in Voltaire's famous essay on religion. (See the feature "Listening to the Past: Voltaire on Religion" on pages 618–619.)

The ultimate strength of the French philosophes lay in their number, dedication, and organization. The philosophes felt keenly that they were engaged in a common undertaking that transcended individuals. Their greatest and most representative intellectual achievement was, quite fittingly, a group effort—the seventeen-volume *Encyclopedia: The Rational Dictionary of the Sciences, the Arts, and the Crafts,* edited by Denis Diderot (1713–1784) and Jean le Rond d'Alembert (1717–1783). They were a curious pair. Diderot began his career as a hack writer, first attracting attention with a skeptical tract on religion that was quickly burned by the judges of Paris.

D'Alembert was one of Europe's leading scientists and mathematicians, the orphaned and illegitimate son of celebrated aristocrats. From different circles and with different interests, the two men set out to find coauthors who would examine the rapidly expanding whole of human knowledge. Even more fundamentally, they set out to teach people how to think critically and objectively about all matters. As Diderot said, he wanted the *Encyclopedia* to "change the general way of thinking."[12]

The editors of the *Encyclopedia* had to conquer innumerable obstacles. After the appearance in 1751 of the first volume, which dealt with such controversial subjects as atheism, the soul, and blind people (all words beginning with *a* in French), the government temporarily banned publication. The pope later placed the work on the Catholic Church's index of forbidden works and pronounced excommunication on all who read or bought it. In an attempt to appease the authorities, the timid publisher watered down some of the articles in the last ten volumes without the editors' consent. Yet Diderot's unwavering belief in the importance of his mission held the encyclopedists together for fifteen years, and the enormous work was completed in 1765. Hundreds of thousands of articles by leading scientists, famous writers, skilled workers, and progressive priests treated every aspect of life and knowledge.

Not every article was daring or original, but the overall effect was little short of revolutionary. Science and the industrial arts were exalted, religion and immortality questioned. Intolerance, legal injustice, and out-of-date social institutions were openly criticized. More generally, the writers of the *Encyclopedia* showed that human beings could use the process of reasoning to expand human knowledge. The encyclopedists were convinced that greater knowledge would result in greater human happiness, for knowledge was useful and made possible economic, social, and political progress. The *Encyclopedia* was widely read, especially in less-expensive reprint editions published in Switzerland, and it was extremely influential in France and throughout western Europe as well. It summed up the new worldview of the Enlightenment.

The Enlightenment Outside of France

For all the importance of Paris as a center of Enlightenment thought, historians now recognize the existence of important strands of Enlightenment thought in other areas of Europe. They have identified distinctive Enlightenment movements in eighteenth-century Italy, Greece, the Balkans, Poland, Hungary, and Russia.

Different areas followed different strands of Enlightenment thinking. In England and Germany, scholars have described a more conservative Enlightenment that tried to integrate the findings of the scientific revolution with religious faith and practices. After the Act of Union with England and Ireland in 1707, Scotland was freed from political crisis to experience a vigorous period of intellectual growth. The Scottish Enlightenment, centered in Edinburgh, was marked by an emphasis on pragmatic and scientific reasoning. Intellectual revival was stimulated by the creation of the first public educational system in Europe. The most important figure in Edinburgh was David Hume (1711–1776), whose carefully argued religious skepticism had a powerful impact at home and abroad.

Building on Locke's teachings on learning, Hume argued that the human mind is really nothing but a bundle of impressions. These impressions originate only in sense experiences and our habits of joining these experiences together. Since our ideas ultimately reflect only our sense experiences, our reason cannot tell us anything about questions that cannot be verified by sense experience (in the form of controlled experiments or mathematics), such as the origin of the universe or the existence of God. Paradoxically, Hume's rationalistic inquiry ended up undermining the Enlightenment's faith in the power of reason.

Urban Culture and the Public Sphere

Enlightenment ideas did not float on air. A series of new institutions and practices emerged in the late seventeenth and eighteenth centuries to facilitate the spread of Enlightenment ideas. First, the European production and consumption of books grew dramatically in the eighteenth century. In Germany the number of new titles appearing annually grew substantially, from roughly six hundred new titles in 1700 to about eleven hundred in 1764 and about twenty-six hundred in 1780. France also witnessed an explosive growth in book consumption. The number of books in the hands of elite readers increased eightfold to tenfold between the 1690s and the 1780s, when the private library of the typical noble contained more than three hundred volumes.

Moreover, the types of books people read changed dramatically. The proportion of religious and devotional books published in Paris declined precipitously, from one-half of the total in the 1690s to one-tenth of the total in the 1780s. History and law held constant, while the proportion of published books treating the arts and sciences surged.

Even these figures understate the shift in French taste because France's unpredictable but pervasive censorship

Illustrating the *Encyclopedia*: "The Print Shop" Diderot wanted to present all valid knowledge—that is, knowledge based on reason and the senses and not on tradition and authority. This plate, one of 3,000 detailed illustrations accompanying the 70,000 essays in the *Encyclopedia,* shows (*from left to right*) compositors setting type, arranging lines, and blocking down completed forms. Printed sheets dry above. (*Division of Rare & Manuscript Collections, Cornell University Library*)

caused many books to be printed abroad and smuggled back into the country for "under-the-cloak" sale. Experts believe that perhaps the majority of French books produced between 1750 and 1789 came from publishing companies outside of France. These publishers, located primarily in the Netherlands and Switzerland but also in England and a few small west German principalities, also smuggled forbidden books in French and other languages into the absolutist states of central, southern, and eastern Europe.

The illegal book trade in France also featured an astonishing growth of scandalmongering denunciations of high political figures and frankly pornographic works. These literary forms frequently came together in scathing pornographic accounts of the moral and sexual depravity of the French court, allegedly mired in luxury, perversion, and adultery. Echoing Montesquieu, a favorite theme was the way that some beautiful but immoral aristocratic

women used their sexual charms to gain power over weak rulers and high officials, thereby corrupting the process of government. These tracts included graphic accounts and images of sexual debauchery among aristocrats and even by the queen herself. Spurred by repeated royal directives, the French police did their best to stamp out this underground literature, but new slanders kept cropping up, with corrosive effects on public confidence in the monarchy.

Reading more books on many more subjects, the educated public in France and throughout Europe increasingly approached reading in a new way. The result was what some scholars have called a **reading revolution.** The old style of reading in Europe had been centered on sacred texts, full of authority, inspiring reverence and teaching earthly duty and obedience to God. Reading had been patriarchal and communal, with the father of the family slowly reading the text aloud and the audience savoring each word. Now reading involved many texts, which were constantly changing and commanded no special respect. Reading became individual, silent, and rapid. The well-educated classes were reading insatiably, skeptically, and carelessly. Subtle but profound, the reading revolution ushered in new ways of relating to the written word.

Conversation, discussion, and debate also played a critical role in the Enlightenment. Paris set the example, and other French and European cities followed. In Paris a number of talented, wealthy women presided over regular social gatherings of the great and near-great in their elegant private drawing rooms, or **salons**. There they encouraged a d'Alembert and a Fontenelle to exchange witty, uncensored observations on literature, science, and philosophy with great aristocrats, wealthy middle-class financiers, high-ranking officials, and noteworthy foreign-

ers. (D'Alembert himself was the illegitimate son of a well-known salon hostess, Madame de Tencin, who abandoned him on the steps of a Parisian church.) Talented hostesses, or *salonnières,* brought the various French elites together and mediated the public's freewheeling examination of Enlightenment thought.

Elite women also exercised an unprecedented feminine influence on artistic taste. Soft pastels, ornate interiors, sentimental portraits, and starry-eyed lovers protected by hovering cupids were all hallmarks of the style they favored. This style, known as **rococo,** was popular throughout Europe in the eighteenth century. It has been argued that feminine influence in the drawing room went hand in hand with the emergence of polite society and the general attempt to civilize a rough military nobility. Similarly, some philosophes championed greater rights and expanded education for women, claiming that the

Selling Books, Promoting Ideas   This appealing bookshop with its intriguing ads for the latest works offers to put customers "Under the Protection of Minerva," the Roman goddess of wisdom. Large packets of books sit ready for shipment to foreign countries. Book consumption surged in the eighteenth century. *(Musée des Beaux-Arts, Dijon/Art Resource, NY)*

Enlightenment Culture   An actor performs the first reading of a new play by Voltaire at the salon of Madame Geoffrin. Voltaire, then in exile, is represented by a bust statue. *(Réunion des Musées Nationaux/Art Resource, NY)*

position and treatment of women were the best indicators of a society's level of civilization and decency.[13] To be sure, for these male philosophes greater rights for women did not mean equal rights, and the philosophes were not particularly disturbed by the fact that elite women remained legally subordinate to men in economic and political affairs. Elite women lacked many rights, but so did most men.

One of the most famous salons was that of Madame Geoffrin, the unofficial godmother of the *Encyclopedia*. Having lost her parents at an early age, she was married at fifteen by her well-meaning grandmother to a rich and boring businessman of forty-eight. After dutifully raising her children, Madame Geoffrin broke out of her gilded cage. With the aid of an aristocratic neighbor and in spite of her husband's loud protests, she developed a twice-weekly salon that counted Fontenelle and Montesquieu among its regular guests. Inheriting a large fortune after her husband's death, Madame Geoffrin gave the encyclopedists generous financial aid and helped save

their enterprise from collapse. Corresponding with the king of Sweden and Catherine the Great of Russia, Madame Geoffrin remained her own woman, a practicing Christian who would not tolerate attacks on the church in her house.

The salon also provided an informal apprenticeship for younger women who aspired to lead salons of their own. One such woman was Julie de Lespinasse. Eventually forming her own highly informal salon and attracting the keenest minds in France and Europe, Lespinasse epitomized the skills of the Enlightenment hostess. As one philosophe wrote:

She could unite the different types, even the most antagonistic, sustaining the conversation by a well-aimed phrase, animating and guiding it at will. . . . Politics, religion, philosophy, news: nothing was excluded. Her circle met daily from five to nine. There one found men of all ranks in the State, the Church, and the Court, soldiers and foreigners, and the leading writers of the day.[14]

As this passage suggests, the salons created a cultural realm free from religious dogma and political censorship. There a diverse but educated public could debate issues and form its own ideas. Through their invitation lists, salon hostesses brought together members of the intellectual, economic, and social elites. In such an atmosphere, the philosophes, the French nobility, and the prosperous middle classes intermingled and influenced one another. Thinking critically about almost any question became fashionable and flourished alongside hopes for human progress through greater knowledge and enlightened public opinion.

Membership at the salons was restricted to the well-born, the well-connected, and the exceptionally talented. A number of institutions emerged for those who aspired to follow, rather than lead, the Enlightenment. Lending libraries served an important function for people who could not afford to buy their own books. The coffee-houses that first appeared in the late seventeenth century became meccas of philosophical discussion. Then, as now, one could linger for hours to read or debate for the price of a cup of coffee. In addition to these institutions, book clubs, Masonic lodges, and journals all played roles in the creation of a new **public sphere** that celebrated open debate informed by critical reason. The public sphere was an idealized space where members of society came together as individuals to discuss issues relevant to the society, economics, and politics of the day.

What of the common people? Did they participate in the Enlightenment? Enlightenment philosophes did not direct their message to peasants or urban laborers. Whether of middling or noble origin, intellectuals sought patronage from the wealthy and powerful. They believed that the masses had no time or talent for philosophical speculation and that elevating them would be a long, slow, potentially dangerous process. Deluded by superstitions and driven by violent passions, they thought, the people were like little children in need of firm parental guidance. French philosophe d'Alembert characteristically made a sharp distinction between "the truly enlightened public" and "the blind and noisy multitude."[15]

There is some evidence, however, that the people were not immune to the words of the philosophes. At a time of rising literacy, book prices were dropping in cities and towns, and many philosophical ideas were popularized in cheap pamphlets. Moreover, even illiterate people had access to written material, through the practice of public reading. The Parisian glass-worker Jacques-Louis Ménétra, whose education consisted of a few years of schooling and his trade apprenticeship, claimed in his autobiography to have cultivated a friendship with Jean-Jacques

Rousseau and to have enjoyed a game of chess and a philosophical discussion with the writer. Although they were barred from salons and academies, ordinary people were not immune to the new ideas in circulation.

Late Enlightenment

After about 1770 a number of thinkers and writers began to attack the Enlightenment's faith in reason, progress, and moderation. The most famous of these was the Swiss Jean-Jacques Rousseau (1712–1778), a brilliant and difficult thinker and an appealing but neurotic individual. Born into a poor family of watchmakers in Geneva, Rousseau went to Paris and was greatly influenced by Diderot and Voltaire. Always extraordinarily sensitive and suspicious, he came to believe that his philosophe friends and the women of the Parisian salons were plotting against him. In the mid-1750s he broke with them personally and intellectually, living thereafter as a lonely outsider with his uneducated common-law wife and going in his own highly original direction.

Like other Enlightenment thinkers, Rousseau was passionately committed to individual freedom. Unlike them, however, he attacked rationalism and civilization as destroying, rather than liberating, the individual. Warm, spontaneous feeling had to complement and correct cold intellect. Moreover, the basic goodness of the individual and the unspoiled child had to be protected from the cruel refinements of civilization. Rousseau's ideals greatly influenced the early romantic movement (see pages 660–661), which rebelled against the culture of the Enlightenment in the late eighteenth century.

Reconfirming Montesquieu's critique of women's influence in public affairs, Rousseau called for a rigid division of gender roles. According to Rousseau, women and men were radically different beings. Destined by nature to assume a passive role in sexual relations, women should also be passive in social life. A woman's role was to care for her children at home and to please her husband with good housekeeping, a modest demeanor, and a fresh, natural appearance. Women's passion for fashion, attending salons, and pulling the strings of power was unnatural and had a corrupting effect on both politics and society. Rousseau thus rejected the sophisticated way of life of elite Parisian women. Against them, he rearticulated conventional stereotypes as a form of natural law, against which debate was impossible. These views had a strong impact on both men and women in the late eighteenth century, contributing to calls for privileged women to abandon their stylish corsets and to breast-feed their children.

Rousseau's contribution to political theory in *The Social Contract* (1762) was equally significant. His contribution was based on two fundamental concepts: the general will and popular sovereignty. According to Rousseau, the **general will** is sacred and absolute, reflecting the common interests of all the people, who have displaced the monarch as the holder of sovereign power. The general will is not necessarily the will of the majority, however. At times the general will may be the authentic, long-term needs of the people as correctly interpreted by a farseeing minority. Little noticed before the French Revolution, Rousseau's concept of the general will appealed greatly to democrats and nationalists after 1789. (The concept has since been used by many dictators who have claimed that they, rather than some momentary majority of the voters, represent the general will.) Rousseau was both one of the most influential voices of the Enlightenment and, in his rejection of rationalism and social discourse, a harbinger of reaction against Enlightenment ideas.

Online Study Center **Improve Your Grade**
Primary Source: Rousseau Espouses Popular
Sovereignty and the General Will

As the reading public developed, it joined forces with the philosophes to call for the autonomy of the printed word. Immanuel Kant (1724–1804), a professor in East Prussia and the greatest German philosopher of his day, posed the question of the age when he published a pamphlet in 1784 entitled *What Is Enlightenment?* Kant answered, "*Sapere Aude!* [dare to know] Have courage to use your own understanding!—that is the motto of enlightenment." He argued that if serious thinkers were granted the freedom to exercise their reason publicly in print, enlightenment would almost surely follow. Kant was no revolutionary; he also insisted that in their private lives, individuals must obey all laws, no matter how unreasonable, and should be punished for "impertinent" criticism. Kant thus tried to reconcile absolute monarchical authority with a critical public sphere. This balancing act characterized experiments with "enlightened absolutism" in the eighteenth century.

Race and the Enlightenment

In addition to criticizing their own societies and political systems, Enlightenment thinkers wrote about society and human nature outside their borders. In recent years, historians have found in the scientific revolution and the Enlightenment a crucial turning point in European ideas about race. Many of the most important thinkers of the Enlightenment devoted substantial attention to comparisons of European and non-European cultures, deriving their understanding of people at home from differences with people abroad. The result was the formation of highly influential new understandings of **racial difference.** As with other strands of Enlightenment thought, the new scientific method, and its apparently neutral, rational thinking, provided intellectual legitimacy for their findings.

A primary catalyst for new ideas about race was the urge to classify nature unleashed by the scientific revolution's insistence on careful empirical observation. In *The System of Nature* (1735) Swedish botanist Carl von Linné argued that nature was organized into a God-given hierarchy, which mankind must uncover and chart meticulously. As scientists developed more elaborate taxonomies of plant and animal species, they also began to classify humans into hierarchically ordered "races" and to investigate the origins of race. The Comte de Buffon argued that humans originated with one species that then developed into distinct races due largely to climactic conditions. In *A Natural History* he describes experiments conducted on African bodies to determine the cause of their "blackness," which was assumed to be an acquired variation from humans' originally white skin.

Using the word *race* to designate biologically distinct groups of humans, akin to distinct animal species, was new. Previously, Europeans grouped other peoples into "nations" based on their historical, political, and cultural affiliations, rather than on supposedly innate physical differences. Unsurprisingly, when European thinkers drew up a hierarchical classification of human species, their own "race" was placed at the top. Europeans had long believed they were culturally superior to "barbaric" peoples in Africa and, since 1492, the New World. Now emerging ideas about racial difference taught them they were biologically superior as well.

Enlightenment thinkers such as David Hume and Immanuel Kant helped popularize these ideas. In *Of Natural Characters* (1748), Hume wrote:

I am apt to suspect the negroes and in general all other species of men (for there are four or five different kinds) to be naturally inferior to the whites. There never was a civilized nation of any other complexion than white, nor even any individual eminent amongst them, no arts, no sciences. . . . Such a uniform and constant difference could not happen, in so many countries and ages if nature had not made an original distinction between these breeds of men.[16]

The Prussian philosopher Immanuel Kant taught and wrote as much about "anthropology" and "geography" as he did about standard philosophical themes such as logic, metaphysics, and moral philosophy. He shared and elaborated Hume's views about race in *On the Different Races of Man* (1775), claiming that there were four human races, each of which had derived from an original race of "white brunette" people. According to Kant, the closest descendants of the original race were the white inhabitants of northern Germany. In deriving new physical characteristics, the other races had degenerated both physically and culturally from this origin.

These ideas did not go unchallenged. James Beattie responded directly to Hume's claims of white superiority by pointing out that Europeans had started out as savage as nonwhites and that many non-European peoples in the Americas, Asia, and Africa had achieved high levels of civilization. Johann von Herder criticized Kant, arguing that humans could not be classified into races based on skin color and that each culture was as intrinsically worthy as any other. These challenges to emerging scientific notions of racial inequality, however, were in the minority. Many other Enlightenment voices agreeing with Kant and Hume—Thomas Jefferson among them—may be found.

Scholars are only at the beginning of efforts to understand links between Enlightenment ideas about race and its notions of equality, progress, and reason. There are clear parallels, though, between the use of science to propagate racial hierarchies and its use to defend social inequalities between men and women. As Rousseau used women's "natural" passivity to argue for their passive role in society, so a Hume and a Kant used non-Europeans' "natural" inferiority to defend slavery and colonial domination. The new powers of science and reason were thus marshaled to imbue traditional stereotypes with the force of natural law.

The Enlightenment and Absolutism

How did the Enlightenment influence political developments? To this important question there is no easy answer. Most Enlightenment thinkers outside of England and the Netherlands believed that political change could best come from above—from the ruler—rather than from below, especially in central and eastern Europe. Royal absolutism was a fact of life, and the kings and queens of Europe's leading states clearly had no intention of giving up their great power. Therefore, the philosophes and their sympathizers realistically concluded that a benevolent absolutism offered the best opportunities for improving society. Critical thinking was

turning the art of good government into an exact science. It was necessary to educate and "enlighten" the monarch, who could then make good laws and promote human happiness.

The philosophes' influence was heightened by the fact that many government officials were attracted to and interested in philosophical ideas. They were among the best-educated and best-informed members of society, and their daily involvement in complex affairs of state made them naturally interested in ideas for improving or reforming human society. Encouraged and instructed by these officials, some absolutist rulers of the later eighteenth century tried to govern in an "enlightened" manner. Yet the actual programs and accomplishments of these rulers varied greatly. It is necessary to examine the evolution of monarchical absolutism at close range before trying to judge the Enlightenment's effect and the meaning of what historians have often called the **enlightened absolutism** of the later eighteenth century.

Enlightenment teachings inspired European rulers in small as well as large states in the second half of the eighteenth century. Absolutist princes and monarchs in several west German and Italian states, as well as in Scandinavia, Spain, and Portugal, proclaimed themselves more enlightened. A few smaller states were actually the most successful in making reforms, perhaps because their rulers were not overwhelmed by the size and complexity of their realms. Denmark, for example, carried out extensive and progressive land reform in the 1780s that practically abolished serfdom and gave Danish peasants secure tenure on their farms. Yet by far the most influential of the new-style monarchs were in Prussia, Russia, and Austria, and they deserve primary attention.

• *What impact did this new way of thinking have on political developments and monarchical absolutism?*

Frederick the Great of Prussia

Frederick II (r. 1740–1786), commonly known as Frederick the Great, built masterfully on the work of his father, Frederick William I (see page 571). This was somewhat surprising, for, like many children with tyrannical parents, he rebelled against his family's wishes in his early years. Rejecting the crude life of the barracks, Frederick embraced culture and literature, even writing poetry and fine prose in French, a language his father detested. After trying unsuccessfully to run away in 1730 at age eighteen, he was virtually imprisoned and compelled to watch as his companion in flight was beheaded at his father's command. Yet like many other rebellious youths, Frederick eventually reconciled with his father, and by the time he came to the throne ten years later Frederick was determined to use the splendid army that his father had left him.

Therefore, when the ruler of Austria, Charles VI, also died in 1740 and his young and charismatic daughter Maria Theresa inherited the Habsburg dominions, Frederick suddenly and without warning invaded her rich, mainly German province of Silesia. This action defied solemn Prussian promises to respect the Pragmatic Sanction, which guaranteed Maria Theresa's succession. Maria Theresa's disunited army was no match for Prussian precision; in 1742, as other greedy powers were falling on her lands in the general European War of the Austrian Succession (1740–1748), she was forced to cede almost all of Silesia to Prussia (see Map 17.2 on page 570). In one stroke Prussia had doubled its population to six million people. Now Prussia unquestionably towered above all the other German states and stood as a European Great Power.

Though successful in 1742, Frederick had to spend much of his reign fighting against great odds to save Prussia from total destruction. Maria Theresa was determined to regain Silesia, and when the ongoing competition between Britain and France for colonial empire brought another great conflict in 1756 (see page 635), Austria fashioned an aggressive alliance with France and Russia. During the Seven Years' War (1756–1763), the aim of the alliance was to conquer Prussia and divide up its territory. Frederick led his army brilliantly, striking repeatedly at vastly superior forces invading from all sides. At times he believed all was lost, but he fought on with stoic courage. In the end he was miraculously saved: Peter III came to the Russian throne in 1762 and called off the attack against Frederick, whom he greatly admired.

In the early years of his reign Frederick II had kept his enthusiasm for Enlightenment culture strictly separated from a brutal concept of international politics. He wrote:

Of all States, from the smallest to the biggest, one can safely say that the fundamental rule of government is the principle of extending their territories. . . . The passions of rulers have no other curb but the limits of their power. Those are the fixed laws of European politics to which every politician submits.[17]

But the terrible struggle of the Seven Years' War tempered Frederick and brought him to consider how more humane policies for his subjects might also strengthen the state. Thus Frederick went beyond a superficial commitment to Enlightenment culture for himself and his circle. He tolerantly allowed his subjects to believe as they wished in religious and philosophical matters. He pro-

moted the advancement of knowledge, improving his country's schools and permitting scholars to publish their findings. Moreover, Frederick tried to improve the lives of his subjects more directly. As he wrote his friend Voltaire, "I must enlighten my people, cultivate their manners and morals, and make them as happy as human beings can be, or as happy as the means at my disposal permit."

The legal system and the bureaucracy were Frederick's primary tools. Prussia's laws were simplified, torture of prisoners was abolished, and judges decided cases quickly and impartially. Prussian officials became famous for their hard work and honesty. After the Seven Years' War ended in 1763, Frederick's government energetically promoted the reconstruction of agriculture and industry in his war-torn country. Frederick himself set a good example. He worked hard and lived modestly, claiming that he was "only the first servant of the state." Thus Frederick justified monarchy in terms of practical results and said nothing of the divine right of kings.

Frederick's dedication to high-minded government went only so far, however. He never tried to change Prussia's existing social structure. True, he condemned serfdom in the abstract, but he accepted it in practice and did not even free the serfs on his own estates. He accepted and extended the privileges of the nobility, which he saw as his primary ally in the defense and extension of his realm. The Junker nobility remained the backbone of the army and the entire Prussian state.

Nor did Frederick listen to thinkers like Moses Mendelssohn (1729–1786), who urged that Jews be given freedom and civil rights. (See the feature "Individuals in Society: Moses Mendelssohn and the Jewish Enlightenment.") As in other German states, Jews in Prussia remained an oppressed group. The vast majority were confined to tiny, overcrowded ghettos, were excluded by law from most business and professional activities, and could be ordered out of the kingdom at a moment's notice. A very few Jews in Prussia did manage to succeed and to obtain the right of permanent settlement, usually by performing some special service for the state. But they were the exception, and Frederick firmly opposed any general emancipation for the Jews, as he did for the serfs.

Catherine the Great of Russia

Catherine the Great of Russia (r. 1762–1796) was one of the most remarkable rulers of her age, and the French philosophes adored her. Catherine was a German princess from Anhalt-Zerbst, a totally insignificant principality sandwiched between Prussia and Saxony. Her father commanded a regiment of the Prussian army, but

Individuals in Society

Moses Mendelssohn and the Jewish Enlightenment

In 1743 a small, humpbacked Jewish boy with a stammer left his poor parents in Dessau in central Germany and walked eighty miles to Berlin, the capital of Frederick the Great's Prussia. According to one story, when the boy reached the Rosenthaler Gate, the only one through which Jews could pass, he told the inquiring watchman that his name was Moses and that he had come to Berlin "to learn." The watchman laughed and waved him through. "Go Moses, the sea has opened before you."* Embracing the Enlightenment and seeking a revitalization of Jewish religious thought, Moses Mendelssohn did point his people in a new and uncharted direction.

Turning in Berlin to a learned rabbi he had previously known in Dessau, the young Mendelssohn studied Jewish law and eked out a living copying Hebrew manuscripts in a beautiful hand. But he was soon fascinated by an intellectual world that had been closed to him in the Dessau ghetto. There, like most Jews throughout central Europe, he had spoken Yiddish— a mixture of German, Polish, and Hebrew. Now, working mainly on his own, he mastered German; learned Latin, Greek, French, and English; and studied mathematics and Enlightenment philosophy. Word of his exceptional abilities spread in Berlin's Jewish community (1,500 of the city's 100,000 inhabitants). He began tutoring the children of a wealthy Jewish silk merchant, and he soon became the merchant's clerk and later his partner. But his great passion remained the life of the mind and the spirit, which he avidly pursued in his off hours.

Gentle and unassuming in his personal life, Mendelssohn was a bold thinker. Reading eagerly in Western philosophy since antiquity, he was, as a pious Jew, soon convinced that Enlightenment teachings need not be opposed to Jewish thought and religion. Indeed, he concluded that reason could complement and strengthen religion, although each would retain its integrity as a separate sphere.† Developing this idea in his first great work, "On the Immortality of the Soul" (1767), Mendelssohn used the neutral setting of a philosophical dialogue between Socrates and his followers in ancient Greece to argue that the human soul lived forever. In refusing to bring religion and critical thinking into conflict, he was strongly influenced by contemporary German philosophers who argued similarly on behalf of Christianity. He reflected the way the German Enlightenment generally supported established religion, in contrast to the French Enlightenment, which attacked it. This was the most important difference in Enlightenment thinking between the two countries.

Mendelssohn's treatise on the human soul captivated the educated German public, which marveled that a Jew could have written a philosophical masterpiece. In the excitement, a Christian zealot named Lavater challenged Mendelssohn in a pamphlet to accept Christianity or to demonstrate how the Christian faith was not "reasonable." Replying politely but passionately, the Jewish philosopher affirmed that all his studies had only strengthened him in the faith of his fathers, although he certainly did not seek to convert anyone not born into Judaism. Rather, he urged toleration in religious matters. He spoke up courageously for his fellow Jews and decried the oppression they endured, and he continued to do so for the rest of his life.

Orthodox Jew and German philosophe, Moses Mendelssohn serenely combined two very different worlds. He built a bridge from the ghetto to the dominant culture over which many Jews would pass, including his novelist daughter Dorothea and his famous grandson, the composer Felix Mendelssohn.

Lavater (right) *attempts to convert Mendelssohn, in a painting by Moritz Oppenheim of an imaginary encounter.* (Collection of the Judah L. Magnes Museum, Berkeley)

Questions for Analysis

1. How did Mendelssohn seek to influence Jewish religious thought in his time?
2. How do Mendelssohn's ideas compare with those of the French Enlightenment?

*H. Kupferberg, *The Mendelssohns: Three Generations of Genius* (New York: Charles Scribner's Sons, 1972), p. 3.
†D. Sorkin, *Moses Mendelssohn and the Religious Enlightenment* (Berkeley: University of California Press, 1996), pp. 8 ff.

Online Study Center **Improve Your Grade**
Going Beyond Individuals in Society

Catherine the Great as Equestrian and Miniature of Count Grigory Grigoryevich Orlov
Catherine conspired with her lover Count Orlov to overthrow her husband Peter III and became
empress of Russia. Strongly influenced by the Enlightenment, she cultivated the French
philosophes and instituted moderate reforms, only to reverse them in the aftermath of Pugachev's
rebellion. This equestrian portrait now hangs above her throne in the palace throne room.
*(left: Musée des Beaux-Arts, Chartres/The Bridgeman Art Library; right: © The State Hermitage Museum,
St. Petersburg)*

her mother was related to the Romanovs of Russia, and
that proved to be Catherine's chance.

Peter the Great had abolished the hereditary succession of tsars so that he could name his successor and thus
preserve his policies. This move opened a period of palace intrigue and a rapid turnover of rulers until Peter's
youngest daughter, Elizabeth, came to the Russian throne
in 1741. A shrewd but crude woman, Elizabeth named
her nephew Peter heir to the throne and chose Catherine
to be his wife in 1744. It was a mismatch from the beginning. The fifteen-year-old Catherine was intelligent
and attractive; her husband shared neither of these qualities. Ignored by her husband, Catherine carefully studied Russian, endlessly read writers such as Bayle and
Voltaire, and made friends at court. Soon she knew what
she wanted: "I did not care about Peter," she wrote in
her *Memoirs,* "but I did care about the crown."[18]

As the old empress Elizabeth approached death, Catherine plotted against her unpopular husband. She selected
as her new lover a dashing young officer named Grigory
Orlov, who with his four officer brothers commanded
considerable support among the soldiers stationed in
St. Petersburg. When Peter came to the throne in 1762,
his decision to withdraw Russian troops from the coalition against Prussia alienated the army. At the end of six
months Catherine and her conspirators deposed Peter III
in a palace revolution, and the Orlov brothers murdered
him. The German princess became empress of Russia.

Catherine had drunk deeply at the Enlightenment well.
Never questioning the common assumption that absolute
monarchy was the best form of government, she set out
to rule in an enlightened manner. She had three main
goals. First, she worked hard to continue Peter the
Great's effort to bring the culture of western Europe to

backward Russia. To do so, she imported Western architects, sculptors, musicians, and intellectuals. She bought masterpieces of Western art in wholesale lots and patronized the philosophes. An enthusiastic letter writer, she corresponded extensively with Voltaire and praised him as the "champion of the human race." When the French government banned the *Encyclopedia*, she offered to publish it in St. Petersburg, and she sent money to Diderot when he needed it. With these and countless similar actions, Catherine won good press in the West for herself and for her country. Moreover, this intellectual ruler, who wrote plays and loved good talk, set the tone for the entire Russian nobility. Peter the Great westernized Russian armies, but it was Catherine who westernized the imagination of the Russian nobility.

Catherine's second goal was domestic reform, and she began her reign with sincere and ambitious projects. Better laws were a major concern. In 1767 she appointed a special legislative commission to prepare a new law code. No new unified code was ever produced, but Catherine did restrict the practice of torture and allowed limited religious toleration. She also tried to improve education and strengthen local government. The philosophes applauded these measures and hoped more would follow.

Online Study Center Improve Your Grade
Primary Source: Catherine the Great's Grand Instruction to the Legislative Commission

Such was not the case. In 1773 a common Cossack soldier named Emelian Pugachev sparked a gigantic uprising of serfs, very much as Stenka Razin had done a century earlier (see page 576). Proclaiming himself the true tsar, Pugachev issued "decrees" abolishing serfdom, taxes, and army service. Thousands joined his cause, slaughtering landlords and officials over a vast area of southwestern Russia. Pugachev's untrained forces eventually proved no match for Catherine's noble-led regular army. Betrayed by his own company, Pugachev was captured and savagely executed.

Pugachev's rebellion was a decisive turning point in Catherine's domestic policy. On coming to the throne, she had condemned serfdom in theory, but Pugachev's rebellion put an end to any intentions she might have had about reforming the system. The peasants were clearly dangerous, and her empire rested on the support of the nobility. After 1775 Catherine gave the nobles absolute control of their serfs. She extended serfdom into new areas, such as Ukraine. In 1785 she formalized the nobility's privileged position, freeing nobles forever from taxes and state service. Under Catherine the Russian nobility attained its most exalted position, and serfdom entered its most oppressive phase.

Catherine's third goal was territorial expansion, and in this respect she was extremely successful. Her armies subjugated the last descendants of the Mongols, the Crimean Tatars, and began the conquest of the Caucasus. Her greatest coup by far was the partition of Poland (see Map 18.1). By 1700 Poland had become a weak and decentralized republic with an elected king (see page 567), and Poland's fate in the late eighteenth century demonstrated the dangers of failing to build a strong absolutist state. All important decisions continued to require the unanimous agreement of all nobles elected to the Polish Diet, which meant that nothing could ever be done to strengthen the state. When, between 1768 and 1772, Catherine's armies scored unprecedented victories against the Turks and thereby threatened to disturb the balance of power between Russia and Austria in eastern Europe, Frederick of Prussia obligingly came forward with a deal. He proposed that Turkey be let off easily and that Prussia, Austria, and Russia each compensate itself by taking a gigantic slice of Polish territory. Catherine jumped at the chance. The first partition of Poland took place in 1772. Two more partitions, in 1793 and 1795, gave all three powers more Polish territory, and the ancient republic of Poland vanished from the map.

Expansion helped Catherine keep the nobility happy, for it provided her with vast new lands to give to her faithful servants. Until the end this remarkable woman—who always believed that, in spite of her domestic setbacks, she was slowly civilizing Russia—kept her zest for life. Fascinated by a new twenty-two-year-old flame when she was a grandmother in her sixties, she happily reported her good fortune to a favorite former lover: "I have come back to life like a frozen fly; I am gay and well."[19]

The Austrian Habsburgs

In Austria two talented rulers did manage to introduce major reforms, although traditional power politics was more important than Enlightenment teachings. One was Joseph II (r. 1780–1790), a fascinating individual. For an earlier generation of historians, he was the "revolutionary emperor," a tragic hero whose lofty reforms were undone by the landowning nobility he dared to challenge. More recent scholarship has revised this romantic interpretation and has stressed how Joseph II continued the state-building work of his mother, the empress Maria Theresa (1740–1780), a remarkable but old-fashioned absolutist.

Mapping the Past

MAP 18.1 The Partition of Poland and Russia's Expansion, 1772–1795 During the sixteenth century the Polish nobility confirmed its right to elect the kings of Poland. The parliament could be blocked by the veto of a single member. In the seventeenth century warfare with Sweden and Russian Cossacks resulted in Poland's loss of the Baltic areas and Ukraine. In 1772 war threatened between Russia and Austria over Russian gains from the Ottoman Empire. To satisfy desires for expansion without fighting, Prussia's Frederick the Great proposed that parts of Poland be divided among Austria, Prussia, and Russia. In 1793 and 1795 the three powers partitioned the remainder, and the ancient republic of Poland vanished from the map. **❶** Why was Poland vulnerable to partition in the latter half of the eighteenth century? What does it say about European politics at the time that a country could simply cease to exist on the map? Could that happen today? **❷** Of the three powers that divided the kingdom of Poland, which benefited the most? How did the partition affect the geographical boundaries of each state, and what was the significance? **❸** What border with the former Poland remained unchanged? Why do you think this was the case?

Emerging from the long War of the Austrian Succession in 1748 with the serious loss of Silesia, Maria Theresa and her closest ministers were determined to introduce reforms that would make the state stronger and more efficient. Three aspects of these reforms were most important. First, Maria Theresa introduced measures aimed at limiting the papacy's political influence in her realm. Second, a whole series of administrative reforms strengthened the central bureaucracy, smoothed out some provincial differences, and revamped the tax system, taxing even the lands of nobles without special exemptions. Third, the government sought to improve the lot of the agricultural population, cautiously reducing the power of lords over their hereditary serfs and their partially free peasant tenants.

Maria Theresa The empress and her husband pose with eleven of their sixteen children at Schönbrunn palace in this family portrait by court painter Martin Meytens (1695–1770). Joseph, the heir to the throne, stands at the center of the star pattern. Wealthy women often had very large families, in part because they, unlike poor women, seldom nursed their babies. *(Réunion des Musées Nationaux/Art Resource, NY)*

Coregent with his mother from 1765 onward and a strong supporter of change, Joseph II moved forward rapidly when he came to the throne in 1780. He controlled the established Catholic Church even more closely in an attempt to ensure that it produced better citizens. He granted religious toleration and civic rights to Protestants and Jews—a radical innovation that impressed his contemporaries. In even more spectacular peasant reforms, Joseph abolished serfdom in 1781, and in 1789 he decreed that all peasant labor obligations be converted into cash payments. This measure was violently rejected not only by the nobility but also by the peasants it was intended to help since their primitive barter economy was woefully lacking in money. When a disillusioned Joseph died prematurely at forty-nine, the entire Habsburg empire was in turmoil. His brother Leopold II (r. 1790–1792) canceled Joseph's radical edicts in order to re-establish order. Peasants once again were required to do forced labor for their lords.

Evaluating "Enlightened Absolutism"

Despite differences, the leading eastern European monarchs of the later eighteenth century all claimed that they were acting on the principles of the Enlightenment. The philosophes generally agreed with this assessment and cheered them on. Beginning in the mid-nineteenth century historians developed the idea of a common "enlightened despotism" or "enlightened absolutism," and they canonized Frederick, Catherine, and Joseph as its most outstanding examples. More recent research has raised doubts about this old interpretation and has led to a fundamental revaluation.

There is general agreement that these absolutists, especially Catherine and Frederick, did encourage and spread the cultural values of the Enlightenment. Perhaps this was their greatest achievement. Skeptical in religion and intensely secular in basic orientation, they unabashedly accepted the here and now and sought their happiness in the enjoyment of it. At the same time, they were proud of their intellectual accomplishments and good taste, and they supported knowledge, education, and the arts. No wonder the philosophes felt that these monarchs were kindred spirits.

Historians also agree that the absolutists believed in change from above and tried to enact needed reforms. Yet the results of these efforts brought only very modest improvements, and the life of the peasantry remained very hard in the eighteenth century. Thus some historians have concluded that these monarchs were not really sincere in their reform efforts. Others disagree, arguing that powerful nobilities blocked the absolutists' genuine commitment to reform. (The old interpretation of Joseph II as the tragic revolutionary emperor forms part of this argument.)

The emerging answer to this controversy is that the later Eastern absolutists were indeed committed to reform but that humanitarian objectives were of secondary importance. Above all, the absolutists wanted reforms that would strengthen the state and allow them to compete militarily with their neighbors. Modern scholarship has therefore stressed how Catherine, Frederick, and Joseph were in many ways simply continuing the state-building of their predecessors, reorganizing armies and expanding bureaucracies to raise more taxes and troops. The reason for this continuation was simple. The international political struggle was brutal, and the stakes were high. First Austria under Maria Theresa and then Prussia under Frederick the Great had to engage in bitter fighting to escape dismemberment, while decentralized Poland was coldly divided and eventually liquidated.

Yet in this drive for more state power, the later absolutists were also innovators, and the idea of an era of enlightened absolutism retains a certain validity. Sharing the Enlightenment faith in critical thinking and believing that knowledge meant power, these absolutists really were more enlightened than their predecessors because they put state-building reforms in a new, broader perspective. Above all, the later absolutists considered how more humane laws and practices could help their populations become more productive and satisfied and thus able to contribute more substantially to the welfare of the state. It was from this perspective that they introduced many of their most progressive reforms, tolerating religious minorities, simplifying legal codes, and promoting practical education.

The primacy of state over individual interests also helps explain some puzzling variations in social policies. For example, Catherine the Great took measures that worsened the peasants' condition because she looked increasingly to the nobility as her natural ally and sought to strengthen it. Frederick the Great basically favored the status quo, limiting only the counterproductive excesses of his trusted nobility against its peasants. Joseph II believed that greater freedom for peasants was the means to strengthen his realm, and he acted accordingly. Each enlightened absolutist sought greater state power, but each believed that a different policy would attain it.

The eastern European absolutists of the later eighteenth century combined old-fashioned state-building with the culture and critical thinking of the Enlightenment. In doing so, they succeeded in expanding the role of the state in the life of society. They perfected bureaucratic machines that were to prove surprisingly adaptive and capable of enduring into the twentieth century. Their failure to implement policies we would recognize as humane and enlightened—such as abolishing serfdom—may reveal inherent limitations in Enlightenment thinking about equality and social justice, rather than in their execution of an Enlightenment program. The fact that leading philosophes supported rather than criticized Eastern rulers' policies suggests some of the blinders of the era.

Chapter Summary

Online Study Center **ACE the Test**

- *What was revolutionary in new attitudes toward the natural world?*
- *How did the new worldview affect the way people thought about society and human relations?*
- *What impact did this new way of thinking have on political developments and monarchical absolutism?*

Decisive breakthroughs in astronomy and physics in the seventeenth century demolished the imposing medieval synthesis of Aristotelian philosophy and Christian theology. These developments had only limited practical consequences at the time, but the impact of new scientific knowledge on intellectual life was enormous. The emergence of modern science was a distinctive characteristic of

Western civilization and became a key element of Western identity. During the eighteenth century scientific thought fostered new ideas about racial differences and provided justifications for belief in Western superiority.

Interpreting scientific findings and Newtonian laws in a manner that was both antitradition and antireligion, Enlightenment philosophes extolled the superiority of rational, critical thinking. This new method, they believed, promised not just increased knowledge but even the discovery of the fundamental laws of human society. Although they reached different conclusions when they turned to social and political realities, they did stimulate absolute monarchs to apply reason to statecraft and the search for useful reforms. Above all, the philosophes succeeded in shaping an emerging public opinion and spreading their radically new worldview.

The ideas of the Enlightenment were an inspiration for monarchs, particularly absolutist rulers in central and eastern Europe who saw in them important tools for reforming and rationalizing their governments. Their primary goal was to strengthen their states and increase the efficiency of their bureaucracies and armies. Enlightened absolutists believed that these reforms would ultimately improve the lot of ordinary people, but this was not their chief concern. With few exceptions, they did not question the institution of serfdom. The fact that leading philosophes supported rather than criticized Eastern rulers' policies suggests some of the limitations of the era.

Key Terms

natural philosophy	skepticism
Copernican	tabula rasa
hypothesis	philosophes
experimental method	separation of powers
law of inertia	reading revolution
law of universal	salons
gravitation	rococo
empiricism	public sphere
Cartesian dualism	general will
scientific community	racial difference
Enlightenment	enlightened
rationalism	absolutism
progress	

 Online Study Center **Improve Your Grade** Flashcards

Suggested Reading

Alexander, John T. *Catherine the Great: Life and Legend.* 1989. The best biography of the famous Russian tsarina.

Beales, Derek. *Joseph II.* 1987. A fine biography of the reforming Habsburg ruler.

Chartier, Roger. *The Cultural Origins of the French Revolution.* 1991. An imaginative analysis of the changing attitudes of the educated public.

Eze, E. Chukwudi, ed. *Race and the Enlightenment: A Reader.* 1997. A pioneering source on the origins of modern racial thinking in the Enlightenment.

Goodman, Dena. *The Republic of Letters: A Cultural History of the Enlightenment.* 1994. An innovative study of the role of salons and salon hostesses in the rise of the Enlightenment.

MacDonogh, Giles. *Frederick the Great.* 2001. An outstanding biography of the Prussian king.

Munck, Thomas. *The Enlightenment: A Comparative History.* 2000. Compares developments in Enlightenment thought in different countries.

Muthu, Sankar. *Enlightenment Against Empire.* 2003. Examines Enlightenment figures' opposition to colonialism.

Outram, Dorinda. *The Enlightenment,* 2d ed. 2006. An outstanding and accessible introduction to Enlightenment debates that emphasizes the Enlightenment's social context and global reach.

Schiebinger, Londa. *The Mind Has No Sex? Women in the Origins of Modern Science.* 1998. Discusses how the new science excluded women.

Shapin, Steven. *The Scientific Revolution.* 2001. A concise and well-informed general introduction to the scientific revolution.

Sorkin, David. *Moses Mendelssohn and the Religious Enlightenment.* 1996. A brilliant study of the Jewish philosopher and of the role of religion in the Enlightenment.

Notes

1. H. Butterfield, *The Origins of Modern Science* (New York: Macmillan, 1951), p. viii.
2. Quoted in A. G. R. Smith, *Science and Society in the Sixteenth and Seventeenth Centuries* (New York: Harcourt Brace Jovanovich, 1972), p. 97.
3. Quoted in Butterfield, *The Origins of Modern Science,* p. 47.
4. Ibid., pp. 115–116.
5. Ibid., p. 120.
6. L. Schiebinger, *The Mind Has No Sex? Women in the Origins of Modern Science* (Cambridge, Mass.: Harvard University Press, 1989), p. 2.
7. Jacqueline Broad, *Women Philosophers of the Seventeenth Century* (Cambridge: Cambridge University Press, 2003), p. 17.
8. Quoted in P. Hazard, *The European Mind, 1680–1715* (Cleveland: Meridian Books, 1963), pp. 304–305.
9. Schiebinger, *The Mind Has No Sex?* p. 64.
10. Quoted in L. M. Marsak, ed., *The Enlightenment* (New York: John Wiley & Sons, 1972), p. 56.
11. Quoted in G. L. Mosse et al., eds., *Europe in Review* (Chicago: Rand McNally, 1964), p. 156.
12. Quoted in P. Gay, "The Unity of the Enlightenment," *History* 3 (1960): 25.
13. See E. Fox-Genovese, "Women in the Enlightenment," in *Becoming Visible: Women in European History,* 2d ed., ed. R. Bridenthal, C. Koonz, and S. Stuard (Boston: Houghton Mifflin, 1987), esp. pp. 252–259, 263–265.
14. Quoted in G. P. Gooch, *Catherine the Great and Other Studies* (Hamden, Conn.: Archon Books, 1966), p. 149.
15. Jean Le Rond d'Alembert, *Eloges lus dans les séances publiques de l'Académie française* (Paris, 1779), p. ix, quoted in Mona Ozouf, "'Public Opinion' at the End of the Old Regime," *The Journal of Modern History* 60, Supplement: Rethinking French Politics in 1788 (September 1988), p. S9.
16. Quoted in Emmanuel Chukwudi Eze, ed., *Race and the Enlightenment: A Reader* (Oxford: Blackwell, 1997), p. 33. This section draws heavily on this reader.
17. Quoted in L. Krieger, *Kings and Philosophers, 1689–1789* (New York: W. W. Norton, 1970), p. 257.
18. Quoted in Gooch, *Catherine the Great,* p. 15.
19. Ibid., p. 53.

Voltaire on Religion

Voltaire was the most renowned and probably
the most influential of the French philosophes. His
biting satirical novel Candide (1759) is still widely
assigned in college courses, and his witty yet serious
Philosophical Dictionary remains a source of pleasure and stimulation. The Dictionary consists of a
series of essays on topics ranging from Adam to
Zoroaster, from certainty to circumcision. The
following passage is taken from the essay on religion.

Voltaire began writing the Philosophical
Dictionary in 1752, at the age of fifty-eight, after
arriving at the Prussian court in Berlin. Frederick
the Great applauded Voltaire's efforts, but Voltaire
put the project aside after leaving Berlin, and the
first of several revised editions was published
anonymously in 1764. It was an immediate and
controversial success. Snapped up by an
"enlightened" public, it was denounced by
religious leaders as a threat to the Christian
community and was burned in Geneva and Paris.

I meditated last night; I was absorbed in the
contemplation of nature; I admired the
immensity, the course, the harmony of those
infinite globes which the vulgar do not know
how to admire.

I admired still more the intelligence which
directs these vast forces. I said to myself: "One
must be blind not to be dazzled by this spectacle;
one must be stupid not to recognize its author;
one must be mad not to worship the Supreme
Being. What tribute of worship should I render
Him? Should not this tribute be the same in the
whole of space, since it is the same Supreme
Power which reigns equally in all space?

"Should not a thinking being who dwells on a
star in the Milky Way offer Him the same homage
as a thinking being on this little globe of ours?
Light is the same for the star Sirius as for us;
moral philosophy must also be the same. If a
feeling, thinking animal on Sirius is born of a

tender father and mother who have been occupied
with his happiness, he owes them as much love
and care as we owe to our parents. If someone in
the Milky Way sees a needy cripple, and if he can
aid him and does not do so, then he is guilty
toward all the globes.

"Everywhere the heart has the same duties:
on the steps of the throne of God, if He has a
throne; and in the depths of the abyss, if there
is an abyss."

I was deep in these ideas when one of those
genii who fill the spaces between the worlds
came down to me. I recognized the same aerial
creature who had appeared to me on another
occasion to teach me that the judgments of God
are different from our own, and how a good
action is preferable to a controversy.

The genie transported me into a desert all
covered with piles of bones. . . . He began with
the first pile. "These," he said, "are the twenty-
three thousand Jews who danced before a calf,
together with the twenty-four thousand who were
killed while fornicating with Midianitish women.
The number of those massacred for such errors
and offences amounts to nearly three hundred
thousand.

"In the other piles are the bones of the
Christians slaughtered by each other because
of metaphysical disputes. They are divided into
several heaps of four centuries each. One heap
would have mounted right to the sky; they had
to be divided."

"What!" I cried, "brothers have treated their
brothers like this, and I have the misfortune to
be of this brotherhood!"

"Here," said the spirit, "are the twelve million
native Americans killed in their own land because
they had not been baptized."

"My God! . . . Why assemble here all these
abominable monuments to barbarism and
fanaticism?"

An impish Voltaire, by the French sculptor Houdon. *(Courtesy of Board of Trustees of the Victoria & Albert Museum)*

"To instruct you. . . . Follow me now." [The genie takes Voltaire to the "heroes of humanity, who tried to banish violence and plunder from the world," and tells Voltaire to question them.]

[At last] I saw a man with a gentle, simple face, who seemed to me to be about thirty-five years old. From afar he looked with compassion upon those piles of whitened bones, through which I had been led to reach the sage's dwelling place. I was astonished to find his feet swollen and bleeding, his hands likewise, his side pierced, and his ribs laid bare by the cut of the lash. "Good God!" I said to him, "is it possible for a just man, a sage, to be in this state? I have just seen one who was treated in a very hateful way, but there is no comparison between his torture and yours. Wicked priests and wicked judges poisoned him; is it by priests and judges that you were so cruelly assassinated?"

With great courtesy he answered, "Yes."

"And who were these monsters?"

"They were hypocrites."

"Ah! that says everything; I understand by that one word that they would have condemned you to the cruelest punishment. Had you then proved to them, as Socrates did, that the Moon was not a goddess, and that Mercury was not a god?"

"No, it was not a question of planets. My countrymen did not even know what a planet was; they were all arrant ignoramuses. Their superstitions were quite different from those of the Greeks."

"Then you wanted to teach them a new religion?"

"Not at all; I told them simply: 'Love God with all your heart and your neighbor as yourself, for that is the whole of mankind's duty.' Judge yourself if this precept is not as old as the universe; judge yourself if I brought them a new religion." . . .

"But did you say nothing, do nothing that could serve them as a pretext?"

"To the wicked everything serves as pretext."

"Did you not say once that you were come not to bring peace, but a sword?"

"It was a scribe's error; I told them that I brought peace and not a sword. I never wrote anything; what I can't have been changed without evil intention."

"You did not then contribute in any way by your teaching, either badly reported or badly interpreted, to those frightful piles of bones which I saw on my way to consult with you?"

"I have only looked with horror upon those who have made themselves guilty of all these murders."

. . . [Finally] I asked him to tell me in what true religion consisted.

"Have I not already told you? Love God and your neighbor as yourself."

"Is it necessary for me to take sides either for the Greek Orthodox Church or the Roman Catholic?"

"When I was in the world I never made any difference between the Jew and the Samaritan."

"Well, if that is so, I take you for my only master." Then he made a sign with his head that filled me with peace. The vision disappeared, and I was left with a clear conscience.

Questions for Analysis

1. Why did Voltaire believe in a Supreme Being? Does this passage reflect the influence of Isaac Newton's scientific system? If so, how?

2. Was Voltaire trying to entertain, teach, or do both? Was he effective? Why?

3. If Voltaire was trying to convey serious ideas about religion and morality, what were those ideas? What was he attacking?

4. If a person today thought and wrote like Voltaire, would that person be called a defender or a destroyer of Christianity? Why?

Source: F. M. Arouet de Voltaire, *Oeuvres complètes,* vol. 8, trans. J. McKay (Paris: Firmin-Didot, 1875), pp. 188–190.

The East India Dock, London (detail), by Samuel Scott, a painting infused with the spirit of maritime expansion. *(© Board of Trustees of the Victoria & Albert Museum)*

Agriculture and the Land
• *What were the causes and effects of the agricultural revolution, and what nations led the way in these developments?*

The Beginning of the Population Explosion
• *Why did European population rise dramatically in the eighteenth century?*

Cottage Industry and Urban Guilds
• *How and why did economic production intensify in the eighteenth century, particularly in the countryside?*

Building the Global Economy
• *How did colonial markets boost Europe's economic and social development, and what conflicts and adversity did world trade entail?*

THE EXPANSION OF EUROPE IN THE EIGHTEENTH CENTURY

The world of absolutism and aristocracy, a combination of raw power and elegant refinement, was a world apart from that of the common people. For most people in the eighteenth century, life remained a struggle with poverty and uncertainty, with the landlord and the tax collector. In 1700 peasants on the land and artisans in their shops lived little better than had their ancestors in the Middle Ages. Only in science and thought, and there only among intellectual elites and their followers, had Western society succeeded in going beyond the great achievements of the High Middle Ages, achievements that in turn owed much to Greece and Rome.

Everyday life was a struggle because European societies still could not produce very much by modern standards. Ordinary men and women might work like their beasts in the fields, but there was seldom enough good food, warm clothing, and decent housing. Life went on; history went on. The wars of religion ravaged Germany in the seventeenth century; Russia rose to become a Great Power; the state of Poland disappeared; monarchs and nobles continually jockeyed for power and wealth. In 1700 the idea of progress, of substantial improvement in the lives of great numbers of people, was still the dream of only a small elite in fashionable salons.

Yet the economic basis of European life was beginning to change. In the course of the eighteenth century the European economy emerged from the long crisis of the seventeenth century, responded to challenges, and began to expand once again. Population resumed its growth, while colonial empires developed and colonial elites prospered. Some areas were more fortunate than others. The rising Atlantic powers—Holland, France, and above all England—and their colonies led the way. The expansion of agriculture, industry, trade, and population marked the beginning of a surge comparable to that of the eleventh- and twelfth-century springtime of European civilization. But this time, broadly based expansion was not cut short. This time the response to new challenges led toward one of the most influential developments in human history, the Industrial Revolution, considered in Chapter 22.

Online Study Center

This icon will direct you to interactive activities and study materials on the website **college.hmco.com/pic/mckaywest9e**

Agriculture and the Land

At the end of the seventeenth century the economy of Europe was agrarian. With the possible exception of Holland, at least 80 percent of the people of all western European countries drew their livelihoods from agriculture. In eastern Europe the percentage was considerably higher. Men and women lavished their attention on the land, plowing fields and sowing seed, reaping harvests and storing grain. Yet even in a rich agricultural region such as the Po Valley in northern Italy, every bushel of wheat sown yielded on average only five or six bushels of grain at harvest during the seventeenth century. By modern standards output was distressingly low.

In most regions of Europe in the sixteenth and seventeenth centuries, climatic conditions produced poor or disastrous harvests every eight or nine years. Unbalanced and inadequate food in famine years made people extremely susceptible to illness. Eating material unfit for human consumption, such as bark or grass, resulted in intestinal ailments of many kinds. Influenza and smallpox preyed on populations weakened by famine. In famine years the number of deaths soared far above normal. A third of a village's population might disappear in a year or two. But new developments in agricultural technology and methods gradually brought an end to the ravages of hunger in western Europe.

- *What were the causes and effects of the agricultural revolution, and what nations led the way in these developments?*

The Open-Field System

These new developments drew on long roots. The great accomplishment of medieval agriculture was the **open-field system** of village farming. That system divided the land to be cultivated by the peasants of a given village into several large fields, which were in turn cut up into long, narrow strips. The fields were open, and the strips were not enclosed into small plots by fences or hedges. Each family followed the same pattern of plowing, sowing, and harvesting in accordance with tradition and the village leaders.

The ever-present problem was soil exhaustion. Wheat planted year after year in a field will deplete the nitrogen in the soil. Since the supply of manure for fertilizer was limited, the only way for the land to recover was to lie fallow for a period of time. In the early Middle Ages a year of fallow was alternated with a year of cropping; then three-year rotations were introduced, especially on more fertile lands. This system permitted a year of wheat or rye to be followed by a year of oats or beans and only then by a year of fallow. Significant gains in agricultural production resulted.

Traditional village rights reinforced communal patterns of farming. In addition to rotating field crops in a uniform way, villages maintained open meadows for hay and natural pasture. These lands were **common lands,** set aside primarily for draft horses and oxen, but open to the cows and pigs of the community as well. After the harvest villagers also pastured their animals on the wheat or rye stubble. In many places such pasturing followed a brief period, also established by tradition, for the gleaning of grain. Poor women would go through the fields picking up the few single grains that had fallen to the ground in the course of the harvest.

In the age of absolutism and nobility, the state and landlords continued to levy heavy taxes and high rents, thereby stripping peasants of much of their meager earnings. The level of exploitation varied. Generally speaking, the peasants of eastern Europe were worst off. As we saw in Chapter 17, they were serfs bound to their lords in hereditary service. In much of eastern Europe, five or six days of unpaid work per week on the lord's land were not uncommon. Well into the nineteenth century individual Russian serfs and serf families were regularly sold with and without land.

Social conditions were better in western Europe, where peasants were generally free from serfdom. In France, western Germany, England, and the Low Countries, they owned land and could pass it on to their children. Yet life in the village was unquestionably hard, and poverty was the great reality for most people. The privileges of Europe's ruling elites weighed heavily on the people of the land.

The Agricultural Revolution

One way for European peasants to improve their difficult position was to take land from those who owned it but did no labor. Yet the social and political conditions that sustained the ruling elites were ancient and deeply rooted, and powerful forces stood ready to crush protest. Only with the coming of the French Revolution were European peasants, mainly in France, able to improve their position by means of radical mass action.

Technological progress offered another possibility. If peasants (and their noble landlords) could replace the idle fallow with crops, they could greatly increase the land under cultivation. So remarkable were the possibilities and the results that historians have often spoken of the progressive elimination of the fallow, which occurred gradually throughout Europe from the mid-seventeenth century on, as an **agricultural revolution.** This revolution, which took longer than historians used to believe, was a great milestone in human development.

Because grain crops exhaust the soil and make fallowing necessary, the secret to eliminating the fallow lies in alternating grain with nitrogen-storing crops. The most important of these land-reviving crops are peas and beans, root crops such as turnips and potatoes, and clovers and grasses. As the eighteenth century went on, the number of crops that were systematically rotated grew. New patterns of organization allowed some farmers to develop increasingly sophisticated patterns of **crop rotation** to suit different kinds of soils. For example, farmers in French Flanders near Lille in the late eighteenth century used a ten-year rotation, alternating a number of grain, root, and hay crops in a given field on a ten-year schedule. Continual experimentation led to more scientific farming.

Improvements in farming had multiple effects. The new crops made ideal feed for animals, and because peasants and larger farmers had more fodder, hay, and root crops for the winter months, they could build up their herds of cattle and sheep. More animals meant more meat and better diets. More animals also meant more manure for fertilizer and therefore more grain for bread and porridge.

Advocates of the new crop rotations, who included an emerging group of experimental scientists, some government officials, and a few big landowners, believed that new methods were scarcely possible within the traditional framework of open fields and common rights. A farmer who wanted to experiment with new methods would have to get all the landholders in a village to agree to the plan. Advocates of improvement argued that innovating agriculturalists needed to enclose and consolidate their scattered holdings into compact, fenced-in fields in order to farm more effectively. In doing so, the innovators also needed to enclose their individual shares of the natural pasture, the common. According to proponents of this movement, known as **enclosure,** a revolution in village life and organization was the necessary price of technical progress.

That price seemed too high to many poor rural people who had small, inadequate holdings or very little land at all. Traditional rights were precious to these poor peasants. They used commonly held pastureland to graze livestock, and marshlands or moorlands outside the village as a source for firewood, berries, and other foraged goods that could make the difference between survival and

Chronology	
ca 1650–1790	Growth of Atlantic economy
ca 1650–1850	Agricultural improvement and revolution
1651–1663	British Navigation Acts
1652–1674	Anglo-Dutch wars; rise of British mercantilism
ca 1690–1780	Enlightenment
1700–1790	Height of Atlantic slave trade; expansion of rural industry in Europe
1701–1713	War of the Spanish Succession
1701–1763	Mercantilist wars of empire
1720–1722	Last of bubonic plague in Europe
1720–1789	Growth of European population
1740–1748	War of the Austrian Succession
1750–1790	Rise of economic liberalism
1756–1763	Seven Years' War
1759	Fall of Quebec
1760–1815	Height of parliamentary enclosure in England
1776	Smith, *Wealth of Nations*
1807	British slave trade abolished

famine in harsh times. Thus when the small landholders and the village poor could effectively oppose the enclosure of the open fields and the common lands, they did so. Moreover, in many countries they found allies among the larger, predominately noble landowners who were also wary of enclosure because it required large investments and posed risks for them as well.

The old system of unenclosed open fields and the new system of continuous rotation coexisted in Europe for a long time. Open fields could be found in much of France and Germany in the early years of the nineteenth century because peasants there had successfully opposed efforts to introduce the new techniques in the late eighteenth century. Until the end of the eighteenth century, the new system was extensively adopted only in the Low Countries and England.

Hendrick Sorgh: Vegetable Market (1662) The wealth and well-being of the industrious, capitalistic Dutch shine forth in this winsome market scene. The market woman's baskets are filled with delicious fresh produce that ordinary citizens can afford—eloquent testimony to the responsive, enterprising character of Dutch agriculture. *(Rijksmuseum, Amsterdam)*

The Leadership of the Low Countries and England

The new methods of the agricultural revolution originated in the Low Countries. Seventeenth-century republican Holland, already the most advanced country in Europe in many areas of human endeavor (see pages 549–553), led the way. By the middle of the seventeenth century intensive farming was well established, and the innovations of enclosed fields, continuous rotation, heavy manuring, and a wide variety of crops were all present. Agriculture was highly specialized and commercialized.

One reason for early Dutch leadership in farming was that the area was one of the most densely populated in Europe. In order to feed themselves and provide employment, the Dutch were forced at an early date to seek maximum yields from their land and to increase the cultivated area through the steady draining of marshes and swamps.

The pressure of population was connected with the second cause: the growth of towns and cities. Stimulated by commerce and overseas trade, Amsterdam grew from thirty thousand to two hundred thousand inhabitants in its golden seventeenth century. The growing urban population provided Dutch peasants with markets for all they could produce and allowed each region to specialize in what it did best. Thus the Dutch could develop their potential, and the Low Countries became "the Mecca of foreign agricultural experts who came . . . to see Flemish agriculture with their own eyes, to write about it and to propagate its methods in their home lands."[1]

The English were the best students. Drainage and water control were one subject in which they received instruction. Large parts of seventeenth-century Holland had once been sea and sea marsh, and the efforts of centuries had made the Dutch the world's leaders in the skills of drainage. In the first half of the seventeenth century Dutch experts made a great contribution to draining the extensive marshes, or fens, of wet and rainy England. The most famous of these Dutch engineers, Cornelius Vermuyden, directed one large drainage project in Yorkshire and another in Cambridgeshire. In the Cambridge fens, Vermuyden and his Dutch workers eventually reclaimed forty thousand acres, which were then farmed intensively in the Dutch manner. Swampy wilderness was converted into thousands of acres of some of the best land in England.

Jethro Tull (1674–1741), part crank and part genius, was an important English innovator. A true son of the early Enlightenment, Tull adopted a critical attitude toward accepted ideas about farming and tried to develop better methods through empirical research. He was especially enthusiastic about using horses, rather than slower-moving oxen, for plowing. He also advocated sowing seed with drilling equipment rather than scattering it by hand. Drilling distributed seed in an even manner and at the proper depth. There were also improvements in livestock, inspired in part by the earlier successes of English country gentlemen in breeding ever-faster horses for the races and fox hunts that were their passions. Selective breeding of ordinary livestock was a marked improvement over the haphazard old pattern.

By the mid-eighteenth century English agriculture was in the process of a long but radical transformation. The eventual result was that by 1870 English farmers were producing 300 percent more food than they had produced in 1700, although the number of people working the land had increased by only 14 percent. This great surge of agricultural production provided food for England's rapidly growing urban population.

Growth in production was achieved in part by land enclosures. About half the farmland in England was enclosed through private initiatives prior to 1700; in the eighteenth century Parliament completed this work. From the 1760s through the Napoleonic wars of the early nineteenth century, a series of acts of Parliament enclosed most of the remaining common land.

By eliminating common rights and greatly reducing the access of poor men and women to the land, the eighteenth-century enclosure movement marked the completion of two major historical developments in England—the rise of market-oriented estate agriculture and the emergence of a landless rural proletariat. By 1815 a tiny minority of wealthy English (and Scottish) landowners held most of the land and pursued profits aggressively, leasing their holdings through agents at competitive prices to middle-size farmers, who relied on landless laborers for their workforce. These landless la-

Enclosure in Streatley, Berkshire County, England   This map shows the results of enclosure in early-nineteenth-century Streatley, a village ten miles west of Reading on the River Thames. The area marked in yellow was the enclosed territory, appropriated mostly by a few large landowners and the city of Reading. The legend provides a detailed list of land ownership, including references to "old inclosures." *(Courtesy, Berkshire Record Office, Ref # Streatley (1817), MRI 256)*

borers worked very long hours, usually following a dawn-to-dusk schedule six days a week all year long. Moreover, landless laborers had lost that bit of independence and self-respect that common rights had provided and were completely dependent on cash wages. In no other European country had this **proletarianization**—this transformation of large numbers of small peasant farmers into landless rural wage earners—gone so far. And England's village poor found the cost of change heavy and unjust.

The Beginning of the Population Explosion

Another factor that affected the existing order of life and forced economic changes in the eighteenth century was the beginning of the "population explosion." Explosive growth continued in Europe until the twentieth century, by which time it was affecting nonwestern areas of the globe. What caused the growth of population, and what did the challenge of more mouths to feed and more hands to employ do to the European economy?

• *Why did European population rise dramatically in the eighteenth century?*

Limitations on Population Growth

Many commonly held ideas about population in the past are wrong. One such mistaken idea is the belief that population was always growing too fast. On the contrary, until 1700 the total population of Europe grew slowly much of the time, and it followed an irregular cyclical pattern (see Figure 19.1). This cyclical pattern had a great influence on many aspects of social and economic life. The terrible ravages of the Black Death caused a sharp drop in population and prices after 1350 and also created a labor shortage throughout Europe. Some economic historians calculate that for those common people in western Europe who managed to steer clear of warfare and of power struggles within the ruling class, the later Middle Ages was an era of exceptional well-being.

But this well-being eroded in the course of the sixteenth century. The second great surge of population growth (see Figure 19.1) outstripped the growth of agricultural production after about 1500. There was less food per person, and food prices rose more rapidly than wages, a development intensified by the inflow of precious metals from the Americas and a general, if uneven, European price revolution. The result was a substantial decline in living standards throughout Europe. By 1600 the pressure of population on resources was severe in much of Europe, and widespread poverty was an undeniable reality.

For this reason, population growth slowed and stopped in seventeenth-century Europe. Births and deaths, fertility and mortality, were in a crude but effective balance. The population grew modestly in normal years at a rate of perhaps 0.5 to 1 percent, or enough to double the population in 70 to 140 years. This is, of course, a generalization encompassing many different patterns. In areas such as Russia and colonial New England, where there was a great deal of frontier to be settled, the annual rate of natural increase, not counting in-migration, might well have exceeded 1 percent. In a country such as France, where the land had long been densely settled, the rate of increase might have been less than 0.5 percent.

FIGURE 19.1 The Growth of Population in England, 1000–1800 England is a good example of both the uneven increase of European population before 1700 and the third great surge of growth, which began in the eighteenth century. (*Source: E. A. Wrigley,* Population and History. *Copyright © 1969 by McGraw-Hill. Reprinted by permission of The McGraw-Hill Companies.)*

Although population growth of even 1 percent per year seems fairly modest, it will produce a very large increase over a long period: in three hundred years it will result in sixteen times as many people. Such gigantic increases simply did not occur in agrarian Europe. In certain abnormal years and tragic periods—the Black Death was only the most extreme example—many more people died than were born. Total population fell sharply, even catastrophically. A number of years of modest growth would then be necessary to make up for those who had died in an abnormal year. Such savage increases in deaths occurred periodically in the seventeenth century on a local and regional scale, and these demographic crises combined to check the growth of population until after 1700.

The grim reapers of demographic crisis were famine, epidemic disease, and war. Famine, the inevitable result of low yields and periodic crop failures, was particularly murderous because it was accompanied by disease. With a brutal one-two punch, famine stunned and weakened a population, and disease finished it off. War was another scourge, and its indirect effects were even more harmful than the organized killing. Soldiers and camp followers passed all manner of contagious diseases throughout the countryside. Armies also requisitioned scarce food supplies and disrupted the agricultural cycle. The Thirty Years' War witnessed all possible combinations of distress. In the German states, the number of inhabitants declined by more than *two-thirds* in some large areas and by at least one-third almost everywhere else.

The Plague at Marseilles in 1720   The last great wave of bubonic plague in Europe occurred at Marseilles in 1720, when a merchant ship from Syria arrived at the Mediterranean port city with infected passengers. The plague spread quickly, killing half the inhabitants of the city. A wall was erected to quarantine the city, but it did not prevent the spread of disease to the surrounding region. Altogether, about a hundred thousand people died before the epidemic ended in 1722. *(Giraudon/Art Resource, NY)*

The New Pattern of the Eighteenth Century

In the eighteenth century the population of Europe began to grow markedly. This increase in numbers occurred in all areas of Europe, western and eastern, northern and southern, dynamic and stagnant. Growth was especially dramatic after about 1750 (see Figure 19.2).

What caused this population growth? In some areas women had more babies than before because new opportunities for employment in rural industry allowed them to marry at an earlier age. But the basic cause for Europe as a whole was a decline in mortality—fewer deaths.

The bubonic plague mysteriously disappeared. Following the Black Death in the fourteenth century, plagues had remained part of the European experience, striking again and again with savage force, particularly in towns.

As late as 1720 a ship from Syria and the Levant brought the disease to Marseilles, killing up to one hundred thousand in the city and surrounding region. By 1722 the epidemic had passed, and that was the last time plague fell on western and central Europe. Exactly why plague disappeared is unknown. Stricter measures of quarantine in Mediterranean ports and along the Austrian border with Turkey helped by carefully isolating human carriers of plague. Chance and plain good luck were probably just as important.

Advances in medical knowledge did not contribute much to reducing the death rate in the eighteenth century. The most important advance in preventive medicine in this period was inoculation against smallpox, and this great improvement was long confined mainly to England, probably doing little to reduce deaths throughout Europe until the latter part of the century. However,

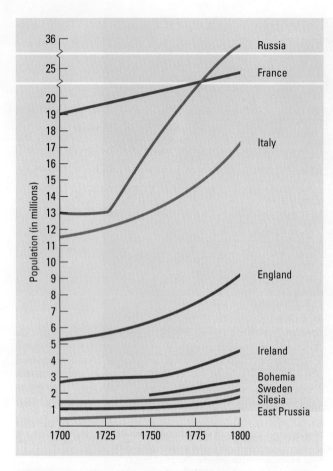

FIGURE 19.2 The Increase of Population in Europe in the Eighteenth Century France's large population continued to support French political and intellectual leadership. Russia emerged as Europe's most populous state because natural increase was complemented by growth from territorial expansion.

improvements in the water supply and sewerage, which were frequently promoted by strong absolutist monarchies, resulted in somewhat better public health and helped reduce such diseases as typhoid and typhus in some urban areas of western Europe. Improvements in water supply and the drainage of swamps also reduced Europe's large insect population. Flies and mosquitoes played a major role in spreading diseases, especially those striking children and young adults. Thus early public health measures helped the decline in mortality that began with the disappearance of plague and continued into the early nineteenth century.

Human beings also became more successful in their efforts to safeguard the supply of food. The eighteenth century was a time of considerable canal and road building in western Europe. These advances in transportation, which were also among the more positive aspects of strong absolutist states, lessened the impact of local crop failure and famine. Emergency supplies could be brought in, and localized starvation became less frequent. Wars became more gentlemanly and less destructive than in the seventeenth century and spread fewer epidemics. New foods, particularly the potato from South America, were introduced. In short, population grew in the eighteenth century primarily because years of abnormal death rates were less catastrophic. Famines, epidemics, and wars continued to occur, but their severity moderated.

Cottage Industry and Urban Guilds

The growth of population increased the number of rural workers with little or no land, and this in turn contributed to the development of industry in rural areas. The poor in the countryside increasingly needed to supplement their agricultural earnings with other types of work, and urban capitalists were eager to employ them, often at lower wages than urban workers were paid. **Cottage industry,** which consisted of manufacturing with hand tools in peasant cottages and work sheds, grew markedly in the eighteenth century and became a crucial feature of the European economy.

To be sure, peasant communities had always made clothing, processed food, and constructed housing for their own use. But medieval peasants did not produce manufactured goods on a large scale for sale in a market. By the eighteenth century, however, the pressures of rural poverty and the need to employ landless proletarians were overwhelming the efforts of urban artisans to maintain their traditional monopoly over industrial production.

Guilds continued to dominate production in towns and cities, providing their masters with economic privileges as well as a fixed social identity. Those excluded from guild membership—women, day laborers, Jews, and foreigners—worked on the margins of the urban economy. Critics attacked the guilds in the second half of the eighteenth century as outmoded institutions that obstructed technical progress and innovation. Until recently, most historians repeated that view. An ongoing re-assessment of guilds now emphasizes their ability to adapt to changing economic circumstances.

• *How and why did economic production intensify in the eighteenth century, particularly in the countryside?*

The Putting-Out System

Cottage industry was often organized through the **putting-out system.** The two main participants in the putting-out system were the merchant capitalist and the rural worker. The merchant loaned, or "put out," raw materials to cottage workers who processed the raw materials in their own homes and returned the finished products to the merchant. There were endless variations on this basic relationship. Sometimes rural workers bought their own raw materials and worked as independent producers before they sold to the merchant. Sometimes whole families were involved in domestic industry; at other times the tasks were closely associated with one gender. Sometimes several workers toiled together to perform a complicated process in a workshop outside the home. The relative importance of earnings from the land and from industry varied greatly for handicraft workers, although industrial wages usually became more important for a given family with time.

As industries grew in scale and complexity, production was often broken into many stages. For example, a merchant would provide raw wool to one group of workers for spinning into thread. He would then pass the thread to another group of workers to be bleached, to another for dying, and to another for weaving into cloth. The merchant paid outworkers by the piece and proceeded to sell the finished product to regional, national, or international markets.

The putting-out system grew because it had competitive advantages. Underemployed labor was abundant, and poor peasants and landless laborers would work for low wages. Since production in the countryside was unregulated, workers and merchants could change procedures and experiment as they saw fit. Because they did not need to meet rigid guild standards, cottage industry became capable of producing many kinds of goods. Textiles; all manner of knives, forks, and housewares; buttons and gloves; and clocks could be produced quite satisfactorily in the countryside. Luxury goods for the rich, such as exquisite tapestries and fine porcelain, demanded special training, close supervision, and centralized workshops. Yet such goods were as exceptional as those who used them. The skills of rural industry were sufficient for everyday articles.

The Weaver's Repose
This painting by Decker Cornelis Gerritz (1594–1637) captures the pleasure of release from long hours of toil in cottage industry. The loom realistically dominates the cramped living space and the family's modest possessions. (*Musées Royaux des Beaux-Arts, Brussels. Copyright A.C.I.*)

Mapping the Past

MAP 19.1 Industry and Population in Eighteenth-Century Europe The growth of cottage manufacturing in rural areas helped country people increase their income and contributed to population growth. The putting-out system began in England, and much of the work was in the textile industry. Cottage industry was also strong in the Low Countries—modern-day Belgium and Holland. ❶ What types of textiles were produced in Europe? How would you account for the distribution of each type of cloth across Europe? ❷ What was the relationship between population density and the growth of textile production? Was this a fixed or variable relationship? What geographical characteristics seem to have played a role in encouraging this industry? ❸ Did metal production draw on different demographic and geographical conditions? Why do you think this was the case?

Online Study Center **Improve Your Grade** Interactive Map: Population and Production in Eighteenth-Century Europe

Rural manufacturing did not spread across Europe at an even rate. It developed most successfully in England, particularly for the spinning and weaving of woolen cloth. By 1500 half of England's textiles were being produced in the countryside. By 1700 English industry was generally more rural than urban and heavily reliant on the putting-out system. Most continental countries, with the exception of Flanders and the Netherlands, developed rural industry more slowly. The latter part of the eighteenth century witnessed a remarkable expansion of rural industry in certain densely populated regions of continental Europe (see Map 19.1).

The Textile Industry

Until the nineteenth century, the industry that employed the most people in Europe was textiles. The making of linen, woolen, and eventually cotton cloth was the typical activity of cottage workers engaged in the putting-out system. A look inside the cottage of the English weaver illustrates a way of life as well as an economic system.

The rural worker lived in a small cottage with tiny windows and little space. Indeed, the worker's cottage was often a single room that served as workshop, kitchen, and bedroom. There were only a few pieces of furniture, of which the weaver's loom was by far the largest and most important. That loom had changed somewhat in the early eighteenth century when John Kay's invention of the flying shuttle enabled the weaver to throw the shuttle back and forth between the threads with one hand. Aside from that improvement, however, the loom was as it had been for much of history and as it would remain until the arrival of mechanized looms in the first decades of the nineteenth century.

Handloom weaving was a family enterprise. All members of the family helped in the work, so that "every person from seven to eighty (who retained their sight and who could move their hands) could earn their bread," as one eighteenth-century English observer put it.[2] Operating the loom was considered a man's job, reserved for the male head of the family. Women and children worked at auxiliary tasks; they prepared the warp (vertical) threads and mounted them on the loom, wound threads on bobbins for the weft (horizontal) threads, and sometimes operated the warp frame while the father passed the shuttle.

There was always a serious imbalance in textile manufacture before mechanization: the work of four or five spinners was needed to keep one weaver steadily employed. Since the weaver's family usually could not produce enough thread, alternate sources of labor were needed. Merchants turned to the wives and daughters of agricultural workers, who took on spinning work in their spare time. Many widows and single women also became "spinsters," so many in fact that the word became a synonym for an unmarried woman. (In other parts of Europe, such as the Rhineland, spinning employed whole families and was not reserved for women.) As the industry expanded and merchants covered ever greater distances in search of workers, they sometimes turned to local shopkeepers to manage the spinners in their villages.

Relations between workers and employers were often marked by sharp conflict. An English popular song written about 1700, called "The Clothier's Delight, or the Rich Men's Joy and the Poor Men's Sorrow," has the merchant boasting of the countless tricks he uses to "beat down wages":

We heapeth up riches and treasure great store
Which we get by griping and grinding the poor.
And this is a way for to fill up our purse
Although we do get it with many a curse.[3]

There were constant disputes over the weights of materials and the quality of finished work. Merchants accused workers of stealing raw materials, and weavers complained that merchants delivered underweight bales. Suspicion abounded.

Conditions were particularly hard for female workers. While men could earn decent wages through long hours of arduous labor, women's wages were always terribly low. In the Yorkshire wool industry, a male wool comber earned a good wage of twelve shillings or more a week, while a spinner could hope for only three-and-a-half shillings.[4] A single or widowed spinner faced a desperate struggle with poverty. Any period of illness or unemployment could spell disaster for her and any dependent children.

There was another problem, at least from the merchant capitalist's point of view. Rural labor was cheap, scattered, and poorly organized. For these reasons it was hard to control. Moreover, the pace of work depended on the agricultural calendar. In spring and late summer planting and haymaking occupied all hands in the rural village, leading to shortages in the supply of thread. Merchants, whose livelihood depended on their ability to meet orders on time, bitterly resented their lack of control over rural labor. They accused workers—especially female spinners—of laziness, intemperance, and immorality. If workers failed to produce enough thread, they reasoned, it must be because their wages were too high and they had little incentive to work. Merchants thus insisted on maintaining the lowest possible wages to force the "idle" poor into productive labor. They also successfully lobbied for, and obtained, new police powers over workers. Imprisonment and public whipping became common punishments for pilfering small amounts of yarn or cloth. For poor workers, their right to hold on to the bits and pieces left over in the production process was akin to the traditional peasant right of gleaning in common lands.

Urban Guilds

The high point of the **guild system** in most of Europe occurred in the seventeenth and eighteenth centuries,

Guild Procession in Seventeenth-Century Brussels   Guilds played an important role in the civic
life of the early modern city. They collected taxes from their members, imposed quality standards
and order on the trades, and represented the interests of commerce and industry to the government.
In return, they claimed exclusive monopolies over their trades and the right to govern their own
affairs. Guilds marched in processions at important moments in the life of the city, proudly displaying their corporate insignia. *(Victoria & Albert Museum, London/Art Resource, NY)*

rather than in the High Middle Ages as previously believed. Guilds grew in number in cities and towns across
Europe during this period. In Louis XIV's France, for example, finance minister Jean-Baptiste Colbert revived the
urban guilds and used them to encourage high-quality
production and to collect taxes. The number of guilds in
the city of Paris grew from 60 in 1672 to 129 in 1691.

Guild masters occupied the summit of the world of
work. Each guild received a detailed set of privileges from
the Crown, including exclusive rights to produce and sell
certain goods, access to restricted markets in raw materials, and the rights to train apprentices, hire workers, and
open shops. Any individual who violated these monopolies could be prosecuted. Guilds also served social and
religious functions, providing a locus of sociability and
group identity to the middling classes of European cities.

To ensure there was enough work to go around, guilds
jealously restricted their membership to local men who

were good Christians, had several years of work experience, paid stiff membership fees, and completed a masterpiece. They also favored family connections. Masters' sons
enjoyed automatic access to their fathers' guilds, while
outsiders were often barred from entering. In the 1720s
Parisian guild masters numbered only about thirty-five
thousand in a population of five hundred thousand. Most
men and women worked in non-guild trades, as domestic servants, as manual laborers, and as vendors of food
and other small goods.

The guilds' ability to enforce their rigid barriers varied
a great deal across Europe. In England, national regulations superseded guild regulations, sapping their importance. In France, the Crown developed an ambiguous
attitude toward guilds, relying on them for taxes and enforcement of quality standards, yet allowing non-guild
production to flourish in the countryside after 1762, and
even in some urban neighborhoods. The Faubourg Saint-

Antoine, an eastern suburb of Paris, maintained freedom from guild privileges through an old legal loophole, acting as a haven for the "false-workers" bitterly denounced by masters. The German guilds were perhaps the most powerful in Europe, and the most conservative. Journeymen in German cities, with their masters' support, violently protested the encroachment of non-guild workers. Whereas French guilds were washed away by the Revolution's attack on royal privilege, guilds persisted in parts of Germany until the second half of the nineteenth century.

Critics of guilds in France derided them as outmoded and exclusionary institutions that obstructed technical innovation and progress. (See the feature "Listening to the Past: The Debate over the Guilds" on pages 650–651.) Many historians have repeated that charge. More recent scholarship, however, has emphasized the flexibility and adaptability of the guild system and its vitality through the eighteenth century. Guild masters adopted new technologies and found creative ways to circumvent impractical rules. For many merchants and artisans, economic regulation did not hinder commerce but instead fostered the confidence necessary to stimulate it. In an economy where buyers' and sellers' access to information was so limited, regulation helped each side trust in the other's good faith.

Online Study Center **Improve Your Grade**
Primary Source: Turgot Abolishes the French Guilds

Over the eighteenth century some guilds grew more accessible to women. This was particularly the case in dressmaking; given the great increase in textile production, more hands were needed to fashion clothing for urban elites. In 1675 Colbert granted seamstresses a new all-female guild in Paris, and soon seamstresses joined tailors' guilds in parts of France, England, and the Netherlands. In the late seventeenth century new vocational training programs were established for poor girls in many European cities, mostly in needlework. There is also evidence that more women were hired as skilled workers by male guilds, often in defiance of official statutes. Like their rural counterparts, urban girls and women were entering the paid labor market in greater numbers. When French guilds received new statutes in 1777, all were formally opened to women. The guilds' final abolition in 1791 makes it impossible to know how this experiment in sexual equality would have fared.

While many artisans welcomed the economic liberalization that followed the Revolution, some continued to espouse the ideals of the guilds. Because they had always been semi-clandestine, journeymen's associations frequently survived into the nineteenth century. They espoused the values of hand craftsmanship and limited competition, in contrast to the proletarianization and loss of skills they endured in mechanized production. Nevertheless, by the middle of the nineteenth century economic deregulation was championed by most European governments and elites.

The Industrious Revolution

One scholar has used the term **industrious revolution** to describe the social and economic changes taking place in Europe in the late seventeenth and early eighteenth centuries.[5] This occurred as households in northwestern Europe reduced leisure time, stepped up the pace of work, and, most importantly, redirected the labor of women and children away from the production of goods for household consumption and toward wage work. By working harder and increasing the number of wageworkers, households could purchase more goods, even in a time of stagnant or falling real wages.

The effect of these changes is still debated. While some scholars lament the encroachment of longer work hours and stricter discipline, others insist that poor families made decisions based on their own self-interests. With more finished goods becoming available at lower prices, households sought cash income to participate in a nascent consumer economy. The role of women and girls in this new economy is particularly controversial. When women entered the labor market, they almost always worked at menial, tedious jobs for very low wages. The fantastic rise of the British textile industry in the eighteenth century was built on the exhausted fingers and blighted eyesight of untold numbers of female cottage workers. Yet when women earned their own wages, they also seem to have taken on a proportionately greater role in household decision making. Most of their scant earnings went for household necessities, items they could no longer produce now that they worked full-time, but there were sometimes a few shillings left for a few ribbons or a new pair of stockings. Women's control over their surplus income thus helped spur the rapid growth of the textile industries in which they labored so hard.

New sources and patterns of labor established important foundations for the Industrial Revolution of the late eighteenth and nineteenth centuries. They created households in which all members worked for wages rather than in a united family business and in which consumption relied on market-produced rather than home-made goods. It was not until the mid-nineteenth century, with rising industrial wages, that a new model emerged in which the male "breadwinner" was expected to earn

The Linen Industry in Ireland Many steps went into making textiles. Here the women are beating away the woody part of the flax plant so that the man can comb out the soft part. The combed fibers will then be spun into thread and woven into cloth by this family enterprise. The increased labor of women and girls from the late seventeenth century helped produce an "industrious revolution." *(Victoria and Albert Museum London/Eileen Tweedy/The Art Archive)*

enough to support the whole family and women and children were relegated back to the domestic sphere. With 77 percent of U.S. women between ages twenty-five and fifty-four in the workforce in the year 2000, today's world is experiencing a second industrious revolution in a similar climate of stagnant wages and increased demand for consumer goods.

Building the Global Economy

In addition to agricultural improvement, population pressure, and growing cottage industry, the expansion of Europe in the eighteenth century was characterized by the growth of world trade. Spain and Portugal revitalized their empires and began drawing more wealth from renewed development. Yet once again the countries of northwestern Europe—the Netherlands, France, and above all Great Britain—benefited most. Great Britain, which was formed in 1707 by the union of England and Scotland into a single kingdom, gradually became the leading maritime power. Thus the British played the

critical role in building a fairly unified Atlantic economy that provided remarkable opportunities for them and their colonists. They also conducted ruthless competition with France and the Netherlands for trade and territory in Asia.

• *How did colonial markets boost Europe's economic and social development, and what conflicts and adversity did world trade entail?*

Mercantilism and Colonial Wars

Britain's commercial leadership in the eighteenth century had its origins in the mercantilism of the seventeenth century (see page 532). European **mercantilism** was a system of economic regulations aimed at increasing the power of the state. As practiced by a leading advocate such as Colbert under Louis XIV, mercantilism aimed particularly at creating a favorable balance of foreign trade in order to increase a country's stock of gold. A country's gold holdings served as an all-important treasure chest that could be opened periodically to pay for war in a violent age. Early English mercantilists shared these views.

The result of the English desire to increase both military power and private wealth was the mercantile system of the **Navigation Acts.** Oliver Cromwell established the first of these laws in 1651, and the restored monarchy of Charles II extended them in 1660 and 1663; these Navigation Acts were not seriously modified until 1786. The acts required that most goods imported from Europe into England and Scotland be carried on British-owned ships with British crews or on ships of the country producing the article. Moreover, these laws gave British merchants and shipowners a virtual monopoly on trade with British colonies. The colonists were required to ship their products on British (or American) ships and to buy almost all European goods from Britain. It was believed that these economic regulations would help British merchants and workers as well as colonial plantation owners and farmers; and the emerging British Empire would develop a shipping industry with a large number of experienced seamen who could serve when necessary in the Royal Navy.

The Navigation Acts were a form of economic warfare. Their initial target was the Dutch, who were far ahead of the English in shipping and foreign trade in the mid-seventeenth century (see page 553). In conjunction with three Anglo-Dutch wars between 1652 and 1674, the Navigation Acts seriously damaged Dutch shipping and commerce. The British seized the thriving Dutch colony of New Amsterdam in 1664 and renamed it "New York." By the late seventeenth century the Netherlands was falling behind England in shipping, trade, and colonies.

Thereafter France stood clearly as England's most serious rival in the competition for overseas empire. Rich in natural resources, with a population three or four times that of England, and allied with Spain, continental Europe's leading military power was already building a powerful fleet and a worldwide system of rigidly monopolized colonial trade. Thus from 1701 to 1763 Britain and France were locked in a series of wars to decide, in part, which nation would become the leading maritime power and claim the profits of Europe's overseas expansion (see Map 19.2).

The first round was the War of the Spanish Succession (see page 534), which started when Louis XIV accepted the Spanish crown willed to his grandson. Besides upsetting the continental balance of power, a union of France and Spain threatened to encircle and destroy the British colonies in North America (see Map 19.2). Defeated by a great coalition of states after twelve years of fighting, Louis XIV was forced in the Peace of Utrecht (1713) to cede Newfoundland, Nova Scotia, and the Hudson Bay territory to Britain. Spain was compelled to give Britain control of its West African slave trade—the so-called *asiento*—and to let Britain send one ship of merchandise into the Spanish colonies annually through Porto Bello on the Isthmus of Panama.

France was still a mighty competitor. The War of the Austrian Succession (1740–1748), which started when Frederick the Great of Prussia seized Silesia from Austria's Maria Theresa (see page 610), gradually became a world war that included Anglo-French conflicts in India and North America. The war ended with no change in the territorial situation in North America.

This inconclusive standoff helped set the stage for the Seven Years' War (1756–1763). In central Europe, Austria's Maria Theresa sought to win back Silesia and crush Prussia, thereby re-establishing the Habsburgs' traditional leadership in German affairs. She almost succeeded in her goals, but Prussia survived with its boundaries intact.

Inconclusive in Europe, the Seven Years' War was the decisive round in the Franco-British competition for colonial empire. The fighting began in North America. The population of New France was centered in Quebec and along the St. Lawrence River, but French soldiers and Canadian fur traders had also built forts and trading posts along the Great Lakes, through the Ohio country, and down the Mississippi to New Orleans (see Map 19.3). Allied with many Native American tribes, the French built more forts in 1753 in what is now western Pennsylvania to protect their claims. The following year a Virginia force attacked a small group of French soldiers, and soon the war to conquer Canada was on.

Although the inhabitants of New France were greatly outnumbered—Canada counted fifty-five thousand inhabitants, as opposed to 1.2 million in the thirteen English colonies—French and Canadian forces under the experienced marquis de Montcalm fought well and scored major victories until 1758. Then, led by their new chief minister, William Pitt, whose grandfather had made a fortune in India, the British diverted men and money from the war in Europe, using superior sea power to destroy the French fleet and choke off French commerce around the world. In 1759 a combined British naval and land force laid siege to Quebec for four long months, defeating Montcalm's army in a dramatic battle that sealed the fate of France in North America.

British victory on all colonial fronts was ratified in the **Treaty of Paris** (1763). France lost its possessions on mainland North America. Canada and all French territory east of the Mississippi River passed to Britain, and France

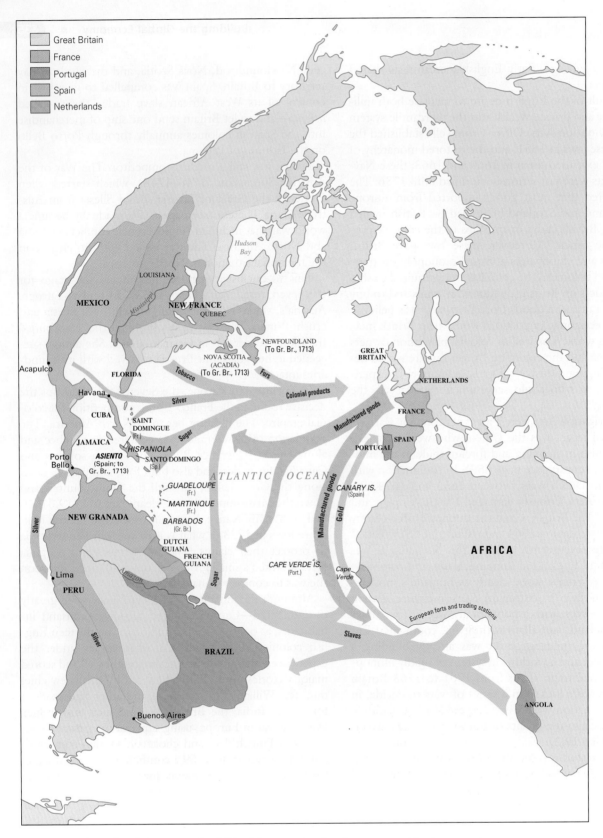

Legend:
- Great Britain
- France
- Portugal
- Spain
- Netherlands

Hudson Bay

LOUISIANA

MEXICO

NEW FRANCE

QUEBEC

NEWFOUNDLAND (To Gr. Br., 1713)

NOVA SCOTIA (ACADIA) (To Gr. Br., 1713)

GREAT BRITAIN

NETHERLANDS

Acapulco

FLORIDA

Tobacco

Furs

Colonial products

FRANCE

Havana

Silver

Manufactured goods

SPAIN

CUBA

SAINT DOMINGUE (Fr.)

Sugar

PORTUGAL

JAMAICA

HISPANIOLA

SANTO DOMINGO (Sp.)

ATLANTIC OCEAN

CANARY IS. (Spain)

Porto Bello

ASIENTO (Spain; to Gr. Br., 1713)

GUADELOUPE (Fr.)

Manufactured goods

Gold

Silver

NEW GRANADA

MARTINIQUE (Fr.)

BARBADOS (Gr. Br.)

DUTCH GUIANA

FRENCH GUIANA

CAPE VERDE IS. (Port.)

Cape Verde

AFRICA

Lima

Amazon

Sugar

PERU

Silver

European forts and trading stations

BRAZIL

Slaves

ANGOLA

Buenos Aires

MAP 19.2 The Atlantic Economy in 1701   The growth of trade encouraged both economic development and military conflict in the Atlantic basin. Four continents were linked together by the exchange of goods and slaves.

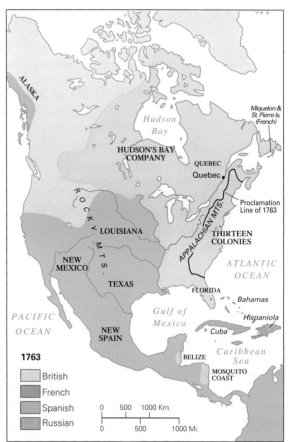

**MAP 19.3 European Claims in North America Before and After the Seven Years' War
(1756–1763)** France lost its vast territories in North America, though the British government
then prohibited colonists from settling west of the Appalachian Mountains in 1763. The
British had raised taxes on themselves and the colonists to pay for the war, and they wanted to
avoid costly conflicts with Native Americans living in the newly conquered territory. One of the
few remaining French colonies in the Americas, Saint Domingue (on the island of Hispaniola)
was the most profitable plantation colony in the New World.

Online Study Center **Improve Your Grade** Interactive Map:
European Claims in North America Before and After the Seven Years' War

ceded Louisiana to Spain as compensation for Spain's
loss of Florida to Britain. France also gave up most of its
holdings in India, opening the way to British dominance
on the subcontinent. By 1763 British naval power, built
in large part on the rapid growth of the British shipping
industry after the passage of the Navigation Acts, had triumphed decisively: Britain had realized its goal of monopolizing a vast trading and colonial empire.

In the eighteenth century, stimulated by trade and empire building, London grew into the West's largest and
richest city. (See the feature "Images in Society: London:

The Remaking of a Great City" on pages 638–639.)
Above all, the rapidly growing and increasingly wealthy
agricultural populations of the mainland colonies provided an expanding market for English manufactured
goods. This situation was extremely fortunate, for England in the eighteenth century was gradually losing, or
only slowly expanding, its sales to many of its traditional
European markets.

As trade with Europe stagnated, protected colonial
markets came to the rescue (see Figure 19.3). English exports of manufactured goods to the Atlantic economy—

Images in Society

London: The Remaking of a Great City

The imperial capital and intercontinental trade center of London dominated Britain and astonished the visitor. Equal in population to Paris with four hundred thousand inhabitants in 1650, the super city of the West grew to nine hundred thousand in 1801, while second-place Paris had six hundred thousand. And as London grew, its citizens created a new urban landscape and style of living.

Image 1 shows the "true profile" of London and its built environment as viewed from the south before the Great Fire of 1666, which raged for four days and destroyed about 80 percent of the old, predominately wooden central city. With the River Thames flowing eastward toward the sea, one sees from left to right pre-Fire St. Paul's Cathedral, London Bridge crowded with houses, ships at the wharves, and the medieval Tower of London. Clearly visible in the distance are the open fields of the large estates surrounding London, while beyond view on the left are the royal palace and adjacent government buildings. Also missing is the famous London smog, the combination of fog and smoke from coal-burning fireplaces that already polluted the metropolis. How would you characterize pre-Fire London?

Reconstruction proceeded quickly after the Great Fire so that people could regain shelter and employ-

ment. Brick construction was made mandatory to prevent fire, but only a few streets were straightened or widened. Thus social classes remained packed together in the rebuilt city. The rich merchant family in a first-class city residence (Image 2), built in the 1670s and still standing in 1939, shared a tiny courtyard and constantly rubbed shoulders with poor and middling people in everyday life.

As London rebuilt and kept growing, big noble landowners followed two earlier examples and sought to increase their incomes by setting up residential developments on their estates west of the city. A landowner would lay out a square with streets and building lots, which he or she would lease to speculative builders who put up fine houses for sale or rent. Soho Square, first laid out in the 1670s and shown in Image 3 as it appeared in 1731, was fairly typical. The spacious square with its gated park is surrounded by three-story row houses set on deep, narrow lots. Set in the country but close to the city, a square like Soho was a kind of elegant "village" with restrictive building codes that catered to aristocrats, officials, and successful professionals who were served by artisans and shopkeepers living in alleys and side streets. Do you see a difference between the houses on the square and on the street behind? How would you compare Soho

Image 1 London Before the Great Fire (*Hulton Archive/Getty Images*)

Image 2 Merchant Family's Residence (built 1670–1680) *(English Heritage/NMR)*

Image 3 Soho Square, 1731 *(Private Collection/The Stapleton Collection/ The Bridgeman Art Library)*

Square with the hills in the distance and with the old London of Images 1 and 2? The classy, new area, known as the West End, contrasted sharply with the shoddy rentals and makeshift shacks of laborers and sailors in the mushrooming East End, which artists rarely painted. Thus residential segregation by income level increased substantially in eighteenth-century London.

As the suburban villages grew and gradually merged together, the West End increasingly attracted the well-to-do from all over England. Rural landowners and provincial notables came for the social season from October to May. Operating out of comfortable second homes purchased or rented in the West End, they played the national market for mortgages, marriages, and recreation. Image 4, showing classy Bloomsbury Square in 1787 and the original country mansion of the enterprising noble developer, provides a glimpse into this well-born culture. How does Image 4 complement Image 3? What message is the artist conveying with the milkmaid and her cows? Some historians believe that London's West End was an important social innovation. Reconsidering these images, do you agree?

Image 4 Bloomsbury Square, 1787 *(HarperCollins Publishers)*

Online Study Center   Improve Your Grade
Going Beyond Images in Society

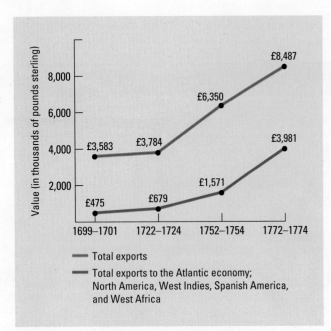

FIGURE 19.3 Exports of English Manufactured Goods, 1700–1774 While trade between England and Europe stagnated after 1700, English exports to Africa and the Americas boomed and greatly stimulated English economic development. *(Source: R. Davis, "English Foreign Trade, 1700–1774," Economic History Review, 2d ser., 15 (1962): 302–303.)*

primarily the mainland colonies of North America and the West Indian sugar islands, with an important assist from West Africa and Latin America—soared from £500,000 to £4.0 million. Sales to other colonies—Ireland and India—also rose substantially in the eighteenth century.

English exports also became more balanced and diversified. To America and Africa went large quantities of metal items—axes to frontier settlers, firearms and chains to slave owners. There were also clocks and coaches, buttons and saddles, china and furniture, musical instruments and scientific equipment, and a host of other things. Foreign trade became the bread and butter of some industries; for example, by 1750 half the nails made in England were going to the colonies. Thus, the mercantilist system achieved remarkable success for England in the eighteenth century, and by the 1770s England stood on the threshold of the epoch-making industrial changes that are described in Chapter 22.

Although they lost many possessions to the English, the French still profited enormously from colonial trade. The colonies of Saint Domingue (modern-day Haiti) and Martinique and Guadeloupe (which remain French departments today) provided immense fortunes in sugar

plantations, coffee, and slave trading during the second half of the eighteenth century. By 1789 the population of Saint Domingue included five hundred thousand slaves whose labor had allowed the colony to become the world's leading producer of coffee and sugar. It was the most profitable plantation colony in the New World and the one that consumed the greatest number of slaves.[6] The wealth generated from colonial trade fostered the confidence of the merchant classes in Paris, Bordeaux, and other large cities, and merchants soon joined other elite groups clamoring for more political responsibility.

Land and Labor in British America

As Britain built its empire in North America, it secured an important outlet for surplus population, so that migration abroad limited poverty at home. The settlers also benefited, for they enjoyed privileged access to virtually free and unlimited land. The situation in the American colonies contrasted sharply with that in the British Isles, where land was already highly concentrated in the hands of the nobility and gentry in 1700. White settlers who came to the colonies as free men and women could obtain their own farms on easy terms, and those who came as indentured servants pledged to work seven years for their passage or as convicts could do so as soon as they had their personal freedom. Unlike the great majority of European peasants, American farmers kept most of what they produced.

Cheap land and the tremendous demand for scarce labor also fostered the growth of slavery in the British colonies. The Spanish and the Portuguese had introduced slavery into the Americas in the sixteenth century. Because Native Americans died in large numbers when enslaved, the Spanish and Portuguese began importing most slaves from Africa. In the seventeenth century the Dutch aggressively followed their example and transported some two hundred thousand Africans to the Americas. There slaves worked on sugar plantations that normally earned large profits for plantation owners and European traders.

As England adopted mercantilist policies after 1650, big investors established valuable sugar plantations in the Caribbean and brought slave laborers from Africa to work them. The small white farmers, who had settled the islands and grew tobacco, generally sold out and migrated to the mainland colonies. Black slaves then became the overwhelming majority of the population, as they were in other European colonies in the Caribbean. By 1700 the pattern of plantations based on slave exploitation had spread to the Virginia lowlands, and by

A Slave Ship and Its Victims This 1827 lithograph of slaves in the hold of a ship bound for Brazil depicts the "scene of horror almost inconceivable" that Equiano encountered in crossing the Atlantic. Inhuman overcrowding of slaves resulted in shocking death rates. The man on the right will be thrown overboard. *(Houghton Library, Harvard University)*

1730 the large plantations there were worked entirely by black slaves. The harsh exploitation of slave labor permitted an astonishing tenfold increase in tobacco production between 1700 and 1774 and created a wealthy planter class in Maryland and Virginia. In 1790, when the U.S. population was approaching 4 million, slaves accounted for almost 20 percent of the total.

Slavery was uncommon in New England and the middle colonies, and in the course of the eighteenth century these areas began to export foodstuffs to the West Indies to feed the slaves. The plantation owners, whether they grew tobacco in Virginia and Maryland or sugar in the West Indies, had the exclusive privilege of supplying the British Isles with their products. Thus white colonists, too, had their place in the protective mercantile system of the Navigation Acts.

The abundance of almost free land resulted in a rapid increase in the colonial population. In a mere three-quarters of a century after 1700, the white population of the mainland colonies multiplied ten times as immigrants arrived and colonial couples raised large families. Rapid population growth did not reduce the white settlers to poverty. On the contrary, agricultural development resulted in fairly high standards of living, and on the eve of the American Revolution white men and women in the mainland British colonies had one of the highest living standards in the world.[7]

The Atlantic Slave Trade

Although the trade in African people was a worldwide phenomenon, the **Atlantic slave trade** became its most significant portion. In the words of a leading historian, by 1700 "it was impossible to imagine the Atlantic system without slavery and the slave trade."[8]

The forced migration of millions of Africans—cruel, unjust, and tragic—remained a key element in the Atlantic system and western European economic expansion

Slaves Harvesting Sugar Cane   In this 1828 print a long line of hard-working slaves systematically harvests the ripe cane on the island of Antigua, while on the right more slaves load cut cane into wagons for refining at the plantation's central crushing mill. The manager on horseback may be ordering the overseer to quicken the work pace, always brutal and unrelenting at harvest time. Slave labor made high-intensity capitalist production of sugar possible in the Americas. *(John Carter Brown Library at Brown University)*

throughout the eighteenth century. Indeed, the brutal trade intensified dramatically after 1700 and especially after 1750. According to one authoritative estimate, European traders purchased and shipped 6.13 million African slaves across the Atlantic between 1701 and 1800—fully 52 percent of the estimated total of 11.7 million Africans transported between 1450 and 1900, not including an additional 10 to 15 percent who died in procurement and transit.[9] By the peak decade of the 1780s, shipments averaged about eighty thousand individuals per year in an attempt to satisfy the constantly rising demand for labor power—and slave owners' profits—in the Americas.

Taken to the Americas in chains, Africans made a decisive contribution to the development of the Atlantic economy. Above all, the labor of enslaved Africans made possible large-scale production of valuable commodities for sale in Europe, for Africans transported to the Americas could not go off and farm for themselves as white settlers did. Indeed, an important recent study concludes

that in the years from 1761 to 1800 Africans and their descendants in Brazil, Spanish America, the Caribbean, and Britain's mainland slave colonies accounted for more than *four-fifths* of all the commodities produced in the Americas for sale in the Atlantic economy.[10] It was this flood of ever-cheaper sugar, coffee, tobacco, rice, and (in the nineteenth century) cotton that generated hard cash in the Americas—cash that paid for manufactured goods and services from Britain and Europe as well as for more slaves from Africa.

Intensification of the slave trade resulted in fundamental changes in its organization. Before 1700 European states waged costly wars with one another through monopolist trading companies in the hope of controlling slave exports. European agents in fortified trading posts tapped into traditional African networks for slaves, who were mainly captives taken in battles between African states, plus some Africans punished with slavery by local societies or secured through small-scale raiding. After

1700, as Britain became the undisputed leader in the slave trade, European governments and ship captains cut back on fighting among themselves and concentrated on commerce. They generally adopted the shore method of trading, which was less expensive. Thus European ships sent boats ashore or invited African dealers to bring traders and slaves out to their ships. This method allowed ships to move easily along the coast from market to market and to depart more quickly for the Americas.

Increasing demand resulted in rising prices for African slaves in the eighteenth century. Some African merchants and rulers who controlled exports profited, and some Africans secured foreign products that they found appealing because of price or quality. But generally such economic returns did not spread very far, and the negative consequences of the expanding slave trade predominated. Wars between Africans to obtain salable captives increased, and leaders purchased more arms and bought relatively fewer textiles and consumer goods.

The kingdom of Dahomey, which entered the slave trade in the eighteenth century and made it a royal monopoly, built up its army, attacked far into the interior, and profited greatly as a major supplier of slaves. More common perhaps was the experience of the kingdom of the Congo in central Africa, where the perpetual Portuguese search for slaves undermined the monarchy, destroyed political unity, and led to constant disorder. All along Africa's western coast small-scale slave raiding also spread far into the interior. There kidnappers seized and enslaved men and women like Olaudah Equiano and his sister, whose tragic separation, exile, and exploitation personified the full horror of the Atlantic slave trade. (See the feature "Individuals in Society: Olaudah Equiano.") Africans who committed crimes had traditionally paid fines, but because of the urgent demand for slaves many misdemeanors became punishable by sale to slave dealers. Finally, while the population of Europe (and Asia) grew substantially in the eighteenth century, that of Africa stagnated or possibly declined.

Online Study Center **Improve Your Grade**
Primary Source: An Eyewitness Describes the Slave Trade in Guinea

Until 1700, and perhaps even 1750, almost all Europeans considered the African slave trade a legitimate business. But shiploads of African slaves never landed in northwestern Europe, partly because cheap labor abounded there. Blacks did arrive in Europe as personal slaves, but if a slave ran away, the courts and the poor often supported the slave, not the slave owner. Runaways merged into London's growing population of free and escaped blacks; unions between blacks and whites were not uncommon. In 1772 a high court ruling, though limited in scope, "clearly doomed the slave status in England."[11]

After 1775 a much broader campaign to abolish slavery developed in Britain, and between 1788 and 1792, according to some recent scholarship, it grew into the first peaceful mass political movement based on the mobilization of public opinion in British history. British women played a critical role in this mass movement, denouncing the immorality of human bondage and stressing the cruel and sadistic treatment of female slaves and slave families. These attacks put the defenders of slavery on the defensive. In 1807 Parliament abolished the British slave trade, although slavery continued in British colonies and the Americas for years.

Revival in Colonial Latin America

When the last Spanish Habsburg, Charles II, died in 1700 (see page 534), Spain's vast empire lay ready for dismemberment. Yet in one of those striking reversals with which history is replete, Spain revived. The empire held together and even prospered, while a European-oriented landowning aristocracy enhanced its position in colonial society. Spain recovered in part because of better leadership. Louis XIV's grandson, who took the throne as Philip V (r. 1700–1746), brought new men and fresh ideas with him from France and rallied the Spanish people to his Bourbon dynasty in the long War of the Spanish Succession. When peace was restored, a series of reforming ministers reasserted royal authority, overhauling state finances and strengthening defense.

Revitalization in Madrid had positive results in the colonies, which defended themselves from numerous British attacks and even increased in size. Spain won Louisiana from France in 1763, and missionaries and ranchers extended Spanish influence all the way to northern California. Political success was matched by economic improvement. After declining markedly in the seventeenth century, silver mining recovered greatly, and in 1800 Spanish America accounted for half the world's silver production. Silver mining also stimulated food production for the mining camps and gave the **Creoles**—people of Spanish blood born in America—the means to purchase more and more European luxuries and manufactured goods. A class of wealthy Creole merchants arose to handle this flourishing trade, which often relied on smuggled goods from Great Britain.

Rivaling officials dispatched from Spain, Creole estate owners controlled much of the land and strove to be-

Forming the Mexican People   A new genre of paintings, called "casta paintings" in English, appeared in eighteenth-century New Spain (Mexico). These paintings, which focused on race and racial mixing, were usually painted as a series of sixteen, each with a mother, a father, and a child representing a different racial category. This painting, by an unknown eighteenth-century artist, shows the union of a Spanish man and a Native American woman that has produced a racially mixed mestizo child on the left, and a group that features a mestizo woman and a Spaniard with their little daughter on the right. Casta paintings reflect contemporary fascination with the spectrum of racial difference produced in the colonies. *(Private Collection, Mexico)*

come a genuine European aristocracy. Estate owners believed that field work was the proper occupation of poor peasants, and the defenseless Native Americans suited their needs. As the indigenous population recovered in numbers, slavery and forced labor gave way to widespread **debt peonage** from 1600 on. Under this system, a planter or rancher would keep the estate's Christianized, increasingly Hispanicized Indians in perpetual debt bondage by advancing food, shelter, and a little money. Debt peonage was a form of serfdom.

The large middle group in Spanish colonies consisted of racially mixed **mestizos,** the offspring of Spanish men and Indian women. The most talented mestizos aspired to join the Creoles, for enough wealth and power could classify one as white. Thus by the end of the colonial era

roughly 20 percent of the population was classified as white and about 30 percent as mestizo. Pure-blooded Indians accounted for most of the remainder, but some black slaves were also found in every part of Spanish America. Great numbers of slaves worked the enormous sugar plantations of Portuguese Brazil, and about half the Brazilian population in the early nineteenth century was of African origin. South America occupied an important place in the expanding Atlantic economy.

Trade and Empire in Asia

As the Atlantic economy took shape, Europeans continued to vie for dominance in the Asian trade. Between 1500 and 1600 the Portuguese had become major play-

Individuals in Society

Olaudah Equiano

The slave trade was a mass migration involving millions of human beings. It was also the sum of individual lives spent partly or entirely in slavery. Although most of those lives remain hidden to us, Olaudah Equiano (1745–1797) is an important exception.

Equiano was born in Benin (modern Nigeria) of Ibo ethnicity. His father, one of the village elders (or chieftains), presided over a large household that included "many slaves," prisoners captured in local wars. All people, slave and free, shared in the cultivation of family lands. One day, when all the adults were in the fields, two strange men and a woman broke into the family compound, kidnapped the eleven-year-old boy and his sister, tied them up, and dragged them into the woods. Brother and sister were separated, and Olaudah was sold several times to various dealers before reaching the coast. As it took six months to walk there, his home must have been far inland.

The slave ship and the strange appearance of the white crew terrified the boy. Much worse was the long voyage from Benin to Barbados in the Caribbean, as Equiano later recounted. "The stench of the [ship's] hold . . . became absolutely pestilential . . . [and] brought on a sickness among the slaves, of which many died. . . . The shrieks of the women and the groans of the dying rendered the whole a scene of horror almost inconceivable." Placed on deck with the sick and dying, Equiano saw two and then three of his "enchained countrymen" escape somehow through the nettings and jump into the sea, "preferring death to such a life of misery."*

Equiano's new owner, an officer in the Royal Navy, took him to England and saw that the lad received some education. Engaged in bloody action in Europe for almost four years as a captain's boy in the Seven Years' War, Equiano hoped that his loyal service and Christian baptism would help secure his freedom. He also knew that slavery was generally illegal in England. But his master deceived him. Docking in London, he and his accomplices forced a protesting and heartbroken Equiano onto a ship bound for the Caribbean.

There he was sold to Robert King, a Quaker merchant from Philadelphia who dealt in sugar and rum. Equiano developed his mathematical skills, worked hard to please as a clerk in King's warehouse, and became first mate on one of King's ships. Allowed to trade on the side for his own profit, Equiano amassed capital, repaid King his original purchase price, and received his deed of manumission at the age of twenty-one. King urged his talented former slave to stay on as a business partner, but Equiano hated the limitations and dangers of black freedom in the colonies—he was almost kidnapped back into slavery while loading a ship in Georgia—and could think only of England. Settling in London, Equiano studied, worked as a hairdresser, and went to sea periodically as a merchant seaman. He developed his ardent Christian faith and became a leading member of London's sizable black community.

Olaudah Equiano, in an engraving from his autobiography. (National Portrait Gallery, Smithsonian Institution/Art Resource, NY)

Equiano loathed the brutal slavery and the vicious exploitation that he saw in the West Indies and Britain's mainland colonies. A complex and sophisticated man, he also respected the integrity of Robert King and admired British navigational and industrial technologies. He encountered white oppressors and made white friends. He once described himself as "almost an Englishman." In the 1780s he joined with white and black activists in the antislavery campaign and wrote *The Interesting Narrative of the Life of Olaudah Equiano Written by Himself*, a well-documented autobiographical indictment of slavery. Above all, he urged Christians to live by the principles they professed and to treat Africans equally as free human beings and children of God. With the success of his widely read book, he carried his message to large audiences across Britain and Ireland and inspired the growing movement to abolish slavery.

Questions for Analysis

1. What aspects of Olaudah Equiano's life as a slave were typical? What aspects were atypical?
2. Describe Equiano's culture and personality. What aspects are most striking? Why?

*Olaudah Equiano, *The Interesting Narrative of the Life of Olaudah Equiano Written by Himself*, ed. with an introduction by Robert J. Allison (Boston: Bedford Books, 1995), pp. 56–57. Recent scholarship has re-examined Equiano's life and thrown some details of his identity into question.

Online Study Center **Improve Your Grade**
Going Beyond Individuals in Society

ers in the Indian Ocean trading world, eliminating Venice as Europe's chief supplier of spices and other Asian luxury goods. The Portuguese dominated but did not fundamentally alter the age-old pattern of Indian Ocean trade, which involved merchants from many areas as more or less autonomous players. This situation changed radically with the intervention of the Dutch and then the English.

In the 1590s Dutch fleets sailed from the Cape of Good Hope and, avoiding Portuguese forts in India, steered directly for Indonesia and its wealth of spices. The voyages were a rousing success. In 1599 a Dutch fleet returned to Amsterdam carrying 600,000 pounds of pepper and 250,000 pounds of cloves and nutmeg. Those who had invested in the expedition received a 100 percent profit. In 1602 the Dutch East India Company was founded with the explicit intention of capturing the spice trade from the Portuguese. In addition to financial assistance, the States General granted the company political sovereignty over the territories it acquired.

The British in India (ca 1785) This Indian miniature shows the wife (*center*) of a British officer attended by many Indian servants. A British merchant (*left*) awaits her attention. The picture reflects the luxurious lifestyle of the British elite in India, many members of which returned home with colossal fortunes. (*Scala/Art Resource, NY*)

In return for assisting Indonesian princes in local conflicts and disputes with the Portuguese, the Dutch won broad commercial concessions. Gradually they gained control of western access to the Indonesian archipelago and eventually of the archipelago itself. In 1619 company forces seized the port of Jakarta in Java. Renamed Batavia, the port became the center of Dutch operations in the Indian Ocean. Exchanging European manufactured goods—armor, firearms, linens, and toys—the Dutch soon captured a monopoly on the lucrative spice trade. Within a few decades they had expelled the Portuguese from Ceylon and other East Indian islands. Unlike the Portuguese, the Dutch transformed the Indian Ocean trading world, turning formerly autonomous business partners into dependents (see Map 16.3 on page 552).

The Dutch hold in Asia faltered in the eighteenth century because of the company's failure to diversify to meet changing consumption patterns. Spices continued to comprise much of its shipping, despite their declining importance in the European diet. Fierce competition from its main rival, the English East India Company (est. 1600), also severely undercut Dutch trade.

Britain initially struggled for a foothold in Asia. With the Dutch monopolizing the Indian Ocean, the British focused on India, where they were minor players throughout the seventeenth century. The English East India Company relied on trade concessions from the powerful Mughal emperor, who granted only piecemeal access to the subcontinent. Finally, in 1716 the Mughals conceded empire-wide trading privileges. To further their economic interests, East India Company agents increasingly intervened in local affairs and made alliances or waged war against Indian princes.

Britain's great rival for influence in India was France. Warfare in Europe in the 1740s spread to British and French forces in India, who supported opposing rulers in local power struggles. Their rivalry was finally resolved by the Treaty of Paris that ended the Seven Years' War in 1763. Among French losses in this war were all of its possessions in India.

With the elimination of the French, British ascendancy in India accelerated. In 1764 company forces defeated the Mughal emperor, leaving him on the throne as a ruler in title only. Robert Clive, a company agent who had led its forces in battle, became the first British governor general of Bengal, in northeast India, with direct authority over the province. By the early 1800s the British had overcome vigorous Indian resistance to gain economic and political dominance of much of the subcontinent, and India was lauded as the "jewel" in the British Empire in the nineteenth century.

Adam Smith and Economic Liberalism

Although mercantilist policies strengthened European colonial empires in the eighteenth century, a strong reaction against mercantilism ultimately set in. Creole merchants chafed at regulations imposed from Madrid. Small English merchants complained loudly about the injustice of handing over exclusive trading rights to great combines such as the East India Company. Wanting a bigger position in overseas commerce, independent merchants in many countries began campaigning against "monopolies" and calling for "free trade."

The general idea of freedom of enterprise in foreign trade was developed by Adam Smith (1723–1790), a professor of philosophy and a leading figure of the Scottish Enlightenment. Smith, whose *Inquiry into the Nature and Causes of the Wealth of Nations* (1776) established the basis for modern economics, was highly critical of eighteenth-century mercantilism. Mercantilism, he said, meant a combination of stifling government regulations and unfair privileges for state-approved monopolies and government favorites. Far preferable was free competition, which would best protect consumers from price gouging and give all citizens a fair and equal right to do what they did best. In keeping with his deep-seated fear of political oppression and with the "system of natural liberty" that he advocated, Smith argued that government should limit itself to "only three duties": it should provide a defense against foreign invasion, maintain civil order with courts and police protection, and sponsor certain indispensable public works and institutions that could never adequately profit private investors.

Smith saw the pursuit of self-interest in a competitive market as the source of an underlying and previously unrecognized harmony that he believed would result in gradual progress. According to Smith:

[Every individual generally] neither intends to promote the public interest, nor knows how much he is promoting it. . . . He is in this case, as in many cases, led by an invisible hand to promote an end which was no part of his intention. Nor is it always the worse for society that it was not part of it. I have never known much good done by those who affected to trade for the public good.[12]

In the nineteenth and twentieth centuries Smith was often seen as an advocate of unbridled capitalism, but his ideas were considerably more complex. In his own mind,

Smith spoke for truth, not for special interests. Unlike many disgruntled merchant capitalists, he applauded the modest rise in real wages of British workers in the eighteenth century and went on to say that "No society can surely be flourishing and happy, of which the far greater part of the members are poor and miserable." Quite realistically, Smith concluded that employers were "always and everywhere in a sort of tacit, but constant and uniform combination, not to raise the wages of labour above their actual rate" and sometimes entered "into particular combinations to sink the wages even below this rate."[13] He also deplored the deadening effects of the division of labor and called for government intervention to raise workers' living standards.

Online Study Center **Improve Your Grade**
Primary Source: *The Wealth of Nations:* A Natural Law of Economy

Smith's provocative work had a great international impact, going through eight editions in English and being translated into several languages within twenty years. It quickly emerged as the classic argument for **economic liberalism.**

Chapter Summary

Online Study Center **ACE the Test**

- *What were the causes and effects of the agricultural revolution, and what nations led the way in these developments?*
- *Why did European population rise dramatically in the eighteenth century?*
- *How and why did economic production intensify in the eighteenth century, particularly in the countryside?*
- *How did colonial markets boost Europe's economic and social development, and what conflicts and adversity did world trade entail?*

While the European educated elite was developing a new view of the world in the eighteenth century, Europe as a whole was experiencing a gradual but far-reaching expansion. As agriculture began showing signs of modest improvement across the continent, first the Low Countries and then England launched changes that gradually revolutionized it. New crops and intensified crop rotation created new food sources for both people and livestock. Enclosure of common land allowed landowners to reap the fruits of agricultural innovation at the cost of excluding poor peasants from their traditional access to the land. The gap between wealthy landowner and landless poor stretched wider in this period.

For reasons historians do not yet understand, the recurring curse of bubonic plague disappeared. Less vulnerable to food shortages and free from the plague, the populations of all European countries grew significantly. During the eighteenth century the European population recovered from the stagnation and losses of the previous century to reach unprecedented new levels.

Population growth encouraged the growth of wage labor, cottage industry, and merchant capitalism. To escape the constraints of urban guilds, merchants transported production to the countryside. Peasant households set up industrial production within their cottages, allocating family members' labor during the slack seasons of agriculture or, in some cases, abandoning farming altogether for a new life of weaving or spinning. The spread of cottage industry was one sign of an "industrious revolution" that helped pave the path of the Industrial Revolution of the late eighteenth century. Women's labor was crucial to the spread of cottage industry and the renewed vitality of the urban trades.

The products of peasant industry were exported across Europe and even across the world. During the eighteenth century Europeans continued their overseas expansion, fighting for empire and profit and, in particular, consolidating their hold on the Americas. A revived Spain and its Latin American colonies participated fully in this expansion. As in agriculture and cottage industry, however, England and its empire proved most successful. The English concentrated much of the growing Atlantic trade in their hands, a development that challenged and enriched

English industry and intensified interest in new methods of production and in an emerging economic liberalism. Thus, by the 1770s England was approaching an economic breakthrough as fully significant as the great political upheaval destined to develop shortly in neighboring France.

Key Terms

open-field system
common lands
agricultural
  revolution
crop rotation
enclosure
proletarianization
cottage industry
putting-out system
guild system

industrious
  revolution
mercantilism
Navigation Acts
Treaty of Paris
Atlantic slave trade
Creoles
debt peonage
mestizos
economic liberalism

 Online Study Center **Improve Your Grade** Flashcards

Suggested Reading

Allen, Robert, et al., eds. *Living Standards in the Past: New Perspectives on Well-Being in Asia and Europe*. 2004. Offers rich comparative perspectives on demographic trends and living standards among common people.

De Vries, Jan, and Ad van der Woude. *The First Modern Economy: Success, Failure, and Perseverance of the Dutch Economy, 1500–1815*. 1997. Examines the early success of the Dutch economy and the challenges it faced in the eighteenth century.

Farr, James R. *Artisans in Europe, 1300–1914*. 2000. Provides an overview of guilds and artisanal labor.

Gullickson, Gary L. *Spinners and Weavers of Auffay: Rural Industry and the Sexual Division of Labor in a French Village, 1750–1850*. 1986. Examines women's labor in cottage industry in northern France.

Harms, Robert W. *The Diligent: A Voyage Through the Worlds of the Slave Trade*. 2002. A deeply moving account of a French slave ship and its victims.

Klein, Herbert S. *The Atlantic Slave Trade*. 1999. An excellent short synthesis on slavery in the Atlantic world.

Liebersohn, Harry. *The Traveler's World: Europe to the Pacific*. 2006. Imaginatively recounts European explorations and imaginations of the Pacific.

Ormrod, David. *The Rise of Commercial Empires: England and the Netherlands in the Age of Mercantilism, 1650–1770*. 2003. Examines the battle for commercial and maritime supremacy in the North Sea.

Overton, Mark. *Agricultural Revolution in England*. 1996. Charts the path of agricultural progress in England.

Porter, Roy. *London: A Social History*. 1994. A sparkling combination of fine scholarship and exciting popular history.

Prak, Maarten, ed. *Early Modern Capitalism: Economic and Social Change in Europe, 1400–1800*. 2001. Collected essays on economic and social developments in early modern Europe.

Rothschild, Emma. *Economic Sentiments: Adam Smith, Condorcet, and the Enlightenment*. 2001. A fascinating reconsideration of Smith and early liberalism.

Notes

1. B. H. Slicher van Bath, *The Agrarian History of Western Europe, A.D. 500–1850* (New York: St. Martin's Press, 1963), p. 240.
2. Quoted in I. Pinchbeck, *Women Workers and the Industrial Revolution, 1750–1850* (New York: F. S. Crofts, 1930), p. 113.
3. Quoted in P. Mantoux, *The Industrial Revolution in the Eighteenth Century* (New York: Harper & Row, 1961), p. 75.
4. Richard J. Soderlund, "'Intended as a Terror to the Idle and Profligate': Embezzlement and the Origins of Policing in the Yorkshire Worsted Industry, c. 1750–1777," *Journal of Social History* 31 (Spring 1998): 658.
5. Ibid. In addition, Jan de Vries, "The Industrial Revolution and the Industrious Revolution," *The Journal of Economic History* 54, 2 (June 1994): 249–270, discusses the second industrious revolution of the second half of the twentieth century.
6. Laurent Dubois and John D. Garrigus, *Slave Revolution in the Caribbean, 1789–1904* (New York: Palgrave, 2006), p. 8.
7. G. Taylor, "America's Growth Before 1840," *Journal of Economic History* 24 (December 1970): 427–444.
8. Seymour Drescher, "Free Labor vs. Slave Labor: The British and Caribbean Cases," in *Terms of Labor: Slavery, Serfdom, and Free Labor*, ed. Stanley L. Engerman (Stanford, Calif.: Stanford University Press, 1999), pp. 52–53.
9. P. E. Lovejoy, *Transformations in Slavery: A History of Slavery in Africa* (Cambridge: Cambridge University Press, 1983), p. 19.
10. J. Inikori, *Africans and the Industrial Revolution in England: A Study in International Trade and Economic Development* (Cambridge: Cambridge University Press, 2002), pp. 481–482.
11. Seymour Drescher, *Capitalism and Antislavery: British Mobilization in Comparative Perspective* (London: Macmillan, 1986), p. 38.
12. Ibid., p. 265.
13. R. Heilbroner, ed., *The Essential Adam Smith* (New York: W. W. Norton, 1986), p. 196.

The Debate over the Guilds

Guilds, also known as trade corporations, claimed that their rules guaranteed fair wages, high-quality goods, and community values. However, both French philosophes and enlightened government officials increasingly disagreed. The first excerpt, from a 1776 law abolishing French guilds by the reform minister Jacques Turgot, is an important example of the liberal critique in action. A vociferous response from the guilds led to the law's repeal only six months later. New guild regulations responded to some of the critiques, for example, by allowing women to join all guilds. In 1791 French revolutionaries definitively abolished the guild system. The second excerpt, from a letter by a Prussian official, explains what it meant "to work free" and testifies to the growth of the putting-out system alongside the guilds in the German states.

Edict Abolishing the Guilds in France

In nearly all the towns of our Kingdom the practice of different arts and crafts is concentrated in the hands of a small number of masters, united in a corporation, who alone have the exclusive right to manufacture and sell particular articles; so that those of our subjects who, through wish or necessity intend to practise in these fields, must have attained the mastership, to which they are admitted only after very long tests which are as difficult as they are useless, and after having satisfied rules or manifold exactions, which absorb part of the funds they need to set up in business or even to exist. . . .

God, in giving man needs, by making work necessary, has made the right to work a universal prerogative, and this is the first, the most sacred and the most indefeasible of all rights.

We regard it as one of the first duties of our law, and one of the acts most worthy of our charity, to free our subjects from all attacks against the inalienable right of mankind. Consequently,

we wish to abolish these arbitrary institutions, which do not allow the poor man to earn his living; which reject a sex whose weakness has given it more needs and fewer resources, and which seem, in condemning it to an inevitable misery, to support seduction and debauchery; which destroy emulation and industry and nullify the talents of those whose circumstances have excluded them from membership of a corporation; which deprive the State and the arts of all the knowledge brought to them by foreigners; which retard the progress of these arts through the innumerable difficulties encountered by inventors with whom different corporations dispute the right to exploit their discoveries . . . which, by the huge expenses artisans are obliged to sustain to obtain the right to work, by their various exactions and frequent fines for alleged illegalities, by all kinds of expenditure, waste and interminable law suits, resulting from the respective claims of all these corporations on the extent of their exclusive privileges, burden industry with an oppressive tax, which bears heavily on the people, and is without benefit to the State; which finally, by the facility they provide for members of corporations to combine to force the poorest members to submit to the laws of the rich, become an instrument of privilege and encourage developments, the effect of which is to raise above their natural level the price of those goods which are most essential for the people.

Breakdown of the Guilds in Germany

Following the repeated complaint of the woollen and worsted weaver named Ast, calling himself a manufacturer of woollen materials, about the runaway apprentice Leder, Your Majesty demanded on 10th and 21st inst. to be informed what the term "to work free" means. It is well known that the [free] woollen and worsted

A German brush maker and guild member shows a customer his wares. *(The Fotomas Index/The Bridgeman Art Library)*

weavers in Germany and abroad are without a guild, that is to say, do not belong to a company which is governed by certain rules or privileges, but follow their trade as woollen and worsted weavers without regulation. For in an organized trade with its own Charter within which it has to operate and which has an assessor appointed whose task it is to see that it is observed, no apprentice may be taken on, unless he first proves by his birth certificate or patent of legitimacy that he was born in wedlock, or legitimized by royal patent. Further, according to the rules of apprenticeship, no apprentice may be given his freedom until his years of apprenticeship are ended according to the registry, and his master declares before the assembled trade when his indenture as journeyman is made out that he has an adequate knowledge of his craft. Similarly, no one can achieve the rights of mastership without having completed two years as journeyman as laid down, and produced the appropriate masterpiece.

All these regulations are omitted in the case of free weavers. For there are really no masters, journeymen and apprentices among them; but if a weaver is able and has resources to set up looms, he sets on workers, usually lads or those who have some knowledge of the trade, who may call themselves apprentices or journeymen, but are not recognized and esteemed as such by those within the guild, since the employer has not produced a masterpiece, the journeymen and apprentices have no indentures or birth certificates, they have no privileges, no assessor, and thus live without a regulation. Such a woollen or worsted weaver will then be called a "free worker." . . .

If such woollen weavers, who have mostly been attracted into the country by the large manufacturers, want to set up here on their own, although they have not been properly brought up within their company, and cannot be accepted as masters, they can receive permission, for themselves only, "to work free." Many of the weavers working "free" have felt the disadvantages of exclusion from their guild, so that some years ago, after some long-drawn-out disputes between the organized and unorganized weavers, they were granted the concession, on certain prescribed conditions, to be accepted as

members of their guilds, whereby the number of unorganized ones has been much reduced, except for the large manufacturers and their workers, who are largely still unorganized.

Such outsiders as have risen to the level of manufacturers, by which it is meant that they man several, perhaps many, looms with unorganized workers, have never been granted this concession, but have, as the term goes, "worked free"; and since they cannot become masters and therefore are not allowed to use the term of master, have termed themselves woollen manufacturers, in order to distinguish themselves from the other excluded, but minor, weavers.

Questions for Analysis

1. How did Turgot justify the abolition of French guilds? Do you think his reasons are valid? How might the guilds respond?

2. How were woolen weavers and their employers organized in Prussia?

3. Do guilds—and modern-day unions—help or hurt workers? Defend your position.

Source: S. Pollard and C. Holmes, eds., *Documents of European Economic History,* vol. 1: *The Process of Industrialization, 1750–1870* (New York: St. Martin's Press, 1968), pp. 53, 55–56. Copyright © S. Pollard and C. Holmes. Reprinted with permission of Palgrave.

A quack doctor uses a snake and a dog to sell a miraculous cure-all in an Italian village market, in a painting (detail) by Michele Graneri (1736–1778). *(Dagli Orti/Private Collection/The Art Archive)*

chapter preview

Marriage and the Family
- *What changes occurred in marriage and the family in the course of the eighteenth century?*

Children and Education
- *What was life like for children, and how did attitudes toward childhood evolve?*

Food, Medicine, and New Consumption Habits
- *How did new patterns of consumption and changing medical care affect people's lives?*

Religion and Popular Culture
- *What were the patterns of popular religion and culture, and how did they interact with the worldview of the educated public and the Enlightenment?*

THE CHANGING LIFE OF THE PEOPLE

T he discussion of agriculture and industry in the last chapter showed the common people at work, straining to make ends meet within the larger context of population growth, gradual economic expansion, and ferocious political competition. The world of work was embedded in a rich complex of family organization, community practices, everyday experiences, and collective attitudes.

In recent years, historians have intensively studied all these aspects of popular life. The challenge has been formidable because regional variations abounded and the common people left few written records. Yet imaginative research has resulted in major findings and much greater knowledge. It is now possible to follow the common people into their homes, workshops, churches, and taverns and to ask, "What were the everyday experiences of ordinary people?"

Marriage and the Family

The basic unit of social organization is the family. It is within the structure of the family that human beings love, mate, and reproduce. It is primarily the family that teaches the child, imparting values and customs that condition an individual's behavior for a lifetime. The family is also an institution woven into the web of history. It evolves and changes, assuming different forms in different times and places.

- *What changes occurred in marriage and the family in the course of the eighteenth century?*

Late Marriage and Nuclear Families

In the previous chapter, we noted the common misconception that populations of the past always grew quickly. Another popular error is that before the modern era people married at a young age and settled in large multigenerational households. In recent years historians have used previ-

Online Study Center
This icon will direct you to interactive activities and study materials on the website **college.hmco.com/pic/mckaywest9e**

ously neglected parish registers of births, deaths, and marriages to uncover details of European family life before the nineteenth century. It is now clear that the extended, three-generation family was a rarity in western and central Europe by 1700. Indeed, the extended family may never have been common in Europe, although it is hard to know about the early Middle Ages because very few records survive. When young European couples married, they normally established their own households and lived apart from their parents. If a three-generation household came into existence, it was usually because a widowed parent moved into the home of a married child.

Moreover, most people did not marry young in the seventeenth and eighteenth centuries. The average person who was neither rich nor aristocratic married surprisingly late, many years after reaching adulthood and many more after beginning to work. In one well-studied, apparently typical English village in the seventeenth and eighteenth centuries, both men and women married for the first time at an average age of twenty-seven or older. A similar pattern existed in eighteenth-century France, where women married around age twenty-five and men around age twenty-seven. A substantial portion of men and women never married at all.

The custom of late marriage combined with a nuclear-family household distinguished European society from other areas of the world. It seems likely that the aggressive dynamism that has characterized European society derived in large part from this marriage pattern. Late marriage joined a mature man and a mature woman—two adults who had already accumulated social and economic capital and could transmit self-reliance and skills to the next generation.

Why was marriage delayed? The main reason was that couples normally did not marry until they could support themselves economically. Peasants often needed to wait until the father's death to inherit land and marry. In the towns, men and women worked to accumulate enough savings to start a small business and establish a household. Most youths began apprenticeships in their mid-teens; given average marriage ages, we may deduce that it took about ten more years of work to earn enough for marriage.

Ten years was a long time for sexually mature young people to wait. Laws and community controls sought to temper impetuous love and physical attraction. In some areas couples needed the legal permission or tacit approval of the local lord or landowner in order to marry. Austria and Germany had legal restrictions on marriage, and well into the nineteenth century poor couples had particular difficulty securing the approval of local offi-

Boucher: The Pretty Cook Increased migration to urban areas in the eighteenth century contributed to a loosening of traditional morals and soaring illegitimacy rates. Young women who worked as servants or shop girls could not be supervised as closely as those who lived at home. The themes of seduction, fallen virtue, and familial conflict were popular in eighteenth-century art, such as this painting by François Boucher (1703–1770), master of the rococo. *(Réunion des Musées Nationaux/Art Resource, NY)*

cials. The officials believed that freedom to marry for the lower classes would mean more landless paupers, more abandoned children, and more money for welfare. Village elders often agreed. Thus prudence, law, and custom combined to postpone the march to the altar. This pattern helped society maintain some kind of balance between the number of people and the available economic resources.

Work Away from Home

Many young people worked within their families until they could start their own households. Boys plowed and wove; girls spun and tended the cows. Many others left home to work elsewhere. In the towns a lad would begin apprenticeship around age fifteen and finish in his late teens or early twenties. During that time he would not be permitted to marry. In most trades he earned little and worked hard, but if he was lucky, he might eventually be admitted to a guild and establish his economic independence. Many poor families could not afford apprenticeship, leaving their sons without the skills and status of guild journeymen. These youths drifted from one tough job to another: hired hand for a small farmer, wage laborer on a new road, carrier of water in a nearby town. They were always subject to economic fluctuations, and unemployment was a constant threat.

Many girls also left their families to work in adolescence. The range of opportunities open to them was more limited, however. Apprenticeship was available in some cities, usually with mistresses in traditionally female occupations like seamstresses, linen drapers, or midwives. With the growth in production of finished goods for the emerging consumer economy during the eighteenth century, demand rose for skilled female labor. Even male guildsmen hired girls and women, despite guild restrictions.

Service in another family's household was by far the most common job for girls, and even middle-class families often sent their daughters into service. The legions of young servant girls worked hard but had little independence. Sometimes the employer paid the girl's wages directly to her parents. Constantly under the eye of her mistress, the servant girl had many tasks—cleaning, shopping, cooking, caring for the baby. Often the work was endless, for there were few laws to limit exploitation. Court records are full of servant girls' complaints of physical mistreatment by their mistresses. There were many like the fifteen-year-old English girl in the early eighteenth century who told the judge that her mistress had not only called her "very opprobrious names, as Bitch, Whore and the like," but also "beat her without provocation and beyond measure."[1]

Male apprentices told similar tales of verbal and physical abuse at their masters' hands. Boys were far less vulnerable, though, to the sexual harassment and assault that threatened female servants. In theory, domestic service offered a young girl protection and security in a new family. But in practice she was often the easy prey of a lecherous master or his sons or friends. Indeed, "the evidence suggests that in all European countries, from Britain to Russia, the upper classes felt perfectly free to exploit sexually girls who were at their mercy."[2] If the girl became pregnant, she could be quickly fired and thrown out in disgrace to make her own way. Prostitution and

Chronology

1717	Elementary school attendance mandatory in Prussia
1720–1780	Government-run foundling homes established
1740–1780	Reign of Maria Theresa in Austria
1740–1786	Reign of Frederick the Great in Prussia
1750–1790	Wesley preaches revival in England
1750–1850	Illegitimacy explosion
1757	Madame du Coudray, *Manual on the Art of Childbirth*
1762	Rousseau advocates more attentive child care in *Emile*
1763	Louis XV orders Jesuits out of France
1775–1783	American Revolution
1789–1799	French Revolution
1796	Jenner performs first smallpox vaccination
1799–1815	Napoleonic era

petty thievery were often the harsh consequences of unwanted pregnancy. "What are we?" exclaimed a bitter Parisian prostitute. "Most of us are unfortunate women, without origins, without education, servants and maids for the most part."[3]

Prostitutes encountered increasingly harsh and repressive laws in the sixteenth and early seventeenth centuries, as officials across Europe began to close licensed brothels and declare prostitution illegal. Despite this repression, prostitution flourished in European cities and towns in the eighteenth century. Most prostitutes were working women who turned to the sex trade when confronted with unemployment or seasonal shortages of work. Such women did not become social pariahs, but retained ties with the communities of laboring poor to which they belonged. If caught by the police, however, they were liable to imprisonment or banishment. Venereal disease was also a constant threat. Farther up the social scale were courtesans whose wealthy protectors provided apartments, servants, beautiful clothing, and cash allowances. After a brilliant, but brief, career, such a woman could descend once more to streetwalking.

Premarital Sex and Community Controls

Did the plight of some former servant girls mean that late marriage in preindustrial Europe went hand in hand with premarital sex and many illegitimate children? For most of western and central Europe until at least 1750, the answer is no. English parish registers seldom listed more than one illegitimate child out of every twenty children baptized. Some French parishes in the seventeenth century had extraordinarily low rates of illegitimacy, with less than 1 percent of the babies born out of wedlock. Illegitimate babies were apparently a rarity, at least as far as the official church records are concerned.

Many unmarried couples satisfied their sexual desires with fondling and petting. Others went further and engaged in premarital intercourse. In one well-studied English village, 33 percent of all first children were conceived before the couple was married, and many were born within three months of the marriage ceremony. In the mid-eighteenth century 20 percent of the women in the French village of Auffay in Normandy were pregnant when they got married, although only 2 percent of all babies in the village were born to unwed mothers. No doubt many of these French and English couples were already betrothed, or at least "going steady," before they entered into intimate relationships, and pregnancy simply set the marriage date once and for all.

The combination of very low rates of illegitimate birth with large numbers of pregnant brides reflects the powerful **community controls** of the traditional village, particularly the open-field village, with its pattern of cooperation and common action. That spirit of common action was rapidly mobilized by the prospect of an unwed (and therefore poor) mother with an illegitimate child, a condition inevitably viewed as a grave threat to the economic, social, and moral stability of the closely knit community. Irate parents, anxious village elders, indignant priests, and stern landlords all combined to pressure young people who wavered about marriage in the face of unexpected pregnancies. In the countryside these controls meant that premarital sex was not entered into lightly and that it was generally limited to those contemplating marriage.

The concerns of the village and the family weighed heavily on most aspects of a couple's life both before and after marriage. Whereas uninvolved individuals today are inclined to stay out of the domestic disputes and marital scandals of their neighbors, the people in peasant communities gave such affairs loud and unfavorable publicity either at the time of the event or during the Carnival season (see page 675). Relying on degrading public rituals, the young men of the village would typically gang up on the person they wanted to punish and force him or her to sit astride a donkey facing backward and holding up the donkey's tail. They would parade the overly brutal spouse-beating husband (or wife), or the couple whose adultery had been discovered, all around the village, loudly proclaiming the offender's misdeeds with scorn and ridicule. The donkey ride and other colorful humiliations ranging from rotten vegetables splattered on the doorstep to obscene and insulting midnight serenades were common punishments throughout much of Europe. They epitomized the community's far-reaching effort to police personal behavior and maintain community standards.

Community controls did not extend to family planning, however. Once a man and a woman married, they generally had several children. Birth control within marriage was not unknown in western and central Europe before the nineteenth century, but it was primitive and quite undependable. The most common method was *coitus interruptus*—withdrawal by the male before ejaculation. The French, who were apparently early leaders in contraception, were using this method extensively to limit family size by the end of the eighteenth century. Mechanical and other means of contraception were also used in the eighteenth century, but mainly by certain sectors of the urban population. The "fast set" of London used the "sheath" regularly, although primarily to protect against venereal disease, not against pregnancy. Prostitutes used various contraceptive techniques to prevent pregnancy, and such information was available in large towns if a person really sought it.

New Patterns of Marriage and Illegitimacy

In the second half of the eighteenth century, the pattern of late marriage and few births out of wedlock began to break down. The number of illegitimate births soared between about 1750 and 1850 as much of Europe experienced an **illegitimacy explosion.** In Frankfurt, Germany, for example, illegitimate births rose steadily from about 2 percent of all births in the early 1700s to a peak of about 25 percent around 1850. In Bordeaux, France, 36 percent of all babies were being born out of wedlock by 1840. Small towns and villages experienced less startling climbs, but between 1750 and 1850 increases from a range of 1 to 3 percent initially to 10 to 20 percent were commonplace. Fewer young people were abstaining from premarital intercourse, and, more important, fewer

David Allan: The Penny Wedding (1795) The spirited merrymaking of a peasant wedding was a popular theme of European artists. In rural Scotland "penny weddings" like this one were common: guests provided cash gifts; any money left after paying for the wedding went to the newlyweds to help them get started. Dancing, feasting, and drinking characterized these community parties, which led the Presbyterian church to oppose them and hasten their decline. *(National Galleries of Scotland)*

young men were marrying the women they got pregnant. Thus a profound sexual and cultural transformation took place.

Historians are still debating the meaning of this transformation, but two interrelated ideas dominate most interpretations. First, the growth of cottage industry created new opportunities for earning a living, opportunities not tied to the land. Cottage industry tended to develop in areas where the land was poor in quality and divided into small, inadequate holdings. As cottage industry took hold in such areas, population grew rapidly because young people attained greater independence and did not have to wait to inherit a farm in order to get married. A scrap of ground for a garden and a cottage for the loom and spinning wheel could be quite enough for a modest living. A contemporary observer of an area of rapidly growing cottage industry in Switzerland at the end of the eighteenth century described these changes:

The increased and sure income offered by the combination of cottage manufacture with farming hastened and multiplied marriages and encouraged the division of landholdings, while enhancing their value; it also promoted the expansion and embellishment of houses and villages.[4]

Cottage workers married not only at an earlier age but also for different reasons. Nothing could be so busi-

nesslike as peasant marriages that were often dictated by the needs of the couples' families. After 1750, however, courtship became more extensive and freer as cottage industry grew. It was easier to yield to the attraction of the opposite sex and fall in love. Members of the older generation were often highly critical of the lack of responsibility they saw in the union of "people with only two spinning wheels and not even a bed." But such scolding did not stop cottage workers from marrying for love rather than for economic considerations as they blazed a path that factory workers would follow in the nineteenth century.

Second, the needs of a growing population sent many young villagers to towns and cities in search of employment. Mobility in turn encouraged new sexual and marital relationships that were less subject to village tradition and more likely to produce illegitimate births. Most young women in urban areas found work only as servants or textile workers. Poorly paid, insecure, and with little possibility of truly independent lives, they looked to marriage and family life as an escape from the vulnerabilities of the single life.

Promises of marriage from a man of the working girl's own class often led to sex, which was viewed as part of serious courtship. In one medium-size French city in 1787–1788, the great majority of unwed mothers stated that sexual intimacy had followed promises of marriage. Their sisters in rural Normandy reported again and again that they had been "seduced in anticipation of marriage."[5] Many soldiers, day laborers, and male servants were no doubt sincere in their proposals. But their lives were also insecure, and many hesitated to take on the burden of a wife and child.

Thus it became increasingly difficult for a woman to convert pregnancy into marriage, and in a growing number of cases the intended marriage did not take place. The romantic, yet practical dreams and aspirations of many young people were frustrated by low wages, inequality, and changing economic and social conditions. Old patterns of marriage and family were breaking down. Only in the late nineteenth century would more stable patterns reappear.

Children and Education

In the traditional framework of agrarian Europe, women married late but then began bearing children rapidly. If a woman married before she was thirty, and if both she and her husband lived to fifty, she would most likely give birth to six or more children. The newborn child entered a dangerous world. Newborns were vulnerable to infectious diseases of the chest and stomach, and many babies died of dehydration brought about by bad bouts of ordinary diarrhea. Of those who survived infancy, many more died in childhood. Even in rich families little could be done for an ailing child. Childbirth could also be dangerous. Women who bore six children faced a cumulative risk of dying in childbirth of 5 to 10 percent, a thousand times as great as the risk in Europe today.[6]

Schools and formal education played only a modest role in the lives of ordinary children, and many boys and many more girls never learned to read. Nevertheless, basic literacy was growing among the popular classes, whose reading habits have been intensively studied in recent years. Attempting to peer into the collective attitudes of the common people and compare them with those of the book-hungry cultivated public, historians have produced some fascinating insights.

● *What was life like for children, and how did attitudes toward childhood evolve?*

Child Care and Nursing

In the countryside, women of the lower classes generally breast-fed their infants for two years or more. Breast-feeding decreases the likelihood of pregnancy for the average woman by delaying the resumption of ovulation. By nursing their babies, women limited their fertility and spaced their children from two to three years apart. If a newborn baby died, nursing stopped, and a new life could be created. Nursing also saved lives: the breast-fed infant received precious immunity-producing substances with its mother's milk and was more likely to survive than when it was given other food.

Women of the aristocracy and upper middle class seldom nursed their own children. The upper-class woman felt that breast-feeding was crude and undignified. Instead, she hired a live-in wet nurse to suckle her child (which usually meant sending the nurse's own infant away to be nursed). Urban mothers of more modest means also relied on wet nurses because they were needed for full-time work. Unable to afford live-in wet nurses, they often turned to the cheaper services of women in the countryside. Rural **wet-nursing** was a widespread business in the eighteenth century, conducted within the framework of the putting-out system. The traffic was in babies rather than in yarn or cloth, and two or three years often passed before the wet-nurse worker in the countryside finished her task. The wet nurse generally had little contact with the family that hired her, and she was expected to privilege the newcomer at the expense of her own nursing child.

Wet-nursing was particularly common in northern France. Whereas the trend was toward more maternal nursing in other parts of Europe, wet-nursing grew substantially in Paris and other northern cities over the eighteenth century. Toward the end of the century roughly twenty thousand babies were born in Paris each year. Almost half were placed with rural wet nurses through a government-supervised distribution network; 20 to 25 percent were placed with Parisian nurses personally selected by their parents; and another 20 to 25 percent were abandoned to foundling hospitals, which would send them to wet nurses in the countryside. The remainder (perhaps 10 percent) were nursed at home by their mothers or live-in nurses.[7]

Reliance on wet nurses contributed to high levels of infant mortality. A study of parish registers in northern France during the late seventeenth and early eighteenth centuries reveals that 35 percent of babies died before their first birthdays, and another 20 percent before age ten.[8] In England, where more mothers nursed, only some 30 percent of children did not reach their tenth birthdays. Frenchwomen also gave birth to more children since nursing tends to slow down the return of fertility after childbirth.

Arrival of the Wet Nurses Wet-nursing was big business in eighteenth-century France, particularly in Paris and the north. Here, rural wet nurses bring their charges back to the city to be reunited with their families after around two years of care. These children were lucky survivors of a system that produced high mortality rates. *(Réunion des Musées Nationaux/Art Resource, NY)*

Why did Frenchwomen send their babies to wet-nurse, given these high mortality rates? Historians have offered several explanations, including parental indifference to the babies' survival. The likeliest explanation appears to be a combination of cultural, socioeconomic, and biological factors. Wet-nursing was a centuries-old tradition in France, so families were merely following well-established patterns. Moreover, in this period migration to the cities, high prices, and stagnant wages pushed more women into the workforce, often into jobs outside the home where it was impossible to nurse their babies. A third factor was that few alternatives existed to breast milk. In an era before germ theory and sterilization, artificial feeding methods were known to be dangerous to the newborn. By turning to wet nurses, mothers who could not nurse sought the safest affordable alternative.

In the second half of the eighteenth century critics mounted a harsh attack against wet-nursing. Upper-class women responded positively to the new mindset, but poor urban women continued to rely on wet nurses until the late-nineteenth-century introduction of sterilized cows' milk and artificial nipples.

Foundlings and Infanticide

The young woman who could not provide for a child had few choices, especially if she had no prospect of marriage. Abortions were illegal, dangerous, and apparently rare. In desperation, some women, particularly in the countryside, hid unwanted pregnancies, delivered in secret, and smothered their newborn infants. If discovered, **infanticide** was punishable by death.

Women in cities had more choices to dispose of babies they could not keep. Foundling homes first took hold in Italy, Spain, and France, spreading to northern and central Europe after 1700. In eighteenth-century England, for example, the government acted on a petition calling for a foundling hospital "to prevent the frequent murders of poor, miserable infants at birth" and "to suppress the inhuman custom of exposing newborn children to perish in the streets." As new homes were established and old ones expanded in the eighteenth century, the number of foundlings being cared for surged. By the end of the century European foundling hospitals were admitting annually about one hundred thousand abandoned children, nearly all of them infants. In the early nineteenth century the foundling home in St. Petersburg had twenty-five thousand children in its care and was receiving five thousand new babies a year. Still, demand always exceeded the supply of places.

Across Europe, foundling homes emerged as a favorite charity of the rich and powerful. At their best eighteenth-century foundling homes were a good example of Christian charity and social concern in an age of great poverty and inequality. Yet the foundling home was no panacea. By the 1770s, one-third of all babies born in Paris were being immediately abandoned to foundling homes by their mothers. Moreover, fully one-third of all those foundlings were abandoned by married couples, a powerful commentary on the standard of living among the working poor, for whom an additional mouth to feed often meant tragedy. The tremendous increase in foundlings resulted not only from a growth in unwanted illegitimate children, but also from the growing tendency of desperately poor parents to abandon children to foundling homes.[9]

Great numbers of babies entered foundling homes, but few left. Even in the best of these homes, 50 percent of the babies normally died within a year. In the worst, fully 90 percent did not survive.[10] They succumbed to long journeys over rough roads, intentional and unintentional neglect by their wet nurses, and customary childhood illnesses. So great were the losses that some contemporaries called the foundling hospitals "legalized infanticide."

Attitudes Toward Children

What were the typical circumstances of children's lives? The topic of parental attitudes toward children in the early modern period remains controversial. Some scholars have claimed that parents did not risk forming emotional attachments to young children because of high mortality

rates. With a reasonable expectation that a child might die, some scholars believe, parents maintained an attitude of indifference, if not downright negligence.

Online Study Center **Improve Your Grade**
Primary Source: Births and Deaths in an English Gentry Family

Certainly, contemporaries were well aware of the dangers of childhood and of the high mortality rates. The great eighteenth-century English historian Edward Gibbon (1737–1794) wrote, with some exaggeration, that "the death of a new born child before that of its parents may seem unnatural but it is a strictly probable event, since of any given number the greater part are extinguished before the ninth year, before they possess the faculties of the mind and the body." Gibbon's father named all his boys Edward after himself, hoping that at least one of them would survive to carry his name. His prudence was not misplaced. Edward the future historian and eldest survived. Five brothers and sisters who followed him all died in infancy.

Emotional prudence could lead to emotional distance. The French essayist, Michel de Montaigne, who lost five of his six daughters in infancy, wrote, "I cannot abide that passion for caressing new-born children, which have neither mental activities nor recognisable bodily shape by which to make themselves loveable and I have never willingly suffered them to be fed in my presence."[11]

In contrast to this harsh picture, however, historians have drawn ample evidence from diaries, letters, and family portraits that many parents did cherish their children and suffered greatly when they died. The English poet Ben Jonson wrote movingly of the death of his six-year-old son Benjamin, which occurred during a London plague outbreak in 1603:

On My First Son
Farewell, thou child of my right hand, and joy;
My sin was too much hope of thee, loved boy.
Seven years thou wert lent to me, and I thee pay,
Exacted by thy fate, on the just day.

In a society characterized by violence and brutality, discipline of children was often severe. The novelist Daniel Defoe (1659–1731), who was always delighted when he saw young children working hard in cottage industry, coined the axiom "Spare the rod and spoil the child." He meant it. So did Susannah Wesley (1669–1742), mother of John Wesley, the founder of Methodism. According to her, the first task of a parent toward her children was "to conquer the will, and bring them to an obedient temper." She reported that her babies were "taught to fear

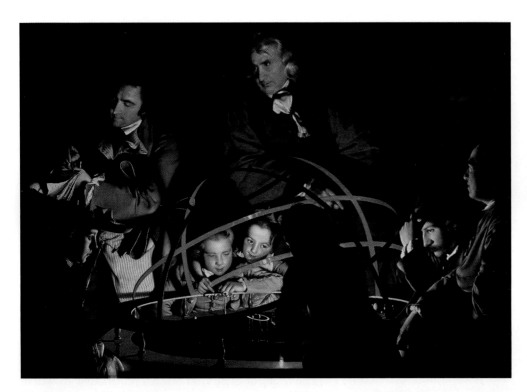

Cultivating the Joy of Discovery This English painting by Joseph Wright of Derby (1734–1797) reflects new attitudes toward child development and education, which advocated greater freedom and direct experience. The children rapturously watch a planetarium, which illustrates the movements and positions of the planets in the solar system. Wise teachers stand by, letting the children learn at their own pace. *(Derby Museum & Art Gallery/The Bridgeman Art Library)*

the rod, and to cry softly; by which means they escaped the abundance of correction they might otherwise have had, and that most odious noise of the crying of children was rarely heard in the house."[12]

The Enlightenment produced an enthusiastic new discourse about childhood and child rearing. Starting around 1760, critics called for greater tenderness toward children and proposed imaginative new teaching methods. In addition to supporting foundling homes and urging women to nurse their babies, these new voices ridiculed the practice of swaddling babies and using rigid whale-boned corsets to form children's bodies properly by "straightening them out." Instead of dressing children in miniature versions of adult clothing, critics called for simpler and more comfortable clothing to allow freedom of movement. These voices belonged to the overall Enlightenment celebration of nature and the natural laws that should guide human behavior. For Enlightenment critics, the best hopes for creating a new society, untrammeled by the prejudices of the past, lay in a radical revision of child-rearing techniques.

One of the century's most influential works on child rearing was Jean-Jacques Rousseau's *Emile*, which fervently advocated breast-feeding and natural dress. Rousseau argued that boys' education should include plenty of fresh air and exercise and that they should be taught practical craft skills in addition to book learning. React-

ing to what he perceived as the vanity and frivolity of upper-class Parisian women, Rousseau insisted girls' education focus on their future domestic responsibilities. For Rousseau, women's "nature" destined them solely for a life of marriage and child rearing. The ideas of Rousseau and other reformers were enthusiastically adopted by elite women, who did not adopt universal nursing but did at least begin to supervise their wet nurses more carefully.

For all his influence, Rousseau also reveals the occasional hypocrisy of Enlightenment thinkers. With regard to the child-rearing techniques he believed would create a better society, Rousseau had extremely high expectations; when it came to the five children he fathered with his common-law wife, however, he abandoned them all in foundling hospitals despite their mother's protests. None are known to have survived. For Rousseau, the idea of creating a natural man was more important than was raising real children.

Schools and Popular Literature

The availability of formal education outside the home increased during the eighteenth century. The aristocracy and the rich led the way in the sixteenth century with special colleges, often run by Jesuits. Schools charged specifically with elementary education of the children of the common people usually did not appear until the

Percentage of bridegrooms able to sign their names on the marriage register, 1786–1790

● Paris

- 80–100
- 50–79
- 20–49
- 0–19
- Unknown

| 0 | 100 | 200 Km. |
| 0 | 100 | 200 Mi. |

Mapping the Past

MAP 20.1 Literacy in France on the Eve of the French Revolution Literacy rates increased but still varied widely between and within states in eighteenth-century Europe. **❶** What trends in French literacy rates does this map reveal? Which regions seem to be ahead? How would you account for the regional variations? **❷** The map is based on the percentage of bridegrooms able to sign their names at marriage. Who is missing from the map? How do you think literacy rates may have varied for people not covered by this source? **❸** Note the areas marked "unknown." Why do you think historians do not know the literacy rates for those areas? What alternate methods might they use to find this information?

seventeenth century. Such schools specialized in teaching seven- to twelve-year-old boys and girls basic literacy, religion, and perhaps some arithmetic for the boys and needlework for the girls.

The religious struggle unleashed by the Protestant and Catholic Reformations promoted popular literacy between 1500 and 1800. Both Protestant and Catholic reformers encouraged reading as a means of instilling their teachings more effectively. Thus literacy was often highest in border areas, such as eastern France, that were open to outside influences and to competition for believers from different churches. The growth of popular education quickened in the eighteenth century, but there was no revolutionary acceleration, and many common people received no formal education.

Prussia led the way in the development of universal education, inspired by the Protestant idea that every believer should be able to read the Bible and by the new idea of a population capable of effectively serving the state. As early as 1717 Prussia made attendance at elementary schools compulsory, and more Protestant German states, such as Saxony and Württemberg, followed in the eighteenth century. Religious motives were also extremely important elsewhere. From the middle of the seventeenth century, Presbyterian Scotland was convinced that the path to salvation lay in careful study of the Scriptures, and it established an effective network of parish schools for rich and poor alike. The Church of England and the dissenting congregations established "charity schools" to instruct poor children, and in 1682 France began setting up Christian schools to teach the catechism and prayers as well as reading and writing. France did less well than the Habsburg state, the only Catholic land to promote elementary education enthusiastically in the eighteenth century. Some elementary education was becoming a reality, and schools were of growing significance in the life of the child.

The result of these efforts was a remarkable growth in basic literacy between 1600 and 1800. Whereas in 1600 only one male in six was barely literate in France and Scotland, and one in four in England, by 1800 almost nine out of ten Scottish males, two out of three French males (see Map 20.1), and more than half of English males were literate. In all three countries, the bulk of the jump occurred in the eighteenth century. Women were also increasingly literate, although they lagged behind men.

The growth in literacy promoted a growth in reading, and historians have carefully examined what the common people read in an attempt to discern what they were thinking. While the Bible remained the overwhelming favorite, especially in Protestant countries, short pamphlets known as chapbooks were the staple of popular literature. Printed on the cheapest paper available, many chapbooks dealt with religious subjects. They featured Bible stories, prayers, devotions, and the lives of saints and exemplary Christians. Promising happiness after death, devotional literature was also intensely practical. It gave the believer moral teachings and a confidence in God that helped in daily living.

Entertaining, often humorous stories formed a second element of popular literature. Fairy tales, medieval romances, true crime stories, and fantastic adventures were some of the delights that filled the peddler's pack as he approached a village. These tales presented a world of danger and magic, of supernatural powers, fairy godmothers, and evil trolls. The significance of these enter-

Raoux: Young Woman Reading a Letter Literacy rates for men and women rose substantially during the eighteenth century. The novel also emerged as a new literary genre in this period. With its focus on emotions, love, and family melodrama, the novel was seen as a particularly feminine genre, and it allowed women writers more access to publication. Writing and reading letters were also associated with women. Some contemporaries worried that women's growing access to reading and writing would excite their imagination and desires, leading to moral dissolution. *(Réunion des Musées Nationaux/Art Resource, NY)*

taining stories for the peasant reader is debated. Many scholars see them reflecting a desire for pure escapism and a temporary flight from harsh everyday reality. Others see the tales reflecting ancient folk wisdom and counseling prudence in a world full of danger and injustice, where wolves dress up like grandmothers and eat Little Red Riding Hoods.

Finally, some popular literature was highly practical, dealing with rural crafts, household repairs, useful plants, and similar matters. Much lore was stored in almanacs, where calendars listing secular, religious, and astrological events were mixed with agricultural schedules, arcane facts, and jokes. The almanac was universal, was not controversial, and was highly appreciated even by many in the comfortable classes. "Anyone who could would read

an almanac."[13] In this way, elites still shared some elements of a common culture with the masses.

While it is safe to say that the vast majority of ordinary people—particularly peasants in isolated villages—did not read the great works of the Enlightenment, that does not mean they were immune to its ideas. Urban working people were exposed to new ideas through the rumor and gossip that spread across city streets, workshops, markets, cafés, taverns, and public gardens. They also had access to cheap broadsides, pamphlets, and newspapers that helped translate Enlightenment critiques into ordinary language. Servants, who usually came from rural areas and traveled home periodically, were well placed to receive ideas from educated employers and disseminate them to the village.

Certainly some ordinary people did assimilate Enlightenment ideals. Thomas Paine, author of some of the most influential texts of the American Revolution, was an English corsetmaker's son who left school at age twelve and carried on his father's trade before emigrating to the colonies. His 1776 pamphlet *Common Sense* attacked the weight of custom and the evils of government against the natural society of men. This text, which sold six hundred thousand copies, is vivid proof of working people's ability to receive Enlightenment ideas; Paine's stirring mastery of them was unique, but his access to them was surely not.

Food, Medicine, and New Consumption Habits

One of the most important developments in European society in the eighteenth century was the emergence of a fledgling consumer culture. Much of the expansion took place in the upper and upper-middle classes, but a boom in cheap reproductions of luxury items also permitted people of modest means to purchase more objects. From food to ribbons and from coal stoves to umbrellas, the material worlds of city dwellers grew richer and more diverse. These developments created new expectations for comfort and hygiene in daily life. Medical practitioners greatly increased in number, although their techniques did not differ much from those of previous generations.

The possibility of picking and choosing among a new variety of consumer goods and provisioners encouraged the development of new notions of individuality and self-expression. A shop girl could stand out from her peers by her choice of a striped jacket, a colored parasol, or simply a new ribbon for her hair. New attitudes about privacy and intimate life also emerged. Whereas families previously shared common living spaces, in the eighteenth century they erected new partitions within their homes to create private nooks. Alongside an upturn in economic production, this "consumer revolution," as it has been called, dramatically changed European life in the eighteenth century. As in other developments, England led the way.

• *How did new patterns of consumption and changing medical care affect people's lives?*

Diets and Nutrition

At the beginning of the eighteenth century, ordinary men and women depended on grain as fully as they had in the past. Bread was quite literally the staff of life. Peasants in the Beauvais region of France ate two pounds of bread a day, washing it down with water, wine, or beer. Their dark bread was made from roughly ground wheat and rye—the standard flour of the common people. The poor also ate grains in soup and gruel. Even peasants normally needed to buy some grain for food, and, in full accord with landless laborers and urban workers, they believed in the moral economy and the idea of the **just price.** That is, they believed that prices should be "fair," protecting both consumers and producers, and that just prices should be imposed by government decree if necessary. When prices rose above this level, they often took action (see page 525).

The rural poor also ate a fair quantity of vegetables. Peas and beans were probably the most common; grown as field crops in much of Europe since the Middle Ages, they were eaten fresh in late spring and summer. Dried, they became the basic ingredients in the soups and stews of the long winter months. In most regions other vegetables appeared in season on the tables of the poor, primarily cabbages, carrots, and wild greens. Fruit was uncommon and limited to the summer months. Milk was used primarily to make cheese and butter, which peasants sold in the market to earn cash for taxes and land rents.

The common people of Europe loved meat and eggs but seldom ate their fill. Indeed, the poor ate less meat in 1700 than in 1500 because their general standard of living had declined as the population surged in the sixteenth century (see page 626) and meat became more expensive. Moreover, harsh game laws in most European countries deprived the poor of the right to hunt and eat game such as rabbits, deer, and partridges. Only nobles and large landowners could legally kill game. Few laws were more bitterly resented—or more frequently broken—by ordinary people than those governing hunting.

The diet of small traders and master craftsmen—the people of the towns and cities—was less monotonous than that of the peasantry. The markets, stocked by market gardens on the outskirts, provided a substantial variety of meats, vegetables, and fruits, although bread and beans still formed the bulk of such families' diets.

The diet of the rich was traditionally quite different from that of the poor. The upper classes were rapacious carnivores, and a truly elegant dinner consisted of an abundance of rich meat and fish dishes, laced with piquant sauces and complemented with sweets, cheeses, and nuts of all kinds. During such dinners, it was common to spend five or more hours at table. There was also an enormous amount of overdrinking. The English squire, for example, who loved to hunt with his hounds loved to drink with a similar passion. Sometimes he ended the evening under the table in a drunken stupor, but very often he did not. Wine and meat were consumed together in long hours of sustained excess, permitting the gentleman and his guests to drink enormous quantities without getting stupefyingly drunk. Gout was a common affliction of the rich. No wonder they were often caricatured as dragging their flabby limbs and bulging bellies to the table to stuff their swollen cheeks and poison their livers.

There were also regional dietary differences in 1700. Generally speaking, northern, Atlantic Europe ate better than southern, Mediterranean Europe. The poor of England and the Netherlands probably ate best of all. Contemporaries on both sides of the Channel often contrasted the English citizen's consumption of meat with the French peasant's greater dependence on bread and vegetables.

Patterns of food consumption changed markedly as the century progressed. There was a general growth of market gardening, and a greater variety of vegetables appeared in towns and cities. This was particularly the case in the Low Countries and England, which pioneered new methods of farming. Introduced into Europe from the Americas—along with corn, squash, tomatoes, and many other useful plants—the humble potato provided an excellent new food source. Containing a good supply of carbohydrates, calories, and vitamins A and C, the potato offset the lack of vitamins from green vegetables in the poor person's diet, and it provided a much higher caloric yield than grain for a given piece of land. After initial resistance, the potato became an important dietary supplement in much of Europe by the end of the century. In the course of the eighteenth century the large towns and cities of maritime Europe also began to receive semitropical fruits, such as oranges and lemons, from Portugal and the West Indies, but they remained expensive.

Royal Interest in the Potato Frederick the Great of Prussia, shown here supervising cultivation of the potato, used his influence and position to promote the new food on his estates and throughout Prussia. Peasants could grow potatoes with the simplest hand tools, but it was backbreaking labor, as this painting by R. Warthmüller suggests. *(Private Collection, Hamburg/akg-images)*

The most remarkable dietary change in the eighteenth century was in the consumption of sugar and tea. No other commodities grew so quickly in consumption. Previously expensive and rare luxury items, they became dietary staples for people of all social classes. This was possible because of the steady drop in prices created by the expansion of colonial production and slave labor. Other colonial goods also became important items of daily consumption in this period, including coffee, tobacco, and chocolate. Part of the motivation for consuming these products was a desire to emulate the habits of "respectable" people. The accelerating pace of work in the eighteenth century also seems to have created new needs for stimulants among working people. (See the feature "Listening to the Past: A Day in the Life of Paris" on pages 678–679.) Whereas the gentry took tea as a leisurely and genteel ritual, the lower classes usually drank tea at work. With the widespread adoption of these products (which turned out to be mildly to extremely addictive), working people in Europe became increasingly dependent on faraway colonial economies. Their understanding of daily necessities and how to procure those necessities shifted definitively, linking them into a globalized capitalism far beyond their ability to shape or control.

Toward a Consumer Society

Along with foodstuffs, all manner of other goods increased in variety and number in the eighteenth century. This proliferation led to a growth in consumption and new attitudes toward consumer goods so wide-ranging that some historians have referred to an eighteenth-century "consumer revolution." The result of this revolution was the birth of a new type of society, in which people had greater access to finished goods and derived their self-identity as much from their consuming practices as from their working lives and place in the production process. The full emergence of a **consumer society** did not take place until much later, but its roots lie in the developments of the eighteenth century.

Increased demand for consumer goods was not merely an innate response to increased supply. Eighteenth-century merchants cleverly pioneered new techniques

The Fashion Merchant's Shop   Shopping in fancy boutiques became a favorite leisure pastime of the rich in the eighteenth century. Whereas shops had previously been dark, cramped spaces, now they were filled with light from large plate-glass windows, staffed by finely dressed attendants, and equipped with chairs and large mirrors for a comfortable shopping experience. Fashion merchants (or milliners) sold hats, shawls, parasols, and an infinite variety of accessories and decorations. (*Courtesy, University of Illinois Library*)

to incite demand: they initiated marketing campaigns, opened fancy boutiques with large windows, and advertised the patronage of royal princes and princesses. By diversifying their product lines and greatly accelerating the turnover of styles, they seized the reins of fashion from the courtiers who had earlier controlled it. Instead of setting new styles, duchesses and marquises now bowed to the dictates of fashion merchants. Fashion also extended beyond court circles to touch many more items and social groups.

Clothing was one of the chief indicators of nascent consumerism. The wiles of entrepreneurs made fashionable clothing seem more desirable, while legions of women entering the textile and needle trades made it ever cheaper. As a result, eighteenth-century western Europe witnessed a dramatic rise in the consumption of clothing, particularly in large cities. One historian has documented an enormous growth in the size and value of Parisians' wardrobes from 1700 to 1789, as well as a new level of diversity in garments and accessories, colors, and fabrics. Colonial economies played an important role, supplying new materials, such as cotton and vegetable dyes, at low cost. Cheaper copies of elite styles made it possible for working people to aspire to follow fashion for the first time.[14] Elite onlookers were bemused by the sight of lower-class people in fashionable dress. In

1784 Mrs. Fanny Cradock described encountering her milkman during an evening stroll "dressed in a fashionable suit, with an embroidered waistcoat, silk knee-breeches and lace cuffs."[15]

Mrs. Cradock's milkman notwithstanding, this was primarily a female phenomenon. Parisian women significantly out-consumed men, acquiring larger and more expensive wardrobes than those of their husbands, brothers, and fathers. This was true across the social spectrum; in ribbons, shoes, gloves, and lace, French working women reaped in the consumer revolution what they had sown in the industrious revolution (see pages 633–634). There were also new gender distinctions in dress. Previously, noblemen vied with noblewomen in the magnificence and ostentation of their dress; by the end of the eighteenth century men had renounced brilliant colors and voluptuous fabrics to don early versions of the plain dark suit that remains standard male formalwear in the West. This was one more aspect of the increasingly rigid opposition drawn between appropriate male and female behavior.

Changes in outward appearances were reflected in inner spaces. Historians have used the probate inventories drawn up by notaries after people's death to peer into ordinary people's homes. In 1700 the cramped home of a modest family consisted of a few rooms, each of which had multiple functions. The same room was used for sleeping, receiving friends, and producing artisanal goods. In the eighteenth century rents rose sharply, making it impossible to gain more space, but families began attributing specific functions to specific rooms. They also began to erect inner barriers within the home to provide small niches in which individuals could seek privacy.

New levels of comfort and convenience accompanied this trend toward more individualized ways of life. In 1700 a meal might be served in a common dish, with each person dipping his or her spoon into the pot. By the end of the eighteenth century even humble households contained a much greater variety of cutlery and dishes, making it possible for each person to eat from his or her own plate. More books and prints, which also proliferated at lower prices, decorated the walls. Improvements in glass-making provided more transparent glass, which allowed daylight to penetrate into gloomy rooms. Cold and smoky hearths were increasingly replaced by more efficient and cleaner coal stoves, which also eliminated the backache of cooking over an open fire. Rooms were warmer, better lit, more comfortable, and more personalized.

The scope of the new consumer economy should not be exaggerated. These developments were concentrated in large cities in northwestern Europe and North America. Even in these centers the elite benefited the most from new modes of life. This was not yet the society of mass consumption that emerged toward the end of the nineteenth century with the full expansion of the Industrial Revolution. The eighteenth century did, however, lay the foundations for one of the most distinctive features of modern Western life: societies based on the consumption of goods and services obtained through the market in which individuals form their identities and self-worth through the goods they consume.

Medical Practitioners

With these advances in daily life, how did the care of sickness, pain, and disease evolve? Medical science continued to struggle in vain against these scourges. Yet the Enlightenment's growing focus on discovering the laws of nature and on human problems did give rise to a great deal of research and experimentation. The century also saw a remarkable rise in the number of medical practitioners. Therefore, when significant breakthroughs in knowledge came in the middle and late nineteenth century, they could be rapidly evaluated and diffused.

Care of the sick in the eighteenth century was the domain of several competing groups: faith healers, apothecaries (or pharmacists), physicians, surgeons, and midwives. Both men and women were prominent in the healing arts, as had been the case since the Middle Ages. But by 1700 the range of medical activities open to women was severely restricted because women were generally denied admission to medical colleges and lacked the diplomas necessary to practice. In the course of the eighteenth century, the position of women as midwives and healers further eroded.

Faith healers remained active. They and their patients believed that demons and evil spirits caused disease by lodging in people and that the proper treatment was to exorcise, or drive out, the offending devil. This demonic view of disease was strongest in the countryside, where popular belief placed great faith in the healing power of religious relics, prayer, and the laying on of hands.

In the larger towns and cities, apothecaries sold a vast number of herbs, drugs, and patent medicines for every conceivable "temperament and distemper." Their prescriptions were incredibly complex—a hundred or more drugs might be included in a single prescription—and often very expensive. Some of the drugs and herbs undoubtedly worked. For example, strong laxatives were given to the rich for their constipated bowels, and regular **purging** of the bowels was considered essential for good health and the treatment of illness. Like all varieties of medical practitioners, apothecaries advertised their wares, their high-class customers, and their miraculous cures in newspapers and commercial circulars. Medicine, like food and fashionable clothing, thus joined the era's new commercial culture.

Physicians, who were invariably men, were apprenticed in their teens to practicing physicians for several years of on-the-job training. This training was then rounded out with hospital work or some university courses. Because such prolonged training was expensive, physicians came mainly from prosperous families, and they usually concentrated on urban patients from similar social backgrounds. They had little contact with urban workers and less with peasants.

Physicians in the eighteenth century were increasingly willing to experiment with new methods, but time-honored practices lay heavily on them. Like apothecaries, they laid great stress on purging, and bloodletting was still considered a medical cure-all. It was the way "bad blood," the cause of illness, was removed and the balance of humors necessary for good health was restored.

Surgeons, in contrast to physicians, made considerable medical and social progress in the eighteenth century. Long considered to be ordinary male artisans comparable to butchers and barbers, surgeons began studying

An Eighteenth-Century Pharmacy   In this lively painting a woman consults an apothecary (in the elegant red suit) while his assistants assemble drugs for new prescriptions. By 1700 apothecaries had emerged as a separate group of state-licensed medical professionals. They drew on published lists and books describing the properties and dosages of their concoctions, but there were many different "recipes" and trade secrets. *(Civico Museo Bibliograco Musicale, Bologna, Italy/ The Bridgeman Art Library)*

anatomy seriously and improved their art. With endless opportunities to practice, army surgeons on gory battlefields led the way. They learned that a soldier with an extensive wound, such as a shattered leg or arm, could perhaps be saved if the surgeon could obtain a flat surface above the wound that could be cauterized with fire. Thus if a soldier (or a civilian) had a broken limb and the bone stuck out, the surgeon amputated so that the remaining stump could be cauterized and the likelihood of death reduced.

The eighteenth-century surgeon (and patient) labored in the face of incredible difficulties. Almost all operations were performed without painkillers, for the anesthesias of the day were hard to control and were believed too dangerous for general use. Many patients died from the agony and shock of such operations. Surgery was also performed in utterly unsanitary conditions, for there was no knowledge of bacteriology and the nature of infection. The simplest wound treated by a surgeon could fester and lead to death.

Midwives continued to deliver the overwhelming majority of babies throughout the eighteenth century. Trained initially by another woman practitioner—and regulated by a guild in many cities—the midwife primarily assisted in labor and delivering babies. She also

treated female problems, such as irregular menstrual cycles, breast-feeding difficulties, infertility, and venereal disease, and ministered to small children.

The midwife orchestrated labor and birth in a woman's world, where friends and relatives offered the pregnant woman assistance and encouragement in the familiar surroundings of her own home. Excluded by tradition and modesty, the male surgeon (and the husband) rarely entered this world, because most births, then as now, were normal and spontaneous. Following the invention of the forceps, which might have helped in exceptionally difficult births, surgeon-physicians used their monopoly over this and other instruments to seek lucrative new business. Attacking midwives as ignorant and dangerous, they persuaded growing numbers of wealthy women of the superiority of their services and sought to undermine faith in midwives.

Recent research suggests that women practitioners successfully defended much but not all of their practice in the eighteenth century. In France one enterprising Parisian midwife secured royal financing for her campaign to teach better birthing techniques to village midwives, which reinforced the position of women practitioners. (See the feature "Individuals in Society: Madame du Coudray, the Nation's Midwife.") In northern Italy state

Individuals in Society

Madame du Coudray, the Nation's Midwife

Plate from Madame du Coudray's manual, illustrating "another incorrect method of delivery." (Rare Books Division, Countway [Francis A.] Library of Medicine)

In 1751 a highly esteemed Parisian midwife left the capital for a market town in central France. Having accepted an invitation to instruct local women in the skills of childbirth, Madame Angelique Marguerite Le Boursier du Coudray soon demonstrated a marvelous ability to teach students and win their respect. The thirty-six-year-old midwife found her mission: she would become the nation's midwife.

For eight years Madame du Coudray taught young women from the impoverished villages of Auvergne. In doing so, she entered into the world of unschooled midwives who typically were solid matrons with several children who relied on traditional birthing practices and folk superstitions. Trained in Paris through a rigorous three-year apprenticeship and imbued with an Enlightenment faith in the power of knowledge, du Coudray had little sympathy for these village midwives. Many peasant mothers told her about their difficult deliveries and their many uterine "infirmities," which they attributed to "the ignorance of the women to whom they had recourse, or to that of some inexperienced village [male] surgeons."* Du Coudray agreed. Botched deliveries by incompetents resulted in horrible deformities and unnecessary deaths.

Determined to raise standards, Madame du Coudray saw that her unlettered pupils learned through the senses, not through books. Thus she made, possibly for the first time in history, a life-size obstetrical model—a "machine"—out of fabric and stuffing for use in her classes. "I had . . . the students maneuver in front of me on a machine . . . which represented the pelvis of a woman, the womb, its opening, its ligaments, the conduit called the vagina, the bladder, and *rectum intestine*. I added an [artificial] child of natural size, whose joints were flexible enough to be able to be put in different positions." Now du Coudray could demonstrate the problems of childbirth, and each student could practice on the model in the "lab session."

As her reputation grew, Madame du Coudray sought to reach a national audience. In 1757 she published the first of several editions of her *Manual on the Art of Childbirth*. Handsomely and effectively illustrated (see the image above), the *Manual* incorporated her hands-on teaching method and served as a text and reference for students and graduates. In 1759 the government authorized Madame du Coudray to carry her instruction "throughout the realm" and promised financial support. Her reception was not always warm, for she was a self-assured and demanding woman who could anger old midwives, male surgeons, and skeptical officials. But aided by servants, a niece, and her husband, this inspired and indefatigable woman took her course from town to town until her retirement in 1784. Typically her students were young peasant women on tiny stipends who came into town from surrounding villages for two to three months of instruction. Classes met mornings and afternoons six days a week, with ample time to practice on the mannequin. After a recuperative break, Madame du Coudray and her entourage moved on.

Teaching thousands of fledgling midwives, Madame du Coudray may well have contributed to the decline in infant mortality and to the increase in population occurring in France in the eighteenth century—an increase she and her royal supporters fervently desired. Certainly she spread better knowledge about childbirth from the educated elite to the common people.

Questions for Analysis

1. How do you account for Madame du Coudray's remarkable success?
2. Does Madame du Coudray's career reflect tensions between educated elites and the common people? If so, how?

*Quotes are from Nina Gelbart, *The King's Midwife: A History and Mystery of Madame du Coudray* (Berkeley: University of California Press, 1998), pp. 60–61. This definitive biography is excellent.

Online Study Center **Improve Your Grade**
Going Beyond Individuals in Society

and church pressures led to major changes in midwife training and certification, but women remained dominant in the birthing trade. It appears that midwives generally lost no more babies than did male doctors, who were still summoned to treat non-elite women only when life-threatening situations required surgery.

Experimentation and the intensified search for solutions to human problems led to some real advances in medicine after 1750. The eighteenth century's greatest medical triumph was the conquest of smallpox. With the progressive decline of bubonic plague, smallpox became the most terrible of the infectious diseases, and it is estimated that 60 million Europeans died of it in the eighteenth century. Fully 80 percent of the population was stricken at some point in life.

The first step in the conquest of this killer in Europe came in the early eighteenth century. An English aristocrat whose beauty had been marred by the pox, Lady Mary Wortley Montagu, learned about the long-established practice of **smallpox inoculation** in the Muslim lands of western Asia while her husband was serving as British ambassador to the Ottoman Empire. She had her own son successfully inoculated with the pus from a smallpox victim and was instrumental in spreading the practice in England after her return in 1722. But inoculation was risky and was widely condemned because about one person in fifty died from it. In addition, people who had been inoculated were infectious and often spread the disease.

Subsequent success in reducing the risks of inoculation and in finding cheaper methods led to something approaching mass inoculation in England in the 1760s. On the continent, the well-to-do were also inoculated, beginning with royal families and then spreading to the middle classes. By the later years of the century smallpox inoculation was playing some part in the decline of the death rate and the general increase in European population.

The final breakthrough against smallpox came at the end of the century. Edward Jenner (1749–1823), a talented country doctor, noted that there was a long-standing belief in the English countryside that dairy maids who had contracted cowpox did not get smallpox. Cowpox produces sores that resemble those of smallpox on the cow's udder and on the hands of the milker, but the disease is mild and is not contagious.

Hospital Life   Patients crowded into hospitals like this one in Hamburg in 1746 had little chance of recovery. A priest by the window administers last rites, while in the center a surgeon coolly saws off the leg of a man who has received no anesthesia. *(Germanisches Nationalmuseum, Nuremberg)*

For eighteen years Jenner practiced a kind of Baconian science, carefully collecting data on protection against smallpox by cowpox. Finally, in 1796 he performed his first vaccination on a young boy using matter taken from a milkmaid with cowpox. After performing more successful vaccinations, Jenner published his findings in 1798. The new method of treatment spread rapidly, and smallpox soon declined to the point of disappearance in Europe and then throughout the world. Jenner eventually received prizes totaling £30,000 from the British government for his great discovery, a fitting recompense for a man who helped lay the foundation for the science of immunology.

Religion and Popular Culture

Though the critical spirit of the Enlightenment made great inroads in the eighteenth century, the majority of ordinary men and women, especially those in rural areas, remained committed Christians. Religious faith promised salvation and eternal life, and it gave comfort and courage in the face of sorrow and death. Religion also remained strong because it was usually embedded in local traditions, everyday social experience, and popular culture.

Yet the popular religion of village Europe was everywhere enmeshed in a larger world of church hierarchies and state power. These powerful outside forces sought to regulate religious life at the local level. Their efforts created tensions that helped set the scene for a vigorous religious revival in Germany and England. Similar tensions arose in Catholic countries, where powerful elites criticized and attacked popular religious practices that their increasingly rationalistic minds deemed foolish and superstitious.

• *What were the patterns of popular religion and culture, and how did they interact with the worldview of the educated public and the Enlightenment?*

The Institutional Church

As in the Middle Ages, the local parish church remained the basic religious unit all across Europe. Still largely coinciding with the agricultural village, the parish fulfilled many needs. The parish church was the focal point of religious devotion, which went far beyond sermons and Holy Communion. It organized colorful processions and pilgrimages to local shrines. Even in Protestant countries, where such activities were severely restricted, congregations gossiped and swapped stories after services, and neighbors came together in church for baptisms, marriages, funerals, and special events. Thus the parish church was woven into the very fabric of community life.

Moreover, the local church had important administrative tasks. Priests and parsons were truly the bookkeepers of agrarian Europe, and it is because parish registers were so complete that historians have learned so much about population and family life. Parishes also normally distributed charity to the destitute, looked after orphans, and provided whatever primary education was available for the common people.

The many tasks of the local church were usually the responsibility of a resident priest or pastor, a full-time professional working with assistants and lay volunteers. All clerics—whether Roman Catholic, Protestant, Greek Orthodox, or Russian Orthodox—also shared the fate of middlemen in a complicated institutional system. Charged most often with ministering to poor peasants, the priest or parson was the last link in a powerful church-state hierarchy that was everywhere determined to control religion down to the grassroots. However, the regulatory framework of belief, which went back at least to the fourth century when Christianity became the official religion of the Roman Empire, had undergone important changes since 1500. The Protestant Reformation had burst forth as a culmination of medieval religiosity and a desire to purify Christian belief. Martin Luther, the most influential of the early reformers, preached that all men and women were saved from their sins and God's damnation only by personal faith in Jesus Christ. The individual could reach God directly, without need of priestly intermediaries.

As the Reformation gathered force, with peasant upheaval and doctrinal competition, German princes and monarchs in northern Europe put themselves at the head of official churches in their territories. Protestant authorities, with generous assistance from state-certified theologians like Luther, then proceeded to regulate their "territorial churches" strictly, selecting personnel and imposing detailed rules. They joined with Catholics to crush the Anabaptists, who, with their belief in freedom of conscience and separation of church and state, had become the real revolutionaries. Thus the Reformation, initially so radical in its rejection of Rome and its stress on individual religious experience, eventually resulted in a bureaucratization of the church and local religious life in Protestant Europe.

The Reformation era also increased the practical power of Catholic rulers over "their" churches, but it was only in the eighteenth century that some Catholic monarchs began to impose striking reforms. These reforms, which had counterparts in Orthodox Russia, had a very "Protestant" aspect. They increased state control over the Catholic Church, making it less subject to papal influence. Spain, a deeply Catholic country with devout rulers, took firm control of ecclesiastical appointments. Papal proclamations could not even be read in Spanish churches without prior approval from the government. Spain also asserted state control over the Spanish Inquisition, which pursued heresy as an independent agency under Rome's direction and went far toward creating a "national" Catholic Church, as France had done earlier.

A more striking indication of state power and papal weakness was the fate of the Society of Jesus, or **Jesuits.** The well-educated Jesuits were extraordinary teachers, missionaries, and agents of the papacy. In many Catholic countries, they exercised tremendous political influence, since individual members held high government positions and Jesuit colleges formed the minds of Europe's Catholic nobility. Yet by playing politics so effectively, the Jesuits eventually elicited a broad coalition of enemies. Bitter controversies led Louis XV to order the Jesuits out of France in 1763 and to confiscate their property. France and Spain then pressured Rome to dissolve the Jesuits completely. In 1773 a reluctant pope caved in, although the order was revived after the French Revolution.

Some Catholic rulers also believed that the clergy in monasteries and convents should make a more practical contribution to social and religious life. Austria, a leader in controlling the church (see page 615) and promoting primary education, showed how far the process could go. Maria Theresa began by sharply restricting entry into "unproductive" orders. In his Edict on Idle Institutions, her successor Joseph II abolished contemplative orders, henceforth permitting only orders that were engaged in teaching, nursing, or other practical work. The state also expropriated the dissolved monasteries and used their wealth for charitable purposes and higher salaries for ordinary priests. These measures recalled the radical transformation of the Protestant Reformation.

Protestant Revival

In their attempt to recapture the vital core of the Christian religion, Protestant reformers had rigorously suppressed medieval practices they considered nonessential or erroneous. For example, they had taken seriously the commandment "Thou shalt not make any graven image" (Exodus 20:4), and their radical reforms had reordered church interiors. Relics and crucifixes were removed, and stained-glass windows were smashed and walls and murals whitewashed. Processions and pilgrimages, saints and shrines—all such practices were eliminated because they had no Scriptural basis. Such revolutionary changes often troubled ordinary churchgoers, but by the late seventeenth century the vast reforms of the Reformation were complete and routinized in most Protestant churches.

Indeed, many official Protestant churches had settled into a smug complacency. In the Reformation heartland, one concerned German minister wrote that the Lutheran church "had become paralyzed in forms of dead doctrinal conformity" and badly needed a return to its original inspiration.[16] His voice was one of many that prepared and then guided a powerful Protestant revival that succeeded because it answered the intense but increasingly unsatisfied needs of common people.

The Protestant revival began in Germany. It was known as **Pietism,** and three aspects helped explain its powerful appeal. First, Pietism called for a warm, emotional religion that everyone could experience. Enthusiasm—in prayer, in worship, in preaching, in life itself—was the key concept. "Just as a drunkard becomes full of wine, so must the congregation become filled with spirit," declared one exuberant writer. Another said simply, "The heart must burn."[17]

Second, Pietism reasserted the earlier radical stress on the priesthood of all believers, thereby reducing the gulf between official clergy and Lutheran laity. Bible reading and study were enthusiastically extended to all classes, and this provided a powerful spur for popular education as well as individual religious development (see page 662). Finally, Pietists believed in the practical power of Christian rebirth in everyday affairs. Reborn Christians were expected to lead good, moral lives and to come from all social classes.

Pietism had a major impact on John Wesley (1703–1791), who served as the catalyst for popular religious revival in England. Wesley came from a long line of ministers, and when he went to Oxford University to prepare for the clergy, he mapped a fanatically earnest "scheme of religion." Like some students during final exams, he organized every waking moment. After becoming a teaching fellow at Oxford, Wesley organized a Holy Club for similarly minded students, who were soon known contemptuously as **Methodists** because they were so methodical in their devotion. Yet like the young Luther, Wesley remained intensely troubled about his own salvation even after his ordination as an Anglican priest in 1728.

Wesley's anxieties related to grave problems of the faith in England. The government shamelessly used the

Hogarth's Satirical View of the Church

William Hogarth (1697–1764) was one of the foremost satirical artists of his day. This image mocks a London Methodist meeting, where the congregation swoons in enthusiasm over the preacher's sermon. The woman in the foreground giving birth to rabbits refers to a hoax perpetrated in 1726 by a servant named Mary Tofts; the credulousness of those who believed Tofts is likened to that of the Methodist congregation. *(HIP/Art Resource, NY)*

trust in Christ, Christ alone for salvation; and an assurance was given me that he had taken away my sins, even mine, and saved me from the law of sin and death.[18]

Wesley's emotional experience resolved his intellectual doubts. Moreover, he was convinced that any person, no matter how poor or uneducated, might have a similarly heartfelt conversion and gain the same blessed assurance.

Wesley took the good news to the people, traveling some 225,000 miles by horseback and preaching more than forty thousand sermons in fifty years. Since existing churches were often overcrowded and the church-state establishment was hostile, Wesley preached in open fields. People came in large numbers. Of critical importance was Wesley's rejection of Calvinist predestination—the doctrine of salvation granted to only a select few. Instead, he preached that *all* men and women who earnestly sought salvation might be saved. It was a message of hope and joy, of free will and universal salvation.

Online Study Center **Improve Your Grade**
Primary Source: Wesley Lays Down the Ground Rules for Methodism

Wesley's ministry won converts, formed Methodist cells, and eventually resulted in a new denomination. And as Wesley had been inspired by the Pietist revival in Germany, so evangelicals in the Church of England and the old dissenting groups now followed Wesley's example, giving impetus to an even broader awakening among the lower classes. In Protestant countries, religion remained a vital force in the lives of the people.

Church of England to provide favorites with high-paying jobs. Building of churches practically stopped while the population grew, and in many parishes there was a shortage of pews. Services and sermons had settled into an uninspiring routine. The separation of religion from local customs and social life was symbolized by church doors that were customarily locked on weekdays. Moreover, Enlightenment skepticism was making inroads among the educated classes, and deism was becoming popular. Some bishops and church leaders seemed to believe that doctrines such as the Virgin Birth were little more than elegant superstitions.

Spiritual counseling from a sympathetic Pietist minister from Germany prepared Wesley for a mystical, emotional "conversion" in 1738. He described this critical turning point in his *Journal:*

In the evening I went to a [Christian] society in Aldersgate Street where one was reading Luther's preface to the Epistle to the Romans. About a quarter before nine, while he was describing the change which God works in the heart through faith in Christ, I felt my heart strangely warmed. I felt I did

Procession of Nuns at Port-Royal des Champs The convent of Port-Royal, located twenty miles southwest of Paris, was a center of Jansenist activity throughout the seventeenth century. Angered by the nuns' defiance, Louis XIV ordered them forcibly relocated in 1709. To generate support, the artist Magdelaine Horthemels painted a series of images depicting the pious and placid religious life at the convent. The convent was nonetheless destroyed by Louis's forces in 1710. This image is one of many copies of Horthemels' work made by Jansenists in the eighteenth century. *(Réunion des Musées Nationaux/Art Resource, NY)*

Catholic Piety

Religion also flourished in Catholic Europe around 1700, but there were important differences from Protestant practice. First, the visual contrast was striking; baroque art had lavished rich and emotionally exhilarating figures and images on Catholic churches, just as Protestants had removed theirs. People in Catholic Europe also remained intensely religious. More than 95 percent of the population probably attended church for Easter Communion, the climax of the Catholic year.

The tremendous popular strength of religion in Catholic countries reflected religion's integral role in community life and popular culture. Thus, although Catholics reluctantly confessed their sins to priests, they enthusiastically joined together in religious festivals to celebrate the passage of the liturgical year. In addition to the great processional days—such as Palm Sunday, the joyful reenactment of Jesus' triumphal entry into Jerusalem—

each parish had its own saints' days, processions, and pilgrimages. Led by its priest, a congregation might march around the village or across the countryside to a local shrine. Before each procession or feast day, the priest explained its religious significance to kindle group piety. But processions were also folklore and tradition, an escape from work, and a form of recreation. A holiday atmosphere sometimes reigned on longer processions, with drinking and dancing and couples disappearing into the woods.

Catholicism did have its own version of the Pietist revivals that shook Protestant Europe. **Jansenism** has been described by one historian as the "illegitimate off-spring of the Protestant Reformation and the Catholic Counter-Reformation."[19] It originated with the Flemish theologian Cornelius Jansen (1585–1638), who called for a return to the austere early Christianity of Saint Augustine. In contrast to the worldly Jesuits, Jansen emphasized the heavy weight of original sin and accepted the doctrine of predestination. Although outlawed by papal and royal edicts as Calvinist heresy, Jansenism attracted Catholic followers eager for religious renewal, particularly in France. Many members of elite French society, especially judicial nobles and some parish priests, became known for their Jansenist piety and spiritual devotion. Such stern religious values encouraged the judiciary's increasing opposition to the monarchy in the second half of the eighteenth century. Among the poor, a different strain of Jansenism took hold. Prayer meetings brought men and women together in ecstatic worship, and some participants fell into convulsions and spoke in tongues.

Jansenism was an urban phenomenon. In the countryside, many peasants in Catholic countries held religious beliefs that were marginal to the Christian faith altogether, often of obscure or even pagan origin. On the Feast of Saint Anthony, for example, priests were expected to bless salt and bread for farm animals to protect them from disease. One saint's relics could help cure a child of fear, and there were healing springs for many ailments. The ordinary person combined strong Christian faith with a wealth of time-honored superstitions.

Inspired initially by the fervor of the Catholic Counter-Reformation and then to some extent by the critical rationalism of the Enlightenment, parish priests and Catholic hierarchies sought increasingly to "purify" popular religious practice. Thus one parish priest in France lashed out at his parishioners, claiming that they were "more superstitious than devout . . . and sometimes appear as baptized idolaters."[20] French priests particularly denounced the "various remnants of paganism" found in popular bonfire ceremonies during Lent, in which young men, "yelling and screaming like madmen," tried to jump over the bonfires in order to help the crops grow and protect themselves from illness. One priest saw rational Christians regressing into pagan animals—"the triumph of Hell and the shame of Christianity."[21]

In contrast with Protestant reformers, many Catholic priests and hierarchies preferred a compromise between theological purity and the people's piety. Thus the severity of the attack on popular Catholicism varied widely by country and region. Where authorities pursued purification vigorously, as in Austria under Joseph II, pious peasants saw only an incomprehensible attack on the true faith and drew back in anger.

Leisure and Recreation

The combination of religious celebration and popular recreation seen in festivals and processions was most strikingly displayed at **Carnival,** a time of reveling and excess in Catholic and Mediterranean Europe. Carnival preceded Lent—the forty days of fasting and penitence before Easter—and for a few exceptional days in February or March, a wild release of drinking, masquerading, and dancing reigned. Moreover, a combination of plays, processions, and rowdy spectacles turned the established order upside down. Peasants dressed up as nobles and men as women, and rich masters waited on their servants at the table. This annual holiday gave people a much-appreciated chance to release their pent-up frustrations and aggressions before life returned to the usual pattern of hierarchy and hard work.

Despite the spread of literacy, the culture of the common people was largely oral rather than written. In the cold, dark winter months, families gathered around the fireplace to talk, sing, tell stories, do craftwork, and keep warm. In some parts of Europe, women would gather together in groups in someone's cottage to chat, sew, spin, and laugh. Sometimes a few young men would be invited so that the daughters (and mothers) could size up potential suitors in a supervised atmosphere. A favorite recreation of men was drinking and talking with buddies in public places, and it was a sorry village that had no tavern. In addition to old favorites such as beer and wine, the common people turned with gusto toward cheap and potent hard liquor, which fell in price because of improved techniques for distilling grain in the eighteenth century.

Towns and cities offered a wide range of amusements. Many of these had to be paid for because the eighteenth century saw a sharp increase in the commercialization of leisure-time activities. Urban fairs featured prepared foods, acrobats, freak shows, open-air performances, optical illusions, and the like. Such entertainments attracted a variety of social classes. So did the growing number of commercial, profit-oriented spectator sports. These ranged from traveling circuses and horse races to boxing matches and bullfights. Modern sports heroes, such as brain-bashing heavyweight champions and haughty matadors, made their appearance on the historical scene.

Blood sports, such as bullbaiting and cockfighting, remained popular with the masses. In bullbaiting the bull, usually staked on a chain in the courtyard of an inn, was attacked by ferocious dogs for the amusement of the innkeeper's clients. Eventually the maimed and tortured animal was slaughtered by a butcher and sold as meat. In cockfighting two roosters, carefully trained by their owners and armed with razor-sharp steel spurs, slashed and clawed each other in a small ring until the victor won—and the loser died. An added attraction of cockfighting was that the screaming spectators could bet on the lightning-fast combat and its uncertain outcome.

Cockfighting in England This engraving by William Hogarth (see also the illustration on page 673) satirizes the popular taste for blood sports, which Hogarth despised and lampooned in his famous *Four Stages of Cruelty*. The central figure in the wildly excited gathering is a blind nobleman who actually existed and seldom missed a fight. Note the steel spurs on the birds' legs. *(Courtesy of the Trustees of the British Museum)*

In trying to place the vibrant popular culture of the common people in broad perspective, historians have stressed the growing criticism levied against it by the educated elites in the second half of the eighteenth century. These elites, which had previously shared the popular enthusiasm for religious festivals, Carnival, drinking in taverns, blood sports, and the like, now tended to see superstition, sin, disorder, and vulgarity.[22] The resulting attack on popular culture, which had its more distant origins in the Protestant clergy's efforts to eliminate frivolity and superstition, was intensified as an educated public embraced the critical worldview of the Enlightenment.

Chapter Summary

Online Study Center **ACE the Test**

- *What changes occurred in marriage and the family in the course of the eighteenth century?*
- *What was life like for children, and how did attitudes toward childhood evolve?*
- *How did new patterns of consumption and changing medical care affect people's lives?*
- *What were the patterns of popular religion and culture, and how did they interact with the worldview of the educated public and the Enlightenment?*

In the current generation, imaginative research has greatly increased our understanding of ordinary life and social patterns of the past. In the eighteenth century the life of the people remained primarily rural and oriented toward the local community. Tradition, routine, and well-established codes of behavior framed much of the everyday experience. Thus just as the three-field agricultural cycle and its pattern of communal rights had determined traditional patterns of grain production, so did community values in the countryside strongly encourage a late marriage age and a low rate of illegitimate births. Yet powerful forces also worked for change. Many came from outside and above, from the aggressive capitalists, educated elites, and government officials discussed in the last two chapters. Closely knit villages began to lose control over families and marital practices, as could be seen in the earlier marriages of cottage workers and in the beginning of the explosion in illegitimate births.

Infancy and childhood were highly vulnerable stages of life. In some parts of Europe fewer than half of all children reached the age of ten. Infant mortality was high in areas, like France, in which wet-nursing was commonly practiced. Treatment of children could be harsh in an early modern society that was characterized by much higher levels of violence and brutality than are Western societies today. The second half of the eighteenth century witnessed a new concern with methods of child raising inspired by Enlightenment efforts to reform human society. Schools for middling and poor children spread across Europe, leading to a growth in literacy rates.

The urban populace benefited from the surge in agricultural and industrial production. People found a greater variety of food products at the market, including new stimulants produced in the colonies that soon became staples of elite and popular consumption. Within homes, standards of comfort and hygiene increased, and the emerging consumer society offered new possibilities for self-expression and individuality. Medical techniques continued to follow traditional patterns, but the number of practitioners grew, and great strides were made against smallpox.

In the background of these changes, patterns of recreation and leisure, from churchgoing and religious festivals to sewing and drinking in groups within an oral culture, reflected and reinforced community ties and values. Many long-standing ideas and beliefs, ranging from obscure religious customs to support for fair prices, remained strong forces and sustained continuity in popular life. A wave of religious revival counteracted the secular tendencies of the Enlightenment, ensuring that religion continued to have a strong hold over the popular classes. The next great wave of change would be inaugurated by revolution in politics.

Key Terms

community controls	smallpox
illegitimacy	inoculation
explosion	Jesuits
wet-nursing	Pietism
infanticide	Methodists
just price	Jansenism
consumer society	Carnival
purging	blood sports

Online Study Center   **Improve Your Grade** Flashcards

Suggested Reading

Brewer, John, and Roy Porter, eds. *Consumption and the World of Goods*. 1993. Pioneering essays from leading scholars on the consumer revolution of eighteenth-century Europe.

Bridenthal, Renate, Susan Mosher Stuard, and Merry Wiesner, eds. *Becoming Visible: Women in European History,* 3d ed. 1998. A valuable starting point for the history of women and gender.

Burke, Peter. *Popular Culture in Early Modern Europe.* 1978. A classic introduction to everyday life, mentalities, and leisure pursuits.

Carrell, Jennifer. *The Speckled Monster: A Historical Tale of Battling Smallpox.* 2003. A lively popular account of the spread of inoculation.

Gelbart, Nina. *The King's Midwife: A History and Mystery of Madame Du Coudray.* 2002. A vivid and accessible biography of the most famous midwife of eighteenth-century France.

Hartman, Mary S. *The Household and the Making of History*. 2004. A bold study of the economic and social ramifications of the European pattern of early marriage.

Kertzer, David I., and Marzio Barbagli, eds. *Family Life in Early Modern Times, 1500–1789.* 2001. A rich collection of essays on the history of the family, women, and children in early modern Europe.

Mintz, Sidney W. *Sweetness and Power: The Place of Sugar in Modern History.* 1985. A fascinating exploration of the shifting cultural significance of sugar and its transformation from elite luxury good to everyday staple.

(continued on page 680)

Listening to the Past

A Day in the Life of Paris

Louis-Sébastien Mercier (1740–1814) was the best chronicler of everyday life in eighteenth-century Paris. His masterpiece was the Tableau de Paris (1781–1788), a multivolume work composed of 1,049 chapters that covered subjects ranging from convents to cafés, bankruptcy to booksellers, the latest fashions to royal laws. As this excerpt demonstrates, he aimed to convey the infinite diversity of people, places, and things he saw around him, and in so doing he left future generations a precious record of the changing dynamics of Parisian society in the second half of the eighteenth century.

Mercier's family belonged to the respectable artisan classes. This middling position ideally suited Mercier for observing the extremes of wealth and poverty around him. Although these volumes contain many wonderful glimpses of daily life, they should not be taken for an objective account. Mercier brought his own moral and political sensibilities, influenced by Jean-Jacques Rousseau, to the task.

Chapter 39: How the Day Goes

It is curious to see how, amid what seems perpetual life and movement, certain hours keep their own characteristics, whether of bustle or of leisure. Every round of the clock-hand sets another scene in motion, each different from the last, though all about equal in length.

Seven o'clock in the morning sees all the gardeners, mounted on their nags and with their baskets empty, heading back out of town again. No carriages are about, and not a presentable soul, except a few neat clerks hurrying to their offices.

Nine o'clock sets all the barbers in motion, covered from head to foot with flour—hence their soubriquet of "whitings"—wig in one hand, tongs in the other. Waiters from the lemonade-shops are busy with trays of coffee and rolls, breakfast for those who live in furnished rooms. . . .

An hour later the Law comes into action; a black cloud of legal practitioners and hangers-on descend upon the Châtelet,* and the other courts; a procession of wigs and gowns and brief-bags, with plaintiffs and defendants at their heels.

Midday is the stockbrokers' hour, and the idlers'; the former hurry off to the Exchange, the latter to the Palais-Royal.† The Saint-Honoré‡ quarter, where all the financiers live, is at its busiest now, its streets are crowded with the customers and clients of the great.

At two o'clock those who have invitations to dine set out, dressed in their best, powdered, adjusted, and walking on tiptoe not to soil their stockings. All the cabs are engaged, not one is to be found on the rank; there is a good deal of competition for these vehicles, and you may see two would-be passengers jumping into a cab together from different sides, and furiously disputing which was first; on which the cabman whips up and drives them both off to the Commissary of Police, who takes the burden of decision off his shoulders.

Three o'clock and the streets are not so full; everyone is at dinner; there is a momentary calm, soon to be broken, for at five fifteen the din is as though the gates of hell were opened, the streets are impassable with traffic going all ways at once, towards the playhouses or the public gardens. Cafés are at their busiest.

Towards seven the din dies down, everywhere and all at once. You can hear the cab-horses' hoofs pawing the stones as they wait—in vain. It is as though the whole town were gagged and bound, suddenly, by an invisible hand. This is the most dangerous time of the whole day for thieves and such, especially towards autumn when the days begin to draw in; for the watch is not yet about, and violence takes its opportunity.

*The main criminal court of Paris.
†The garden surrounded by arcades with shops and cafés constructed by the Duke of Orléans.
‡The neighborhood around the rue Saint-Honoré, between the Palais-Royal and the Place Vendôme; a fashionable quarter for the wealthy.

Night falls; and, while scene-shifters set to work at the play-houses, swarms of other workmen, carpenters, masons and the like, make their way towards the poorer quarters. They leave white footprints from the plaster on their shoes, a trail that any eye can follow. They are off home, and to bed, at the hour which finds elegant ladies sitting down to their dressing-tables to prepare for the business of the night.

At nine this begins; they all set off for the play. Houses tremble as the coaches rattle by, but soon the noise ceases; all the fine ladies are making their evening visits, short ones, before supper. Now the prostitutes begin their night parade, breasts uncovered, heads tossing, colour high on their cheeks, and eyes as bold as their hands. These creatures, careless of the light from shop-windows and street lamps, follow and accost you, trailing through the mud in their silk stockings and low shoes, with words and gestures well matched for obscenity. . . .

By eleven, renewed silence. People are at supper, private people, that is; for the cafés begin at this hour to turn out their patrons, and to send the various idlers and workless and poets back to their garrets for the night. A few prostitutes still linger, but they have to use more circumspection, for the watch is about, patrolling the streets, and this is the hour when they "gather em in"; that is the traditional expression.

A quarter after midnight, a few carriages make their way home, taking the non–card players back to bed. These lend the town a sort of transitory life; the tradesman wakes out of his first sleep at the sound of them, and turns to his wife, by no means unwilling. More than one young Parisian must owe his existence to this sudden passing rattle of wheels. Thunder sends up the birth-rate here too, as it does everywhere else.

At one in the morning six thousand peasants arrive, bringing the town's provision of vegetables and fruits and flowers, and make straight for the Halles;§ their beasts have come eighteen leagues perhaps, and are weary. As for the market itself, it never sleeps. Morpheus never shakes his poppy-seed there. Perpetual noise, perpetual motion, the curtain never rings down on the enormous stage; first come the fishmongers, and after these the egg-dealers, and after these the retail buyers; for the Halles keep all the other markets of Paris going; they are the warehouses whence these draw their supplies. The food of the whole city is

§The city's central wholesale food market.

shifted and sorted in high-piled baskets; you may see eggs, pyramids of eggs, moved here and there, up steps and down, in and out of the throngs, miraculous; not one is ever broken. . . .

This impenetrable din contrasts oddly with the sleeping streets, for at that hour none but thieves and poets are awake.

Twice a week, at six, those distributors of the staff of life, the bakers of Gonesse,** bring in an enormous quantity of loaves to the town, and may take none back through the barriers. And at this same hour workmen take up their tools, and trudge off to their day's labour. Coffee with milk is, unbelievably, the favoured drink among these stalwarts nowadays.

At street-corners, where the pale light from a street lamp falls, the coffee women stand, carrying their tin urns on their backs; they sell their coffee in earthenware cups, two sous a cup, one penny, and not too well sugared at that; but our workmen find it very much to their taste. . . .

So coffee-drinking has become a habit, and one so deep-rooted that the working classes will start the day on nothing else. It is not costly, and has more flavour to it, and more nourishment too, than anything else they can afford to drink; so they consume immense quantities, and say that if a man can only have coffee for breakfast it will keep him going till nightfall. They take only two meals in the twenty-four hours; that at midday and the evening snack of supper, what they call the *persillade*.

Questions for Analysis

1. What different social groups does Mercier describe in Paris? On what basis does he categorize people?

2. What is Mercier's attitude toward the poor and the rich? Does he approve or disapprove of Parisian society as he describes it?

3. How does the division of the day in 1780s Paris compare to your lifestyle today?

**A suburb of Paris, famous for the excellent bread baked there.

Ramsey, Matthew. *Professional and Popular Medicine in France, 1770–1830: The Social World of Medical Practice.* 1988. A good introduction to the medical profession.

Sussman, George D. *Selling Mother's Milk: The Wet-Nursing Business in France, 1715–1914.* 1982. An engrossing account of the large-scale organization of wet-nursing in eighteenth-century France.

Wrightson, Keith. *Earthly Necessities: Economic Lives in Early Modern Britain.* 2000. Examines the economics of everyday life.

Notes

1. Quoted in J. M. Beattie, "The Criminality of Women in Eighteenth-Century England," *Journal of Social History* 8 (Summer 1975): 86.
2. W. L. Langer, "Infanticide: A Historical Survey," *History of Childhood Quarterly* 1 (Winter 1974): 357.
3. Quoted in R. Cobb, *The Police and the People: French Popular Protest, 1789–1820* (Oxford: Clarendon Press, 1970), p. 238.
4. Quoted in D. S. Landes, ed., *The Rise of Capitalism* (New York: Macmillan, 1966), pp. 56–57.
5. G. Gullickson, *Spinners and Weavers of Auffay: Rural Industry and the Sexual Division of Labor in a French Village, 1750–1850* (Cambridge: Cambridge University Press, 1986), p. 186. See also L. A. Tilly, J. W. Scott, and M. Cohen, "Women's Work and European Fertility Patterns," *Journal of Interdisciplinary History* 6 (Winter 1976): 447–476.
6. Pier Paolo Viazzo, "Mortality, Fertility, and Family," in *Family Life in Early Modern Times, 1500–1789,* ed. David I. Kertzer and Marzio Barbagli (New Haven: Yale University Press, 2001), p. 180.
7. George Sussman, *Selling Mothers' Milk: The Wet-Nursing Business in France, 1715–1914* (Urbana: University of Illinois Press, 1982), p. 22.
8. Robert Woods, "Did Montaigne Love His Children? Demography and the Hypothesis of Parental Indifference," *Journal of Interdisciplinary History* 33, 3 (2003): 426.
9. P. Viazzo, "Mortality, Fertility, and Family," in *The History of the European Family,* vol. 1, ed. D. Kertzer and M. Barbagli (New Haven: Yale University Press, 2001), pp. 176–178.
10. Alysa Levene, "The Estimation of Mortality at the London Foundling Hospital, 1741–99," *Population Studies* 59, 1 (2005): 87–97.
11. Cited in Woods, "Did Montaigne Love His Children?," p. 421.
12. Ibid., pp. 13, 16.
13. E. Kennedy, *A Cultural History of the French Revolution* (New Haven: Yale University Press, 1989), p. 47.
14. Daniel Roche, *The Culture of Clothing: Dress and Fashion in the Ancien Regime.* Translated by Jean Birrell (Cambridge: Cambridge University Press, 1996).
15. Quoted in Cissie Fairchilds, "The Production and Marketing of Populuxe Goods in Eighteenth-Century Paris," in *Consumption and the World of Goods*, ed. John Brewer and Roy Porter (London: Routledge, 1993), p. 228.
16. Quoted in K. Pinson, *Pietism as a Factor in the Rise of German Nationalism* (New York: Columbia University Press, 1934), p. 13.
17. Ibid., pp. 43–44.
18. Quoted in S. Andrews, *Methodism and Society* (London: Longmans, Green, 1970), p. 327.
19. Dale Van Kley, "The Rejuvenation and Rejection of Jansenism in History and Historiography," *French Historical Studies* 29 (Fall 2006): 649–684.
20. Quoted in I. Woloch, *Eighteenth-Century Europe: Tradition and Progress, 1715–1789* (New York: W. W. Norton, 1982), p. 292.
21. Quoted in T. Tackett, *Priest and Parish in Eighteenth-Century France* (Princeton, N.J.: Princeton University Press, 1977), p. 214.
22. Woloch, *Eighteenth-Century Europe,* pp. 220–221; see also pp. 214–220 for this section.

In this painting by the female artist Nanine Vallain, the figure of Liberty bears a copy of the Declaration of the Rights of Man and of the Citizen in one hand and a pike to defend them in the other. The painting hung in the Jacobin club until its fall from power. *(Musée de la Revolution Française, Vizille/The Bridgeman Art Library)*

THE REVOLUTION IN POLITICS, 1775–1815

The last years of the eighteenth century were a time of great upheaval. A series of revolutions and revolutionary wars challenged the old order of monarchs and aristocrats. The ideas of freedom and equality, ideas that have not stopped shaping the world since that era, flourished and spread. The revolutionary era began in North America in 1775. Then in 1789 France, the most influential country in Europe, became the leading revolutionary nation. It established first a constitutional monarchy, then a radical republic, and finally a new empire under Napoleon. Inspired by both the ideals of the Revolution and internal colonial conditions, the slaves of Saint-Domingue rose up in 1791. Their rebellion led to the creation of the new independent nation of Haiti in 1805.

The armies of France violently exported revolution beyond the nation's borders in an effort to establish new governments throughout much of Europe. The world of modern domestic and international politics was born.

Background to Revolution

Since July 1789 the origins of the French Revolution have been one of the most debated topics in history. Historians long explained the Revolution as a clash between the rising bourgeoisie and the entrenched nobility in which the former asserted its right to political power commensurate with its new economic strength. It is now apparent that such a simplistic explanation cannot account for the complexity of an event that spanned several decades and involved millions of people and numerous nations. In uncovering the path to revolution, numerous interrelated factors must be taken into account. These include deep social changes in France, a long-term political crisis that eroded monarchical legitimacy, the impact of new political ideas derived from the Enlightenment, the emergence of a "public sphere" in which such opinions were formed and shared, and, perhaps most importantly, a financial crisis created by France's participation in expensive overseas wars.

Online Study Center

This icon will direct you to interactive activities and study materials on the website **college.hmco.com/pic/mckaywest9e**

While these developments built a thirst for fundamental political reform, there was nothing inevitable in the unfolding of the Revolution. As in many historical events, chance played a significant role in leading the French to revolution and in the course of events after its outbreak. Examining the background of institutions, events, and ideas helps explain how the fascinating and complex phenomenon known as the French Revolution came into being.

• *What social, political, and economic factors formed the background to the French Revolution?*

Legal Orders and Social Change

As in the Middle Ages, France's 25 million inhabitants were still legally divided into three orders, or **estates**— the clergy, the nobility, and everyone else. As the nation's first estate, the clergy numbered about one hundred thousand and had important privileges. It owned about 10 percent of the land and paid only a "voluntary gift," rather than regular taxes, to the government every five years. Moreover, the church levied a tax (the tithe) on landowners, which averaged somewhat less than 10 percent.

The second estate consisted of some four hundred thousand nobles, the descendants of "those who fought" in the Middle Ages. Nobles owned about 25 percent of the land in France outright, and they too were lightly taxed. Moreover, nobles continued to enjoy certain **manorial rights,** or privileges of lordship, that dated back to medieval times. These included exclusive rights to hunt and fish, village monopolies on baking bread and pressing grapes for wine, fees for justice, and a host of other "useful privileges." In addition, nobles had "honorific privileges" such as the right to precedence on public occasions and the right to wear swords. These rights conspicuously proclaimed the nobility's legal superiority and exalted social position.

Everyone else was a commoner, legally a member of the third estate. A few commoners—prosperous merchants, lawyers, and officials—were well educated and rich, and they might even have purchased manorial rights as a way of obtaining profit and social honor. The vast majority of the third estate consisted of peasants and agricultural workers in the countryside and urban artisans and unskilled day laborers. Thus the third estate was a conglomeration of very different social groups united only by their shared legal status as distinct from the nobility and clergy.

The Three Estates In this political cartoon from 1789 a peasant of the third estate struggles under the crushing burden of a happy clergyman and a plumed nobleman. The caption—"Let's hope this game ends soon"—sets forth a program of reform that any peasant could understand. (*Réunion des Musées Nationaux/Art Resource, NY*)

In discussing the origins of the French Revolution, historians long focused on growing tensions between the nobility and the comfortable members of the third estate, the *bourgeoisie* or upper middle class. Increasing in size, wealth, culture, and self-confidence, this rising bourgeoisie became progressively exasperated by archaic "feudal" laws restraining the economy and by the pretensions of a reactionary nobility that was closing ranks against middle-class aspirations. As a result, the French bourgeoisie eventually rose up to lead the entire third estate in a great social revolution that destroyed feudal privileges and established a capitalist order based on individualism and a market economy.

In recent years, a flood of new research has challenged these accepted views. Above all, revisionist historians have questioned the existence of growing social conflict between a progressive capitalistic bourgeoisie and a reactionary feudal nobility in eighteenth-century France. Instead, they see both bourgeoisie and nobility as highly fragmented, riddled with internal rivalries. The ancient sword nobility, for example, was profoundly separated from the newer robe nobility by differences in wealth, education, and worldview. Differences within the bourgeoisie—between wealthy financiers and local lawyers, for example—were no less profound. Rather than standing as unified blocs against each other, nobility and bourgeoisie formed two parallel social ladders increasingly linked together at the top by wealth, marriage, and Enlightenment culture.

Revisionist historians stress three developments in particular. First, the nobility remained a fluid and relatively open order. Throughout the eighteenth century substantial numbers of successful commoners continued to seek and obtain noble status through government service and purchase of expensive positions conferring nobility. Second, key sections of the nobility were no less liberal than the middle class, and until revolution actually began, both groups generally supported the judicial opposition to the government led by the Parlement of Paris. Third, the nobility and the bourgeoisie were not really at odds in the economic sphere. Investment in land and government service were the preferred activities of both groups, and the ideal of the merchant capitalist was to gain enough wealth to retire from trade, purchase an estate, and live nobly as a large landowner. At the same time, wealthy nobles often acted as aggressive capitalists, investing especially in mining, metallurgy, and foreign trade.

Revisionists have clearly shaken the belief that the bourgeoisie and the nobility were inevitably locked in growing conflict before the Revolution. But in stressing the similarities between the two groups, especially at the top, revisionists have also reinforced the view that the Old Regime had ceased to correspond with social reality by the 1780s. Legally, society was still based on rigid orders inherited from the Middle Ages. In reality, France had already moved far toward being a society based on wealth and education in which an emerging elite that included both aristocratic and bourgeois notables was frustrated by a bureaucratic monarchy that continued to claim the right to absolute power.

Chronology

1773	Boston Tea Party
1775	Paine, *Common Sense*
1775–1783	American Revolution
1786–1789	Financial crisis in France
1789	Feudalism abolished in France; ratification of U.S. Constitution; storming of the Bastille
1789–1799	French Revolution
1790	Burke, *Reflections on the Revolution in France*
1791	Slave insurrection in Saint-Domingue
1792	Wollstonecraft, *A Vindication of the Rights of Woman*
1793	Execution of Louis XVI
1793–1794	Economic controls to help poor in France; Robespierre's Reign of Terror
1794	Robespierre deposed and executed
1794–1799	Thermidorian reaction
1799–1815	Napoleonic era
1805	Haitian republic declares independence
1812	Napoleon invades Russia
1814–1815	Napoleon defeated and exiled

The Crisis of Political Legitimacy

Overlaying these social changes was a century-long political and fiscal struggle between the monarchy and its opponents that was primarily enacted in the law courts. When Louis XIV finally died in 1715 and was succeeded by his five-year-old great-grandson, Louis XV (r. 1715–1774), the Sun King's elaborate system of absolutist rule was challenged. Favored by the duke of Orléans (1674–1723), who governed as regent until 1723, a number of institutions retrieved powers they had lost under Louis XIV. Instead of assuming personal rule, the regent reinstated councils of state to aid in decision making.

Most important, in 1715 the duke restored to the high courts of France—the parlements—the ancient right to evaluate royal decrees publicly in writing before they were registered and given the force of law. The restoration of this right, which had been suspended under Louis XIV, was a fateful step. The magistrates of the parlements were leaders of the robe nobility. In 1604 Henry IV had created the paulette (see page 528) on royal offices as a way to raise desperately needed revenue. The unintended consequence of this act was to transform royal offices, including judicial positions, into a form of private property passed down from father to son. By allowing a well-entrenched and highly articulate branch of the nobility to evaluate the king's decrees before they became law, the duke of Orléans sanctioned a counterweight to absolute power.

These implications became clear when the heavy expenses of the War of the Austrian Succession plunged France into financial crisis. In 1748 Louis XV appointed a finance minister who decreed a 5 percent income tax on every individual regardless of social status. Exemption from most taxation had long been a hallowed privilege of the nobility, and other important groups—the clergy, the large towns, and some wealthy bourgeoisie—had also gained special tax advantages over time. The result was a vigorous protest from many sides led by the influential Parlement of Paris. The monarchy retreated; the new tax was dropped.

Following the disastrously expensive Seven Years' War (see pages 635–637), the conflict re-emerged. The government tried to maintain emergency taxes after the war ended; the Parlement of Paris protested and even challenged the basis of royal authority, claiming that the king's power had to be limited to protect liberty. Once again the government caved in and withdrew the taxes. The judicial opposition then asserted that the king could not levy taxes without the consent of the Parlement of Paris, which was acting as the representative of the entire nation.

After years of attempting to compromise with the parlements, Louis XV roused himself for a determined defense of his absolutist inheritance. "The magistrates," he angrily told the Parlement of Paris in a famous face-to-face confrontation, "are my officers. . . . In my person only does the sovereign power rest."[1] In 1768 Louis appointed a tough career official named René de Maupeou as chancellor and ordered him to crush the judicial opposition.

Maupeou abolished the existing parlements and exiled the vociferous members of the Parlement of Paris to the provinces. He created a new and docile parlement of royal officials, known as the **Maupeou parlements,** and he began once again to tax the privileged groups. A few

philosophes applauded these measures: the sovereign was using his power to introduce badly needed reforms that had been blocked by a self-serving aristocratic elite. Most philosophes, and public opinion as a whole, sided with the old parlements, however, and there was widespread criticism of "royal despotism."

Learned dissent was accompanied by scandalous libels. Known as Louis *le bien-aimé* (beloved Louis) in his youth, the king found his people turning against him for moral as well as political reasons. Kings had always maintained mistresses who were invariably chosen from the court nobility. Louis XV broke that pattern with Madame de Pompadour, daughter of a disgraced bourgeois financier. As favorite from 1745 to 1750, Pompadour exercised tremendous influence over literature, art, and the decorative arts, using her patronage to support Voltaire and promote the rococo style. Even after their love affair ended, Pompadour wielded considerable influence over the king, helping bring about the alliance with Austria that resulted in the Seven Years' War. Pompadour's low birth and hidden political influence generated a stream of resentful pamphleteering.

After Pompadour, the king appeared to sink ever lower in licentiousness; his last favorite, Madame du Barry, was derided as a common streetwalker, and the king was accused of maintaining a brothel of teenage girls at Versailles to serve his lusts. The illegal stream of scandal-mongering became a torrent. Lurid and pornographic depictions of the court ate away at the foundations of royal authority, especially among the common people in turbulent Paris. The king was being stripped of the sacred aura of God's anointed on earth and was being reinvented in the popular imagination as a degenerate.

Despite this progressive **desacralization** of the monarchy, its power was still great enough to ride over the opposition, and Louis XV would probably have prevailed if he had lived to a ripe old age, but he died in 1774. The new king, Louis XVI (r. 1774–1792), was a shy twenty-year-old with good intentions. Taking the throne, he is reported to have said, "What I should like most is to be loved."[2] The eager-to-please monarch yielded in the face of vehement opposition from France's educated elite. He dismissed chancellor Maupeou and repudiated the strong-willed minister's work. Louis also waffled on the economy, dismissing controller-general Turgot when his attempts to liberalize the economy drew fire. A weakened but unreformed monarchy now faced a judicial opposition that claimed to speak for the entire French nation. Increasingly locked in stalemate, the country was drifting toward renewed financial crisis and political upheaval.

The Impact of the American Revolution

Coinciding with the first years of Louis XVI's reign, the American Revolution had an enormous impact on France both in practical and ideological terms. French expenses to support the colonists bankrupted the Crown, while the ideals of liberty and equality provided heady inspiration for political reform.

Like the French Revolution, the American Revolution had its immediate origins in struggles over increased taxes. The high cost of the Seven Years' War—fought with little financial contribution from the colonies—doubled the British national debt. When the government tried to recoup some of the losses in increased taxes on the colonies in 1765, the colonists reacted with anger.

The key questions were political rather than economic. To what extent could the home government assert its power while limiting the authority of colonial legislatures and their elected representatives? Accordingly, who should represent the colonies, and who had the right to make laws for Americans? The British government replied that Americans were represented in Parliament, albeit indirectly (like most British people themselves), and that the absolute supremacy of Parliament throughout the empire could not be questioned. Many Americans felt otherwise.

In 1773 the dispute over taxes and representation flared up again after the British government awarded a monopoly on Chinese tea to the East India Company, suddenly excluding colonial merchants from a lucrative business. In response, Boston men disguised as Indians held a rowdy "tea party" and threw the company's tea into the harbor. This led to extreme measures. The so-called Coercive Acts closed the port of Boston, curtailed local elections, and greatly expanded the royal governor's power. County conventions in Massachusetts protested vehemently and urged that the acts be "rejected as the attempts of a wicked administration to enslave America." Other colonial assemblies joined in the denunciations. In September 1774 the First Continental Congress met in Philadelphia, where the more radical members argued successfully against concessions to the Crown. Compromise was also rejected by the British Parliament, and in April 1775 fighting began at Lexington and Concord.

The fighting spread, and the colonists moved slowly but inevitably toward open rebellion and a declaration of independence. The uncompromising attitude of the British government and its use of German mercenaries dissolved long-standing loyalties to the home country and rivalries among the separate colonies. Some colonists

Toward Revolution in Boston The Boston Tea Party was only one of many angry confrontations between British officials and Boston patriots. On January 27, 1774, an angry crowd seized a British customs collector and tarred and feathered him. This French engraving of 1784 commemorates the defiant and provocative action. *(The Granger Collection, New York)*

remained loyal to the Crown; large numbers of these Loyalists emigrated to the northern colonies of Canada.

On July 4, 1776, the Second Continental Congress adopted the Declaration of Independence. Written by Thomas Jefferson, it boldly listed the tyrannical acts committed by George III (r. 1760–1820) and confidently proclaimed the natural rights of mankind and the **sovereignty** of the American states. Sometimes called the world's greatest political editorial, the Declaration of Independence in effect universalized the traditional rights of English people and made them the rights of all mankind. It stated that "all men are created equal. . . . They are endowed by their Creator with certain unalienable rights. . . . Among these are life, liberty, and the pursuit of happiness."

On the international scene, the French wanted revenge for the humiliating defeats of the Seven Years' War.

They sympathized with the rebels and supplied guns and gunpowder from the beginning. By 1777 French volunteers were arriving in Virginia, and a dashing young nobleman, the marquis de Lafayette (1757–1834), quickly became one of George Washington's most trusted generals. In 1778 the French government offered a formal alliance to the American ambassador in Paris, Benjamin Franklin, and in 1779 and 1780 the Spanish and Dutch declared war on Britain. Catherine the Great of Russia helped organize the League of Armed Neutrality in order to protect neutral shipping rights, which Britain refused to recognize.

Thus by 1780 Great Britain was engaged in an imperial war against most of Europe as well as against the thirteen colonies. In these circumstances, and in the face of severe reverses, a new British government decided to cut its losses and offered peace on extremely generous terms. By the Treaty of Paris of 1783, Britain recognized the independence of the thirteen colonies and ceded all its territory between the Allegheny Mountains and the Mississippi River to the Americans. Out of the bitter rivalries of the Old World, the Americans snatched dominion over a vast territory.

Europeans who dreamed of a new era were fascinated by the political lessons of the American Revolution. The Americans had begun with a revolutionary defense against tyrannical oppression, and they had been victorious. They had then shown how rational beings could assemble together to exercise sovereignty and write a permanent constitution—a new social contract. All this gave greater reality to the concepts of individual liberty and representative government and reinforced one of the primary ideas of the Enlightenment: that a better world was possible.

No country felt the consequences of the American Revolution more directly than France. Hundreds of French officers served in America and were inspired by the experience, the marquis de Lafayette chief among them. French intellectuals and publicists engaged in passionate analysis of the new federal Constitution as well as the constitutions of the various states of the new United States. Perhaps more importantly, the expenses of supporting the revolutionary forces provided the last nail in the coffin for the French treasury.

Financial Crisis

The French Revolution thus had its immediate origins in the financial difficulties of the government. The efforts of Louis XV's ministers to raise taxes had been thwarted by the high courts, led by the Parlement of Paris, which was strengthened in its opposition by widespread popular support. When renewed efforts to reform the tax system met a similar fate in 1776, the government was forced to finance all of its enormous expenditures during the American war with borrowed money. As a result, the national debt and the annual budget deficit soared.

By the 1780s, fully 50 percent of France's annual budget went for interest payments on the debt. Another 25 percent went to maintain the military, while 6 percent was absorbed by the king and his court at Versailles. Less than 20 percent of the entire national budget was available for the productive functions of the state, such as transportation and general administration. This was an impossible financial situation.

One way out would have been for the government to declare partial bankruptcy, forcing its creditors to accept greatly reduced payments on the debt. The Spanish monarchy had regularly repudiated large portions of its debt in earlier times, and France had done likewise after an attempt to establish a national bank ended in financial disaster in 1720. Yet by the 1780s the French debt was being held by an army of aristocratic and bourgeois creditors, and the French monarchy, though absolute in theory, had become too weak for such a drastic and unpopular action.

Nor could the king and his ministers print money and create inflation to cover their deficits. Unlike England and Holland, which had far larger national debts relative to their populations, France had no central bank, no paper currency, and no means of creating credit. French money was good gold coin. Therefore, when a depressed economy and public distrust made it increasingly difficult for the government to obtain new gold loans in 1786, it had no alternative but to try to increase taxes. Since France's tax system was unfair and out-of-date, increased revenues were possible only through fundamental reform. Such reforms, which would affect all groups in France's complex and fragmented society, opened a Pandora's box of social and political demands.

The Revolution was looming by 1787, though no one could have realized what was to follow. Spurred by a depressed economy and falling tax receipts, Louis XVI's minister of finance revived old proposals to impose a general tax on all landed property as well as to form provincial assemblies to help administer the tax, and he convinced the king to call an **Assembly of Notables** to gain support for the idea. The notables, who were mainly important noblemen and high-ranking clergy, opposed the new tax. In exchange for their support, they demanded that control over all government spending be given to the provincial assemblies. When the government refused, the notables responded that such sweeping tax changes required the approval of the Estates General, the representative body of all three estates, which had not met since 1614.

Facing imminent bankruptcy, the king tried to reassert his authority. He dismissed the notables and established new taxes by decree. In stirring language, the judges of the Parlement of Paris promptly declared the royal initiative null and void. When the king tried to exile the judges, a tremendous wave of protest swept the country. Frightened investors also refused to advance more loans to the state. Finally, in July 1788, Louis XVI bowed to public opinion and called for a spring session of the Estates General.

Revolution in Metropole and Colony, 1789–1791

Although inspired by the ideals of the American Revolution, the French Revolution did not mirror the American example. It was more radical and more complex, more influential and more controversial, more loved and more hated. For Europeans and most of the rest of the world, it was the great revolution of the eighteenth century, *the* revolution that opened the modern era in politics. In turn, the slave insurrection in Saint-Domingue—which ultimately resulted in the second independent republic of the Americas—inspired liberation movements across the world.

• *What were the immediate events that sparked the Revolution, and how did they result in the formation of a constitutional monarchy in France? How did the ideals and events of the early Revolution raise new aspirations in the colonies?*

The Formation of the National Assembly

Once Louis had agreed to hold the **Estates General,** following precedent, he set elections for the three orders. As at previous meetings of the Estates General, local assemblies were to prepare a list of grievances for their representatives to bring to the next electoral level. This request, as traditional as it was, set off a flood of debate, criticism, and demands throughout France. All across the country, clergy, nobles, and commoners came together in their respective orders to draft petitions for change and to elect delegates to the Estates General. These documents reveal the main complaints French subjects had on

the eve of revolution. The local assemblies of the clergy showed considerable dissatisfaction with the church hierarchy. The nobles were politically divided. A conservative majority was drawn from the poorer and more numerous provincial nobility, but fully one-third of the nobility's representatives were liberals committed to major changes.

As for the third estate, there was great popular participation in the elections. Almost all male commoners twenty-five years of age and older had the right to vote. However, most of the representatives selected by the third estate were well-educated, prosperous members of the middle class. Most were not businessmen but rather lawyers and government officials. Social status and prestige were matters of particular concern to this economic elite. No delegates from the great mass of laboring poor—the peasants and urban artisans—were elected.

The petitions for change coming from the three estates showed a surprising degree of consensus. There was general agreement that royal absolutism should give way to a constitutional monarchy in which laws and taxes would require the consent of the Estates General in regular meetings. All agreed that individual liberties would have to be guaranteed by law and that economic regulations should be loosened. The striking similarities in the grievance petitions of the clergy, nobility, and third estate reflected a shared commitment to a basic reform platform among the educated elite.

Online Study Center **Improve Your Grade**
Primary Source: The Third Estate Speaks: The Cahier de Doleances of the Carcassonne

Yet an increasingly bitter quarrel undermined this consensus during the intense electoral campaign: *how* would the Estates General vote, and precisely *who* would lead in the political reorganization that was generally desired? The Estates General of 1614 had sat as three separate houses. Each house held one vote, despite the enormous numerical discrepancies between the estates in the general population. Given the close ties between them, the nobility and clergy would control all decisions. As soon as the estates were called, the aristocratic Parlement of Paris, mainly out of respect for tradition but partly out of a desire to enhance the nobility's political position, ruled that the Estates General should once again sit separately. The ruling was quickly denounced by some intellectuals, who demanded instead a single assembly dominated by the third estate to ensure fundamental reforms. In his famous 1789 pamphlet *What Is the Third Estate?* the abbé Emmanuel Joseph Sieyès argued that the nobility was a tiny, overprivileged minority and that the neglected third estate constituted the true strength of the French nation. When the government agreed that the third estate should have as many delegates as the clergy and the nobility combined but then rendered this act meaningless by upholding voting by separate order, reform-minded critics saw fresh evidence of an aristocratic conspiracy.

In May 1789 the twelve hundred delegates of the three estates paraded in medieval pageantry through the streets of Versailles to an opening session resplendent with feudal magnificence. The estates were almost immediately deadlocked. Delegates of the third estate refused to transact any business until the king ordered the clergy and nobility to sit with them in a single body. Finally, after a six-week war of nerves, a few parish priests began to go over to the third estate, which on June 17 voted to call itself the **National Assembly.** On June 20 the delegates of the third estate, excluded from their hall because of "repairs," moved to a large indoor tennis court. There they swore the famous Oath of the Tennis Court, pledging not to disband until they had written a new constitution.

The king's response was ambivalent. On June 23 he made a conciliatory speech urging reforms to a joint session, and four days later he ordered the three estates to meet together. At the same time, the vacillating and indecisive monarch apparently followed the advice of relatives and court nobles who urged him to dissolve the Estates General by force. The king called an army of eighteen thousand troops toward Versailles, and on July 11 he dismissed his finance minister and his other more liberal ministers. As Louis XVI belatedly reasserted his "divine right" to rule, middle-class delegates and their allies from the liberal nobility resigned themselves to being disbanded at bayonet point. One third-estate delegate reassured a worried colleague, "You won't hang—you'll only have to go back home."[3]

The Revolt of the Poor and the Oppressed

While delegates of the third estate pressed for political rights, economic hardship gripped the common people. Grain was the basis of the diet of ordinary people in the eighteenth century, and in 1788 the harvest had been extremely poor. The price of bread began to soar. In Paris, where bread was regularly subsidized by the government in an attempt to prevent popular unrest, the price rose to 4 sous. The poor could scarcely afford to pay 2 sous per pound, for even at that price a laborer with a wife and three children had to spend half his wages on the family's bread.

Harvest failure and high bread prices unleashed a classic economic depression of the preindustrial age. With food so expensive and with so much uncertainty, the demand for manufactured goods collapsed. Thousands of artisans and small traders were thrown out of work. By the end of 1789 almost half of the French people would be in need of relief. One person in eight was a pauper living in extreme want. In Paris perhaps 150,000 of the city's 600,000 people were without work in July 1789.

Against this background of poverty and ongoing political crisis, the people of Paris entered decisively onto the revolutionary stage. They believed in a general, though ill-defined, way that the economic distress had human causes. They believed that they should have steady work and enough bread at fair prices to survive. Specifically, they feared that the dismissal of the king's moderate finance minister would put them at the mercy of aristocratic landowners and grain speculators. Rumors that the king's troops would sack the city began to fill the air. Angry crowds formed, and passionate voices urged action. On July 13 the people began to seize arms for the defense of the city as the king's armies moved toward Paris, and on July 14 several hundred people marched to the Bastille to search for weapons and gunpowder.

A medieval fortress with walls ten feet thick and eight great towers each one hundred feet high, the Bastille had long been used as a royal prison. It was guarded by eighty retired soldiers and thirty Swiss mercenaries. The governor of the fortress-prison refused to hand over the powder, panicked, and ordered his men to resist, killing ninety-eight people attempting to enter. Cannon were brought to batter the main gate, and fighting continued until the prison surrendered. The governor of the prison was later hacked to death, and his head was stuck on a pike and paraded through the streets. The next day a committee of citizens appointed the marquis de Lafayette commander of the city's armed forces. Paris was lost to the king, who was forced to recall the finance minister and disperse his troops. The popular uprising had broken the power monopoly of the royal army and thereby saved the National Assembly.

Online Study Center **Improve Your Grade**
Primary Source: The Taking of the Bastille and Its Aftermath: An English Perspective

As the delegates resumed their inconclusive debates at Versailles, the countryside sent them a radical and unmistakable message. Throughout France peasants began to rise in insurrection against their lords, ransacking manor houses and burning feudal documents that recorded their obligations. In some areas peasants reinstated traditional village practices, undoing recent enclosures and re-occupying old common lands. They seized forests, and taxes went unpaid. Fear of vagabonds and outlaws—called the **Great Fear** by contemporaries—seized the countryside and fanned the flames of rebellion. The long-suffering peasants were doing their best to free themselves from manorial rights and exploitation.

Faced with chaos, yet afraid to call on the king to restore order, some liberal nobles and middle-class delegates at Versailles responded to peasant demands with a surprise maneuver on the night of August 4, 1789. The duke of Aiguillon, also notably one of France's greatest noble landowners, declared that

in several provinces the whole people forms a kind of league for the destruction of the manor houses, the ravaging of the lands, and especially for the seizure of the archives where the title deeds to feudal properties are kept. It seeks to throw off at last a yoke that has for many centuries weighted it down.[4]

He urged equality in taxation and the elimination of feudal dues. In the end, all the old noble privileges—peasant serfdom where it still existed, exclusive hunting rights, fees for justice, village monopolies, the right to make peasants work on the roads, and a host of other dues—were abolished. Thus the French peasantry, which already owned about 30 percent of all the land, achieved an unprecedented victory in the early days of revolutionary upheaval. Henceforth, French peasants would seek mainly to protect and consolidate their triumph. As the Great Fear subsided in the countryside, they became a force for order and stability.

A Limited Monarchy

The National Assembly moved forward. On August 27, 1789, it issued the Declaration of the Rights of Man and of the Citizen, which stated, "Men are born and remain free and equal in rights." The declaration also maintained that mankind's natural rights are "liberty, property, security, and resistance to oppression" and that "every man is presumed innocent until he is proven guilty." As for law, "it is an expression of the general will; all citizens have the right to concur personally or through their representatives in its formation. . . . Free expression of thoughts and opinions is one of the most precious rights of mankind: every citizen may therefore speak, write, and publish freely." In short, this clarion call of the liberal revolutionary ideal guaranteed equality before the law, representative government for a sovereign people, and individual freedom. This revolutionary credo, only two

pages long, was disseminated throughout France and Europe and around the world.

Online Study Center **Improve Your Grade**
Primary Source: The Declaration of the Rights of Man and of the Citizen

Moving beyond general principles to draft a constitution proved difficult. The questions of how much power the king should retain and whether he could permanently veto legislation led to another deadlock. Once again the decisive answer came from the poor—in this instance, the poor women of Paris.

Women customarily bought the food and managed the poor family's slender resources. In Paris great numbers of women also worked for wages, making garments and luxury items destined for an aristocratic and international clientele. Immediately after the fall of the Bastille, many of France's great court nobles began to leave Versailles for foreign lands, so that a plummeting demand for luxuries intensified the general economic crisis. International markets also declined. The church was no longer able to give its traditional grants of food and money to the poor. Increasing unemployment and hunger put tremendous pressure on household managers, and the result was another popular explosion.

On October 5 some seven thousand desperate women marched the twelve miles from Paris to Versailles to demand action. A middle-class deputy looking out from the Assembly saw "multitudes arriving from Paris including fishwives and bullies from the market, and these people wanted nothing but bread." This great crowd invaded the Assembly, "armed with scythes, sticks and pikes." One tough old woman defiantly shouted into the debate, "Who's that talking down there? Make the chatterbox shut up. That's not the point: the point is that we want bread."[5] Hers was the genuine voice of the people, essential to any understanding of the French Revolution.

The women invaded the royal apartments, slaughtered some of the royal bodyguards, and furiously searched for the queen, Marie Antoinette, who was widely despised for her frivolous and supposedly immoral behavior. "We are going to cut off her head, tear out her heart, fry her liver, and that won't be the end of it," they shouted, surging through the palace in a frenzy. It seems likely that only the intervention of Lafayette and the National Guard saved the royal family. But the only way to calm the disorder was for the king to live in Paris, as the crowd demanded.

The next day the royal family left for Paris in the midst of a strange procession. The heads of two aristocrats, stuck on pikes, led the way. They were followed by the

The Women of Paris March to Versailles   On October 5, 1789, a large group of Parisian market women marched to Versailles to protest the price of bread. For the people of Paris, the king was the baker of last resort, responsible for feeding his people during times of scarcity. The crowd forced the royal family to return with them and to live in Paris, rather than remain isolated from their subjects at court. *(Erich Lessing/Art Resource, NY)*

remaining members of the royal bodyguard, unarmed and mocked by fierce men holding sabers and pikes. A mixed and victorious multitude surrounded the carriage of the captured royal family, hurling crude insults at the queen. There was drinking and eating among the women, who had emerged as a major element in the Parisian revolutionary crowd.[6]

The National Assembly followed the king to Paris, and the next two years, until September 1791, saw the consolidation of the liberal revolution. Under middle-class leadership, the National Assembly abolished the French nobility as a legal order and pushed forward with the creation of a **constitutional monarchy,** which Louis XVI reluctantly agreed to accept in July 1790. In the final constitution, the king remained the head of state, but all lawmaking power was placed in the hands of the National Assembly, elected by the economic upper half of French males.

New laws broadened women's rights to seek divorce, to inherit property, and to obtain financial support for illegitimate children from fathers. But women were not allowed to vote or hold political office for at least two reasons. First, the great majority of comfortable, well-educated males in the National Assembly believed that women should be limited to child rearing and domestic duties and should leave politics and most public activities to men, as Rousseau had advocated in his influential writings (see page 607). Second, the delegates to the National Assembly were convinced that political life in absolutist France had been profoundly corrupt and that a prime example of this corruption was the way that some talented but immoral aristocratic women had used their sexual charms to manipulate weak rulers and their ministers. Thus delegates argued that excluding women from politics would help create the civic virtue that had been missing: pure, home-focused wives would raise the high-minded sons needed to govern the nation.

The National Assembly replaced the complicated patchwork of historic provinces with eighty-three departments of approximately equal size. The jumble of weights and measures that varied from province to province was reformed, leading to the introduction of the metric system in 1793. Monopolies, guilds, and workers' associations were prohibited, and barriers to trade within France were abolished in the name of economic liberty. Thus the National Assembly applied the critical spirit of the Enlightenment in a thorough reform of France's laws and institutions.

The Assembly also imposed a radical reorganization on the country's religious life. It granted religious freedom to the small minority of French Jews and Protestants. Of greater impact, it then nationalized the Catholic Church's property and abolished monasteries as useless relics of a distant past. The government used all former church property as collateral to guarantee a new paper currency, the assignats, and then sold the property in an attempt to put the state's finances on a solid footing. Although the church's land was sold in large blocks, peasants eventually purchased much when it was subdivided. These purchases strengthened their attachment to the new revolutionary order in the countryside.

The religious reorganization of France brought the new government into conflict with the Catholic Church and many sincere Christians, especially in the countryside. Imbued with the rationalism and skepticism of the eighteenth-century philosophes, many delegates distrusted popular piety and "superstitious religion." Thus they established a national church, with priests chosen by voters. The National Assembly then forced the Catholic clergy to take a loyalty oath to the new government. The pope formally condemned this attempt to subjugate the church, and only half the priests of France swore the oath. The result was a deep religious divide within the country and the clergy. The attempt to remake the Catholic Church, like the Assembly's abolition of guilds and workers associations, sharpened the conflict between the educated classes and the common people that had been emerging in the eighteenth century. This policy toward the church was the revolutionary government's first important failure.

Revolutionary Aspirations in Saint-Domingue

The French Revolution radically transformed not only the territorial nation of France but its overseas colonies as well. On the eve of the Revolution, Saint-Domingue—the most profitable of all Caribbean colonies—was even more rife with social tensions than France itself. In addition to distinctions between noble and commoner or rich and poor, Saint-Domingue harbored divisions between free and unfree and a racial spectrum that included black, mixed race, and white people.

The colony's slave population was at least five hundred thousand, in comparison to a white population of approximately forty thousand. Because the brutal conditions created very high death rates among slaves, traders brought a constant stream of new arrivals from Africa. In 1789 up to two-thirds of slaves in Saint-Domingue had been born in Africa, most in the west-central region of the continent. Many were veterans of wars in Africa.

The free population was divided by color and by wealth. The European population included French colonial officials, wealthy planters and merchants, and poor immigrants. A sizable population of free people of African and mixed African European descent also existed, who referred to themselves as "free coloreds" or **free people of color.** They varied from modest artisans, to plantation managers and clerks, to wealthy established planters who owned slaves themselves. Failing to achieve their dreams of a colonial fortune, poor whites bitterly resented the privileges of the others, especially the free-colored elite. The white elite harbored its own grudges against France's monopoly on colonial trade and the royal government's attempts in the 1780s to impose legislation requiring humane treatment of slaves.

The 1685 *Code noir* (Black Code) that set the parameters of slavery had granted free people of color the same legal status as whites: they could own property, live where they wished, and pursue any education or career they desired. From the 1760s on, however, colonial administrators began rescinding these rights, and by the time of the Revolution, myriad aspects of free coloreds' lives—from the professions they could practice, to the names they could adopt, to the clothes they could wear—were ruled by discriminatory laws. White planters eagerly welcomed these laws, convinced that the best defense of slavery was a rigid color line.

The political and intellectual turmoil of the 1780s, with its growing rhetoric of liberty, equality, and fraternity, raised new challenges and possibilities for each of these groups. For slaves, news of abolitionist movements in France, and the royal government's own attempts to rein in the worst abuses of slavery, led to hopes that the mother country might grant them freedom. Free people of color found in such rhetoric the principles on which to base a defense of their legal and political rights. They looked to political reforms in Paris as a means of gaining political enfranchisement and reasserting equal status with whites. The white elite, not surprisingly, saw matters very differently. Infuriated by talk of abolition and determined to protect their way of life, they looked to revolutionary ideals of representative government for the chance to gain control of their own affairs, as had the American colonists before them. The meeting of the Estates General and the Declaration of the Rights of Man and of the Citizen raised these conflicting colonial aspirations to new levels.

The National Assembly, however, frustrated the hopes of all these groups. Cowed by colonial representatives who claimed that support for free coloreds would result in slave insurrection and independence, the Assembly refused to extend French constitutional safeguards to the colonies. Instead, it ruled that each colony would draft its own constitution, with free rein over decisions on slavery and the enfranchisement of free people of color. After dealing this blow to the aspirations of slaves and free coloreds, the committee also reaffirmed French monopolies over colonial trade, thereby angering planters as well.

In July 1790 Vincent Ogé, a free man of color, returned to Saint-Domingue from Paris determined to redress these issues. He raised an army of several hundred, occupied the town of Grande-Rivière, and sent letters to the new Provincial Assembly of Saint-Domingue demanding political rights for all free citizens, a statute already passed in France. After initial victories, his army was defeated, and Ogé himself was tortured and executed. In an attempt to forge compromise, in May 1791 the National Assembly granted political rights to free people of color born to two free parents who possessed sufficient property. When news of this legislation arrived in Saint-Domingue, the white elite was furious and the colonial governor refused to enact it. Violence now erupted between groups of whites and free coloreds in parts of the colony. The liberal revolution had failed to satisfy the contradictory ambitions in the colonies.

World War and Republican France, 1791–1799

When Louis XVI accepted the final version of the National Assembly's constitution in September 1791, a young and still obscure provincial lawyer and delegate named Maximilien Robespierre (1758–1794) concluded, "The Revolution is over." Robespierre was both right and wrong. He was right in the sense that the most constructive and lasting reforms were in place. Nothing substantial in the way of liberty and fundamental reform would be gained in the next generation. He was wrong in the sense that a much more radical stage lay ahead. New heroes and new ideologies were to emerge in revolutionary wars and international conflict in which Robespierre himself would play a central role.

● *How and why did the Revolution take a radical turn at home and in the colonies?*

Foreign Reactions and the Beginning of War

The outbreak and progress of revolution in France produced great excitement and a sharp division of opinion in Europe and the United States. Liberals and radicals saw a mighty triumph of liberty over despotism. In Great Britain especially, they hoped that the French example would lead to a fundamental reordering of Parliament, which was in the hands of the aristocracy and a few wealthy merchants. After the French Revolution began, conservative leaders such as Edmund Burke (1729–1797) were deeply troubled by the aroused spirit of reform. In 1790 Burke published *Reflections on the Revolution in France,* one of the great defenses of European conservatism. He defended inherited privileges in general and those of the English monarchy and aristocracy. He glorified the unrepresentative Parliament and predicted that thoroughgoing reform like that occurring in France would lead only to chaos and tyranny. Burke's work sparked much debate.

One passionate rebuttal came from a young writer in London, Mary Wollstonecraft (1759–1797). Born into the middle class, Wollstonecraft was schooled in adversity by a mean-spirited father who beat his wife and squandered his inherited fortune. Determined to be independent in a society that expected women of her class to become obedient wives, she struggled for years to earn her living as a governess and a teacher—practically the only acceptable careers for single, educated women—before attaining success as a translator and author. Incensed by Burke's book, Wollstonecraft immediately wrote a blistering, widely read attack, *A Vindication of the Rights of Man* (1790).

Then she made a daring intellectual leap, developing for the first time the logical implications of natural-law philosophy in her masterpiece, *A Vindication of the Rights of Woman* (1792). To fulfill the still-unrealized potential of the French Revolution and to eliminate the sexual inequality she had felt so keenly, she demanded that

the Rights of Women be respected . . . [and] JUSTICE for one-half of the human race. . . . It is time to effect a revolution in female manners, time to restore to them their lost dignity, and make them, as part of the human species, labor, by reforming themselves, to reform the world.

Setting high standards for women—"I wish to persuade women to endeavor to acquire strength, both of mind and body"—Wollstonecraft broke with those who had a low opinion of women's intellectual potential. She advocated rigorous coeducation, which would make women better wives and mothers, good citizens, and economically independent. Women could manage businesses and enter politics if only men would give them the chance. Men themselves would benefit from women's rights, for Wollstonecraft believed that "the two sexes mutually corrupt and improve each other."[7] Wollstonecraft's analysis testified to the power of the Revolution to excite and inspire outside of France. Paralleling ideas put forth independently in France by Olympe de Gouges (1748–1793), a self-taught writer and woman of the people (see the feature "Listening to the Past: Revolution and Women's Rights" on pages 714–715), Wollstonecraft's work marked the birth of the modern women's movement for equal rights, and it was ultimately very influential.

Online Study Center **Improve Your Grade**
Primary Source: A Feminist Analysis of Natural Law and the Rights of Women

The kings and nobles of continental Europe, who had at first welcomed the revolution in France as weakening a competing power, began to feel no less threatened than did Burke and his supporters. In June 1791, Louis XVI and Marie Antoinette were arrested and returned to Paris after trying unsuccessfully to slip out of France. The shock of this arrest led the monarchs of Austria and Prussia to issue the Declaration of Pillnitz in August 1791. This carefully worded statement declared their willingness to intervene in France in certain circumstances and was expected to have a sobering effect on revolutionary France without causing war.

But the crowned heads of Europe misjudged the revolutionary spirit in France. When the National Assembly disbanded, it sought popular support by decreeing that none of its members would be eligible for election to the new Legislative Assembly. This meant that when the new representative body convened in October 1791, it had a different character. The great majority of the legislators were still prosperous, well-educated middle-class men, but they were younger and less cautious than their predecessors. Many of the deputies belonged to a political club called the **Jacobin club,** after the name of the former monastery in which they held their meetings. Such clubs had proliferated in Parisian neighborhoods since the beginning of the Revolution, drawing men and women to debate the burning political questions of the day.

The Capture of Louis XVI, June 1791 This painting commemorates a dramatic turning point in the French Revolution, the midnight arrest of Louis XVI and the royal family as they tried to flee France in disguise and reach counter-revolutionaries in the Austrian Netherlands. Recognized and stopped at Varennes, just forty miles from the border, the king still nearly succeeded, telling municipal officers that dangerous mobs controlled Paris and securing promises of safe passage. But within hours the local leaders reversed themselves, and by morning Louis XVI was headed back to Paris. (*Bibliothèque nationale de France*)

The new representatives to the Assembly were passionately committed to the Revolution and distrustful of monarchy after Louis's attempted flight. They increasingly lumped "useless aristocrats" and "despotic monarchs" together, and they whipped themselves into a patriotic fury with bombastic oratory. If the courts of Europe were attempting to incite a war of kings against France, then "we will incite a war of people against kings. . . . Ten million Frenchmen, kindled by the fire of liberty, armed with the sword, with reason, with eloquence would be able to change the face of the world and make the tyrants tremble on their thrones."[8] Only Robespierre and a very few others argued that people would not welcome liberation at the point of a gun. Such warnings were brushed aside. France would "rise to the full height of her mission," as one deputy urged. In April 1792 France declared war on Francis II, the Habsburg monarch.

France's crusade against tyranny went poorly at first. Prussia joined Austria in the Austrian Netherlands (present-day Belgium), and French forces broke and fled at their first encounter with armies of this First Coalition. The road to Paris lay open, and it is possible that only conflict between the Eastern monarchs over the division of Poland saved France from defeat.

Military reversals and patriotic fervor led the Legislative Assembly to declare the country in danger. Volunteer armies from the provinces streamed through Paris, fraternizing with the people and singing patriotic songs like the stirring "Marseillaise," later the French national anthem. In this supercharged wartime atmosphere, rumors of treason by the king and queen spread in Paris. On August 10, 1792, a revolutionary crowd attacked the royal palace at the Tuileries, capturing it after heavy fighting with the Swiss Guards. The king and his family fled for their lives to the nearby Legislative Assembly, which suspended the king from all his functions, imprisoned him, and called for a new National Convention to be elected by universal male suffrage. Monarchy in France was on its deathbed, mortally wounded by war and popular upheaval.

The Second Revolution

The fall of the monarchy marked a rapid radicalization of the Revolution, a phase that historians often call the **second revolution.** Louis's imprisonment was followed by the September Massacres. Wild stories that imprisoned counter-revolutionary aristocrats and priests were plotting with the allied invaders seized the city. As a result, angry crowds invaded the prisons of Paris and slaughtered half the men and women they found. In late

September 1792 the new, popularly elected National Convention proclaimed France a republic.

The republic sought to create a new popular culture, fashioning compelling symbols that broke with the past and glorified the new order. It adopted a brand-new revolutionary calendar, which eliminated saints' days and renamed the days and the months after the seasons of the year. The republic energetically promoted broad, open-air, democratic festivals. These spectacles brought the entire population together and sought to redirect the people's traditional enthusiasm for Catholic religious celebrations to secular holidays instilling republican virtue and a love of nation. These spectacles were less successful in villages than in cities, where popular interest in politics was greater and Catholicism was weaker.

All the members of the National Convention were republicans, and at the beginning almost all belonged to the Jacobin club of Paris. But the Jacobins themselves were increasingly divided into two bitterly competitive groups—the **Girondists,** named after a department in southwestern France that was home to several of their leaders, and **the Mountain,** led by Robespierre and another young lawyer, Georges Jacques Danton. The Mountain was so called because its members sat on the uppermost benches on the left side of the assembly hall. A majority of the indecisive Convention members, seated in the "Plain" below, floated back and forth between the rival factions.

This division emerged clearly after the National Convention overwhelmingly convicted Louis XVI of treason. The Girondists accepted his guilt but did not wish to put the king to death. By a narrow majority, the Mountain carried the day, and Louis was executed on January 21, 1793, on the newly invented guillotine. One of his last statements was "I am innocent and shall die without fear. I would that my death might bring happiness to the French, and ward off the dangers which I foresee."[9]

Both the Girondists and the Mountain were determined to continue the "war against tyranny." The Prussians had been stopped at the Battle of Valmy on September 20, 1792, one day before the republic was proclaimed. French armies then invaded Savoy and captured Nice, moved into the German Rhineland, and by November 1792 were occupying the entire Austrian Netherlands. Everywhere they went French armies of occupation chased the princes, "abolished feudalism," and found support among some peasants and middle-class people.

But the French armies also lived off the land, requisitioning food and supplies and plundering local treasures. The liberators looked increasingly like foreign invaders.

International tensions mounted. In February 1793 the National Convention, at war with Austria and Prussia, declared war on Britain, Holland, and Spain as well. Republican France was now at war with almost all of Europe, a great war that would last almost without interruption until 1815.

As the forces of the First Coalition drove the French from the Austrian Netherlands, peasants in western France revolted against being drafted into the army. They were supported and encouraged in their resistance by devout Catholics, royalists, and foreign agents. In Paris the National Convention was locked in a life-and-death political struggle between the Girondists and the Mountain. Both groups were sincere republicans, hating privilege and wanting to temper economic liberalism with social concern. Yet personal hatreds ran deep. The Girondists feared a bloody dictatorship by the Mountain, and the Mountain was no less convinced that the more moderate Girondists would turn to conservatives and even royalists in order to retain power.

With the middle-class delegates so bitterly divided, the laboring poor of Paris emerged as the decisive political factor. The laboring men and women of Paris always constituted—along with the peasantry in the summer of 1789—the elemental force that drove the Revolution forward. It was the artisans, day laborers, market women, and garment workers who had stormed the Bastille, marched on Versailles, driven the king from the Tuileries, and carried out the September Massacres. The laboring poor and the petty traders were often known as the **sans-culottes,** "without breeches," because sans-culottes men wore trousers instead of the knee breeches of the aristocracy and the solid middle class. The immediate interests of the sans-culottes were mainly economic, and in spring 1793 rapid inflation, unemployment, and food shortages were again weighing heavily on poor families.

Moreover, by spring 1793 the sans-culottes had become keenly interested in politics. Encouraged by the so-called angry men, such as the passionate young ex-priest and journalist Jacques Roux, sans-culottes men and women were demanding radical political action to guarantee them their daily bread. At first the Mountain joined the Girondists in rejecting these demands. But in the face of military defeat, peasant revolt, and hatred of the Girondists, the Mountain and especially Robespierre became more sympathetic. The Mountain joined with sans-culottes activists in the city government to engineer a popular uprising that forced the Convention to arrest thirty-one Girondist deputies for treason on June 2. All power passed to the Mountain.

Robespierre and others from the Mountain joined the recently formed Committee of Public Safety, to which the Convention had given dictatorial power to deal with the national emergency. These developments in Paris triggered revolt in leading provincial cities, such as Lyons and Marseilles, where moderates denounced Paris and demanded a decentralized government. The peasant revolt spread, and the republic's armies were driven back on all fronts. By July 1793 only the areas around Paris and on the eastern frontier were firmly held by the central government. Defeat seemed imminent.

Total War and the Terror

A year later, in July 1794, the Austrian Netherlands and the Rhineland were once again in the hands of conquering French armies, and the First Coalition was falling apart. This remarkable change of fortune was due to the revolutionary government's success in harnessing, for perhaps the first time in history, the explosive forces of a planned economy, revolutionary terror, and modern nationalism in a total war effort.

Robespierre and the Committee of Public Safety advanced with implacable resolution on several fronts in 1793 and 1794. First, they collaborated with the fiercely patriotic and democratic sans-culottes, who retained the common people's traditional faith in fair prices and a moral economic order and who distrusted most wealthy capitalists and all aristocrats. Thus Robespierre and his coworkers established, as best they could, a **planned economy** with egalitarian social overtones. Rather than let supply and demand determine prices, the government set maximum allowable prices for key products. Though the state was too weak to enforce all its price regulations, it did fix the price of bread in Paris at levels the poor could afford. Rationing was introduced, and bakers were permitted to make only the "bread of equality"—a brown bread made of a mixture of all available flours. White bread and pastries were outlawed as luxuries. The poor of Paris may not have eaten well, but at least they ate.

They also worked, mainly to produce arms and munitions for the war effort. The government told craftsmen what to produce, nationalized many small workshops, and requisitioned raw materials and grain. Sometimes planning and control did not go beyond orders to meet the latest emergency. But failures to control and coordinate were failures of means and not of desire. The second revolution and the ascendancy of the sans-culottes had produced an embryonic emergency socialism, which thoroughly frightened Europe's propertied classes and

Contrasting Visions of the Sans-Culottes The woman on the left, with her playful cat and calm simplicity, suggests how the French sans-culottes saw themselves as democrats and virtuous citizens. The ferocious sans-culotte harpy on the right, a creation of wartime England's vivid counter-revolutionary imagination, screams for more blood, more death: "I am the Goddess of Liberty! Long live the guillotine!" *(Bibliothèque nationale de France)*

had great influence on the subsequent development of socialist ideology.

Second, while radical economic measures supplied the poor with bread and the armies with weapons, the **Reign of Terror** (1793–1794) used revolutionary terror to solidify the home front. Special revolutionary courts responsible only to Robespierre's Committee of Public Safety tried rebels and "enemies of the nation" for political crimes. Drawing on popular support centered in the local Jacobin clubs, these local courts ignored normal legal procedures and judged severely. Some forty thousand French men and women were executed or died in prison. Another three hundred thousand suspects were arrested.

Robespierre's Reign of Terror is one of the most controversial phases of the French Revolution. Most historians now believe that the Reign of Terror was not directed against any single class. Rather, it was a political weapon directed impartially against all who might oppose the revolutionary government. For many Europeans of the

time, however, the Reign of Terror represented a frightening perversion of the generous ideals of 1789, strengthening the belief that France had foolishly replaced a weak king with a bloody dictatorship.

The third and perhaps most decisive element in the French republic's victory over the First Coalition was its ability to draw on the explosive power of patriotic dedication to a national state and a national mission. An essential part of modern **nationalism,** this commitment was something new in history. With a common language and a common tradition newly reinforced by the ideas of popular sovereignty and democracy, large numbers of French people were stirred by a common loyalty. They developed an intense emotional commitment to the defense of the nation, and they imagined the nation as a great loving family that included all right-thinking patriots. In such circumstances war was no longer the gentlemanly game of the eighteenth century, but rather total war, a life-and-death struggle between good and evil.

The French Revolution

May 5, 1789	Estates General convene at Versailles.
June 17, 1789	Third estate declares itself the National Assembly.
June 20, 1789	Oath of the Tennis Court is sworn.
July 14, 1789	Storming of the Bastille occurs.
July–August 1789	Great Fear ravages the countryside.
August 4, 1789	National Assembly abolishes feudal privileges.
August 27, 1789	National Assembly issues Declaration of the Rights of Man and of the Citizen.
October 5, 1789	Women march on Versailles and force royal family to return to Paris.
November 1789	National Assembly confiscates church lands.
July 1790	Civil Constitution of the Clergy establishes a national church. Louis XVI reluctantly agrees to accept a constitutional monarchy.
June 1791	Royal family is arrested while attempting to flee France.
August 1791	Austria and Prussia issue the Declaration of Pillnitz. Slave insurrections break out in Saint-Domingue.
April 1792	France declares war on Austria. Legislative Assembly enfranchises free people of color.
August 1792	Parisian mob attacks the palace and takes Louis XVI prisoner.
September 1792	September Massacres occur. National Convention declares France a republic and abolishes monarchy.
January 1793	Louis XVI is executed.
February 1793	France declares war on Britain, Holland, and Spain. Revolts take place in some provincial cities.
March 1793	Bitter struggle occurs in the National Convention between Girondists and the Mountain.
April–June 1793	Robespierre and the Mountain organize the Committee of Public Safety and arrest Girondist leaders.
September 1793	Price controls are instituted to aid the sans-culottes and mobilize the war effort. British troops invade Saint-Domingue.
1793–1794	Reign of Terror darkens Paris and the provinces.
February 1794	National Convention abolishes slavery in all French territories.
Spring 1794	French armies are victorious on all fronts.
July 1794	Robespierre is executed. Thermidorian reaction begins.
1795–1799	The Directory rules.
1795	Economic controls are abolished, and suppression of the sans-culottes begins. Toussaint L'Ouverture named brigadier general.
1797	Napoleon defeats Austrian armies in Italy and returns triumphant to Paris.
1798	Austria, Great Britain, and Russia form the Second Coalition against France.
1799	Napoleon overthrows the Directory and seizes power.

Everyone had to participate in the national effort. According to a famous decree of August 23, 1793:

The young men shall go to battle and the married men shall forge arms. The women shall make tents and clothes, and shall serve in the hospitals; children shall tear rags into lint. The old men will be guided to the public places of the cities to kindle the courage of the young warriors and to preach the unity of the Republic and the hatred of kings.

The all-out mobilization of French resources under the Terror combined with the fervor of modern nationalism to create an awesome fighting machine. After August 1793 all unmarried young men were subject to the draft, and by January 1794 the French had about eight hundred thousand soldiers on active duty in fourteen armies. A force of this size was unprecedented in the history of European warfare, and recent research concludes that the French armed forces outnumbered their enemies almost four to one.[10] Well trained, well equipped, and constantly indoctrinated, the enormous armies of the re-

public were led by young, impetuous generals. These generals often had risen from the ranks, and they personified the opportunities the Revolution offered gifted sons of the people. Following orders from Paris to attack relentlessly, French generals used mass assaults at bayonet point to overwhelm the enemy. "No maneuvering, nothing elaborate," declared the fearless General Hoche. "Just cold steel, passion and patriotism."[11] By spring 1794 French armies were victorious on all fronts. The republic was saved.

Revolution in Saint-Domingue

The second stage of revolution in Saint-Domingue also resulted from decisive action from below. In August 1791 slaves, previously fettered witnesses to the confrontation between whites and free coloreds, took events into their own hands. Groups of slaves held a series of nighttime meetings to plan a mass insurrection. These meetings reportedly included religious ceremonies in

Slave Revolt on Saint-Domingue Starting in August 1791 the slaves of Saint-Domingue rose in revolt. *(Giraudon/Art Resource, NY)*

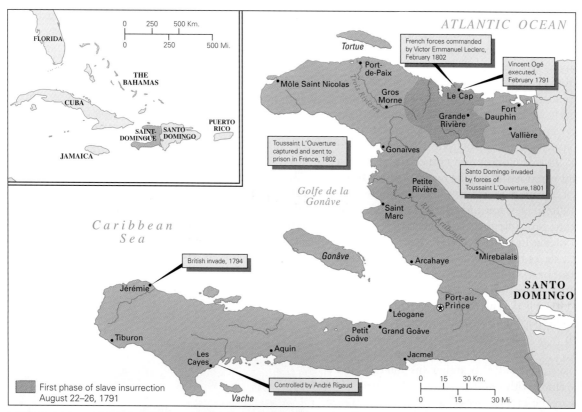

MAP 21.1 The Haitian Revolution Neighbored by the Spanish colony of Santo Domingo, Saint-Domingue was the most profitable European colony in the Caribbean. In 1770 the French transferred the capital from Le Cap to Port-au-Prince, which became capital of the newly independent Haiti in 1804. Slave revolts erupted in the north, near Le Cap, in 1791.

which participants made ritual offerings and swore a sacred oath of secrecy and revenge. The rituals belonged to the religious practices, later known as "voodoo," that slaves had created on Saint-Domingue plantations from a combination of Catholicism and African cults. French soldiers later reported that religious incantations and African songs accompanied rebel slaves into combat. African culture thus played an important role in the Saint-Domingue revolution, alongside Enlightenment ideals of freedom and equality.

Revolts began on a few plantations on the night of August 22; within a few days the uprising had swept much of the northern plain, creating a slave army estimated at around 2,000 individuals. By August 27 it was "10,000 strong, divided into 3 armies, of whom 700 or 800 are on horseback, and tolerably well-armed."[12] During the next month slaves attacked and destroyed hundreds of sugar and coffee plantations.

On April 4, 1792, as war loomed with the European states, the National Assembly issued a new decree enfranchising all free blacks and free people of color, but not slaves. The loyalty of free men of color, the Paris government reasoned, was crucial to defeating the slave rebellion and stabilizing the colony.

Warfare in Europe soon spread to Saint-Domingue (see Map 21.1), adding another complicating factor to its racial and political conflicts. Since the beginning of the slave insurrection, the Spanish in neighboring Santo Domingo had supported rebel slaves, and in early 1793 they began to bring slave leaders and their soldiers into the Spanish army. Toussaint L'Ouverture, a freed slave who had joined the slave revolt, was named a Spanish officer. The British navy also blockaded the colony, and invading British troops captured French territory on the island. For the Spanish and British, revolutionary chaos provided a tempting opportunity to capture a profitable colony.

Desperate for forces to oppose France's enemies, the commissioners sent by the newly elected National Convention turned to slaves. They began by promising freedom to those who fought for France. By October 1793 they had abolished slavery throughout the colony. On February 4, 1794, the Convention ratified the **abolition of slavery** and extended it to all French territories, including the Caribbean colonies of Martinique and Guadeloupe. The new constitution of 1795 reaffirmed abolition and the principle that the same laws would apply in the colonies as in metropolitan France. In just four years insurgent slaves had ended centuries of bondage in the French Caribbean and won full political rights.

For the future, the problem loomed of how these rights would be applied. The most immediate question, however, was whether France would be able to retain the colony, which was still under attack by Spanish and British forces. The tide began to turn when Toussaint L'Ouverture switched sides, bringing his military and political skills, along with four thousand well-trained soldiers, to support the French war effort.

By 1796 the French had gradually regained control of the colony, and L'Ouverture had emerged as the key leader of the combined slave and free colored forces. In May 1796 he was named commander of the western province of Saint-Domingue (see Map 21.1). The increasingly conservative nature of the French government during the Thermidorian reaction, however, threatened to undo the gains made by former slaves and free people of color. As exiled planters gained a stronger voice in French policymaking, L'Ouverture and other local leaders grew ever more wary of what the future might hold.

Online Study Center **Improve Your Grade**
Primary Source: A Black Revolutionary Leader in Haiti: Toussaint L'Ouverture

The Thermidorian Reaction and the Directory, 1794–1799

The success of the French armies led Robespierre and the Committee of Public Safety to relax the emergency economic controls, but they extended the political Reign of Terror. In March 1794, to the horror of many sans-culottes, Robespierre's Terror wiped out many of the angry men who had been criticizing Robespierre for being

soft on the wealthy and who were led by the radical social democrat Jacques Hébert. Two weeks later, Robespierre sent many of his long-standing collaborators, including the famous orator Danton, up the steps to the guillotine. A strange assortment of radicals and moderates in the Convention, knowing that they might be next, organized a conspiracy. They howled down Robespierre when he tried to speak to the National Convention on 9 Thermidor (July 27, 1794). The next day it was Robespierre's turn to be shaved by the revolutionary razor.

As Robespierre's closest supporters followed their leader to the guillotine, France unexpectedly experienced a thorough reaction to the despotism of the Reign of Terror. In a general way, this **Thermidorian reaction** recalled the early days of the Revolution. The respectable middle-class lawyers and professionals who had led the liberal revolution of 1789 reasserted their authority, drawing support from their own class, the provincial

The Execution of Robespierre The guillotine was painted red and was completely wooden except for the heavy iron blade. Large crowds witnessed the executions in a majestic public square in central Paris, then known as the Place de la Révolution and now called the Place de la Concorde (Harmony Square). *(Snark/Art Resource, NY)*

cities, and the better-off peasants. The National Convention abolished many economic controls, let prices rise sharply, and severely restricted the local political organizations in which the sans-culottes had their strength.

The collapse of economic controls, coupled with runaway inflation, hit the working poor very hard. The sans-culottes accepted private property, but they believed passionately in small business, decent wages, and economic justice. Increasingly disorganized after Robespierre purged radical leaders, the common people of Paris finally revolted against the emerging new order in early 1795. The Convention quickly used the army to suppress these insurrections and made no concessions to the poor. In the face of all these reversals, the revolutionary fervor of the laboring poor in Paris finally subsided. Excluded and disillusioned, the urban poor would have little interest in and influence on politics until 1830.

In villages and small towns there arose a great cry for peace and a turning toward religion, especially from women, who had seldom experienced the political radicalization of sans-culottes women in the big cities. Instead, these women had tenaciously defended their culture and religious beliefs against the often heavy-handed attacks of antireligious revolutionary officials after 1789. As the government began to retreat on the religious question from 1796 to 1801, the women of rural France brought back the Catholic Church and the open worship of God.

As for the middle-class members of the National Convention, in 1795 they wrote yet another constitution that they believed would guarantee their economic position and political supremacy. As in previous elections, the mass of the population voted only for electors, whose number was cut back to men of substantial means. Electors then elected the members of a reorganized legislative assembly as well as key officials throughout France. The new assembly also chose a five-man executive—the Directory.

The Directory continued to support French military expansion abroad. War was no longer so much a crusade as a means to meet ever-present, ever-unsolved economic problems. Large, victorious French armies reduced unemployment at home and were able to live off the territories they conquered and plundered.

The unprincipled action of the Directory reinforced widespread disgust with war and starvation. This general dissatisfaction revealed itself clearly in the national elections of 1797, which returned a large number of conservative and even monarchist deputies who favored peace at almost any price. The members of the Directory, fearing for their skins, used the army to nullify the elections

and began to govern dictatorially. Two years later Napoleon Bonaparte ended the Directory in a coup d'état and substituted a strong dictatorship for a weak one. The effort to establish stable representative government had failed.

The Napoleonic Era, 1799–1815

For almost fifteen years, from 1799 to 1814, France was in the hands of a keen-minded military dictator of exceptional ability. One of history's most fascinating leaders, Napoleon Bonaparte (1769–1821) realized the need to put an end to civil strife in France in order to create unity and consolidate his rule. And he did. But Napoleon saw himself as a man of destiny, and the glory of war and the dream of universal empire proved irresistible. For years he spiraled from victory to victory, but in the end he was destroyed by a mighty coalition united in fear of his restless ambition.

• *Why did Napoleon Bonaparte assume control of France, and what factors led to his downfall? How did the new republic of Haiti gain independence from France?*

Napoleon's Rule of France

In 1799 when he seized power, young General Napoleon Bonaparte was a national hero. Born in Corsica into an impoverished noble family in 1769, Napoleon left home and became a lieutenant in the French artillery in 1785. After a brief and unsuccessful adventure fighting for Corsican independence in 1789, he returned to France as a French patriot and a dedicated revolutionary. Rising rapidly in the new army, Napoleon was placed in command of French forces in Italy and won brilliant victories there in 1796 and 1797. His next campaign, in Egypt, was a failure, but Napoleon returned to France before the fiasco was generally known, and his reputation remained intact.

Napoleon soon learned that some prominent members of the legislature were plotting against the Directory. The dissatisfaction of these plotters stemmed not so much from the fact that the Directory was a dictatorship as from the fact that it was a weak dictatorship. Ten years of upheaval and uncertainty had made firm rule much more appealing than liberty and popular politics to these disillusioned revolutionaries. The abbé Sieyès personified this evolution in thinking. In 1789 he had written that the nobility was grossly overprivileged and that the entire people should rule the French nation. Now Sieyès's

The Napoleonic Era

November 1799	Napoleon overthrows the Directory.
December 1799	French voters overwhelmingly approve Napoleon's new constitution.
1800	Napoleon founds the Bank of France.
1801	France defeats Austria and acquires Italian and German territories in the Treaty of Lunéville.
	Napoleon signs the Concordat with the pope.
1802	France signs the Treaty of Amiens with Britain.
	French forces arrive in Saint-Domingue.
April 1803	Toussaint L'Ouverture dies in France.
January 1804	Jean Jacques Dessalines declares Haitian independence.
March 1804	Napoleonic Code comes into force.
December 1804	Napoleon crowns himself emperor.
May 1805	First Haitian constitution promulgated.
October 1805	Britain defeats the French and Spanish fleet at the Battle of Trafalgar.
December 1805	Napoleon defeats Austria and Russia at the Battle of Austerlitz.
1807	Napoleon redraws the map of Europe in the treaties of Tilsit.
1810	The Grand Empire is at its height.
June 1812	Napoleon invades Russia with 600,000 men.
Fall–Winter 1812	Napoleon makes a disastrous retreat from Russia.
March 1814	Russia, Prussia, Austria, and Britain sign the Treaty of Chaumont, pledging alliance to defeat Napoleon.
April 1814	Napoleon abdicates and is exiled to Elba.
February–June 1815	Napoleon escapes from Elba and rules France until he is defeated at the Battle of Waterloo.

motto was "Confidence from below, authority from above."

Like the other members of his group, Sieyès wanted a strong military ruler. The flamboyant thirty-year-old Napoleon was ideal. Thus the conspirators and Napoleon organized a takeover. On November 9, 1799, they ousted the Directors, and the following day soldiers disbanded the legislature at bayonet point. Napoleon was named first consul of the republic, and a new constitution consolidating his position was overwhelmingly approved in a plebiscite in December 1799. Republican appearances were maintained, but Napoleon was already the real ruler of France.

The essence of Napoleon's domestic policy was to use his great and highly personal powers to maintain order and end civil strife. He did so by working out unwritten agreements with powerful groups in France whereby the groups received favors in return for loyal service. Napoleon's bargain with the solid middle class was codified in the famous Civil Code of 1804, which reasserted two of the fundamental principles of the liberal and essentially moderate revolution of 1789: equality of all male citizens before the law and absolute security of wealth and private property. Napoleon and the leading bankers of Paris established the privately owned Bank of France, which loyally served the interests of both the state and the financial oligarchy. Napoleon's defense of the new economic order also appealed successfully to peasants, who had gained both land and status from the revolutionary changes. Thus Napoleon reconfirmed the gains of the peasantry and reassured the solid middle class, which had lost a large number of its revolutionary illusions in the face of social upheaval.

At the same time Napoleon accepted and strengthened the position of the French bureaucracy. Building on the solid foundations that revolutionary governments had inherited from the Old Regime, he perfected a thoroughly centralized state. As recent scholarship shows, Napoleon consolidated his rule by recruiting disillusioned revolutionaries for the network of ministers, prefects, and centrally appointed mayors that depended on him and came to serve him well. Only former revolutionaries who leaned too far to the left or to the right were pushed to the sidelines.[13] Nor were members of the old nobility slighted. In 1800 and again in 1802 Napoleon granted amnesty to one hundred thousand émigrés on the condition that they return to France and take a loyalty oath. Members of this returning elite soon ably occupied many high posts in the expanding centralized state. Only one thousand die-hard monarchists were exempted and remained abroad. Napoleon also created a new imperial nobility in order to reward his most talented generals and officials.

Napoleon's skill in gaining support from important and potentially hostile groups is illustrated by his treatment of the Catholic Church in France. In 1800 the French clergy was still divided into two groups: those who had taken an oath of allegiance to the revolutionary government and those in exile or hiding who had refused to do so. Personally uninterested in religion, Napoleon wanted to heal the religious division so that a united Catholic Church could serve as a bulwark of order and social peace in France. After arduous negotiations, Napoleon and Pope Pius VII (1800–1823) signed the Concordat of 1801. The pope gained the precious right for French Catholics to practice their religion freely, but Napoleon gained political power: his government now nominated bishops, paid the clergy, and exerted great influence over the church in France.

The domestic reforms of Napoleon's early years were his greatest achievement. Much of his legal and administrative reorganization has survived in France to this day. More generally, Napoleon's domestic initiatives gave the great majority of French people a welcome sense of stability and national unity.

Order and unity had a price: Napoleon's authoritarian rule. Women, who had often participated in revolutionary politics without having legal equality, lost many of the gains they had made in the 1790s. Under the law of the new Napoleonic Code, women were dependents of either their fathers or their husbands, and they could not make contracts or even have bank accounts in their own names. Indeed, Napoleon and his advisers aimed at re-establishing a family monarchy, where the power of the husband and father was as absolute over the wife and the children as that of Napoleon was over his subjects.

Free speech and freedom of the press were continually violated. By 1811 only four newspapers were left, and they were little more than organs of government propaganda. The occasional elections were a farce. Later laws prescribed harsh penalties for political offenses. These changes in the law were part of the creation of a police state in France. Since Napoleon was usually busy making war, this task was largely left to Joseph Fouché, an unscrupulous opportunist who had earned a reputation for brutality during the Reign of Terror. As minister of police, Fouché organized a ruthlessly efficient spy system that kept thousands of citizens under continual police surveillance. People suspected of subversive activities were arbitrarily detained, placed under house arrest, or consigned to insane asylums. After 1810 political suspects were held in state prisons, as they had been during the Terror. There were about twenty-five hundred such political prisoners in 1814.

Napoleon's Expansion in Europe

Napoleon was above all a military man, and a great one. After coming to power in 1799 he sent peace feelers to Austria and Great Britain, the two remaining members of the Second Coalition that had been formed against France in 1798. When these overtures were rejected, French armies led by Napoleon decisively defeated the Austrians. In the Treaty of Lunéville (1801) Austria accepted the loss of almost all its Italian possessions, and German territory on the west bank of the Rhine was incorporated into France. Once more, as in 1797, the British were alone, and war-weary, like the French.

Still seeking to consolidate his regime domestically, Napoleon concluded the Treaty of Amiens with Great Britain in 1802. France remained in control of Holland, the Austrian Netherlands, the west bank of the Rhine, and most of the Italian peninsula. The Treaty of Amiens was clearly a diplomatic triumph for Napoleon, and peace with honor and profit increased his popularity at home.

In 1802 Napoleon was secure but unsatisfied. Ever a romantic gambler as well as a brilliant administrator, he could not contain his power drive. Aggressively redrawing the map of Germany so as to weaken Austria and encourage the secondary states of southwestern Germany to side with France, Napoleon tried to restrict British trade with all of Europe. After deciding to renew war

The Coronation of Napoleon, 1804 (detail)   In this grandiose painting by Jacques-Louis David, Napoleon prepares to crown his wife, Josephine, in an elaborate ceremony in Notre Dame Cathedral. Napoleon, the ultimate upstart, also crowned himself. Pope Pius VII, seated glumly behind the emperor, is reduced to being a spectator. *(Louvre/Réunion des Musées Nationaux/Art Resource, NY)*

with Britain in May 1803, Napoleon concentrated his armies in the French ports on the Channel in the fall and began making preparations to invade England. Great Britain remained dominant on the seas, and when Napoleon tried to bring his Mediterranean fleet around Gibraltar to northern France, a combined French and Spanish fleet was virtually annihilated by Lord Nelson at the Battle of Trafalgar on October 21, 1805. Invasion of England was henceforth impossible. Renewed fighting had its advantages, however, for the first consul used the wartime atmosphere to have himself proclaimed emperor in late 1804.

Austria, Russia, and Sweden joined with Britain to form the Third Coalition against France shortly before the Battle of Trafalgar. Actions such as Napoleon's assumption of the Italian crown had convinced both Alexander I of Russia and Francis II of Austria that

Napoleon was a threat to their interests and to the European balance of power. Yet the Austrians and the Russians were no match for Napoleon, who scored a brilliant victory over them at the Battle of Austerlitz in December 1805. Alexander I decided to pull back, and Austria accepted large territorial losses in return for peace as the Third Coalition collapsed.

Napoleon then proceeded to reorganize the German states to his liking. In 1806 he abolished many of the tiny German states as well as the ancient Holy Roman Empire and established by decree the German Confederation of the Rhine, a union of fifteen German states minus Austria, Prussia, and Saxony. Naming himself "protector" of the confederation, Napoleon firmly controlled western Germany.

Napoleon's intervention in German affairs alarmed the Prussians, who mobilized their armies after more than a decade of peace with France. Napoleon attacked and won two more brilliant victories in October 1806 at Jena and Auerstädt, where the Prussians were outnumbered two to one. The war with Prussia, now joined by Russia, continued into the following spring, and after Napoleon's larger armies won another victory, Alexander I of Russia wanted peace.

For several days in June 1807 the young tsar and the French emperor negotiated face to face on a raft anchored in the middle of the Niemen River. All the while, the helpless Frederick William III of Prussia rode back and forth on the shore anxiously awaiting the results. As the German poet Heinrich Heine said later, Napoleon had but to whistle and Prussia would have ceased to exist. In the subsequent treaties of Tilsit, Prussia lost half of its population, while Russia accepted Napoleon's reorganization of western and central Europe and promised to enforce Napoleon's economic blockade against British goods.

The War of Haitian Independence

In the midst of these victories, Napoleon was forced to accept defeat overseas. With Toussaint L'Ouverture acting increasingly as an independent ruler of the western province of Saint-Domingue, another general, André Rigaud, set up his own government in the southern peninsula, which had long been more isolated from France than the rest of the colony. Both leaders maintained policies, initially established by the French, of requiring former slaves to continue to work on their plantations. They believed that reconstructing the plantation economy was crucial to maintaining their military and political victories, and they harshly suppressed resistance from former slaves.

Tensions mounted, however, between L'Ouverture and Rigaud. While L'Ouverture was a freed slave of African descent, Rigaud belonged to the free colored elite. This elite resented the growing power of former slaves like L'Ouverture, who in turn accused them of adopting the racism of white settlers. Civil war broke out between the two sides in 1799, when L'Ouverture's forces, led by his lieutenant Jean Jacques Dessalines, invaded the south. Victory over Rigaud gave Toussaint control of the entire colony. (See the feature "Individuals in Society: Toussaint L'Ouverture.")

This victory was soon challenged by Napoleon's arrival in power. Napoleon intended to reinvigorate the Caribbean plantation economy as a basis for expanding French power. His new constitution of 1799 opened the way for a re-establishment of slavery much feared in the colony. When the colonial assembly of Saint-Domingue, under L'Ouverture's direction, drafted its own constitution—which reaffirmed the abolition of slavery and granted L'Ouverture governorship for life—Napoleon viewed it as a seditious act. He ordered his brother-in-law General Charles-Victor-Emmanuel Leclerc to lead an expedition to the island to crush the new regime. Napoleon placed a high premium on bringing the colony to heel, writing to Leclerc: "Once the blacks have been disarmed and the principal generals sent to France, you will have done more for the commerce and civilization of Europe than we have done in our most brilliant campaigns." An officer sent to serve in the colony had a more cynical interpretation, writing that he was being sent to "fight with the Negroes for their own sugar."[14]

In 1802 Leclerc landed in Saint-Domingue. Although Toussaint L'Ouverture cooperated with the French and turned his army over to them, Leclerc had him arrested and deported to France, along with his family, where he died in 1803. After arresting L'Ouverture, Leclerc moved to defuse the threat posed by former slaves by taking away their arms. This effort aroused armed resistance on the plantations and led to the defection of the remnants of L'Ouverture's army. Jean Jacques Dessalines united the resistance under his command and led them to a crushing victory over the French forces. Of the fifty-eight thousand French soldiers, fifty thousand were lost in combat and to disease. On January 1, 1804, Dessalines formally declared the independence of Saint-Domingue and the creation of the new sovereign nation of Haiti, the name used by the pre-Columbian inhabitants of the island. (The remaining French Caribbean colonies—Guadeloupe, Martinique, and French Guiana—remained part of France. Slavery was re-established and remained in force until 1848.)

Haiti, the second independent state in the Americas and the first in Latin America, was thus born from the first successful large-scale slave revolt in history. Fearing the spread of slave rebellion to the United States, President Thomas Jefferson refused to recognize Haiti. Both the American and the French Revolutions thus exposed their limits by acting to protect economic interests at the expense of revolutionary ideals of freedom and equality. Yet, Haitian independence had fundamental repercussions for world history. As one recent historian of the Haitian revolution commented:

The slave insurrection of Saint-Domingue led to the expansion of citizenship beyond racial barriers despite the massive political and economic investment in the slave system at the time. If we live in a world in which democracy is meant to exclude no one, it is in no small part because of the actions of those slaves in Saint-Domingue who insisted that human rights were theirs too.[15]

The Grand Empire and Its End

Napoleon resigned himself to the loss of Saint-Domingue, but he still maintained imperial ambitions in Europe. Increasingly, he saw himself as the emperor of Europe and not just of France. The so-called **Grand Empire** he built had three parts. The core, or first part, was an ever-expanding France, which by 1810 included Belgium, Holland, parts of northern Italy, and much German territory on the east bank of the Rhine. Beyond French borders Napoleon established the second part: a number of dependent satellite kingdoms, on the thrones of which he placed (and replaced) the members of his large family. The third part comprised the independent but allied states of Austria, Prussia, and Russia. After 1806 both satellites and allies were expected to support Napoleon's continental system and to cease trade with Britain.

The impact of the Grand Empire on the peoples of Europe was considerable. In the areas incorporated into France and in the satellites (see Map 21.2), Napoleon introduced many French laws, abolishing feudal dues and serfdom where French revolutionary armies had not already done so. Some of the peasants and middle class benefited from these reforms. Yet Napoleon had to put the prosperity and special interests of France first in order to safeguard his power base. Levying heavy taxes in money and men for his armies, he came to be regarded more as a conquering tyrant than as an enlightened liberator. Thus French rule sparked patriotic upheavals and encouraged the growth of reactive nationalism, for individuals in different lands learned to identify emotionally with their own embattled national families as the French had done earlier.

Online Study Center **Improve Your Grade**
Interactive Map: Napoleonic Europe, 1810

The first great revolt occurred in Spain. In 1808 a coalition of Catholics, monarchists, and patriots rebelled against Napoleon's attempts to make Spain a French satellite with a Bonaparte as its king. French armies occupied Madrid, but the foes of Napoleon fled to the hills and waged uncompromising guerrilla warfare. Spain was a clear warning: resistance to French imperialism was growing.

Yet Napoleon pushed on, determined to hold his complex and far-flung empire together. In 1810, when the Grand Empire was at its height, Britain still remained at war with France, helping the guerrillas in Spain and Portugal. The continental system, organized to exclude British goods from the continent and force that "nation of shopkeepers" to its knees, was a failure. Instead, it was France that suffered from Britain's counter-blockade, which created hard times for French artisans and the middle class. Perhaps looking for a scapegoat, Napoleon turned on Alexander I of Russia, who in 1811 openly repudiated Napoleon's war of prohibitions against British goods.

Napoleon's invasion of Russia began in June 1812 with a force that eventually numbered 600,000, probably the largest force yet assembled in a single army. Only one-third of this Great Army was French, however; nationals of all the satellites and allies were drafted into the operation. Originally planning to winter in the Russian city of Smolensk if Alexander did not sue for peace, Napoleon reached Smolensk and recklessly pressed on toward Moscow. The great Battle of Borodino that followed was a draw, and the Russians retreated in good order. Alexander ordered the evacuation of Moscow, which then burned in part, and he refused to negotiate. Finally, after five weeks in the abandoned city, Napoleon ordered a retreat. That retreat was one of the greatest military disasters in history. The Russian army, the Russian winter, and starvation cut Napoleon's army to pieces. When the frozen remnants staggered into Poland and Prussia in December, 370,000 men had died and another 200,000 had been taken prisoner.[16]

Leaving his troops to their fate, Napoleon raced to Paris to raise yet another army. Possibly he might still have saved his throne if he had been willing to accept a France reduced to its historical size—the proposal offered by Austria's foreign minister, Prince Klemens von Metternich. But Napoleon refused. Austria and Prussia deserted Napoleon and joined Russia and Great Britain in the Treaty of Chaumont in March 1814, by which the four powers pledged allegiance to defeat the French emperor. All across Europe patriots called for a "war of liberation" against Napoleon's oppression, and the well-disciplined regular armies of Napoleon's enemies closed in for the kill. Less than a month later, on April 4, 1814, a defeated Napoleon abdicated his throne. After this unconditional abdication, the victorious allies granted Napoleon the island of Elba off the coast of Italy as his own tiny state. Napoleon was even allowed to keep his imperial title, and France was required to pay him a yearly income of 2 million francs.

The allies also agreed to the restoration of the Bourbon dynasty, in part because demonstrations led by a few

Individuals in Society

Toussaint L'Ouverture

Little is known of the early life of the brilliant military and political leader Toussaint L'Ouverture. He was born in 1743 on a plantation outside Le Cap owned by the Count de Bréda. According to tradition, Toussaint was the eldest son of a captured African prince from modern-day Benin. Toussaint Bréda, as he was then called, occupied a privileged position among slaves. Instead of performing backbreaking labor in the fields, he served his master as a coachman and livestock keeper. He also learned to read and write French and some Latin, but he was always more comfortable with the Creole dialect.

During the 1770s the plantation manager emancipated Toussaint, who subsequently leased his own small coffee plantation, worked by slaves. He married Suzanne Simone, who already had one son, and the couple had another son during their marriage.

Toussaint L'Ouverture entered history in 1791 when he joined the slave uprisings that swept Saint-Domingue. (At some point he took on the cryptic *nom de guerre* "l'ouverture" meaning "the opening.") Toussaint rose to prominence among rebel slaves allied with Spain and by early 1794 controlled his own army. In 1794 he defected to the French side and led his troops to a series of victories against the Spanish. In 1795 the National Convention promoted L'Ouverture to brigadier general.

Over the next three years L'Ouverture successively eliminated rivals for authority on the island. First he freed himself of the French commissioners sent to govern the colony. With a firm grip on power in the northern province, Toussaint defeated General André Rigaud in 1800 to gain control in the south. His army then marched on the capital of Spanish Santo Domingo on the eastern half of the island, meeting little resistance. The entire island of Hispaniola was now under his command.

As one historian has described him, L'Ouverture was a "small, wiry man, very black, with mobile, penetrating eyes; he greatly impressed most who met him, even those who thought him ugly. He had lost his upper set of front teeth in battle and his ears were deformed by wearing heavy gold earrings, but his presence was commanding and suggested enormous self-control."[*] A devout Catholic who led a frugal and ascetic life, L'Ouverture impressed others with his enormous physical energy, intellectual acumen, and air of mystery.

With control of Saint-Domingue in his hands, L'Ouverture was confronted with the challenge of building a post-emancipation society, the first of its kind. The task was made even more difficult by the chaos wreaked by war, the destruction of plantations, and bitter social and racial tensions. For L'Ouverture the most pressing concern was to re-establish the plantation economy. Without revenue to pay his army, the gains of the rebellion could be lost. He therefore encouraged white planters to return and reclaim their property. He also adopted harsh policies toward former slaves, forcing them back to their plantations and restricting their ability to acquire land. When they resisted, he sent troops across the island to enforce submission.

In 1801 L'Ouverture convened a colonial assembly to draft a new constitution that reaffirmed his draconian labor policies. The constitution named L'Ouverture governor for life, leaving Saint-Domingue as a colony in name alone. When news of the constitution arrived in France, an angry Napoleon dispatched General Leclerc to re-establish French control. In June 1802 Leclerc's forces arrested L'Ouverture and took him to France. He was jailed at Fort de Joux in the Jura Mountains near the Swiss border, where he died of pneumonia on April 7, 1803. It was left to his lieutenant, Jean Jacques Dessalines, to win independence for the new Haitian nation.

Equestrian portrait of Toussaint L'Ouverture. (Réunion des Musées Nationaux/Art Resource, NY)

Questions for Analysis

1. Toussaint L'Ouverture was both slave and slave owner. How did each experience shape his life and actions?
2. Despite their differences, what did Toussaint L'Ouverture and Napoleon Bonaparte have in common? Why did they share a common fate?

[*] David Patrick Geggus, *Haitian Revolutionary Studies* (Bloomington: Indiana University Press, 2002), p. 22.

Online Study Center   **Improve Your Grade**
Going Beyond Individuals in Society

The War in Spain   This unforgettable etching by the Spanish painter Francisco Goya (1746–1828) comes from his famous collection "The Disasters of the War." A French firing squad executes captured Spanish rebels almost as soon as they are captured, an everyday event in a war of atrocities on both sides. Do you think these rebels are "terrorists" or "freedom fighters"? *(Foto Marburg/Art Resource, NY)*

Mapping the Past

MAP 21.2 Napoleonic Europe in 1810   Only Great Britain remained at war with Napoleon at the height of the Grand Empire. Many British goods were smuggled through Helgoland, a tiny but strategic British possession off the German coast. Compare this map with Map 16.2, which shows the division of Europe in 1715. **❶** How had the balance of power shifted in Europe from 1715 to 1810? What changed, and what remained the same? **❷** Why did Napoleon succeed in achieving vast territorial gains where Louis XIV did not? **❸** In comparing Map 16.2 with this map, what was the impact of Napoleon's wars on Germany and the Italian peninsula? What significance do you think this had for these regions in the nineteenth century?

Online Study Center   **Improve Your Grade** Interactive Map: Napoleonic Europe, 1810

dedicated French monarchists indicated some support among the French people for that course of action. The new monarch, Louis XVIII (r. 1814–1824), tried to consolidate that support by issuing the Constitutional Charter, which accepted many of France's revolutionary changes and guaranteed civil liberties. Indeed, the charter gave France a constitutional monarchy roughly similar to that established in 1791, although far fewer people had the right to vote for representatives to the resurrected Chamber of Deputies. Moreover, in an attempt to strengthen popular support for Louis XVIII's new government, France was treated leniently by the allies, which agreed to meet in Vienna to work out a general peace settlement.

Yet Louis XVIII—old, ugly, and crippled by gout—totally lacked the glory and magic of Napoleon. Hearing of political unrest in France and diplomatic tensions in Vienna, Napoleon staged a daring escape from Elba in February 1815. Landing in France, he issued appeals for support and marched on Paris with a small band of followers. French officers and soldiers who had fought so long for their emperor responded to the call. Louis XVIII fled, and once more Napoleon took command. But Napoleon's gamble was a desperate long shot, for the allies were united against him. At the end of a frantic period known as the Hundred Days, they crushed his forces at Waterloo on June 18, 1815, and imprisoned him on the rocky island of St. Helena, far off the western coast of Africa. Louis XVIII returned again and recommenced his reign. The allies now dealt more harshly with the apparently incorrigible French. As for Napoleon, he took revenge by writing his memoirs, skillfully nurturing the myth that he had been Europe's revolutionary liberator, a romantic hero whose lofty work had been undone by oppressive reactionaries. An era had ended.

Chapter Summary

- *What social, political, and economic factors formed the background to the French Revolution?*
- *What were the immediate events that sparked the Revolution, and how did they result in the formation of a constitutional monarchy in France? How did the ideals and events of the early Revolution raise new aspirations in the colonies?*
- *How and why did the Revolution take a radical turn at home and in the colonies?*
- *Why did Napoleon Bonaparte assume control of France, and what factors led to his downfall? How did the new republic of Haiti gain independence from France?*

The French Revolution was forged by multiple and complex factors. Whereas an earlier generation of historians was convinced that the origins of the Revolution lay in class struggle between the entrenched nobility and the rising bourgeoisie, it is now clear that many other factors were involved. Certainly, French society had undergone significant transformations during the eighteenth century, which dissolved many economic and social differences among elites without removing the legal distinction between them. These changes were accompanied by political struggles between the monarchy and its officers, particularly in the high law courts. Emerging public opinion focused on the shortcomings of monarchical rule, and a rising torrent of political theory, cheap pamphlets, gossip, and innuendo offered scathing and even pornographic depictions of the king and his court. With their sacred royal aura severely tarnished, Louis XV and his successor Louis XVI found themselves unable to respond to the financial crises generated by French involvement in the Seven Years' War and the American Revolution. Louis XVI's half-hearted efforts to redress the situation were quickly overwhelmed by elite and popular demands for fundamental reform.

Forced to call a meeting of the Estates General for the first time in almost two centuries, Louis XVI fell back on the traditional formula of one vote for each of the three orders of society. Debate over the composition of the assembly called forth a bold new paradigm: that the Third Estate in itself constituted the French nation. By 1791 the National Assembly had eliminated Old Regime privileges and had established a constitutional monarchy. Talk in France of liberty, equality, and fraternity raised new and contradictory aspirations in the colony of Saint-Domingue. White planters lobbied for increased colonial autonomy; free people of color sought the return of legal equality; slaves of African birth or descent took direct action on revolutionary ideals by rising in rebellion against their masters.

With the execution of the royal couple and the declaration of terror as the order of the day, the French Revolution took an increasingly radical turn from the end of 1792. Popular fears of counter-revolutionary conspiracy combined with the outbreak of war against a mighty alliance of European monarchs convinced many that the Revolution was vulnerable and must be defended against its multiple enemies. In a spiraling cycle of accusations and executions, the Jacobins eliminated political opponents and then factions within its own party. The Directory government that took power after the fall of Robespierre restored political equilibrium at the cost of the radical platform of social equality he had pursued.

Wearied by the weaknesses of the Directory, a group of conspirators gave Napoleon Bonaparte control of France. His brilliant reputation as a military leader and his charisma and determination made him seem ideal to lead France to victory over its enemies. As is so often the case in history, Napoleon's relentless ambitions ultimately led to his downfall. His story is paralleled by that of Toussaint L'Ouverture, another soldier who emerged to the political limelight from the chaos of revolution only to endure exile and defeat.

As complex as its origins are the legacies of the French Revolution. These include liberalism, assertive nationalism, radical democratic republicanism, embryonic socialism, self-conscious conservatism, abolitionism, decolonization, and movements for racial and sexual equality. The Revolution also left a rich and turbulent history of electoral competition, legislative assemblies, and even mass politics. Thus the French Revolution and conflicting interpretations of its significance presented a whole range of political options and alternative visions of the future. For this reason, it was truly the revolution in modern European politics.

Key Terms

estates
manorial rights
Maupeou parlements
desacralization
sovereignty
Assembly of Notables
Estates General
National Assembly
Great Fear
constitutional
  monarchy
free people of color

Jacobin club
second revolution
Girondists
the Mountain
sans-culottes
planned economy
Reign of Terror
nationalism
abolition of slavery
Thermidorian
  reaction
Grand Empire

 Online Study Center **Improve Your Grade** Flashcards

Suggested Reading

Bell, David A. *The Cult of the Nation in France: Inventing Nationalism, 1680–1800.* 2001. Traces early French nationalism through its revolutionary culmination.

Blanning, T. C. W. *The French Revolutionary Wars (1787–1802).* 1996. A masterful account of the revolutionary wars that also places the French Revolution in its European context.

Broers, Michael. *Europe Under Napoleon.* 2002. Probes Napoleon's impact on the territories he conquered.

Connelly, Owen. *The French Revolution and Napoleonic Era.* 1991. An excellent introduction to the French Revolution and Napoleon.

Desan, Suzanne. *The Family on Trial in Revolutionary France.* 2004. Studies the effects of revolutionary law on the family, including the legalization of divorce.

Dubois, Laurent. *Avengers of the New World: The Story of the Haitian Revolution.* 2004. An excellent and highly readable account of the revolution that transformed the French colony of Saint-Domingue into the independent state of Haiti.

Englund, Steven. *Napoleon: A Political Life.* 2004. A good biography of the French emperor.

Hunt, Lynn. *Politics, Culture and Class in the French Revolution,* 2d ed. 2004. A pioneering examination of the French Revolution as a cultural phenomenon that generated new festivals, clothing, and songs and even a new calendar.

Landes, John B. *Visualizing the Nation: Gender, Representation, and Revolution in Eighteenth-Century France.* 2001. Analyzes images of gender and the body in revolutionary politics.

Schechter, Ronald. *Obstinate Hebrews: Representations of Jews in France, 1715–1815.* 2003. An illuminating study of Jews and attitudes toward them in France from Enlightenment to emancipation.

Sutherland, Donald. *France, 1789–1815.* 1986. An overview of the French Revolution that emphasizes its many opponents, as well as its supporters.

Tackett, Timothy. *When the King Took Flight.* 2003. An exciting re-creation of the royal family's doomed effort to escape from Paris.

Notes

1. Quoted in R. R. Palmer, *The Age of Democratic Revolution,* vol. 1 (Princeton, N.J.: Princeton University Press, 1959), pp. 95–96.
2. Quoted in G. Wright, *France in Modern Times,* 4th ed. (New York: W. W. Norton, 1987), p. 34.
3. G. Lefebvre, *The Coming of the French Revolution* (New York: Vintage Books, 1947), p. 81.
4. P. H. Beik, ed., *The French Revolution* (New York: Walker, 1970), p. 89.
5. G. Pernoud and S. Flaisser, eds., *The French Revolution* (Greenwich, Conn.: Fawcett, 1960), p. 61.
6. O. Hufton, *Women and the Limits of Citizenship in the French Revolution* (Toronto: University of Toronto Press, 1992), pp. 3–22.
7. Quotations from Wollstonecraft are drawn from E. W. Sunstein, *A Different Face: The Life of Mary Wollstonecraft* (New York: Harper & Row, 1975), pp. 208, 211; and H. R. James, *Mary Wollstonecraft: A Sketch* (London: Oxford University Press, 1932), pp. 60, 62, 69.
8. Quoted in L. Gershoy, *The Era of the French Revolution, 1789–1799* (New York: Van Nostrand, 1957), p. 150.
9. Pernoud and Flaisser, *The French Revolution,* pp. 193–194.
10. T. Blanning, *The French Revolutionary Wars, 1787–1802* (London: Arnold, 1996), pp. 116–128.
11. Quoted ibid., p. 123.
12. Quoted in Laurent Dubois, *Avengers of the New World: The Story of the Haitian Revolution* (Cambridge: Harvard University Press, 2004), p. 97.
13. I. Woloch, *Napoleon and His Collaborators: The Making of a Dictatorship* (New York: W. W. Norton, 2001), pp. 36–65.
14. Quoted in Dubois, *Avengers of the New World,* pp. 255–256.
15. Ibid., p. 3.
16. D. Sutherland, *France, 1789–1815: Revolution and Counterrevolution* (New York: Oxford University Press, 1986), p. 420.

Revolution and Women's Rights

The 1789 Declaration of the Rights of Man and of the Citizen was a revolutionary call for legal equality, representative government, and individual freedom. But the new rights were strictly limited to men; Napoleon tightened further the subordination of French women. Among those who saw the contradiction in granting supposedly universal rights to only half the population was Marie Gouze (1748–1793), known to history as Olympe de Gouges. The daughter of a provincial butcher and peddler, she pursued a literary career in Paris after the death of her husband. Between 1790 and 1793 she wrote more than two dozen political pamphlets under her new name. De Gouges's great work was her "Declaration of the Rights of Woman" (1791). Excerpted here, de Gouges's manifesto went beyond the 1789 Rights of Man. It called on males to end their oppression of women and to give women equal rights. A radical on women's issues, de Gouges sympathized with the monarchy and criticized Robespierre in print. Convicted of sedition, she was guillotined in November 1793.

. . . Man, are you capable of being just? . . . Tell me, what gives you sovereign empire to oppress my sex? Your strength? Your talents? Observe the Creator in his wisdom . . . and give me, if you dare, an example of this tyrannical empire. Go back to animals, consult the elements, study plants . . . and distinguish, if you can, the sexes in the administration of nature. Everywhere you will find them mingled; everywhere they cooperate in harmonious togetherness in this immortal masterpiece.

Man alone has raised his exceptional circumstances to a principle. . . . [H]e wants to command as a despot a sex which is in full possession of its intellectual faculties; he pretends to enjoy the Revolution and to claim his rights to equality in order to say nothing more about it.

DECLARATION OF THE RIGHTS OF WOMAN AND THE FEMALE CITIZEN

For the National Assembly to decree in its last sessions, or in those of the next legislature:

Preamble

Mothers, daughters, sisters and representatives of the nation demand to be constituted into a national assembly. Believing that ignorance, omission, or scorn for the rights of woman are the only causes of public misfortunes and of the corruption of governments, [the women] have resolved to set forth in a solemn declaration the natural, inalienable, and sacred rights of woman. . . .

. . . the sex that is as superior in beauty as it is in courage during the sufferings of maternity recognizes and declares in the presence and under the auspices of the Supreme Being, the following Rights of Woman and of Female Citizens:

I. Woman is born free and lives equal to man in her rights. Social distinctions can be based only on the common utility.

II. The purpose of any political association is the conservation of the natural and imprescriptible rights of woman and man; these rights are liberty, property, security, and especially resistance to oppression.

III. The principle of all sovereignty rests essentially with the nation, which is nothing but the union of woman and man. . . .

IV. Liberty and justice consist of restoring all that belongs to others; thus, the only limits on the exercise of the natural rights of woman are perpetual male tyranny; these limits are to be reformed by the laws of nature and reason.

V. Laws of nature and reason proscribe all acts harmful to society. . . .

VI. The law must be the expression of the general will; all female and male citizens must contribute either personally or through their representatives to its formation; it must be the same for all: male and female citizens, being equal in the eyes of the law, must be equally admitted to all honors, positions, and public employment according to their capacity and without other distinctions besides those of their virtues and talents.

VII. No woman is an exception; she is accused, arrested, and detained in cases determined by law. Women, like men, obey this rigorous law.

VIII. The law must establish only those penalties that are strictly and obviously necessary. . . .

IX. Once any woman is declared guilty, complete rigor is [to be] exercised by the law.

X. No one is to be disquieted for his very basic opinions; woman has the right to mount the scaffold; she must equally have the right to mount the rostrum, provided that her demonstrations do not disturb the legally established public order.

XI. The free communication of thoughts and opinions is one of the most precious rights of woman, since that liberty assures the recognition of children by their fathers. Any female citizen thus may say freely, I am the mother of a child which belongs to you, without being forced by a barbarous prejudice to hide the truth. . . .

XIII. For the support of the public force and the expenses of administration, the contributions of woman and man are equal; she shares all the duties . . . and all the painful tasks; therefore, she must have the same share in the distribution of positions, employment, offices, honors, and jobs. . . .

XIV. Female and male citizens have the right to verify, either by themselves or through their representatives, the necessity of the public contribution. This can only apply to women if they are granted an equal share, not only of wealth, but also of public administration. . . .

XV. The collectivity of women, joined for tax purposes to the aggregate of men, has the right to demand an accounting of his administration from any public agent.

XVI. No society has a constitution without the guarantee of rights and the separation of powers; the constitution is null if the majority of individuals comprising the nation have not cooperated in drafting it.

XVII. Property belongs to both sexes whether united or separate; for each it is an inviolable and sacred right. . . .

Postscript

Women, wake up. . . . Discover your rights. . . . Oh, women, women! When will you cease to be

Olympe de Gouges in 1784; aquatint by Madame Aubry (1748–1793). *(Musée de la Ville de Paris, Musée Carnavalet, Paris, France/The Bridgeman Art Library)*

blind? What advantage have you received from the Revolution? A more pronounced scorn, a more marked disdain. . . . [If men persist in contradicting their revolutionary principles,] courageously oppose the force of reason to the empty pretensions of superiority . . . and you will soon see these haughty men, not groveling at your feet as servile adorers, but proud to share with you the treasure of the Supreme Being. Regardless of what barriers confront you; it is in your power to free yourselves; you have only to want to. . . .

Questions for Analysis

1. On what basis did de Gouges argue for gender equality? Did she believe in natural law?

2. What consequences did "scorn for the rights of woman" have for France, according to de Gouges?

3. Did de Gouges stress political rights at the expense of social and economic rights? If so, why?

Source: Olympe de Gouges, "Declaration of the Rights of Woman," in Darline G. Levy, Harriet B. Applewhite, and Mary D. Johnson, eds., *Women in Revolutionary Paris, 1789–1795* (Urbana: University of Illinois Press, 1979), pp. 87–96. Copyright © 1979 by the Board of Trustees, University of Illinois. Used with permission.

A colorful timetable poster lists the trains from London to Folkstone, the English Channel's gateway port to the European continent, and proudly proclaims the speed of the journey. *(Private Collection/The Bridgeman Art Library)*

The Industrial Revolution in Britain

● *What were the origins of the Industrial Revolution in Britain, and how did it develop between 1780 and 1850?*

Industrialization in Continental Europe

● *How after 1815 did continental countries respond to the challenge of industrialization?*

Relations Between Capital and Labor

● *How did the Industrial Revolution affect social classes, the standard of living, and patterns of work? What measures were taken to improve the conditions of workers?*

THE REVOLUTION IN ENERGY AND INDUSTRY,
CA 1780–1860

While the revolution in France was opening a new political era, another revolution was beginning to transform economic and social life. This was the Industrial Revolution, which began in Great Britain around the 1780s and started to influence continental Europe after 1815. Because the Industrial Revolution was less dramatic than the French Revolution, some historians see industrial development as basically moderate and evolutionary. But from a longer perspective, it was rapid and brought about numerous radical changes. Quite possibly only the development of agriculture during Neolithic times had a comparable impact and significance.

The Industrial Revolution profoundly modified much of human experience. It changed patterns of work, transformed the social class structure and the way people thought about class, and eventually even altered the international balance of political power. The Industrial Revolution also helped ordinary people gain a higher standard of living as the widespread poverty of the preindustrial world was gradually reduced.

Unfortunately, the improvement in the European standard of living was quite limited until about 1850 for at least two reasons. First, even in Britain, only a few key industries experienced a technological revolution. Many more industries continued to use old methods, especially on the continent, and this held down the increase in total production. Second, the increase in total population, which began in the eighteenth century (see pages 625–628), continued all across Europe as the era of the Industrial Revolution unfolded. As a result, the rapid growth in population threatened to eat up the growth in production and to leave most individuals poorer than ever. As a consequence, rapid population growth provided a somber background for European industrialization and made the wrenching transformation all the more difficult.

Online Study Center

This icon will direct you to interactive activities and study materials on the website **college.hmco.com/pic/mckaywest9e**

The Industrial Revolution in Britain

The Industrial Revolution began in Great Britain, that historic union of Scotland, Wales, and England—the wealthiest and the dominant part of the country. It was something new in history, and it was quite unplanned. With no models to copy and no idea of what to expect, Britain had to pioneer not only in industrial technology but also in social relations and urban living. Between 1793 and 1815, these formidable tasks were complicated by almost constant war with France. As the trailblazer in economic development, as France was in political change, Britain must command special attention.

- *What were the origins of the Industrial Revolution in Britain, and how did it develop between 1780 and 1850?*

Eighteenth-Century Origins

Although many aspects of the British Industrial Revolution are still matters for scholarly debate, it is generally agreed that the industrial changes that did occur grew out of a long process of development. First, the expanding Atlantic economy of the eighteenth century served mercantilist Britain remarkably well. The colonial empire that Britain aggressively built, augmented by a strong position in Latin America and in the African slave trade, provided a growing market for British manufactured goods. So did the domestic market. In an age when it was much cheaper to ship goods by water than by land, no part of England was more than twenty miles from navigable water. Beginning in the 1770s, a canal-building boom greatly enhanced this natural advantage (see Map 22.1). Rivers and canals provided easy movement of England's and Wales's enormous deposits of iron and coal, resources that would be critical raw materials in Europe's early industrial age. Nor were there any tariffs within the country to hinder trade, as there were in France before 1789 and in politically fragmented Germany.

Second, agriculture played a central role in bringing about the Industrial Revolution in Britain. English farmers in particular were second only to the Dutch in productivity in 1700, and they were continually adopting new methods of farming as the century went on. The result, especially before 1760, was a period of bountiful crops and low food prices. The ordinary English family did not have to spend almost everything it earned just to

MAP 22.1 Cottage Industry and Transportation in Eighteenth-Century England England had an unusually good system of navigable rivers. From about 1770 to 1800 a canal-building boom linked these rivers together and greatly improved inland transportation.

Online Study Center **Improve Your Grade** Interactive Map: Cottage Industry and Transportation in Eighteenth-Century England

buy bread. It could spend more on, for example, manufactured goods—leather shoes or a razor for the man, a bonnet or a shawl for the woman, toy soldiers for the son, and a doll for the daughter. Thus demand for goods within the country complemented the demand from the colonies.

Third, Britain had other assets that helped give rise to industrial leadership. Unlike eighteenth-century France, Britain had an effective central bank and well-developed credit markets. The monarchy and the aristocratic oligarchy, which had jointly ruled the country since 1688, provided stable and predictable government. At the same time, the government let the domestic economy operate with few controls, encouraging personal initiative, technical change, and a free market. Finally, Britain had long had a large class of hired agricultural laborers, rural proletarians whose numbers were further increased by the second great round of enclosures in the late eighteenth century. These rural wage earners were relatively mobile—compared to village-bound peasants in France and western Germany, for example—and along with cottage workers they formed a potential industrial labor force for capitalist entrepreneurs.

All these factors combined to initiate the **Industrial Revolution,** a term first coined by awed contemporaries in the 1830s to describe the burst of major inventions and technical changes they had witnessed in certain industries. This technical revolution went hand in hand with an impressive quickening in the annual rate of industrial growth in Britain. Whereas industry had grown at only 0.7 percent between 1700 and 1760 (before the Industrial Revolution), it grew at the much higher rate of 3 percent between 1801 and 1831 (when industrial transformation was in full swing).[1] The decisive quickening of growth probably came in the 1780s, after the American War of Independence and just before the French Revolution.

Therefore, the great economic and political revolutions that shaped the modern world occurred almost simultaneously, though they began in different countries. The Industrial Revolution was, however, a longer process than the political upheavals. It was not complete in Britain until 1850 at the earliest, and it had no real impact on continental countries until after 1815.

The First Factories

The pressure to produce more goods for a growing market was directly related to the first decisive breakthrough of the Industrial Revolution—the creation of the world's first large factories in the British cotton textile industry. Technological innovations in the manufacture of cotton cloth led to a new system of production and social relationships. Since no other industry experienced such a rapid or complete transformation before 1830, these trailblazing developments deserve special consideration.

Although the putting-out system of merchant capitalism (see page 629) was expanding all across Europe in the eighteenth century, this pattern of rural industry was most fully developed in Britain. There, under the pressure of growing demand, the system's limitations began to outweigh its advantages for the first time. This was especially true in the British textile industry after about 1760.

Chronology	
ca 1765	Hargreaves invents spinning jenny
1769	Watt creates modern steam engine
1775–1783	American Revolution
1780s–1850	Industrial Revolution
1780–1851	Population boom in England
1789–1799	French Revolution
1798	Malthus, *Essay on the Principle of Population*
1799	Combination Acts passed
1810	Strike of Manchester cotton spinners
1824	Combination Acts repealed
1830s	Industrial banks in Belgium
1830	Stephenson's *Rocket*; first important railroad
1833	Factory Act
1841	List, *National System of Political Economy*
1842	Mines Act
1844	Engels, *The Condition of the Working Class in England*
1851	Great Exhibition held at Crystal Palace

A constant shortage of thread in the textile industry focused attention on ways of improving spinning. Many a tinkering worker knew that a better spinning wheel promised rich rewards. It proved hard to spin the traditional raw materials—wool and flax—with improved machines, but cotton was different. Cotton textiles had first been imported into Britain from India by the East India Company, and by 1760 there was a tiny domestic industry in northern England. After many experiments over a generation, a gifted carpenter and jack-of-all-trades, James Hargreaves, invented his cotton-spinning jenny about 1765. At almost the same moment, a barber-turned-manufacturer named Richard Arkwright invented (or possibly pirated) another kind of spinning machine, the water frame. These breakthroughs produced an explosion in the infant cotton textile industry in the 1780s, when it was increasing the value of its output at an unprecedented rate of about 13 percent each year. By 1790 the new machines were producing ten times as much cotton yarn as had been made in 1770.

Woman Working a Hargreaves's Spinning Jenny The loose cotton strands on the slanted bobbins passed up to the sliding carriage and then on to the spindles in back for fine spinning. The worker, almost always a woman, regulated the sliding carriage with one hand, and with the other she turned the crank on the wheel to supply power. By 1783 one woman could spin by hand a hundred threads at a time on an improved model. *(Mary Evans Picture Library)*

Online Study Center **Improve Your Grade**
Primary Source: Manchester Becomes a Thriving Industrial City

Hargreaves's **spinning jenny** was simple and inexpensive. In early models, from six to twenty-four spindles were mounted on a sliding carriage, and each spindle spun a fine, slender thread. The woman moved the carriage back and forth with one hand and turned a wheel to supply power with the other. Now it was the male weaver who could not keep up with the vastly more efficient female spinner.

Arkwright's **water frame** employed a different principle. It quickly acquired a capacity of several hundred spindles and demanded much more power—waterpower. The water frame thus required large specialized mills, factories that employed as many as one thousand workers from the very beginning. The water frame could spin only coarse, strong thread, which was then put out for respinning on hand-powered cottage jennies. Around 1790 an alternative technique invented by Samuel Crompton also began to require more power than the human arm could supply. After that time, all cotton spinning was gradually concentrated in factories.

The first consequences of these revolutionary developments were more beneficial than is generally believed.

Cotton goods became much cheaper, and they were bought and treasured by all classes. In the past, only the wealthy could afford the comfort and cleanliness of underwear, which was called **body linen** because it was made from expensive linen cloth. Now millions of poor people, who had earlier worn nothing underneath their coarse, filthy outer garments, could afford to wear cotton slips and underpants as well as cotton dresses and shirts.

Families using cotton in cottage industry were freed from their constant search for adequate yarn from scattered, part-time spinners, since all the thread needed could be spun in the cottage on the jenny or obtained from a nearby factory. The wages of weavers, now hard-pressed to keep up with the spinners, rose markedly until about 1792. Weavers were among the best-paid workers in England. They were known to walk proudly through the streets with 5-pound notes stuck in their hatbands, and they dressed like the middle class. As a result, large numbers of agricultural laborers became hand-loom weavers, while mechanics and capitalists sought to invent a power loom to save on labor costs. This Edmund Cartwright achieved in 1785. But the power looms of the factories worked poorly at first, and hand-loom weavers continued to receive good wages until at least 1800.

Working conditions in the early factories were less satisfactory than those of cottage weavers and spinners, and people were reluctant to work in them. Therefore, factory owners often turned to young children who had been abandoned by their parents and put in the care of local parishes. Parish officers often "apprenticed" such unfortunate foundlings to factory owners. The parish thus saved money, and the factory owners gained workers over whom they exercised almost the authority of slave owners.

Apprenticed as young as five or six years of age, boy and girl workers were forced by law to labor for their "masters" for as many as fourteen years. Housed, fed, and locked up nightly in factory dormitories, the young workers received little or no pay. Hours were appalling— commonly thirteen or fourteen hours a day, six days a week. Harsh physical punishment maintained brutal discipline. To be sure, poor children typically worked long hours and frequently outside the home for brutal masters. But the wholesale coercion of orphans as factory apprentices constituted exploitation on a truly unprecedented scale. This exploitation ultimately piqued the conscience of reformers and reinforced more humanitarian attitudes toward children and their labor in the early nineteenth century.

The creation of the world's first modern factories in the British cotton textile industry in the 1770s and 1780s, which grew out of the putting-out system of cottage production, was a major historical development. Both symbolically and substantially, the big new cotton mills marked the beginning of the Industrial Revolution in Britain. By 1831 the largely mechanized cotton textile industry towered above all others, accounting for fully 22 percent of the country's entire industrial production.

The Problem of Energy

The growth of the cotton textile industry might have been stunted or cut short, however, if water from rivers and streams had remained the primary source of power for the new factories. But this did not occur. Instead, an epoch-making solution was found to the age-old problem of energy and power. This solution permitted continued rapid development in cotton textiles, the gradual generalization of the factory system, and the triumph of the Industrial Revolution in Britain.

Human beings have long used their toolmaking abilities to construct machines that convert one form of energy into another for their own benefit. In the medieval period, people began to develop water mills to grind their grain and windmills to pump water and drain swamps. More efficient use of water and wind in the sixteenth and seventeenth centuries enabled human beings to accomplish more; intercontinental sailing ships were a prime example. Nevertheless, even into the eighteenth century,

society continued to rely for energy mainly on plants, and human beings and animals continued to perform most work. This dependence meant that Western civilization remained poor in energy and power.

Lack of power lay at the heart of the poverty that afflicted the large majority of people. The man behind the plow and the woman at the spinning wheel could employ only horsepower and human muscle in their labor. No matter how hard they worked, they could not produce very much.

The shortage of energy had become particularly severe in Britain by the eighteenth century. Because of the growth of population, most of the great forests of medieval Britain had long ago been replaced by fields of grain and hay. Wood was in ever-shorter supply, yet it remained tremendously important. It served as the primary source of heat for all homes and industries and as a basic raw material. Processed wood (charcoal) was the fuel that was mixed with iron ore in the blast furnace to produce pig iron. The iron industry's appetite for wood was enormous, and by 1740 the British iron industry was stagnating. Vast forests enabled Russia to become the world's leading producer of iron, much of which was exported to Britain. But Russia's potential for growth was limited, too, and in a few decades Russia would reach the barrier of inadequate energy that was already holding England back.

The Steam Engine Breakthrough

As this early energy crisis grew worse, Britain looked toward its abundant and widely scattered reserves of coal as an alternative to its vanishing wood. Coal was first used in Britain in the late Middle Ages as a source of heat. By 1640 most homes in London were heated with it, and it also provided heat for making beer, glass, soap, and other products. Coal was not used, however, to produce mechanical energy or to power machinery. It was there that coal's potential was enormous, as a simple example shows.

A hard-working miner can dig out 500 pounds of coal a day using hand tools. Even an extremely inefficient converter, which transforms only 1 percent of the heat energy in coal into mechanical energy, will produce 27 horsepower-hours of work from that 500 pounds of coal. The miner, by contrast, produces only about 1 horsepower-hour in the course of a day. Early steam engines were powerful but still inefficient converters of energy.

As more coal was produced, mines were dug deeper and deeper and were constantly filling with water. Mechanical pumps, usually powered by animals walking in circles at the surface, had to be installed. At one mine, fully five hundred horses were used in pumping. Such power was expensive and bothersome. In an attempt to

Manchester, England, 1851 The development of the steam engine enabled industry to concentrate in towns and cities. Manchester mushroomed from a town of 20,000 in 1750 into "Cottonopolis," cotton city, with 400,000 inhabitants in 1850. In this painting the artist contrasts the smoky city and its awesome power with the idealized beauty of the suburbs, where the new rich settled and built their mansions. *(The Royal Collection, © 2007 Her Majesty Queen Elizabeth II)*

overcome these disadvantages, Thomas Savery in 1698 and Thomas Newcomen in 1705 invented the first primitive **steam engines.** Both engines were extremely inefficient. Both burned coal to produce steam, which was then used to operate a pump. However, by the early 1770s, many of the Savery engines and hundreds of the Newcomen engines were operating successfully, though inefficiently, in English and Scottish mines.

In the early 1760s, a gifted young Scot named James Watt (1736–1819) was drawn to a critical study of the steam engine. Watt was employed at the time by the University of Glasgow as a skilled craftsman making scientific instruments. The Scottish universities were pioneers in practical technical education, and in 1763 Watt was called on to repair a Newcomen engine being used in a physics course. After a series of observations, Watt saw that the Newcomen engine's waste of energy could be reduced by adding a separate condenser. This splendid invention, patented in 1769, greatly increased the efficiency of the steam engine.

To invent something in a laboratory is one thing; to make it a practical success is quite another. Watt needed skilled workers, precision parts, and capital, and the relatively advanced nature of the British economy proved essential. A partnership with a wealthy English toymaker provided risk capital and a manufacturing plant. In the craft tradition of locksmiths, tinsmiths, and millwrights, Watt found skilled mechanics who could install, regulate, and repair his sophisticated engines. From ingenious manufacturers such as the cannonmaker John Wilkinson, Watt was gradually able to purchase precision parts. This support allowed him to create an effective vacuum and regulate a complex engine. In more than twenty years of constant effort, Watt made many further improvements. By the late 1780s, the steam engine had become a practical and commercial success in Britain.

The steam engine of Watt and his followers was the Industrial Revolution's most fundamental advance in technology. For the first time in history, humanity had, at least for a few generations, almost unlimited power at its disposal. For the first time, inventors and engineers could devise and implement all kinds of power equipment to aid people in their work. For the first time, abundance was at least a possibility for ordinary men and women.

The steam engine was quickly put to use in several industries in Britain. It drained mines and made possible the production of ever more coal to feed steam engines elsewhere. The steam-power plant began to replace waterpower in the cotton-spinning mills during the 1780s, contributing greatly to that industry's phenomenal rise. Steam also took the place of waterpower in flour mills, in the malt mills used in breweries, in the flint mills supplying the china industry, and in the mills exported by Britain to the West Indies to crush sugar cane.

Steam power promoted important breakthroughs in other industries. The British iron industry was radically transformed. The use of powerful, steam-driven bellows in blast furnaces helped ironmakers switch over rapidly from limited charcoal to unlimited **coke** (which is made from coal) in the smelting of pig iron after 1770. In the 1780s, Henry Cort developed the puddling furnace, which allowed pig iron to be refined in turn with coke. Strong, skilled ironworkers—the puddlers—"cooked" molten pig iron in a great vat, raking off globs of refined iron for further processing. Cort also developed heavy-duty, steam-powered rolling mills, which were capable of spewing out finished iron in every shape and form.

The economic consequence of these technical innovations was a great boom in the British iron industry. In 1740 annual British iron production was only 17,000 tons. With the spread of coke smelting and the first impact of Cort's inventions, production reached 68,000 tons in 1788, 125,000 tons in 1796, and 260,000 tons in 1806. In 1844 Britain produced 3 million tons of iron. This was a truly amazing expansion. Once scarce and expensive, iron became the cheap, basic, indispensable building block of the economy.

The Coming of the Railroads

The second half of the eighteenth century saw extensive construction of hard and relatively smooth roads, particularly in France before the Revolution. Yet it was passenger traffic that benefited most from this construction. Overland shipment of freight, relying solely on horsepower, was still quite limited and frightfully expensive;

James Nasmyth's Mighty Steam Hammer Nasmyth's invention was the forerunner of the modern pile driver, and its successful introduction in 1832 epitomized the rapid development of steam power technology in Britain. In this painting by the inventor himself, workers manipulate a massive iron shaft being hammered into shape at Nasmyth's foundry near Manchester. *(Science & Society Picture Library, London)*

The Saltash Bridge   Railroad construction presented innumerable challenges, such as the building of bridges to span rivers and gorges. Civil engineers responded with impressive feats, and their profession bounded ahead. This painting portrays the inauguration of I. K. Brunel's Saltash Bridge, where the railroad crosses the Tamar River into Cornwall in southwest England. The high spans allow large ships to pass underneath. *(Elton Collection, Ironbridge Gorge Museum Trust)*

shippers used rivers and canals for heavy freight whenever possible. It was logical, therefore, that inventors would try to use steam power.

As early as 1800, an American ran a "steamer on wheels" through city streets. Other experiments followed. In the 1820s, English engineers created steam cars capable of carrying fourteen passengers at ten miles an hour—as fast as the mail coach. But the noisy, heavy steam automobiles frightened passing horses and damaged themselves as well as the roads with their vibrations. For the rest of the century, horses continued to reign on highways and city streets.

The coal industry had long been using plank roads and rails to move coal wagons within mines and at the surface. Rails reduced friction and allowed a horse or a human being to pull a heavier load. Thus once a rail capable of supporting a heavy locomotive was developed in 1816, all sorts of experiments with steam engines on rails went forward. In 1825 after ten years of work, George

Stephenson built an effective locomotive. In 1830 his *Rocket* sped down the track of the just-completed Liverpool and Manchester Railway at sixteen miles per hour. This was the world's first important railroad, fittingly steaming in the heart of industrial England. The line from Liverpool to Manchester was a financial as well as a technical success, and many private companies were quickly organized to build more rail lines. Within twenty years, they had completed the main trunk lines of Great Britain. Other countries were quick to follow.

The significance of the railroad was tremendous. The railroad dramatically reduced the cost and uncertainty of shipping freight overland. This advance had many economic consequences. Previously, markets had tended to be small and local; as the barrier of high transportation costs was lowered, markets became larger and even nationwide. Larger markets encouraged larger factories with more sophisticated machinery in a growing number of industries. Such factories could make goods more cheaply and gradually subjected most cottage workers and many urban artisans to severe competitive pressures.

In all countries, the construction of railroads created a strong demand for unskilled labor and contributed to the growth of a class of urban workers. Hard work on construction gangs was done in the open air with animals and hand tools. Many landless farm laborers and poor peasants, long accustomed to leaving their villages for temporary employment, went to build railroads. By the time the work was finished, life back home in the village often seemed dull and unappealing, and many men drifted to towns in search of work. By the time they sent for their wives and sweethearts to join them, they had become urban workers.

The railroad changed the outlook and values of the entire society. The last and culminating invention of the Industrial Revolution, the railroad dramatically revealed the power and increased the speed of the new age. Racing down a track at sixteen miles per hour or, by 1850, at a phenomenal fifty miles per hour was a new and awesome experience. As a French economist put it after a ride on the Liverpool and Manchester in 1833, "There are certain impressions that one cannot put into words!"

Some great painters, notably Joseph M. W. Turner (1775–1851) and Claude Monet (1840–1926), succeeded in expressing this sense of power and awe. So did the massive new train stations, the cathedrals of the industrial age. Leading railway engineers such as Isambard Kingdom Brunel and Thomas Brassey, whose tunnels pierced mountains and whose bridges spanned valleys, became public idols—the astronauts of their day. Everyday speech absorbed the images of railroading. After you got up a "full head of steam," you "highballed" along. And if you didn't "go off the track," you might "toot your own whistle." The railroad fired the imagination.

Industry and Population

In 1851 London was the site of a famous industrial fair. This Great Exhibition was held in the newly built **Crystal Palace,** an architectural masterpiece made entirely of glass and iron, both of which were now cheap and abundant. For the millions who visited, one fact stood out: the little island of Britain was the "workshop of the world." It alone produced two-thirds of the world's coal and more than one-half of its iron and cotton cloth. More generally, it has been carefully estimated that in 1860 Britain produced a truly remarkable 20 percent of the entire world's output of industrial goods, whereas it had produced only about 2 percent of the world total in 1750.[2] Experiencing revolutionary industrial change, Britain became the first industrial nation (see Map 22.2).

MAP 22.2 The Industrial Revolution in England, ca 1850 Industry concentrated in the rapidly growing cities of the north and the Midlands, where rich coal and iron deposits were in close proximity.

Online Study Center **Improve Your Grade**
Interactive Map: Industrialization in England, ca 1850

As the British economy significantly increased its production of manufactured goods, the gross national product (GNP) rose roughly fourfold at constant prices between 1780 and 1851. In other words, the British people as a whole increased their wealth and their national income dramatically. At the same time, the population of Britain boomed, growing from about 9 million in 1780 to almost 21 million in 1851. Thus growing numbers consumed much of the increase in total production. According to one important study, average consumption per person increased by only 75 percent between 1780 and 1851, as the growth in the total population ate up a large part of the fourfold increase in GNP in those years.[3]

Although the question is still debated, many economic historians now believe that rapid population growth in

The Crystal Palace The Great Exhibition of 1851 attracted more than six million visitors, many of whom journeyed to London on the newly built railroads. Countries and companies from all over the world displayed their products and juries awarded prizes in the strikingly modern Crystal Palace, an architectural marvel built using the cheap iron and glass of the industrial age. In this illustration visitors stroll through the domed hall and peruse the 1500 exhibits. *(Courtesy of the Trustees of the British Museum)*

Great Britain was not harmful because it facilitated industrial expansion. More people meant a more mobile labor force, with a wealth of young workers in need of employment and ready to go where the jobs were. Contemporaries were much less optimistic. In his famous and influential *Essay on the Principle of Population* (1798), Thomas Malthus (1766–1834) argued that population would always tend to grow faster than the food supply. In Malthus's opinion, the only hope of warding off such "positive checks" to population growth as war, famine, and disease was "prudential restraint." That is, young men and women had to limit the growth of population by the old tried-and-true means of marrying late in life. But Malthus was not optimistic about this possibility. The powerful attraction of the sexes would cause most people to marry early and have many children.

Online Study Center **Improve Your Grade**
Primary Source: Malthus Predicts Gloomy Prospects for the Human Condition

Wealthy English stockbroker and leading economist David Ricardo (1772–1823) coldly spelled out the pessimistic implications of Malthus's thought. Ricardo's depressing **iron law of wages** posited that because of the pressure of population growth, wages would always sink to subsistence level. That is, wages would be just high enough to keep workers from starving. With Malthus and Ricardo setting the tone, economics was soon dubbed "the dismal science."

Malthus, Ricardo, and their many followers were proved wrong—in the long run. However, until the 1820s, or even the 1840s, contemporary observers might reasonably have concluded that the economy and the total population were racing neck and neck, with the outcome very much in doubt. The closeness of the race added to the difficulties inherent in the journey toward industrial civilization.

There was another problem as well. Perhaps workers, farmers, and ordinary people did not get their rightful share of the new wealth. Perhaps only the rich got richer, while the poor got poorer or made no progress. We will turn to this great issue after looking at the process of industrialization in continental countries.

Industrialization in Continental Europe

The new technologies developed in the British Industrial Revolution were adopted rather slowly by businesses in continental Europe. Yet by the end of the nineteenth century, several European countries as well as the United States had also industrialized their economies to a considerable but variable degree. This meant that the process of Western industrialization proceeded gradually, with uneven jerks and national (and regional) variations.

Scholars are still struggling to explain these variations, especially since good answers may offer valuable lessons in our own time for poor countries seeking to improve their material condition through industrialization and economic development. The latest findings on the Western experience are encouraging. They suggest that there were alternative paths to the industrial world in the nineteenth century and that, today as then, there was no need to follow a rigid, predetermined British model.

• *How after 1815 did continental countries respond to the challenge of industrialization?*

National Variations

European industrialization, like most economic developments, requires some statistical analysis as part of the effort to understand it. Comparative data on industrial production in different countries over time help give us an overview of what happened. One set of data, the work of a Swiss scholar, compares the level of industrialization on a per capita basis in several countries from 1750 to 1913. These data are far from perfect because there are gaps in the underlying records. But they reflect basic trends and are presented in Table 22.1 for closer study.

As the heading of Table 22.1 makes clear, this is a per capita comparison of levels of industrialization—a comparison of how much industrial product was produced, on average, for each person in a given country in a given

year. Therefore, all the numbers in Table 22.1 are expressed in terms of a single index number of 100, which equals the per capita level of industrial goods in Great Britain (and Ireland) in 1900. Every number in the table is thus a percentage of the 1900 level in Britain and is directly comparable with other numbers. The countries are listed in roughly the order that they began to use large-scale, power-driven technology.

What does this overview of European industrialization tell us? First, and very significantly, one sees in the first column that in 1750 all countries were fairly close together and that Britain was only slightly ahead of its archenemy, France. Second, the column headed 1800 shows that Britain had opened up a noticeable lead over all continental countries by 1800, and that gap progressively widened as the British Industrial Revolution accelerated to 1830 and reached full maturity by 1860. The British level of per capita industrialization was twice the French level in 1830, for example, and more than three times the French level in 1860. All other large countries (except the United States) had fallen even further behind Britain than France had at both dates.

Third, variations in the timing and in the extent of industrialization in the continental powers and the United States are also apparent. Belgium, independent in 1831 and rich in iron and coal, led in adopting Britain's new technology, and it experienced a truly revolutionary surge between 1830 and 1860. France developed factory production more gradually, and most historians now detect no burst in French mechanization and no acceleration in the growth of overall industrial output that may accurately be called revolutionary. They stress instead France's relatively good pattern of early industrial growth, which was unjustly tarnished by the spectacular rise of Germany and the United States after 1860. In general, eastern and southern Europe began the process of modern industrialization later than northwestern and central Europe. Nevertheless, these regions made real progress in the late nineteenth century, as growth after 1880 in Austria-Hungary, Italy, and Russia suggests.

Finally, the late but substantial industrialization in eastern and southern Europe meant that all European states (as well as the United States, Canada, and Japan) managed to raise per capita industrial levels in the nineteenth century. These continent-wide increases stood in stark contrast to the large and tragic decreases that occurred at the same time in many non-Western countries, most notably in China and India, as Table 22.1 clearly shows. European countries industrialized to a greater or lesser extent even as most of the non-Western world *de*-industrialized. Thus differential rates of wealth- and power-creating industrial development, which heightened disparities within Europe,

Table 22.1 Per Capita Levels of Industrialization, 1750–1913

	1750	1800	1830	1860	1880	1900	1913
Great Britain	10	16	25	64	87	100	115
Belgium	9	10	14	28	43	56	88
United States	4	9	14	21	38	69	126
France	9	9	12	20	28	39	59
Germany	8	8	9	15	25	52	85
Austria-Hungary	7	7	8	11	15	23	32
Italy	8	8	8	10	12	17	26
Russia	6	6	7	8	10	15	20
China	8	6	6	4	4	3	3
India	7	6	6	3	2	1	2

Note: All entries are based on an index value of 100, equal to the per capita level of industrialization in Great Britain in 1900. Data for Great Britain are actually for the United Kingdom, thereby including Ireland with England, Wales, and Scotland.

Source: P. Bairoch, "International Industrialization Levels from 1750 to 1980," *Journal of European Economic History* 11 (Spring 1982): 294. Reprinted with permission.

also greatly magnified existing inequalities between Europe and the rest of the world. We shall return to this momentous change in world economic relationships in Chapter 26.

The Challenge of Industrialization

The different patterns of industrial development suggest that the process of industrialization was far from automatic. Indeed, building modern industry was an awesome challenge. To be sure, throughout Europe the eighteenth century was an era of agricultural improvement, population increase, expanding foreign trade, and growing cottage industry. Thus when the pace of British industry began to accelerate in the 1780s, continental businesses began to adopt the new methods as they proved their profitability. British industry enjoyed clear superiority, but at first the continent was close behind.

By 1815, however, the situation was quite different. In spite of wartime difficulties, British industry maintained the momentum of the 1780s and continued to grow and improve between 1789 and 1815. On the continent, the

upheavals that began with the French Revolution had another effect: they disrupted trade, created runaway inflation, and fostered social anxiety. War severed normal communications between Britain and the continent, severely handicapping continental efforts to use new British machinery and technology. Moreover, the years from 1789 to 1815 were, even for the privileged French economy receiving special favors from Napoleon, a time of "national catastrophe"—in the graphic words of a famous French scholar.[4] Thus France and the rest of Europe were further behind Britain in 1815 than in 1789.

This widening gap made it more difficult, if not impossible, for other countries to follow the British pattern in energy and industry after peace was restored in 1815. Above all, in the newly mechanized industries, British goods were being produced very economically, and these goods had come to dominate world markets completely while the continental states were absorbed in war between 1792 and 1815. In addition, British technology had become so advanced and complicated that very few engineers or skilled technicians outside England understood it. Moreover, the technology of steam power had grown much more expensive. It involved large investments in the iron and coal industries and, after 1830, required the existence of railroads, which were very costly. Continental business people had great difficulty finding the large sums of money the new methods demanded, and there was a shortage of laborers accustomed to working in factories. All these disadvantages slowed the spread of modern industry (see Map 22.3).

After 1815, however, when continental countries began to face up to the British challenge, they had at least three important advantages. First, most continental countries had a rich tradition of putting-out enterprise, merchant capitalists, and skilled urban artisans. Such a tradition gave continental firms the ability to adapt and survive in the face of new market conditions. Second, continental capitalists did not need to develop their own

Mapping the Past

MAP 22.3 Continental Industrialization, ca 1850 Although continental countries were beginning to make progress by 1850, they still lagged far behind Britain. For example, continental railroad building was still in an early stage, whereas the British rail system was essentially complete (review Map 22.2, page 725). Coal played a critical role in nineteenth-century industrialization both as a power source for steam engines and as a raw material for making iron and steel. ❶ Locate the major exposed (that is, known) coal deposits in 1850. Which countries and areas appear rich in coal resources, and which appear poor? Is there a difference between northern and southern Europe? ❷ What is the relationship between known coal deposits and emerging industrial areas?

advanced technology. Instead, they could simply "borrow" the new methods developed in Great Britain, as well as engineers and some of the financial resources these countries lacked. European countries such as France and Russia also had a third asset that many non-Western areas lacked in the nineteenth century. They had strong independent governments, which did not fall under foreign political control. These governments could fashion economic policies to serve their own interests, as they proceeded to do. They would eventually use the power of the state to promote industry and catch up with Britain.

Agents of Industrialization

The British realized the great value of their technical discoveries and tried to keep their secrets to themselves. Until 1825 it was illegal for artisans and skilled mechanics to leave Britain; until 1843 the export of textile machinery and other equipment was forbidden. Many talented, ambitious workers, however, slipped out of the country illegally and introduced the new methods abroad.

One such man was William Cockerill, a Lancashire carpenter. He and his sons began building cotton-spinning equipment in French-occupied Belgium in 1799. In 1817 the most famous son, John Cockerill, purchased the old summer palace of the deposed bishops of Liège in southern Belgium. Cockerill converted the palace into a large industrial enterprise, which produced machinery, steam engines, and then railway locomotives. He also established modern ironworks and coal mines.

Cockerill's plants in the Liège area became an industrial nerve center, continually gathering new information and transmitting it across Europe. Many skilled British workers came illegally to work for Cockerill, and some went on to found their own companies throughout Europe. Newcomers brought the latest plans and secrets, so Cockerill could boast that ten days after an industrial advance occurred in Britain, he knew all about it in Belgium. Thus British technicians and skilled workers were a powerful force in the spread of early industrialization.

A second agent of industrialization were talented entrepreneurs such as Fritz Harkort, a business pioneer in the German machinery industry. Serving in England as a Prussian army officer during the Napoleonic wars, Harkort was impressed and enchanted with what he saw. He concluded that Germany had to match all these English achievements as quickly as possible. Setting up shop in an abandoned castle in the still-tranquil Ruhr Valley, Harkort felt an almost religious calling to build steam engines and become the "Watt of Germany."

Harkort's basic idea was simple, but it was enormously difficult to carry out. Lacking skilled laborers to do the job, Harkort turned to England for experienced, though expensive, mechanics. Getting materials also posed a great problem. He had to import the thick iron boilers that he needed from England at great cost. In spite of all these problems, Harkort built and sold engines, winning fame and praise. His ambitious efforts over sixteen years also resulted in large financial losses for himself and his partners, and in 1832 he was forced out of his company by his financial backers, who cut back operations to reduce losses. His career illustrates both the great efforts of a few important business leaders to duplicate the British achievement and the difficulty of the task.

Entrepreneurs like Harkort were obviously exceptional. Most continental businesses adopted factory technology slowly, and handicraft methods lived on. Indeed, continental industrialization usually brought substantial but uneven expansion of handicraft industry in both rural and urban areas for a time. Artisan production of luxury items grew in France as the rising income of the international middle class created foreign demand for silk scarfs, embroidered needlework, perfumes, and fine wines.

Government Support and Corporate Banking

Another major force in continental industrialization was government, which often helped business people in continental countries to overcome some of their difficulties. **Tariff protection** was one such support. For example, after Napoleon's wars ended in 1815, France was suddenly flooded with cheaper and better British goods. The French government responded by laying high tariffs on many British imports in order to protect the French economy. After 1815 continental governments bore the cost of building roads and canals to improve transportation.

They also bore to a significant extent the cost of building railroads. Belgium led the way in the 1830s and 1840s. In an effort to tie the newly independent nation together, the Belgian government decided to construct a state-owned system. Built rapidly as a unified network, Belgium's state-owned railroads stimulated the development of heavy industry and made the country an early industrial leader. Several of the smaller German states also built state systems.

The Prussian government provided another kind of invaluable support. It guaranteed that the state treasury would pay the interest and principal on railroad bonds if the closely regulated private companies in Prussia were

A German Ironworks, 1845 This big business enterprise, the Borsig ironworks in Berlin, mastered the new British method of smelting iron ore with coke. Germany, and especially the state of Prussia, was well endowed with both iron and coal, and the rapid exploitation of these resources after 1840 transformed a poor agricultural country into an industrial powerhouse. *(akg-images)*

unable to do so. Thus railroad investors in Prussia ran little risk, and capital was quickly raised. In France the state shouldered all the expense of acquiring and laying roadbed, including bridges and tunnels. Finished roadbed was leased to a carefully supervised private company, which usually benefited from a state guarantee of its debts. In short, governments helped pay for railroads, the all-important leading sector in continental industrialization.

The career of German journalist and thinker Friedrich List (1789–1846) reflects government's greater role in industrialization on the continent than in England. List considered the growth of modern industry of the utmost importance because manufacturing was a primary means of increasing people's well-being and relieving their poverty. Moreover, List was a dedicated nationalist. He wrote that the "wider the gap between the backward and advanced nations becomes, the more dangerous it is to remain behind." An agricultural nation was not only poor but

also weak, increasingly unable to defend itself and maintain its political independence. To promote industry was to defend the nation.

The practical policies that List focused on in articles and in his influential *National System of Political Economy* (1841) were railroad building and the tariff. List supported the formation of a customs union, or *Zollverein*, among the separate German states. Such a tariff union came into being in 1834, allowing goods to move between the German member states without tariffs, while erecting a single uniform tariff against other nations. List wanted a high protective tariff, which would encourage infant industries, allowing them to develop and eventually hold their own against their more advanced British counterparts. List denounced the British doctrine of free trade as little more than Britain's attempt "to make the rest of the world, like the Hindus, its serfs in all industrial and commercial relations." By the 1840s List's economic nationalism had become increasingly popular in Germany and elsewhere.

Finally, banks, like governments, also played a larger and more creative role on the continent than in Britain. Previously, almost all banks in Europe had been private, organized as secretive partnerships. Because of the possibility of unlimited financial loss, the partners of private banks tended to be quite conservative and were content to deal with a few rich clients and a few big merchants. They generally avoided industrial investment as being too risky.

In the 1830s, two important Belgian banks pioneered in a new direction. They received permission from the growth-oriented government to establish themselves as corporations enjoying limited liability. That is, a stockholder could lose only his or her original investment in the bank's common stock and could not be assessed for any additional losses. Publicizing the risk-reducing advantage of limited liability, these Belgian banks were able to attract many shareholders, large and small. They mobilized impressive resources for investment in big companies, became industrial banks, and successfully promoted industrial development.

Similar corporate banks became important in France and Germany in the 1850s and 1860s. Usually working in collaboration with governments, they established and developed many railroads and many companies working in heavy industry, which were increasingly organized as limited liability corporations. The most famous such bank was the Crédit Mobilier of Paris, founded by Isaac and Emile Pereire, two young Jewish journalists from Bordeaux. The Crédit Mobilier advertised extensively. It used the savings of thousands of small investors as well as the resources of big ones. The activities of the bank were far-reaching; it built railroads all over France and Europe. As Emile Pereire had said in 1835, "It is not enough to outline gigantic programs on paper. I must write my ideas on the earth."

The combined efforts of skilled workers, entrepreneurs, governments, and industrial banks meshed successfully between 1850 and the financial crash of 1873. This was a period of unprecedentedly rapid economic growth on the continent. In Belgium, Germany, and France, key indicators of modern industrial development—such as railway mileage, iron and coal production, and steam-engine capacity—increased at average annual rates of 5 to 10 percent. As a result, rail networks were completed in western and much of central Europe, and the leading continental countries mastered the industrial technologies that had first been developed in Great Britain. In the early 1870s, Britain was still Europe's most industrial nation, but a select hand-

ful of countries were closing the gap that had been opened up by the Industrial Revolution.

Relations Between Capital and Labor

Industrial development brought new social relations and intensified long-standing problems between capital and labor in both urban workshops and cottage industry (see pages 628–631). A new group of factory owners and industrial capitalists arose. These men and women and their families strengthened the wealth and size of the middle class, which had previously been made up mainly of merchants and professional people. The nineteenth century became the golden age of the middle class. Modern industry also created a much larger group, the factory workers. For the first time, large numbers of men, women, and children came together under one roof to work with complicated machinery for a single owner or a few partners in large companies.

The growth of new occupational groups in industry stimulated new thinking about social relations. Often combined with reflections on the French Revolution, this thinking led to the development of a new overarching interpretation—a new paradigm—regarding social relationships (see Chapter 23). Briefly, this paradigm argued, with considerable success, that individuals were members of economically determined classes, which had conflicting interests. Accordingly, the comfortable, well-educated "public" of the eighteenth century came increasingly to see itself as the backbone of the middle class (or the middle classes), and the "people" gradually transformed themselves into the modern working class (or working classes). And if the new class interpretation was more of a deceptive simplification than a fundamental truth for some critics, it appealed to many because it seemed to explain what was happening. Therefore, conflicting classes existed, in part, because many individuals came to believe they existed and developed an appropriate sense of class feeling—what Marxists call **class-consciousness.**

• *How did the Industrial Revolution affect social classes, the standard of living, and patterns of work? What measures were taken to improve the conditions of workers?*

The New Class of Factory Owners

Early industrialists operated in a highly competitive economic system. As the careers of Watt and Harkort illus-

Ford Maddox Brown: Work This midcentury painting provides a rich visual representation of the new concepts of social class that became common by 1850. The central figures are the colorful laborers, endowed by the artist with strength and nobility. Close by, a poor girl minds her brother and sister for her working mother. On the right, a middle-class minister and a social critic observe and do intellectual work. What work does the couple on horseback perform? *(Birmingham Museums and Art Gallery/ The Bridgeman Art Library)*

trate, there were countless production problems, and success and large profits were by no means certain. Manufacturers therefore waged a constant battle to cut their production costs and stay afloat. Much of the profit had to go back into the business for new and better machinery. "Dragged on by the frenzy of this terrible life," according to one of the dismayed critics, the struggling manufacturer had "no time for niceties. He must conquer or die, make a fortune or drown himself."[5]

Most early industrialists drew upon their families and friends for labor and capital, but they came from a variety of backgrounds. Many, such as Harkort, were from well-established merchant families, which provided a rich network of contacts and support. Others, such as Watt and Cockerill, were of modest means, especially in the early days. Artisans and skilled workers of exceptional ability had unparalleled opportunities. Members of ethnic and religious groups who had been discriminated against in the traditional occupations controlled by the landed aristocracy jumped at the new chances and often helped each other. Scots, Quakers, and other Protestant dissenters were tremendously important in Britain; Protestants and Jews dominated banking in Catholic France. Many of the industrialists were newly rich, and, not surprisingly, they were very proud and self-satisfied.

As factories and firms grew larger, opportunities declined, at least in well-developed industries. It became considerably harder for a gifted but poor young mechanic to start a small enterprise and end up as a wealthy manufacturer. Formal education (for sons and males) became more important as a means of success and advancement, and formal education at the advanced level was expensive. In Britain by 1830 and in France and Germany by 1860, leading industrialists were more likely to have inherited their well-established enterprises, and they were financially much more secure than their struggling fathers and mothers had been. They also had a greater sense of class-consciousness, fully aware that ongoing industrial development had widened the gap between themselves and their workers.

The wives and daughters of successful businessmen also found fewer opportunities for active participation in Europe's increasingly complex business world. Rather than contributing as vital partners in a family-owned enterprise, as so many middle-class women such as Elizabeth Strutt had done (see the feature "Individuals in Society: The Strutt Family"), these women were increasingly valued for their ladylike gentility. By 1850 some influential women writers and most businessmen assumed that middle-class wives and daughters should steer clear of undignified work in offices and factories. Rather, a middle-class lady should protect and enhance her femininity. She should concentrate on her proper role as wife and mother, preferably in an elegant residential area far removed from ruthless commerce and the volatile working class.

The New Factory Workers

The social consequences of the Industrial Revolution have long been hotly debated. The condition of British workers during the transformation has always generated the most controversy among historians because Britain was the first country to industrialize and because the social consequences seemed harshest there. Before 1850 other countries had not proceeded very far with industrialization, and almost everyone agrees that the economic conditions of European workers improved after 1850. Thus the experience of British workers to about 1850 deserves special attention. (Industrial growth also promoted rapid urbanization, with its own awesome problems, as will be shown in Chapter 24.)

From the beginning, the Industrial Revolution in Britain had its critics. Among the first were the romantic poets. William Blake (1757–1827) called the early factories "satanic mills" and protested against the hard life of the London poor. William Wordsworth (1770–1850) lamented the destruction of the rural way of life and the pollution of the land and water. Some handicraft workers—notably the **Luddites,** who attacked whole factories in northern England in 1812 and after—smashed the new machines, which they believed were putting them out of work. Doctors and reformers wrote eloquently of problems in the factories and new towns, while Malthus and Ricardo concluded that workers would earn only enough to stay alive.

Online Study Center **Improve Your Grade**
Primary Source: Yorkshire Luddites Threaten the
   Owner of a Mechanized Factory

This pessimistic view was accepted and reinforced by Friedrich Engels (1820–1895), the future revolutionary and colleague of Karl Marx. After studying conditions in northern England, this young middle-class German published in 1844 *The Condition of the Working Class in England,* a blistering indictment of the middle classes. "At the bar of world opinion," he wrote, "I charge the English middle classes with mass murder, wholesale robbery, and all the other crimes in the calendar." The new poverty of industrial workers was worse than the old poverty of cottage workers and agricultural laborers, according to Engels. The culprit was industrial capitalism, with its relentless competition and constant technical change. Engels's extremely influential charge of middle-class exploitation and increasing worker poverty was embellished by Marx and later socialists.

Meanwhile, other observers believed that conditions were improving for the working people. Andrew Ure wrote in 1835 in his study of the cotton industry that conditions in most factories were not harsh and were even quite good. Edwin Chadwick, a great and conscientious government official well acquainted with the problems of the working population, concluded that the "whole mass of the laboring community" was increasingly able "to buy more of the necessities and minor luxuries of life."[6] Nevertheless, if all the contemporary assessments had been counted up, those who thought conditions were getting worse for working people would probably have been the majority.

In an attempt to go beyond the contradictory judgments of contemporaries, some historians have looked at different kinds of sources. Statistical evidence is one such source. If working people suffered a great economic decline, as Engels and later socialists asserted, then the purchasing power of the working person's wages must have declined drastically.

Scholarly statistical studies have weakened the idea that the condition of the working class got much worse

Individuals in Society

The Strutt Family

For centuries economic life in Europe revolved around hundreds of thousands of small family enterprises. These family enterprises worked farms, crafted products, and traded goods. They built and operated the firms and factories of the early industrial era, with the notable exceptions of the capital-hungry railroads and a few big banks. Indeed, until late in the nineteenth century, close-knit family groups continued to control most successful businesses, including those organized as corporations.

One successful and fairly well-documented family enterprise began with the marriage of Jedediah Strutt (1726–1797) and Elizabeth Woollat (1729–1774) in Derbyshire in northern England in 1755. The son of a farmer, Jedediah fell in love with Elizabeth when he was apprenticed away from home as a wheelwright and lodged with her parents. Both young people grew up in the close-knit dissenting Protestant community, which did not accept the doctrines of the state-sponsored Church of England, and the well-educated Elizabeth worked in a local school for dissenters and then for a dissenter minister in London. Indecisive and self-absorbed, Jedediah inherited in 1754 a small stock of animals from an uncle and finally married Elizabeth the following year.

Aided by Elizabeth, who was "obviously a very capable woman" and who supplied some of the drive her husband had previously lacked, Jedediah embarked on a new career.[*] He invented a machine to make handsome, neat-fitting ribbed silk stockings, which had previously been made by hand. He secured a patent, despite strong opposition from competitors, and went into production. Elizabeth helped constantly in the enterprise, which was nothing less than an informal partnership between husband and wife.[†]

In 1757, for example, when Jedediah was fighting to uphold his patent in the local court, Elizabeth left her son of nine months and journeyed to London to seek a badly needed loan from her former employer. She also canvassed her London relatives and dissenter friends for orders for stockings and looked for sales agents and sources of capital. Elizabeth's letters reveal a detailed knowledge of ribbed stockings and the prices and quality of different kinds of thread. The family biographers, old-line economic historians writing without a trace of feminist concerns, conclude that her husband "owed much of his success to her energy and counsel." Elizabeth was always "active in the business—

a partner in herself."[‡] Historians have often overlooked such invaluable contributions from wives like Elizabeth, partly because the legal rights and consequences of partnership were denied to married women in Britain and Europe in the eighteenth and nineteenth centuries.

The Strutt enterprise grew and gradually prospered, but it always retained its family character. The firm built a large silk mill and then went into cotton spinning in partnership with Richard Arkwright, the inventor of the water frame (see page 720). The brothers of both Jedediah and Elizabeth worked for the firm, and their eldest daughter worked long hours in the warehouse. Bearing three sons, Elizabeth fulfilled yet another vital task because the typical family firm looked to its own members for managers and continued success. All three sons entered the business and became cotton textile magnates. Elizabeth never saw these triumphs. The loyal and talented wife in the family partnership died suddenly at age forty-five while in London with Jedediah on a business trip.

Jedediah Strutt (ca 1790), by Joseph Wright of Derby. (Derby Museum & Art Gallery/ The Bridgeman Art Library)

Questions for Analysis

1. How and why did the Strutts succeed?
2. What does Elizabeth's life tell us about the role of British women in the early Industrial Revolution?

[*]R. Fitton and A. Wadsworth, *The Strutts and the Arkwrights, 1758–1830: A Study of the Early Factory System* (Manchester, England: Manchester University Press, 1958), p. 23.
[†]See the excellent discussion by C. Hall, "Strains in the 'Firm of Wife, Children and Friends'? Middle-Class Women and Employment in Early Nineteenth-Century England," in P. Hudson and W. Lee, eds., *Women's Work and the Family Economy in Historical Perspective* (Manchester, England: Manchester University Press, 1990), pp. 106–132.
[‡]Fitton and Wadsworth, *The Strutts*, pp. 110–111.

Online Study Center **Improve Your Grade**
Going Beyond Individuals in Society

with industrialization. But the most recent studies also confirm the view that the early years of the Industrial Revolution were hard ones for British workers. There was little or no increase in the purchasing power of the average British worker from about 1780 to about 1820. The years from 1792 to 1815, a period of almost constant warfare with France, were particularly difficult. Food prices rose faster than wages, and the living conditions of the laboring poor declined. Only after 1820, and especially after 1840, did real wages rise substantially, so that the average worker earned and consumed roughly 50 percent more in real terms in 1850 than in 1770.[7] In short, there was considerable economic improvement for workers throughout Great Britain by 1850, but that improvement was hard won and slow in coming.

This important conclusion must be qualified, however. First, the hours in the average workweek increased, as some economic historians now believe it had been increasing in parts of northern Europe since the seventeenth century. Thus, to a large extent, workers earned more simply because they worked more. Indeed, significant recent research shows that in England nonagricultural workers labored about 250 days per year in 1760 as opposed to 300 days per year in 1830, while the normal workday remained an exhausting eleven hours throughout the entire period. In 1760 nonagricultural workers still observed many religious and public holidays by not working, and Monday was popularly known as "Saint Monday" because so many workers took the day off. These days of leisure and relaxation declined rapidly after 1760, and by 1830 nonagricultural workers had joined landless agricultural laborers in toiling six rather than five days a week.[8]

Second, the wartime decline in the average worker's standard of living was very important. The difficult war years were formative years for the new factory labor force, and they colored the early experience of modern industrial life in somber tones.

Another way to consider the workers' standard of living is to look at the goods that they purchased. Again the evidence is somewhat contradictory. Speaking generally, workers ate somewhat more food of higher nutritional quality as the Industrial Revolution progressed, except during wartime. Diets became more varied; people ate more potatoes, dairy products, fruits, and vegetables. Clothing improved, but housing for working people probably deteriorated somewhat. In short, per capita use of specific goods supports the position that the standard of living of the working classes rose, at least moderately, after the long wars with France.

Conditions of Work

What about working conditions? Did workers eventually earn more only at the cost of working longer and harder? Were workers exploited harshly by the new factory owners?

The first factories were cotton mills, which began functioning along rivers and streams in the 1770s. Cottage workers, accustomed to the putting-out system, were reluctant to work in the new factories even when they received relatively good wages because factory work was unappealing. In the factory, workers had to keep up with the machine and follow its tempo. They had to show up every day and work long, monotonous hours. Factory workers had to adjust their daily lives to the shrill call of the factory whistle.

Cottage workers were not used to that kind of life and discipline. All members of the family worked hard and long, but in spurts, setting their own pace. They could interrupt their work when they wanted to. Women and children could break up their long hours of spinning with other tasks. On Saturday afternoon the head of the family delivered the week's work to the merchant manufacturer and got paid. Saturday night was a time of relaxation and drinking, especially for the men. Recovering from his hangover on Tuesday, the weaver bent to his task on Wednesday and then worked frantically to meet his deadline on Saturday. Like some students today, he might "pull an all-nighter" on Thursday or Friday in order to get his work in.

Also, early factories resembled English poorhouses, where totally destitute people went to live at public expense. Some poorhouses were industrial prisons, where the inmates had to work in order to receive their food and lodging. The similarity between large brick factories and large stone poorhouses increased the cottage workers' fear of factories and their hatred of factory discipline.

It was cottage workers' reluctance to work in factories that prompted the early cotton mill owners to turn to abandoned and pauper children for their labor. As we have seen, these owners contracted with local officials to employ large numbers of these children, who had no say in the matter. Pauper children were often badly treated and terribly overworked in the mills, as they were when they were apprenticed as chimney sweeps, market girls, shoemakers, and so forth. In the eighteenth century, semiforced child labor seemed necessary and was socially accepted. From our modern point of view, it was cruel exploitation and a blot on the record of the new industrial system.

Workers at a Large Cotton Mill This 1833 engraving shows adult women operating power looms under the supervision of a male foreman, and it accurately reflects both the decline of family employment and the emergence of a gender-based division of labor in many English factories. The jungle of belts and shafts connecting the noisy looms to the giant steam engine on the ground floor created a constant din. *(Time Life Pictures/Getty Images)*

By 1790 the early pattern was rapidly changing. The use of pauper apprentices was in decline, and in 1802 it was forbidden by Parliament. Many more factories were being built, mainly in urban areas, where they could use steam power rather than waterpower and attract a workforce more easily than in the countryside. The need for workers was great. Indeed, people came from near and far to work in the cities, both as factory workers and as laborers, builders, and domestic servants. Yet as they took these new jobs, working people did not simply give in to a system of labor that had formerly repelled them. Rather, they helped modify the system by carrying over old, familiar working traditions.

For one thing, they often came to the mills and the mines as family units. This was how they had worked on farms and in the putting-out system. The mill or mine owner bargained with the head of the family and paid him or her for the work of the whole family. In the cotton mills, children worked for their mothers or fathers, collecting scraps and "piecing" broken threads together. In the mines, children sorted coal and worked the ventilation equipment. Their mothers hauled coal in the tunnels below the surface, while their fathers hewed with pick and shovel at the face of the seam.

The preservation of the family as an economic unit in the factories from the 1790s on made the new surroundings more tolerable, both in Great Britain and in other countries, during the early stages of industrialization. Parents disciplined their children, making firm measures socially acceptable, and directed their upbringing.

The presence of the whole family meant that children and adults worked the same long hours (twelve-hour shifts were normal in cotton mills in 1800). In the early years, some very young children were employed solely to keep the family together. For example, Jedediah Strutt (see page 735) believed children should be at least ten years old to work in his mills, but he reluctantly employed seven-year-olds to satisfy their parents. Adult workers were not particularly interested in limiting the minimum working age or hours of their children as long as family members worked side by side. Only when technical changes threatened to place control and discipline in the hands of impersonal managers and overseers did adult workers protest against inhuman conditions in the name of their children.

Some enlightened employers and social reformers in Parliament definitely felt otherwise. They argued that more humane standards were necessary, and they used widely circulated parliamentary reports to influence public opinion. For example, Robert Owen (1771–1858), a very successful manufacturer in Scotland, testified in 1816 before an investigating committee on the basis of his experience. He stated that "very strong facts" demonstrated that employing children under ten years of age as factory workers was "injurious to the children, and not beneficial to the proprietors."[9] Workers also provided graphic testimony at such hearings as the reformers pressed Parliament to pass corrective laws. They scored some important successes.

Their most significant early accomplishment was the **Factory Act of 1833.** It limited the factory workday for children between nine and thirteen to eight hours and that of adolescents between fourteen and eighteen to twelve hours, although the act made no effort to regulate the hours of work for children at home or in small businesses. Children under nine were to be enrolled in the elementary schools that factory owners were required to establish. The employment of children declined rapidly. Thus the Factory Act broke the pattern of whole families working together in the factory because efficiency required standardized shifts for all workers.

Ties of blood and kinship were important in other ways in Great Britain in the formative years between about 1790 and 1840. Many manufacturers and builders hired workers through subcontractors. They paid the subcontractors on the basis of what the subcontractors and their crews produced—for smelting so many tons of pig iron or moving so much dirt or gravel for a canal or roadbed. Subcontractors in turn hired and fired their own workers, many of whom were friends and relations. The subcontractor might be as harsh as the greediest capitalist, but the relationship between subcontractor and work crew was close and personal. This kind of personal relationship had traditionally existed in cottage industry and in urban crafts, and it was more acceptable to many workers than impersonal factory discipline. This system also provided people with an easy way to find a job. Even today, a friend or relative who is a supervisor is frequently worth a host of formal application forms.

Ties of kinship were particularly important for newcomers, who often traveled great distances to find work. Many urban workers in Great Britain were from Ireland. Forced out of rural Ireland by population growth and deteriorating economic conditions from 1817 on, Irish in search of jobs could not be choosy; they took what they could get. As early as 1824, most of the workers in the Glasgow cotton mills were Irish; in 1851 one-sixth of the population of Liverpool was Irish. Like many other immigrant groups held together by ethnic and religious ties, the Irish worked together, formed their own neighborhoods, and not only survived but also thrived.

The Sexual Division of Labor

The era of the Industrial Revolution witnessed major changes in the sexual division of labor. In preindustrial Europe most people generally worked in family units. By tradition, certain jobs were defined by gender—women and girls for milking and spinning, men and boys for plowing and weaving—but many tasks might go to either sex. Family employment carried over into early factories and subcontracting, but it collapsed as child labor was restricted and new attitudes emerged. A different sexual division of labor gradually arose to take its place. The man emerged as the family's primary wage earner, while the woman found only limited job opportunities. Generally denied good jobs at good wages in the growing urban economy, women were expected to concentrate on unpaid housework, child care, and craftwork at home.

This new pattern of "separate spheres" had several aspects. First, all studies agree that married women from the working classes were much less likely to work full-time for wages outside the house after the first child arrived, although they often earned small amounts doing putting-out handicrafts at home and taking in boarders. Second, when married women did work for wages outside the house, they usually came from the poorest families, where the husbands were poorly paid, sick, unemployed, or missing. Third, these poor married (or widowed) women were joined by legions of young unmarried women, who worked full-time but only in certain jobs. Fourth, all women were generally confined to low-paying, dead-end jobs. Virtually no occupation open to women paid a wage sufficient for a person to live independently. Men predominated in the better-paying, more promising employments. Evolving gradually, but largely in place by 1850, the new sexual division of labor in Britain constituted a major development in the history of women and of the family.

If the reorganization of paid work along gender lines is widely recognized, there is no agreement on its causes. One school of scholars sees little connection with industrialization and finds the answer in the deeply ingrained sexist attitudes of a "patriarchal tradition," which predated the economic transformation. These scholars stress the role of male-dominated craft unions in denying working women access to good jobs and relegating them to unpaid housework. Other scholars, stressing that the gender roles of women and men can vary enormously with time and culture, look more to a combination of economic and biological factors in order to explain the emergence of a sex-segregated division of labor.

Three ideas stand out in this more recent interpretation. First, the new and unfamiliar discipline of the clock and the machine was especially hard on married women of the laboring classes. Above all, relentless factory discipline conflicted with child care in a way that labor on the farm or in the cottage had not. A woman operating ear-splitting spinning machinery could mind a child of seven or eight working beside her (until such work was outlawed), but she could no longer pace herself through pregnancy or breast-feed her baby on the job. Thus a working-class woman had strong incentives to concentrate on child care within her home if her family could afford it.

Second, running a household in conditions of primitive urban poverty was an extremely demanding job in its own right. There were no supermarkets or public transportation. Everything had to be done on foot. Shopping and feeding the family constituted a never-ending challenge. The woman marched from one tiny shop to another, dragging her tired children (for who was to watch them?) and struggling valiantly with heavy sacks and tricky shopkeepers. Yet another brutal job outside the house—a "second shift"—had limited appeal for the average married woman. Thus women might well have accepted the emerging division of labor as the best available strategy for family survival in the industrializing society.[10]

Third, why were the women who did work for wages outside the home segregated and confined to certain "women's jobs"? No doubt the desire of males to monopolize the best opportunities and hold women down provides part of the answer. Yet as some feminist scholars have argued, sex-segregated employment was also a collective response to the new industrial system. Previously, at least in theory, young people worked under a watchful parental eye. The growth of factories and mines brought unheard-of opportunities for girls and boys to mix on the job, free of familial supervision. Continuing to mix after work, they were "more likely to form liaisons, initiate courtships, and respond to advances."[11] Such intimacy also led to more unplanned pregnancies and fueled the illegitimacy explosion that had begun in the late eighteenth century and that gathered force until at least 1850 (see pages 656–657). Thus segregation of jobs by gender was partly an effort by older people to help control the sexuality of working-class youths.

Investigations into the British coal industry before 1842 provide a graphic example of this concern. (See the feature "Listening to the Past: The Testimony of Young Mine Workers" on pages 744–745.) The middle-class men leading the inquiry, who expected their daughters and wives to pursue ladylike activities, often failed to appreciate the physical effort of the girls and women who dragged with belt and chain the unwheeled carts of coal along narrow underground passages. But they professed horror at the sight of girls and women working without shirts, which was a common practice because of the heat, and they quickly assumed the prevalence of licentious sex with the male miners, who also wore very little clothing. In fact, most girls and married women worked for related males in a family unit that provided considerable protection and restraint. Yet many witnesses from the working class also believed that "blackguardism and debauchery" were common and that "they are best out of the pits, the lasses." Some miners stressed particularly the danger of sexual aggression for girls working past puberty. As one explained: "I consider it a scandal for girls to work in the pits. Till they are 12 or 14 they may work very well but after that it's an abomination. . . . The work of the pit does not hurt them, it is the effect on their morals that I complain of."[12] The **Mines Act of 1842** prohibited underground work for all women as well as for boys under ten.

Some women who had to support themselves protested against being excluded from coal mining, which paid higher wages than most other jobs open to working-class women. But provided they were part of families that could manage economically, the girls and the women who had worked underground were generally pleased with the law. In explaining her satisfaction in 1844, one mother of four provided a real insight into why many women accepted the emerging sexual division of labor:

While working in the pit I was worth to my [miner] husband seven shillings a week, out of which we had to pay 2½ shillings to a woman for looking after the younger children. I used to take them to her house at 4 o'clock in the morning, out of their own beds, to put them into hers. Then there was one shilling a week for washing; besides, there was mending to pay for, and other things. The house was not guided. The other children broke things; they did not go to school when they were sent; they would be playing about, and get ill-used by other children, and their clothes torn. Then when I came home in the evening, everything was to do after the day's labor, and I was so tired I had no heart for it; no fire lit, nothing cooked, no water fetched, the house dirty, and nothing comfortable for my husband. It is all far better now, and I wouldn't go down again.[13]

The Early Labor Movement in Britain

Many kinds of employment changed slowly during and after the Industrial Revolution in Great Britain. In 1850 more British people still worked on farms than in any other occupation. The second-largest occupation was domestic service, with more than one million household servants, 90 percent of whom were women. Thus many old, familiar jobs outside industry lived on and provided alternatives for individual workers. This helped ease the transition to industrial civilization.

Within industry itself, the pattern of artisans working with hand tools in small shops remained unchanged in many trades, even as some others were revolutionized by technological change. For example, as in the case of cotton and coal, the British iron industry was completely dominated by large-scale capitalist firms by 1850. Many large ironworks had more than one thousand people on their payrolls. Yet the firms that fashioned iron into small metal goods, such as tools, tableware, and toys, employed on average fewer than ten wage workers, who used time-honored handicraft skills. Only gradually after 1850 did some owners find ways to reorganize some handicraft industries with new machines and new patterns of work. The survival of small workshops gave many workers an alternative to factory employment.

Working-class solidarity and class-consciousness developed in small workshops as well as in large factories. In the northern factory districts, where thousands of "hired hands" looked across at a tiny minority of managers and owners, anticapitalist sentiments were frequent by the 1820s. Commenting in 1825 on a strike in the woolen center of Bradford and the support it had gathered from other regions, one paper claimed with pride that "it is all the workers of England against a few masters of Bradford."[14] Modern technology had created a few versus a many.

The transformation of some traditional trades by organizational changes, rather than technological innovations, could also create ill will and class feeling. The liberal concept of economic freedom gathered strength in the late eighteenth and early nineteenth centuries. As in France during the French Revolution, the British government attacked monopolies, guilds, and workers combinations in the name of individual liberty. In 1799 Parliament passed the **Combination Acts,** which outlawed unions and strikes. In 1813 and 1814, Parliament repealed the old and often disregarded law of 1563 regulating the wages of artisans and the conditions of apprenticeship. As a result of these and other measures, certain skilled artisan workers, such as bootmakers and high-quality tailors, found aggressive capitalists ignoring traditional work rules and flooding their trades with unorganized women workers and children to beat down wages.

Celebrating Skilled Labor This handsome engraving embellished the membership certificate of the British carpenters union, one of the leading "new model unions" that represented skilled workers effectively after 1850. The upper panel shows carpenters building the scaffolding for a great arch; the lower panel captures the spirit of a busy workshop. *(HIP/Art Resource, NY)*

The liberal capitalist attack on artisan guilds and work rules was bitterly resented by many craftworkers, who subsequently played an important part in Great Britain and in other countries in gradually building a modern labor movement to improve working conditions and to serve worker needs. The Combination Acts were widely disregarded by workers. Printers, papermakers, carpenters, tailors, and other such craftsmen continued to take collective action, and societies of skilled factory workers also organized unions. Unions sought to control the number of skilled workers, limit apprenticeship to members' own children, and bargain with owners over wages. They were not afraid to strike; there was, for example, a general strike of adult cotton spinners in Manchester in 1810. In the face of widespread union activity, Parliament repealed the Combination Acts in 1824, and unions were tolerated, though not fully accepted, after 1825.

The next stage in the development of the British trade-union movement was the attempt to create a single large national union. This effort was led not so much by working people as by social reformers such as Robert Owen. Owen, a self-made cotton manufacturer (see page 738), had pioneered in industrial relations by combining firm discipline with concern for the health, safety, and hours of his workers. After 1815 he experimented with cooperative and socialist communities, including one at New Harmony, Indiana. Then in 1834 Owen organized one of the largest and most visionary of the early national unions, the **Grand National Consolidated Trades Union.** When this and other grandiose schemes collapsed, the British labor movement moved once again after 1851 in the direction of craft unions. The most famous of these "new model unions" was the Amalgamated Society of Engineers, which represented skilled machinists. These unions won real benefits for members by fairly conservative means and thus became an accepted part of the industrial scene.

British workers also engaged in direct political activity in defense of their own interests. After the collapse of Owen's national trade union, many working people went into the Chartist movement, which sought political democracy. The key Chartist demand—that all men be given the right to vote—became the great hope of millions of aroused people. Workers were also active in campaigns to limit the workday in factories to ten hours and to permit duty-free importation of wheat into Great Britain to secure cheap bread. Thus working people developed a sense of their own identity and played an active role in shaping the new industrial system. They were neither helpless victims nor passive beneficiaries.

Chapter Summary

Online Study Center   **ACE the Test**

- *What were the origins of the Industrial Revolution in Britain, and how did it develop between 1780 and 1850?*
- *How after 1815 did continental countries respond to the challenge of industrialization?*
- *How did the Industrial Revolution affect social classes, the standard of living, and patterns of work? What measures were taken to improve the conditions of workers?*

Western society's industrial breakthrough grew out of a long process of economic and social change in which the rise of capitalism, overseas expansion, and the growth of rural industry stood out as critical preparatory developments. Eventually taking the lead in all of these developments, and also profiting from stable government, abundant natural resources, and a flexible labor force, Britain experienced between the 1780s and the 1850s an epoch-making transformation, one that is still aptly termed the Industrial Revolution.

Building on technical breakthroughs, power-driven equipment, and large-scale enterprise, the Industrial Revolution in England greatly increased output in certain radically altered industries, stimulated the large handicraft and commercial sectors, and speeded up overall economic growth. Rugged Scotland industrialized at least as fast as England, and Great Britain became the first industrial nation. By 1850 the level of British per capita industrial production was surpassing continental levels by a growing margin, and Britain savored a near monopoly in world markets for mass-produced goods.

Continental countries inevitably took rather different paths to the urban industrial society. They relied more on handicraft production in both towns and villages. Only in the 1840s did railroad construction begin to create the strong demand for iron, coal, and railway equipment that speeded up the process of industrialization in the 1850s and 1860s.

The rise of modern industry had a profound impact on people and their lives. In the early stages, Britain again led the way, experiencing in a striking manner the long-term social changes accompanying the economic transformation. Factory discipline and Britain's stern capitalist economy weighed heavily on working people, who, however, actively fashioned their destinies and refused to be passive victims. Improvements in the standard of living came slowly, but they were substantial by 1850. The era of industrialization fostered new attitudes toward child labor, encouraged protective factory legislation, and called forth a new sense of class feeling and an assertive labor movement. It also promoted a more rigid division of roles and responsibilities within the family that was detrimental to women, another gradual but profound change of revolutionary proportions.

Key Terms

Industrial Revolution	economic
spinning jenny	nationalism
water frame	class-consciousness
body linen	Luddites
steam engines	Factory Act of 1833
coke	Mines Act of 1842
Rocket	Combination Acts
Crystal Palace	Grand National
iron law of wages	Consolidated
tariff protection	Trades Union

Online Study Center **Improve Your Grade** Flashcards

Suggested Reading

Cameron, Rondo, and Larry Neal. *A Concise Economic History of the World,* 4th ed. 2003. Provides an introduction to key issues related to the Industrial Revolution and has a carefully annotated bibliography.

Clapham, J. H. *Economic Development of France and Germany.* 1963. A classic study.

Davidoff, Leonore, and Catherine Hall. *Family Fortunes: Men and Women of the English Middle Class, 1750–1850,*

rev. ed. 2003. Examines both economic activities and cultural beliefs with great skill.

Fuchs, Rachel G. *Gender and Poverty in Nineteenth-Century Europe.* 2005. Provides a broad comparative perspective.

Gaskell, Elizabeth. *Mary Barton.* 1848. Gaskell's novel offers a realistic portrayal of the new industrial society.

Goodman, Jordan, and Katrina Honeyman. *Gainful Pursuits: The Making of Industrial Europe, 1600–1914.* 1988. An excellent general treatment of European industrial growth.

Kemp, Tom. *Industrialization in Europe,* 2d ed. 1985. A useful overview.

Landes, David. *Dynasties: Fortunes and Misfortunes of the World's Great Family Businesses.* 2006. A collection offering fascinating and insightful histories of famous enterprises and leading capitalists.

Pomeranz, Kenneth. *The Great Divergence: China, Europe, and the Making of the Modern World Economy.* 2000. A sophisticated reconsideration of why western Europe underwent industrialization and China did not.

Stearns, Peter N. *The Industrial Revolution in World History,* 3d ed. 2007. A useful brief survey.

Thompson, E. P. *The Making of the English Working Class.* 1963. A fascinating book in the Marxian tradition that is rich in detail and early working-class lore.

Valenze, Deborah. *The First Industrial Woman.* 1995. A gender study that reinvigorates the debate between "optimists" and "pessimists" about the consequences of industrialization in Britain.

Walton, Whitney. *France and the Crystal Palace: Bourgeois Taste and Artisan Manufacture in the 19th Century.* 1992. Examines the gradual transformation of handicraft techniques and their persistent importance in the international economy.

Wrigley, E. A. *Continuity, Chance and Change: The Character of the Industrial Revolution in England.* 1994. An important reconsideration stressing resources and population.

Notes

1. N. F. R. Crafts, *British Economic Growth During the Industrial Revolution* (Oxford: Oxford University Press, 1985), p. 32.
2. P. Bairoch, "International Industrialization Levels from 1750 to

1980," *Journal of European Economic History* 11 (Spring 1982): 269–333.

3. Crafts, *British Economic Growth,* pp. 45, 95–102.

4. M. Lévy-Leboyer, *Les banques européennes et l'industrialisation dans la première moitié du XIXe siècle* (Paris: Presses Universitaires de France, 1964), p. 29.

5. J. Michelet, *The People,* trans. with an introduction by J. P. McKay (Urbana: University of Illinois Press, 1973; original publication, 1846), p. 64.

6. Quoted in W. A. Hayek, ed., *Capitalism and the Historians* (Chicago: University of Chicago Press, 1954), p. 126.

7. Crafts, *British Economic Growth,* p. 95.

8. H-J. Voth, *Time and Work in England, 1750–1830* (Oxford: Oxford University Press, 2000), pp. 268–270; also pp. 118–133.

9. Quoted in E. R. Pike, *"Hard Times": Human Documents of the Industrial Revolution* (New York: Praeger, 1966), p. 109.

10. See especially J. Brenner and M. Rama, "Rethinking Women's Oppression," *New Left Review* 144 (March–April 1984): 33–71, and sources cited there.

11. J. Humphries, ". . . 'The Most Free from Objection' . . . : The Sexual Division of Labor and Women's Work in Nineteenth-Century England," *Journal of Economic History* 47 (December 1987): 948.

12. Ibid., p. 941; Pike, *"Hard Times,"* p. 266.

13. Pike, *"Hard Times,"* p. 208.

14. Quoted in D. Geary, ed., *Labour and Socialist Movements in Europe Before 1914* (Oxford: Berg, 1989), p. 29.

The Testimony of Young Mine Workers

The use of child labor in British industrialization quickly attracted the attention of humanitarians and social reformers. This interest led to investigations by parliamentary commissions, which resulted in laws limiting the hours and the ages of children working in large factories. Designed to build a case for remedial legislation, parliamentary inquiries gave large numbers of workers a rare chance to speak directly to contemporaries and to historians.

The moving passages that follow are taken from testimony gathered in 1841 and 1842 by the Ashley Mines Commission. Interviewing employers and many male and female workers, the commissioners focused on the physical condition of the youth and on the sexual behavior of workers far underground. The subsequent Mines Act of 1842 sought to reduce immoral behavior and sexual bullying by prohibiting underground work for all women (and for boys younger than ten).

Mr. Payne, coal master:

That children are employed generally at nine years old in the coal pits and sometimes at eight. In fact, the smaller the vein of coal is in height, the younger and smaller are the children required; the work occupies from six to seven hours per day in the pits; they are not ill-used or worked beyond their strength; a good deal of depravity exists but they are certainly not worse in morals than in other branches of the Sheffield trade, but upon the whole superior; the morals of this district are materially improving; Mr. Bruce, the clergyman, has been zealous and active in endeavoring to ameliorate their moral and religious education. . . .

Ann Eggley, hurrier, 18 years old:

I'm sure I don't know how to spell my name. We go at four in the morning, and sometimes at half-past four. We begin to work as soon as we get down. We get out after four, sometimes at five, in the evening. We work the whole time except an hour for dinner, and sometimes we haven't time to eat. I hurry [move coal wagons underground] by myself, and have done so for long. I know the corves [small coal wagons] are very heavy, they are the biggest corves anywhere about. The work is far too hard for me; the sweat runs off me all over sometimes. I am very tired at night. Sometimes when we get home at night we have not power to wash us, and then we go to bed. Sometimes we fall asleep in the chair. Father said last night it was both a shame and a disgrace for girls to work as we do, but there was naught else for us to do. I began to hurry when I was seven and I have been hurrying ever since. I have been 11 years in the pits. The girls are always tired. I was poorly twice this winter; it was with headache. I hurry for Robert Wiggins; he is not akin to me. . . . We don't always get enough to eat and drink, but we get a good supper. I have known my father go at two in the morning to work . . . and he didn't come out till four. I am quite sure that we work constantly 12 hours except on Saturdays. We wear trousers and our shifts in the pit and great big shoes clinkered and nailed. The girls never work naked to the waist in our pit. The men don't insult us in the pit. The conduct of the girls in the pit is good enough sometimes and sometimes bad enough. I never went to a day-school. I went a little to a Sunday-school, but I soon gave it over. I thought it too bad to be confined both Sundays and week-days. I walk about and get the fresh air on Sundays. I have not learnt to read. I don't know my letters. I never learnt naught. I never go to church or chapel; there is no church or chapel at Gawber, there is none nearer than a mile. . . . I have never heard that a good man came into the world who was God's son to save sinners. I never

This illustration of a girl dragging a coal wagon was one of several that shocked public opinion and contributed to the Mines Act of 1842. *(The British Library)*

heard of Christ at all. Nobody has ever told me about him, nor have my father and mother ever taught me to pray. I know no prayer; I never pray.

Patience Kershaw, aged 17:

My father has been dead about a year; my mother is living and has ten children, five lads and five lasses; the oldest is about thirty, the youngest is four; three lasses go to mill; all the lads are colliers, two getters and three hurriers; one lives at home and does nothing; mother does nought but look after home.

All my sisters have been hurriers, but three went to the mill. Alice went because her legs swelled from hurrying in cold water when she was hot. I never went to day-school; I go to Sunday-school, but I cannot read or write; I go to pit at five o'clock in the morning and come out at five in the evening; I get my breakfast of porridge and milk first; I take my dinner with me, a cake, and eat it as I go; I do not stop or rest any time for the purpose; I get nothing else until I get home, and then have potatoes and meat, not every day meat. I hurry in the clothes I have now got on, trousers and ragged jacket; the bald place upon my head is made by thrusting the corves; my legs have never swelled, but sisters' did when they went to mill; I hurry the corves a mile and more under ground and back; they weigh 300; I hurry 11 a day; I wear a belt and chain at the workings to get the corves out; the putters [miners] that I work for are *naked* except their caps; they pull off all their clothes; I see them at work when I go up; sometimes they beat me, if I am not quick enough, with their hands; they strike me upon my back; the boys take liberties with me, sometimes, they pull me about; I am the only girl in the pit; there are about 20 boys and 15 men; all the men are naked; I would rather work in mill than in coal-pit.

Isabel Wilson, 38 years old, coal putter:

When women have children thick [fast] they are compelled to take them down early. I have been married 19 years and have had 10 bairns [children]; seven are in life. When on Sir John's work was a carrier of coals, which caused me to miscarry five times from the strains, and was gai [very] ill after each. Putting is no so oppressive; last child was born on Saturday morning, and I was at work on the Friday night.

Once met with an accident; a coal brake my cheek-bone, which kept me idle some weeks.

I have wrought below 30 years, and so has the guid man; he is getting touched in the breath now.

None of the children read, as the work is no regular. I did read once, but no able to attend to it now; when I go below lassie 10 years of age keeps house and makes the broth or stir-about.

Questions for Analysis

1. To what extent are the testimonies of Ann Eggley and Patience Kershaw in harmony with that of Payne?

2. Describe the work of Eggley and Kershaw. What do you think of their work? Why?

3. What strikes you most about the lives of these workers?

4. The witnesses were responding to questions from middle-class commissioners. What did the commissioners seem interested in? Why?

Source: J. Bowditch and C. Ramsland, eds., *Voices of the Industrial Revolution.* Copyright © 1961, 1989 by the University of Michigan. Reprinted by permission.

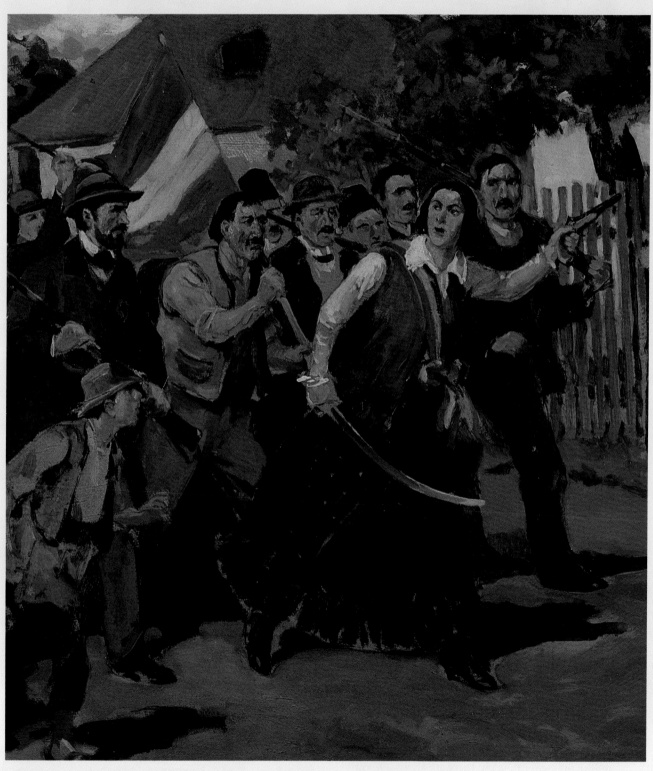

Revolutionaries in Transylvania. Ana Ipatescu, of the first group of revolutionaries in Transylvania against
Russia, 1848. *(National Historical Museum, Bucharest/The Art Archive)*

IDEOLOGIES AND UPHEAVALS, 1815–1850

The momentous economic and political transformation of modern times began in the late eighteenth century with the Industrial Revolution in England and then the French Revolution. Until about 1815, these economic and political revolutions were separate, involving different countries and activities and proceeding at very different paces. After peace returned in 1815, the situation changed. Economic and political changes tended to fuse, reinforcing each other and bringing about what historian Eric Hobsbawm has incisively called the **dual revolution.** For instance, the growth of the industrial middle class encouraged the drive for representative government, and the demands of the French sans-culottes in 1793 and 1794 inspired many socialist thinkers. Gathering strength, the dual revolution rushed on to alter completely first Europe and then the rest of the world. Much of world history in the past two centuries can be seen as the progressive unfolding of the dual revolution.

In Europe in the nineteenth century, as in Asia and Africa in more recent times, the interrelated economic and political transformation was built on complicated histories, strong traditions, and highly diverse cultures. Radical change was eventually a constant, but the particular results varied enormously. In central and eastern Europe especially, the traditional elites—the monarchs, noble landowners, and bureaucrats—proved capable of defending their privileges and eventually using nationalism as a way to respond to the dual revolution and to serve their interests, as we shall see in Chapter 25.

The dual revolution also posed a tremendous intellectual challenge. The meanings of the economic, political, and social changes that were occurring, as well as the ways they would be shaped by human action, were anything but clear. These changes fascinated observers and stimulated the growth of new ideas and powerful ideologies. The most important of these ideological forces were revitalized conservatism and three ideologies of change—liberalism, nationalism, and socialism. All played critical roles in the political and social battles of the era and the great popular upheaval that eventually swept across Europe in the revolutions of 1848.

Online Study Center

This icon will direct you to interactive activities and study materials on the website **college.hmco.com/pic/mckaywest9e**

Kingdom of Prussia

Austrian Empire

Boundary of German Confederation

RUSSIAN EMPIRE

Moscow

St. Petersburg

Kiev

Dnieper

FINLAND

Riga

UKRAINE

BESSARABIA

MOLDAVIA

WALLACHIA

Danube

BULGARIA

Black Sea

Constantinople

OTTOMAN EMPIRE

ALBANIA

GREECE

Athens

GALICIA

KINGDOM OF
SWEDEN AND
NORWAY

Oslo

Stockholm

Baltic Sea

Danzig

Vistula

Warsaw

KINGDOM OF
POLAND
(Russia)

Cracow

Copenhagen

DENMARK

SCHLESWIG

HOLSTEIN

HANOVER

KINGDOM OF PRUSSIA

Berlin

Elbe

SAXONY

Prague
BOHEMIA

Troppau

Pest

Buda

HUNGARY

AUSTRIAN EMPIRE

Vienna

CROATIA

SERBIA

BOSNIA

Adriatic Sea

Sea

MALTA
(Gr. Br.)

SICILY

KINGDOM OF THE
TWO SICILIES

NAPLES

Rome

PAPAL
STATES

TUSCANY

ELBA

CORSICA
(Fr.)

LUCCA

MODENA

PARMA

Venice

VENETIA

Milan

LOMBARDY

PIEDMONT

KINGDOM OF
SARDINIA

SARDINIA

Mediterranean

North Sea

UNITED KINGDOM
OF GREAT BRITAIN
AND IRELAND

SCOTLAND

Manchester

ENGLAND

London

Dublin

IRELAND

Amsterdam

KINGDOM OF THE
NETHERLANDS

Cologne

Rhine

Waterloo

Luxembourg

LORRAINE

ALSACE

BADEN

SWITZERLAND

Frankfurt

WÜRTTEMBERG

Munich

BAVARIA

Seine

Paris

FRANCE

Loire

Marseilles

Rhône

Ebro

SPAIN

Madrid

PORTUGAL

GIBRALTAR
(Gr. Br.)

ATLANTIC
OCEAN

400 Mi.

400 Km.

200

200

0

0

The Peace Settlement

The eventual triumph of revolutionary economic and political forces was by no means certain as the Napoleonic era ended. Quite the contrary. The conservative, aristocratic monarchies of Russia, Prussia, Austria, and Great Britain—the Quadruple Alliance—had finally defeated France and reaffirmed their determination to hold France in line. But many other international questions were outstanding, and the allies agreed to meet at the **Congress of Vienna** to fashion a general peace settlement.

Most people felt a profound longing for peace. The great challenge for political leaders in 1814 was to construct a settlement that would last and not sow the seeds of another war. Their efforts were largely successful and contributed to a century unmarred by destructive, generalized war (see Map 23.1).

• *How did the victorious allies fashion a general peace settlement, and how did Metternich uphold a conservative European order?*

The European Balance of Power

The allied powers were concerned first and foremost with the defeated enemy, France. Agreeing to the restoration of the Bourbon dynasty (see page 708), the allies were quite lenient toward France after Napoleon's abdication. The first Peace of Paris gave to France the boundaries it possessed in 1792, which were larger than those of 1789, and France did not have to pay any war reparations. Thus the victorious powers did not foment a spirit of injustice and revenge in the defeated country.

When the four allies of the Quadruple Alliance met together at the Congress of Vienna, assisted in a minor way

Chronology

1790s–1840s	Romantic movement in literature and the arts
1809–1848	Metternich serves as Austrian foreign minister
1810	Staël, *On Germany*
1815	Holy Alliance formed; revision of Corn Laws in Britain
1819	Carlsbad Decrees issued by German Confederation
1830	Greece wins independence from Turks
1830–1848	Reign of Louis Philippe in France
1832	Reform Bill in Britain
1839	Blanc, *Organization of Work*
1845–1851	Great Famine in Ireland
1847	Ten Hours Act in Britain
1848	Revolutions in France, Austria, and Prussia; Marx and Engels, *The Communist Manifesto*

by a host of delegates from the smaller European states, they also agreed to raise a number of formidable barriers against renewed French aggression. The Low Countries—Belgium and Holland—were united under an enlarged Dutch monarchy capable of opposing France more effectively. Above all, Prussia received considerably more territory on France's eastern border so as to stand as the "sentinel on the Rhine" against France. In these ways, the Quadruple Alliance combined leniency toward France with strong defensive measures.

In their moderation toward France, the allies were motivated by self-interest and traditional ideas about the balance of power. To Klemens von Metternich and Robert Castlereagh, the foreign ministers of Austria and Great Britain, respectively, as well as their French counterpart, Charles Talleyrand, the balance of power meant an international equilibrium of political and military forces that would discourage aggression by any combination of states or, worse, the domination of Europe by any single state.

The Great Powers—Austria, Britain, Prussia, Russia, and France—used the balance of power to settle their own dangerous disputes at the Congress of Vienna. There was general agreement among the victors that

Mapping the Past

MAP 23.1 Europe in 1815 Europe's leaders re-established a balance of political power after the defeat of Napoleon. Prussia gained territory on the Rhine and in Saxony, consolidating its position as a Great Power. Austria gained the Italian provinces of Lombardy and Venetia as well as Galicia and land along the Adriatic Sea. In 1815 Europe contained many different states, but international politics was dominated by the five Great Powers (or six, if one includes the Ottoman Empire). Trace the political boundaries of each Great Power, and compare their geographical strengths and weaknesses. **1** In which directions might the different Great Powers seek to expand further and gain more people and territory? **2** At what points might these states then come into conflict with one another?

Adjusting the Balance   The Englishman on the left uses his money to counterbalance the people that the Prussian and the fat Metternich are gaining in Saxony and Italy. Alexander I sits happily on his prize, Poland. This cartoon captures the essence of how most people thought about balance-of-power diplomacy at the Congress of Vienna. *(Bibliothèque nationale de France)*

each of them should receive compensation in the form of territory for their successful struggle against the French. Great Britain had already won colonies and strategic outposts during the long wars. Metternich's Austria gave up territories in Belgium and southern Germany but expanded greatly elsewhere, taking the rich provinces of Venetia and Lombardy in northern Italy as well as former Polish possessions and new lands on the eastern coast of the Adriatic (see Map 23.1).

One ticklish question almost led to renewed war in January 1815, however. The vaguely progressive, impetuous Tsar Alexander I of Russia wanted to restore the ancient kingdom of Poland, on which he expected to bestow the benefits of his rule. The Prussians agreed, provided they could swallow up the large and wealthy kingdom of Saxony, their German neighbor to the south. These demands were too much for Castlereagh and Metternich, who feared an unbalancing of forces in central Europe. In an astonishing about-face, they turned for diplomatic sup-

port to the wily Talleyrand and the defeated France he represented, signing a secret alliance directed against Russia and Prussia. War seemed imminent. But the threat of war caused the rulers of Russia and Prussia to moderate their demands. Russia accepted a small Polish kingdom, and Prussia took only part of Saxony (see Map 23.1). This compromise was very much within the framework of balance-of-power ideology.

Unfortunately for France, Napoleon suddenly escaped from his "comic kingdom" on the island of Elba. Yet the second Peace of Paris, concluded after Napoleon's final defeat at Waterloo, was still relatively moderate toward France. Fat old Louis XVIII was restored to his throne for a second time. France lost only a little territory, had to pay an indemnity of 700 million francs, and had to support a large army of occupation for five years.

The rest of the settlement already concluded at the Congress of Vienna was left intact. The members of the Quadruple Alliance, however, did agree to meet periodically to discuss their common interests and to consider appropriate measures for the maintenance of peace in Europe. This agreement marked the beginning of the European "congress system," which lasted long into the nineteenth century and settled many international crises through international conferences and balance-of-power diplomacy.

Intervention and Repression

There was also a domestic political side to the reestablishment of peace. Within their own countries, the leaders of the victorious states were much less flexible. In 1815 under Metternich's leadership, Austria, Prussia, and Russia embarked on a crusade against the ideas and politics of the dual revolution. This crusade lasted until 1848. The first step was the **Holy Alliance,** formed by Austria, Prussia, and Russia in September 1815. First proposed by Russia's Alexander I, the alliance soon became a symbol of the repression of liberal and revolutionary movements all over Europe.

In 1820 revolutionaries succeeded in forcing the monarchs of Spain and the southern Italian kingdom of the Two Sicilies to grant liberal constitutions against their wills. Metternich was horrified: revolution was rising once again. Calling a conference at Troppau in Austria under the provisions of the Quadruple Alliance, he and Alexander I proclaimed the principle of active intervention to maintain all autocratic regimes whenever they were threatened. Austrian forces then marched into Naples in 1821 and restored Ferdinand I to the throne of the Two Sicilies, while French armies likewise restored the Spanish regime.

In the following years, Metternich continued to battle against liberal political change. Sometimes he could do little, as in the case of the new Latin American republics that broke away from Spain. Nor could he undo the dynastic changes of 1830 and 1831 in France and Belgium. Nonetheless, until 1848 Metternich's system proved quite effective in central Europe, where his power was the greatest.

Metternich's policies dominated not only Austria and the Italian peninsula but also the entire German Confederation, which the peace settlement of Vienna had called into being. The confederation was composed of thirty-eight independent German states, including Prussia and Austria (see Map 23.1). These states met in complicated assemblies dominated by Austria, with Prussia a willing junior partner in the execution of repressive measures.

It was through the German Confederation that Metternich had the infamous **Carlsbad Decrees** issued in 1819. These decrees required the thirty-eight German member states to root out subversive ideas in their universities and newspapers. The decrees also established a permanent committee with spies and informers to investigate and punish any liberal or radical organizations.

Metternich and Conservatism

Metternich's determined defense of the status quo made him a villain in the eyes of most progressive, optimistic historians of the nineteenth century. Yet rather than denounce the man, we can try to understand him and the general conservatism he represented.

Born into the middle ranks of the landed nobility of the Rhineland, Prince Klemens von Metternich (1773–1859) was an internationally oriented aristocrat who made a brilliant diplomatic career in Austria. Austrian foreign minister from 1809 to 1848, the cosmopolitan Metternich always remained loyal to his class and jealously defended its rights and privileges. Like most other conservatives of his time, he did so with a clear conscience. The nobility was one of Europe's most ancient institutions, and conservatives regarded tradition as the basic source of human institutions. In their view, the proper state and society remained those of pre-1789 Europe, which rested on a judicious blend of monarchy, bureaucracy, aristocracy, and respectful commoners.

Metternich firmly believed that liberalism, as embodied in revolutionary America and France, had been responsible for a generation of war with untold bloodshed and suffering. Like many other conservatives then and since, Metternich blamed liberal middle-class revolutionaries for stirring up the lower classes, which he believed desired nothing more than peace and quiet.

The threat of liberalism appeared doubly dangerous to Metternich because it generally went with national aspirations. Liberals believed that each people, each national group, had a right to establish its own independent government and seek to fulfill its own destiny. The idea of national self-determination was repellent to Metternich. It not only threatened the primacy of the aristocracy but also threatened to destroy the Austrian Empire and revolutionize central Europe.

The vast Austrian Empire of the Habsburgs was a great dynastic state. Formed over centuries by war, marriage, and luck, it was made up of many peoples (see Map 23.2). The Germans had long dominated the empire, yet they accounted for only one-fourth of the population. The Magyars (Hungarians), a substantially smaller group, dominated the kingdom of Hungary, though they did not account for a majority of the population in that part of the Austrian Empire.

MAP 23.2 Peoples of the Habsburg Monarchy, 1815 The old dynastic state was a patchwork of nationalities. Note the widely scattered pockets of Germans and Hungarians.

Legend:
- Germans
- Hungarians
- Italians
- Romanians
- Poles
- Czechs
- Carpatho-Ukrainians (Ruthenians)
- Serbs and Croats
- Slovaks
- Slovenes
- Habsburg Monarchy boundaries

RUSSIA

GALICIA

POLAND

SILESIA

MORAVIA

BOHEMIA

Prague

GERMAN STATES

BAVARIA

TYROL

SWITZERLAND

SALZBURG

AUSTRIA

Vienna

CARINTHIA

STYRIA

Danube

Tisza

HUNGARY

Budapest

TRANSYLVANIA

ROMANIA

Danube

OTTOMAN EMPIRE

SERBIA

BOSNIA

CROATIA-SLAVONIA

ILLYRIA

Adriatic Sea

VENETIA

Venice

LOMBARDY

Milan

Po

ITALIAN STATES

100 Km.

100 Mi.

Metternich This portrait by Sir Thomas Lawrence reveals much about Metternich the man. Handsome, refined, and intelligent, Metternich was a great aristocrat who was passionately devoted to the defense of his class and its interests. *(The Royal Collection, © 2007 Her Majesty Queen Elizabeth II)*

The Czechs, the third major group, were concentrated in Bohemia and Moravia. There were also large numbers of Italians, Poles, and Ukrainians as well as smaller groups of Slovenes, Croats, Serbs, Ruthenians, and Romanians. The various Slavic peoples, together with the Italians and the Romanians, represented a widely scattered and completely divided majority in an empire dominated by Germans and Hungarians. Different ethnic groups often lived in the same provinces and even in the same villages. Thus the different parts and provinces of the empire differed in languages, customs, and institutions.

The multiethnic state Metternich served was both strong and weak. It was strong because of its large population and vast territories; it was weak because of its many and potentially dissatisfied nationalities. In these circumstances, Metternich virtually had to oppose liberalism

and nationalism, for Austria was simply unable to accommodate these ideologies of the dual revolution.

In his efforts to hold back liberalism and nationalism Metternich was supported by the Russian Empire and, to a lesser extent, by the Ottoman Empire. Bitter enemies and often at war with each other, these far-flung empires also shared several basic characteristics. Both were absolutist states with powerful armies and long traditions of expansion and conquest. Both were multinational empires made up of many peoples, languages, and religions, but in each case most of the ruling elite came from the dominant ethnic group—the Orthodox Christian Russians centered in central and northern Russia, and the Muslim Ottoman Turks of Anatolia (much of modern Turkey). After 1815, both multinational, absolutist states worked to preserve their respective traditional, conservative orders. Only in the middle of the nineteenth century did each in turn experience a profound crisis and embark on a program of fundamental reform and modernization, as we shall see in Chapter 25.

Radical Ideas and Early Socialism

In the years following the peace settlement of 1815 intellectuals and social observers sought to understand the revolutionary changes that had occurred and were still taking place. These efforts led to ideas that still motivate the world.

Almost all of these basic ideas were radical. In one way or another, they rejected the old, deeply felt conservatism, with its stress on tradition, a hereditary monarchy, a strong and privileged landowning aristocracy, and an official church. Instead, they developed and refined alternative visions—alternative ideologies—and tried to convince society to act on them. With time, they were very successful.

• *What were the basic tenets of liberalism, nationalism, and socialism, and what groups were most attracted to these ideologies?*

Liberalism

The principal ideas of **liberalism**—liberty and equality—were by no means defeated in 1815. First realized successfully in the American Revolution and then achieved in part in the French Revolution, this political and social philosophy continued to pose a radical challenge to revived conservatism. Liberalism demanded representative government as opposed to autocratic monarchy, equality before the law as opposed to legally separate classes. The idea of liberty also meant specific individual freedoms: freedom of the press, freedom of speech, freedom of assembly, and freedom from arbitrary arrest. In Europe only France with Louis XVIII's Constitutional Charter and Great Britain with its Parliament and historic rights of English men and women had realized much of the liberal program in 1815. Even in those countries, liberalism had not fully succeeded.

Although liberalism retained its cutting edge, it was seen by many as being a somewhat duller tool than it had been. The reasons for this were that liberalism faced more radical ideological competitors in the early nineteenth century. Opponents of liberalism especially criticized its economic principles, which called for unrestricted private enterprise and no government interference in the economy. This philosophy was popularly known as the doctrine of **laissez faire.** (This form of liberalism is often called "classical" liberalism in the United States in order to distinguish it sharply from modern American liberalism, which usually favors more government programs to meet social needs and to regulate the economy.)

The idea of a free economy had first been persuasively formulated by Scottish philosophy professor Adam Smith, whose *Inquiry into the Nature and Causes of the Wealth of Nations* (1776) founded modern economics. Smith was highly critical of eighteenth-century mercantilism and its attempt to regulate trade and economic activity. Far preferable were free competition and the "invisible hand" of the self-regulating market, which would give all citizens a fair and equal opportunity to do what they did best. Smith argued effectively that freely competitive private enterprise would result in greater income for everyone, not just the rich.

Online Study Center **Improve Your Grade**
Primary Source: The Wealth of Nations: A Natural Law of Economy

In early-nineteenth-century Britain this economic liberalism, which promoted continued economic growth in the Industrial Revolution, was embraced most enthusiastically by business groups and became a doctrine associated with business interests. Businessmen used the doctrine to defend their right to do as they wished in their factories. Labor unions were outlawed because they supposedly restricted free competition and the individual's "right to work."

In the early nineteenth century, liberal political ideals also became more closely associated with narrow class interests. Early nineteenth-century liberals favored repre-

sentative government, but they generally wanted property qualifications attached to the right to vote. In practice, this meant limiting the vote to well-to-do aristocratic landowners, substantial businessmen, and successful members of the professions. Workers and peasants, as well as the lower middle class of shopkeepers, clerks, and artisans, did not own the necessary property and thus could not vote.

As liberalism became increasingly identified with the middle class after 1815, some intellectuals and foes of conservatism felt that liberalism did not go nearly far enough. Inspired by memories of the French Revolution and the example of Jacksonian democracy in the young American republic, they called for universal voting rights, at least for males, and for democracy. These democrats and republicans were more radical than the liberals, and they were more willing than most liberals to endorse violent upheaval to achieve goals. All of this meant that liberals and radical, democratic republicans could join forces against conservatives only up to a point.

Nationalism

Nationalism was a second radical idea in the years after 1815—an idea destined to have an enormous influence in the modern world. Nationalism had its immediate origins in the French Revolution and the Napoleonic wars, and there were already hints of its remarkable ability to spread and develop.

Early advocates of the "national idea" argued that each people had its own genius and its own *cultural* unity. For nationalists this cultural unity was basically self-evident, manifesting itself especially in a common language, history, and territory. In fact, in the early nineteenth century such cultural unity was more a dream than a reality as far as most nationalities were concerned. Within each ethnic grouping only an elite spoke a standardized written language. Local dialects abounded, and peasants from nearby villages often failed to understand each other. As for historical memory, it divided the inhabitants of the different German or Italian states as much as it unified them. Moreover, a variety of ethnic groups shared the territory of most states.

Despite these basic realities, sooner or later European nationalists usually sought to turn the cultural unity that they perceived into a *political* reality. They sought to make the territory of each people coincide with well-defined boundaries in an independent nation-state. It was this political goal that made nationalism so explosive in central and eastern Europe after 1815, when there were either too few states (Austria, Russia, and the Ottoman

Building German Nationalism   As popular upheaval in France spread to central Europe in March 1848, Germans from the solid middle classes came together in Frankfurt to draft a constitution for a new united Germany. This woodcut commemorates the solemn procession of delegates entering Saint Paul's Cathedral in Frankfurt, where the delegates would have their deliberations. Festivals, celebrations, and parades helped create a feeling of belonging to a large unseen community, a nation binding millions of strangers together. *(akg-images)*

Empire) or too many (the Italian peninsula and the German Confederation) and when different peoples overlapped and intermingled.

In recent years scholars have been trying to understand how the nationalist vision, often fitting so poorly with existing conditions and promising so much upheaval, was so successful in the long run. Certain interrelated ideas stand out.

Of fundamental importance in the rise of nationalism was the epoch-making development of complex industrial and urban society, which required much better communication between individuals and groups.[1] These communication needs promoted the use of a standardized national language within many countries, creating at least a superficial cultural unity as it eventually encompassed the entire population through mass education.

When a minority population was large and concentrated, the nationalist campaign for a standardized language often led to a push for a separate nation-state.

Many scholars also argue that nations are recent creations, the product of the new, self-conscious nationalist ideology. Thus nation-states emerged in the nineteenth century as "imagined communities," communities seeking to bind millions of strangers together around the abstract concept of an all-embracing national identity. This meant bringing citizens together with emotionally charged symbols and ceremonies, such as independence holidays and patriotic parades. On such fleeting occasions the imagined nation of spiritual equals might celebrate its most hallowed traditions, which were often recent inventions.[2]

Historians also stress the dynamic, ever-changing character of nationalism. Industrialism and mass education, so important in the later nineteenth century, played only a minor role before 1850. In those years the faith in nationhood was fresh, idealistic, and progressive.

Between 1815 and 1850 most people who believed in nationalism also believed in either liberalism or radical, democratic republicanism. A common faith in the creativity and nobility of the people was perhaps the single most important reason for the linking of these two concepts. Liberals and especially democrats saw the people as the ultimate source of all government. Yet liberals and nationalists agreed that the benefits of self-government would be possible only if the people were united by common traditions that transcended local interests and even class differences.

Early nationalists usually believed that every nation, like every citizen, had the right to exist in freedom and to develop its character and spirit. They were confident that a symphony of nations would promote the harmony and ultimate unity of all peoples. The great Italian patriot Guiseppe Mazzini (1805–1872) believed that "in laboring according to the true principles of our country we are laboring for Humanity." Thus the liberty of the individual and the love of a free nation overlapped greatly in the early nineteenth century.

Yet early nationalists also stressed the differences among peoples. Even early nationalism developed a strong sense of "we" and "they." To this "we-they" outlook, it was all too easy for nationalists to add two highly volatile ingredients: a sense of national mission and a sense of national superiority. Even the French historian Jules Michelet, so alive to the national aspirations of other peoples, could not help speaking in 1846 of the "superiority of France"; the principles espoused in the French Revolution had made France the "salvation of mankind." (See the feature "Individuals in Society: Jules Michelet" on page 769.)

Russian and German nationalists had a very different opinion of France. In the narratives they constructed, the French often seemed oppressive, as the Russians did to the Poles and as the Germans did to the Czechs. (See the feature "Listening to the Past: Speaking for the Czech Nation" on pages 776–777.) Thus "they" often emerged as the enemy.

Early nationalism was ambiguous. Its main thrust was liberal and democratic. But below the surface lurked ideas of national superiority and national mission that could lead to aggression and conflict.

French Utopian Socialism

Socialism, the new radical doctrine after 1815, began in France, despite the fact that France lagged far behind Great Britain in developing modern industry. Early French socialist thinkers were acutely aware that the political revolution in France, the rise of laissez faire, and the emergence of modern industry in Britain were transforming society. They were disturbed because they saw these developments as fomenting selfish individualism and splitting the community into isolated fragments. There was, they believed, an urgent need for a further reorganization of society to establish cooperation and a new sense of community.

Early French socialists believed in economic planning. Inspired by the emergency measures of 1793 and 1794 in France, they argued that the government should rationally organize the economy and not depend on destructive competition to do the job. Early socialists also shared an intense desire to help the poor, and they preached that the rich and the poor should be more nearly equal economically. Finally, socialists believed that private property should be strictly regulated by the government or that it should be abolished and replaced by state or community ownership. Planning, greater economic equality, and state regulation of property—these were the key ideas of early French socialism and of all socialism since.

One of the most influential early socialist thinkers was a nobleman, Count Henri de Saint-Simon (1760–1825). Saint-Simon optimistically proclaimed the tremendous possibilities of industrial development: "The age of gold is before us!" The key to progress was proper social organization. Such an arrangement of society required the **parasites**—the court, the aristocracy, lawyers, and churchmen—to give way, once and for all, to the **doers**—the leading scientists, engineers, and industrialists. The doers would carefully plan the economy and

guide it forward by undertaking vast public works projects and establishing investment banks. Saint-Simon also stressed in highly moralistic terms that every social institution ought to have as its main goal improved conditions for the poor.

After 1830 the socialist critique of capitalism became sharper. Charles Fourier (1772–1837), a lonely, saintly man with a tenuous hold on reality, envisaged a socialist utopia of mathematically precise, self-sufficient communities, each made up of 1,620 people. Fourier was also an early proponent of the total emancipation of women. Extremely critical of middle-class family life, Fourier believed that most marriages were only another kind of prostitution. According to Fourier, young single women were shamelessly "sold" to their future husbands for dowries and other financial considerations. Therefore, Fourier called for the abolition of marriage, free unions based only on love, and sexual freedom. Many middle-class men and women found these ideas, which were shared and even practiced by some followers of Saint-Simon, shocking and immoral. The socialist program for the liberation of women as well as workers appeared to them as doubly dangerous and revolutionary.

Louis Blanc (1811–1882), a sharp-eyed, intelligent journalist, focused on practical improvements. In his *Organization of Work* (1839), he urged workers to agitate for universal voting rights and to take control of the state peacefully. Blanc believed that the state should set up government-backed workshops and factories to guarantee full employment. The right to work had to become as sacred as any other right.

Finally, there was Pierre Joseph Proudhon (1809–1865), a self-educated printer who wrote a pamphlet in 1840 titled *What Is Property?* His answer was that it was nothing but theft. Property was profit that was stolen from the worker, who was the source of all wealth. Unlike most socialists, Proudhon feared the power of the state and was often considered an anarchist.

Of great importance, the message of French utopian socialists interacted with the experiences of French urban workers. Workers cherished the memory of the radical phase of the French Revolution, and they became violently opposed to laissez-faire laws that denied workers the right to organize. Developing a sense of class in the process, workers favored collective action and government intervention in economic life. Thus the aspirations of workers and utopian theorists reinforced each other, and a genuine socialist movement emerged in Paris in the 1830s and 1840s. To Karl Marx was left the task of establishing firm foundations for modern socialism.

The Birth of Marxian Socialism

In 1848 the thirty-year-old Karl Marx (1818–1883) and the twenty-eight-year-old Friedrich Engels (1820–1895) published *The Communist Manifesto,* which became the bible of socialism. The son of a Jewish lawyer who had converted to Christianity, the atheistic young Marx had studied philosophy at the University of Berlin before turning to journalism and economics. He read widely in French socialist thought, and like Fourier he looked forward to the emancipation of women and the abolition of the family. By the time Marx was twenty-five, he was developing his own socialist ideas.

Early French socialists often appealed to the middle class and the state to help the poor. Marx ridiculed such appeals as naive. He argued that the interests of the middle class and those of the industrial working class were inevitably opposed to each other. Indeed, according to the *Manifesto,* the "history of all previously existing society is the history of class struggles." In Marx's view, one class had always exploited the other, and with the advent of modern industry, society was split more clearly than ever before: between the middle class (the **bourgeoisie**) and the modern working class (the **proletariat**).

Just as the bourgeoisie had triumphed over the feudal aristocracy, Marx predicted that the proletariat would conquer the bourgeoisie in a violent revolution. While a tiny minority owned the means of production and grew richer, the ever-poorer proletariat was constantly growing in size and in class-consciousness. In this process, the proletariat was aided, according to Marx, by a portion of the bourgeoisie who had gone over to the proletariat and who (like Marx and Engels) "had raised themselves to the level of comprehending theoretically the historical moment." The critical moment, Marx thought, was very near. "Let the ruling classes tremble at a Communist revolution. The proletarians have nothing to lose but their chains. They have a world to win. WORKING MEN OF ALL COUNTRIES, UNITE!" So ends *The Communist Manifesto.*

Online Study Center **Improve Your Grade**
Primary Source: "Working Men of All Countries, Unite!"

Marx's ideas united sociology, economics, and all human history in a vast and imposing edifice. He synthesized in his socialism not only French utopian schemes but also English classical economics and German philosophy—the major intellectual currents of his day.

Marx's debt to England was great. He was the last of the classical economists. Following David Ricardo, who

Karl Marx Active in the revolution of 1848, Marx fled from Germany in 1849 and settled in London. There he wrote *Capital,* the weighty exposition of his socialist theories, and worked to organize the working class. Marx earned a modest living as a journalist, supplemented by financial support from his coauthor, Friedrich Engels. *(The Granger Collection, New York)*

had taught that labor was the source of all value, Marx went on to argue that profits were really wages stolen from the workers. Moreover, Marx incorporated Engels's charges of terrible oppression of the new class of factory workers in England; thus Marx's doctrines seemed to be based on hard facts.

Marx's theory of historical evolution was built on the philosophy of the German Georg Hegel (1770–1831). Hegel believed that each age is characterized by a dominant set of ideas, which produces opposing ideas and eventually a new synthesis. The idea of being had been dominant initially, for example, and it had produced its antithesis, the idea of nonbeing. This idea in turn had resulted in the synthesis of becoming. Thus history has pattern and purpose.

Marx retained Hegel's view of history as a dialectic process of change but made economic relationships between classes the driving force. This dialectic explained the decline of agrarian feudalism and the rise of industrial capitalism. Marx stressed repeatedly that the "bourgeoisie, historically, has played a most revolutionary part. . . . During its rule of scarcely one hundred years the bourgeoisie has created more massive and more colossal productive forces than have all preceding generations together." Marx's next idea, that it was now the bourgeoisie's turn to give way to the socialism of revolutionary workers, appeared to many the irrefutable capstone of a brilliant interpretation of humanity's long development. Thus Marx pulled together powerful ideas and insights to create one of the great secular religions out of the intellectual ferment of the early nineteenth century.

The Romantic Movement

Radical concepts of politics and society were accompanied by comparable changes in literature and other arts during the dual revolution. The early nineteenth century marked the acme of the romantic movement, which profoundly influenced the arts and enriched European culture immeasurably.

The romantic movement was in part a revolt against classicism and the Enlightenment. Classicism was essentially a set of artistic rules and standards that went hand in glove with the Enlightenment's belief in rationality, order, and restraint. The classicists believed that the ancient Greeks and Romans had discovered eternally valid aesthetic rules and that playwrights and painters should continue to follow them. Classicists could enforce these rules in the eighteenth century because they dominated the courts and academies for which artists worked.

Forerunners of the romantic movement appeared from about 1750 on. Of these, Rousseau (see page 607)—the passionate advocate of feeling, freedom, and natural goodness—was the most influential. Romanticism then crystallized fully in the 1790s, primarily in England and Germany. The French Revolution kindled the belief that radical reconstruction was also possible in cultural and artistic life (even though many early English and German romantics became disillusioned with events in France and turned from liberalism to conservatism in politics). Romanticism gained strength until the 1840s.

● *What were the characteristics of the romantic movement, and who were some of the great romantic artists?*

Romanticism's Tenets

Romanticism was characterized by a belief in emotional exuberance, unrestrained imagination, and spontaneity in both art and personal life. In Germany early romantics of the 1770s and 1780s called themselves the **Sturm und Drang** ("Storm and Stress"), and many romantic artists of the early nineteenth century lived lives of tremendous emotional intensity. Suicide, duels to the death, madness, and strange illnesses were not uncommon among leading romantics. Romantic artists typically led bohemian lives, wearing their hair long and uncombed in preference to powdered wigs and living in cold garrets rather than frequenting stiff drawing rooms. They rejected materialism and sought to escape to lofty spiritual heights through their art. Great individualists, the romantics believed the full development of one's unique human potential to be the supreme purpose in life.

Nowhere was the break with classicism more apparent than in romanticism's general conception of nature. Classicism was not particularly interested in nature. In the words of the eighteenth-century English author Samuel Johnson, "A blade of grass is always a blade of grass; men and women are my subjects of inquiry." Nature was portrayed by classicists as beautiful and chaste, like an eighteenth-century formal garden. The romantics, in contrast, were enchanted by nature. For some it was awesome and tempestuous, while others saw nature as a source of spiritual inspiration. As the great English landscape artist John Constable declared, "Nature is Spirit visible."

Most romantics saw the growth of modern industry as an ugly, brutal attack on their beloved nature and on the human personality. They sought escape—in the unspoiled Lake District of northern England, in exotic North Africa, in an idealized Middle Ages.

Fascinated by color and diversity, the romantic imagination turned toward history with a passion. Beautiful, exciting, and important, history was the art of change over time—the key to a universe that was now perceived to be organic and dynamic, not mechanical and static as the Enlightenment had believed. Historical studies promoted the growth of national aspirations, fanning the embers of memory and encouraging entire peoples to seek in the past their special destinies.

Literature

Britain was the first country where romanticism flowered fully in poetry and prose, and the British romantic writers were among the most prominent in Europe. Wordsworth,

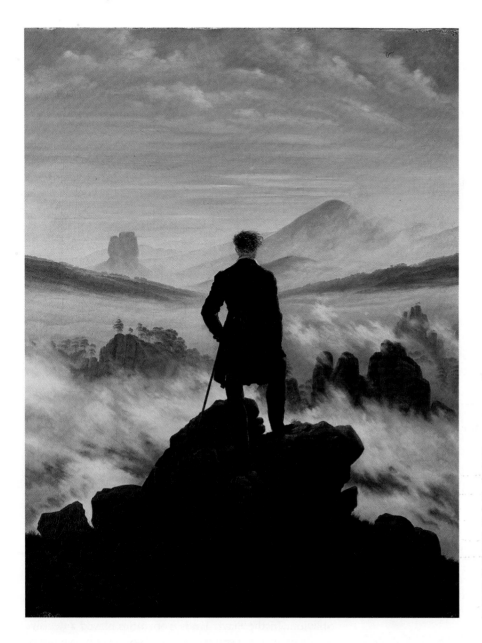

Nature and the Meaning of Life
Caspar David Friedrich (1774–1840) was Germany's greatest romantic painter, and his *Traveler Looking over a Sea of Fog* (1815) is a representative masterpiece. Friedrich's paintings often focus on dark, silhouetted figures silently contemplating an eerie landscape. Friedrich came to believe that humans were only an insignificant part of an all-embracing higher unity. *(Bildarchiv Preussischer Kulturbesitz/Art Resource, NY)*

Coleridge, and Scott were all active by 1800, to be followed shortly by Byron, Shelley, and Keats. All were poets: romanticism found its distinctive voice in poetry, as the Enlightenment had in prose.

A towering leader of English romanticism, William Wordsworth (1770–1850) traveled in France after his graduation from Cambridge. There he fell passionately in love with a Frenchwoman, who bore him a daughter. Deeply influenced by Rousseau and the spirit of the early French Revolution, Wordsworth returned to England and settled in the countryside with his sister, Dorothy,

and Samuel Taylor Coleridge (1772–1834). In 1798 the two poets published their *Lyrical Ballads,* which abandoned flowery classical conventions for the language of ordinary speech and endowed simple subjects with the loftiest majesty.

One of the best examples of Wordsworth's romantic credo and genius is "Daffodils":

I wandered lonely as a cloud
That floats on high o'er vales and hills,
When all at once I saw a crowd,

A host, of golden daffodils;
Beside the lake, beneath the trees,
Fluttering and dancing in the breeze.

. . . .

The waves beside them danced, but they
Out-did the sparkling waves in glee:
A poet could not but be gay,
In such a jocund company:
I gazed—and gazed—but little thought
What wealth the show to me had brought:

For oft, when on my couch I lie
In vacant or in pensive mood,
They flash upon that inward eye
Which is the bliss of solitude;
And then my heart with pleasure fills,
And dances with the daffodils.

Here indeed are simplicity and love of nature in commonplace forms, which could be appreciated by everyone. Wordsworth's conception of poetry as the "spontaneous overflow of powerful feeling recollected in tranquility" is well illustrated by the last stanza.

Born in Edinburgh, Walter Scott (1771–1832) personified the romantic movement's fascination with history. Raised on his grandfather's farm, Scott fell under the spell of the old ballads and tales of the Scottish border. He was also deeply influenced by German romanticism, particularly by the immortal poet and dramatist Johann Wolfgang von Goethe (1749–1832). Scott translated Goethe's famous *Gotz von Berlichingen,* a play about a sixteenth-century knight who revolted against centralized authority and championed individual freedom—at least in Goethe's romantic drama. A natural storyteller, Scott composed long narrative poems and a series of historical novels. Scott excelled in re-creating the spirit of bygone ages and great historical events, especially those of Scotland.

Classicism remained strong in France under Napoleon and inhibited the growth of romanticism there. In 1813 Germaine de Staël (1766–1817), a Franco-Swiss writer living in exile, urged the French to throw away their worn-out classical models. Her study *On Germany* (1810) extolled the spontaneity and enthusiasm of German writers and thinkers, and it had a powerful impact on the post-1815 generation in France. Between 1820 and 1850, the romantic impulse broke through in the poetry and prose of Lamartine, de Vigny, Hugo, Dumas, and Sand. Of these, Victor Hugo (1802–1885) was the greatest in both poetry and prose.

Son of a Napoleonic general, Hugo achieved an amazing range of rhythm, language, and image in his lyric poetry. His powerful novels exemplified the romantic fascination with fantastic characters, exotic historical settings, and human emotions. The hero of Hugo's famous *Hunchback of Notre Dame* (1831) is the great cathedral's deformed bell-ringer, a "human gargoyle" overlooking the teeming life of fifteenth-century Paris. Renouncing his early conservatism, Hugo equated freedom in literature with liberty in politics and society. Hugo's political evolution was thus exactly the opposite of Wordsworth's, in whom youthful radicalism gave way to middle-aged caution. As the contrast between the two artists suggests, romanticism was a cultural movement compatible with many political beliefs.

Amandine Aurore Lucie Dupin (1804–1876), generally known by her pen name, George Sand, defied the narrow conventions of her time in an unending search for self-fulfillment. After eight years of unhappy marriage she abandoned her husband and took her two children to Paris to pursue a career as a writer. There Sand soon achieved fame and wealth, eventually writing over eighty novels on a variety of romantic and social themes. George Sand's striking individualism went far beyond her flamboyant preference for men's clothing and her notorious affairs. Her semi-autobiographical novel *Lélia* was shockingly modern, delving deeply into her tortuous quest for sexual and personal freedom.

In central and eastern Europe, literary romanticism and early nationalism often reinforced each other. Seeking a unique greatness in every people, well-educated romantics plumbed their own histories and cultures. Like modern anthropologists, they turned their attention to peasant life and transcribed the folk songs, tales, and proverbs that the cosmopolitan Enlightenment had disdained. The brothers Jacob and Wilhelm Grimm were particularly successful at rescuing German fairy tales from oblivion. In the Slavic lands, romantics played a decisive role in converting spoken peasant languages into modern written languages. The greatest of all Russian poets, Aleksander Pushkin (1799–1837), rejecting eighteenth-century attempts to force Russian poetry into a classical straitjacket, used his lyric genius to mold the modern literary language.

Art and Music

The greatest and most moving romantic painter in France was Eugène Delacroix (1798–1863), probably the illegitimate son of French foreign minister Talleyrand. Delacroix was a master of dramatic, colorful scenes that stirred the emotions. He was fascinated with remote and exotic subjects, whether lion hunts in Morocco or dreams of languishing, sensuous women in a sultan's harem. Yet he was also a passionate spokesman for freedom.

In England the most notable romantic painters were Joseph M. W. Turner (1775–1851) and John Constable (1776–1837). Both were fascinated by nature, but their interpretations of it contrasted sharply, aptly symbolizing the tremendous emotional range of the romantic movement. Turner depicted nature's power and terror; wild storms and sinking ships were favorite subjects. Constable painted gentle Wordsworthian landscapes in which human beings were at one with their environment, the comforting countryside of unspoiled rural England.

It was in music that romanticism realized most fully and permanently its goals of free expression and emotional intensity. Abandoning well-defined structures, the great romantic composers used a wide range of forms to create a thousand musical landscapes and evoke a host of powerful emotions. Romantic composers also transformed the small classical orchestra, tripling its size by adding wind instruments, percussion, and more brass and strings. The crashing chords evoking the surge of the masses in Chopin's Revolutionary Etude, and the bottomless despair of the funeral march in Beethoven's Third Symphony—such were the modern orchestra's musical paintings that plumbed the depths of human feeling.

This range and intensity gave music and musicians much greater prestige than in the past. Music no longer simply complemented a church service or helped a nobleman digest his dinner. Music became a sublime end in itself, most perfectly realizing the endless yearning of the soul. The unbelievable one-in-a-million performer—the great virtuoso who could transport the listener to ecstasy and hysteria—became a cultural hero. People swooned for Franz Liszt (1811–1886), the greatest pianist of his age, as they scream for rock stars today.

Though romanticism dominated music until late in the nineteenth century, no composer ever surpassed its first great master, Ludwig van Beethoven (1770–1827). Extending and breaking open classical forms, Beethoven used contrasting themes and tones to produce dramatic conflict and inspiring resolutions. As one contemporary admirer wrote, "Beethoven's music sets in motion the lever of fear, of awe, of horror, of suffering, and awakens just that infinite longing which is the essence of Romanticism." Beethoven's range and output were tremendous. At the peak of his fame, he began to lose his hearing. He

considered suicide but eventually overcame despair: "I will take fate by the throat; it will not bend me completely to its will."[3] Beethoven continued to pour out immortal music, although his last years were silent, spent in total deafness.

Reforms and Revolutions

While the romantic movement was developing, liberal, national, and socialist forces battered against the conservatism of 1815. In some countries, change occurred gradually and peacefully. Elsewhere, pressure built up like steam in a pressure cooker without a safety valve and eventually caused an explosion in 1848. Three important countries—Greece, Great Britain, and France—experienced variations on this basic theme between 1815 and 1848.

- *How after 1815 did liberal, national, and socialist forces challenge conservatism in Greece, Great Britain, and France?*

National Liberation in Greece

National, liberal revolution, frustrated in Italy and Spain by conservative statesmen, succeeded first after 1815 in Greece. Since the fifteenth century, the Greeks had been living under the domination of the Ottoman Turks. In spite of centuries of foreign rule, the Greeks had survived as a people, united by their language and the Greek Orthodox religion. It was perfectly natural that the general growth of national aspirations and a desire for independence would inspire some Greeks in the early nineteenth century. This rising national movement led to the formation of secret societies and then to revolt in 1821, led by Alexander Ypsilanti, a Greek patriot and a general in the Russian army.

The Great Powers, particularly Metternich, were opposed to all revolution, even revolution against the Islamic Turks. They refused to back Ypsilanti and supported the Ottoman Empire. Yet for many Europeans, the Greek cause became a holy one. Educated Americans and Europeans were in love with the culture of classical Greece; Russians were stirred by the piety of their Orthodox brethren. Writers and artists, moved by the romantic impulse, responded enthusiastically to the Greek national struggle. The famous English romantic poet Lord Byron even joined the Greeks and died fighting "that Greece may yet be free."

Delacroix: Massacre at Chios The Greek struggle for freedom and independence won the enthusiastic support of liberals, nationalists, and romantics. The Ottoman Turks were portrayed as cruel oppressors who were holding back the course of history, as in this moving masterpiece by Delacroix. *(Réunion des Musées Nationaux/Art Resource, NY)*

The Greeks, though often quarreling among themselves, battled on against the Turks and hoped for the eventual support of European governments. In 1827 Great Britain, France, and Russia responded to popular demands at home and directed Turkey to accept an armistice. When the Turks refused, the navies of these three powers trapped the Turkish fleet at Navarino and destroyed it. Russia then declared another of its periodic wars of expansion against the Turks. This led to the establishment of a Russian protectorate over much of present-day Romania, which had also been under Turkish rule. Great Britain, France, and Russia finally declared Greece independent in 1830 and installed a German prince as king of the new country in 1832. In the end, the Greeks had won: a small nation had gained its independence in a heroic war of liberation against a foreign empire.

Liberal Reform in Great Britain

Eighteenth-century British society had been both flexible and remarkably stable. It was dominated by the land-owning aristocracy, but that class was neither closed nor rigidly defined. Successful business and professional people could buy land and become gentlefolk, while the common people had more than the usual opportunities of the preindustrial world. Basic civil rights for all were balanced by a tradition of deference to one's social superiors. Parliament was manipulated by the king and was thoroughly undemocratic. Only about 8 percent of the population could vote for representatives to Parliament, and by the 1780s there was growing interest in some kind of political reform.

But the French Revolution threw the British aristocracy into a panic for a generation, making it extremely hostile to any attempts to change the status quo. The Tory Party, completely controlled by the landed aristocracy, was particularly fearful of radical movements at home and abroad. After 1815 the aristocracy defended its ruling position by repressing every kind of popular protest.

The first step in this direction began with revision of the **Corn Laws** in 1815. Corn Laws to regulate the foreign grain trade had long existed, but they were not needed during a generation of war with France because the British had been unable to import cheap grain from eastern Europe, leading to high prices and large profits for the landed aristocracy. Peace meant that grain could be imported again and that the price of wheat and bread would go down, benefiting almost everyone except the aristocracy. The aristocracy, however, rammed far-reaching changes in the Corn Laws through Parliament. The new regulation prohibited the importation of foreign grain unless the price at home rose to improbable levels. Seldom has a class legislated more selfishly for its own narrow economic advantage or done more to promote a class-based view of political action.

The change in the Corn Laws, coming as it did at a time of widespread unemployment and postwar economic distress, resulted in protests and demonstrations by urban laborers, who were supported by radical intellectuals. In 1817 the Tory government responded by temporarily suspending the traditional rights of peaceable assembly and habeas corpus. Two years later, Parliament passed the infamous Six Acts, which, among other things, placed controls on a heavily taxed press and practically eliminated all mass meetings. These acts followed an enormous but orderly protest, at Saint Peter's Fields in Manchester, that had been savagely broken up by armed cavalry. Nicknamed the **Battle of Peterloo,** in scornful reference to the British victory at Waterloo, this incident demonstrated the government's determination to repress and stand fast.

Strengthened by ongoing industrial development, the new manufacturing and commercial groups insisted on a place for their new wealth alongside the landed wealth of the aristocracy in the framework of political power and social prestige. They called for many kinds of liberal reform: reform of town government, organization of a new police force, more rights for Catholics and dissenters, and reform of the Poor Laws that provided aid to some low-paid workers. In the 1820s, a less frightened Tory government moved in the direction of better urban administration, greater economic liberalism, civil equality for Catholics, and limited imports of foreign grain. These actions encouraged the middle classes to press on for reform of Parliament so they could have a larger say in government.

The Whig Party, though led like the Tories by great aristocrats, had by tradition been more responsive to commercial and manufacturing interests. In 1830 a Whig ministry introduced "an act to amend the representation of the people of England and Wales." Defeated, then passed by the House of Commons, this reform bill was rejected by the House of Lords. But when in 1832 the Whigs got the king to promise to create enough new peers to pass the law, the House of Lords reluctantly gave in rather than see its snug little club ruined by upstart manufacturers and plutocrats. A mighty surge of popular protest had helped the king and lords make up their minds.

The Reform Bill of 1832 had profound significance. The House of Commons had emerged as the all-important legislative body. The new industrial areas of the country gained representation in the Commons, and many old "rotten boroughs"—electoral districts that had very few voters and that the landed aristocracy had bought and sold—were eliminated.

The redistribution of seats reflected the shift in population to the northern manufacturing counties and the gradual emergence of an urban society. As a result of the Reform Bill of 1832, the number of voters increased by about 50 percent, giving about 12 percent of adult men in Britain and Ireland the right to vote. Comfortable middle-class groups in the urban population, as well as some substantial farmers who leased their land,

Hayter: The House of Commons, 1833 This collective portrait of the first parliament elected after the Reform Bill of 1832 was painted over several years. The arrangement of the members reflects Britain's historic two-party system, with the majority on one side and the "loyal opposition" on the other. Most European countries developed multiparty systems and coalition politics, with competing groups seated in a large half circle. *(Trustees of the National Portrait Gallery, London)*

received the vote. Thus the pressures building in Great Britain were successfully—though only temporarily—released. A major reform had been achieved peacefully. Continued fundamental reform within the system appeared difficult but not impossible.

The principal radical program was embodied in the "People's Charter" of 1838 and the Chartist movement (see page 741). Partly inspired by the economic distress of the working class in the 1830s and 1840s, the Chartists' core demand was universal male (but not female) suffrage. They saw complete political democracy and rule by the common people as the means to a good and just society. Hundreds of thousands of people signed gigantic petitions calling on Parliament to grant all men the right to vote, first and most seriously in 1839, again in 1842, and yet again in 1848. Parliament rejected all three petitions. In the short run, the working poor failed with their Chartist demands, but they learned a valuable lesson in mass politics.

While calling for universal male suffrage, many working-class people joined with middle-class manufacturers in the Anti–Corn Law League, founded in Manchester in 1839. Mass participation made possible a popular crusade led by fighting liberals, who argued that lower food prices and more jobs in industry depended on repeal of the Corn Laws. Much of the working class agreed. When Ireland's potato crop failed in 1845 and famine prices for food seemed likely in England, Tory prime minister Robert Peel joined with the Whigs and a minority of his own party to repeal the Corn Laws in 1846 and allow free imports of grain. England escaped famine. Thereafter the liberal doctrine of free trade became almost sacred dogma in Great Britain.

Online Study Center **Improve Your Grade**
Primary Source: A Denunciation of the Corn Laws

The following year, the Tories passed a bill designed to help the working classes, but in a different way. The Ten

The Prelude to 1848

March 1814	Russia, Prussia, Austria, and Britain form the Quadruple Alliance to defeat France.
April 1814	Napoleon abdicates.
May–June 1814	Bourbon monarchy is restored; Louis XVIII issues the Constitutional Charter providing for civil liberties and representative government.
	First Peace of Paris: allies combine leniency with a defensive posture toward France.
October 1814– June 1815	Congress of Vienna peace settlement establishes balance-of-power principle and creates the German Confederation.
February 1815	Napoleon escapes from Elba and marches on Paris.
June 1815	Napoleon defeated at the Battle of Waterloo.
September 1815	Austria, Prussia, and Russia form the Holy Alliance to repress liberal and revolutionary movements.
November 1815	Second Peace of Paris and renewal of Quadruple Alliance punish France and establish the European "congress system."
1819	In Carlsbad Decrees, Metternich imposes harsh measures throughout the German Confederation.
1820	Revolution occurs in Spain and the kingdom of the Two Sicilies.
	At the Congress of Troppau, Metternich and Alexander I of Russia proclaim the principle of intervention to maintain autocratic regimes.
1821	Austria crushes a liberal revolution in Naples and restores the Sicilian autocracy.
	Greeks revolt against the Ottoman Turks.
1823	French armies restore the Spanish regime.
1824	Reactionary Charles X succeeds Louis XVIII in France.
1830	Charles X repudiates the Constitutional Charter; insurrection and collapse of the government follow. Louis Philippe succeeds to the throne and maintains a narrowly liberal regime until 1848.
	Greece wins independence from the Ottoman Empire.
1832	Reform Bill expands British electorate and encourages the middle class.
1839	Louis Blanc publishes *Organization of Work*.
1840	Pierre Joseph Proudhon publishes *What Is Property?*
1846	Jules Michelet publishes *The People*.
1848	Karl Marx and Friedrich Engels publish *The Communist Manifesto*.

Hours Act of 1847 limited the workday for women and young people in factories to ten hours. Tory aristocrats continued to champion legislation regulating factory conditions. They were competing vigorously with the middle class for the support of the working class. This healthy competition between a still-vigorous aristocracy and a strong middle class was a crucial factor in Great Britain's peaceful evolution. The working classes could make temporary alliances with either competitor to better their own conditions.

Ireland and the Great Famine

The people of Ireland did not benefit from the political competition in Britain. The great mass of the population (outside of the northern counties of Ulster, which were partly Presbyterian) were Irish Catholics, who rented their land from a tiny minority of Church of England Protestants. These landlords were content to use their power to grab as much as possible.

The result was that the condition of the Irish peasantry around 1800 was abominable. The typical peasant lived in a wretched cottage and could afford neither shoes nor stockings. Hundreds of shocking accounts describe hopeless poverty. Yet in spite of terrible conditions, population growth sped onward. The 3 million of 1725 reached 4 million in 1780 and doubled to 8 million by 1840. Between 1780 and 1840, 1.75 million people left Ireland for Britain and America.

The population grew so quickly for three reasons: extensive cultivation of the potato, early marriage, and exploitation of peasants by landlords. The cultivation of the potato, introduced into Ireland (and all of Europe) in the late sixteenth century, was originally a response to the pressure of numbers. Once peasants began to cultivate potatoes, many more people could exist. A single acre of land spaded and planted with potatoes could feed an Irish family of six for a year, whereas two to four acres of grain and pasture were needed to feed the same number. The potato also could thrive on boggy wastelands.

Needing only a big potato patch to survive, Irish men and women married early. Setting up housekeeping was easy, for a cabin of mud and stone could be slapped together with the help of friends and relatives in a few days. A mat for a bed, chairs and a table, and an iron pot to boil potatoes were easily acquired. To be sure, the young couple was embracing a life of extreme poverty. They would literally live on potatoes—ten pounds a day for an average male—moistened at best with a cup of milk.

Yet the decision to marry and have large families made sense. Landlords leased land for short periods only. Peasants had no incentive to make permanent improvements because anything beyond what was needed for survival would quickly be taken by higher rent. Rural poverty was inescapable and better shared with a spouse, while a dutiful son or a loving daughter was an old person's best hope of escaping destitution.

Daniel McDonald: The Discovery of the Potato Blight
Although the leaves of diseased plants usually shriveled and died, they could also look deceptively healthy. This Irish family has dug up its potato harvest and just discovered to its horror that the blight has rotted the crop. Like thousands of Irish families, this family now faces the starvation and the mass epidemics of the Great Famine. *(Department of Irish Folklore, University College, Dublin)*

As population and potato dependency grew, conditions became more precarious. From 1820 onward deficiencies and diseases in the potato crop became more common. In 1845 and 1846, and again in 1848 and 1851, the potato crop failed in Ireland.

The result was unmitigated disaster—the **Great Famine.** Blight attacked the young plants, the leaves withered, and the tubers rotted. Widespread starvation and mass fever epidemics followed. Yet the British government, committed to rigid laissez-faire ideology, was slow to act. When it did, its relief efforts were tragically inadequate. Moreover, the government continued to collect taxes, and landlords demanded their rents. Tenants who could not pay were evicted and their homes destroyed. Famine or no, Ireland remained the conquered jewel of foreign landowners.

Online Study Center **Improve Your Grade**
Primary Source: The Misery That Was Ireland: The Potato Famine

The Great Famine shattered the pattern of Irish population growth. Fully 1 million emigrants fled the famine between 1845 and 1851, and at least 1.5 million died or went unborn because of the disaster. Alone among the countries of Europe, Ireland experienced a declining population in the nineteenth century, from about 8 million in 1845 to 4.4 million in 1911. Ireland became a land of continuous out-migration, late marriage, and widespread celibacy.

The Great Famine also intensified anti-British feeling and promoted Irish nationalism, for the bitter memory of starvation, exile, and British inaction was burned deeply into the popular consciousness. Patriots could call on powerful collective emotions in their campaigns for land reform, home rule, and, eventually, Irish independence.

The Revolution of 1830 in France

Louis XVIII's Constitutional Charter of 1814—theoretically a gift from the king but actually a response to political pressures—was basically a liberal constitution (see page 711). The economic and social gains made by sections of the middle class and the peasantry in the French Revolution were fully protected, great intellectual and artistic freedom was permitted, and a parliament with upper and lower houses was created. Immediately after Napoleon's abortive Hundred Days, the moderate, worldly king refused to bow to the wishes of die-hard aristocrats such as his brother Charles, who wished to sweep away all the revolutionary changes and return to a bygone age of royal absolutism and aristocratic pretension. Instead,

Louis appointed as his ministers moderate royalists, who sought and obtained the support of a majority of the representatives elected to the lower Chamber of Deputies between 1816 and Louis's death in 1824.

Louis XVIII's charter was anything but democratic. Only about 100,000 of the wealthiest males out of a total population of 30 million had the right to vote for the deputies who, with the king and his ministers, made the laws of the nation. Nonetheless, the "notable people" who did vote came from very different backgrounds. There were wealthy businessmen, war profiteers, successful professionals, ex-revolutionaries, large landowners from the old aristocracy and the middle class, Bourbons, and Bonapartists.

The old aristocracy, with its pre-1789 mentality, was a minority within the voting population. It was this situation that Louis's successor, Charles X (r. 1824–1830), could not abide. Crowned in a lavish, utterly medieval, five-hour ceremony in the cathedral of Reims in 1824, Charles was a true reactionary. He wanted to re-establish the old order in France. Increasingly blocked by the opposition of the deputies, Charles's government turned in 1830 to military adventure in an effort to rally French nationalism and gain popular support. A long-standing economic and diplomatic dispute with Muslim Algeria, a vassal state of the Ottoman Empire, provided the opportunity.

In June 1830, a French force of 37,000 crossed the Mediterranean, landed to the west of Algiers, and took the capital city in three short weeks. Victory seemed complete, but in 1831 tribes in the interior revolted and waged a fearsome war until 1847, when French armies finally subdued the country. Bringing French, Spanish, and Italian settlers to Algeria and leading to the expropriation of large tracts of Muslim land, the conquest of Algeria marked the rebirth of French colonial expansion.

Emboldened by the good news from Algeria, which actually had limited impact in Paris, Charles repudiated the Constitutional Charter in an attempted coup in July 1830. He issued decrees stripping much of the wealthy middle class of its voting rights, and he censored the press. The immediate reaction, encouraged by journalists and lawyers, was an insurrection in the capital by printers, other artisans, and small traders. In "three glorious days," the government collapsed. Paris boiled with revolutionary excitement, and Charles fled. Then the upper middle class, which had fomented the revolt, skillfully seated Charles's cousin, Louis Philippe, duke of Orléans, on the vacant throne.

Louis Philippe (r. 1830–1848) accepted the Constitutional Charter of 1814; adopted the red, white, and blue flag of the French Revolution; and admitted

The Fall of Algiers, July 1830 France assembled more than six hundred ships for its attack on the Ottoman dependency of Algeria, and this contemporary engraving depicts the ferocious naval bombardment that destroyed the capital's last remaining fortifications. However, after the surrender French soldiers rampaged through the city, and news of this brutal behavior encouraged Muslims in the interior to revolt and fight on until 1847. *(Musée de la Ville de Paris, Musée Carnavalet, Paris, France/Lauros/Giraudon/The Bridgeman Art Library)*

that he was merely the "king of the French people." In spite of such symbolic actions, the situation in France remained fundamentally unchanged. The vote was extended only from 100,000 to 170,000 citizens. The wealthy notable elite actually tightened its control as the old aristocracy retreated to the provinces to sulk harmlessly. For the upper middle class, there had been a change in dynasty in order to protect the status quo and the narrowly liberal institutions of 1815. Republicans, democrats, social reformers, and the poor of Paris were bitterly disappointed. They had made a revolution, but it seemed for naught. The social and political divisions that so troubled Jules Michelet in the 1840s were clear for all to see. (See the feature "Individuals in Society: Jules Michelet.")

The Revolutions of 1848

In 1848 revolutionary political and social ideologies combined with severe economic crisis and the romantic impulse to produce a vast upheaval across Europe. Only the most advanced and the most backward major countries—reforming Great Britain and immobile Russia—escaped untouched. Governments toppled; monarchs and ministers bowed or fled. National independence, liberal-democratic constitutions, and social reform: the lofty aspirations of a generation seemed at hand. Yet in the end, the revolutions failed.

● *Why in 1848 did revolution triumph briefly throughout most of Europe, and why did it fail almost completely?*

Individuals in Society

Jules Michelet

Famous proponent of democratic nationalism and generally recognized as France's pre-eminent romantic historian, Jules Michelet (1798–1874) was born and educated in Paris, the only child in a loving family of poor printers. Largely self-taught in the family print shop in his early years, the awkward apprentice-turned-student entered the prestigious Charlemagne College in 1813 and had to repeat his first year. Then he sped forward, winning prizes and building a brilliant academic career. Yet Michelet remained true to his roots in the common people, and he drew from history a vision of a generous France that would embrace all its children and heal their social divisions.

The young Michelet was strongly influenced by the still largely ignored Italian philosopher Giovanni Battista Vico (1668–1744), who viewed history as the development of societies and human institutions, as opposed to the biographies of great men or the work of divine providence. Translating and popularizing Vico's work and quickly writing three general histories, Michelet was rewarded with a professorship in Paris. He then launched an in-depth study of French society in the Middle Ages.

Motivated by the Gothic revival and romantic nationalism, Michelet was also inspired by his appointment as historical director of the National Archives after the revolution of 1830. This enabled him to combine teaching and writing with intense research in still largely unexplored documentary collections and present what he believed to be the first genuine history of his country and its people. Many historians, though not Michelet himself, believe that his history of France in the Middle Ages—published between 1833 and 1844 and becoming the first six volumes in his multivolume *History of France* (1833–1867)—is his most solid, useful, and lasting accomplishment. They single out his vast knowledge of the sources, his uncanny evocation of times and places, and his empathic and balanced understanding of different views and individuals. His treatment of the national revival under Joan of Arc in the fifteenth century is a famous example of his early work.

Finishing his study of the Middle Ages and shaken by his wife's death, Michelet became eager to write the history of the French Revolution as the ultimate achievement, the time the French people reached maturity and began the long-delayed liberation of mankind. Yet, confronted by growing social divisions and seeing "France sinking hour by hour," he tried first to write a book that would save France. Published in 1846, *The People* drew on personal experience, history, and contemporary debates, painting a vivid picture of French society and the social dislocation that afflicted all classes. Rejecting socialism as an unrealistic fantasy, Michelet pleaded instead for national unity: "One people! one country! one France! Never, never, I beg you, must we become two nations! Without unity, we perish!"* He also called for universal secular education, which would teach the revolution in 1789 and anchor France in a culture of republican democracy. Michelet's book was widely read and discussed.

Sickened by the failure of the revolution of 1848 and refusing to swear allegiance to Louis Napoleon, Michelet lost his government positions and turned to full-time writing. He completed his seven-volume history of the French Revolution, filled in the early modern period history of France with another eleven volumes, and wrote popular impressions of nature and anticlerical polemics. Michelet's later history is often criticized for being overly emotional and biased against the monarchy, the nobility, and the clergy while idealizing popular forces and revolutionary upheaval. A great individualist, Michelet was a gifted writer with a grand, heartfelt historical narrative of compassionate nationhood for a noble people.

Jules Michelet, in a portrait by Joseph Court. (Photo12.com)

Questions for Analysis

1. How would you describe Michelet's conception of history, and how did it evolve over time?
2. Does the study of history help solve contemporary problems? Debate this question, and defend your position.

*Jules Michelet, *The People*, trans. with an introduction by John P. McKay (Urbana: University of Illinois Press, 1973), p. 21.

Online Study Center **Improve Your Grade**
Going Beyond Individuals in Society

A Democratic Republic in France

The late 1840s in Europe were hard economically and tense politically. The potato famine in Ireland in 1845 and 1846 had many echoes on the continent. Bad harvests jacked up food prices and caused misery and unemployment in the cities. "Prerevolutionary" outbreaks occurred all across Europe: an abortive Polish revolution in the northern part of Austria in 1846, a civil war between radicals and conservatives in Switzerland in 1847, and an armed uprising in Naples, Italy, in January 1848. Revolution was almost universally expected, but it took revolution in Paris—once again—to turn expectations into realities.

Louis Philippe's "bourgeois monarchy" had been characterized by stubborn inaction and complacency. There was a glaring lack of social legislation, and politics was dominated by corruption and selfish special interests. With only the rich voting for deputies, many of the deputies were docile government bureaucrats.

The government's stubborn refusal to consider electoral reform heightened a sense of class injustice among middle-class shopkeepers, skilled artisans, and unskilled working people, and it eventually touched off a popular revolt in Paris. Barricades went up on the night of February 22, 1848, and by February 24 Louis Philippe had abdicated in favor of his grandson. But the common people in arms would tolerate no more monarchy. This refusal led to the proclamation of a provisional republic, headed by a ten-man executive committee and certified by cries of approval from the revolutionary crowd.

A generation of historians and journalists had praised the First French Republic, and their work had borne fruit: the revolutionaries were firmly committed to a republic (as opposed to any form of constitutional monarchy), and they immediately set about drafting a constitution for France's Second Republic. Moreover, they wanted a truly popular and democratic republic so that the healthy, life-giving forces of the common people—the peasants, the artisans, and the unskilled workers—could reform society

The Triumph of Democratic Republics   This French illustration constructs a joyous, optimistic vision of the initial revolutionary breakthrough in 1848. The peoples of Europe, joined together around their respective national banners, are achieving republican freedom, which is symbolized by the statue of liberty and the discarded crowns. The woman wearing pants—very radical attire—represents feminist hopes for liberation. *(Archive of Arnoldo Mondadori Editore, Milan)*

with wise legislation. In practice, building such a republic meant giving the right to vote to every adult male, and this was quickly done. Revolutionary compassion and sympathy for freedom were expressed in the freeing of all slaves in French colonies, the abolition of the death penalty, and the establishment of a ten-hour workday for Paris.

Yet there were profound differences within the revolutionary coalition in Paris. On the one hand, there were the moderate, liberal republicans of the middle class. They viewed universal male suffrage as the ultimate concession to be made to popular forces, and they strongly opposed any further radical social measures. On the other hand, there were radical republicans and hard-pressed artisans. Influenced by a generation of utopian socialists, and appalled by the poverty and misery of the urban poor, the radical republicans were committed to some kind of socialism. So were many artisans, who hated the unrestrained competition of cutthroat capitalism and who advocated a combination of strong craft unions and worker-owned businesses.

Worsening depression and rising unemployment brought these conflicting goals to the fore in 1848. Louis Blanc, who along with a worker named Albert represented the republican socialists in the provisional government, pressed for recognition of a socialist right to work. Blanc asserted that permanent government-sponsored cooperative workshops should be established for workers. Such workshops would be an alternative to capitalist employment and a decisive step toward a new, noncompetitive social order.

The moderate republicans wanted no such thing. They were willing to provide only temporary relief. The resulting compromise set up national workshops—soon to become little more than a vast program of pick-and-shovel public works—and established a special commission under Blanc to "study the question." This satisfied no one. The national workshops were, however, better than nothing. An army of desperate poor from the French provinces and even from foreign countries streamed into Paris to sign up. As the economic crisis worsened, the number enrolled in the workshops soared from 10,000 in March to 120,000 by June, and another 80,000 were trying unsuccessfully to join.

While the workshops in Paris grew, the French masses went to the election polls in late April. Voting in most cases for the first time, the people of France elected to the new Constituent Assembly about five hundred moderate republicans, three hundred monarchists, and one hundred radicals who professed various brands of socialism. One of the moderate republicans was the author of *Democracy in America,* Alexis de Tocqueville (1805–

1859), who had predicted the overthrow of Louis Philippe's government. To this brilliant observer, socialism was the most characteristic aspect of the revolution in Paris.

This socialist revolution was evoking a violent reaction not only among the frightened middle and upper classes but also among the bulk of the population—the peasants. The French peasants owned land, and according to Tocqueville, "private property had become with all those who owned it a sort of bond of fraternity."[4] Returning from Normandy to take his seat in the new Constituent Assembly, Tocqueville saw that a majority of the members were firmly committed to the republic and strongly opposed to the socialists and their artisan allies, and he shared their sentiments.

This clash of ideologies—of liberal capitalism and socialism—became a clash of classes and arms after the elections. The new government's executive committee dropped Blanc and thereafter included no representative of the Parisian working class. Fearing that their socialist hopes were about to be dashed, artisans and unskilled workers invaded the Constituent Assembly on May 15 and tried to proclaim a new revolutionary state. But the government was ready and used the middle-class National Guard to squelch this uprising. As the workshops continued to fill and grow more radical, the fearful but powerful propertied classes in the Assembly took the offensive. On June 22, the government dissolved the national workshops in Paris, giving the workers the choice of joining the army or going to workshops in the provinces.

The result was a spontaneous and violent uprising. Frustrated in attempts to create a socialist society, masses of desperate people were now losing even their life-sustaining relief. As a voice from the crowd cried out when the famous astronomer François Arago counseled patience, "Ah, Monsieur Arago, you have never been hungry!"[5] Barricades sprang up in the narrow streets of Paris, and a terrible class war began. Working people fought with the courage of utter desperation, but the government had the army and the support of peasant France. After three terrible "June Days" and the death or injury of more than ten thousand people, the republican army under General Louis Cavaignac stood triumphant in a sea of working-class blood and hatred.

The revolution in France thus ended in spectacular failure. The February coalition of the middle and working classes had in four short months become locked in mortal combat. In place of a generous democratic republic, the Constituent Assembly completed a constitution featuring a strong executive. This allowed Louis Napoleon, nephew of Napoleon Bonaparte, to win a landslide victory in the election of December 1848. The appeal of his great name as well as the desire of the propertied classes for order at any cost had produced a semi-authoritarian regime.

The Austrian Empire in 1848

Throughout central Europe, the first news of the upheaval in France evoked feverish excitement and eventually revolution. Liberals demanded written constitutions, representative government, and greater civil liberties from authoritarian regimes. When governments hesitated, popular revolts followed. Urban workers and students served as the shock troops, but they were allied with middle-class liberals and peasants. In the face of this united front, monarchs collapsed and granted almost everything. The popular revolutionary coalition, having secured great and easy victories, then broke down as it had in France. The traditional forces—the monarchy, the aristocracy, the regular army—recovered their nerve, reasserted their authority, and took back many, though not all, of the concessions. Reaction was everywhere victorious.

The revolution in the Austrian Empire began in Hungary, where nationalistic Hungarians demanded national autonomy, full civil liberties, and universal suffrage. When the monarchy in Vienna hesitated, Viennese students and workers took to the streets, and peasant disorders broke out in parts of the empire. The Habsburg emperor Ferdinand I (r. 1835–1848) capitulated and promised reforms and a liberal constitution. Metternich fled in disguise toward London. The old absolutist order seemed to be collapsing with unbelievable rapidity.

The coalition of revolutionaries was not stable, however. The Austrian Empire was overwhelmingly agricultural, and serfdom still existed. On March 20, as part of its capitulation before upheaval, the monarchy abolished serfdom, with its degrading forced labor and feudal services. Feeling they had won a victory reminiscent of that in France in 1789, newly free men and women of the land then lost interest in the political and social questions agitating the cities. Meanwhile, the coalition of urban revolutionaries also broke down. When artisan workers and the urban poor rose in arms and presented their own demands for socialist workshops and universal voting rights for men, the prosperous middle classes recoiled in alarm.

The coalition of March was also weakened, and ultimately destroyed, by conflicting national aspirations. In March the Hungarian revolutionary leaders pushed through an extremely liberal, almost democratic, constitution. But the Hungarian revolutionaries also sought to transform the mosaic of provinces and peoples that was the kingdom of Hungary into a unified, centralized, Hungarian nation. To the minority groups that formed half of the population—the Croats, Serbs, and Romanians—such unification was completely unacceptable. Each felt entitled to political autonomy and cultural independence. The Habsburg monarchy in Vienna exploited the fears of the minority groups, and they were soon locked in armed combat with the new Hungarian government. In a somewhat similar way, Czech nationalists based in Bohemia and the city of Prague came into conflict with German nationalists. (See the feature "Listening to the Past: Speaking for the Czech Nation" on pages 776–777.) Thus conflicting national aspirations within the Austrian Empire enabled the monarchy to play off one ethnic group against the other.

Finally, the conservative aristocratic forces gathered around Emperor Ferdinand I regained their nerve and reasserted their great strength. The archduchess Sophia, a conservative but intelligent and courageous Bavarian princess married to the emperor's brother, provided a rallying point. Deeply ashamed of the emperor's collapse before a "mess of students," she insisted that Ferdinand, who had no heir, abdicate in favor of her son, Francis Joseph.[6] Powerful nobles who held high positions in the government, the army, and the church agreed completely. They organized around Sophia in a secret conspiracy to reverse and crush the revolution.

Their first breakthrough came when the army bombarded Prague and savagely crushed a working-class revolt there on June 17. Other Austrian officials and nobles began to lead the minority nationalities of Hungary against the revolutionary government proclaimed by the Hungarian patriots. At the end of October, the well-equipped, predominantly peasant troops of the regular Austrian army attacked the student and working-class radicals in Vienna and retook the city at the cost of more than four thousand casualties. Thus the determination of the Austrian aristocracy and the loyalty of its army were the final ingredients in the triumph of reaction and the defeat of revolution.

When Francis Joseph (r. 1848–1916) was crowned emperor of Austria immediately after his eighteenth birthday in December 1848, only Hungary had yet to be brought under control. But another determined conservative, Nicholas I of Russia (r. 1825–1855), obligingly lent his iron hand. On June 6, 1849, 130,000 Russian troops poured into Hungary and subdued the country after bitter fighting. For a number of years, the Habsburgs ruled Hungary as a conquered territory.

Prussia and the Frankfurt Assembly

After Austria, Prussia was the largest and most influential German kingdom. Prior to 1848, the goal of middle-class Prussian liberals had been to transform absolutist Prussia into a liberal constitutional monarchy, which would lead the thirty-eight states of the German Confederation into the liberal, unified nation desired by liberals throughout the German states. The agitation following the fall of Louis Philippe encouraged Prussian liberals to press their demands. When the artisans and factory workers in Berlin exploded in March and joined temporarily with the middle-class liberals in the struggle against the monarchy, the autocratic yet paternalistic Frederick William IV (r. 1840–1861) vacillated and finally caved in. On March 21, he promised to grant Prussia a liberal constitution and to merge Prussia into a new national German state that was to be created. But urban workers wanted much more and the Prussian aristocracy wanted much less than the moderate constitutional liberalism

Street Fighting in Frankfurt, 1848 Workers and students could tear up the cobblestones, barricade a street, and make it into a fortress. But urban revolutionaries were untrained and poorly armed. They were no match for professional soldiers led by tough officers who were sent against them after frightened rulers had recovered their nerve. *(The Granger Collection, New York)*

the king conceded. The workers issued a series of demo-cratic and vaguely socialist demands that troubled their middle-class allies, and the conservative clique gathered around the king to urge counter-revolution.

As an elected Prussian Constituent Assembly met in Berlin to write a constitution for the Prussian state, a self-appointed committee of liberals from various German states successfully called for a national assembly to begin writing a federal constitution for a unified German state. Meeting in Frankfurt in May, the National Assembly was a curious revolutionary body. It was a really serious middle-class body of lawyers, professors, doctors, offi-cials, and businessmen.

Convened to write a constitution, the learned body was soon absorbed in a battle with Denmark over the provinces of Schleswig and Holstein, an extremely com-plicated issue from a legal point of view. The provinces were inhabited primarily by Germans but were ruled by the king of Denmark, although Holstein was a member of the German Confederation. When Frederick VII, the new nationalistic king of Denmark, tried to integrate both provinces into the rest of his state, the Germans in these provinces revolted. Hypnotized by this conflict, the Na-tional Assembly at Frankfurt debated ponderously and fi-nally called on the Prussian army to oppose Denmark in the name of the German nation. Prussia responded and

began war with Denmark. As the Schleswig-Holstein is-sue demonstrated, the national ideal was a crucial factor motivating the German middle classes in 1848.

In March 1849, the National Assembly finally com-pleted its drafting of a liberal constitution and elected King Frederick William of Prussia emperor of the new German national state (minus Austria and Schleswig-Holstein). By early 1849, however, reaction had been successful almost everywhere. Frederick William had re-asserted his royal authority, disbanded the Prussian Con-stituent Assembly, and granted his subjects a limited, essentially conservative constitution. Reasserting that he ruled by divine right, Frederick William contemptuously refused to accept the "crown from the gutter." Bogged down by their preoccupation with nationalist issues, the reluctant revolutionaries in Frankfurt had waited too long and acted too timidly.

When Frederick William, who really wanted to be em-peror but only on his own authoritarian terms, tried to get the small monarchs of Germany to elect him emperor, Austria balked. Supported by Russia, Austria forced Prus-sia to renounce all its schemes of unification in late 1850. The German Confederation was re-established. Attempts to unite the Germans—first in a liberal national state and then in a conservative Prussian empire—had failed completely.

Chapter Summary

Online Study Center **ACE the Test**

- *How did the victorious allies fashion a general peace settlement, and how did Metternich uphold a conservative European order?*
- *What were the basic tenets of liberalism, nationalism, and socialism, and what groups were most attracted to these ideologies?*
- *What were the characteristics of the romantic move-ment, and who were some of the great romantic artists?*
- *How after 1815 did liberal, national, and socialist forces challenge conservatism in Greece, Great Britain, and France?*
- *Why in 1848 did revolution triumph briefly throughout most of Europe, and why did it fail almost completely?*

In 1814 the victorious allied powers sought to restore peace and stability in Europe. Dealing moderately with France and wisely settling their own differences, the allies laid the foundations for beneficial international coopera-tion throughout much of the nineteenth century. Led by Metternich, the conservative powers also sought to pre-vent the spread of subversive ideas and radical changes in domestic politics. Yet European thought has seldom been more powerfully creative than after 1815, and ide-ologies of liberalism, nationalism, and socialism all devel-oped to challenge the existing order in this period of early industrialization and rapid population growth. The romantic movement, breaking decisively with the dic-tates of classicism, reinforced the spirit of change and revolutionary anticipation.

All of these forces shaped European development after 1815, and they culminated in the liberal and nationalistic revolutions of 1848. Political, economic, and social pressures that had been building since 1815 exploded dramatically and rocked the continent. Yet the upheavals of 1848 were abortive, and very few revolutionary goals were realized. The moderate, nationalistic middle classes were unable to consolidate their initial victories in France or elsewhere in Europe. Instead, they drew back when artisans, factory workers, and radical socialists rose up to present their own much more revolutionary demands. This retreat facilitated the efforts of dedicated aristocrats in central Europe to reassert their power. And it made possible the crushing of Parisian workers by a coalition of solid bourgeoisie and landowning peasantry in France. A host of fears, a sea of blood, and a torrent of disillusion had drowned the lofty ideals and utopian visions of a generation. The age of romantic revolution was over. Soon tough-minded realists would take command to confront the challenges of the dual revolution.

Key Terms

dual revolution	doers
Congress of Vienna	bourgeoisie
Holy Alliance	proletariat
Carlsbad Decrees	romanticism
liberalism	Sturm und Drang
laissez faire	Corn Laws
nationalism	Battle of Peterloo
socialism	Great Famine
parasites	

Online Study Center   **Improve Your Grade** Flashcards

Suggested Reading

Berger, Stefan, ed. *A Companion to Nineteenth-Century Europe, 1789–1914.* 2006. A useful study with an up-to-date bibliography.

Chadwick, Owen. *The Secularization of the European Mind in the Nineteenth Century.* 1976. Considers the important place of religion in nineteenth-century thought.

Gildea, Robert. *Barricades and Borders: Europe, 1800–1914,* 2d ed. 1996. A recommended general study.

Greene, Abigail. *Fatherlands: State-Building and Nationhood in Nineteenth-Century Germany.* 2001. A brilliant discussion of the smaller German states.

Lindemann, Albert S. *A History of European Socialism.* 1983. A stimulating survey of early socialism and Marxism.

Malia, Martin, and Terence Emmons. *History's Locomotives: Revolutions and the Making of the Modern World.* 2006. An ambitious comparative work of high quality.

Mann, Thomas. *Buddenbrooks.* A wonderful historical novel that traces the rise and fall of a prosperous German family over three generations.

Merriman, John. *Police Stories: Building the French State, 1815–1851.* 2006. An outstanding and innovative compendium.

Pilbeam, Pamela. *French Socialists Before Marx: Workers, Women, and the Social Question.* 2000. Shows the significant role of women in utopian socialism.

Price, Roger. *A Social History of Nineteenth-Century France.* 1987. A fine synthesis.

Rubinstein, W. D. *Britain's Century: A Political and Social History, 1815–1905.* 1998. An excellent English history.

Sheehan, James J. *German History, 1770–1866.* 1993. A stimulating general history that skillfully incorporates recent research.

Shelley, Mary. *Frankenstein.* A great nineteenth-century romantic novel that draws an almost lovable picture of the famous monster and is highly recommended.

Sperber, Jonathan. *The European Revolutions, 1848–1851.* 1993. A solid synthesis of the great revolutionary upheaval.

Notes

1. E. Gellner, *Nations and Nationalism* (Oxford: Basil Blackwell, 1983), especially pp. 19–39.
2. This paragraph draws on the influential views of B. Anderson, *Imagined Communities: Reflections on the Origins and Spread of Nationalism,* rev. ed. (London/New York: Verso, 1991), and E. J. Hobsbawm and T. Ranger, eds., *The Invention of Tradition* (Cambridge: Cambridge University Press, 1983).
3. Quoted in F. B. Artz, *From the Renaissance to Romanticism: Trends in Style in Art, Literature, and Music, 1300–1830* (Chicago: University of Chicago Press, 1962), pp. 276, 278.
4. A. de Tocqueville, *Recollections* (New York: Columbia University Press, 1949), p. 94.
5. M. Agulhon, *1848* (Paris: Éditions du Seuil, 1973), pp. 68–69.
6. W. L. Langer, *Political and Social Upheaval, 1832–1852* (New York: Harper & Row, 1969), p. 361.

Listening to the Past

Speaking for the Czech Nation

The creation of national consciousness and nationalism often began with a cultural revival that focused on a people's language and history, which led to calls for cultural autonomy and political independence. In Austria, the influential historian Frantisek Palacky (1798–1876) inspired the Czech cultural and political revival, re-creating the Czechs in his books as progressive and democratic before the Counter-Reformation and the long process of Germanization under Habsburg rule.

In the revolution of 1848, when the German National Assembly in Frankfurt assumed that Austrian provinces that were part of the German Confederation would also join a united Germany, it asked Palacky to represent Czech Bohemia. In the famous letter that follows Palacky rejected this invitation. Asserting the reality of a Czech nation and warning of both Russian and German expansionism, he proposed a "union of equals" in a radically transformed Austria. A version of Palacky's proposal was passed by Austria's constituent assembly in 1849, but the resurgent absolutist government vetoed it.

. . . I am a Czech of Slav descent and with all the little I own and possess I have devoted myself wholly and for ever to the service of my nation. That nation is small, it is true, but from time immemorial it has been an independent nation with its own character; its rulers have participated since old times in the federation of German princes, but the nation never regarded itself nor was it regarded by others throughout all the centuries, as part of the German nation. The whole union of the Czech lands first with the Holy German Empire and then with the German Confederation was always a purely dynastic one of which the Czech nation, the Czech Estates, hardly wished to know and which they hardly noticed. . . . If anyone asks that the Czech nation should now unite with the German nation,

beyond this heretofore existing federation between princes, this is then a new demand which has no historical legal basis. . . . The second reason which prevents me from participating in your deliberations is the fact that . . . you . . . are . . . aiming to undermine Austria forever as an independent empire and to make its existence impossible—an empire whose preservation, integrity and consolidation is, and must be, a great and important matter not only for my own nation but for the whole of Europe, indeed for mankind and civilization itself. Allow me kindly to explain myself briefly on this point.

You know, gentlemen, what power it is that holds the whole great eastern part of our continent; you know that this power [Russia] which now already has grown to vast dimensions, increases and expands by its own strength every decade . . . has for a long time been a threat to its neighbours; and . . . that every further step which it will take forward on this path threatens at an ever accelerated pace to produce and found a *universal monarchy,* that is to say, an infinite and inexpressible evil, a misfortune without measure or bound which I, though heart and soul a Slav, would nonetheless deeply regret for the good of mankind even though that monarchy proclaimed itself a Slav one. . . . The bare possibility of a Russian universal monarchy has no more determined opponent or adversary than myself, not because that monarchy would be Russian but because it would be universal.

You know that in south-east Europe, along the frontiers of the Russian empire, there live many nations widely different in origin, language, history and habits—Slavs, Rumanians, Magyars [Hungarians] and Germans, not to speak of Greeks, Turks and Albanians—none of whom is strong enough by itself to be able to resist successfully for all time the superior neighbour to the east; they could do it only if a close and firm tie bound them all together. The vital artery of this necessary union of nations is the Danube; the focus of its power must never be removed far from this river, if the union is to be effective at all and to remain so. Certainly, if the Austrian state had not existed for ages, we would be obliged in the interests of Europe and even of mankind to endeavor to create it as fast as possible.

But why have we seen this state, which by nature and history is destined to be the bulwark and guardian of Europe against Asiatic elements of every kind—why have we seen it in a critical moment helpless and almost unadvised in the face of the advancing storm? It is because in an unhappy blindness which has lasted for very long, Austria has not recognized the real legal and moral foundation of its existence and has denied it: the fundamental rule that all the nationalities united under its scepter should enjoy complete equality of rights and respect. The right of nations is truly a natural right; no nation on earth has the right to demand that its neighbour should sacrifice itself for its benefit, no nation obliged to deny or sacrifice itself for the good of its neighbour. Nature knows neither ruling nor subservient nations. If the union which unites several different nations is to be firm and lasting, no nation must have cause to fear that by that union it will lose any of the goods which it holds most dear; on the contrary each must have the certain hope that it will find in the central authority defense and protection against possible violations of equality by neighbours; then every nation will do its best to strengthen that central authority so that it can successfully provide the aforesaid defense. I am convinced that even now it is not too late for the Austrian empire to proclaim openly and sincerely this fundamental rule of justice, the sacred anchor for a ship in danger of floundering and to carry it out energetically in common and in every respect; but every moment is precious; for God's sake do not let us delay another hour with this! . . .

When I look behind the Bohemian frontiers, then natural and historical reasons make me turn not to Frankfurt but to Vienna to seek there the center which is fitted and destined to ensure and defend the peace, the liberty and the right of my nation. Your efforts, gentlemen, seem to me now to be directed as I have already stated, not only

Frantisek Palacky, in a frontispiece portrait accompanying his most important work on Czech history. (*Visual Connection Archive*)

towards ruinously undermining, but even utterly destroying that center from whose might and strength I expect the salvation not only of the Czech land. . . . For the sake of Europe, Vienna must not sink to the role of a provincial town. If there are in Vienna itself such people who demand to have your Frankfurt as their capital, then we must cry: Lord, forgive them, for they know not what they ask!

Questions for Analysis

1. Why did Palacky refuse to participate in the German National Assembly?

2. What is Palacky's attitude toward Russia? Why?

3. In a famous epigram inspired by Voltaire, Palacky writes, "If the Austrian state had not existed for ages, we would be obliged . . . to create it as fast as possible." What does he mean?

4. How has Austria failed to perform its mission? Why?

Source: Slightly adapted from Hans Kohn, *Pan-Slavism: Its Ideology and History*, pp. 65–69. Copyright © 1953. Reprinted by permission of the University of Notre Dame Press.

John Perry, *A Bill-poster's Fantasy* (1855), explores the endless diversity of big-city entertainment.
(dunhill Museum & Archive, 48 Germyn Street, St. James's, London)

24

Taming the City
- *What was life like in the cities, and how did urban life change in the nineteenth century?*

Rich and Poor and Those in Between
- *What did the emergence of urban industrial society mean for rich and poor and those in between?*

The Changing Family
- *How did families change as they coped with the challenges and the opportunities of the developing urban civilization?*

Science and Thought
- *What major changes in science and thought reflected and influenced the new urban society?*

LIFE IN THE EMERGING URBAN SOCIETY IN THE NINETEENTH CENTURY

T he era of intellectual and political upheaval that culminated in the revolutions of 1848 was also an era of rapid urbanization. After 1848 Western political development veered off in a novel and uncharted direction, but the growth of towns and cities rushed forward with undiminished force. Thus Western society was urban and industrial in 1900 as surely as it had been rural and agrarian in 1800. The urbanization of society was both a result of the Industrial Revolution and a reflection of its enormous long-term impact.

Taming the City

The growth of industry posed enormous challenges for all elements of Western society, from young factory workers confronting relentless discipline to aristocratic elites maneuvering to retain political power. As we saw in Chapter 22, the early consequences of economic transformation were mixed and far-reaching and by no means wholly negative. By 1850 at the latest, working conditions were improving and real wages were rising for the mass of the population, and they continued to do so until 1914. Thus given the poverty and uncertainty of preindustrial life, some historians maintain that the history of industrialization in the nineteenth century is probably better written in terms of increasing opportunities than in terms of greater hardships.

Critics of this relatively optimistic view of industrialization claim that it neglects the quality of life in urban areas. They stress that the new industrial towns and cities were awful places where people, especially poor people, suffered from bad housing, lack of sanitation, and a sense of hopelessness. They ask if these drawbacks did not more than cancel out higher wages and greater opportunity. An examination of the development of

Online Study Center

This icon will direct you to interactive activities and study materials on the website **college.hmco.com/pic/mckaywest9e**

Mapping the Past

MAP 24.1 European Cities of 100,000 or More, 1800 and 1900 There were more large cities in Great Britain in 1900 than in all of Europe in 1800. A careful comparison of these historical snapshots reveals key aspects of nineteenth-century urbanization. ❶ In 1800, what common characteristics were shared by many large European cities? (For example, how many big cities were capitals and/or leading ports?) ❷ Compare the spatial distribution of cities in 1800 with the distribution in 1900. Where and why in 1900 are many large cities concentrated in two clusters?

cities in the nineteenth century provides some answers to this complex question.

● *What was life like in the cities, and how did urban life change in the nineteenth century?*

Industry and the Growth of Cities

Since the Middle Ages, European cities had been centers of government, culture, and large-scale commerce. They had also been congested, dirty, and unhealthy. People were packed together almost as tightly as possible within the city limits. The typical city was a "walking city": for all but the wealthiest classes, walking was the only available form of transportation.

Infectious disease spread with deadly speed in cities, and people were always more likely to die in the city than in the countryside. In the larger towns, more people died each year than were born, on average, and urban populations were able to maintain their numbers only because newcomers were continually arriving from rural areas. Little could be done to improve these conditions, given the pervasive poverty, absence of urban transportation, lack of medical knowledge, and deadly overcrowding.

Clearly, deplorable urban conditions did not originate with the Industrial Revolution. What the Industrial Revolution did was to reveal those conditions more nakedly than ever before. The steam engine freed industrialists from dependence on the energy of fast-flowing streams and rivers so that by 1800 there was every incentive to build new factories in urban areas. Cities had better shipping facilities than the countryside and thus better supplies of coal and raw materials. There were also many hands wanting work in the cities, for cities drew people like a magnet. And it was a great advantage for a manufacturer to have other factories nearby to supply the business's needs and buy its products. Therefore, as industry grew, there was also a rapid expansion of already over-crowded and unhealthy cities.

The challenge of the urban environment was felt first and most acutely in Great Britain. The number of people living in cities of 20,000 or more in England and Wales jumped from 1.5 million in 1801 to 6.3 million in 1851 and reached 15.6 million in 1891. Such cities accounted for 17 percent of the total English population in 1801, 35 percent as early as 1851, and fully 54 percent in 1891. Other countries duplicated the English pattern as they industrialized (see Map 24.1). An American observer was hardly exaggerating when he wrote in 1899 that "the most remarkable social phenomenon of the present century is the concentration of population in cities."[1]

In the 1820s and 1830s, people in Britain and France began to worry about the condition of their cities. In those years, the populations of a number of British cities were increasing by 40 to 70 percent each decade. With urban areas expanding at such previously undreamed-of rates, people's fatalistic acceptance of overcrowded, unsanitary urban living conditions began to give way to active concern. Something urgently needed to be done.

On one point everyone could agree: except on the outskirts, each town or city was using every scrap of land to the fullest extent. Parks and open areas were almost nonexistent. Buildings were erected on the smallest possible lots in order to pack the maximum number of people into a given space. Narrow houses were built wall to wall in long rows. These row houses had neither front nor back yards, and only a narrow alley in back separated one row from the next. Or buildings were built around tiny courtyards completely enclosed on all four sides. Many people lived in extremely small, often overcrowded cellars or attics. "Six, eight, and even ten occupying one room is anything but uncommon," wrote a doctor from Aberdeen in Scotland for a government investigation in 1842.

These highly concentrated urban populations lived in extremely unsanitary and unhealthy conditions. Open drains and sewers flowed alongside or down the middle of unpaved streets. Toilet facilities were primitive in the extreme. In parts of Manchester, as many as two hundred people shared a single outhouse. Such privies filled up rapidly, and since they were infrequently emptied, sewage often overflowed and seeped into cellar dwellings. Moreover, some courtyards in poorer neighborhoods became dunghills, collecting excrement that was sometimes sold as fertilizer. By the 1840s there was among the better-off classes a growing, shocking "realization that, to put it as mildly as possible, millions of English men, women, and children were living in shit."[2]

Who or what was responsible for these awful conditions? The crucial factors were the tremendous pressure of more people and the *total* absence of public transportation. People simply had to jam themselves together if they were to be able to walk to shops and factories. Another factor was that government in Great Britain, both local and national, was slow to provide sanitary facilities and establish adequate building codes. This slow pace was probably attributable more to a need to explore and identify what precisely should be done than to rigid middle-class opposition to government action. Certainly, Great Britain had no monopoly on overcrowded and unhealthy urban

conditions; many continental cities with stronger traditions of municipal regulation were every bit as bad.

Most responsible of all was the sad legacy of rural housing conditions in preindustrial society combined with appalling ignorance. As one authority concludes, "the decent cottage was the exception, the hovel the rule."[3] Thus housing was far down on the newcomer's list of priorities, and ordinary people generally took dirt and filth for granted. One English miner told an investigator, "I do not think it usual for the lasses [in the coal mines] to wash their bodies; my sisters never wash themselves." As for the men, "their legs and bodies are as black as your hat."[4]

Public Health and the Bacterial Revolution

Although cleanliness was not next to godliness in most people's eyes, it was becoming so for some reformers. The most famous of these was Edwin Chadwick, one of the commissioners charged with the administration of relief to paupers under Britain's revised Poor Law of 1834. Chadwick was a good **Benthamite**—that is, a follower of radical philosopher Jeremy Bentham (1748–1832). Bentham had taught that public problems ought to be dealt with on a rational, scientific basis and according to the

Chronology

ca 1850–1870	Modernization of Paris
1850–1914	Condition of working classes improves
1854	Pasteur studies fermentation and develops pasteurization
1854–1870	Development of germ theory
1857	Flaubert, *Madame Bovary*
1859	Darwin, *On the Origin of Species*
1859–1870	Unification of Italy
1861–1865	U.S. Civil War
1866	Austro-Prussian War
1869	Mendeleev creates periodic table
1870–1871	Franco-Prussian War
1880–1881	Dostoevski, *The Brothers Karamazov*
1880–1913	Birthrate steadily declines in Europe
1890s	Electric streetcars introduced in Europe

A COURT FOR KING CHOLERA.

Filth and Disease This 1852 drawing from *Punch* tells volumes about the unhealthy living conditions of the urban poor. In the foreground children play with a dead rat and a woman scavenges a dung heap. Cheap rooming houses provide shelter for the frightfully overcrowded population. *(The British Library)*

"greatest good for the greatest number." Applying these principles, Chadwick soon became convinced that disease and death actually caused poverty simply because a sick worker was an unemployed worker and orphaned children were poor children. Most important, Chadwick believed that disease could be prevented by cleaning up the urban environment. That was his "sanitary idea."

Chadwick collected detailed reports from local Poor Law officials on the "sanitary conditions of the laboring population" and published his hard-hitting findings in 1842. This mass of widely publicized evidence proved

that disease was related to filthy environmental conditions, which were in turn caused largely by lack of drainage, sewers, and garbage collection.

Chadwick correctly believed that the stinking excrement of communal outhouses could be dependably carried off by water through sewers at less than one-twentieth the cost of removing it by hand. The cheap iron pipes and tile drains of the industrial age would provide running water and sewerage for all sections of town, not just the wealthy ones. In 1848, with the cause strengthened by the cholera epidemic of 1846, Chadwick's report became the basis of

Great Britain's first public health law, which created a national health board and gave cities broad authority to build modern sanitary systems.

The public health movement won dedicated supporters in the United States, France, and Germany from the 1840s on. Governments accepted at least limited responsibility for the health of all citizens, and their programs broke decisively with the age-old fatalism of urban populations in the face of shockingly high mortality. By the 1860s and 1870s, European cities were making real progress toward adequate water supplies and sewerage systems, city dwellers were beginning to reap the reward of better health, and death rates began to decline (see Figure 24.1).

Still, effective control of communicable disease required a great leap forward in medical knowledge and biological theory. Early reformers such as Chadwick were seriously handicapped by the prevailing **miasmatic theory** of disease—the belief that people contract disease when they breathe the bad odors of decay and putrefying excrement. Keen observation by doctors and public health officials in the 1840s and 1850s pinpointed the role of bad drinking water in the transmission of disease and suggested that contagion was *spread through* filth and not caused by it, thus weakening the miasmatic idea.

The breakthrough was the development of the **germ theory** of disease by Louis Pasteur (1822–1895), a French chemist who began studying fermentation in 1854 at the request of brewers. Using his microscope to develop a simple test that brewers could use to monitor the fermentation process and avoid spoilage, Pasteur found that fermentation depended on the growth of living organisms and that the activity of these organisms could be suppressed by heating the beverage—by **pasteurization.** The breathtaking implication was that specific diseases were caused by specific living organisms—germs—and that those organisms could be controlled in people as well as in beer, wine, and milk.

By 1870 the work of Pasteur and others had demonstrated the general connection between germs and disease. When, in the middle of the 1870s, German country doctor Robert Koch and his coworkers developed pure cultures of harmful bacteria and described their life cycles, the dam broke. Over the next twenty years, researchers—mainly Germans—identified the organisms responsible for disease after disease. These discoveries led to the development of a number of effective vaccines.

Acceptance of the germ theory brought about dramatic improvements in the deadly environment of hospitals and surgery. In 1865, when Pasteur showed that the air was full of bacteria, English surgeon Joseph Lister (1827–1912) immediately grasped the connection be-

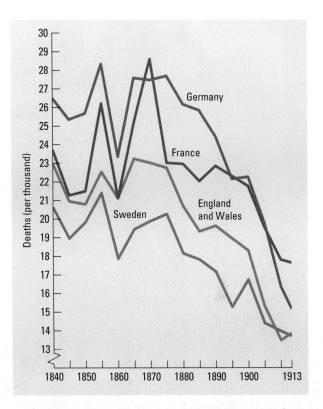

FIGURE 24.1 The Decline of Death Rates in England and Wales, Germany, France, and Sweden, 1840–1913 A rising standard of living, improvements in public health, and better medical knowledge all contributed to the dramatic decline of death rates in the nineteenth century.

tween aerial bacteria and the problem of wound infection. He reasoned that a chemical disinfectant applied to a wound dressing would "destroy the life of the floating particles." Lister's **antiseptic principle** worked wonders. In the 1880s, German surgeons developed the more sophisticated practice of sterilizing not only the wound but also everything—hands, instruments, clothing—that entered the operating room.

The achievements of the bacterial revolution coupled with the ever more sophisticated public health movement saved millions of lives, particularly after about 1880. Mortality rates began to decline dramatically in European countries (see Figure 24.1) as the awful death sentences of the past—diphtheria, typhoid, typhus, cholera, yellow fever—became vanishing diseases. City dwellers benefited especially from these developments. By 1910 a great silent revolution had occurred: the death rates for people of all ages in urban areas were generally no greater than those for people in rural areas, and sometimes they were less.

MAP 24.2 The Modernization of Paris, ca 1850–1870 Broad boulevards, large parks, and grandiose train stations transformed Paris. The cutting of the new north-south axis—known as the Boulevard Saint-Michel—was one of Haussmann's most controversial projects. It razed much of Paris's medieval core and filled the Île de la Cité with massive government buildings.

Urban Planning and Public Transportation

More effective urban planning was one of the keys to improving the quality of urban life. Urban planning was in decline by the early nineteenth century, but after 1850 its practice was revived and extended. France took the lead during the rule of Napoleon III (r. 1848–1870), who sought to stand above class conflict and promote the welfare of all his subjects through government action. He believed that rebuilding much of Paris would provide employment, improve living conditions, and testify to the power and glory of his empire. In the baron Georges Haussmann (1809–1884), an aggressive, impatient Alsatian whom he placed in charge of Paris, Napoleon III found an authoritarian planner capable of bulldozing both buildings and opposition. In twenty years, Paris was transformed (see Map 24.2).

The Paris of 1850 was a labyrinth of narrow, dark streets, the results of desperate overcrowding. In a central city not twice the size of New York's Central Park lived more than

Apartment Living in Paris This drawing shows how different social classes lived close together in European cities in about 1850. Passing the middle-class family on the first floor (American second floor), the economic condition of the tenants declined until one reached abject poverty in the garret. *(Bibliothèque nationale de France)*

one-third of the city's 1 million inhabitants. Terrible slum conditions and extremely high death rates were facts of life. There were few open spaces and only two public parks for the entire metropolis. Public transportation played a very small role in this enormous walking city.

Haussmann and his fellow planners proceeded on many interrelated fronts. With a bold energy that often shocked their contemporaries, they razed old buildings in order to cut broad, straight, tree-lined boulevards through the center of the city as well as in new quarters on the outskirts (see Map 24.2). These boulevards, designed in part to prevent the easy construction and defense of barricades by revolutionary crowds, permitted traffic to flow freely and afforded impressive vistas. Their creation also demolished some of the worst slums. New streets stimulated the construction of better housing, especially for the middle classes. Small neighborhood parks and open spaces were created throughout the city, and two very large parks suitable for all kinds of holiday activities were developed—one on the wealthy west side and one on the poor east side of the city. The city also improved its sewers, and a system of aqueducts more than doubled the city's supply of good fresh water.

Rebuilding Paris provided a new model for urban planning and stimulated modern urbanism throughout Europe, particularly after 1870. In city after city, public authorities mounted a coordinated attack on many of the interrelated problems of the urban environment. As in Paris, improvements in public health through better water supply and waste disposal often went hand in hand with new boulevard construction. Cities such as Vienna and Cologne followed the Parisian example of tearing down old walled fortifications and replacing them with broad, circular boulevards on which office buildings, town halls, theaters, opera houses, and museums were erected. These ring roads and the new boulevards that radiated out from them toward the outskirts eased movement and encouraged urban expansion (see Map 24.2). Zoning expropriation laws, which allowed a majority of the owners of land in a given quarter of the city to impose major street or sanitation improvements on a reluctant minority, were an important mechanism of the new urbanism.

The development of mass public transportation was also of great importance in the improvement of urban living conditions. In the 1870s, many European cities authorized private companies to operate horse-drawn streetcars, which had been developed in the United States, to carry riders along the growing number of major thoroughfares. Then in the 1890s, the real revolution occurred: European countries adopted another American transit innovation, the electric streetcar.

Electric streetcars were cheaper, faster, more dependable, and more comfortable than their horse-drawn counterparts. Service improved dramatically. Millions of Europeans—workers, shoppers, schoolchildren—hopped on board during the workweek. And on weekends and holidays, streetcars carried millions on happy outings to parks and countryside, racetracks and music halls. In 1886 the horse-drawn streetcars of Austria-Hungary, France, Germany, and Great Britain were carrying about 900 million riders. By 1910 electric streetcar systems in the four countries were carrying 6.7 billion riders.[5] Each man, woman, and child was using public transportation four times as often in 1910 as in 1886.

Good mass transit helped greatly in the struggle for decent housing. The new boulevards and horse-drawn streetcars had facilitated a middle-class move to better housing in the 1860s and 1870s; after 1890 electric streetcars gave people of modest means access to new, improved housing. The still-crowded city was able to expand and become less congested. In England in 1901, only 9 percent of the urban population was "overcrowded" in terms of the official definition of more than two persons per room. On the continent, many city governments in the early twentieth century were building electric streetcar systems that provided transportation to new public and private housing developments in outlying areas of the city for the working classes.

Rich and Poor and Those in Between

General improvements in health and in the urban environment had beneficial consequences for all kinds of people. Yet differences in living conditions among social classes remained gigantic.

- *What did the emergence of urban industrial society mean for rich and poor and those in between?*

Social Structure

How much did the almost-completed journey to an urban, industrialized world change the social framework of rich and poor and those in between? The first great change was a substantial and undeniable increase in the standard of living for the average person. The real wages of British workers, for example, which had already risen by 1850, almost doubled between 1850 and 1906. Similar increases occurred in continental countries as indus-

The Urban Landscape: Madrid in 1900   This wistful painting of a Spanish square on a rainy day, by Enrique Martinez Cubells y Ruiz (1874–1917), includes a revealing commentary on public transportation. Coachmen wait atop their expensive hackney cabs for a wealthy clientele, while modern electric streetcars that carry the masses converge on the square from all directions. *(Museo Municipal, Madrid/The Bridgeman Art Library)*

trial development quickened after 1850. Ordinary people took a major step forward in the centuries-old battle against poverty, reinforcing efforts to improve many aspects of human existence.

There is another side to the income coin, however. Greater economic rewards for the average person did *not* eliminate hardship and poverty, nor did they make the wealth and income of the rich and the poor significantly more equal. In almost every advanced country around 1900, the richest 5 percent of all households in the population received 33 percent of all national income. The richest 20 percent of households received anywhere from 50 to 60 percent of all national income, while the entire

bottom 80 percent received only 40 to 50 percent. Moreover, the bottom 30 percent of households received 10 percent or less of all income. These enormous differences are illustrated in Figure 24.2.

The middle classes, smaller than they are today, accounted for less than 20 percent of the population; thus the statistics show that the upper and middle classes alone received more than 50 percent of all income. The poorest 80 percent—the working classes, including peasants and agricultural laborers—received less altogether than the two richest classes. Moreover, income taxes on the wealthy were light or nonexistent. Thus the gap between rich and poor remained enormous at the beginning of the

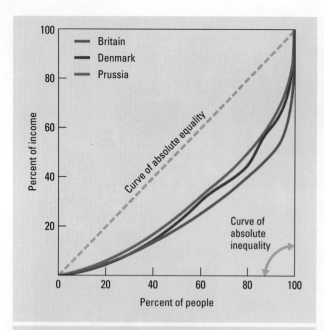

Distribution of Income

	Richest 5%	Richest 10%	Richest 20%	Poorest 60%
Britain	43%		59%	
Denmark	30%	39%	55%	31%
Prussia	30%		50%	33%

FIGURE 24.2 The Distribution of Income in Britain, Denmark, and Prussia in 1913 The so-called Lorenz curve is useful for showing the degree of economic inequality in a given society. The closer the actual distribution of income lies to the (theoretical) curve of absolute equality, where each 20 percent of the population receives 20 percent of all income, the more incomes are nearly equal. European society was very far from any such equality before World War I. Notice that incomes in Prussia were somewhat more equal than those in Britain. *(Source: S. Kuznets,* Modern Economic Growth, *pp. 208–209. Copyright © 1966 by Yale University Press. Reprinted by permission of Yale University Press.)*

twentieth century. It was probably almost as great as it had been in the age of agriculture and aristocracy before the Industrial Revolution.

The great gap between rich and poor endured, in part, because industrial and urban development made society more diverse and less unified. By no means did society split into two sharply defined opposing classes, as Marx had predicted. Instead, economic specialization enabled society to produce more effectively and in the process

created more new social groups than it destroyed. There developed an almost unlimited range of jobs, skills, and earnings; one group or subclass shaded off into another in a complex, confusing hierarchy. Thus the tiny elite of the very rich and the sizable mass of the dreadfully poor were separated from each other by a range of subclasses, each filled with individuals struggling to rise or at least to hold their own in the social order. In this atmosphere of competition and hierarchy, neither the middle classes nor the working classes acted as a unified force. This social and occupational hierarchy developed enormous variations, but the age-old pattern of great economic inequality remained firmly intact.

The Middle Classes

By the beginning of the twentieth century, the diversity and range within the urban middle class were striking. Indeed, it is more meaningful to think of a confederation of middle classes loosely united by occupations requiring mental, rather than physical, skill.

At the top stood the upper middle class, composed mainly of the most successful business families from banking, industry, and large-scale commerce. As people in the upper middle class gained in income and progressively lost all traces of radicalism after the trauma of 1848, they were almost irresistibly drawn toward the aristocratic lifestyle. And although the genuine hereditary aristocracy constituted only a tiny minority in every European country, it retained imposing wealth, unrivaled social prestige, and substantial political influence. This was especially true in central and eastern Europe, where the monarch—the highest-ranking noble of them all—continued to hold great political power.

As the aristocracy had long divided the year between palatial country estates and lavish townhouses during "the season," so the upper middle class purchased country places or built beach houses for weekend and summer use. The number of servants was an important indicator of wealth and standing for the middle class, as it had always been for the aristocracy. Private coaches and carriages, ever-expensive items in the city, were also signs of rising social status.

The topmost reaches of the upper middle class tended to shade off into the old aristocracy to form a new upper class of at most 5 percent of the population. Much of the aristocracy welcomed this development. Having experienced a sharp decline in its relative income in the course of industrialization, the landed aristocracy had met big business coming up the staircase and was often delighted to trade titles, country homes, and snobbish elegance for good hard cash. Some of the best bargains were made through marriages to American heiresses. Correspondingly, wealthy aristocrats tended increasingly to exploit their agricultural and mineral resources as if they were business people. Bismarck was not the only proud nobleman to make a fortune distilling brandy on his estates.

Below the wealthy upper middle class were much larger, much less wealthy, and increasingly diversified middle-class groups. Here one found the moderately successful industrialists and merchants as well as professionals in law and medicine. This was the middle middle class, solid and quite comfortable but lacking great wealth. Below it were independent shopkeepers, small traders, and tiny manufacturers—the lower middle class. Both of these traditional elements of the middle class expanded modestly in size with economic development.

Meanwhile, the traditional middle class was gaining two particularly important additions. The expansion of industry and technology created a growing demand for experts with specialized knowledge. The most valuable of the specialties became solid middle-class professions. Engineering, for example, emerged from the world of skilled labor as a full-fledged profession of great importance, considerable prestige, and many branches. Architects, chemists, accountants, and surveyors, to name only a few, first achieved professional standing in this period. They established criteria for advanced training and certification and banded together in organizations to promote and defend their interests.

Management of large public and private institutions also emerged as a kind of profession as governments provided more services and as very large corporations such as railroads came into being. Government officials and many private executives were not capitalists in the sense that they owned business enterprises. But public and private managers did have specialized knowledge and the capacity to earn a good living. And they shared most of the values of the business-owning entrepreneurs and the older professionals.

Industrialization also expanded and diversified the lower middle class. The number of independent, property-owning shopkeepers and small business people grew, and so did the number of white-collar employees—a mixed group of traveling salesmen, bookkeepers, store managers, and clerks who staffed the offices and branch stores of large corporations. White-collar employees were property-less and often earned no more than the better-paid skilled or semiskilled workers did. Yet white-collar workers were fiercely committed to the middle class and to the ideal of moving up in society. In the Balkans, for example, clerks let their fingernails grow very long to distinguish themselves from people who worked with their hands. The tie, the suit, and soft, clean hands were no-less-subtle marks of class distinction than wages.

Relatively well educated but without complex technical skills, many white-collar groups aimed at achieving professional standing and the accompanying middle-class status. Elementary school teachers largely succeeded in this effort. From being miserably paid part-time workers in the early nineteenth century, teachers rode the wave of mass education to respectable middle-class status and income. Nurses also rose from the lower ranks of unskilled labor to precarious middle-class standing. Dentistry was taken out of the hands of working-class barbers and placed in the hands of highly trained (and middle-class) professionals.

Middle-Class Culture

In spite of growing occupational diversity and conflicting interests, the middle classes were loosely united by a certain style of life and culture. Food was the largest item in the household budget, for middle-class people liked to eat very well. The European middle classes consumed meat in abundance, and a well-off family might spend 10 percent of its substantial earnings on meat and fully 25 percent of its income on food and drink. Spending on food was also great because the dinner party was this class's favored social occasion. A wealthy family might give a lavish party for eight to twelve almost every week, whereas more modest households would settle for once a month.

The middle-class wife could cope with this endless procession of meals, courses, and dishes because she had both servants and money at her disposal. Indeed, the employment of at least one enormously helpful full-time maid to cook and clean was the best single sign that a family had crossed the cultural divide separating the working classes from what some contemporary observers called the "servant-keeping classes." The greater a family's income, the greater the number of servants it employed. Food and servants together absorbed about 50 percent of income at all levels of the middle class.

Well fed and well served, the middle classes were also well housed by 1900. Many quite prosperous families rented, rather than owned, their homes. Apartment living, complete with tiny rooms for servants under the eaves of the top floor, was commonplace, and wealthy investors and speculative builders found good profits in middle-class housing. By 1900 the middle classes were also quite clothes-conscious. The factory, the sewing machine, and the department store had all helped reduce the cost and expand the variety of clothing. Middle-class women were particularly attentive to the fickle dictates of fashion. (See the feature "Images in Society: Class and Gender Boundaries in Women's Fashion, 1850–1914" on pages 792–793.)

Education was another growing expense, as middle-class parents tried to provide their children with ever more crucial advanced education. The keystones of culture and leisure were books, music, and travel. The long realistic novel, the heroics of composers Wagner and Verdi, the diligent striving of the dutiful daughter at the piano, and the packaged tour to a foreign country were all sources of middle-class pleasure.

Finally, the middle classes were loosely united by a shared code of expected behavior and morality. This code was strict and demanding. It laid great stress on hard work, self-discipline, and personal achievement. Men and women who fell into crime or poverty were generally assumed to be responsible for their own circumstances. Traditional Christian morality was reaffirmed by this code and was preached tirelessly by middle-class people. Drunkenness and gambling were denounced as vices; sexual purity and fidelity were celebrated as virtues. In short, the middle-class person was supposed to know right from wrong and was expected to act accordingly.

The Working Classes

About four out of five people belonged to the working classes at the turn of the century. Many members of the working classes—that is, people whose livelihoods depended on physical labor and who did not employ domestic servants—were still small landowning peasants and hired farm hands. This was especially true in eastern Europe. In western and central Europe, however, the typical worker had left the land. In Great Britain, less than 8 percent of the people worked in agriculture, and in rapidly industrializing Germany only 25 percent were employed in agriculture and forestry. Even in less industrialized France, less than 50 percent of the people depended on the land in 1900.

The urban working classes were even less unified and homogeneous than the middle classes. In the first place, economic development and increased specialization expanded the traditional range of working-class skills, earnings, and experiences. Meanwhile, the old sharp distinction between highly skilled artisans and unskilled manual workers gradually broke down. To be sure, highly skilled

"A Corner of the Table" With photographic precision, the French academic artist Paul-Émile Chabas (1869–1937) idealizes the elegance and intimacy of a sumptuous dinner party. Throughout Europe, such dinners were served in eight or nine separate courses, beginning with appetizers and ending with coffee and liqueurs. *(Archives Charmet/The Bridgeman Art Library)*

printers and masons as well as unskilled dockworkers and common laborers continued to exist. But between these extremes there appeared ever more semiskilled groups, many of which were composed of factory workers and machine tenders (see Figure 24.3).

In the second place, skilled, semiskilled, and unskilled workers developed widely divergent lifestyles and cultural values, and their differences contributed to a keen sense of social status and hierarchy within the working classes. The result was great variety and limited class unity.

Highly skilled workers, who made up about 15 percent of the working classes, became a real **labor aristocracy.** These workers earned only about two-thirds of the income of the bottom ranks of the servant-keeping classes, but that was fully twice as much as the earnings of unskilled workers. The most "aristocratic" of the highly skilled workers were construction bosses and factory foremen, men who had risen from the ranks and were fiercely proud of their achievement. The labor aristocracy also included members of the traditional highly skilled handicraft trades that had not been mechanized or placed in factories, like cabinetmakers, jewelers, and printers.

This group as a whole was under constant long-term pressure. Irregularly but inexorably, factory methods were being extended to more crafts, and many skilled artisans were being replaced by lower-paid semiskilled factory workers. Traditional woodcarvers and watchmakers virtually disappeared, for example, as the making of furniture and timepieces now took place in the factory. At the same time, the labor aristocracy was consistently being enlarged by new kinds of skilled workers such as shipbuilders and railway locomotive engineers. Thus the labor elite remained in a state of flux as individuals and whole crafts moved in and out of it.

To maintain this precarious standing, the upper working class adopted distinctive values and strait-laced, almost puritanical behavior. Like the middle classes, the labor aristocracy was strongly committed to the family and to economic improvement. Families in the upper working class saved money regularly, worried about their children's education, and valued good housing. Despite these similarities, skilled workers viewed themselves not as aspirants to the middle class but as the pacesetters and natural leaders of all the working classes. Well aware of the degradation not so far below them, they practiced self-discipline and stern morality.

The upper working class in general frowned on heavy drinking and sexual permissiveness. An organized temperance movement was strong in the countries of northern Europe. As one German labor aristocrat somberly

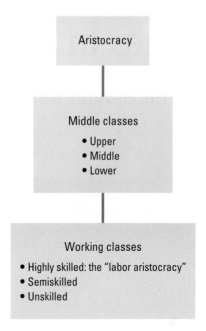

FIGURE 24.3 The Urban Social Hierarchy

warned, "The path to the brothel leads through the tavern" and from there quite possibly to drastic decline or total ruin for person and family.[6] Men and women of the labor aristocracy were also quick to find fault with those below them who failed to meet their standards. Finally, many members of the labor aristocracy had definite political and philosophical beliefs, which further strengthened their firm moral code.

Below the labor aristocracy stood semiskilled and unskilled urban workers. The enormous complexity of this sector of the world of labor is not easily summarized. Workers in the established crafts—carpenters, bricklayers, pipe fitters—stood near the top of the semiskilled hierarchy, often flirting with (or sliding back from) the labor elite. A large number of the semiskilled were factory workers who earned highly variable but relatively good wages and whose relative importance in the labor force was increasing.

Below the semiskilled workers was a larger group of unskilled workers that included day laborers such as longshoremen, wagon-driving teamsters, teenagers, and every kind of "helper." Many of these people had real skills and performed valuable services, but they were unorganized and divided, united only by the common fate of meager earnings. The same lack of unity characterized street vendors and market people—self-employed workers who competed savagely with each other and with the established shopkeepers of the lower middle class.

Images in Society

Class and Gender Boundaries in Women's Fashion, 1850–1914

Women's fashion was big business in the nineteenth century. Long the dominant industrial pursuit in human history, the production of textiles took off with the Industrial Revolution. In the later nineteenth century fashionable clothing, especially for middle-class women, became the first modern consumer industry as careful buyers snapped up the constantly changing ready-to-wear goods sold by large department stores.

In the nineteenth century, before society fragmented into many different groups expressing themselves in many dress styles, clothing patterns focused mainly on perceived differences in class and gender. The four illustrations presented here allow one to analyze the social information communicated through women's clothing. As you study these illustrations, note the principal characteristics and then try to draw out the larger implications. What does the impractical, restrictive clothing in these images reveal about society's view of women during this period? What is the significance of the emergence of alternative styles of well-groomed dress?

Most changes in women's fashion originated in Paris in the nineteenth century. Image 1 shows the attire worn by French aristocratic and wealthy middle-class women in the 1850s and 1860s. Note that these expensive dresses, flawlessly tailored by an army of skilled seamstresses, abound in elaborate embroidery, rich velvety materials, and fancy accessories. The circular spread of these floor-sweeping gowns is due to the crinoline, a slip with metal hoops that holds the skirt out on all sides. These women also are wearing the corset, the century's most characteristic women's undergarment, which was laced up tightly in back and pressed unmercifully from the breasts to the hips. What does this image tell you about the life of these women (their work, leisure activities, and so on)?

The intriguing 1875 painting by Atkinson Grimshaw, *Summer* (Image 2), shows a middle-class interior and the evolution of women's summer fashion two decades

later. The corset still binds, but crinoline hoops have given way to the bustle, a cotton fan with steel reinforcement that pushes the dress out in back and exaggerates gender differences. The elaborate costume of the wealthy elite, available in cheaper ready-to-wear versions sold through department stores and mail-order catalogues throughout Europe, had become the standard for middle-class women. Emulating the elite in style, conventional middle-class women shopped carefully, scouting for sales, and drew a boundary separating themselves from working-class women in their simple cotton clothes. What implications, if any, do you see this having on class distinctions?

The young middle-class Englishwoman in an 1893 photo (Image 3) has chosen a woman's tailored suit, the only major English innovation in nineteenth-

Image 1 Crinoline Dresses, Paris, 1859. *(The Illustrated London News Picture Library)*

Image 2 Summer Dress with Bustle, England, 1875. *(Roy Miles, Esq./The Bridgeman Art Library)*

Image 3 Alternative Fashion, England, 1893. *(Manchester City Art Galleries)*

Image 4 Loose-fitting Dress, France, 1910. *(© Corbis)*

century women's fashion. This "alternative dress" combines the tie, suit jacket, vest, and straw hat—all initially items of male attire—with typical feminine elements, such as the skirt and gloves. This practical, socially accepted alternative dress appealed to the growing number of women in paid employment in the 1890s. The historian Diana Crane has argued that this departure from the dominant style can be seen as a symbolic, nonverbal assertion of independence and equality with men.* Do you agree with this? If so, what was the significance of the pre-1914 turn from stifling corset to the more flexible brassiere and the mainstream embrace of loose-fitting garments, such as the 1910 dress in Image 4? Did the greater freedom of movement in clothing reflect the emerging emancipation of Western women? Or was the coquettish femininity of these loose, flowing dresses only a repackaging of the dominant culture's sharply defined gender boundaries?

*Diana Crane, *Fashion and Its Social Agendas: Class, Gender, and Identity in Clothing* (Chicago: University of Chicago Press, 2000), pp. 99–114.

The Labor Aristocracy This group of British foremen is attending the International Exhibition in Paris in 1862. Their "Sunday best" includes the silk top hats and long morning coats of the propertied classes, but they definitely remain workers, the proud leaders of laboring people. (*© The Board of Trustees of the Victoria & Albert Museum*)

One of the largest components of the unskilled group was domestic servants, whose numbers grew steadily in the nineteenth century. In advanced Great Britain, for example, one out of every seven employed persons was a domestic servant in 1911. The great majority were women; indeed, one out of every three girls in Britain between the ages of fifteen and twenty was a domestic servant. Throughout Europe and America, a great many female domestics in the cities were recent migrants from rural areas. As in earlier times, domestic service was still hard work at low pay with limited personal independence and the danger of sexual exploitation. For the full-time general maid in a lower-middle-class family, there was an unending routine of baby-sitting, shopping, cooking, and cleaning. In the great households, the girl was at the bottom of a rigid hierarchy of status-conscious butlers and housekeepers.

Nonetheless, domestic service had real attractions for "rough country girls" with strong hands and few specialized skills. Marriage prospects were better, or at least more varied, in the city. And though wages were low, they were higher and more regular than in hard agricultural work. Finally, as one London observer noted, young girls and other migrants were drawn to the city by

the contagion of numbers, the sense of something going on, the theaters and the music halls, the brightly lighted streets and busy crowds—all, in short, that makes the difference between the Mile End fair on a Saturday night, and a dark and muddy country lane, with no glimmer of gas and with nothing to do.[7]

Many young domestics from the countryside made a successful transition to working-class wife and mother. Yet with an unskilled or unemployed husband and a growing family, such a woman often had to join the broad ranks of workingwomen in the "sweated industries." These industries flowered after 1850 and resembled the old putting-out and cottage industries of earlier times. The women normally worked at home, paid by the piece and not by the hour. They and their young daughters, for whom organization and collective action were virtually impossible, earned pitiful wages and lacked any job security.

Some women did hand-decorating of every conceivable kind of object; the majority, however, made clothing, especially after the advent of the sewing machine. By 1900 only a few such tailors lingered on in high-priced "tailor-made" shops. An army of poor women accounted for the bulk of the inexpensive "ready-made" clothes displayed on department store racks and in tiny shops.

Working-Class Leisure and Religion

Notwithstanding the rise and fall of groups and individuals, the urban working classes sought fun and recreation, and they found both. Across the face of Europe, drinking remained unquestionably the favorite leisure-time activity of working people. For many middle-class moralists as well as moralizing historians since, love of drink has been a curse of

A School for Servants   Although domestic service was poorly paid, there was always plenty of competition for the available jobs. Schools sprang up to teach young women the manners and the household skills that employers in the "servant-keeping classes" demanded. (*Corporation of London: London Metropolitan Archives*)

Big City Nightlife The most famous dance hall and cabaret in Paris was the Moulin Rouge. There La Goulue ("the Glutton"), who is featured on this poster, performed her provocative version of the cancan and reigned as the queen of Parisian sensuality. This is one of many colorful posters done by Henri de Toulouse-Lautrec (1864–1901), who combined stupendous creativity and dedicated debauchery in his short life. *(Bridgeman-Giraudon/Art Resource, NY)*

the modern age—a sign of social dislocation and popular suffering. Certainly, drinking was deadly serious business. One English slum dweller recalled that "drunkenness was by far the commonest cause of dispute and misery in working class homes. On account of it one saw many a decent family drift down through poverty into total want."[8]

Generally, however, heavy "problem" drinking declined in the late nineteenth century as it became less and less socially acceptable. This decline reflected in part the moral leadership of the upper working class. At the same time, drinking became more public and social. Cafés and pubs became increasingly bright, friendly places. Working-class political activities, both moderate and radical, were also concentrated in taverns and pubs. Moreover, social drink-

ing in public places by married couples and sweethearts became an accepted and widespread practice for the first time. This greater participation by women undoubtedly helped civilize the world of drink and hard liquor.

The two other leisure-time passions of the working classes were sports and music halls. A great decline in "cruel sports," such as bullbaiting and cockfighting, had occurred throughout Europe by the late nineteenth century. Their place was filled by modern spectator sports, of which racing and soccer were the most popular. There was a great deal of gambling on sports events, and for many a working person a desire to decipher racing forms provided a powerful incentive toward literacy. Music halls and vaudeville theaters, the working-class counterparts of middle-class opera and classical theater, were enormously popular throughout Europe. In 1900 there were more than fifty such halls and theaters in London alone. Music hall audiences were thoroughly mixed, which may account for the fact that drunkenness, sexual intercourse and pregnancy before marriage, marital difficulties, and problems with mothers-in-law were favorite themes of broad jokes and bittersweet songs.

In more serious moments, religion and Christian churches continued to provide working people with solace and meaning. The eighteenth-century vitality of popular religion in Catholic countries and the Protestant rejuvenation exemplified by German Pietism and English Methodism (see pages 672–673) carried over into the nineteenth century. Indeed, many historians see the early nineteenth century as an age of religious revival. Yet historians also recognize that by the last two or three decades of the nineteenth century, a considerable decline in both church attendance and church donations was occurring in most European countries. And it seems clear that this decline was greater for the urban working classes than for their rural counterparts or for the middle classes.

What did the decline in working-class church attendance really mean? Some have argued that it accurately reflected a general decline in faith and religious belief. Others disagree, noting correctly that most working-class families still baptized their children and considered themselves Christians. Although more research is necessary, it appears that the urban working classes in Europe did become more secular and less religious in the late nineteenth and early twentieth centuries. They rarely repudiated the Christian religion, but it tended to play a diminishing role in their daily lives.

Part of the reason for this change was that the construction of churches failed to keep up with the rapid growth of urban population, especially in new working-class neighborhoods. Thus the vibrant, materialistic urban environment undermined popular religious impulses, which were poorly served in the cities. Equally important, however, was the fact that throughout the nineteenth century both Catholic and Protestant churches were normally seen as they saw themselves—as conservative institutions defending social order and custom. Therefore, as the European working classes became more politically conscious, they tended to see the established (or quasi-established) "territorial church" as defending what they wished to change and as allied with their political opponents. Especially the men of the urban working classes developed vaguely anti-church attitudes, even though they remained neutral or positive toward religion. They tended to regard regular church attendance as "not our kind of thing"—not part of urban working-class culture.

The pattern was different in the United States. There, most churches also preached social conservatism in the nineteenth century. But because church and state had always been separate and because there was always a host of competing denominations and even different religions, working people identified churches much less with the political and social status quo. Instead, individual churches in the United States were often closely identified with an ethnic group rather than with a social class, and churches thrived, in part, as a means of asserting ethnic identity. This same process did occur in Europe if the church or synagogue had never been linked to the state and served as a focus for ethnic cohesion. Irish Catholic churches in Protestant Britain and Jewish synagogues in Russia were outstanding examples.

The Changing Family

Urban life wrought many fundamental changes in the family. Although much is still unknown, it seems clear that in the second half of the nineteenth century the family had stabilized considerably after the disruption of the late eighteenth and early nineteenth centuries. The home became more important for both men and women. The role of women and attitudes toward children underwent substantial change, and adolescence emerged as a distinct stage of life. These are but a few of the transformations that affected all social classes in varying degrees.

- *How did families change as they coped with the challenges and the opportunities of the developing urban civilization?*

Premarital Sex and Marriage

By 1850 the preindustrial pattern of lengthy courtship and mercenary marriage was pretty well dead among the working classes. In its place, the ideal of romantic love had triumphed. Couples were ever more likely to come from different, even distant, towns and to be more nearly the same age, further indicating that romantic sentiment was replacing tradition and financial considerations.

Economic considerations in marriage remained more important to the middle classes than to the working classes after 1850. In France dowries and elaborate legal marriage contracts were common practice among the middle classes in the later nineteenth century, and marriage was for many families one of life's most crucial financial transactions. A popular author advised young Frenchmen that "marriage is in general a means of increasing one's credit and one's fortune and of insuring one's success in the world."[9] This preoccupation with money led many middle-class men in

France and elsewhere to marry late, after they had been established economically, and to choose women considerably younger than themselves. These differences between husband and wife became a source of tension in many middle-class marriages.

A young woman of the middle class found her romantic life carefully supervised by her well-meaning mother, who schemed for a proper marriage and guarded her daughter's virginity like the family's credit. (See the feature "Listening to the Past: Middle-Class Youth and Sexuality" on pages 812–813.) After marriage, middle-class morality sternly demanded fidelity.

Middle-class boys were watched, too, but not as vigilantly. By the time they reached late adolescence, they had usually attained considerable sexual experience with maids or prostitutes.

In the early nineteenth century, sexual experimentation before marriage also triumphed, as did illegitimacy. There was an **illegitimacy explosion** between 1750 and 1850 (see page 656). By the 1840s, one birth in three was occurring outside of wedlock in many large cities of western, northern, and central Europe. In Vienna and Stockholm, one out of every two births was illegitimate. Although poverty and economic uncertainty undoubtedly prevented many lovers from marrying, there were also many among the poor and propertyless who saw little wrong with having illegitimate offspring. Thus the pattern of romantic ideals, premarital sexual activity, and widespread illegitimacy was firmly established by mid-century among the urban working classes.

Some regions, especially those little touched by industrialization and urbanization, did not experience an illegitimacy explosion. Neither did certain churches and religious communities that strictly prohibited premarital sex. "The Catholic Church in Ireland and many southern European regions, Calvinist communities in the Netherlands, Moslems in the Balkans, and Jewish communities throughout Europe seem to have been successful in enforcing this norm."[10] Although these religious groups exercised strict external control, they succeeded in large part because their young people internalized the values they were taught and acted accordingly.

In western, northern, and central Europe, the rising rate of illegitimacy was reversed in the second half of the nineteenth century: more babies were born to married mothers. Some observers have argued that this shift reflected the growth of puritanism and a lessening of sexual permissiveness among the unmarried. This explanation, however, is unconvincing.

The percentage of brides who were pregnant continued to be high and showed little or no tendency to decline after 1850. In many parts of urban Europe around 1900, as many as one woman in three was going to the altar an expectant mother. Moreover, unmarried people almost certainly used the cheap condoms and diaphragms the industrial age had made available to prevent pregnancy, at least in predominately Protestant countries.

Thus unmarried young people were probably engaging in just as much sexual activity as their parents and grandparents who had created the illegitimacy explosion of 1750 to 1850. But in the later nineteenth century, pregnancy for a young single woman led increasingly to marriage and the establishment of a two-parent household. This important development reflected the growing respectability of the working classes as well as their gradual economic improvement. Skipping out was less acceptable, and marriage was less of an economic challenge. Thus the urban working-class couple became more stable, and that stability strengthened the family as an institution.

Prostitution

In Paris alone, 155,000 women were registered as prostitutes between 1871 and 1903, and 750,000 others were suspected of prostitution in the same years. Men of all classes visited prostitutes, but the middle and upper classes supplied much of the motivating cash. Thus, though many middle-class men abided by the publicly professed code of stern puritanical morality, others indulged their appetites for prostitutes and sexual promiscuity.

My Secret Life, the anonymous eleven-volume autobiography of an English sexual adventurer from the servant-keeping classes, provides a remarkable picture of such a man. Beginning at an early age with a maid, the author becomes progressively obsessed with sex and devotes his life to living his sexual fantasies. In almost every one of his innumerable encounters all across Europe, this man of wealth simply buys his pleasure. Usually meetings are arranged in a businesslike manner: regular and part-time prostitutes quote their prices; working-class girls are corrupted by hot meals and baths.

At one point, he offers a young girl a sixpence for a kiss and gets it. Learning that the pretty, unskilled working girl earns nine pence a day, he offers her the equivalent of a week's salary for a few moments of fondling. When she finally agrees, he savagely exults that "*her* want was my opportunity." Later he offers more money for more gratification, and when she refuses, he tries unsuccessfully to rape her in a hackney cab. On another occasion he takes a farm worker by force.[11]

Obviously atypical in its excesses, *My Secret Life* does reveal the dark side of sex and class in urban society. Frequently thinking of their wives largely in terms of money, family, and social position, the men of the comfortable classes often purchased sex and even affection from poor girls both before and after marriage. Moreover, the great continuing differences between rich and poor made for every kind of debauchery and sexual exploitation. Brutal sexist behavior was part of life—a part the sternly moral women (and men) of the upper working class detested and tried to shield their daughters from. For many poor young women, prostitution, like domestic service, was a stage of life and not a permanent employment. Having done it for a while in their twenties, they went on to marry (or live with) men of their own class and establish homes and families.

Kinship Ties

Within working-class homes, ties to relatives after marriage—kinship ties—were in general much stronger than many social observers have recognized. Most newlyweds tried to live near their parents, though not in the same house. Indeed, for many married couples in later-nineteenth-century cities, ties to mothers and fathers, uncles and aunts, were more important than ties to unrelated acquaintances.

People turned to their families for help in coping with sickness, unemployment, death, and old age. Although governments were generally providing more welfare services by 1900, the average couple and its children inevitably faced crises. Funerals, for example, brought sudden demands, requiring a large outlay for special clothes, carriages, and burial services. Unexpected death or desertion could leave the bereaved or abandoned, especially widows and orphans, in need of financial aid or perhaps a foster home. Relatives responded hastily to such cries, knowing full well that their own time of need and repayment would undoubtedly come.

Relatives were also valuable at less tragic moments. If a couple was very poor, an aged relation often moved in to cook and mind the children so that the wife could earn badly needed income outside the home. Sunday dinners were often shared, as were outgrown clothing and useful information. Often the members of a large family group all lived in the same neighborhood.

Gender Roles and Family Life

Industrialization and the growth of modern cities brought great changes to the lives of European women. These changes were particularly consequential for married women, and most women did marry in the nineteenth century.

After 1850 the work of most wives became increasingly distinct and separate from that of their husbands. Husbands became wage earners in factories and offices, while wives tended to stay home and manage households and care for children. The preindustrial pattern among both peasants and cottage workers, in which husbands and wives worked together and divided up household duties and child rearing, declined. Only in a few occupations, such as retail trade, did married couples live where they worked and struggle together to make their mom-and-pop operations a success. Factory employment for married women also declined as the early practice of hiring entire families in the factory disappeared.

As economic conditions improved, most men expected married women to work outside the home only in poor families. One old English worker recalled that "the boy wanted to get into a position that would enable him to keep a wife and family, as it was considered a thoroughly unsatisfactory state of affairs if the wife had to work to help maintain the home."[12] The ideal became a strict division of labor by gender and rigidly constructed **separate spheres:** the wife as mother and homemaker, the husband as wage earner.

This rigid gender division of labor meant that married women faced great injustice when they needed—or wanted—to move into the man's world of employment outside the home. Husbands were unsympathetic or hostile. Well-paying jobs were off-limits to women, and a woman's wage was almost always less than a man's, even for the same work.

Moreover, married women were subordinated to their husbands by law and lacked many basic legal rights. In England the situation in the early nineteenth century was summed up in a famous line from jurist William Blackstone: "In law husband and wife are one person, and the husband is that person." Thus a wife in England had no legal identity and hence no right to own property in her own name. Even the wages she might earn belonged to her husband. In France the Napoleonic Code (see pages 704–705) also enshrined the principle of female subordination and gave the wife few legal rights regarding property, divorce, and custody of the children. Legal inferiority for women permeated Western society.

With all women facing discrimination in education and employment and with middle-class women suffering especially from a lack of legal rights, there is little wonder that some women rebelled and began the long-continuing fight for equality of the sexes and the rights of women. Their struggle proceeded on two main fronts. First, following in the steps of women such as Mary Wollstonecraft (see page 694), organizations founded by middle-class feminists campaigned for equal legal rights for women as well as access to higher education and professional employment. These middle-class feminists argued that unmarried women and middle-class widows with inadequate incomes simply had to have more opportunities to support themselves. Middle-class feminists also recognized that paid (as opposed to unpaid) work could relieve the monotony that some women found in their sheltered middle-class existence and put greater meaning into their lives.

In the later nineteenth century, these organizations scored some significant victories, such as the 1882 law giving English married women full property rights. More women found professional and white-collar employment, especially after about 1880. But progress was slow and hard won. For example, in Germany before 1900, women were not admitted as fully registered students at a single university, and it was virtually impossible for a woman to receive certification and practice as a lawyer or doctor. (See the feature "Individuals in Society: Franziska Tiburtius.") In the years before 1914, middle-class feminists increasingly focused their attention on political action and fought for the right to vote for women.

Women inspired by utopian and especially Marxian socialism blazed a second path. Often scorning the programs of middle-class feminists, socialist women leaders argued that the liberation of working-class women would come only with the liberation of the entire working class through revolution. In the meantime, they championed the cause of workingwomen and won some practical improvements, especially in Germany, where the socialist movement was most effectively organized. In a general way, these different approaches to women's issues reflected the diversity of classes in urban society.

◈ *Online Study Center* **Improve Your Grade**
Primary Source: A Socialist Solution to the Question of Women's Rights

If the ideology and practice of rigidly separate spheres undoubtedly narrowed women's horizons and caused some women to rebel, there was a brighter side to the same coin. As home and children became the typical wife's main concerns in the late nineteenth century, her control and influence there apparently became increasingly strong throughout Europe. Among the English working classes, it was the wife who generally determined how the family's money was spent. In many families, the husband gave all his earnings to his wife to manage, whatever the law might read. She returned to him only a small allowance for carfare, beer, tobacco, and union dues. All the major domestic decisions, from the children's schooling and religious instruction to the selection of new furniture or a new apartment, were hers. In France women had even greater power in their assigned domain. One English feminist noted in 1908 that "though legally women occupy a much inferior status than men [in France], in practice they constitute the superior sex. They are the power behind the throne."[13]

Women ruled at home partly because running the urban household was a complicated, demanding, and valuable task. Twice-a-day food shopping, penny-pinching, economizing, and the growing crusade against dirt—not to mention child rearing—were a full-time occupation. Nor were there any laborsaving appliances to help, and even when servants were present, they had to be carefully watched and supervised. Working yet another job for wages outside the home had limited appeal for most married women unless such earnings were essential for family survival. Many married women in the working classes did make a monetary contribution to family income by taking in boarders or doing piecework at home in the sweated industries (see page 794).

The wife also guided the home because a good deal of her effort was directed toward pampering her husband as he expected. In countless humble households, she saw that he had meat while she ate bread, that he relaxed by the fire while she did the dishes.

The woman's guidance of the household went hand in hand with the increased emotional importance of home and family. The home she ran was idealized as a warm shelter in a hard and impersonal urban world. For a child of the English slums in the early 1900s,

home, however poor, was the focus of all love and interests, a sure fortress against a hostile world. Songs about its beauties were ever on people's lips. "Home, sweet home," first heard in the 1870s, had become "almost a second national anthem." Few walls in lower-working-class houses lacked "mottoes"—colored strips of paper, about nine inches wide and eighteen inches in length, attesting to domestic joys: EAST, WEST, HOME'S BEST; BLESS OUR HOME; GOD IS MASTER OF THIS HOUSE; HOME IS THE NEST WHERE ALL IS BEST.[14]

By 1900 home and family were what life was all about for millions of people of all classes.

Married couples also developed stronger emotional ties to each other. Even in the comfortable classes, marriages in the late nineteenth century were based more on sentiment and sexual attraction than they had been earlier in the century, as money and financial calculation declined in importance. Affection and eroticism became more central to the couple after marriage. Gustave Droz, whose bestseller *Mr., Mrs., and Baby* went through 121

Individuals in Society

Franziska Tiburtius

Why did a small number of women in the late nineteenth century brave great odds and embark on professional careers? And how did a few of those manage to reach their objectives? The career and personal reflections of Franziska Tiburtius, a pioneer in German medicine, suggest that talent, determination, and economic necessity were critical ingredients.*

Like many women of her time who would study and pursue professional careers, Franziska Tiburtius (1843–1927) was born into a property-owning family of modest means. The youngest of nine children on a small estate in northeastern Germany, the sensitive child wilted under a harsh governess but flowered with a caring teacher and became an excellent student.

Graduating at sixteen and needing to support herself, Tiburtius had few opportunities. A young woman from a "proper" background could work as a governess or a teacher without losing her respectability and spoiling her matrimonial prospects, but that was about it. She tried both avenues. Working for six years as a governess in a noble family and no doubt learning that poverty was often one's fate in this genteel profession, she then turned to teaching. Called home from her studies in Britain in 1871 to care for her brother, who had contracted typhus as a field doctor in the Franco-Prussian War, she found her calling. She decided to become a medical doctor.

Supported by her family, Tiburtius's decision was truly audacious. In all Europe, only the University of Zurich in republican Switzerland accepted female students. Moreover, if it became known that she had studied medicine and failed, she would never get a job as a teacher. No parent would entrust a daughter to an "emancipated" radical who had carved up dead bodies!

Although the male students at the university sometimes harassed the women with crude pranks, Tiburtius thrived. The revolution of the microscope and the discovery of microorganisms was rocking Zurich, and she was fascinated by her studies. She became close friends with a fellow female medical student from Germany, Emilie Lehmus, with whom she would form a lifelong partnership in medicine. She did her internship with families of cottage workers around Zurich and loved her work.

Graduating at age thirty-three in 1876, Tiburtius went to stay with her brother the doctor in Berlin. Though well qualified to practice, she ran into pervasive discrimination. She was not even permitted to take the state medical exams and could practice only as an unregulated (and unprofessional) "natural healer." But after persistent fighting with the bureaucrats, she was able to display her diploma and practice as "Franziska Tiburtius, M.D. University of Zurich." She and Lehmus were in business.

Franziska Tiburtius, pioneering woman physician in Berlin. (Ullstein Bilderdienst/The Granger Collection, New York)

Soon the two women realized their dream and opened a clinic, subsidized by a wealthy industrialist, for women factory workers. The clinic filled a great need and was soon treating many patients. A room with beds for extremely sick women was later expanded into a second clinic.

Tiburtius and Lehmus became famous. For fifteen years, they were the only women doctors in all Berlin. An inspiration for a new generation of women, they added the wealthy to their thriving practice. But Tiburtius's clinics always concentrated on the poor, providing them with subsidized and up-to-date treatment. Talented, determined, and working with her partner, Tiburtius experienced the joys of personal achievement and useful service, joys that women and men share in equal measure.

Questions for Analysis

1. How does Franziska Tiburtius's life reflect both the challenges and the changing roles of middle-class women in the later nineteenth century?
2. In what ways was Tiburtius's career related to improvements in health in urban society and to the expansion of the professions?

*This portrait draws on Conradine Lück, *Frauen: Neun Lebensschicksale* (Reutlingen: Ensslin & Laiblin, n.d.), pp. 153–185.

Online Study Center   Improve Your Grade
Going Beyond Individuals in Society

editions between 1866 and 1884, saw love within marriage as the key to human happiness. He condemned men who made marriage sound dull and practical, men who were exhausted by prostitutes and rheumatism and who wanted their young wives to be little angels. He urged women to follow their hearts and marry men more nearly their own age:

A husband who is stately and a little bald is all right, but a young husband who loves you and who drinks out of your glass without ceremony, is better. Let him, if he ruffles your dress a little and places a kiss on your neck as he passes. Let him, if he undresses you after the ball, laughing like a fool. You have fine spiritual qualities, it is true, but your little body is not bad either and when one loves, one loves completely. Behind these follies lies happiness.[15]

Many French marriage manuals of the late 1800s stressed that women had legitimate sexual needs, such as the "right to orgasm." Perhaps the French were a bit more enlightened in these matters than other nationalities. But the rise of public socializing by couples in cafés and music halls as well as franker affection within the family suggests a more erotic, pleasurable intimate life for women throughout Western society. This, too, helped make the woman's role as mother and homemaker acceptable and even satisfying.

Child Rearing

One striking sign of deepening emotional ties within the family was the growing love and concern that mothers gave their tiny infants. Because so many babies died so early in life, mothers in preindustrial Western society often avoided making a strong emotional commitment to a newborn in order to shield themselves from recurrent heartbreak. Early emotional bonding and a willingness to make real sacrifices for the welfare of the infant were beginning to spread among the comfortable classes by the end of the eighteenth century, but the ordinary mother of modest means adopted new attitudes only as the nineteenth century progressed. The baby became more important, and women became better mothers.

Mothers increasingly breast-fed their infants, for example, rather than paying wet nurses to do so. Breast-feeding involved sacrifice—a temporary loss of freedom, if nothing else. Yet in an age when there was no good alternative to mother's milk, it saved lives. This surge of maternal feeling also gave rise to a wave of specialized books on child rearing and infant hygiene, such as Droz's phenomenally successful book. Droz urged fathers to get into the act and pitied those "who do not know how to

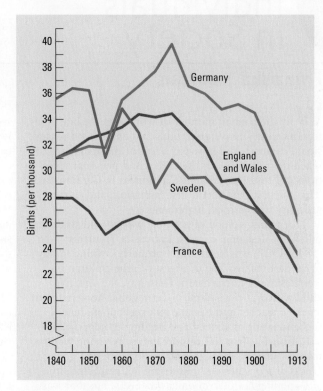

FIGURE 24.4 The Decline of Birthrates in England and Wales, France, Germany, and Sweden, 1840–1913
Women had fewer babies for a variety of reasons, including the fact that their children were increasingly less likely to die before reaching adulthood. Compare with Figure 24.1 on page 783.

roll around on the carpet, play at being a horse and a great wolf, and undress their baby."[16] Another sign, from France, of increased affection is that fewer illegitimate babies were abandoned as foundlings after about 1850. Moreover, the practice of swaddling disappeared completely. Instead, ordinary mothers allowed their babies freedom of movement and delighted in their spontaneity.

The loving care lavished on infants was matched by greater concern for older children and adolescents. They, too, were wrapped in the strong emotional ties of a more intimate and protective family. For one thing, European women began to limit the number of children they bore in order to care adequately for those they had. It was evident by the end of the nineteenth century that the birthrate was declining across Europe, as Figure 24.4 shows, and it continued to do so until after World War II. The Englishwoman who married in the 1860s, for example, had an average of about six children; her daughter marrying in the 1890s had only four; and her granddaughter marrying in the 1920s had only two or possibly three.

A Working-Class Home, 1875 Emotional ties within ordinary families grew stronger in the nineteenth century. Parents gave their children more love and better care. *(Illustrated London News Library)*

The most important reason for this revolutionary reduction in family size, in which the comfortable and well-educated classes took the lead, was parents' desire to improve their economic and social position and that of their children. Children were no longer an economic asset in the later nineteenth century. By having fewer youngsters, parents could give those they had valuable advantages, from music lessons and summer vacations to long, expensive university educations and suitable dowries. A young German skilled worker with only one child spoke for many in his class when he said, "We want to get ahead, and our daughter should have things better than my wife and sisters did."[17] Thus the growing tendency of couples in the late nineteenth century to use a variety of contraceptive methods—rhythm method, withdrawal method, and mechanical devices—certainly reflected increased concern for children.

Indeed, many parents, especially in the middle classes, probably became *too* concerned about their children, unwittingly subjecting them to an emotional pressure cooker of almost unbearable intensity. The result was that many children and especially adolescents came to feel trapped and in need of greater independence.

Prevailing biological and medical theories led parents to believe in the possibility that their own emotional characteristics were passed on to their offspring and that they were thus directly responsible for any abnormality in a child. The moment the child was conceived was thought to be of enormous importance. "Never run the risk of conception when you are sick or over-tired or unhappy," wrote one influential American woman. "For the bodily condition of the child, its vigor and magnetic qualities, are much affected by conditions ruling this great moment."[18] So might the youthful "sexual excess" of the father curse future generations. Although this was true in the case of syphilis, which could be transmitted to unborn children, the rigid determinism of such views left little scope for the child's individual development.

Another area of excessive parental concern was the sexual behavior of the child. Masturbation was viewed with horror, for it represented an act of independence and even defiance. Diet, clothing, games, and sleeping were carefully regulated. Girls were discouraged from riding horses and bicycling because rhythmic friction simulated masturbation. Boys were dressed in trousers with shallow and widely separated pockets. Between 1850 and 1880, there were surgical operations for children who persisted in masturbating. Thereafter until about 1905, various restraining apparatuses were more often used.

These and less blatant attempts to repress the child's sexuality were a source of unhealthy tension, often made worse by the rigid division of gender roles within the family. It was widely believed that mother and child loved each other easily but that relations between father and child were necessarily difficult and often tragic. The father was a stranger; his world of business was far removed from the maternal world of spontaneous affection. Moreover, the father was demanding, often expecting the child to succeed where he himself had failed and making his love conditional on achievement. Little wonder that the imaginative literature of the late nineteenth century came to deal with the emotional and destructive elements of father-son relationships. In the Russian Feodor Dostoevski's great novel *The Brothers Karamazov* (1880–1881), for example, four sons work knowingly or unknowingly to destroy their father. Later at the murder trial, one of the brothers claims to speak for all mankind and screams out, "Who doesn't wish his father dead?"

Sigmund Freud (1856–1939), the Viennese founder of psychoanalysis, formulated the most striking analysis of the explosive dynamics of the family, particularly the middle-class family in the late nineteenth century. A physician by training, Freud began his career treating mentally ill patients. He noted that the hysteria of his patients appeared to originate in bitter early-childhood experiences wherein the child had been obliged to repress strong feelings. When these painful experiences were recalled and reproduced under hypnosis or through the patient's free association of ideas, the patient could be brought to understand his or her unhappiness and eventually deal with it.

One of Freud's most influential ideas concerned the Oedipal tensions resulting from the son's instinctive competition with the father for the mother's love and affection. More generally, Freud postulated that much of human behavior is motivated by unconscious emotional needs whose nature and origins are kept from conscious awareness by various mental devices he called **defense mechanisms.** Freud concluded that much unconscious psychological energy is sexual energy, which is repressed and precariously controlled by rational thinking and moral rules. If Freud exaggerated the sexual and familial

roots of adult behavior, that exaggeration was itself a reflection of the tremendous emotional intensity of family life in the late nineteenth century.

The working classes probably had more avenues of escape from such tensions than did the middle classes. Unlike their middle-class counterparts, who remained economically dependent on their families until a long education was finished or a proper marriage secured, working-class boys and girls went to work when they reached adolescence. Earning wages on their own, they could bargain with their parents for greater independence within the household by the time they were sixteen or seventeen. If they were unsuccessful, they could and did leave home to live cheaply as paying lodgers in other working-class homes. Thus the young person from the working classes broke away from the family more easily when emotional ties became oppressive. In the twentieth century, middle-class youths would follow this lead.

Science and Thought

Major changes in Western science and thought accompanied the emergence of urban society. Two aspects of these complex intellectual developments stand out as especially significant. First, scientific knowledge expanded rapidly, influencing the Western worldview even more profoundly than ever before and spurring the creation of new products and whole industries. Second, between about the 1840s and the 1890s, European literature underwent a shift from soaring romanticism to tough-minded realism.

• *What major changes in science and thought reflected and influenced the new urban society?*

The Triumph of Science

As the pace of scientific advance quickened and as theoretical advances resulted in great practical benefits, science exercised growing influence on human thought. The intellectual achievements of the scientific revolution had resulted in few such benefits, and theoretical knowledge had also played a relatively small role in the Industrial Revolution in England. But breakthroughs in industrial technology enormously stimulated basic scientific inquiry, as researchers sought to explain theoretically how such things as steam engines and blast furnaces actually worked. The result was an explosive growth of fundamental scientific discoveries from the 1830s onward. And in contrast to earlier periods, these theoretical discoveries were increasingly transformed into material improvements for the general population.

A perfect example of the translation of better scientific knowledge into practical human benefits was the work of Louis Pasteur and his followers in biology and the medical sciences. Another was the development of the branch of physics known as **thermodynamics.** Building on Isaac Newton's laws of mechanics and on studies of steam engines, thermodynamics investigated the relationship between heat and mechanical energy. By midcentury, physicists had formulated the fundamental laws of thermodynamics, which were then applied to mechanical engineering, chemical processes, and many other fields. The *law of conservation of energy* held that different forms of energy—such as heat, electricity, and magnetism—could be converted but neither created nor destroyed. Nineteenth-century thermodynamics demonstrated that the physical world was governed by firm, unchanging laws.

Chemistry and electricity were two other fields characterized by extremely rapid scientific progress. And in both fields, "science was put in the service of industry," as the influential economist Alfred Marshall (1842–1924) argued at the time.

Chemists devised ways of measuring the atomic weight of different elements, and in 1869 the Russian chemist Dmitri Mendeleev (1834–1907) codified the rules of chemistry in the periodic law and the periodic table. Chemistry was subdivided into many specialized branches, such as **organic chemistry**—the study of the compounds of carbon. Applying theoretical insights gleaned from this new field, researchers in large German chemical companies discovered ways of transforming the dirty, useless coal tar that accumulated in coke ovens into beautiful, expensive synthetic dyes for the world of fashion. The basic discoveries of Michael Faraday (1791–1867) in electromagnetism in the 1830s and 1840s resulted in the first dynamo (generator) and opened the way for the subsequent development of the telegraph, electric motor, electric light, and electric streetcar.

The successful application of scientific research in the fast-growing electrical and organic chemical industries promoted solid economic growth between 1880 and 1913 and provided a model for other industries. Systematic "R & D"—research and development—was born in the late nineteenth century.

The triumph of science and technology had at least three more significant consequences. First, though ordinary citizens continued to lack detailed scientific knowledge, everyday experience and innumerable popularizers impressed the importance of science on the popular mind.

Second, as science became more prominent in popular thinking, the philosophical implications of science formulated in the Enlightenment spread to broad sections of the population. Natural processes appeared to be determined by rigid laws, leaving little room for either divine intervention or human will. Yet scientific and technical advances had also fed the Enlightenment's optimistic faith in human progress, which now appeared endless and automatic to many middle-class minds.

Third, the methods of science acquired unrivaled prestige after 1850. For many, the union of careful experiment and abstract theory was the only reliable route to truth and objective reality. The "unscientific" intuitions of poets and the revelations of saints seemed hopelessly inferior.

Social Science and Evolution

From the 1830s onward, many thinkers tried to apply the objective methods of science to the study of society. In some ways, these efforts simply perpetuated the critical thinking of the philosophes. Yet there were important differences. The new "social scientists" had access to the massive sets of numerical data that governments had begun to collect on everything from children to crime, from population to prostitution. In response, social scientists developed new statistical methods to analyze these facts "scientifically" and supposedly to test their theories. And the systems of the leading nineteenth-century social scientists were more unified, all-encompassing, and dogmatic than those of the philosophes. Marx was a prime example (see pages 757–758).

Another extremely influential system builder was French philosopher Auguste Comte (1798–1857). Initially a disciple of the utopian socialist Saint-Simon (see page 756), Comte wrote the six-volume *System of Positive Philosophy* (1830–1842), which was largely overlooked during the romantic era. But when the political failures of 1848 completed the swing to realism, Comte's philosophy came into its own. Its influence has remained great to this day.

Comte postulated that all intellectual activity progresses through predictable stages:

The great fundamental law . . . is this:—that each of our leading conceptions—each branch of our knowledge—passes successively through three different theoretical conditions: the Theological, or fictitious; the Metaphysical, or abstract; and the Scientific, or positive. . . . The first is the necessary point of departure of human understanding, and the third is the fixed and definitive state. The second is merely a transition.[19]

By way of example, Comte noted that the prevailing explanation of cosmic patterns had shifted, as knowledge of astronomy developed, from the will of God (the

DARWIN! — PAR GILL

Satirizing Darwin's Ideas   The heated controversies over Darwin's theory of evolution also spawned innumerable jokes and cartoons. This cartoon depicts a bearded Charles Darwin and the atheistic materialist Emile Littré performing as monkeys in a circus. *(Musée de la Ville de Paris, Musée Carnavalet/Archives Charmet/The Bridgeman Art Library)*

theological) to the will of an orderly nature (the metaphysical) to the rule of unchanging laws (the scientific). Later, this same intellectual progression took place in increasingly complex fields—physics, chemistry, and, finally, the study of society. Comte believed that by applying the scientific method, also called the **positivist method,** his new discipline of sociology would soon discover the eternal laws of human relations. This colossal achievement would in turn enable expert social scientists to impose a disciplined harmony and well-being on less

enlightened citizens. Dismissing the "fictions" of traditional religions, Comte became the chief priest of the religion of science and rule by experts.

Comte's stages of knowledge exemplify the nineteenth-century fascination with the idea of **evolution** and dynamic development. Thinkers in many fields, such as the romantic historians and "scientific" Marxists, shared and applied this basic concept. In geology, Charles Lyell (1797–1875) effectively discredited the long-standing view that the earth's surface had been formed by short-lived cataclysms, such as biblical floods and earthquakes. Instead, according to Lyell's principle of uniformitarianism, the same geological processes that are at work today slowly formed the earth's surface over an immensely long time. The evolutionary view of biological development, first proposed by the Greek Anaximander in the sixth century B.C., reemerged in a more modern form in the work of Jean Baptiste Lamarck (1744–1829). Lamarck asserted that all forms of life had arisen through a long process of continuous adjustment to the environment.

Lamarck's work was flawed—he believed that the characteristics parents acquired in the course of their lives could be inherited by their children—and was not accepted, but it helped prepare the way for Charles Darwin (1809–1882), the most influential of all nineteenth-century evolutionary thinkers. As the official naturalist on a five-year scientific cruise to Latin America and the South Pacific beginning in 1831, Darwin carefully collected specimens of the different animal species he encountered on the voyage. Back in England, convinced by fossil evidence and by his friend Lyell that the earth and life on it were immensely ancient, Darwin came to doubt the general belief in a special divine creation of each species of animal. Instead, he concluded, all life had gradually evolved from a common ancestral origin in an unending "struggle for survival." After long hesitation, Darwin published his research, which immediately attracted wide attention.

Darwin's great originality lay in suggesting precisely *how* biological evolution might have occurred. His theory is summarized in the title of his work *On the Origin of Species by the Means of Natural Selection* (1859). Decisively influenced by Thomas Malthus's gloomy theory that populations naturally grow faster than their food supplies (see page 726), Darwin argued that chance differences among the members of a given species help some survive while others die. Thus the variations that prove useful in the struggle for survival are selected naturally and gradually spread to the entire species through reproduction. Darwin did not explain why such variations occurred in the first place, and not until the early twentieth century did the study of genetics and the concept of mutation provide some answers.

Online Study Center **Improve Your Grade**
Primary Source: The Theory of Natural Selection and the Evolution of Species

As the capstone of already-widespread evolutionary thinking, Darwin's theory had a powerful and many-sided influence on European thought and the European middle classes. Darwin was hailed as the great scientist par

excellence, the "Newton of biology," who had revealed once again the powers of objective science. Darwin's findings also reinforced the teachings of secularists such as Comte and Marx, who scornfully dismissed religious belief in favor of agnostic or atheistic materialism. In the great cities especially, religion was on the defensive. Finally, many writers applied the theory of biological evolution to human affairs. Herbert Spencer (1820–1903), an English disciple of Auguste Comte, saw the human race as driven forward to ever-greater specialization and progress by the brutal economic struggle. According to Spencer, this unending struggle efficiently determined the "survival of the fittest." The poor were the ill-fated weak; the prosperous were the chosen strong. Understandably, Spencer and other **Social Darwinists** were especially popular with the upper middle class.

Online Study Center **Improve Your Grade**
Primary Source: Survival of the Fittest Applied to Human Kind

Realism in Literature

In literature, the key themes of **realism** emerged in the 1840s and continued to dominate Western culture and style until the 1890s. Realist writers believed that literature should depict life exactly as it was. Forsaking poetry for prose and the personal, emotional viewpoint of the romantics for strict, scientific objectivity, the realists simply observed and recorded—content to let the facts speak for themselves.

The major realist writers focused their extraordinary powers of observation on contemporary everyday life. Emphatically rejecting the romantic search for the exotic and the sublime, they energetically pursued the typical and the commonplace. Beginning with a dissection of the middle classes, from which most of them sprang, many realists eventually focused on the working classes, especially the urban working classes, which had been neglected in imaginative literature before this time. The realists put a microscope to many unexplored and taboo subjects—sex, strikes, violence, alcoholism—and hastened to report that slums and factories teemed with savage behavior. Many shocked middle-class critics denounced realism as ugly sensationalism wrapped provocatively in pseudoscientific declarations and crude language.

The realists' claims of objectivity did not prevent the elaboration of a definite worldview. Unlike the romantics, who had gloried in individual freedom and an unlimited universe, realists were strict determinists. Human beings,

Manet: Emile Zola   The young novelist's sensitivity and strength of character permeate this famous portrait by the great French painter Edouard Manet. Focusing on nuances and subtle variations, Manet was at first denounced by the critics, and after Zola lost a newspaper job defending Manet they became close friends. Manet was strongly influenced by Japanese prints, seen in the background. *(Erich Lessing/Art Resource, NY)*

like atoms, were components of the physical world, and all human actions were caused by unalterable natural laws. Heredity and environment determined human behavior; good and evil were merely social conventions.

The realist movement began in France, where romanticism had never been completely dominant, and three of its greatest practitioners—Balzac, Flaubert, and Zola—were French. Honoré de Balzac (1799–1850) spent thirty years writing a vastly ambitious panorama of postrevolutionary French life. Known collectively as *The Human Comedy,* this series of nearly one hundred books vividly portrays more than two thousand characters from virtually all sectors of French society. Balzac pictures urban society as grasping, amoral, and brutal, characterized by a Darwinian struggle for wealth and power. In *Le*

Père Goriot (1835), the hero, a poor student from the provinces, eventually surrenders his idealistic integrity to feverish ambition and society's pervasive greed.

Madame Bovary (1857), the masterpiece of Gustave Flaubert (1821–1880), is far narrower in scope than Balzac's work but unparalleled in its depth and accuracy of psychological insight. Unsuccessfully prosecuted as an outrage against public morality and religion, Flaubert's carefully crafted novel tells the ordinary, even banal, story of a frustrated middle-class housewife who has an adulterous love affair and is betrayed by her lover. Without moralizing, Flaubert portrays the provincial middle class as petty, smug, and hypocritical.

Emile Zola (1840–1902) was most famous for his seamy, animalistic view of working-class life. But he also wrote gripping, carefully researched stories featuring the stock exchange, the big department store, and the army, as well as urban slums and bloody coal strikes. Like many later realists, Zola sympathized with socialism, a sympathy evident in his overpowering novel *Germinal* (1885).

Realism quickly spread beyond France. In England, Mary Ann Evans (1819–1880), who wrote under the pen name George Eliot, brilliantly achieved a more deeply felt, less sensational kind of realism. "It is the habit of my imagination," George Eliot wrote, "to strive after as full a vision of the medium in which a character moves as one of the character itself." Her great novel *Middlemarch: A Study of Provincial Life* (1871–1872) examines masterfully the ways in which people are shaped by their social medium as well as their own inner strivings, conflicts, and moral choices. Thomas Hardy (1840–1928) was more in the Zola tradition. His novels, such as *Tess of the D'Urbervilles* (1891) and *The Return of the Native* (1878), depict men and women frustrated and crushed by fate and bad luck.

The greatest Russian realist, Count Leo Tolstoy (1828–1910), combined realism in description and character development with an atypical moralizing, which came to dominate his later work. Tolstoy's greatest work is *War and Peace* (1864–1869), a monumental novel set against the historical background of Napoleon's invasion of Russia in 1812. Tolstoy probed deeply into the lives of a multitude of unforgettable characters, such as the ill-fated Prince Andrei; the shy, fumbling Pierre; and the enchanting, level-headed Natasha. Tolstoy went to great pains to develop his fatalistic theory of history, which regards free will as an illusion and the achievements of even the greatest leaders as only the channeling of historical necessity. Yet Tolstoy's central message is one that most of the people discussed in this chapter would have readily accepted: human love, trust, and everyday family ties are life's enduring values.

Thoroughgoing realism (or "naturalism," as it was often called) arrived late in the United States, most arrestingly in the work of Theodore Dreiser (1871–1945). His first novel, *Sister Carrie* (1900), a story of an ordinary farm girl who does well going wrong in Chicago, so outraged conventional morality that the publisher withdrew the book. The United States subsequently became a bastion of literary realism in the twentieth century after the movement had faded away in Europe.

"Life Is Everywhere" The simple but profound joys of everyday life infuse this outstanding example of Russia's powerful realist tradition. Painted in 1888 by N. A. Yaroshenko, this representation of the mother and child and adoring men also draws on the classic theme of the infant Jesus and the holy family. *(Sovfoto)*

Chapter Summary

Online Study Center   ACE the Test

- *What was life like in the cities, and how did urban life change in the nineteenth century?*
- *What did the emergence of urban industrial society mean for rich and poor and those in between?*
- *How did families change as they coped with the challenges and the opportunities of the developing urban civilization?*
- *What major changes in science and thought reflected and influenced the new urban society?*

The revolution in industry had a decisive influence on the urban environment. The populations of towns and cities grew rapidly because it was economically advantageous to locate factories and offices in urban areas. This rapid growth worsened long-standing overcrowding and unhealthy living conditions and posed a frightening challenge for society. Eventually government leaders, city planners, reformers, scientists, and ordinary citizens responded. They took effective action in public health and provided themselves with other badly needed urban services. Gradually they tamed the ferocious savagery of the traditional city.

As the quality of urban life improved, the class structure became more complex and diversified than before. Urban society featured many distinct social groups, which existed in a state of constant flux and competition. The gap between rich and poor remained enormous and really quite traditional in mature urban society, although there were countless gradations between the extremes. Large numbers of poor women in particular continued to labor as workers in sweated industries, as domestic servants, and as prostitutes in order to satisfy the demands of their masters in the servant-keeping classes.

Major changes in family life accompanied the more complex and diversified class system. Especially among the working classes, family life became more stable, more loving, and less mercenary. These improvements had a price, however. Gender roles for men and women became sharply defined and rigidly separate. Women especially tended to be locked into a subordinate and stereotypical role. Nonetheless, on balance, the quality of family life improved for all family members. Better, more stable family relations reinforced the benefits for the masses of

higher real wages, increased social security, political participation, and education. Urban society in the late nineteenth century represented a long step forward for humanity, but it remained very unequal.

Inequality was a favorite theme of realist novelists such as Balzac and Zola. More generally, literary realism reflected Western society's growing faith in science, material progress, and evolutionary thinking. The emergence of urban, industrial civilization accelerated the secularization of the Western worldview.

Key Terms

Benthamite	defense mechanisms
miasmatic theory	thermodynamics
germ theory	organic chemistry
pasteurization	positivist method
antiseptic principle	evolution
labor aristocracy	Social Darwinists
illegitimacy explosion	realism
separate spheres	

Online Study Center   Improve Your Grade Flashcards

Suggested Reading

Anderson, Bonnie S., and Judith P. Zinsser. *A History of Their Own: Women in Europe from Prehistory to the Present*, vol. 2, rev. ed. 2000. An excellent, wide-ranging survey.

Barnes, David S. *The Great Stink of Paris and the Nineteenth-Century Struggle Against Filth and Germs.* 2006. An excellent introduction to sanitary developments and attitudes toward public health.

Coontz, Stephanie. *Marriage, a History: From Obedience to Intimacy, or How Love Conquered Marriage.* 2005. A lively investigation of the historical background to current practice.

Crane, Diana. *Fashion and Its Social Agendas: Class, Gender, and Identity.* 2001. An innovative and extremely helpful historical investigation.

Gottlieb, Beatrice. *The Family in the Western World.* 1993. A wide-ranging synthesis.

Hunt, Tristram. *Building Jerusalem: The Rise and Fall of the Victorian City.* 2006. Considers British urban life and civic pride.

Maynes, Mary Jo. *Taking the Hard Road: Life Course in French and German Workers' Biographies in the Era of Industrialization.* 1995. Includes fascinating stories that provide insight into how workers saw themselves.

Olsen, Donald J. *The City as a Work of Art: London, Paris, and Vienna.* 1988. An architectural feast.

Perrot, Michelle, ed. *A History of Private Life.* 1990. A fascinating multivolume work.

Pilbeam, Pamela. *The Middle Classes in Europe, 1789–1914: France, Germany, Italy, and Russia.* 1990. A stimulating introduction to middle-class life.

Schmiechen, James, and Kenneth Carls. *The British Market Hall: A Social and Architectural History.* 1999. A pathbreaking and beautiful study of Britain's enclosed markets and how they revolutionized the sale of food.

Thompson, F. M. L. *The Rise of Respectable Society: A Social History of Victorian Britain, 1830–1900.* 1986. A laudable survey.

Weiner, Jonathan. *The Beak of the Finch: The Story of Evolution in Our Time.* 1994. A prize-winning, highly readable account of Darwin and evolution.

Zeldin, Theodore. *France, 1848–1945,* 2 vols. 1973, 1977. A pioneering social history that opened many new lines of inquiry.

Notes

1. A. Weber, *The Growth of Cities in the Nineteenth Century* (New York: Columbia University Press, 1899), p. 1.

2. S. Marcus, "Reading the Illegible," in *The Victorian City: Images and Realities,* ed. H. J. Dyos and Michael Wolff, vol. 1 (London: Routledge & Kegan Paul, 1973), p. 266.

3. E. Gauldie, *Cruel Habitations: A History of Working-Class Housing, 1780–1918* (London: George Allen & Unwin, 1974), p. 21.

4. Quoted in E. Chadwick, *Report on the Sanitary Condition of the Labouring Population of Great Britain,* ed. M. W. Flinn (Edinburgh: University of Edinburgh Press, 1965; original publication, 1842), pp. 315–316.

5. J. P. McKay, *Tramways and Trolleys: The Rise of Urban Mass Transport in Europe* (Princeton, N.J.: Princeton University Press, 1976), p. 81.

6. Quoted in R. P. Neuman, "The Sexual Question and Social Democracy in Imperial Germany," *Journal of Social History* 7 (Winter 1974): 276.

7. Quoted in J. A. Banks, "The Contagion of Numbers," in *The Victorian City: Images and Realities,* ed. H. J. Dyos and Michael Wolff, vol. 1 (London: Routledge & Kegan Paul, 1973), p. 112.

8. Quoted in R. Roberts, *The Classic Slum: Salford Life in the First Quarter of the Century* (Manchester, England: University of Manchester Press, 1971), p. 95.

9. Quoted in T. Zeldin, *France, 1848–1945,* vol. 1 (Oxford: Clarendon Press, 1973), p. 288.

10. J. Ehmer, "Marriage," in *The History of the European Family,* ed. D. Kertzer and M. Barbagli, vol. 2 (New Haven: Yale University Press, 2002), p. 319.

11. S. Marcus, *The Other Victorians: A Study of Sexuality and Pornography in Mid-Nineteenth-Century England* (New York: Basic Books, 1966), p. 142.

12. Quoted in G. S. Jones, "Working-Class Culture and Working-Class Politics in London, 1870–1900: Notes on the Remaking of a Working Class," *Journal of Social History* 7 (Summer 1974): 486.

13. Quoted in Zeldin, *France,* p. 346.

14. Roberts, *The Classic Slum,* p. 35.

15. Quoted in Zeldin, *France,* p. 295.

16. Quoted ibid., p. 328.

17. Quoted in Neuman, "The Sexual Question," p. 281.

18. Quoted in S. Kern, "Explosive Intimacy: Psychodynamics of the Victorian Family," *History of Childhood Quarterly* 1 (Winter 1974): 439.

19. A. Comte, *The Positive Philosophy of Auguste Comte,* trans. H. Martineau, vol. 1 (London: J. Chapman, 1853), pp. 1–2.

Middle-Class Youth and Sexuality

Growing up in Vienna in a prosperous Jewish family, Stephan Zweig (1881–1942) became an influential voice calling for humanitarian values and international culture in early-twentieth-century Europe. Passionately opposed to the First World War, Zweig wrote poetry, plays, and novels. But he was most famous for many outstanding biographies, which featured shrewd psychological portraits of intriguing historical figures such as Magellan and Marie Antoinette. After Hitler came to power in Germany in 1933, Zweig lived in exile until his death in 1942.

Zweig's last work was The World of Yesterday (1943), one of the truly fascinating autobiographies of the twentieth century. In the following passage taken from that work, Zweig recalls and also interprets the romantic experiences and the sexual separation of middle-class youth before the First World War.

During the eight years of our higher schooling [beyond grade school], something had occurred which was of great importance to each one of us: we ten-year-olds had grown into virile young men of sixteen, seventeen, and eighteen, and Nature began to assert its rights. . . . It did not take us long to discover that those authorities in whom we had previously confided—school, family, and public morals—manifested an astonishing insincerity in this matter of sex. But what is more, they also demanded secrecy and reserve from us in this connection. . . .

This "social morality," which on the one hand privately presupposed the existence of sexuality and its natural course, but on the other would not recognize it openly at any price, was doubly deceitful. While it winked one eye at a young man and even encouraged him with the other "to sow his wild oats," as the kindly language of the home put it, in the case of a woman it studiously shut both eyes and acted as if it were blind. That a man could experience desires, and was permitted to

experience them, was silently admitted by custom. But to admit frankly that a woman could be subject to similar desires, or that creation for its eternal purposes also required a female polarity, would have transgressed the conception of the "sanctity of womanhood." In the pre-Freudian era, therefore, the axiom was agreed upon that a female person could have no physical desires as long as they had not been awakened by man, and that, obviously, was officially permitted only in marriage. But even in those moral times, in Vienna in particular, the air was full of dangerous erotic infection, and a girl of good family had to live in a completely sterilized atmosphere, from the day of her birth until the day when she left the altar on her husband's arm. In order to protect young girls, they were not left alone for a single moment. . . . Every book which they read was inspected, and above all else, young girls were constantly kept busy to divert their attention from any possible dangerous thoughts. They had to practise the piano, learn singing and drawing, foreign languages, and the history of literature and art. They were educated and overeducated. But while the aim was to make them as educated and as socially correct as possible, at the same time society anxiously took great pains that they should remain innocent of all natural things to a degree unthinkable today. A young girl of good family was not allowed to have any idea of how the male body was formed, or to know how children came into the world, for the angel was to enter into matrimony not only physically untouched, but completely "pure" spiritually as well. "Good breeding," for a young girl of that time, was identical with ignorance of life; and this ignorance ofttimes lasted for the rest of their lives. . . .

What possibilities actually existed for a young man of the middle-class world? In all the others, in the so-called lower classes, the problem was no problem at all. . . . In most of our Alpine villages the number of natural children greatly exceeded the legitimate ones. Among the proletariat, the worker, before he could get married, lived with another worker in free love. . . . It was only in our middle-class society that such a remedy as an early marriage was scorned. . . . And so there was an artificial interval of six, eight, or ten years between actual manhood and manhood as society accepted it; and in this interval the young man had to take care of his own "affairs" or adventures.

Those days did not give him too many opportunities. Only a very few particularly rich young men could afford the luxury of keeping a mistress, that is, taking an apartment and paying her expenses. And only a very few fortunate young men achieved the literary ideal of love of the times—the only one which it was permitted to describe in novels—an affair with a married woman. The others helped themselves for the most part with shopgirls and waitresses, and this offered little inner satisfaction. . . . But, generally speaking, prostitution was still the foundation of the erotic life outside of marriage; in a certain sense it constituted a dark underground vault over which rose the gorgeous structure of middle-class society with its faultless, radiant façade.

The present generation has hardly any idea of the gigantic extent of prostitution in Europe before the [First] World War. Whereas today it is as rare to meet a prostitute on the streets of a big city as it is to meet a wagon in the road, then the sidewalks were so sprinkled with women for sale that it was more difficult to avoid than to find them. To this was added the countless number of "closed houses," the night clubs, the cabarets, the dance parlours with their dancers and singers, and the bars with their "come-on" girls. At that time female wares were offered for sale at every hour and at every price. . . . And this was the same city, the same society, the same morality, that was indignant when young girls rode bicycles, and declared it a disgrace to the dignity of science when Freud in his calm, clear, and penetrating manner established truths that they did not wish to be true. The same world that so pathetically defended the purity of womanhood allowed this cruel sale of women, organized it, and even profited thereby.

We should not permit ourselves to be misled by sentimental novels or stories of that epoch. It was a bad time for youth. The young girls were

An elegant ball for upper-class youth, with debutantes, junior officers, and vigilant chaperons watching in the background. *(State Russian Museum, St. Petersburg, Russia/The Bridgeman Art Library)*

hermetically locked up under the control of the family, hindered in their free bodily as well as intellectual development. The young men were forced to secrecy and reticence by a morality which fundamentally no one believed or obeyed. Unhampered, honest relationships—in other words, all that could have made youth happy and joyous according to the laws of Nature—were permitted only to the very few.

Questions for Analysis

1. According to Zweig, how did the sex lives of young middle-class women and young middle-class men differ? What accounted for these differences?

2. Was there nonetheless a basic underlying unity in the way society treated both the young men and the young women of the comfortable middle class? If so, what was that unity?

3. Zweig ends this passage with a value judgment: "It was a bad time for youth." Do you agree or disagree? Why?

Source: The World of Yesterday by Stephan Zweig, translated by Helmut Ripperger. Translation copyright 1943 by the Viking Press, Inc. Used with permission of Viking Penguin, a division of Penguin Group (USA) Inc.

France's Napoleon III and Empress Eugénie greet Britain's Queen Victoria and Prince Albert in a dazzling ceremony in Paris in 1855. *(The Royal Collection, © 2007 Her Majesty Queen Elizabeth II)*

THE AGE OF NATIONALISM, 1850–1914

The revolutions of 1848 closed one era and opened another. Urban industrial society began to take a strong hold on the continent and in the young United States, as it already had in Great Britain. Internationally, the repressive peace and diplomatic stability of Metternich's time were replaced by a period of war and rapid change. In thought and culture, exuberant romanticism gave way to hardheaded realism. In the Atlantic economy, the hard years of the 1840s were followed by good times and prosperity throughout most of the 1850s and 1860s. Perhaps most important of all, Western society progressively developed, for better or worse, a new and effective organizing principle capable of coping with the many-sided challenge of the dual revolution and the emerging urban civilization. That principle was nationalism—dedication to an identification with the nation-state.

The triumph of nationalism is an enormously significant historical development that was by no means completely predictable. After all, nationalism had been a powerful force since at least 1789, but it had repeatedly failed to realize its goals, most spectacularly so in 1848. Yet by 1914 nationalism had become in one way or another an almost universal faith in Europe and in the United States, a faith that had evolved to appeal not only to predominately middle-class liberals but also to the broad masses of society. To understand this fateful evolution is the task of this chapter.

Napoleon III in France

Early nationalism was generally liberal and idealistic and often democratic and radical as well. The ideas of nationhood and popular sovereignty posed a fearful revolutionary threat to conservatives like Metternich. Yet from the vantage point of the twenty-first century, it is clear that nationalism wears many masks: it may be narrowly liberal or democratic and radical, as it was for Mazzini and Michelet, but it can also flourish in dictatorial states, which may be conservative, fascist, or communist. Napoleon I's France had already combined national feeling with authoritarian rule. Significantly, it

Online Study Center

This icon will direct you to interactive activities and study materials on the website **college.hmco.com/pic/mckaywest9e**

was Napoleon's nephew, Louis Napoleon, who revived and extended this merger. In doing so, he provided a model for political leaders elsewhere.

• *How in France did Napoleon III seek to reconcile popular and conservative forces in an authoritarian nation-state?*

The Second Republic and Louis Napoleon

Although Louis Napoleon Bonaparte had played no part in French politics before 1848, universal male suffrage gave him three times as many votes as the four other presidential candidates combined in the French presidential election of December 1848. This outcome occurred for several reasons. First, Louis Napoleon had the great name of his uncle, whom romantics had transformed from a dictator into a demigod as they created a Napoleonic legend after 1820. Second, as Karl Marx stressed at the time, middle-class and peasant property owners feared the socialist challenge of urban workers, and they wanted a tough ruler to provide protection. Third, in late 1848 Louis Napoleon had a positive "program" for France, which had been elaborated in widely circulated pamphlets before the election and which guided him through his long reign.

Above all, Louis Napoleon believed that the government should represent the people and that it should try hard to help them economically. But how were these tasks to be done? Parliaments and political parties were not the answer, according to Louis Napoleon. French politicians represented special-interest groups, particularly middle-class ones. The answer was a strong, even authoritarian, national leader, like the first Napoleon, who would serve all the people, rich and poor. This leader would be linked

Paris in the Second Empire The flash and glitter of unprecedented prosperity in the Second Empire come alive in this vibrant contemporary painting. Writers and intellectuals chat with elegant women and trade witticisms with financiers and government officials at the Café Tortoni, a favorite rendezvous for fashionable society. Horse-drawn omnibuses with open top decks mingle with cabs and private carriages on the broad new boulevard. *(Lauros/Giraudon/ The Bridgeman Art Library)*

to each citizen by direct democracy, his sovereignty uncorrupted by politicians and legislative bodies. These political ideas went hand in hand with Louis Napoleon's vision of national unity and social progress. The state and its leader had a sacred duty to provide jobs and stimulate the economy. All classes would benefit by such action.

Louis Napoleon's political and social ideas were at least vaguely understood by large numbers of French peasants and workers in December 1848. To many common people, he appeared to be a strong man *and* a forward-looking champion of their interests, and that is why they voted for him.

Online Study Center **Improve Your Grade**
Primary Source: The French Elect Another Bonaparte: Louis Napoleon Bonaparte

Elected to a four-year term, President Louis Napoleon had to share power with a conservative National Assembly. But in 1851, after the Assembly failed to change the constitution so he could run for a second term, Louis Napoleon began to conspire with key army officers. On December 2, 1851, he illegally dismissed the Assembly and seized power in a coup d'état. There was some armed resistance in Paris and widespread insurrection in the countryside in southern France, but these protests were crushed by the army. Restoring universal male suffrage, Louis Napoleon called on the French people, as his uncle had done, to legalize his actions. They did: 92 percent voted to make him president for ten years. A year later, 97 percent in a plebiscite made him hereditary emperor; for the third time, and by the greatest margin yet, the authoritarian Louis Napoleon was overwhelmingly elected to lead the French nation.

Napoleon III's Second Empire

Louis Napoleon—now proclaimed Emperor Napoleon III—experienced both success and failure between 1852 and 1870. His greatest success was with the economy, particularly in the 1850s. His government encouraged the new investment banks and massive railroad construction that were at the heart of the Industrial Revolution on the continent. The government also fostered general economic expansion through an ambitious program of public works, which included the rebuilding of Paris to improve the urban environment (see page 784). The profits of business people soared with prosperity, and unemployment declined greatly.

Louis Napoleon always hoped that economic progress would reduce social and political tensions. This hope was

Chronology

1852–1871	Reign of Napoleon III in France
1859–1870	Unification of Italy
1860–1900	Industrialization of Russia
1861	Freeing of Russian serfs
1861–1865	U.S. Civil War
1866	Austro-Prussian War
1870–1871	Franco-Prussian War
1870–1878	Kulturkampf, Bismarck's attack on Catholic Church
1880s	Educational reforms affect Catholic schools in France
1883	First social security laws to help workers in Germany
1905	Bloody Sunday in Russia
1908	Young Turks in power

at least partially realized. Until the mid-1860s there was considerable support from France's most dissatisfied group, the urban workers. Napoleon III's regulation of pawnshops and his support of credit unions and better housing for the working classes were evidence of positive concern in the 1850s. In the 1860s, he granted workers the right to form unions and the right to strike—important economic rights denied by earlier governments.

At first, political power remained in the hands of the emperor. He alone chose his ministers, and they had great freedom of action. At the same time, Napoleon III restricted but did not abolish the Assembly. Members were elected by universal male suffrage every six years, and Louis Napoleon and his government took the parliamentary elections very seriously. They tried to entice notable people, even those who had opposed the regime, to stand as government candidates in order to expand the base of support. Moreover, the government used its officials and appointed mayors to spread the word that the election of the government's candidates—and the defeat of the opposition—was the key to roads, tax rebates, and a thousand other local concerns.

In 1857 and again in 1863, Louis Napoleon's system worked brilliantly and produced overwhelming electoral victories. Yet in the 1860s, Napoleon III's electoral system gradually disintegrated. A sincere nationalist, Napoleon had wanted to reorganize Europe on the principle of nationality and gain influence and territory for France and himself in the process. Instead, problems in Italy and the rising power of Prussia led to increasing criticism at home from his Catholic and nationalist supporters. With increasing effectiveness, the middle-class liberals who had always wanted a less authoritarian regime continued to denounce his rule.

Napoleon was always sensitive to the public mood. Public opinion, he once said, always wins the last victory. Thus in the 1860s, he progressively liberalized his empire. He gave the Assembly greater powers and the opposition candidates greater freedom, which they used to good advantage. In 1869 the opposition, consisting of republicans, monarchists, and liberals, polled almost 45 percent of the vote.

The next year, a sick and weary Louis Napoleon again granted France a new constitution, which combined a basically parliamentary regime with a hereditary emperor as chief of state. In a final great plebiscite on the eve of the disastrous war with Prussia, 7.5 million Frenchmen voted in favor of the new constitution, and only 1.5 million opposed it. Napoleon III's attempt to reconcile a strong national state with universal male suffrage was still evolving and was doing so in a democratic direction.

Nation Building in Italy and Germany

Louis Napoleon's triumph in 1848 and his authoritarian rule in the 1850s provided the old ruling classes of Europe with a new model in politics. To what extent might the expanding urban middle classes and even portions of the growing working classes rally to a strong and essentially conservative national state? This was one of the great political questions in the 1850s and 1860s. In central Europe, a resounding answer came with the national unification of Italy and Germany.

• *How did the process of unification in Italy and Germany create conservative nation-states?*

Italy to 1850

Italy had never been united prior to 1850. Part of Rome's great empire in ancient times, the Italian peninsula was divided in the Middle Ages into competing city-states that led the commercial and cultural revival of the West with amazing creativity. A battleground for Great Powers after 1494, Italy was reorganized in 1815 at the Congress of Vienna. The rich northern provinces of Lombardy and

Venetia were taken by Metternich's Austria. Sardinia and Piedmont were under the rule of an Italian monarch, and Tuscany, with its famous capital Florence, shared north-central Italy with several smaller states. Central Italy and Rome were ruled by the papacy, which had always considered an independent political existence necessary to fulfill its spiritual mission. Naples and Sicily were ruled, as they had been for almost a hundred years, by a branch of the Bourbons. Metternich was not wrong in dismissing Italy as "a geographical expression" (see Map 25.1).

Between 1815 and 1848, the goal of a unified Italian nation captured the imaginations of many Italians. There were three basic approaches. The first was the radical program of the idealistic patriot Giuseppe Mazzini, who preached a centralized democratic republic based on universal male suffrage and the will of the people (see page 755). The second was that of Vincenzo Gioberti, a Catholic priest who called for a federation of existing states under the presidency of a progressive pope. The third was the program of those who looked for leadership to the autocratic kingdom of Sardinia-Piedmont, much as many Germans looked to Prussia.

The third alternative was strengthened by the failures of 1848, when Austria smashed Mazzini's republicanism. Almost by accident, Sardinia's monarch, Victor Emmanuel, retained the liberal constitution granted under duress in March 1848. This constitution provided for a fair degree of civil liberties and real parliamentary government, with deputies elected by a limited franchise based on income. To the Italian middle classes, Sardinia appeared to be a liberal, progressive state ideally suited to achieve the goal of national unification. By contrast, Mazzini's brand of democratic republicanism seemed quixotic and too radical.

As for the papacy, the initial cautious support by Pius IX (r. 1846–1878) for unification had given way to fear and hostility after he was temporarily driven from Rome during the upheavals of 1848. For a long generation, the papacy would stand resolutely opposed not only to national unification but also to most modern trends. In 1864 in the *Syllabus of Errors,* Pius IX strongly denounced rationalism, socialism, separation of church and state, and religious liberty, denying that "the Roman pontiff can and ought to reconcile and align himself with progress, liberalism, and modern civilization."

Cavour and Garibaldi in Italy

Sardinia had the good fortune of being led by a brilliant statesman, Count Camillo Benso di Cavour, the dominant figure in the Sardinian government from 1850 until his death in 1861. Indicative of the coming tacit alliance

MAP 25.1 The Unification of Italy, 1859–1870   The leadership of Sardinia-Piedmont, nationalist fervor, and Garibaldi's attack on the kingdom of the Two Sicilies were decisive factors in the unification of Italy.

between the aristocracy and the solid middle class under the banner of the strong nation-state, Cavour came from a noble family, and he made a substantial fortune in business before entering politics. Cavour's national goals were limited and realistic. Until 1859 he sought unity only for the states of northern and perhaps central Italy in a greatly expanded kingdom of Sardinia.

In the 1850s, Cavour worked to consolidate Sardinia as a liberal constitutional state capable of leading northern Italy. His program of highways and railroads, of civil liberties and opposition to clerical privilege, increased support for Sardinia throughout northern Italy. Yet Cavour realized that Sardinia could not drive Austria out of Lombardy and Venetia and unify northern Italy under Victor Emmanuel without the help of a powerful ally. Accordingly, he worked for a secret diplomatic alliance with Napoleon III against Austria.

Finally, in July 1858 Cavour succeeded and goaded Austria into attacking Sardinia in 1859. Napoleon III came to Sardinia's defense. Then after the victory of the combined Franco-Sardinian forces, Napoleon III did a sudden about-face. Deciding it was not in his interest to have too strong a state on his southern border and criticized by French Catholics for supporting the pope's declared enemy, Napoleon III abandoned Cavour. He made a compromise peace with the Austrians at Villafranca in July 1859. Sardinia would receive only Lombardy, the area around Milan. The rest of the map of Italy would remain essentially unchanged. Cavour resigned in a rage.

Yet Cavour's plans were salvaged by the skillful maneuvers of his allies in the moderate nationalist movement. While the war against Austria had raged in the north, pro-Sardinian nationalists in central Italy had fanned popular revolts and driven out their easily toppled princes. Using and controlling the popular enthusiasm, the middle-class nationalist leaders in central Italy called for fusion with Sardinia. This was not at all what France and the other Great Powers wanted, but the nationalists held firm. Cavour returned to power in early 1860 and gained Napoleon III's support by ceding Savoy and Nice to France. The people of central Italy then voted overwhelmingly to join a greatly enlarged kingdom of Sardinia. Cavour had achieved his original goal of a northern Italian state (see Map 25.1).

Garibaldi and Victor Emmanuel The historic meeting in Naples between the leader of Italy's revolutionary nationalists and the king of Sardinia sealed the unification of northern and southern Italy in a unitary state. With only the sleeve of his red shirt showing, Garibaldi offers his hand—and his conquests—to the uniformed king and his moderate monarchical government. *(Scala/Art Resource, NY)*

For superpatriots such as Giuseppe Garibaldi (1807–1882), the job of unification was still only half done. The son of a poor sailor, Garibaldi personified the romantic, revolutionary nationalism and republicanism of Mazzini and 1848. Leading a corps of volunteers against Austria in 1859, Garibaldi emerged in 1860 as an independent force in Italian politics.

Partly to use him and partly to get rid of him, Cavour secretly supported Garibaldi's bold plan to "liberate" the kingdom of the Two Sicilies. Landing on the shores of Sicily in May 1860, Garibaldi's guerrilla band of a thousand **Red Shirts** captured the imagination of the Sicilian peasantry. Outwitting the twenty-thousand-man royal army, the guerrilla leader won battles, gained volunteers, and took Palermo. Then he and his men crossed to the mainland, marched triumphantly toward Naples, and prepared to attack Rome and the pope. But the wily Cavour quickly sent Sardinian forces to occupy most of the Papal States (but not Rome) and to intercept Garibaldi.

Cavour realized that an attack on Rome would bring about war with France, and he also feared Garibaldi's radicalism and popular appeal. Thus he immediately organized a plebiscite in the conquered territories. Despite the urging of some radical supporters, the patriotic Garibaldi did not oppose Cavour, and the people of the south voted to join Sardinia. When Garibaldi and Victor Emmanuel rode through Naples to cheering crowds, they symbolically sealed the union of north and south, of monarch and nation-state.

Cavour had succeeded. He had controlled Garibaldi and had turned popular nationalism in a conservative direction. The new kingdom of Italy, which expanded to include Venice in 1866 and Rome in 1870, was a parliamentary monarchy under Victor Emmanuel, neither radical nor democratic. Despite political unity, only a small minority of Italian males had the right to vote. The propertied classes and the common people were divided. A great and growing social and cultural gap separated the progressive, industrializing north from the stagnant, agrarian south. The new Italy was united on paper, but profound divisions remained.

Germany Before Bismarck

In the aftermath of 1848, the German states were locked in a political stalemate. After Austria and Russia blocked Frederick William's attempt to unify Germany "from above," tension grew between Austria and Prussia as each power sought to block the other within the German Confederation (see pages 751 and 773–774). Stalemate also prevailed in the domestic politics of the individual states in the 1850s.

At the same time, powerful economic forces were undermining the political status quo. Modern industry grew rapidly within the German customs union, or **Zollverein**, founded in 1834 to stimulate trade and increase the revenues of member states. The Zollverein had not included Austria, and after 1848 this exclusion became a crucial factor in the Austro-Prussian rivalry.

The Zollverein's tariff duties were substantially reduced so that Austria's highly protected industry could not bear to join. In retaliation, Austria tried to destroy the Zollverein, but without success. Indeed, by the end of 1853 all the German states except Austria had joined the customs union. A new Germany excluding Austria was becoming an economic reality. Middle-class and business groups in the Zollverein were enriching themselves and finding solid economic reasons to bolster their idealistic support of national unification. Prussia's leading role within the Zollverein gave it a valuable advantage in its struggle against Austria's supremacy in German political affairs.

The national uprising in Italy in 1859 made a profound impression in the German states. In Prussia great political change and war—perhaps with Austria, perhaps with France—seemed quite possible. Along with his top military advisers, the tough-minded William I of Prussia (r. 1861–1888), who had replaced the unstable Frederick William IV as regent in 1858 and become king himself in 1861, was convinced of the need for major army reforms. William I wanted to double the size of the highly disciplined regular army. Army reforms meant a bigger defense budget and higher taxes.

Prussia had emerged from 1848 with a parliament of sorts, which was in the hands of the liberal middle class by 1859. The wealthy middle class wanted society to be less, not more, militaristic. Above all, middle-class representatives wanted to establish once and for all that the parliament, not the king, had the ultimate political power and that the army was responsible to Prussia's elected representatives. These demands were popular. The parliament rejected the military budget in 1862, and the liberals triumphed completely in new elections. King William then called on Count Otto von Bismarck to head a new ministry and defy the parliament. This was a momentous choice.

Bismarck and the Austro-Prussian War, 1866

The most important figure in German history between Luther and Hitler, Otto von Bismarck (1815–1898) has been the object of enormous interest and debate. A great hero to some, a great villain to others, Bismarck was above all a master of politics. Born into the Prussian landowning aristocracy, the young Bismarck was a wild and tempestuous student given to duels and drinking. Proud of his Junker heritage and always devoted to his Prussian sovereign, Bismarck had a strong personality and an unbounded desire for power. Yet in his drive to secure power for himself and for Prussia, Bismarck was extraordinarily flexible and pragmatic. "One must always have two irons in the fire," he once said. He kept his options open, pursuing one policy and then another as he moved with skill and cunning toward his goal.

Bismarck first honed his political skills as a high-ranking diplomat for the Prussian government. When he took office as chief minister in 1862, he made a strong but unfavorable impression. His speeches were a sensation and a scandal. Declaring that the government would rule without parliamentary consent, Bismarck lashed out at the middle-class opposition: "The great questions of the day will not be decided by speeches and resolutions—that was the blunder of 1848 and 1849—but by blood and iron." Denounced for this view that "might makes right," Bismarck had the Prussian bureaucracy go right on collecting taxes, even though the parliament refused to approve the budget. Bismarck reorganized the army. And for four years, from 1862 to 1866, the voters of Prussia continued to express their opposition by sending large liberal majorities to the parliament.

Opposition at home spurred the search for success abroad. The ever-knotty question of Schleswig-Holstein provided a welcome opportunity. In 1864, when the Danish king tried again, as in 1848, to bring the provinces into a more centralized Danish state against the will of the German Confederation, Prussia joined Austria in a short and successful war against Denmark. However, Bismarck was convinced that Prussia had to control completely the northern, predominately Protestant part of the German Confederation, which meant expelling Austria from German affairs. After the victory over Denmark, Bismarck's skillful maneuvering had Prussia in a position to force Austria out by war, if necessary. Bismarck knew that a war with Austria would have to be a localized one that would not provoke a mighty alliance against Prussia. By skillfully neutralizing Russia and France, he was in a position to engage in a war of his own making.

The Austro-Prussian War of 1866 lasted only seven weeks. Utilizing railroads to mass troops and the new breechloading needle gun to achieve maximum firepower, the reorganized Prussian army overran northern Germany and defeated Austria decisively at the Battle of Sadowa in Bohemia. Anticipating Prussia's future needs, Bismarck offered Austria realistic, even generous, peace terms. Austria paid no reparations and lost no territory to Prussia, although Venetia was ceded to Italy. But the German Confederation was dissolved, and Austria agreed to withdraw from German affairs. The states north of the Main River were grouped in the new North German Confederation, led by an expanded Prussia. The mainly Catholic states of the south remained independent while forming alliances with Prussia. Bismarck's fundamental goal of Prussian expansion was being realized (see Map 25.2).

The Taming of the Parliament

Bismarck had long been convinced that the old order he so ardently defended should make peace, on its own terms, with the liberal middle class and the nationalist movement. He realized that nationalism was not necessarily hostile to conservative, authoritarian government. Moreover, Bismarck believed that because of the events of 1848, the German middle class could be led to prefer the reality of national unity under conservative leadership to a long, uncertain battle for truly liberal institutions. During the constitutional struggle over army reform and parliamentary authority, he had delayed but not abandoned this goal. Thus during the attack on Austria in 1866, he increasingly identified Prussia's fate with the "national development of Germany."

In the aftermath of victory, Bismarck fashioned a federal constitution for the new North German Confederation. Each state retained its own local government, but the king of Prussia became president of the confederation, and the chancellor—Bismarck—was responsible only to the president. The federal government—William I and Bismarck—controlled the army and foreign affairs. There was also a legislature with members of the lower house elected by universal, single-class, male suffrage. With this radical innovation, Bismarck opened the door to popular participation and the possibility of going over the head of the middle class directly to the people, much as Napoleon III had done in France. All the while, however, ultimate power rested in the hands of Prussia and its king and army.

In Prussia itself, Bismarck held out an olive branch to the parliamentary opposition. Marshaling all his diplomatic skill, Bismarck asked the parliament to pass a special indemnity bill to approve after the fact all the government's spending between 1862 and 1866. Most of the liberals jumped at the chance to cooperate. With German unity in sight, they repented their "sins." The constitutional struggle was over, and the German middle class was accepting respectfully the monarchical authority and the aristocratic superiority that Bismarck represented. In the

Mapping the Past

MAP 25.2 The Unification of Germany, 1866–1871 This map shows how Prussia expanded and a new German empire was created through two wars, the Austro-Prussian War of 1866 and the Franco-Prussian War of 1870–1871. It deserves careful study because it highlights how central Europe was remade and the power of Prussia-Germany was greatly increased. **①** What were the results of the Austro-Prussian War? Specifically, how did Prussia treat its neighbors in the north, such as Hanover and Saxony? **②** What losses did Austria experience in 1866? **③** What were the results of the Franco-Prussian War for France and for the predominately Catholic states of southern Germany, such as Bavaria and Württemberg?

Online Study Center **Improve Your Grade**
Interactive Map: Unification of Germany, 1866–1871

Proclaiming the German Empire, January 1871 This commemorative painting by Anton von Werner testifies to the nationalistic intoxication in Germany after the victory over France. William I of Prussia stands on a platform surrounded by princes and generals in the famous Hall of Mirrors in the palace of Versailles, while officers from all the units around a besieged Paris cheer and salute him with uplifted swords as emperor of a unified Germany. Bismarck, like a heroic white knight, stands between king and army. *(akg-images)*

years before 1914, the values of the aristocratic Prussian army officer increasingly replaced those of the middle-class liberal in public esteem and set the social standard.[1]

The Franco-Prussian War, 1870–1871

The final act in the drama of German unification followed quickly. Bismarck realized that a patriotic war with France would drive the south German states into his arms. The French obligingly played their part. The apparent issue—whether a distant relative of Prussia's William I (and France's Napoleon III) might become king of Spain—was only a diplomatic pretext. By 1870 the French

leaders of the Second Empire, goaded by Bismarck and alarmed by their powerful new neighbor on the Rhine, had decided on a war to teach Prussia a lesson.

As soon as war against France began in 1870, Bismarck had the wholehearted support of the south German states. With other governments standing still—Bismarck's generosity to Austria in 1866 was paying big dividends—German forces under Prussian leadership decisively defeated the main French army at Sedan on September 1, 1870. Louis Napoleon himself was captured and humiliated. Three days later, French patriots in Paris proclaimed yet another French republic and vowed to continue fighting. But after five months, in January 1871, a starving Paris surrendered, and France went on to accept Bismarck's harsh peace terms. By this time, the south German states had agreed to join a new German Empire. The victorious William I was proclaimed emperor of Germany in the Hall of Mirrors in the palace of Versailles. Europe had a nineteenth-century German "sun king." As in the 1866 constitution, the king of Prussia and his ministers had ultimate power in the new German Empire, and the lower house of the legislature was elected by universal male suffrage.

Bismarck and the German Empire imposed a harsh peace on France. France was forced to pay a colossal indemnity of 5 billion francs and to cede the rich eastern province of Alsace and part of Lorraine to Germany. The German general staff asserted that this annexation would enhance military security, and German nationalists claimed that the Alsacians, who spoke a German dialect as well as French, wanted to rejoin the fatherland after more than two hundred years. But both cases were weak, and revenge for France's real and imagined aggression in the past was probably the decisive factor. In any event, French men and women of all classes viewed the seizure of Alsace and Lorraine as a terrible crime. They could never forget and never forgive, and thus relations between France and Germany after 1871 were tragically poisoned.

The Franco-Prussian War, which Europeans generally saw as a test of nations in a pitiless Darwinian struggle for existence, released an enormous surge of patriotic feeling in Germany. Bismarck's genius, the invincible Prussian army, the solidarity of king and people in a unified nation—these and similar themes were trumpeted endlessly during and after the war. The weakest of the Great Powers in 1862 (after Austria, Britain, France, and Russia), Prussia had become, with fortification by the other German states, the most powerful state in Europe in less than a decade. Most Germans were enormously proud, blissfully imagining themselves the fittest and best of the European species. Semi-authoritarian nationalism and a "new conservatism," which was based on an alliance of the propertied classes and sought the active support of the working classes, had triumphed in Germany.

Nation Building in the United States

• *In what ways did the United States experience the full drama of nation building?*

Closely linked to European developments in the nineteenth century, the United States experienced the full drama of bloody nation building. The "United" States was divided by slavery from its birth, as economic development in the young republic carried free and slaveholding states in very different directions. Northerners extended family farms westward and began building English-model factories in the Northeast. By 1850 an industrializing, urbanizing North was also building a system of canals and railroads and attracting most of the European immigrants. In sharp contrast, industry and cities did not develop in the South, and newcomers avoided the region. And even though three-quarters of all Southern white families were small farmers and owned no slaves in 1850, plantation owners holding twenty or more slaves dominated the economy and society. These profit-minded slave owners used gangs of black slaves to claim a vast new kingdom across the Deep South where cotton was king (see Map 25.3). By 1850, this kingdom produced 5 million bales a year and satisfied an apparently insatiable demand from textile mills in Europe and New England.

The rise of the cotton empire revitalized slave-based agriculture, spurred exports, and played a key role in igniting rapid U.S. economic growth. The large profits flowing from cotton also led influential Southerners to defend slavery. In doing so, Southern whites developed a strong cultural identity and came to see themselves as a closely knit "we" distinct from the Northern "they." Northern whites viewed their free-labor system as being no less economically and morally superior. Thus regional antagonisms intensified.

These antagonisms came to a climax after 1848 when a defeated Mexico ceded to the United States a vast area stretching from west Texas to the Pacific Ocean. Debate over the extension of slavery in this new territory caused attitudes to harden on both sides. In Abraham Lincoln's famous words, the United States was a "house divided" by slavery, contradictory economic systems, conflicting values, and regional loyalties.

Lincoln's election as president in 1860 gave Southern "fire-eaters" the chance they had been waiting for. Eventually eleven states left the Union, determined to win their own independence, and formed the Confederate States of America. When Southern troops fired on a Union fort in South Carolina's Charleston harbor, war began.

The long Civil War (1861–1865) was the bloodiest conflict in all of American history, but in the end the South was decisively defeated and the Union preserved. The vastly superior population, industry, and transportation of the North placed the South at a great, probably fatal, disadvantage. Yet less obvious factors tied to morale and national purpose were also extremely important. The enormous gap between the slave-owning elite and the poor whites also made it impossible for the South to build effectively on the

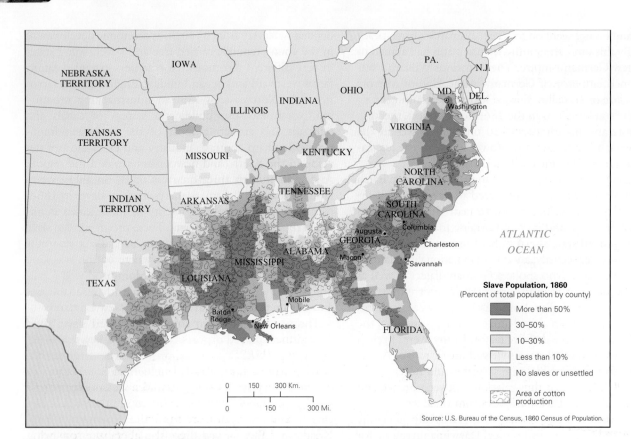

MAP 25.3 Slavery in the United States, 1860   This map illustrates the nation on the eve of the Civil War. Although many issues contributed to the developing opposition between North and South, slavery was the fundamental, enduring force that underlay all others. Lincoln's prediction, "I believe this government cannot endure permanently half slave and half free," tragically proved correct. (*Source: Carol Berkin et al.,* Making America: A History of the United States, *2d ed., p. 322. Copyright © 1999 by Houghton Mifflin Company. Reprinted with permission.*)

patriotism of 1861. As the war ground on, many ordinary whites felt that the burden was falling mainly on their shoulders as big planters resisted taxation and used loopholes to avoid the draft. Desertions from Southern armies mounted rapidly from 1863 on as soldiers became disillusioned.

In the North, by contrast, many people prospered during the war years. Enthusiasm remained high, and certain dominant characteristics of American life and national culture took shape. Powerful business corporations emerged, steadfastly supported by the Republican Party during and after the war. The **Homestead Act** of 1862, which gave western land to settlers, and the Thirteenth Amendment of 1865, which ended slavery, reinforced the concept of free labor taking its chances in a market economy. Finally, the success of Lincoln and the North in holding the Union together seemed to confirm that the "manifest destiny" of the United States was indeed to straddle a continent as a great world power. Thus a new American

nationalism grew out of the war to prevent the realization of Southern nationhood.

Online Study Center **Improve Your Grade**
Primary Source: "Four Score and Seven Years Ago . . ."

The Modernization of Russia and the Ottoman Empire

The Russian and the Ottoman empires also experienced profound political crises in the mid-nineteenth century. These crises were unlike those occurring in Italy and Germany, for neither Russia nor the Ottoman Empire aspired to build a single powerful state out of a jumble of principalities. Both empires were already vast multinational states, built on long traditions of military conquest and absolutist rule by elites from the dominant ethnic groups—the Russians and the Ottoman Turks. In the early nineteenth century these governing elites in both states were strongly opposed to representative government and national self-determination, and they continued to concentrate on absolutist rule and competition with other Great Powers.

For both states relentless power politics led to serious trouble. It became clear to the leaders of both empires that they had to embrace the process of **modernization,** defined narrowly and usefully as the changes that enable a country to compete effectively with the leading countries at a given time. This limited conception of modernization fits Russia after the Crimean War particularly well, and it helps explain developments in the Ottoman Empire.

• *What steps did Russia and the Ottoman Turks take toward modernization, and how successful were they?*

The "Great Reforms"

In the 1850s, Russia was a poor agrarian society with a rapidly growing population. Industry was little developed, and almost 90 percent of the population lived off the land. Agricultural techniques were backward, and serfdom was still the basic social institution. Bound to the lord on a hereditary basis, the peasant serf was little more than a slave. Serfs were obliged to furnish labor services or money payments as the lord saw fit. Moreover, the lord could choose freely among the serfs for army recruits, who had to serve for twenty-five years, and he could punish a serf with deportation to Siberia. Sexual exploitation of female serfs by their lords was common.

Serfdom had become the great moral and political issue for the government by the 1840s. Then the Crimean War of 1853 to 1856, arising out of a dispute with France over who should protect certain Christian shrines in the Ottoman Empire, brought crisis. Because the fighting was concentrated in the Crimean peninsula on the Black Sea, Russia's transportation network of rivers and wagons failed to supply the distant Russian armies adequately. France and Great Britain, aided by Sardinia and the Ottoman Empire, inflicted a humiliating defeat on Russia.

This military defeat marked a turning point in Russian history because it demonstrated that Russia had fallen behind the rapidly industrializing nations of western Europe in many areas. At the very least, Russia needed railroads, better armaments, and reorganization of the army if it was to maintain its international position. Moreover, the disastrous war had caused hardship and raised the specter of massive peasant rebellion. Reform of serfdom was imperative. Military disaster thus forced Alexander II

(r. 1855–1881) and his ministers along the path of rapid social change and general modernization.

The first and greatest of the reforms was the freeing of the serfs in 1861. Human bondage was abolished forever, and the emancipated peasants received, on average, about half of the land. Yet they had to pay fairly high prices for their land, and because the land was owned collectively, each peasant village was jointly responsible for the payments of all the families in the village. Collective ownership and responsibility made it very difficult for individual peasants to improve agricultural methods or leave their villages. Thus old patterns of behavior predominated, and the effects of reform were limited.

Most of the later reforms were also halfway measures. In 1864 the government established a new institution of local government, the **zemstvo.** Members of this local assembly were elected by a three-class system of towns, peasant villages, and noble landowners. A zemstvo executive council dealt with local problems. Russian liberals hoped that this reform would lead to an elected national parliament, but they were soon disappointed. The local zemstvo remained subordinate to the traditional bureaucracy and the local nobility. More successful was reform of the legal system, which established independent courts and equality before the law. Education and policies toward Russian Jews were also liberalized somewhat, and censorship was relaxed but not removed.

Until the twentieth century, Russia's greatest strides toward modernization were economic rather than political. Industry and transport, both so vital to the military, were transformed in two industrial surges. The first of these came after 1860. The government encouraged and subsidized private railway companies, and construction boomed. In 1860 the empire had only about 1,250 miles of railroads; by 1880 it had about 15,500 miles. The railroads enabled agricultural Russia to export grain and thus earn money for further industrialization. Industrial suburbs grew up around Moscow and St. Petersburg, and a class of modern factory workers began to take shape.

Industrial development strengthened Russia's military forces and gave rise to territorial expansion to the south and east. Imperial expansion greatly excited many ardent Russian nationalists and superpatriots, who became some of the government's most enthusiastic supporters. Industrial development also contributed mightily to the spread of Marxian thought and the transformation of the Russian revolutionary movement after 1890.

In 1881 Alexander II was assassinated by a small group of terrorists. The era of reform came to an abrupt end, for the new tsar, Alexander III (r. 1881–1894), was a determined reactionary. Nevertheless, economic modernization

The Fruits of Terrorism, 1881   In the late 1870s a small group of revolutionaries believed that killing the tsar could destroy the Russian state. Succeeding in blowing up the reforming Alexander II after several near misses, the five assassins, including one woman, were quickly caught and hanged. Russia entered an era of reaction and harsh authoritarian rule. *(Visual Connection Archive)*

sped forward in the massive industrial surge of the 1890s. Nationalism played a decisive role, as it had after the Crimean War. The key leader was Sergei Witte, the tough, competent minister of finance from 1892 to 1903. Inspired by the writings of Friedrich List (see pages 731–732), Witte believed that the harsh reality of industrial backwardness was threatening Russia's power and greatness.

Therefore, under Witte's leadership the government built state-owned railroads rapidly, doubling the network to thirty-five thousand miles by the end of the century. Witte established high protective tariffs to build Russian industry, and he put the country on the gold standard of the "civilized world" in order to strengthen Russian finances.

Witte's greatest innovation was to use the West to catch up with the West. He aggressively encouraged for-

eigners to build great factories in backward Russia, and this policy was brilliantly successful, especially in southern Russia. There, in eastern Ukraine, foreign capitalists and their engineers built an enormous and very modern steel and coal industry.[2] In 1900 peasants still constituted the great majority of the population, but a fiercely autocratic and independent Russia was industrializing and catching up with the advanced nations of the West.

The Revolution of 1905

Catching up partly meant vigorous territorial expansion, for this was the age of Western imperialism. By 1903 Russia had established a sphere of influence in Chinese Manchuria and was casting greedy eyes on northern Korea. When the diplomatic protests of equally imperialistic Japan were ignored, the Japanese launched a surprise attack in February 1904. To the amazement of self-confident Europeans, Japan scored repeated victories, and Russia was forced in September 1905 to accept a humiliating defeat.

As is often the case, military disaster abroad brought political upheaval at home. The business and professional classes had long wanted to match economic with political modernization. Their minimal goal was to turn the last of Europe's absolutist monarchies into a liberal, representative regime. Factory workers, strategically concentrated in the large cities, had all the grievances of early industrialization and were organized in a radical and still illegal labor movement. Peasants had gained little from the era of reforms and were suffering from poverty and overpopulation. At the same time, nationalist sentiment was emerging among the empire's minorities. The politically and culturally dominant ethnic Russians were only about 45 percent of the population, and by 1900 some intellectuals among the subject nationalities were calling for self-rule and autonomy. Separatist nationalism was strongest among the Poles and Ukrainians. With the army pinned down in Manchuria, all these currents of discontent converged in the **revolution of 1905.**

The beginning of the revolution pointed up the incompetence of the government. On a Sunday in January 1905, a massive crowd of workers and their families converged peacefully on the Winter Palace in St. Petersburg to present a petition to the tsar. Suddenly troops opened fire, killing and wounding hundreds. The **Bloody Sunday** massacre turned ordinary workers against the tsar and produced a wave of general indignation.

Outlawed political parties came out into the open, and by the summer of 1905 strikes, peasant uprisings, revolts among minority nationalities, and troop mutinies were sweeping the country. The revolutionary surge culminated in October 1905 in a great paralyzing general strike, which forced the government to capitulate. The tsar issued the **October Manifesto,** which granted full civil rights and promised a popularly elected Duma (parliament) with real legislative power. The manifesto split the opposition. Frightened middle-class leaders helped the government repress the uprising and survive as a constitutional monarchy.

On the eve of the opening of the first **Duma** in May 1906, the government issued the new constitution, the Fundamental Laws. The tsar retained great powers. The Duma, elected indirectly by universal male suffrage, and a largely appointive upper house could debate and pass laws, but the tsar had an absolute veto. As in Bismarck's Germany, the emperor appointed his ministers, who did not need to command a majority in the Duma.

The disappointed, predominately middle-class liberals, the largest group in the newly elected Duma, saw the Fundamental Laws as a step backward. Efforts to cooperate with the tsar's ministers soon broke down. After months of deadlock, the tsar dismissed the Duma. Thereupon he and his reactionary advisers unilaterally rewrote the electoral law so as to increase greatly the weight of the propertied classes at the expense of workers, peasants, and national minorities.

The new law had the intended effect. With landowners assured half the seats in the Duma, the government secured a loyal majority in 1907 and again in 1912. Thus armed, the tough, energetic chief minister, Peter Stolypin, pushed through important agrarian reforms designed to break down collective village ownership of land and encourage the more enterprising peasants—his "wager on the strong." In 1914, Russia was partially modernized, a conservative constitutional monarchy with a peasant-based but industrializing economy.

Decline and Reform in the Ottoman Empire

Although the Ottoman Empire began to decline slowly after reaching its high point of development under Suleiman the Magnificent in the sixteenth century, the Ottomans began in the eighteenth century to fall rapidly behind western Europe in science, industrial skill, and military technology. At the same time, Russia's powerful westernized army pushed southward, overrunning and occupying Ottoman provinces on the Danube River. The danger that the Great Powers of Europe would gradually conquer the Ottoman Empire and divide up its vast territories was real.

Caught up in the Napoleonic wars and losing more territory to Russia, the Ottomans were forced in 1816 to grant Serbia local autonomy. In 1830, the Greeks won their national independence, while French armies began their long and bloody conquest of the Arabic-speaking province of Algeria (see pages 776–777). French efforts to strip Algerians of their culture and identity were brutal and persistent, eventually resulting in one of Africa's most bitter anticolonial struggles after 1945.

Ottoman weakness reflected the decline of the sultan's "slave army," the so-called **janissary corps.** In the sixteenth century the Ottoman sultans levied an annual slave tax of one thousand to three thousand male children on the conquered Christian provinces in the Balkans. The boys and other slaves were raised in Turkey as Muslims, were trained to fight and administer, and joined the elite corps of the Ottoman infantry. With time, however, the janissaries became a corrupt and privileged hereditary caste. A transformation of the army was absolutely necessary to battle the Europeans more effectively, as well as to enhance the sultanate's authority within the empire.

The reform-minded Mahmud III (r. 1808–1839) proceeded cautiously, picking loyal officers and building up his dependable artillery corps. In 1826 his council ordered the janissaries to drill in the European manner. As expected, the janissaries revolted and charged the palace, where they were mowed down by the waiting artillery corps.

The destruction of the janissaries cleared the way for building a new army, but it came too late to stop the rise of Muhammad Ali, the Ottoman governor in Egypt (see

pages 853–854). In 1831, and again in 1839, his French-trained forces occupied the Ottoman provinces of Syria and then Iraq and appeared ready to depose Mahmud II. The Ottoman sultan survived, but only because the European powers forced Muhammad Ali to withdraw. The European powers, minus France, preferred a weak and dependent Ottoman state to a strong and revitalized Muslim entity under a dynamic leader such as Muhammad Ali.

Realizing their precarious position, liberal Ottoman statesmen launched in 1839 an era of radical reforms, which lasted with fits and starts until 1876 and culminated in a constitution and a short-lived parliament. Known as the **Tanzimat** (literally, regulations or orders), these reforms were designed to remake the empire on a

Pasha Halim Receiving Archduke Maximilian of Austria As this painting suggests, Ottoman leaders became well versed in European languages and culture. They also mastered the game of power politics, playing one European state off against another and securing the Ottoman Empire's survival. The black servants on the right may be slaves from Sudan. *(Miramare Palace Trieste/Dagli Orti/The Art Archive)*

western European model. New decrees called for the equality of Muslims, Christians, and Jews before the law and a modernized administration and military. New commercial laws allowed free importation of foreign goods and permitted foreign merchants to operate freely throughout the empire. Of great importance for later developments, growing numbers among the elite and the upwardly mobile embraced Western education and accepted secular values to some extent.

Intended to bring revolutionary modernization such as that experienced by Japan in the Meiji era (see pages 870–872), the Tanzimat permitted partial recovery but fell short of its goals for several reasons. First, the liberal reforms failed to halt the growth of nationalism among Christian subjects in the Balkans (see Chapter 29), which resulted in crises and defeats that undermined all reform efforts. Second, the Ottoman initiatives did not curtail the appetite of Western imperialism, which secured a stranglehold on the Ottoman economy.

Finally, equality before the law for all citizens and religious communities actually increased religious disputes, which were in turn exacerbated by the relentless interference of the European powers. This development embittered relations between the religious communities, distracted the government from its reform mission, and split Muslims into secularists and religious conservatives. These Islamic conservatives became the most dependable support of Sultan Abdülhamid (r. 1876–1909), who abandoned the model of European liberalism in his long and repressive reign.

The combination of declining international power and conservative tyranny eventually led to a powerful resurgence of the modernizing impulse among idealistic Turkish exiles in Europe and young army officers in Istanbul. These fervent patriots, the so-called **Young Turks,** seized power in the revolution of 1908, and they forced the sultan to implement reforms. Failing to stop the rising tide of anti-Ottoman nationalism in the Balkans, the Young Turks helped prepare the way for the birth of modern secular Turkey after the defeat and collapse of the Ottoman Empire in World War I (see pages 889–890).

The Responsive National State, 1871–1914

For central and western Europe, the unification of Italy and Germany by "blood and iron" marked the end of a dramatic period of nation building. After 1871 the heartland of Europe was organized into strong national states. Only on the borders of Europe—in Ireland and Russia, in Austria-Hungary and the Ottoman Empire—did subject peoples still strive for political unity and independence.

- *Why after 1871 did ordinary citizens feel a growing loyalty to their governments?*

General Trends

Despite some major differences between countries, European domestic politics after 1871 had a common framework, the firmly established national state. The common themes within that framework were the emergence of mass politics and growing mass loyalty toward the national state.

For good reason, ordinary people—the masses of an industrializing, urbanizing society—felt increasing loyalty to their governments. More people could vote. By 1914 universal male suffrage had become the rule rather than the exception. This development had as much psychological as political significance. Ordinary men were no longer denied the right to vote because they lacked wealth or education. They felt that they counted; they could influence the government to some extent. They were becoming "part of the system."

Women also began to demand the right to vote. The women's suffrage movement achieved its first success in the western United States, and by 1913 women could vote in twelve states. Europe, too, moved slowly in this direction. In 1914 Norway gave the vote to most women. Elsewhere, women such as the English Emmeline Pankhurst were very militant in their demands. They heckled politicians and held public demonstrations. These efforts generally failed before 1914, but they prepared the way for the triumph of the women's suffrage movement immediately after World War I.

As the right to vote spread, politicians and parties in national parliaments represented the people more responsively. The multiparty system prevailing in most countries meant that parliamentary majorities were built on shifting coalitions of different parties, and this gave individual parties leverage to obtain benefits for their supporters. Governments also passed laws to alleviate general problems, thereby acquiring greater legitimacy and appearing more worthy of support.

There was a less positive side to building support for strong nation-states after 1871. Governments found that they could manipulate national feeling to create a sense of unity and to divert attention away from underlying class conflicts. Conservative and moderate leaders found that workers who voted socialist would rally around the flag in a diplomatic crisis or cheer when distant territory of

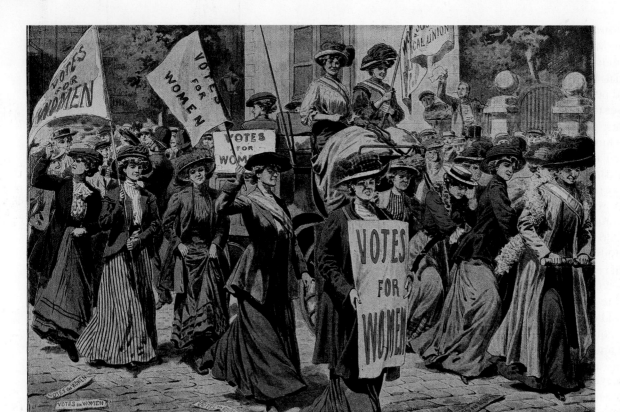

"Votes for Women!"   The long-simmering campaign for women's suffrage in England came to a rapid boil after 1903, as militants took to the streets, disrupted political meetings, and tried to storm Parliament. Manhandled by the police and often jailed, some activists responded by damaging public property and going on hunger strikes in prison. This 1908 illustration shows demonstrators giving a hero's welcome to Mary Leigh, the first suffragette imprisoned for property damage after she threw rocks through the windows of the prime minister's house. *(The Art Archive)*

doubtful value was seized in Africa or Asia (see Chapter 26). Therefore, after 1871 governing elites frequently used antiliberal and militaristic policies to help manage domestic conflicts, but at the expense of increasing the international tensions that erupted in 1914 in cataclysmic war and revolution (see Chapter 27).

In these same years some fanatics and demagogic political leaders also sought to build extreme nationalist movements by whipping up popular animosity toward imaginary enemies, especially the Jews. The growth of modern anti-Semitism after 1880 epitomized the most negative aspects of European nationalism before the First World War.

The German Empire

Politics in Germany after 1871 reflected many of the general developments. The new German Empire was a federal union of Prussia and twenty-four smaller states. Much of the everyday business of government was conducted by the separate states, but there was a strong national government with a chancellor—until 1890, Bismarck—and a popularly elected lower house, called the **Reichstag.** Although Bismarck refused to be bound by a parliamentary majority, he tried nonetheless to maintain one. This situation gave the political parties opportunities. Until 1878 Bismarck relied mainly on the National Liberals, who had rallied to him after 1866. They supported legislation useful for further economic and legal unification of the country.

Less wisely, they backed Bismarck's attack on the Catholic Church, the so-called **Kulturkampf,** or "struggle for civilization." Like Bismarck, the middle-class National Liberals were particularly alarmed by Pius IX's declaration of papal infallibility in 1870. That dogma seemed to ask German Catholics to put loyalty to their church above loyalty to their nation. Only in Protestant Prussia did the Kulturkampf have even limited success. Catholics throughout the country generally voted for the Catholic Center Party, which blocked passage of national laws hostile to the church. Finally, in 1878 Bismarck abandoned his attack. Indeed, he and the Catholic Center Party entered into an uneasy but mutually advantageous alliance. Their reasons for doing so were largely economic.

Bismarck moved to enact high tariffs on cheap grain from the United States, Canada, and Russia, against which less efficient European producers could not compete. This won over not only the Catholic Center, whose supporters were small farmers in western and southern Germany, but also the Protestant Junkers, who had large landholdings in the east. With the tariffs, then, Bismarck won Catholic and conservative support.

Bismarck had been looking for a way to increase taxes, and the solution he chose was higher tariffs. Many other governments acted similarly. The 1880s and 1890s saw a widespread return to protectionism. France, in particular, established very high tariffs to protect agriculture and industry, peasants and manufacturers, from foreign competition. Thus the German government and other governments responded effectively to a major economic problem and won greater loyalty. The general rise of protectionism in this period was also an outstanding example of the dangers of self-centered nationalism: new tariffs led to international name-calling and nasty trade wars.

As for socialism, Bismarck tried to stop its growth in Germany because he genuinely feared its revolutionary language and allegiance to a movement transcending the nation-state. In 1878, after two attempts on the life of William I by radicals (though not socialists), Bismarck used a carefully orchestrated national outcry to ram through the Reichstag a law that strictly controlled socialist meetings and publications and outlawed the Social Democratic Party, which was thereby driven underground. However, German socialists displayed a discipline and organization worthy of the Prussian army itself. Bismarck decided to try another tack.

Thus Bismarck's essentially conservative nation-state pioneered with social measures designed to win the support of working-class people. In 1883 he pushed through the Reichstag the first of several modern social security laws to help wage earners. The laws of 1883 and 1884 established national sickness and accident insurance; the law of 1889 established old-age pensions and retirement benefits. Henceforth sick, injured, and retired workers could look forward to some regular benefits from the state. This national social security system, paid for through compulsory contributions by wage earners and employers as well as grants from the state, was the first of its kind

anywhere. Bismarck's social security system did not wean workers from voting socialist, but it did give them a small stake in the system and protect them from some of the uncertainties of the complex urban industrial world. This enormously significant development was a product of political competition and government efforts to win popular support.

Online Study Center **Improve Your Grade**
Primary Source: The Welfare State Is Born

Increasingly, the great issues in German domestic politics were socialism and the Marxian Social Democratic Party. In 1890 the new emperor, the young, idealistic, and unstable William II (r. 1888–1918), opposed Bismarck's attempt to renew the law outlawing the Social Democratic Party. Eager to rule in his own right and to earn the support of the workers, William II forced Bismarck to resign. After the "dropping of the pilot," German foreign policy changed profoundly and mostly for the worse, but the government did pass new laws to aid workers and to legalize socialist political activity.

Yet William II was no more successful than Bismarck in getting workers to renounce socialism. Indeed, socialist ideas spread rapidly, and more and more Social Democrats were elected to the Reichstag in the 1890s. After opposing a colonial war in German Southwest Africa in 1906 that led to important losses in the general elections of 1907, the German Social Democratic Party broadened its base and adopted a more patriotic tone. In 1912 the party scored a great electoral victory, becoming the largest single party in the Reichstag. This victory shocked aristocrats and their wealthy conservative middle-class allies, heightening the fears of an impending socialist upheaval in both groups. Yet the "revolutionary" socialists were actually becoming less radical in Germany. In the years before World War I, the strength of socialist opposition to greater military spending and imperialist expansion declined substantially, for example. German socialists identified increasingly with the German state, and they concentrated on gradual social and political reform.

Republican France

Although Napoleon III's reign made some progress in reducing antagonisms between classes, the war with Prussia undid these efforts, and in 1871 France seemed hopelessly divided once again. The patriotic republicans who proclaimed the Third Republic in Paris after the military disaster at Sedan refused to admit defeat. They defended Paris with great heroism for weeks, living off rats and zoo animals until they were starved into submission by German armies in January 1871. When national elections then sent a large majority of conservatives and monarchists to the National Assembly and France's new leaders decided they had no choice but to surrender Alsace and Lorraine to Germany, the traumatized Parisians exploded in patriotic frustration and proclaimed the Paris Commune in March 1871. Vaguely radical, the leaders of the Commune wanted to govern Paris without interference from the conservative French countryside. The National Assembly, led by aging politician Adolphe Thiers, would hear none of it. The Assembly ordered the French army into Paris and brutally crushed the Commune. Twenty thousand people died in the fighting. As in June 1848, it was Paris against the provinces, French against French.

Out of this tragedy, France slowly formed a new national unity, achieving considerable stability before 1914.

How is one to account for this? Luck played a part. Until 1875 the monarchists in the "republican" National Assembly had a majority but could not agree who should be king. The compromise Bourbon candidate refused to rule except under the white flag of his ancestors—a completely unacceptable condition. In the meantime, Thiers's destruction of the radical Commune and his other firm measures showed the fearful provinces and the middle class that the Third Republic might be moderate and socially conservative. France therefore retained the republic, though reluctantly. As President Thiers cautiously said, this was "the government which divides us least."

Another stabilizing factor was the skill and determination of the moderate republican leaders in the early years. The most famous of these was Léon Gambetta, the son of an Italian grocer, a warm, easygoing, unsuccessful lawyer who had turned professional politician. By 1879 the great majority of members of both the upper and the lower houses of the National Assembly were republicans, and the Third Republic had firm foundations after almost a decade.

The moderate republicans sought to preserve their creation by winning the hearts and minds of the next generation. Trade unions were fully legalized, and France acquired a colonial empire. More important, a series of laws between 1879 and 1886 established free compulsory elementary education for both girls and boys. At the same time, they greatly expanded the state system of public tax-supported schools. In France and elsewhere the general expansion of public education served as a critical nation-building tool throughout the Western world in the late nineteenth century. In France most elementary and much secondary education had traditionally been in the parochial schools of the Catholic Church, which had long been hostile to republics and to much of secular life. Free compulsory elementary education in France became secular republican education.

Although the educational reforms of the 1880s disturbed French Catholics, many of them rallied to the republic in the 1890s. The limited acceptance of the modern world by the more liberal Pope Leo XIII (1878–1903) eased tensions between church and state. Unfortunately, the **Dreyfus affair** changed all that.

Captain Alfred Dreyfus Leaving an 1899 reconsideration of his original court martial, Dreyfus receives an insulting "guard of dishonor" from soldiers whose backs are turned. Top army leaders were determined to brand Dreyfus a traitor. (*Roger-Viollet/Getty Images*)

Alfred Dreyfus, a Jewish captain in the French army, was falsely accused and convicted of treason. His family never doubted his innocence and fought to reopen the case, enlisting the support of prominent republicans and intellectuals such as novelist Emile Zola. In 1898 and 1899, the case split France apart. On one side was the army, which had manufactured evidence against Dreyfus, joined by anti-Semites and most of the Catholic establishment. On the other side stood the civil libertarians and most of the more radical republicans.

Online Study Center **Improve Your Grade**
Primary Source: "J'Accuse" the French Army

This battle, which eventually led to Dreyfus's being declared innocent, revived republican feeling against the church. Between 1901 and 1905, the government severed all ties between the state and the Catholic Church after centuries of close relations. The salaries of priests and bishops were no longer paid by the government, and all churches were given to local committees of lay Catholics. Catholic schools were put on their own financially and soon lost a third of their students. The state school system's power of indoctrination was greatly strengthened. In France only the growing socialist movement, with its very different and thoroughly secular ideology, stood in opposition to patriotic, republican nationalism.

Great Britain and Ireland

Britain in the late nineteenth century has often been seen as a shining example of peaceful and successful political evolution, where an effective two-party parliament skillfully guided the country from classical liberalism to full-fledged democracy with hardly a misstep. This view of Great Britain is not so much wrong as it is incomplete. After the right to vote was granted to males of the solid middle class in 1832, opinion leaders and politicians wrestled with the uncertainties of a further expansion of the franchise. In 1867 Benjamin Disraeli and the Conservatives extended the vote to all middle-class males and the best-paid workers in the Second Reform Bill, in order to broaden the Conservative Party's traditional base of aristocratic and landed support. After 1867 English political parties and electoral campaigns became more modern, and the "lower orders" appeared to vote as responsibly as their "betters." Hence the Third Reform Bill of 1884 gave the vote to almost every adult male.

While the House of Commons was drifting toward democracy, the House of Lords was content to slumber nobly. Between 1901 and 1910, however, that bastion of aristocratic conservatism tried to reassert itself. Acting as

supreme court of the land, it ruled against labor unions in two important decisions. And after the Liberal Party came to power in 1906, the Lords vetoed several measures passed by the Commons, including the so-called **People's Budget,** which was designed to increase spending on social welfare services. The Lords finally capitulated, as they had done in 1832, when the king threatened to create enough new peers to pass the bill.

Aristocratic conservatism yielded to popular democracy once and for all. The result was that extensive social welfare measures, slow to come to Great Britain, were passed in a spectacular rush between 1906 and 1914. During those years, the Liberal Party, inspired by the fiery Welshman David Lloyd George (1863–1945), substantially raised taxes on the rich as part of the People's Budget. This income helped the government pay for national health insurance, unemployment benefits, old-age pensions, and a host of other social measures. The state was integrating the urban masses socially as well as politically.

This record of accomplishment was only part of the story, however. On the eve of World War I, the unanswered question of Ireland brought Great Britain to the brink of civil war. The terrible Irish famine fueled an Irish revolutionary movement. Thereafter, the English slowly granted concessions, such as the abolition of the privileges of the Anglican Church and rights for Irish peasants. Liberal prime minister William Gladstone (1809–1898), who had proclaimed twenty years earlier that "my mission is to pacify Ireland," introduced bills to give Ireland self-government in 1886 and in 1893. They failed to pass. After two decades of relative quiet, Irish nationalists in the British Parliament saw their chance. They supported the Liberals in their battle for the People's Budget and received a home-rule bill for Ireland in return.

Thus Ireland, the emerald isle, was on the brink of achieving self-government. Yet Ireland was composed of two peoples. As much as the Irish Catholic majority in the southern counties wanted home rule, precisely that much did the Irish Protestants of the northern counties of Ulster come to oppose it. Motivated by the accumulated fears and hostilities of generations, the Protestants of Ulster refused to submerge themselves in a Catholic Ireland, just as Irish Catholics had refused to submit to a Protestant Britain.

The Ulsterites vowed to resist home rule in northern Ireland. By December 1913 they had raised 100,000 armed volunteers, and they were supported by much of English public opinion. Thus in 1914 the Liberals in the House of Lords introduced a compromise home-rule bill that did not apply to the northern counties. This bill,

"No Home Rule" Posters like this one helped to foment pro-British, anti-Catholic sentiment in the northern Irish counties of Ulster before the First World War. The rifle raised defiantly and the accompanying rhyme are a thinly veiled threat of armed rebellion and civil war. *(Reproduced with the kind permission of the Trustees of the National Museums & Galleries of Northern Ireland. Photograph © Ulster Museum, Belfast)*

which openly betrayed promises made to Irish nationalists, was rejected, and in September the original home-rule bill was passed but simultaneously suspended for the duration of the hostilities—the momentous Irish question had been overtaken by an earth-shattering world war in August 1914.

Irish developments illustrated once again the power of national feeling and national movements in the nineteenth century. Moreover, they were proof that governments could not elicit greater loyalty unless they could capture and control that elemental current of national

feeling. Though Great Britain had much going for it—power, Parliament, prosperity—none of these availed in the face of the conflicting nationalisms created by Catholics and Protestants in northern Ireland. Similarly, progressive Sweden was powerless to stop the growth of the Norwegian national movement, which culminated in Norway's breaking away from Sweden and becoming a fully independent nation in 1905. In this light, one can also see how hopeless was the case of the Ottoman Empire in Europe in the later nineteenth century. It was only a matter of time before the Serbs, Bulgarians, and Romanians would break away, and they did.

The Austro-Hungarian Empire

The dilemma of conflicting nationalisms in Ireland also helps one appreciate how desperate the situation in the Austro-Hungarian Empire had become by the early twentieth century. In 1849 Magyar nationalism had driven Hungarian patriots to declare an independent Hungarian republic, which was savagely crushed by Russian and Austrian armies (see page 772). Throughout the 1850s, Hungary was ruled as a conquered territory, and Emperor Francis Joseph and his bureaucracy tried hard to centralize the state and Germanize the language and culture of the different nationalities.

Then in the wake of defeat by Prussia in 1866, a weakened Austria was forced to strike a compromise and establish the so-called dual monarchy. The empire was divided in two, and the nationalistic Magyars gained virtual independence for Hungary. Henceforth each half of the empire agreed to deal with its own "barbarians"—its own minorities—as it saw fit. The two states were joined only by a shared monarch and common ministries for finance, defense, and foreign affairs.

In Austria ethnic Germans were only one-third of the population, and in 1895 many Germans saw their traditional dominance threatened by Czechs, Poles, and other Slavs. A particularly emotional issue in the Austrian parliament was the language used in government and elementary education at the local level. From 1900 to 1914 the parliament was so divided that ministries generally could not obtain a majority and ruled instead by decree. Efforts by both conservatives and socialists to defuse national antagonisms by stressing economic issues that cut across ethnic lines were largely unsuccessful.

In Hungary the Magyar nobility in 1867 restored the constitution of 1848 and used it to dominate both the Magyar peasantry and the minority populations until 1914. Only the wealthiest one-fourth of adult males had the right to vote, making the parliament the creature of the Magyar elite. Laws promoting the use of the Magyar (Hungarian) language in schools and government were rammed through and bitterly resented, especially by the Croatians and Romanians. While Magyar extremists campaigned loudly for total separation from Austria, the radical leaders of the subject nationalities dreamed in turn of independence from Hungary. Unlike most major countries, which harnessed nationalism to strengthen the state after 1871, the Austro-Hungarian Empire was progressively weakened and destroyed by it.

Jewish Emancipation and Modern Anti-Semitism

Revolutionary changes in political principles and the triumph of the nation-state brought equally revolutionary changes in Jewish life in western and central Europe. Beginning in France in 1791, Jews gradually gained their civil rights, although the process was slow and uneven. The decisive turning point came in 1848, when Jews formed part of the revolutionary vanguard in Vienna and Berlin and the Frankfurt Assembly endorsed full rights for German Jews. Important gains in 1848 survived the conservative reaction, and throughout the 1850s and 1860s liberals in Austria, Italy, and Prussia pressed successfully for legal equality. In 1871 the constitution of the new German Empire consolidated the process of Jewish emancipation in central Europe. It abolished all restrictions on Jewish marriage, choice of occupation, place of residence, and property ownership. Exclusion from government employment and discrimination in social relations remained. However, according to one leading historian, by 1871 "it was widely accepted in Central Europe that the gradual disappearance of anti-Jewish prejudice was inevitable."[3]

The process of emancipation presented Jews with challenges and opportunities. Traditional Jewish occupations, such as court financial agent, village moneylender, and peddler, were undermined by free-market reforms, but careers in business, the professions, and the arts were opening to Jewish talent. Many Jews responded energetically and successfully. Active in finance and railroad building, European Jews excelled in wholesale and retail trade, consumer industries, journalism, medicine, and law. By 1871 a majority of Jewish people in western and central Europe had improved their economic situation and entered the middle classes. Most Jewish people also identified strongly with their respective nation-states and with good reason saw themselves as patriotic citizens.

Vicious anti-Semitism reappeared after the stock market crash of 1873, beginning in central Europe. Drawing on long traditions of religious intolerance, ghetto exclusion, and periodic anti-Jewish riots and expulsions, this anti-Semitism was also a modern development. It built on the general reaction against liberalism and its economic and political policies. Modern anti-Semitism whipped up resentment against Jewish achievement and Jewish "financial control," while fanatics claimed that the Jewish race (rather than the Jewish religion) posed a biological threat to the German people. Anti-Semitic beliefs were particularly popular among conservatives, extremist nationalists, and people who felt threatened by Jewish competition, such as small shopkeepers, officeworkers, and professionals.

Anti-Semites also created modern political parties to attack and degrade Jews. In 1893, the prewar electoral high

Edmond de Rothschild Visits Palestine Born into the French branch of modern Europe's most famous banking family, Baron Edmond de Rothschild played an important role in early Jewish settlements in the Ottoman province of Palestine. Beginning in the 1880s, Rothschild purchased large tracts of land from Arab landowners, and on several occasions he visited the Jewish colonists that he continued to support. Seen here in a long coat on a Turkish train, he is flanked by Ottoman officials. *(Courtesy, Central Zionist Archive, Jerusalem)*

point in Germany, small anti-Semitic parties secured 2.9 percent of the votes cast. However, in Austrian Vienna in the early 1890s, Karl Lueger and his "Christian socialists" won striking electoral victories, spurring Theodor Herzl to turn from German nationalism and advocate political **Zionism** and the creation of a Jewish state. (See the feature "Individuals in Society: Theodor Herzl.") Lueger, the popular mayor of Vienna from 1897 to 1910, combined fierce anti-Semitic rhetoric with municipal ownership of basic services, and he appealed especially to the German-speaking lower middle class—and an unsuccessful young artist named Adolf Hitler.

Before 1914 anti-Semitism was most oppressive in eastern Europe, where Jews also suffered from terrible poverty. In the Russian empire, where there was no Jewish emancipation and 4 million of Europe's 7 million Jewish people lived in 1880, officials used anti-Semitism to channel popular discontent away from the government and onto the Jewish minority. Russian Jews were denounced as foreign exploiters who corrupted national traditions, and in 1881–1882 a wave of violent pogroms commenced in southern Russia. The police and the army stood aside for days while peasants looted and destroyed Jewish property. Official harassment continued in the following decades, and quotas were placed on Jewish residency, education, and participation in the professions. As a result, some Russian Jews turned toward self-emancipation and the vision of a Zionist settlement in Palestine. Large numbers also emigrated to western Europe and the United States. About 2.75 million Jews left eastern Europe between 1881 and 1914.

Online Study Center **Improve Your Grade**
Primary Source: A Russian Zionist Makes the Case for a Jewish Homeland

Marxism and the Socialist Movement

Nationalism served, for better or worse, as a new unifying principle. But what about socialism? Socialist parties, which were generally Marxian parties dedicated to an international proletarian revolution, grew rapidly in these years. Did this mean that national states had failed to gain the support of workers? Certainly, many prosperous and conservative citizens were greatly troubled by the socialist movement. And numerous historians have portrayed the years before 1914 as a time of increasing conflict between revolutionary socialism, on the one hand, and a nationalist alliance of the conservative aristocracy and the prosperous middle class, on the other.

● *Why did the socialist movement grow, and how revolutionary was it?*

The Socialist International

Socialism appealed to large numbers of workingmen and workingwomen in the late nineteenth century, and the growth of socialist parties after 1871 was phenomenal. (See the feature "Listening to the Past: The Making of a Socialist" on pages 844–845.) Neither Bismarck's antisocialist laws nor his extensive social security system checked the growth of the German Social Democratic Party, which espoused the Marxian ideology. By 1912 it had millions of followers and was the largest party in the Reichstag. Socialist parties also grew in other countries, though nowhere else with such success. In 1883 Russian exiles in Switzerland founded the Russian Social Democratic Party, which grew rapidly after 1890 despite internal disputes. In France various socialist parties re-emerged in the 1880s after the carnage of the Paris Commune. They were finally unified in 1905 in an increasingly powerful Marxian party called the French Section of the Workers International. Belgium and Austria-Hungary also had strong socialist parties.

As the name of the French party suggests, Marxian socialist parties were eventually linked together in an international organization. As early as 1848, Marx had laid out his intellectual system in *The Communist Manifesto* (see pages 757–758). He had declared that "the working men have no country," and he had urged proletarians of all nations to unite against their governments. Joining the flood of radicals and republicans who fled continental Europe for England and America after the unsuccessful revolutions of 1848, Marx settled in London. Poor and depressed, he lived on his meager earnings as a journalist and on the gifts of his friend Friedrich Engels. Marx never stopped thinking of revolution. Digging deeply into economics and history, he concluded that revolution follows economic crisis and tried to prove this in his greatest theoretical work, *Capital* (1867).

The bookish Marx also excelled as a practical organizer. In 1864 he played an important role in founding the First International of socialists—the International Working Men's Association. In the following years, he battled successfully to control the organization and used its annual meetings as a means of spreading his realistic, "scientific" doctrines of inevitable socialist revolution. Then Marx enthusiastically embraced the passionate, vaguely radical patriotism of the Paris Commune and its terrible conflict with the French National Assembly as a

Individuals in Society

Theodor Herzl

In September 1897, only days after his vision and energy had called into being the First Zionist Congress in Basel, Switzerland, Theodor Herzl (1860–1904) assessed the results in his diary: "If I were to sum up the Congress in a word—which I shall take care not to publish—it would be this: At Basel I founded the Jewish state. If I said this out loud today I would be greeted by universal laughter. In five years perhaps, and certainly in fifty years, everyone will perceive it."* Herzl's buoyant optimism, which so often carried him forward, was prophetic. Leading the Zionist movement until his death at age forty-four in 1904, Herzl guided the first historic steps toward modern Jewish political nationhood and the creation of Israel in 1948.

Theodor Herzl was born in Budapest, Hungary, into an upper-middle-class, German-speaking Jewish family. When Herzl was eighteen, his family moved to Vienna, where he studied law. As a university student, he soaked up the liberal beliefs of most well-to-do Viennese Jews, who also championed the assimilation of German culture. Wrestling with his nonreligious Jewishness and his strong pro-German feeling, Herzl embraced German nationalism and joined a German dueling fraternity. There he discovered that full acceptance required openly anti-Semitic attitudes and a repudiation of all things Jewish. This Herzl could not tolerate, and he resigned. After receiving his law degree, he embarked on a literary career. In 1889 Herzl married into a wealthy Viennese Jewish family, but he and his socialite wife were mismatched and never happy together.

Herzl achieved considerable success as both a journalist and a playwright. His witty comedies focused on the bourgeoisie, including Jewish millionaires trying to live like aristocrats. Accepting many German stereotypes, Herzl sometimes depicted eastern Jews as uneducated and grasping. But as a dedicated, highly educated liberal, he mainly believed that the Jewish shortcomings he perceived were the results of age-old persecution and would disappear through education and assimilation. Herzl also took a growing pride in Jewish steadfastness in the face of victimization and suffering. He savored memories of his early Jewish education and going with his father to the synagogue.

The emergence of modern anti-Semitism shocked Herzl, as it did many acculturated Jewish Germans. Moving to Paris in 1891 as the correspondent for Vienna's leading liberal newspaper, Herzl studied politics and pondered recent historical developments. He then came to a bold conclusion, published in 1896 as *The Jewish State: An Attempt at a Modern Solution to the Jewish Question.* According to Herzl, Jewish assimilation had failed, and attempts to combat anti-Semitism would never succeed. Only by building an independent Jewish state could the Jewish people achieve dignity and renewal. As recent scholarship shows, Herzl developed his political nationalism, or Zionism, before the anti-Jewish agitation accompanying the Dreyfus affair, which only strengthened his faith in his analysis.

Theodor Herzl.
(Library of Congress)

Generally rebuffed by skeptical Jewish elites in western and central Europe, Herzl turned for support to youthful idealists and the poor Jewish masses. He became an inspiring man of action, rallying the delegates to the annual Zionist congresses, directing the growth of the worldwide Zionist organization, and working himself to death. Herzl also understood that national consciousness required powerful emotions and symbols, such as a Jewish flag. Flags build nations, he said, because people "live and die for a flag."

Putting the Zionist vision before non-Jews and world public opinion, Herzl believed in international diplomacy and political agreements. He traveled constantly to negotiate with European rulers and top officials, seeking their support in securing territory for a Jewish state, usually in the Ottoman Empire. Aptly described by an admiring contemporary as "the first Jewish statesman since the destruction of Jerusalem," Herzl proved most successful in Britain. He paved the way for the 1917 Balfour Declaration, which solemnly pledged British support for a "Jewish homeland" in Palestine.

Questions for Analysis

1. Describe Theodor Herzl's background and early beliefs. Do you see a link between Herzl's early German nationalism and his later Zionism?
2. How did Herzl work as a leader to turn his Zionist vision into a reality?

*Quotes are from Theodor Herzl, *The Diaries of Theodor Herzl,* trans. and ed. with an introduction by Marvin Lowenthal (New York: Grosset & Dunlap, 1962), pp. 224, 22, xxi.

Online Study Center **Improve Your Grade**
Going Beyond Individuals in Society

giant step toward socialist revolution. This impetuous action frightened many of his early supporters, especially the more moderate British labor leaders. The First International collapsed.

Yet international proletarian solidarity remained an important objective for Marxists. In 1889, as the individual parties in different countries grew stronger, socialist leaders came together to form the Second International, which lasted until 1914. The International was only a federation of national socialist parties, but it had a great psychological impact. Every three years, delegates from the different parties met to interpret Marxian doctrines and plan coordinated action. May 1 (May Day) was declared an annual international one-day strike, a day of marches and demonstrations. A permanent executive for the International was established. Many feared and many others rejoiced in the growing power of socialism and the Second International.

Unions and Revisionism

Was socialism really radical and revolutionary in these years? On the whole, it was not. Indeed, as socialist parties grew and attracted large numbers of members, they looked more and more toward gradual change and steady improvement for the working class and less and less toward revolution. The mainstream of European socialism became militantly moderate; that is, socialists increasingly combined radical rhetoric with sober action.

Workers themselves were progressively less inclined to follow radical programs. There were several reasons for this. As workers gained the right to vote and to partici-

"Greetings from the May Day Festival"   Workers participated enthusiastically in the annual one-day strike on May 1 to honor internationalist socialist solidarity, as this postcard from a happy woman visitor to her cousin suggests. Speeches, picnics, and parades were the order of the day, and workers celebrated their respectability and independent culture. Picture postcards developed with railroads and mass travel. *(akg-images)*

pate politically in the nation-state, they focused their attention more on elections than on revolutions. And as workers won real, tangible benefits, this furthered the process. Workers were also not immune to patriotic education and indoctrination during military service, and many responded positively to drum-beating parades and aggressive foreign policy as they loyally voted for socialists. Nor were workers a unified social group.

Perhaps most important of all, workers' standard of living rose gradually but substantially after 1850 as the promise of the Industrial Revolution was at least partially realized. In Great Britain, for example, workers could buy almost twice as much with their wages in 1906 as in 1850, and most of the increase came after 1870. Workers experienced similar gradual increases in most continental countries after 1850, though much less strikingly in late-developing Russia. Improvement in the standard of living was much more than merely a matter of higher wages. The quality of life improved dramatically in urban areas. For all these reasons, workers tended more and more to become militantly moderate: they demanded gains, but they were less likely to take to the barricades in pursuit of them.

The growth of labor unions reinforced this trend toward moderation. In the early stages of industrialization, modern unions were generally prohibited by law. A famous law of the French Revolution had declared all guilds and unions illegal in the name of "liberty" in 1791. In Great Britain, attempts by workers to unite were considered criminal conspiracies after 1799. Other countries had similar laws, and these obviously hampered union development. In France, for example, about two hundred workers were imprisoned each year between 1825 and 1847 for taking part in illegal combinations. Unions were considered subversive bodies, only to be hounded and crushed.

From this sad position workers struggled to escape. Great Britain led the way in 1824 and 1825 when unions won the right to exist but (generally) not the right to strike. After the collapse of Robert Owen's attempt to form one big union in the 1830s (see page 741), new and more practical kinds of unions appeared. Limited primarily to highly skilled workers such as machinists and carpenters, the "new model unions" avoided both radical politics and costly strikes. Instead, their sober, respectable leaders concentrated on winning better wages and hours for their members through collective bargaining and compromise. This approach helped pave the way to full acceptance in Britain in the 1870s, when unions won the right to strike without being held legally liable for the financial damage inflicted on employers. After 1890 unions for unskilled workers developed, and between 1901 and 1906 the legal position of British unions was further strengthened.

Germany was the most industrialized, socialized, and unionized continental country by 1914. German unions were not granted important rights until 1869, and until the antisocialist law was repealed in 1890, they were frequently harassed by the government as socialist fronts. Nor were socialist leaders particularly interested in union activity, believing as they did in the iron law of low wages and the need for political revolution. The result was that as late as 1895, there were only about 270,000 union members in a male industrial workforce of nearly 8 million. Then, with German industrialization still storming ahead and almost all legal harassment eliminated, union membership skyrocketed, reaching roughly 3 million in 1912.

This great expansion both reflected and influenced the changing character of German unions. Increasingly, unions in Germany focused on bread-and-butter issues—wages, hours, working conditions—rather than on the dissemination of pure socialist doctrine. Genuine collective bargaining, long opposed by socialist intellectuals as a "sellout," was officially recognized as desirable by the German Trade Union Congress in 1899. When employers proved unwilling to bargain, a series of strikes forced them to change their minds.

Between 1906 and 1913, successful collective bargaining gained a prominent place in German industrial relations. In 1913 alone, over ten thousand collective bargaining agreements affecting 1.25 million workers were signed. Gradual improvement, not revolution, was becoming the primary goal of the German trade-union movement.

The German trade unions and their leaders were in fact, if not in name, thoroughgoing revisionists. **Revisionism**—that most awful of sins in the eyes of militant Marxists in the twentieth century—was an effort by various socialists to update Marxian doctrines to reflect the realities of the time. Thus the socialist Edward Bernstein (1850–1932) argued in 1899 in his *Evolutionary Socialism* that Marx's predictions of ever-greater poverty for workers and ever-greater concentration of wealth in ever-fewer hands had been proved false. Therefore, Bernstein suggested, socialists should reform their doctrines and tactics. They should combine with other progressive forces to win gradual evolutionary gains for workers through legislation, unions, and further economic development. These views were denounced as heresy by the German Social Democratic Party and later by the entire Second International. Yet the revisionist, gradualist approach continued to gain the tacit acceptance of many German socialists, particularly in the trade unions.

Moderation found followers elsewhere. In France the great socialist leader Jean Jaurès (1859–1914) formally repudiated revisionist doctrines in order to establish a unified socialist party, but he remained at heart a gradualist and optimistic secular humanist. Questions of revolution split Russian Marxists.

Socialist parties before 1914 had clear-cut national characteristics. Russians and socialists in the Austro-Hungarian Empire tended to be the most radical. The German party talked revolution and practiced reformism, greatly influenced by its enormous trade-union movement. The French party talked revolution and tried to practice it, un-restrained by a trade-union movement that was both very weak and very radical. In England the socialist but non-Marxian Labour Party, reflecting the well-established union movement, was formally committed to gradual reform. In Spain and Italy, Marxian socialism was very weak. There anarchism, seeking to smash the state rather than the bourgeoisie, dominated radical thought and action.

In short, socialist policies and doctrines varied from country to country. Socialism itself was to a large extent "nationalized" behind the imposing façade of international unity. This helps explain why when war came in 1914, almost all socialist leaders supported their governments.

Chapter Summary

Online Study Center   **ACE the Test**

- *How in France did Napoleon III seek to reconcile popular and conservative forces in an authoritarian nation-state?*
- *How did the process of unification in Italy and Germany create conservative nation-states?*
- *In what ways did the United States experience the full drama of nation building?*
- *What steps did Russia and the Ottoman Turks take toward modernization, and how successful were they?*
- *Why after 1871 did ordinary citizens feel a growing loyalty to their governments?*
- *Why did the socialist movement grow, and how revolutionary was it?*

After 1850, Western society became nationalistic as well as urban and industrial. Conservative monarchical governments, recovering from the revolutionary trauma of 1848, learned to remodel early so as to build stronger states with greater popular support. Napoleon III in France led the way, combining authoritarian rule with economic prosperity and positive measures for the poor. In Italy, Cavour joined traditional diplomacy with national revolt in the north and Garibaldi's revolutionary patriotism in the south, expanding the liberal Sardinian monarchy into a conservative nation-state. Bismarck also combined traditional statecraft with national feeling to expand the power of Prussia and its king in a new German Empire.

In the midcentury years, the United States, Russia, and the Ottoman Empire also experienced crises of nation building. The United States overcame sectionalism in a war that prevented an independent South and seemed to confirm America's destiny as a great world power. In autocratic Russia, defeat in the Crimean War led to the emancipation of the serfs, economic modernization with railroad building and industrialization, and limited political reform. The Ottoman Empire also sought to modernize to protect the state, but it was considerably less successful.

Nation-states gradually enlisted widespread popular support, providing men and women with a greater sense of belonging and giving them specific political, social, and economic improvements. Even the growing socialist movement became increasingly national in orientation, gathering strength as a champion of working-class interests in domestic politics. Yet even though nationalism served to unite peoples, it also drove them apart—obvious not only in the United States before the Civil War and in Austria-Hungary and Ireland, but also throughout Europe. There the universal national faith, which usually reduced social tensions within states, promoted a bitter, almost Darwinian, competition between states and thus threatened the progress and unity it had helped to build, as we shall see in Chapters 26 and 27.

Key Terms

Red Shirts
Zollverein
Homestead Act
modernization
zemstvo
revolution of 1905
Bloody Sunday
October Manifesto
Duma

janissary corps
Tanzimat
Young Turks
Reichstag
Kulturkampf
Dreyfus affair
People's Budget
Zionism
revisionism

Online Study Center **Improve Your Grade** Flashcards

Suggested Reading

Berend, Ivan T. *History Derailed: Central and Eastern Europe in the Long Nineteenth Century.* 2003. Focuses on industrialization and its consequences.

Blanning, T. C. W. *Oxford Illustrated History of Modern Europe.* 1996. A heavily illustrated text that provides useful surveys of the entire nineteenth century.

Boyce, D. George. *Nationalism in Ireland*, 2d ed. 1991. Provides an excellent account of the Irish struggle for nationhood.

Clyman, Toby W., and Judith Vowles, eds. *Russia Through Women's Eyes: Autobiographies from Tsarist Russia.* 1999. An eye-opening collection detailing women's experiences in Russia.

Fink, Carole. *Defending the Rights of Others: The Great Powers, the Jews, and the International Protection, 1878–1938.* 2004. Skilled consideration of the cruelty and tragedy of ethnic conflict and minority oppression.

Geary, Dick, ed. *Labour and Socialist Movements in Europe Before 1914.* 1989. An excellent collection that examines labor movements in several different countries.

Hobsbawm, Eric. *The Age of Empire, 1875–1914.* 1987. An outstanding interpretative work.

Kitchen, Martin. *The Cambridge Illustrated History of Germany.* 1996. Features handsome pictures and a readable text.

Quataert, Donald. *The Ottoman Empire, 1700–1900*, 2d ed. 2005. An excellent introduction.

Ridley, Jasper. *Phoenix: Garibaldi.* 2001. A thorough study of the world-renowned revolutionary nationalist.

Rogger, Hans. *Russia in the Age of Modernisation and Revolution, 1881–1917.* 1983. A fine study on Russian development that includes an excellent bibliography.

Schulze, Hagen, and William E. Yuill. *States, Nations and Nationalism: From the Middle Ages to the Present.* 1996. An important study that explores the resurgence of European nationalism since the fall of communism.

Slezkine, Yuri. *The Jewish Century.* 2004. A brilliant interpretation of Jewish achievement in the modern era.

Tombs, Robert. *France, 1814–1914.* 1996. An impressive survey with a useful bibliography.

Vital, David. *A People Apart: The Jews in Europe, 1789–1939.* 1999. An engaging and judicious survey.

Notes

1. H. Schulze, *States, Nations and Nationalism: From the Middle Ages to the Present* (Oxford: Blackwell, 1994), pp. 222–223, 246–247.
2. J. McKay, *Pioneers for Profit: Foreign Entrepreneurship and Russian Industrialization, 1885–1913* (Chicago: University of Chicago Press, 1970), pp. 112–157.
3. R. Seltzer, *Jewish People, Jewish Thought: The Jewish Experience in History* (New York: Macmillan, 1980), p. 533.

The Making of a Socialist

Nationalism and socialism appeared locked in bitter competition in Europe before 1914, but they actually complemented each other in many ways. Both faiths were secular as opposed to religious, and both fostered political awareness. A working person who became interested in politics and developed nationalist beliefs might well convert to socialism at a later date.

This was the case for Adelheid Popp (1869–1939), a self-taught workingwoman who became an influential socialist leader. Born into a desperately poor working-class family in Vienna and remembering only a "hard and gloomy childhood," she was forced by her parents to quit school at age ten to begin full-time work. She struggled with low-paying piecework for years before she landed a solid factory job, as she recounts in the following selection from her widely read autobiography.

Always an avid reader, Popp became the editor of a major socialist newspaper for German working-women. She then told her life story so that all workingwomen might share her truth: "Socialism could change and strengthen others, as it did me."

[Finally] I found work again; I took everything that was offered me in order to show my willingness to work, and I passed through much. But at last things became better. [At age fifteen] I was recommended to a great factory which stood in the best repute. Three hundred girls and about fifty men were employed. I was put in a big room where sixty women and girls were at work. Against the windows stood twelve tables, and at each sat four girls. We had to sort the goods which had been manufactured, others had to count them, and a third set had to brand on them the mark of the firm. We worked from 7 A.M. to 7 P.M. We had an hour's rest at noon, half-an-hour in the afternoon. . . . I had never yet been paid so much. . . .

I seemed to myself to be almost rich. . . . [Yet] from the women of this factory one can judge how sad and full of deprivation is the lot of a factory worker. In none of the neighbouring factories were the wages so high; we were envied everywhere. Parents considered themselves fortunate if they could get their daughters of fourteen in there on leaving school. . . . And even here, in this paradise, all were badly nourished. Those who stayed at the factory for the dinner hour would buy themselves for a few pennies a sausage or the leavings of a cheese shop. . . . In spite of all the diligence and economy, every one was poor, and trembled at the thought of losing her work. All humbled themselves, and suffered the worst injustice from the foremen, not to risk losing this good work, not to be without food. . . .

I did not only read novels and tales; I had begun . . . to read the classics and other good books. I also began to take an interest in public events. . . . I was not democratically inclined. I was full of enthusiasm then for emperors, and kings and highly placed personages played no small part in my fancies. . . . I bought myself a strict Catholic paper, that criticised very adversely the workers' movement, which was attracting notice. Its aim was to educate in a patriotic and religious direction. . . . I took the warmest interest in the events that occurred in the royal families, and I took the death of the Crown Prince of Austria so much to heart that I wept a whole day. . . . Political events [also] held me in suspense. The possibility of a war with Russia roused my patriotic enthusiasm. I saw my brother already returning from the battlefield covered with glory. . . .

When a particularly strong anti-Semitic feeling was noticeable in political life, I sympathised with it for a time. A broad sheet, "How Israel Attained

Power and Sovereignty over all the Nations of the Earth," fascinated me. . . .

About this time an Anarchist group was active. Some mysterious murders which had taken place were ascribed to the Anarchists, and the police made use of them to oppress the rising workmen's movement. . . . I followed the trial of the Anarchists with passionate sympathy. I read all the speeches, and because, as always happens, Social Democrats, whom the authorities really wanted to attack, were among the accused, I learned their views. I became full of enthusiasm. Every single Social Democrat . . . seemed to me a hero. . . .

There was unrest among the workers . . . and demonstrations of protest followed. When these were repeated the military entered the "threatened" streets. . . . In the evenings I rushed in the greatest excitement from the factory to the scene of the disturbance. The military did not frighten me; I only left the place when it was "cleared."

Later on my mother and I lived with one of my brothers who had married. Friends came to him, among them some intelligent workmen. One of these workmen was particularly intelligent, and . . . could talk on many subjects. He was the first Social Democrat I knew. He brought me many books, and explained to me the difference between Anarchism and Socialism. I heard from him, also for the first time, what a republic was, and in spite of my former enthusiasm for royal dynasties, I also declared myself in favour of a republican form of government. I saw everything so near and so clearly, that I actually counted the weeks which must still elapse before the revolution of state and society would take place.

From this workman I received the first Social Democratic party organ. . . . I first learned from it to understand and judge of my own lot. I learned to see that all I had suffered was the result not of a divine ordinance, but of an unjust organization of society. . . .

In the factory I became another woman. . . . I told my [female] comrades all that I had read of the workers' movement. Formerly I had often told stories when they had begged me for them. But instead of narrating . . . the fate of some queen, I now held forth on oppression and exploitation. I told of accumulated wealth in the

1890 engraving of a meeting of workers in Berlin. *(Bildarchiv Preussischer Kulturbesitz/Art Resource, NY)*

hands of a few, and introduced as a contrast the shoemakers who had no shoes and the tailors who had no clothes. On breaks I read aloud the articles in the Social Democratic paper and explained what Socialism was as far as I understood it. . . . [While I was reading] it often happened that one of the clerks passing by shook his head and said to another clerk: "The girl speaks like a man."

Questions for Analysis

1. How did Popp describe and interpret work in the factory?

2. To what extent did her socialist interpretation of factory life fit the facts she described?

3. What were Popp's political interests before she became a socialist?

4. How and why did she become a Social Democrat?

5. Was this account likely to lead other workingwomen to socialism? Why or why not?

Source: Slightly adapted from A. Popp, *The Autobiography of a Working Woman,* trans. E. C. Harvey (Chicago: F. G. Browne, 1913), pp. 29, 34–35, 39, 66–69, 71, 74, 82–90.

Africans in Madagascar transport a French diplomat in 1894, shortly before France annexed the island.
(Snark/Art Resource, NY)

THE WEST AND THE WORLD, 1815–1914

While industrialization and nationalism were transforming urban life and Western society, Western society itself was reshaping the world. At the peak of its power and pride, the West entered the third and most dynamic phase of the aggressive expansion that had begun with the Crusades and continued with the great discoveries and the rise of seaborne colonial empires. An ever-growing stream of products, people, and ideas flowed out of Europe in the nineteenth century. Hardly any corner of the globe was left untouched. The most spectacular manifestations of Western expansion came in the late nineteenth century when the leading European nations established or enlarged their far-flung political empires. The political annexation of territory in the 1880s—the "new imperialism," as it is often called by historians—was the capstone of a profound underlying economic and technological process.

Industrialization and the World Economy

The Industrial Revolution created, first in Great Britain and then in continental Europe and North America, a growing and tremendously dynamic economic system. In the course of the nineteenth century, that system was extended across the face of the earth. Some of this extension into non-Western areas was peaceful and beneficial for all concerned, for the West had many products and techniques the rest of the world desired. If peaceful methods failed, however, Europeans did not stand on ceremony. They used their superior military power to force non-Western nations to open their doors to Western economic interests. In general, Westerners fashioned the global economic system so that the largest share of the ever-increasing gains from trade, technology, and migration flowed to the West and its propertied classes.

• *What were some of the global consequences of European industrialization between 1815 and 1914?*

Online Study Center

This icon will direct you to interactive activities and study materials on the website **college.hmco.com/pic/mckaywest9e**

The Rise of Global Inequality

The Industrial Revolution in Europe marked a momentous turning point in human history. Indeed, only by placing Europe's economic breakthrough in a global perspective can one truly appreciate its revolutionary implications and consequences.

From such a global perspective, the ultimate significance of the Industrial Revolution was that it allowed those regions of the world that industrialized in the nineteenth century to increase their wealth and power enormously in comparison to those that did not. As a result, a gap between the industrializing regions (mainly Europe and North America) and the nonindustrializing ones (mainly Africa, Asia, and Latin America) opened up and grew steadily throughout the nineteenth century. Moreover, this pattern of uneven global development became institutionalized, or built into the structure of the world economy. Thus we evolved a "lopsided world," a world of rich lands and poor.

In recent years historical economists have begun to chart the long-term evolution of this gap with some precision. Figure 26.1 summarizes the important findings of one such study. It compares the long-term evolution of average income per person in today's "developed" (or industrialized) regions—defined as Europe, North America, and Japan—with that found in Africa, Asia, and Latin America, also often known as the **Third World.** To get these individual income figures, researchers estimate a country's gross national product (GNP) at different points in time, convert those estimates to some common currency, and divide by the total population.

Figure 26.1 highlights three main points. First, in 1750 the average standard of living was no higher in Europe as a whole than in the rest of the world. In 1750 Europe was still a poor agricultural society. By 1970, however, the average person in the wealthiest countries had an income fully twenty-five times as great as that received by the average person in the poorest countries of Africa and Asia.

Second, it was industrialization that opened the gaps in average wealth and well-being among countries and regions. One sees that Great Britain had jumped well above the European average by 1830, when the first industrial nation was well in advance of its continental competitors. One also sees how Great Britain's lead gradually narrowed as other European countries and the United States successfully industrialized in the course of the nineteenth century.

Third, income per person stagnated in the Third World before 1913, in striking contrast to the industrializing regions. Only after 1945, in the era of political independence and decolonization, did Third World countries finally make some real economic progress, beginning in their turn the critical process of industrialization.

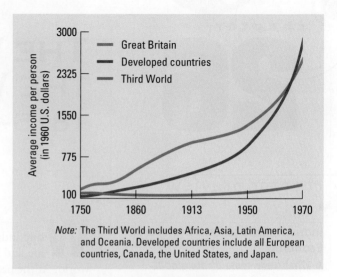

FIGURE 26.1 The Growth of Average Income per Person in the Third World, Developed Countries, and Great Britain, 1750–1970 Growth is given in 1960 U.S. dollars and prices. (*Source: P. Bairoch and M. Lévy-Leboyer, eds.,* Disparities in Economic Development Since the Industrial Revolution. *Copyright © 1981. Reprinted by permission of Palgrave Macmillan, UK.)*

The rise of these enormous income disparities, which are poignant indicators of equal disparities in food and clothing, health and education, life expectancy and general material well-being, has generated a great deal of debate. One school of interpretation stresses that the West used science, technology, capitalist organization, and even its critical worldview to create its wealth and greater physical well-being. Another school argues that the West used its political and economic power to steal much of its riches, continuing in the nineteenth (and twentieth) century the rapacious colonialism born of the era of expansion.

These issues are complex, and there are few simple answers. As noted in Chapter 22, the wealth-creating potential of technological improvement and more intensive capitalist organization was indeed great. At the same time, those breakthroughs rested, in part, on Great Britain's having already used political force to dominate part of the world economy by the late eighteenth century. In the nineteenth century other industrializing countries joined with Britain to extend Western domination over the entire world economy. Wealth—unprecedented wealth—was indeed created, but the lion's share of that new wealth flowed to the West and its propertied classes.

The World Market

Commerce between nations has always been a powerful stimulus to economic development. Never was this more true than in the nineteenth century, when world trade grew prodigiously. In 1913 the value of world trade was roughly $38 billion, or about *twenty-five* times what it had been in 1800, even though prices of both manufactured goods and raw materials were lower in 1913 than in 1800. In a general way, the enormous increase in international commerce summed up the growth of an interlocking world economy centered in and directed by Europe.

Great Britain played a key role in using trade to tie the world together economically. In 1815 Britain already had a colonial empire, for India, Canada, Australia, and other scattered areas remained British possessions after American independence. The technological breakthroughs of the Industrial Revolution allowed Britain to manufacture cotton textiles, iron, and other goods more cheaply and to far outstrip domestic demand for such products. Thus British manufacturers sought export markets first in Europe and then around the world.

Take the case of cotton textiles. By 1820 Britain was exporting 50 percent of its production. Europe bought 50 percent of these cotton textile exports, while India bought only 6 percent. Then as European nations and the United States erected protective tariff barriers and promoted domestic industry, British cotton textile manufacturers aggressively sought and found other foreign markets in non-Western areas. By 1850 India was buying 25 percent and Europe only 16 percent of a much larger total. As a British colony, India could not raise tariffs to protect its ancient cotton textile industry, and thousands of Indian weavers lost their livelihoods.

After the repeal of the Corn Laws in 1846 (see page 764), Britain became the world's single best market. Until 1914 Britain remained the world's emporium, where not only agricultural products and raw materials but also manufactured goods entered freely. Free access to Britain's market stimulated the development of mines and plantations in many non-Western areas.

The growth of trade was facilitated by the conquest of distance. The earliest railroad construction occurred in Europe (including Russia) and in America north of the Rio Grande; other parts of the globe saw the building of rail lines after 1860. By 1920 more than one-quarter of the world's railroads were in Latin America, Asia, Africa, and Australia. Wherever railroads were built, they drastically reduced transportation costs, opened new economic opportunities, and called forth new skills and attitudes. Much of the railroad construction undertaken in Latin

Chronology

1853	Perry "opens" Japan for trade
1863–1879	Reign of Ismail in Egypt
1865–1909	Reign of Leopold II in Belgium
1867	Meiji Restoration in Japan
1869	Completion of Suez Canal
1898	United States takes over Philippines; hundred days of reform in China
1899	Kipling, "The White Man's Burden"
1902	Conrad, *Heart of Darkness*; Hobson, *Imperialism*

America, Asia, and Africa connected seaports with inland cities and regions, as opposed to linking and developing cities and regions within a given country. Thus railroads dovetailed admirably with Western economic interests, facilitating the inflow and sale of Western manufactured goods and the export and the development of local raw materials.

The power of steam revolutionized transportation by sea as well as by land. Steam power, long used to drive paddle wheelers on rivers, particularly in Russia and North America, finally began to supplant sails on the oceans of the world in the late 1860s. Lighter, stronger, cheaper steel replaced iron, which had replaced wood. Screw propellers superseded paddle wheels, while mighty compound steam engines cut fuel consumption by half. Passenger and freight rates tumbled, and the intercontinental shipment of low-priced raw materials became feasible.

An account of an actual voyage by a typical tramp freighter highlights nineteenth-century developments in global trade. The ship left England in 1910 carrying rails and general freight to western Australia. From there it carried lumber to Melbourne in southeastern Australia, where it took on harvester combines for Argentina. In Buenos Aires it loaded wheat for Calcutta, and in Calcutta it took on jute for New York. From New York it carried a variety of industrial products to Australia before returning to England with lead, wool, and wheat after a voyage of approximately seventy-two thousand miles to six continents in seventeen months.

The revolution in land and sea transportation helped European pioneers open up vast new territories and produce agricultural products and raw materials there for sale in Europe. Improved transportation enabled Asia, Africa, and Latin America to ship not only the traditional tropical products—

British Ships and Shipbuilders The British continued to dominate international trade before the First World War. This handsome membership certificate of the British shipbuilders union features the vessels that drew the world together and were Britain's pride. Britain's thriving shipbuilding industry was concentrated in southern Scotland along the Clyde. (*Trade Union Congress, London/The Bridgeman Art Library*)

spices, tea, sugar, coffee—but also new raw materials for industry, such as jute, rubber, cotton, and coconut oil.

Intercontinental trade was enormously facilitated by the Suez and Panama Canals. Of great importance, too, was large and continual investment in modern port facilities, which made loading and unloading cheaper, faster, and more dependable. Finally, transoceanic telegraph cables inaugurated rapid communications among the financial centers of the world. While a British tramp freighter steamed from Calcutta to New York, a broker in London was arranging by telegram for it to carry an American

cargo to Australia. World commodity prices were also instantaneously conveyed by the same network of communications.

The growth of trade and the conquest of distance encouraged the expanding European economy to make massive foreign investments beginning about 1840. By the outbreak of World War I in 1914, Europeans had invested more than $40 billion abroad. Great Britain, France, and Germany were the principal investing countries (see Map 26.1). The great gap between rich and poor within Europe meant that the wealthy and moderately well-to-do could and did send great sums abroad in search of interest and dividends.

Most of the capital exported did not go to European colonies or protectorates in Asia and Africa. About three-quarters of total European investment went to other European countries, the United States and Canada, Australia and New Zealand, and Latin America. Europe found its most profitable opportunities for investment in construction of the railroads, ports, and utilities that were necessary to settle and develop the almost-vacant lands in such places as Australia and the Americas. By lending money for a foreign railroad, Europeans also enabled white settlers to buy European rails and locomotives and developed sources of cheap food and raw materials. Much of this investment was peaceful and mutually beneficial for lenders and borrowers. The victims were Native American Indians and Australian aborigines, who were decimated by the diseases, liquor, and weapons of an aggressively expanding Western society.

The Opening of China and Japan

Europe's relatively peaceful development of robust offshoots in sparsely populated North America, Australia, and much of Latin America absorbed huge quantities of goods, investments, and migrants. From a Western point of view, that was the most important aspect of Europe's global thrust. Yet Europe's economic and cultural penetration of old, densely populated civilizations was also profoundly significant, especially for the non-European peoples affected by it. With such civilizations Europeans also increased their trade and profit, and they were prepared to use force, if necessary, to attain their desires. This was what happened in China and Japan, two crucial examples of the general pattern of intrusion into non-Western lands.

Traditional Chinese civilization was self-sufficient. For centuries China had sent more goods and inventions to Europe than it had received, and this was still the case in the early nineteenth century. Trade with Europe was care-

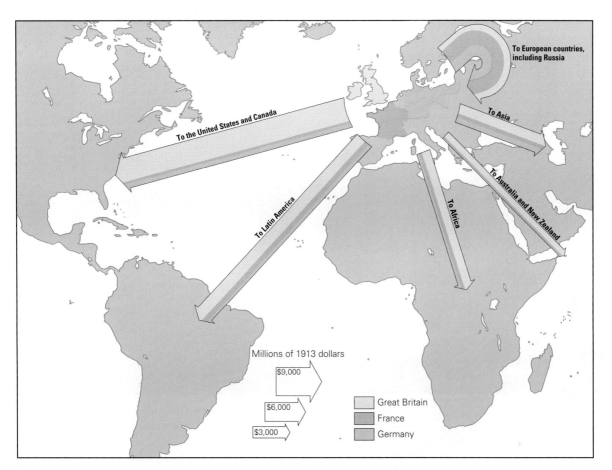

MAP 26.1 European Investment to 1914   Foreign investment grew rapidly after 1850, and Britain, France, and Germany were the major investing nations. As this map suggests, most European investment was not directed to the African and Asian areas seized by the "new imperialism" after 1880.

fully regulated by the Chinese imperial government—the Qing (or Manchu) Dynasty—which required all foreign merchants to live in the southern city of Canton and to buy from and sell to only the local merchant monopoly. Practices considered harmful to Chinese interests, such as the sale of opium, were strictly forbidden.

For years the little community of foreign merchants in Canton had to accept the Chinese system. By the 1820s, however, the dominant group, the British, were flexing their muscles. Moreover, in the smoking of opium—that "destructive and ensnaring vice" denounced by Chinese decrees—they had found something the Chinese really wanted. Grown legally in British-occupied India, opium was smuggled into China by means of fast ships and bribed officials. By 1836 the aggressive goal of the British merchants in Canton was an independent British colony in

China and "safe and unrestricted liberty" in trade. Spurred on by economic motives, they pressured the British government to take decisive action and enlisted the support of British manufacturers with visions of vast Chinese markets to be opened.

At the same time, the Qing government decided that the **opium trade** had to be stamped out. It was ruining the people and stripping the empire of its silver, which was going to British merchants to pay for the opium. The government began to prosecute Chinese drug dealers vigorously and in 1839 it ordered the foreign merchants to obey China's laws. The British merchants refused and were expelled, whereupon war soon broke out.

Using troops from India and being in control of the seas, the British occupied several coastal cities and forced China to surrender. In the Treaty of Nanking in 1842,

Britain and China at War, 1841   Britain capitalized on its overwhelming naval superiority, and this British aquatint celebrates a dramatic moment in a crucial battle near Guangzhou. Having received a direct hit from a steam-powered British ironclad, a Chinese sailing ship explodes into a wall of flame. The Chinese lost eleven ships and five hundred men in the two-hour engagement; the British suffered only minor damage. *(National Maritime Museum, London)*

the imperial government was forced to cede the island of Hong Kong to Britain forever, pay an indemnity of $100 million, and open up four large cities to foreign trade with low tariffs.

Thereafter the opium trade flourished, and Hong Kong developed rapidly as an Anglo-Chinese enclave. China continued to accept foreign diplomats in Beijing (Peking), the imperial capital. Finally, there was a second round of foreign attack between 1856 and 1860, culminating in the occupation of Beijing by seventeen thousand British and French troops and the intentional burning of the emperor's summer palace. Another round of harsh treaties gave European merchants and missionaries greater privileges and protection and forced the Chinese to accept trade and investment on unfavorable terms for several more cities. Thus did Europeans use military aggression to blow a hole in the wall of Chinese seclusion and open the country to foreign trade and foreign ideas.

China's neighbor Japan had its own highly distinctive

civilization and even less use for Westerners. European traders and missionaries first arrived in Japan in the sixteenth century. By 1640 Japan had reacted quite negatively to their presence. The government decided to seal off the country from all European influences in order to preserve traditional Japanese culture and society. When American and British whaling ships began to appear off Japanese coasts almost two hundred years later, the policy of exclusion was still in effect. An order of 1825 commanded Japanese officials to "drive away foreign vessels without second thought."[1]

Japan's unbending isolation seemed hostile and barbaric to the West, particularly to the United States. It complicated the practical problems of shipwrecked American sailors and the provisioning of whaling ships and China traders sailing in the eastern Pacific. It also thwarted the hope of trade and profit. Moreover, Americans shared the self-confidence and dynamism of expanding Western society, and they felt destined to play a great role in the

Pacific. To Americans it seemed the duty of the United States to force the Japanese to share their ports and behave as a "civilized" nation.

After several unsuccessful American attempts to establish commercial relations with Japan, Commodore Matthew Perry steamed into Edo (now Tokyo) Bay in 1853 and demanded diplomatic negotiations with the emperor. Japan entered a grave crisis. Some Japanese warriors urged resistance, but senior officials realized how defenseless their cities were against naval bombardment. Shocked and humiliated, they reluctantly signed a treaty with the United States that opened two ports and permitted trade. Over the next five years, more treaties spelled out the rights and privileges of the Western nations and their merchants in Japan. Japan was "opened." What the British had done in China with war, the Americans had done in Japan with only the threat of war.

Western Penetration of Egypt

Egypt's experience illustrates not only the explosive power of the expanding European economy and society but also their seductive appeal in non-Western lands. European involvement in Egypt also led to a new model of formal political control, which European powers applied widely in Africa and Asia after 1882.

Of great importance in African and Middle Eastern history, the ancient land of the pharaohs had since 525 B.C. been ruled by a succession of foreigners, most recently by the Ottoman Turks. In 1798 French armies under young General Napoleon Bonaparte invaded the Egyptian part of the Ottoman Empire and occupied the territory for three years. Into the power vacuum left by the French withdrawal stepped an extraordinary Albanian-born Turkish general, Muhammad Ali (1769–1849).

First appointed governor of Egypt by the Turkish sultan, Muhammad Ali set out to build his own state on the strength of a large, powerful army organized along European lines. He drafted for the first time the illiterate, despised peasant masses of Egypt, and he hired French and Italian army officers to train these raw recruits and their Turkish officers. The government was also reformed, new lands were cultivated, and communications were improved. By the time of his death in 1849, Muhammad Ali had established a strong and virtually independent Egyptian state, to be ruled by his family on a hereditary basis within the Turkish empire.

Muhammad Ali's policies of modernization attracted large numbers of Europeans to the banks of the Nile. The port city of Alexandria had more than fifty thousand Europeans by 1864. Europeans served not only as army officers but also as engineers, doctors, government officials, and police officers. Others turned to trade, finance, and shipping.

To pay for his ambitious plans, Muhammad Ali encouraged the development of commercial agriculture. This development had profound implications. Egyptian peasants were poor but largely self-sufficient, growing food for their own consumption on state-owned lands allotted to them by tradition. Faced with the possibility of export agriculture, high-ranking officials and members of Muhammad Ali's family began carving large private landholdings out of the state domain. The new landlords made the peasants their tenants and forced them to grow cash crops geared to European markets. Thus Egyptian landowners "modernized" agriculture, but to the detriment of peasant well-being.

These trends continued under Muhammad Ali's grandson Ismail, who in 1863 began his sixteen-year rule as Egypt's **khedive,** or prince. Educated at France's leading military academy, Ismail was a westernizing autocrat. The large irrigation networks he promoted caused cotton production and exports to Europe to boom, and with his support the Suez Canal was completed by a French company in 1869. The Arabic of the masses replaced the Turkish of the conquerors as the official language. Young Egyptians educated in Europe spread new skills, and Cairo acquired modern boulevards and Western hotels. As Ismail proudly declared, "My country is no longer in Africa, we now form part of Europe."[2]

Yet Ismail was too impatient and reckless. His projects were enormously expensive, and by 1876 Egypt owed foreign bondholders a colossal debt that it could not pay. Rather than let Egypt go bankrupt and repudiate its loans, the governments of France and Great Britain intervened politically to protect the European bondholders. They forced Ismail to appoint French and British commissioners to oversee Egyptian finances so that the Egyptian debt would be paid in full. This momentous decision implied direct European political control and was a sharp break with the previous pattern of trade and investment. Throughout most of the nineteenth century, Europeans had used military might and political force primarily to make sure that non-Western lands would accept European trade and investment. Now Europeans were going to determine the state budget and effectively rule Egypt.

Foreign financial control evoked a violent nationalistic reaction among Egyptian religious leaders, young intellectuals, and army officers. In 1879, under the leadership of Colonel Ahmed Arabi, they formed the Egyptian

The Opening of the Suez Canal   A long procession of eighty ships passed through the Suez Canal when it was opened in November 1869, and thousands of spectators lined the shores and joined in the celebrations. The building of the hundred-mile canal was a momentous event, cutting in half the length of the journey between Europe and Asia. *(Archives Charmet/The Bridgeman Art Library)*

Nationalist Party. Continuing diplomatic pressure, which forced Ismail to abdicate in favor of his weak son, Tewfiq (r. 1879–1892), resulted in bloody anti-European riots in Alexandria in 1882. A number of Europeans were killed, and Tewfiq and his court had to flee to British ships for safety. When the British fleet bombarded Alexandria, more riots swept the country, and Colonel Arabi led a revolt. But a British expeditionary force put down the rebellion and occupied all of Egypt.

The British said their occupation was temporary, but British armies remained in Egypt until 1956. They maintained the façade of the khedive's government as an autonomous province of the Ottoman Empire, but the khedive was a mere puppet. British rule did result in tax reforms and somewhat better conditions for peasants, while foreign bondholders received their interest and Egyptian nationalists nursed their injured pride.

British rule in Egypt provided a new model for European expansion in densely populated lands. Such expansion was based on military force, political domination, and a self-justifying ideology of beneficial reform. This

model was to predominate until 1914. Thus did Europe's Industrial Revolution lead to tremendous political as well as economic expansion throughout the world after 1880.

The Great Migration

A poignant human drama was interwoven with economic expansion: millions of people pulled up stakes and left their ancestral lands in the course of history's greatest migration. To millions of ordinary people, for whom the opening of China and the interest on the Egyptian debt had not the slightest significance, this great movement was the central experience in the saga of Western expansion. It was, in part, because of this **great migration** that the West's impact on the world in the nineteenth century was so powerful and many-sided.

• *How was massive migration an integral part of Western expansion?*

The Pressure of Population

In the early eighteenth century, the growth of European population entered its third and decisive stage, which continued unabated until the early twentieth century (see Figure 26.2). Birthrates eventually declined in the nineteenth century, but so did death rates, mainly because of the rising standard of living and secondarily because of the medical revolution. Thus the population of Europe (including Asiatic Russia) more than doubled, from approximately 188 million in 1800 to roughly 432 million in 1900.

These figures actually understate Europe's population explosion, for between 1815 and 1932 more than 60 million people left Europe. These migrants went primarily to the "areas of European settlement"—North and South America, Australia, New Zealand, and Siberia—where they contributed to a rapid growth in numbers. Since population grew more slowly in Africa and Asia than in Europe and the Americas, as Figure 26.2 shows, Europeans and people of predominately European origin jumped from about 22 percent of the world's total to about 38 percent on the eve of World War I.

The growing number of Europeans provided further impetus for Western expansion. It was a driving force behind emigration. As in the eighteenth century, the rapid increase in numbers put pressure on the land and led to land hunger and relative overpopulation in area after area. In most countries, migration increased twenty years after a rapid growth in population, as many children of the baby boom grew up, saw little available land and few opportunities, and migrated. This pattern was especially prevalent when rapid population increase predated extensive industrial development, which offered the best long-term hope of creating jobs within the country and reducing poverty. Thus millions of country folk went abroad as well as to nearby cities in search of work and economic opportunity.

Before looking at the people who migrated, let us consider three facts. First, the number of men and women who left Europe increased rapidly before World War I. As Figure 26.3 shows, more than 11 million left in the first decade of the twentieth century, over five times the number departing in the 1850s. The outflow of migrants was clearly an enduring characteristic of European society for the entire period.

Second, different countries had very different patterns of movement. As Figure 26.3 also shows, people left Britain and Ireland (which are not distinguished in the British figures) in large numbers from the 1840s on. This

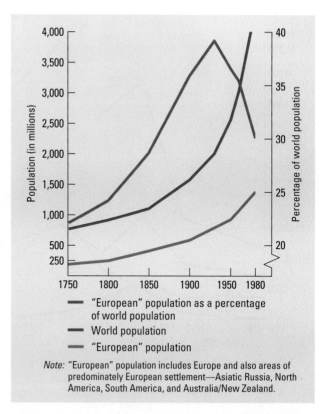

FIGURE 26.2 The Increase of European and World Populations, 1750–1980 (*Sources: W. Woodruff,* Impact of Western Man: A Study of Europe's Role in the World Economy. *St. Martin's Press, New York, 1967, p. 103; United Nations,* Statistical Yearbook, 1982, *1985, pp. 2–3.*)

emigration reflected not only rural poverty but also the movement of skilled, industrial technicians and the preferences shown to British migrants in the British Empire. Ultimately, about one-third of all European migrants between 1840 and 1920 came from the British Isles. German migration was quite different. It grew irregularly after about 1830, reaching a first peak in the early 1850s and another in the early 1880s. Thereafter it declined rapidly, for Germany's rapid industrialization was providing adequate jobs at home. This pattern contrasted sharply with that of Italy. More and more Italians left the country right up to 1914, reflecting severe problems in Italian villages and relatively slow industrial growth. Thus migration patterns mirrored social and economic conditions in the various European countries and provinces.

Third, although the United States absorbed the largest number of European migrants, less than half of all migrants went to the United States. Asiatic Russia, Canada, Argentina, Brazil, Australia, and New Zealand also attracted

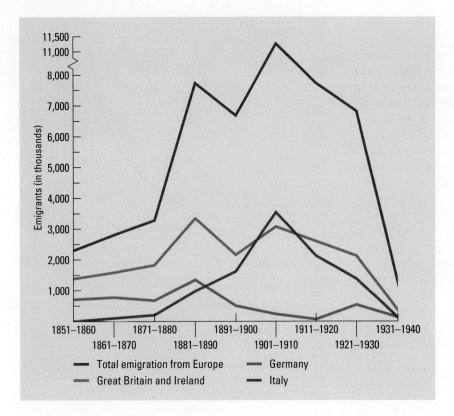

FIGURE 26.3 Emigration from Europe by Decades, 1851–1940 *(Source: Copyright © W. Woodruff, from* Impact of Western Man, *by W. Woodruff, 1982. Reprinted with permission of University Press of America.)*

large numbers, as Figure 26.4 shows. Moreover, migrants accounted for a larger proportion of the total population in Argentina, Brazil, and Canada than in the United States. The common American assumption that European migration meant migration to the United States is quite inaccurate.

European Migrants

What kind of people left Europe, and what were their reasons for doing so? The European migrant was most often a small peasant landowner or a village craftsman whose traditional way of life was threatened by too little land, estate agriculture, and cheap, factory-made goods. German peasants who left the Rhineland and southwestern Germany between 1830 and 1854, for example, felt trapped by what Friedrich List called the "dwarf economy," with its tiny landholdings and declining craft industries. Selling out and moving to buy much cheaper land in the American Midwest became a common response. Thus the European migrant was generally an energetic small farmer or skilled artisan trying hard to stay ahead of poverty, not a desperately impoverished landless peasant or urban proletarian.

Determined to maintain or improve their status, mi-

grants were a great asset to the countries that received them. This was doubly so because the vast majority were young and very often unmarried. They came in the prime of life and were ready to work hard in the new land, at least for a time. Many Europeans moved but remained within Europe, settling temporarily or permanently in another European country. Jews from eastern Europe and peasants from Ireland migrated to Great Britain, Russians and Poles sought work in Germany, and Latin peoples from Spain, Portugal, and Italy entered France. Many Europeans were truly migrants as opposed to immigrants— that is, they returned home after some time abroad. One in two migrants to Argentina and probably one in three to the United States eventually returned to their native land.

The likelihood of repatriation varied greatly by nationality. People who migrated from the Balkans, for instance, were much more likely to return to their countries than people from Ireland and eastern European Jews. Once again, the possibility of buying land in the old country was of central importance. In Ireland (as well as in England and Scotland) land was tightly held by large, often absentee landowners, and little land was available for purchase. In Russia most land was held by non-Jews. Therefore, when Russian Jewish artisans began in the 1880s to escape both factory competition and oppression by mi-

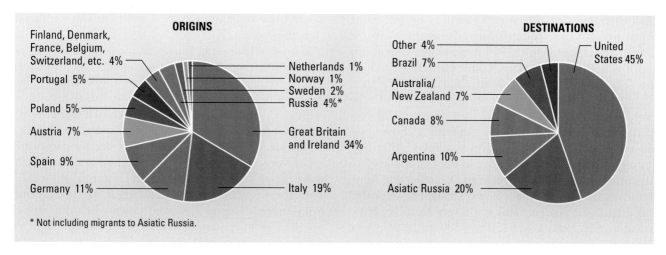

FIGURE 26.4 Origins and Destinations of European Emigrants, 1851–1960 *(Source:*
Copyright © W. Woodruff, from Impact of Western Man, *by W. Woodruff, 1982. Reprinted with*
permission of University Press of America.)

grating, it was basically a once-and-for-all departure. Non-Jewish migrants from Russia had access to land and returned much more frequently to their peasant villages in central Russia, Poland, and Ukraine.

The mass movement of Italians illustrates many of the characteristics of European migration. As late as the 1880s, three of every four Italians depended on agriculture. With the influx of cheap North American wheat, many small

An Italian Custom in Argentina Italian immigrants introduced the game of boccia to Argentina, where it took hold and became a popular recreation for men. Dressed up in their Sunday best, these Argentinian laborers are totally focused on the game, which is somewhat like horseshoes or shuffleboard. *(Hulton Archive/ Getty Images)*

landowning peasants whose standard of living was falling began to leave their country. Many Italians went to the United States, but before 1900 more went to Argentina and Brazil. In Brazil the large coffee planters, faced with the collapse of black slavery, attracted Italians to their plantations with subsidized travel and promises of relatively high wages.

Many Italians had no intention of settling abroad permanently. Some called themselves **swallows.** After harvesting their own wheat and flax in Italy, they "flew" to Argentina to harvest wheat between December and April. Returning to Italy for the spring planting, they repeated this exhausting process. This was a very hard life, but a frugal worker could save $250 to $300 in the course of a season.

Ties of family and friendship played a crucial role in the movement of peoples. Many people from a given province or village settled together in rural enclaves or tightly knit urban neighborhoods thousands of miles away. Very often a strong individual—a businessman, a religious leader—

would blaze the way and others would follow, forming a "migration chain."

Many landless young European men and women were spurred to leave by a spirit of revolt and independence. In Sweden and in Norway, in Jewish Russia and in Italy, these young people felt frustrated by the small privileged classes, which often controlled both church and government and resisted demands for change and greater opportunity. Many a young Norwegian seconded the passionate cry of Norway's national poet, Martinius Bjørnson: "Forth will I! Forth! I will be crushed and consumed if I stay."[3] Thus for many, migration was a radical way to "get out from under." Migration slowed down when the people won basic political and social reforms, such as the right to vote and social security.

Asian Migrants

Not all migration was from Europe. A substantial number of Chinese, Japanese, Indians, and Filipinos—to name

Vaccinating Migrants Bound for Hawaii, 1904   First Chinese, then Japanese, and finally Koreans and Filipinos went in large numbers across the Pacific to labor in Hawaii on American-owned sugar plantations in the late nineteenth century. The native Hawaiians had been decimated by disease, preparing the way for the annexation of Hawaii by the United States in 1898. *(Corbis)*

only four key groups—responded to rural hardship with temporary or permanent migration. At least 3 million Asians (as opposed to more than 60 million Europeans) moved abroad before 1920. Most went as indentured laborers to work under incredibly difficult conditions on the plantations or in the gold mines of Latin America, southern Asia, Africa, California, Hawaii, and Australia. White estate owners very often used Asians to replace or supplement blacks after the suppression of the slave trade.

In the 1840s, for example, there was a strong demand for field hands in Cuba, and the Spanish government actively recruited Chinese laborers. Between 1853 and 1873, when such migration was stopped, more than 130,000 Chinese laborers went to Cuba. The majority spent their lives as virtual slaves. The great landlords of Peru also brought in more than 100,000 workers from China in the nineteenth century, and there were similar movements of Asians elsewhere.

Such migration from Asia would undoubtedly have grown to much greater proportions if planters and mine owners in search of cheap labor had been able to hire as many Asian workers as they wished. But they could not. Asians fled the plantations and gold mines as soon as possible, seeking greater opportunities in trade and towns. There they came into conflict with local populations, whether in Malaya, East Africa, or areas settled by Europeans. These European settlers demanded a halt to Asian migration. By the 1880s, Americans and Australians were building **great white walls**—discriminatory laws designed to keep Asians out.

A crucial factor in the migrations before 1914 was, therefore, the general policy of "whites only" in the open lands of possible permanent settlement. This, too, was part of Western dominance in the increasingly lopsided world. Largely successful in monopolizing the best overseas opportunities, Europeans and people of European ancestry reaped the main benefits from the great migration. By 1913 people in Australia, Canada, and the United States all had higher average incomes than people in Great Britain, still Europe's wealthiest nation.

Western Imperialism, 1880–1914

The expansion of Western society reached its apex between about 1880 and 1914. In those years, the leading European nations not only continued to send massive streams of migrants, money, and manufactured goods around the world, but also rushed to create or enlarge vast *political* empires abroad. This political empire build-

ing contrasted sharply with the economic penetration of non-Western territories between 1816 and 1880, which had left a China or a Japan "opened" but politically independent. By contrast, the empires of the late nineteenth century recalled the old European colonial empires of the seventeenth and eighteenth centuries and led contemporaries to speak of the **new imperialism.**

Characterized by a frantic rush to plant the flag over as many people and as much territory as possible, the new imperialism had momentous consequences. It resulted in new tensions among competing European states, and it led to wars and rumors of war with non-European powers. The new imperialism was aimed primarily at Africa and Asia. It put millions of black, brown, and yellow peoples directly under the rule of whites.

• *How and why after 1875 did European nations rush to build political empires in Africa and Asia?*

The Scramble for Africa

The most spectacular manifestation of the new imperialism was the seizure of Africa, which broke sharply with previous patterns and fascinated contemporary Europeans and Americans. As late as 1880, European nations controlled only 10 percent of the African continent, and their possessions were hardly increasing. The French had begun conquering Algeria in 1830, and by 1880 substantial numbers of French, Italian, and Spanish colonists had settled among the overwhelming Arab majority.

At the other end of the continent, in South Africa, the British had taken possession of the Dutch settlements at Cape Town during the wars with Napoleon I. This takeover had led disgruntled Dutch cattle ranchers and farmers in 1835 to make their so-called Great Trek into the interior, where they fought the Zulu and Xhosa peoples for land. After 1853, while British colonies such as Canada and Australia were beginning to evolve toward self-government, the Boers, or **Afrikaners** (as the descendants of the Dutch in the Cape Colony were beginning to call themselves), proclaimed their political independence and defended it against British armies. By 1880 Afrikaner and British settlers, who detested each other, had wrested control of much of South Africa from the Zulu, Xhosa, and other African peoples.

European trading posts and forts dating back to the Age of Discovery and the slave trade dotted the coast of West Africa. The Portuguese proudly but ineffectively held their old possessions in Angola and Mozambique. Elsewhere over the great mass of the continent, Europeans did not rule.

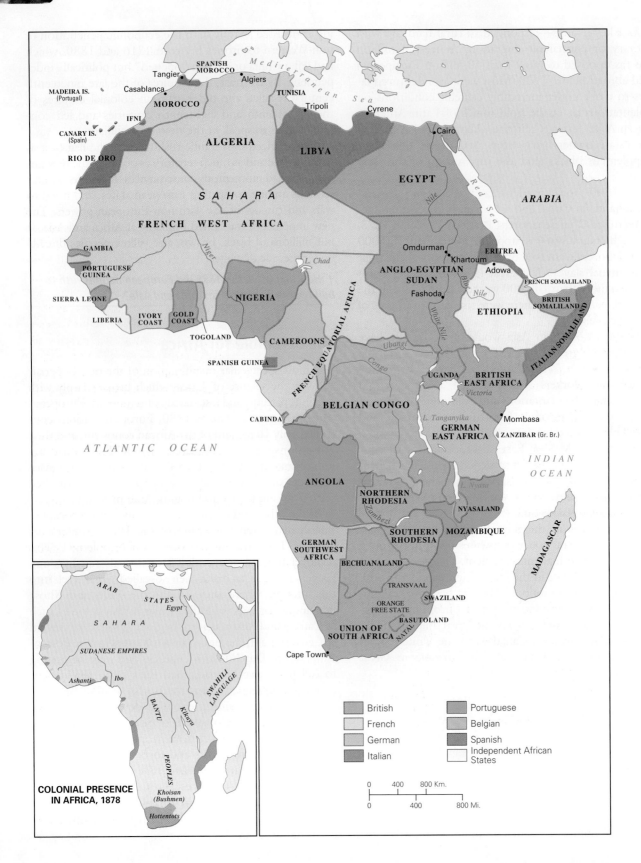

Tangier
SPANISH MOROCCO
Algiers
MADEIRA IS.
(Portugal)
Casablanca
IFNI
MOROCCO
CANARY IS.
(Spain)
RIO DE ORO
TUNISIA
Tripoli
Cyrene
Cairo
ALGERIA
LIBYA
EGYPT
SAHARA
Nile
ARABIA
FRENCH WEST AFRICA
Red Sea
GAMBIA
Niger
L. Chad
Omdurman
ERITREA
Khartoum
ANGLO-EGYPTIAN
SUDAN
Adowa
FRENCH SOMALILAND
PORTUGUESE
GUINEA
SIERRA LEONE
NIGERIA
Fashoda
Blue Nile
ETHIOPIA
BRITISH
SOMALILAND
LIBERIA
IVORY
COAST
GOLD
COAST
White Nile
TOGOLAND
Ubangi
CAMEROONS
FRENCH EQUATORIAL AFRICA
ITALIAN SOMALILAND
SPANISH GUINEA
Congo
UGANDA
BRITISH
EAST AFRICA
CABINDA
BELGIAN CONGO
L. Victoria
L. Tanganyika
Mombasa
GERMAN
EAST AFRICA
ZANZIBAR (Gr. Br.)
ATLANTIC OCEAN
INDIAN
OCEAN
ANGOLA
L. Nyasa
NORTHERN
RHODESIA
NYASALAND
Zambezi
SOUTHERN
RHODESIA
MOZAMBIQUE
GERMAN
SOUTHWEST
AFRICA
MADAGASCAR
BECHUANALAND
TRANSVAAL
SWAZILAND
ORANGE
FREE STATE
BASUTOLAND
UNION OF
SOUTH AFRICA
NATAL
Cape Town
Mediterranean Sea

ARAB
STATES
Egypt
SAHARA
SUDANESE EMPIRES
Ashanti
Ibo
BANTU
Kikuyu
SWAHILI LANGUAGE
PEOPLES
Khoisan
(Bushmen)
Hottentots

**COLONIAL PRESENCE
IN AFRICA, 1878**

	British		Portuguese
	French		Belgian
	German		Spanish
	Italian		Independent African States

0   400   800 Km.

0   400   800 Mi.

Between 1880 and 1900, the situation changed drastically. Britain, France, Germany, and Italy scrambled for African possessions as if their national livelihoods depended on it (see Map 26.2). By 1900 nearly the whole continent had been carved up and placed under European rule: only Ethiopia in northeast Africa, which repulsed Italian invaders, and Liberia on the West African coast, which had been settled by freed slaves from the United States, remained independent. In the years before 1914, the European powers tightened their control and established colonial governments to rule their gigantic empires.

Online Study Center **Improve Your Grade**
Primary Source: European Imperialism in Africa: A Veteran Explains the Rules of the Game

The Dutch settler republics also succumbed to imperialism, but the final outcome was quite different. The British, led by Cecil Rhodes in the Cape Colony, leapfrogged over the Afrikaner states in the early 1890s and established protectorates over Bechuanaland (now Botswana) and Rhodesia (now Zimbabwe and Zambia), named in honor of its freelance imperial founder. Trying unsuccessfully to undermine the stubborn Afrikaners in the Transvaal, where English-speaking capitalists like Rhodes were developing fabulously rich gold mines, the British conquered their white rivals in the bloody South African War (1899–1902). In 1910 their territories were united with the old Cape Colony and the eastern province of Natal in a new Union of South Africa, established— unlike any other territory in Africa—as a largely "self-governing" colony. This enabled the defeated Afrikaners to use their numerical superiority over the British settlers to gradually take political power, as even the most

Mapping the Past

MAP 26.2 The Partition of Africa   The European powers carved up Africa after 1880 and built vast political empires. European states also seized territory in Asia in the nineteenth century, although some Asian states and peoples managed to maintain their political independence, as may be seen on Map 26.3, page 864. The late nineteenth century was the high point of European imperialism. Compare the patterns of European imperialism in Africa and Asia, using this map and Map 26.3. ❶ What European countries were leading imperialist states in both Africa and Asia, and what lands did they hold? ❷ What countries in Africa and Asia maintained their political independence? ❸ From an imperialist perspective, what in 1914 did the United States and Japan, two very different countries, have in common in Africa and Asia?

Online Study Center **Improve Your Grade**
Interactive Map: Africa in 1914

educated nonwhites lost the right to vote outside the Cape Colony. (See the feature "Individuals in Society: Cecil Rhodes.")

In the complexity of the European seizure of Africa, certain events and individuals stand out. Of enormous importance was the British occupation of Egypt in 1882, which established the new model of formal political control. There was also the role of Leopold II of Belgium (r. 1865–1909), an energetic, strong-willed monarch with a lust for distant territory. "The sea bathes our coast, the world lies before us," he had exclaimed in 1861. "Steam and electricity have annihilated distance, and all the non-appropriated lands on the surface of the globe can become the field of our operations and of our success."[4] By 1876 Leopold was focusing on central Africa. Subsequently, he formed a financial syndicate under his personal control to send Henry M. Stanley, a sensation-seeking journalist and part-time explorer, to the Congo basin. Stanley was able to establish trading stations, sign "treaties" with African chiefs, and plant Leopold's flag. Leopold's actions alarmed the French, who quickly sent out an expedition under Pierre de Brazza. In 1880 de Brazza signed a treaty of protection with the chief of the large Teke tribe and began to establish a French protectorate on the north bank of the Congo River.

Leopold's buccaneering intrusion into the Congo area raised the question of the political fate of Africa. By 1882 Europe had caught "African fever." There was a gold rush mentality, and the race for territory was on.

To lay down some basic rules for this new and dangerous game of imperialist competition in sub-Saharan Africa, Jules Ferry of France and Otto von Bismarck of Germany arranged an international conference on Africa in Berlin in 1884 and 1885. The conference established the principle that European claims to African territory had to rest on "effective occupation" in order to be recognized by other states. This meant that Europeans would push relentlessly into interior regions from all sides and that no single European power would be able to claim the entire continent. The conference recognized Leopold's personal rule over a neutral Congo free state and agreed to work to stop slavery and the slave trade in Africa.

The **Berlin conference** coincided with Germany's sudden emergence as an imperial power. Prior to about 1880, Bismarck, like many other European leaders at the time, had seen little value in colonies. Colonies reminded him, he said, of a poor but proud nobleman who wore a fur coat when he could not afford a shirt underneath. Then in 1884 and 1885, as political agitation for expansion increased, Bismarck did an abrupt about-face, and Germany established protectorates over a number of

European Imperialism at Its Worst This 1908 English cartoon, "Leopold, King of the Congo, in his national dress," focuses on the barbaric practice of cutting off the hands and feet of Africans who refused to gather as much rubber as Leopold's company demanded. In 1908 an international human rights campaign forced the Belgian king to cede his personal fief to the Belgian state. *(The Granger Collection, New York)*

small African kingdoms and tribes in Togo, Cameroons, southwest Africa, and, later, East Africa. In acquiring colonies, Bismarck cooperated against the British with France's Ferry, who was as ardent for empire as he was for education. With Bismarck's tacit approval, the French pressed southward from Algeria, eastward from their old forts on the Senegal coast, and northward from their protectorate on the Congo River.

Meanwhile, the British began enlarging their West African enclaves and impatiently pushing northward from the Cape Colony and westward from Zanzibar. Their thrust southward from Egypt was blocked in Sudan by fiercely independent Muslims who massacred a British force at Khartoum in 1885.

A decade later, another British force, under General Horatio H. Kitchener, moved cautiously and more successfully up the Nile River, building a railroad to supply arms and reinforcements as it went. Finally, in 1898 these British troops met their foe at Omdurman (see Map 26.2), where Muslim tribesmen armed with spears charged time and time again, only to be cut down by the recently invented machine gun. For one smug participant, the young British officer Winston Churchill, it was "like a pantomime scene" in a play. "These extraordinary foreign figures . . . march up one by one from the darkness of Barbarism to the footlights of civilization . . . and their conquerors, taking their possessions, forget even their names." For another, more somber English observer, "It was not a battle but an execution. The bodies were not in heaps . . . but they spread evenly over acres and acres."[5] In the end, eleven thousand brave Muslim tribesmen lay dead, while only twenty-eight Britons had been killed.

Continuing up the Nile after the Battle of Omdurman, Kitchener's armies found that a small French force had already occupied the village of Fashoda. Locked in imperial competition with Britain ever since the British occupation of Egypt, France had tried to beat the British to one of Africa's last unclaimed areas—the upper reaches of the Nile. The result was a serious diplomatic crisis and even the threat of war. Eventually, wracked by the Dreyfus affair (see page 834) and unwilling to fight, France backed down and withdrew its forces, allowing the British to take over.

The British conquest of Sudan exemplifies the general process of empire building in Africa. The fate of the Muslim force at Omdurman was eventually inflicted on all native peoples who resisted European rule: they were blown away by vastly superior military force. But however much the European powers squabbled for territory and privilege around the world, they always had the sense

Individuals in Society

Cecil Rhodes

Cecil Rhodes (1853–1902) epitomized the dynamism and the ruthlessness of the new imperialism. He built a corporate monopoly, claimed vast tracts in Africa, and established the famous Rhodes scholarships to develop colonial (and American) leaders who would love and strengthen the British Empire. But to Africans, he left a bitter legacy.

Rhodes came from a large middle-class family and at seventeen went to southern Africa to seek his fortune. He soon turned to diamonds, newly discovered at Kimberley, picked good partners, and was wealthy by 1876. But Rhodes, often called a dreamer, wanted more. He entered Oxford University, while returning periodically to Africa, and his musings crystallized in a belief in progress through racial competition and territorial expansion. "I contend," he wrote, "that we [English] are the finest race in the world and the more of the world we inhabit the better it is for the human race."*

Rhodes's belief in British expansion never wavered. In 1880 he formed the De Beers Mining Company, and by 1888 his firm monopolized southern Africa's diamond production and earned fabulous profits. Rhodes also entered the Cape Colony's legislature and became the all-powerful prime minister from 1890 to 1896. His main objective was to dominate the Afrikaner republics and to impose British rule on as much land as possible beyond their northern borders. Working through a state-approved private company financed in part by De Beers, Rhodes's agents forced and cajoled African kings to accept British "protection," then put down rebellions with Maxim machine guns. Britain thus obtained a great swath of empire on the cheap.

But Rhodes, like many high achievers obsessed with power and personal aggrandizement, went too far. He backed, and then in 1896 declined to call back, a failed invasion of the Transvaal, which was designed to topple the Dutch-speaking republic. Repudiated by top British leaders who had encouraged his plan, Rhodes had to resign as prime minister. In declining health, he continued to agitate against the Afrikaner republics. He died at age forty-nine as the South African War (1899–1902) ended.

In accounting for Rhodes's remarkable but flawed achievements, both sympathetic and critical biographers stress his imposing size, enormous energy, and powerful personality. His ideas were commonplace, but he believed in them passionately, and he could persuade and inspire others to follow his lead. Rhodes the idealist was nonetheless a born negotiator, a crafty

Cecil Rhodes, after crushing the last African revolt in Rhodesia in 1896. (Brown Brothers)

dealmaker who believed that everyone could be had for a price. According to his best biographer, Rhodes's homosexuality—discreet, partially repressed, and undeniable—was also "a major component of his magnetism and his success."† Never comfortable with women, he loved male companionship. He drew together a "band of brothers," both gay and straight, to share in the pursuit of power.

Rhodes cared nothing for the rights of blacks. Ever a combination of visionary and opportunist, he looked forward to an eventual reconciliation of Afrikaners and British in a united white front. Therefore, as prime minister of the Cape Colony, he broke with the colony's liberal tradition and supported Afrikaner demands to reduce drastically the number of black voters and limit black freedoms. This helped lay the foundation for the Union of South Africa's brutal policy of racial segregation known as *apartheid* after 1948.

Questions for Analysis

1. How did Rhodes relate to Afrikaners and to black Africans? How do you account for the differences and the similarities?
2. In what ways does Rhodes's career throw additional light on the debate over the causes of the new imperialism?

*Robert Rotberg, *The Founder: Cecil Rhodes and the Pursuit of Power* (New York: Oxford University Press, 1988), p. 150.
†Ibid., p. 408.

Online Study Center   **Improve Your Grade**
Going Beyond Individuals in Society

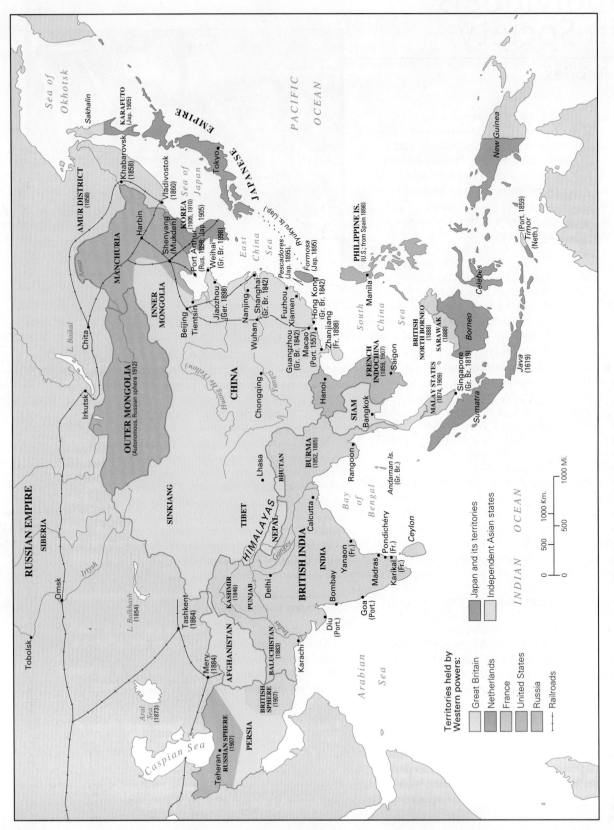

MAP 26.3 Asia in 1914 India remained under British rule, while China precariously preserved its political independence. The Dutch empire in modern-day Indonesia was old, but French control of Indochina was a product of the new imperialism.

Territories held by Western powers:
- Great Britain
- Netherlands
- France
- United States
- Russia
- Railroads

Japan and its territories

Independent Asian states

RUSSIAN EMPIRE

SIBERIA

Tobolsk

Omsk

Irtysh

L. Balkhash (1854)

Tashkent (1864)

Aral Sea (1873)

Merv (1884)

Caspian Sea

Teheran

PERSIA

RUSSIAN SPHERE (1907)

BRITISH SPHERE (1907)

BALUCHISTAN (1883)

AFGHANISTAN

Karachi

Diu (Port.)

Goa (Port.)

Arabian Sea

Delhi

PUNJAB

KASHMIR (1846)

SINKIANG

Indus

Bombay

INDIA

BRITISH INDIA

Yanaon (Fr.)

Madras

Pondichéry (Fr.)

Karikal (Fr.)

Ceylon

Bay of Bengal

Andaman Is. (Gr. Br.)

INDIAN OCEAN

Ganges

NEPAL

HIMALAYAS

TIBET

Lhasa

BHUTAN

BURMA (1852, 1885)

Rangoon

Calcutta

L. Baikal

Irkutsk

Chita

OUTER MONGOLIA (Autonomous, Russian sphere 1912)

INNER MONGOLIA

CHINA

Huang He (Yellow)

Chongqing

Yangzi

Wuhan

Beijing

Tientsin

Jiaozhou (Ger. 1898)

Nanjing

Shanghai (Gr. Br. 1842)

Fuzhou

Xiamen

Guangzhou (Gr. Br. 1842)

Macao (Port. 1557)

Hong Kong (Gr. Br. 1842)

Zhanjiang (Fr. 1898)

Hanoi

FRENCH INDOCHINA (1859, 1907)

Saigon

SIAM

Bangkok

South China Sea

MANCHURIA

Harbin

Shenyang (Mukden)

Port Arthur (Rus. 1898; Jap. 1905)

Weihai (Gr. Br. 1898)

KOREA (1905, 1910)

Khabarovsk (1858)

Vladivostok (1860)

AMUR DISTRICT (1858)

Amur

Sea of Okhotsk

Sakhalin

KARAFUTO (Jap. 1905)

Sea of Japan

Tokyo

JAPANESE EMPIRE

Ryukyu Is. (Jap.)

East China Sea

Pescadores (Jap. 1895)

Formosa (Jap. 1895)

PACIFIC OCEAN

PHILIPPINE IS. (U.S.: from Spain 1898)

Manila

BRITISH NORTH BORNEO (1888)

SARAWAK (1888)

Borneo

MALAY STATES (1874, 1909)

Singapore (Gr. Br. 1819)

Sumatra

Java (1619)

Celebes

New Guinea

(Port. 1859)

Timor (Neth.)

1000 Mi.

1000 Km.

500

0

to stop short of actually fighting each other. Imperial ambitions were not worth a great European war.

Imperialism in Asia

Although the sudden division of Africa was more spectacular, Europeans also extended their political control in Asia. In 1815 the Dutch ruled little more than the island of Java in the East Indies. Thereafter they gradually brought almost all of the three-thousand-mile archipelago under their political authority, though—in good imperialist fashion—they had to share some of the spoils with Britain and Germany. In the critical decade of the 1880s, the French under the leadership of Ferry took Indochina. India, Japan, and China also experienced a profound imperialist impact (see Map 26.3).

Two other great imperialist powers, Russia and the United States, also acquired rich territories in Asia. Russia moved steadily forward on two fronts throughout the nineteenth century. Russians conquered Muslim areas to the south in the Caucasus and in Central Asia and also proceeded to nibble greedily on China's outlying provinces in the Far East, especially in the 1890s.

The United States's great conquest was the Philippines, taken from Spain in 1898 after the Spanish-American War. When it quickly became clear that the United States had no intention of granting independence, Philippine patriots rose in revolt and were suppressed only after long, bitter fighting. Some Americans protested the taking of the Philippines, but to no avail. Thus another great Western power joined the imperialist ranks in Asia.

Causes of the New Imperialism

Many factors contributed to the late-nineteenth-century rush for territory and empire, which was in turn one aspect of Western society's generalized expansion in the age of industry and nationalism. It is little wonder that controversies have raged over interpretation of the new imperialism, especially since authors of every persuasion have often exaggerated particular aspects in an attempt to prove their own theories. Yet despite complexity and controversy, basic causes are clearly identifiable.

Economic motives played an important role in the extension of political empires, especially the British Empire. By the late 1870s, France, Germany, and the United States were industrializing rapidly behind rising tariff barriers. Great Britain was losing its early lead and facing increasingly tough competition in foreign markets. In this new economic situation, Britain came to value old possessions, especially its vast colony of India, which it

had exploited most profitably for more than a century. When continental powers began to grab territory in the 1880s, the British followed suit immediately. They feared that France and Germany would seal off their empires with high tariffs and restrictions and that future economic opportunities would be lost forever.

Actually, the overall economic gains of the new imperialism proved quite limited before 1914. The new colonies were simply too poor to buy much, and they offered few immediately profitable investments. Nonetheless, even the poorest, most barren desert was jealously prized, and no territory was ever abandoned. Colonies became important for political and diplomatic reasons. Each leading country saw colonies as crucial to national security, military power, and international prestige. For instance, safeguarding the Suez Canal played a key role in the British occupation of Egypt, and protecting Egypt in turn led to the bloody conquest of Sudan. Far-flung possessions guaranteed ever-growing navies the safe havens and the dependable coaling stations they needed in time of crisis or war.

Many people were convinced that colonies were essential to great nations. "There has never been a great power without great colonies," wrote one French publicist in 1877. "Every virile people has established colonial power," echoed the famous nationalist historian of Germany, Heinrich von Treitschke. "All great nations in the fullness of their strength have desired to set their mark upon barbarian lands and those who fail to participate in this great rivalry will play a pitiable role in time to come."[6]

Treitschke's harsh statement reflects not only the increasing aggressiveness of European nationalism after Bismarck's wars of German unification but also Social Darwinian theories of brutal competition among races. As one prominent English economist argued, the "strongest nation has always been conquering the weaker . . . and the strongest tend to be best." Thus European nations, which were seen as racially distinct parts of the dominant white race, had to seize colonies to show they were strong and virile. Moreover, since racial struggle was nature's inescapable law, the conquest of "inferior" peoples was just. "The path of progress is strewn with the wreck . . . of inferior races," wrote one professor in 1900. "Yet these dead peoples are, in very truth, the stepping stones on which mankind has risen to the higher intellectual and deeper emotional life of today."[7] Social Darwinism and harsh racial doctrines fostered imperialist expansion.

So did the industrial world's unprecedented technological and military superiority. Three aspects were crucial. First, the rapidly firing machine gun, so lethal at Omdurman in Sudan, was an ultimate weapon in many another unequal battle. Second, newly discovered quinine proved no less effective in controlling attacks of malaria, which had previously decimated whites in the tropics whenever they left breezy coastal enclaves and dared to venture into mosquito-infested interiors. Third, the combination of the steamship and the international telegraph permitted Western powers to quickly concentrate their firepower in a given area when it was needed. Never before—and never again after 1914—would the technological gap between the West and non-Western regions of the world be so great.

Social tensions and domestic political conflicts also contributed mightily to overseas expansion. In Germany, in Russia, and in other countries to a lesser extent, contemporary critics of imperialism charged conservative political leaders with manipulating colonial issues in order to divert popular attention from the class struggle at home and to create a false sense of national unity. Thus imperial propagandists relentlessly stressed that colonies benefited workers as well as capitalists, providing jobs and cheap raw materials that raised workers' standard of living. Government leaders and their allies in the tabloid press successfully encouraged the masses to savor foreign triumphs and glory in the supposed increase in national prestige. In short, conservative leaders defined imperialist development as a national necessity, which they used to justify the status quo and their hold on power.

Finally, certain special-interest groups in each country were powerful agents of expansion. Shipping companies wanted lucrative subsidies. White settlers demanded more land and greater protection. Missionaries and humanitarians wanted to spread religion and stop the slave trade. Military men and colonial officials, whose role has often been overlooked, foresaw rapid advancement and high-paid positions in growing empires. The actions of such groups pushed the course of empire forward.

A Missionary School A Swahili schoolboy leads his classmates in a reading lesson in Dar es Salaam in German East Africa before 1914, as portraits of Emperor William II and his wife look down on the classroom. Europeans argued that they were spreading the benefits of a superior civilization with schools like this one, which is unusually solid because of its strategic location in the capital city. *(Ullstein Bilderdienst/The Granger Collection, New York)*

A "Civilizing Mission"

Western society did not rest the case for empire solely on naked conquest and a Darwinian racial struggle or on power politics and the need for naval bases on every ocean. Imperialists developed additional arguments in order to satisfy their consciences and answer their critics.

A favorite idea was that Europeans could and should "civilize" more primitive, nonwhite peoples. According to this view, nonwhites would eventually receive the benefits of modern economies, cities, advanced medicine, and higher standards of living. In time, they might be ready for self-government and Western democracy. Thus the French spoke of their sacred "civilizing mission." In 1899 Rudyard Kipling (1865–1936), who wrote masterfully of Anglo-Indian life and was perhaps the most influential British writer of the 1890s, exhorted Europeans (and Americans in the United States) to unselfish service in distant lands:

Take up the White Man's Burden—
  Send forth the best ye breed—
Go bind your sons to exile
  To serve your captives' need,
To wait in heavy harness,
  On fluttered folk and wild—
Your new-caught, sullen peoples
  Half-devil and half-child.[8]

Many Americans accepted the ideology of the **white man's burden.** It was an important factor in the decision to rule, rather than liberate, the Philippines after the Spanish-American War. Like their European counterparts, these Americans sincerely believed that their civilization had reached unprecedented heights and that they had unique benefits to bestow on all "less advanced" peoples. Another argument was that imperial government protected natives from tribal warfare as well as cruder forms of exploitation by white settlers and business people.

Peace and stability under European control also facilitated the spread of Christianity. In Africa Catholic and Protestant missionaries competed with Islam south of the Sahara, seeking converts and building schools to spread the Gospel. Many Africans' first real contact with whites was in mission schools. Some peoples, such as the Ibo in Nigeria, became highly Christianized.

Such occasional successes in black Africa contrasted with the general failure of missionary efforts in India, China, and the Islamic world. There Christians often preached in vain to peoples with ancient, complex religious beliefs. Yet the number of Christian believers around the world did increase substantially in the nineteenth century, and missionary groups kept trying. Unfortunately, "many missionaries had drunk at the well of European racism," and this probably prevented them from doing better.[9]

Critics of Imperialism

The expansion of empire aroused sharp, even bitter, critics. A forceful attack was delivered in 1902, after the unpopular South African War, by radical English economist J. A. Hobson (1858–1940) in his *Imperialism,* a work that influenced Lenin and others. Hobson contended that the rush to acquire colonies was due to the economic needs of unregulated capitalism, particularly the need of the rich to find outlets for their surplus capital. Yet, Hobson argued, imperial possessions did not pay off economically for the country as a whole. Only unscrupulous special-interest groups profited from them, at the expense of both the European taxpayer and the natives. Moreover, Hobson argued that the quest for empire diverted popular attention away from domestic reform and the need to reduce the great gap between rich and poor. These and similar arguments were not very persuasive, however. Most people then (and now) were sold on the idea that imperialism was economically profitable for the homeland, and a broad and genuine enthusiasm for empire developed among the masses.

Hobson and many other critics struck home, however, with their moral condemnation of whites imperiously ruling nonwhites. They rebelled against crude Social Darwinian thought. "O Evolution, what crimes are committed in thy name!" cried one foe. Another sardonically coined a new beatitude: "Blessed are the strong, for they shall prey on the weak."[10] Kipling and his kind were lampooned as racist bullies whose rule rested on brutality, racial contempt, and the Maxim machine gun. Henry Labouchère, a member of Parliament and prominent spokesman for this position, mocked Kipling's famous poem:

Pile on the Brown Man's burden!
And if ye rouse his hate,
Meet his old-fashioned reasons
With Maxims up to date,
With shells and Dum-Dum bullets
A hundred times plain
The Brown Man's loss must never
Imply the White Man's gain.[11]

Similarly, in 1902 in *Heart of Darkness* Polish-born novelist Joseph Conrad (1857–1924) castigated the "pure selfishness" of Europeans in "civilizing" Africa; the main character, once a liberal scholar, turns into a savage brute.

Critics charged Europeans with applying a degrading double standard and failing to live up to their own noble ideals. At home Europeans had won or were winning representative government, individual liberties, and a certain equality of opportunity. In their empires, Europeans imposed military dictatorships on Africans and Asians; forced them to work involuntarily, almost like slaves; and discriminated against them shamelessly. Only by renouncing imperialism, its critics insisted, and giving captive peoples the freedoms Western society had struggled for since the French Revolution would Europeans be worthy of their traditions. Europeans who denounced the imperialist tide provided colonial peoples with a Western ideology of liberation.

Responding to Western Imperialism

To peoples in Africa and Asia, Western expansion represented a profoundly disruptive assault. Everywhere it threatened traditional ruling classes, traditional economies, and traditional ways of life. Christian missionaries and European secular ideologies challenged established beliefs and values. Non-Western peoples experienced a crisis of identity, one made all the more painful by the power and arrogance of the white intruders.

● *What was the general pattern of non-Western responses to Western expansion, and how did India, Japan, and China meet the imperialist challenge?*

The Pattern of Response

Generally, the initial response of African and Asian rulers to aggressive Western expansion was to try to drive the unwelcome foreigners away. This was the case in China, Japan, and upper Sudan, as we have seen. Violent anti-foreign reactions exploded elsewhere again and again, but the superior military technology of the industrialized West almost invariably prevailed. Beaten in battle, many Africans and Asians concentrated on preserving their cultural traditions at all costs. Others found themselves forced to reconsider their initial hostility. Some (such as Ismail of Egypt) concluded that the West was indeed superior in some ways and that it was therefore necessary to reform their societies and copy some European achievements, especially if they wished to escape full-blown Western political rule. Thus it is possible to think of responses to the Western impact as a spectrum, with "traditionalists" at one end, "westernizers" or "modernizers" at the other, and many shades of opinion in between. Both before and after European domination, the struggle among these groups was often intense. With

time, however, the modernizers tended to gain the upper hand.

When the power of both the traditionalists and the modernizers was thoroughly shattered by superior force, the great majority of Asians and Africans accepted imperial rule. Political participation in non-Western lands was historically limited to small elites, and the masses were used to doing what their rulers told them. In these circumstances Europeans, clothed in power and convinced of their righteousness, governed smoothly and effectively. They received considerable support from both traditionalists (local chiefs, landowners, religious leaders) and modernizers (Western-educated professional classes and civil servants).

Nevertheless, imperial rule was in many ways an imposing edifice built on sand. Support for European rule among the conforming and accepting millions was shallow and weak. Thus the conforming masses followed with greater or lesser enthusiasm a few determined personalities who came to oppose the Europeans. Such leaders always arose, both when Europeans ruled directly and when they manipulated native governments, for at least two basic reasons.

First, the nonconformists—the eventual anti-imperialist leaders—developed a burning desire for human dignity. They came to feel that such dignity was incompatible with foreign rule. Second, potential leaders found in the Western world the ideologies and justification for their protest. They discovered liberalism, with its credo of civil liberty and political self-determination. They echoed the demands of anti-imperialists in Europe and America that the West live up to its own ideals. Above all, they found themselves attracted to modern nationalism, which asserted that every people had the right to control its own destiny. After 1917 anti-imperialist revolt would find another weapon in Lenin's version of Marxian socialism. Thus the anti-imperialist search for dignity drew strength from Western thought and culture, as is apparent in the development of three major Asian countries—India, Japan, and China.

Empire in India

India was the jewel of the British Empire, and no colonial area experienced a more profound British impact. Unlike Japan and China, which maintained a real or precarious independence, and unlike African territories, which were annexed by Europeans only at the end of the nineteenth century, India was ruled more or less absolutely by Britain for a very long time.

Arriving in India on the heels of the Portuguese in the seventeenth century, the British East India Company had conquered the last independent native state by 1848. The

Imperial Complexities in India Britain permitted many native princes to continue their rule, if they accepted British domination. This photo shows a road-building project designed to facilitate famine relief in a southern native state. Officials of the local Muslim prince and their British "advisers" watch over workers drawn from the Hindu majority. *(Nizam's Good Works Project—Famine Relief: Road Building, Aurangabad 1895–1902, from Judith Mara Gutman, Through Indian Eyes. Courtesy, Private Collection)*

last "traditional" response to European rule—the attempt by the established ruling classes to drive the white man out by military force—was broken in India in 1857 and 1858. Those were the years of the **Great Rebellion** (which the British called a "mutiny"), when an insurrection by Muslim and Hindu mercenaries in the British army spread throughout northern and central India before it was finally crushed, primarily by loyal native troops from southern India. Thereafter Britain ruled India directly.

After 1858 India was ruled by the British Parliament in London and administered by a tiny, all-white civil service in India. In 1900 this elite consisted of fewer than 3,500 top officials, for a population of 300 million. The white elite, backed by white officers and native troops, was competent and generally well-disposed toward the welfare of the Indian peasant masses. Yet it practiced strict job discrimination and social segregation, and most of its members quite frankly considered the jumble of Indian peoples and castes to be racially inferior. As Lord Kitchener, one of the most distinguished top military commanders in India, stated:

It is this consciousness of the inherent superiority of the European which has won for us India. However well educated and clever a native may be, and however brave he may prove himself, I believe that no rank we can bestow on him would cause him to be considered an equal of the British officer.[12]

British women played an important part in the imperial enterprise, especially after the opening of the Suez Canal in 1869 made it much easier for civil servants and businessmen to bring their wives and children with them to India. These British families tended to live in their own separate communities, where they occupied large houses with well-shaded porches, handsome lawns, and a multitude of servants. It was the wife's responsibility to manage this complex household. Many officials' wives learned to relish their duties, and they directed their households and servants with the same self-confident authoritarianism that characterized British political rule in India. (See the feature "Listening to the Past: A British Woman in India" on pages 876–877.)

A small minority of British women—many of them feminists, social reformers, or missionaries, both married and single—sought to go further and shoulder the "white women's burden" in India, as one historian has described it.[13] These women tried especially to improve the lives of Indian women, both Hindu and Muslim, and to move them closer through education and legislation to the better conditions that they believed Western women had attained. Their greatest success was educating some elite Hindu women who took up the cause of reform.

With British men and women sharing a sense of mission as well as strong feelings of racial and cultural superiority, the British acted energetically and introduced many desirable changes to India. Realizing that they needed well-educated Indians to serve as skilled subordinates in the government and army, the British established a modern system of progressive secondary education in which all instruction was in English. Thus through education and government service, the British offered some Indians excellent opportunities for both economic and social advancement. High-caste Hindus, particularly quick to respond, emerged as skillful intermediaries between the British rulers and the Indian people, and soon they formed a new elite profoundly influenced by Western thought and culture.

This new bureaucratic elite played a crucial role in modern economic development, which was a second result of British rule. Irrigation projects for agriculture, the world's third-largest railroad network for good communications, and large tea and jute plantations geared to the world economy were all developed. Unfortunately, the lot of the Indian masses improved little, for the increase in production was eaten up by population increase.

Finally, with a well-educated, English-speaking Indian bureaucracy and modern communications, the British created a unified, powerful state. They placed under the same general system of law and administration the different Hindu and Muslim peoples and the vanquished kingdoms of the entire subcontinent—groups that had fought each other for centuries and had been repeatedly conquered by Muslim and Mongol invaders. It was as if Europe, with its many states and varieties of Christianity, had been conquered and united in a single great empire.

In spite of these achievements, the decisive reaction to European rule was the rise of nationalism among the Indian elite. No matter how anglicized and necessary a member of the educated classes became, he or she could never become the white ruler's equal. The top jobs, the best clubs, the modern hotels, and even certain railroad compartments were sealed off to brown-skinned Indians. The peasant masses might accept such inequality as the latest version of age-old oppression, but the well-educated, English-speaking elite eventually could not. For the elite, racial discrimination meant injured pride and bitter injustice. It flagrantly contradicted those cherished Western concepts of human rights and equality. Moreover, it was based on dictatorship, no matter how benign.

By 1885, when educated Indians came together to found the predominately Hindu Indian National Congress, demands were increasing for the equality and self-government that Britain had already granted white-settler colonies, such as Canada and Australia. By 1907, emboldened in part by Japan's success (see the next section), the radicals in the Indian National Congress were calling for complete independence. Even the moderates were demanding home rule for India through an elected parliament. Although there were sharp divisions between Hindus and Muslims, Indians were finding an answer to the foreign challenge. The common heritage of British rule and Western ideals, along with the reform and revitalization of the Hindu religion, had created a genuine movement for national independence.

The Example of Japan

When Commodore Matthew Perry arrived in Japan in 1853 with his crude but effective gunboat diplomacy,

Japan was a complex feudal society. At the top stood a figurehead emperor, but real power was in the hands of a hereditary military governor, the **shogun**. With the help of a warrior nobility known as **samurai**, the shogun governed a country of hard-working, productive peasants and city dwellers. Often poor and restless, the intensely proud samurai were humiliated by the sudden American intrusion and the unequal treaties with Western countries.

When foreign diplomats and merchants began to settle in Yokohama, radical samurai reacted with a wave of antiforeign terrorism and antigovernment assassinations between 1858 and 1863. The imperialist response was swift and unambiguous. An allied fleet of American, British, Dutch, and French warships demolished key forts, further weakening the power and prestige of the shogun's government. Then in 1867, a coalition led by patriotic samurai seized control of the government with hardly any bloodshed and restored the political power of the emperor. This was the Meiji Restoration, a great turning point in Japanese development.

The immediate, all-important goal of the new government was to meet the foreign threat. The battle cry of the Meiji reformers was "Enrich the state and strengthen the armed forces." Yet how were these tasks to be done? In an about-face that was one of history's most remarkable chapters, the young but well-trained, idealistic but flexible leaders of Meiji Japan dropped their antiforeign attacks. Convinced that Western civilization was indeed superior in its military and industrial aspects, they initiated from above a series of measures to reform Japan along modern lines. In the broadest sense, the Meiji leaders tried to harness the power inherent in Europe's dual revolution in order to protect their country and catch up with the West.

In 1871 the new leaders abolished the old feudal structure of aristocratic, decentralized government and formed a strong unified state. Following the example of the French Revolution, they dismantled the four-class legal system and declared social equality. They decreed freedom of movement in a country where traveling abroad had been a most serious crime. They created a free, competitive, government-stimulated economy. Japan began to build railroads and modern factories. Thus the new generation adopted many principles of a free, liberal society, and, as in Europe, such freedom resulted in a tremendously creative release of human energy.

Yet the overriding concern of Japan's political leadership was always a powerful state, and to achieve this, more than liberalism was borrowed from the West. A powerful modern navy was created, and the army was completely reorganized along European lines, with three-year military service for all males and a professional officer corps.

The Rapid Modernization of the Japanese Army This woodcut from about 1870 shows Japanese soldiers outfitted in Western uniforms and marching in Western formation. Japanese reformers, impressed by Prussian discipline and success on the battlefield, looked to Germany for their military models. *(Ryogoku Tsuneo Tamba Collection/Laurie Platt Winfrey)*

This army of draftees effectively put down disturbances in the countryside, and in 1877 it was used to crush a major rebellion by feudal elements protesting the loss of their privileges. Japan also borrowed rapidly and adapted skillfully the West's science and modern technology, particularly in industry, medicine, and education. Many Japanese were encouraged to study abroad, and the government paid large salaries to attract foreign experts. These experts were always carefully controlled, however, and replaced by trained Japanese as soon as possible.

By 1890, when the new state was firmly established, the

wholesale borrowing of the early restoration had given way to more selective emphasis on those things foreign that were in keeping with Japanese tradition. Following the model of the German Empire, Japan established an authoritarian constitution and rejected democracy. The power of the emperor and his ministers was vast, that of the legislature limited.

Japan successfully copied the imperialism of Western society. Expansion not only proved that Japan was strong; it also cemented the nation together in a great mission. Having "opened" Korea with the gunboat diplomacy of imperialism in 1876, Japan decisively defeated China in a war over Korea in 1894 and 1895 and took Formosa (modern-day Taiwan). In the next years, Japan competed aggressively with the leading European powers for influence and territory in China, particularly Manchuria. There Japanese and Russian imperialism met and collided. In 1904 Japan attacked Russia without warning, and after a bloody war, Japan emerged with a valuable foothold in China, Russia's former protectorate over Port Arthur (see Map 26.3). By 1910, with the annexation of Korea, Japan had become a major imperialist power.

Japan became the first non-Western country to use an ancient love of country to transform itself and thereby meet the many-sided challenge of Western expansion. Moreover, Japan demonstrated convincingly that a modern Asian nation could defeat and humble a great Western power. Many Chinese nationalists were fascinated by Japan's achievement. A group of patriots in French-ruled southern Vietnam sent Vietnamese students to Japan to learn the island empire's secret of success. Japan provided patriots throughout Asia and Africa with an inspiring example of national recovery and liberation.

Toward Revolution in China

In 1860 the two-hundred-year-old Qing Dynasty in China appeared on the verge of collapse. Efforts to repel foreigners had failed, and rebellion and chaos wracked the country. Yet the government drew on its traditional strengths and made a surprising comeback that lasted more than thirty years.

Two factors were crucial in this reversal. First, the traditional ruling groups temporarily produced new and effective leadership. Loyal scholar-statesmen and generals quelled disturbances such as the great Tai Ping rebellion. The empress dowager Tzu Hsi, a truly remarkable woman, governed in the name of her young son and combined shrewd insight with vigorous action to revitalize the bureaucracy.

Second, destructive foreign aggression lessened, for the Europeans had obtained their primary goal of commercial and diplomatic relations. Indeed, some Europeans contributed to the dynasty's recovery. A talented Irishman effectively reorganized China's customs office and increased the government tax receipts, while a sympathetic American diplomat represented China in foreign lands and helped strengthen the central government. Such efforts dovetailed with the dynasty's efforts to adopt some aspects of Western government and technology while maintaining traditional Chinese values and beliefs.

The parallel movement toward domestic reform and limited cooperation with the West collapsed under the blows of Japanese imperialism. The Sino-Japanese War of 1894 to 1895 and the subsequent harsh peace treaty revealed China's helplessness in the face of aggression, triggering a rush for foreign concessions and protectorates in China. At the high point of this rush in 1898, it appeared that the European powers might actually divide China among themselves, as they had recently divided Africa. Probably only the jealousy each nation felt toward its imperialist competitors saved China from partition, although the U.S. Open Door policy, which opposed formal annexation of Chinese territory, may have helped tip the balance. In any event, the tempo of foreign encroachment greatly accelerated after 1894.

So, too, did the intensity and radicalism of the Chinese reaction. Like the leaders of the Meiji Restoration, some modernizers saw salvation in Western institutions. In 1898 the government launched a desperate **hundred days of reform** in an attempt to meet the foreign challenge. More radical reformers, such as the revolutionary Sun Yat-sen (1866–1925), who came from the peasantry and was educated in Hawaii by Christian missionaries, sought to overthrow the dynasty altogether and establish a republic.

On the other side, some traditionalists turned back toward ancient practices, political conservatism, and fanatical hatred of the "foreign devils." "Protect the country, destroy the foreigner" was their simple motto. Such conservative, antiforeign patriots had often clashed with foreign missionaries, whom they charged with undermining reverence for ancestors and thereby threatening the Chinese family and the entire society. In the agony of defeat and unwanted reforms, secret societies such as the Boxers rebelled. In northeastern China, more than two hundred foreign missionaries and several thousand Chinese Christians were killed. Once again the imperialist response was swift and harsh. Peking was occupied and plundered by foreign armies. A heavy indemnity was imposed.

The years after the Boxer Rebellion (1900–1903) were

The Empress Dowager Tzu Hsi (1835–1908) Tzu Hsi drew on conservative forces, like the court eunuchs surrounding her here, to maintain her power. Three years after her death in 1908, a revolution broke out and forced the last Chinese emperor, a boy of six, to abdicate. *(Freer Gallery of Art and Arthur M. Sackler Gallery Archives, Smithsonian Institution. Photographer: Hsun-ling. Negative no. 261)*

ever more troubled. Anarchy and foreign influence spread as the power and prestige of the Qing Dynasty declined still further. Antiforeign, antigovernment revolutionary groups agitated and plotted. Finally in 1912, a spontaneous uprising toppled the Qing Dynasty. After thousands of years of emperors and empires, a loose coalition of revolutionaries proclaimed a Western-style republic and called for an elected parliament. The transformation of China under the impact of expanding Western society entered a new phase, and the end was not in sight.

Chapter Summary

Online Study Center **ACE the Test**

- What were some of the global consequences of European industrialization between 1815 and 1914?
- How was massive migration an integral part of Western expansion?
- How and why after 1875 did European nations rush to build political empires in Africa and Asia?
- What was the general pattern of non-Western responses to Western expansion, and how did India, Japan, and China meet the imperialist challenge?

Key Terms

Third World	Afrikaners
opium trade	Berlin conference
khedive	white man's burden
great migration	Great Rebellion
swallows	shogun
great white walls	samurai
new imperialism	hundred days of reform

Online Study Center **Improve Your Grade** Flashcards

In the nineteenth century, the industrializing West entered the third and most dynamic phase of its centuries-old expansion into non-Western lands. In so doing, Western nations promoted a prodigious growth of world trade, forced reluctant countries such as China and Japan into the globalizing economy, and profitably subordinated many lands to their economic interests. Western nations also sent forth millions of emigrants to the sparsely populated areas of European settlement, which generally limited migration from Asia.

After 1875, Western countries grabbed vast political empires in Africa and rushed to establish political influence in Asia. The reasons for this culminating surge were many, but the economic thrust of robust industrial capitalism, an ever-growing lead in technology, and the competitive pressures of European nationalism were particularly important.

Western expansion had far-reaching consequences. For the first time in human history, the world became in many ways a single unit. Moreover, European expansion diffused the ideas and techniques of a highly developed civilization. Yet the West relied on force to conquer and rule, and it treated non-Western peoples as racial inferiors. Thus non-Western elites, often armed with Western doctrines, gradually responded to the Western challenge. As the histories of India, Japan, and China show, non-Western elites launched a national, anti-imperialist struggle for dignity, genuine independence, and modernization. This struggle would emerge as a central drama of world history after the great European civil war of 1914 to 1918, which reduced the West's technological advantage and shattered its self-confidence and complacent moral superiority.

Suggested Reading

Aldrich, Robert. *Greater France: A History of French Overseas Expansion*. 1996. A well-balanced study.

Bagchi, Amiya Kumar. *Perilous Passage: Mankind and the Ascendancy of Capital*. 2005. A spirited radical critique of the "rise of the West."

Conklin, Alice. *A Mission to Civilize: The French Republican Ideal and West Africa, 1895–1930*. 1997. An outstanding examination of French imperialism.

Conrad, Joseph. *Heart of Darkness*. A novel that unforgettably probes European imperial motives.

Cook, Scott B. *Colonial Encounters in the Age of High Imperialism*. 1996. A stimulating overview with a very readable account of the explorer Stanley and central Africa.

Crews, Robert. *For Prophet and Tsar: Islam and Empire in Russia and Central Asia*. 2006. Considers neglected aspects of Russian imperialism.

Curtin, P., et al. *African History: From Earliest Times to Independence,* 2d ed. 1995. An excellent brief introduction to Africa in the age of imperialism.

Ebrey, Patricia Buckley. *The Cambridge Illustrated History of China*. 1999. A lively and beautiful work by a leading specialist.

Fage, J. D. *A History of Africa*, 3d ed. 1995. A highly recommended account.

Goodlad, Graham. *British Foreign and Imperial Policy, 1865–1919*. 2000. A lively examination of Britain's leading position in European imperialism.

Hochshild, Adam. *King Leopold's Ghost: A Story of Greed, Terror, and Heroism in Colonial Africa, 1895–1930*. 1997. A chilling account of Belgian imperialism in the Congo.

Maier, Charles S. *Among Empires: American Ascendancy and Its Predecessors*. 2006. Examines imperial power in history and how well America measures up.

Marshall, P. J., ed. *Cambridge Illustrated History of the British Empire*. 1996. A stunning pictorial history.

Midgley, Clare, ed. *Gender and Imperialism*. 1998. Examines the complex questions related to European women and imperialism.

Rotberg, Robert I. *The Founder: Cecil Rhodes and the Pursuit of Power*. 1988. Examines the imperialist's mind and times with great acuity.

Said, Edward. *Orientalism*. 1978. An exceedingly influential cultural study of imperialism and non-Europeans.

Notes

1. Quoted in J. W. Hall, *Japan, from Prehistory to Modern Times* (New York: Delacorte Press, 1970), p. 250.
2. Quoted in Earl of Cromer, *Modern Egypt* (London, 1911), p. 48.
3. Quoted in T. Blegen, *Norwegian Migration to America,* vol. 2 (Northfield, Minn.: Norwegian-American Historical Association, 1940), p. 468.
4. Quoted in W. L. Langer, *European Alliances and Alignments, 1871–1890* (New York: Vintage Books, 1931), p. 290.
5. Quoted in J. Ellis, *The Social History of the Machine Gun* (New York: Pantheon Books, 1975), pp. 86, 101.
6. Quoted in G. H. Nadel and P. Curtis, eds., *Imperialism and Colonialism* (New York: Macmillan, 1964), p. 94.
7. Quoted in W. L. Langer, *The Diplomacy of Imperialism,* 2d ed. (New York: Alfred A. Knopf, 1951), pp. 86, 88.
8. Rudyard Kipling, *The Five Nations* (London, 1903).
9. E. H. Berman, "African Responses to Christian Mission Education," *African Studies Review* 17 (1974): 530.
10. Quoted in Langer, *The Diplomacy of Imperialism,* p. 88.
11. Quoted in Ellis, *The Social History of the Machine Gun,* pp. 99–100.
12. Quoted in K. M. Panikkar, *Asia and Western Dominance: A Survey of the Vasco da Gama Epoch of Asian History* (London: George Allen & Unwin, 1959), p. 116.
13. A. Burton, "The White Women's Burden: British Feminists and 'The Indian Women,' 1865–1915," in *Western Women and Imperialism: Complicity and Resistance,* ed. N. Chauduri and M. Strobel (Bloomington: Indiana University Press, 1992), pp. 137–157.

A British Woman in India

Guides for housekeeping became popular in Europe in the nineteenth century as middle-class women funneled great energy into their homes. A British woman in India probably consulted The Complete Indian Housekeeper and Cook by Flora Annie Steel and Grace Gardiner, a bestseller published in 1888 and frequently updated.

Steel (1847–1929) moved to India in 1867 with her husband, a civil engineer, and lived there until the family returned to England in 1889. Accustomed to directing a large household with several Indian servants, Steel believed herself well qualified to offer advice "to English girls to whom fate may assign the task of being house-mothers in our Eastern empire." The following passage focuses on how the British mistress should manage her Indian servants, and along with practical suggestions it lays bare some basic attitudes and assumptions of Europeans in colonial settings. Steel subsequently wrote books on India, education, and women's issues.

Housekeeping in India, when once the first strangeness has worn off, is a far easier task in many ways than it is in England, though it none the less requires time, and, in this present transitional period, an almost phenomenal patience. . . .

And, first it must be distinctly understood that it is not necessary, or in the least degree desirable, that an educated woman should waste the best years of her life in scolding and petty supervision. Life holds higher duties, and it is indubitable that friction and over-zeal is a sure sign of a bad housekeeper. . . .

Easy, however, as the actual housekeeping is in India, the personal attention of the mistress is quite as much needed here as at home. The Indian servant, it is true, learns more readily, and is guiltless of the sniffiness with which Mary Jane [the servant in England] receives suggestions, but a few days of absence or neglect on the part of the mistress, results in the servants falling into their old habits with the inherited conservatism of dirt. This is, of course, disheartening, but it has to be

faced as a necessary condition of life, until a few generations of training shall have started the Indian servant on a new inheritance of habit. It must never be forgotten that at present those mistresses who aim at anything beyond keeping a good table are in the minority, and that pioneering is always arduous work.

The first duty of a mistress is, of course, to be able to give intelligible orders to her servants; therefore it is necessary she should learn to speak Hindustani. No sane Englishwomen would dream of living, say, for twenty years, in Germany, Italy, or France, without making the *attempt,* at any rate, to learn the language. . . .

The next duty is obviously to insist on her orders being carried out. And here we come to the burning question: "How is this to be done?" Certainly, there is at present very little to which we can appeal in the average Indian servant, but then, until it is implanted by training, there is very little sense of duty in a child; yet in some well-regulated nurseries obedience is a foregone conclusion. The secret lies in making rules, and *keeping to them.* The Indian servant is a child in everything save age, and should be treated as a child; that is to say, kindly, but with the greatest firmness. The laws of the household should be those of the Medes and Persians, and first faults should never go unpunished. By overlooking a first offence, we lose the only opportunity we have of preventing it becoming a habit.

But it will be asked, How are we to punish our servants when we have no hold either on their minds or bodies? . . .

In their own experience the authors have found a system of rewards and punishments perfectly easy of attainment. One of them has for years adopted the plan of engaging her servants at so much a month—the lowest rate at which such servant is obtainable—and so much extra as *buksheesh* [a bonus], conditional on good service. For instance, a *khitmutgâr* [male table servant] is engaged permanently on Rs. 9 a month, but the additional rupee which makes the wage up to that usually demanded by good servants is a fluctuating assessment! . . . That plan has never been objected to, and . . . the household quite enters into the spirit of the idea, infinitely preferring it to volcanic eruptions of fault-finding. . . .

In regard to actual housekeeping, the authors emphatically deny the common assertion that it must necessarily run on different lines to what it does in England. Economy, prudence, efficiency are the same all over the world, and because butcher meat is cheap, that is no excuse for its being wasted. Some modification, of course, there must be, *but as little as possible.* . . .

A good mistress in India will try to set a good example to her servants in routine, method, and tidiness. Half-an-hour after breakfast should be sufficient for the whole arrangements for the day; but that half-hour should be given as punctually as possible. An untidy mistress invariably has *untidy,* a weak one, *idle* servants. It should never be forgotten that—though it is true in both hemispheres that if you want a thing done you should do it yourself—still, having to do it is a distinct confession of failure in your original intention. Anxious housewifes are too apt to accept defeat in this way; the result being that the lives of educated women are wasted in doing the work of lazy servants.

The authors' advice is therefore—

"Never do work which an ordinarily good servant ought to be able to do. If the one you have will not or cannot do it, get another who can." . . .

Having thus gone generally into the duties of the mistress, we may detail what in our opinion should be the daily routine.

The great object is to secure three things—smooth working, quick ordering, and subsequent peace and leisure to the mistress. It is as well, therefore, with a view to the preservation of temper, to eat your breakfast in peace before venturing into the pantry and cookroom; it is besides a mistake to be constantly on the worry.

Inspection parade should begin, then, immediately after breakfast, or as near ten o'clock as circumstances will allow. The cook should be waiting—in clean raiment—with a pile of plates, and his viands for the day spread out on a table. With everything *en evidence,* it will not take five minutes to decide on what is best, while a very constant occurrence at Indian tables—the serving up of stale, sour, and unwholesome food—will be avoided. It is perhaps *not* pleasant to go into such details, but a good mistress will remember the breadwinner who requires blood-forming nourishment, and the children whose constitutions are

An English lady attended by her Indian servants. *(Stapleton Collection, UK/The Bridgeman Art Library)*

being built up day by day, sickly or healthy, according to the food given them; and bear in mind the fact that, in India especially, half the comfort of life depends on clean, wholesome, digestible food. . . .

We do not wish to advocate an unholy haughtiness; but an Indian household can no more be governed peacefully, without dignity and prestige, than an Indian Empire. For instance, if the mistress wishes to teach the cook a new dish, let her give the order for everything, down to charcoal, to be ready at a given time, and the cook in attendance; and let her do nothing herself that the servants can do, if only for this reason, that the only way of teaching is to *see* things done, not to let others see *you* do them.

Questions for Analysis

1. What challenges does the British housekeeper face in India? How, according to Steel, should she meet them?

2. In what ways do Steel's comments and housekeeping policies reflect the attitudes of European imperialism?

Source: F. A. Steel and G. Gardiner, *The Complete Indian Housekeeper and Cook* (London: William Heinemann, 1902), chap. 1. Reprinted in L. DiCaprio and M. Wiesner, eds., *Lives and Voices: Sources in European Women's History* (Boston: Houghton Mifflin, 2001), pp. 323–328.

French soldiers in the trenches man a machine gun, the weapon that killed so many, in this chilling work by Christopher Nevinson. *(© Tate, London 2007/Art Resource, NY)*

THE GREAT BREAK: WAR AND REVOLUTION, 1914–1919

I n the summer of 1914, the nations of Europe went willingly to war. They believed they had no other choice. Moreover, both peoples and governments confidently expected a short war leading to a decisive victory. Such a war, they believed, would "clear the air," and European society would be able to go on as before.

These expectations were almost totally mistaken. The First World War was long, indecisive, and tremendously destructive. To the shell-shocked generation of survivors, it was known simply as the Great War: the war of unprecedented scope and intensity. From today's perspective, it is clear that the First World War marked a great break in the course of Western historical development since the French and Industrial Revolutions. A noted British political scientist has gone so far as to say that even in victorious and relatively fortunate Great Britain, the First World War was *the* great turning point in government and society, "as in everything else in modern British history. . . . There's a much greater difference between the Britain of 1914 and, say, 1920, than between the Britain of 1920 and today."[1] This strong statement contains a great amount of truth, for all of Europe as well as for Britain. World War I was a revolutionary conflict of gigantic proportions.

The First World War

The First World War was extremely long and destructive because it involved all the Great Powers and because it quickly degenerated into a senseless military stalemate. Like evenly matched boxers in a championship bout, the two sides tried to wear each other down. But there was no referee to call a draw, only the blind hammering of a life-or-death struggle.

• *What caused the Great War, and why did it have such revolutionary consequences?*

Online Study Center

This icon will direct you to interactive activities and study materials on the website **college.hmco.com/pic/mckaywest9e**

The Bismarckian System of Alliances

The Franco-Prussian War and the founding of the German Empire opened a new era in international relations. France was decisively defeated in 1871 and forced to pay a large war indemnity and give up Alsace-Lorraine. In ten short years, from 1862 to 1871, Bismarck had made Prussia-Germany—traditionally the weakest of the Great Powers—the most powerful nation in Europe (see pages 821–825).

Yet, as Bismarck never tired of repeating after 1871, Germany was a "satisfied" power. Within Europe, Germany had no territorial ambitions and wanted only peace.

But how was peace to be preserved? Bismarck's first concern was to keep an embittered France diplomatically isolated and without military allies. His second concern was the threat to peace posed from the east, from Austria-Hungary and from Russia. Those two enormous multinational empires had many conflicting interests, particularly

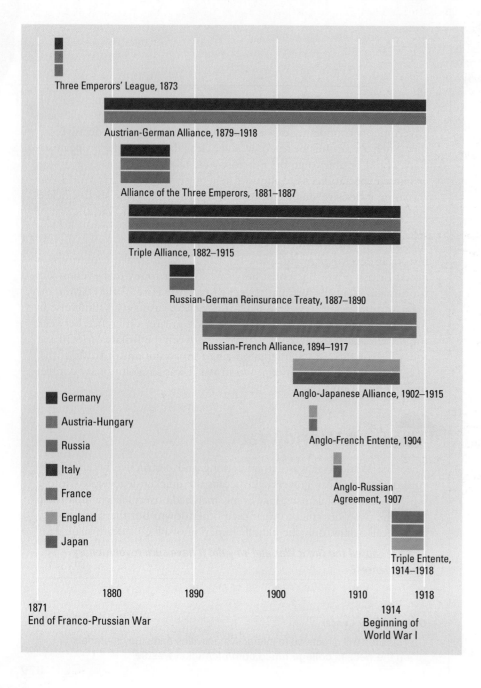

FIGURE 27.1 The Alliance System After 1871 Bismarck's subtle diplomacy maintained reasonably good relations among the eastern monarchies—Germany, Russia, and Austria-Hungary—and kept France isolated. The situation changed dramatically in 1891, when the Russian-French Alliance divided the Great Powers into two fairly equal military blocs.

in southeastern Europe, where the strength of the Ottoman Empire was ebbing fast. There was a real threat that Germany might be dragged into a great war between the two rival empires. Bismarck's solution was a system of alliances (see Figure 27.1) to restrain both Russia and Austria-Hungary, to prevent conflict between them, and to isolate a hostile France, which could never forget the loss of Alsace-Lorraine.

A first step was the creation in 1873 of the conservative **Three Emperors' League,** which linked the monarchs of Austria-Hungary, Germany, and Russia in an alliance against radical movements. In 1877 and 1878, when Russia's victories in a war with the Ottoman Empire threatened the balance of Austrian and Russian interests in the Balkans and the balance of British and Russian interests in the entire Middle East, Bismarck played the role of sincere peacemaker. But his balancing efforts at the Congress of Berlin in 1878 infuriated Russian nationalists, and this led Bismarck to conclude a defensive military alliance with Austria against Russia in 1879. This alliance lasted until 1918 and the end of World War I. Motivated by tensions with France, Italy joined Germany and Austria in 1882, thereby forming what became known as the Triple Alliance.

Bismarck continued to work for peace in eastern Europe, seeking to neutralize tensions between Austria-Hungary and Russia. In 1881 he capitalized on their mutual fears and cajoled them both into a secret alliance with Germany. This Alliance of the Three Emperors lasted until 1887.

Bismarck also maintained good relations with Britain and Italy, while encouraging France in Africa but keeping France isolated in Europe. In 1887 Russia declined to renew the Alliance of the Three Emperors because of new tensions in the Balkans. Bismarck craftily substituted the Russian-German Reinsurance Treaty, by which both states promised neutrality if the other was attacked.

Bismarck's accomplishments in foreign policy after 1871 were great. For almost a generation, he maintained German leadership in international affairs, and he worked successfully for peace by managing conflicts and by restraining Austria-Hungary and Russia with defensive alliances.

The Rival Blocs

In 1890 the young, impetuous Emperor William II dismissed Bismarck, in part because of the chancellor's friendly policy toward Russia since the 1870s. William then adamantly refused to renew the Russian-German Reinsurance Treaty, in spite of Russian willingness to do so. This fateful departure in foreign affairs prompted long-

Chronology

1912	First Balkan War
1914	Assassination of Archduke Francis Ferdinand
1914–1918	World War I
1915	Italy and Bulgaria enter World War I; Ministry of Munitions established in Britain
1916	German males between seventeen and sixty required to work only for war effort; Rasputin murdered
1916–1918	Growth of antiwar movement throughout Europe
1917	Russian Revolution
1919	Treaty of Versailles

isolated republican France to court absolutist Russia, offering loans, arms, and friendship. In both countries, there were enthusiastic public demonstrations of friendship in 1891, and in early 1894 France and Russia became military allies. This alliance (see Figure 27.1) was to remain in effect as long as the Triple Alliance of Austria, Germany, and Italy existed. As a result, continental Europe was dangerously divided into two rival blocs.

Online Study Center **Improve Your Grade**
Primary Source: Bismarck's Worst Nightmare: A Franco-Russian Rapprochement

Great Britain's foreign policy became increasingly crucial. Long content with "splendid isolation" and no permanent alliances, Britain after 1891 was the only uncommitted Great Power. Could Britain afford to remain isolated, or would it feel compelled to take sides? Many Germans and some Britons felt that a "natural alliance" united the advanced, racially related Germanic and Anglo-Saxon peoples. However, the generally good relations that had prevailed between Prussia and Great Britain ever since the mid-eighteenth century gave way to a bitter Anglo-German rivalry.

There were several reasons for this tragic development. Commercial rivalry in world markets between Germany and Great Britain increased sharply in the 1890s, and Germany's pursuit of world power unsettled the British. Above all, Germany's decision in 1900 to expand greatly its battle fleet posed a challenge to Britain's long-standing naval supremacy. This decision coincided with the hard-fought South African War (1899–1902) between the British and the tiny Dutch republics of southern Africa,

German Warships Under Full Steam   As these impressive ships engaged in battle exercises in 1907 suggest, Germany did succeed in building a large modern navy. But Britain was equally determined to maintain its naval superiority, and the spiraling arms race helped poison relations between the two countries. *(Archives Charmet/Bibliothèque des Arts Décoratifs/ Archives Charmet/The Bridgeman Art Library)*

which brought into the open widespread anti-British feeling, as editorial writers in many nations denounced this latest manifestation of British imperialism. Thus British leaders prudently set about shoring up their exposed position with alliances and agreements.

Britain improved its often-strained relations with the United States and in 1902 concluded a formal alliance with Japan (see Figure 27.1). Britain then responded favorably to the advances of France's skillful foreign minister, Théophile Delcassé, who wanted better relations with Britain and was willing to accept British rule in Egypt in return for British support of French plans to dominate Morocco. The resulting Anglo-French Entente of 1904 settled all outstanding colonial disputes between Britain and France.

Frustrated by Britain's turn toward France in 1904,

Germany's leaders decided to test the strength of the entente. They foolishly rattled their swords by insisting in 1905 on an international conference on the whole Moroccan question. But Germany's crude bullying forced France and Britain closer together, and the conference left Germany empty-handed and isolated (except for Austria-Hungary).

The result of the Moroccan crisis was something of a diplomatic revolution. Britain, France, Russia, and even the United States began to see Germany as a potential threat, a would-be intimidator that might seek to dominate all Europe. At the same time, German leaders began to see sinister plots to "encircle" Germany and block its development as a world power. In 1907 Russia, battered by its disastrous war with Japan and the revolution of 1905, agreed to settle its quarrels with Great Britain in

Persia and Central Asia with the Anglo-Russian Agreement (see Figure 27.1).

Germany's decision to add a large, enormously expensive fleet of big-gun battleships to its already expanding navy also heightened tensions after 1907. German nationalists, led by the extremely persuasive Admiral Alfred von Tirpitz, saw a large navy as the legitimate mark of a great world power and as a source of pride and patriotic unity. But British leaders such as David Lloyd George saw it as a detestable military challenge, which forced them to spend the "People's Budget" (see page 835) on battleships rather than social welfare. Unscrupulous journalists and special-interest groups in both countries also portrayed healthy competition in foreign trade and investment as a form of economic warfare. In 1909 the mass-circulation London *Daily Mail* hysterically informed its readers in a series of reports that "Germany is deliberately preparing to destroy the British Empire."[2] By then Britain was psychologically, if not officially, in the Franco-Russian camp. The leading nations of Europe were divided into two hostile blocs, both ill-prepared to deal with upheaval on Europe's southeastern frontier.

The Outbreak of War

In the early years of the twentieth century, war in the Balkans was as inevitable as anything can be in human history. The reason was simple: nationalism was destroying the Ottoman Empire in Europe and threatening to break up the Austro-Hungarian Empire. The only questions were what kinds of wars would occur and where they would lead.

Greece had long before led the struggle for national liberation, winning its independence in 1832. In 1875 widespread nationalist rebellion in the European provinces of the sprawling Ottoman Empire had resulted in Turkish repression, Russian intervention, and Great Power tensions. Bismarck had helped resolve this crisis at the 1878 Congress of Berlin, which worked out the partial division of Turkish possessions in Europe. Austria-Hungary obtained the right to "occupy and administer" Bosnia and Herzegovina. Serbia and Romania won independence, and a part of Bulgaria won local autonomy. The Ottoman Empire retained important Balkan holdings, for Austria-Hungary and Russia each feared the other's domination of totally independent states in the area (see Map 27.1).

By 1903, however, nationalism in southeastern Europe was on the rise once again. Serbia led the way, becoming openly hostile toward both Austria-Hungary and the Ottoman Empire. The Serbs, a Slavic people, looked to Slavic Russia for support of their national aspirations. To block Serbian expansion and to take advantage of Russia's weakness after the revolution of 1905, Austria in 1908 formally annexed Bosnia and Herzegovina, with their large Serbian, Croatian, and Muslim populations. The kingdom of Serbia erupted in rage but could do nothing without Russian support.

Then, in 1912, in the First Balkan War, Serbia joined Greece and Bulgaria to attack the Ottoman Empire and then quarreled with Bulgaria over the spoils of victory—a dispute that led in 1913 to the Second Balkan War. Austria intervened in 1913 and forced Serbia to give up Albania. After centuries, nationalism had finally destroyed the Ottoman Empire in Europe (see Map 27.2). This sudden but long-awaited event elated the Balkan nationalists and dismayed the leaders of multinational Austria-Hungary. The former hoped and the latter feared that Austria might be next to be broken apart.

Within this tense context, Archduke Francis Ferdinand, heir to the Austrian and Hungarian thrones, and his wife, Sophie, were assassinated by Serbian revolutionaries living in Bosnia on June 28, 1914, during a state visit to the Bosnian capital of Sarajevo. After some hesitation, the leaders of Austria-Hungary concluded that Serbia was implicated and had to be severely punished once and for all. On July 23 Austria-Hungary finally presented Serbia with an unconditional ultimatum. The Serbian government had forty-eight hours in which to agree to demands that would amount to ceding control of the Serbian state. When Serbia replied moderately but evasively, Austria began to mobilize and then declared war on Serbia on July 28. Thus a desperate multinational Austria-Hungary deliberately chose war in a last-ditch attempt to stem the rising tide of hostile nationalism within its borders and save the existing state. The "Third Balkan War" had begun.

Of prime importance in Austria-Hungary's fateful decision was Germany's unconditional support. Emperor William II and his chancellor, Theobald von Bethmann-Hollweg, realized that war between Austria and Russia was the most probable result, for a resurgent Russia could not stand by, as in the Bosnian crisis, and simply watch the Serbs be crushed. Yet Bethmann-Hollweg apparently hoped that while Russia (and therefore France) would go to war, Great Britain would remain neutral, unwilling to fight for "Russian aggression" in the distant Balkans.

In fact, the diplomatic situation was already out of control. Military plans and timetables began to dictate policy. Russia, a vast country, would require much longer to mobilize its armies than Germany and Austria-Hungary. All the complicated mobilization plans of the Russian general staff had assumed a war with both Austria and Germany: Russia could not mobilize against one without

MAP 27.1 The Balkans After the Congress of Berlin, 1878 The Ottoman Empire suffered large territorial losses but remained a power in the Balkans.

MAP 27.2 The Balkans in 1914 Ethnic boundaries did not follow political boundaries, and Serbian national aspirations threatened Austria-Hungary.

mobilizing against the other. Therefore, on July 29 Tsar Nicholas II ordered full mobilization and in effect declared general war.

The German general staff had also thought only in terms of a two-front war. The staff's plan for war called for knocking out France first with a lightning attack through neutral Belgium before turning on Russia. So German armies attacked Belgium, whose neutrality had been solemnly guaranteed in 1839 by all the great states including Prussia. Thus Germany's terrible, politically disastrous response to a war in the Balkans was an all-out invasion of France by way of the plains of neutral Belgium on August 3. In the face of this act of aggression, Great Britain joined France and declared war on Germany the following day. The First World War had begun.

Online Study Center **Improve Your Grade**
Primary Source: The British Rationale for Entering World War I

Reflections on the Origins of the War

In reflecting on the origins of the First World War, it seems clear that Austria-Hungary deliberately started the Third Balkan War. A war for the right to survive was Austria-Hungary's desperate, though understandable, response to the aggressive, yet understandable, revolutionary drive of Serbian nationalists to unify their people in a single state. Moreover, in spite of Russian intervention in the quarrel, it is clear that from the beginning of the crisis, Germany not only pushed and goaded Austria-Hungary but also was re-

Nationalist Opposition in the Balkans   This band of well-armed and determined guerrillas from northern Albania was typical of groups fighting against Ottoman rule in the Balkans. Balkan nationalists succeeded in driving the Ottoman Turks out of most of Europe, but their victory increased tensions with Austria-Hungary and among the Great Powers. *(Roger-Viollet/Getty Images)*

sponsible for turning a little war into the Great War by means of a sledgehammer attack on Belgium and France. Why Germany was so aggressive in 1914 is less certain.

Diplomatic historians stress that German leaders lost control of the international system after Bismarck's resignation in 1890. They felt increasingly that Germany's status as a world power was declining, while that of Britain, France, Russia, and the United States was growing. Indeed, the powers of what officially became in August 1914 the **Triple Entente**—Great Britain, France, and Russia—were checking Germany's vague but real aspirations as well as working to strangle Austria-Hungary, Germany's only real ally. Germany's aggression in 1914 reflected the failure of all European leaders, not just those in Germany, to incorporate Bismarck's mighty empire permanently and peacefully into the international system.

A more controversial interpretation argues that domestic conflicts and social tensions lay at the root of German aggression. Determined to hold on to power and frightened by the rising socialist movement, the German ruling class was willing to gamble on diplomatic victory and even on war as the means of rallying the masses to its side and preserving its privileged position. Historians have also discerned similar, if less clear-cut, behavior in Great Britain, where leaders faced civil war in northern Ireland, and in Russia, where the revolution of 1905 had brought tsardom to its knees.

This debate over social tensions and domestic political factors correctly suggests that the triumph of nationalism was a crucial underlying precondition of the Great War. Nationalism was at the heart of the Balkan wars, in the form of Serbian aspirations and the grandiose pan-German versus pan-Slavic racism of some fanatics. Nationalism also drove the spiraling arms race. Broad popular commitment

MAP 27.3 The First World War in Europe Trench warfare on the western front was concentrated in Belgium and northern France, while the war in the east encompassed an enormous territory.

"Never Forget!" This 1915 French poster with its passionate headline dramatizes Germany's brutal invasion of Belgium in 1914. Neutral Belgium is personified as a traumatized mother, assaulted and ravished by savage outlaws. The "rape of Belgium" featured prominently—and effectively—in anti-German propaganda. *(Mary Evans Picture Library)*

Stalemate and Slaughter

When the Germans invaded Belgium in August 1914, they and everyone else believed that the war would be short, for urban society rested on the food and raw materials of the world economy: "The boys will be home by Christmas." The Belgian army heroically defended its homeland, however, and fell back in good order to join a rapidly landed British army corps near the Franco-Belgian border. Instead of quickly capturing Paris in a vast encircling movement, by the end of August dead-tired German soldiers were advancing along an enormous front in the scorching summer heat.

On September 6 the French attacked a gap in the German line at the Battle of the Marne. For three days, France threw everything into the attack. At one point, the French government desperately requisitioned all the taxis of Paris to rush reserves to the troops at the front. Finally, the Germans fell back. Paris and France had been miraculously saved (see Map 27.3).

Soon, with the armies stalled, both sides began to dig trenches to protect themselves from machine-gun fire. By November 1914, an unbroken line of trenches extended from the Belgian ports through northern France, past the fortress of Verdun, and on to the Swiss frontier. In the face of this unexpected stalemate, slaughter on the western front began in earnest. The defenders on both sides dug in behind rows of trenches, mines, and barbed wire. For days and even weeks, ceaseless shelling by heavy artillery supposedly "softened up" the enemy in a given area (and also signaled the coming attack). Then young draftees and their junior officers went "over the top" of the trenches in frontal attacks on the enemy's line.

The cost in lives of this **trench warfare** was staggering, the gains in territory minuscule. The massive French and British offensives during 1915 never gained more than 3 miles of blood-soaked earth from the enemy. In the Battle of the Somme in the summer of 1916, the British and French gained an insignificant 125 square miles at the cost of 600,000 dead or wounded, while the Germans lost 500,000 men. In that same year the unsuccessful German campaign against Verdun cost 700,000 lives on both sides. British poet Siegfried Sassoon (1886–1967) wrote of the Somme offensive, "I am staring at a sunlit picture of Hell."

The year 1917 was equally terrible. The hero of Erich Remarque's great novel *All Quiet on the Western Front* (1929) describes one attack:

We see men living with their skulls blown open; we see soldiers run with their two feet cut off. . . . Still the little piece of convulsed earth in which we lie is held. We have yielded no

to "my country right or wrong" weakened groups that thought in terms of international communities and consequences. In each country, the great majority of the population enthusiastically embraced the outbreak of war in August 1914. In each country, people believed that their country had been wronged, and they rallied to defend it. Patriotic nationalism brought unity in the short run.

In all of this, the wealthy governing classes certainly underestimated the risk of war to themselves in 1914. They had forgotten that great wars and great social revolutions very often go hand in hand. Metternich's alliance of conservative forces in support of international peace and the social status quo had become only a distant memory.

The Tragic Absurdity of Trench Warfare   Soldiers charge across a scarred battlefield and overrun an enemy trench. The dead defender on the right will fire no more. But this is only another futile charge that will yield much blood and little land. A whole generation is being decimated by the slaughter. *(By courtesy of the Trustees of the Imperial War Museum)*

more than a few hundred yards of it as a prize to the enemy. But on every yard there lies a dead man.

Such was war on the western front.

Trench warfare shattered an entire generation of young men. Millions who could have provided political creativity and leadership after the war were forever missing. Moreover, those who lived through the slaughter were maimed, shell-shocked, embittered, and profoundly disillusioned. The young soldiers went to war believing in the world of their leaders and elders—the pre-1914 world of order, progress, and patriotism. Then, in Remarque's words, the

"first bombardment showed us our mistake, and under it the world as they had taught it to us broke in pieces."

The Widening War

On the eastern front, slaughter did not degenerate into suicidal trench warfare. With the outbreak of the war, the "Russian steamroller" immediately moved into eastern Germany. Very badly damaged by the Germans under Generals Paul von Hindenburg and Erich Ludendorff at the Battles of Tannenberg and the Masurian Lakes in August and September 1914, Russia never threatened

The Armenian Atrocities When in 1915 some Armenians welcomed Russian armies as liberators after years of persecution, the Ottoman government ordered a genocidal mass deportation of its Armenian citizens from their homeland in the empire's eastern provinces. This photo, taken in Kharpert in 1915 by a German businessman from his hotel window, shows Turkish guards marching Armenian men off to a prison, where they will be tortured to death. A million Armenians died from murder, starvation, and disease during World War I. *(Courtesy of the Armenian Library, Watertown, Mass.)*

Germany again. On the Austrian front, enormous armies seesawed back and forth, suffering enormous losses. Austro-Hungarian armies were repulsed twice by Serbia in bitter fighting. But with the help of German forces, they reversed the Russian advances of 1914 and forced the Russians to retreat deep into their own territory in the eastern campaign of 1915. A staggering 2.5 million Russians were killed, wounded, or taken prisoner that year.

These changing tides of victory and hopes for territorial gains brought neutral countries into the war (see Map 27.3). Italy, a member of the Triple Alliance since 1882, had declared its neutrality in 1914 on the grounds that Austria had launched a war of aggression. Then in May 1915, Italy joined the Triple Entente of Great Britain, France, and Russia in return for promises of Austrian territory. In October 1914 the Ottoman Empire joined with Austria and Germany, by then known as the Central Powers. The following September Bulgaria decided to follow the Ottoman Empire's lead in order to settle old scores with Serbia. The Balkans, with the exception of Greece, came to be occupied by the Central Powers.

The entry of the Ottoman Turks carried the war into the Middle East. Heavy fighting between the Ottomans and the Russians saw battle lines seesawing back and forth and enveloping the Armenians, who lived on both sides of the border and had experienced brutal repression by the Turks in 1909 (see Map 27.5 on page 906). When in 1915 some Armenians welcomed Russian armies as liberators, the Ottoman government ordered a genocidal mass deportation of its Armenian citizens from their homeland. A million Armenians died from murder, starvation, and disease during World War I. In 1915 British forces tried to take the Dardanelles and Constantinople from the Ottomans but were badly defeated.

The British were more successful at inciting the Arabs to revolt against their Turkish overlords. They bargained with the foremost Arab leader, Hussein ibn-Ali (1856–1931), who was a direct descendant of the prophet Muhammad and the chief magistrate (*sharif*) of Mecca, the holiest city in the Muslim world. Controlling much of the Ottoman Empire's territory along the Red Sea, an area known as the Hejaz (see Map 27.5), Hussein managed in 1915 to win vague British commitments for an independent Arab kingdom. Thus in 1916 Hussein revolted against the Turks, proclaiming himself king of the Arabs. He joined forces with the British under T. E. Lawrence, who in 1917 led Arab tribesmen and Indian soldiers in a highly successful guerrilla war against the Turks on the Arabian peninsula.

Similar victories were eventually scored in the Ottoman province of Iraq. Britain occupied the southern Iraqi city of Basra in 1914 and captured Baghdad in 1917. In September 1918 British armies and their Arab allies rolled into Syria. This offensive culminated in the triumphal entry of Hussein's son Faisal into Damascus. Throughout Syria and Iraq there was wild Arab rejoicing. Many patriots expected a large, unified Arab nation-state to rise from the dust of the Ottoman collapse.

As world war engulfed and revolutionized the Middle East, it also spread to some parts of East Asia and Africa. Instead of revolting as the Germans hoped, the colonial subjects of the British and French generally supported their foreign masters, providing crucial supplies and fighting in Europe and the Ottoman Empire. They also helped local British and French commanders seize Germany's colonies around the globe. The Japanese, allied in Asia with the British since 1902, similarly used the war to grab German outposts in the Pacific Ocean and on the Chinese mainland, infuriating Chinese patriots and heightening long-standing tensions between China and Japan. More than a million Africans and Asians served in the various armies of the warring powers; more than double that number served as porters to carry equipment. The French, facing a shortage of young men, made especially heavy use of colonial troops.

In April 1917 the United States declared war on Germany, another crucial development in the expanding conflict. American intervention grew out of the war at sea, sympathy for the Triple Entente, and the increasing desperation of total war. At the beginning of the war, Britain and France had established a total naval blockade to strangle the Central Powers. No neutral ship was permitted to sail to Germany with any cargo. In early 1915 Germany retaliated with a counter-blockade using the murderously effective submarine, a new weapon that violated traditional niceties of fair warning under international law. In May 1915 a German submarine sank the British passenger liner **Lusitania,** claiming more than 1,000 lives, among them 139 Americans. President Woodrow Wilson protested vigorously. Germany was forced to relax its submarine warfare for almost two years; the alternative was almost certain war with the United States.

Early in 1917, the German military command—confident that improved submarines could starve Britain into submission before the United States could come to its rescue—resumed unrestricted submarine warfare. Like the invasion of Belgium, this was a reckless gamble. "German submarine warfare against commerce," President Wilson had told a sympathetic Congress and people, "is a warfare against mankind." Thus the last uncommitted great nation, as fresh and enthusiastic as Europe had been in 1914, entered the world war in April 1917, almost three years after it began. Eventually the United States was to tip the balance in favor of the Triple Entente and its allies.

The Home Front

Before looking at the last year of the Great War, let us turn our attention to the people on the home front. They were tremendously involved in the titanic struggle. War's impact on them was no less massive than on the men crouched in the trenches.

- *What was the impact of total war on civilian populations?*

Mobilizing for Total War

In August 1914, most people greeted the outbreak of hostilities enthusiastically. In every country, the masses believed that their nation was in the right and defending itself from aggression. With the exception of a few extreme left-wingers, even socialists supported the war. Everywhere the support of the masses and working class contributed to national unity and an energetic war effort.

By mid-October generals and politicians had begun to realize that more than patriotism would be needed to win the war, whose end was not in sight. Each country experienced a relentless, desperate demand for men and weapons. In each country, economic life and organization had to change and change fast to keep the war machine from sputtering to a stop. And change they did.

In each country, a government of national unity began to plan and control economic and social life in order to wage **total war.** Free-market capitalism was abandoned, at least "for the duration." Instead, government planning boards established priorities and decided what was to be produced and consumed. Rationing, price and wage controls, and even restrictions on workers' freedom of movement were imposed by government. Only through such regimentation could a country make the greatest possible military effort. Thus, though there were national variations, the great nations all moved toward planned economies commanded by the established political leadership.

The economy of total war blurred the old distinction between soldiers on the battlefield and civilians at home. The war was a war of whole peoples and entire populations. Based on tremendously productive industrial economies not confined to a single nation, total war yielded an effective— and therefore destructive—war effort on all sides.

However awful the war was, the ability of governments to manage and control highly complicated economies strengthened the cause of socialism. With the First World War, state socialism became for the first time a realistic economic blueprint rather than a utopian program. Germany illustrates the general trend. It also went furthest in developing a planned economy to wage total war.

As soon as war began, Walter Rathenau, the talented, foresighted Jewish industrialist in charge of Germany's largest electric company, convinced the government to set up the **War Raw Materials Board** to ration and distribute raw materials. Under Rathenau's direction, every useful material from foreign oil to barnyard manure was inventoried and rationed. Moreover, the board launched successful attempts to produce substitutes such as synthetic rubber and synthetic nitrates, needed to make explosives and essential to the blockaded German war machine. An aggressive recycling campaign, including everything from fruit peels to women's hair, augmented these efforts.

Food was also rationed in accordance with physical need. Men and women doing hard manual work were given extra rations. During the last two years of the war, only children and expectant mothers received milk rations. At the same time, Germany failed to tax the war profits of private firms heavily enough. This failure contributed to massive deficit financing, inflation, the growth of a black market, and the eventual re-emergence of class conflict.

Following the terrible Battles of Verdun and the Somme in 1916, Chancellor Bethmann-Hollweg was driven from office in 1917 by military leaders Hindenburg and Ludendorff, who became the real rulers of Germany. They

Hair for the War Effort Blockaded and cut off from overseas supplies, Germany mobilized effectively to find substitutes at home. This poster calls on German women—especially young women with long flowing tresses—to donate their hair, which was used to make rope. Children were organized by their teachers into garbage brigades to collect every scrap of useful material. *(akg-images)*

decreed the ultimate mobilization for total war. Germany, said Hindenburg, could win only "if all the treasures of our soil that agriculture and industry can produce are used exclusively for the conduct of War. . . . All other considerations must come second."[3] Thus in December 1916, military leaders rammed through the Reichstag the Auxiliary Service Law, which required all males between seventeen and sixty to work only at jobs considered critical to the war effort.

Although women and children were not specifically mentioned, this forced-labor law was also aimed at them. Many women already worked in war factories, mines, and steel mills, where they labored, like men, at the heaviest and most dangerous jobs. With the passage of the Auxiliary Service Law, many more women followed. People averaged little more than one thousand calories a day. Thus in Germany total war led to the establishment of history's first "totalitarian" society, and war production increased while some people starved to death.

Great Britain mobilized for total war less rapidly and less completely than Germany, for it could import materials from its empire and from the United States. By 1915, however, a serious shortage of shells had led to the establishment of the Ministry of Munitions under David Lloyd George. The ministry organized private industry to produce for the war, controlled profits, allocated labor, fixed wage rates, and settled labor disputes. By December 1916, when Lloyd George became prime minister, the British economy was largely planned and regulated. Great Britain had followed successfully in Germany's footsteps.

The Social Impact

The social impact of total war was no less profound than the economic impact, though again there were important national variations. The millions of men at the front and the insatiable needs of the military created a tremendous demand for workers. Jobs were available for everyone. This situation—seldom, if ever, seen before 1914, when unemployment and poverty had been facts of urban life—brought about momentous changes.

One such change was greater power and prestige for labor unions. Having proved their loyalty in August 1914, labor unions cooperated with war governments on work rules, wages, and production schedules in return for real participation in important decisions. This entry of labor leaders and unions into policymaking councils paralleled the entry of socialist leaders into the war governments.

The role of women changed dramatically. In every country, large numbers of women left home and domestic service to work in industry, transportation, and offices. Moreover, women became highly visible—not only as munitions workers but as bank tellers, mail carriers, even police officers. Women also served as nurses and doctors at the front. (See the feature "Individuals in Society: Vera Brittain.") In general, the war greatly expanded the range of women's activities and changed attitudes toward women. As a direct result of women's many-sided war ef-

Waging Total War   A British war plant strains to meet the insatiable demand for trench-smashing heavy artillery shells. Quite typically, many of these defense workers are women.
(By courtesy of the Trustees of the Imperial War Museum)

Individuals in Society

Vera Brittain

Although the Great War upended millions of lives, it struck Europe's young people with the greatest force. For Vera Brittain (1893–1970), as for so many in her generation, the war became life's defining experience, which she captured forever in her famous autobiography, *Testament of Youth* (1933).

Brittain grew up in a wealthy business family in northern England, bristling at small-town conventions and discrimination against women. Very close to her brother Edward, two years her junior, Brittain read voraciously and dreamed of being a successful writer. Finishing boarding school and beating down her father's objections, she prepared for Oxford's rigorous entry exams and won a scholarship to its women's college. Brittain also fell in love with Roland Leighton, an equally brilliant student from a literary family and her brother's best friend. All three, along with two more close friends, Victor Richardson and Geoffrey Thurlow, confidently prepared to enter Oxford in late 1914.

When war suddenly approached in July 1914, Brittain shared with millions of Europeans a thrilling surge of patriotic support for her government, a pro-war enthusiasm she later played down in her published writings. She wrote in her diary that her "great fear" was that England would declare its neutrality and commit the "grossest treachery" toward France.* She seconded Roland's decision to enlist, agreeing with her sweetheart's glamorous view of war as "very ennobling and very beautiful." Later, exchanging anxious letters in 1915 with Roland in France, Vera began to see the conflict in personal, human terms. She wondered if any victory or defeat could be worth Roland's life.

Struggling to quell her doubts, Brittain redoubled her commitment to England's cause and volunteered as an army nurse. For the next three years she served with distinction in military hospitals in London, Malta, and northern France, repeatedly torn between the vision of noble sacrifice and the reality of human tragedy. She lost her sexual inhibitions caring for mangled male bodies, and she longed to consummate her love with Roland. Awaiting his return on leave on Christmas Day in 1915, she was greeted instead with a telegram: Roland had been killed two days before.

Roland's death was the first of the devastating blows that eventually overwhelmed Brittain's idealistic patriotism. In 1917, first Geoffrey and then Victor died from gruesome wounds. In early 1918, as the last great German offensive covered the floors of her war-zone hospital with maimed and dying German prisoners, the bone-weary Vera felt a common humanity and saw only more victims. A few weeks later brother Edward—her last hope—died in action. When the war ended, she was, she said, a "complete automaton," with "my deepest emotions paralyzed if not dead."

Returning to Oxford and finishing her studies, Brittain gradually recovered. She formed a deep, restorative friendship with another talented woman writer, Winifred Holtby, published novels and articles, and became a leader in the feminist campaign for gender equality. She also married and had children. But her wartime memories were always there. Finally, Brittain succeeded in coming to grips with them in *Testament of Youth,* her powerful antiwar autobiography. The unflinching narrative spoke to the experiences of an entire generation and became a runaway bestseller. Above all perhaps, Brittain captured the ambivalent, contradictory character of the war, when millions of young people found excitement, courage, and common purpose but succeeded only in destroying their lives with their superhuman efforts and futile sacrifices. Becoming ever more committed to pacifism, Brittain opposed England's entry into World War II.

Vera Brittain, marked forever by her wartime experiences.
(Vera Brittain Archive, William Ready Division of Archives and Research Collections, McMaster University Library)

Questions for Analysis

1. What were Brittain's initial feelings toward the war? How did they change as the conflict continued? Why did they change?
2. Why did Brittain volunteer as a nurse, as many women did? Judging from her account, how might wartime nursing have influenced women of her generation?
3. In portraying the ambivalent, contradictory character of World War I for Europe's youth, was Brittain describing the contradictory character of all modern warfare?

*Quoted in the excellent study by P. Berry and M. Bostridge, *Vera Brittain: A Life* (London: Virago Press, 2001), p. 59; additional quotes are from pp. 80 and 136. This work is highly recommended.

Online Study Center **Improve Your Grade**
Going Beyond Individuals in Society

fort, Britain, Germany, and Austria granted women the right to vote immediately after the war. Women also showed a growing spirit of independence during the war, as they started to bob their hair, shorten their skirts, and smoke in public.

Online Study Center **Improve Your Grade**
Primary Source: A British Feminist Analyzes the Impact of the War on Women

War promoted greater social equality, blurring class distinctions and lessening the gap between rich and poor. This blurring was most apparent in Great Britain, where wartime hardship was never extreme. In fact, the bottom third of the population generally lived *better* than they ever had, for the poorest gained most from the severe shortage of labor. In continental countries, greater equality was reflected in full employment, rationing according to physical needs, and a sharing of hardships. There, too, society became more uniform and more egalitarian, in spite of some war profiteering.

Finally, death itself had no respect for traditional social distinctions. It savagely decimated the young aristocratic officers who led the charge, and it fell heavily on the mass of drafted peasants and unskilled workers who followed. Yet death often spared the aristocrats of labor, the skilled workers and foremen. Their lives were too valuable to squander at the front, for they were needed to train the newly recruited women and older unskilled men laboring valiantly in war plants at home.

Growing Political Tensions

During the first two years of war, most soldiers and civilians supported their governments. Belief in a just cause, patriotic nationalism, the planned economy, and a sharing of burdens united peoples behind their various national leaders.

Each government employed rigorous censorship to control public opinion, and each used both crude and subtle propaganda to maintain popular support. German propaganda hysterically pictured black soldiers from France's African empire raping German women, while German atrocities in Belgium and elsewhere were ceaselessly recounted and exaggerated by the French and British. Patriotic posters and slogans, slanted news, and biased editorials inflamed national hatreds and helped sustain superhuman efforts.

By the spring of 1916, however, people were beginning to crack under the strain of total war. In April 1916, Irish nationalists in Dublin tried to take advantage of this situation and rose up against British rule in their great Easter Rebellion. A week of bitter fighting passed before the rebels were crushed and their leaders executed. On May 1, 1916, several thousand demonstrators in Berlin heard the radical socialist leader Karl Liebknecht (1871–1919) shout, "Down with the government! Down with the war!" Liebknecht was immediately arrested and imprisoned, but his daring action electrified Europe's far left. Strikes and protest marches over inadequate food began to flare up on every home front.

Soldiers' morale also began to decline. Italian troops mutinied. Numerous French units refused to fight after the disastrous French offensive of May 1917. Only tough military justice for leaders and a tacit agreement with the troops that there would be no more grand offensives enabled the new general in chief, Henri Philippe Pétain, to restore order. A rising tide of war-weariness and defeatism also swept France's civilian population before Georges Clemenceau emerged as a ruthless and effective wartime leader in November 1917. Clemenceau (1841–1929) established a virtual dictatorship, pouncing on strikers and jailing without trial journalists and politicians who dared to suggest a compromise peace with Germany.

The strains were worse for the Central Powers. In October 1916, the chief minister of Austria was assassinated by a young socialist crying, "Down with Absolutism! We want peace!"[4] The following month, when feeble old Emperor Francis Joseph died, a symbol of unity disappeared. In spite of absolute censorship, political dissatisfaction and conflicts among nationalities grew. In April 1917, Austria's chief minister summed up the situation in the gloomiest possible terms. The country and army were exhausted. Another winter of war would bring revolution and disintegration. Both Czech and Yugoslav leaders demanded autonomous democratic states for their peoples. The British blockade kept tightening; people were starving.

The strain of total war and of the Auxiliary Service Law was also evident in Germany. In the winter of 1916 to 1917, Germany's military position appeared increasingly desperate. Stalemates and losses in the west were matched by temporary Russian advances in the east: hence the military's insistence on an all-or-nothing gamble of unrestricted submarine warfare when the Triple Entente refused in December 1916 to consider peace on terms favorable to the Central Powers.

Also, the national political unity of the first two years of war was collapsing as the social conflict of prewar Germany re-emerged. A growing minority of moderate socialists in the Reichstag called for a compromise "peace without annexations or reparations." Such a peace was unthinkable for conservatives and military leaders. So also was the surge in revolutionary agitation and strikes by war-weary workers that occurred in early 1917. When the bread ration was further reduced in April, more than 200,000 workers struck and demonstrated for a week in Berlin, returning to work only under the threat of prison and military discipline. Thus militaristic Germany, like its ally Austria-Hungary (and its enemy France), was beginning to crack in 1917. Yet it was Russia that collapsed first and saved the Central Powers—for a time.

The Russian Revolution

The Russian Revolution of 1917 was one of modern history's most momentous events. Directly related to the growing tensions of World War I, it had a significance far beyond the wartime agonies of a single European nation. The Russian Revolution opened a new era. For some, it was Marx's socialist vision come true; for others, it was the triumph of dictatorship. To all, it presented a radically new prototype of state and society.

- *Why did World War I bring socialist revolution in Russia?*

The Fall of Imperial Russia

Like its allies and its enemies, Russia embraced war with patriotic enthusiasm in 1914. At the Winter Palace, while throngs of people knelt and sang, "God save the tsar," Tsar Nicholas II (r. 1894–1917) repeated the oath Alexander I had sworn in 1812 and vowed never to make peace as long as the enemy stood on Russian soil. Russia's lower house, the Duma, voted war credits. Conservatives anticipated expansion in the Balkans, while liberals and most socialists believed alliance with Britain and France would bring democratic reforms. For a moment, Russia was united.

Unprecedented artillery barrages used up Russia's supplies of shells and ammunition, and better-equipped German armies inflicted terrible losses. In 1915 substantial numbers of Russian soldiers were sent to the front without rifles; they were told to find their arms among the dead. There were 2 million Russian casualties in 1915 alone. Nevertheless, Russia's battered peasant army did not collapse but continued to fight courageously, and Russia moved toward full mobilization on the home front. The Duma and organs of local government took the lead, setting up special committees to coordinate defense, industry, transportation, and agriculture. These efforts improved the military situation. Yet there were many failures, and Russia mobilized less effectively for total war than the other warring nations.

The great problem was leadership. Under the constitution resulting from the revolution of 1905 (see pages 828–829), the tsar had retained complete control over the bureaucracy and the army. Legislation proposed by the Duma, which was weighted in favor of the wealthy and conservative classes, was subject to the tsar's veto. Moreover, Nicholas II fervently wished to maintain the sacred inheritance of supreme royal power. A kindly, slightly stupid man, Nicholas failed to form a close partnership with his citizens in order to fight the war more effectively. He came to rely instead on the old bureaucratic apparatus, distrusting the moderate Duma, rejecting popular involvement, and resisting calls to share power.

As a result, the Duma, the educated middle classes, and the masses became increasingly critical of the tsar's leadership. In September 1915 parties ranging from conservative to moderate socialist formed the Progressive bloc, which called for a completely new government responsible to the Duma instead of the tsar. In answer, Nicholas temporarily adjourned the Duma and announced that he was traveling to the front in order to lead and rally Russia's armies.

His departure was a fatal turning point. With the tsar in the field with the troops, control of the government was taken over by the hysterical empress, Tsarina Alexandra, and a debauched adventurer and self-proclaimed holy man, Rasputin. Nicholas's wife was a strong-willed woman with a hatred of parliaments. Having constantly urged her husband to rule absolutely, Alexandra tried to do so herself in his absence. She seated and unseated the top ministers. Her most trusted adviser was "our Friend Grigori," an uneducated Siberian preacher who was appropriately nicknamed "Rasputin"—the "Degenerate."

Rasputin's influence rested on mysterious healing powers. Alexis, Alexandra's fifth child and heir to the throne, suffered from the rare blood disease hemophilia, and only Rasputin could miraculously stop the bleeding, perhaps through hypnosis.

In a desperate attempt to right the situation and end unfounded rumors that Rasputin was the empress's lover, three members of the high aristocracy murdered Rasputin in December 1916. The empress went into semipermanent shock. Food shortages in the cities worsened; morale declined. On March 8, women calling for bread in Petrograd (formerly St. Petersburg) started riots, which spontaneously spread to the factories and then elsewhere throughout the city. From the front, the tsar ordered troops to restore order, but discipline broke down, and the soldiers joined the revolutionary crowd. The Duma responded by declaring a provisional government on March 12, 1917. Three days later, Nicholas abdicated.

"The Russian Ruling House" This wartime cartoon captures the ominous, spellbinding power of Rasputin over Tsar Nicholas II and his wife, Alexandra. Rasputin's manipulations disgusted Russian public opinion and contributed to the monarchy's collapse. *(Stock Montage)*

The Provisional Government

The March revolution was the result of an unplanned uprising of hungry, angry people in the capital, but it was joyfully accepted throughout the country. The patriotic upper and middle classes rejoiced at the prospect of a more determined and effective war effort, while workers happily anticipated better wages and more food. All classes and political parties called for liberty and democracy. They were not disappointed. As Vladimir Lenin said, Russia became the freest country in the world. After generations of arbitrary authoritarianism, the provisional government quickly established equality before the law; freedom of religion, speech, and assembly; the right of unions to organize and strike; and the rest of the classic liberal program.

Yet both liberal and moderate socialist leaders of the provisional government rejected social revolution. The reorganized government formed in May 1917 included the fiery agrarian socialist Alexander Kerensky, who became prime minister in July. He refused to confiscate large landholdings and give them to peasants, fearing that such drastic action in the countryside would only complete the disintegration of Russia's peasant army. For the patriotic Kerensky, as for other moderate socialists, the continuation of war was still the all-important national duty. Human suffering and war-weariness grew, sapping the limited strength of the provisional government.

From its first day, the provisional government had to share power with a formidable rival—the **Petrograd Soviet** (or council) of Workers' and Soldiers' Deputies. Modeled on the revolutionary soviets of 1905, the Petrograd Soviet was a huge, fluctuating mass meeting of two thousand to three thousand workers, soldiers, and socialist intellectuals. Seeing itself as a true grassroots revolutionary democracy, this counter- or half-government suspiciously watched the provisional government and issued its own radical orders, further weakening the provisional government. Most famous of these was **Army Order No. 1,** issued to all Russian military forces as the provisional government was forming.

Army Order No. 1 stripped officers of their authority and placed power in the hands of elected committees of common soldiers. Designed primarily to protect the revolution from some counter-revolutionary Bonaparte on horseback, the order instead led to a total collapse of army discipline. Many an officer was hanged for his sins. Meanwhile, following the foolhardy summer offensive, masses of peasant soldiers began "voting with their feet," to use Lenin's graphic phrase. That is, they began returning to their villages to help their families get a share of the land, which peasants were simply seizing as they settled old scores in a great agrarian upheaval. All across the country, liberty was turning into anarchy in the summer of 1917. It was an unparalleled opportunity for the most radical and most talented of Russia's many socialist leaders, Vladimir Ilyich Lenin (1870–1924).

Lenin and the Bolshevik Revolution

From his youth, Lenin's whole life had been dedicated to the cause of revolution. Born into the middle class, Lenin became an implacable enemy of imperial Russia when his older brother was executed for plotting to kill the tsar in

The Russian Revolution

1914	Russia enthusiastically enters the First World War.
1915	Russia suffers 2 million casualties.
	Progressive bloc calls for a new government responsible to the Duma rather than to the tsar.
	Tsar Nicholas adjourns the Duma and departs for the front; Alexandra and Rasputin exert a strong influence on the government.
December 1916	Rasputin is murdered.
March 8, 1917	Bread riots take place in Petrograd (St. Petersburg).
March 12, 1917	Duma declares a provisional government.
March 15, 1917	Tsar Nicholas abdicates without protest.
April 3, 1917	Lenin returns from exile and denounces the provisional government.
May 1917	Reorganized provisional government, including Kerensky, continues the war.
	Petrograd Soviet issues Army Order No. 1, granting military power to committees of common soldiers.
Summer 1917	Agrarian upheavals: peasants seize estates; peasant soldiers desert the army to participate.
October 1917	Bolsheviks gain a majority in the Petrograd Soviet.
November 6, 1917	Bolsheviks seize power; Lenin heads the new "provisional workers' and peasants' government."
November 1917	Lenin accepts peasant seizure of land and worker control of factories; all banks are nationalized.
January 1918	Lenin permanently disbands the Constituent Assembly.
February 1918	Lenin convinces the Bolshevik Central Committee to accept a humiliating peace with Germany in order to safeguard the revolution.
March 1918	Treaty of Brest-Litovsk: Russia loses one-third of its population.
	Trotsky as war commissar begins to rebuild the Russian army.
	Government moves from Petrograd to Moscow.
1918–1920	Great civil war takes place.
Summer 1918	Eighteen regional governments compete for power.
	White armies oppose the Bolshevik Revolution.
1919	White armies are on the offensive but divided politically; they receive little benefit from Allied intervention.
1920	Lenin and the Red Army are victorious, retaking Belorussia and Ukraine.

1887. As a law student, Lenin found a revolutionary faith in Marxian socialism, which began to win converts among radical intellectuals as industrialization surged forward in Russia in the 1890s. Exiled to Siberia for three years, Lenin studied Marxian doctrines with religious in-tensity. After his release, this young priest of socialism then joined fellow socialists in western Europe and developed his own revolutionary interpretations of the body of Marxian thought.

Three interrelated ideas were central for Lenin. First, like other eastern European radical socialists after 1900, he turned to the early fire-breathing Marx of 1848 and *The Communist Manifesto* for inspiration. Thus Lenin stressed that capitalism could be destroyed only by violent revolution. He tirelessly denounced all revisionist theories of a peaceful evolution to socialism as betraying Marx's message of unending class conflict. Lenin's second, more original idea was that under certain conditions a socialist revolution was possible even in a relatively backward country like Russia. There the industrial working class was small, but peasants were poor and thus potential revolutionaries.

Lenin believed that at a given moment revolution was determined more by human leadership than by vast historical laws. Thus was born his third basic idea: the necessity of a highly disciplined workers' party, strictly controlled by a dedicated elite of intellectuals and full-time revolutionaries like Lenin himself. Unlike ordinary workers and trade-union officials, this elite would never be seduced by short-term gains. It would not stop until revolution brought it to power.

Lenin's theories and methods did not go unchallenged by other Russian Marxists. At meetings of the Russian Social Democratic Labor Party in London in 1903, matters came to a head. Lenin demanded a small, disciplined, elitist party, while his opponents wanted a more democratic party with mass membership. The Russian party of Marxian socialism promptly split into two rival factions. Lenin's camp was called **Bolsheviks,** or "majority group"; his opponents were *Mensheviks,* or "minority group." Lenin's majority did not last, but Lenin did not care. He kept the fine-sounding name Bolshevik and developed the party he wanted: tough, disciplined, revolutionary.

Online Study Center Improve Your Grade
Primary Source: What Is to Be Done with Russia?

Unlike most other socialists, Lenin did not rally round the national flag in 1914. Observing events from neutral Switzerland, he saw the war as a product of imperialistic rivalries and as a marvelous opportunity for class war and socialist upheaval. After the March revolution the German government provided the impatient Lenin, his wife, and about twenty trusted colleagues with safe passage across Germany and back into Russia in April 1917. The Germans hoped that Lenin would undermine the sagging war effort of the world's freest society. They were not disappointed.

Arriving triumphantly at Petrograd's Finland Station on April 3, Lenin attacked at once. To the great astonishment of the local Bolsheviks, he rejected all cooperation with the "bourgeois" provisional government of the liberals and moderate socialists. His slogans were radical in the extreme: "All power to the soviets"; "All land to the peasants"; "Stop the war now." Never a slave to Marxian determinism, the brilliant but not unduly intellectual Lenin was a superb tactician. The moment was now.

Yet Lenin almost overplayed his hand. An attempt by the Bolsheviks to seize power in July collapsed, and Lenin fled and went into hiding. He was charged with being a German agent, and indeed he and the Bolsheviks were getting money from Germany.[5] But no matter. Intrigue between Kerensky, who became prime minister in July, and his commander in chief, General Lavr Kornilov, resulted in Kornilov's leading a feeble attack against the provisional government in September. In the face of this rightist "counter-revolutionary" threat, the Bolsheviks were rearmed and redeemed. Kornilov's forces disintegrated, but Kerensky lost all credit with the army, the only force that might have saved him and democratic government in Russia.

Trotsky and the Seizure of Power

Throughout the summer, the Bolsheviks had appealed very effectively to the workers and soldiers of Petrograd, markedly increasing their popular support. Party membership had soared from 50,000 to 240,000, and in October the Bolsheviks gained a fragile majority in the Petrograd Soviet. It was now Lenin's supporter Leon Trotsky (1879–1940), a spellbinding revolutionary orator and independent radical Marxist, who brilliantly executed the Bolshevik seizure of power.

Painting a vivid but untruthful picture of German and counter-revolutionary plots, Trotsky first convinced the Petrograd Soviet to form a special military-revolutionary committee in October and make him its leader. Military power in the capital passed into Bolshevik hands. Then, on the night of November 6, militants from Trotsky's committee joined with trusty Bolshevik soldiers to seize government buildings and pounce on members of the provisional government. Then they went on to the congress of soviets. There a Bolshevik majority—roughly 390 of 650 turbulent delegates—declared that all power had passed to the soviets and named Lenin head of the new government.

The Bolsheviks came to power for three key reasons. First, by late 1917 democracy had given way to anarchy: power was there for those who would take it. Second, in Lenin and Trotsky the Bolsheviks had an utterly determined and truly superior leadership, which both the tsarist government and the provisional government lacked. Third, in 1917 the Bolsheviks succeeded in appealing to many soldiers and urban workers, people who were exhausted by war and eager for socialism. With time, many workers would become bitterly disappointed, but for the moment they had good reason to believe that they had won what they wanted.

Dictatorship and Civil War

History is full of short-lived coups and unsuccessful revolutions. The truly monumental accomplishment of Lenin, Trotsky, and the rest of the Bolsheviks was not taking power but keeping it. In the next four years, the Bolsheviks went on to conquer the chaos they had helped create, and they began to build their kind of dictatorial socialist society. The conspirators became conquerors. How was this done?

Lenin had the genius to profit from developments over which he and the Bolsheviks had no control. Since summer, a peasant revolution had been sweeping across Russia as the tillers of the soil invaded and divided among themselves the estates of the landlords and the church. Peasant seizure of the land—a Russian 1789—was not very Marxian, but it was quite unstoppable in 1917. Thus Lenin's first law, which supposedly gave land to the peasants, actually merely approved what peasants were already doing. Urban workers' great demand in November was direct control of individual factories by local workers committees. This, too, Lenin ratified with a decree in November.

Unlike many of his colleagues, Lenin acknowledged that Russia had lost the war with Germany and that the only realistic goal was peace at any price. That price was very high. Germany demanded in December 1917 that the Soviet government give up all its western territories. These areas were inhabited by Poles, Finns, Lithuanians, and other non-Russians—all those people who had been conquered by the tsars over three centuries and put into the "prisonhouse of nationalities," as Lenin had earlier called the Russian empire.

At first, Lenin's fellow Bolsheviks would not accept such great territorial losses. But when German armies resumed their unopposed march into Russia in February 1918, Lenin had his way in a very close vote in the Central Committee of the party. "Not even his greatest enemy can deny that at this moment Lenin towered like a giant over his Bolshevik colleagues."[6] A third of old Russia's population was sliced away by the German meat ax in the Treaty of Brest-Litovsk in March 1918. With peace, Lenin had escaped the certain disaster of continued war and could pursue his goal of absolute political power for the Bolsheviks—now renamed Communists—within Russia.

In November 1917, the Bolsheviks had cleverly proclaimed their regime only a "provisional workers' and peasants' government," promising that a freely elected

Lenin Rallies Worker and Soldier Delegates   At a midnight meeting of the Petrograd Soviet, the Bolsheviks rise up and seize power on November 6, 1917. This painting from the 1940s idealizes Lenin, but his great talents as a revolutionary leader are undeniable. In this re-creation Stalin, who actually played only a small role in the uprising, is standing behind Lenin, already his trusty right-hand man. *(Sovfoto)*

Constituent Assembly would draw up a new constitution. But free elections produced a stunning setback for the Bolsheviks, who won less than one-fourth of the elected delegates. The Socialist Revolutionaries—the peasants' party—had a clear majority. The Constituent Assembly met for only one day, on January 18, 1918. It was then permanently disbanded by Bolshevik soldiers acting under Lenin's orders. Thus even before the peace with Germany, Lenin was forming a one-party government.

The destruction of the democratically elected Constituent Assembly helped feed the flames of civil war. People who had risen up for self-rule in November saw that once again they were getting dictatorship from the capital. For the next three years, "Long live the [democratic] soviets; down with the Bolsheviks" was to be a popular slogan. The officers of the old army took the lead in organizing the so-called White opposition to the Bolsheviks in southern Russia, Ukraine, Siberia, and west of Petrograd. The

"You! Have You Volunteered?" A Red Army soldier makes a compelling direct appeal to the ordinary citizen and demands all-out support for the Bolshevik cause in this 1920 poster by Dmitri Moor, a popular Soviet artist. Lenin recognized the importance of visual propaganda in a vast country with limited literacy, and mass-produced posters like this one were everywhere during the civil war of 1918–1920. *(Stephen White, University of Glasgow)*

Whites came from many social groups and were united only by their hatred of the Bolsheviks—the Reds.

By the summer of 1918, fully eighteen self-proclaimed regional governments—several of which represented minority nationalities—were competing with Lenin's Bolsheviks in Moscow. By the end of the year, White armies were on the attack. In October 1919, it appeared they might triumph, as they closed in on Lenin's government from three sides. Yet they did not. By the spring of 1920, the White armies had been almost completely defeated, and the Bolshevik Red Army had retaken Belorussia and Ukraine. The following year, the Communists also reconquered the independent nationalist governments of the Caucasus. The civil war was over; Lenin had won.

Lenin and the Bolsheviks won for several reasons. Strategically, they controlled the center, while the Whites were always on the fringes and disunited. Moreover, the poorly defined political program of the Whites was vaguely conservative, and it did not unite all the foes of the Bolsheviks under a progressive, democratic banner. Most important, the Communists quickly developed a better army, an army for which the divided Whites were no match.

Once again, Trotsky's leadership was decisive. The Bolsheviks had preached democracy in the army and elected officers in 1917. But beginning in March 1918, Trotsky as war commissar re-established the draft and the most drastic discipline for the newly formed Red Army. Soldiers deserting or disobeying an order were summarily shot. Moreover, Trotsky made effective use of former tsarist army officers, who were actively recruited and given unprecedented powers of discipline over their troops. In short, Trotsky formed a disciplined and effective fighting force.

The Bolsheviks also mobilized the home front. Establishing **war communism**—the application of the total war concept to a civil conflict—they seized grain from peasants, introduced rationing, nationalized all banks and industry, and required everyone to work. Although these measures contributed to a breakdown of normal economic activity, they also served to maintain labor discipline and to keep the Red Army supplied.

"Revolutionary terror" also contributed to the Communist victory. The old tsarist secret police was re-established as the **Cheka,** which hunted down and executed thousands of real or supposed foes, such as the tsar and his family and other "class enemies." Moreover, people were shot or threatened with being shot for minor nonpolitical failures. The terror caused by the secret police became a tool of the government. The Cheka sowed fear, and fear silenced opposition.

Finally, foreign military intervention in the civil war ended up helping the Communists. After Lenin made peace with Germany, the Allies (United States, Britain, Japan) sent troops to Archangel and Vladivostok to prevent war materiel they had sent the provisional government from being captured by the Germans. After the Soviet government nationalized all foreign-owned factories without compensation and refused to pay all of Russia's foreign debts, Western governments, particularly France, began to support White armies in the south and west. Yet these efforts were small and halfhearted. In 1919 Western peoples were sick of war, and few Western politicians believed in a military crusade against the Bolsheviks. Thus Allied intervention in the civil war did not aid the Whites effectively, though it did permit the Communists to appeal to the patriotic nationalism of ethnic Russians, in particular former tsarist army officers. Allied intervention was both too little and too much.

Together, the Russian Revolution and the Bolshevik triumph were one of the reasons the First World War was such a great turning point in modern history. A radically new government, based on socialism and one-party dictatorship, came to power in a great European state, maintained power, and eagerly encouraged worldwide revolution. Although halfhearted constitutional monarchy in Russia was undoubtedly headed for some kind of political crisis before 1914, it is hard to imagine the triumph of the most radical proponents of change and reform except in a situation of total collapse. That was precisely what happened to Russia in the First World War.

The Peace Settlement

Victory over revolutionary Russia boosted sagging German morale, and in the spring of 1918 the Germans launched their last major attack against France. Yet this offensive failed, just as those before it had. With breathtaking rapidity, the United States, Great Britain, and France decisively defeated Germany militarily. The guns of world war finally fell silent. Then as civil war spread in Russia and as chaos engulfed much of eastern Europe, the victorious Western Allies came together in Paris to establish a lasting peace.

Expectations were high; optimism was almost unlimited. The Allies labored intensively and soon worked out terms for peace with Germany and for the creation of the peacekeeping League of Nations. Nevertheless, the hopes of peoples and politicians were soon disappointed, for the peace settlement of 1919 turned out to be a failure. Rather than creating conditions for peace, it sowed the seeds of another war. Surely this was the ultimate tragedy of the Great War, a war that directly and indirectly cost $332 billion and left 10 million dead and another 20 million wounded.

• *How did the Allies fashion a peace settlement, and why was it unsuccessful?*

The End of the War

In early 1917, the strain of total war was showing everywhere. After the Russian Revolution in March, there were major strikes in Germany. In July a coalition of moderates passed a "peace resolution" in the Reichstag, calling for peace without territorial annexations. To counter this moderation born of war-weariness, the German military established a virtual dictatorship. The military also aggressively exploited the collapse of Russian armies, winning great concessions in the Treaty of Brest-Litovsk in March 1918.

With victory in the east quieting German moderates, General Ludendorff and company fell on France once more in the great spring offensive of 1918. For a time, German armies pushed forward, coming within thirty-five miles of Paris. But Ludendorff's exhausted, overextended forces never broke through. They were decisively stopped in July at the second Battle of the Marne, where 140,000 fresh American soldiers saw action. Adding 2 million men in arms to the war effort by August, the late but massive American intervention decisively tipped the scales in favor of Allied victory.

By September British, French, and American armies were advancing steadily on all fronts, and a panicky General Ludendorff realized that Germany had lost the war. Yet he insolently insisted that moderate politicians shoulder the shame of defeat, and on October 4 the emperor formed a new, more liberal German government to sue for peace. As negotiations over an armistice dragged on, an angry and frustrated German people finally rose up. On November 3, sailors in Kiel mutinied, and throughout northern Germany soldiers and workers began to establish revolutionary councils on the Russian soviet model. The same day, Austria-Hungary surrendered to the Allies and began breaking apart. Revolution broke out in Germany, and masses of workers demonstrated for peace in Berlin. With army discipline collapsing, the emperor abdicated and fled to Holland. Socialist leaders in Berlin proclaimed a German republic on November 9 and simultaneously agreed to tough Allied terms of surrender. The armistice went into effect on November 11, 1918. The war was over.

Revolution in Germany

Military defeat brought political revolution to Germany and Austria-Hungary, as it had to Russia. In Austria-Hungary the revolution was primarily nationalistic and republican in character. Having started the war to preserve an antinationalistic dynastic state, the Habsburg empire had perished in the attempt. In its place, independent Austrian, Hungarian, and Czechoslovakian republics were proclaimed, while a greatly expanded Serbian monarchy united the South Slavs and took the name Yugoslavia. The prospect of firmly establishing the new national states overrode class considerations for most people in east-central Europe.

The German Revolution of November 1918 resembled the Russian Revolution of March 1917. In both cases, a genuine popular uprising welled up from below, toppled an authoritarian monarchy, and brought the establishment of a liberal provisional republic. In both countries, liberals and moderate socialists took control of the central government, while workers' and soldiers' councils formed a counter-government. In Germany, however, the moderate socialists and their liberal allies won, and the Lenin-like radical revolutionaries in the councils lost. In communist terms, the liberal, republican revolution in Germany in 1918 was only half a revolution: a bourgeois political revolution without a communist second installment. It was Russia without Lenin's Bolshevik triumph.

There were several reasons for the German outcome. The great majority of Marxian socialist leaders in the Social Democratic Party were, as before the war, really pink and not red. They wanted to establish real political democracy and civil liberties, and they favored the gradual elimination of capitalism. They were also German nationalists, appalled by the prospect of civil war and revolutionary terror. Moreover, there was less popular support among workers, soldiers, and peasants.

Of crucial importance was the fact that the moderate German Social Democrats, unlike Kerensky and company, accepted defeat and ended the war the day they took power. This act ended the decline in morale among soldiers and prevented the regular army, with its conservative officer corps, from disintegrating. When radicals headed by Karl Liebknecht and Rosa Luxemburg and their supporters in the councils tried to seize control of the government in Berlin in January, the moderate socialists called on the army to crush the uprising. Liebknecht and Luxemburg were arrested and then brutally murdered by army leaders. Their murders, widely believed to have had government support, caused many working-class activists in the Social Democratic Party to break away in anger and join the pro-Lenin German Communist Party that Liebknecht's group had just founded. Finally, even if the moderate socialists had followed Liebknecht and Luxemburg on the Leninist path, it is very unlikely they would have succeeded. Civil war in Germany would certainly have followed. And the Allies, who were already occupying western Germany according to the terms of the armistice, would have marched on to Berlin and ruled Germany directly.

The Treaty of Versailles

The peace conference opened in Paris in January 1919 with seventy delegates representing twenty-seven victorious nations. There were great expectations. A young British diplomat later wrote that the victors "were convinced that they would never commit the blunders and iniquities of the Congress of Vienna [of 1815]." Then the "misguided, reactionary, pathetic aristocrats" had cynically

shuffled populations; now "we believed in nationalism, we believed in the self-determination of peoples." Indeed, "we were journeying to Paris . . . to found a new order in Europe. We were preparing not Peace only, but Eternal Peace."[7] This general optimism and idealism had been greatly strengthened by President Wilson's January 1918 peace proposal, the Fourteen Points, which stressed national self-determination and the rights of small countries.

Online Study Center **Improve Your Grade**
Primary Source: A New Diplomacy: The Fourteen Points

The real powers at the conference were the United States, Great Britain, and France, for Germany was not allowed to participate and Russia was locked in civil war and did not attend. Italy was considered part of the Big Four, but its role was quite limited. Almost immediately the three great Allies began to quarrel. President Wilson, who was wildly cheered by European crowds as the spokesman for a new idealistic and democratic international cooperation, was almost obsessed with creating the **League of Nations.** Wilson insisted that this question come first, for he passionately believed that only a permanent international organization could protect member states from aggression and avert future wars. Wilson had his way, although Lloyd George of Great Britain and especially Clemenceau of France were unenthusiastic. They were primarily concerned with punishing Germany.

Playing on British nationalism, Lloyd George had already won a smashing electoral victory in December on the popular platform of making Germany pay for the war. "We shall," he promised, "squeeze the orange until the pips squeak." Personally inclined to make a somewhat moderate peace with Germany, Lloyd George was to a considerable extent a captive of demands for a total victory worthy of the sacrifices of total war against a totally depraved enemy. As Kipling summed up the general British feeling at the end of the war, the Germans were "a people with the heart of beasts."[8]

France's Georges Clemenceau, "the Tiger" who had broken wartime defeatism and led his country to victory, wholeheartedly agreed. Like most French people, Clemenceau wanted old-fashioned revenge. He also wanted lasting security for France. This, he believed, required the creation of a buffer state between France and Germany, the permanent demilitarization of Germany, and vast German reparations. He feared that sooner or later Germany with its 60 million people would attack France with its 40 million unless the Germans were permanently weakened. Moreover, France had no English Channel (or Atlantic Ocean) as a reassuring barrier against German aggression. Wilson, supported by Lloyd George, would hear none of this. Clemenceau's demands seemed vindictive, violating morality and the principle of national self-determination. By April the countries attending the conference were deadlocked on the German question, and Wilson packed his bags to go home.

In the end, convinced that France could not afford to face Germany alone in the future, Clemenceau agreed to a compromise. He gave up the French demand for a Rhineland buffer state in return for a formal defensive alliance with the United States and Great Britain. Under the terms of this alliance, both Wilson and Lloyd George promised that their countries would come to France's aid in the event of a German attack. Thus Clemenceau appeared to win his goal of French security, as Wilson had won his of a permanent international organization. The Allies moved quickly to finish the settlement, believing that any adjustments would later be possible within the dual framework of a strong Western alliance and the League of Nations (see Map 27.4).

The **Treaty of Versailles** between the Allies and Germany was the key to the settlement, and the terms were not unreasonable as a first step toward re-establishing international order. Had Germany won, it seems certain that France and Belgium would have been treated with greater severity, as Russia had been at Brest-Litovsk. Germany's colonies were given to France, Britain, and Japan as League of Nations mandates. Germany's territorial losses within Europe were minor, thanks to Wilson. Alsace-Lorraine was returned to France. Parts of Germany inhabited primarily by Poles were ceded to the new Polish state, in keeping with the principle of national self-determination. Predominately German Danzig was also placed within the Polish tariff lines, but as a self-governing city under League of Nations protection. Germany had to limit its army to 100,000 men and agree to build no military fortifications in the Rhineland.

More harshly, the Allies declared that Germany (with Austria) was responsible for the war and had therefore to pay reparations equal to all civilian damages caused by the war. This unfortunate and much-criticized clause expressed inescapable popular demands for German blood, but the actual figure was not set, and there was the clear possibility that reparations might be set at a reasonable level in the future when tempers had cooled.

When presented with the treaty, the German government protested vigorously. But there was no alternative, especially considering that Germany was still starving because the Allies had not yet lifted their naval blockade. On June 28, 1919, German representatives of the ruling moderate Social Democrats and the Catholic Party signed the treaty in the Sun King's Hall of Mirrors at Versailles, where Bismarck's empire had been joyously proclaimed almost fifty years before.

Online Study Center **Improve Your Grade**
Primary Source: A Defeated Germany Contemplates the Peace Treaty

Separate peace treaties were concluded with the other defeated European powers—Austria, Hungary, and Bulgaria. For the most part, these treaties merely ratified the existing situation in east-central Europe following the breakup of the Austro-Hungarian Empire. Like Austria, Hungary was a particularly big loser, as its "captive" nationalities (and some interspersed Hungarians) were ceded to Romania, Czechoslovakia, Poland, and Yugoslavia. Italy got some Austrian territory.

The Peace Settlement in the Middle East

Although Allied leaders at Versailles focused mainly on European questions, they also imposed a political settlement on what had been the Ottoman Empire. This settlement brought radical changes to the Middle East, and it became very controversial. Basically, the Ottoman Empire was broken up, Britain and France expanded their power and influence in the Middle East, and Arab nationalists felt cheated and betrayed.

The British government had encouraged the wartime Arab revolt against the Ottoman Turks (see page 890) and had even made vague promises of an independent Arab kingdom. However, when the fighting stopped, the British and the French chose instead to honor secret wartime agreements to divide and rule the Ottoman lands. Most important, in 1916 Britain and France had agreed that France would receive modern-day Lebanon and Syria, and much of southern Turkey, and Britain would receive Palestine, Transjordan, and Iraq. This agreement contradicted British (and later Wilsonian) promises concerning Arab independence after the war. When Britain and France set about implementing their secret plans after the armistice, Arab nationalists felt they were being double-crossed.

British plans for the old Ottoman province of Palestine also angered Arab nationalists. The **Balfour Declaration** of November 1917, made by the British foreign secretary Arthur Balfour, had declared that Britain favored a "National Home for the Jewish People" in Palestine, but without prejudicing the civil and religious rights of the non-Jewish communities already living in Palestine.

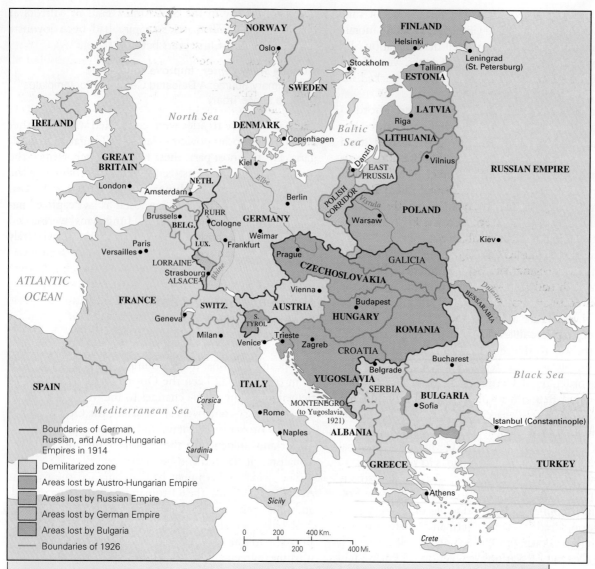

Mapping the Past

MAP 27.4 Shattered Empires and Territorial Changes After World War I   The Great War brought tremendous changes in eastern Europe. New nations and new boundaries were established, generally on the principle of national self-determination. A dangerous power vacuum was created by the new, usually small states established between Germany and Soviet Russia. ❶ Identify the boundaries of Germany, Austria-Hungary, and Russia in 1914, and note carefully the changes caused by the war. ❷ What territory did Germany lose, and why did France, Poland, and even Denmark receive it? Why was Austria sometimes called a head without a body in the 1920s? ❸ What new independent states (excluding disputed Bessarabia) were formed from the old Russian empire, and what nationalities lived in these states?

Some members of the British cabinet believed the declaration would appeal to German, Austrian, and American Jews and thus help the British war effort. Others sincerely supported the Zionist vision of a Jewish homeland (pages 838–839), which they hoped would also help Britain maintain control of the Suez Canal. In any event, Palestinian Arabs were dismayed.

In 1914 Jews accounted for about 11 percent of the predominately Arab population in the three Ottoman administrative units that would subsequently be lumped together by the British to form Palestine. The "National Home for the Jewish People" mentioned in the Balfour Declaration implied to the Arabs—and to the Zionist Jews as well—the establishment of some kind of Jewish state that would be incompatible with majority rule. Moreover, a state founded on religious and ethnic exclusivity was out of keeping with both Islamic and Ottoman tradition, which had historically been more tolerant of religious diversity and minorities than had the Christian monarchs or nation-states in Europe.

Despite strong French objections, Hussein of the Hejaz (see page 890) was allowed to send his son Faisal (1885–1933) as his representative to the Versailles Peace Conference. Yet Hussein's efforts to secure Arab independence came to nothing. President Wilson wanted to give the Arab case serious consideration, but the British and the French were determined to rule Syria, Iraq, Transjordan, and Palestine as League of Nations mandates, and they confirmed only the independence of Hussein's kingdom of Hejaz (see Map 27.5). In response Arab nationalists came together in Damascus as the General Syrian Congress in 1919 and unsuccessfully called again for political independence. (See the feature "Listening to the Past: Arab Political Aspirations in 1919" on pages 910–911.) Brushing aside Arab opposition, the British mandate in Palestine formally incorporated the Balfour Declaration and its commitment to a Jewish national home. When Faisal returned to Syria, his followers repudiated the agreement he had reluctantly accepted. In March 1920 they met as the Syrian National Congress and proclaimed Syria independent, with Faisal as king. A similar congress declared Iraq an independent kingdom.

Prince Faisal at the Versailles Peace Conference, 1919 Standing in front, Faisal is supported by his allies and black slave. Nur-as-Said, an officer in the Ottoman army who joined the Arab revolt, is second from the left, and the British officer T. E. Lawrence—popularly known as Lawrence of Arabia—is fourth from the left in back. Faisal failed to win political independence for the Arabs, as the British backed away from the vague promises they had made during the war. *(Courtesy of the Trustees of the Imperial War Museum)*

MAP 27.5 The Partition of the Ottoman Empire, 1914–1923 By 1914 the Ottoman Turks had been pushed out of the Balkans, and their Arab provinces were on the edge of revolt. That revolt, in alliance with the British, erupted in the First World War and contributed greatly to the Ottomans' defeat. Refusing to grant independence to the Arabs, the Allies established League of Nations mandates and replaced Ottoman rulers in Syria, Iraq, Transjordan, and Palestine.

Western reaction to events in Syria and Iraq was swift and decisive. A French army stationed in Lebanon attacked Syria, taking Damascus in July 1920. Faisal fled, and the French took over. Meanwhile, the British put down an uprising in Iraq with bloody fighting and established effective control there. Western imperialism, in the form of League of Nations mandates, appeared to have replaced Ottoman rule in the Arab Middle East (see Map 27.5).

The Allies sought to impose even harsher terms on the defeated Turks than on the "liberated" Arabs. A treaty forced on the helpless Ottoman sultan dismembered the Turkish heartland. Great Britain and France occupied parts of modern-day Turkey, and Italy and Greece also claimed shares. There was a sizable Greek minority in western Turkey, and Greek nationalists wanted to build a

modern Greek empire modeled on long-dead Christian Byzantium. In 1919 Greek armies carried by British ships landed on the Turkish coast at Smyrna and advanced unopposed into the interior. Turkey seemed finished.

But Turkey produced a great leader and revived to become an inspiration for many modernizing reformers. Mustafa Kemal (1881–1938), later known as **Atatürk,** which means "father of the Turks," was a military man who had directed the successful defense of the Dardanelles against British attack. Watching the Allies' aggression and the sultan's cowardice after the armistice, in early 1919 he moved to central Turkey and gradually unified the Turkish resistance. Refusing to acknowledge the Allied dismemberment of their country, the Turks battled on through 1920 despite staggering defeats. The

Mustafa Kemal Surnamed Atatürk, meaning "father of the Turks," Mustafa Kemal and his supporters imposed revolutionary changes aimed at modernizing and westernizing Turkish society and the new Turkish government. Dancing here with his adopted daughter at her high-society wedding, Atatürk often appeared in public in elegant European dress— a vivid symbol for the Turkish people of his radical break with traditional Islamic teaching and custom. *(Hulton Archive/Getty Images)*

next year they won a great victory in central Turkey, and the Greeks and their British allies sued for peace. After long negotiations, the resulting Treaty of Lausanne (1923) solemnly abolished the hated Capitulations, which the European powers had imposed over the centuries to give their citizens special privileges in the Ottoman Empire, and recognized the territorial integrity of a truly independent Turkey. Turkey lost only its former Arab provinces.

Mustafa Kemal, a nationalist without religious faith, believed that Turkey should modernize and secularize along Western lines. He established a republic, had him-

self elected president, and created a one-party system— partly inspired by the Bolshevik example—in order to transform his country. The most radical reforms pertained to religion and culture. For centuries most of the intellectual and social activities of believers had been regulated by Islamic religious authorities. Profoundly influenced by the example of western Europe, Mustafa Kemal set out to limit the place of religion and religious leaders in daily affairs. He decreed a revolutionary separation of church and state, promulgated law codes inspired by European models, and established a secular public school system. Women received rights that they never had before. By the time of his death in 1938, Mustafa Kemal had implemented successfully much of his revolutionary program. He had moved Turkey much closer to Europe, foretelling current efforts by Turkey to join the European Union as full-fledged member.

American Rejection of the Versailles Treaty

The rapidly concluded Versailles treaty of early 1919 was not perfect, but within the context of war-shattered Europe it was an acceptable beginning. The principle of national self-determination, which had played such a large role in starting the war, was accepted for Europe and served as an organizing framework. Germany had been punished but not dismembered. A new world organization complemented a traditional defensive alliance of satisfied powers. The serious remaining problems could be worked out in the future. Moreover, Allied leaders had seen speed as essential for another reason: they detested Lenin and feared that his Bolshevik Revolution might spread. They realized that their best answer to Lenin's unending calls for worldwide upheaval was peace and tranquillity for war-weary peoples.

There were, however, two great interrelated obstacles to such peace: Germany and the United States. Plagued by communist uprisings, reactionary plots, and popular disillusionment with losing the war at the last minute, Germany's moderate socialists and their liberal and Catholic supporters faced an enormous challenge. Like French republicans after 1871, they needed time (and luck) if they were to establish firmly a peaceful and democratic republic. Progress in this direction required understanding but firm treatment of Germany by the victorious Western Allies, particularly by the United States.

However, the U.S. Senate and, to a lesser extent, the American people rejected Wilson's handiwork. Republican senators led by Henry Cabot Lodge refused to ratify the

Treaty of Versailles without changes in the articles creating the League of Nations. The key issue was the League's power—more apparent than real—to require member states to take collective action against aggression. Lodge and others believed that this requirement gave away Congress's constitutional right to declare war. In failing health, Wilson, with narrow-minded self-righteousness, rejected all attempts at compromise. In doing so, he ensured that the treaty would never be ratified by the United States in any form and that the United States would never join the League of Nations. Moreover, the Senate refused to ratify Wilson's treaties forming a defensive alliance with France and Great Britain. America turned its back on Europe.

The Wilson-Lodge fiasco and the newfound gospel of isolationism represented a tragic and cowardly renunciation of America's responsibility. Using America's action as an excuse, Great Britain, too, refused to ratify its defensive alliance with France. Bitterly betrayed by its allies, France stood alone. Very shortly France was to take actions against Germany that would feed the fires of German resentment and seriously undermine democratic forces in the new republic. The great hopes of early 1919 had turned to ashes by the end of the year. The Western alliance had collapsed, and a grandiose plan for permanent peace had given way to a fragile truce. For this and for what came later, the United States must share a large part of the guilt.

Chapter Summary

Online Study Center   **ACE the Test**

- *What caused the Great War, and why did it have such revolutionary consequences?*
- *What was the impact of total war on civilian populations?*
- *Why did World War I bring socialist revolution in Russia?*
- *How did the Allies fashion a peace settlement, and why was it unsuccessful?*

World War I had truly revolutionary consequences because, first and foremost, it was a war of committed peoples. In France, Britain, and Germany in particular, governments drew on genuine popular support. This support reflected in part the diplomatic origins of the war, which citizens saw as growing out of an unwanted crisis in the Balkans and an inflexible alliance system of opposing blocs. More importantly, popular support reflected the way western European society had been unified under the nationalist banner in the later nineteenth century, despite the fears that the growing socialist movement aroused in conservatives.

The relentlessness of total war helps explain why so many died, why so many were crippled physically and psychologically, and why Western civilization would in so many ways never be the same again. More concretely, the war swept away monarchs and multinational empires. National self-determination apparently triumphed across Europe, not only in Austria-Hungary but also in many of Russia's west-

ern borderlands. Except in Ireland and parts of Soviet Russia (and the Arab Middle East), the revolutionary dream of national unity, born of the French Revolution, had finally come true.

Two other revolutions were products of the war. In Russia the Bolsheviks established a radical regime, smashed existing capitalist institutions, and stayed in power with a new kind of authoritarian rule. Whether the new Russian regime was truly Marxian or socialist was questionable, but it indisputably posed a powerful, ongoing revolutionary challenge to Europe and its colonial empires.

More subtle but quite universal in its impact was an administrative revolution. This revolution, born of the need to mobilize entire societies and economies for total war, greatly increased the power of government. Freewheeling market capitalism and a well-integrated world economy were among the many casualties of the administrative revolution, and greater social equality was everywhere one of its results. Thus even in European countries where a communist takeover never came close to occurring, society still experienced a great revolution.

Finally, the "war to end war" did not bring peace—only a fragile truce. In the West, the Allies failed to maintain their wartime solidarity. Germany remained unrepentant and would soon have more grievances to nurse. Moreover, the victory of national self-determination in eastern Europe created small, weak states and thus a power vacuum between a still-powerful Germany and a potentially mighty communist Russia. A vast area lay open to military aggression from two sides.

Key Terms

Three Emperors'
  League
Triple Entente
trench warfare
Lusitania
total war
War Raw Materials
  Board
Petrograd Soviet
Army Order No. 1

Bolsheviks
Constituent
  Assembly
war communism
Cheka
League of Nations
Treaty of Versailles
Balfour
  Declaration
Atatürk

Online Study Center   **Improve Your Grade** Flashcards

Suggested Reading

Davis, Belinda J. *Home Fires Burning: Food, Politics, and Everyday Life in Berlin in World War I.* 2000. A moving account of women struggling to feed their families.

Eksteins, Modris. *Rites of Spring: The Great War and the Birth of the Modern Age.* 1989. An imaginative cultural investigation that has won critical acclaim.

Fromkin, David. *A Peace to End All Peace.* 2001. A brilliant reconsideration of the collapse of the Ottoman Empire and its division by the Allies.

Gatrell, Peter. *Russia's First World War: A Social and Economic History.* 2005. An excellent resource for students and specialists.

Herwig, Holger H. *The First World War: Germany and Austria, 1914–1918.* 1997. Ably follows the hard road to defeat and collapse.

Higonnet, Margaret R., Jane Jenson, Sonya Michel, and Margaret Collins Weitz, eds. *Behind the Lines: Gender and the Two World Wars.* 1989. Examines the changes that the war brought for women and for relations between the sexes.

Hobsbawm, Eric. *The Age of Extremes: A History of the World, 1914–1991.* 1996. A provocative interpretation by a famous historian, with a good discussion of war and revolution.

Howard, Michael. *The First World War: A Very Short Introduction.* 2007. A fine brief introduction.

Macmillan, Margaret. *Paris, 1919: Six Months That Changed the World.* 2001. A comprehensive, exciting account of all aspects of the peace conference.

Neiberg, Michael S. *Fighting the Great War: A Global History.* 2006. A lively and up-to-date account.

Read, Christopher. *From Tsar to Soviets: The Russian People and Their Revolution, 1917–1921.* 1996. A highly recommended account of the Russian Revolution.

Remarque, Erich Maria. *All Quiet on the Western Front.* Originally published in 1928, this novel remains one of the most moving fictional treatments of World War I.

Tucker, Jonathan. *War of Nerves: Chemical Warfare from World War I to Al-Qaeda.* 2007. A comprehensive and informative survey of chemical warfare.

Winter, J. M. *The Experience of World War I.* 1988. A striking illustrated history of the war.

Zuckerman, Larry. *The Rape of Belgium: The Untold Story of World War I.* 2004. A poignant examination of German atrocities.

Notes

1. M. Beloff, quoted in *U.S. News & World Report,* March 8, 1976, p. 53.
2. Quoted in J. Remak, *The Origins of World War I* (New York: Holt, Rinehart & Winston, 1967), p. 84.
3. Quoted in F. P. Chambers, *The War Behind the War, 1914–1918* (London: Faber & Faber, 1939), p. 168.
4. Quoted in R. O. Paxton, *Europe in the Twentieth Century* (New York: Harcourt Brace Jovanovich, 1975), p. 109.
5. A. B. Ulam, *The Bolsheviks* (New York: Collier Books, 1968), p. 349.
6. Ibid., p. 405.
7. H. Nicolson, *Peacemaking 1919* (New York: Grosset & Dunlap Universal Library, 1965), pp. 8, 31–32.
8. Quoted ibid., p. 24.

Listening to the Past

Arab Political Aspirations in 1919

Great Britain and France had agreed to divide up the Arab lands, and the British also had made conflicting promises to Arab and Jewish nationalists. However, President Wilson insisted at Versailles that the right of self-determination should be applied to the conquered Ottoman territories, and he sent an American commission of inquiry to Syria, even though the British and French refused to participate. The commission canvassed political views throughout greater Syria, and its long report with many documents reflected public opinion in the region in 1919.

To present their view to the Americans, Arab nationalists from present-day Syria, Lebanon, Israel, and Jordan came together in Damascus as the General Syrian Congress, and they passed the following resolution on July 2, 1919. In addition to the Arab call for political independence, the delegates addressed the possibility of French rule under a League of Nations mandate and the establishment of a Jewish national home.

We the undersigned members of the General Syrian Congress, meeting in Damascus on Wednesday, July 2nd, 1919, . . . provided with credentials and authorizations by the inhabitants of our various districts, Moslems, Christians, and Jews, have agreed upon the following statement of the desires of the people of the country who have elected us to present them to the American Section of the International Commission; the fifth article was passed by a very large majority; all the other articles were accepted unanimously.

1. We ask absolutely complete political independence for Syria within these boundaries. [Describes the area including the present-day states of Syria, Lebanon, Israel, and Jordan.]

2. We ask that the Government of this Syrian country should be a democratic civil constitutional Monarchy on broad decentralization principles, safeguarding the rights of minorities, and that the King be the Emir Faisal, who carried on a glorious struggle in the cause of our liberation and merited our full confidence and entire reliance.

3. Considering the fact that the Arabs inhabiting the Syrian area are not naturally less gifted than other more advanced races and that they are by no means less developed than the Bulgarians, Serbians, Greeks, and Roumanians at the beginning of their independence, we protest against Article 22 of the Covenant of the League of Nations, placing us among the nations in their middle stage of development which stand in need of a mandatory power.

4. In the event of the rejection by the Peace Conference of this just protest for certain considerations that we may not understand, we, relying on the declarations of President Wilson that his object in waging war was to put an end to the ambition of conquest and colonization, can only regard the mandate mentioned in the Covenant of the League of Nations as equivalent to the rendering of economical and technical assistance that does not prejudice our complete independence. And desiring that our country should not fall a prey to colonization and believing that the American Nation is farthest from any thought of colonization and has no political ambition in our country, we will seek the technical and economical assistance from the United States of America, provided that such assistance does not exceed 20 years.

5. In the event of America not finding herself in a position to accept our desire for assistance, we will seek this assistance from Great Britain, also provided that such assistance does not infringe the complete independence and unity of our country and that the duration of such assistance does not exceed that mentioned in the previous article.

Palestinian Arabs protest against large-scale Jewish migration into Palestine. *(Roger-Viollet/ Getty Images)*

6. We do not acknowledge any right claimed by the French Government in any part whatever of our Syrian country and refuse that she should assist us or have a hand in our country under any circumstances and in any place.

7. We oppose the pretensions of the Zionists to create a Jewish commonwealth in the southern part of Syria, known as Palestine, and oppose Zionist migration to any part of our country; for we do not acknowledge their title but consider them a grave peril to our people from the national, economical, and political points of view. Our Jewish compatriots shall enjoy our common rights and assume the common responsibilities.

8. We ask that there should be no separation of the southern part of Syria, known as Palestine, nor of the littoral western zone, which includes Lebanon, from the Syrian country. We desire that the unity of the country should be guaranteed against partition under whatever circumstances.

9. We ask complete independence for emancipated Mesopotamia [today's Iraq] and that there should be no economical barriers between the two countries.

10. The fundamental principles laid down by President Wilson in condemnation of secret treaties impel us to protest most emphatically against any treaty that stipulates the partition of our Syria country and against any private engagement aiming at the establishment of Zionism in the southern part of Syria; therefore we ask the complete annulment of these conventions and agreements.

The noble principles enunciated by President Wilson strengthen our confidence that our desires emanating from the depths of our hearts, shall be the decisive factor in determining our future; and that President Wilson and the free American people will be our supporters for the realization of our hopes, thereby proving their sincerity and noble sympathy with the aspiration of the weaker nations in general and our Arab people in particular.

We also have the fullest confidence that the Peace Conference will realize that we would not have risen against the Turks, with whom we had participated in all civil, political, and representative privileges, but for their violation of our national rights, and so will grant us our desires in full in order that our political rights may not be less after the war than they were before, since we have shed so much blood in the cause of our liberty and independence.

We request to be allowed to send a delegation to represent us at the Peace Conference to defend our rights and secure the realization of our aspirations.

Questions for Analysis

1. What kind of state did the delegates want?

2. How did the delegates want to modify an unwanted League of Nations mandate to make it less objectionable?

3. Did the delegates view their "Jewish compatriots" and the Zionists in different ways? Why?

Source: "Resolution of the General Syrian Congress at Damascus, 2 July 1919," from the King-Crane Commission Report, in *Foreign Relations of the United States: Paris Peace Conference*, 1919, 12: 780–781.

This detail of George Grosz's *Draussen und Drinnen* (Outside and Inside) captures the uncertainty and anxiety of the 1920s. *(akg-images)*

THE AGE OF ANXIETY,
CA 1900–1940

When Allied diplomats met in Paris in early 1919 with their optimistic plans for building a lasting peace, most people looked forward to happier times. They hoped that life would return to normal after the terrible trauma of total war. They hoped that once again life would make sense in the familiar prewar terms of peace, prosperity, and progress. These hopes were in vain. The Great Break—the First World War and the Russian Revolution—had mangled too many things beyond repair. Life would no longer fit neatly into the old molds.

Instead, great numbers of men and women felt themselves increasingly adrift in a strange, uncertain, and uncontrollable world. They saw themselves living in an age of anxiety, an age of continual crisis (this age lasted until at least the early 1950s). In almost every area of human experience, people went searching for ways to put meaning back into life.

Uncertainty in Modern Thought

A complex revolution in thought and ideas was under way before the First World War, but only small, unusual groups were aware of it. After the war, these new and upsetting ideas began to spread through the entire population. Western society as a whole began to question and even abandon many cherished values and beliefs that had guided it since the eighteenth-century Enlightenment and the nineteenth-century triumph of industrial development, scientific advances, and evolutionary thought.

• *In what ways did new and disturbing ideas in philosophy, physics, psychology, and literature reflect the general crisis in Western thought?*

The "Cruelly Injured Mind"

Before 1914 most people still believed in progress, reason, and the rights of the individual. Progress was a daily reality, apparent in the rising standard of living, the taming of the city, and the steady increase in popular education. Such developments also encouraged the comforting belief in the logical universe of Newtonian physics as well as faith in the ability of a rational human mind to understand that universe through intellectual investigation. And just as there were laws of science, so were there laws of society that rational human beings could discover and then wisely act on. At the same time, the rights of the individual were not just taken for granted; they were actually increasing. Well-established political rights were gradually spreading to women and workers, and new "social rights," such as old-age pensions, were emerging. In short, before World War I most Europeans had a moderately optimistic view of the world, and with good reason.

Nevertheless, since the 1880s, a small band of serious thinkers and creative writers had been attacking these well-worn optimistic ideas. These critics rejected the general faith in progress and the power of the rational human mind. An expanding chorus of thinkers echoed and enlarged their views after the experience of history's most destructive war—a war that suggested to many that human beings were a pack of violent, irrational animals quite capable of tearing the individual and his or her rights to shreds. Disorientation and pessimism were particularly acute in the 1930s, when the rapid rise of harsh dictatorships and the Great Depression transformed old certainties into bitter illusions, as we shall see in Chapter 29.

No one expressed this state of uncertainty better than French poet and critic Paul Valéry (1871–1945) in the early 1920s. Speaking of the "crisis of the mind," Valéry noted that Europe was looking at its future with dark foreboding:

The storm has died away, and still we are restless, uneasy, as if the storm were about to break. Almost all the affairs of men remain in a terrible uncertainty. We think of what has disappeared, and we are almost destroyed by what has been destroyed; we do not know what will be born, and we fear the future, not without reason. . . . Doubt and disorder are in us and with us. There is no thinking man, however shrewd or learned he may be, who can hope to dominate this anxiety, to escape from this impression of darkness.[1]

In the midst of economic, political, and social disruptions, Valéry saw the "cruelly injured mind," besieged by doubts and suffering from anxieties. This was the general intellectual crisis of the twentieth century, which touched almost every field of thought. The implications of new

Kollwitz: The Grieving Parents After the renowned German artist Kathe Kollwitz learned in October 1914 that her son Peter had died in battle, the heartbroken mother conceived of a sculpture to honor his memory. Yet her efforts were repeatedly overwhelmed by sorrow. Only in 1931 could she complete this graveside memorial in a military cemetery, a telling indication of the war's ongoing devastation for millions. The grieving father and mother are finally reunited with their son, and they beg forgiveness for the mad war their generation inflicted on its children. *(John Parker, photographer, © 2007 Artists Rights Society [ARS], New York/VG Bild-Kunst, Bonn)*

ideas and discoveries in philosophy, physics, psychology, and literature played a central role in this crisis, disturbing "thinking people" everywhere.

Modern Philosophy

Among the small band of thinkers in the late nineteenth century who challenged the belief in progress and the general faith in the rational human mind, German philosopher Friedrich Nietzsche (1844–1900) was particularly influential. The son of a Lutheran minister, Nietzsche rejected Christianity and became a professor of classical languages until ill health forced him to retire at an early age. Never a systematic philosopher, Nietzsche wrote as a prophet in a provocative and poetic style. His first great work in 1872 argued that ever since classical Athens, the West had overemphasized rationality and stifled the passion and animal instinct that drive human activity and true creativity. Nietzsche went on to question all values. He claimed that Christianity embodied a "slave morality" that glorified weakness, envy, and mediocrity. In Nietzsche's most famous line, a wise fool proclaims that "God is dead," dead because he has been murdered by lackadaisical modern Christians who no longer really believe in him. Nietzsche viewed the pillars of conventional morality—reason, democracy, progress, respectability—as outworn social and psychological constructs whose influence was suffocating self-realization and excellence.

Online Study Center **Improve Your Grade**
Primary Source: God Is Dead, the Victim of Science

Nietzsche painted a dark world, foreshadowing perhaps his loss of sanity in 1889. The West was in decline; false values had triumphed. The death of God left people disoriented and depressed. The only hope for the individual was to accept the meaninglessness of human existence and then make that very meaninglessness a source of self-defined personal integrity and hence liberation. This would at least be possible for a few superior individuals who could free themselves from the humdrum thinking of the masses and become true heroes. Little read during his active years, Nietzsche attracted growing attention in the early twentieth century, especially from German radicals who found inspiration in Nietzsche's ferocious assault on the conventions of pre-1914 imperial Germany. Subsequent generations have each discovered new Nietzsches, and his influence remains enormous to this day.

This growing dissatisfaction with established ideas before 1914 was apparent in other important thinkers. In the 1890s, French philosophy professor Henri Bergson

Chronology

1919 Treaty of Versailles; Freudian psychology gains popular attention; Keynes, *Economic Consequences of the Peace*; Rutherford splits the atom

1920s Existentialism gains prominence

1920s–1930s Dadaism and surrealism (artistic movements)

1922 Eliot, *The Waste Land*; Joyce, *Ulysses*; Woolf, *Jacob's Room*; Wittgenstein writes on logical empiricism

1923 French and Belgian armies occupy the Ruhr

1924 Dawes Plan

1925 Berg's opera *Wozzeck* first performed; Kafka, *The Trial*

1926 Germany joins League of Nations

1927 Heisenberg's principle of uncertainty

1928 Kellogg-Briand Pact

1929 Faulkner, *The Sound and the Fury*

1929–1939 Great Depression

1930 Van der Rohe becomes director of Bauhaus

1932 Franklin Roosevelt elected U.S. president

1934 Riefenstahl's documentary film *The Triumph of the Will*

1935 Creation of WPA as part of New Deal

1936 Formation of Popular Front in France

(1859–1941) convinced many young people through his writing that immediate experience and intuition were as important as rational and scientific thinking for understanding reality. Indeed, according to Bergson, a religious experience or a mystical poem was often more accessible to human comprehension than a scientific law or a mathematical equation.

Another thinker who agreed about the limits of rational thinking was French socialist Georges Sorel (1847–1922). Sorel frankly characterized Marxian socialism as an inspiring but unprovable religion rather than a rational scientific truth. Socialism would come to power, he believed, through a great, general strike of all working people, which would shatter capitalist society. Sorel rejected democracy and believed that the masses of the new socialist society

Friedrich Nietzsche   This colored photograph of the German philosopher was taken in 1882, when he was at the height of his creative powers. A brilliant iconoclast, Nietzsche debunked European values and challenged the optimistic faith in human rationality before World War I. *(akg-images)*

would have to be tightly controlled by a small revolutionary elite.

The First World War accelerated the revolt against established certainties in philosophy, but that revolt went in two very different directions. In English-speaking countries, the main development was the acceptance of logical empiricism (or logical positivism) in university circles. In continental countries, the primary development in philosophy was existentialism.

Logical empiricism was truly revolutionary. It quite simply rejected most of the concerns of traditional philosophy, from the existence of God to the meaning of happiness, as nonsense and hot air. This outlook began primarily with Austrian philosopher Ludwig Wittgenstein (1889–1951), who later immigrated to England, where he trained numerous disciples.

Wittgenstein argued in his pugnacious *Tractatus Logico-Philosophicus* (Essay on Logical Philosophy) in 1922 that philosophy is only the logical clarification of thoughts, and therefore it becomes the study of language, which expresses thoughts. The great philosophical issues of the ages—God, freedom, morality, and so on—are quite literally senseless, a great waste of time, for statements about them can be neither tested by scientific experiments nor demonstrated by the logic of mathematics. Statements about such matters reflect only the personal preferences of a given individual. As Wittgenstein put it in the famous last sentence of his work, "Of what one cannot speak, of that one must keep silent." Logical empiricism, which has remained dominant in England and the United States to this day, drastically reduced the scope of philosophical inquiry. Anxious people could find few, if any, answers in this direction.

Some looked for answers in **existentialism.** Highly diverse and even contradictory, existential thinkers were loosely united in a courageous search for moral values in a world of terror and uncertainty. Theirs were true voices of the age of anxiety.

Most existential thinkers in the twentieth century were atheists. Often inspired by Nietzsche, who had already proclaimed the death of God and called for new values, they did not believe a supreme being had established humanity's fundamental nature and given life its meaning. In the words of the famous French existentialist Jean-Paul Sartre (1905–1980), human beings simply exist: "They turn up, appear on the scene." Only after they "turn up" do they seek to define themselves. Honest human beings are terribly alone, for there is no God to help them. They are hounded by despair and the meaninglessness of life. The crisis of the existential thinker epitomized the modern intellectual crisis—the shattering of beliefs in God, reason, and progress.

Existentialists did recognize that human beings, unless they kill themselves, must act. Indeed, in the words of Sartre, "man is condemned to be free." There is therefore the possibility—indeed, the necessity—of giving meaning to life through actions, of defining oneself through choices. To do so, individuals must become "engaged" and choose their own actions courageously and consistently and in full awareness of their inescapable responsibility for their own behavior. In the end, existentialists argued, human beings can overcome life's absurdity.

Modern existentialism first attained prominence in Germany in the 1920s when philosophers Martin Heidegger and Karl Jaspers found a sympathetic audience among disillusioned postwar university students. But it was in France during and immediately after World War II that existentialism came of age. The terrible conditions of the war (see Chapter 29) reinforced the existential view of and approach to life. On the one hand, the armies of the German dictator Hitler had conquered most of Europe and unleashed a hideous reign of barbarism. On the other, men and women had more than ever to define themselves by their actions. Specifically, each individual had to choose whether to join the resistance against Hitler or accept and even abet tyranny. The writings of Sartre, who along with Albert Camus (1913–1960) was the leading French existentialist, became enormously influential. Himself active in the French resistance, Sartre and his colleagues offered a powerful answer to profound moral issues and the contemporary crisis.

The Revival of Christianity

The loss of faith in human reason and in continual progress also led to a renewed interest in the Christian view of the world. Christianity and religion in general had been on the defensive in intellectual circles since the Enlightenment. In the years before 1914, some theologians, especially Protestant ones, had felt the need to interpret Christian doctrine and the Bible so that they did not seem to contradict science, evolution, and common sense. Christ was therefore seen primarily as the greatest moral teacher, and the "supernatural" aspects of his divinity were strenuously played down. Indeed, some modern theologians were embarrassed by the miraculous, unscientific aspects of Christianity and turned away from them.

Especially after World War I, a number of thinkers and theologians began to revitalize the fundamentals of Christianity. Sometimes described as Christian existentialists because they shared the loneliness and despair of atheistic existentialists, they stressed human beings' sinful nature, the need for faith, and the mystery of God's forgiveness. The revival of fundamental Christian belief after World War I was fed by rediscovery of the work of nineteenth-century Danish religious philosopher Søren Kierkegaard (1813–1855), whose ideas became extremely influential. Having rejected formalistic religion, Kierkegaard had eventually resolved his personal anguish over his imperfect nature by making a total religious commitment to a remote and majestic God.

Similar ideas were brilliantly developed by Swiss Protestant theologian Karl Barth (1886–1968), whose many influential writings after 1920 sought to re-create the religious intensity of the Reformation. For Barth, the basic fact about human beings is that they are imperfect, sinful creatures whose reason and will are hopelessly flawed. Religious truth is therefore made known to human beings only through God's grace. People have to accept God's word and the supernatural revelation of Jesus Christ with awe, trust, and obedience. Lowly mortals should not expect to "reason out" God and his ways.

Among Catholics, the leading existential Christian thinker was Gabriel Marcel (1887–1973). Born into a cultivated French family, where his atheistic father was "gratefully aware of all that . . . art owed to Catholicism but regarded Catholic thought itself as obsolete and tainted with absurd superstitions,"[2] Marcel found in the Catholic Church an answer to what he called the postwar "broken world." Catholicism and religious belief provided the hope, humanity, honesty, and piety for which he hungered. Flexible and gentle, Marcel and his countryman Jacques Maritain (1882–1973) denounced anti-Semitism and supported closer ties with non-Catholics.

After 1914 religion became much more relevant and meaningful to thinking people than it had been before the war. In addition to Marcel and Maritain, many other illustrious individuals turned to religion between about 1920 and 1950. Poets T. S. Eliot and W. H. Auden, novelists Evelyn Waugh and Aldous Huxley, historian Arnold Toynbee, Oxford professor C. S. Lewis, psychoanalyst Karl Stern, physicist Max Planck, and philosopher Cyril Joad were all either converted to religion or attracted to it for the first time. Religion, often of a despairing, existential variety, was one meaningful answer to terror and anxiety. In the words of a famous Roman Catholic convert, English novelist Graham Greene, "One began to believe in heaven because one believed in hell."[3]

The New Physics

Ever since the scientific revolution of the seventeenth century, scientific advances and their implications had greatly influenced the beliefs of thinking people. By the late nineteenth century, science was one of the main pillars supporting Western society's optimistic and rationalistic view of the world. The Darwinian concept of evolution had been accepted and assimilated in most intellectual circles. Progressive minds believed that science, unlike religion and philosophical speculation, was based on hard facts and controlled experiments. Science seemed to have achieved an unerring and almost complete picture of reality. Unchanging natural laws seemed to determine physical processes and permit useful solutions to more and more problems. All this was comforting, especially to people who were no longer committed to traditional religious beliefs. And all this was challenged by the new physics.

An important first step toward the new physics was the discovery at the end of the nineteenth century that atoms were not like hard, permanent little billiard balls. They were actually composed of many far-smaller, fast-moving particles, such as electrons and protons. Polish-born physicist Marie Curie (1867–1934) and her French husband, Pierre, discovered that radium constantly emits subatomic particles and thus does not have a constant atomic weight. Building on this and other work in radiation, German physicist Max Planck (1858–1947) showed in 1900 that subatomic energy is emitted in uneven little spurts, which Planck called "quanta," and not in a steady stream, as previously believed. Planck's discovery called into question the old sharp distinction between matter and energy; the implication was that matter and energy might be different forms of the same thing. The old view of atoms as the stable, basic building blocks of nature, with a different kind of unbreakable atom for each of the ninety-two chemical elements, was badly shaken.

In 1905 the German-Jewish genius Albert Einstein (1879–1955) went further than the Curies and Planck in undermining Newtonian physics. His famous theory of special relativity postulated that time and space are relative to the viewpoint of the observer and that only the speed of light is constant for all frames of reference in the universe. In order to make his revolutionary and paradoxical idea somewhat comprehensible to the nonmathematical layperson, Einstein later used analogies involving moving trains. For example, if a woman in the middle of a moving car got up and walked forward to the door, she had gone, relative to the train, a half car length. But relative to an observer on the embankment, she had gone farther. The closed framework of Newtonian physics was quite limited compared to that of Einsteinian physics, which unified an apparently infinite universe with the incredibly small, fast-moving subatomic world. Moreover, Einstein's theory stated clearly that matter and energy are interchangeable and that even a particle of matter contains enormous levels of potential energy.

The 1920s opened the "heroic age of physics," in the apt words of one of its leading pioneers, Ernest Rutherford (1871–1937). Breakthrough followed breakthrough. In 1919 Rutherford showed that the atom could be split. By 1944 seven subatomic particles had been identified, of which the most important

Unlocking the Power of the Atom Many of the fanciful visions of science fiction came true in the twentieth century, although not exactly as first imagined. This 1927 cartoon satirizes a professor who has split the atom and unwittingly destroyed his building and neighborhood in the process. In the Second World War the professors harnessed the atom in bombs and decimated faraway cities and foreign civilians. *(Mary Evans Picture Library)*

was the **neutron.** The neutron's capacity to pass through other atoms allowed for even more intense experimental bombardment of matter, leading to chain reactions of unbelievable force. This was the road to the atomic bomb.

Although few nonscientists understood this revolution in physics, the implications of the new theories and discoveries, as presented by newspapers and popular writers, were disturbing to millions of men and women in the 1920s and 1930s. The new universe was strange and troubling. It lacked any absolute objective reality. Everything was "relative," that is, dependent on the observer's frame of reference. Moreover, the universe was uncertain and undetermined, without stable building blocks. In 1927 German physicist Werner Heisenberg (1901–1976) formulated the "principle of uncertainty," which postulates that because it is impossible to know the position and speed of an individual electron, it is therefore impossible to predict its behavior. Instead of Newton's dependable, rational laws, there seemed to be only tendencies and probabilities in an extraordinarily complex and uncertain universe.

Moreover, a universe described by abstract mathematical symbols seemed to have little to do with human experience and human problems. When, for example, Planck was asked what science could contribute to resolving conflicts of values, his response was simple: "Science is not qualified to speak to this question." Physics, the queen of the sciences, no longer provided people easy, optimistic answers—for that matter, it did not provide any answers at all.

Giorgio de Chirico: The Song of Love De Chirico strongly influenced the surrealist painters of the 1920s and 1930s, who saw civilization in crisis and found inspiration in Freudian theories of human thought and action. In this 1914 painting De Chirico tightly groups unrelated images—a classical head, a glove, a ball, a building—in a fantastic, dreamlike combination that fascinates and puzzles. What mysterious significance, if any, lies behind this reordering of everyday reality? (*Digital image © The Museum of Modern Art/Licensed by Scala/Art Resource, NY/© 2007 Artists Rights Society [ARS], New York/SIAE, Rome*)

Freudian Psychology

With physics presenting an uncertain universe so unrelated to ordinary human experience, questions regarding the power and potential of the human mind assumed special significance. The findings and speculations of leading psychologist Sigmund Freud (see page 804) were particularly disturbing.

Before Freud, poets and mystics had probed the unconscious and irrational aspects of human behavior. But most professional, "scientific" psychologists assumed that a single, unified conscious mind processed sense experiences in a rational and logical way. Human behavior in turn was the result of rational calculation—of "thinking"—by the conscious mind. Basing his insights on the analysis of dreams

and of hysteria, Freud developed a very different view of the human psyche beginning in the late 1880s.

According to Freud, human behavior is basically irrational. The key to understanding the mind is the primitive, irrational unconscious, which he called the **id.** The unconscious is driven by sexual, aggressive, and pleasure-seeking desires and is locked in a constant battle with the other parts of the mind: the rationalizing conscious (the **ego**), which mediates what a person *can* do, and ingrained moral values (the **superego**), which specify what a person *should* do. Human behavior is a product of a fragile compromise between instinctual drives and the controls of rational thinking and moral values. Since the instinctual drives are extremely powerful, the ever-present danger for individuals and whole societies is that unacknowledged drives will overwhelm the control mechanisms in a violent, distorted way. Yet Freud also agreed with Nietzsche that the mechanisms of rational thinking and traditional moral values can be too strong. They can repress sexual desires too effectively, crippling individuals and entire peoples with guilt and neurotic fears.

Freudian psychology and clinical psychiatry had become an international movement by 1910, but only after 1918 did they receive popular attention, especially in the Protestant countries of northern Europe and in the United States. Many opponents and even some enthusiasts interpreted Freud as saying that the first requirement for mental health is an uninhibited sex life. Thus after the First World War, the popular interpretation of Freud reflected and encouraged growing sexual experimentation, particularly among middle-class women. For more serious students, the psychology of Freud and his followers drastically undermined the old, easy optimism about the rational and progressive nature of the human mind.

Twentieth-Century Literature

The general intellectual climate of pessimism, relativism, and alienation was also articulated in literature. Novelists developed new techniques to express new realities. The great nineteenth-century novelists had typically written as all-knowing narrators, describing realistic characters and their relationship to an understandable, if sometimes harsh, society. In the twentieth century, most major writers adopted the limited, often confused viewpoint of a single individual. Like Freud, these novelists focused their attention on the complexity and irrationality of the human mind, where feelings, memories, and desires are forever scrambled. The great French novelist Marcel Proust (1871–1922), in his semi-autobiographical *Remembrance of Things Past* (1913–1927), recalled bittersweet memories of childhood and youthful love and tried to discover their innermost meaning. To do so, Proust lived like a hermit in a soundproof Paris apartment for ten years, withdrawing from the present to dwell on the past.

Serious novelists also used the **stream-of-consciousness technique** to explore the psyche. In *Jacob's Room* (1922), Virginia Woolf (1882–1941) created a novel made up of a series of internal monologues, in which ideas and emotions from different periods of time bubble up as randomly as from a patient on a psychoanalyst's couch. William Faulkner (1897–1962), perhaps America's greatest twentieth-century novelist, used the same technique

in *The Sound and the Fury* (1929), much of whose intense drama is confusedly seen through the eyes of an idiot. The most famous stream-of-consciousness novel—and surely the most disturbing novel of its generation—is *Ulysses,* which Irish novelist James Joyce (1882–1941) published in 1922. Into an account of an ordinary day in the life of an ordinary man, Joyce weaves an extended ironic parallel between his hero's aimless wanderings through the streets and pubs of Dublin and the adventures of Homer's hero Ulysses on his way home from Troy. Abandoning conventional grammar and blending foreign words, puns, bits of knowledge, and scraps of memory together in bewildering confusion, the language of *Ulysses* is intended to mirror modern life itself: a gigantic riddle waiting to be unraveled.

As creative writers turned their attention from society to the individual and from realism to psychological relativity, they rejected the idea of progress. Some even described "anti-utopias," nightmare visions of things to come. In 1918 an obscure German high school teacher named Oswald Spengler (1880–1936) published *The Decline of the West,* which quickly became an international sensation. According to Spengler, every culture experiences a life cycle of growth and decline. Western civilization, in Spengler's opinion, was in its old age, and death was approaching in the form of conquest by the yellow race. T. S. Eliot (1888–1965), in his famous poem *The Waste Land* (1922), depicts a world of growing desolation, although after his conversion to Anglo-Catholicism in 1927, Eliot came to hope cautiously for humanity's salvation. No such hope appears in the work of Franz Kafka (1883–1924), whose novels *The Trial* (1925) and *The Castle* (1926), as well as several of his greatest short stories, portray helpless individuals crushed by inexplicably hostile forces. The German-Jewish Kafka died young, at forty-one, and so did not see the world of his nightmares materialize in the Nazi state.

Englishman George Orwell (1903–1950), however, had seen both that reality and its Stalinist counterpart by 1949, when he wrote perhaps the ultimate in anti-utopian literature: *1984.* Orwell set the action in the future, in 1984. Big Brother—the dictator—and his totalitarian state use a new kind of language, sophisticated technology, and psychological terror to strip a weak individual of his last shred of human dignity. The supremely self-confident chief of the Thought Police tells the tortured, broken, and framed Winston Smith, "If you want a picture of the future, imagine a boot stamping on a human face—forever."[4] A phenomenal bestseller, *1984* spoke to millions of people in the closing years of the age of anxiety.

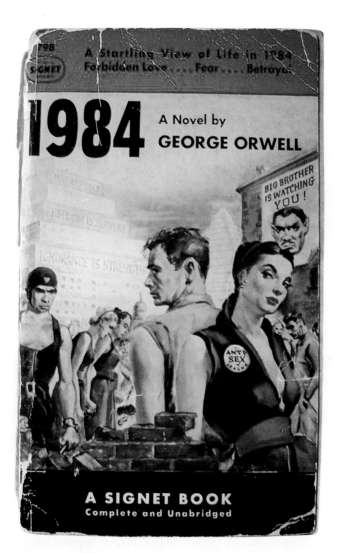

1984 This intriguing cover for an early edition of Orwell's brilliant novel hints at the tragic love affair between Winston and Julia. Considered a crime in Orwell's totalitarian dictatorship of the future, the love affair leads to the couple's arrest, torture, and betrayal. No one can escape the scrutiny of Big Brother and the Thought Police. *(Signet Books/New American Library photo)*

Modern Art and Music

Throughout the twentieth century, there was considerable unity in the arts. Even today the "modernism" of the immediate prewar years and the 1920s still seems strikingly modern. Like the scientists and creative artists who were partaking of the same culture, creative artists rejected old forms and old values. Modernism in art and music meant constant experimentation and a search for new kinds of expression. And though many people find the numerous and varied modern visions of the arts strange, disturbing, and even ugly, the first half of the twentieth century, so dismal in many respects, will probably stand as one of Western civilization's great artistic eras.

• *How did modernism revolutionize architecture, painting, and music?*

Architecture and Design

Modernism in the arts was loosely unified by a revolution in architecture. This revolution intended nothing less than a transformation of the physical framework of urban society according to a new principle: **functionalism.** Buildings, like industrial products, should be useful and "functional"—that is, they should serve, as well as possible, the purpose for which they were made. Thus architects and designers had to work with engineers, town planners, and even sanitation experts. Moreover, they had to throw away useless ornamentation and find beauty and aesthetic pleasure in the clean lines of practical constructions and efficient machinery. Franco-Swiss genius Le Corbusier (1887–1965) insisted that "a house is a machine for living in."[5]

The United States, with its rapid urban growth and lack of rigid building traditions, pioneered in the new architecture. In the 1890s, the Chicago school of architects, led by Louis H. Sullivan (1856–1924), used cheap steel, reinforced concrete, and electric elevators to build skyscrapers and office buildings lacking almost any exterior ornamentation. In the first decade of the twentieth century, Sullivan's student Frank Lloyd Wright (1869–1959) built a series of radically new and truly modern houses featuring low lines, open interiors, and mass-produced building materials. Europeans were inspired by these and other American examples of functional construction, like the massive, unadorned grain elevators of the Midwest.

In Europe architectural leadership centered in German-speaking countries until Hitler took power in 1933. In 1911 twenty-eight-year-old Walter Gropius (1883–1969) broke sharply with the past in his design of the Fagus shoe factory at Alfeld, Germany—a clean, light, elegant building of glass and iron. After the First World War, Gropius merged the schools of fine and applied arts at Weimar into a single, interdisciplinary school, the **Bauhaus.** The Bauhaus brought together many leading modern architects, designers, and theatrical innovators. Working as

Walter Gropius: The Fagus Shoe Factory, 1911 The factory's sleek exterior is inspired by the revolutionary principles of functionalism. The striking glass façade creates a feeling of lightness and eliminates the traditional separation between interior and exterior. The glass façade also provides workers with healthy natural light—a practical, "functional" concern. *(Vanni/Art Resource, NY)*

an effective, inspired team, they combined the study of fine art, such as painting and sculpture, with the study of applied art in the crafts of printing, weaving, and furniture making. Throughout the 1920s, the Bauhaus, with its stress on functionalism and good design for everyday life, attracted enthusiastic students from all over the world. It had a great and continuing impact.

Another leader in the "international" style, Ludwig Mies van der Rohe (1886–1969), followed Gropius as director of the Bauhaus in 1930 and immigrated to the United States in 1937. His classic Lake Shore Apartments in Chicago, built between 1948 and 1951, symbolized the triumph of steel-frame and glass-wall modern architecture in the great building boom after the Second World War.

Modern Painting

Modern painting grew out of a revolt against French impressionism. The *impressionism* of such French painters

as Claude Monet (1840–1926), Pierre Auguste Renoir (1841–1919), and Camille Pissarro (1830–1903) was, in part, a kind of "superrealism." Leaving exact copying of objects to photography, these artists sought to capture the momentary overall feeling, or impression, of light falling on a real-life scene before their eyes. By 1890, when impressionism was finally established, a few artists known as *postimpressionists,* or sometimes as *expressionists,* were already striking out in new directions. After 1905 art increasingly took on a nonrepresentational, abstract character, a development that reached its high point after World War II.

Though individualistic in their styles, postimpressionists were united in their desire to know and depict worlds other than the visible world of fact. Like the early-nineteenth-century romantics, they wanted to portray unseen, inner worlds of emotion and imagination. Like modern novelists, they wanted to express a complicated psychological view of reality as well as an overwhelming emotional intensity. In

The Starry Night (1889), for example, the great Dutch expressionist Vincent van Gogh (1853–1890) painted the moving vision of his mind's eye (see the illustration below). Paul Gauguin (1848–1903), the French stockbroker-turned-painter, pioneered in expressionist techniques, though he used them to infuse his work with tranquillity and mysticism. In 1891 he fled to the South Pacific in search of unspoiled beauty and a primitive way of life. Gauguin believed that the form and design of a picture were important in themselves and that the painter need not try to represent objects on canvas as the eye actually saw them.

Fascination with form, as opposed to light, was char-

acteristic of postimpressionism and expressionism. Paul Cézanne (1839–1906), who had a profound influence on twentieth-century painting, was particularly committed to form and ordered design. He told a young painter, "You must see in nature the cylinder, the sphere, and the cone."[6] As Cézanne's later work became increasingly abstract and nonrepresentational, it also moved away from the traditional three-dimensional perspective toward the two-dimensional plane, which has characterized so much of modern art. The expressionism of a group of painters led by Henri Matisse (1869–1954) was so extreme that an exhibition of their work in Paris in 1905 prompted

Van Gogh: The Starry Night Van Gogh absorbed impressionism in Paris, but under the burning sun of southern France he went beyond the portrayal of external reality. In *The Starry Night* (1889) flaming cypress trees, exploding stars, and a comet-like Milky Way swirl together in one great cosmic rhythm. Painting an inner world of intense emotion and wild imagination, van Gogh contributed greatly to the rise of expressionism in modern art. *(Digital image © The Museum of Modern Art/Licensed by Scala/Art Resource, NY)*

Images in Society

Pablo Picasso and Modern Art

Pablo Picasso (1881–1973) was probably the most significant artist of the early twentieth century. For more than seventy years, he personified the individuality, freedom, and revolutionary creativity of the modern artist.

Born at Málaga in southern Spain, Picasso quickly demonstrated a precocious talent. At nineteen he headed for Paris, Europe's art capital. Suffering from poverty and falling into depression, he painted the weak and the poor in somber blue and purple tones. These pessimistic paintings of Picasso's "Blue Period" (1901–1904) are masterpieces in the tradition of Spanish realism.

Yet the young Picasso soon sought a new visual reality. In 1907 his arduous struggle to create a new style resulted in *Les Demoiselles d'Avignon* (Image 1), a painting originating in memories of a brothel scene in Barcelona. This work was considered a revolutionary upheaval in art. Since the Renaissance, artists had been expected to follow established rules, seeing objects in an orderly perspective from a single viewpoint and creating "beauty" and unified human forms. Do the faces of the central figures in this work conform to these rules? Regard the figures on either side, who were painted later. Notice how the light fails to combine with the shadow to create bodies with continuous, three-dimensional contours. The figures appear broken into large, flat planes with heads that are twisted, fractured dislocations. Do

you see the magical violence of a pictorial breakthrough or a grotesque, ugly departure?

Picasso extended his revolutionary experiments, and after 1910 he was joined by others. A critic called the new school cubism because these artists used many geometric forms in intersecting planes. Objects, viewed from many shifting viewpoints, often emerged as purely abstract designs.

Three Musicians (Image 2), painted in 1921, represents mature cubism. Many people believe that it marks the culmination of Picasso's cubist style. What similarities and differences do you see between this picture and Image 1? Notice the limited number of viewpoints, with the white clown, the harlequin, the monk, their

Image 1 Les Demoiselles d'Avignon (1907). *(Digital image © The Museum of Modern Art/Licensed by Scala/Art Resource, NY/© 2004 Estate of Pablo Picasso/Artists Rights Society [ARS], New York)*

instruments, and the table in front cut up into rectangular shapes and reassembled in recognizable form on a shallow series of planes. What is the effect of the bright primary colors and the harmonious, decorative order? Picasso had been making the sets for Sergei Diaghilev's famous Russian dance company in Paris, and these three jagged figures from traditional Italian comedy seem to convey the atmosphere of the theater and the dissonant, syncopated rhythm of modern music. Picasso always drew back from pure abstraction because he began with real objects and used models.

Picasso's passionate involvement in his times infuses his immense painting *Guernica* (Image 3), often considered his greatest work. Painted for the Spanish pavilion at the Paris International Exhibition in 1937, this mural, with its mournful white, black, and blue colors, was inspired by the Spanish civil war and the deadly terror bombing of Guernica by fascist planes in a single night. In this complex work, a shrieking woman falls from a burning house on the far right. On the left, a woman holds a dead child, while toward the center are fragments of a warrior and a screaming horse pierced by a spear. Do cubist techniques heighten the effect? Picasso also draws on other aspects of the modernist revolution here. Compare *Guernica* with the expressionist work on page 923. Surrealists were fascinated with grotesque subject matter and apparently unrelated objects in surprising situations. Are these elements also

Image 2 Three Musicians (1921). *(Digital image © The Museum of Modern Art/Licensed by Scala/Art Resource, NY/© 2004 Estate of Pablo Picasso/Artists Rights Society [ARS], New York)*

present here? Picasso wanted his painting to be an unforgettable attack on "brutality and darkness." Did he succeed? How do the works presented here enhance your understanding of modern art?

Image 3 Guernica (1937). *(Bridgeman-Giraudon/Art Resource, NY/© 2004 Estate of Pablo Picasso/Artists Rights Society [ARS], New York)*

shocked critics to call them *les fauves*—"the wild beasts." Matisse and his followers still painted real objects, but their primary concern was the arrangement of color, line, and form as an end in itself.

In 1907 a young Spaniard in Paris, Pablo Picasso (1881–1973), founded another movement—*cubism*. (See the feature "Images in Society: Pablo Picasso and Modern Art" on pages 924–925.) Cubism concentrated on a complex geometry of zigzagging lines and sharply angled, overlapping planes. About three years later came the ultimate stage in the development of abstract, nonrepresentational art. Artists such as the Russian-born Wassily Kandinsky (1866–1944) turned away from nature completely. "The observer," said Kandinsky, "must learn to look at [my] pictures . . . as form and color combinations . . . as a representation of mood and not as a representation of *objects*."[7] On the eve of the First World War, extreme expressionism and abstract painting were developing rapidly not only in Paris but also in Russia and Germany. Modern art had become international.

In the 1920s and 1930s, the artistic movements of the prewar years were extended and consolidated. The most notable new developments were *dadaism* and *surrealism*. **Dadaism** attacked all accepted standards of art and behavior, delighting in outrageous conduct. Its name, from the French word *dada*, meaning "hobbyhorse," is deliberately nonsensical. A famous example of dadaism is a reproduction of Leonardo da Vinci's *Mona Lisa* in which the famous woman with the mysterious smile sports a mustache and is ridiculed with an obscene inscription. After 1924 many dadaists were attracted to surrealism, which became very influential in art in the late 1920s and 1930s. Surrealists painted a fantastic world of wild dreams and complex symbols, where watches melted and giant metronomes beat time in precisely drawn but impossible alien landscapes. Refusing to depict ordinary visual reality, surrealist painters made powerful statements about the age of anxiety.

Modern Music

Developments in modern music were strikingly parallel to those in painting. Composers, too, were attracted by the emotional intensity of expressionism. The ballet *The Rite of Spring* by composer Igor Stravinsky (1882–1971) practically caused a riot when it was first performed in Paris in 1913 by Sergei Diaghilev's famous Russian dance company. The combination of pulsating, dissonant rhythms from the orchestra pit and an earthy representation of lovemaking by the dancers on the stage seemed a shocking, almost pornographic enactment of a primitive fertility rite.

After the experience of the First World War, when irrationality and violence seemed to pervade the human experience, expressionism in opera and ballet flourished. One of the most famous and powerful examples was the opera *Wozzeck*, by Alban Berg (1885–1935), first performed in Berlin in 1925. Blending a half-sung, half-spoken kind of dialogue with harsh, atonal music, *Wozzeck* is a gruesome tale of a soldier driven by Kafka-like inner terrors and vague suspicions of unfaithfulness to murder his mistress.

Some composers turned their backs on long-established musical conventions. As abstract painters arranged lines and color but did not draw identifiable objects, so modern composers arranged sounds without creating recognizable harmonies. Led by Viennese composer Arnold Schönberg (1874–1951), they abandoned traditional harmony and tonality. The musical notes in a given piece were no longer united and organized by a key; instead they were independent and unrelated. Schönberg's twelve-tone music of the 1920s arranged all twelve notes of the scale in an abstract, mathematical pattern, or "tone row." This pattern sounded like no pattern at all to the ordinary listener and could be detected only by a highly trained eye studying the musical score. Accustomed to the harmonies of classical and romantic music, audiences generally resisted modern atonal music. Only after the Second World War did it begin to win acceptance.

Movies and Radio

• **In what ways did movies and radio become mainstays of popular culture?**

Until after World War II at the earliest, these revolutionary changes in art and music appealed mainly to a minority of "highbrows" and not to the general public. That public was primarily and enthusiastically wrapped up in movies and radio. The long-declining traditional arts and amusements of people in villages and small towns almost vanished, replaced by standardized, commercial entertainment.

Moving pictures were first shown as a popular novelty in naughty peepshows—"What the Butler Saw"—and penny arcades in the 1890s, especially in Paris. The first movie houses date from an experiment in Los Angeles in 1902. They quickly attracted large audiences and led to the production of short, silent action films such as the eight-minute *Great Train Robbery* of 1903. American directors and business people then set up "movie factories," at first in the New York area and then after 1910 in Los

Angeles. These factories churned out two short films each week. On the eve of the First World War, full-length feature films such as the Italian *Quo Vadis* and the American *Birth of a Nation,* coupled with improvements in the quality of pictures, suggested the screen's vast possibilities.

During the First World War, the United States became the dominant force in the rapidly expanding silent-film industry. In the 1920s, Mack Sennett (1884–1960) and his zany Keystone Kops specialized in short, slapstick comedies noted for frantic automobile chases, custard-pie battles, and gorgeous bathing beauties. Screen stars such as Mary Pickford and Lillian Gish, Douglas Fairbanks and Rudolf Valentino, became household names, with their own "fan clubs." Yet Charlie Chaplin (1889–1978), a funny little Englishman working in Hollywood, was unquestionably the king of the "silver screen" in the 1920s. In his enormously popular role as the lonely Little Tramp, complete with baggy trousers, battered derby, and an awkward, shuffling walk, Chaplin symbolized the "gay spirit of laughter in a cruel, crazy world."[8] Chaplin also demonstrated that in the hands of a genius, the new medium could combine mass entertainment and artistic accomplishment.

The early 1920s were also the great age of German films. Protected and developed during the war, the large German studios excelled in bizarre expressionist dramas, beginning with *The Cabinet of Dr. Caligari* in 1919. Unfortunately, their period of creativity was short-lived. By 1926 American money was drawing the leading German talents to Hollywood and consolidating America's international domination. Film making was big business, and European theater owners were forced to book whole blocks of American films to get the few pictures they really wanted. This system put European producers at a great disadvantage until "talkies" permitted a revival of national film industries in the 1930s, particularly in France.

Whether foreign or domestic, motion pictures became the main entertainment of the masses until after the Second World War. In Great Britain one in every four adults went to the movies twice a week in the late 1930s, and two in five went at least once a week. Continental countries had similar figures. The greatest appeal of motion pictures was that they offered ordinary people a temporary escape from the hard realities of everyday life. The appeal of escapist entertainment was especially strong during the Great Depression. Millions flocked to musical comedies featuring glittering stars such as Ginger Rogers and Fred Astaire and to the fanciful cartoons of Mickey Mouse and his friends.

Radio became possible with the transatlantic "wireless" communication of Guglielmo Marconi (1874–1937) in 1901 and the development of the vacuum tube in 1904, which permitted the transmission of speech and music.

The Great Dictator In 1940 the renowned actor and director Charlie Chaplin abandoned the Little Tramp role to satirize the "great dictator," Adolf Hitler. Chaplin had strong political views and made a number of films with political themes as the escapist fare of the Great Depression gave way to the reality of the Second World War. *(The Museum of Modern Art/Still Film Archives)*

But only in 1920 were the first major public broadcasts of special events made in Great Britain and the United States. Lord Northcliffe, who had pioneered in journalism with the inexpensive, mass-circulation *Daily Mail,* sponsored a broadcast of "only one artist . . . the world's very best, the soprano Nellie Melba."[9] Singing from London in English, Italian, and French, Melba was heard simultaneously all over Europe on June 16, 1920. This historic event captured the public's imagination. The meteoric career of radio was launched.

Every major country quickly established national broadcasting networks. In the United States such networks were privately owned and financed by advertising. In Great Britain Parliament set up an independent, public corporation, the British Broadcasting Corporation (BBC), supported by licensing fees. Elsewhere in Europe the typical pattern was direct control by the government.

Whatever the institutional framework, radio became popular and influential. By the late 1930s, more than three out of every four households in both democratic Great Britain and dictatorial Germany had at least one cheap, mass-produced radio.

Radio in unscrupulous hands was particularly well suited for political propaganda. Dictators such as Mussolini and Hitler controlled the airwaves and could reach enormous national audiences with their frequent, dramatic speeches. In democratic countries, politicians such as President Franklin Roosevelt and Prime Minister Stanley Baldwin effectively used informal "fireside chats" to bolster their support.

Motion pictures also became powerful tools of indoctrination, especially in countries with dictatorial regimes. Lenin himself encouraged the development of Soviet film making, believing that the new medium was essential to the social and ideological transformation of the country. Beginning in the mid-1920s, a series of epic films, the most famous of which were directed by Sergei Eisenstein (1898–1948), brilliantly dramatized the communist view of Russian history.

In Germany Hitler turned to a young and immensely talented woman film maker, Leni Riefenstahl (1902–2003), for a masterpiece of documentary propaganda, *The Triumph of the Will,* based on the Nazi Party rally at Nuremberg in 1934. Riefenstahl combined stunning aerial photography, joyful crowds welcoming Hitler, and mass processions of young Nazi fanatics. Her film was a brilliant and all-too-powerful documentary of Germany's "Nazi rebirth." The new media of mass culture were potentially dangerous instruments of political manipulation.

The Search for Peace and Political Stability

As established patterns of thought and culture were challenged and mangled by the ferocious impact of World War I, so also was the political fabric stretched and torn by the consequences of the great conflict. The Versailles settlement had established a shaky truce, not a solid peace. Thus national leaders faced a gigantic task as they struggled with uncertainty and sought to create a stable international order within the general context of intellectual crisis and revolutionary artistic experimentation.

The pursuit of real and lasting peace proved difficult for many reasons. Germany hated the Treaty of Versailles. France was fearful and isolated. Britain was undependable, and the United States had turned its back on European problems. Eastern Europe was in ferment, and no one could predict the future of communist Russia. Moreover, the international economic situation was poor and greatly complicated by war debts and disrupted patterns of trade. Yet for a time, from 1925 to late 1929, it appeared that peace and stability were within reach. When the subsequent collapse of the 1930s mocked these hopes and brought the rise of brutal dictators, the disillusionment of liberals in the democracies was intensified.

● *How did the democratic leaders of the 1920s deal with deep-seated instability and try to establish real peace and prosperity?*

Germany and the Western Powers

Germany was the key to lasting peace. Yet to Germans of all political parties, the Treaty of Versailles represented a harsh, dictated peace, to be revised or repudiated as soon as possible. The treaty had neither broken nor reduced Germany, which was potentially still the strongest country in Europe. Thus the treaty had fallen between two stools: too harsh for a peace of reconciliation, too soft for a peace of conquest.

Moreover, with ominous implications for the future, France and Great Britain did not see eye to eye on Germany. By the end of 1919, France wanted to stress the harsh elements in the Treaty of Versailles. Most of the war in the west had been fought on French soil, and the expected costs of reconstruction, as well as repaying war debts to the United States, were staggering. Thus French politicians believed that massive reparations from Germany were a vital economic necessity. Also, having compromised with President Wilson only to be betrayed by America's failure to ratify the treaty, many French leaders saw strict implementation of all provisions of the Treaty of Versailles as France's last best hope. Large reparation payments could hold Germany down indefinitely, and France would realize its goal of security.

The British soon felt differently. Prewar Germany had been Great Britain's second-best market in the entire world, and after the war a healthy, prosperous Germany appeared to be essential to the British economy. Indeed, many English people agreed with the analysis of the young English economist John Maynard Keynes (1883–1946), who eloquently denounced the Treaty of Versailles in his famous *Economic Consequences of the Peace* (1919). According to

Keynes's interpretation, astronomical reparations and harsh economic measures would impoverish Germany and also increase economic hardship in all countries. Only a complete revision of the foolish treaty could save Germany—and Europe. Keynes's attack exploded like a bombshell and became very influential. It stirred deep guilt feelings about Germany in the English-speaking world, feelings that often paralyzed English and American leaders in their relations with Germany and its leaders between the First and Second World Wars.

Online Study Center **Improve Your Grade**
Primary Source: An Economist Analyzes the Versailles Treaty and Finds It Lacking

The British were also suspicious of France's army—the largest in Europe, and authorized at Versailles to occupy the German Rhineland until 1935—and France's foreign policy. Ever since 1890, France had looked to Russia as a powerful ally against Germany. But with Russia hostile and communist, and with Britain and the United States unwilling to make any firm commitments, France turned to the newly formed states of eastern Europe for diplomatic support. In 1921 France signed a mutual defense pact with Poland and associated itself closely with the so-called Little Entente, an alliance that joined Czechoslovakia, Romania, and Yugoslavia against defeated and bitter Hungary.

While French and British leaders drifted in different directions, the Allied reparations commission completed its work. In April 1921, it announced that Germany had to pay the enormous sum of 132 billion gold marks ($33 billion) in annual installments of 2.5 billion gold marks. Facing possible occupation of more of its territory, the young German republic—generally known as the Weimar Republic—made its first payment in 1921. Then in 1922, wracked by rapid inflation and political assassinations and motivated by hostility and arrogance as well, the Weimar Republic announced its inability to pay more. It proposed a moratorium on reparations for three years, with the clear implication that thereafter reparations would be either drastically reduced or eliminated entirely.

The British were willing to accept a moratorium on reparations, but the French were not. Led by their tough-minded prime minister, Raymond Poincaré (1860–1934), they decided they had to either call Germany's bluff or see the entire peace settlement dissolve to France's great disadvantage. So, despite strong British protests, in early January 1923, armies of France and its ally Belgium moved out of the Rhineland and began to occupy the Ruhr district, the heartland of industrial Germany, creating the most serious international crisis of the 1920s. If forcible collection proved impossible, France would use occupation to paralyze Germany and force it to accept the Treaty of Versailles.

Strengthened by a wave of patriotism, the German government ordered the people of the Ruhr to stop working and start passively resisting the French occupation. The coal mines and steel mills of the Ruhr grew silent, leaving 10 percent of Germany's total population in need of relief. The French answer to passive resistance was to seal off the Ruhr and the entire Rhineland from the rest of Germany, letting in only enough food to prevent starvation.

By the summer of 1923, France and Germany were engaged in a great test of wills. French armies could not collect reparations from striking workers at gunpoint. But French occupation was indeed paralyzing Germany and its economy and had turned rapid German inflation

"Hands Off the Ruhr"   The French occupation of the Ruhr to collect reparations payments raised a storm of patriotic protest in Germany. This anti-French poster of 1923 turns Marianne, the personification of French republican virtue, into a vicious harpy. *(International Instituut voor Sociale Geschiedenis)*

into runaway inflation. Faced with the need to support the striking Ruhr workers and their employers, the German government began to print money to pay its bills. Prices soared. People went to the store with a big bag of paper money; they returned home with a handful of groceries. German money rapidly lost all value.

Runaway inflation brought about a social revolution. The accumulated savings of many retired and middle-class people were wiped out. Catastrophic inflation cruelly mocked the old middle-class virtues of thrift, caution, and self-reliance. Many Germans felt betrayed. They hated and blamed the Western governments, their own government, big business, the Jews, the workers, and the communists for their misfortune. They were psychologically prepared to follow radical leaders in a crisis.

In August 1923, as the mark fell and political unrest grew throughout Germany, Gustav Stresemann (1878–1929) assumed leadership of the government. Stresemann adopted a compromising attitude. He called off passive resistance in the Ruhr and in October agreed in principle to pay reparations but asked for a re-examination of Germany's ability to pay. Poincaré accepted. His hard line was becoming increasingly unpopular with French citizens, and it was hated in Britain and the United States. (See the feature "Individuals in Society: Gustav Stresemann.")

More generally, in both Germany and France, power was finally passing to the moderates, who realized that continued confrontation was a destructive, no-win situation. Thus after five long years of hostility and tension, culminating in a kind of undeclared war in the Ruhr in 1923, Germany and France decided to give compromise and cooperation a try. The British, and even the Americans, were willing to help. The first step was a reasonable agreement on the reparations question.

Hope in Foreign Affairs, 1924–1929

The reparations commission appointed an international committee of financial experts headed by American banker Charles G. Dawes to re-examine reparations from a broad perspective. The resulting **Dawes Plan** (1924) was accepted by France, Germany, and Britain. Germany's yearly reparations were reduced and depended on the level of German economic prosperity. Germany would also receive large loans from the United States to promote German recovery. In short, Germany would get private loans from the United States and pay reparations to France and Britain, thus enabling those countries to repay the large sums they owed the United States.

This circular flow of international payments was complicated and risky, but for a while it worked. The German republic experienced a spectacular economic recovery. With prosperity and large, continual inflows of American capital, Germany easily paid about $1.3 billion in reparations in 1927 and 1928, enabling France and Britain to pay the United States. In this way the Americans belatedly played a part in the general economic settlement that, though far from ideal, facilitated the worldwide recovery of the late 1920s.

This economic settlement was matched by a political settlement. In 1925 the leaders of Europe signed a number of agreements at Locarno, Switzerland. Germany and France solemnly pledged to accept their common border, and both Britain and Italy agreed to fight either France or Germany if one invaded the other. Stresemann also agreed to settle boundary disputes with Poland and Czechoslovakia by peaceful means, and France promised those countries military aid if Germany attacked them. For years, a "spirit of Locarno" gave Europeans a sense of growing security and stability in international affairs.

Other developments also strengthened hopes. In 1926 Germany joined the League of Nations, where Stresemann continued his "peace offensive." In 1928 fifteen countries signed the Kellogg-Briand Pact, initiated by French prime minister Aristide Briand and U.S. secretary of state Frank B. Kellogg. This multinational pact "condemned and renounced war as an instrument of national policy." The signing states agreed to settle international disputes peacefully. Often seen as idealistic nonsense because it made no provisions for action in case war actually occurred, the pact was still a positive step. It fostered the cautious optimism of the late 1920s and also encouraged the hope that the United States would accept its responsibilities as a great world power and contribute to European stability.

Hope in Democratic Government

Domestic politics also offered reason to hope. During the occupation of the Ruhr and the great inflation, republican government in Germany had appeared on the verge of collapse. In 1923 communists momentarily entered provincial governments, and in November an obscure nobody named Adolf Hitler leaped onto a table in a beer hall in Munich and proclaimed a "national socialist revolution." But Hitler's plot to seize control of the government was poorly organized and easily crushed, and Hitler was sentenced to prison, where he outlined his theories and program in his book **Mein Kampf** (My Strug-

Individuals in Society

Gustav Stresemann

The German foreign minister Gustav Stresemann (1878–1929) is a controversial historical figure. Hailed by many as a hero of peace, he was denounced as a traitor by radical German nationalists and then by Hitler's Nazis. After World War II, revisionist historians stressed Stresemann's persistent nationalism and cast doubt on his peaceful intentions. Weimar Germany's most renowned leader is a fascinating example of the restless quest for convincing historical interpretation.

Stresemann's origins were modest. His parents were Berlin innkeepers and retailers of bottled beer, and only Gustav of their five children was able to attend high school. Attracted first to literature and history, Stresemann later turned to economics, earned a doctoral degree, and quickly reached the top as a manager and director of German trade associations. A highly intelligent extrovert with a knack for negotiation, Stresemann entered the Reichstag in 1907 as a business-oriented liberal and nationalist. When World War I erupted, he believed, like most Germans, that Germany had acted defensively and was not at fault. He emerged as a strident nationalist and urged German annexation of conquered foreign territories. Germany's collapse in defeat and revolution devastated Stresemann. He seemed a prime candidate for the hateful extremism of the far right.

Yet although Stresemann opposed the Treaty of Versailles as an unjust and unrealistic imposition, he turned back toward the center. He accepted the new Weimar Republic and played a growing role in the Reichstag as the leader of his own small probusiness party. His hour came in the Ruhr crisis, when French and Belgian troops occupied the district. Named chancellor in August 1923, he called off passive resistance and began talks with the French. His government also quelled communist uprisings; put down rebellions in Bavaria, including Hitler's attempted coup; and ended runaway inflation with a new currency. Stresemann fought to preserve German unity, and he succeeded.

Voted out as chancellor in November 1923, Stresemann remained as foreign minister in every government until his death in 1929. Proclaiming a policy of peace and agreeing to pay reparations, he achieved his greatest triumph in the Locarno agreements of 1925 (see page 930). But the interlocking guarantees of existing French and German borders (and the related agreements to resolve peacefully all disputes with Poland and Czechoslovakia) did not lead the French to make any further concessions that might have disarmed Stresemann's extremist foes. Working himself to death, he made little additional progress in achieving international reconciliation and sovereign equality for Germany.

Stresemann was no fuzzy pacifist. Historians debunking his "legend" are right in seeing an enduring love of nation in his defense of German interests. But Stresemann, like his French counterpart Aristide Briand, was a statesman of goodwill

Foreign Minister Gustav Stresemann of Germany (right) *leaves a meeting with Aristide Briand, his French counterpart.* (Corbis)

who wanted peace through mutually advantageous compromise. A realist trained by business and politics in the art of the possible, Stresemann also reasoned that Germany had to be a satisfied and equal partner if peace was to be secure. His unwillingness to guarantee Germany's eastern borders (see Map 27.4 on page 904), which is often criticized, reflects his conviction that keeping some Germans under Polish and Czechoslovak rule created a ticking time bomb in Europe. Stresemann was no less convinced that war on Poland would almost certainly re-create the Allied coalition that had crushed Germany in 1918.* His insistence on the necessity of peace in the east as well as the west was prophetic. Hitler's 1939 invasion of Poland resulted in an even mightier coalition that almost annihilated Germany in 1945.

Questions for Analysis

1. What did Gustav Stresemann do to promote reconciliation in Europe? How did his policy toward France differ from that toward Poland and Czechoslovakia?
2. What is your interpretation of Stresemann? Does he arouse your sympathy or your suspicion and hostility? Why?

*Robert Grathwol, "Stresemann: Reflections on His Foreign Policy," *Journal of Modern History* 45 (March 1973): 52–70.

Online Study Center **Improve Your Grade**
Going Beyond Individuals in Society

gle). Throughout the 1920s, Hitler's National Socialist Party attracted support only from a few fanatical anti-Semites, ultranationalists, and disgruntled ex-servicemen. In 1928 his party had an insignificant twelve seats in the Reichstag. Indeed, after 1923 democracy seemed to take root in Weimar Germany. A new currency was established, and the economy boomed.

The moderate businessmen who tended to dominate the various German coalition governments were convinced that economic prosperity demanded good relations with the Western Powers, and they supported parliamentary government at home. Stresemann himself was a man of this class, and he was the key figure in every government until his death in 1929. Elections were held regularly, and republican democracy appeared to have growing support among a majority of Germans.

There were, however, sharp political divisions in the country. Many unrepentant nationalists and monarchists populated the right and the army. Members of Germany's recently formed Communist Party were noisy and active on the left. The Communists, directed from Moscow, reserved their greatest hatred and sharpest barbs for their cousins the Social Democrats, whom they endlessly accused of betraying the revolution. The working classes were divided politically, but a majority supported the nonrevolutionary but socialist Social Democrats.

The situation in France had numerous similarities to that in Germany. Communists and Socialists battled for the support of the workers. After 1924 the democratically elected government rested mainly in the hands of coalitions of moderates, and business interests were well represented. France's great accomplishment was rapid rebuilding of its war-torn northern region. The expense of this undertaking led, however, to a large deficit and substantial inflation. By early 1926, the franc had fallen to 10 percent of its prewar value, causing a severe crisis. Poincaré was recalled to office, while Briand remained minister for foreign affairs. The Poincaré government proceeded to slash spending and raise taxes, restoring confidence in the economy. The franc was "saved," stabilized at about one-fifth of its prewar value. Good times prevailed until 1930.

Despite political shortcomings, France attracted artists and writers from all over the world in the 1920s. Much of the intellectual and artistic ferment of the times flourished in Paris. As writer Gertrude Stein (1874–1946), a leader of the large colony of American expatriates living in Paris, later recalled, "Paris was where the twentieth century was."[10] More generally, France appealed to foreigners and the French as a harmonious combination of small businesses and family farms, of bold innovation and solid traditions.

Britain, too, faced challenges after 1920. The wartime trend toward greater social equality continued, however, helping maintain social harmony. The great problem was unemployment. Many of Britain's best markets had been lost during the war. In June 1921, almost 2.2 million people—23 percent of the labor force—were out of work, and throughout the 1920s unemployment hovered around 12 percent. Yet the state provided unemployment benefits of equal size to all those without jobs and supplemented those payments with subsidized housing, medical aid, and increased old-age pensions. These and other measures kept living standards from seriously declining, defused

American Jazz in Paris This woodcut from a 1928 French book on cafés and nightclubs suggests how black musicians took Europe by storm, although the blacks are represented stereotypically. One French critic concluded that American blacks had attained a "pre-eminent" place in music since the war, "for they have impressed the entire world with their vibrating or melancholy rhythms." *(akg-images)*

class tensions, and pointed the way toward the welfare state Britain established after World War II.

Relative social harmony was accompanied by the rise of the Labour Party as a determined champion of the working classes and of greater social equality. Committed to the kind of moderate, "revisionist" socialism that had emerged before World War I (see pages 840–842), the Labour Party replaced the Liberal Party as the main opposition to the Conservatives. The new prominence of the Labour Party reflected the decline of old liberal ideals of competitive capitalism, limited government control, and individual responsibility. In 1924 and 1929, the Labour Party under Ramsay MacDonald (1866–1937) governed the country with the support of the smaller Liberal Party. Yet Labour moved toward socialism gradually and democratically, so that the middle classes were not overly frightened as the working classes won new benefits.

The Conservatives under Stanley Baldwin (1867–1947) showed the same compromising spirit on social issues. The last line of Baldwin's greatest speech in March 1925 summarized his international and domestic programs: "Give us peace in our time, O Lord." In spite of such conflicts as the 1926 strike by hard-pressed coal miners, which ended in an unsuccessful general strike, social unrest in Britain was limited in the 1920s and in the 1930s as well. In 1922 Britain granted southern, Catholic Ireland full autonomy after a bitter guerrilla war, thereby removing another source of prewar friction. Thus developments in both international relations and the domestic politics of the leading democracies gave cause for optimism in the late 1920s.

The Great Depression, 1929–1939

Like the Great War, the **Great Depression** must be spelled with capital letters. Economic depression was nothing new. Depressions occurred throughout the nineteenth century with predictable regularity, as they recur in the form of recessions and slumps to this day. What was new about this depression was its severity and duration. It struck the entire world with ever-greater intensity from 1929 to 1933, and recovery was uneven and slow. Only with the Second World War did the depression disappear in much of the world.

The social and political consequences of prolonged economic collapse were enormous. The depression shattered the fragile optimism of political leaders in the late 1920s. Mass unemployment and failing farms made insecurity a reality for millions of ordinary people, who had paid little attention to the intellectual crisis or to new directions in art and ideas (see Map 28.1). In desperation, people looked for leaders who would "do something."

- *What caused the Great Depression, and how did the Western democracies respond to this challenge?*

The Economic Crisis

There is no agreement among historians and economists about why the Great Depression was so deep and lasted so long. Thus it is best to trace the course of the great collapse before trying to identify what caused it.

Though economic activity was already declining moderately in many countries by early 1929, the crash of the stock market in the United States in October of that year triggered the collapse into the Great Depression. The American economy had prospered in the late 1920s, but there were large inequalities in income and a serious imbalance between "real" investment and stock market speculation. Thus net investment—in factories, farms, equipment, and the like—actually fell from $3.5 billion in 1925 to $3.2 billion in 1929. In the same years, as money flooded into stocks, the value of shares traded on the exchanges soared from $27 billion to $87 billion. As a financial historian concluded in an important study, "It should have been clear to everybody concerned that a crash was inevitable under such conditions."[11] Of course it was not. Irving Fisher, one of America's most brilliant economists, was highly optimistic in 1929 and fully invested in stocks. He then lost his entire fortune and would have been forced from his house if his university had not bought it and rented it to him.

The American stock market boom was built on borrowed money. Many wealthy investors, speculators, and people of modest means had bought stocks by paying only a small fraction of the total purchase price and borrowing the remainder from their stockbrokers. Such buying "on margin" was extremely dangerous. When prices started falling, the hard-pressed margin buyers either had to put up more money, which was often impossible, or sell their shares to pay off their brokers. Thus thousands of people started selling all at once. The result was a financial panic. Countless investors and speculators were wiped out in a matter of days or weeks.

The general economic consequences were swift and severe. Stripped of wealth and confidence, battered investors and their fellow citizens started buying fewer goods. Prices fell, production began to slow down, and unemployment began to rise. Soon the entire American economy was caught in a spiraling decline.

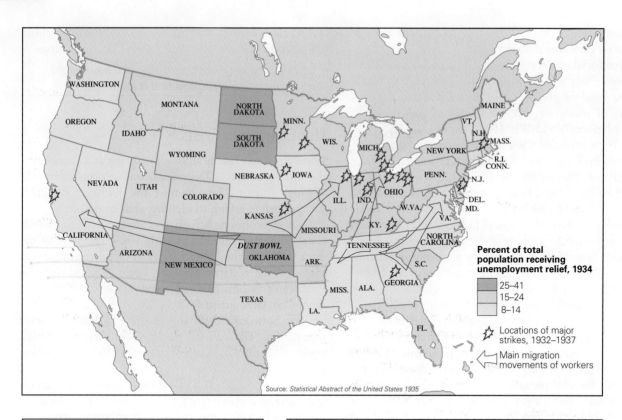

Percent of total
population receiving
unemployment relief, 1934

25–41
15–24
8–14

☆ Locations of major
  strikes, 1932–1937

⇦ Main migration
  movements of workers

Source: *Statistical Abstract of the United States 1935*

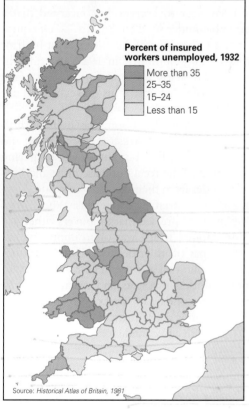

Percent of insured
workers unemployed, 1932

More than 35
25–35
15–24
Less than 15

Source: *Historical Atlas of Britain, 1981*

Percent of workers unemployed, 1932

25–32
15–24

No comparable data available

Source: *European Historical Statistics, 1790–1970*
Monthly Labor Review, U.S. Dept. of Labor, 1934, vol. 39

The financial panic in the United States triggered a worldwide financial crisis. Throughout the 1920s, American bankers and investors had lent large amounts of capital to many countries. Many of these loans were short-term, and once panic broke, New York bankers began recalling them. Gold reserves thus began to flow out of European countries, particularly Germany and Austria, toward the United States. It became very hard for European business people to borrow money, and the panicky public began to withdraw its savings from the banks. These banking problems eventually led to the crash of the largest bank in Austria in 1931 and then to general financial chaos. The recall of private loans by American bankers also accelerated the collapse in world prices, as business people around the world dumped industrial goods and agricultural commodities in a frantic attempt to get cash to pay what they owed.

The financial crisis led to a general crisis of production: between 1929 and 1933, world output of goods fell by an estimated 38 percent. As this happened, each country turned inward and tried to go it alone. In 1931, for example, Britain went off the gold standard, refusing to convert bank notes into gold, and reduced the value of its money. Britain's goal was to make its goods cheaper and therefore more salable in the world market. But because more than twenty nations, including the United States in 1934, also went off the gold standard, few countries gained a real advantage. Similarly, country after country followed the example of the United States when in 1930 it raised protective tariffs to their highest levels ever and tried to seal off shrinking national markets for American producers only. Within this context of fragmented and destructive economic nationalism, recovery finally began in 1933.

Mapping the Past

MAP 28.1 The Great Depression in the United States, Britain, and Europe These maps show that unemployment was high almost everywhere, but that national and regional differences were also substantial. With this in mind: ❶ In the United States, what in 1934 were the main channels of migration for workers? ❷ In Britain, why do you think unemployment was higher in south Wales than in the greater London area? (*Hints*: First locate both regions on Map 22.1 on page 718; assume that Map 22.2 on page 725 provides clues regarding the kinds of work that might be available in 1932; and integrate this information with the discussion in the text on Britain's changing economy in the 1920s and 1930s.) ❸ Which European countries in 1932 had the highest rate of unemployment (usually considered a good indicator of the level of economic hardship)?

Although opinions differ, two factors probably best explain the relentless slide to the bottom from 1929 to early 1933. First, the international economy lacked a leadership able to maintain stability when the crisis came. Specifically, as a noted American economic historian concluded, the seriously weakened British, the traditional leaders of the world economy, "couldn't and the United States wouldn't" stabilize the international economic system in 1929.[12] The United States, which had momentarily played a positive role after the occupation of the Ruhr, cut back its international lending and erected high tariffs.

The second factor was poor national economic policy in almost every country. Governments generally cut their budgets and reduced spending when they should have run large deficits in an attempt to stimulate their economies. After World War II, such a "counter-cyclical policy," advocated by John Maynard Keynes, became a well-established weapon against downturn and depression. But in the 1930s, Keynes's prescription was generally regarded with horror by orthodox economists.

Mass Unemployment

The need for large-scale government spending was tied to mass unemployment. As the financial crisis led to cuts in production, workers lost their jobs and had little money to buy goods. In Britain unemployment had averaged 12 percent in the 1920s; between 1930 and 1935, it averaged more than 18 percent. Far worse was the case of the United States, where unemployment had averaged only 5 percent in the 1920s. In 1932 unemployment soared to about 33 percent of the entire labor force: 14 million people were out of work (see Map 28.1). Only by pumping new money into the economy could the government increase demand and break the vicious cycle of decline.

Along with economic effects, mass unemployment posed a great social problem. Poverty increased dramatically, although in most countries unemployed workers generally received some kind of meager unemployment benefits or public aid that prevented starvation. (See the feature "Listening to the Past: Life on the Dole in Great Britain" on pages 942–943.) Millions of people lost their spirit, condemned to an apparently hopeless search for work or to idle boredom. Homes and ways of life were disrupted in millions of personal tragedies. Young people postponed marriages, and birthrates fell sharply. There was an increase in suicide and mental illness. Poverty or the threat of

Isaac Soyer: Employment Agency (1937)   The frustration and agony of looking for work against long odds are painfully evident in this American masterpiece. The time-killing, pensive resignation and dejection seen in the three figures are only aspects of the larger problem. One of three talented brothers born in Russia and trained as artists in New York, Isaac Soyer worked in the tradition of American realism and concentrated on people and the influence of their environment. *(Oil on canvas, 34¼ × 45 in. Whitney Museum of American Art, New York; Purchase 37.44. Courtesy, Estate of artist, Isaac Soyer)*

poverty became a grinding reality. In 1932 the workers of Manchester, England, appealed to their city officials—a typical plea echoed throughout the Western world:

We tell you that thousands of people . . . are in desperate straits. We tell you that men, women, and children are going hungry. . . . We tell you that great numbers are being rendered distraught through the stress and worry of trying to exist without work. . . .

If you do not do this—if you do not provide useful work for the unemployed—what, we ask, is your alternative? Do not

imagine that this colossal tragedy of unemployment is going on endlessly without some fateful catastrophe. Hungry men are angry men.[13]

Only strong government action could deal with mass unemployment, a social powder keg preparing to explode.

The New Deal in the United States

Of all the major industrial countries, only Germany was harder hit by the Great Depression, or reacted more radically to it, than the United States (see Chapter 29). The depression was so traumatic in the United States because the 1920s had been a period of complacent optimism. The Great Depression and the response to it marked a major turning point in American history.

President Herbert Hoover (1895–1972) and his administration initially reacted to the stock market crash and economic decline with dogged optimism and limited action. But when the full force of the financial crisis struck Europe in the summer of 1931 and boomeranged back to the United States, people's worst fears became reality. Banks failed; unemployment soared. Between 1929 and 1932, industrial production fell by about 50 percent.

In these tragic circumstances, Franklin Delano Roosevelt (1882–1945), an inspiring wheelchair-bound aristocrat previously crippled by polio, won a landslide electoral victory in 1932 with grand but vague promises of a "**New Deal** for the forgotten man."

Roosevelt's basic goal was to reform capitalism in order to preserve it. Roosevelt rejected socialism and government ownership of industry in 1933. To right the situation, he chose forceful government intervention in the economy. In this choice, Roosevelt was flexible, pragmatic, and willing to experiment. He and his "brain trust" of advisers adopted policies echoing the American experience in World War I, when the American economy had been thoroughly planned and regulated.

Innovative programs promoted agricultural recovery, a top priority. Almost half of the American population still lived in rural areas, and American farmers were hard hit by the depression. Roosevelt's decision to leave the gold standard and devalue the dollar was designed to raise American prices and rescue farmers. The Agricultural Adjustment Act of 1933 also aimed at raising prices and farm income by limiting production. These planning measures worked for a while, and farmers repaid Roosevelt in 1936 with overwhelming support.

The most ambitious attempt to control and plan the economy was the National Recovery Administration (NRA). Intended to reduce competition and fix prices and wages for everyone's benefit, the NRA broke with the cherished American tradition of free competition and aroused conflicts among business people, consumers, and bureaucrats. It did not work well and was declared unconstitutional in 1935.

Roosevelt and his advisers then attacked the key problem of mass unemployment directly. The federal government accepted the responsibility of employing directly as many people as financially possible. New agencies were created to undertake a vast range of projects. The most

famous of these was the Works Progress Administration (**WPA**), set up in 1935. One-fifth of the entire labor force worked for the WPA at some point in the 1930s, constructing public buildings, bridges, and highways. The WPA was enormously popular, and the hope of a government job helped check the threat of social revolution in the United States.

Relief programs like the WPA were part of the New Deal's most fundamental commitment, the commitment to use the federal government to provide for the welfare of all Americans. This commitment marked a profound shift from the traditional stress on family support and community responsibility. Embraced by a large majority in the 1930s, this shift in attitudes proved to be one of the New Deal's most enduring legacies.

Other social measures aimed in the same direction. Following the path blazed by Germany's Bismarck in the 1880s, the U.S. government in 1935 established a national social security system, with old-age pensions and unemployment benefits, to protect many workers against some of life's uncertainties. The National Labor Relations Act of 1935 gave union organizers the green light by declaring collective bargaining to be the policy of the United States. Union membership more than doubled, from 4 million in 1935 to 9 million in 1940. In general, between 1935 and 1938 government rulings and social reforms chipped away at the privileges of the wealthy and tried to help ordinary people.

Yet despite undeniable accomplishments in social reform, the New Deal was only partly successful as a response to the Great Depression. At the height of the recovery in May 1937, 7 million workers were still unemployed, as opposed to a high of 15 million in 1933. The economic situation then worsened seriously in the recession of 1937 and 1938, and unemployment was still a staggering 10 million when war broke out in Europe in September 1939. The New Deal never did pull the United States out of the depression.

The Scandinavian Response to the Depression

Of all the Western democracies, the Scandinavian countries under Social Democratic leadership responded most successfully to the challenge of the Great Depression. Having grown steadily in number in the late nineteenth century, the **Social Democrats** became the largest political party in Sweden and then in Norway after the First World War. In the 1920s, they passed important social reform legislation for both peasants and workers, gained practical administrative experience, and developed a unique kind of socialism. Flexible and nonrevolutionary, Scandinavian socialism grew out of a strong tradition of cooperative community action. Even before 1900, Scandinavian agricultural cooperatives had shown how individual peasant families could join together for everyone's benefit. Labor leaders and capitalists were also inclined to work together.

When the economic crisis struck in 1929, socialist governments in Scandinavia built on this pattern of cooperative social action. Sweden in particular pioneered in the use of large-scale deficits to finance public works and thereby maintain production and employment. Scandinavian governments also increased social welfare benefits, from old-age pensions and unemployment insurance to subsidized housing and maternity allowances. All this spending required a large bureaucracy and high taxes, first on the rich and then on practically everyone. Yet both private and cooperative enterprise thrived, as did democracy. Some observers saw Scandinavia's welfare socialism as an appealing "middle way" between sick capitalism and cruel communism or fascism.

Recovery and Reform in Britain and France

In Britain MacDonald's Labour government and then, after 1931, the Conservative-dominated coalition government followed orthodox economic theory. The budget was balanced, but unemployed workers received barely enough welfare to live. Despite government lethargy, the economy recovered considerably after 1932. By 1937 total production was about 20 percent higher than in 1929. In fact, for Britain the years after 1932 were actually somewhat better than the 1920s had been, quite the opposite of the situation in the United States and France.

This good but by no means brilliant performance reflected the gradual reorientation of the British economy. After going off the gold standard in 1931 and establishing protective tariffs in 1932, Britain concentrated increasingly on the national, rather than the international, market. The old export industries of the Industrial Revolution, such as textiles and coal, continued to decline, but new industries, such as automobiles and electrical appli-

Oslo Breakfast Scandinavian socialism championed cooperation and practical welfare measures, playing down strident rhetoric and theories of class conflict. The Oslo Breakfast exemplified the Scandinavian approach. It provided every schoolchild in the Norwegian capital with a good breakfast free of charge. (*Courtesy, Directorate for Health and Social Affairs, Oslo*)

ances, grew in response to British home demand. More-over, low interest rates encouraged a housing boom. By the end of the decade, there were highly visible differ-ences between the old, depressed industrial areas of the north and the new, growing areas of the south. These de-velopments encouraged Britain to look inward and avoid unpleasant foreign questions.

Online Study Center **Improve Your Grade**
Primary Source: The Great Depression in Britain: The "Special Areas"

Because France was relatively less industrialized and more isolated from the world economy, the Great De-pression came late. But once the depression hit France, it stayed and stayed. Decline was steady until 1935, and a short-lived recovery never brought production or em-ployment back up to predepression levels. Economic stag-nation both reflected and heightened an ongoing political crisis. There was no stability in government. As before 1914, the French parliament was made up of many polit-ical parties, which could never cooperate for very long. In 1933, for example, five coalition cabinets formed and fell in rapid succession.

The French lost the underlying unity that had made government instability bearable before 1914. Fascist-type organizations agitated against parliamentary democracy and looked to Mussolini's Italy and Hitler's Germany for inspiration (see Chapter 29). In February 1934, French fascists and semifascists rioted and threatened to overturn the republic. At the same time, the Communist Party and many workers opposed to the existing system were look-ing to Stalin's Russia for guidance. The vital center of moderate republicanism was sapped from both sides.

Frightened by the growing strength of the fascists at home and abroad, the Communists, the Socialists, and the Radicals formed an alliance—the **Popular Front**—for the national elections of May 1936. Their clear victory reflected the trend toward polarization. The number of Communists in the parliament jumped dramatically from 10 to 72, while the Socialists, led by Léon Blum, became the strongest party in France, with 146 seats. The really quite moderate Radicals slipped badly, and the conserv-atives lost ground to the semifascists.

In the next few months, Blum's Popular Front gov-ernment made the first and only real attempt to deal with the social and economic problems of the 1930s in France. Inspired by Roosevelt's New Deal, the Popular Front encouraged the union movement and launched a far-reaching program of social reform, complete with paid vacations and a forty-hour workweek. Popular with workers and the lower middle class, these measures were quickly sabotaged by rapid inflation and cries of revolution from fascists and frightened conservatives. Wealthy people sneaked their money out of the country, labor unrest grew, and France entered a severe financial crisis. Blum was forced to announce a "breathing spell" in social reform.

The fires of political dissension were also fanned by civil war in Spain. Communists demanded that France support the Spanish republicans, while many French con-servatives would gladly have joined Hitler and Mussolini in aiding the attack of Spanish fascists. Extremism grew, and France itself was within sight of civil war. Blum was forced to resign in June 1937, and the Popular Front quickly collapsed. An anxious and divided France drifted aimlessly once again, preoccupied by Hitler and German rearmament.

Chapter Summary

• In what ways did new and disturbing ideas in philosophy, physics, psychology, and literature reflect the general crisis in Western thought?

• How did modernism revolutionize architecture, painting, and music?

• In what ways did movies and radio become mainstays of popular culture?

• How did the democratic leaders of the 1920s deal with deep-seated instability and try to establish real peace and prosperity?

• What caused the Great Depression, and how did the Western democracies respond to this challenge?

Online Study Center **ACE the Test**

After the First World War, Western society entered a complex and difficult era—truly an age of anxiety. Intellectual life underwent a crisis marked by pessimism, uncertainty, and fascination with irrational forces. Ceaseless experimentation and rejection of old forms characterized art and music, while motion pictures and radio provided new, standardized entertainment for the masses. Intellectual and artistic developments that had been confined to small avant-garde groups before 1914, along with the insecure state of mind they expressed, gained wider currency.

Politics and economics were similarly disrupted. In the 1920s, political leaders groped to create an enduring peace and rebuild the prewar prosperity, and for a brief period late in the decade, they even seemed to have succeeded. Then the Great Depression, growing out of the complicated international financial system and the speculative boom and bust in the U.S. stock market, shattered that fragile stability. Uncertainty returned with redoubled force in the 1930s. The international economy collapsed, and unemployment struck millions worldwide. The democracies turned inward as they sought to cope with massive domestic problems and widespread disillusionment. Generally speaking, they were not very successful, although relief measures and social concern eased distress and prevented revolutions in the leading Western nations. The old liberal ideals of individual rights and responsibilities, elected government, and economic freedom declined and seemed outmoded to many. And in many countries of central and eastern Europe, these ideas were abandoned completely, as we shall see in the next chapter.

Key Terms

logical empiricism	Bauhaus
existentialism	dadaism
neutron	Dawes Plan
id, ego, and	*Mein Kampf*
superego	Great Depression
stream-of-	New Deal
consciousness	WPA
technique	Social Democrats
functionalism	Popular Front

Online Study Center **Improve Your Grade** Flashcards

Suggested Reading

Berend, Ivan T. *Decades of Crisis: Central and Eastern Europe Before World War II*. 2001. An up-to-date study of this complex region.

Berghahn, Volker R. *Europe in the Era of Two World Wars: From Militarism and Genocide to Civil Society*. 2006. A short and stimulating account.

Bullock, Alan, ed. *The Twentieth Century: A Promethean Age*. 1971. Particularly noteworthy because it is a lavish visual feast combined with penetrating essays on major developments.

Burrow, J. W. *The Crisis of Reason: European Thought, 1848–1914*. 2002. A rewarding intellectual history.

Cawood, Ian. *Britain in the Twentieth Century*. 2003. A useful national survey.

Crossman, Richard, ed. *The God That Failed*. 1950. Features famous Western writers telling why they were attracted to and later repelled by communism.

Jules-Rossette, Bennetta. *Josephine Baker in Art and Life: The Icon and the Image*. 2007. Tells the fascinating story of the African American dancer who won fame and fortune in Paris.

Kertzer, David I., and Marzio Barbagli, eds. *The History of the European Family,* Vol. 3: *Family Life in the Twentieth Century.* 2003. A distinguished collection of essays by experts.

McMillan, James F. *Twentieth-Century France: Politics and Society, 1898–1991.* 1992. A recommended national survey.

Paxton, Robert O. *Europe in the Twentieth Century.* 2004. An excellent account of contemporary history with a liberal viewpoint.

Winders, James A. *European Culture Since 1848: From Modernism to Postmodern and Beyond.* 1998. A lively and accessible account.

Notes

1. P. Valéry, *Variety,* trans. M. Cowley (New York: Harcourt Brace, 1927), pp. 27–28.

2. Quoted in S. Hughes, *The Obstructed Path: French Social Thought in the Years of Desperation, 1930–1960* (New York: Harper & Row, 1967), p. 82.

3. G. Greene, *Another Mexico* (New York: Viking Press, 1939), p. 3.

4. G. Orwell, *1984* (New York: New American Library, 1950), p. 220.

5. C. E. Jeanneret-Gris (Le Corbusier), *Towards a New Architecture* (London: J. Rodker, 1931), p. 15.

6. Quoted in A. H. Barr Jr., *What Is Modern Painting?* 9th ed. (New York: Museum of Modern Art, 1966), p. 27.

7. Quoted ibid., p. 25.

8. R. Graves and A. Hodge, *The Long Week End: A Social History of Great Britain, 1918–1939* (New York: Macmillan, 1941), p. 131.

9. Quoted in A. Briggs, *The Birth of Broadcasting,* vol. 1 (London: Oxford University Press, 1961), p. 47.

10. Quoted in R. J. Sontag, *A Broken World, 1919–1939* (New York: Harper & Row, 1971), p. 129.

11. Dietmar Rothermund, *The Global Impact of the Great Depression, 1929–1939* (London: Routledge, 1996), p. 50.

12. C. P. Kindleberger, *The World in Depression, 1929–1939* (Berkeley: University of California Press, 1973), p. 292.

13. Quoted in S. B. Clough et al., eds., *Economic History of Europe: Twentieth Century* (New York: Harper & Row, 1968), pp. 243–245.

Life on the Dole in Great Britain

Periodic surges in unemployment were an old story in capitalist economies, but the long-term joblessness of millions in the Great Depression was something new and unexpected. In Britain especially, where the depression followed a weak postwar recovery, large numbers suffered involuntary idleness for years at a time. Whole families lived "on the dole," the weekly welfare benefits paid by the government.

One of the most insightful accounts of unemployed workers was written by the British journalist and novelist George Orwell (1903–1950), who studied the conditions in northern England and wrote The Road to Wigan Pier *(1937), an excerpt of which follows. An independent socialist who distrusted rigid Marxism, Orwell believed that socialism could triumph in Britain if it came to mean "justice and liberty" for a commonsense majority. Orwell's disillusionment with authoritarian socialism and communism pervades his most famous work,* 1984 *(1949).*

When you see the unemployment figures quoted at two millions, it is fatally easy to take this as meaning that two million people are out of work and the rest of the population is comparatively comfortable. . . . [Adding in the destitute,] you might take the number of underfed people in England (for *everyone* on the dole or thereabouts is underfed) as being, at the very most, five millions.

This is an enormous under-estimate, because, in the first place, the only people shown on unemployment figures are those actually drawing the dole—that is, in general, heads of families. An unemployed man's dependants do not figure on the list unless they too are drawing a separate allowance. . . . In addition there are great numbers of people who are in work but who, from a financial point of view, might equally be unemployed, because they are not drawing anything that can be described as a living wage. Allow for these and their dependants, throw in as

before the old-age pensioners, the destitute and other nondescripts, and you get an *underfed* population of well over ten millions. . . .

Take the figures for Wigan, which is typical enough of the industrial and mining districts. . . . The total population of Wigan is a little under 87,000; so that at any moment more than one person in three out of the whole population—not merely the registered workers—is either drawing or living on the dole. . . .

Nevertheless, in spite of the frightful extent of unemployment, it is a fact that poverty—extreme poverty—is less in evidence in the industrial North than it is in London. Everything is poorer and shabbier, there are fewer motor-cars and fewer well-dressed people; but also there are fewer people who are obviously destitute. . . . In the industrial towns the old communal way of life has not yet broken up, tradition is still strong and almost everyone has a family—potentially, therefore, a home. In a town of 50,000 or 100,000 inhabitants there is no casual and as it were unaccounted-for population; nobody sleeping in the streets, for instance. Moreover, there is just this to be said for the unemployment regulations, that they do not discourage people from marrying. A man and wife on twenty-three shillings a week are not far from the starvation line, but they can make a home of sorts; they are vastly better off than a single man on fifteen shillings. . . .

But there is no doubt about the deadening, debilitating effect of unemployment upon everybody, married or single, and upon men more than upon women. . . . Everyone who saw Greenwood's play *Love on the Dole* must remember that dreadful moment when the poor, good, stupid working man beats on the table and cries out, "O God, send me some work!" This was not dramatic exaggeration, it was a touch from life. That cry must have been uttered, in almost those words, in tens of thousands, perhaps hundreds of thousands of English homes, during the past fifteen years.

But, I think not again—or at least, not so often. . . . When people live on the dole for years at a time they grow used to it, and drawing the dole, though it remains unpleasant, ceases to be shameful. Thus the old, independent, workhouse-fearing tradition is undermined. . . .

So you have whole populations settling down, as it were, to a lifetime of the P.A.C. . . . Take, for instance, the fact that the working class think nothing of getting married on the dole. . . . Life is still fairly normal, more normal than one really has the right to expect. Families are impoverished, but the family-system has not broken up. The people are in effect living a reduced version of their former lives. Instead of raging against their destiny they have made things tolerable by lowering their standards.

But they don't necessarily lower their standards by cutting out luxuries and concentrating on necessities; more often it is the other way about— the more natural way, if you come to think of it. Hence the fact that in a decade of unparalleled depression, the consumption of all cheap luxuries has increased. The two things that have probably made the greatest difference of all are the movies and the mass-production of cheap smart clothes since the war. The youth who leaves school at fourteen and gets a blind-alley job is out of work at twenty, probably for life; but for two pounds ten on the hire-purchase system he can buy himself a suit which, for a little while and at a little distance, looks as though it had been tailored in Savile Row. The girl can look like a fashion plate at an even lower price. . . . You can stand on the street corner, indulging in a private daydream of yourself as Clark Gable or Greta Garbo, which compensates you for a great deal. . . .

Trade since the war has had to adjust itself to meet the demands of underpaid, underfed people, with the result that a luxury is nowadays almost always cheaper than a necessity. One pair of plain solid shoes costs as much as two ultra-smart pairs. . . . And above all there is gambling, the cheapest of all luxuries. Even people on the verge of starvation can buy a few days' hope ("Something to live for," as they call it) by having a penny on a sweepstake. . . . Twenty million people are underfed but literally everyone in England has access to a radio. What we have lost in food we have gained in electricity. Whole sections of the working class who have been plundered of all they really need are being compensated, in part, by cheap luxuries which mitigate the surface of life.

Do you consider all this desirable? No, I don't. But it may be that the psychological adjustment

Poster used in the election campaign of 1931, when unemployment rose to a new record high. (*Conservative Research Department/The Bridgeman Art Library*)

which the working class are visibly making is the best they could make in the circumstances. They have neither turned revolutionary nor lost their self-respect; merely they have kept their tempers and settled down to make the best of things on a fish-and-chip standard. The alternative would be God knows what continued agonies of despair; or it might be attempted insurrections which, in a strongly governed country like England, could only lead to futile massacres and a régime of savage repression.

Questions for Analysis

1. According to Orwell, "extreme poverty" was less visible in the northern industrial towns than in London. Were family relations important in this regard?

2. What were the consequences of long-term unemployment for English workers? Were some of the consequences surprising?

3. Judging from Orwell's description, did radical revolution seem likely in England in the Great Depression? Why?

Source: Excerpts from Chapter V in *The Road to Wigan Pier* by George Orwell, copyright © 1958 and renewed 1986 by the Estate of Sonia B. Orwell. Reprinted by permission of Harcourt, Inc.

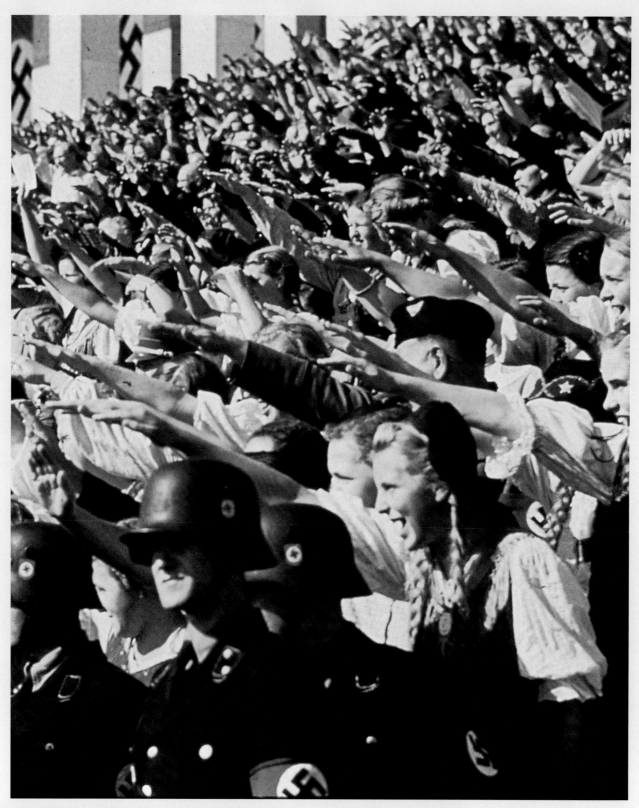

Hugo Jager's photograph of a crowd of enthusiastic Hitler supporters. *(Time Life Pictures/Getty Images)*

29

DICTATORSHIPS AND THE SECOND WORLD WAR, 1919–1945

---

chapter preview

Authoritarian States
• *What was the nature of radical totalitarian dictatorship, and how did it differ from conservative authoritarianism?*

Stalin's Soviet Union
• *How did Stalin and the Communist Party build a modern totalitarian state in the Soviet Union?*

Mussolini and Fascism in Italy
• *How did Mussolini's dictatorship come to power and govern in Italy?*

Hitler and Nazism in Germany
• *How did Hitler gain power, what policies did totalitarian Nazi Germany pursue, and why did they lead to World War II?*

The Second World War
• *How did Germany and Japan create enormous empires that were defeated by the Allies—Britain, the Soviet Union, and the United States?*

T he era of anxiety and economic depression was also a time of grow- ing strength for political dictatorship. Popularly elected govern- ments and basic civil liberties declined drastically in Europe. On the eve of the Second World War, liberal democratic governments were surviving only in Great Britain, France, the Low Countries, the Scandinavian na- tions, and Switzerland. Elsewhere in Europe, various kinds of "strong- men" ruled. Dictatorship seemed the wave of the future. Thus the intellectual and economic crisis discussed in Chapter 28 and the decline in liberal political institutions and rise of dictatorship to be considered in this chapter were interrelated elements in the general crisis of European civilization.

The era of dictatorship is a highly disturbing chapter in the history of Western civilization. The key development was not only the resurgence of authoritarian rule but also the rise of a particularly ruthless and dy- namic tyranny. This new kind of tyranny reached its full realization in the Soviet Union and Nazi Germany in the 1930s. Stalin and Hitler mobi- lized their peoples for enormous undertakings and ruled with unprece- dented severity. Hitler's mobilization was ultimately directed toward racial aggression and territorial expansion, and his sudden attack on Poland in 1939 started World War II.

Nazi armies were defeated by a great coalition, and today we want to believe that the era of totalitarian dictatorship was a terrible accident, that Stalin's slave-labor camps and Hitler's gas chambers "can't happen again." Yet the cruel truth is that horrible atrocities continue to plague the world in our time. The Khmer Rouge inflicted genocide on its people in Kampuchea, and civil war in Bosnia and in Rwanda led to racially mo- tivated atrocities recalling the horrors of World War II. And there are other examples. Thus it is all the more vital that we understand Europe's era of brutal and aggressive dictatorship in order to guard against the pos- sibility of its recurrence in the future.

Online Study Center

This icon will direct you to interactive activities and study materials on the website **college.hmco.com/pic/mckaywest9e**

Authoritarian States

Both conservative and radical dictatorships swept through Europe in the 1920s and 1930s. Although these two types of dictatorship shared some characteristics and sometimes overlapped in practice, they were in essence profoundly different. Conservative authoritarian regimes were an old story in Europe. Radical, totalitarian dictatorships were a new and frightening development.

- *What was the nature of radical totalitarian dictatorship, and how did it differ from conservative authoritarianism?*

Conservative Authoritarianism

The traditional form of antidemocratic government in European history was conservative authoritarianism. Like Catherine the Great in Russia and Metternich in Austria, the leaders of such governments tried to prevent major changes that would undermine the existing social order. To do so, they relied on obedient bureaucracies, vigilant police departments, and trustworthy armies. Popular participation in government was forbidden or limited to such natural allies as landlords, bureaucrats, and high church officials. Liberals, democrats, and socialists were persecuted as subversive radicals, often finding themselves in jail or exile.

Yet old-fashioned authoritarian governments were limited in their power and in their objectives. They had neither the ability nor the desire to control many aspects of their subjects' lives. Nor did they wish to do so. Preoccupied with the goal of mere survival, these governments largely limited their demands to taxes, army recruits, and passive acceptance. As long as the people did not try to change the system, they often had considerable personal independence.

After the First World War, this kind of authoritarian government revived, especially in the less-developed eastern part of Europe. There the parliamentary regimes that had been founded on the wreckage of empires in 1918 fell one by one. By early 1938, only economically and socially advanced Czechoslovakia remained true to liberal political ideals. Conservative dictators also took over in Spain and Portugal.

There were several reasons for this development. These lands lacked a strong tradition of self-government, with its necessary restraint and compromise. Moreover, many of these new states, such as Yugoslavia, were torn by ethnic conflicts that threatened their very existence. Dictatorship appealed to nationalists and military leaders

as a way to repress such tensions and preserve national unity. Large landowners and the church were still powerful forces in these largely agrarian areas, and they often looked to dictators to save them from progressive land reform or communist agrarian upheaval. So did some members of the middle class, which was small and weak in eastern Europe. Finally, though some kind of democracy managed to stagger through the 1920s in Austria, Bulgaria, Romania, Greece, Estonia, and Latvia, the Great Depression delivered the final blow to those countries by 1936.

Although some of the conservative authoritarian regimes adopted certain Hitlerian and fascist characteristics in the 1930s, their general aims were limited. They were concerned more with maintaining the status quo than with forcing society into rapid change or war. This tradition continued into the twenty-first century, especially in some of the military dictatorships that ruled in Latin America until the late 1980s.

Radical Totalitarian Dictatorships

Conservative authoritarianism predominated in the smaller states of central and eastern Europe by the mid-1930s, but a new kind of radical dictatorship emerged in the Soviet Union, Germany, and, to a lesser extent, Italy. Almost all scholars agree that the leaders of these radical dictatorships violently rejected parliamentary restraint and liberal values. Scholars also agree that these dictatorships exercised unprecedented control over the masses and sought to mobilize them for action. However, there has always been controversy over the interpretation of these regimes.

One extremely useful approach relates the radical dictatorships to the rise of modern totalitarianism. The concept of **totalitarianism** emerged in the 1920s and 1930s, although it is frequently and mistakenly seen as developing only after 1945 as part of anti-Soviet propaganda during the cold war. In 1924 Benito Mussolini spoke of the "fierce totalitarian will" of his movement in Italy. In the 1930s more and more British, American, and German exiled writers used the concept of totalitarianism to describe what they saw happening before their eyes. They linked Italian and especially German fascism with Soviet communism in "a 'new kind of state' that could be called totalitarian." With the alliance between Hitler and Stalin in 1939, "all doubts" about the totalitarian nature of both dictatorships "were swept away for most Americans."[1]

Early writers believed that modern totalitarian dictatorship burst on the scene with the revolutionary total war effort of 1914–1918. The war called forth a tendency to subordinate all institutions and all classes to the state in order to achieve one supreme objective: victory. As the French thinker Elie Halévy put it in 1936 in his influential *The Era of Tyrannies,* the varieties of modern totalitarian tyranny—fascism, Nazism, and communism—could be thought of as "feuding brothers" with a common father: the nature of modern war.[2]

Writers such as Halévy believed that the crucial experience of World War I was carried further by Lenin and the Bolsheviks during the Russian civil war. Lenin showed how a dedicated minority could achieve victory over a less determined majority and subordinate institutions and human rights to the needs of a single group—the Communist Party—and its leader. Providing a model for single-party dictatorship, Lenin inspired imitators, including Adolf Hitler. The modern totalitarian state reached maturity in the 1930s in the Stalinist U.S.S.R. and Nazi Germany.

Embellishing on early insights, numerous Western political scientists and historians argued in the 1950s and 1960s that the totalitarian state used modern technology and communications to exercise complete political power. But it did not stop there. Increasingly, the state took over and tried to control just as completely the economic, social, intellectual, and cultural aspects of people's lives. Deviation from the norm, even in art or family behavior, could become a crime.

This vision of total state represented a radical revolt against liberalism. Classical liberalism (see page 753) sought to limit the power of the state and protect the rights of the individual. Moreover, liberals stood for rationality, peaceful progress, economic freedom, and a strong middle class. All of that disgusted totalitarians as sentimental slop. They believed in willpower, preached conflict, and worshiped violence. The individual was infinitely less valuable than the state.

Unlike old-fashioned authoritarianism, modern totalitarianism was based not on an elite but on people who had already become engaged in the political process, most notably through commitment to nationalism and socialism. Thus totalitarian societies were fully mobilized societies moving toward some goal and possessing boundless dynamism. As soon as one goal was achieved at the cost of enormous sacrifice, another arose at the leader's command to take its place. Thus totalitarianism was a *permanent* revolution, an *unfinished* revolution, in which rapid, profound change imposed from on high went on forever.

In developing the concept of totalitarianism, scholars recognized that there were major differences between Stalin's communist U.S.S.R. and Hitler's Nazi Germany. Soviet communism, growing out of Marxian socialism, seized all private property (except personal property) for

Chronology

1921	New Economic Policy (NEP) in U.S.S.R.
1922	Mussolini seizes power in Italy
1924–1929	Buildup of Nazi Party in Germany
1927	Stalin comes to power in U.S.S.R.
1928	Stalin's first five-year plan
1929	Lateran Agreement; start of collectivization in Soviet Union
1929–1939	Great Depression
1932–1933	Famine in Ukraine
1933	Hitler appointed chancellor in Germany; Nazis begin to control intellectual life and blacklist authors
1934	Sergei Kirov, Stalin's number-two man, murdered
1935	Mussolini invades Ethiopia
1936	Start of great purges under Stalin; Halévy, *The Era of Tyrannies,* analyzes totalitarianism
1939	Germany occupies Czech lands; Germany invades Poland; Britain and France declare war on Germany
1941	SS stops Jewish emigration from Europe; Germany invades Soviet Union; bombing of Pearl Harbor; U.S. enters war
1941–1945	Six million Jews killed in death camps
1944	Allied invasion at Normandy
1945	Atomic bombs dropped on Japan; end of war

the state and crushed the middle classes. Nazi Germany, growing out of extreme nationalism and racism, criticized big landowners and industrialists, but both private property and the middle classes survived. This difference in property and class relations led some scholars to speak of "totalitarianism of the left"—Stalinist Russia—and "totalitarianism of the right"—Nazi Germany.

A second group of writers in the 1930s approached radical dictatorships outside the Soviet Union through the concept of **fascism**. A term of pride for Mussolini and Hitler, who used it to describe the supposedly "total" and revolutionary character of their movements, fascism was severely criticized by these writers and linked to decaying capitalism and domestic class conflict. Orthodox Marxists, generally sympathetic to the Soviet Union and

Nazi Mass Rally, 1936 This picture captures the essence of the totalitarian interpretation of dynamic modern dictatorship. The uniformed members of the Nazi Party have willingly merged themselves into a single force and await the command of the godlike leader. *(AP/Wide World Photos)*

the socialism it established, argued that fascism was the way powerful capitalists sought to create a mass movement capable of destroying the revolutionary working class and thus protect their enormous profits.

Scholarly interest in fascism declined in the 1950s but revived thereafter. Comparative studies of fascist movements all across Europe showed that they shared many characteristics, including extreme, often expansionist nationalism; an antisocialism aimed at destroying working-class movements; alliances with powerful capitalists and landowners; a dynamic and violent leader; and glorification of war and the military. Yet these studies also highlighted how fascist movements generally failed to gain political power.

In recent years, many historians have tended to adopt a third approach, emphasizing the uniqueness of developments in each country. This is especially true for Hitler's Germany, where some elements of the totalitarian interpretation have been nuanced and revised, as we shall see. A similar revaluation of Stalin's U.S.S.R. began after the fall of communism opened the former Soviet Union's archives to new research. For many of today's historians, the differences within broad historical patterns often seem more important than the similarities.

In summary, these conclusions seem appropriate. First, although the concept of totalitarianism has been questioned, it remains a valuable tool for historical understanding. It correctly highlights that both Hitler's Germany and Stalin's Soviet Union made an unprecedented "total claim" on the belief and behavior of their respective citizens, as a noted scholar has recently concluded.[3] Second, antidemocratic, antisocialist fascist movements sprang up all over Europe, but only in Italy and Germany (and some would say Spain) were they able to take power. Studies of fascist movements seeking to gain power locate important common elements, but they do not explain what fascist governments in Italy and Germany actually did. Finally, it is important to remember that the problem of Europe's radical dictatorships is complex and that there are few easy answers.

Stalin's Soviet Union

Lenin's harshest critics claim that he established the basic outlines of a modern totalitarian dictatorship after the Bolshevik Revolution and during the Russian civil war. If this is so, then Joseph Stalin (1879–1953) certainly finished the job. A master of political infighting, Stalin cautiously consolidated his power and eliminated his enemies in the mid-1920s. Then in 1928, as undisputed leader of the ruling Communist Party, he launched the first **five-year plan**—the "revolution from above," as he so aptly termed it.

The five-year plans were extremely ambitious. Often incorrectly considered a mere set of economic measures to speed up the Soviet Union's industrial development, the five-year plans actually marked the beginning of a renewed attempt to mobilize and transform Soviet society along socialist lines. The ultimate goal of the plans was to generate new attitudes, new loyalties, and a new socialist humanity. The means Stalin and the small Communist Party elite chose in order to do so were constant propaganda, enormous sacrifice by the people, and the concentration of all power in party hands. Thus the Soviet Union in the 1930s became a dynamic, modern totalitarian state.

• *How did Stalin and the Communist Party build a modern totalitarian state in the Soviet Union?*

From Lenin to Stalin

By spring 1921, Lenin and the Bolsheviks had won the civil war, but they ruled a shattered and devastated land. Many farms were in ruins, and food supplies were exhausted. In southern Russia, drought combined with the ravages of war to produce the worst famine in generations. Industrial production also broke down completely. The Bolsheviks had destroyed the economy as well as their foes.

In the face of economic disintegration, riots by peasants and workers, and an open rebellion by previously pro-Bolshevik sailors at Kronstadt, the tough but ever-flexible Lenin changed course. In March 1921, he announced the **New Economic Policy (NEP),** which re-established limited economic freedom in an attempt to rebuild agriculture and industry. During the civil war, the Bolsheviks had simply seized grain without payment. Now peasant producers were permitted to sell their surpluses in free markets, and private traders and small handicraft manufacturers were allowed to reappear. Heavy industry, railroads, and banks, however, remained wholly nationalized.

The NEP was shrewd and successful both politically and economically. Politically, it was a necessary but temporary compromise with the Soviet Union's overwhelming peasant majority. Realizing that his government was not strong enough to take land from the peasants and turn them into state workers, Lenin made a deal with the only force capable of overturning his government. Economically, the NEP brought rapid recovery. In 1926 industrial output surpassed the level of 1913, and Soviet peasants were producing almost as much grain as before the war.

As the economy recovered and the government partially relaxed its censorship and repression, an intense struggle for power began in the inner circles of the Communist Party, for Lenin had left no chosen successor when he died in 1924. The principal contenders were the stolid Stalin and the flamboyant Trotsky.

The son of a shoemaker, Joseph Dzhugashvili—later known as Stalin—studied for the priesthood but was expelled from his theological seminary, probably for rude rebelliousness. By 1903 he was a Bolshevik revolutionary in southern Russia.

Stalin was a good organizer but a poor speaker and writer, with no experience outside of Russia. Trotsky, a great and inspiring leader who had planned the 1917 takeover (see page 898) and then created the victorious Red Army, appeared to have all the advantages. Yet it was Stalin who succeeded Lenin. Stalin won because he was more effective at gaining the all-important support of the party, the only genuine source of power in the one-party state. Rising to general secretary of the party's Central Committee just before Lenin's first stroke in 1922, Stalin used his office to win friends and allies with jobs and promises.

The practical Stalin also won because he appeared better able than the brilliant Trotsky to relate Marxian teaching to Soviet realities in the 1920s. Stalin developed a theory of "socialism in one country" that was more appealing to the majority of communists than Trotsky's doctrine of "permanent revolution." Stalin argued that the Russian-dominated Soviet Union had the ability to build socialism on its own. Trotsky maintained that

Kazimir Malevich: Suprematism, ca 1917 Russian artists occupied a prominent position in the international avant-garde in the early twentieth century, and the Ukrainian-born Malevich is widely recognized as a leading figure in the development of modern abstract art. Malevich originated the theory of suprematism, whereby he abandoned images from nature and painted pure forms that were beautiful in themselves, as in this outstanding example. When the Bolsheviks condemned abstraction and demanded "socialist realism," Malevich returned to more recognizable forms and taught design. *(Erich Lessing/Art Resource, NY)*

against his allies, the moderates, and destroyed them as well. Stalin's final triumph came at the party congress of December 1927, which condemned all "deviation from the general party line" formulated by Stalin. The dictator and his followers were then ready to launch the revolution from above—the real revolution for millions of ordinary citizens.

The Five-Year Plans

The party congress of 1927, which ratified Stalin's consolidation of power, marked the end of the NEP and the beginning of the era of socialist five-year plans. Building on planning models developed by Soviet economists in the 1920s, the first five-year plan had staggering economic objectives. In just five years, total industrial output was to increase by 250 percent. Heavy industry, the preferred sector, was to grow even faster. Agricultural production was slated to increase by 150 percent, and one-fifth of the peasants in the Soviet Union were scheduled to give up their private plots and join socialist collective farms. By 1930 economic and social change was sweeping the country.

Stalin unleashed his "second revolution" for a variety of interrelated reasons. There were, first of all, ideological considerations. Like Lenin, Stalin

socialism in the Soviet Union could succeed only if revolution occurred quickly throughout Europe. To many Russian communists, Trotsky's views seemed to sell their country short and to promise risky conflicts with capitalist countries by recklessly encouraging revolutionary movements around the world. Stalin's willingness to break with the NEP and "build socialism" at home appealed to young militants in the party, who detested the capitalist-appearing NEP.

With cunning skill, Stalin gradually achieved supreme power between 1922 and 1927. First, he allied with Trotsky's personal enemies to crush Trotsky, and then he aligned with the moderates to suppress Trotsky's radical followers. Third, having defeated all the radicals, he turned

and his militant supporters were deeply committed to socialism as they understood it. They feared a gradual restoration of capitalism, and they burned to stamp out the NEP's private traders, independent artisans, and property-owning peasants. Purely economic motivations were also important. Although the economy had recovered, it seemed to have stalled in 1927 and 1928. A new socialist offensive seemed necessary if industry and agriculture were to grow rapidly.

Political considerations were most important. Internationally, there was the old problem, remaining from pre-revolutionary times, of catching up with the advanced and presumably hostile capitalist nations of the West. Stalin said in 1931, when he pressed for ever-greater speed and sacrifice, "We are fifty or a hundred years be-hind the advanced countries. We must make good this distance in ten years. Either we do it, or we shall go un-der." (See the feature "Listening to the Past: Stalin Justi-fies the Five-Year Plan" on pages 978–979.)

Domestically, there was the problem of the peasants. For centuries the peasants had wanted to own the land, and finally they had it. Sooner or later, the communists reasoned, the peasants would become conservative little capitalists and pose a threat to the regime. At the same time, the mainly urban communists believed that the feared and despised "class enemy" in the villages could be squeezed to provide the enormous sums needed for all-out industrialization. Thus Stalin decided on a war against the peasantry in order to bring it under the con-trol of the state and to make it pay the costs of the new socialist offensive.

That war was **collectivization**—the forcible consolida-tion of individual peasant farms into large, state-controlled enterprises. Beginning in 1929, peasants all over the So-viet Union were ordered to give up their land and ani-mals and become members of collective farms, although they continued to live in their own homes. As for the **kulaks,** the better-off peasants, Stalin instructed party workers to "liquidate them as a class." Stripped of land and livestock, the kulaks were generally not even permit-ted to join the collective farms. Many starved or were de-ported to forced-labor camps for "re-education."

Since almost all peasants were in fact poor, the term *kulak* soon meant any peasant who opposed the new system. Whole villages were often attacked. One conscience-stricken colonel in the secret police confessed to a foreign journalist,

I am an old Bolshevik. I worked in the underground against the Tsar and then I fought in the Civil War. Did I do all that

Life in a Forced-Labor Camp   This rare photo from about 1933 shows the reality of de-ported peasants and other political prisoners building the Stalin–White Sea Canal in far north-ern Russia, with their bare hands and under the most dehumanizing conditions. In books and plays Stalin's followers praised the project as a model for the regeneration of "reactionaries" and "kulak exploiters" through the joys of socialist work. (*David King Collection*)

in order that I should now surround villages with machine guns and order my men to fire indiscriminately into crowds of peasants? Oh, no, no![4]

Forced collectivization of the peasants led to economic and human disaster. Large numbers of peasants slaughtered their animals and burned their crops in sullen, hopeless protest. Between 1929 and 1933, the number of horses, cattle, sheep, and goats in the Soviet Union fell by at least half. Nor were the state-controlled collective farms more productive. The output of grain barely increased between 1928 and 1938. Collectivized agriculture was unable to make any substantial financial contribution to Soviet industrial development in the first five-year plan.

The human dimension of the tragedy was absolutely staggering. As one leading historian writes in outrage, "The number dying in Stalin's war against the peasants was higher than the total deaths of all the countries in World War I." Yet, he notes, in Stalin's war only one side was armed and the other side bore almost all the casualties, many of whom were women, children, and the old.[5]

Online Study Center **Improve Your Grade**
Primary Source: Stalinist Interrogation Techniques Revealed

In Ukraine the drive against peasants snowballed into a general assault on Ukrainians as reactionary nationalists and enemies of socialism. Thus in 1932, as collectivization and deportations continued, Stalin and his associates set levels of grain deliveries for the Ukrainian collective at excessively high levels, and they refused to relax those quotas or even allow food relief when Ukrainian communist leaders reported that starvation was occurring. The result was a terrible man-made famine in Ukraine in 1932 and 1933, which probably claimed 6 million lives.

Collectivization, justly called the "second serfdom," was a cruel but real victory for communist ideologues. By the end of 1932, fully 60 percent of peasant families had been herded onto collective farms; by 1938, 93 percent. Regimented as employees of the state and dependent on the state-owned tractor stations, the collectivized peasants were no longer even a potential political threat to Stalin and the Communist Party.

Peasants fought back with indirect daily opposition and forced the supposedly all-powerful state to make modest compromises. Peasants secured the right to limit a family's labor on the state-run farms and to cultivate tiny family plots, which provided them with much of their food. In 1938 these family plots produced 22 per-

cent of all Soviet agricultural produce on only 4 percent of all cultivated land.

The industrial side of the five-year plans was more successful—indeed, quite spectacular. Soviet industry produced about four times as much in 1937 as it had in 1928. No other major country had ever achieved such rapid industrial growth. Heavy industry led the way; consumer industry grew quite slowly. A new heavy industrial complex was built almost from scratch in western Siberia. Industrial growth also went hand in hand with urban development, and more than 25 million people migrated to cities during the 1930s.

The great industrialization drive, concentrated between 1928 and 1937, was an awe-inspiring achievement purchased at enormous sacrifice. The sudden creation of dozens of new factories required a great increase in total investment. The money for investment was collected from the people by means of heavy, hidden sales taxes.

Two other factors contributed importantly to rapid industrialization: firm labor discipline and foreign engineers. Between 1930 and 1932, trade unions lost most of their power. The government could assign workers to any job anywhere in the country, and individuals could not move without the permission of the police. When factory managers needed more hands, they called on their counterparts on the collective farms, who sent them millions of "unneeded" peasants over the years.

Foreign engineers were hired to plan and construct many of the new factories. Highly skilled American engineers, hungry for work in the depression years, were particularly important until newly trained Soviet experts began to replace them after 1932. The gigantic mills of the new Siberian steel industry were modeled on America's best. Thus Stalin's planners harnessed even the skill and technology of capitalist countries to promote the surge of socialist industry.

Life and Culture in Soviet Society

The aim of Stalin's five-year plans was to create a new kind of society and human personality as well as a strong industrial economy and a powerful army. Stalin and his helpers were good Marxian economic determinists. Once everything was owned by the state, they believed, a socialist society and a new kind of human being would inevitably emerge. Their utopian vision of a new humanity floundered, but they did build a new society, whose broad outlines existed into the mid-1980s. Life in this society had both good and bad aspects.

Because consumption was reduced to pay for investment, there was no improvement in the average standard of living. Indeed, the most careful studies show that the average nonfarm wage apparently purchased only about half as many goods in 1932 as in 1928. After 1932 real wages rose slowly, so that in 1937 workers could buy about 60 percent of what they had bought in 1928 and less than in 1913. Collectivized peasants experienced greater declines.

Life was hard in Stalin's Soviet Union. The masses of people lived primarily on black bread and wore old, shabby clothing. There were constant shortages in the stores, although very heavily taxed vodka was always readily available. A shortage of housing was a particularly serious problem. Millions were moving into the cities, but the government built few new apartments. A relatively lucky family received one room for all its members and shared both a kitchen and a toilet with others on the floor.

Life was hard but by no means hopeless. Idealism and ideology had real appeal for many communists, who saw themselves heroically building the world's first socialist society while capitalism crumbled in a worldwide depression and degenerated into fascism in the West. This optimistic belief in the future of the Soviet Union also attracted many disillusioned Westerners to communism in the 1930s.

On a more practical level, Soviet workers did receive some important social benefits, such as old-age pensions, free medical services, free education, and day-care centers for children. Unemployment was almost unknown. Finally, there was the possibility of personal advancement.

The keys to improving one's position were specialized skills and technical education. Rapid industrialization required massive numbers of trained experts, such as skilled workers, engineers, and plant managers. Thus the Stalinist state broke with the egalitarian policies of the 1920s and provided tremendous incentives to those who could serve its needs. It paid the mass of unskilled workers and collective farmers very low wages, but it dangled high salaries and many special privileges before its growing technical and managerial elite. This elite joined with the political and artistic elites in a new upper class, whose members were rich, powerful, and insecure. Thus millions struggled for an education.

The radical transformation of Soviet society had a profound impact on women's lives. Marxists had traditionally believed that both capitalism and the middle-class husband exploited women. The Russian Revolution of 1917 immediately proclaimed complete equality of rights for women. In the 1920s, divorce and abortion were made easily available, and women were urged to work outside the home and

ОРУЖИЕМ МЫ ДОБИЛИ ВРАГА
ТРУДОМ МЫ ДОБУДЕМ ХЛЕБ
ВСЕ ЗА РАБОТУ, ТОВАРИЩИ!

"Let's All Get to Work, Comrades!" Art in the Stalinist era generally followed the official doctrine of socialist realism, representing objects in a literal style and celebrating Soviet achievements. Characteristically, this poster glorifies the working class, women's equality (in hard labor at least), mammoth factories, and the Communist Party (represented by the hammer and sickle by the woman's foot). Assailed by propaganda, Soviet citizens often found refuge in personal relations and deep friendships. *(From* Art of the October Revolution, *Mikhail Guerman [Aurora Publishers, Leningrad]. Reproduced by permission of Mikhail Guerman)*

liberate themselves sexually. The most prominent Bolshevik feminist, Alexandra Kollontai, went so far as to declare that the sex act had no more significance than "drinking a glass of water."[6] After Stalin came to power, sexual and familial liberation was played down, and the most lasting changes for women involved work and education.

Young women were constantly told that they had to be fully equal to men. Peasant women continued to work on farms, and millions of women now toiled in factories and in heavy construction, building dams, roads, and steel mills in summer heat and winter frost. Determined women pursued their studies and entered the ranks of the better-paid specialists in industry and science. Medicine practically became a woman's profession. By 1950, 75 percent of all doctors in the Soviet Union were women.

Soviet society also demanded great sacrifices from women. The vast majority of women simply *had* to work outside the home. Wages were so low that it was almost impossible for a family or couple to live only on the husband's earnings. Men continued to dominate the very best jobs. Finally, rapid change and economic hardship led to many broken families, creating further physical and emotional strains for women. In any event, the massive mobilization of women was a striking characteristic of the Soviet state.

Culture lost its autonomy in the 1930s and became thoroughly politicized through constant propaganda and indoctrination. Party activists lectured workers in factories and peasants on collective farms, while newspapers, films, and radio broadcasts endlessly recounted socialist achievements and capitalist plots. Whereas the 1920s had seen considerable experimentation in modern art and theater, intellectuals were ordered by Stalin to become "engineers of human minds." Writers and artists who could effectively combine genuine creativity and political propaganda became the darlings of the regime. It became increasingly important for the successful writer and artist to glorify Russian nationalism. Russian history was rewritten so that early tsars such as Ivan the Terrible and Peter the Great became worthy forerunners of the greatest Russian leader of all—Stalin.

Stalin seldom appeared in public, but his presence was everywhere—in portraits, statues, books, and quotations from his "sacred" writings. Although the government persecuted religion and turned churches into "museums of atheism," the state had both an earthly religion and a high priest—Marxism-Leninism and Joseph Stalin.

Stalinist Terror and the Great Purges

In the mid-1930s, the great offensive to build socialism and a new socialist personality culminated in ruthless police terror and a massive purging of the Communist Party. First used by the Bolsheviks in the civil war to maintain their power, terror as state policy was revived in the collectivization drive against the peasants. The top members of the party and government publicly supported Stalin's initiatives, but there was some grumbling in the party. At a small gathering in November 1932, even Stalin's wife complained bitterly about the misery

of the people and the horrible famine in Ukraine. Stalin showered her with insults, and she died that same night, apparently by her own hand. In late 1934, Stalin's number-two man, Sergei Kirov, was suddenly and mysteriously murdered. Although Stalin himself probably ordered Kirov's murder, he used the incident to launch a reign of terror.

In August 1936, sixteen prominent Old Bolsheviks confessed to all manner of plots against Stalin in spectacular public trials in Moscow. Then in 1937 the secret police arrested a mass of lesser party officials and newer members, also torturing them and extracting more confessions for more show trials. In addition to the party faithful, union officials, managers, intellectuals, army officers, and countless ordinary citizens were struck down. In all, at least 8 million people were probably arrested, and millions of these were executed or never returned from prisons and forced-labor camps.

Stalin and the remaining party leadership recruited 1.5 million new members to take the place of those purged. Thus more than half of all Communist Party members in 1941 had joined since the purges. "These new men were 'thirty-something' products of the Second Revolution of the 1930s, Stalin's upwardly mobile yuppies, so to speak."[7] Often sons (and daughters) of workers, they had usually studied in the new technical schools, and they soon proved capable of managing the government and large-scale production. A product of the great purges, this new generation of Stalin-formed communists would serve the leader effectively until his death in 1953, and they would govern the Soviet Union until the early 1980s.

Stalin's mass purges remain baffling, for almost all historians believe that those purged posed no threat and confessed to crimes they had not committed. Certainly the highly publicized purges sent a warning to the people: no one was secure; everyone had to serve the party and its leader with redoubled devotion. Some Western scholars have also argued that the terror reflected a fully developed totalitarian state, which must always be fighting real or imaginary enemies.

The long-standing Western interpretation that puts the blame for the great purges on Stalin, which became very popular in Russia after the fall of communism, has nevertheless been challenged. Some historians argue that Stalin's fears were exaggerated but real. Moreover, these fears and suspicions were shared by many in the party and in the general population. Bombarded with ideology and political slogans, the population responded energetically to Stalin's directives. Investigations and trials snowballed into a mass hysteria, a new witch-hunt that claimed millions of victims.[8] In short, in this view of the 1930s, a deluded Stalin found large numbers of willing collaborators for crime as well as for achievement.

Mussolini and Fascism in Italy

Mussolini's movement and his seizure of power in 1922 were important steps in the rise of dictatorships in Europe between the two world wars. Like all the future dictators, the young Mussolini hated liberalism and wanted to destroy it in Italy. But although Mussolini began as a revolutionary socialist, like Stalin, he turned against the working class and successfully sought the support of conservatives. At the same time, Mussolini and his supporters were the first to call themselves "fascists"—revolutionaries determined to create a certain kind of totalitarian state. Yet few scholars today would argue that Mussolini succeeded. His dictatorship was brutal and theatrical, but it remained a halfway house between conservative authoritarianism and dynamic totalitarianism.

- **How did Mussolini's dictatorship come to power and govern in Italy?**

The Seizure of Power

In the early twentieth century, Italy was a liberal state with civil rights and a constitutional monarchy. On the eve of the First World War, the parliamentary regime finally granted universal male suffrage, and Italy appeared to be moving toward democracy. But there were serious problems. Much of the Italian population was still poor, and many peasants were more attached to their villages and local interests than to the national state. Moreover, the papacy, many devout Catholics, conservatives, and landowners remained strongly opposed to liberal institutions and to the heirs of Cavour and Garibaldi—the middle-class lawyers and politicians who ran the country largely for their own benefit. Relations between church and state were often tense. Class differences were also extreme, and a powerful revolutionary socialist movement had developed. Only in Italy among the main European countries did the radical left wing of the Socialist Party gain the leadership as early as 1912, and only in Italy did the Socialist Party unanimously oppose the war from the very beginning.[9]

The war worsened the political situation. Having fought on the side of the Allies almost exclusively for purposes of territorial expansion, the parliamentary government bitterly disappointed Italian nationalists with Italy's modest gains at Versailles. Workers and peasants also felt cheated: to win their support during the war, the government had promised social and land reform, which it did not deliver after the war.

The Russian Revolution inspired and energized Italy's revolutionary socialist movement. The Socialist Party quickly lined up with the Bolsheviks, and radical workers and peasants began occupying factories and seizing land in 1920. These actions scared and mobilized the property-owning classes. Moreover, after the war the pope lifted his ban on participation by Catholics in Italian politics, and a strong Catholic party quickly emerged. Thus by 1921 revolutionary socialists, antiliberal conservatives, and frightened property owners were all opposed—though for different reasons—to the liberal parliamentary government.

Into these crosscurrents of unrest and fear stepped the blustering, bullying Benito Mussolini (1883–1945). Son of a village schoolteacher and a poor blacksmith, Mussolini began his political career as a Socialist Party leader and radical newspaper editor before World War I. In 1914, powerfully influenced by antidemocratic cults of violent action, the young Mussolini urged that Italy join the Allies, a stand for which he was expelled from the Italian Socialist Party. Later Mussolini fought at the front and was wounded in 1917. Returning home, he began organizing bitter war veterans like himself into a band of fascists—from the Italian word for "a union of forces."

At first Mussolini's program was a radical combination of nationalist and socialist demands, including territorial expansion, benefits for workers, and land reform for peasants. As such, it competed directly with the well-organized Socialist Party and failed to get off the ground. When Mussolini saw that his violent verbal assaults on rival Socialists won him growing support from conservatives and the frightened middle classes, he shifted gears in 1920. In thought and action, Mussolini was a striking example of the turbulent uncertainty of the age of anxiety.

Mussolini and his growing private army of **Black Shirts** began to grow violent. Typically, a band of fascist toughs would roar off in trucks at night and swoop down on a few isolated Socialist organizers, beating them up and force-feeding them almost deadly doses of castor oil. Few people were killed, but socialist newspapers, union halls, and local Socialist Party headquarters were destroyed. Mussolini's toughs pushed Socialists out of the city governments of northern Italy.

A skillful politician, Mussolini allowed his followers to convince themselves that they were not just opposing the

"Reds" but also making a real revolution of their own, forging a strong, dynamic movement that would help the little people against the established interests. With the government breaking down in 1922, largely because of the chaos created by his direct-action bands, Mussolini stepped forward as the savior of order and property. Striking a conservative note in his speeches and gaining the sympathetic neutrality of army leaders, Mussolini demanded the resignation of the existing government and his own appointment by the king. In October 1922, to force matters, a large group of fascists marched on Rome to threaten the king and force him to call on Mussolini. The threat worked. Victor Emmanuel III (r. 1900–1946), who had no love for the old liberal politicians, asked Mussolini to form a new cabinet. Thus, after widespread violence and a threat of armed uprising, Mussolini seized power "legally." He was immediately granted dictatorial authority for one year by the king and the parliament.

The Regime in Action

Mussolini became dictator on the strength of Italians' rejection of parliamentary government coupled with fears of Soviet-style revolution. Yet what he intended to do with his power was by no means clear until 1924. Some of his dedicated supporters pressed for a "second revolution." Mussolini's ministers, however, included old conservatives, moderates, and even two reform-minded Socialists. A new electoral law was passed giving two-thirds of the representatives in the parliament to the party that won the most votes, a change that allowed the Fascist Party and its allies to win an overwhelming majority in 1924. Shortly thereafter, five of Mussolini's thugs kidnapped and murdered Giacomo Matteotti, the leader of the Socialists in the parliament. In the face of this outrage, the opposition demanded that Mussolini's armed squads be dissolved and all violence be banned.

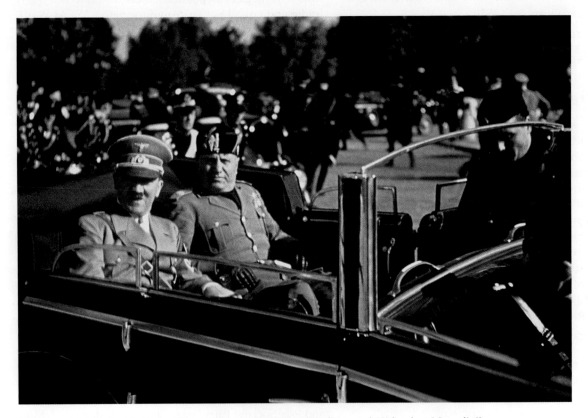

Hitler and Mussolini in Italy, May 1938 At first Mussolini distrusted Hitler, but Mussolini's conquest of Ethiopia in 1936 and Hitler's occupation of the Rhineland brought the two dictators together in a close alliance. State visits by Mussolini to Berlin in 1937 and by Hitler to Rome in 1938 included gigantic military reviews, which were filmed to impress the whole world. Uniformed Italian fascists accompany this motorcade. *(Time Life Pictures/Getty Images)*

Although Mussolini may or may not have ordered Matteotti's murder, he stood at the crossroads of a severe political crisis. After some hesitation, he charged forward. Declaring his desire to "make the nation Fascist," he imposed a series of repressive measures. Freedom of the press was abolished, elections were fixed, and the government ruled by decree. Mussolini arrested his political opponents, disbanded all independent labor unions, and put dedicated Fascists in control of Italy's schools. Moreover, he created a fascist youth movement, fascist labor unions, and many other fascist organizations. Mussolini trumpeted his goal in a famous slogan of 1926: "Everything in the state, nothing outside the state, nothing against the state." By the end of that year, Italy was a one-party dictatorship under Mussolini's unquestioned leadership.

Mussolini, however, did not complete the establishment of a modern totalitarian state. His Fascist Party never became all-powerful. It never destroyed the old power structure, as the Communists did in the Soviet Union, or succeeded in dominating it, as the Nazis did in Germany. Membership in the Fascist Party was more a sign of an Italian's respectability than a commitment to radical change. Interested primarily in personal power, Mussolini was content to compromise with the old conservative classes that controlled the army, the economy, and the state. He never tried to purge these classes or even move very vigorously against them. He controlled and propagandized labor but left big business to regulate itself, profitably and securely. There was no land reform.

Mussolini also drew increasing support from the Catholic Church. In the **Lateran Agreement** of 1929, he recognized the Vatican as a tiny independent state, and he agreed to give the church heavy financial support. The pope expressed his satisfaction and urged Italians to support Mussolini's government.

Nothing better illustrates Mussolini's unwillingness to harness everyone and everything for dynamic action than his treatment of women. He abolished divorce and told women to stay at home and produce children. To promote that goal, he decreed a special tax on bachelors in 1934. In 1938 women were limited by law to a maximum of 10 percent of the better-paying jobs in industry and government. Italian women appear not to have changed their attitudes or behavior in any important way under fascist rule.

Mussolini's government did not pass racial laws until 1938 and did not persecute Jews savagely until late in the Second World War, when Italy was under Nazi control. Nor did Mussolini establish a truly ruthless police state.

Only twenty-three political prisoners were condemned to death between 1926 and 1944. In spite of much pompous posing by the chauvinist leader and in spite of mass meetings, salutes, and a certain copying of Hitler's aggression in foreign policy after 1933, Mussolini's fascist Italy, though repressive and undemocratic, was never really totalitarian.

Hitler and Nazism in Germany

The most frightening dictatorship developed in Nazi Germany. A product of Hitler's evil genius as well as of Germany's social and political situation and the general attack on liberalism and rationality in the age of anxiety, the Nazi movement shared some of the characteristics of Mussolini's Italian model and was a form of fascism. But Nazi dictatorship smashed or took over most independent organizations, mobilized the economy, and violently persecuted the Jewish population. Thus Nazism asserted an unlimited claim over German society and proclaimed the ultimate power of its endlessly aggressive leader—Adolf Hitler. Truly totalitarian in its aspirations, the dynamism of Hitler and the Nazi elite was ultimately directed to war, territorial expansion, and racial aggression.

• *How did Hitler gain power, what policies did totalitarian Nazi Germany pursue, and why did they lead to World War II?*

The Roots of Nazism

Nazism grew out of many complex developments, of which the most influential were extreme nationalism and racism. These two ideas captured the mind of the young Hitler, and it was he who dominated Nazism for as long as it lasted.

Born the fourth child of a successful Austrian customs official and an indulgent mother, Adolf Hitler (1889–1945) spent his childhood in small towns in Austria. A good student in grade school, Hitler did poorly on reaching high school and dropped out at age fourteen following the death of his father. After four years of unfocused loafing, Hitler finally left for Vienna, where he lived a comfortable, lazy life on his generous orphan's pension and found most of the perverted beliefs that guided his life.

In Vienna Hitler soaked up extreme German nationalism, which was particularly strong there. Austro-German nationalists believed Germans to be a superior people and the natural rulers of central Europe. They often advocated union with Germany and violent expulsion of "inferior" peoples as the means of maintaining German domination of the Austro-Hungarian Empire.

Hitler was deeply impressed by Vienna's mayor, Karl Lueger (1844–1910). With the help of the Catholic trade unions, Lueger had succeeded in winning the support of the little people of Vienna, and he showed Hitler the enormous potential of anticapitalist and antiliberal propaganda. From Lueger and others, Hitler eagerly absorbed virulent anti-Semitism, racism, and hatred of Slavs. He developed an unshakable belief in the crudest, most exaggerated distortions of the Darwinian theory of survival, the superiority of Germanic races, and the inevitability of racial conflict. Thus anti-Semitism and racism became Hitler's most passionate convictions, his explanation for everything. The Jews, he claimed, directed an international conspiracy of finance capitalism and Marxian socialism against German culture, German unity, and the German race. Hitler's belief was totally irrational, but he never doubted it.

Although he moved to Munich in 1913 to avoid being drafted in the Austrian army, the lonely Hitler greeted the outbreak of the First World War as a salvation. He later wrote in his autobiography, *Mein Kampf*, that, "overcome by passionate enthusiasm, I fell to my knees and thanked heaven out of an overflowing heart." The struggle and discipline of war gave life meaning, and Hitler served bravely as a dispatch carrier on the western front.

When Germany was suddenly defeated in 1918, Hitler's world was shattered. Not only was he a fanatical nationalist, but war was also his reason for living. Convinced that Jews and Marxists had "stabbed Germany in the back," he vowed to fight on.

In late 1919, Hitler joined a tiny extremist group in Munich called the German Workers' Party. In addition to denouncing Jews, Marxists, and democrats, the German Workers' Party promised unity under a uniquely German "national socialism" that would abolish the injustices of capitalism and create a mighty "people's community." By 1921 Hitler had gained absolute control of this small but growing party. He was already a master of mass propaganda and political showmanship. His most effective tool was the mass rally, where he often worked his audience into a frenzy with wild, demagogic attacks on the Versailles treaty, the Jews, the war profiteers, and Germany's Weimar Republic.

Party membership multiplied tenfold after early 1922. In late 1923, the Weimar Republic seemed on the verge of collapse, and Hitler, inspired by Mussolini's recent easy victory, decided on an armed uprising in Munich. Despite the failure of the poorly organized plot and Hitler's arrest, Nazism had been born.

Hitler's Road to Power

At his trial, Hitler violently denounced the Weimar Republic, and he gained enormous publicity and attention. Moreover, he learned from his unsuccessful revolt. Hitler concluded that he had to undermine, rather than overthrow, the government and come to power legally through electoral competition. He forced his more violent supporters to accept his new strategy. He also used his brief prison term to dictate *Mein Kampf*. There he expounded on his basic themes: "race," with a stress on anti-Semitism; "living space," with a sweeping vision of war and conquered territory; and the leader-dictator (**Führer**), with unlimited, arbitrary power.

In the years of prosperity and relative stability between 1924 and 1929, Hitler concentrated on building his National Socialist German Workers' Party, or Nazi Party. By 1928 the party had 100,000 highly disciplined members under Hitler's absolute control. To appeal to the middle-class voters, Hitler de-emphasized the anticapitalist elements of national socialism and vowed to fight Bolshevism. Yet the Nazis remained a small splinter group in 1928, when they received only 2.6 percent of the vote in the general elections and twelve seats in the Reichstag. There the Nazi deputies pursued the legal strategy of using democracy to destroy democracy.

The Great Depression, shattering economic prosperity from 1929 on, presented Hitler with a fabulous opportunity. Unemployment jumped from 1.3 million in 1929 to 5 million in 1930. By the end of 1932, an incredible 43 percent of the labor force was unemployed. Industrial production fell by one-half between 1929 and 1932. No factor contributed more to Hitler's success than the economic crisis. Never very interested in economics before, Hitler began promising German voters economic as well as political and international salvation.

Above all, Hitler rejected free-market capitalism and advocated government programs to bring recovery. Hitler pitched his speeches especially to middle- and lower-middle-class groups—small business people, officeworkers, artisans, and peasants—as well as to skilled workers striving for middle-class status. Seized by panic as bankruptcies increased, unemployment soared, and the Communists made dramatic election gains, great numbers of middle- and lower-middle-class people "voted their pocketbooks"[10] and deserted the conservative and moderate parties for the Nazis. In the election of 1930, the Nazis won 6.5 million votes and 107 seats, and in July 1932 they gained 14.5 million votes—38 percent of the total—and became the largest party in the Reichstag.

The appeal to pocketbook interests was particularly

The Great Depression in Germany   As unemployment increased almost fourfold from 1929 to 1930, millions of Germans felt the lash of poverty and hunger. This soup kitchen, operated by the Salvation Army in Berlin in 1930, is serving up free meals to a broad cross section of society—young and old, weak and able-bodied. *(Ullstein Bilderdienst/The Granger Collection, New York)*

effective in the early 1930s because Hitler appeared more mainstream, playing down his anti-Jewish hatred and racist nationalism. A master of mass propaganda and psychology, he had written in *Mein Kampf* that the masses were the "driving force of the most important changes in this world" and were themselves driven by fanaticism and not by knowledge. To arouse such hysterical fanaticism, he believed that all propaganda had to be limited to a few simple, endlessly repeated slogans. But now when he harangued vast audiences with wild oratory and simple slogans, he featured "national rebirth" and the "crimes" of the Versailles treaty. And many uncertain individuals, surrounded by thousands of enthralled listeners, found a sense of belonging as well as hope for better times.

Online Study Center **Improve Your Grade**
Primary Source: The Art of Propaganda: A Master Reveals His Secrets (Hitler, 1924)

Hitler and the Nazis also appealed strongly to German youth. Indeed, in some ways the Nazi movement was a mass movement of young Germans. Hitler himself was only forty in 1929, and he and most of his top aides were much younger than other leading German politicians. "National Socialism is the organized will of the youth," proclaimed the official Nazi slogan, and the battle cry of Gregor Strasser, a leading Nazi organizer, was "Make way, you old ones."[11] In 1931 almost 40 percent of Nazi party members were under thirty, compared with 20 percent of Social Democrats. National recovery, exciting and rapid change, and personal advancement were the appeals of Nazism to millions of German youths.

Another reason Hitler came to power was that normal democratic government broke down as early as May 1930. Unable to gain the support of a majority in the Reichstag, Chancellor (chief minister) Heinrich Brüning convinced the president, the aging war hero General Hindenburg, to authorize rule by decree. Intending to use this emergency measure indefinitely, Brüning was determined to overcome the economic crisis by cutting back government spending and ruthlessly forcing down prices and wages. Brüning's ultra-orthodox policies not only intensified the economic collapse in Germany but also convinced many voters that the country's republican leaders were stupid and corrupt, thereby adding to Hitler's appeal.

The continuation of the struggle between the Social Democrats and the Communists, right up until the moment Hitler took power, was another aspect of the breakdown of democratic government. The Communists refused to cooperate with the Social Democrats, even though the two parties together outnumbered the Nazis in the Reichstag, even after the elections of 1932. German Communists (and the still complacent Stalin) were blinded by hatred of socialists and by ideology: the Communists believed that Hitler's fascism represented the last agonies of monopoly

Reaching a National Audience This poster ad promotes the VE-301 receiver, "the world's cheapest radio," and claims that "All Germany listens to the Führer on the people's receiver." Constantly broadcasting official views and attitudes, the state-controlled media also put the Nazis' favorite entertainment—gigantic mass meetings that climaxed with Hitler's violent theatrical speeches—on an invisible stage for millions. (*Bundesarchiv Koblenz Plak 003-022-025*)

capitalism and that a communist revolution would soon follow his taking power. Disunity on the left was undoubtedly another nail in the republic's coffin.

Finally, Hitler excelled in the dirty, backroom politics of the decaying Weimar Republic. That, in fact, brought him to power. In complicated infighting in 1932, he cleverly succeeded in gaining additional support from key people in the army and big business. These people thought they could use Hitler for their own advantage to get increased military spending, fat contracts, and tough measures against workers. Many conservative and nationalistic politicians thought similarly. They thus accepted Hitler's demand to join the government only if he became chancellor. There would be only two other National Socialists and nine solid conservatives as ministers, and in such a coalition government, they reasoned, Hitler could be used and controlled. On January 30, 1933, Adolf Hitler, leader of the largest party in Germany, was legally appointed chancellor by Hindenburg.

The Nazi State and Society

Hitler moved rapidly and skillfully to establish an unshakable dictatorship. Continuing to maintain legal appearances, he immediately called for new elections. In the midst of a violent electoral campaign, the Reichstag building was partly destroyed by fire. Hitler screamed that the Communist Party was responsible, and he convinced President Hindenburg to sign dictatorial emergency acts that practically abolished freedom of speech and assembly as well as most personal liberties.

When the Nazis won only 44 percent of the vote in the elections, Hitler immediately outlawed the Communist Party and arrested its parliamentary representatives. Then on March 23, 1933, the Nazis pushed through the Reichstag the so-called **Enabling Act,** which gave Hitler absolute dictatorial power for four years. Armed with the Enabling Act, Hitler and the Nazis moved to smash or control all independent organizations. Their deceitful stress on legality, coupled with divide-and-conquer techniques, disarmed the opposition until it was too late for effective resistance.

Germany soon became a one-party state. Only the Nazi Party was legal. Elections were farces. The Reichstag was jokingly referred to as the most expensive glee club in the country, for its only function was to sing hymns of praise to the Führer. Hitler and the Nazis took over the government bureaucracy intact, installing many Nazis in top positions. At the same time, they created a series of overlapping Nazi Party organizations responsible solely to Hitler.

As research in recent years shows, the resulting system of dual government was riddled with rivalries, contradictions, and inefficiencies. Thus the Nazi state was sloppy and often disorganized, lacking the all-encompassing unity that its propagandists claimed. Yet this fractured system suited Hitler and his purposes. He could play the established bureaucracy against his private, personal "party government" and maintain his freedom of action. Hitler could concentrate on general principles and the big decisions, which he always made.

In the economic sphere, one big decision outlawed strikes and abolished independent labor unions, which were replaced by the Nazi Labor Front. Professional people—doctors and lawyers, teachers and engineers—also saw their previously independent organizations swallowed up by Nazi associations. Publishing houses were put under Nazi control, and universities and writers were quickly brought into line. Democratic, socialist, and Jewish literature was put on ever-growing blacklists. Passionate students and pitiful professors burned forbidden books in public squares. Modern art and architecture were ruthlessly prohibited. Life became violently anti-intellectual. By 1934 a brutal dictatorship characterized by frightening dynamism and obedience to Hitler was already largely in place.

Only the army retained independence, and Hitler moved brutally and skillfully to establish his control there, too. The Nazi storm troopers (the SA), the quasi-military band of 3 million toughs in brown shirts who had fought communists and beaten up Jews before the Nazis took power, expected top positions in the army and even talked of a "second revolution" against capitalism. Hitler decided that the SA leaders had to be eliminated. Needing to preserve good relations with the army as well as with big business, he struck on the night of June 30, 1934. Hitler's elite personal guard—the SS—arrested and shot without trial roughly a thousand SA leaders and assorted political enemies. Shortly thereafter army leaders swore a binding oath of "unquestioning obedience . . . to the Leader of the German State and People, Adolf Hitler." The SS grew rapidly. Under its methodical, inhuman leader, Heinrich Himmler (1900–1945), the SS joined with the political police, the Gestapo, to expand its network of special courts and concentration camps. Nobody was safe.

From the beginning, Jews were a special object of Nazi persecution. By the end of 1934, most Jewish lawyers, doctors, professors, civil servants, and musicians had lost their jobs and the right to practice their professions. In 1935 the infamous Nuremberg Laws classified as Jewish anyone having one or more Jewish grandparents and deprived Jews of all rights of citizenship. By 1938 roughly 150,000 of Germany's half a million Jews had emigrated, sacrificing almost all their property in order to leave Germany.

Online Study Center **Improve Your Grade**
Primary Source: The Centerpiece of Nazi Racial Legislation: The Nuremberg Laws

In late 1938, the attack on the Jews accelerated. A well-organized wave of violence, known to history as "Kristallnacht," smashed windows, looted shops, and destroyed homes and synagogues. German Jews were then rounded up and made to pay for the damage. Another 150,000 Jews fled Germany. Some Germans privately opposed these outrages, but most went along or looked the other way. This lack of opposition reflected anti-Semitism to a degree still being debated by historians, but it certainly reflected the strong popular support Hitler's government enjoyed.

Hitler's Popularity

Hitler had promised the masses economic recovery—"work and bread"—and he delivered. Breaking with Brüning's do-nothing policies, Hitler launched a large public works program to help pull Germany out of the depression. Work began on superhighways, offices, gigantic sports stadiums, and public housing. Hitler also appointed as Germany's central banker a well-known conservative named Hjalmar Schacht, who skillfully restored credit and business. In 1936 an openly aggressive Hitler broke with Schacht, and Germany turned decisively toward rearmament and preparation for war. As a result of these policies (and plain good luck), unemployment dropped steadily, from 6 million in January 1933 to about 1 million in late 1936. By 1938 there was a shortage of workers, as unemployment fell to 2 percent, and women began to take jobs previously denied them by the antifeminist Nazis. Thus between 1932 and 1938, the standard of living for the average employed worker increased moderately. The profits of business rose sharply. For millions of people, economic recovery was tangible evidence that Nazi promises were more than show and propaganda.

For the masses of ordinary German citizens who were not Jews, Slavs, Gypsies, Jehovah's Witnesses, communists, or homosexuals, Hitler's government meant greater equality and more opportunities. In 1933 the position of the traditional German elites—the landed aristocracy, the wealthy capitalists, and the well-educated professional classes—was still very strong. Barriers between classes were generally high. Hitler's rule introduced changes that lowered these barriers. For example, stiff educational requirements, which favored the well-to-do, were relaxed. The new Nazi elite included many young and poorly educated dropouts, rootless lower-middle-class people like Hitler who rose to the top with breathtaking speed. More generally, the Nazis tolerated privilege and wealth only as long as they served the needs of the party. Even big business was constantly ordered around.

Yet few historians today believe that Hitler and the Nazis brought about a real social revolution, as an earlier generation of scholars often argued. Millions of modest middle-class and lower-middle-class people *felt* that Germany was becoming more open and equal, as Nazi propagandists constantly claimed. But quantitative studies show that the well-educated classes held on to most of their advantages and that only a modest social leveling occurred in the Nazi years. It is significant that the Nazis shared with the Italian fascists the stereotypic view of women as housewives and mothers. Only under the relentless pressure of war did they reluctantly mobilize large numbers of German women for work in offices and factories.

Hitler's rabid nationalism, which had helped him gain power, continued to appeal to Germans after 1933. Ever since the wars against Napoleon, many Germans had believed in a special mission for a superior German nation. The successes of Bismarck had furthered such feelings, and near-victory in World War I made nationalists eager for renewed expansion in the 1920s. Thus when Hitler went from one foreign triumph to another and a great German Empire seemed within reach, as we shall see, the majority of the population was delighted and kept praising the Führer's actions well into World War II.

Not all Germans supported Hitler, however, and a number of German groups actively resisted him after 1933. Tens of thousands of political enemies were imprisoned, and thousands were executed. But opponents of the Nazis pursued various goals, and they were never unified, a fact that helps account for their ultimate lack of success. In the first years of Hitler's rule, the principal resisters were the communists and the socialists in the trade unions. But the expansion of the SS system of terror after 1935 smashed most of these leftists. A second group of opponents arose in the Catholic and Protestant churches. However, their efforts were directed primarily at preserving genuine religious life, not at overthrowing Hitler. Finally in 1938 (and again in 1942–1944), some high-ranking army officers, who feared the consequences of Hitler's reckless aggression, plotted against him, unsuccessfully.

Aggression and Appeasement, 1933–1939

Although economic recovery and somewhat greater opportunity for social advancement won Hitler support, they were only byproducts of the Nazi regime. The guid-

ing and unique concepts of Nazism remained space and race—the territorial expansion of the superior German race. As we shall see, German expansion was facilitated by the uncertain and divided Western democracies, which tried to buy off Hitler to avoid war.

Hitler realized that his aggressive policies had to be carefully camouflaged at first, for Germany's army was limited by the Treaty of Versailles to only one hundred thousand men. As he told a group of army commanders in February 1933, the early stages of his policy of "conquest of new living space in the East and its ruthless Germanization" had serious dangers. If France had real leaders, Hitler said, it would "not give us time but attack us, presumably with its eastern satellites."[12] Thus, although Hitler loudly proclaimed his peaceful intentions, Germany's withdrawal from the League of Nations in October 1933 indicated that Gustav Stresemann's policy of peaceful cooperation (see pages 930–932) was dead.

Following this action, Hitler sought to incorporate independent Austria into a greater Germany. But a worried Mussolini threatened to fight, and Hitler backed down. When in March 1935 Hitler established a general military draft and declared the "unequal" disarmament clauses of the Treaty of Versailles null and void, other countries appeared to understand the danger. With France taking the lead, Italy and Great Britain protested strongly and warned against future aggressive actions.

Yet the emerging united front against Hitler quickly collapsed. Of crucial importance, Britain adopted a policy of **appeasement,** granting Hitler everything he could reasonably want (and more) in order to avoid war. The first step was an Anglo-German naval agreement in June 1935 that broke Germany's isolation. The second step came in March 1936 when Hitler suddenly marched his armies into the demilitarized Rhineland, brazenly violating the Treaties of Versailles and Locarno. This was the last good chance to stop the Nazis, but an uncertain France would not move without British support, and Britain refused to act (Map 29.1).

British appeasement, which practically dictated French policy, lasted far into 1939. It was motivated by British feelings of guilt toward Germany and the pacifism of a population still horrified by the memory of the First World War. As in Germany, many powerful conservatives in Britain underestimated Hitler. They believed that Soviet communism was the real danger and that Hitler could be used to stop it. Such strong anticommunist feelings made an alliance between the Western Powers and Stalin unlikely.

As Britain and France opted for appeasement and the Soviet Union watched all developments suspiciously, Hitler found powerful allies. In 1935 the bombastic

MAP 29.1 The Growth of Nazi Germany, 1933–1939 Until March 1939, Hitler brought ethnic Germans into the Nazi state; then he turned on the Slavic peoples he had always hated. He stripped Czechoslovakia of its independence and prepared for an attack on Poland in September 1939.

Mussolini attacked the independent African kingdom of Ethiopia. The Western Powers and the League of Nations piously condemned Italian aggression, but Hitler supported Italy energetically and overcame Mussolini's lingering doubts about the Nazis. The result in late 1936 was an agreement on close cooperation between Italy and Germany, the so-called Rome-Berlin Axis. Japan, which had been expanding into Manchuria since 1931, soon joined the Axis alliance.

At the same time, Germany and Italy intervened in the Spanish civil war (1936–1939), which broke out in July 1936. Their support eventually helped General Francisco Franco's fascist movement defeat republican Spain. Spain's only official aid came from the Soviet Union, for public opinion in Britain and especially in France was hopelessly divided on the Spanish question.

In late 1937 Hitler moved forward with plans to crush Austria and Czechoslovakia at the earliest possible moment

Events Leading to World War II

1919	Treaty of Versailles is signed; J. M. Keynes publishes *Economic Consequences of the Peace.*
1919–1920	U.S. Senate rejects the Treaty of Versailles.
1921	Germany is billed $33 billion in reparations.
1922	Mussolini seizes power in Italy; Germany proposes a moratorium on reparations.
January 1923	France and Belgium occupy the Ruhr; Germany orders passive resistance to the occupation.
October 1923	Stresemann agrees to reparations based on Germany's ability to pay.
1924	Dawes Plan: German reparations are reduced and put on a sliding scale. Large U.S. loans to Germany are recommended to promote German recovery; Adolf Hitler dictates *Mein Kampf.*
1924–1929	Spectacular German economic recovery occurs; circular flow of international funds enables sizable reparations payments.
1925	Treaties of Locarno promote European security and stability.
1926	Germany joins the League of Nations.
1928	Kellogg-Briand Pact renounces war as an instrument of international affairs.
1929	U.S. stock market crashes and triggers worldwide financial crisis.
1929–1939	Great Depression rages.
1931	Japan invades Manchuria.
1932	Nazis become the largest party in the Reichstag.
January 1933	Hitler is appointed chancellor of Germany.
March 1933	Reichstag passes the Enabling Act, granting Hitler absolute dictatorial power.
October 1933	Germany withdraws from the League of Nations.
1935	Nuremberg Laws deprive Jews of all rights of citizenship.
March 1935	Hitler announces German rearmament.
June 1935	Anglo-German naval agreement is signed.
October 1935	Mussolini invades Ethiopia and receives Hitler's support.
March 1936	German armies move unopposed into the demilitarized Rhineland.
July 1936	Civil war breaks out in Spain.
1937	Japan invades China; Rome-Berlin Axis in effect.
March 1938	Germany annexes Austria.
September 1938	Munich Conference: Britain and France agree to German seizure of the Sudetenland from Czechoslovakia.
March 1939	Germany occupies the rest of Czechoslovakia; appeasement ends in Britain.
August 1939	Nazi-Soviet nonaggression pact is signed.
September 1, 1939	Germany invades Poland.
September 3, 1939	Britain and France declare war on Germany.

Hitler's Success with Aggression
This biting criticism of appeasing leaders by the cartoonist David Low appeared shortly after Hitler remilitarized the Rhineland. Appeasement also appealed to millions of ordinary citizens in Britain and France, who wanted to avoid at any cost another great war. *(Solo Syndication/Associated Newspapers)*

as the first step in his long-contemplated drive to the east for living space. By threatening Austria with invasion, Hitler forced the Austrian chancellor in March 1938 to put local Nazis in control of the government. The next day, German armies moved in unopposed, and Austria became two more provinces of Greater Germany (see Map 29.1).

Simultaneously, Hitler began demanding that the pro-Nazi, German-speaking minority of western Czechoslovakia—the Sudetenland—be turned over to Germany. Yet democratic Czechoslovakia was prepared to defend itself. Moreover, France had been Czechoslovakia's ally since 1924; and if France fought, the Soviet Union was pledged to help. War appeared inevitable, but appeasement triumphed again. In September 1938, Chamberlain flew to Germany three times in fourteen days. In these negotiations, to which the U.S.S.R. was deliberately not invited, Chamberlain and the French agreed with Hitler that the Sudetenland should be ceded to Germany immediately. Returning to London from the Munich Conference, Chamberlain told cheering crowds that he had secured "peace with honor . . . peace for our time." Sold out by the Western Powers, Czechoslovakia gave in.

Confirmed once again in his opinion of the Western democracies as weak and racially degenerate, Hitler accelerated his aggression. His armies occupied the Czech lands in March 1939. The effect on Western public opinion was electrifying. For the first time, there was no possible rationale of self-determination for Nazi aggression since Hitler was seizing Czechs and Slovaks as captive peoples. Thus when Hitler used the question of German minorities in Danzig as a pretext to confront Poland, a suddenly militant Chamberlain declared that Britain and France would fight if Hitler attacked his eastern neighbor. Hitler did not take these warnings seriously and decided to press on.

In an about-face that stunned the world, Hitler offered and Stalin signed a ten-year Nazi-Soviet nonaggression pact in August 1939. Each dictator promised to remain neutral if the other became involved in war. An attached secret protocol, which became known only after the war, ruthlessly divided eastern Europe into German and Soviet zones, "in the event of a political territorial reorganization." The nonaggression pact itself was enough to make Britain and France cry treachery, for they, too, had been negotiating with Stalin. But Stalin had remained distrustful of Western intentions, and Hitler had offered immediate territorial gain.

For Hitler, everything was set. He told his generals on the day of the nonaggression pact, "My only fear is that at the last moment some dirty dog will come up with a mediation plan." On September 1, 1939, German armies and warplanes smashed into Poland from three sides.

Two days later, Britain and France, finally true to their word, declared war on Germany. The Second World War had begun.

The Second World War

War broke out in both western and eastern Europe because Hitler's ambitions were essentially unlimited. On both war fronts, Nazi soldiers scored enormous successes until late 1942, establishing a vast empire of death and destruction. Hitler's victories increased tensions in Asia between Japan and the United States and prompted Japan to attack the United States and overrun much of Southeast Asia. Yet reckless aggression by Germany and Japan also raised a mighty coalition determined to smash the aggressors. Led by Britain, the United States, and the Soviet Union, the Grand Alliance—to use Winston Churchill's favorite name for it—functioned quite effectively in military terms. Thus the Nazi and Japanese empires proved short-lived.

● **How did Germany and Japan create enormous empires that were defeated by the Allies—Britain, the Soviet Union, and the United States?**

Hitler's Empire, 1939–1942

Using planes, tanks, and trucks in the first example of a **blitzkrieg,** or "lightning war," Hitler's armies crushed Poland in four weeks. While the Soviet Union quickly took its part of the booty—the eastern half of Poland and the independent Baltic states of Lithuania, Estonia, and Latvia—French and British armies dug in in the west. They expected another war of attrition and economic blockade.

In spring 1940, the lightning war struck again. After occupying Denmark, Norway, and Holland, German motorized columns broke through southern Belgium, split the Franco-British forces, and trapped the entire British army on the beaches of Dunkirk. By heroic efforts, the British withdrew their troops but not their equipment.

France was taken by the Nazis. Aging Marshal Henri-Philippe Pétain formed a new French government—the so-called Vichy government—to accept defeat, and German armies occupied most of France. By July 1940, Hitler ruled practically all of western continental Europe; Italy was an ally, and the Soviet Union and Spain were friendly neutrals. Only Britain, led by the uncompromising Winston Churchill (1874–1965), remained unconquered.

London, 1940 Hitler believed that his relentless terror bombing of London—the "blitz"—could break the will of the British people. He was wrong. The blitz caused enormous destruction, but Londoners went about their business with courage and calm determination, as this unforgettable image of a milkman in the rubble suggests. (*Corbis*)

Online Study Center Improve Your Grade
Primary Source: "This Was Their Finest Hour"

Germany sought to gain control of the air, the necessary first step toward an amphibious invasion of Britain. In the Battle of Britain, up to a thousand German planes attacked British airfields and key factories in a single day, dueling with British defenders high in the skies. Losses were heavy on both sides. Then in September Hitler angrily turned from military objectives to indiscriminate bombing of British cities in an attempt to break British morale. British aircraft factories increased production, and the heavily bombed people of London defiantly dug in. In September and October 1940, Britain was beating Germany three to one in the air war. There was no possibility of an immediate German invasion of Britain.

Turning from Britain and moving into the Balkans by April 1941, Hitler now allowed his lifetime obsession with a vast eastern European empire for the "master race" to dictate policy. In June 1941, German armies suddenly attacked the Soviet Union along a vast front (see Map 29.2). By October Leningrad was practically surrounded, Moscow was besieged, and most of Ukraine had been conquered. But the Soviets did not collapse, and when a severe winter struck German armies outfitted in summer uniforms, the invaders were stopped.

Stalled in Russia, Hitler ruled over a vast European empire stretching from the outskirts of Moscow to the English Channel. Hitler, the Nazi leadership, and the loyal German army were positioned to greatly accelerate construction of their "New Order" in Europe, and they continued their efforts until their final collapse in 1945. In doing so, they showed what Nazi victory would have meant.

Hitler's **New Order** was based firmly on the guiding principle of Nazi totalitarianism: racial imperialism. Within this New Order, the Nordic peoples—the Dutch, Norwegians, and Danes—received preferential treatment, for they were racially related to the master race, the Germans. The French, an "inferior" Latin people, occupied a middle position. All the occupied territories of western and northern Europe were exploited with increasing intensity. Material shortages and both mental and physical suffering afflicted millions of people.

Slavs in the conquered territories to the east were treated with harsh hatred as "subhumans." At the height of his success in 1941 and 1942, Hitler set the tone. He painted for his intimate circle the fantastic vision of a vast eastern colonial empire where Poles, Ukrainians, and Russians would be enslaved and forced to die out, while Germanic peasants resettled the resulting abandoned lands. But he needed countless helpers and many ambitious initiators to turn his dreams into reality. These accomplices came forth. Himmler and the elite corps of SS volunteers shared Hitler's ideology of barbarous racial imperialism, and they rarely wavered in their efforts to realize his goals.[13] Supported (or condoned) by military commanders and German policemen in the occupied territories, the SS corps pressed relentlessly to implement the program of destruction and to create a "mass settlement space" for Germans. Many Poles, captured communists, Gypsies, and Jehovah's Witnesses were murdered in cold blood.

The Holocaust

The ultimate abomination of Nazi racism was the condemnation of all European Jews to extermination in the Holocaust. After the fall of Warsaw, the Nazis stepped up their expulsion campaign and began deporting all German Jews to occupied Poland. There they and Jews from all over Europe were concentrated in ghettos, compelled to wear the Jewish star, and turned into slave laborers.

Online Study Center Improve Your Grade
Primary Source: The Ghettoization of the Jews: Prelude to the Final Solution

In 1941, as part of the "war of annihilation" in the Soviet Union, expulsion spiraled into extermination. On the Russian front, Himmler's special SS killing squads and also regular army units forced Soviet Jews to dig giant pits, which became mass graves as the victims were lined up on the edge and cut down by machine guns. Then in late 1941, Hitler and the Nazi leadership, in some still-debated combination, ordered the SS to stop all Jewish emigration from Europe and speeded up planning for mass murder. As one German diplomat put it, "The Jewish Question must be resolved in the course of the war, for only so can it be solved without a worldwide outcry."[14] The "final solution of the Jewish question"—the murder of every single Jew—had begun. Jews were systematically arrested, packed like cattle onto freight trains, and dispatched to extermination camps. Many Jews could hardly imagine the enormity of the crime that lay before them.

Arriving at their destination, small numbers of Jews were sent to nearby slave labor camps, where they were starved and systematically worked to death. But most of the victims were moved immediately to the death camps, where they were taken by force or deception to "shower rooms" that were actually gas chambers. These gas chambers, first perfected in the quiet, efficient execution

Hitler's Greater Germany

Allied with Germany

Occupied by Germany and its allies

Grand Alliance

Neutral nations

X **Major battles**

SOVIET UNION

Russian front, Nov. 1942

Siege of Stalingrad, Aug. 21, 1942–Jan. 31, 1943

Stalingrad

Russian front, Dec. 1941

Baku

Volga

Don

Moscow

Tula

Smolensk

Russian front, Spring 1944

Kiev

UKRAINE

Dnieper

Leningrad

Siege of Leningrad, Sept. 1941–Jan. 1944

FINLAND

Helsinki

Riga

Minsk

SWEDEN

Stockholm

Baltic Sea

NORWAY

Oslo

DENMARK

Copenhagen

Posen

Warsaw

SLOVAKIA

Cracow

Russian front, Feb. 1945

Vistula

Berlin

GERMANY

Elbe

Vienna

HUNGARY

Budapest

CROATIA

YUGOSLAVIA

SERBIA

ROMANIA

Bucharest

Danube

BULGARIA

Sofia

GREECE

Athens

ALBANIA

Black Sea

Yalta

TURKEY

Ankara

CYPRUS

SYRIA

TRANS-JORDAN (Br. Mandate)

PALESTINE (Br. Mandate)

Suez Canal

Nile

Cairo

EGYPT

El Alamein, Summer 1942

Mediterranean Sea

Crete

Sicily

MALTA (Gr. Br.)

Sicily, July 1943

Salerno, Sept. 1943

Allies invade Sicily and Italy, July–Sept. 1943

Monte Cassino, May 1944

ITALY

Italian front, Feb. 1945

Rome

Bologna

Po

SWITZERLAND

Western front, Feb. 1945

Rhine Crossing, March 7, 1945

German surrender Reims, May 7, 1945 Berlin, May 8, 1945

NETHERLANDS

Dunkirk

BELGIUM

Battle of the Bulge, Dec. 1944

Rhine

Paris

FRANCE

Vichy

VICHY FRANCE (occupied Nov. 1942)

Allies land in Provence, Aug. 15, 1944

Axis troops occupy Vichy France, Nov. 10 and 11, 1942

Invasion of Normandy, June 6, 1944

London

GREAT BRITAIN

Battle of Britain, Fall 1940

NORTHERN IRELAND

IRELAND

North Sea

ATLANTIC OCEAN

PORTUGAL

Lisbon

SPAIN

Madrid

GIBRALTAR (Gr. Br.)

SP. MOROCCO

Ebro

Casablanca, Nov. 1942

FRENCH MOROCCO

ALGERIA (Vichy France)

TUNISIA

Rommel defeated in Tunisia; Axis troops evacuated, May 1943

LIBYA

400 Mi.

400 Km.

200

200

0

0

Prelude to Murder This photo captures the terrible inhumanity of Nazi racism and the Holocaust. Frightened and bewildered families from the soon-to-be-destroyed Warsaw Ghetto are being forced out of their homes by German soldiers for deportation to concentration camps. There they face murder in the gas chambers. *(Hulton Archive/Getty Images)*

of seventy thousand mentally ill Germans between 1938 and 1941, permitted rapid, hideous, and thoroughly bureaucratized mass murder. For fifteen to twenty minutes came the terrible screams and gasping sobs of men,

women, and children choking to death on poison gas. Then, only silence. Special camp workers quickly yanked the victims' gold teeth from their jaws, and the bodies were then cremated or sometimes boiled for oil to make soap. At Auschwitz-Birkenau, the most infamous of the Nazi death factories, as many as twelve thousand human beings were slaughtered each day. The extermination of European Jews was the ultimate monstrosity of Nazi racism and racial imperialism. By 1945, 6 million Jews had been murdered. (See the feature "Individuals in Society: Primo Levi.")

Who was responsible for this terrible crime? An older generation of historians usually laid most of the guilt on Hitler and the Nazi leadership. Ordinary Germans had little knowledge of the extermination camps, it was argued, and those who cooperated had no alternative given the brutality of Nazi terror and totalitarian control. But in recent years, many studies have revealed a much broader participation of German people in the Holocaust and popular indifference (or worse) to the fate of the Jews. Yet exactly why so many perpetrated or condoned Nazi crimes has remained unclear.

In a controversial work, the American historian Daniel

Mapping the Past

MAP 29.2 World War II in Europe The map shows the extent of Hitler's empire before the Battle of Stalingrad in late 1942 and the subsequent advances of the Allies until Germany surrendered on May 7, 1945. This map, combined with Map 29.1 on page 963, can be used to trace the rise and fall of the Nazi empire over time. **1** First, using Map 29.1, what was the first country to be conquered by Hitler (and divided with the Soviet Union)? **2** Second, locate Germany's advance and retreat on the Russian front at different dates: December 1941, November 1942, Spring 1944, and February 1945. Locate the position of British and American forces on the battlefield at similar points in time, and then compare the respective Russian and British-American positions. What implications might the battle lines on February 1945 have for the postwar settlement in Europe?

Online Study Center **Improve Your Grade** Interactive Map: WWII in Europe

Goldhagen reignited discussion of Nazi crimes by arguing that, above all, the extreme anti-Semitism of "ordinary Germans" led them to respond to Hitler and to become his "willing executioners" in World War II.[15] Yet in most occupied countries, local non-German officials also cooperated in the arrest and deportation of Jews to a large extent. As in Germany, only a few exceptional bystanders did not turn a blind eye. Thus some scholars have concluded that the key for most Germans (and most people in occupied countries) was that they felt no personal responsibility for Jews and therefore were not prepared to help them. This meant that many individuals, conditioned by Nazi racist propaganda but also influenced by peer pressure and brutalizing wartime violence, were psychologically prepared to join the SS ideologues and perpetrate ever-greater crimes. They were ready to plumb the depths of evil and to spiral downward from mistreatment to arrest to mass murder.

Japan's Empire in Asia

By late 1938, 1.5 million Japanese troops were bogged down in China, holding a great swath of territory but unable to defeat the Nationalists and the Communists (see Map 29.3). Nor had Japan succeeded in building a large, self-sufficient Asian economic zone, for it still depended on oil and scrap metal from the Netherlands East Indies and the United States. Thus Japanese leaders followed events in Europe closely, looking for alliances and actions that might improve their position in Asia. At home they gave free rein to the anti-Western ultranationalism that had risen in the 1920s and 1930s. In speeches, schools, and newspapers ultranationalists proclaimed Japan's liberating mission in Asia, glorified the warrior virtues of honor and sacrifice, and demanded absolute devotion to the semidivine emperor.

The outbreak of war in Europe in 1939 and Hitler's early victories opened up opportunities for the Japanese in Southeast Asia, where European empires appeared vulnerable. Expanding the war in China, the Japanese also pressured the Dutch to surrender control of the Netherlands East Indies and its rich oil fields, but Dutch colonial officials, backed by the British and the Americans, refused. The United States had repeatedly condemned Japanese aggression in China, and it now feared that embattled Britain would collapse if it lost the support of its Asian colonies.

Japan's invasion of southern Indochina in July 1941 further worsened relations with the United States. President Franklin Roosevelt demanded that Japan withdraw from China, which was completely unacceptable to the Japanese, and they refused. The United States responded with strong action, cutting off the sale of U.S. oil to Japan and thereby reducing Japan's oil supplies by 90 percent. Japanese leaders believed increasingly that war with the United States was inevitable, for Japan's battle fleet would run out of fuel in eighteen months, and its industry would be crippled. After much debate and almost in desperation, Japanese leaders decided to launch a surprise attack on the United States. They hoped to cripple their Pacific rival, gain time to build a defensible Asian empire, and eventually win an ill-defined compromise peace.

The Japanese attack on the U.S. naval base at Pearl Harbor in the Hawaiian Islands was a complete surprise but a limited success. On December 7, 1941, the Japanese sank or crippled every American battleship, but by chance all the all-important American aircraft carriers were at sea and escaped unharmed. More important, Pearl Harbor humiliated Americans and brought them together in a spirit of anger and revenge.

Hitler immediately declared war on the United States. Simultaneously, Japanese armies successfully attacked European and American colonies in Southeast Asia. Japanese armies were small (because most soldiers remained in China), but they were well trained, highly motivated, and very successful. By May 1942 Japan held a vast empire in Southeast Asia and the western Pacific (see Map 29.3).

The Japanese claimed that they were freeing Asians from Western imperialism, and they called their empire the Greater East Asian Co-prosperity Sphere. Some—perhaps many—Japanese army officers and officials sincerely believed that they were creating a mutually advantageous union for the long-term development of Asia. Initially they tapped currents of nationalist sentiment, and most local populations were glad to see the Western Powers go. But Asian faith in "co-prosperity" and support for Japan steadily declined as the war went on. Why was this so?

First of all, although the Japanese set up anticolonial governments and promised genuine independence, real power always rested with Japanese military commanders and their superiors in Tokyo. The "independent" governments were basically shams. Second, the Japanese never really delivered on their promises because they were constantly improvising a frantic defense of their far-flung conquests from relentless attack by a determined foe with vastly superior resources. Thus, as living standards plummeted in Japan and heavy industry sputtered, the Japanese occupiers exploited local peoples for Japan's wartime needs. Finally, the Japanese often exhibited

Individuals in Society

Primo Levi

Most Jews deported to Auschwitz were murdered as soon as they arrived, but the Nazis made some prisoners into slave laborers and a few of these survived. Primo Levi (1919–1987), an Italian Jew, became one of the most influential witnesses to the Holocaust and its death camps.

Like much of Italy's small Jewish community, Levi's family belonged to the urban professional classes. The young Primo graduated in 1941 from the University of Turin with highest honors in chemistry. But since 1938, when Italy introduced racial laws, he had faced growing discrimination, and two years after graduation he joined the antifascist resistance movement. Quickly captured, he was deported to Auschwitz with 650 Italian Jews in February 1944. Stone-faced SS men picked only ninety-six men and twenty-nine women to work in their respective labor camps. Primo was one of them.

Nothing prepared Levi for what he encountered. The Jewish prisoners were kicked, punched, stripped, branded with tattoos, crammed into huts, and worked unmercifully. Hoping for some sign of prisoner solidarity in this terrible environment, Levi found only a desperate struggle of each against all and enormous status differences among prisoners. Many stunned and bewildered newcomers, beaten and demoralized by their bosses—the most privileged prisoners—simply collapsed and died. Others struggled to secure their own privileges, however small, because food rations and working conditions were so abominable that ordinary Jewish prisoners perished in two to three months.

Sensitive and noncombative, Levi found himself sinking into oblivion. But instead of joining the mass of the "drowned," he became one of the "saved"—a complicated surprise with moral implications that he would ponder all his life. As Levi explained in *Survival in Auschwitz* (1947), the usual road to salvation in the camps was some kind of collaboration with German power.* Savage German criminals were released from prison to become brutal camp guards; non-Jewish political prisoners competed for jobs entitling them to better conditions, and, especially troubling for Levi, a small number of Jewish men plotted and struggled for the power of life and death over other Jewish prisoners. Though not one of these Jewish bosses, Levi believed that he himself, like almost all survivors, had entered the "gray zone" of moral compromise. Only a very few superior individuals, "the stuff of saints and martyrs," survived the death camps without shifting their moral stance.

For Levi, compromise and salvation came from his profession. Interviewed by a German technocrat for the camp's synthetic rubber program, Levi performed brilliantly in scientific German and savored his triumph as a Jew over Nazi racism. Work in the warm camp laboratory offered Levi opportunities to pilfer equipment that could then be traded for food and necessities with other prisoners. Levi also gained critical support from three saintly prisoners, who refused to do wicked and hateful acts. And he counted "luck" as essential for his survival: in the camp infirmary with scarlet fever in February 1945 as advancing Russian armies prepared to liberate the camp, Levi was not evacuated by the Nazis and shot to death like most Jewish prisoners.

After the war Primo Levi was forever haunted by the nightmare that the Holocaust would be ignored or forgotten. Always ashamed that so many people whom he considered better than himself had perished, he wrote and lectured tirelessly to preserve the memory of Jewish victims and guilty Nazis. Wanting the world to understand the Jewish genocide in all its complexity so that never again would people tolerate such atrocities, he grappled tirelessly with his vision of individual choice and moral compromise in a hell designed to make the victims collaborate and persecute each other.

Primo Levi, who never stopped thinking, writing, and speaking about the Holocaust.
(Giansanti/Corbis Sygma)

Questions for Analysis

1. Describe Levi's experience at Auschwitz. How did camp prisoners treat each other? Why?
2. What does Levi mean by the "gray zone"? How is this concept central to his thinking?
3. Will a vivid historical memory of the Holocaust help to prevent future genocide?

*Primo Levi, *Survival in Auschwitz: The Nazi Assault on Humanity,* rev. ed. 1958 (London: Collier Books, 1961), pp. 79–84, and *The Drowned and the Saved* (New York: Summit Books, 1988). These powerful testimonies are highly recommended.

Online Study Center **Improve Your Grade**
Going Beyond Individuals in Society

MAP 29.3 World War II in the Pacific Japanese forces overran an enormous amount of territory in 1942, which the Allies slowly recaptured in a long, bitter struggle. As this map shows, Japan still held a large Asian empire in August 1945, when the unprecedented devastation of atomic warfare suddenly forced it to surrender.

Online Study Center **Improve Your Grade** Interactive Map: WWII in the Pacific

great cruelty toward prisoners of war and civilians, as they had toward the Chinese since 1937. Recurring cruel behavior aroused local populations against the invaders.

The Grand Alliance

While the Nazis and the Japanese built their savage empires, the Allies faced the hard fact that chance, rather than choice, had brought them together. Stalin had been cooperating fully with Hitler between August 1939 and June 1941, and only the Japanese attack on Pearl Harbor in December 1941 had overwhelmed powerful isolationism in the United States.

As a first step toward building an unshakable alliance, U.S. president Franklin D. Roosevelt accepted the contention of British prime minister Winston Churchill that the United States should agree on a policy of **Europe first.** Only after Hitler was defeated would the Allies turn toward the Pacific for an all-out attack on Japan, the lesser threat. The Allies also put immediate military needs first, postponing until after the war tough political questions relating to the eventual peace settlement that might have split the alliance.

To further encourage mutual trust, the Allies adopted the principle of the "unconditional surrender" of Germany and Japan. This policy cemented the Grand Alliance because it denied Hitler any hope of dividing his foes. It also meant that victorious Soviet and Anglo-American armies would almost certainly come together to divide all of Germany, and that Japan would fight to the bitter end.

The military resources of the Grand Alliance were awesome. The strengths of the United States were its mighty industry, its large population, and its national unity. Gearing up rapidly for all-out war in 1942, the United States acquired a unique capacity to wage global war. In 1943 it outproduced not only Germany, Italy, and Japan but also all of the rest of the world combined.

Britain continued to make a great contribution as well. The British economy was totally and effectively mobilized, and the sharing of burdens through rationing and heavy taxes on war profits maintained social harmony. By early 1943 the Americans and the British were combining small aircraft carriers with radar-guided bombers to rid the Atlantic of German submarines. Britain, the impregnable floating fortress, became a gigantic frontline staging area for the decisive blow to the heart of Germany.

As for the Soviet Union, so great was its strength that it might well have defeated Germany without Western help. In the face of the German advance, whole factories and populations were successfully evacuated to eastern Russia and Siberia. There war production was reorganized and expanded, and the Red Army was increasingly well supplied and well led. Above all, Stalin drew on the massive support and heroic determination of the Soviet people, especially those in the central Russian heartland. Broad-based Russian nationalism, as opposed to narrow communist ideology, became the powerful unifying force in what the Soviet people appropriately called the "Great Patriotic War of the Fatherland."

Finally, the United States, Britain, and the Soviet Union had the resources of much of the world at their command. They were also aided by a growing resistance movement against the Nazis throughout Europe, even in Germany. After the Soviet Union was invaded in June 1941, communists throughout Europe took the lead in the underground resistance, joined by a growing number of patriots, Christians, and agents sent by governments-in-exile in London.

The War in Europe, 1942–1945

Barely halted at the gates of Moscow and Leningrad in 1941, the Germans renewed their offensive against the Soviet Union in July 1942, driving toward the southern city of Stalingrad and occupying most of the city in a month of incredibly savage house-to-house fighting.

Then, in November 1942, Soviet armies counterattacked. They rolled over Romanian and Italian troops to the north and south of Stalingrad, quickly closing the trap and surrounding the entire German Sixth Army of 300,000 men. The surrounded Germans were systematically destroyed, until by the end of January 1943 only 123,000 soldiers were left to surrender. Hitler, who had refused to allow a retreat, had suffered a catastrophic defeat. In summer 1943, the larger, better-equipped Soviet armies took the offensive and began moving forward (see Map 29.2).

Not yet prepared to attack Germany directly through France, the Western Allies saw heavy fighting in North Africa from 1940 onward (see Map 29.2). In May 1942, combined German and Italian armies were finally defeated by British forces only seventy miles from Alexandria at the Battle of El Alamein. Almost immediately thereafter, an Anglo-American force landed in Morocco and Algeria. These French possessions, which were under the control of Pétain's Vichy government, quickly went over to the side of the Allies.

Having driven the Axis powers from North Africa by spring 1943, Allied forces maintained the initiative by invading Sicily and then mainland Italy. Mussolini was deposed by a war-weary people, and the new Italian government publicly accepted unconditional surrender in September 1943. Italy, it seemed, was liberated. Yet German commandos rescued Mussolini in a daring raid and put him at the head of a puppet government. German armies seized Rome and all of northern Italy. Fighting continued in Italy.

Indeed, bitter fighting continued in Europe for almost two years. Germany, less fully mobilized for war than Britain in 1941, applied itself to total war in 1942 and enlisted millions of German women and millions of prisoners of war and slave laborers from all across occupied Europe in that effort. Between early 1942 and July 1944, German war production actually tripled in spite of heavy bombing by the British and American air forces. German resistance against Hitler also failed. After an unsuccessful attempt on Hitler's life in July 1944, SS fanatics brutally liquidated thousands of Germans. Terrorized at home and frightened by the prospect of unconditional surrender, the Germans fought on with suicidal stoicism.

On June 6, 1944, American and British forces under General Dwight Eisenhower landed on the beaches of Normandy, France, in history's greatest naval invasion. In a hundred dramatic days, more than 2 million men and almost half a million vehicles pushed inland and broke through German lines. Rejecting proposals to strike straight at Berlin in a massive attack, Eisenhower moved forward cautiously on a broad front. Not until March 1945 did American troops cross the Rhine and enter Germany.

The Soviets, who had been advancing steadily since July 1943, reached the outskirts of Warsaw by August 1944. For the next six months, they moved southward into Romania, Hungary, and Yugoslavia. In January 1945, the Red Army again moved westward through Poland, and on April 26 it met American forces on the Elbe River. The Allies had closed their vise on Nazi Germany and overrun Europe. As Soviet forces fought their way into Berlin, Hitler committed suicide in his bunker, and on May 7 the remaining German commanders capitulated.

The War in the Pacific, 1942–1945

In Asia, as gigantic armies clashed in Europe, the greatest naval battles in history decided the fate of warring nations. First, in the Battle of the Coral Sea in May 1942, an American carrier force fought its Japanese counterpart to a draw, thereby stopping the Japanese advance on Port Moresby and relieving Australia from the threat of invasion. This engagement was followed in June 1942 by the Battle of Midway, in which American carrier-based pilots sank all four of the attacking Japanese aircraft carriers and established overall naval equality with Japan in the Pacific. In August 1942 American marines attacked and took Guadalcanal in the Solomon Islands in heavy fighting.

Hampered by the policy of "Europe first," the United States gradually won control of the sea and air as it geared up massive production of aircraft carriers, submarines, and fighter planes. By 1943 the United States was producing one hundred thousand aircraft a year, almost twice as many as Japan produced in the entire war. In July 1943 the Americans and their Australian allies opened an "island hopping" campaign toward Japan. Pounding Japanese forces on a given island with satura-

"Follow Me!" This painting by Charles McBarron, Jr., shows the action at Red Beach on October 20, 1944, in the Battle of Leyte Gulf in the Philippine Islands. It captures the danger and courage of U.S. troops, which had to storm well-fortified Japanese positions again and again in their long island-hopping campaign. The officer exhorts his men, and death is all around. *(The Granger Collection, New York)*

tion bombing, American army and marine units would then hit the beaches with rifles and flame throwers and secure victory in hand-to-hand combat. Many islands were bypassed, and their Japanese defenders were blockaded and left to starve.

The war in the Pacific was extremely brutal—a "war without mercy," in the words of a leading American scholar—and atrocities were committed on both sides.[16] Knowing of Japanese atrocities in China and the Philippines, the U.S. Marines and Army troops seldom took Japanese prisoners after the Battle of Guadalcanal, killing even those rare Japanese soldiers who offered to surrender. A product of spiraling violence, mutual hatred, and dehumanizing racial stereotypes, the war without mercy intensified as it moved toward Japan.

In June 1944 giant U.S. bombers began a relentless bombing campaign that intensified steadily until the end of the war. In October 1944, as Allied advances in the Pacific paralleled those in Europe, American forces won a great victory in the four-day Battle of Leyte Gulf, the greatest battle in naval history, with 282 ships involved. The Japanese navy was practically finished.

In spite of all their defeats, Japanese troops continued to fight with enormous courage and determination. Indeed, the bloodiest battles of the Pacific war took place on Iwo Jima in February 1945 and on Okinawa in June 1945. American commanders believed the conquest of Japan might cost a million American casualties and claim 10 to 20 million Japanese lives. In fact, Japan was almost helpless, its industry and dense, fragile wooden cities largely destroyed by incendiary bombing and uncontrollable hurricanes of fire. Yet the Japanese seemed determined to fight on, ever ready to die for a hopeless cause.

On August 6 and 9, 1945, the United States dropped atomic bombs on Hiroshima and Nagasaki in Japan. Mass bombing of cities and civilians, one of the terrible new practices of World War II, had ended in the final nightmare—unprecedented human destruction in a single blinding flash. On August 14, 1945, the Japanese announced their surrender. The Second World War, which had claimed the lives of more than 50 million soldiers and civilians, was over.

Chapter Summary

Online Study Center **ACE the Test**

- *What was the nature of radical totalitarian dictatorship, and how did it differ from conservative authoritarianism?*
- *How did Stalin and the Communist Party build a modern totalitarian state in the Soviet Union?*
- *How did Mussolini's dictatorship come to power and govern in Italy?*
- *How did Hitler gain power, what policies did totalitarian Nazi Germany pursue, and why did they lead to World War II?*
- *How did Germany and Japan create enormous empires that were defeated by the Allies—Britain, the Soviet Union, and the United States?*

The Second World War marked the climax of the tremendous practical and spiritual maladies of the age of anxiety, which led in many lands to the rise of dictatorships. Many of these dictatorships were variations on conservative authoritarianism, but there was also a fateful innovation—a new kind of totalitarian dictatorship that was dynamic and theoretically unlimited in its actions. Liberals especially have fastened on the violent, profoundly antiliberal, and apparently totalitarian character of these brutal new dictatorships, linking the one-party socialism of Lenin and Stalin with the one-party fascism of Mussolini and Hitler.

Surely Stalin's Soviet Union asserted a total claim on the lives of its citizens. It posed ambitious goals in the form of rapid state-directed industrialization and savage collectivization of agriculture. And it found enthusiastic supporters who believed that Stalin and the Communist Party were building their kind of socialism and a new socialist personality at home. As for Mussolini's Italy, it also proclaimed its revolutionary, "totalitarian" character, but it retained many elements of conservative authoritarianism, such as compromising with the Catholic Church and keeping women in traditional roles.

Coming to power legally with cunning skill, Hitler also quickly established a one-party totalitarian regime with ambitious goals and widespread popular support. But whereas Stalin concentrated on building socialism at home, Hitler and the Nazi elite aimed at unlimited territorial and racial aggression on behalf of a master race. Economic recovery was only a means to that heinous end. Nazi racism and unlimited aggression made war inevitable, first with the western European democracies, then with hated eastern neighbors, and finally with the United States. Joined by Japan after Pearl Harbor, Hitler's forces overran much of western and eastern Europe, annihilated millions of Jews, and plunged Europe into the ultimate nightmare. But unlimited aggression unwittingly forged a mighty coalition led by Britain, the Soviet Union, and the United States. This Grand Alliance held together and smashed the racist Nazi empire and its leader. The United States also destroyed Japan's vast, overextended empire in the Pacific, thus bringing to a close history's most destructive war.

Key Terms

totalitarianism	Lateran Agreement
fascism	Nazism
five-year plan	Führer
New Economic Policy (NEP)	Enabling Act
collectivization	appeasement
kulaks	blitzkrieg
Black Shirts	New Order
	Europe first

Online Study Center **Improve Your Grade** Flashcards

Suggested Reading

Applebaum, Anne. *Gulag: A History*. 2004. An excellent study of Soviet police terror.

Bosworth, R. J. B. *Mussolini's Italy: Life Under the Fascist Dictatorship, 1915–1945*. 2007. An outstanding study of Italy under Mussolini.

Browning, Christopher R. *Ordinary Men: Reserve Police Battalion 101 and the Final Solution in Poland*, 2d ed. 2001. A carefully researched, unnerving account of Polish police atrocities during World War II.

Bullock, Alan. *Hitler and Stalin: Parallel Lives*. 1998. A fascinating comparison by a master biographer.

Burleigh, Michael. *The Third Reich: A New History*. 2001. A splendid accomplishment that includes a refurbishing of the concept of totalitarianism.

Conquest, Robert. *The Great Terror: A Reassessment*. 1991. An excellent account of Stalin's purges of the 1930s.

Frank, Anne. *The Diary of Anne Frank*. A remarkable first-person account by a Jewish girl in hiding during the Nazi occupation of Holland.

Friedrich, Jorg. *The Fire: The Bombing of Germany, 1940–1945*. 2006. Presents the Allied fire bombing in harrowing detail.

Marrus, Michael R. *The Holocaust in History*. 1989. An excellent interpretive survey.

Merridale, Catherine. *Ivan's War: Life and Death in the Red Army, 1939–1945*. 2007. A moving account of ordinary Soviet soldiers.

Ransel, David L. *Village Mothers: Three Generations of Change in Russia and Tataria*. 2005. A pathbreaking study based on oral histories made in the 1990s.

Service, Robert. *Lenin: A Biography*. 2002. A major work using recently available sources.

Weinberg, Gerhard L. *World at Arms: A Global History of World War II*, new ed. 2005. A masterful interconnected overview.

Notes

1. A. Gleason, *Totalitarianism: The Inner History of the World War* (New York: Oxford University Press, 1995), p. 50.

2. E. Halévy, *The Era of Tyrannies* (Garden City, N.Y.: Doubleday, 1965), pp. 265–316, esp. p. 300.

3. I. Kershaw, *The Nazi Dictatorship: Problems and Perspectives of Interpretation,* 2d ed. (London: Edward Arnold, 1989), p. 34.

4. Quoted in I. Deutscher, *Stalin: A Political Biography,* 2d ed. (New York: Oxford University Press, 1967), p. 325.

5. R. Conquest, *The Harvest of Sorrow: Soviet Collectivization and the Terror-Famine* (New York: Oxford University Press, 1986), pp. 4, 303.

6. Quoted in B. Rosenthal, "Women in the Russian Revolution and After," in *Becoming Visible: Women in European History,* ed. R. Bridenthal and C. Koonz (Boston: Houghton Mifflin, 1976), p. 383.

7. M. Malia, *The Soviet Tragedy: A History of Socialism in Russia* (New York: Free Press, 1994), p. 248.

8. R. Thurston, *Life and Terror in Stalin's Russia, 1934–1941* (New Haven, Conn.: Yale University Press, 1996), esp. pp. 16–106; also Malia, *The Soviet Tragedy,* pp. 227–270.

9. R. Vivarelli, "Interpretations on the Origins of Fascism," *Journal of Modern History* 63 (March 1991): 41.

10. W. Brustein, *The Logic of Evil: The Social Origins of the Nazi Party, 1925–1933* (New Haven, Conn.: Yale University Press, 1996), pp. 52, 182.

11. Quoted in K. D. Bracher, *The German Dictatorship: The Origins, Structure and Effects of National Socialism* (New York: Praeger, 1970), pp. 146–147.

12. Quoted ibid., p. 289.

13. R. Allen, *The Business of Genocide: The SS, Slave Labor, and the Concentration Camps* (Chapel Hill: University of North Carolina Press, 2002), pp. 270–285.

14. Quoted in M. Marrus, *The Holocaust in History* (Hanover, N.H.: University Press of New England, 1987), p. 28.

15. D. Goldhagen, *Hitler's Willing Executioners: Ordinary Germans and the Holocaust* (New York: Vintage Books, 1997).

16. J. Dower, *War Without Mercy: Race and Power in the Pacific War* (New York: Pantheon, 1986).

Stalin Justifies the Five-Year Plan

On *February 4, 1931, Joseph Stalin delivered the following address, entitled "No Slowdown in Tempo!" to the First Conference of Soviet Industrial Managers. Published the following day in* Pravda, *the newspaper of the Communist Party, and widely publicized at home and abroad, Stalin's speech reaffirmed the leader's commitment to the breakneck pace of industrialization and collectivization set forth in the first five-year plan. Arguing that more sacrifices were necessary, Stalin sought to rally the people and generate support for the party's program. His address captures the spirit of Soviet public discourse in the early 1930s.*

Stalin's concluding idea, that Bolsheviks needed to master technology and industrial management, reflected another major development. The Soviet Union was training a new class of communist engineers and technicians, who were beginning to replace foreign engineers and "bourgeois specialists," Russian engineers trained in tsarist times who were grudgingly tolerated after the revolution.

It is sometimes asked whether it is not possible to slow down the tempo somewhat, to put a check on the movement. No, comrades, it is not possible! The tempo must not be reduced! On the contrary, we must increase it as much as is within our powers and possibilities. This is dictated to us by our obligations to the workers and peasants of the U.S.S.R. This is dictated to us by our obligations to the working class of the whole world.

To slacken the tempo would mean falling behind. And those who fall behind get beaten. But we do not want to be beaten. No, we refuse to be beaten! One feature of the history of old Russia was the continual beatings she suffered because of her backwardness. She was beaten by the Mongol khans, . . . the Turkish beys, . . . and the Japanese barons. All beat her—because of her backwardness, cultural backwardness, political backwardness, industrial backwardness, agricultural backwardness. They beat her because to do so was profitable and could be done with impunity. . . . Such is the law of the exploiters—to beat the backward and the weak. It is the jungle law of capitalism. You are backward, you are weak—therefore you are wrong; hence you can be beaten and enslaved. You are mighty—therefore you are right; hence we must be wary of you.

That is why we must no longer lag behind.

In the past we had no fatherland, nor could we have had one. But now that we have overthrown capitalism and power is in our hands, in the hands of the people, we have a fatherland, and we will uphold its independence. Do you want our socialist fatherland to be beaten and to lose its independence? If you do not want this, you must put an end to its backwardness in the shortest possible time and develop a genuine Bolshevik tempo in building up its socialist economy. There is no other way. That is why Lenin said on the eve of the October Revolution: "Either perish, or overtake and outstrip the advanced capitalist countries."

We are fifty or a hundred years behind the advanced countries. We must make good this distance in ten years. Either we do it, or we shall go under.

That is what our obligations to the workers and peasants of the U.S.S.R. dictate to us.

But we have yet other, more serious and more important, obligations. They are our obligations to the world proletariat. . . . We achieved victory not solely through the efforts of the working class of the U.S.S.R., but also thanks to the support of the working class of the world. Without this support we would have been torn to pieces long ago. . . . Why does the international proletariat support us? How did we merit this support? By the fact that we were the first to hurl ourselves into the battle against capitalism, we were the first to establish working-class state power, we were the first to begin building socialism. By the fact that we are engaged on a cause which, if successful, will transform the whole world and free the entire working class. But what is needed for success? The elimination of our backwardness, the development of a high Bolshevik tempo of construction. We must march forward in such a way that the working class of the whole world, looking at us, may say: There you have my advanced detachment, my shock brigade, my working-class state power, my fatherland; they are engaged on their cause, *our* cause, and they are working well; let us support them against the capitalists and promote the cause of the world revolution. Must we not justify the hopes of the world's working class, must we not fulfill our obligations to them? Yes, we must if we do not want to utterly disgrace ourselves.

Such are our obligations, internal and international.

As you see, they dictate to us a Bolshevik tempo of development.

I will not say that we have accomplished nothing in regard to management of production during these years. In fact, we have accomplished a good deal. . . . But we could have accomplished still more if we had tried during this period really to master production, the technique of production, the financial and economic side of it.

In ten years at most we must make good the distance that separates us from the advanced capitalist countries. We have all the "objective" possibilities for this. The only thing lacking is the ability to make proper use of these possibilities. And that depends on us. *Only* on us! . . . If you are a factory manager—interfere in all the affairs of the factory, look into everything, let nothing escape you, learn and learn again. Bolsheviks must master technique. It is time Bolsheviks themselves became experts. . . .

It is said that it is hard to master technique. That is not true! There are no fortresses that Bolsheviks cannot capture. We have solved a number of most difficult problems. We have overthrown capitalism. We have assumed power. We have built up a huge socialist industry. We have transferred the middle peasants on the path of socialism. We have already accomplished what is most important from the point of view of construction. What remains to be done is not so

"Our program is realistic," Stalin proclaims on this poster, "because it is you and me working together."
(David King Collection)

much: to study technique, to master science. And when we have done that we shall develop a tempo of which we dare not even dream at present.

And we shall do it if we really want to.

Questions for Analysis

1. What reasons does Stalin give to justify an unrelenting "Bolshevik" tempo of industrial and social change? In the light of history, which reason seems most convincing? Why?

2. Imagine that the year is 1931 and you are a Soviet student reading Stalin's speech. Would Stalin's determination inspire you, frighten you, or leave you cold? Why?

3. Some historians argue that Soviet socialism was a kind of utopianism—that zealots believed that the economy, the society, and even human beings could be completely remade and perfected. What utopian elements do you see in Stalin's declaration?

Source: Joseph Stalin, "No Slowdown in Tempo!," *Pravda,* February 5, 1931.

The youth revolution. London, ca 1980. *(Wellcome Photo Library/Anthea Seiveking)*

30

The Division of Europe
- *What were the causes of the cold war?*

The Western Renaissance, 1945–1968
- *Why did western Europe recover so successfully? How did colonial peoples win political independence and American blacks triumph in the civil rights movement?*

Soviet Eastern Europe, 1945–1968
- *What was the pattern of postwar rebuilding and development in the Soviet Union and Communist eastern Europe?*

Postwar Social Transformations, 1945–1968
- *How did changing patterns in technology, class relations, women's work, and youth culture bring major social transformations?*

Conflict and Challenge in the Late Cold War, 1968–1985
- *What were the key aspects of political conflict, economic stagnation, and the feminist movement in the late cold war?*

COLD WAR CONFLICTS AND SOCIAL TRANSFORMATIONS, 1945–1985

T he total defeat of the Nazis and their allies in 1945 laid the basis for one of Western civilization's most remarkable recoveries. A battered western Europe dug itself out from under the rubble and fashioned a great renaissance, building strong democracies, vibrant economies, and new societies. The United States also made solid progress, and the Soviet Union became more humane and less dictatorial. Yet there was also a tragic setback. The Grand Alliance against Hitler gave way to an apparently endless cold war in which tension between East and West threatened world peace.

In the late 1960s and early 1970s, the postwar Western renaissance came to an end. First, as cold war competition again turned very hot in Vietnam, postwar certainties such as domestic political stability and social harmony evaporated, and several countries experienced major crises. Second, the astonishing postwar economic advance came to a halt, and this had serious social consequences. Third, new roles for women after World War II led to a powerful "second wave" of feminist thought and action in the 1970s, resulting in major changes for women and gender relations. Thus the long cold war created an underlying unity for the years 1945–1985, but the first half of the cold war era was quite different from the second.

The Division of Europe

In 1945 triumphant American and Russian soldiers came together and embraced on the banks of the Elbe River in the heart of vanquished Germany. At home, in the United States and in the Soviet Union, the soldiers' loved ones erupted in joyous celebration. Yet victory was flawed.

Online Study Center

This icon will direct you to interactive activities and study materials on the website **college.hmco.com/pic/mckaywest9e**

The Allies could not cooperate politically in peacemaking. Motivated by different goals and hounded by misunderstandings, the United States and the Soviet Union soon found themselves at loggerheads. By the end of 1947, Europe was rigidly divided. It was West versus East in a cold war that was waged around the world for forty years.

● *What were the causes of the cold war?*

The Origins of the Cold War

The most powerful allies in the wartime coalition—the Soviet Union and the United States—began to quarrel almost as soon as the unifying threat of Nazi Germany disappeared. A tragic disappointment for millions of people, the hostility between the Eastern and Western superpowers was the sad but logical outgrowth of military developments, wartime agreements, and long-standing political and ideological differences.

In the early phases of the Second World War, the Americans and the British made military victory their highest priority. They consistently avoided discussion of Stalin's war aims and the shape of the eventual peace settlement. Stalin received only a military alliance and no postwar commitments. Yet the United States and Britain did not try to take advantage of the Soviet Union's precarious position in 1942, because they feared that hard bargaining would encourage Stalin to consider making a separate peace with Hitler. They focused instead on the policy of unconditional surrender to solidify the alliance.

By late 1943, discussion about the shape of the postwar world could no longer be postponed. The conference that Stalin, Roosevelt, and Churchill held in the Iranian capital of Teheran in November 1943 thus proved of crucial importance in determining subsequent events. There, the **Big Three** jovially reaffirmed their determination to crush Germany and searched for the appropriate military strategy. Churchill, fearful of the military dangers of a direct attack, argued that American and British forces should follow up their Italian campaign with an indirect attack on Germany through the Balkans. Roosevelt, however, agreed with Stalin that an American-British frontal assault through France would be better. This agreement was part of Roosevelt's general effort to

The Big Three In 1945 a triumphant Winston Churchill, an ailing Franklin Roosevelt, and a determined Joseph Stalin met at Yalta in southern Russia to plan for peace. Cooperation soon gave way to bitter hostility. (*Franklin D. Roosevelt Presidential Library*)

meet Stalin's wartime demands whenever possible, and it had momentous political implications. It meant that the Soviet and the American-British armies would come together in defeated Germany along a north-south line and that only Soviet troops would liberate eastern Europe. Thus the basic shape of postwar Europe was emerging even as the fighting continued.

When the Big Three met again in February 1945 at Yalta on the Black Sea in southern Russia, advancing Soviet armies were within a hundred miles of Berlin. The Red Army had occupied not only Poland but also Bulgaria, Romania, Hungary, part of Yugoslavia, and much of Czechoslovakia. The temporarily stalled American-British forces had yet to cross the Rhine into Germany. Moreover, the United States was far from defeating Japan. In short, the Soviet Union's position was strong and America's weak.

There was little the increasingly sick and apprehensive Roosevelt could do but double his bet on Stalin's peaceful intentions. It was agreed at Yalta that Germany would be divided into zones of occupation and would pay heavy reparations to the Soviet Union. At American insistence, Stalin agreed to declare war on Japan after Germany was defeated. As for Poland and eastern Europe—"that Pandora's Box of infinite troubles," according to American secretary of state Cordell Hull—the Big Three struggled to reach an ambiguous compromise at Yalta: eastern European governments were to be freely elected but pro-Russian.

The Yalta compromise over eastern Europe broke down almost immediately. Even before the Yalta Conference, Bulgaria and Poland were controlled by communists who arrived home with the Red Army. Elsewhere in eastern Europe, pro-Soviet "coalition" governments of several parties were formed, but the key ministerial posts were reserved for Moscow-trained communists.

At the postwar Potsdam Conference of July 1945, the long-avoided differences over eastern Europe finally surged to the fore. The compromising Roosevelt had died and been succeeded by the more determined President Harry Truman, who demanded immediate free elections throughout eastern Europe. Stalin refused point-blank. "A freely elected government in any of these East European countries would be anti-Soviet," he admitted simply, "and that we cannot allow."[1]

Here, then, is the key to the much-debated origins of the cold war. American ideals, pumped up by the crusade against Hitler, and American politics, heavily influenced by millions of voters from eastern Europe, demanded free elections in Soviet-occupied eastern Europe. Stalin, who

Chronology

1945–1962	U.S. takes lead in Big Science
1945–1960s	Decolonization of Asia and Africa
1947	Truman Doctrine; Marshall Plan
1949	Formation of NATO; Stalin launches verbal attack on Soviet Jews; Beauvoir, *The Second Sex*
1950–1953	Korean War
1953–1964	De-Stalinization of Soviet Union
1956	Pasternak, *Doctor Zhivago*
1957	Formation of Common Market
1961	Building of Berlin Wall
1962	Cuban missile crisis; Solzhenitsyn, *One Day in the Life of Ivan Denisovich*
1964	Civil Rights Act in the United States
1964–1973	U.S. involvement in Vietnam War
1966	Formation of National Organization for Women (NOW)
1968	Soviet invasion of Czechoslovakia; student protests in Paris
1969	First Apollo moon landing
1972	Watergate break-in
1973	OPEC oil embargo
1979	Margaret Thatcher becomes British prime minister

had lived through two enormously destructive German invasions, wanted absolute military security from Germany and its potential Eastern allies. Suspicious by nature, he believed that only communist states could be truly dependable allies, and he realized that free elections would result in independent and possibly hostile governments on his western border. Moreover, by the middle of 1945, there was no way short of war that the United States could determine political developments in eastern Europe, and war was out of the question. Stalin was bound to have his way.

West Versus East

The American response to Stalin's exaggerated conception of security was to "get tough." In May 1945, Truman abruptly cut off all aid to the U.S.S.R. In October he declared that the United States would never recognize any government established by force against the free will of its people. In March 1946, former British prime minister Churchill ominously informed an American audience that an "iron curtain" had fallen across the continent, dividing Germany and all of Europe into two antagonistic camps. Emotional, moralistic denunciations of Stalin and communist Russia emerged as part of American political life. Yet the United States also responded to the popular desire to "bring the boys home" and demobilized its troops with great speed. Some historians have argued that American leaders believed that the atomic bomb gave the United States all the power it needed, but "getting tough" really meant "talking tough."

Stalin's agents quickly reheated what they viewed as the "ideological struggle against capitalist imperialism." The large, well-organized Communist Parties of France and Italy obediently started to uncover "American plots" to take over Europe and challenged their own governments with violent criticisms and large strikes. The Soviet Union also put pressure on Iran, Turkey, and Greece, while a bitter civil war raged in China. By the spring of 1947, it appeared to many Americans that Stalin was determined to export communism by subversion throughout Europe and around the world.

The United States responded to this challenge with the Truman Doctrine, which was aimed at "containing" communism to areas already occupied by the Red Army. Truman told Congress in March 1947, "I believe it must be the policy of the United States to support free people who are resisting attempted subjugation by armed minorities or by outside pressure." To begin, Truman asked Congress for military aid to Greece and Turkey, countries that Britain, weakened by war and financially overextended, could no longer protect. Then, in June, Secretary of State George C. Marshall offered Europe economic aid—the **Marshall Plan**—to help it rebuild.

Online Study Center **Improve Your Grade**
Primary Source: An American Plan to Rebuild a Shattered Europe

Stalin refused Marshall Plan assistance for all of eastern Europe. He purged the last remaining noncommunist elements from the coalition governments of eastern Europe and established Soviet-style, one-party communist dictatorships. The seizure of power in Czechoslovakia in February 1948 was particularly antidemocratic, and it greatly strengthened Western fears of limitless communist expansion. Thus, when Stalin blocked all traffic through the Soviet zone of Germany to Berlin, the former capital, which the occupying powers had also divided into sectors at the end of the war, the Western allies acted firmly but not provocatively. Hundreds of planes began flying over the Soviet roadblocks around the clock, supplying provisions to the people of West Berlin and thwarting Soviet efforts to swallow up the West Berliners. After 324 days, the Soviets backed down: containment seemed to work. In 1949, therefore, the United States formed an anti-Soviet military alliance of Western governments: the North Atlantic Treaty Organization (**NATO**). Stalin countered by tightening his hold on his satellites, later united in the Warsaw Pact. Europe was divided into two hostile blocs.

In late 1949, the communists triumphed in China, frightening and angering many Americans, who saw new evidence of a powerful worldwide communist conspiracy. When the Russian-backed communist army of North Korea invaded South Korea in 1950, President Truman acted swiftly. American-led United Nations forces under General Douglas MacArthur intervened. Initially, the North Koreans almost conquered the entire peninsula, but the South Koreans and the Americans rallied and advanced until China suddenly entered the war. The bitter, bloody contest then seesawed back and forth near where it had begun, as President Truman rejected General MacArthur's call to attack China and fired him instead. In 1953 a fragile truce was negotiated, and the fighting stopped. Thus the United States extended its policy of containment to Asia but drew back from an attack on communist China and possible nuclear war.

The rapid descent from victorious Grand Alliance to bitter **cold war** was directly connected to the tragic fate of eastern Europe. After 1933, when the eastern European power vacuum invited Nazi racist imperialism, the appeasing Western democracies mistakenly did nothing. They did, however, have one telling insight: how, they asked themselves, could they unite with Stalin to stop Hitler without giving Stalin great gains on his western borders? After Hitler's invasion of the Soviet Union, the Western Powers preferred to ignore this question and hope for the best. But when Stalin later began to claim the spoils of victory, the United States began to protest and professed outrage. This belated opposition quite possibly encouraged even more aggressive measures by the always-suspicious Stalin, and it helped explode the quarrel over eastern Europe into a global confrontation. Thus the Soviet-American confrontation became institutionalized and formed the bedrock of the long cold war

The Berlin Airlift   Standing in the rubble of their bombed-out city, a German crowd in the American sector awaits the arrival of a U.S. transport plane flying in over the Soviet blockade in 1948. The crisis over Berlin was a dramatic indication of growing tensions among the Allies, which resulted in the division of Europe into two hostile camps. *(Time Life Pictures/Getty Images)*

era, which lasted until the mid-1980s despite intermittent periods of relaxation.

The Western Renaissance, 1945–1968

As the cold war divided Europe into two blocs, the future appeared bleak on both sides of the iron curtain. European economic conditions were the worst in generations, and Europe was weak and divided, a battleground for cold war ambitions. Moreover, western European empires were crumbling in the face of nationalism in Asia and Africa. Yet Europe recovered, and the nations of western Europe led the way. In less than a generation, western Europe achieved unprecedented economic prosperity and peaceful social transformation, while the United States boomed and eventually experienced a wholesome social revolution. It was an amazing rebirth—a true renaissance.

• *Why did western Europe recover so successfully? How did colonial peoples win political independence and American blacks triumph in the civil rights movement?*

The Postwar Challenge

After the war, economic conditions in western Europe were terrible. Runaway inflation and black markets testified to severe shortages and hardships. Many people believed that Europe was quite simply finished.

Suffering was most intense in defeated Germany. The major territorial change of the war had moved the Soviet Union's border far to the west. Poland was in turn compensated for this loss to the Soviets with land taken from Germany (see Map 30.1). To solidify these changes in boundaries, 13 million Germans were driven from their homes and forced to resettle in a greatly reduced Germany. The Russians were also seizing factories and equipment as reparations in their zone, even tearing up railroad tracks and sending the rails to the Soviet Union.

In 1945 and 1946, conditions were not much better in the Western zones, for the Western allies also treated the German population with severity at first. Countless Germans sold prized possessions to American soldiers to buy food. By the spring of 1947, refugee-clogged, hungry, prostrate Germany was on the verge of total collapse and threatening to drag down the rest of Europe. Yet western

MAP 30.1 The Results of World War II in Europe Millions of refugees fled westward because of war and territorial changes. The Soviet Union and Poland took land from Germany, which the Allies partitioned into occupation zones. Those zones subsequently formed the basis of the East and West German states, as the iron curtain fell to divide both Germany and Europe. Austria was detached from Germany, but the Soviets subsequently permitted Austria to reunify as a neutral state.

Postwar national boundaries, to 1989
Allied occupation of Germany and Austria 1945–1955
Territory lost by Germany
Territory gained by Soviet Union
1945 Year communist control of government gained
"Iron Curtain" to 1989
Baltic
Czech
Finns
Germans
Poles
Russians
Peoples settled by International Refugee Organization

Berlin Wall (1961–1989)

EAST GERMANY
Soviet Sector
East Berlin
French Sector
British Sector
West Berlin
U.S. Sector
Potsdam

SOVIET UNION 1917

FINLAND
Leningrad
Helsinki
From Finland, 1940–1956

NORWAY
Oslo
SWEDEN
Stockholm
Copenhagen
DENMARK

ESTONIA to U.S.S.R. 1940
LATVIA to U.S.S.R. 1940
LITHUANIA to U.S.S.R. 1940
Incorporated into U.S.S.R. 1945

Baltic Sea

Gdansk (Danzig)
Incorporated into Poland, 1945
POLAND 1947
From Poland, 1940–1947
Brest
UKRAINE
Warsaw
From Czechoslovakia, 1945–1947
BESSARABIA
From Romania, 1940–1947
From Romania, 1940
Yalta
Black Sea
TURKEY
Istanbul
Cyprus

ROMANIA 1947
Bucharest
BULGARIA 1946
Sofia
HUNGARY 1949
Budapest
CZECHOSLOVAKIA 1948
Prague
Vienna
Soviet Zone
AUSTRIA
British Zone
U.S. Zone
From Italy, 1945
French Zone
YUGOSLAVIA 1945
Belgrade
ALBANIA 1944
Tiranë
GREECE
Athens

EAST GERMANY 1949
Berlin
Soviet Zone
Bremen
British Zone
U.S. Zone
Amsterdam
NETHERLANDS
Brussels
BEL.
LUX.
WEST GERMANY 1949
Bonn
Munich
French Zone
U.S. Zone
SWITZERLAND
Bern

ITALY
Rome
Milan
Adriatic Sea
Corsica (Fr.)
Sardinia (Italy)
Mediterranean Sea
Sicily
Crete

GREAT BRITAIN
London
IRELAND
North Sea
ATLANTIC OCEAN
FRANCE
Paris
SPAIN
Madrid

400 Mi.
400 Km.
200
200
0
0

Europe was not finished. The Nazi occupation and the war had discredited old ideas and old leaders. All over Europe, many people were willing to change and experiment, and new groups and new leaders were coming to the fore to guide these aspirations. Progressive Catholics and revitalized Catholic political parties—the **Christian Democrats**—were particularly influential.

In Italy the Christian Democrats emerged as the leading party in the first postwar elections in 1946, and in early 1948 they won an absolute majority in the parliament in a landslide victory. Their very able leader was Alcide De Gasperi, a courageous antifascist firmly committed to political democracy, economic reconstruction, and moderate social reform. In France, too, the Catholic Party also provided some of the best postwar leaders after January 1946, when General Charles de Gaulle, the inspiring wartime leader of the Free French, resigned after having re-established the free and democratic Fourth Republic. As Germany was partitioned by the cold war, a purified Federal Republic of Germany (as West Germany was officially known) found new and able leadership among its Catholics. In 1949 Konrad Adenauer, the former mayor of Cologne and a long-time anti-Nazi, began his long, highly successful democratic rule; the Christian Democrats became West Germany's majority party for a generation. In providing effective leadership for their respective countries, the Christian Democrats were inspired and united by a common Christian and European heritage. They steadfastly rejected authoritarianism and narrow nationalism and placed their faith in democracy and cooperation.

The socialists and the communists, active in the resistance against Hitler, also emerged from the war with increased power and prestige, especially in France and Italy. They, too, provided fresh leadership and pushed for social change and economic reform. In the immediate postwar years, welfare measures such as family allowances, health insurance, and increased public housing were enacted throughout continental Europe. Britain followed the same trend, as the newly elected socialist Labour Party established a "welfare state." Many British industries were nationalized, and the government provided free medical service. Thus all across Europe, social reform complemented political transformation, creating solid foundations for a great European renaissance.

The United States also supplied strong and creative leadership, providing western Europe with both massive economic aid and ongoing military protection. Economic aid was channeled through the Marshall Plan, and military security was provided through NATO, which featured American troops stationed permanently in Europe and the American nuclear umbrella. Thus the United States assumed the international responsibilities it had shunned after 1919.

As Marshall Plan aid poured in, the battered economies of western Europe began to turn the corner in 1948. The outbreak of the Korean War in 1950 further stimulated economic activity, and Europe entered a period of rapid economic progress that lasted into the late 1960s. Never before had the European economy grown so fast. There were many reasons for western Europe's brilliant economic performance. American aid helped the process get off to a fast start. Moreover, economic growth became a basic objective of all western European governments, for leaders and voters were determined to avoid a return to the dangerous and demoralizing stagnation of the 1930s. Thus governments generally accepted Keynesian economics (see pages 928 and 935) and sought to stimulate their economies. They also adopted a variety of imaginative and successful strategies.

In postwar West Germany, Minister of Economy Ludwig Erhard, a roly-poly, cigar-smoking former professor, broke decisively with the straitjacketed Nazi economy. Erhard bet on the free-market economy while maintaining the extensive social welfare network inherited from the Hitler era. He and his teachers believed not only that capitalism was more efficient but also that political and social freedom could thrive only if there were real economic freedom. Erhard's first step was to reform the currency and abolish rationing and price controls in 1948. He boldly declared, "The only ration coupon is the Mark."[2] West Germany's success renewed respect for free-market capitalism.

The French innovation was a new kind of planning. Under the guidance of Jean Monnet, an economic pragmatist and apostle of European unity, a planning commission set ambitious but flexible goals for the French economy and used the nationalized banks to funnel money into key industries. Thus France combined flexible planning and a "mixed" state and private economy to achieve the most rapid economic development in its long history.

In most countries, there were many people ready to work hard for low wages and the hope of a better future. Moreover, although many consumer products had been invented or perfected since the late 1920s, few Europeans had been able to buy them. In 1945 the electric refrigerator, the washing machine, and the automobile were rare luxuries. There was a great potential demand, which the economic system moved to satisfy. Finally, western European nations abandoned protectionism and gradually created a large unified market known as the "Common Market." This historic action, which certainly

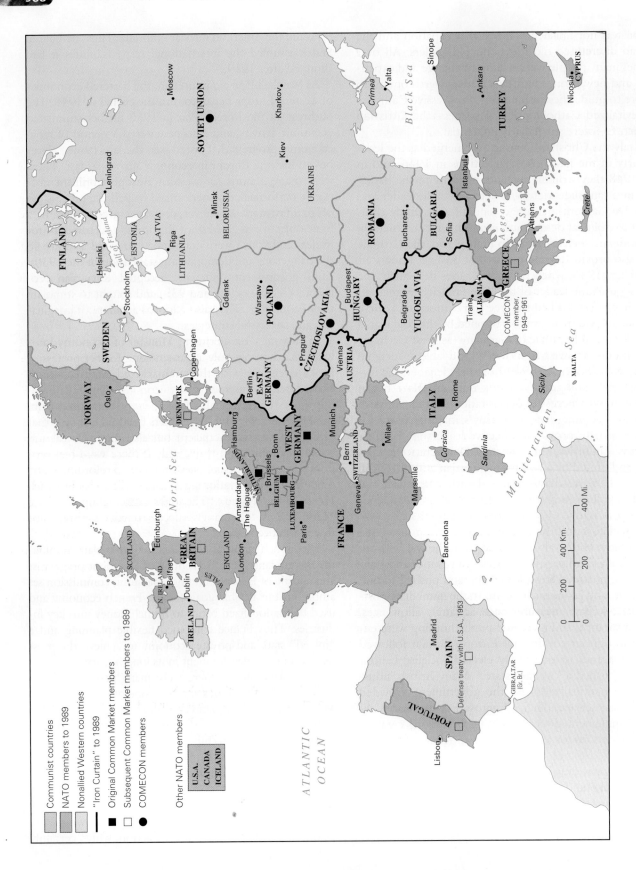

Moscow

SOVIET UNION

Leningrad

Kharkov

Sinope

Yalta

Crimea

Black Sea

Ankara

TURKEY

Nicosia• CYPRUS

Kiev

UKRAINE

Minsk

BELORUSSIA

Riga

LATVIA

ESTONIA

LITHUANIA

Istanbul

Aegean Sea

Crete

FINLAND

Helsinki

Gulf of Finland

Stockholm

SWEDEN

Gdansk

Warsaw•

POLAND

Prague•

CZECHOSLOVAKIA

Budapest•

HUNGARY

Vienna•

AUSTRIA

ROMANIA

Bucharest•

BULGARIA

•Sofia

YUGOSLAVIA

Belgrade•

Tiranë•

ALBANIA

GREECE

Athens•

COMECON member, 1949–1961

MALTA Sea

NORWAY

Oslo•

DENMARK

Copenhagen•

Berlin•

EAST GERMANY

Hamburg

Bonn•

WEST GERMANY

Munich•

Milan•

ITALY

Rome•

Corsica

Sardinia

Sicily

Mediterranean Sea

North Sea

NETHERLANDS

Amsterdam•

The Hague•

Brussels•

BELGIUM

LUXEMBOURG

Paris•

FRANCE

Bern•

SWITZERLAND

Geneva•

Marseille•

SCOTLAND

Edinburgh•

GREAT BRITAIN

ENGLAND

London•

WALES

N. IRELAND

Belfast•

Dublin•

IRELAND

Barcelona•

Madrid•

SPAIN

Defense treaty with U.S.A. 1953

GIBRALTAR (Gr. Br.)

PORTUGAL

Lisbon•

ATLANTIC OCEAN

0   200   400 Km.

0   200   400 Mi.

Communist countries

NATO members to 1989

Nonallied Western countries

"Iron Curtain" to 1989

Original Common Market members

Subsequent Common Market members to 1989

COMECON members

Other NATO members

U.S.A.
CANADA
ICELAND

stimulated the economy, was part of a larger search for European unity.

Toward European Unity

Western Europe's political recovery was spectacular in the generation after 1945. Republics were re-established in France, West Germany, and Italy. Constitutional monarchs were restored in Belgium, Holland, and Norway. Democratic governments, often within the framework of multiparty politics and shifting parliamentary coalitions, took root again and thrived. National self-determination was accompanied by civil liberties and individual freedom.

A similarly extraordinary achievement was the march toward a united Europe. The Christian Democrats, with their shared Catholic heritage, were particularly committed to "building Europe," and other groups shared their dedication. Many Europeans believed that only unity in a new "European nation" could reassert western Europe's influence in world affairs.

The close cooperation among European states required by the Americans for Marshall Plan aid led to the creation of both the Organization of European Economic Cooperation (OEEC) and the Council of Europe in 1948. European federalists hoped that the Council of Europe would quickly evolve into a true European parliament with sovereign rights, but this did not happen. Britain, with its empire and its "special relationship" with the United States, consistently opposed giving any real political power—any sovereignty—to the council. Many continental nationalists and communists felt similarly.

Frustrated in the direct political approach, European federalists turned toward economics as a way of working toward genuine unity. Two far-seeing French statesmen, the planner Jean Monnet and Foreign Minister Robert Schuman, took the lead in 1950 and called for a special international organization to control and integrate all European steel and coal production. West Germany,

Italy, Belgium, the Netherlands, and Luxembourg accepted the French idea in 1952; the British would have none of it. The immediate economic goal—a single steel and coal market without national tariffs or quotas—was rapidly realized. The more far-reaching political goal was to bind the six member nations so closely together economically that war among them would eventually become unthinkable and virtually impossible.

In 1957 the six nations of the Coal and Steel Community signed the Treaty of Rome, which created the European Economic Community, generally known as the **Common Market** (see Map 30.2). The first goal of the treaty was a gradual reduction of all tariffs among the six in order to create a single market almost as large as that of the United States. Other goals included the free movement of capital and labor and common economic policies and institutions. The Common Market was a great success, encouraging companies and regions to specialize in what they did best.

The development of the Common Market fired imaginations and encouraged hopes of rapid progress toward political as well as economic union. In the 1960s, however, these hopes were frustrated by a resurgence of more traditional nationalism. France took the lead. Mired in a bitter colonial war in Algeria, the French turned in 1958 to General de Gaulle, who established the Fifth Republic and ruled as its president until 1969. De Gaulle was at heart a romantic nationalist, and he viewed the United States as the main threat to genuine French (and European) independence. He withdrew all French military forces from the "American-controlled" NATO, developed France's own nuclear weapons, and vetoed the scheduled advent of majority rule within the Common Market. Thus throughout the 1960s, the Common Market thrived economically but remained a union of sovereign states.

Decolonization in East Asia

In the postwar era, Europe's long-standing overseas expansion was dramatically reversed. Future generations will almost certainly see this rolling back of Western expansion as one of world history's great turning points (see Map 30.3).

The most basic cause of imperial collapse—what Europeans called **decolonization**—was the rising demand of Asian and African peoples for national self-determination, racial equality, and personal dignity. This demand spread from intellectuals to the masses in nearly every colonial territory after the First World War. As a result, colonial empires had already been shaken by 1939, and the way

Mapping the Past

MAP 30.2 European Alliance Systems, 1949–1989
After the cold war divided Europe into two hostile military alliances, six western European countries formed the Common Market in 1957. The Common Market grew later to include most of western Europe. The communist states organized their own economic association—COMECON. **1** Identify the countries that were the original members of the Common Market. What do they have in common? **2** Identify the members of COMECON. What communist country or countries did not join COMECON? Why? **3** Which non-allied nations had joined the Common Market by 1989?

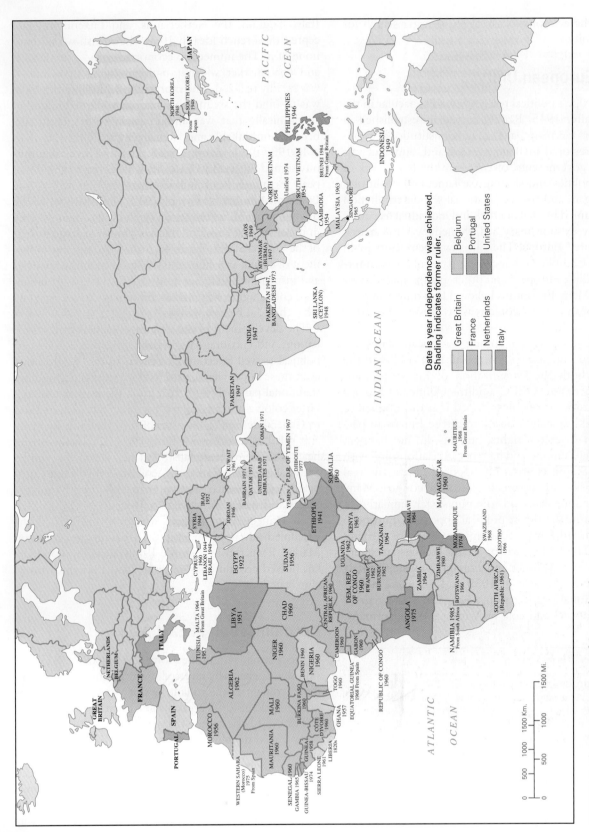

MAP 30.3 **The New States in Africa and Asia**   Divided primarily along religious lines into two states, British India led the way to political independence in 1947. Most African territories achieved statehood by the mid-1960s, as European empires passed away, unlamented.

Online Study Center **Improve Your Grade** Interactive Map: Decolonization and Independence was prepared for the eventual triumph of independence movements.

European empires had been based on an enormous power differential between the rulers and the ruled, a difference that had greatly declined by 1945. Not only was western Europe poor and battered immediately after the war, but imperial rulers had been driven from large parts of South Asia by the Japanese, and in these areas Europeans now faced strong nationalist movements that had developed under the Japanese occupation.

Many Europeans also regarded their empires very differently after 1945 than before 1914, or even before 1939. Empire had rested on self-confidence and self-righteousness; Europeans had believed their superiority to be not only technical and military but also spiritual and moral. The horrors of the Second World War destroyed such complacent arrogance and gave opponents of imperialism much greater influence in Europe. With their political power and moral authority in tatters in 1945, many

Europeans had little taste for bloody colonial wars and wanted to concentrate on rebuilding at home.

India, Britain's oldest, largest, and most lucrative non-white possession, played a key role in decolonization. Nationalist opposition to British rule coalesced after the First World War under the leadership of British-educated lawyer Mohandas "Mahatma" Gandhi (1869–1948), one of the twentieth century's most significant and influential figures. In the 1920s and 1930s Gandhi built a mass movement preaching nonviolent "noncooperation" with the British. In 1935 Gandhi wrested from the frustrated and unnerved British a new constitution that was practically a blueprint for independence. When the Labour Party came to power in Great Britain in 1945, it was ready to relinquish sovereignty. British socialists had always been critical of imperialism, and the heavy cost of governing India had become a large financial burden. The obstacle to India's independence posed by conflict between India's Hindu and Muslim populations was

Gandhi Arrives in Delhi, October 1939 A small frail man, Gandhi possessed enormous courage and determination. His campaign of nonviolent resistance to British rule inspired the Indian masses and nurtured national identity and self-confidence. Here he arrives for talks with the British viceroy after the outbreak of World War II. *(Corbis)*

resolved in 1947 through the creation of two states, predominately Hindu India and Muslim Pakistan.

If Indian nationalism drew on Western parliamentary liberalism, Chinese nationalism developed and triumphed in the framework of Marxist-Leninist ideology. In the turbulent early 1920s, a broad alliance of nationalist forces within the Soviet-supported Guomindang (Kuomintang, or National People's Party) was dedicated to unifying China and abolishing European concessions. But in 1927 Chiang Kai-shek (1887–1975), successor to Sun Yat-sen (see page 872) and leader of the Guomindang, broke with his more radical communist allies, headed by Mao Zedong (Mao Tse-tung), and tried to destroy them.

In 1931, to escape Guomindang armies closing in for the kill, Mao (1893–1976) led his followers on an incredible 5,000-mile march to remote northern China and built up an independent power base there. Even war could not force Mao and Chiang to cooperate. By late 1945 their long-standing quarrel had erupted in civil war. Stalin gave Mao some aid, and the Americans gave Chiang much more. Winning the support of the peasantry by promising to expropriate the big landowners, the tougher, better-organized communists forced the Nationalists to withdraw to the island of Taiwan in 1949.

Mao and the communists united China's 550 million inhabitants in a strong centralized state, expelled foreigners, and began building a new society along Soviet lines, with mass arrests, forced-labor camps, and ceaseless propaganda. The peasantry was collectivized, and the inevitable five-year plans concentrated successfully on the expansion of heavy industry.

Most Asian countries followed the pattern of either India or China. In 1946 the Philippines achieved independence peacefully from the United States. Britain quickly granted Sri Lanka (Ceylon) and Burma independence in 1948. However, Indonesian nationalists had to beat off attempts by the Dutch to reconquer the Dutch East Indies before Indonesia emerged in 1949 as a sovereign state.

The French also tried their best to re-establish colonial rule in Indochina, but despite American aid, they were defeated in 1954 by forces under the communist and nationalist guerrilla leader Ho Chi Minh (1890–1969), who was supported by the Soviet Union and China. But Indochina was not unified, and two independent Vietnamese states came into being, which led to civil war and subsequent intervention by the United States (see page 1006).

Decolonization in the Middle East and Africa

In the Middle East, the movement toward political independence continued after World War II (see Map 30.3).

In 1944 the French gave up their League of Nations mandates in Syria and Lebanon. In British-mandated Palestine, where after 1918 the British government established a Jewish homeland alongside the Arab population, violence and terrorism mounted on both sides. In 1947 the frustrated British decided to leave Palestine, and the United Nations then voted in a nonbinding resolution to divide Palestine into two states—one Arab and one Jewish, which became Israel. The Jews accepted the plan but the Arabs did not, and in 1948 they attacked the Jewish state as soon as it was proclaimed. The Israelis drove off the invaders and conquered more territory, as roughly 900,000 Arabs fled or were expelled. Holocaust survivors from Europe streamed into Israel, as Theodor Herzl's Zionist dream came true (see page 839). The next fifty years saw four more wars between the Israelis and the Arab states and innumerable clashes between the Israelis and the Palestinians.

The Arab defeat in 1948 triggered a powerful nationalist revolution in Egypt in 1952, where a young army officer named Gamal Abdel Nasser (1918–1970) drove out the pro-Western king. In 1956 Nasser abruptly nationalized the foreign-owned Suez Canal Company, the last symbol and substance of Western power in the Middle East. Infuriated, the British and the French, along with the Israelis, invaded Egypt. This was, however, the dying gasp of traditional imperial power: the Americans joined with the Soviets to force the British, French, and Israelis to withdraw. Nasser and anti-Western Egyptian nationalism triumphed.

The failure of Britain and France to unseat Nasser in 1956 encouraged Arab nationalists in Algeria. The country's large French population considered colonial Algeria an integral part of France and was determined to stay in Algeria and continue dominating the Arab majority. This settler determination made the Algerian war for independence long, bloody, and dirty, with systematic torture and numerous atrocities on both sides. In the end, General de Gaulle, who had returned to power as part of the movement to keep Algeria French, accepted the principle of Algerian self-determination. In 1962, after more than a century of French rule, Algeria became independent and its European population quickly fled to France.

In much of Africa south of the Sahara, decolonization proceeded much more smoothly. Beginning in 1957, Britain's colonies achieved independence with little or no bloodshed and then entered a very loose association with Britain as members of the British Commonwealth of Nations. In 1958 the clever de Gaulle offered the leaders of French black Africa the choice of a total break with France or immediate independence within a kind of

Nationalizing the Suez Canal Nasser's 1956 takeover of the Suez Canal, cheered here by a huge crowd in Cairo, was wildly popular throughout Egypt and the Arab world. Jubilation quickly turned to humiliation as invading forces from Israel, Britain, and France crushed the Egyptian army, and a shell-shocked Nasser offered to resign. But the Egyptian masses demanded he stay, enabling the charismatic Nasser to emerge triumphant with American support. *(Hulton-Deutsch Collection/Corbis)*

French commonwealth. All but one of the new states chose association with France. African leaders did so because they identified with French culture and because they wanted aid from France. The French were eager to help—provided their former colonies would accept close ties with France on French terms. As in the past, the French and their Common Market partners, who helped foot the bill, saw themselves as continuing their civilizing mission in sub-Saharan Africa. More important, they saw in Africa untapped markets for their industrial goods, raw materials for their factories, outlets for profitable investment, and good temporary jobs for their engineers and teachers. The British acted somewhat similarly.

As a result, western European countries actually managed to increase their economic and cultural ties with their former African colonies in the 1960s and 1970s.

Above all, they used the lure of special trading privileges and heavy investment in French- and English-language education to enhance a powerful Western presence in the new African states. This situation led a variety of leaders and scholars to charge that western Europe (and the United States) had imposed a system of neocolonialism on the former colonies. According to this view, **neocolonialism** was a system designed to perpetuate Western economic domination and undermine the promise of political independence, thereby extending to Africa (and much of Asia) the economic subordination that the United States had established in Latin America in the nineteenth century. At the very least, enduring influence in sub-Saharan Africa testified to western Europe's resurgent economic and political power in international relations.

The March on Washington, August 1963   The march marked a dramatic climax in the civil rights struggle. More than 200,000 people gathered at the Lincoln Memorial to hear the young Martin Luther King, Jr., deliver his greatest address, the "I have a dream" speech. *(Time Life Pictures/Getty Images)*

America's Civil Rights Revolution

The Second World War cured the depression in the United States and brought about an economic boom. Despite fears that peace would bring renewed depression, conversion to a peacetime economy went smoothly. As in western Europe, the U.S. economy proceeded to advance fairly steadily for a long generation.

Belatedly and reluctantly, postwar America did experience a genuine social revolution. After a long struggle, African Americans (and their white supporters) threw off a deeply entrenched system of segregation, discrimination, and repression. Eloquent lawyers challenged school segregation and in 1954 won a landmark decision in the Supreme Court, which ruled in *Brown v. Board of Education* that "separate educational facilities are inherently unequal." Blacks effectively challenged institutionalized inequality with bus boycotts, sit-ins, and demonstrations. As civil rights leader Martin Luther King, Jr. (1929–1968), told the white power struc-

ture, "We will not hate you, but we will not obey your evil laws."[3]

In key northern states, African Americans used their growing political power to gain the support of the liberal wing of the Democratic Party. A liberal landslide elected Lyndon Johnson (1908–1973) president in 1964. The Civil Rights Act of 1964 prohibited discrimination in public services and on the job; the Voting Rights Act of 1965 guaranteed all blacks the right to vote. By the 1970s, substantial numbers of blacks had been elected to public and private office throughout the southern states, proof positive that dramatic changes had occurred in American race relations.

President Johnson also declared "unconditional war on poverty," and Congress and the administration created a host of antipoverty programs intended to aid all poor Americans and bring greater economic equality. Thus the United States promoted in the mid-1960s the kind of fundamental social reform that western Europe had embraced immediately after the Second World War. The United States became more of a welfare state, as government spending for social benefits rose dramatically and approached European levels.

Soviet Eastern Europe, 1945–1968

While western Europe surged ahead economically after the Second World War and increased its political power as American influence gradually waned, eastern Europe followed a different path. The Soviet Union first tightened its grip on the "liberated" nations of eastern Europe under Stalin and then refused to let go. Thus postwar economic recovery in eastern Europe proceeded along Soviet lines, and political and social developments were strongly influenced by changes in the Soviet Union.

- *What was the pattern of postwar rebuilding and development in the Soviet Union and Communist eastern Europe?*

Stalin's Last Years, 1945–1953

Americans were not the only ones who felt betrayed by Stalin's postwar actions. The "Great Patriotic War of the Fatherland" had fostered Russian nationalism and a relaxation of dictatorial terror. It also had produced a rare but real unity between Soviet rulers and most Russian people. Having made a heroic war effort, the vast major-

ity of the Soviet people hoped in 1945 that a grateful party and government would grant greater freedom and democracy. Such hopes were soon crushed.

Even before the war ended, Stalin was moving his country back toward rigid dictatorship. As early as 1944, the leading members of the Communist Party were being given a new motivating slogan: "The war on Fascism ends, the war on capitalism begins."[4] By early 1946, Stalin was publicly singing the old tune that war was inevitable as long as capitalism existed. Stalin's new foreign foe in the West provided an excuse for re-establishing a harsh dictatorship. Many returning soldiers and ordinary citizens were purged in 1945 and 1946, as Stalin revived the terrible forced-labor camps of the 1930s.

Culture and art were also purged in violent campaigns that reimposed rigid anti-Western ideological conformity. Many artists were denounced, including the composers Sergei Prokofiev and Dimitri Shostakovich and the film director Sergei Eisenstein. In 1949 Stalin launched a savage verbal attack on Soviet Jews, accusing them of being pro-Western and antisocialist.

In the political realm, Stalin reasserted the Communist Party's complete control of the government and his absolute mastery of the party. Five-year plans were reintroduced to cope with the enormous task of economic reconstruction. Once again, heavy industry and the military were given top priority, and consumer goods, housing, and collectivized agriculture were neglected. Everyday life was very hard. In short, it was the 1930s all over

Sergei Eisenstein: Ivan the Terrible
Eisenstein's final masterpiece—one of the greatest films ever—was filmed during the Second World War and released in two parts in 1946. In this chilling scene, the crafty paranoid tyrant, who has saved Russia from foreign invaders, invites the unsuspecting Prince Vladimir to a midnight revel that will lead to his murder. The increasingly demonic Ivan seemed to resemble Stalin, and Eisenstein was censored and purged. *(David King Collection)*

again in the Soviet Union, although police terror was less intense.

Stalin's prime postwar innovation was to export the Stalinist system to the countries of eastern Europe. The Communist Parties of eastern Europe had established one-party states by 1948, thanks to the help of the Red Army and the Russian secret police. Rigid ideological indoctrination, attacks on religion, and a lack of civil liberties were soon facts of life. Industry was nationalized, and the middle class was stripped of its possessions. Economic life was then faithfully recast in the Stalinist mold. Forced industrialization lurched forward without regard for human costs. The collectivization of agriculture began.

Only Josip Broz Tito (1892–1980), the resistance leader and Communist chief of Yugoslavia, was able to resist Soviet domination successfully. Tito stood up to Stalin in 1948, and since there was no Russian army in Yugoslavia, he got away with it. Yugoslavia prospered as a multiethnic state until it began to break apart in the 1980s. Tito's proclamation of independence infuriated Stalin. Popular Communist leaders who, like Tito, had led the resistance against Germany were purged as Stalin sought to create absolutely obedient instruments of domination in eastern Europe.

Reform and De-Stalinization, 1953–1964

In 1953 the aging Stalin finally died, and the dictatorship that he had built began to change. Even as Stalin's heirs struggled for power, they realized that reforms were necessary because of the widespread fear and hatred of Stalin's political terrorism. The power of the secret police was curbed, and many of the forced-labor camps were gradually closed. Change was also necessary for economic reasons. Moreover, Stalin's belligerent foreign policy had led directly to a strong Western alliance, which isolated the Soviet Union.

On the question of just how much change should be permitted in order to preserve the system, the Communist leadership was badly split. Conservatives wanted to make as few changes as possible. Reformers, who were led by Nikita Khrushchev, argued for major innovations. Khrushchev (1894–1971), who had joined the party as an uneducated coal miner in 1918 and risen to a high-level position in the 1930s, emerged as the new ruler in 1955.

To strengthen his position and that of his fellow reformers within the party, Khrushchev launched an all-out attack on Stalin and his crimes at a closed session of the Twentieth Party Congress in 1956. In gory detail, he de-

scribed to the startled Communist delegates how Stalin had tortured and murdered thousands of loyal Communists, how he had trusted Hitler completely and bungled the country's defense, and how he had "supported the glorification of his own person with all conceivable methods." Khrushchev's "secret speech" was read at Communist Party meetings held throughout the country, and it strengthened the reform movement.

The liberalization—or **de-Stalinization,** as it was called in the West—of the Soviet Union was genuine. The Communist Party jealously maintained its monopoly on political power, but Khrushchev shook up the party and brought in new members. Some resources were shifted from heavy industry and the military toward consumer goods and agriculture, and Stalinist controls over workers were relaxed. The Soviet Union's very low standard of living finally began to improve and continued to rise substantially throughout the booming 1960s.

De-Stalinization created great ferment among writers and intellectuals who hungered for cultural freedom. The poet Boris Pasternak (1890–1960) finished his great novel *Doctor Zhivago* in 1956. Published in the West but not in Russia, *Doctor Zhivago* is both a literary masterpiece and a powerful challenge to communism. It tells the story of a prerevolutionary intellectual who rejects the violence and brutality of the revolution of 1917 and the Stalinist years. Even as he is destroyed, he triumphs because of his humanity and Christian spirit. Pasternak was denounced—but he was not shot. Other talented writers followed Pasternak's lead, and courageous editors let the sparks fly.

The writer Aleksandr Solzhenitsyn (b. 1918) created a sensation when his *One Day in the Life of Ivan Denisovich* was published in the Soviet Union in 1962. Solzhenitsyn's novel portrays in grim detail life in a Stalinist concentration camp—a life to which Solzhenitsyn himself had been unjustly condemned—and is a damning indictment of the Stalinist past.

Online Study Center **Improve Your Grade**
Primary Source: *One Day in the Life of Ivan Denisovich* Describes the Stalinist Gulag

Khrushchev also de-Stalinized Soviet foreign policy. "Peaceful coexistence" with capitalism was possible, he argued, and great wars were not inevitable. Khrushchev even made concessions, agreeing in 1955 to real independence for a neutral Austria after ten long years of Allied occupation. Thus there was considerable relaxation of cold war tensions between 1955 and 1957. At the same time, Khrushchev began wooing the new nations of Asia and Africa—even if they were not communist—with promises and aid.

De-Stalinization stimulated rebelliousness in the eastern European satellites. Having suffered in silence under Stalin, communist reformers and the masses were quickly emboldened to seek much greater liberty and national independence. Poland took the lead in 1956, when extensive rioting brought a new government that managed to win greater autonomy.

Hungary experienced a real and tragic revolution. Led by students and workers—the classic urban revolutionaries—the people of Budapest installed a liberal communist reformer as their new chief in October 1956. Soviet troops were forced to leave the country. But after the new government promised free elections and renounced Hungary's military alliance with Moscow, the Russian leaders ordered an invasion and crushed the national and democratic revolution. Fighting was bitter until the end, for the Hungarians hoped that the United States would come to their aid. When this did not occur, most people in eastern Europe concluded that their only hope was to strive for small domestic gains while following Russia obediently in foreign affairs.

The End of Reform

By late 1962, opposition in party circles to Khrushchev's policies was strong, and in 1964 Khrushchev fell in a bloodless palace revolution. Under Leonid Brezhnev (1906–1982), the Soviet Union began a period of stagnation and limited "re-Stalinization." The basic reason for this development was that Khrushchev's Communist colleagues saw de-Stalinization as a dangerous threat to the dictatorial authority of the party. The party had to tighten up considerably while there was still time. Khrushchev had to go.

Another reason for conservative opposition was that Khrushchev's policy toward the West was erratic and ultimately unsuccessful. In 1958 he ordered the Western allies to evacuate West Berlin within six months. In response, the allies reaffirmed their unity in West Berlin, and Khrushchev backed down. Then in 1961, as relations with communist China deteriorated dramatically, Khrushchev ordered the East Germans to build a wall between East and West Berlin, thereby sealing off West Berlin in clear violation of existing access agreements between the Great Powers. The recently elected U.S. president, John F. Kennedy, acquiesced to the construction of the Berlin Wall. Emboldened and seeing a chance to change the balance of military power decisively, Khrushchev ordered missiles with nuclear warheads installed in Fidel Castro's communist Cuba in 1962. President Kennedy countered with a naval blockade of Cuba. After a tense diplomatic crisis, Khrushchev agreed to remove the Soviet missiles in return for American pledges not to disturb Castro's regime. Khrushchev looked like a bumbling buffoon; his influence, already slipping, declined rapidly after the Cuban fiasco.

In 1964, Brezhnev and his supporters took over. Almost immediately they started talking quietly of Stalin's "good points" and ignoring his crimes. This change informed Soviet citizens that further liberalization could not be expected at home. Soviet leaders, determined never to suffer Khrushchev's humiliation in the face of American nuclear superiority, also launched a massive arms buildup. Yet Brezhnev and company proceeded cautiously in the mid-1960s and avoided direct confrontation with the United States.

In the wake of Khrushchev's reforms, the 1960s brought modest liberalization and more consumer goods to eastern Europe, as well as somewhat greater national autonomy, especially in Poland and Romania. In January 1968, the reform elements in the Czechoslovak Communist Party gained a majority and voted out the long-time Stalinist leader in favor of Alexander Dubček (1921–1992), whose new government launched dramatic reforms.

Educated in Moscow, Dubček was a dedicated Communist. But he and his allies believed that they could reconcile genuine socialism with personal freedom and internal party democracy. Thus local decision making by trade unions, managers, and consumers replaced rigid bureaucratic planning, and censorship was relaxed. The reform program proved enormously popular.

Although Dubček remembered the lesson of the Hungarian revolution and constantly proclaimed his loyalty to the Warsaw Pact, the determination of the Czechoslovak reformers to build what they called "socialism with a human face" frightened hard-line Communists. These fears were particularly strong in Poland and East Germany, where leaders knew full well that they lacked popular support. Moreover, the Soviet Union feared that a liberalized Czechoslovakia would eventually be drawn to neutrality or even to the democratic West. Thus the Eastern bloc countries launched a concerted campaign of intimidation against the Czechoslovak leaders, and in August 1968, 500,000 Russian and allied eastern European troops suddenly occupied Czechoslovakia. The Czechoslovaks made no attempt to resist militarily, and the arrested leaders surrendered to Soviet demands. The reform program was abandoned, and the Czechoslovak experiment in humanizing communism came to an end. Shortly after the invasion of Czechoslovakia, Brezhnev declared the so-called **Brezhnev Doctrine,** according to which the Soviet Union and its allies had the right to intervene in any socialist country whenever they saw the need.

The Invasion of Czechoslovakia   Armed with Czechoslovakian flags, courageous Czechs in downtown Prague try to stop a Soviet tank and repel the invasion and occupation of their country by the Soviet Union and its eastern European allies. This dramatic confrontation marked a high point, because the Czechs and the Slovaks realized that military resistance would be suicidal. *(AP/Wide World Photos)*

The 1968 invasion of Czechoslovakia was the crucial event of the Brezhnev era, which really lasted beyond the aging leader's death in 1982 until the emergence in 1985 of Mikhail Gorbachev. The invasion demonstrated the determination of the ruling elite to maintain the status quo throughout the Soviet bloc. Only in the 1980s, with Poland taking the lead, would a strong current of reform and opposition develop again to challenge Communist rule.

The Soviet Union to 1985

Determined to maintain firm control of eastern Europe, Soviet leaders set the example at home. There was a certain **re-Stalinization** of the U.S.S.R., but now dictatorship was collective rather than personal, and coercion replaced terror. This compromise seemed to suit the leaders and a majority of the people.

A slowly rising standard of living for ordinary people contributed to the apparent stability in the Soviet Union, although long lines and innumerable shortages persisted. Ambitious individuals had a tremendous incentive to do as the state wished in order to gain access to special, well-stocked stores, to attend special schools, and to travel abroad.

Another source of stability was the enduring nationalism of ordinary Great Russians. Party leaders successfully identified themselves with Russian patriotism, stressing their role in saving the country during the Second World War and protecting it now from foreign foes, including eastern European "counter-revolutionaries." Moreover, the politically dominant Great Russians, who were concentrated in the central Russian heartland, generally feared that greater freedom might result in demands for autonomy and even independence not only by eastern European nationalities but also by the non-Russian nationalities within the Soviet Union itself.

The strength of the government was expressed in the re-Stalinization of culture and art. Critical free expression disappeared. Acts of open nonconformity and public protest were severely punished, but by sophisticated, cunning methods. Most frequently, dissidents were blacklisted and thus rendered unable to find decent jobs since the government was the only employer. This fate was enough to keep most in line. More determined protesters were quietly imprisoned, while celebrated nonconformists such as Aleksandr Solzhenitsyn were permanently expelled from the country. Eliminating the worst aspects of Stalin's dictatorship strengthened the regime, and almost all Western experts concluded that rule by a self-perpetuating Communist Party elite in the Soviet Union appeared to be quite solid in the 1970s and early 1980s.

Yet beneath the dreary immobility of political life in the Brezhnev era, the Soviet Union was actually experiencing profound changes. Three of these changes, which were seldom appreciated by Western observers at the time, were particularly significant.

First, the growth of the urban population, which had raced forward at breakneck speed in the Stalin years, continued rapidly in the 1960s and 1970s. In 1985 two-thirds of all Soviet citizens lived in cities, and one-quarter lived in big cities. Of great significance, this expanding urban population lost its old peasant ways, exchanging them for more education, better job skills, and greater sophistication.

Second, the number of highly trained scientists, managers, and specialists expanded prodigiously, increasing fourfold between 1960 and 1985. Thus the class of well-educated, pragmatic, and self-confident experts, which played such an important role in restructuring industrial societies after World War II (see the discussion in the next section), continued to develop rapidly in the Soviet Union after 1968.

Third, education and freedom for experts in their special areas helped foster the gradual growth of Soviet public opinion. Educated people read, discussed, and formed definite ideas on important issues, many of which could be approached and debated in "nonpolitical" terms. Developing ideas on such questions as environmental pollution and urban transportation, educated urban people increasingly saw themselves as worthy of having a voice in society's decisions, even its political decisions. While Brezhnev and his aging colleagues slept, a revolution was in the making.

Postwar Social Transformations, 1945–1968

While Europe staged its astonishing political and economic recovery from the Nazi nightmare, the patterns of everyday life and the structure of Western society were changing no less rapidly and remarkably. Epoch-making inventions and new technologies profoundly affected human existence. Important groups in society formulated new attitudes and demands, which were closely related to the changing class structure and social reforms. The structure of women's lives changed dramatically. An international youth culture took shape and rose to challenge established lifestyles and even governments.

• *How did changing patterns in technology, class relations, women's work, and youth culture bring major social transformations?*

Science and Technology

Ever since the scientific revolution of the seventeenth century and the Industrial Revolution at the end of the eighteenth century, scientific and technical developments had powerfully influenced attitudes, society, and everyday life. Never was this influence stronger than after about 1940. Science and technology proved so productive and influential because, for the first time in history, "pure theoretical" science and "practical" technology (or "applied" science) were effectively joined together on a massive scale.

With the advent of the Second World War, pure science lost its impractical innocence. Most leading university scientists went to work on top-secret projects to help their governments fight the war. The development by British scientists of radar to detect enemy aircraft was a particularly important outcome of this new kind of sharply focused research. A radically improved radar system played a key role in Britain's victory in the battle for air supremacy in 1940. The air war also greatly stimulated the development of jet aircraft and spurred further research on electronic computers, which calculated the complex mathematical relationships between fast-moving planes and anti-aircraft shells to increase the likelihood of a hit.

The most spectacular result of directed scientific research during the war was the atomic bomb. In August 1939, physicist Albert Einstein wrote to President Franklin Roosevelt that recent work in physics suggested that "it may become possible to set up a nuclear chain reaction in a large mass of uranium" and to construct "extremely powerful bombs of a new type."[5] This letter and ongoing experiments by nuclear physicists led to the top-secret Manhattan Project, which ballooned into a mammoth crash program. After three years of intensive effort, the first atomic bomb was successfully tested in July 1945. In August 1945, two bombs were dropped on Hiroshima and Nagasaki, thereby ending the war with Japan.

Online Study Center **Improve Your Grade**
Primary Source: Witness to the Birth of the Atomic Age

The atomic bomb showed the world both the awesome power and the heavy moral responsibilities of modern science and its high priests. As one Los Alamos scientist exclaimed as he watched the first mushroom cloud rise over the American desert, "We are all sons-of-bitches now!"[6]

The spectacular results of directed research during World War II inspired a new model for science—**Big Science.** By combining theoretical work with sophisticated engineering in a large organization, Big Science could attack extremely difficult problems, from better products for consumers to new and improved weapons for the military. Big Science was extremely expensive, requiring large-scale financing from governments and large corporations.

Populous, victorious, and wealthy, the United States took the lead in Big Science after World War II. Between 1945 and 1965, spending on scientific research and development in the United States grew five times as fast as the national income, and by 1965 such spending took 3 percent of all U.S. income. It was generally accepted that government should finance science heavily in both the "capitalist" United States and the "socialist" Soviet Union.

One reason for the parallel between the two countries was that science was not demobilized in either country after the war. Scientists remained a critical part of every major military establishment, and a large portion of all postwar scientific research went for "defense." New weapons such as rockets, nuclear submarines, and spy satellites demanded breakthroughs no less remarkable than those of radar and the first atomic bomb. After 1945 roughly one-quarter of all men and women trained in science and engineering in the West—and perhaps more in the Soviet Union—were employed full-time in the production of weapons to kill other humans.

Sophisticated science, lavish government spending, and military needs all came together in the space race of the 1960s. In 1957 the Soviets used long-range rockets developed in their nuclear weapons program to put a satellite in orbit. In 1961 they sent the world's first cosmonaut circling the globe. Embarrassed by Soviet triumphs, the United States made an all-out U.S. commitment to catch up with the Soviets and landed a crewed spacecraft on the moon in 1969. Four more moon landings followed by 1972.

The rapid expansion of government-financed research in the United States attracted many of Europe's best scientists during the 1950s and 1960s. Thoughtful Europeans lamented this "brain drain" and feared that Europe was falling hopelessly behind the United States in science and technology. In fact, a revitalized Europe was already responding to the American challenge, with countries pooling their efforts on such Big Science projects as the Concorde supersonic passenger airliner and the peaceful uses of atomic energy.

The rise of Big Science and of close ties between science and technology greatly altered the lives of scientists. The scientific community grew much larger than ever before. There were about four times as many scientists in Europe and North America in 1975 as in 1945. Scientists, technologists, engineers, and medical specialists were counted after 1945, in part because there were so many of them.

One consequence of the growth of science was its high degree of specialization, for no one could possibly master a broad field such as physics or medicine. Intense specialization in new disciplines and subdisciplines increased the rates at which both basic knowledge was acquired and practical applications were made.

Highly specialized modern scientists and technologists normally had to work as members of a team, which completely changed the work and lifestyle of modern scientists. A great deal of work therefore went on in large bureaucratic organizations, where the individual was very often a small cog in a great machine. The growth of large scientific bureaucracies in government and private enterprise suggested how scientists and technologists permeated the entire society and many aspects of life.

Modern science became highly, even brutally, competitive. This competitiveness is well depicted in Nobel Prize winner James Watson's fascinating book *The Double Helix,* which tells how in 1953 Watson and an Englishman, Francis Crick, discovered the structure of DNA, the molecule of heredity. A brash young American Ph.D. in his twenties, Watson seemed almost obsessed by the idea that some other research team would find the solution first and thereby deprive him of the fame and fortune he desperately wanted. With so many thousands of like-minded researchers in the wealthy countries of the world, scientific and technical knowledge rushed forward in the postwar era.

The Changing Class Structure

Rapid economic growth went a long way toward creating a new society in Europe after the Second World War. European society became more mobile and more democratic. Old class barriers relaxed, and class distinctions became fuzzier.

Changes in the structure of the middle class were particularly influential in the general drift toward a less rigid class structure. In the nineteenth and early twentieth centuries, the model for the middle class had been the independent, self-employed individual who owned a business or practiced a liberal profession such as law or medicine. Ownership of property—very often inherited property—and strong family ties had often been the keys to wealth and standing within the middle class. After 1945 this pattern declined drastically in western Europe. A new breed of managers and experts replaced traditional property owners as the leaders of the middle class. Ability to serve the needs of a big organization largely replaced inherited property and family connections in determining an individual's social position in the middle and upper middle classes. At the same time, the middle class grew massively and became harder to define.

There were several reasons for these developments. Rapid industrial and technological expansion created in large corporations and government agencies a powerful demand for technologists and managers. Moreover, the old propertied middle class lost control of many family-owned businesses, and many small businesses (including family farms) simply passed out of existence as their former owners joined the ranks of salaried employees.

Top managers and ranking civil servants therefore represented the model for a new middle class of salaried specialists. Well paid and highly trained, often with backgrounds in engineering or accounting, these experts increasingly came from all social classes, even the working class. Pragmatic and realistic, they were primarily concerned with efficiency and practical solutions to concrete problems. This new middle class was more open, democratic, and insecure than the old propertied middle class.

The structure of the lower classes also became more flexible and open. There was a mass exodus from farms and the countryside, as one of the most traditional and least mobile groups in European society drastically declined. Meanwhile, the industrial working class ceased to expand and began to decline, while job opportunities for white-collar and service employees grew rapidly. Such employees bore a greater resemblance to the new middle class of salaried specialists than to industrial workers, who were also better educated and more specialized.

European governments were reducing class tensions with a series of social security reforms. Many of these reforms—such as increased unemployment benefits and more extensive old-age pensions—simply strengthened social security measures first pioneered in Bismarck's Ger-

many before the First World War (see page 833). Other programs were new, like comprehensive national health systems directed by the state. Most countries introduced family allowances—direct government grants to parents to help them raise their children. These allowances helped many poor families make ends meet. Most European governments also gave maternity grants and built inexpensive public housing for low-income families and individuals. These and other social reforms provided a humane floor of well-being. Reforms also promoted greater equality because they were expensive and were paid for in part by higher taxes on the rich.

Consumers on the Move In the early postwar years the Italians had their motor scooters and the French their motorbikes. This ad promises young people that "sooner or later" they will have a "Velo," and it subtly assures housewives that the bike is safe. In small towns and villages the slow-moving motorbike could be a godsend for errands and daily shopping. (*Roger Perrin/The Bridgeman Art Library*)

The rising standard of living and the spread of standardized consumer goods also worked to level Western society, as the percentage of income spent on food and drink declined substantially. For example, the European automobile industry expanded phenomenally after lagging far behind the United States since the 1920s. In 1948 there were only 5 million cars in western Europe, but in 1965 there were 44 million. Car ownership was democratized and came within the range of better-paid workers.

Europeans took great pleasure in the products of the "gadget revolution" as well. Like Americans, Europeans filled their houses and apartments with washing machines, vacuum cleaners, refrigerators, dishwashers, radios, TVs, and stereos. The purchase of consumer goods was greatly facilitated by installment purchasing, which allowed people to buy on credit. With the expansion of social security safeguards, reducing the need to accumulate savings for hard times and old age, ordinary people were increasingly willing to take on debt. This change had far-reaching consequences.

Leisure and recreation occupied an important place in consumer societies. The most astonishing leisure-time development was the blossoming of mass travel and tourism. With month-long paid vacations required by law in most European countries and widespread automobile ownership, beaches and ski resorts came within the reach of the middle class and much of the working class. By the late 1960s, packaged tours with cheap group flights and bargain hotel accommodations had made even distant lands easily accessible. A French company grew rich building imitation Tahitian paradises around the world. At Swedish nudist colonies on secluded West African beaches, officeworkers from Stockholm fleetingly worshiped the sun in the middle of the long northern winter. Truly, consumerism had come of age.

New Roles for Women

A growing emancipation of women in Europe and North America was unquestionably one of the most significant transformations of the cold war era. This historic development grew out of long-term changes in the basic patterns of motherhood and paid work outside the home. These changing patterns altered women's experiences and expectations, preparing the way for the success of a new generation of feminist thinkers and a militant women's movement in the 1970s and 1980s (see pages 1009–1010).

Before the Industrial Revolution, most Europeans married late. Once a woman was married, however, she usually had children as long as she was fertile. By the late nineteenth century, improved diet, higher incomes, and the use of contraception within marriage were producing the

demographic transition from high birthrates and death rates to low birthrates and death rates.

These trends continued in the twentieth century. In the 1950s and 1960s, the typical woman in the West married early and bore her children quickly. The postwar baby boom did make for larger families and a fairly rapid population growth of 1 to 1.5 percent per year in many European countries. However, in the 1960s the long-term decline in birthrates resumed, and from the mid-1970s on in many European countries, the total population practically stopped growing from natural increase, with limited subsequent growth coming mainly from immigation.

The postwar culmination of the trends toward early marriage, early childbearing, and small family size in wealthy urban societies had revolutionary implications for women. Above all, pregnancy and child care occupied a much smaller portion of a woman's life than in earlier times. By the early 1970s, about half of Western women were having their last baby by the age of twenty-six or twenty-seven. When the youngest child trooped off to kindergarten, the average mother had more than forty years of life in front of her.

This was a momentous change. Throughout history male-dominated society insisted on defining most women as mothers or potential mothers, and motherhood was very demanding. In the postwar years, however, motherhood no longer absorbed the energies of a lifetime, and more and more married women looked for new roles in the world of work outside the family.

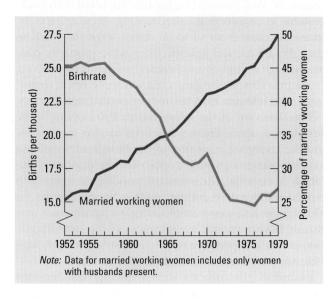

Note: Data for married working women includes only women with husbands present.

FIGURE 30.1 The Decline of the Birthrate and the Increase of Married Working Women in the United States, 1952–1979 The challenge of working away from home encouraged American wives to prefer fewer children and helped lower the birthrate.

For centuries before the Industrial Revolution, ordinary women worked hard and long on farms and in home industries while caring for their large families. With the growth of modern industry and much more rigid gender roles, few middle-class women worked outside the home for wages, although charity work was socially acceptable. Young unmarried women continued to work as wage earners, but poor married women typically earned their money at home in low-paid crafts as they looked after their children.

In the twentieth century and especially after World War II, the ever-greater complexity of the modern economy meant that almost all women had to go outside the home to find cash income. Three major forces helped women searching for jobs. First, the economy boomed from about 1950 to 1973 and created a strong demand for labor. Second, the economy continued its gradual shift away from the old, male-dominated heavy industries, such as coal, steel, and shipbuilding, to the more dynamic, "white-collar" service industries, such as government, education, trade, and health care. Some women had always worked in these service fields. Third, young Western women shared fully in the postwar education revolution and could

Celebrating Women's History Judy Chicago's multimedia creation *The Dinner Party* features thirty-nine handcrafted placemats and ceramic plates, each embellished with a painted motif associated with the woman being honored. Begun in 1974 and completed in 1978 with the participation of more than one hundred women, *The Dinner Party* was intended to represent the "historic struggle of women to participate in all the aspects of society." It attracted enormous crowds. *(© 2007 Judy Chicago/Artists Rights Society [ARS], New York)*

take advantage of the growing need for officeworkers and well-trained professionals. Thus more and more married women became full-time and part-time wage earners.

The trend went the furthest in communist eastern Europe, where women accounted for almost half of all employed persons. In noncommunist western Europe and North America, there was a good deal of variation, with the percentage of married women in the workforce rising from a range of roughly 20 to 25 percent in 1950 to a range of 40 to 70 percent in the early 1980s.

Rising employment for married women went hand in hand with the decline of the birthrate (see Figure 30.1). Women who worked outside the home had significantly fewer children than women of the same age who did not. Raising a family while holding down a full-time job was a tremendous challenge and often resulted in a woman's being grossly overworked. The multiple demands of job, motherhood, and marriage became more manageable with fewer children.

Married women entering (or re-entering) the labor force faced widespread, long-established discrimination in pay, advancement, and occupational choice in comparison to men. Moreover, many women could find only part-time work. As the divorce rate rose in the 1960s, part-time work, with its low pay and scanty benefits, meant poverty for many women with teenage children. Finally, in the best of circumstances, married working women still carried most of the child-raising and housekeeping responsibilities. A reason for many to accept part-time employment, this gendered imbalance meant an exhausting "double day"—on the job and at home—for the full-time worker.

The injustices that married women encountered as wage earners contributed greatly to the subsequent movement for women's equality and emancipation. A young unmarried woman of a hundred years ago was more likely to accept such problems as temporary nuisances because she looked forward to marriage and motherhood for fulfillment. In the postwar era, a married wage earner in her thirties gradually developed a very different perspective. She saw employment as a permanent condition within which she, like her male counterpart, sought not only income but also psychological satisfaction. Sexism and discrimination in the workplace—and in the home—grew loathsome and evoked the sense of injustice that drives revolutions and reforms. When powerful voices arose to challenge the system, they found widespread support among working women.

Youth and the Counterculture

Economic prosperity and a more democratic class structure had a powerful impact on youth throughout the Western world. The bulging cohort of youth born after World War II developed a distinctive and very international youth culture, which eventually became a "counterculture" that rebelled against parents, authority figures, and the status quo.

Young people in the United States took the lead. American college students in the 1950s were often dismissed as the "Silent Generation," but by the late 1950s the "beat" movement was stoking the fires of revolt in selected urban enclaves, such as the Near North Side of Chicago. There the young (and the not-so-young) fashioned a highly pub-

licized subculture that blended radical politics, unbridled personal experimentation (with drugs and communal living, for example), and new artistic styles. This subculture quickly spread to major American and western European cities. The young folksinger Bob Dylan summed up the increasingly radical political and cultural aspirations of the "younger generation" in lyrics that became a rallying cry, "the times they are a'changing."[7]

Certainly the sexual behavior of young people appeared to change dramatically in the 1960s and into the 1970s. More young people engaged in sexual intercourse, and they did so at an earlier age, in part because the discovery of safe and effective contraceptive pills could eliminate the risk of unwanted pregnancy. A 1973 study reported that only 4.5 percent of West German youths born in 1945 and 1946 had experienced sexual relations before their seventeenth birthday but that 32 percent of those born in 1953 and 1954 had done so.[8] Perhaps even more significant was the growing tendency of young unmarried people to live together in a separate

Woodstock, 1969   The brainchild of four young entrepreneurs, Woodstock snowballed into the world's biggest rock concert, a three-day bash in upstate New York that drew 450,000 guests and caused twenty-mile traffic jams. Standout performers included the guitarist Jimi Hendrix, Janis Joplin, and Joe Cocker. A high point for the youth culture, with antiwar and free love overtones, Woodstock spawned many myths and conflicting interpretations. *(© Lisa Law)*

Student Rebellion in Paris   These rock-throwing students in the Latin Quarter of Paris are trying to force education reforms and even to topple de Gaulle's government. Throughout May 1968 students clashed repeatedly with France's tough riot police in bloody street fighting. De Gaulle remained in power, but a major reform of French education did follow. *(Bruno Barbey/Magnum Photos)*

household on a semipermanent basis, with little thought of getting married or having children. Thus many youths, especially middle-class youths, defied social custom, claiming in effect that the long-standing monopoly of married couples on legitimate sexual unions was dead.

Several factors contributed to the emergence of the international youth culture in the 1960s. First, mass communications and youth travel linked countries and continents together. Second, the postwar baby boom meant that young people became an unusually large part of the population and could therefore exercise exceptional influence on society as a whole. Third, postwar prosperity and greater equality gave young people more purchasing power than ever before. This enabled them to set their own trends and patterns of consumption, which fostered generational loyalty. Finally, prosperity meant that good jobs were readily available. Students and young job seekers had little need to fear punishment from strait-laced employers for unconventional behavior.

The youth culture practically fused with the counterculture in opposition to the established order in the late 1960s. Student protesters embraced romanticism and revolutionary idealism, dreaming of complete freedom and simpler, purer societies. The materialistic West was hopelessly rotten, but better societies were being built in the newly independent countries of Asia and Africa, or so many young radicals believed. Thus the Vietnam War took on special significance. Many politically active students believed that the older generation was fighting an immoral and imperialistic war against a small and heroic people. As the war in Vietnam intensified, so did worldwide student opposition to it.

Student protests in western Europe also highlighted more general problems of youth, education, and a society of specialists. In contrast to the United States, high school and university educations in Europe had been limited for centuries to a small elite. Whereas 22 percent of the American population was going on to some form of higher education in 1950, only 3 to 4 percent of western European youths were doing so. Then enrollments skyrocketed. By 1960 at least three times as many students were going to some kind of university as had attended before the war, and the number continued to rise sharply until the 1970s. Reflecting the development of a more democratic class structure and a growing awareness that higher education was the key to success, European universities gave more scholarships and opened their doors to more students from the lower middle and lower classes.

The rapid expansion of higher education meant that classes were badly overcrowded. Competition for grades became intense. Moreover, although more practical areas of study were gradually added, many students felt that they were not getting the kind of education they needed for jobs in the modern world. At the same time, some reflective students feared that universities would soon do nothing but turn out docile technocrats both to stock and to serve "the establishment."

The many tensions within the exploding university population came to a head in the late 1960s and early 1970s. As in the United States, European university students rose to challenge their university administrations and even their governments. The most far-reaching of these revolts occurred in France in 1968. Students occupied buildings and took over the University of Paris, which led to violent clashes with police. Rank-and-file workers ignored the advice of their cautious union officials, and a more or less spontaneous general strike spread across France in May 1968. It seemed certain that President de Gaulle's Fifth Republic would collapse.

In fact, de Gaulle stiffened, like an old-fashioned irate father. He moved troops toward Paris and called for new elections. Thoroughly frightened by the student-sparked upheaval and fearing an eventual communist takeover, the masses of France voted overwhelmingly for de Gaulle's party and a return to law and order. Workers went back to work, and the mini-revolution collapsed. Yet the proud de Gaulle and the postwar European renaissance that he represented had been shaken, and within a year he resigned. Growing out of the counterculture and youthful idealism, the student rebellion of 1968 signaled the end of an era and the return of unrest and uncertainty in the 1970s and early 1980s.

Conflict and Challenge in the Late Cold War, 1968–1985

Similar to but more important than the student upheaval in France and the crushing of socialist reform in Czechoslovakia, the Vietnam War marked the beginning of a new era of challenges and uncertainties in the late 1960s. The Vietnam War and its aftermath divided the people of the United States, shook the ideology of containment, and weakened the Western alliance. A second challenge affecting the whole world appeared when the great postwar economic boom came to a close in 1973, opening a long period of economic stagnation, widespread unemployment, and social dislocation.

• *What were the key aspects of political conflict, economic stagnation, and the feminist movement in the late cold war?*

The United States and Vietnam

President Johnson wanted to go down in history as a master reformer and a healer of old wounds. Instead, he opened new ones with the Vietnam War.

Although many student radicals believed that imperialism was the main cause, American involvement in Vietnam was more clearly a product of the cold war and the policy of containment (see page 984). From the late 1940s on, most Americans and their leaders viewed the world in terms of a constant struggle to stop the spread of communism. As western Europe began to revive and China established a communist government in 1949, efforts to contain communism shifted to Asia. The bloody Korean War (1950–1953) ended in stalemate, but the United States did succeed in preventing a communist victory in South Korea. After the defeat of the French in Vietnam in 1954, the Eisenhower administration refused to sign the Geneva Accords that temporarily divided the country into two zones pending national unification by means of free elections. President Eisenhower then acquiesced in the refusal of the anticommunist South Vietnamese government to accept the verdict of elections and provided it with military aid. President Kennedy greatly increased the number of American "military advisers" to sixteen thousand.

After winning the 1964 election on a peace platform, President Johnson greatly expanded the American role in the Vietnam conflict. American strategy was to "escalate" the war sufficiently to break the will of the North Vietnamese and their southern allies without resorting to "overkill," which might risk war with the entire Communist bloc. Thus South Vietnam received massive military aid, American forces in the South gradually grew to half a million men, and the United States bombed North Vietnam with ever-greater intensity. But there was no invasion of the North or naval blockade. In the end, the American strategy of limited warfare backfired. It was the American people who grew weary and the American leadership that cracked.

The undeclared war in Vietnam, fought nightly on American television, eventually divided the nation. Initial support was strong. The politicians, the media, and the population as a whole saw the war as part of a legitimate defense against communist totalitarianism in all poor countries. But an antiwar movement quickly emerged on college campuses, where the prospect of being drafted to fight savage battles in Asian jungles made male stomachs churn. In October 1965, student protesters joined forces with old-line socialists, New Left intellectuals, and pacifists in antiwar demonstrations in fifty American cities. By 1967 a growing number of critics denounced the war as a criminal intrusion into a complex and distant civil war.

Criticism reached a crescendo after the Vietcong Tet Offensive in January 1968. This, the communists' first comprehensive attack with conventional weapons on major cities in South Vietnam, failed militarily: the Vietcong suffered heavy losses, and the attack did not spark a mass uprising. But Washington had been claiming that victory in South Vietnam was in sight, and U.S. critics of the Vietnam War quickly interpreted the bloody combat as a decisive American defeat. America's leaders lost heart. In 1968, after a narrow victory in the New Hampshire primary, President Johnson called for negotiations with North Vietnam and announced that he would not stand for re-election.

Elected by a razor-slim margin in 1968, President Richard Nixon (1913–1994) sought to gradually disengage America from Vietnam and the accompanying national crisis. Intensifying the continuous bombardment of the enemy while simultaneously pursuing peace talks with the North Vietnamese, Nixon suspended the draft, so hated on college campuses, and cut American forces in Vietnam from 550,000 to 24,000 in four years. The cost of the war dropped dramatically. Moreover, President Nixon launched a flank attack in diplomacy. He journeyed to China in 1972 and reached a spectacular if limited reconciliation with the People's Republic of China. In doing so, Nixon took advantage of China's growing fears of the Soviet Union and undermined North Vietnam's position.

Fortified by the overwhelming endorsement of the voters in his 1972 electoral triumph, President Nixon and Secretary of State Henry Kissinger finally reached a peace agreement with North Vietnam. The agreement allowed remaining American forces to complete their withdrawal, and the United States reserved the right to resume bombing if the accords were broken. Fighting declined markedly in South Vietnam, where the South Vietnamese army appeared to hold its own against the Vietcong. The storm of crisis in the United States seemed to have passed.

On the contrary, the country reaped the **Watergate** whirlwind. Like some other recent American presidents, Nixon authorized spying activities that went beyond the law. Going further than his predecessors, he allowed special units to use various illegal means to stop the leaking of government documents to the press. One such group broke into the Democratic Party headquarters in Washington's Watergate complex in June 1972 and was promptly arrested. Nixon and many of his assistants then tried to hush up the bungled job, but the media and the machinery of congressional investigation eventually exposed the administration's web of lies and lawbreak-

Seymour Chwast: End Bad Breath   Antiwar messages came in every shape and form as opposition to the Vietnam War heated up. This vibrant poster assumes, quite reasonably, that the American viewer is steeped in the popular culture of the mass media. It ridicules American military involvement with a sarcastic parody of familiar television commercials. *(Courtesy, Seymour Chwast/Push Pin Group)*

ing. In 1974 a beleaguered Nixon was forced to resign in disgrace.

The consequences of renewed political crisis flowing from the Watergate affair were profound. First, Watergate resulted in a major shift of power away from the presidency and toward Congress, especially in foreign affairs. Therefore, as American aid to South Vietnam diminished in 1973 and as an emboldened North Vietnam launched a general invasion against South Vietnamese armies in early 1974, Congress refused to permit any American military response. A second consequence of the U.S. crisis was that after more than thirty-five years of battle, the Vietnamese communists unified their country in 1975 as a harsh dictatorial state. Third, the belated fall of South Vietnam in the wake of Watergate shook America's postwar confidence and left the country divided and uncertain about its proper role in world affairs.

Détente or Cold War?

One alternative to the badly damaged policy of containing communism was the policy of détente, or the progressive piecemeal relaxation of cold war tensions. Thus while the cold war continued to rage outside Europe and generally defined superpower relations between the Soviet Union and the United States, West Germany took a major step toward genuine peace in Europe.

West German chancellor Willy Brandt (1913–1992) took the lead when in December 1970 he flew to Poland for the signing of a historic treaty of reconciliation. In a dramatic moment rich in symbolism, Brandt laid a wreath at the tomb of the Polish unknown soldier and another at the monument commemorating the armed uprising of Warsaw's Jewish ghetto against occupying Nazi armies. Standing before the ghetto memorial, a somber Brandt fell to his knees and knelt as if in prayer. "I wanted," Brandt said later, "to ask pardon in the name of our people for a million-fold crime which was committed in the misused name of the Germans."[9]

Brandt's gesture at the Warsaw Ghetto memorial and the treaty with Poland were part of his policy of reconciliation with eastern Europe. Indeed, Brandt aimed at nothing less than a comprehensive peace settlement for central Europe and the two German states established after 1945. The Federal Republic of Germany (West Germany) had long claimed that the communist German Democratic Republic (East Germany) lacked free elections and hence any legal or moral basis. West Germany also refused to accept the loss of German territory taken by Poland and the Soviet Union after 1945. But Brandt, the popular socialist mayor of West Berlin when the Berlin Wall was built in 1961, believed that the wall showed the painful limitations of West Germany's official hard line toward communist eastern Europe. A new foreign policy was needed.

Winning the chancellorship in 1969, Brandt negotiated treaties with the Soviet Union, Poland, and Czechoslovakia that formally accepted existing state boundaries in return for a mutual renunciation of force or the threat of force. Using the imaginative formula of "two German states within one German nation," Brandt's government also broke decisively with the past and entered into direct relations with East Germany. He aimed for modest practical improvements rather than reunification, which at that point was completely impractical.

The policy of détente reached its high point when all European nations (except isolationist Albania), the United States, and Canada signed the Final Act of the Helsinki Conference in 1975. The thirty-five nations participating agreed that Europe's existing political frontiers could not be changed by force. They also solemnly accepted numerous provisions guaranteeing the human rights and political freedoms of their citizens.

Online Study Center **Improve Your Grade**
Primary Source: The Helsinki Final Act: Human Rights and Fundamental Freedoms Enunciated

Optimistic hopes for détente in international relations gradually faded in the later 1970s. Brezhnev's Soviet Union ignored the human rights provisions of the Helsinki agreement, and East-West political competition remained very much alive outside Europe. Many Americans became convinced that the Soviet Union was taking advantage of détente, steadily building up its military might and pushing for political gains and revolutions in Africa, Asia, and Latin America. The Soviet invasion of Afghanistan in December 1979, which was designed to save an increasingly unpopular Marxist regime, was especially alarming. Many Americans feared that the oil-rich states of the Persian Gulf would be next, and once again they looked to the Atlantic alliance and military might to thwart communist expansion.

President Jimmy Carter (b. 1924), elected in 1976, tried to lead the Atlantic alliance beyond verbal condemnation and urged economic sanctions against the Soviet Union. Yet only Great Britain among the European allies supported the American initiative. The alliance showed the same lack of concerted action when the Solidarity movement rose in Poland. Some observers concluded that the alliance had lost the will to think and act decisively in dealing with the Soviet bloc.

The Atlantic alliance endured, however. The U.S. military buildup launched by Carter in his last years in office was greatly accelerated by President Ronald Reagan (1911–2004), who was swept into office in 1980 by a wave of patriotism and economic discontent. The new American leadership acted as if the military balance had tipped in favor of the Soviet Union, which Reagan anathematized as the "evil empire." Increasing defense spending enormously, the Reagan administration concentrated on nuclear arms and an expanded navy as keys to American power in the post-Vietnam age.

A broad swing in the historical pendulum toward greater conservatism in the 1980s gave Reagan invaluable allies in western Europe. In Great Britain a strong-willed Margaret Thatcher worked well with Reagan and was a forceful advocate for a revitalized Atlantic alliance. After a strongly pro-American Helmut Kohl (b. 1930) came to power with the conservative Christian Democrats in 1982, West Germany and the United States once again effectively coordinated military and political policy toward the Soviet bloc.

Passing in the 1970s and early 1980s from détente to confusion to regeneration, the Atlantic alliance bent, but it did not break. In maintaining the alliance, the Western nations gave indirect support to ongoing efforts to liberalize authoritarian communist eastern Europe and probably helped convince the Soviet Union's Mikhail Gorbachev that endless cold war conflict was foolish and dangerous.

The Women's Movement

The 1970s marked the birth of a broad-based feminist movement devoted to securing genuine gender equality and promoting the general interests of women. Three basic reasons accounted for this major development. First, ongoing changes in underlying patterns of motherhood and paid work created novel conditions and new demands (see pages 1002–1004). Second, a vanguard of feminist intellectuals articulated a powerful critique of gender relations, which stimulated many women to rethink their assumptions and challenge the status quo. Third, taking a lesson from the civil rights movement in the United States and worldwide student protest against the Vietnam War, dissatisfied individuals recognized that they had to band together if they were to influence politics and secure fundamental reforms.

One of the most influential works produced by this new feminist wave was *The Second Sex* (1949) by the French writer and philosopher Simone de Beauvoir (1908–1986). Characterizing herself as a "dutiful daughter" of the bourgeoisie in childhood, the adolescent Beauvoir came to see her pious and submissive mother as foolishly renouncing any self-expression outside of home and marriage and showing Beauvoir the dangers of a life she did not want. A brilliant university student, Beauvoir began at the Sorbonne a complex relationship with Jean-Paul Sartre, the future philosopher who became her lifelong intellectual companion and sometime lover.

Beauvoir analyzed the position of women within the framework of existential thought (see pages 916–917). She argued that women—like all human beings—were in essence free but that they had almost always been trapped by particularly inflexible and limiting conditions. (See the feature "Listening to the Past: A Feminist Critique of Marriage" on pages 1016–1017.) Only by means of courageous action and self-assertive creativity could a woman become a completely free person and escape the role of the inferior "other" that men had constructed for her gender. Drawing on history, philosophy, psychology, biology, and literature, Beauvoir's massive investigation inspired a generation of women intellectuals.

Online Study Center **Improve Your Grade**
Primary Source: *The Second Sex*: Existential Feminism

One such woman was Betty Friedan (b. 1924), who played a key role in reopening a serious discussion of women's issues in the United States. As a working wife and the mother of three small children in the 1950s, Friedan became acutely aware of the conflicting pressures of career and family. Conducting an in-depth survey of her classmates at Smith College fifteen years after their graduation, she concluded that many well-educated women shared her growing dissatisfaction. In her pathbreaking study *The Feminine Mystique* (1963), Friedan identified this dissatisfaction as the "problem that has no name." According to Friedan, the cause of this nameless problem was a crisis of identity. Women were not permitted to become mature adults and genuine human beings. Instead, they were expected to conform to a false, infantile pattern of femininity and live (like Beauvoir's mother) for their husbands and children. In short, women faced what feminists would soon call *sexism*, a pervasive social problem that required drastic reforms.

When long-standing proposals to treat sex discrimination as seriously as race discrimination fell again on deaf ears, Friedan took the lead in 1966 in founding the National Organization for Women (NOW) to press for women's rights. NOW flourished, growing from seven hundred members in 1967 to forty thousand in 1974. Many other women's organizations of varying persuasions rose to follow NOW in Europe and the United States. Throughout the 1970s, a proliferation of publications, conferences, and institutions devoted to women's issues reinforced the emerging international movement.

Although national peculiarities abounded, this movement generally shared the common strategy of entering the political arena and changing laws regarding women. First, advocates of women's rights pushed for new statutes in the workplace: laws against discrimination, "equal pay for equal work," and measures such as maternal leave and affordable day care designed to help women combine careers and family responsibilities. Second, the movement concentrated on gender and family questions, including the right to divorce (in some Catholic countries), legalized abortion, the needs of single mothers, and protection from rape and physical violence. In almost every country, the effort to decriminalize abortion served as a catalyst in mobilizing an effective, self-conscious women's movement (and in creating an opposition to it, as in the United States).

In countries that had long placed women in a subordinate position, the legal changes were little less than revolutionary. In Italy, for example, new laws abolished restrictions on divorce and abortion, which had been strengthened by Mussolini and defended energetically by the Catholic Church in the postwar era. By 1988 divorce

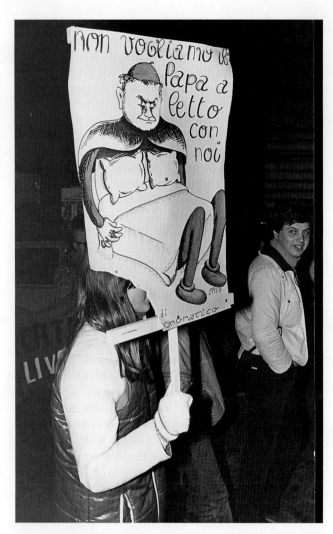

Italian Feminists These women demonstrate in Rome in 1981 for the passage of legislation legalizing abortion, which the pope and the Catholic Church have steadfastly opposed. This woman's provocative sign says that she does not want the pope in her bed. *(Giansanti/Corbis Sygma)*

and abortion were common in Italy, which had the lowest birthrate in Europe. More generally, the sharply focused women's movement of the 1970s won new rights for women. Subsequently, the movement became more diffuse, a victim of both its successes and the resurgence of an antifeminist opposition.

The accomplishments of the women's movement encouraged mobilization by many other groups. Gay men and lesbian women pressed their own demands, organizing politically and calling for an end to legal discrimination and social harassment. People with physical disabilities joined together to promote their interests. Thus many subordinate groups challenged the dominant majorities,

and the expansion and redefinition of human liberty— one of the great themes of modern Western and world history—continued.

The Troubled Economy

For twenty years after 1945, most Europeans were pre-occupied with the possibilities of economic progress and consumerism. The more democratic class structure also helped to reduce social tension, and ideological conflict went out of style. In the late 1960s, sharp criticism and social conflict re-emerged, however, marking the passing of postwar stability.

Yet it was the reappearance of economic crisis in the early 1970s that brought the most serious challenges for the average person. The postwar international monetary system was based on the American dollar, valued in gold at $35 an ounce. Giving foreign aid and fighting foreign wars, the United States sent billions abroad. By early 1971, it had only $11 billion in gold left, and Europe had accumulated U.S. $50 billion. Foreigners then panicked and raced to exchange their dollars for gold. President Richard Nixon responded by stopping the sale of American gold. The value of the dollar fell sharply, and inflation accelerated worldwide. Fixed rates of exchange were abandoned, and great uncertainty replaced postwar predictability in international trade and finance.

Even more damaging was the dramatic reversal in the price and availability of energy. The great postwar boom was fueled by cheap oil from the Middle East, which permitted energy-intensive industries—automobiles, chemicals, and electric power—to expand rapidly and lead other sectors of the economy forward. By 1971 the Arab-led Organization of Petroleum Exporting Countries (**OPEC**) had watched the price of crude oil decline consistently compared with the rising price of manufactured goods and had decided to reverse that trend by presenting a united front against the oil companies. The stage was set for a revolution in energy prices during the fourth Arab-Israeli war in October 1973, when Egypt and Syria launched a surprise attack on Israel. OPEC then declared an embargo on oil shipments to the United States, Israel's ally, and within a year crude oil prices quadrupled. Western nations realized that the rapid price rise was economically destructive, but they did nothing. Thus governments, industry, and individuals had no other choice than to deal piecemeal with the so-called oil shock—a "shock" that turned out to be an earthquake.

Coming on the heels of upheaval in the international monetary system, the revolution in energy prices plunged the world into its worst economic decline since the 1930s.

The energy-intensive industries that had driven the economy up in the 1950s and 1960s now dragged it down. Unemployment rose; productivity and living standards declined. By 1976 a modest recovery was in progress. But when a fundamentalist Islamic revolution struck Iran and oil production collapsed in that country, the price of crude oil doubled in 1979 and the world economy succumbed to its second oil shock. Unemployment and inflation rose dramatically before another uneven recovery began in 1982. In 1985 the unemployment rate in western Europe rose to its highest level since the Great Depression. Nineteen million people were unemployed.

One telling measure of the troubled economy was the **misery index,** which combined rates of inflation and unemployment in a single, powerfully emotional number. Figure 30.2 shows a comparison of misery indexes for the United States, Japan, and the Common Market countries between 1970 and 1986. "Misery" increased on both sides of the Atlantic, but the increase was substantially greater in western Europe, where these hard times were often referred to simply as "the crisis." Japan did better than both Europe and the United States in this period.

Throughout the 1970s and 1980s, anxious observers, recalling the disastrous consequences of the Great Depression, worried that the Common Market would disintegrate in the face of severe economic dislocation and that economic nationalism would halt steps toward European unity. Yet the Common Market—now officially known as the European Economic Community—continued to attract new members. In 1973 Denmark and Iceland, in addition to Britain, finally joined. Greece joined in 1981, and Portugal and Spain entered in 1986. The nations of the European Economic Community also cooperated more closely in international undertakings, and the movement toward unity for western Europe stayed alive.

Society in a Time of Economic Uncertainty

The most pervasive consequences of economic stagnation in the 1970s and early 1980s were probably psychological and attitudinal. Optimism gave way to pessimism; romantic utopianism yielded to sober realism. This drastic change in mood—a complete surprise only to those who had never studied history—affected states, institutions, and individuals in countless ways.

To be sure, there were heartbreaking human tragedies—lost jobs, bankruptcies, homelessness, and mental breakdowns. But on the whole, the welfare system fashioned in the postwar era prevented mass suffering and degradation

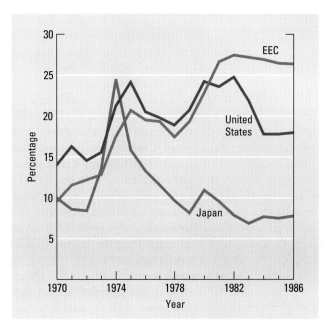

FIGURE 30.2 The Misery Index, 1970–1986 Combining rates of unemployment and inflation provided a simple but effective measure of economic hardship. This particular index represents the sum of two times the unemployment rate plus the inflation rate, reflecting the widespread belief that joblessness causes more suffering than higher prices. EEC = European Economic Community, or Common Market countries. (*Source: OECD data, as given in* The Economist, *June 15, 1985, p. 69.)*

through extended benefits for the unemployed, pensions for the aged, free medical care and special allowances for the needy, and a host of lesser supports. The responsive, socially concerned national state undoubtedly contributed to the preservation of political stability and democracy in the face of economic difficulties that might have brought revolution and dictatorship in earlier times.

The energetic response of governments to social needs helps explain the sharp increase in total government spending in most countries during the 1970s and early 1980s. In 1982 western European governments spent an average of more than 50 percent of all national income, as compared to only 37 percent fifteen years earlier. In all countries, people were much more willing to see their governments increase spending than raise taxes. This imbalance contributed to the rapid growth of budget deficits, national debts, and inflation. By the late 1970s, a powerful reaction against government's ever-increasing role had set in, however, and Western governments were gradually forced to introduce austerity measures to slow the growth of public spending and the welfare state.

Part of a broad cultural shift toward greater conservatism, growing voter dissatisfaction with government and government spending helped bring Margaret Thatcher (b. 1925) to power in Britain in 1979. Thatcher was determined to scale back the role of government in Britain, and in the 1980s—the "Thatcher years"—she pushed through a series of controversial "free-market" policies that transformed postwar Britain. In one of its most popular actions, Thatcher's Conservative government encouraged low- and moderate-income renters in state-owned housing projects to buy their apartments at rock-bottom prices. This initiative, part of Thatcher's broader privatization campaign, created a whole new class of property owners, thereby eroding the electoral base of Britain's socialist Labour Party. (See the feature "Individuals in Society: Margaret Thatcher.")

President Ronald Reagan's success in the United States was more limited. With widespread popular support and the agreement of most congressional Democrats as well as Republicans, Reagan in 1981 pushed through major cuts in income taxes all across the board. But Reagan and Congress failed to cut government spending, which increased as a percentage of national income in the course of his presidency. Reagan's massive military buildup was partly responsible, but spending on social programs also grew rapidly. The harsh recession of the early 1980s required that the government spend more on unemployment benefits, welfare benefits, and medical treatment for the poor. Moreover, Reagan's antiwelfare rhetoric mobilized the liberal opposition and eventually turned many moderates against him. Thus the budget deficit soared and the U.S. government debt tripled in a decade.

The most striking temporary exception to the general trend toward greater frugality was François Mitterrand (1916–1996) of France. After his election as president in 1981, Mitterrand led his Socialist Party on a lurch to the left, launching a vast program of nationalization and public investment designed to spend France out of economic stagnation. By 1983 this attempt had clearly failed. Mitterrand's Socialist government was then compelled to impose a wide variety of austerity measures and to maintain those policies for the rest of the decade.

When governments were forced to restrain spending, large scientific projects were often singled out for cuts. These reductions reinforced the ongoing computer revolution, which increased the efficiency of small businesses and stimulated new ventures by young innovative entrepreneurs. Big organizations lost some of their advantages over small firms.

Individuals felt the impact of austerity at an early date, for unlike governments, they could not pay their bills by printing money and going ever further into debt. The energy crisis of the 1970s forced them to re-examine not only their fuel bills but also the whole pattern of self-indulgent materialism in the postwar years. A growing number of experts and citizens concluded that the world was running out of resources and decried wasteful industrial practices and environmental pollution. In West Germany young activists known as the Greens in 1979 founded a political party to fight for environmental causes. The German Green movement elected some national and local representatives, and similar parties developed throughout Europe as environmentalism became a leading societal concern.

Another consequence of austerity in both Europe and North America was a leaner, tougher lifestyle in the 1970s and early 1980s, featuring more attention to nutrition and a passion for exercise. Correspondingly, there was less blind reliance on medical science for good health and a growing awareness that individuals had to accept a large portion of the responsibility for illness and disease. More people began to realize that they could substantially increase their life spans simply by eating regular meals, sleeping seven or eight hours each night, exercising two or three times a week, maintaining moderate weight, forgoing smoking, and using alcohol only in moderation.

Economic troubles also strengthened the new trends within the family. Men and women were encouraged to postpone marriage until they had put their careers on a firm foundation, so the age of marriage rose sharply for both sexes in many Western countries. Indeed, the very real threat of unemployment—or "underemployment" in a dead-end job—seemed to shape the outlook of a whole generation. College students of the 1980s were serious, practical, and often conservative. As one young woman at a French university told a reporter in 1985, "Jobs are the big worry now, so everyone wants to learn something practical."[10] In France as elsewhere, the shift away from the romantic visions and the political activism of the late 1960s was astonishing.

Harder times also help explain why ever more women entered or remained in the workforce after they did marry. Although attitudes related to personal fulfillment were one reason for the continuing increase—especially for well-educated, upper-middle-class women—many wives in poor and middle-class families simply had to work outside the home because of economic necessity. As in preindustrial Europe, the wife's earnings provided the margin of survival for millions of hard-pressed families.

Individuals in Society

Margaret Thatcher

Margaret Thatcher (b. 1925), the first woman elected to lead a major European state, stands as one of the most significant leaders of the late twentieth century. The controversial "Iron Lady" attacked socialism, promoted capitalism, and changed the face of modern Britain.

Born Margaret Roberts in a small city in southeastern England, her father was a small shopkeeper who instilled in his daughter the classic lower-middle-class virtues—hard work, personal responsibility, and practical education. A scholarship student at a local girls school, she entered Oxford in 1943 to study chemistry but soon found that politics was her passion. Elected president of student Conservatives, she ran in 1950 for Parliament in a solidly Labour district to gain experience. Articulate and attractive, she also gained the attention of Denis Thatcher, a wealthy businessman who drove her to campaign appearances in his Jaguar. Married a year later, the new Mrs. Thatcher abandoned chemistry, went to law school, gave birth to twins, and practiced as a tax attorney. In 1959, she returned to politics and won a seat in the Conservative triumph.

For the next fifteen years Mrs. Thatcher served in Parliament and held various ministerial posts when the Conservatives governed. In 1974, as the economy soured and the Conservatives lost two close elections, a rebellious Margaret Thatcher adroitly ran for the leadership position of the Conservative Party and won. In the 1979 election, as the Labour government faced rampant inflation and crippling strikes, Mrs. Thatcher promised to reduce union power, lower taxes, and promote free markets. Attracting swing votes from skilled workers, she won and became prime minister.

A self-described "conviction politician," Thatcher rejected postwar Keynesian efforts to manage the economy, arguing that governments had created inflation by printing too much money. Thus her government reduced the supply of money and credit, and it refused to retreat as interest rates and unemployment soared. Her popularity plummeted. But Thatcher was saved by good luck—and courage. In 1982, the generals ruling Argentina suddenly seized the Falkland Islands off the Argentine coast, the home of 1,800 British citizens. Ever a staunch nationalist, Thatcher detached a naval armada that recaptured the Falklands without a hitch. Britain loved Thatcher's determination, and the "Iron Lady" was re-elected in 1983.

Thatcher's second term was the high point of her success and influence. Her whole-hearted commitment to privatization changed the face of British industry.

More than fifty state-owned companies, ranging from the state tele-phone monopoly to the nationalized steel trust, were sold to private investors. Small investors were offered shares at bargain prices to promote "people's capitalism." Thatcher also curbed the power of British labor unions with various laws and actions. Most spectacularly, when in 1984 the once-mighty coal miners rejected more mine closings and doggedly struck for a year, Thatcher stood firm and beat them. This outcome had a profound psychological impact on the public.

Margaret Thatcher as prime minister.
(AP Images/Staff-Caulkin)

Elected again in 1987, Thatcher became increasingly stubborn, overconfident, and uncaring. Working well with her ideological soul mate, U.S. president Ronald Reagan, she opposed greater political and economic unity within the European Community. This, coupled with an unpopular effort to assert financial control over city governments, proved her undoing. In 1990, as in 1974, party stalwarts suddenly revolted and elected a new Conservative leader. Raised to the peerage by Queen Elizabeth II, the new Lady Thatcher then sat in the largely ceremonial House of Lords. The transformational changes of the Thatcher years endured, consolidated by her Conservative successor and largely accepted by the "New Labour" prime minister, the moderate Tony Blair.

Questions for Analysis

1. Why did Margaret Thatcher want to change Britain, and how did she do it?
2. Historians have often debated whether great leaders determine the course of history, or whether they only ride successfully the major forces of their time. Which view of history is supported by Thatcher's achievements? Why?

Online Study Center   **Improve Your Grade**
Going Beyond Individuals in Society

German Greens Supporting Poland's Solidarity   Best known for its passionate commitment to the environment, the German Green Party has also supported many progressive causes and campaigned against militarism and communism. These Greens are protesting in 1982 against the crackdown on Solidarity, the trade union movement that challenged Communist rule in Poland in the 1980s. The Greens are now Germany's third-largest political party, and they exercise real influence. *(Time Life Pictures/Getty Images)*

Chapter Summary

Online Study Center   **ACE the Test**

- *What were the causes of the cold war?*
- *Why did western Europe recover so successfully? How did colonial peoples win political independence and American blacks triumph in the civil rights movement?*
- *What was the pattern of postwar rebuilding and development in the Soviet Union and Communist eastern Europe?*
- *How did changing patterns in technology, class relations, women's work, and youth culture bring major social transformations?*
- *What were the key aspects of political conflict, economic stagnation, and the feminist movement in the late cold war?*

The recovery of western Europe after World War II was one of the most striking chapters in the long, uneven course of Western civilization. Although the dangerous tensions of the cold war frustrated hopes for a truly peaceful international order, the transition from imperi-

alism to decolonization proceeded rapidly, surprisingly smoothly, and without serious damage to western Europe. Genuine political democracy gained unprecedented strength in western Europe, and rapid economic progress marked a generation.

Fundamental social changes accompanied the political recovery and economic expansion after World War II. Pure science combined with applied technology to achieve remarkable success. The triumphs of applied science contributed not only to economic expansion but also to a more fluid, less antagonistic class structure, in which specialized education was the high road to advancement for men and women. Married women entered the labor force in growing numbers.

Postwar developments in eastern Europe displayed both similarities to and differences from developments in western Europe and North America. Perhaps the biggest difference was that Stalin imposed harsh one-party rule in the lands occupied by his armies, which led to the bitter cold war. Nevertheless, the Soviet Union became less dictatorial under Khrushchev, and the standard of living in the Soviet Union improved markedly in the 1950s and 1960s.

In the late 1960s and early 1970s, Europe and North America entered a time of crisis. Many nations, from France to Czechoslovakia to the United States, experienced major political difficulties, as cold war conflicts and ideological battles divided peoples and shook governments. Beginning with the oil shocks of the 1970s, severe economic problems added to the turmoil and brought real hardship to millions of people. Yet in western Europe and North America, the welfare system held firm, and both democracy and the movement toward European unity successfully passed through the storm. The women's movement also mobilized effectively and won expanded rights in the best tradition of Western civilization. Finally, efforts to achieve détente in central Europe while still maintaining a strong Atlantic alliance met some success. This modest progress helped lay the foundations for the sudden end of the cold war and the opening of a new era.

Key Terms

Big Three	de-Stalinization
Marshall Plan	Brezhnev Doctrine
NATO	re-Stalinization
cold war	Big Science
Christian Democrats	Watergate
Common Market	détente
decolonization	OPEC
neocolonialism	misery index

Online Study Center **Improve Your Grade** Flashcards

Suggested Reading

Bernstein, Serge. *The Republic of de Gaulle, 1958–1969.* 2006. An outstanding work on France.

Caute, David. *The Year of the Barricades: A Journey Through 1968.* 1990. A high-energy examination that brings the 1968 upheavals to life.

Chamberlain, M. E. *Decolonization: The Fall of European Empires,* 2d ed. 1999. A clear, up-to-date account.

de Grazia, Victoria. *Irresistible Empire: America's Advance Through Twentieth-Century Europe.* 2005. Lively, provocative account of Europe's "Americanization."

de Senarclens, Pierre. *From Yalta to the Iron Curtain: The Great Powers and the Origins of the Cold War.* 1995. A valuable work on the cold war.

Eksteins, Modris. *Walking Since Daybreak: A Story of Eastern Europe, World War II, and the Heart of Our Cen-*

tury. 2000. A powerful, partly autobiographical account that is highly recommended.

Gillingham, John. *European Integration, 1950–2003: Superstate or New Market Economy?* 2003. A brilliant interpretive history.

Hitchcock, William I. *The Struggle for Europe: The Turbulent History of a Divided Continent, 1945 to the Present.* 2004. A valuable general study with extensive bibliographies.

Jaraush, Konrad. *After Hitler: Recivilizing Germans, 1945–1995.* 2006. A stimulating survey by a distinguished historian.

Judt, Tony. *Postwar: A History of Europe Since 1945.* 2005. A masterful reconsideration, especially strong on smaller countries.

Reitan, Earl. *Tory Radicalism: Margaret Thatcher, John Major, and the Transformation of Modern Britain, 1979–1997.* 1997. Clear, concise, and very useful.

Scott, Joan W. *Only Paradoxes to Offer: French Feminists and the Rights of Man.* 1997. An important study of French feminism.

Tipton, Frank B., and Robert Aldrich. *An Economic and Social History of Europe from 1939 to the Present.* 1987. An interesting, wide-ranging account.

Westad, Odd Arne. *The Global Cold War: Third World Interventions and the Making of Our Times.* 2007. Up-to-date study of the cold war's global impact.

Notes

1. Quoted in N. Graebner, *Cold War Diplomacy, 1945–1960* (Princeton, N.J.: Van Nostrand, 1962), p. 17.
2. Quoted in J. Hennessy, *Economic "Miracles"* (London: Andre Deutsch, 1964), p. 5.
3. Quoted in S. E. Morison et al., *A Concise History of the American Republic* (New York: Oxford University Press, 1977), p. 697.
4. Quoted in D. Treadgold, *Twentieth Century Russia,* 5th ed. (Boston: Houghton Mifflin, 1981), p. 442.
5. Quoted in J. Ziman, *The Force of Knowledge: The Scientific Dimension of Society* (Cambridge: Cambridge University Press, 1976), p. 128.
6. Quoted in S. Toulmin, *The Twentieth Century: A Promethean Age,* ed. A. Bullock (London: Thames & Hudson, 1971), p. 294.
7. Quoted in N. Cantor, *Twentieth-Century Culture: Modernism to Deconstruction* (New York: Peter Lang, 1988), p. 252.
8. M. Mitterauer, *The History of Youth* (Oxford: Basil Blackwell, 1992), p. 40.
9. Quoted in Kessing's Research Report, *Germany and East Europe Since 1945: From the Potsdam Agreement to Chancellor Brandt's "Ostpolitik"* (New York: Charles Scribner's Sons, 1973), pp. 284–285.
10. *Wall Street Journal,* June 28, 1985, p. 1.

A Feminist Critique of Marriage

Having grown up in Paris in a middle-class family and become a teacher, novelist, and intellectual, Simone de Beauvoir (1908–1986) turned increasingly to feminist concerns after World War II. Her most influential work was The Second Sex (1949), a massive declaration of independence for contemporary women.

As an existentialist, Beauvoir believed that all individuals must accept responsibility for their lives and strive to overcome the tragic dilemmas they face. Studying the experience of women since antiquity, Beauvoir argued that men had generally used education and social conditioning to create a dependent "other," a negative nonman who was not permitted to grow and strive for freedom.

Marriage—on men's terms—was part of this unjust and undesirable process. Beauvoir's conclusion that some couples could establish free and equal unions was based in part on her experience with philosopher Jean-Paul Sartre, Beauvoir's encouraging companion and sometime lover.

Every human existence involves transcendence and immanence at the same time; to go forward, each existence must be maintained, for it to expand toward the future it must integrate the past, and while intercommunicating with others it should find self-confirmation. These two elements—maintenance and progression—are implied in any living activity, and for *man* marriage permits precisely a happy synthesis of the two. In his occupation and his political life he encounters change and progress, he senses his extension through time and the universe; and when he is tired of such roaming, he gets himself a home, a fixed location, and an anchorage in the world. At evening he restores his soul in the home, where his wife takes care of his furnishings and children and guards the things of the past that she keeps in store. But she has no other job than to maintain and provide for life in pure and unvarying generality; she perpetuates the species without change, she ensures the even rhythm of the days and the continuity of the home, seeing to it that the doors are locked. But she is allowed no direct influence upon the future nor upon the world; she reaches out beyond herself toward the social group only through her husband as intermediary.

Marriage today still retains, for the most part, this traditional form. . . . The male is called upon for action, his vocation is to produce, fight, create, progress, to transcend himself toward the totality of the universe and the infinity of the future; but traditional marriage does not invite woman to transcend herself with him; it confines her in immanence, shuts her up within the circle of herself. She can thus propose to do nothing more than construct a life of stable equilibrium in which the present as a continuance of the past avoids the menaces of tomorrow—that is, construct precisely a life of happiness. . . .

In domestic work, with or without the aid of servants, woman makes her home her own, finds social justification, and provides herself with an occupation, an activity, that deals usefully and satisfyingly with material objects—shining stoves, fresh, clean clothes, bright copper, polished furniture—but provides no escape from immanence and little affirmation of individuality. . . . Few tasks are more like the torture of Sisyphus than housework, with its endless repetition: the clean becomes soiled, the soiled is made clean, over and over, day after day. The housewife wears herself out marking time: she makes nothing, simply perpetuates the present. She never senses conquest of a positive Good, but rather indefinite struggle against negative Evil. . . . Washing, ironing, sweeping, ferreting out rolls of lint from under wardrobes— all this halting of decay is also the denial of life;

for time simultaneously creates and destroys, and only its negative aspect concerns the housekeeper. . . .

Thus woman's work within the home gives her no autonomy; it is not directly useful to society, it does not open out on the future, it produces nothing. It takes on meaning and dignity only as it is linked with existent beings who reach out beyond themselves, transcend themselves, toward society in production and action. That is, far from freeing the matron, her occupation makes her dependent upon husband and children; she is justified through them; but in their lives she is only an inessential intermediary. . . .

The tragedy of marriage is not that it fails to assure woman the promised happiness—there is no such thing as assurance in regard to happiness—but that it mutilates her; it dooms her to repetition and routine. The first twenty years of woman's life are extraordinarily rich, as we have seen; she discovers the world and her destiny. At twenty or thereabouts mistress of a home, bound permanently to a man, a child in her arms, she stands with her life virtually finished forever. Real activities, real work, are the prerogative of her man: she has mere things to occupy her which are sometimes tiring but never fully satisfying. . . .

Marriage should be a combining of two whole, independent existences, not a retreat, an annexation, a flight, a remedy. . . . The couple should not be regarded as a unit, a close cell; rather each individual should be integrated as such in society at large, where each (whether male or female) could flourish without aid; then attachments could be formed in pure generosity with another individual equally adapted to the group, attachments that would be founded upon the acknowledgment that both are free.

This balanced couple is not a utopian fancy: such couples do exist, sometimes even within the frame of marriage, most often outside it. Some mates are united by a strong sexual love that leaves them free in their friendships and in their work; others are held together by a friendship that does not preclude sexual liberty; more rare are those who are at once lovers and friends but do not seek in each other their sole reasons for living. Many nuances are possible in the relations between a man and a woman: in comradeship, pleasure, trust, fondness, co-operation, and love, they can be for each other the most abundant

Simone de Beauvoir as a teacher in 1947, when she was writing *The Second Sex*. *(Hulton-Deutsch Collection/Corbis)*

source of joy, richness, and power available to human beings.

Questions for Analysis

1. How did Beauvoir analyze marriage and marriage partners in terms of existential philosophy?

2. To what extent does a married woman benefit from a "traditional" marriage, according to Beauvoir? Why?

3. What was Beauvoir's solution to the situation she described? Was her solution desirable? Realistic?

4. What have you learned about the history of women that supports or challenges Beauvoir's analysis? Include developments since World War II and your own reflections.

Source: Simone de Beauvoir, *The Second Sex,* trans. H. M. Parshley. Copyright © 1952 and renewed 1980 by Alfred A. Knopf, a division of Random House, Inc. Used by permission of Alfred A. Knopf, a division of Random House, Inc.

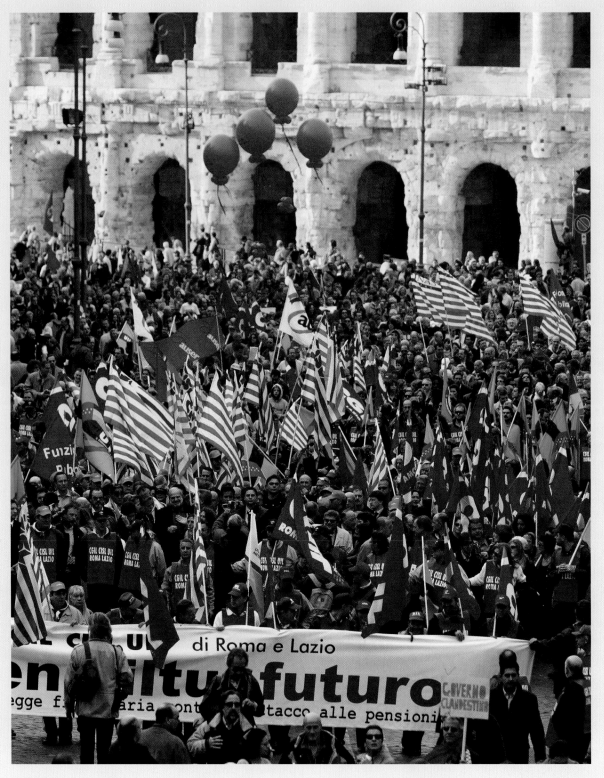

Italians protesting government economic policies gather in front of the Roman Coliseum during a nationwide strike in October 2003. *(Philippe Desmazes/AFP/Getty Images)*

chapter

31

---

chapter preview

The Decline of Communism in Eastern Europe

● *In what ways did Solidarity confront the communist system in Poland, and how did Mikhail Gorbachev try to reverse the decline of communism in the Soviet Union?*

The Revolutions of 1989

● *How did anticommunist revolutions sweep through eastern Europe in 1989, and what were the immediate consequences?*

Building a New Europe in the 1990s

● *How, in the 1990s, did the different parts of a reunifying Europe meet the challenges of postcommunist reconstruction, resurgent nationalism, and economic union?*

New Challenges in the Twenty-first Century

● *Why did the prospect of population decline, the reality of large-scale immigration, and concern for human rights emerge as critical issues in contemporary Europe?*

The West and the Islamic World

● *How and why did relations between the West and the Islamic world deteriorate dramatically in the early twenty-first century?*

The Future in Perspective

● *What does the study of history have to tell us about the future?*

REVOLUTION, REBUILDING, AND NEW CHALLENGES: 1985 TO THE PRESENT

In the late twentieth century, massive changes swept through eastern Europe and opened a new era in human history. In the 1980s a broad movement to transform the communist system took root in Poland, and efforts to reform and revitalize the communist system in the Soviet Union snowballed out of control. In 1989 revolutions swept away communist rule throughout the entire Soviet bloc. The cold war came to a spectacular end, West Germany absorbed East Germany, and the Soviet Union broke into fifteen independent countries. Thus after forty years of cold war division, Europe regained an underlying unity, as faith in democratic government and some kind of market economy became the common European creed. In 1991 hopes for peaceful democratic progress throughout Europe were almost universal.

The post–cold war years saw the realization of some of these hopes, but the new era brought its own problems and tragedies. The cold war division of Europe had kept a lid on ethnic conflicts and nationalism, which suddenly burst into the open and led to a disastrous civil war in the former Yugoslavia. Moreover, most western European economies were plagued by high unemployment and struggling to adapt to the wide-open global economy, which undermined cherished social benefits and complicated the task of working together with the former communist states. Thus in eastern Europe, the process of rebuilding shattered societies was more difficult than optimists had envisioned in 1991, and in western Europe, the road toward greater unity and eastward expansion proved bumpy. Nevertheless, the will to undo the cold war division prevailed, and in 2004 eight former communist countries as well as the islands of Cyprus and Malta joined the European Union—a historic achievement.

Online Study Center

This icon will direct you to interactive activities and study materials on the website **college.hmco.com/pic/mckaywest9e**

The new century brought a growing awareness of a new set of fundamental challenges, which were related to the prospect of population decline, the reality of large-scale immigration, and the promotion of human rights. These challenges promised to preoccupy Western society for years to come.

More dramatically, the old, often contentious question of relations with the Islamic world suddenly re-emerged as a critical issue after the attack on New York's World Trade Center and the Pentagon in 2001. After the West united in a quick response against the Taliban in Afghanistan, the subsequent war in Iraq divided western Europe and threatened the future of Western cooperation in world affairs. The war in Iraq also complicated the ongoing integration of Europe's rapidly growing Muslim population.

The Decline of Communism in Eastern Europe

Following the 1968 invasion of Czechoslovakia, the crucial event of the Brezhnev era (pages 997–999), the Soviet Union repeatedly demonstrated that it remained a harsh and aggressive dictatorship. It paid only lip service to egalitarian ideology at home and was determined to uphold its rule throughout eastern Europe. Thus the Soviet Union eventually crushed the Solidarity movement in Poland, the powerful, peaceful challenge to Communist rule in Poland in the early 1980s. Periodic efforts to achieve fundamental political change were doomed to failure sooner or later—or so it seemed to most Western experts into the mid-1980s.

And then Mikhail Gorbachev burst on the scene. The new Soviet leader opened an era of reform that was as sweeping as it was unexpected. Although many believed that Gorbachev would soon fall from power, his reforms rapidly transformed Soviet culture and politics, and they drastically reduced cold war tensions. But communism, which Gorbachev wanted so desperately to revitalize in order to save it, continued to decline as a functioning system throughout the Soviet bloc.

- *In what ways did Solidarity confront the communist system in Poland, and how did Mikhail Gorbachev try to reverse the decline of communism in the Soviet Union?*

Solidarity in Poland

Gorbachev's reforms interacted with a resurgence of popular protest in the Soviet Union's satellite empire. Developments in Poland were most striking and significant.

Poland had been an unruly satellite from the beginning. Stalin said that introducing communism to Poland was like putting a saddle on a cow. Efforts to saddle the cow—really a spirited stallion—led to widespread riots in 1956 (see page 997). As a result, Polish Communists dropped their efforts to impose Soviet-style collectivization on the peasants and to break the Roman Catholic Church. Most agricultural land remained in private hands, and the Catholic Church thrived. Thus the Communists failed to monopolize society.

They also failed to manage the economy effectively. Even the booming 1960s saw little economic improvement. In 1970 Poland's working class rose again in angry protest. A new Communist leader came to power, and he wagered that massive inflows of Western capital and technology, especially from rich and now-friendly West Germany (see page 1008), could produce a Polish "economic miracle." Instead, bureaucratic incompetence and the first oil shock in 1973 put the economy into a nosedive. Workers, intellectuals, and the church became increasingly restive. Then the real Polish miracle occurred: Cardinal Karol Wojtyla, archbishop of Cracow, was elected pope in 1978. In June 1979, he returned from Rome, preaching love of Christ and country and the "inalienable rights of man." Pope John Paul II drew enormous crowds and electrified the Polish nation. The economic crisis became a moral and spiritual crisis as well.

In August 1980, the sixteen thousand workers at the gigantic Lenin Shipyards in Gdansk (formerly known as Danzig) laid down their tools and occupied the plant. As other workers joined "in solidarity," the strikers advanced revolutionary demands, including the right to form free-trade unions, freedom of speech, release of political prisoners, and economic reforms. After eighteen days of shipyard occupation, the government gave in and accepted the workers' demands in the **Gdansk Agreement.** In a state where the Communist Party claimed to rule on behalf of the proletariat, a working-class revolt had won an unprecedented victory.

Online Study Center   **Improve Your Grade**
Primary Source: The "Twenty-one Demands": A Call for Workers' Rights and Freedom in a Socialist State

Led by feisty Lenin Shipyards electrician and devout Catholic Lech Walesa (b. 1943), the workers proceeded to organize their free and democratic trade union. They called it **Solidarity.** Joined by intellectuals and supported by the Catholic Church, Solidarity became the union of a nation. By March 1981, a full-time staff of 40,000 linked 9.5 million union members together as Solidarity published its own newspapers and cultural and intellectual freedom blossomed in Poland. Solidarity's leaders had tremendous support, and the ever-present threat of calling a nationwide strike gave them real power in on-going negotiations with the Communist bosses.

But if Solidarity had power, it did not try to take the reins of government in 1981. History, the Brezhnev Doctrine, and virulent attacks from communist neighbors all seemed to guarantee the intervention of the Red Army and a terrible bloodbath if Polish Communists "lost control." Thus the Solidarity revolution remained a "self-limiting revolution" aimed at defending the cultural and trade-union freedoms won in the Gdansk Agreement, and it refused to use force to challenge directly the Communist monopoly of political power.

Solidarity's combination of strength and moderation postponed a showdown, as the Soviet Union played a waiting game of threats and pressure. After a confrontation in March 1981, Walesa settled for minor government concessions, and Solidarity dropped plans for a massive general strike. Criticism of Walesa's moderate leadership grew, and Solidarity lost its cohesiveness. The worsening economic crisis also encouraged grassroots radicalism, as the Polish Communist leadership shrewdly denounced Solidarity for promoting economic collapse and provoking Soviet invasion. In December 1981, Communist leader General Wojciech Jaruzelski suddenly struck, proclaiming martial law, arresting Solidarity's leaders, and "saving" the nation.

Outlawed and driven underground, Solidarity fought successfully to maintain its organization and to voice the aspirations of the Polish masses after 1981. Part of the reason for the union's survival was the government's unwillingness (and probably its inability) to impose full-scale terror. Moreover, millions of Poles decided to continue acting as if they were free, even though they were not. Cultural and intellectual life remained extremely vigorous as the faltering Polish economy continued to deteriorate. Thus popular support for outlawed Solidarity remained strong under martial law in the 1980s, preparing the way for the union's political rebirth toward the end of the decade.

The rise and survival of Solidarity showed the desire of millions of eastern Europeans for greater political liberty and the enduring appeal of cultural freedom, trade-union rights, patriotic nationalism, and religious feeling. Not least, Solidarity's challenge encouraged fresh thinking in the Soviet Union, ever the key to lasting change in the Eastern bloc.

Chronology

1985 Glasnost leads to greater freedom of speech and expression in the Soviet Union

1985– Decline in birthrate in industrialized nations continues

1986 Single European Act lays groundwork for single currency

August 1989 Solidarity gains power in Poland

November 1989 Collapse of the Berlin Wall

November–December 1989 Velvet Revolution ends communism in Czechoslovakia

October 1990 Reunification of Germany

1990–1991 First war with Iraq

July 1991 Failed coup against Gorbachev in Russia

December 1991 Dissolution of the Soviet Union

1991 Maastricht treaty sets financial criteria for European monetary union

1991–2000 Resurgence of nationalism and ethnic conflict in eastern Europe

1991–2001 Civil war in Yugoslavia

1992–1997 "Shock therapy" in Russia causes decline of the economy

1993 Creation of the European Union; growth of illegal immigration in Europe

1996 Cronin, *The World the Cold War Made*

1998– Growing support for global human rights in Europe

1999 Russian economy booms

September 2001 Terrorist attack on the United States

2001 War in Afghanistan

January 2002 New euro currency goes into effect in the European Union

2003 Second war in Iraq begins

2004 Ten new states join European Union

November 2005 Young Muslims riot in France

2006 Murderous sectarian conflict in Iraq increases

Lech Walesa and Solidarity   An inspiration for fellow workers at the Lenin Shipyards in the dramatic and successful strike against the Communist bosses in August 1980, Walesa played a key role in Solidarity before and after it was outlawed. Speaking here to old comrades at the Lenin Shipyards after Solidarity was again legalized in 1988, Walesa personified an enduring opposition to Communist rule in eastern Europe. *(G. Merrillon/Gamma Presse/EYEDEA)*

Gorbachev's Reforms in the Soviet Union

Fundamental change in Russian history has often come in short, intensive spurts, which contrast vividly with long periods of immobility. The era of reform launched by Mikhail Gorbachev in 1985 was one such decisive transformation. Gorbachev's initiatives brought political and cultural liberalization to the Soviet Union, and they then permitted democracy and national self-determination to triumph spectacularly in the old satellite empire and eventually in the Soviet Union itself, although this was certainly not Gorbachev's original intention.

As we have seen (page 998), the Soviet Union's Communist Party elite seemed secure in the early 1980s as far as any challenge from below was concerned. The long-established system of administrative controls continued to stretch downward from the central ministries and state committees to provincial cities, and from there to facto-

ries, neighborhoods, and villages. At each level of this massive state bureaucracy, the overlapping hierarchy of the Communist Party, with its 17.5 million members, continued to watch over all decisions and manipulate every aspect of national life. Organized opposition was impossible, and average people simply left politics to the bosses.

Yet the massive state and party bureaucracy was a mixed blessing. It safeguarded the elite, but it promoted apathy in the masses. Therefore, when the ailing Brezhnev finally died in 1982, his successor, the long-time chief of the secret police, Yuri Andropov (1914–1984), tried to invigorate the system. Relatively little came of these efforts, but they combined with a sharply worsening economic situation to set the stage for the emergence in 1985 of Mikhail Gorbachev (b. 1931), the most vigorous Soviet leader in a generation.

Trained as a lawyer and working his way up as a Communist Party official in the northern Caucasus, Gorbachev was smart, charming, and tough. Gorbachev believed in communism, but he realized it was failing to keep up with Western capitalism and technology. This was eroding the Soviet Union's status as a superpower. Thus Gorbachev (and his intelligent, influential wife, Raisa, a dedicated professor of Marxist-Leninist thought) wanted to save the Soviet system by revitalizing it with fundamental reforms. Gorbachev was also an idealist. He wanted to improve conditions for ordinary citizens. Understanding that the endless waste and expense of the cold war arms race had had a disastrous impact on living conditions in the Soviet Union, he realized that improvement at home required better relations with the West.

In his first year in office, Gorbachev attacked corruption and incompetence in the bureaucracy, and he consolidated his power. He attacked alcoholism and drunkenness, which were deadly scourges of Soviet society, and elaborated his ambitious reform program.

The first set of reform policies was designed to transform and restructure the economy, in order to provide for the real needs of the Soviet population. To accomplish this economic "restructuring," or **perestroika,** Gorbachev and his supporters permitted an easing of government price controls on some goods, more independence for state enterprises, and the setting up of profit-seeking private cooperatives to provide personal services for consumers. These timid economic reforms initially produced a few improvements, but shortages then grew as the economy stalled at an intermediate point between central planning and free-market mechanisms. By late 1988, widespread consumer dissatisfaction posed a serious threat to Gorbachev's leadership and the entire reform program.

Online Study Center **Improve Your Grade**
Primary Source: The Last Heir of Lenin Explains His Reform Plans: Perestroika and Glasnost

Gorbachev's bold and far-reaching campaign "to tell it like it is" was much more successful. Very popular in a country where censorship, dull uniformity, and outright lies had long characterized public discourse, the new-found "openness," or **glasnost,** of the government and the media marked an astonishing break with the past. Long-banned and vilified émigré writers sold millions of copies of their works in new editions, while denunciations of Stalin and his terror became standard fare in plays and movies. Thus initial openness in government pronouncements quickly went much further than Gorbachev intended and led to something approaching free speech and free expression, a veritable cultural revolution.

Democratization was the third element of reform. Beginning as an attack on corruption in the Communist Party, it led to the first free elections in the Soviet Union

Mikhail Gorbachev In his acceptance speech before the Supreme Soviet (the U.S.S.R.'s parliament), newly elected president Mikhail Gorbachev vowed to assume "all responsibility" for the success or failure of perestroika. Previous parliaments were no more than tools of the Communist Party, but this one actively debated and even opposed government programs. (*Vlastimir Shone/Gamma Presse/EYEDEA*)

since 1917. Gorbachev and the party remained in control, but a minority of critical independents was elected in April 1989 to a revitalized Congress of People's Deputies. Millions of Soviets then watched the new congress for hours on television as Gorbachev and his ministers saw their proposals debated and even rejected. Thus

MAP 31.1 Democratic Movements in Eastern Europe, 1989 With Gorbachev's repudiation of the Brezhnev Doctrine, the revolutionary drive for freedom and democracy spread throughout eastern Europe. Countries that had been satellites in the orbit of the Soviet Union began to set themselves free to establish their own place in the universe of free nations.

sion. Thus nationalist demands continued to grow in the non-Russian Soviet republics.

Finally, the Soviet leader brought "new political thinking" to the field of foreign affairs and acted on it. He withdrew Soviet troops from Afghanistan and sought to reduce East-West tensions. Of enormous importance, he sought to halt the arms race with the United States and convinced President Ronald Reagan of his sincerity. In December 1987, the two leaders agreed in a Washington summit to eliminate all land-based intermediate-range missiles in Europe, setting the stage for more arms reductions. Gorbachev also encouraged reform movements in Poland and Hungary and pledged to respect the political choices of the peoples of eastern Europe, repudiating the Brezhnev Doctrine. By early 1989, it seemed that if Gorbachev held to his word, the tragic Soviet occupation of eastern Europe might well wither away, taking the long cold war with it once and for all.

The Revolutions of 1989

Instead, history accelerated. In 1989 Gorbachev's plan to reform communism in order to save it snowballed out of control. A series of largely peaceful revolutions swept across eastern Europe (see Map 31.1), overturning existing communist regimes and ending the communists' monopoly of power. Watched on television in the Soviet Union and around the world, these stirring events marked the triumph and the transformation of long-standing opposition to communist rule and foreign domination in eastern Europe.

The revolutions of 1989 had momentous consequences. First, the peoples of eastern Europe joyfully re-entered the mainstream of contemporary European life and culture, after having been conquered and brutalized by Nazis and communists for almost sixty years. Second, Gorbachev's reforms boomeranged, and a complicated anticommunist revolution swept through the Soviet Union, as the multinational empire broke into a large Russia and

millions of Soviet citizens took practical lessons in open discussion, critical thinking, and representative government. The result was a new political culture at odds with the Communist Party's monopoly of power and control.

Democratization ignited demands for greater autonomy and even for national independence by non-Russian minorities, especially in the Baltic region and in the Caucasus. In April 1989, troops with sharpened shovels charged into a rally of Georgian separatists in Tbilisi and left twenty dead. But whereas China's Communist leaders brutally massacred similar prodemocracy demonstrators in Beijing in June 1989 and reimposed rigid authoritarian rule, Gorbachev drew back from represfourteen other independent states. Third, West Germany quickly absorbed its East German rival and emerged as the most influential country in Europe. Finally, the long cold war came to an abrupt end, and the United States suddenly stood as the world's only superpower.

• *How did anticommunist revolutions sweep through eastern Europe in 1989, and what were the immediate consequences?*

The Collapse of Communism in Eastern Europe

Solidarity and the Polish people led the way to revolution in eastern Europe. In 1988 widespread labor unrest, raging inflation, and the outlawed Solidarity's refusal to cooperate with the military government had brought Poland to the brink of economic collapse. Thus Solidarity skillfully pressured Poland's frustrated Communist leaders into another round of negotiations that might work out a sharing of power to resolve the political stalemate and the economic crisis. The subsequent agreement in early 1989 legalized Solidarity and declared that a large minority of representatives to the Polish parliament would be chosen by free elections in June 1989. Still guaranteed a parliamentary majority and expecting to win many of the contested seats, the Communists believed that their rule was guaranteed for four years and that Solidarity would keep the workers in line.

Lacking access to the state-run media, Solidarity succeeded nonetheless in mobilizing the country and winning most of the contested seats in an overwhelming victory. Moreover, many angry voters crossed off the names of unopposed party candidates, so that the Communist Party failed to win the majority its leaders had anticipated. Solidarity members jubilantly entered the Polish parliament, and a dangerous stalemate quickly developed. But Solidarity leader Lech Walesa, a gifted politician who always repudiated violence, adroitly obtained a majority by securing the allegiance of two minor procommunist parties that had been part of the coalition government after World War II. In August 1989, the editor of Solidarity's weekly newspaper was sworn in as Poland's new noncommunist leader.

In its first year and a half, the new Solidarity government cautiously introduced revolutionary political changes. It eliminated the hated secret police, the Communist ministers in the government, and finally Jaruzelski himself, but it did so step by step in order to avoid confrontation with the army or the Soviet Union. However, in economic affairs, the Solidarity-led government was radical from the beginning. It applied **shock therapy** designed to make a clean break with state planning and move quickly to market mechanisms and private property. Thus the Solidarity government abolished controls on many prices on January 1, 1990, and reformed the monetary system with a "big bang."

Hungary followed Poland. Hungary's Communist Party boss, János Kádár, had permitted liberalization of the rigid planned economy after the 1956 uprising in exchange for political obedience and continued Communist control. In May 1988, in an effort to retain power by granting modest political concessions, the party replaced Kádár with a reform communist. But opposition groups rejected piecemeal progress, and in the summer of 1989 the Hungarian Communist Party agreed to hold free elections in early 1990. Welcoming Western investment and moving rapidly toward multiparty democracy, Hungary's Communists now enjoyed considerable popular support, and they believed, quite mistakenly it turned out, that they could defeat the opposition in the upcoming elections. In an effort to strengthen their support at home and also put pressure on East Germany's hard-line Communist regime, the Hungarians opened their border to East Germans and tore down the barbed-wire "iron curtain" with Austria. Thus tens of thousands of dissatisfied East German "vacationers" began pouring into Hungary, crossed into Austria as refugees, and continued on to immediate resettlement in thriving West Germany.

The flight of East Germans led to the rapid growth of a homegrown protest movement in East Germany. Intellectuals, environmentalists, and Protestant ministers took the lead, organizing huge candlelight demonstrations and arguing that a democratic but still socialist East Germany was both possible and desirable. These "stayers" failed to convince the "leavers," however, who continued to flee the country en masse. In a desperate attempt to stabilize the situation, the East German government opened the Berlin Wall in November 1989, and people danced for joy atop that grim symbol of the prison state. East Germany's aging Communist leaders were swept aside, and a reform government took power and scheduled free elections.

In Czechoslovakia, communism died quickly in November–December 1989 in an almost good-humored ousting of Communist bosses. This so-called **Velvet Revolution** grew out of popular demonstrations led by students, intellectuals, and a dissident playwright turned moral revolutionary named Václav Havel. The protesters practically took control of the streets and forced the Communists into a power-sharing arrangement, which quickly resulted in the resignation of the Communist

Demonstrators During the Velvet Revolution   Hundreds of thousands of Czechoslovakian citizens flooded the streets of Prague in peaceful, daily protests after the police savagely beat student demonstrators in mid-November 1989. On the night of November 24, three hundred thousand people roared "Dubček-Havel" when Alexander Dubček, the aging reformer ousted in 1968 by the Soviets, stood on a balcony with Václav Havel, the leading opponent of communism. That night the communists agreed to share power, and a few days later they resigned from the government. *(Corbis)*

government. As 1989 ended, the Czechoslovakian assembly elected Havel president.

Only in Romania was revolution violent and bloody. There ironfisted Communist dictator Nicolae Ceaușescu (1918–1989) had long combined Stalinist brutality with stubborn independence from Moscow. Faced with mass protests in December, Ceaușescu, alone among eastern European bosses, ordered his ruthless security forces to slaughter thousands, thereby sparking a classic armed uprising. After Ceaușescu's forces were defeated, the tyrant and his wife were captured and executed by a military court. A coalition government emerged from the fighting, although the legacy of Ceaușescu's oppression left a very troubled country.

The Disintegration of the Soviet Union

As 1990 began, revolutionary changes had triumphed in all but two eastern European states—tiny Albania and the vast Soviet Union. The great question now became whether the Soviet Union would follow its former satellites and whether reform communism would give way to a popular anticommunist revolution.

In February 1990, as competing Russian politicians noisily presented their programs, and nationalists in the non-Russian republics demanded autonomy or independence from the Soviet Union, the Communist Party suffered a stunning defeat in local elections throughout the country. As in the eastern European satellites, democrats and anticommunists won clear majorities in the leading cities of the Russian Federation. Moreover, in Lithuania the people elected an uncompromising nationalist as president, and the newly chosen parliament declared Lithuania an independent state. Gorbachev responded by placing an economic embargo on Lithuania, but he refused to use the army to crush the separatist government. The result was a tense political stalemate, which undermined popular support for Gorbachev. Separating himself further from Communist hardliners, Gorbachev asked Soviet citizens to ratify a new constitution, which formally abolished the Communist Party's monopoly of political power and expanded the power of the Congress of People's Deputies. Retaining his post as party secretary, Gorbachev convinced a majority of deputies to elect him president of the Soviet Union.

Gorbachev's eroding power and his unwillingness to risk a universal suffrage election for the presidency strengthened his great rival, Boris Yeltsin (1931–2007). A radical reform communist who had been purged by party conservatives in 1987, Yeltsin embraced the democratic movement, and in May 1990 he was elected leader of the Russian Federation's parliament. He boldly announced that Russia would put its interests first and declare its independence from the Soviet Union, thereby broadening the base of the anticommunist movement as he joined the patriotism of ordinary Russians with the democratic aspirations of big-city intellectuals. Gorbachev tried to save the Soviet Union with a new treaty that would link the member republics in a looser, freely accepted confederation, but six of the fifteen Soviet republics rejected Gorbachev's pleas.

The Fall of the Berlin Wall   The sudden opening of the Berlin Wall in November 1989 dramatized the spectacular collapse of communism throughout eastern Europe. Built by the Soviet leader Nikita Khrushchev in 1961, the hated barrier had stopped the flow of refugees from East Germany to West Germany. *(Patrick Piel/Gamma Presse/EYEDEA)*

Celebrating Victory, August 1991   A Russian soldier flashes the victory sign in front of the Russian parliament, as the last-gasp coup attempt of Communist hardliners is defeated by Boris Yeltsin and an enthusiastic public. The soldier has cut the hammer and sickle out of the Soviet flag, consigning those famous symbols of proletarian revolution to what Trotsky once called the "garbage can of history." *(Filip Horvat/Corbis Saba)*

Opposed by democrats and nationalists, Gorbachev was also challenged again by the Communist old guard. Defeated at the Communist Party congress in July 1990, a gang of hardliners kidnapped a vacationing Gorbachev and his family in the Caucasus and tried to seize the Soviet government in August 1991. But the attempted coup collapsed in the face of massive popular resistance, which rallied around Yeltsin, recently elected president of the Russian Federation by universal suffrage. As the world watched spellbound on television, Yeltsin defiantly denounced the rebels from atop a stalled tank in central Moscow and declared the "rebirth of Russia." The army supported Yeltsin, and Gorbachev was rescued and returned to power as head of the Soviet Union.

The leaders of the coup wanted to preserve Communist power, state ownership, and the multinational Soviet Union, but they succeeded only in destroying all three. An anticommunist revolution swept the Russian Federation as Yeltsin and his supporters outlawed the Communist Party and confiscated its property. Locked in a personal and political duel with Gorbachev, Yeltsin and his democratic allies declared Russia independent and withdrew from the Soviet Union. All the other Soviet republics also left. The Soviet Union—and Gorbachev's job—ceased to exist on December 25, 1991 (see Map 31.2). The independent republics of the old Soviet Union then established a loose confederation, the Commonwealth of Independent States, which played only a minor role in the 1990s.

German Unification and the End of the Cold War

The sudden death of communism in East Germany in 1989 reopened the "German question" and raised the

MAP 31.2 Russia and the Successor States After the attempt in August 1991 to depose Gorbachev failed, an anticommunist revolution swept the Soviet Union. Led by Russia and Boris Yeltsin, the republics that formed the Soviet Union declared their sovereignty and independence. Eleven of the fifteen republics then formed a loose confederation called the Commonwealth of Independent States, but the integrated economy of the Soviet Union dissolved into separate national economies, each with its own goals and policies.

threat of renewed cold war conflict over Germany. Taking power in October 1989, East German reform communists, enthusiastically supported by leading East German intellectuals and former dissidents, wanted to preserve socialism by making it genuinely democratic and responsive to the needs of the people. They argued for a **third way,** which would go beyond the failed Stalinism they had experienced and the ruthless capitalism they saw in the West. These reformers supported closer ties with West Germany, but they feared unification and wanted to preserve a distinct East German identity.

These efforts failed, and within a few months East Germany was absorbed into an enlarged West Germany, much like a faltering company is merged into a stronger rival and ceases to exist. Three factors were particularly important in this sudden absorption. First, in the first week after the Berlin Wall was opened, almost 9 million East Germans—roughly one-half of the total population—

poured across the border into West Germany. Almost all returned to their homes in the East, but the joy of warm welcomes from long-lost friends and loved ones and the exhilarating experience of shopping in the well-stocked stores of the much wealthier West aroused long-dormant hopes of unity among ordinary citizens.

Second, West German chancellor Helmut Kohl and his closest advisers skillfully exploited the historic opportunity on their doorstep. Sure of support from the United States, whose leadership he had steadfastly followed, in November 1989 Kohl presented a ten-point plan for a step-by-step unification in cooperation with both East Germany and the international community. Kohl then promised the struggling citizens of East Germany an immediate economic bonanza—a one-for-one exchange of all East German marks in savings accounts and pensions into much more valuable West German marks. This generous offer helped a well-financed conservative-liberal **Alliance for**

Germany, which was set up in East Germany and was closely tied to Kohl's West German Christian Democrats to overwhelm those who argued for the preservation of some kind of independent socialist society in East Germany. In March 1990, the Alliance outdistanced the Socialist Party and won almost 50 percent of the votes in an East German parliamentary election. (The Communists ignominiously fell to fringe-party status.) The Alliance for Germany quickly negotiated an economic union on favorable terms with Chancellor Kohl.

Finally, in the summer of 1990, the crucial international aspect of German unification was successfully resolved. Unification would once again make Germany the strongest state in central Europe and would directly affect the security of the Soviet Union. But Gorbachev swallowed hard—Western cartoonists showed Stalin turning over in his grave—and negotiated the best deal he could. In a historic agreement signed by Gorbachev and Kohl in July 1990, a uniting Germany solemnly affirmed its peaceful intentions and pledged never to develop nuclear, biological, or chemical weapons. Germany also sweetened the deal by promising to make enormous loans to the hard-pressed Soviet Union. In October 1990, East Germany merged into West Germany, forming henceforth a single nation under the West German laws and constitution.

The peaceful reunification of Germany accelerated the pace of agreements to liquidate the cold war. In November 1990, delegates from twenty-two European countries joined those from the United States and the Soviet Union in Paris and agreed to a scaling down of all their armed forces. The delegates also solemnly affirmed that all existing borders in Europe—from unified Germany to the newly independent Baltic republics—were legal and valid. The **Paris Accord** was for all practical purposes a general peace treaty, bringing an end to World War II and the cold war that followed.

Peace in Europe encouraged the United States and the Soviet Union to scrap a significant portion of their nuclear weapons in a series of agreements. In September 1991, a confident President George H. W. Bush also canceled the around-the-clock alert status for American bombers outfitted with atomic bombs, and a floundering Gorbachev quickly followed suit. For the first time in four decades, Soviet and American nuclear weapons were no longer standing ready to destroy capitalism, communism, and life itself.

The Gulf War of 1991

As anticommunist revolutions swept eastern Europe and East-West tensions rapidly disappeared, the Soviet Union lost both the will and the means to be a global superpower. Yet the United States retained the strength and the desire to influence political and economic developments on a global scale. Thus the United States, still flanked by many allies, emerged rather suddenly as the world's only surviving superpower.

In 1991 the United States used its military superiority on a grand scale in a quick war with Iraq in western Asia. Emerging in 1988 from an eight-year war with neighboring Iran with a big, tough army equipped by the Soviet bloc, western Europe, and the United States, Iraq's strongman Saddam Hussein (1937–2006) set out to make himself the leader of the entire Arab world. Eyeing the great oil wealth of his tiny southern neighbor, Saddam Hussein's forces suddenly invaded Kuwait in August 1990 and proclaimed the annexation of Kuwait.

Reacting vigorously to free Kuwait, the United States mobilized the U.N. Security Council, which in August 1990 imposed a strict naval blockade on Iraq. Receiving the support of some Arab states, as well as of Great Britain and France, the United States also landed 500,000 American soldiers in Saudi Arabia near the border of Kuwait. When a defiant Saddam Hussein refused to withdraw from Kuwait, the Security Council authorized the U.S.-led military coalition to attack Iraq. The American army and air force then smashed Iraqi forces in a lightning-quick desert campaign, although the United States stopped short of toppling Saddam because it feared a sudden disintegration of Iraq more than Saddam's hanging on to power.

The defeat of Iraqi armies in the Gulf War demonstrated the awesome power of the U.S. military, rebuilt and revitalized by the spending and patriotism of the 1980s. Little wonder that in the flush of yet another victory, the first President Bush spoke of a **"new world order,"** an order that would apparently feature the United States and a cooperative United Nations working together to impose stability throughout the world.

Building a New Europe in the 1990s

The fall of communism, the end of the cold war, and the collapse of the Soviet Union opened a new era in European and world history. The dimensions and significance of this new era, opening suddenly and unexpectedly, are subject to debate. We are so close to what is going on that we lack vital perspective. Yet the historian must take a stand.

First, it seems clear that Europe took giant strides toward a loose unification of fundamental institutions and beliefs and that many broad economic, social, and political trends operated all across the continent in the 1990s. We shall focus on three of the most important trends: the pressure on national economies increasingly caught up in global capitalism; the defense of social achievements under attack; and a resurgence of nationalism and ethnic conflict. Second, with these common themes providing an organizational framework, we shall examine the course of development in the three overlapping but still distinct regions of contemporary Europe. These are Russia and the western states of the old Soviet Union, previously communist eastern Europe, and western Europe.

• *How, in the 1990s, did the different parts of a reunifying Europe meet the challenges of postcommunist reconstruction, resurgent nationalism, and economic union?*

Common Patterns and Problems

The end of the cold war and the disintegration of the Soviet Union ended the division of Europe into two opposing camps with two different political and economic systems. Thus, although Europe in the 1990s was a collage of diverse peoples with their own politics, cultures, and histories, the entire continent shared an underlying network of common developments and challenges.

Of critical importance, in economic affairs European leaders embraced, or at least accepted, a large part of the neoliberal, free-market vision of capitalist development. This was most strikingly the case in eastern Europe, where states such as Poland and Hungary implemented market reforms and sought to create vibrant capitalist economies. Thus postcommunist governments in eastern Europe freed prices, turned state enterprises over to private owners, and sought to move toward strong currencies and balanced budgets. Milder doses of this same free-market medicine were administered by politicians and big business to the lackluster economies of western Europe. These initiatives and proposals for further changes marked a considerable modification in western Europe's still-dominant welfare capitalism, which featured government intervention, high taxes, and high levels of social benefits.

Two factors were particularly important in accounting for this ongoing shift from welfare state activism to tough-minded capitalism. First, Europeans were only following practices and ideologies revived and enshrined in the 1980s in the United States and Great Britain (see page 1012). Western Europeans especially took American prescriptions more seriously because U.S. prestige and power were so high after the United States "won the cold war" and because the U.S. economy continued to

outperform its western European counterparts in the Clinton years. Second, the deregulation of markets and the privatization of state-controlled enterprises were an integral part of the powerful trend toward a wide-open, wheeler-dealer global economy. The rules of the global economy, which were laid down by Western governments, multinational corporations, and international financial organizations such as the International Monetary Fund (IMF), called for the free movement of capital and goods and services, as well as low inflation and limited government deficits. Accepting these rules and attempting to follow them was the price of full participation in the global economy.

The ongoing computer and electronics revolution strengthened the move toward a global economy. That revolution thrived on the diffusion of ever-cheaper computational and informational capacity to small research groups and private businesses, which were both cause and effect of the revolution itself. By the 1990s, an inexpensive personal computer had the power of a 1950s mainframe that filled a room and cost hundreds of thousands of dollars. The computer revolution reduced the costs of distance, speeding up communications and helping businesses tap cheaper labor overseas. Reducing the friction of distance made threats of moving factories abroad ring true and helped hold down wages at home.

Globalization, the emergence of a freer global economy, probably did speed up world economic growth as enthusiasts invariably claimed, but it also had powerful and quite negative social consequences. Millions of ordinary citizens in western Europe believed that global capitalism and freer markets were undermining hard-won social achievements. As in the United States and Great Britain in the 1980s, the public in other countries generally associated globalization with the increased unemployment that accompanied corporate downsizing, the efforts to reduce the power of labor unions, and, above all, government plans to reduce social benefits. The reaction was particularly intense in France and Germany, where unions remained strong and socialists championed a minimum of change in social policies.

Indeed, the broad movement toward neoliberal global development sparked a powerful counterattack as the 1990s ended. Financial crises, which devastated many of Asia's smaller economies and threatened to spread, triggered this reaction. Many critics and protesters argued increasingly that globalization damaged poor countries as much as wealthy ones. Above all, critics insisted that globalization hurt the world's poor, because multinational corporations destroyed local industries and paid pitiful wages, and because international financial organizations

Santiago Calatrava: Tenerife Concert Hall, 2003   One of the most celebrated of the "postmodern" architects, who go beyond the modernism that dominated from the 1920s to the 1970s, Calatrava is known for swooping shapes and unusual spaces that convey a sense of motion to his buildings. The enormous, free-standing "roof" of this concert hall rises on a waterfront property like a cresting, crashing wave, linking the ocean with the city and beckoning tourists to Tenerife and Portugal's Canary Islands. Postmodern architects rely heavily on three-dimensional computer modeling to fashion complex forms and translate them into construction blueprints. *(Barbara Burg and Oliver Schuh/Palladium Photodesign, Cologne, Germany)*

demanded harsh balanced budgets and deep cuts in government social programs. These attacks shook global neoliberalism, but it remained dominant.

Political developments across Europe also were loosely unified by common patterns and problems. The demise of European communism brought the apparent triumph of liberal democracy everywhere. All countries embraced genuine electoral competition, with elected presidents and legislatures and the outward manifestations of representative liberal governments. With some notable exceptions, such as discrimination against Gypsies, countries also guaranteed basic civil liberties. Thus, for the first time since before the French Revolution, almost all of

Europe followed the same general political model, although the variations were endless.

The triumph of the liberal democratic program led the American scholar Francis Fukuyama to discern in 1992 the "end of history" in his influential book by that title. According to Fukuyama, first fascism and Nazism and then communism had been definitively bested by liberal democratic politics and market economics. Conversely, as James Cronin perceptively noted in 1996 in *The World the Cold War Made*, the fall of communism also marked the return of nationalism and national history.[1] The cold war and the superpowers generally kept their allies and clients in line, either by force or by granting them conditional aid. As soon as the cold war was over, nationalism and ethnic conflict re-emerged, and history, as the story of different peoples, began again.

The resurgence of nationalism in the 1990s led to terrible tragedy and bloodshed in parts of eastern Europe, as it did in several hot spots in Africa and Asia. During the civil wars in Yugoslavia, many observers feared that national and ethnic hatreds would spread throughout eastern Europe and infect western Europe in the form of racial hostility toward minorities and immigrants. Yet if nationalist and racist incidents were a recurring European theme, they remained limited in the extent of their damage. Of critical importance in this regard was the fact that all European states wished to become or remain full-fledged members of the European society of nations and to join eventually an ever-expanding European Community, renamed the **European Union** in 1993. States that embraced national hatred and ethnic warfare, most notably Serbia, were branded as outlaws and boycotted and isolated by the European Union and the international community. The process of limiting resurgent nationalism in Europe was almost as significant as the resurgence itself.

Recasting Russia

Politics and economics were closely intertwined in Russia after the attempted Communist coup in 1991 and the dissolution of the Soviet Union. President Boris Yeltsin, his democratic supporters, and his economic ministers wanted to create conditions that would prevent forever a return to communism and would also right the faltering economy. Following the example of some postcommunist governments in eastern Europe and agreeing with those Western advisers who argued that private economies were always best, the Russian reformers opted in January 1992 for breakneck liberalization. Their "shock therapy" freed prices on 90 percent of all Russian goods, with the exception of bread, vodka, oil, and public transportation. The government also launched a rapid privatization of industry and turned thousands of factories and mines over to new private companies. Each citizen received a voucher worth 10,000 rubles (about $22) to buy stock in private companies, but control of the privatized companies usually remained in the hands of the old bosses, the managers and government officials from the communist era.

President Yeltsin and his economic reformers believed that shock therapy would revive production and bring prosperity after a brief period of hardship. The results of the reforms were in fact quite different. Prices increased 250 percent on the very first day, and they kept on soaring, increasing twenty-six times in the course of 1992. At the

same time, Russian production fell a staggering 20 percent. Nor did the situation stabilize quickly. Throughout 1995 rapid but gradually slowing inflation raged, and output continued to fall. According to most estimates, in 1996 the Russian economy produced at least one-third and possibly as much as one-half less than in 1991. Only in 1997 did the economy stop declining, before crashing yet again in 1998 in the wake of Asia's financial crisis.

Rapid economic liberalization worked poorly in Russia for several reasons. Soviet industry had been highly monopolized and strongly tilted toward military goods. Production of many items had been concentrated in one or two gigantic factories or in interconnected combines that supplied the entire economy. With privatization these powerful state monopolies became powerful private monopolies, which cut production and raised prices in order to maximize their financial returns. Moreover, powerful managers and bureaucrats forced Yeltsin's government to hand out enormous subsidies and credits to reinforce the positions of big firms and to avoid bankruptcies and the discipline of a free market. The managerial elite also combined with criminal elements to intimidate would-be rivals and prevent the formation of new businesses. Not that most ordinary Soviet citizens were eager to start businesses. In the end, enterprise directors and politicians succeeded in eliminating worker ownership and converted large portions of previously state-owned industry into their own private property.

Runaway inflation and poorly executed privatization brought a profound social revolution to Russia. A new capitalist elite acquired great wealth and power, while large numbers of people fell into abject poverty, and the majority struggled in the midst of decline to make ends meet.

Managers, former officials, and financiers who came out of the privatization process with large shares of the old state monopolies stood at the top of the reorganized elite. The richest plums were found in Russia's enormous oil and natural resources industries, where unscrupulous enterprise directors pocketed enormous dishonest gains. The new elite was more highly concentrated than ever before. By 1996 Moscow, with 5 percent of Russia's population, accounted for 35 percent of the country's national income and controlled 80 percent of its capital resources.

At the other extreme, the vast majority saw their savings become practically worthless. Pensions lost much of their value, and whole markets were devoted to people selling off their personal goods to survive. Perhaps the most telling statistic, summing up millions of hardships and tragedies, was the truly catastrophic decline in the life expectancy of the average Russian male from sixty-nine years in 1991 to only fifty-eight years in 1996.

Rapid economic decline in 1992 and 1993 and rising popular dissatisfaction encouraged a majority of communists, nationalists, and populists in the Russian parliament to oppose Yeltsin and his coalition of democratic reformers and big-business interests. The erratic, increasingly hard-drinking Yeltsin would accept no compromise and insisted on a strong presidential system. Winning in April 1993 the support of 58 percent of the population in a referendum on his proposed constitution, Yeltsin then brought in tanks to crush a parliamentary mutiny in October 1993 and literally blew away the opposition. Subsequently, Yeltsin consolidated his power, and in 1996 he used his big-business cronies in the media to win an impressive come-from-behind victory. But effective representative government failed to develop, and many Russians came to equate "democracy" with the corruption, poverty, and national decline they experienced throughout the 1990s.

This widespread disillusionment set the stage for the "managed democracy" of Vladimir Putin, first elected president as Yeltsin's chosen successor in 2000 and re-elected in a landslide in March 2004. An officer in the secret police in the communist era, Putin maintained relatively free markets in the economic sphere but re-established semi-authoritarian political rule. Aided greatly by high oil prices for Russia's most important export, this combination worked well and seemed to suit most Russians. In 2007, the Russian economy had been growing rapidly for eight years, the Russian middle class was expanding, and the elected parliament supported Putin overwhelmingly. Proponents of liberal democracy were in retreat, while conservative Russian intellectuals were on the offensive, arguing

Russia's Leading Capitalist on Trial, 2004 Mikhail Khodorkovsky emerged from the privatization of Russian industry as the progressive chief and largest shareholder of Yukos, Russia's most successful oil company. But after he supported liberal opposition parties in 2002, an increasingly authoritarian President Putin jailed the billionaire, charged him with tax fraud, and confiscated his wealth before the trial even began. Putin's behavior was widely criticized in the West, but most ordinary Russians applauded because they believed the super rich had plundered the Russian state. *(Alexander Natruskin/Reuters/Corbis)*

that free markets and capitalism required strong political rule to control corruption and prevent chaos. Historians saw a reassertion of Russia's long authoritarian tradition.

Putin's forceful, competent image in world affairs also soothed the country's injured pride and symbolized its national resurgence. Nor did the government permit any negative television reports on the civil war in Chechnya, the tiny republic of 1 million Muslims on Russia's southern border, which in 1991 had declared its independence from the Russian Federation (see Map 31.2). The savage conflict in Chechnya continued, largely unreported, with numerous atrocities on both sides.

Progress in Eastern Europe

Developments in eastern Europe shared important similarities with those in Russia, as many of the problems were the same. Thus the postcommunist states of the former satellite empire worked to replace state planning and socialism with market mechanisms and private property. Western-style electoral politics also took hold, and as in Russia, these politics were marked by intense battles between presidents and parliaments and by weak political parties. The social consequences of these revolutionary changes were similar to those in Russia. Ordinary citizens and the elderly were once again the big losers, while the young and the ex-Communists were the big winners. Inequalities between richer and poorer regions also increased. Capital cities such as Warsaw, Prague, and Budapest concentrated wealth, power, and opportunity as never before, while provincial centers stagnated and old industrial areas declined. Crime and gangsterism increased in the streets and in the executive suites.

Yet the 1990s saw more than a difficult transition, with high social costs, to market economies and freely elected governments in eastern Europe. Many citizens had never fully accepted communism, which they equated with Russian imperialism and the loss of national independence. The joyous crowds that toppled communist regimes in 1989 believed that they were liberating the nation as well as the individual. Thus communism died and nationalism was reborn.

The surge of nationalism in eastern Europe recalled a similar surge of state creation after World War I. Then, too, authoritarian multinational empires had come crashing down in defeat and revolution. Then, too, nationalities with long histories and rich cultures had drawn upon ideologies of popular sovereignty and national self-determination to throw off foreign rule and found new democratic states.

The response to this opportunity in the former communist countries was quite varied in the 1990s, but most observers agreed that Poland, the Czech Republic, and Hungary were the most successful (see Map 31.3). Each of these three countries met the critical challenge of economic reconstruction more successfully than Russia, and each could claim to be the economic leader in eastern Europe, depending on the criteria selected. The reasons for these successes included considerable experience with limited market reforms before 1989, flexibility and lack of dogmatism in government policy, and an enthusiastic embrace of capitalism by a new entrepreneurial class. In the first five years of reform, Poland created twice as many new businesses as Russia, with a total population only one-fourth as large.

The three northern countries in the former Soviet bloc also did far better than Russia in creating new civic institutions, legal systems, and independent broadcasting networks that reinforced political freedom and national revival. Lech Walesa in Poland and Václav Havel in Czechoslovakia were elected presidents of their countries and proved as remarkable in power as in opposition. After Czechoslovakia's "Velvet Revolution" in 1989, Havel and the Czech parliament accepted a "velvet divorce" in 1993 when Slovakian nationalists wanted to break off and form their own state. All three northern countries managed to control national and ethnic tensions that might have destroyed their postcommunist reconstruction.

Above all, and in sharp contrast to Russia, the popular goal of "rejoining the West" reinforced political moderation and compromise. Seeing themselves as heirs to medieval Christendom and liberal democratic values in the 1920s, Poles, Hungarians, and Czechs hoped to find security in NATO membership and economic prosperity in western Europe's ever-tighter union. Membership required many proofs of character and stability, however. Providing these proofs and endorsed by the Clinton administration, Poland, Hungary, and the Czech Republic were accepted into the NATO alliance in 1997. Gaining admission to the European Union (EU) proved more difficult, because candidates also had to accept and be ready to apply all the rules and regulations that the EU had developed since 1956—an awesome task.

Romania and Bulgaria were the eastern European laggards in the postcommunist transition. Western traditions were much weaker there, and both countries were much poorer than neighbors to the north. In 1993 Bulgaria and Romania had per capita national incomes of $1,140, in contrast to Hungary ($3,830) and the Czech Republic ($2,710). Although Romania and Bulgaria eventually made progress in the late 1990s, full membership for both countries in either NATO or the EU still lay far in the future.

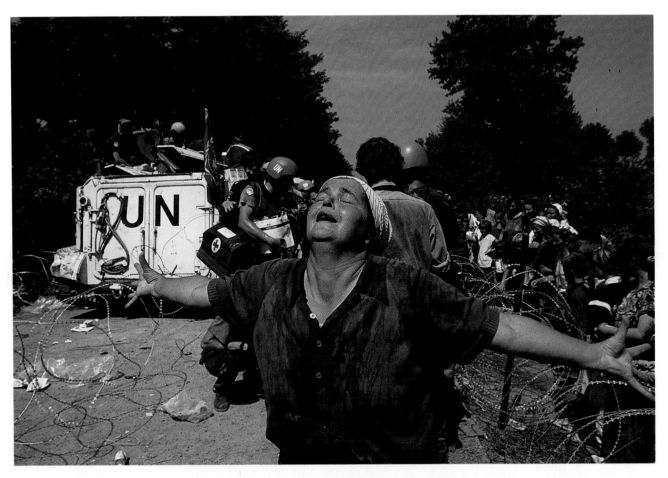

Escape from Srebrenica A Bosnian Muslim refugee arrives at the United Nations base in Tuzla and with her anguished screams tells the world of the Serbian atrocities. Several thousand civilians were murdered at Srebrenica, and Western public opinion finally demanded decisive action. Efforts continue to arrest those Serbs believed responsible and to try them for crimes against humanity. *(J. Jones/Corbis Sygma)*

Mapping the Past

MAP 31.3 Contemporary Europe No longer divided by ideological competition and the cold war, today's Europe features a large number of independent states. Several of these states were previously part of the Soviet Union and Yugoslavia, both of which broke into many different countries. Czechoslovakia also divided on ethnic lines, while a reunited Germany emerged, once again, as the dominant nation in central Europe. ❶ Which countries shown here were previously part of the Soviet Union? ❷ Which countries were part of Yugoslavia? ❸ Where did the old "iron curtain" run? (See Map 30.2, page 988, if necessary.)

Tragedy in Yugoslavia

The great postcommunist tragedy was Yugoslavia, which under Josip Tito had been a federation of republics and regions under strict communist rule (see page 996). After Tito's death in 1980, power passed increasingly to the sister republics, which encouraged a revival of regional and ethnic conflicts that were exacerbated by charges of ethnically inspired massacres during World War II and a dramatic economic decline in the mid-1980s.

The revolutions of 1989 accelerated the breakup of Yugoslavia. Serbian president Slobodan Milosevic intended to grab land from other republics and unite all Serbs, regardless of where they lived, in a "greater Serbia." In 1989 Milosevic arbitrarily abolished self-rule in the Serbian province of Kosovo, where Albanian-speaking people

MAP 31.4 The Ethnic Composition of Yugoslavia, 1991
Yugoslavia had the most ethnically diverse population in eastern Europe. The Republic of Croatia had substantial Serbian and Muslim minorities. Bosnia-Herzegovina had large Muslim, Serbian, and Croatian populations, none of which had a majority. In June 1991, Serbia's brutal effort to seize territory and unite all Serbs in a single state brought a tragic civil war.

constituted the overwhelming majority. Milosevic's moves strengthened the cause of separatism, and in June 1991 Slovenia and Croatia declared their independence. Slovenia repulsed a Serbian attack, but Milosevic's armies managed to take about 30 percent of Croatia. In 1992 the civil war spread to Bosnia-Herzegovina, which had declared its independence. Serbs—about 30 percent of that region's population—refused to live under the more numerous Bosnian Muslims (see Map 31.4). Yugoslavia had once been a tolerant and largely successful multiethnic state, with different groups living side by side and often intermarrying. The Bosnian civil war unleashed ruthless brutality, with murder, rape, destruction, and the herding of refugees into concentration camps.

While scenes of horror shocked the world, the Western nations had difficulty formulating an effective response. The turning point came in July 1995, when Bosnian Serbs overran Srebrenica—a Muslim city previously declared a United Nations "safe area"—and killed several thousand civilians. World outrage prompted NATO to bomb Bosnian Serb military targets intensively, and the

Croatian army drove all the Serbs from Croatia. In November 1995, President Bill Clinton helped the warring sides hammer out a complicated accord that gave the Bosnian Serbs about 49 percent of Bosnia and the Muslim-Croatian peoples the rest. Troops from NATO countries patrolled Bosnia to try to keep the peace.

The Albanian Muslims of Kosovo had been hoping for a restoration of self-rule, but they gained nothing from the Bosnian agreement. In early 1998, frustrated Kosovar militants formed the **Kosovo Liberation Army (KLA)** and began to fight for independence. Serbian repression of the Kosovars increased, and in 1998 Serbian forces attacked both KLA guerrillas and unarmed villagers, displacing 250,000 people within Kosovo. By January 1999, the Western Powers, led by the United States, were threatening Milosevic with heavy air raids if he did not withdraw Serbian armies from Kosovo and accept self-government (but not independence) for Kosovo. Milosevic refused, and in March 1999 NATO began bombing Yugoslavia. Serbian paramilitary forces responded by driving about 780,000 Kosovars into exile. NATO redoubled its highly destructive bombing campaign, which eventually forced Milosevic to withdraw and allowed the joyous Kosovars to regain their homeland. The impoverished Serbs eventually voted the still-defiant Milosevic out of office, and in July 2001 a new pro-Western Serbian government turned him over to the war crimes tribunal in the Netherlands, to stand trial for crimes against humanity. The civil wars in the former Yugoslavia were a monument to human cruelty and evil in the worst tradition of the twentieth century. But ongoing efforts to preserve peace, repatriate refugees, and try war criminals also testified to the regenerative power of liberal values and human rights as the twenty-first century unfolded.

Unity and Identity in Western Europe

The movement toward western European unity, which since the late 1940s had inspired practical politicians seeking economic recovery and idealistic visionaries imagining a European identity that transcended destructive national rivalries, received a powerful second wind in the mid-1980s. The Single European Act of 1986 laid down a detailed legal framework for establishing a single market, which would add the free movement of labor, capital, and services to the existing free trade in goods. With work proceeding vigorously toward the single market, which went into effect in 1993 as the European Community proudly rechristened itself the European Union (EU), French president François Mitterrand and German chancellor Helmut Kohl took the lead in pushing for a monetary union of EU members. After long negotiations and compromises, designed especially to overcome Britain's long-standing reluctance to cede aspects of sovereignty, in December 1991 the member states reached an agreement in the Dutch town of Maastricht. The **Maastricht treaty** set strict financial criteria for joining the proposed monetary union, with its single currency, and set 1999 as the target date for its establishment. The treaty also anticipated the development of common policies on defense and foreign affairs after achieving monetary union.

Western European elites and opinion makers generally supported the decisive step toward economic integration embodied in the Maastricht treaty. They saw monetary union as a means of coping with Europe's ongoing economic problems, imposing financial discipline, cutting costs, and reducing high unemployment. European elites also viewed monetary union as a historic, irreversible step toward a basic political unity. This unity would allow western Europe as a whole to regain its rightful place in world politics and to deal with the United States as an equal.

The Maastricht plan for monetary union encountered widespread skepticism and considerable opposition from ordinary people, leftist political parties, and patriotic nationalists. Ratification votes were close, especially when the public rather than the politicians could vote yes or no on the question.

There were several interrelated reasons for this widespread popular opposition. Many people resented the unending flow of rules handed down by the EU's ever-growing bureaucracy in Brussels, which sought to impose common standards on everything from cheese to day care and undermined national practices and local traditions. Moreover, increased unity meant yielding still more power to distant "Eureaucrats" and political insiders, thereby undermining popular sovereignty and democratic control through national politics and electoral competition. Above all, many ordinary citizens feared that the new Europe was being made at their expense. Joining the monetary union required national governments to meet stringent fiscal standards and impose budget cuts. The resulting reductions in health care and social benefits hit ordinary citizens and did nothing to reduce western Europe's high unemployment rate.

Events in France dramatically illustrated these developments. Mitterrand's Socialist government had been forced to adopt conservative financial policies in the 1980s (see page 1012), and in early 1993 a coalition of conservatives and moderates won an overwhelming victory by promising a vigorous attack on unemployment. However, the Maastricht criteria soon forced the new government to resume deficit-reducing cuts in health benefits and transportation services. France's powerful unions and railroad workers responded with a crippling national strike that shut down rail traffic throughout France for almost a month. Yet despite the enormous inconvenience and economic damage, many people felt that the transport workers were also fighting for them. The government had to back down, and soon the Socialists returned to power. The Socialists quickly passed a controversial new law to reduce the legal workweek to thirty-five hours in an attempt to reduce France's stubborn 12 percent unemployment rate without budget-busting spending. More generally, much of the western European public increasingly saw laws to cut the workweek and share the work as a way to reconcile desires for social welfare and a humane market economy with financial discipline and global competition.

Battles over budgets and high unemployment throughout the European Union in the 1990s raised profound questions about the meaning of European unity and identity. Would the European Union expand as promised to include the postcommunist nations of eastern Europe, and if it did, how could Muslim Turkey's longstanding application be ignored? How could a European Union of twenty-five to thirty countries have any real cohesion and common identity? Conversely, would a large, cohesive Europe remain closely linked with the United States in the NATO alliance and with an evolving Western tradition?

The merging of East Germany into the German Federal Republic suggested the enormous difficulties of full East-West integration under the best conditions. After 1991 Helmut Kohl's Germany pumped massive investments into its new eastern provinces, but Germans in the east still saw factories closed and social dislocation. Unemployment in Germany reached a postwar high of 12.8 percent in late 1997, and it soared to 20 percent in the eastern region. Germany's generous social benefits cushioned the economic difficulties, but many ordinary citizens felt hurt and humiliated.

Eastern German women suffered in particular. Before unification, the overwhelming majority had worked outside the home, effectively supported by cheap child care, flexible hours, and the prevailing socialist ideology. Now they faced expensive child care and a variety of pressures to stay at home and let men take the hard-to-find jobs. Many of these women, who had found autonomy and self-esteem in paid work, felt a keen sense of loss. They helped vote Kohl out of office in 1998.

Instructed by the serious difficulties of unification in Germany, western Europeans proceeded cautiously in considering new requests for EU membership. Sweden, Finland, and Austria were admitted because they had strong capitalist economies and because they no longer needed to maintain the legal neutrality that the Soviet Union had required during the cold war.

Turkey's Struggle for EU Membership   Turkish elites and the general population want to "join Europe," but the road to EU membership is proving long and difficult. The EU has required Turkey to make many constitutional reforms and give greater autonomy to Turkish Kurds. Yet the Turks face ever more demands, and many now believe that the real roadblock is Europe's anti-Muslim feeling. *(CartoonStock Limited)*

At the same time the former communist states pressed toward meeting the EU's detailed criteria for membership. In December 2000, the EU's fifteen members agreed to begin final negotiations with the eight leading eastern candidates in the near future. The very smooth establishment of the euro on January 1, 2002, when brand-new euros entered the billfolds of all euro-zone citizens as their unified common currency, built confidence and brought an acceleration of arduous but triumphant negotiations. Thus on May 1, 2004, the European Union added 70 million people and expanded to include 455 million citizens in twenty-five different countries. The largest newcomer by far was Poland, followed in descending size by the Czech Republic, Hungary, Slovenia, Slovakia, Estonia, Lithuania, Latvia, Malta, and Cyprus.

In June 2004, more than two years after charging a special commission to write "a new constitution for European citizens," the leaders of the European Union reached agreement on the final document. Above all, the new constitution, with almost 350 articles, established a single rulebook to replace the complex network of treaties concluded by the member states since the 1957 creation of the European Economic Community. The EU constitution created a president, a foreign minister, and a voting system weighted to reflect the number of people in the different states. The result of intense debate and many compromises, the constitution moved toward a more centralized federal system in several fields, but each state retained veto power in the most sensitive areas, such as taxation, social policy, and foreign affairs. In order for the constitution to take effect, each and every EU country needed to ratify it.

Nine countries, led by Germany, Italy, and seven eastern European members, soon ratified the constitution by parliamentary action, while seven states planned to go beyond the political elites and let the voters decide. The referendum campaigns were noisy and contentious, as generally well-informed citizens debated whether the new constitution surrendered too much national sovereignty to an emerging central European government in Brussels. British voters were considered most likely to vote no, but both the French and the Dutch beat them to it, rejecting the new constitution by clear majorities. Nationalist fears about losing sovereignty were matched by fears that an unwieldy European Union would grow to include Ukraine, Georgia, and Muslim Turkey—countries with cultures and histories that were very different from those in western Europe. Thus the long postwar march toward ever greater European unity stopped, or at least stalled, and the European Union concentrated on fully integrating the new eastern European members.

New Challenges in the Twenty-first Century

As the twenty-first century opened and the historic movement toward European unity began to include post-communist eastern Europe, European society faced new uncertainties. Of great significance, Europe continued to experience a remarkable **baby bust,** as birthrates fell to levels that seemed to promise a shrinking and aging population in the future. At the same time, the peaceful, wealthy European Union attracted rapidly growing numbers of refugees and illegal immigrants from the former Soviet Union, the Middle East, Africa, and Asia. The unexpected arrival of so many newcomers raised many perplexing questions and prompted serious thinking about European identity, Europe's humanitarian mission, and Europe's place in the world.

• *Why did the prospect of population decline, the reality of large-scale immigration, and concern for human rights emerge as critical issues in contemporary Europe?*

The Prospect of Population Decline

Population is still growing rapidly in many poor countries, but this is not the case in the world's industrialized nations. In 2000, women in developed countries had only 1.6 children on average; only in the United States did women have, almost exactly, the 2.1 children necessary to maintain a stable population. In European countries, where women have been steadily having fewer babies since the 1950s, national fertility rates ranged from 1.2 to 1.8 children per woman. Italy, once renowned for big Catholic families, had achieved the world's lowest birthrate—a mere 1.2 babies per woman. In 2006, the European fertility rate was little changed at about 1.4 children per woman.

If the current baby bust continues, the long-term consequences could be dramatic, though hardly predictable. At the least, Europe's population would decline and age. Projections for Germany are illustrative. Total German population, barring much greater immigration, would gradually decline from 82 million in 2001 to only 62 million around 2050. The number of people of working age would drop by a third, and almost half of the population would be over sixty. Social security taxes paid by the shrinking labor force would need to soar for the skyrocketing costs of pensions and health care for seniors to be met—a recipe for generational tension and conflict. As the premier of Bavaria, Germany's biggest state, has warned, the prospect of demographic decline was a "ticking time bomb under our social welfare system and entire economy."[2]

Why, in times of peace, were Europeans failing to reproduce themselves? Certainly the uneven, uninspiring European economic conditions of the 1980s and much of the 1990s played some role. High unemployment fell heavily on young people and often frustrated their plans to settle down and have children. Some observers also argued that a partial rejection of motherhood and parenting was critical. They noted that many women chose to have no children or only one child. By 2000, 30 percent of German women born in 1965 were childless, whereas 90 percent would have had children in earlier generations. In the Catholic countries of southern Europe, where strong pressures to have children still exist, a quarter of the couples were fulfilling their "social duty" with a single child.

In our view, the ongoing impact of careers for married women and the related drive for gender equality remained the decisive factors in the long-term decline of postwar birthrates. After World War II, Western women married early, had their children early, and then turned increasingly to full-time employment, where they suffered from the discrimination that drove the women's movement (see pages 1009–1010). As the twenty-first century opened, women had attained many (but not all) of their objectives. They did as well as or better than men in school, and educated young women earned almost as much as their male counterparts.

Research showed that European women (and men) in their twenties, thirties, and early forties still wanted to have two or even three children—about the same number as their parents had wanted. But unlike their parents, young couples did not realize their ideal family size. Many women postponed the birth of their first child into their thirties in order to finish their education and establish themselves in their careers. Then, finding that raising even one child was more difficult and time-consuming than anticipated, new mothers tended to postpone and eventually forgo a second child. This was especially true of professional women. The better educated and the more economically successful a woman was, the more likely she was to stop with a single child or to have no children at all.

By 2005 some population experts believed that European women were no longer postponing having children. At the least, birthrates appeared to have stabilized. Moreover, the frightening implications of dramatic population decline had emerged as a major public issue. Opinion leaders, politicians, and the media started to press the case for more babies and more support for families with chil-

dren. Europeans may respond with enough vigor to limit the extent of their population decline and avoid societal disaster.

The Growth of Immigration

As European demographic vitality waned in the 1990s, a surge of migrants from Africa, Asia, and eastern Europe headed for western Europe. Some migrants entered the European Union legally, but increasing numbers were smuggled in past beefed-up border patrols. Large-scale immigration emerged as a contentious and critical challenge.

Historically a source rather than a destination of immigrants, booming western Europe drew heavily on North Africa and Turkey for manual laborers from about 1960 until about 1973, when unemployment started to rise and governments abruptly stopped the inflow. Many foreign workers stayed on, however, eventually bringing their families to western Europe and establishing permanent immigrant communities there.

A new and different surge of migration into western Europe began in the 1990s. The collapse of communism in the East and savage civil wars in Yugoslavia sent hundreds of thousands of refugees fleeing westward. Equally brutal conflicts in Afghanistan, Iraq, Somalia, and Rwanda—to name only four countries—brought thousands more from Asia and Africa. Illegal immigration into the European Union also exploded, rising from an estimated 50,000 people in 1993 to perhaps 500,000 a decade later. This movement exceeded the estimated 300,000 unauthorized foreigners entering the United States each year.

In the early twenty-first century, many migrants still applied for political asylum and refugee status, but most were eventually rejected and classified as illegal job seekers. Certainly, greater economic opportunities exerted a powerful pull. Germans earned on average five times more than neighboring Poles, who in turn earned much more than people farther east and in North Africa.

Illegal immigration also soared because powerful criminal gangs turned to "people smuggling" for big, low-risk profits. Ruthless Russian-speaking gangs played an important role in the trade, passing their human cargo across Russia and through the Balkans to western Europe. A favorite final leg involved Albanian smugglers with speedy motorboats, who slipped across the narrow Adriatic Sea past Italian coastal patrols and landed their high-paying passengers on the beaches of southern Italy. From there new arrivals could head off unimpeded in al-

Illegal Immigrants from Eritrea Italian police have just rescued these young immigrants from an overloaded boat off the coast of Italy. Fleeing civil war and desperate for work, the immigrants are weary because of the long and dangerous voyage from Libya. Every year thousands of illegal immigrants try to reach Italy and Spain from North Africa. Many are found dead on the shoreline. *(Mimi Mollica/Corbis)*

most any direction, because in 1998 the European Union abolished all border controls between member states. After 2000, growing numbers from Africa and the Middle East tried similar entries across the Strait of Gibraltar into southern Spain.

A large portion of the illegal immigrants were young women from eastern Europe, especially Russia and Ukraine. Often lured by criminals promising jobs as maids or waitresses and sometimes simply kidnapped and sold like slaves from hand to hand for a few thousand dollars, these women were smuggled into the most prosperous parts of central Europe and into the European Union and forced into prostitution or worse.

Illegal immigration generated intense discussion and controversy in western Europe. A majority opposed the newcomers, who were accused of taking jobs from the unemployed and somehow undermining national unity. The idea that cultural and ethnic diversity could be a force for vitality and creativity ran counter to deep-seated beliefs. Concern about illegal migration in general often fused with fears of Muslim immigrants and Muslim residents who had grown up in Europe. As busy mosques came to outnumber dying churches in parts of some European cities, rightist politicians especially tried to exploit widespread doubts that immigrant populations from Muslim countries would ever assimilate to the different national cultures. These doubts increased after the attack on New York's World Trade Center, as we shall see later in the chapter.

An articulate minority challenged the anti-immigrant campaign and its racist overtones. They argued that Europe badly needed newcomers—preferably talented newcomers—to limit the impending population decline and provide valuable technical skills. European leaders also focused on improved policing of EU borders and tougher common procedures to combat people smuggling and punish international crime. Above all, growing illegal immigration pushed Europeans to examine the whys of this dramatic human movement and to consider how it related to Europe's proper role in world affairs.

Promoting Human Rights

The tide of refugees and illegal job seekers made thinking people in western Europe acutely aware of their current good fortune, the sweet fruit of more than fifty years of peace, security, and rising standards of living. The nearby agonies of barbarism and war in the former Yugoslavia vividly recalled the horrors of World War II, and they cast in bold relief the ever-present reality of collective violence in today's world. At the same time, western European countries were generally doing their best to limit or expel the foreigners arriving at their gates, as we have seen. This ongoing rejection gave some Europeans a guilty conscience and a feeling that they needed to do more when they had so much and so many others had so little. As a result, European intellectuals and opinion makers began to envision a new historic mission for Europe—the promotion of domestic peace and human rights in those lands plagued by instability, violence, and oppression.

European leaders and humanitarians believed that Europe's mission required more global agreements and new international institutions to set moral standards and to regulate countries, political leaders, armies, corporations, and individuals. In practice, this meant more curbs on the sovereign rights of the world's states, just as the states of the European Union had imposed increasingly strict standards of behavior on themselves in order to secure the rights and welfare of EU citizens. As Nicole Gnesotto, the director of the European Union's institute, concluded, the EU has a "historical responsibility" to make morality "a basis of policy," because "human rights are more important than states' rights."[3] In general, the United States reacted coolly to the idea of preferring human rights to states' rights. American leaders stressed the preservation of U.S. freedom of action in world affairs, particularly after George W. Bush was elected president in 2000.

In practical terms, western Europe's evolving human rights mission meant, first of all, humanitarian interventions to stop civil wars and to prevent tyrannical governments from slaughtering their own people. Thus the European Union joined with the United States to inter-

Fighting the AIDS Epidemic These women, financed in part by the European Union, are treating an AIDS patient at his home in Mozambique. In 2004 the United Nations estimated that about 42 million persons were infected with HIV, the virus that causes AIDS. AIDS is the fourth-leading cause of death in the world. (*Black Star/stockphoto.com*)

vene militarily to stop the killing in Bosnia, Kosovo, and Macedonia and to protect the rights of embattled minorities (see pages 1037–1039). The states of the EU also vigorously supported UN-sponsored conferences and treaties that sought to verify the compliance of anti–germ warfare conventions, outlawed the use of hideously destructive land mines, and established a new international court to prosecute war criminals.

Europeans also pushed for broader definitions of individual rights. Abolishing the death penalty in the European Union, for example, they condemned its continued use in China, the United States, Saudi Arabia, and some other countries as inhumane and uncivilized. Rights for Europeans in their personal relations also continued to expand. In the pacesetting Netherlands, for example, a growing network of laws gave prostitutes (legally recognized since 1917) pensions and full workers' rights and legalized gay and lesbian marriages, the smoking of pot in licensed coffee shops, and assisted suicide (euthanasia) for the terminally ill.

As the twenty-first century opened, western Europeans also pushed as best they could to extend their broad-based concept of social and economic rights to the world's poor countries. These efforts were related to sharp criticism of globalization and unrestrained capitalism (see pages 1031–1032), criticism that helped socialists regain power in several countries in the European Union. Quite typically, Europe's moderate social democrats combined with human rights campaigners in 2001 to help African governments secure drastic price cuts from the big international drug companies on the drug cocktails needed to combat Africa's AIDS crisis. Strong advocates of greater social equality and state-funded health care, European socialists embraced morality as a basis for action and the global expansion of human rights as a primary goal.

The West and the Islamic World

A hundred years from now, when historians assess developments in the early twenty-first century, they will almost certainly highlight the dramatic deterioration in the long, rich, up-and-down relationship between the West and the Islamic world. They will examine the reasons that the peaceful conclusion of the cold war and the joyful reunification of a divided continent gave way to spectacular terrorist attacks, Western invasions of Muslim countries, and new concern about Muslims living in the West. Unfortunately, we lack the perspective and the full range of source materials that future historians will have at their disposal.

Yet we are deeply involved in this momentous historical drama, and we must try to find insight and understanding.

• *How and why did relations between the West and the Islamic world deteriorate dramatically in the early twenty-first century?*

The al-Qaeda Attack of September 11, 2001

On the morning of September 11, 2001, two hijacked passenger planes from Boston crashed into and destroyed the World Trade Center towers in New York City. Shortly thereafter a third plane crashed into the Pentagon, and a fourth, believed to be headed for the White House or the U.S. Capitol, crashed into a field in rural Pennsylvania. These terrorist attacks took the lives of more than three thousand people from many countries and put the personal safety of ordinary citizens at the top of the West's agenda. Stunned and horrified, the peoples and governments of the world joined Americans in heartfelt solidarity.

The United States, led by President George W. Bush, launched a military campaign to destroy the perpetrators of the crime—Saudi-born millionaire Osama bin Laden's al-Qaeda network of terrorists and Afghanistan's reactionary Muslim government, the Taliban. Drawing on the world's sympathy and building a broad international coalition that included western Europe, Russia, and Pakistan, the United States joined its tremendous airpower with the faltering Northern Alliance in Afghanistan, which had been fighting the Taliban for years. By mid-October 2001 American special forces on the ground were directing precision air strikes that devastated Taliban and al-Qaeda troops, and a rejuvenated Northern Alliance took the offensive. In mid-November the Taliban collapsed, and jubilant crowds in the capital of Kabul welcomed Northern Alliance soldiers as liberators. Afghan opposition leaders and United Nations mediators worked out plans for a new broad-based government, while American planes, ground troops, and tribal fighters searched for bin Laden and his die-hard supporters in their mountain hideaways. In 2002 foreign governments, aid organizations, and the United Nations turned to the arduous task of helping the Afghans get themselves back on their feet after a generation of conflict and civil war following the 1979 Soviet invasion of their country.

In trying to make some sense out of the heinous attack of September 11, 2001, and the current wave of terrorist action in general, it is helpful to realize that civil war and terrorism often went hand in hand in the twentieth century. Beginning in the 1920s and peaking in the 1960s, many nationalist movements used terrorism in their battles to achieve political independence and decolonization. This was the case in several new states, including Algeria, Cyprus, Ireland, Israel, and Yemen.[4] Those fighting for independence and political power often targeted police forces for assassination campaigns, thereby breaking down confidence in the colonial government and provoking counter-atrocities that generated increased support for the independence movement.

In the Vietnam War era, a second wave of terrorism saw some far-left supporters of the communist Vietcong, such as the American Weathermen, the German Red Army Faction, and the Italian Red Brigade, practicing "revolutionary terror" in an effort to cripple the Western heartland. These groups engineered a series of deadly bombings, assassinations, and kidnappings. These terrorists also hijacked airplanes—more than one hundred each

year in the 1970s—in order to take hostages and blackmail governments into meeting some demand, such as the release of convicted fellow terrorists. Some terrorists trained in the facilities of the PLO (the Palestine Liberation Organization) operated international networks and targeted Israel and U.S. installations abroad. This second wave receded in the 1980s as painstaking police work and international cooperation defeated these "revolutionaries" in country after country.

In recent years a third wave has been building, leading toward al-Qaeda's attack on the World Trade Center and the Pentagon on September 11, 2001. In analyzing this third wave, many commentators were quick to stress the role of extreme Islamic fundamentalism as a motivating factor. But the most perceptive scholars noted that recent deadly attacks had been committed by terrorists inspired by several religious faiths and religious sects and were by no means limited to Islamic extremists.[5] These scholars noted that the different terrorist movements in today's

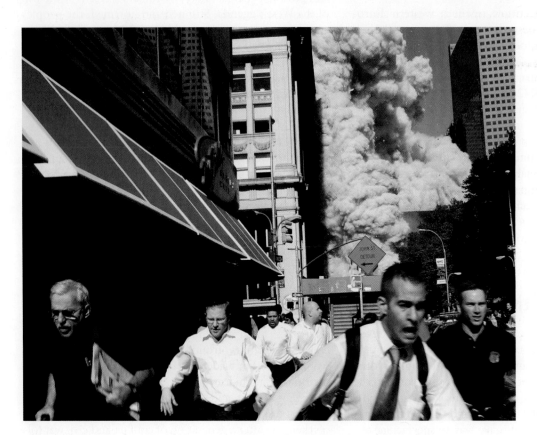

New York, September 11, 2001   Pedestrians race for safety as the World Trade Center towers collapse after being hit by jet airliners. Al-Qaeda terrorists with box cutters hijacked four aircraft and used three of them as suicide missiles to perpetrate their unthinkable crime. Heroic passengers on the fourth plane realized what was happening and forced their hijackers to crash in a field. *(AP Images/Suzanne Plunkett)*

world need to be linked to underlying political conflicts and civil wars for meaningful understanding.

When this perspective is applied to Osama bin Laden and al-Qaeda members, two stages stand out. First, in the long bitter fighting against the Soviet Union and the local communists in Afghanistan, bin Laden and like-minded "holy warriors" developed terrorist skills and a narrow-minded, fanatical Islamic puritanism. They also developed a hatred of most existing Arab governments, which they viewed as corrupt, un-Islamic, and unresponsive to the needs of ordinary Muslims. The objects of their hostility included the absolute monarchy of oil-rich Saudi Arabia (bin Laden's own country), pro-Western but undemocratic Egypt, and the secular, one-party dictatorship of Saddam Hussein.

Second, when these Islamic extremists returned home from Afghanistan and began to organize, they usually met the fate of many earlier Islamic extremists and were jailed or forced into exile, often in tolerant Europe. There they blamed the United States for being the supporter and corrupter of existing Arab governments, and they organized murderous plots against the United States—a despised proxy for the Arab rulers they could not reach. This development set the stage for the 1998 bombing of the U.S. embassy in Nairobi, Kenya, which claimed nearly 200 lives, the World Trade Center atrocity, and the U.S.-led counterattack on al-Qaeda in Afghanistan.

The War in Iraq

Unfortunately, Western unity in Afghanistan soon turned into bitter quarreling and international crisis over the prospect of war with Iraq. As soon as he was elected in 2000, President Bush and his most influential advisers, led by Vice President Dick Cheney and Secretary of Defense Donald Rumsfeld, began to consider how to overthrow Iraq's Saddam Hussein and remake the Middle East. Paul O'Neill, Bush's secretary of the treasury, summed up discussions on Iraq by the president and his cabinet this way: "From the start, they were building the case against Hussein and looking at how we could take him out and change Iraq into a new country. And, if we did that, it would solve everything."[6] And indeed, many in the administration believed that the United States could create a democratic, pro-American Iraq, an Iraq that would transform the Middle East, make peace with Israel, provide easy access to the world's second-largest oil reserves, and show small states the folly of opposing the United States. The most effective prowar argument, however, played on American fears of renewed terrorism and charged that Saddam Hussein was still developing weapons of mass destruction in flagrant disregard of his promise to end all such programs following the first war with Iraq, in 1991 (see page 1030). Saddam had used chemical weapons in his war with Iran in the 1980s and against the Kurdish population of northern Iraq, and the Bush administration argued that sooner or later he would probably use these terrible weapons against the United States and its allies or would give them to anti-American fanatics like those who struck New York on September 11, 2001.

In August 2002, Vice President Cheney promised Iraqi exiles that the United States would depose Saddam, although according to the United Nations charter, the Security Council has the sole authority to use armed force, except in self-defense, and Iraq, impoverished by a decade of tough United Nations sanctions, gave no indication of attacking any of its neighbors, much less the United States. Moreover, large numbers of Americans shared widespread doubts in Europe about the legality—and wisdom—of an American attack on Iraq and argued for a peaceful settlement of the Iraqi weapons crisis. So the Bush administration reluctantly agreed to new Security Council resolutions requiring Iraq to accept the return of United Nations weapons inspectors and destroy any remaining prohibited weapons. Iraq accepted the inspectors, declaring it had destroyed all prohibited weapons.

As 2003 opened, the inspectors operated freely in Iraq and found no weapons of mass destruction. However, the United States and Britain said Iraq was hiding prohibited weapons, moved armies to the Middle East, and lobbied for a new United Nations resolution authorizing immediate military action against Iraq. The world followed the debates in the Security Council with unprecedented interest and generally opposed an attack on Iraq. France, Russia, China, Germany, and a majority of the smaller states argued for continued weapons inspections. Western governments became bitterly divided, and the Security Council deadlocked and failed to act.

In March 2003 the United States and Britain invaded Iraq from bases in Kuwait and quickly overwhelmed the Iraqi army. Yet even as Saddam's dictatorship collapsed, the confident expectation of a long and peaceful occupation in a pro-American Iraq was impaired by serious errors of American judgment. As chaos spread and looters stripped government buildings and hospitals of everything from computers to faucets, American and British troops simply turned a blind eye and took no action. Disbanding the Iraqi army also alienated the population, worsened security, and created mass unemployment, while the failure to seize huge stocks of weapons left Iraqi

The Golden Mosque of Samarra: Before and After Built to commemorate two of Shi'ite Islam's most revered saints, the Golden Mosque drew countless Shi'ite pilgrims. Then, on June 13, 2006, insurgents dressed as Iraqi policemen entered the mosque, overwhelmed the guards, and detonated two bombs that collapsed the golden dome and destroyed the mosque. Sectarian conflict exploded. (A second terrorist bombing in June 2007 levelled the two minarets seen on the right.) *(AP Images/Khalid Mohammed, Hameed Rasheed)*

insurgents with guns and explosives for subsequent counterattacks. The allies found no weapons of mass destruction, which raised many questions about a prewar manipulation of intelligence data.

American efforts to establish a stable, pro-American Iraq proved difficult if not impossible. Poor postwar planning and management by President Bush and his top aides was one factor, but there were others. Modern Iraq, a creation of Western imperialism after World War I (see page 906), is a fragile state with three distinct groups: non-Arab Kurds, and Sunnis and Shi'ites—Arab Muslims who were forever divided by a great schism in the seventh century. Saddam's dictatorship preached Arab and Iraqi nationalism, but it relied heavily on the Sunni minority—20 percent of the population—and repressed the Shi'ites, who made up 60 percent of the population. Jailed or ousted from their positions by American forces, top Sunnis quickly turned against the occupation, rallied their supporters, and launched an armed insurgency. By late 2004, radical Sunnis and al-Qaeda converts were slipping into Iraq, where they directed horrendous suicide bombings at American soldiers, Iraqi security forces, and defenseless Shi'ite civilians.

Believing in democracy and representative institutions, the Americans restored Iraqi sovereignty in July 2004, formed a provisional government, and held relatively free national elections in January 2005. Boycotted by the Sunnis, these elections brought the Shi'ite majority to power and marked the high point of Iraqi and American hopes for security and a gradual reconciliation with the Sunni population. Instead, Sunni fighters and jihadist extremists stepped up their deadly campaign. Then, in February 2005 in a carefully planned operation, they blew up the beautiful Golden Mosque of Samarra, one of the most sacred shrines of Shi'ite Islam. This outrage touched off violent retaliation. Shi'ite militias became death squads, killing Sunnis and driving them from their homes. By 2006 a deadly sectarian conflict had taken hold of Baghdad. American soldiers, continuing loyally to do their duty, were increasingly caught in the crossfire. In 2007, as President Bush faced widespread opposition at home, it seemed unlikely that yet another intensification of American efforts to create stability in Iraq would succeed.

The West and Its Muslim Citizens

The attack on the World Trade Center and the long war in Iraq, signaling a dramatic worsening of relations between the West and the Islamic world, had major repercussions in Western countries. In the United States there were great fears of more terrorist attacks, but to almost everyone's surprise Europe received the extremists' next blows. In May 2004 Moroccan Muslims living in Spain exploded bombs planted on morning trains bound for Madrid and killed 252 commuters. A year later a similar attack was carried out in London by British citizens of Pakistani descent, young men who had grown up in Britain and seemed to be ordinary fellows.

Even more traumatic for the tolerant Dutch and many other Europeans was the repeated stabbing and brutal murder of Theo van Gogh by a young Dutch Muslim. Van Gogh, a provocative filmmaker, had joined an anti-Islamic feminist and refugee from East Africa in making a vulgar ten-minute film that mocked the prophet Muhammad and denounced Islam's treatment of women. For his "blasphemy," van Gogh was "executed" by the son of Moroccan immigrants, who proudly explained his action to the court in colloquial Dutch.

These spectacular attacks and lesser actions by Islamic militants sharpened the European debate on immigration (see pages 1042–1044). A shrill chorus warned that, in addition to the security danger, Europe's rapidly growing Muslim population posed a dire threat to the West's entire Enlightenment tradition, which embraced freedom of thought, representative government, toleration, separation of church and state, and, more recently, equal rights for women and gays. Islamic extremists and radical clerics settled in Europe were, the critics claimed, rejecting these fundamental Western values and preaching instead the supremacy of Islamic laws for Muslims living in Europe, and even for non-Muslim Europeans on some issues. Moreover, the critics claimed, many "moderate" Islamic teachers were really anti-Western radicals playing for time. (See the feature "Individuals in Society: Tariq Ramadan.") And time was on the side of Euro-Islam. Europe's Muslim population, estimated at 15 million in 2006, appeared likely to double to 30 million by 2025, and it would increase rapidly thereafter as the number of non-Europeans plummeted (see pages 1041–1042).

Admitting that Islamic extremism could pose a serious challenge, many mainstream observers focused instead on the problem of immigrant integration. Whereas the first generation of Muslim immigrants—predominately Turks in Germany, Algerians in France, Pakistanis in Britain, and Moroccans in the Netherlands—had found jobs as unskilled workers in Europe's great postwar boom, they and their children had been hard hit after 1973 by the general economic downturn. Immigrants also suffered from the ongoing decline of European manufacturing due to globalization. Provided for modestly by the welfare state and housed minimally in ugly housing projects, many Muslims of the second and third generations were finding themselves locked out in their adopted countries. In short, economics, inadequate job training, and discrimination trumped religion and extremist teachings.

This argument was strengthened by widespread rioting in France in November 2005 that saw hundreds of young second- and third-generation Muslim immigrants go on a rampage. Almost always French by birth, language, and education, marauding groups of "Arabs" torched hundreds of automobiles night after night in Paris suburbs and large cities. (See the feature "Listening to the Past: The French Riots: Will They Change Anything?" on pages 1054–1055.) The rioters complained bitterly of very high unemployment, systematic discrimination, and exclusion. Religious ideology appeared almost nonexistent in their thinking. Studies sparked by the rioting in France found poor, alienated Muslims in unwholesome ghettos throughout western Europe.

Although Muslim immigrants in the United States certainly experienced increased hostility after the September 11 attack, it was generally recognized that they were integrating more successfully with their adopted homeland than were their European counterparts. This is partly because the United States believes that it has always been a nation of immigrants, whereas the European ideal remains the homogeneous national state. Equally important, Muslim immigrants to the United States have often been well educated, have come from several countries speaking different languages, and have spread out within cities and across the country. Muslim immigrants to western Europe, usually a larger percentage of the host country's population than in America, have generally been poor rural people with limited education who came to do manual labor. In each of the leading host countries, they came mainly from a single Muslim country and then lived together on the fringes of the largest cities. Muslim immigrants to the United States brought more "human capital," and this facilitated more successful integration.

Finally, the fact that Americans and western Europeans have gone their separate ways on religion probably impacts their relations with their Muslim citizens. A large though declining number of Americans still take religion seriously, whereas western Europeans have largely abandoned Christianity, with less than 5 percent of the population attending church on most Sundays. Thus many Americans still can—or should—understand and even appreciate the power of Islam for devout Muslims, whereas western Europeans tend to find all traditional religious belief irrational and out-of-date. This is why, in addition to determined efforts to root out anti-Muslim discrimination, the renowned French scholar Olivier Roy argues, Europe must recognize that Islam is now a European religion and a vital part of European life. This recognition, he argues, will open the way to eventual full acceptance of European Muslims in both political and cultural terms. It will head off the resentment that can drive Europe's Muslim believers to separatism and acts of terror.

The Future in Perspective

● *What does the study of history have to tell us about the future?*

For centuries astrologers and scientists, experts and ordinary people, have sought to peek into the future. And although it may seem that the study of the past has little to say about the future, the study of history over a long period is actually very useful in this regard. It helps put the future in perspective.

Certainly, history is full of erroneous predictions, a few of which we have mentioned in this book. Yet lack of success has not diminished the age-old desire to look into the future. Self-proclaimed experts even pretend that they have created a new science of futurology. With great pomposity, they often act as if their hunches and guesses about future human development are inescapable realities. Yet the study of history teaches healthy skepticism regarding such predictions, however scientific and learned they may appear. Past results suggest that most such predictions will simply not come true, or at least not in the anticipated ways. Thus history provides some psychological protection from the visions of modern prognosticators.

This protection is particularly valuable when we realize that views of the future tend to swing between pessimistic and optimistic extremes from one generation, or even from one decade, to the next. These swings back and forth between optimism and pessimism, which one historian has aptly called "the great seesaw" in the development of the Western world, reflect above all the current situation of the observers.[7] Thus in the economic stagnation and revived cold war of the 1970s and 1980s, many projections into the future were quite pessimistic, just as they were very optimistic in the 1950s and 1960s. Many people in the Western world feared that conditions were going to get worse rather than better. For example, there were fears that pollution would destroy the environment and that the traditional family would disappear. Some gloomy experts predicted that twenty to thirty states might well have nuclear weapons by the end of the twentieth century. Many forecasters and politicians predicted

that the energy crisis—in the form of skyrocketing oil prices—meant disaster in the form of lower standards of living at best and the collapse of civilization at worst. In fact, oil prices collapsed in the early 1980s and generally stayed low until the second Iraq war in 2003. It was heartening in that time of pessimism to know that most dire predictions do not prove true, just as the same knowledge of likely error is sobering in times of optimistic expectations.

Optimistic visions of the future were certainly in the air after the end of the cold war. The pendulum had definitely swung, most notably in the United States. Untroubled in the late 1990s by the high unemployment and the early stages of corporate downsizing that soured the mood in western Europe, the United States celebrated its dynamic economy and its booming stock market. U.S. military power, leadership in world affairs, and excellence in advanced technologies also encouraged optimism and rosy projections.

In 2000 the American mood shifted. The dot-com bubble burst, and in 2001 the U.S. economy slid into a recession. The al-Qaeda attack on New York and the tragic war in Iraq, with its endless carnage and suicide bombings, led to many pessimistic forecasts of a long uphill struggle against global extremism, especially Islamic extremism. Most frightening of all were grim warnings by some self-described experts who predicted that terrorist groups were likely to succeed in developing or buying biological and nuclear weapons of mass destruction, which they would then turn on millions of innocent people with unspeakable cruelty. Such nightmare scenarios are not impossible, but we should remember that modern governments possess tremendous resources that they can mobilize to control individuals and opposition groups, especially when the leading states decide to work together, as they did immediately after September 11, 2001. Once again, just as it is sobering to know that the rosiest predictions in optimistic times usually do not prove true, so is it heartening to know that the direst projections in pessimistic times normally do not come to pass.

Whatever does or does not happen, the study of history puts the future in perspective in other ways. We have seen that every age has its problems and challenges. Others before us have trodden the paths of uncertainty and crisis. This knowledge helps save us from exaggerated self-pity in the face of our own predicaments.

Perhaps our Western heritage may rightly inspire us with pride and measured self-confidence. We stand, momentarily, at the head of the long procession of Western civilization. Sometimes the procession has wandered, or backtracked, or done terrible things. But it has also

Individuals in Society

Tariq Ramadan

Religious teacher, activist professor, and media star, Tariq Ramadan (b. 1962) is Europe's most famous Muslim intellectual. He is also a controversial figure, praised by many as a moderate bridge-builder and denounced by others as an Islamic militant in clever disguise.

Born in Switzerland of Egyptian ancestry, Ramadan is the grandson of Hassan al-Banna, the charismatic founder of the powerful Muslim Brotherhood. Al-Banna fought to reshape Arab nationalism within a framework of Islamic religious orthodoxy and anti-British terrorism until he himself was assassinated in 1949. Growing up in Geneva, where his father sought refuge in 1954 after Nasser's anti-Islamic crackdown in Egypt, the young Tariq attended mainstream public schools, played soccer, and absorbed a wide-ranging Islamic heritage. For example, growing up fluent in French and Arabic, he learned English mainly from listening to Pakistani Muslims discuss issues with his father, who represented the Muslim Brotherhood and its ideology in Europe.

Ramadan studied philosophy and French literature as an undergraduate at the University of Geneva, and he then earned a doctorate in Arabic and Islamic studies. Marrying a Swiss woman who converted to Islam, Ramadan moved his family to Cairo in 1991 to study Islamic law and philosophy. It proved to be a pivotal experience. Eagerly anticipating the return to his Muslim roots, Ramadan gradually realized that only in Europe did he feel truly "at home." In his personal experience he found his message: that Western Muslims should feel equally "at home" and that they should participate fully as active citizens in their adopted countries.

In developing his message, Ramadan left the classroom and focused on creating non-scholarly books, audio cassettes that sell in the tens of thousands, and media events. Slim and elegant in well-tailored suits and open collars, Ramadan is a brilliant speaker. His public lectures in French and English draw hundreds of Muslims (and curious non-Muslims).

Ramadan argues that Western Muslims basically live in security, have fundamental legal rights, and can freely practice their religion. He notes that Muslims in the West are often more secure than are believers in the Muslim world, where governments are frequently repressive and arbitrary. According to Ramadan, Islamic teaching requires Western Muslims to obey Western laws, although in rare cases they may need to plead "conscientious objection" and disobey on religious

grounds. Becoming full citizens and refusing to live in parallel as the foreign Other, Muslims should work with non-Muslims on matters of common concern, such as mutual respect, better schools, and economic justice.* Ramadan is most effective with second- or third-generation college

Tariq Ramadan.
(AP Images/Keystone/Salvatore Di Nolfi)

graduates. He urges them to think for themselves and distinguish the sacred revelation of Islam from the nonessential cultural aspects that their parents brought from African and Asian villages.

With growing fame has come growing controversy. In 2004, preparing to take up a professorship in the United States, he was denied an entry visa on the grounds that he had contributed to a Palestinian charity with ties to terrorists. Defenders disputed the facts and charged that his criticism of Israeli policies and the invasion of Iraq were the real reasons. Ramadan's critics also claim that he says different things to different groups: hard-edged criticism of the West found on tapes for Muslims belies the reasoned moderation of his books. Some critics also argue that his recent condemnation of Western capitalism and globalization is an opportunistic attempt to win favor with European leftists and does not reflect a self-proclaimed Islamic passion for justice. Yet, on balance, Ramadan's reputation remains intact.† An innovative bridge-builder, he symbolizes the growing importance of Europe's Muslim citizens.

Questions for Analysis

1. What is Ramadan's message to Western Muslims? How did he reach his conclusions?
2. Do you think Ramadan's ideas are realistic? Why?

*See, especially, Tariq Ramadan, *Western Muslims and the Future of Islam* (Oxford: Oxford University Press, 2004).
†See Ian Buruma, *The New York Times Magazine*, February 4, 2007.

Online Study Center **Improve Your Grade**
Going Beyond Individuals in Society

carried the efforts and sacrifices of generations of toiling, struggling ancestors. Through no effort of our own, we are the beneficiaries of those sacrifices and achievements. Now that it is our turn to carry the torch onward, we may remember these ties with our forebears.

To change the metaphor, we in the West are like a card player who has been dealt many good cards. Some of them are obvious, such as our technical and scientific heritage or our commitment to human rights, religious freedom, and the individual. Others are not so obvious, sometimes half-forgotten or even hidden up the sleeve. Think, for example, of the Christian Democrats, the moderate Catholic party that emerged after World War II to play such an important role in the western European renaissance. And in the almost miraculous victory of peaceful revolution in eastern Europe in 1989—in what Czech playwright-turned-president Václav Havel called "the power of the powerless"—we see again the regenerative strength of the Western ideals of individual rights,

representative government, and nationhood in the European homeland. We hold a good hand.

Our study of history, of mighty struggles and fearsome challenges, of shining achievements and tragic failures, gives a sense of the essence of life itself: the process of change over time. Again and again we have seen how peoples and societies evolve, influenced by ideas, human passions, and material conditions. As surely as anything is sure, this process of change over time will continue as the future becomes the present and then the past. And students of history are better prepared to make sense of this unfolding process because they have already observed it. They know how change is rooted in existing historical forces, and their projections will probably be better than many of the trendy speculations of futurologists. Students of history are also prepared for the new and unexpected in human development, for they have already seen great breakthroughs and revolutions. They have an understanding of how things really happen.

Demonstrating for Peace   Millions long for peace, but history and current events suggest that bloody conflicts will continue. Yet there is cause for some cautious optimism: since 1945 wars have been localized and cataclysmic catastrophes like World Wars I and II have been averted. Holding torches, some 3,500 people form the sign of peace in an antiwar, antiviolence rally in Heroes Square in central Budapest. The rally marked the third anniversary of the U.S.-led invasion of Iraq. *(Peter Kollanyi/epa/Corbis)*

Chapter Summary

Online Study Center **ACE the Test**

- *In what ways did Solidarity confront the communist system in Poland, and how did Mikhail Gorbachev try to reverse the decline of communism in the Soviet Union?*
- *How did anticommunist revolutions sweep through eastern Europe in 1989, and what were the immediate consequences?*
- *How, in the 1990s, did the different parts of a reunifying Europe meet the challenges of postcommunist reconstruction, resurgent nationalism, and economic union?*
- *Why did the prospect of population decline, the reality of large-scale immigration, and concern for human rights emerge as critical issues in contemporary Europe?*
- *How and why did relations between the West and the Islamic world deteriorate dramatically in the early twenty-first century?*
- *What does the study of history have to tell us about the future?*

The rise of Solidarity in Poland showed again that the communist system in eastern Europe depended ultimately on Soviet armies. Therefore, when the Russian leader Mikhail Gorbachev refused to use force abroad and his ambitious reforms at home spiraled out of control, the peoples of eastern Europe rose and overturned communist rule in the spectacular, peaceful revolutions of 1989. In a dramatic finale, the democratic movement triumphed in the Soviet Union, the two Germanies joined in a single state, the cold war ended, and the United States remained the only superpower.

In the 1990s, post–cold war Europe grappled with neoliberal market economies, welfare systems under continuing attack, and globalization. Social and economic reconstruction in Russia was less successful than it was in eastern Europe, with the glaring exception of the former Yugoslavia, which was destroyed by resurgent ethnic nationalism. Eastern Europe's rebuilding and its determination to "rejoin Europe" stimulated the long postwar movement toward European unity, and the newly named European Union expanded to include almost all of Eu-

rope west of Russia, Ukraine, and the Caucasus. This triumph was the shining achievement of the post–cold war era.

The twenty-first century highlighted critical issues, and we have seen how the European baby bust, the growth of illegal immigration, and the increased commitment to human rights were all interrelated. The most disturbed development was the renewed hostility between the West and the Islamic world, which was marked indelibly by the al-Qaeda attack of 2001, the campaign to punish Afghanistan, and the American and British invasion of Iraq. Essentially an effort to remake Iraq (and the Arab world) along Western lines, the war in Iraq saw American soldiers run up against a potent combination of Arab nationalism, Islamic extremism, and sectarian conflict. War in the Middle East encouraged shrill cries about an ominous Muslim threat from immigrants living in western Europe, but a study of history would suggest that these fears were greatly exaggerated.

Key Terms

Gdansk Agreement	Paris Accord
Solidarity	"new world order"
perestroika	globalization
glasnost	European Union
shock therapy	Kosovo Liberation
Velvet Revolution	Army (KLA)
third way	Maastricht treaty
Alliance for	baby bust
Germany	

Online Study Center **Improve Your Grade** Flashcards

Suggested Reading

Bernstein, Richard B. *Out of the Blue: A Narrative of September 11, 2001*. 2003. A gripping account by a talented journalist.

Brubaker, Rogers. *Nationalism Reframed: Nationhood and the National Question*. 1996. An excellent analysis of the contemporary resurgence of nationalism.

(continued on page 1056)

The French Riots: Will They Change Anything?

In late November 2005, young Muslim males rioted for several nights in the suburbs of Paris and other French cities. Receiving saturation coverage from the media, this explosion of car-burning and arson ignited controversy and debate throughout France and across Europe. What caused the riots? What could and should be done? How did the conditions of second- and third-generation Muslims in France compare with conditions of Muslims in other Western countries?

One penetrating commentary, aimed at an American audience and reprinted here, came from William Pfaff, a noted author and political columnist with many years of European experience. As you read Pfaff's analysis, note in particular the contrast he draws between the French government's policy toward Muslims and the policy pursued in Britain and the Netherlands.

The rioting in France's ghetto suburbs is a phenomenon of futility—but a revelation nonetheless. It has no ideology and no purpose other than to make a statement of distress and anger. It is beyond politics. It broke out spontaneously and spread in the same way, communicated by televised example, ratified by the huge attention it won from the press and television and the politicians, none of whom had any idea what to do.

It has been an immensely pathetic spectacle, whose primary meaning has been that it happened. It has been the most important popular social phenomenon in France since the student uprisings of 1968. But those uprisings . . . had consequences for power. The new riots have nothing to do with power.

They started with the accidental electrocutions of two boys hiding from the police, who they thought were after them. The police say there was no pursuit and they had no interest in the boys. However, under the policies of the minister of interior—the presidential candidate Nicolas Sarkozy—there had been a general police crackdown in these ugly suburban clusters of deteriorating high-rise apartments built years ago to house immigrant workers. They were meant to be machines for living. The police attention meant random identity checks, police suspicion, and harassment of young men hanging about—maybe dealing in drugs, maybe simply doing nothing because there is nothing for them to do. (In the past, they at least had to do national military service, which was a strong integrative force, but now France has a professional army.)

Their grandfathers came to France, mostly from North Africa, to do the hard labor in France's industrial reconstruction after the Second World War. Their fathers saw the work gradually dry up as Europe's economies slowed, following the first oil shock in the early 1970s. After that came unemployment. The unemployment rate in the zones where there has been the most violence is nearly 40 percent and among young people it is higher. Many of the young men in these places have never been offered a job. When they applied, their names often excluded them.

Their grandfathers were hard-working men. Their fathers saw their manhood undermined by unemployment. These young men are doomed to be boys. They often take their frustration out on their sisters and girlfriends, who are more likely to have done well in school and found jobs—and frequently a new life—outside the ghetto. . . .

The Muslim mothers and wives of the French ghetto are often confined in the home. Drugs are big business in the American ghetto; they are not that big in France. The crimes of the French ghetto are robbery and shoplifting, stealing mobile phones, stealing cars for joyrides, burning them afterward to eliminate fingerprints, or burning cars just for the hell of it, as well as robbing middle-class students in the city and making trouble on suburban trains, looking for excitement.

Religion is important . . . in the French ghetto, it provides the [shell] that protects against the France that excludes Muslims. To the European Muslim, it seems that all of the powerful in the world are in collusion to exclude Muslims—or are at war with them. The war in Iraq, on television, is the constant backdrop to Muslim life in Europe. There are itinerant imams who can put the young ghetto Muslim on the road to danger and adventure in Afghanistan, Pakistan, Iraq—or elsewhere. There are plenty more who preach a still deeper ghettoization: a retreat inside Islamic fundamentalism, totally shutting out a diabolized secular world.

One would think there would be a revolutionary potential in these ghettos, vulnerability to a mobilizing ideology. This seems not to be so. We may be living in a religious age, but it is not one of political ideology. In any case, it is difficult to imagine how the marginalized, thirteen- to twenty-three-year-old children of the Muslim immigration could change France other than by what they are doing, which is to demonstrate that the French model of assimilating immigrants as citizens, and not as members of religious or ethnic groups, has failed for them. It has failed because it has not seriously been tried.

The ghettoization of immigrant youth in France is the consequence of negligence. It has been as bad as the ghettoization through political correctness of Muslims in Britain and the Netherlands, where many people who thought of themselves as enlightened said that assimilation efforts were acts of cultural aggression. The immigrant in France is told that he or she is a citizen just like everyone else, with all the rights and privileges of citizenship—including the right to be unemployed.

Nicolas Sarkozy's zero tolerance of crime and of the petty mafias in the ghetto contributed to touching off these riots, but until recently he was the only French politician to say there has to be affirmative action to get an immigrant elite out of the ghettos and into important roles in French life, where they can pull their communities after them. Some affirmative action has been attempted in recruiting candidates for the elite *grandes écoles* [state schools] that train the French administrative and political class, where the cultural hurdles are

French police face off with young rioters, silhouetted against the flames of burning automobiles. *(Reuters/Corbis)*

immense for candidates. Virtually no children of the Muslim immigration are prominent in mainstream electoral politics; the political parties have yet to make a serious effort to include them. The present government has one junior minister of Algerian origin. I am not aware of any Muslims of immigrant origin in French diplomacy or the top ranks of police and military.

President Jacques Chirac has announced a civilian national service agency to give training and employment to 50,000 young people from the troubled zones by 2007. The age of apprenticeship has been lowered to fourteen, with a corresponding drop in the age of compulsory academic schooling and new measures to support apprenticeships. There will be more money for schools, local associations, and housing construction and renovation. This is change. Whether it is enough, and in time, is another matter.

Questions for Analysis

1. Describe the situation of young Muslims in France. What elements of their situation strike you most forcefully? Why?

2. France has maintained that, since all citizens are equal, they should all be treated the same way. Why has this policy failed for French Muslims? What alternatives would you suggest? Why?

Source: William Pfaff, "The French Riots: Will They Change Anything?" *The New York Review of Books,* December 15, 2005, pp. 88–89. Reprinted with permission from The New York Review of Books. Copyright © 2005 NYREV, Inc.

Buruma, Ian. *Murder in Amsterdam: The Death of Theo van Gogh and the Limits of Toleration*. 2006. A masterful, very readable investigation of the crime that electrified Europe.

Dobbs, Michael. *Down with Big Brother: The Fall of the Soviet Empire*. 1998. A superb firsthand study by an inspired journalist.

Johnson, Lonnie R. *Central Europe: Enemies, Neighbors, Friends*. 2001. A book that ably interprets developments in eastern Europe before and after the revolutions of 1989.

Lampe, John R. *Yugoslavia as History: Twice There Was a Country,* 2d ed. 2003. An excellent, judicious work on the tragedy in Yugoslavia.

Lucassen, Leo. *The Immigrant Threat: The Integration of Old and New Immigrants in Western Europe Since 1850*. 2005. Argues effectively that Muslims are assimilating as rapidly as previous immigrants.

Reid, T. R. *The United States of Europe: The New Superpower and the End of American Supremacy*. 2005. A lively, informative examination by a perceptive American.

Ross, George. *Jacques Delors and European Integration*. 1995. Analyzes the controversies surrounding the European Union in the 1990s.

Sakwa, Richard. *Putin: Russia's Choice*. 2003. Puts the Russian leader in social and historical context.

Shore, Zachary. *Breeding Bin Ladens: America, Islam, and the Future of Europe*. 2006. A comprehensive overview of the Muslim question in Europe.

Stiglitz, Joseph E. *Making Globalization Work*. 2006. An excellent overview of the successes and failures of globalization by a distinguished economist.

Suny, Ronald Grigor. *The Soviet Experiment: Russia, the USSR, and the Successor States*. 1998. An outstanding history of Russia in the 1990s.

Viorst, Milton. *Storm from the East: The Struggle Between the Arab World and the Christian West*. 2007. Recommended short study of twentieth-century developments within a broad historical perspective.

Woodward, Bob. *State of Denial: Bush at War, Part III*. 2006. Best-selling account based on extensive interviews.

Notes

1. F. Fukuyama, *The End of History and the Last Man* (New York: Free Press, 1992); and J. Cronin, *The World the Cold War Made: Order, Chaos, and Return of History* (New York: Routledge, 1996), pp. 267–281.
2. Quoted in *The Economist,* January 6, 2001, p. 6.
3. Quoted by Flora Lewis, *International Herald Tribune,* June 15, 2001, p. 6.
4. D. Rappaport, "The Fourth Wave: September 11 in the History of Terrorism," *Current History,* December 2001, pp. 419–424.
5. Ibid.
6. R. Suskind, *The Price of Loyalty: George W. Bush, the White House, and the Education of Paul O'Neill* (New York: Simon and Schuster, 2004), p. 86.
7. G. Blainey, *The Great Seesaw: A New View of the Western World* (London: Macmillan, 1988).

Index

Ptah (god), 105(illus.)

Ptolemies (Egypt), 98, 105(illus.); trade and, 108; agriculture and, 109; gold mining and, 109; intellectual thought under, 114; Rome and, 133, 144. *See also* Egypt (ancient)

Ptolemy, Claudius (scientist), 114, 494, 494(illus.), 591

Publicans (tax collectors), 160

Public education: in Enlightenment, 603. *See also* Education

Public health, 628, 781–783

Public opinion: in Hundred Years' War, 382–383; Napoleon III on, 818; before First World War, 883

Public sphere, 607

Public transportation, 786, 787(illus.)

Public works programs: of Hitler, 961. *See also* New Deal (U.S.)

Puddling furnace, 723

Pugachev, Emelian, 613

Punic Wars, 109, 132–133

Punishment: in Hammurabi's Code, 17; on manors, 299; for heresy, 362

Purgatory, 313, 448

Purges: in Soviet Union, 954–955

Purging, 667

Puritans, 463, 465, 544, 545(illus.); occupations of, 545(illus.); English absolutism of, 546–547

"Purple People," 38

Pushkin, Aleksander, 760

Putin, Vladimir, 1034, 1034(illus.)

Putting-out system, 629–630, 650–651, 719, 721, 729

Pylos, 60; battle at, 73

Pyramids, 21; in Egypt, 21; of Giza, 21, 23(illus.); Nubian, 37(illus.), 38

Pyrenees, Treaty of the, 537

Pyrrhic victory, 132

Pyrrhus (Epirus), 132

Pythian games, 84

al- Qanun (Avicenna), 230

Qing (Manchu) Dynasty (China), 851, 872, 873

Quadruple Alliance: at Congress of Vienna, 749–750

Quaestors (Rome), 129

Quakers, 454

Quanta, 918

Quarantines, 381, 627

Quebec, 501, 532, 635

Queens, *see* Monarchy; specific individuals

Quinine, 866

Quinto, 539

Quo Vadis (film), 927

Qur'an, 224, 226, 313

Ra (god), 20, 20(illus.), 21

Rabbis: Jewish, 351

Race and racism: categorizing people by, 399, 429–431; meanings of, 429–431; anti-Semitism and, 439; ideas about, 513–514; Enlightenment and, 608–609; imperialism and, 865, 967; nationalism and, 885; Nazis and, 957–958, 969(illus.); in 1990s, 1033. *See also* Ethnic groups; Holocaust; Slaves and slavery; specific groups

Racial difference, 608

Racine, Jean, 542

Racing, 796; chariot, 170

Radar, 999

Radegund (Franks), 217

Radical Reformation, 451–454

Radicals (France), 939

Radicals and radicalism, 753–758, 915–916

Radio, 927, 960(illus.)

Railroads, 849; in England, 716(illus.), 723–725; continental, 730–731, 732; in Russia, 827; investment in, 850; in India, 870

Raison d'état, 530

Rákóczy, Francis, 567

Ralph (bishop of Bath and Wells), 379

Ramadan, 225, 1051

Rameses II (Egypt), 28

R&D, *see* Research, and development (R&D)

Raoux, 663(illus.)

Rape, 1009; in Rome, 125–126; in Middle Ages, 394–395

"Rape of the Sabine women," 125

Raphael, 415(illus.), 425

Rapprochement policy: of Urban II, 279

Rashi (Solomon bar Isaac), 350–351

Rasputin, Grigori, 895, 896(illus.)

Rastrelli, Bartolomeo, 580

Ratification: of EU constitution, 1041

Rationalism, 598, 603, 607

Rationing: in First World War, 891, 894–895

Ravaillac, François, 529

Ravenna: mosaic from, 162(illus.); Ostrogoths in, 212

Raw materials: transportation of, 849–850; rationing of (First World War), 891

Raymond of Toulouse, 279, 364(illus.)

al-Razi, 230

Razin, Stenka, 576

Reading: in Enlightenment, 603–607; revolution in, 604–605; popular literature and, 662–663

Reagan, Ronald, 1008, 1012, 1024

Realism: in Renaissance painting, 422, 423; in literature, 804, 807–809; Comte and, 805; in painting, 809(illus.); in art, 924

Rearmament: by Nazi Germany, 961

Reason: Thomas Aquinas on, 349–350; use of term, 589; Descartes and, 595–596, 598; in Enlightenment, 598, 603; race and, 609. *See also* Enlightenment

Rebellions, *see* Revolts and rebellions

Recession: of early 1980s, 1012

Reconciliation treaty (West Germany), 1008

Reconquista (Spain), 266–267, 266(illus.), 279, 436

Record-keeping: financial, 343

Recreation: medieval, 352; postwar, 1002

Red Army (Soviet Union), 900(illus.), 949, 973, 974, 983

Red Army Faction (Germany), 1046

Red Brigade (Italy), 1046

Reds: in Russian civil war, 899–900, 900(illus.)

Red Sea region, 484, 487; Egypt and, 37–38

Red Shirts, 821

Reflections on the Revolution in France (Burke), 694

Reform(s): Spartan, 67–68; in Rome, 130, 141–143, 165; in High Middle Ages, 274–276; of papacy, 274–276, 278, 467; of Christian Church, 391, 445; Erasmus on, 418; by Peter the Great (Russia), 576–578; in Prussia, 609–610; in Russia, 612–613, 827; in Austria, 614–615; central and eastern European, 615–616; in churches, 672; in France, 688, 692–693; in 19th century, 761–768; in England, 763–765, 835; Ottoman, 830–831; after Second World War, 987; in West Germany, 987; in United States, 994–995; in Soviet Union, 996–997; in Czechoslovakia, 997; by Gorbachev, 1020, 1022–1024, 1024–1025. *See also* Protestant Reformation; Reformation; specific reforms

Reformation: of Christian church, 445–457; Protestant, 449–454, 455–459; radical, 451–454; arts in, 452–453, 452(illus.), 453(illus.); marriage and, 455–457; women and, 457; German politics and, 457–459; in eastern Europe, 465–466; Catholic, 466–472; witchcraft trials and, 475; church regulation and, 671–672. *See also* Counter-Reformation; Protestant Reformation

Reform Bill (England, 1832), 763

Reformed church: of Calvin, 465

Refugees: religious, in Geneva, 465; after Second World War, 985, 986(map); in 1990s, 1042–1043

Regents: Dutch, 549

Regular clergy, 199

Reichstag (Germany), 832, 833, 891, 901, 932; Hitler and, 958

Reign of Terror: in French Revolution, 698–700, 702–703

Reinhart, Anna, 455

Relativity theory, 918

Relics: in churches, 208(illus.), 360–361; of saints, 307, 314

Relief (tax), 268

Relief programs: in Great Depression, 935, 937, 959(illus.); Orwell on, 942–943

Timeline A History of Western Society: A Brief Overview

	Government	Society and Economy
3200 B.C.	Dominance of Sumerian cities in Mesopotamia, ca 3200–2340 Unification of Egypt; Archaic Period, ca 3100–2660 Old Kingdom of Egypt, ca 2660–2180 Dominance of Akkadian empire in Mesopotamia, ca 2331–2200 Middle Kingdom in Egypt, ca 2080–1640	Neolithic peoples rely on settled agriculture, while others pursue nomadic life, ca 7000–ca 3000 Development of wheeled transport in Mesopotamia, by ca 3200 Expansion of Mesopotamian trade and culture into modern Turkey, the Middle East, and Iran, ca 2600
2000 B.C.	Babylonian empire, ca 2000–1595 Hyksos invade Egypt, ca 1640–1570 Hittite Empire, ca 1600–1200 New Kingdom in Egypt, ca 1570–1075	First wave of Indo-European migrants, by 2000 Extended commerce in Egypt, by ca 2000 Horses introduced into western Asia, by ca 2000
1500 B.C.	Third Intermediate Period in Egypt, ca 1100–700 Unified Hebrew Kingdom under Saul, David, and Solomon, ca 1025–925	Use of iron increases in western Asia, by ca 1300–1100 Second wave of Indo-European migrants, by ca 1200
1000 B.C.	Hebrew Kingdom divided into Israel and Judah, 925 Assyrian Empire, ca 900–612 Phoenicians found Carthage, 813 Kingdom of Kush conquers and reunifies Egypt, 8th c. Medes conquers Persia, 710 Babylon wins independence from Assyria, 626 Dracon issues law code at Athens, 621 Cyrus the Great conquers Medes, founds Persian Empire, 550 Solon's reforms at Athens, ca 549 Persians complete conquest of ancient Near East, 521–464 Reforms of Cleisthenes in Athens, 508	Concentration of landed wealth in Greece, ca 750–600 Greek overseas expansion, ca 750–550 Beginning of coinage in western Asia, ca 640
500 B.C.	Battle of Marathon, 490 Xerxes' invasion of Greece, 480–479 Delian Confederacy, 478/7 Twelve Tables in Rome, 451/0 Valerio-Horatian laws in Rome, 449 Peloponnesian War, 431–404 Rome captures Veii, 396 Gauls sack Rome, 390 Roman expansion in Italy, 390–290 Conquests of Alexander the Great, 334–323 Punic Wars, 264–146 Reforms of the Gracchi, 133–121	Building of the Via Appia begins, 312 Growth of Hellenistic trade and cities, ca 300–100 Beginning of Roman silver coinage, 269 Growth of slavery, decline of small farmers in Rome, ca 250–100 Agrarian reforms of the Gracchi, 133–121

Religion and Philosophy	Science and Technology	Arts and Letters
Growth of anthropomorphic religion in Mesopotamia, ca 3000–2000	Development of wheeled transport in Mesopotamia, by ca 3200	Sumerian cuneiform writing, ca 3200
Emergence of Egyptian polytheism and belief in personal immortality, ca 2660	Use of widespread irrigation in Mesopotamia and Egypt, ca 3000	Egyptian hieroglyphic writing, ca 3100
Spread of Mesopotamian and Egyptian religious ideas as far north as modern Anatolia and as far south as central Africa, ca 2600	Construction of the first pyramid in Egypt, ca 2600	
Emergence of Hebrew monotheism, ca 1700	Construction of the first ziggurats in Mesopotamia, ca 2000	*Epic of Gilgamesh,* ca 1900
Mixture of Hittite and Near Eastern religious beliefs, ca 1595	Widespread use of bronze in the ancient Near East, ca 1900	Code of Hammurabi, ca 1790
	Babylonian mathematical advances, ca 1800	
Exodus of the Hebrews from Egypt into Palestine, 13th c.	Hittites introduce iron technology, ca 1400	Phoenicians develop alphabet, ca 1400
Religious beliefs of Akhenaten, ca 1367		Naturalistic art in Egypt under Akhenaten, ca 1367
		Egyptian Book of the Dead, ca 1300
Era of the prophets in Israel, ca 1100–500	Babylonian astronomical advances, ca 750–400	Beginning of the Hebrew Bible, ca 9th c.
Intermixture of Etruscan and Roman religious cults, ca 753–509		First Olympic Games, 776
Growing popularity of local Greek religious cults, ca 700 B.C.–A.D. 337		Babylonian astronomical advances, ca 750–400
Babylonian Captivity of the Hebrews, 586–539		Homer, traditional author of the *Iliad* and *Odyssey,* ca 700
		Hesiod, author of the *Theogony* and *Works and Days,* ca 700
		Archilochos, lyric poet, 648
		Aeschylus, first significant Athenian tragedian, 525/4–456
Pre-Socratic philosophers, 5th c.	Hippocrates, formal founder of medicine ca 430	Sophocles, tragedian who used his plays to explore moral and political problems, ca 496–406
Socrates, 469–399	Theophrastus, founder of botany, ca 372–288	Euripides, the most personal of the Athenian tragedians, ca 480–406
Plato, 429–347	Aristarchos of Samos, advances in astronomy, ca 310–230	Thucydides, historian of the Peloponnesian War, ca 460–400
Diogenes, leading proponent of cynicism, ca 412–323	Euclid codifies geometry, ca 300	Aristophanes, the greatest writer of Old Comedy, ca 457–ca 385
Aristotle, 384–322	Herophilus, discoveries in medicine, ca 300–250	Herodotus, the father of history, ca 450
Epicurus, 340–270	Archimedes, works on physics and hydrologics, ca 287–212	
Zeno, founder of Stoic philosophy, 335–262		
Emergence of Mithraism, ca 300		
Spread of Hellenistic mystery religions, 2nd c.		
Greek cults brought to Rome, ca 200		

	Government	Society and Economy
100 B.C.	Dictatorship of Sulla, 88–79 Civil war in Rome, 78–27 Dictatorship of Caesar, 45–44 Principate of Augustus, 31 B.C.–A.D. 14	Reform of the Roman calendar, 46
A.D. 300	Constantine removes capital of Roman Empire to Constantinople, ca 315 Visigoths defeat Roman army at Adrianople (378), signaling massive German invasions into the empire Bishop Ambrose asserts church's independence from the state, 380 Death of emperor Romulus Augustus marks end of Roman Empire in the West, 476 Clovis issues Salic law of the Franks, ca 490	Growth of serfdom in Roman Empire, ca 200–500 Economic contraction in Roman Empire, 3rd c.
500	Law Code of Justinian, 529 Dooms of Ethelbert, king of Kent, ca 604 Spread of Islam across Arabia, the Mediterranean region, Spain, North Africa, and Asia as far as India, ca 630–733	Gallo-Roman aristocracy intermarries with Germanic chieftains Decline of towns and trade, ca 500–700 Agrarian economy predominates in the West, ca 500–1800
700	Charles Martel defeats Muslims at Tours, 732 Pippin III anointed king of the Franks, 754 Charlemagne secures Frankish crown, r. 768–814	Height of Muslim commercial activity, ca 700–1300, with western Europe
800	Imperial coronation of Charlemagne, Christmas 800 Treaty of Verdun, 843 Viking, Magyar, and Muslim invasions, ca 845–900	Byzantine commerce and industry, ca 800–1000 Invasions and unstable conditions lead to increase of serfdom
1000	Seljuk Turks conquer Muslim Baghdad, 1055 Norman conquest of England, 1066 Penance of Henry IV at Canossa, 1077	Decline of Byzantine free peasantry, ca 1025–1100 Growth of towns and trade in the West, ca 1050–1300 Domesday Book, 1086
1100	Henry I of England, r. 1100–1135 Louis VI of France, r. 1108–1137 Frederick I of Germany, r. 1152–1190 Henry II of England, r. 1154–1189 Thomas Becket murdered, 1170 Philip Augustus of France, r. 1180–1223	Henry I of England establishes the Exchequer, 1130 Beginnings of the Hanseatic League, 1159

Religion and Philosophy	Science and Technology	Arts and Letters
Mithraism spreads to Rome, 27 B.C.–A.D. 270 Dedication of the Ara Pacis Augustae, 9 Traditional birth of Jesus, ca 3	Pliny the Elder, student of natural history, 23 B.C.–A.D. 79 Frontinus, engineering advances in Rome, 30 B.C.–A.D. 104	Virgil, 70–19 B.C. Livy, ca 59 B.C.–A.D. 17 Ovid, 43 B.C.–A.D. 17
Constantine legalizes Christianity, 312 Theodosius declares Christianity the official state religion, 380 Donatist heretical movement at its height, ca 400 St. Augustine, *The City of God,* ca 425 Clovis adopts Roman Christianity, 496		St. Jerome publishes the Latin *Vulgate,* late 4th c. St. Augustine, *Confessions,* ca 390 Byzantines preserve Greco-Roman culture, ca 400–1000
Rule of St. Benedict, 529 Monasteries established in Anglo-Saxon England, 7th c. Muhammad preaches reform, ca 610 Publication of the Qu'ran, 651 Synod of Whitby, 664	Using watermills, Benedictine monks exploit energy of fast-flowing rivers and streams Heavy plow and improved harness facilitate use of multiple-ox teams; harrow widely used in northern Europe	Boethius, *The Consolation of Philosophy,* ca 520 Justinian constructs church of Santa Sophia, 532–537 Pope Gregory the Great publishes *Dialogues, Pastoral Care, Moralia,* 590–604
Missionary work of St. Boniface in Germany, ca 710–750 Iconoclastic controversy in Byzantine Empire, 726–843 Pippin III donates Papal States to the papacy, 756	Byzantines successfully use "Greek fire" in naval combat against Arab fleets attacking Constantinople, 673, 717	Lindisfarne Gospel Book, ca 700 Bede, *Ecclesiastical History of the English Nation,* ca 700 *Beowulf,* ca 700 Carolingian Renaissance, ca 780–850
Foundation of abbey of Cluny, 909 Byzantine conversion of Russia, late 10th c.	Stirrup and nailed horseshoes become widespread in shock combat Paper, invented in China ca 2d c., enters Europe through Muslim Spain in 10th c.	Byzantines develop the Cyrillic script, late 10th c.
Beginning of reformed papacy, 1046 Schism between Roman and Greek Orthodox churches, 1054 Pope Gregory VII, 1073–1085 Peter Abelard, 1079–1142 St. Bernard of Clairvaux, 1090–1153 First Crusade, 1095–1099	Arab conquests bring new irrigation methods, cotton cultivation, and manufacture to Spain, Sicily, southern Italy Avicenna, Arab scientist, d. 1037	Romanesque style in architecture and art, ca 1000–1200 *Song of Roland,* ca 1095 Muslim musicians introduce lute, rebec—stringed instruments and ancestors of violin
Universities begin, ca 1100–1300 Concordat of Worms ends investiture controversy, 1122 Height of Cistercian monasticism, 1125–1175 Aristotle's works translated into Latin, ca 1140–1260 Third Crusade, 1189–1192 Pope Innocent III, 1198–1216	In castle construction Europeans, copying Muslim and Byzantine models, erect rounded towers and crenelated walls Windmill invented, ca 1180 Some monasteries, such as Clairvaux and Canterbury Cathedral Priory, supplied by underground pipes with running water and indoor latrines, elsewhere rare until 19th c.	*Rubaiyat of Umar Khayyam,* ca 1120 Dedication of abbey church of Saint-Denis launches Gothic style, 1144 Hildegard of Bingen, 1098–1179 Court of troubador poetry, especially that of Chrétien de Troyes, circulates widely

	Government	Society and Economy
1200	Spanish victory over Muslims at Las Navas de Tolosa, 1212 Frederick II of Germany and Sicily, r. 1212–1250 Magna Carta, 1215 Louis IX of France, r. 1226–1270 Mongols end Abbasid caliphate, 1258 Edward I of England, r. 1272–1307 Philip IV (the Fair) of France, r. 1285–1314 England and France at war, 1296	Economic revival, growth of towns, clearing of wasteland contribute to growth of personal freedom, 13th c. Crusaders capture Constantinople (Fourth Crusade) and spur Venetian economy, 1204 Agricultural expansion leads to population growth, ca 1225–1300
1300	Philip IV orders arrest of Pope Boniface at Anagni, 1303 Hundred Years' War, 1337–1453 Political disorder in Germany, ca 1350–1450 Merchant oligarchies or despots rule Italian city-states	European economic depression, ca 1300–1450 Black Death appears ca 1347; returns intermittently until 18th c. Height of the Hanseatic League, 1350–1450 Peasant and working-class revolts: Flanders, 1302; France, 1358; Florence, 1378; England, 1381
1400	Joan of Arc rallies French monarchy, 1429–1431 Medici domination of Florence begins, 1434 Princes in Germany consolidate power, ca 1450–1500 Ottoman Turks under Mahomet II capture Constantinople, May 1453 Wars of the Roses in England, 1453–1471 Ferdinand and Isabella complete reconquista in Spain, 1492 French invasion of Italy, 1494	Population decline, peasants' revolts, high labor costs contribute to decline of serfdom in western Europe Christopher Columbus reaches the Americas, October 1492 Portuguese gain control of East Indian spice trade, 1498–1511 Flow of Balkan slaves into eastern Mediterranean; of African slaves into Iberia and Italy, ca 1400–1500
1500	Charles V, Holy Roman emperor, 1519–1556 Imperial sack of Rome, 1527 Philip II of Spain, r. 1556–1598 Revolt of the Netherlands, 1566–1609 St. Bartholomew's Day massacre, August 24, 1572 Defeat of the Spanish Armada, 1588 Henry IV of France issues Edict of Nantes, 1598	Balboa discovers the Pacific, 1513 Magellan's crew circumnavigates the earth, 1519–1522 Spain and Portugal gain control of regions of Central and South America, ca 1520–1550 Peasants' Revolt in Germany, 1524–1525 "Time of Troubles" in Russia, 1598–1613
1600	Thirty Years' War, 1618–1648 Richelieu dominates French government, 1624–1643 Frederick William, Elector of Brandenburg, r. 1640–1688 English Civil War, 1642–1649	Chartering of British East India Company, 1600 Famine and taxation lead to widespread revolts, decline of serfdom in western Europe, ca 1600–1650 English Poor Law, 1601

Religion and Philosophy	Science and Technology	Arts and Letters
Maimonides, d. 1204 Founding of Franciscan order, 1210 Fourth Lateran Council, 1215 Founding of Dominican order, 1216 Thomas Aquinas (1225–1274) marks height of Scholasticism Pope Boniface VIII, 1294–1303	*Notebooks* of Villard de Honnecourt, a master mason (architect), a major source for Gothic engineering, ca 1250 Development of double-entry bookkeeping in Florence and Genoa, ca 1250–1340 Venetians purchase secrets of glass manufacture from Syria, 1277 Mechanical clock invented, ca 1290	*Parzifal, Roman de la Rose, King Arthur and the Round Table* celebrate virtues of knighthood Height of Gothic style, ca 1225–1300
Babylonian Captivity of the papacy, 1307–1377 John Wyclif, ca 1330–1384 Great Schism in the papacy, 1377–1418	Edward III of England uses cannon in siege of Calais, 1346	Petrarch, 1304–1374 Paintings of Giotto, ca 1305–1337 Dante, *Divine Comedy,* ca 1310 Boccaccio, *The Decameron,* ca 1350 Jan van Eyck, 1366–1441 Brunelleschi, 1377–1446 Chaucer, *Canterbury Tales,* ca 1385–1400
Council of Constance, 1414–1418 Pragmatic Sanction of Bourges, 1438 Expulsion of Jews from Spain, 1492	Water-powered blast furnaces operative in Sweden, Austria, the Rhine Valley, Liège, ca 1400 Leonardo Fibonacci's *Liber Abaci* (1202) popularizes use of Hindu-Arabic numerals, "a major factor in the rise of science in the Western world" Paris and largest Italian cities pave streets, making street cleaning possible Printing and movable type, ca 1450	Masaccio, 1401–1428 Botticelli, 1444–1510 Leonardo da Vinci, 1452–1519 Albrecht Dürer, 1471–1528 Michelangelo, 1475–1564 Raphael, 1483–1520 Rabelais, ca 1490–1553
Lateran Council attempts reforms of church abuses, 1512–1517 Machiavelli, *The Prince,* 1513 Concordat of Bologna, 1516 More, *Utopia,* 1516 Luther, *Ninety-five Theses,* 1517 Henry VIII of England breaks with Rome, 1532–1534 Loyola establishes Society of Jesus, 1540 Calvin establishes theocracy in Geneva, 1541 Merici establishes Ursuline order for education of women, 1544 Council of Trent, 1545–1563 Peace of Augsburg, 1555 Hobbes, 1588–1679 Descartes, 1596–1650	Copernicus, *On the Revolutions of the Heavenly Bodies,* 1543 Galileo, 1564–1642 Kepler, 1571–1630 Harvey, 1578–1657	Erasmus, *The Praise of Folly,* 1509 Castiglione, *The Courtier,* 1528 Cervantes, 1547–1616 Baroque movement in the arts, ca 1550–1725 Shakespeare, 1564–1616 Rubens, 1577–1640 Montaigne, *Essays,* 1598 Velazquez, 1599–1660
Huguenot revolt in France, 1625	Bacon, *The Advancement of Learning,* 1605 Boyle, 1627–1691 Leeuwenhoek, 1632–1723	Rembrandt van Rijn, 1606–1669 Golden Age of Dutch culture, 1625–1675 Vermeer, 1632–1675 Racine, 1639–1699

	Government	Society and Economy
1600 (cont.)	Louis XIV, r. 1643–1715 Peace of Westphalia, 1648 The Fronde in France, 1648–1660	Chartering of Dutch East India Company, 1602 Height of Dutch commercial activity, ca 1630–1665
1650	Protectorate in England, 1653–1658 Leopold I, Habsburg emperor, r. 1658–1705 Treaty of the Pyrenees, 1659 English monarchy restored, 1660 Ottoman Siege of Vienna, 1683 Glorious Revolution in England, 1688–1689 Peter the Great of Russia, r. 1689–1725	Height of mercantilism in Europe, ca 1650–1750 Principle of peasants' "hereditary subjugation" to their lords affirmed in Prussia, 1653 Colbert's economic reforms in France, ca 1663–1683 Cossack revolt in Russia, 1670–1671
1700	War of the Spanish Succession, 1701–1713 Peace of Utrecht, 1713 Frederick William I of Prussia, r. 1713–1740 Louis XV of France, r. 1715–1774 Maria Theresa of Austria, r. 1740–1780 Frederick the Great of Prussia, r. 1740–1786	Foundation of St. Petersburg, 1701 Last appearance of bubonic plague in western Europe, ca 1720 Enclosure movement in England, ca 1730–1830 Jeremy Bentham, 1748–1823
1750	Seven Years' War, 1756–1763 Catherine the Great of Russia, r. 1762–1796 Partition of Poland, 1772–1795 Louis XVI of France, r. 1774–1792 American Revolution, 1776–1783 Beginning of the French Revolution, 1789	Start of general European population increase, ca 1750 Growth of illegitimate births, ca 1750–1850 Adam Smith, *The Wealth of Nations*, 1776 Thomas Malthus, *Essay of the Principle of Population*, 1798
1800	Napoleonic era, 1799–1815 Congress of Vienna, 1814–1815 "Battle of Peterloo," Great Britain, 1819	European economic imperialism, ca 1816–1880
1825	Greece wins independence, 1830 French conquest of Algeria, 1830 Revolution in France, 1830 Great Britain: Reform Bill of 1832; Poor Law reform, 1834; Chartists, repeal of Corn Laws, 1838–1848 British complete occupation of India, 1848 Revolutions in Europe, 1848	Height of French utopian socialism, 1830s–1840s German Zollverein founded, 1834 European capitalists begin large-scale foreign investment, 1840s Great Famine in Ireland, 1845–1851 Marx, *Communist Manifesto*, 1848
1850	Second Empire in France, 1852–1870 Crimean War, 1853–1856 Unification of Italy, 1859–1870 Civil War, United States, 1861–1865 Bismarck leads Germany, 1862–1890 Unification of Germany, 1864–1871 Britain's Second Reform Bill, 1867 Third Republic in France, 1870–1940	Crédit Mobilier founded in France, 1852 Japan opened to European influence, 1853 Mill, *On Liberty*, 1859 Russian serfs emancipated, 1861 First Socialist International, 1864–1871 Marx, *Das Capital*, 1867

Religion and Philosophy	Science and Technology	Arts and Letters
Patriarch Nikon's reforms split Russian Orthodox church, 1652 Test Act in England excludes Roman Catholics from public office, 1673 Revocation of Edict of Nantes, 1685 James II tries to restore Catholicism as state religion, 1685–1688 Montesquieu, 1689–1755 Locke, *Second Treatise on Civil Government,* 1690 Pierre Bayle, *Historical and Critical Dictionary,* 1697	Tull (1674–1741) encourages innovation in English agriculture Newton, *Principia Mathematica,* 1687 Newcomen develops steam engine, 1705	Construction of baroque palaces and remodeling of capital cities throughout central and eastern Europe, ca 1650–1725 J. S. Bach, 1685–1750 Fontenelle, *Conversations on the Plurality of Worlds,* 1686 The Enlightenment, ca 1690–1790 Voltaire, 1694–1778
Wesley, 1703–1791 Hume, 1711–1776 Diderot, 1713–1784 Condorcet, 1743–1794	Charles Townsend introduces four-year crop rotation, 1730	Montesquieu, *The Spirit of Laws,* 1748
Ricardo, 1772–1823 Fourier, 1772–1837 Papacy dissolves the Jesuits, 1773 Church reforms of Joseph II in Austria, 1780s Reorganization of the church in France, 1790s	Hargreaves's spinning jenny, ca 1765 Arkwright's water frame, ca 1765 Watt's steam engine promotes industrial breakthroughs, 1780s War widens the gap in technology between Britain and the continent, 1792–1815 Jenner's smallpox vaccine, 1796	*Encyclopedia,* edited by Diderot and d'Alembert, published, 1751–1765 Mozart, 1756–1791 Rousseau, *The Social Contract,* 1762 Beethoven, 1770–1827 Wordsworth, 1770–1850 Romanticism, ca 1790–1850 Wollstonecraft, *A Vindication of the Rights of Women,* 1792
Napoleon signs Concordat with Pope Pius VII regulating Catholic church in France, 1801 Spencer, 1820–1903		Staël, *On Germany,* 1810 Liszt, 1811–1886
Comte, *System of Positive Philosophy,* 1830–1842 List, *National System of Political Economy,* 1841 Nietzsche, 1844–1900 Sorel, 1847–1922	First railroad, Great Britain, 1825 Faraday studies electromagnetism, 1830–1840s	Balzac, *The Human Comedy,* 1829–1841 Delacroix, *Liberty Leading the People,* 1830 Hugo, *Hunchback of Notre Dame,* 1831
Decline in church attendance among working classes, ca 1850–1914 Pope Pius IX, *Syllabus of Errors,* denounces modern thoughts, 1864 Doctrine of papal infallibility, 1870	Modernization of Paris, ca 1850–1870 Great Exhibition, London, 1851 Darwin, *Origin of Species,* 1859 Pasteur develops germ theory of disease, 1860s Suez Canal opened, 1869 Mendeleev develops the periodic table, 1869	Realism, ca 1850–1870 Freud, 1856–1939 Flaubert, *Madame Bovary,* 1857 Tolstoy, *War and Peace,* 1869 Impressionism in art, ca 1870–1900 Eliot (Mary Ann Evans), *Middlemarch,* 1872

	Government	Society and Economy
1875	Congress of Berlin, 1878 European "scramble for Africa," 1880–1900 Britain's Third Reform Bill, 1884 Dreyfus affair in France, 1894–1899 Spanish-American War, 1898 Boer War, 1899–1902	Full property rights for women, Great Britain, 1882 Social welfare legislation, Germany, 1883–1889 Second Socialist International, 1889–1914 Witte directs modernization of Russian economy, 1892–1899
1900	Russo-Japanese War, 1904–1905 Revolution in Russia, 1905 Balkan wars, 1912–1913	Women's suffrage movement, England, ca 1900–1914 Social welfare legislation, France, 1904, 1910; England, 1906–1914 Agrarian reforms in Russia, 1907–1912
1914	World War I, 1914–1918 Armenian genocide, 1915 Easter Rebellion, 1916 U.S. declares war on Germany, 1917 Bolshevik Revolution, 1917–1918 Treaty of Versailles, 1919	Planned economics in Europe, 1914 Auxiliary Service Law in Germany, 1916 Bread riots in Russia, March 1917
1920	Mussolini seizes power, 1922 Stalin uses forced collectivization, police terror, ca 1929–1939 Hitler gains power, 1933 Rome-Berlin Axis, 1936 Nazi-Soviet Non-Aggression Pact, 1939 World War II, 1939–1945	New Economic Policy in the Soviet Union, 1921 Dawes Plan for reparations and recovery, 1924 The Great Depression, 1929–1939 Rapid industrialization in Soviet Union, 1930s Roosevelt's "New Deal," 1933
1940	United Nations, 1945 Cold war begins, 1947 Fall of colonial empires, 1947–1962 Communist government in China, 1949 Korean War, 1950–1953 "De-Stalinization," 1955–1962	The Holocaust, 1941–1945 Marshall Plan, 1947 European economic progress, ca 1950–1969 European Coal and Steel Community, 1952 European Economic Community, 1957
1960	The Berlin Wall goes up, 1961 United States in Vietnam, ca 1961–1973 Student rebellion in France, 1968 Soviet tanks end Prague Spring, 1968 Détente, 1970s Soviets in Afghanistan, 1979	Civil rights movement in United States, 1960s Collapse of postwar monetary system, 1971 OPEC oil price increases, 1973 and 1979 Stagflation, 1970s Women's movement, 1970s
1980	U.S. military buildup, 1980s Solidarity in Poland, 1980 Unification of Germany, 1989 Revolutions in eastern Europe, 1989–1990 End of Soviet Union, 1991 War in former Yugoslavia, 1991–1995 War in Chechnya, 1991–present	Growth of debt, 1980s Economic crisis in Poland, 1988 Maastricht Treaty proposes monetary union, 1990 European Community becomes European Union, 1993 Migration to western Europe grows, 1990s
2000	Terrorist attack on U.S., Sept. 11, 2001 War in Afghanistan, 2001 War in Iraq, 2003–present	Euro note enters circulation, 2002 Voters reject new constitution for the European Union, 2005 Immigrant riots in France, 2005

Religion and Philosophy	Science and Technology	Arts and Letters
Growth of public education in France, ca 1880–1900 Growth of mission schools in Africa, 1890–1914	Emergence of modern immunology, ca 1875–1900 Trans-Siberian Railroad, 1890s Marie Curie, discovery of radium, 1898 Electrical industry: lighting and streetcars, 1880–1900	Zola, *Germinal,* 1885 Kipling, "The White Man's Burden," 1899
Separation of church and state, France, 1901–1905 Jean-Paul Sartre, 1905–1980	Planck develops quantum theory, ca 1900 First airplane flight, 1903 Einstein develops relativity theory, 1905–1910	"Modernism," ca 1900–1929 Conrad, *Heart of Darkness,* 1902 Cubism in art, ca 1905–1930 Proust, *Remembrance of Things Past,* 1913–1927
Schweitzer, *Quest of the Historical Jesus,* 1906	Submarine warfare, 1915 Ernest Rutherford splits the atom, 1919	Spengler, *The Decline of the West,* 1918
Emergence of modern existentialism, 1920s Wittgenstein, *Essay on Logical Philosophy,* 1922 Revival of Christianity, 1920s and 1930s	"Heroic age of physics," 1920s First major public radio broadcasts in Great Britain and the United States, 1920 Heisenberg, "principle of uncertainty," 1927 Talking movies, 1930 Radar system in England, 1939	Gropius, the Bauhaus, 1920s Dadaism and surrealism, 1920s Woolf, *Jacob's Room,* 1922 Joyce, *Ulysses,* 1922 Eliot, *The Waste Land,* 1922 Remarque, *All Quiet on the Western Front,* 1929 Picasso, *Guernica,* 1937
De Beauvoir, *The Second Sex,* 1949 Communists fail to break Catholic church in Poland, 1950s	Oppenheimer, 1904–1967 "Big Science" in United States, ca 1940–1970 U.S. drops atomic bombs on Japan, 1945 Watson and Crick discover structure of DNA molecule, 1953 Russian satellite in orbit, 1957	Cultural purge in Soviet Union, 1946–1952 Van der Rohe, Lake Shore Apartments, 1948–1951 Orwell, *1984,* 1949 Pasternak, *Doctor Zhivago,* 1956 The "beat" movement in the U.S., late 1950s
Catholic church opposes the legalization of divorce and abortion, 1970 to present Pope John Paul II electrifies Poland, 1979	European Council for Nuclear Research (CERN), 1960 Space race, 1960s Russian cosmonaut first to orbit globe, 1961 American astronaut first person on the moon, 1969	The Beatles, 1960s Solzhenitsyn, *One Day in the Life of Ivan Denisovitch,* 1962 Friedan, *The Feminine Mystique,* 1963 Servan-Schreiber, *The American Challenge,* 1967
Revival of religion in Soviet Union, 1985 to present Fukuyama proclaims "end of history," 1991 Growth of Islam in Europe, 1990s	Reduced spending on Big Science, 1980s Computer revolution continues, 1980s and 1990s U.S. Genome Project begins, 1990 First WWW server/browser, 1991 Pentium processor invented, 1993 "Dolly," first genetically cloned sheep, 1996	Solzhenitsyn returns to Russia, 1994 Author Salman Rushdie is exiled from Iran, 1989 Gehry, Guggenheim Museum, Bilbao, 1997
Ramadan, *Western Muslims and the Future of Islam,* 2004 Conservative elected as Pope Benedict XVI, 2005	Growing concern about global warming, 2000s First hybrid car, 2003	Calatrava, Tenerife Concert Hall, 2003

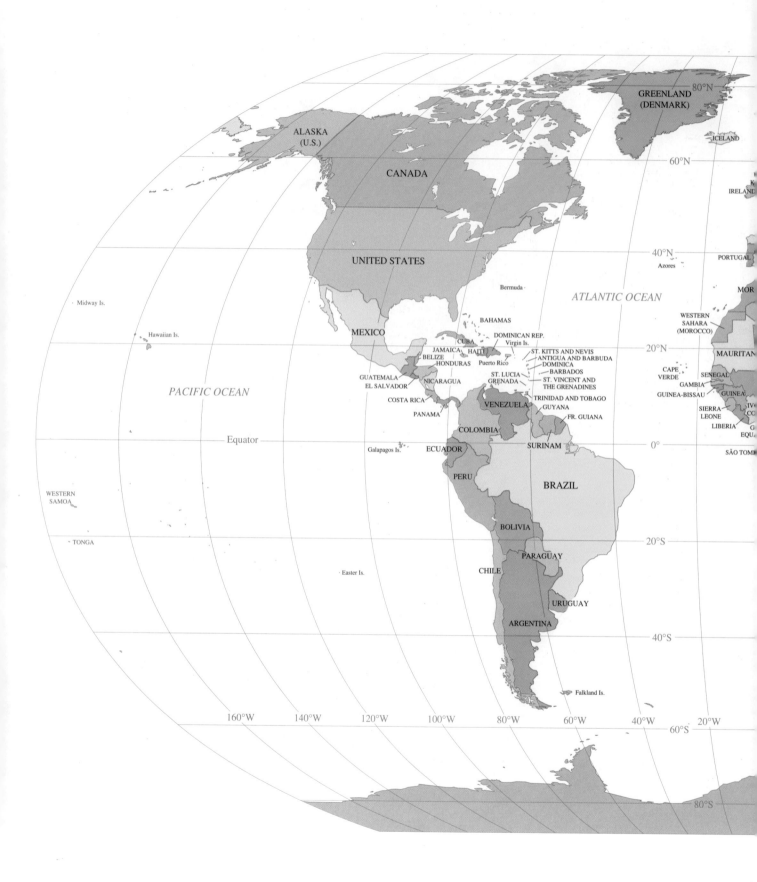